NEW WORLD VISION.
SEEKERS, AND CREATORS WITH
CZECHOSLOVAK ROOTS

Also Authored or Edited by Miloslav Rechcigl, Jr.

Scholarly Publications:
The Rechcigl Genealogy
Keep Them in 'Czech'
Notable Czech and Slovak Americans. From Explorers and Pioneer Colonists
Notable Americans of Czechoslovak Ancestry in Arts and Letters and Education
American Men and Women in Medicine, Applied Sciences and Engineering with Roots in Czechoslovakia
American Learned Men and Women with Czechoslovak Roots
Celebrities and Less Famed Americans Married to Women of Bohemian and Czech Ancestry and their Progeny
Notable American Women with Czechoslovak Roots
Notable Americans with Slovak Roots
American Jews with Czechoslovak Roots
Czechs Won't Get Lost in the World, Let Alone in America
Beyond the Sea of Beer. History of Immigration of Bohemians and Czechs to the New World
Encyclopedia of Bohemian and Czech-American Biography 3 vols.
Czech It Out. Czech American Biography Sourcebook
Czech American Timetable. Chronology of Milestones in the History of Czechs in America.
Czech American Bibliography. A Comprehensive Listing
Czechmate. From Bohemian Paradise to American Haven. A Personal Memoir
On Behalf of their Homeland: Fifty Years of SVU
Czechs and Slovaks in America
Czech and Slovak American Archival Materials and their Preservation
Czechoslovak American Archivalia 2 vols.
Czech-American Historic Sites, Monuments, and Memorials
US Legislators with Czechoslovak Roots
Educators with Czechoslovak Roots
Deceased Members of the Czechoslovak Society of Arts and Sciences
Czechoslovak Society of Arts and Sciences Directory: 8 editions
Studies in Czechoslovak History 2 vols.
Czechoslovakia Past and Present 2 vols.
The Czechoslovak Contribution to World Culture

Scientific Monographs:
Nutrition and the World Food Problem
Comparative Animal Nutrition. Vol. 1. Carbohydrates, Lipids, and Accessory Growth Factors

Comparative Animal Nutrition. Vol. 2 Nutrient Elements and Toxicants
Comparative Animal Nutrition. Vol. 3. Nitrogen, Electrolytes, Water and Energy Metabolism
Comparative Animal Nutrition. Vol. 4. Physiology of Growth and Nutrition
Man, Food and Nutrition. Strategies and Technol. Measures for Alleviating the World Food Problem
World Food Problem: A Selective Bibliography of Reviews
Food, Nutrition and Health. A Multidisciplinary Treatise
Enzyme Synthesis and Degradation in Mammalian Systems
Microbodies and Related Particles

Handbook Series in Nutrition and Food: 18 vols.

Czech Publications:
Češi se ve světě neztratí, natož v Americe
Tam za tím mořem piva aneb Naše Amerika, jak ji málokdo zná
Pro Vlast. Padesát let Společnosti pro vědy a umění
Postavy naší Ameriky

NEW WORLD VISIONARIES, SEEKERS, AND CREATORS WITH CZECHOSLOVAK ROOTS

Miloslav Rechcigl, Jr.

Scholar-in-Residence and Past President of the Czechoslovak Society of Arts and Sciences (SVU)

Author's Tranquility Press
ATLANTA, GEORGIA

Copyright © 2024 by Miloslav Rechcigl, Jr.

All rights reserved. No part of this publication may be reproduced, distributed or transmitted in any form or by any means, including photocopying, recording, or other electronic or mechanical methods, without the prior written permission of the publisher, except in the case of brief quotations embodied in critical reviews and certain other noncommercial uses permitted by copyright law. For permission requests, write to the publisher, addressed "Attention: Permissions Coordinator," at the address below.

Miloslav Rechcigl, Jr./Author's Tranquility Press
3900 N Commerce Dr. Suite 300 #1255
Atlanta, GA 30344, USA
www.authorstranquilitypress.com

Ordering Information:
Quantity sales. Special discounts are available on quantity purchases by corporations, associations, and others. For details, contact the "Special Sales Department" at the address above.

New World Visionaries, Seekers, and Creators with Czechoslovak Roots / Miloslav Rechcigl, Jr.
Hardback: 978-1-966088-10-3
Paperback: 978-1-966088-90-5
eBook: 978-1-965463-75-8

In affection to my late amiable and devoted wife Eva,
loving and accomplished children Jack and Karen,
adorable and brilliant grandchildren Kristin, Paul, Lindsey, Kevin and Greg,
our cutest great-grandchildren James and Evelyn,
dear daughter-in-law Nancy
and in memory of our beloved parents

Contents

FOREWORD iii
PREFACE v
PROLOGUE xi
I. Information Resources 1
    A. Archivists, Bibliophiles, Bibliographers and Encyclopedists 1
    B. Librarians 6
    C. Media 8
    D. Publishing 43
II. The Mythical New World 55
III. Pioneers 57
    A. Early Colonists 57
    B. Jesuit Missionaries 61
    C. Moravian Brethren 68
IV. Wanderers 88
    A. Explorers 88
    B. Astronauts 95
    C. Aviators & Navigators 97
    D. Adventurers, Globetrotters, Daredevils 100
    E. Spies 103
V. The Society 110
    A. Education & Learning 110
    B. Economy & Business 118
    C. Religion 140
    D. Law 179
    E. Medicine 211
    F. Agriculture 218
VI. Public Life 233
    A. Executive Branch Officials 233
    B. Diplomats 240
    C. US Legislators 246
    D. Federal Judges 256
    E. Governors 259
    F. Mayors 263
    G. Military 271

- VII. Advocacy & Activism 306
  - A. Loyalists 306
  - B. Abolitionists 310
  - C. Freethinkers 312
  - D. Suffragists 314
  - E. Civil and Human Rights Activists 317
  - F. Social Activists & Reformers 321
  - G. Political Activists 327
  - H. Zionists 341
  - I. Socialists & Radicals 347
  - J. Environmentalists & Conservationists 353
  - K. Anarchists 356
  - L. Futurists 357
- VIII. Culture: Arts & Letters 360
  - A. Creative Writing 360
  - B. Music 376
  - C. Dramatic Art 518
  - D. Visual Art 648
- IX. Humanities 799
  - A. History 799
  - B. Philosophers 836
  - C. Languages and Literature 858
- X. Science 925
  - A. Biological Sciences 925
  - B. Physical Sciences 935
  - C. Earth Sciences 946
  - D. Social Sciences 967
- XI. Technology 987
  - A. Engineering 987
  - B. Invention 993
  - C. Computing 1012
  - D. Artificial Intelligence 1034
- REFERENCES 1036
- ABOUT THE AUTHOR 1042
- NAME INDEX 1049

PREFACE

The Czechs, or the Bohemians,[1] as they used to be called, from the times of the ancient Kingdom of Bohemia to the onset of the 20th century, have had the reputation as being considered among the highest accomplishers and achievers possible.[2] This is a reflection of the Czech culture and traditions, developed throughout centuries in their ancestral home. The industrial nature, skill, workmanship, and precision were attributes that made the Czech tradesmen famous throughout Europe.

Some people likened the characteristics of the Czech people,[3] such as realism, pragmatism, independence and love for liberty and democracy to Americans and called them Yankees of Europe.

The desire to travel to America manifested itself soon after the discovery of the New World, for which they were prepared, by the works of Bohemian humanists, even before Columbus.[4]

As surprising, as it may appear, according to some scholars, Czechs could actually claim some credit for the discovery of the New World. Thus, the German author Franz Löher[5] maintained that Martin Behaim, was the discoverer of America. Löher celebrates Behaim, whom he considers to be a German,[6] not only as the first European to view the coast of America off Brazil in the year 1483 but also as the instructor in the western navigation of both putative discoverers and explorers, Columbus and Magellan.

Although his claim was later disputed, Behaim was known to take part in the expedition of Diego Cap (1485-1486) which followed the coast of Africa to Cape Cross. His most important work was terrestrial globe, the earliest extant known, which has been

---

[1] Bohemia comes from the name of the Keltic tribe Boi who occupied the territory in Central Europe, before the Czechs settled there.
[2] Slovakia in those ancient times, known as Upper Hungary, was ruled by the Hungarians and the subjugation existed until the creation of Czechoslovakia, which imclude Slovakia as one of its provinces.
[3] Miloslav Rechcigl, Jr., "The Czech American Character," in: Beyond the Sea of Beer. History of Immigration of Bohemians and Czechs to the New World and their Contribution. Bloomington, IN: AuthorHouse, 2017, pp. 422-426.
[4] Miloslav Rechcigl, Jr., Beyond the Sea of Beer. History of Immigration of Bohemians and Czechs to the New World and their Contribution, op. cit., p. 3.
[5] See his *Geschichte und Zusande der Deutschen in Amerika*. Cincinnati, OH: Eggers und Wallop, 1847.
[6] As the name indicates, Behaim was not a German, at all, but rather a Bohemian. The name Behaim is the old German equivalent of the later used term Boehme, i.e., Bohemian. His family actually moved from Bohemia to Nuremberg after the death of the Czech Duke Vratislav I.

preserved in Nuremberg. What role the globe played in the actual discovery of the New World is not known.

Czech immigrants, including Bohemian Jews, have brought to the New World their talents, their ingenuity, their technical and their scientific knowhow, and their humanistic and spiritual upbringing, reflecting upon the richness of their culture and traditions, developed throughout centuries in their ancestral home. This accounts for the remarkable success and achievements of these settlers in their new home, transcending through their descendants.

Johan Berger, born around 1502 in Osoblaha (Hotzenplotz), Moravia, has the distinction, as being the first colonist from the Czechlands in the New World, when he took part as a soldier in the expedition of Hernan Cortes against the Aztecs in 1519.

The first documented instance of a Bohemian setting foot on North American shores is that of Joachim Gans of Prague, who came to Roanoke, NC in 1585, with the expedition of Sir Walter (1552–1618). Gans was a scientist and metallurgist who mastered the skills of dressing and smelting copper. Master Youngham, as he was affectionately called by the English, was held in considerable esteem by his fellow colonists, which is not surprising, considering his extraordinary knowledge of metallurgy and the fact that one of the goals of the expedition was to search for exploitable deposits of precious metals.

All evidence seems to indicate that the first visitors from the Czechlands to the Western Hemisphere were sent there because of their particular technical or scientific skills. This was the case of the Jáchymov miners, employed by the banking house of the Welser family, who were dispatched, before 1528, to Little Naples (the present Venezuela) in order to establish silver mines there.[7] Latin America was also opened for missionary work to Bohemian Jesuits in the second half of the 17th century. At least half of these missionaries were skilled craftsmen or members of learned professions, including scientists.[8]

Rev. Kenneth D. Miller,[9] a recognized authority on Czech Americans, wrote the following about their character: "The charge that the immigrants are undermining the moral standards of America cannot be brought against the Czecho-Slovaks." According to

---

[7] Josef Polišenský, "Prameny a problem déjin českého a slovenského vystěhovalectví do Latinské Ameriky," *Český lid*, 88, No. 1 (1981), p. 5.

[8] Otakar Odložilík, "Czech Missionaries in New Spain," *Hispanic American Historical Review* 25 (1945), pp. 428–454; Miloslav Rechcigl, Jr., "Bohemian Jesuits," in: *Beyond the Sea of Beer. History of Bohemians and Czechs to the New World and their Contributions*, Bloomington, IN: AuthorHouse, 2017, pp. 11–17.

[9] Kenneth D. Miller, The Czecho-Slovaks in America. New York: George H. Doren Co., 1922, pp. 70–71.

him, the Czechs are conspicuously quiet, industrious and law-abiding. With reference to life style, he states that family life among the Czechs is generally stable and marked by unusual faithfulness on the part of man and wife." Rev. Miller then concludes that the Czechs are well fitted to understand the genius of American life. He believes that this is because both their background and mental equipment give them splendid preparation for life in America. Liberty, equality, democracy, justice and such ideals find ready acceptance in the heart and minds of Czech people.[10]

You would hardly ever find an individual among them, suffering from an inferiority or minority complex. Actually, the opposite may be true. Most Czechs are very proud people who have a good opinion and good feelings about themselves. American sociologist Robert L. Skrabanek, [11] who was born in the Czech community of Snook, TX, where the Czech farmers led a distinctive and fiercely proud way of life, described it well in his book. According to him, 'We're Czechs, they are Americans.' was an expression commonly used in his home, often accentuated with the additional admonition – 'and don't forget it!'

In this comprehensive compendium, notable Americans with roots on the territory of Czechoslovakia are viewed from the perspective of their unique characteristics as Visionaries, Seekers, and Creators in the New World, encompassing such Activists as Advocates, Explorers, Pathfinders, Leaders, Reformers, Innovators, Inventors and Futurists.

The monograph is organized into sections by subject matter, i.e., The Mythical New World, Pioneers, Wanderers, The Society, Law, Public Life, Advocacy & Activism, Culture: Arts & Letters, Humanities, and Science & Technology.

Considering the intriguing and exclusive title of the book, the reader may be perplexed by the seemingly unassuming headings of the respective sections. Frankly, I have done it on purpose to demonstrate that the Visionaries and other Activists were not limited to a few individuals, but rather, that they could be found in just about every area of human endeavor, in numbers that would surprise you. There is such as a plethora of them which would literally fill hundreds of pages, many of whom the readers would not even suspect what their ethnic origin is. As an illustration, would you know the answers to the following queries regarding ethnic origin of these eminent individuals:

a nobleman who envisioned the existence of the New World

---

[10] Kenneth D. Miller, *op. cit.*, pp. 106–107.

[11] Robert L. Skrabanek, *We're Czech*. College Station, TC: Texas A&M University Press, 1988, p. 3 and ff.

PREFACE

the first Jew who came to America

First Lord of Bohemia Manor

the wealthiest individual in New Amsterdam

the founder of Bethlehem, PA

the first American male Saint

the founder of the American Reform Judaism

first American Bishop of the Moravian Church (the renewed Unitas fratrum)

woman responsible for amending the Constitution to allow women to vote

internationally known Tragedienne

First Lady of the USA who descended from Moravian Brethren

President of the USA who was the son of the above

lawyer appointed by President a chief director of TVA

a Founding Father of the USA who served as the first Chief Justice of the USA

Delaware abolitionist and politician who signed the US Constitution

US Supreme Court Justice noted for his devotion to freedom of speech

US Supreme Court Justice who took strong stand on individual civil rights

literary scholar regarded as a founder of comparative literature and literary criticism

Catholic priest considered one of the leading 20th century experts on Slavic and Byzantine history

American Hyperpolyglot

Director of the National Conservatory of Music in New York City

composer who set Hollywood in music

most famous dancer in the world

educator credited with major reform of medical education in the US pioneer in the field of public relations and propaganda

psychologist who proposed that the U.S. Treasury start collecting income taxes through a withholding, pay-as-you-go, system.

first woman named to the post of the US Secretary of State

epidemiologist who found the cure for pellagra

greatest logician since Aristoteles

virologist awarded Nobel Price for discovering etiology of the disease kuru

actress who invented Wi-Fi

nuclear physicist credited with the development and production of the first atomic bomb

woman pediatrician who found the cure for the blue baby syndrome

the only one husband-wife team to become the Nobel Prize Laureates

chemist award Nobel Prize for the discovery of catalytic properties of RNA

immunologist who discovered human blood groups

ophthalmologist who introduced cocaine as a local antiseptic in eye

plastic surgeon who pioneered the first full-face transplantation

engineer specializing in the design and construction of airships

engineer considered discoverer of radio astronomy

electrical engineer credited with the development of the Global Positioning System (GPS)

astronaut who walked most recently on the Moon

physicist considered developer of nuclear magnetic resonance imaging (MRI)

innovative manufacturer of commercially produced yeast

entrepreneur and the founder of the McDonald's empire

corporate executive who became CEO and Chairman of the Board of the Walt Disney Co.

beauty queen and the founder of the pioneering cosmetics co.

Believe it or not, or have you guessed it? – They are all Americans with roots in Czechoslovakia. Frankly, I could have go on and on and on. The book is really about the Best and about the Firsts! Have a Good Read!

The reader will find lots of information in this book which may be new. I hope the book will not only bring you information, but also pleasure, and that it will correct frequently distorted views about the Czech and Slovak Americans. Hopefully, it will inspire the readers to seek higher horizon in their work, just as these self-made immigrants achieved, often under most wearisome conditions.

PROLOGUE

Although the mass migration from the territory of the former Czechoslovakia had its start only after the Revolutionary Year of 1848, there are a number records indicating that individuals began to appear on the soil of the New World much earlier, in fact, soon after its discovery.

The first visitors were most certainly attracted by a desire for adventure, but what is more probable, that they were sent there by the rulers or aristocracy, or by Religious Orders, for their specific knowledge and ability, to assist with settlement. That was the case of the Jáchymov miners, who were sent to Venezuela before 1528, to start mining of silver. Similarly, Joachim Gans from Prague, who took part in the first English colonizing expedition to Roanoke, North Carolina, was selected for his metallurgical knowhow. The same could be said about the Bohemian Jesuits in Latin America, as well as in some states of the US, i.e., Arizona and California, who were as a rule trained as tradesmen technicians, specialist in architecture, medicine or astronomy.

Augustine Heřman from Prague is usually considered to be the first documented case of Bohemian immigrant who settled permanently on the territory of the US. He was no soldier of fortune but rather a skillful surveyor and cartographer, who mastered a number of languages, to such an extent that the governor of the Dutch Province sent him on several diplomatic assignments, be it with the English or the Indians. Similarly, Heřman's contemporary, Frederick Philipse, originally from a Bohemian aristocratic family, was a skillful tradesman and unusually able businessman, who was considered one of the wealthiest men in New Amsterdam. Just like Heřman, so did Philipse, leave extensive number of descendants, some of whom have lived to date. Among them, one could find Senators, Congressmen, Governors, Judges, lawyers, physicians, businessmen and professionals of all kinds.

Mass migration in the second half of the 19th century was preceded by a numerous emigration wave of the followers of the *Unitas fratrum*, who immigrated to Georgia and Pennsylvania, starting in 1735. These so called 'Moravian Brethren' were probably carefully selected for emigration, since they were predominately trained tradesmen and craftsmen.

At the onset of the 19th century Bohemian Jews began to immigrate to America, whose number gradually grew, especially around the year of 1848. They were mostly educated people, who applied themselves well in America. A number of their families founded the whole dynasties of important personalities, as was the case, for example, with the Taussig and Flexner families.

The emigration around the year 1848, known as 'Forty-Eighters,' was political in character, consisting primarily of intellectuals. Besides politicians, there were also some students among them, like Vojta Náprstek or František Korbel.

The mass migration was largely instigated for economic reasons. The immigrants were mostly farmers, or better said peasants and cottagers, from the rural area and tradesmen from the cities. The New York Harbor was the usually the first place on the American soil, where the Czech immigrants first stepped on the American soil. Very few of them remained there, however, preferring to move into the interior of the US.

Most people don't realize that the most numerous Bohemian colonies in America was first in the state of Wisconsin. Similarly, it is not known that that the first Bohemian Metropolis in the US was neither New York nor Chicago, but rather St. Louis, Missouri. Only after the railroad was built, connecting the East with Chicago, Chicago became the largest Czech Metropolis in the US, which grew into such proportions that only Czech Vienna could compete with it. In the nineties of the 19th century, the largest city after Chicago was Cleveland, OH.

Besides large cities, where the tradesmen mainly settled, a large percentage of the Czech immigrants moved to rural states, such as Wisconsin, Nebraska, Texas, Iowa, Michigan, Minnesota, Kansas, Dakota Territory and later also Oklahoma. Of all the states, Iowa reminded the Czech immigrants most their native ho country most. As one can learn from this publication, Czechs also settled in other states, including Maryland, Pennsylvania, Georgia, Louisiana, New Jersey, North and South Carolina, Kentucky, Virginia, California and others.

Starting with Augustine Heřman, he wanted to establish a 'New Bohemia' on his Bohemia Manor. There were also efforts among the Czech settlers to establish their own Czech colony, but the idea was never realized, just as the Germans and other ethnic groups failed in their efforts. Nevertheless, the Czechs founded many villages, bearing Czech names, with predominately Czech inhabitants.

The beginnings of Czech immigrants in America were hard, if not harsh. After arrival in America, a Czech immigrant had to face a number of typical immigrants' problems, e.g. little money, lack of agricultural equipment, distant market, where they could convert their produce for money or exchange for other goods, etc. In a prairie state like Nebraska, they had 'dig a dugout' in the ground or build a 'sod house,' while in Wisconsin they constructed a log cabin. In Texas, under cruel and inhumane conditions they constructed dwellings from fallen trees, with the floor formed from rammed down soil and hearth in the middle of the room. For livelihood they had nothing but their hands, courage and perseverance. Instead of yoke of oxen, individual members of the family were used like draught horses, to pull logs.

The first Czech immigrants, just as other ethnic groups, lived in their own enclaves, where they helped each other and, of course, spoke Czech. They had their Czech schools, and they organized their benevolent insurance, cultural and social associations. There was hardly a single larger Czech community which would not have its own Czech newspaper. A newspaper editor was considered their most important cultural representative. Czech settlers never suffered from any inferiority complexes.

As for religion, although they were originally from greater extent Catholics, after coming to America, a number of them transferred to Protestants or left their faith entirely. A sizeable group among them, especially among the intellectuals, formed Freethinkers clubs. There were frequent quarrels between the believers and not believers and this unsettling situation lasted until the Czech Americans became involved in the struggle for liberalization of the Czech Nation from the Austrian rule and tyranny which brought them together.

Although Czechs were engaged organizationally in their communities, in which women played an important role, they did not care much for politics. Only toward the end of the 19th century news began appear in print about naming Czech Americans to various public offices. In the 20th century one could find Czechs also among the congressmen, Mayors and Governors.

It is remarkable how the Czech immigrants were able to overcome the initial hardships and in time succeeded in building for themselves better conditions for livelihood and were able to attain tremendous success in their careers. From peasants and cottagers evolved farmers and agribusinessmen, from peddlers and salesmen, wholesalers, from tradesmen, manufacturers and entrepreneurs, and so on.

In the cultural and science world, the situation was similar. From teachers became university professors, from pharmacists, specialized physicians, from musicians, composers and conductors, from builders, architects, from attorneys, Justices of the Supreme Court, etc. There has not been a single area in which the Czechs would not have succeeded. Among the religious dignitaries, mention needs to be made of John Nepomucene Neumann, the first American male Saint, or David Nitschmann, the first

Bishop of the renewed *Unitas fratrum*, Rabbi Isaac M. Wise, the founder of the modern Reform Judaism in the US.

Among writers, Paul Albieri, Rudolf Pšenka, Jan Havlasa, Theodore Dreiser, Egon Hostovský, and more recently Arnošt Lustig and Josef Škvorecký excelled.

In humanities there were a number of outstanding personalities, including René Wellek, the founder of comparative literature, Francis Dvorník, a Byzantine and Slavic historian of world repute, Hans Kohn, world authority on history of nationalism, Erich Heller, critical essayist and expert on German literature, Henry Kučera, a quantitative linguist, Benno Landsberger, authority on Assyriology, Herbert Feigl, philosopher of science, etc.

In social sciences, Czech American pioneers in economics and econometrics excelled (Taussig, Schumpeter), the founder of gestalt psychology (Wertheimer), the creator of normative theory of Law (Kelsen), the founder of modern empiric sociology (Lazarsfeld), quantitative innovator of political; science (Deutsch), the father of public relations and the spin (Bernays), reformer of income tax system (Ruml), and many others.

Among American scientists, inventors and reformers, there has been a number of Czech Americans, including the discoverer of local anesthesia, the founder of radio astronomy, founder of cardiac pediatrics, pioneer in American bacteriology, the discoverer of dysentery bacillus, pioneer of airship building, a reformer of medical education and many others. There is also a multiple number of Nobel Prize laureates among the Czech Americans, in comparison with the number of those in the land of their ancestors.

Soon after the Czechoslovak Republic was established, the influx of new immigrants from their homeland ceased, which led to the talk about twilight of Czech American community. That was a premature conclusion. The coming of Nazism and the World War II brought to America a plethora of new immigrants, especially from the intellectual circles, among whom, was a large number of Jews. A few years after the end of the World War, Czechoslovakia was taken over by communists, which led to another wave of refugees, most of whom found refuge in the US. Similarly, the same happened after the Prague Spring and after the occupation of Czechoslovakia by the Soviet troops.

After the Velvet Revolution in 1989, democracy returned to Czechoslovakia and its successor states, the Czech and the Slovak Republics, resulting also to in the renewal of relations between America and the old country. This has had a beneficial salutary effect on the status of Czech communities throughout America. Besides frequent travel to the Czech Republic and Slovakia, the interest in the Czech culture has been greatly enhanced, the children again begin to learn Czech and almost in every larger community Czech festivals are being held. Famous Americans of Czech descent openly and proudly boast of their Czech origin, which undoubtedly enhances the self-confidence of the Czech American branch and brings the image of Czech culture and with it the Czechlands themselves to higher horizons.

In conclusion, which is also apparent from this publication, the Czechs in America made a difference and considerably contributed to the growth and development of their new homeland. By the way, do you know that English word robot was coined by the Czechs, as was the word dollar which had its origin in the Czech thaler.

To be sure, the Czechoslovak immigration history is most certainly also a component of their ancestral home's history and is a business card for the entire Czech Republic and Slovakia.

I. Information Resources

A. Archivists, Bibliophiles, Bibliographers and Encyclopedists

Franz Bader (1903–1994), b. Vienna, of Moravian father, became a bookseller and by the mid-1930s owned the oldest bookstore in Vienna, the Wallishausser'sche Buchhandlung. Following the German annexation of Austria in March 1938, Bader, like other Jews, lost his business, and he and his first wife, Antonia, known as Tony, were fortunate to escape to the United States. On arriving in Washington, DC, he worked in James Whyte's bookstore, selling foreign language books and maps as well as modern art. After the war, Bader opened his own art gallery, where he also sold art and foreign language books. Tony Bader died in 1966, and in 1971, Franz married Virginia Forman. He believed his role as a gallery owner was to reveal hidden artistic talent to the public. He wanted to continue this work after his death and decided, with his wife, Virginia, to establish a fund to help mature artists to continue working to develop their talent.

Adelaide Fries (1871–1949), b. Salem, NC, of Moravian ancestry, was the foremost scholar of the history and genealogy of the Moravians in the southern United States. She made important contributions to the field as archivist, translator, author and editor. Among other, she edited 8 volumes of *Records of the Moravians in North Carolina*. One of Fries' best-known books is *The Road To Salem* (1944), an account of the life of Anna Catharina (Antes) Ernst (1726–1816). Another well-known book, *The Moravians in Georgia*, has entered the public domain and is available online. Her *Forsyth County* was revised and updated in 1949, and a further revision and update was issued in 1976.

Paul Horecký (1913–1999), b. Trutnov, Czech., attended the Sorbonne and received a Doctorate in law and political science from University of Prague (JUDr., 1936). He also received a Master's degree in political science from Harvard University (M.A., 1951). During World War II, he served in Czechoslovak army units under British command. After the war, he worked on war crimes investigations and was a trial attorney at the Nuremberg trials. He also edited trial records for publication by the U.S. Army. He worked for the Library of Congress for 26 years before retiring in 1977, as chief of what was then its Slavic of Slavic and Central Europe Div. (1972–77). After retiring from the library, he was a senior research fellow at George Washington University's Sino-Russian Studies Institute. He also taught for a time in Japan. He was author and editor of *Libraries and Bibliographic Centers in the Soviet Union* (1959), *Basic Russian Publications* (1962), *Russia and the Soviet Union. A Bibliographic Guide to Western-Language Publications* (1966), *East Central Europe: A Guide to Basic Publications* (1969). *Southeastern Europe, A Guide to Basic Publications* (1969),

East Central and Southeastern Europe: Handbook of Library and Archival Resources in North America (1976).

Hans Peter Kraus (1907–1988), b. Vienna, of Bohemian father (Dr. Emil Kraus of Karlovy Vary), was a book dealer described as "without doubt the most successful and dominant rare book dealer in the world in the second half of the 20th century" and in a league with other rare book dealers such as Bernard Quaritch, Guillaume de Bure and A.S.W. Rosenbach. Kraus specialized in medieval illuminated manuscripts, incunables (books printed before 1501), and rare books of the 16th and 17th centuries, but would purchase and sell almost any book that came his way that was rare, valuable and important. He prided himself in being "the only bookseller in history…to have owned a Gutenberg Bible and the Psalters of 1457 and 1459 simultaneously," stressing that "'own' here is the correct word, as they were bought not for a client's account but for stock." He started his own rare book business in 1932, which prospered despite the Depression. In 1938, after the German annexation of Austria, Kraus was arrested for being Jewish and sent to the Dachau concentration camp. After several months, he was transferred to Buchenwald. After eight months in Buchenwald, he was released, returned to Vienna and ordered to leave Austria within two months. Kraus restarted his rare book business in New York, which soon began to prosper. Over the years, Kraus bought and sold major medieval illuminated manuscripts, incunables and assorted rare books and manuscripts.

Adolf K. Placzek (1913–2000), b. Vienna, of Moravian ancestry, was a distinguished architectural librarian, historian, editor and preservationist and adjunct professor of architecture at Columbia University. Placzek transformed the Avery Architectural Library at Columbia University, where he spent 32 years, including 20 as the director, into one of the world's finest repositories of architectural books, drawings, and other archival materials. He was editor-in-chief of the four-volume *Macmillan Encyclopedia of Architects*, published in 1982, a collection of biographies of more than 2,000 architects, from builders of ancient Egypt to avant-garde 20th-century architects. In 1986, he was named co-editor of *The Buildings of the United States*, a voluminous series published by Oxford University Press under the editorial direction of the Society of Architectural Historians, of which Mr. Placzek was a past president. Five volumes of the proposed 600 have been published during his lifetime.

Gustav Pollak (1848–1919), b. Vienna, of Moravian ancestry, was an editor and author, educated in Vienna. He immigrated to the US at the age of seventeen. He was a contributor to the Evening Post, In New York, and the Nation, for 40 years, chiefly on foreign politics and literary matters. In 1884, he was editor of *Babyhood*. He assisted in editing four encyclopedias, i.e., *The Century Cyclopaedia of Names, New International Encyclopaedia,*

Nelson's Encyclopaedia and Appleton' *New American Cyclopaedia*. He was the author of *Fifty Years of American Idealism* and other books. In 1892, he was one of the founders of the German-American Reform Union.

Miloslav 'Mila' Rechcigl (1930–), b. Mladá Boleslav, Czech., is a biochemist, trained at Cornell University (B.S., M.N.S., Ph.D.), and science administrator. He was one of the founders and past President, for many years, of the Czechoslovak Society of Arts and Sciences (SVU). Beyond his scientific career, he is also a noted bibliographer, historian, archivist and encyclopedist. In 2007, he was named SVU Scholar-in Residence and SVU Archivist. Among other, he was editor-in-chief of multiple monograph series, *CRC Handbook Series in Nutrition and Food* (18 volumes) and the author of a 3-volume *Encyclopedia of Bohemian and Czech-American Biography* (2016). He also authored a 2-volume *Czechoslovak American Archivalia,* bearing on the Czech presence in in the United States (2014). In 2012, he was awarded, by the Minister of Interior of the Czech Republic Jan Kubice, a medal for his lifetime contributions to the Czech archival science.

Jiřina Rybáčková (1942–), b. Prague, Czech.; editor and nonfiction writer. Received her education in the Philosophical Faculty of Charles University. After the Soviet invasion in August 1968, left for France and then moved to the US. She first worked at Princeton University, as research assistant, editor and the head of the Latin American collections in the University Library Firestone. Since the end of the 70s, she was engaged as an editor with a number of American publishing firms, such as Scribners, Grolier, Oxford University Press and Princeton University Press. One of her largest projects was a 13-volume *Dictionary of the Middle Ages,* in which 1400 leading American and European historians were involved. After the fall of communism in Czechoslovakia, she was appointed director of the American Czech and Slovak Fund (ACSEF), which provided the Czech and Slovak universities with thousands of books and hundreds of computers, at the value of almost $5 million. In 1993, she moved to Prague, where she soon began working as an executive editor of the thematic encyclopedia *Larousse*. Since 2007, she has been director of the International Antonin Dvořák Society. Throughout these times she has published a number of nonfiction books.

Isidore Singer (1859–1939), b. Hranice, Moravia, resided in the US s. 1895. He studied at the University of Vienna and the Humboldt University of Berlin, receiving his Ph.D. in 1884. Singer moved to New York City in 1895, where he raised the money for the *Jewish Encyclopedia* he had envisioned and subsequently edited the twelve-volume work (1901–06) himself. Singer was also managing editor of the *International Insurance Encyclopedia* (1909) and co-editor of *German Classics of the Nineteenth and Twentieth Centuries* (20 vols.). He was founder (1922) and literary director of the denominational Amos Soc., a monotheistic world league for better understanding among peoples. Singer was a prolific writer in three languages. He also edited *The World's Debt to the Jews* (6 vols.) and translated books from French into German. Over the course of his career, Singer also proposed many other projects which never won backing, including a multi-million-dollar loan to aid the Jews of Eastern Europe, a Jewish university open to students of any background, various encyclopedias about secular topics, and a 25-volume publication series of Hebrew classics. He was also a founder of the American League for the Rights of Man.

M. Mark Stolarik (1943–), b. St. Martin, Czech., is Professor of History and holder of the Chair in Slovak History and Culture at the University of Ottawa. From 1979 to 1991, he was President and CEO of the Balch Institute for Ethnic Studies in Philadelphia, and Director of its press. He is a specialist in the history of immigration and ethnic groups in North America, with emphasis on the Slovak experience. Apart from history, he also has written on Slovak bibliography and historiography.

Allan J. Stypeck (1950–), b. Brooklyn, NY, of Czech ancestry, is the President of Second Story Books, Inc., the Washington, D.C. area's largest used-and-rare bookstore. "Best Used Bookstore", *Washingtonian Magazine*, "One of 10 Best Used Bookstores in the U.S.", *USA Today*, and the cover story of the April 4, 2017 *Washington Post Magazine*. Second Story Books, Inc. has two locations: 2000 P St., NW, Washington, D.C. 20036 and 12160 Parklawn Drive, Rockville, MD 20852.

Mr. Stypeck graduated in 1972 from the American University School of Government and International Service in Washington, D.C. with a B.A. in Economics and a B.A. in Political Science.

He is a Senior Member of the American Society of Appraisers (ASA) accredited in Books and Manuscripts; member of the Antiquarian Booksellers Association of America (ABAA), the International League of Antiquarian Booksellers (ILAB) and The Manuscript Society. Mr. Stypeck serves as an expert witness in all judicial court systems, both federal and state. He has worked on criminal and civil cases with the FBI, U.S. Post Office Inspector General, Library of Congress, the Inspector General of the State of Connecticut and has worked with the police and judicial systems of Maryland, Pennsylvania, Virginia, and the District of Columbia. Stypeck has prepared over 4,000 appraisals for donation, risk management, insurance, estate and sale purposes since 1974. He appraises all printed material, including books, maps, manuscripts and stamps, as well as photography, phonograph records, fine art, antiquities, Oriental art and objects d'art. Mr. Stypeck conducts appraisals for the Library of Congress, Smithsonian Institution, Federal Bureau of Investigation, United States Department of State, National Park Service, the Senate, House of Representatives, White

House, Supreme Court, National Archives, U.S. Holocaust Memorial Museum, Corcoran Museum of Art, Folger Shakespeare Library, Georgetown University, George Washington University, the University of Maryland, Catholic University of America, the National Library of Medicine at NIH, the Peabody Conservatory of Music as well as colleges, universities, major museums, institutions and corporations throughout North America.

Josef G. Svoboda (1930-2006), b. Czech., was a graduate of University of Toronto (B.A., 1930) and studied history at American University (M.A., 1963). He initially worked as an archivist at Case Institute of Technology, Cleveland, Ohio. In 1968, he became an archivist and head, University Archives - Special Collections, University of Nebraska, Lincoln. One of Svoboda's more significant accomplishments included the early development of the Czech Heritage Collections. These collections include documents associated with Czech immigrants to Nebraska and those who experienced World War II and the Prague Spring of 1968 in Czechoslovakia. The University of Nebraska Foundation provided funding for Svoboda to create oral histories and he eventually recorded 65 interviews with Nebraskans of Czech descent.

Katharine Prescott Wormeley (1830-1908), b. Ipswich, England, desc. from Augustine Heřman, was an author, editor, and translator of French language literary works. She was one of the best-known translators of her time, having translated from the French language the *Complete Works of Honoré de Balzac* (40 vols., 1883-97) for American readers. She also translated the *Narrative of Marie-Thérèse Charlotte de France*, the *Memoirs of Madame de Motteville on Anne of Austria and her Court*, as well as works by Molière (6 vols., 1892); Louis de Rouvroy, duc de Saint-Simon; Alphonse Daudet; and Alexandre Dumas, among others.

Robert Owen Zeleny (1930-), b. Chicago, IL, of Bohemian ancestry, was reared in New Orleans, and then returned to work to Chicago, where he secured his place and made a success of his career in book editing and publishing. A graduate of Tulane University, majoring in journalism and political science, he joined the Navy soon after graduation and spent 3½ years as a communications officer aboard a minesweeper during the Korean War. He went back to Chicago after his discharge and attended graduate school at the University of Chicago. While there, he took a part time job at *The World Book* as assistant editor and decided to stay (s. 1956), for 37 years. He became sr. science editor (1957-58), managing editor (1964-65), vice president and executive editor (1965-72). He was also sr. vice president and editor of *Childcraft* (1967-83); sr. vice president and editor-in-chief of *World Book, Inc.* (1983-91); and publisher of *World Book International* (s. 1992).

B. Librarians

Jewel Drickamer (orig. Weidenthal) (1917–2005), b. Cleveland, OH, of Bohemian ancestry, was one of the pioneers in the development of Rhode Island's State library network and Statewide library development, in general. She served at the Department of State Library Services as deputy director from 1964–1975 and then as director from 1975, until she retired in 1980. Before coming to Rhode Island, Ms. Drickamer worked in a variety of library settings including the Cleveland Public Library, the Hartford Public Library, the National Association of Broadcasters.

Jennie Mass Flexner (1882–1944), from Louisville, KY, of Bohemian ancestry, was probably the first significant librarian of Czech origin in the US. She became the head of the circulation department in the Louisville Public Library from 1912 through 1928, publishing *Circulation Work in Libraries* (1927), a long standard text for library students. In 1928, she was hired as the readers' adviser at the New York Public Library, a post she retained until the end of her life. When the influx of European refugees, escaping Fascism, began to arrive in the 1930s, Jennie Flexner was active helping them find new resources for their professional and intellectual lives.

Paul Horecký (1913–1999), of Trutnov, Bohemia, was with Library of Congress since 1951, as Chief of Slavic and Central European Division since 1977. He was editor of *East Central Europe: A Guide to Basic Publications* (1969), *Southeastern Europe. A Guide to Basic Publications* (1969) and *East Central and Southeastern Europe: Handbook of Library and Archival Resources in North America* (1976).

Esther Jerabek (1897–1979), born in Silver Lake, MN, of Czech immigrant parents, was a teacher and a librarian. In 1929, she joined the library technical services staff of the Minnesota Historical Society, where she served as cataloguer until her retirement in 1963. Her major publication was *Czechs and Slovaks in North America: a Bibliography* (1972).

Edward Kasinec (1945–), b. New York, NY, of Rusyn descent, was a reference librarian, curator of Slavic-Baltic Division, New York Public Library (1984–2009), visiting fellow of Hoover Institution, research scholar with Harriman Institute, Columbia University.

Fern Long (1905–), of Cleveland OH, of Czech ancestry, received her training at Charles University, Prague. She was associated the Cleveland Public Library, working in a variety of areas, including literature, the John G. White Collection, philosophy, religion and as a reader's advisor. In 1944, she became the Supervisor of the Adult Education Department serving until 1970. Dedicated to responsible library service for the elderly, she helped create the Live Long and Like It Club in 1946. From January to September 1970, Long was acting director of the Cleveland Public Library. From September 1970 to January 1974, she was deputy director. Finally, between January 1974 and December 31, 1975, she became interim director.

Susan K. Martin (née Orowan) (1942-), born in Cambridge, England, of Slovak grandfather, is an American librarian. She holds a Doctorate from the University of California, Berkley. She held important positions at Harvard University, Johns Hopkins University, Princeton University and Tufts University, and Georgetown University.

Adolf K. Placzek (1913-2000), born in Vienna, of Moravian ancestry, was a distinguished architectural librarian, historian, editor and preservationist and adjunct professor of architecture at Columbia University.

Felix Pollak (1909-1987), a native of Vienna, of Bohemian mother, was curator of rare books at the University of Wisconsin Memorial Library, Madison.

Hana Pyro (née Stádníková) (1947-), a native of Prague, Czech., gradually progressed from library assistant and cataloguer in the Slavic Division to the position of Slavic librarian at Harvard University. With learning a number of Slavic languages, she has been acquiring up to 3,000 titles per year, building on the great collections at Harvard in these languages. She has also developed Czech and Slovak Samizdat collection at Harvard.

Tatjana Sahanek (1922-2013), a native of Prague, Czech, trained as a librarian, had a varied career. She started as a cataloger at Toronto Public Library and then became employed at Ontario Legislation Library, Toronto. Subsequently, she became head of the catalog and classification division at Harvard Law School Library, Cambridge, MA; head of the catalog department at Law Library of the University Michigan, Ann Arbor; translator and interpreter with Dow Chemical International, Midland, MI; library-translator with Dow Chemical Co., Freeport, TX; assistant librarian at Antioch School Law, Washington (1972-74); editor and indexer of legal periodicals for H. W. Wilson Co., Bronx, NY; coordinator at Saginaw Medical Center, MI (1978-79); and acquisitions librarian at the Executive Office of President Information Center, Washington, DC.

Jozef Staško (1917-1999) b. Sedliacka Dubová, Slovakia, trained as a lawyer, was a politician. He immigrated to the US in 1961 and became a librarian in NYC. He was also an editor and writer for the *SKS Bulletin* and for the periodical *Horizont*.

Edward R. Strážnický (1820-1976), from Moravia, became assistant librarian in Astor Library, New York City and, in 1872, he was elected superintendent. He was secretary of the American Geographical Society.

Sister M. Martina Tybor (1908-1998), b. Bridgeport, CT, of Slovak descent; professed in Sisters of SS Cyril and Methodius (s. 1928). She was a teacher, translator, and the founder and the first director of Jankola Library and Slovak Museum, Danville, PA (s. 1968).

Otto Wierer (1912-2001), a native of Prague, Bohemia, became, consecutively, a cataloguer at New York Public Library, assistant head of language division, Queensboro Public Library, cataloguer at Gibb College, head of international information center, SUNY, Oyster Bay and university librarian and lecturer at US International University, San Diego.

C. Media

1. Czech-Language Journalists

Bartoš Bittner (1861-1912), b. Milavče, Bohemia, served as editor of the *Svornost* in Chicago. He then moved to New York, where he became editor of *Duch Času* in 1890 and in 1893, he began publishing his satirical weekly, the *Šotek* (Imp), which soon achieved marked success.

Joseph Buňata (1846-1934), b. Křesetice, near Kutná Hora, Bohemia, at his time, was the oldest Czech editor living in the US. He came to this country in 1870, to New York and he divided his time between working on newspapers, most of which had a precarious existence, and his trade of cigar making. He was editor of the *Dělnické Listy* in New York in 1877, of the *Slovan* in La Grange, Texas in 1888 (the first Czech paper in that state), in 1898 of the *New Yorské Listy* in New York, in 1899 of the *Pokrok Zapadu* in Omaha, later of the *Pravda* in Cedar Rapids, Iowa, and the *Svornost* in Chicago, IL.

Jan Vratislav Čapek (1842-1909), b. Krastovice, nr. Strakonice, Bohemia, in 1871 was invited to Cleveland to assume editorship of *Pokrok*. Within a year he established his own paper, a satirical weekly *Diblík* which in 1873, he was forced to change into a political weekly *Národní Noviny*. He then moved to NYC to take over editorship of *New Yorské Listy* which he subsequently bought and changed into a daily. For a time, he also co-published a weekly *Patriot*.

Antonín Cekota (1899-1995), b. Napajedla, Moravia, attended industrial school in Pardubice. He worked for the Czechoslovak Baťa Enterprises as publicity director and publisher of several newspapers and magazines, published by Baťa interests from 1929-39. He entered Canada in 1939, became research director of the Bata Organization operating in the Free World. He was the author of several books dealing with the work and life of Tomáš Baťa, the founder of the Baťa Enterprises, including *Tomáš Baťa Entrepreneur Extraordinaire* (1968). In addition, he had written technical papers on the manufacturing of shoes and industrial relations. He also translated John Masefield's poetry into Czech.

Otakar Charvát (1885-1956), b. Pelhřimov, Bohemia, after coming to US in 1905, became editor of *St. Louiské Listv* and later *Český Oklahoman* in Oklahoma City. In 1906, he removed to Omaha, NE as editor of *Pokrok Západu* and remained there until his death. He was also editor of the *Nová Doba* and the *Národní Pokrok*, both in Omaha.

Ludvík W. Dongres (1872-1932), b. Kralovice, Bohemia, came to US in 1891, settling in Texas. He became editor of *Hospodář* and *Dělnické Listy*, Omaha; *Hospodářské Listy,* Chicago; magazine *Komenský,* Lincoln; *Hlasatel*, Chicago; *Česko-Americký Venkov*, Omaha; and others. He wrote many articles for various papers and fiction and poems, sometimes under the pseudonym of Just-a-Man, also translated poetry.

Hynek Dostál (1871-1943), b. Boršice, Moravia, accepted the post in Chicago of an editor of the Czech Catholic daily *Národ* (1900-02). Since 1902, he edited the oldest Czech Catholic paper in the US, *Hlas,* a semi-weekly and women's journal *Česká Žena* (a weekly).

Anna Dostálová (pseud., A. Čechová) (1876-1919), b. Německý Brod, Czech. She was editor of the newspaper *Česká Žena* (Czech Woman), for Czech Catholic women and girls in America, published in St. Louis, MO, and co-editor of the paper *Hlas* (The Voice); her husband H. Dostal was editor of *Hlas*. She also wrote a number of informative and patriotic papers for both papers and some of them also were published in Bohemia. She came to America in September 1899 and has been actively writing since 1903.

Vojtěch Duben (actually Vojtěch Nevlud) (1920-2005), b. Fryčovice, Czech., was educated in Czechoslovakia, where he was a member of the editorial staff of various dailies. He left in 1948 for West Germany, where he edited a Czech weekly and directed a press service. He entered the US in 1950 and became editor of a Czech daily in New York. Subsequently, he joined the Voice of America, where he held the position of foreign language information specialist. He specialized in Czechoslovak political affairs, the history and the status of Czech and Slovak journalism and labor relations. He was the author of *Czech and Slovak Periodical Press outside Czechoslovakia* (1962) and of *Ledy se hnuly: Československý kulturní a politický kvas 1963* (1964).

Josef Falta (1895-1973), b. Železný Brod., Bohemia, in 1919, he volunteered to serve in the Czechoslovak Army during the invasion of the communist Béla Kun in Slovakia. When the fighting was over, Falta joined the Social Democratic Party (SDP) and wrote for SDP newspapers. From 1927 to 1931, he served as a chief editor of *Ruch*, published at Brno. Between 1921 and 1935, Falta worked as the parliamentary editor of the daily *Právo Lidu*. From 1935 until 1939, he served as secretary to František Soukup, the president of the Czechoslovak Senate. In 1939, Falta fled to the US and settled in Chicago, Illinois in 1941. During WWII he did weekly broadcasts for the radio station WEDC. Falta also worked for the Czechoslovak Information Service and the Czechoslovak American National Council. From 1945 to 1948, he edited the monthly *Svobodné Československo* published by the Czech National Committee. From 1951 to 1970, he edited the Czech daily *Denní Hlasatel* published in Chicago.

František Fišera (1864–), b. Studenec, nr. Jilemnice, Bohemia, in 1888 came to US, settling first in Chicago. He was the editor of *Čechoslovan, Chičázské Listy, Denní Hlasatel, Národ* and *Jednota*, then at the *Osvěta* in Omaha and the *Pravda* in Cedar Rapids. He was also a co-editor of *Lidové Noviny*.

Joseph Hessoun (1830–1906), b. Písek, Bohemia, R.C. priest, "Little Father," founded in 1868 the weekly *Katolické Noviny* in Chicago. However, the paper became extinct after a few months. Not discouraged, Hessoun established the Czech Literary Society in St. louis, and in 1871, the Society under his leadership began to publish a new Catholic weekly, *Hlas*, which was distributed widely in America. Most of the works published in it have been written by Hessoun who also wrote numerous articles for the old homeland papers.

Frank J. Hlaváček (1853–1937), b. Renčov, Bohemia, was a journalist by trade. In 1866, he left for America, settling in NYC, where he was offered a position on editorial staff of *Proletář* and *Diblík*. At demise of *Proletář*, he continued working for *Hlas Lidu* and in 1893, he with his friends set up a radical newspaper *Dělnické Listy*, the publisher of which was the International Workingmen's Union. In 1896, he arrived in Chicago and joined staff of the weekly *Pochodeň*. In 1900, he founded a weekly *Spravedlnost* and remained its editor until 1921.

Jiří Hochman (1926–2012), b. Prague, Czech., was a Czech journalist and publicist. After graduating from the Commercial Academy, he became editor of *Obrana lidu* (1950–54), *Rudé právo* (1954–66) and then a correspondent in Geneva, Paris, Havana, Washington, DC and Peking. He was considered a leading Czechoslovak political journalist in the 2nd half of the 50s and in the 60s. During 1968–69, he became editor and commentator of the weekly *Reportér* and engaged himself in the democratization process. In 1969, he was forced out of the journalistic profession and due to personal persecution, he emigrated to the US in 1974. He was engaged as a professor at several universities and also authored several books. Among others, he edited and published memoirs of Alexander Dubček under the title *Hope Dies Last: The Autobiography of Alexander Dubček* (1993). He also authored *Český Happening* (1978), and *Soviet Union and the Failure of Collective Security, 1934-1938* (1984) and co-authored *Historical Dictionary of the Czech State* (2009).

Josephine Humpal-Zeman (1870–1906), b. Sušice, Bohemia, was a newspaper writer and suffragist. While studying at Western Reserve Univ., she became chief editor of the college paper *College Folio* which she helped to establish. In 1984, she founded a weekly paper the *Ženské Listy* (Women's Gazette). Some journalists referred to her as 'Mrs. General.' In 1897, at the Congress of Slavic Journalists she was elected executive secretary.

Charles (Karel) Jonáš (1840-1896), b. Malešov, Bohemia, 'the first Čech in America,' at invitation of publisher Frank Kořízek, came to Racine, WI to take over editorship of his paper *Slavie*, even though he was barely twenty-three. He soon assumed the responsibilities of editor, which position he held for thirty-two years. Among his colleagues, he attained an exceptional position; they looked up to him as an authority, and his views on matters relating to the national life of Czechs in America were regarded as final.

Ladimír Klácel (orig. František Matouš) (1808-1882), b. Česká Třebová, Bohemia, a former monk, outstanding Czech teacher and author of a number of poetic and philosophical works, came to the US in 1869, at the invitation of Jan Bárta Letovský, to edit his *Slovan Amerikánský* (later renamed *Slovan Americký*), published in Iowa City. They soon parted company and in 1871, he accepted editorship of *Hlas Jednoty Svobodomyslných*, organ of the Czech Freethinkers. In the same year, Klácel also began publishing a new periodical *Svojan*, which did not last long.

Leopold Kochman (1847-1919), b. Nové Strašecí, Bohemia, arrived in NY in 1882, where he joined the editorial staff of Škarda's *Dělnické Listy*. He then transferred to more radical *Dělník Americký* and *Zábavné Listy*. In 1884, he founded a revolutionary periodical *Proletář* which he also edited. In 1886, he joined the editorial staff of the *Hlas lidu* and became its editor, where he remained for a total of thirty-two years.

Valentine Kohlbeck (1864-1937), b. Bedřichovice, Bohemia, R.C. priest, became managing editor of the Bohemian daily *Národ* (Nation), Chicago and the semi-weekly *Katolík* (1896-1919).

Josef Jiří Král (1870-1951), b. Loužná, Bohemia, although trained as a lawyer, became a journalist in the US. He was co-publisher and editor of the *Slavie*, Racine (1894-1904), and editor of the socialist daily *Spravedlnost* (1905-11). He was considered one of the most talented journalists among the freethinkers.

Frank Jaroslav Kuták (1872-1910), b. Blatenka, Bohemia, after coming to US in 1887, worked as a member of newspapers in New York, Cleveland, Chicago, and Omaha. In Omaha he published weekly *Osvěta* and in Cleveland a monthly *Rozhledy*. Subsequently, he was engaged in Cleveland on the editorial staff of the *Orgán Bratrstva*.

I. INFORMATION RESOURCES

Jan Bárta Letovský (1821–1898), b. Letovice, Moravia, immigrated to America, settling in Racine, WI but soon removed to Iowa. He farmed in Jefferson Township until 1859, but subsequently moved back to Racine, to assist František Kořízek with publishing the paper *Slowan Amerikánský*, the first Czech newspaper in America, as an editor. In 1869, he founded a new paper, *Slovan Amerikánský*, in Cedar Rapids, which was later moved to Iowa City, IA and subsequently renamed *Slovan Americký*. He was an ardent Russophile, who in 1860s left for Asian Russia to determine whether the basin of the Amur River would be suitable for Czech American colonists.

Antonín J. Liehm (1924–2020), b. Prague, Czech., was a journalist, cultural publicist, and film critic. During 1966–68, he represented Czechoslovak state film in Paris. He then remained abroad and taught at various universities in France and in the US. He now lives in Paris. In 1984, he founded an international periodical *Lettre Internationale*. He is the author of several important books about the Czech films, including *The Politics of Culture* (1968), *Closely Watched Films: The Czechoslovak Experience* (1974), *The Miloš Forman Stories* (1975), *The Most Important Art: Eastern European Film after 1945* (1977), *Czech New Filmmakers in Interviews* (2002).

Joseph Martínek (1889–1980), b. Poděbrady, Bohemia, enjoyed a long and varied career as a newspaper editor, labor organizer, gymnastics instructor, author, and poet. He settled in Cleveland and since 1912, held position of editor of *Americké Dělnické Listy* and since 1921, also edited the paper's annual revue *Ročenka*. In 1934, he returned to his old country where he was made editor of *Právo Lidu* in Prague. Active in the anti-Nazi movement, Martinek was forced to flee his native country in 1938 following the German annexation of the Sudetenland. After his return to the United States, he served as executive secretary of the Czechoslovak National Council in Chicago, Illinois, from 1939 until 1945. In 1947, Martinek moved to Tucson, Arizona, where he focused on his writing career. He published six books of poetry between 1944 and 1968 and wrote scripts for Radio Free Europe and the Voice of America, radio programs broadcast in Europe.

Alena Martinů (1957–), Prague, Czech., obtained her degree (M.S., 1981) in civil engineering (steel constructions) from Czech Technical University in Prague. After moving with her family to Canada in 1988, she studied psychology and comparative religion at Concordia Univ. (B.A., 1997). In 2001, she became editor-in-chief of the *Montrealský věstník* and, since 2009, she has been member of the editorial board of *Nový Domov*. At the same time, she pursued her career as a writer. She published her first book *Scream of Silence and Other Stories* (2011), and second book, a romance *A Prayer to Tangaroa* (2014).

Vojta Mašek (1839–1907), b. Phořovice, Bohemia, a student at Technical Univ. in Prague, was jailed during the Prague riots, together with Karel Jonáš. He came to America in 1860, settling in Racine, WI, where before the arrival of Jonáš, the future editor of *Slavie,* he served as editor-in-chief of *Slavie.* Together with Kořízek, he was also a co-publisher of the entertaining monthly *Zvony* (Bells), published in Racine in 1863. He soon left journalism, moved to Kewaunne, WI and became a successful businessman.

John V. Matějka (1855–1904), b. Kladruby, nr. Zbiroh, Bohemia, was associated with various newspapers as an editor. He also founded and established several new periodicals but most of them did not survive long. The only exception was a periodical *Chicágské Listy* which was published in Chicago from 1882–93.

Václav J. Miniberger (1883–1969), b. Písek, Bohemia, a Presbyteral minister, was a journalist, writer, and publicist. He immigrated to America in 1902. In 1904, he studied at Fremont College, NE and from 1904 to 1907 attended the Presbyterial Theological Seminary, Omaha, NE. He was Pastor in South Omaha (1907–09), then in Racine, WI, until 1913, when he became superintendent of an immigrant home in Baltimore, MD. Later, he published the *Čecho-Američan* weekly and in 1919 became editor of the *Spravedlnost* daily in Chicago. Since 1926, he had been on the editorial staff of the daily *Spravedlnost* and since 1931 he had been editor of the *Age of Reason,* a weekly published by the Czechoslovak Rationalist Federation of America. Apart from his journalistic career, he was the author of several novels, including *In the Mists* and *Malat.*

František Mráček (1828–1896), b. Nenakonice, nr. Olomouc, Moravia, after spending his first 6 years in New York as a cigar maker, became editor of *Národní Noviny* in St. Louis, MO. When the paper was combined with *Slowan Amerikánský* under the name, Slavie, he became its chief editor.

Ferdinand L. Musil (1888–1959), b. Moravia, was a Czech-American journalist, poet, and writer. He came to America in 1910, settling first in Omaha for three years and, in 1913, moving to Chicago. He edited *Komenský* monthly (1914–18), the *Nové Směry* monthly (1915), the *Poselství* monthly (1919–21) and, since 1923, was member of editorial staff for *Denní Hlasatel* and editor of *Sokol Americký.* He also served on advisory board of *Přírodní Lékař* monthly and was a member of editorial staff of *Věstník Sokolský,* both published in Prague.

Vojtěch 'Vojta' Náprstek (1826–1894), a native of Prague, Bohemia, interestingly, years before Kořízek's achievement, had striven hard to establish here a newspaper in the Czech language. In 1857, he had addressed meeting of interested parties in St. Louis on the subject. He urged New Yorkers and Chicagoans to help and even outlined the future policy of such paper. Náprstek's return to Europe in 1857 alone, prevented him from realizing this pet project. It is for this reason that Náprstek is considered 'father of Czech-American journalism.'

Antonin Novotný (1886-1932), b. Královy Městec, Bohemia, a baker by trade, after coming to Chicago, became a part-time editor of Czech daily *Spravedlnost*, dedicated to the cause of workingman. In 1911, he moved to Cleveland to assume editorship of *Americké Dělnické Llisty*. In 1920, he moved to New York and became editor of *Práce,* publication of amalgamated tailors. In 1932, he became editor of *Spravedlnost* in Chicago.

Jan A. Oliverius (1843-1904), b. Kralovice, nr. Plzeň, Bohemia, came to US in 1865, settling in St. Louis, where he became editor of *Pozor Americký*. He published and/or edited as many as 16 periodicals which earned him nickname 'newspaper grave digger.'

Lev J. Palda (1897-1913), b. Vodňany, Bohemia, came to US in 1867. After a few difficult years, he was offered editorship of *Národní Noviny*, in which he announced, in its first issue, that the paper will have socialist orientation. In 1875, he became an editor of *Dělnické Listy* in Cleveland, which he co-founded with Frank Škarda, who, in turn, became the paper's publisher. The paper was later moved to New York.

Josef Pastor (1841-1899), b. Hostokreje, Bohemia, arrived in New York in 1866. There he earned 'niggardly' living at cigar making. Later he entered the service of the New York *Staatszeitung* as a stenographer. His letters to *Slavie* attracted the attention of Jonáš and Kořízek, who offered him the editorship of *Pokrok* (Progress) (1867). He resigned the following year and became editor of *Národní Noviny* (1868) and later of *Nová Doba* (1871). Wearied of the miseries of journalism, Pastor removed to Hamburg, Germany, where he established himself as a steamship ticket agent. During his residence in Hamburg, he issued a periodical *České osady v Americe* (Czech settlements in America) (1884-89), containing much useful statistical information.

Josef Boleslav Pecka (1849-1897), b. Prague, Bohemia, was a leader in the Czech labor movement. In 1885, he moved to Chicago, where he became editor of *Budoucnost* (1886-87), *Prace* (1887), *Dělnické Listy* (1887-92), *Pravda Lidu* (1893-94).

Jožka Pejskar (1912-1999), b. Malá Skalice, Bohemia, served as Secretary of the Czechoslovak National Party (1935-38) and after the war, he became editor of *Slovo národa* (The Word of the Nation) in Brno. Following the communist putsch in 1968, he was dismissed. After escaping to Germany, he worked as editor for Radio Free Europe in New York and then in Munich (1951-79). He also co-founded the exile periodical *České slovo* (The Czech Word). He also authored a number of books, including *Pronásledovaní vlastenci* (The Persecuted Patriots)

(1987) and *Poslední pocta* (The Last Honor) (1982-89) and *Útěky železnou oponou* (Gateways through the Iron Curtain) (1989).

Ferdinand Peroutka (1895-1978), b. Prague, Czechoslovakia, was an eminent Czech-American journalist and writer. Beginning in the early 1950s, Peroutka took an active part in building Radio Free Europe. He was chief editor of Czechoslovak broadcasting and wrote more than a thousand commentaries called 'Sunday Talks' that were beamed to Czechoslovakia. He was also a dramatist and novelist.

Rudolf Jaromír Pšenka (orig. Pšenička) (1875-1939), b. Jindřichův Hradec, Bohemia, was a Czech-American, journalist, writer, and playwright. He was a Post Office employee in Poděbrady and Tábor (1893-95), soldier of the French Foreign Legion at Algiers (1895-99) and teacher of French, and guide and organizer of excursions from Bohemia to Paris (1900-01). Accepting a call from August Geringer, publisher of *Daily Svornost*, he came to Chicago in 1901. From 1901 to 1906, he was a member of the administrative staff, from 1906 to 1909, reporter, and since 1909, he had been editor-in-chief of *Daily Svornost*. He had also been the author of a number of novels, such as *Washington Závora, Mlhami Jitra, A přece Cech, Dabel Kalinský, Čisťoucký Pationo, Versus Čermák, Šarlatánka, Veřím v člověka, Marabut, Dolary a krev*, and *Martin Carson*. He was also president of the Bohemian Arts Club of Chicago and president of the Smetana Singing Society of Chicago. He was co-founder and editor-secretary of the Bohemian American Press Bureau (1909-15) and one of the leaders of the movement for the Czech independence and founding of Czechoslovakia.

František K. Ringsmuth (1858-1937), b. Dobříš, Bohemia, in 1885, came to Omaha, NE, where for 2 years edited the *Květy Americké*, for which he also wrote a number of poems. Later he was associated with the weeklies *Nová Doba* and *Svit* in Schuyler, NE.

Věra Marie Rollerová (1940-2011), b. Zlín, Czech.; in Canada s. 1979; was a journalist and writer. She was educated at Charles University in cultural sociology (Dipl., 1973). She worked as a freelance journalist for Radio Free Europe. In 1990, he was appointed a chief editor of Czech Canadian paper, *Nový Domov*. Her interests included: cultural sociology, adult education and writing short stories.

Rose Rosicky (aka Rosická) (1875-1954), b. Crete, NE, of Czech ancestry (daughter of Jan Rosický), after her father's death, became associate editor of *Osvěta Americká, Hospodář* and *Květy Americké*. She edited five volumes of the almanac *Pioneer* for which she prepared translations.

Václav Šnajdr (1847-1920), b. České Budějovice, Bohemia, came to America in 1869, where he became journalist. He first worked for *Slavie* in Racine, WI, then for *Pokrok Západu* in

Omaha, NE and then in Cleveland, OH. In 1873, he founded in Cleveland a radical paper *Dennice Novověku* (Morning Star of the New Era) which he edited until 1910. Under his editorship, the *Dennice Novověku* clearly became the most literate of all Czech language papers published in US at that time. Later he also published a Sunday paper, *Jednota Osvojených* (1883-86) and from 1891 to 1896, he published *Orgán Bratrstva*. He also wrote poetry. With the exception of Jonáš, Šnajdr was clearly the most influential Czech American journalist.

Jaroslav E. S. Vojan (1872-1944), b. Prague. Bohemia, although trained as a lawyer and economist, he had has chosen the career of a journalist, and publicist and cultural worker. After receiving his law degree at Charles University (1898), he became Professor of national economics at the Czechoslovak Commercial College in Prague (1809-1904). During 1903-04, he edited *Nová Česká Revue* and, for 4 years, was a member of the Central Committee of the Ustřední matice školská, for two years was Secretary of the Národní jednota severočeská and Secretary of the Commercial Museum in Prague. In 1904, he arrived in New York and became a member of the editorial staff of *New Yorské Listy* and *Hlas Lidu* and contributor to *Osvěta Americká*. He founded the Society of Friends of Czech Literature and assisted in organizing a Czech department in Webster's Public Library. In 1909, he was appointed General Manager of the Czech-American Press Bureau in Chicago. There he also edited *Organ Bratrstva ČSPS* for nine years and for four years edited weekly *Slavie*. During the World War, he organized the first conference of the Czech National Association in Cleveland with the cooperation of others, he founded the *V boj!* periodical. In 1916, he became advertising manager of Joseph Triner Co. In 1912, he organized the Bohemian Arts Club and had been its president many times since. He was also chairman of the Program Committee of the Czechoslovak Group of A Century of Progress and was editor of the *World's Fair Czechoslovak Memorial* booklet. He was also one of the leaders of the Czech Rationalistic Movement which had been started by Vojta Náprstek in 1849 and since 1924, had been Secretary of the National Executive Committee of the Czechoslovak Rationalistic Federation of America.

F. B. Zdrůbek (1842-1911), b. Bezdědice, Bohemia, educated as a Protestant minister, became one of the early editors of the *Pokrok Západu*. For many years, he was editor of the Chicago daily *Svornost*.

2. Slovak-Language Journalists

Anton Štefan Ambrose (Ambrosi) (1867-1941), b. Kobyly, Bardejov District, Slovakia, was a pioneer journalist and cultural worker. He came to the US in 1882. He founded the oldest Slovak magazine *Slovák in America* (1889, Plymouth). He was also a co-founder of the National Slovak Association (1890), serving as its chairman (1901-12). During the First World War, he activated the Czech-Slovak foreign resistance through the Slovak League in America and recruited volunteers from the ranks of American Slovaks into the Czechoslovak army in France. In 1921-38, he served as Press Secretary of the Czechoslovak Government in Prague, responsible for information for the expatriate press. In 1938, he returned to the USA.

Julius Behul (fl. 2012), a Slovak Canadian, was the editor-in-chief of *Kanadsky Slovák*.

Charles (Karol) Belohlavek (1886-1942), b. Holíč, Slovakia, was a printer, publisher, and a journalist. In 1912, Belohlavek settled in Pittsburgh, where he became the editor of *Slovensky Hlasnik*, the newspaper of the Slovak Evangelical Union. He also worked in the editorial offices of the National Slovak Society. Before and during World War I, Belohlavek was a leader in the movement to establish an independent Czechoslovak Republic. He moved to Detroit in 1944, where he founded the Slovak Radio Circle and hosted a half-hour radio program. In 1952, Belohlavek and his second wife, Maria Jergo Belohlavek, founded Slovak Garden, a retirement community for American Slovaks in Maitland, Florida. He was also a publisher and editor of *Floridsky Slovak*.

Ivan Bielek (1886-1941), b. Slovakia, was a businessman, journalist and Fraternalist. He was vice-president and director of the Czechoslovak Commercial Corp. of America, an import company. He was editor of *The National News*, Pittsburgh, PA; president of Slovak League of America, and signatory of the Pittsburgh Agreement.

Ján E. Bor (pseudonym of Dr. Ernest Žatko) (1907-1991), b. Žabokreky, Slovakia, trained as a linguist, he held the post of professor of Roman literature at University of Bratislava. He became a columnist and traveled abroad; in 1948 he immigrated to Argentina, where he remained, working as a journalist.

John Cieker (1912-1993), Slovak American, resided in Parma and then in Cleveland, OH. He was editor, of *Živena,* monthly, Pittsburgh, PA.

John Denďúr (1898-1988), b. Petrovec, Yugoslavia, of Slovak ancestry, was a printer, teacher, journalist, and publisher. In 1920, he came to America and in 1923 settled in Chicago. From 1923 to 1930, he was teacher in the Slovak Workers School, Cicero, IL. He was Secretary of the Slovak Socialist Federation (1923-26) and linotype operator for *Rovnost Ludu* and *Spravedlnost* (1926-30). Subsequently, he became editor of *Náš Svet*, a Slovak weekly. He was also educator and dramatic director of the Slovak Workers Society. He was editor of *Náš Svet*, a Slovak weekly, and dramatic director of the Slovak Worker's Society.

Rudolf Dilong (1905-1986), b. Trstená, Slovakia, R.C. priest, O.F.M. was author and journalist. He was an editor of *Listy svatého Františka* (Leaflets of Saint Francis), monthly, Pittsburgh, PA

Ján Eliáš (1910-), b. Jaklovce, Slovakia, was a teacher and editor of *Slovenska Ocine* (1961-64). He was a contributor to Slovak periodicals in Canada.

John Adolf Feriencik (1865-1925), b. Zvolen, Slovakia; in US s. 1894; journalist, writer; editor of *Slovenský Hlásnik* (Slovak Herald), the weekly publication of the Slavonic Evangelical Union of America. He was also the founder of the *Osveta* magazine in Cleveland.

Jozef Filek (1867-1905), b. Slovakia, was a journalist. He was editor, *Slovenské katolicke noviny* (Hazelton, PA).

Milan Alexander Getting (1878-1951), b. Bytča, Slovakia, was a journalist and politician. He immigrated to Pittsburgh in 1902. In the years 1905-1919, he published the newspaper *Slovenský Sokol*. In the years 1914-1918, he organized a campaign in the USA, which prepared the visit of TG Masaryk, and during his visit, he was one of the signatories of the Pittsburgh Agreement of 1918. In 1919, at the invitation of Vavro Šrobár, he returned temporarily to Czechoslovakia, and later returned to the United States as head of the press department of the Czechoslovak Embassy in Washington. He then served as Czechoslovak Consul in Western Pennsylvania (1924-32).

Thomas B. Harnyak (1894-1987), b. South Side, PA, of Slovak descent; R.C. priest, pastor of churches in Fairchance and Shoaf and Whitaker, before moving to St. Joachim at Greenfield, PA; editor of *Svornost* (Harmony), bi-monthly, Pittsburgh, PA.

Stefan Hreha (1918-2015), b. Čemerné, Slovakia; in Canada since 1936; founder of the weekly *Kanadský Slovak* (The Canadian Slovak) and its first editor (1942-53). This was the official organ of the Canadian Slovak League, which has the distinction of being the only surviving Slovak weekly in North America that has been published, without interruption, for over 70 years. In 1952, he was hired by *Crane Canada* where he rose to the position of Advertising Production Manager.

Philip Anthony Hrobak (1904-1964), b. Cleveland, OH, of Slovak descent; editor of *Jednota*, manager of *Jednota* printery, and author, Middletown, PA.

Joseph Hušek (1880-1947), b. Ružomberok, Slovakia, was a journalist. He emigrated to the US in 1903 and worked in journalism and the Slovak League of America. He was editor and manager of *Jednota* (s. 1904).

Stephen Huska (1888-1973), b. Brezová, Slovakia, was a Fraternalist, teacher, and journalist. He went to Vienna in 1902 and attended a trade school for two years. Then worked in Budapest for two years and attended another trades school. Coming to America in 1906, he worked for different concerns and was active in the Slovak Sokol organizations. In 1918, he became teacher of Sokol gymnastics, then Division Director in Chicago, Assistant General Director of the Slovak Gymnastic Union Sokol (1910-16) and from 1917 to 1920, General Director of that organization. At the same time, he was editor of the technical section of the Slovensky Sokol periodical. In 1915, he was in starting the *Tatran* monthly and in March 1918, he was co-founder of the *Nové Časy*, a Slovak national weekly. In 1920, he became the editor of this periodical. His office was in Chicago on south Halsted Street.

Teresa 'Terri' Ivanec (1954-), b. Cleveland, OH, of Slovak descent; her grandmother was born in Orava, Slovakia; a holder of a Master's degree in English from the University of Kansas. She spent a decade in Atlanta, Georgia, where she honed her skills as an in-house magazine editor and senior writer for Dun & Bradstreet Software. Returning to Cleveland in 1990s, she worked as an article writer, newsletter editor, and magazine contributor for some of the Midwest's premier manufacturers, healthcare organizations, advertising and public relations agencies, and community leaders. Since January 2000, she has held the position of editor of Slovak newspaper *Jednota*.

Ján Janček, Jr. (1881-1933), b. Ružomberok, Slovakia; news editor, writer; founder and editor *Slovenský Sokol* (1905).

Matúš Jankola (1872-1916), b. Budapest, of Slovak parents, R.C. priest, was a writer, playwright, editor, publisher and leading expatriate national official and organizer of the life of American Slovaks. He emigrated to the US in 1893. He was a long-time chief official and chairman of the First Slovak Catholic Women's Union, a publisher and for a short time also the editor of its press organ *Jednota* (1910). He contributed to compatriot newspapers, magazines and calendars, his journalistic work was predominantly religious in nature, but also fulfilled national awareness goals.

J. Jesenský, b. Slovakia, was a journalist. He was first editor of *Rovnosť ľudu* (Equality of People), Chicago, IL (s. 1906). It was the oldest Slovak-language labor union periodical in America. He supported the radical Social Democratic Party in America.

Ondrej E. Komara (1883-1932), b. Levoča, Slovakia, R.C. priest, was editor and writer. He helped found magazine *Ave Mária* and *Božské Srdce Ježiša* (Sacred Heart of Jesus).

Martin Kopunek (1889-1959), Slovak American, was a Fraternal leader, editor of *Dobrý Pastier* (Good Shepherd), the periodical of the Slovak Catholic Federation.

Edward Kovac (1901-), b. Zvolen, Slovakia, was editor of *Narodne Noviny* (National News), semi-monthly, Pittsburgh (s. 1910); and editor of *Slovenska Obrana*.

I. INFORMATION RESOURCES

John Kovacik (1905-2000), b. Necpaly, Slovakia, Lutheran minister, was a co-editor of *Sion* (Zion), monthly, Pittsburgh, PA.

Joseph Charles Krajsa (1917-1998), b. Allentown, PA, of Slovak ancestry, was a Slovak Fraternalist, editor of *Jednota* (Union), Catholic Slovak weekly, Middletown, PA (s. 1964); and also, editor of *Kalendar* and Annual *Furdek* (s. 1964).

Jozef Borivoj Krčméry (1865-1925), b. Badín, Slovakia, was a publicist, journalist, and banker, Pittsburgh, PA.

Michal Laucik (1878-1965), b. Vrbica, Slovakia, was a grocer, journalist, and teacher. He immigrated to the US, in 1901, settling in Chicago. He was connected with the Superior Tanning Co. (1911-13); with the Jonas Greenbaum Tanning Co. (1911-24) and the owner of a grocery store (1924-25). Subsequently, he became Elder of the Young Folk's Circle of the National Slovak Society of America and editor of its organ, the *Kruh Mládeže*. He was a contributor to *Národné Noviny*, the *Nové Časy* and the Almanc of the National Slovak Society. He had also been instructor for twenty-five years in the Slovak National Evening School.

George Stephen Luba (1897-1961), b. Budapest, of Slovak descent, R.C. priest, O.S.B., was a teacher, St. Procopius Academy (1917-27); founder and principal of Benedictine HS, Cleveland (s. 1927); pastor, St. Andrew's, Cleveland (1929-30); prior, St. Andrew's Abbey (1935-48); editor of *Ave Maria* (Slovak monthly) (s. 1936), *Ženská Jednota* bi-monthly (s. 1937)

Hubert Macko (1899-1971), b. Jaklovce, Slovakia; R.C. priest, O.S.B., was a pastor, teacher and editor of the Slovak Catholic weekly *Slovenský Svet* (s. 1926)

John Matlocha (1879-1944), b. Zvolen, Slovakia, was editor and publisher. He immigrated to the US in 1903, settling in Chicago in 1905. He was educated in the public and night schools of Zvolen and Banska Bystrica. He was a trustee of the Národný Slovenský Spolok and a member of the Slovak Gymnastic Union, the Tatran Slovak Union, etc. He was a co-founder of *Rovnosť Ludu*, a monthly with socialistic leanings up to the World War; he was its editor from 1912 to 1918. He was editor of *Tatran*, a monthly journal, a contributor to *Nové Časy* and a member of the Publication Committee for the Almancs of the National Slovak Society. He was also the owner of the Mally Press, Printers and Binders Co., residing in Chicago. He was the author of *Album Nového Slovenska* and *Co sa stalo v Národnom Slovenskem Spolku*. His office was in Chicago, on South Halstead Street.

Stanislav Mečiar (1910-1971), b. Previdza, Slovakia, was editor, poet, essayist, literary critic, historian, and translator. He worked for Matica slovenská in Martin (s. 1934). Since 1949, he resided in Argentina.

Ján Okáľ (1915-1990), b. Hubová, Slovakia, was a teacher, writer, and editor. He was Matica Slovenska employee. He emigrated to Italy, then to USA in 1950. He was editor, *Slovák v Amerike* (1951-58), *Literary Almanac of Slovak in America*, the *Bulletin of the World Congress of the Slovaks* (1979-90). He wrote prose, poetry, and books for children.

Stephen J. Palickar (1885-1955), b. Olyphant, PA, of Slovak immigrant parents; they came from Stropkov, Slovakia. He was professional journalist and writer.

Ján Pankúch (1869-1952), b. Prešov, Slovakia, was a newspaper editor and publisher. He was a long-time editor and publisher of *Hlas* (The Voice), Cleveland's only Slovak newspaper.

Draga Paučo (1922-2003), b. Slovakia, was editor, *Slovak v Amerike*, weekly, Middletown, PA (s. 1889).

Jaroslav John Pelikan, Sr. (1898-1974), b. Slovakia, was a Lutheran minister. He was pastor, Trinity Slovak Lutheran Church, Chicago, IL; president of the Slovak Alliance; editor, *Svedok* (The Witness), monthly, Pittsburgh, PA.

John Porubský (1874-1953), b. Zniev, Slovakia; R.C. priest, was a prolific writer and journalist.

František Pucher-Čiernovodský (1861-1905), b. Svätý Jur, Slovakia, was a journalist. He was editor of *Slovak v Amerike*.

Stephen Reistetter (1914-2006), b. Lipany, Slovakia, came to Canada in 1948 and worked for General Motors until his retirement. He edited *Kanadsky Slovak*. In 1955, he helped found the Nitra Folk Dancing group. He was charged with kidnapping of 3,000 Slovakian Jews in 1942 in Bardejov, Slovakia, but was acquitted for lack of evidence.

Peter Víťazoslav Rovnianek (1867-1933), b. Dolný Hričov, Slovakia, was a businessman, banker, journalist and the founder of Slovaktown, AR. He was the founder of the first Slovak newspaper in America; editor of several Slovak papers, especially the first Slovak daily in Pittsburgh.

Fedor Ivan Salva (1901-1988), b. Ružomberok, Slovakia, son of Karol Salva, was a journalist and national activist. He was an editor of *Slovenská Obrana* (Scranton) and *Národné Noviny*. He was a member of the Slovak delegation which visited President Roosevelt in 1937.

Karol Salva (1849-1913), b. Liptovská Sielnica, Slovakia, was a teacher, journalist, publicist, and publisher. He was editor of *Amerikánsko-Slovenské Novíny, Rarášek* and *Slovenský Denník*, published in Pittsburgh.

Edward Schwartz-Markovič (1850–1933), b. Ťepla, Slovakia, was a pioneer journalist in Streator, IL. He was publisher of *Nova Vlast* (New Home).

John C. Sciranka (1902–1980), b. Allegheny City, PA, of Slovak descent, was an outstanding Slovak American Fraternalist and a journalist. He was editor of *Katolicky Sokol*, residing in Passaic, NJ.

Ján 'Janko' Slovenský (1856–1900), b. Krompachy, Slovakia, originally a Slovak businessman, he became a journalist, editor and prominent figure among the compatriots in the US. He was the founder of mimeographed weekly *Bulletin,* Pittsburgh, PA. Together with Julius Wolf, they published *Amerikanszko-Szlovenszke Noviny* (American-Slovak News).

Joseph Staško (1917–1997), b. Sedliacka Dubová, Slovakia, was a journalist and retired librarian. He was editor and writer for the *SKS Bulletin* and for the periodical *Horizont*.

Anna Chladek Sutherland (1954–2019), b. Spišská Nova Ves, Slovakia, was an editor of Slovak section, *Jednota* newspaper.

Anthony X. Sutherland (1944–), b. Stony Point, NY, of Slovak descent, was a historian and editor of Slovak-American newspaper *Jednota* (1995–2009).

Adalbert Tholt-Veľkoštiavnický (1852–1940), b. Ružomberok, Slovakia, was editor of several Slovak-American newspapers, including *Slovenská svornosť*, Connelsville, PA (1896), *Slovák v Amerike, Slovenský denník* and, in 1905–1909, he was editor of *Amerikánsko-ruský viestnik*.

Stephen J. Tkach (1894–1981), was editor of *Bratrstvo* (Brotherhood), monthly, Wilkes-Barre, PA (s. 1899).

Wendel Tylka (1889–1977), b. Námestovo, Slovakia, was a journalist and editor. He immigrated to the US in 1913. He studied printing at St. Procopius, Lisle, IL; founded Tylka Brothers Press, Chicago; and edited, with Peter Hletko, a Catholic weekly, *Osadné hlasy* (Community Voice).

Stephen Varzaly (1890–1957), b. Fulianka, Slovakia, was a leading priest, journalist, and cultural activist for Rusyns in the United States. From 1930 to 1937, Varzaly served as editor-in-chief of *Amerikansky Russky Viestnik* (1892–1952), the longest-running Rusyn-American newspaper in America and the official publication of the Greek Catholic Union of Rusyn Brotherhoods, a fraternal benefit society based in Pennsylvania. Many Carpatho-Rusyns, including Varzaly, believed clerical celibacy to be so inherently unnatural as to lead inevitably to promiscuity and sexual abuse. During the celibacy conflict, Varzaly used the newspaper to argue against *Cum Data Fuerit* and for continuation of a traditional married clergy within the Church. He joined, eventually, with the other clergy and laity to formally fight the Pope's decree.

Július Wolf (1860–1930), b. Krompachy, Slovakia, a journalist, together with Ján Slovenský, was publisher of *Amerikanszko-Szlovenszke Noviny* (American-Slovak News). It was written in eastern dialect with Magyar orthography with pro-Hungarian political leaning.

Jozef Žák-Marušiak (1885–1979), b. Laksárska Nová Ves, Slovakia, was editor of *Národné Noviny*, Pittsburgh and *Rovnost Ľudu*, Chicago.

Julius Žorna-Horský (1865–1902), b. Slovakia; editor, *Americko-Slovenské Noviny*, Cleveland (s. 1886); *Bulletin*, Pittsburgh 1885–86); *Americký Slovak*, Cleveland (s. 1892); *Bratrstvo* (s. 1899).

3. English-Language Journalists

Anton Štefan Ambrose (Ambrosi) (1867–1941), b. Kobyly, Bardejov District, Slovakia, lived in the US s. 1882. He was a pioneer journalist, the founder of *Slovak v Amerike*, the oldest newspaper and still in print in the US.

Robert Lyman 'Bob' Adren (1940–2008), b. Wyeville, WI, of Czech ancestry, graduated from Denver High School before attending the University of Iowa. He began his career in journalism as a reporter for United Press International in Indianapolis and Detroit. He later worked in public relations for General Electric in Schenectady, N.Y., and Louisville, Ky., then relocated to Des Moines, Iowa, as an editor for the Meredith Publishing Co. After moving to Sarasota, FL in 1976, he became director of public affairs at the John and Mabel Ringling Museum of Art, where he was also curator of the Ringling Circus Museum for a time. He was a museum employee for 16 years. For 20 years, Adren wrote a weekly column for the *Tampa Tribune* called 'Suncoast Shelter' about the Southwest Florida housing industry. He was also a contributing writer for Sarasota magazine and for *The Islander* newspaper on Anna Maria Island. In 1994, he joined the Pelican Press, a weekly newspaper based on Siesta Key, as a reporter and columnist. He wrote extensively about the city of Sarasota in news articles and his twice-monthly column, 'Main Street Beat,' covering life and events in downtown Sarasota. He expressed his longtime interest in local waters, boating and the environment in another twice-monthly Pelican column, 'Sarasota Waters.' He was the recipient of multiple writing awards from the Florida Press Association. He was a former president of the Florida Attractions Association and a founding member of the Sarasota-Manatee Press Club.

Meyer Berger (1898–1960), New York City, of Czech immigrant father, was an American journalist, considered one of the finest newspaper reporters. He was also known for "About New York", a long-running column in *The New York Times*, and for his centennial history of that paper. Since the year after his death, Columbia School of Journalism annually gives the Berger Award to a reporter for outstanding local reporting. Berger won the annual Pulitzer Prize for Local Reporting in 1950.

Jonas (ben Abraham) Bondi (1804-1874), b. Dresden, of Bohemian ancestry, was American Rabbi and journalist. He became the proprietor and editor of the Jewish paper, *The Hebrew Leader*, published in English and German.

(Oscar) Henry Brandon (1916-1993), b. Liberec, Bohemia, was educated at the Universities of Prague and Lausanne, Switz., and moved to London in 1939. He joined *The Sunday Times* as a freelance contributor, then served as a war correspondent (1943-45), Paris correspondent (1945-46), and roving diplomatic correspondent (1947-49) before moving to Washington, DC. A man of natural charm and discretion, Brandon cultivated close ties with US presidents and Cabinet members. In 1983, Brandon retired from *The Sunday Times,* of which he had been associate editor from 1963, but he remained at the center of things as a columnist for *The New York Times World Syndicate* and a guest scholar with the Brookings Institution (1983-93). Brandon's books include *The Retreat of American Power* (1973) and *Special Relationships* (1989). He was made Commander of the Order of the British Empire in 1985.

Helen Epstein (1947-), b. Prague, Czech., is a journalist and nonfiction author. She grew up in New York City, and graduated from Hunter College High School, Hebrew University, and the Columbia Graduate School of Journalism. She became a journalist at the age of 20, while caught in the Soviet Invasion of Czechoslovakia. Her account was published in *The Jerusalem Post* and she has been a journalist ever since. Her articles and reviews have appeared in many major American publications and include profiles of art historian Meyer Schapiro and musicians Vladimir Horowitz and Leonard Bernstein. She was the first tenured woman journalism professor in New York University (1981) and taught about 1000 students over 12 years. She guest lectures extensively at universities, libraries and religious institutions in North America and abroad. She is the author, coauthor, translator or editor of ten books of narrative non-fiction including the memoirs *Children of the Holocaust* and *Where She Came From: A Daughter's Search for Her Mother's History*; the biography of theater producer Joseph Papp; Heda Kovaly's *Under a Cruel Star*, Paul Ornstein's *Looking Back: Memoir of a Psychoanalyst*, and the tribute anthology *Archivist on a Bicycle*. Her most recent book, published January 8, 2018, is *The Long Half Lives of Love and Trauma*. It was published in English and Czech in 2018. She is married to Patrick Mehr (ca. 1945) and they have 2 children.

Martha Gellhorn (1908-1998), b. St. Louis, of Bohemian ancestry, was an American novelist, travel writer, and journalist, considered by *The London Daily Telegraph*, among others, to be one of the greatest war correspondents of the 20th century. She reported on virtually every major world conflict that took place during her 60-year career. Gellhorn was also the third wife of American novelist Ernest Hemingway, from 1940 to 1945.

Francis Grund (1805–1863), b. Liberec, Bohemia, was a pioneer American journalist and editor. He wrote for such newspapers as *Standard*, the German-language *Der Pennsylvanisch Deutsche*, *Mercury* and *Evening Journal*, *Public Ledger*, and *Sun*.

Nikole Sheri Hannah-Jones (1976–), b. Waterloo, IA, of Czech mother and African American father, is an American investigative journalist, known for her coverage of civil rights in the United States. In April 2015, she became a staff writer for *The New York Times*. In 2017, she was awarded a MacArthur Fellowship and in 2020, she won the Pulitzer Prize for Commentary for her work on the controversial 'The 1619 Project'. Hannah-Jones is the inaugural Knight Chair in Race and Journalism at the Howard University School of Communications, where she will also find the Center for Journalism and Democracy.

Wanda Jablonski (1920–1992), b. Moravia, Czech., was an American journalist who covered the global petroleum industry. She founded *Petroleum Intelligence Weekly* in 1961, which came to be known as the "bible of the oil industry" and ran it until 1988. She was called "the most influential oil journalist of her time."

Edward Victor Koterba (1919–1961), b. Omaha, NE, of Czech ancestry, was a columnist for the Scripps-Howard newspapers and United Features Syndicate. Before that, he was reporter and feature writer with the *Washington Rimes Herald* and *Washington Post*. He traveled widely with John F. Kennedy during the latter's campaign for the Presidency.

David Krajicek (1955–), b Omaha, NE, of Czech ancestry, is a writer, newspaper columnist, and journalism professor. In 1991, he joined the faculty at Columbia's Graduate School of Journalism. He is a special correspondent for the *New York Daily News*, for which he writes 'The Justice Story,' a long-running Sunday crime feature.

Arne Laurin (1889–1945), b. Hrnčíř, near Prague, Bohemia, was editor-in-chief of the *Prager Presse,* official Czech. govt. organ (1918–39). In 1939, he came to the US, where he became in charge of the Index Dept., Czechoslovak Information Service in NYC.

Isidor Lewi (1850–1939), b. Albany, of Bohemian father, was initiated to news-gathering on the old *Albany Morning Express*. Later he became a correspondent for the *Albany Argus*. In 1891, he joined the staff of *The New York Tribune*. He began as a reporter and then became special writer, copy editor and a contributor to the editorial page.

Teresa Mahoney (ca. 1987–), b. Portland, OR, daughter of Daniela Šípková (1955–) from Prague, Czech., and Patrick Michael Mahoney, is a video journalist at *The Oregonian*, producing everything from animated investigative explainers to social-friendly, breaking news and feature videos. Teresa came to *The Oregonian* after working as a video manager and trainer at *Mint* newspaper in New Delhi, India's second largest financial daily. There, she oversaw a team of video producers and animators and taught the newsroom to shoot video with cell phones and DSLR cameras. She previously taught multimedia journalism including video, audio, and basic web development as a digital media fellow at the Columbia Graduate School of Journalism, from where she graduated in 2012. Teresa won first place 2016 National Headliner Award for online videography and was nominated for a 2016 regional Emmy for her explanatory video on how *Salmonella* spreads. She won two gold medal MarCom awards in the corporate image and self-promotion categories for a corporate video she produced. Her work has been screened at The Craft Film Festival in London.

Janet Malcolm (1934–2031), b. Prague, Czech., journalist, New Yorker staff writer, an American writer, staff journalist at *The New Yorker* magazine, and collagist, who fled antisemitic persecution in Nazi-occupied Prague just before it became impossible to escape. She was the author of *Psychoanalysis: The Impossible Profession* (1981), *In the Freud Archives* (1984), and *The Journalist and the Murderer* (1990). Malcolm wrote frequently about psychoanalysis and explored the relationship between journalist and subjects. She was known for her prose style and for polarizing criticism of her profession, especially in her most contentious work, *The Journalist and the Murderer*, which has become a staple of journalism-school curricula.

Rudolph 'Rudy' Joseph Maxa, Jr. (1949–), b. Cleveland, OH, of Czech ancestry, was a columnist and reporter for 13 years with the *Washington Post*, a senior writer and columnist for nine years with *Washingtonian* magazine, and Washington bureau chief of *SPY* magazine for two years. A member of the Writer's Guild of America, Mr. Maxa has written dramatic scripts for the ABC TV series *Capital News* and hosted for several years a four-hour, Saturday morning talk show on the NBC-owned-and-operated station in Washington, WRC-AM. He then began covering the travel industry for public radio's evening business show, *Marketplace* where his bi-weekly commentaries under his moniker, "The Savvy Traveler", were then heard by nearly five million listeners. His award-winning, 65-part public television series, *Smart Travels: Europe with Rudy Maxa*, aired on public television stations coast-to-coast.

Mark R. Neuzil (1958–), b. Eldora, IA, of Czech ancestry, studied journalism and political science at Iowa State (Univ. (B.A., 1980) and mass communications at Univ. of Minnesota (M.A., 1991; Ph.D., 1993). He was asst. sports editor with *Ames Daily Tribune* (1980-82); reporter for *Quad-City Times*, Davenport (1982-87); reporter for *Cedar Rapids Gazette* (1987–

89); newsman for *Associate Press*, Minneapolis (1992-93) and editor/reporter for *Minneapolis Star Tribune* (1997-98, 2003-04). Since 1993, he has held the position of professor at Univ. of St. Thomas, St. Paul. He specializes in environmental journalism, environmental policy, communications history and nature writing. He authored a number of books, including *Environmental Crises in Central Asia: From Steppes to Seas, from Deserts to Glaciers* (with Eric Freedman), *A Cultural History of the North American Canoe* (with Norman Sims), *The Environment and the Press: From Adventure Writing to Advocacy* (2008), *A Spiritual Field Guide: Meditations for the Outdoors* (with Bernard Brady) (2005), *Views on the Mississippi: The Photographs of Henry Peter Bosse* (2001), *Writing Across the Media* (with K. Bunton, D. Nimmer, T. Connery and S. Kanihan) (1999), *Mass Media and Environmental Conflict: America's Green Crusades* (with William Kovarik) (1996). He was named the 2013 Univ. of St. Thomas Professor of the Year and in 2008, he was a recipient of the James A. Tankard Award for the best book from the Assn. for Education in Journalism and Mass Communication.

Barnet Phillips (1826-1905), b. Philadelphia, PA, of Bohemian ancestry, was an American journalist, long been regarded as among the ablest writers for the press. Since 1872, Phillips has occupied an important position on *The New York Times*. His work has been that of literary editor, and many a brilliant article has borne evidence to his scholarship and critical acumen. He has likewise written works of fiction.

Robert Reguly (1931-2011), b. Fort William, Ont., Canada, of Slovak parents, was a three-time National Newspaper Award-winning journalist. He was one of Canada's top news reporters in the 1950s and 1960s. He was at the forefront of the mid-20th century news war between the *Toronto Telegram* and the *Toronto Star*. In 1981, he became a spokesperson for the Ontario Ministry of the Environment. After his retirement, he became a successful freelance writer, writing mainly for outdoors magazines.

Edward Rosewater (1841-1906), b. Bukovany, Bohemia, was a newspaper editor and politician. He was the founder of the daily *The Omaha Daily Bee* which developed into the largest and most influential newspaper of the mid-west.

Rosa Sonneschein (1847-1932), b. Prostějov, Moravia, a rebbetzin and journalist, as one of the best-known society women in St. Louis, a prominent figure in literary circles, and an active worker in the field of charity, independent of creed or nationality. In 1879, she founded the Pioneers, a Jewish women's literary society. Modeled on similar Christian women's clubs, the Pioneers devoted themselves not to studying Jewish literature but to cultivating general literary taste and knowledge. In 1895 (through 1899), she founded the *American Jewess*, the first English-language magazine for Jewish women in the US, to be voice and forum for American Jewish women. Throughout the run of the magazine, Sonneschein was an advocate for the expansion of women's role in the synagogue and the Jewish community. She pushed Temple Isaiah, Chicago to become the world's first synagogue to admit women to full membership without restrictions. She was also among the US first Zionists and advocated for Zionism in the *American Jewess* pages. She viewed Zionism as a potential source of relief for oppressed Jews in Eastern Europe and a source of pride and countermeasure to assimilation for Jews in America and Eastern Europe.

Linda Steiner (1950–), b. Schenectady, NY, of Czech immigrant parents, attended Smith College and earned her Doctorate at the Institute of Communications Research at the University of Illinois, Urbana Champaign (Ph.D., 1979). Her first full-time faculty position was at Governors State University, in Illinois. (1978-91). She was then with Rutgers Univ. (1991-2006), until her appointment as professor at Merrill College of Journalism, Univ. of Maryland (s. 2006). Her research areas include public and citizen journalism, media history, the alternative and new media, and, most centrally, women in the media, and feminist ethics. Steiner is a coauthor of *And Baby Makes Two: Motherhood without Marriage* (1984) and *Women and Journalism* (2004); and author of a monograph *Conceptions of Gender in Reporting Textbooks, 1890-1990* (1992). She has co-edited three books, most recently *The Routledge Companion to Media and Gender* (2013). In 2011, she was named Outstanding Woman of the Year in Journalism and Mass Communication Education by the Association for Education in Journalism and Mass Communication.

Mike Stoklasa (1978–), b. Illinois, US, of Czech descent, is a director, actor, and creator of Red Letter Media. He is best known for *The Phantom Menace Review* (2009), *Attack of the Clones Review* (2010) and *Revenge of the Sith Review* (2010). His great-grandparents were Václav Stoklasa from Chotusice and Josefa Brčková from Jestřebice.

Judith Sulzberger (Judith Peixotto Sulzberger) (1923-2011), b. New York, NY, of Czech Jewish descent, was an American physician and philanthropist. Her family has been associated with *The New York Times* since her grandfather, Adolph Ochs purchased the paper in 1896. She was the director of *The New York Times* from 1974 to 2000. She authored a book *Younger* (2003). In the early 1990s, she provided financing for what became the J. P. Sulzberger Genome Center at Columbia's College of Physicians and Surgeons, her alma mater.

Lester Tanzer (1929-2004), of Bohemian ancestry, was reporter for *Wall Street Journal* (1952-59); assoc. editor, *Changing Times* magazine, Washington (1959-64); with *US News and World Report*, Washington, DC (1964-76), managing editor (1976-85). He was also a founding editor, *Cosmos Journal* (1990-93).

André Vltchek (1963-2020), b. Leningrad, Soviet Union, of Czech father, was an American political analyst, journalist, and a filmmaker. Vltchek was born in Leningrad but later became a naturalized U.S. citizen after being granted asylum there in his 20s. He was raised in Plzeň, Czechoslovakia before emigrating to the United States. Until his death, he was based in Asia and Africa. He lived in the United States, Chile, Peru, Mexico, Vietnam, Samoa, and Indonesia. Vltchek covered armed conflicts in Peru, Kashmir, Mexico, Bosnia, Sri Lanka, Congo, India, South Africa, East Timor, Indonesia, Turkey, and the Middle East. He traveled to more than 140 countries, and wrote articles for *Der Spiegel*, Japanese newspaper *The Asahi Shimbun*, *The Guardian*, ABC News and the Czech Republic daily *Lidové noviny*. From 2004, Vltchek served as a senior fellow at the Oakland Institute. He appeared on television and radio shows, including those broadcasts by France 24, China Radio International, the Voice of Russia, CCTV, Ulusal Kanal (Turkey), Al Mayadeen (Pan-Arabic network), Radio Pacifika, Radio Cape, among others.

Marilyn vos Savant (1946-), b. St. Louis, MO is the daughter of Joseph Mach and Mariana vos Savant, the former being of Czech descent, having descended from the noted physicist and philosopher Ernst Mach from Brno, Moravia. Marilyn is an American magazine columnist, author, lecturer, and playwright. She best known for having the highest recorded intelligence quotient (IQ) in the *Guinness Book of Records*. Since 1986, she has written "Ask Marilyn," a *Parade* magazine Sunday column where she solves puzzles and answers questions on various subjects. Among them was a discussion of the Monty Hall problem, to which she postulated an answer in 1990. After marrying Robert Jarvik (1946-), the developer of artificial heart, she was made Chief Financial Officer of Jarvik Heart, Inc. Toastmasters International named her one of "Five Outstanding Speakers of 1999", and in 2003 she was awarded an honorary Doctor of Letters degree from The College of New Jersey.

Leo Weidenthal (1878-1967), b. Cleveland, of Bohemian ancestry, was a journalist who worked for the *Cleveland World, Cleveland Leader*, then the *Plain Dealer*, for 11 years where he covered City Hall. On the death of his brother Maurice, he took over the *Jewish Independent* and was its publisher-editor for 47 years. They dubbed him 'Leo the Lion of Willowdale' for his journalistic tenacity; when he got on to a story or a cause, he never let go.

Jeffrey 'Jeff' Dean Zeleny (1973-), Exeter, NE, son of Robert Dean Zeleny and Diane Naomi Yeck, an American journalist and the chief national affairs correspondent for CNN. He previously was senior Washington correspondent for ABC News. During his newspaper career, he won a Pulitzer Prize with the *Chicago Tribune*.

4. German-Language Journalists

Oskar Benjamin Frank (1881–1955), b. Kroměříž, Moravia, was a writer educated at Univ. of Berlin and Vienna. He was in US s. 1941. He was a member of the staff on broadcasting questions, Office of Research, Columbia Univ.; later lecturer, Rand School of Social Science; and freelance journalist. He was the founder and exec. of Emerson-Goethe Society.

Heinrich Glücksmann (1864–1947), b. Rakšice, nearby Moravský Krumlov, was a Moravian-born author who lived in Argentina. He began his literary career at 16, one of his first writings being 'Aufsätze über Frauensitten und Unsitten,' which appeared in the *Wiener Hausfrauen-Zeitung* under the pseudonym Henriette Namskilg (other pseudonym is Fortunatus). He then became a teacher in the Vienna School of Acting. From 1882 to 1885, he was editor of the *Fünfkirchner Zeitung* (of Pécs), and from 1884 to 1886, held similar positions with the *Neue Pester Journal* and the *Polit'sche Volksblatt* of Budapest. In 1886, Glücksmann published an illustrated biographical edition of the works of Michael von Zichy, the painter; and in the same year he published a biography of Munkàcsy. Since that time, he had been active as a feuilletonist and dramatist.

Egon Erwin Kisch (1885–1948), b. Prague, Bohemia, was widely regarded as one of the most outstanding journalists of the 20th century. In 1939, he and his wife sailed for New York where he was initially denied entry. Since he only had a transit visa, he moved to Mexico in 1939. He remained in Mexico for the next five years. In this period of exile, Kisch's work regularly returned to the themes of his Prague home and his Jewish roots.

Anna Krommer (1924–), b. Dolný Kubín, Czech., of Moravian father, was a journalist. Until 1933, she resided in Berlin, then she immigrated to Prague and in 1939 to UK. In 1940–43, she studied at Technical Coll., Guildford, Surrey and in 1943–45, she studied history of art and drawing at School of Arts, London. In 1952, she immigrated to the US, living first in Boston, since 1953 in New York, and since 1962 in Washington, DC. She contributed to *Aufbau, New Yorker Staatszeitung* and *Herold, Literatur und Kritik, Frankfurter Hefte, Washington Journal, Mnemosyne* (Klagenfurt), *Mit der Ziehharmonika, Decision* (Hamburg).

Anne Laurin (1889–1945), b. Hrnčíře, near Prague, Bohemia, was editor-in-chief, *Prager Presse*, official Govt. organ (1918–39). She came to US in 1939. In US, she was in charge of index dept., Czechoslovak Information Service in NYC.

Alfred V. Krusenstiern (1929–2007), b. Prague, Czech., was a distinguished newspaper journalist who covered the United States for German readers. A man of great intellect and ironic wit, he spent the last 25 years of his career in New York writing for the German newspaper group Springer News (Axel Springer AG). He served as the bureau chief in New

York for *Springer Foreign News* from 1968 until 1989 and thereafter as the special correspondent to the US and Canada.

Anton Kuh (1890–1941), b. Vienna, of Bohemian parents, was a journalist and essayist. A monocle-wearing Bohemian, Kuh constructed his identity according to the concept of supranational Empire, timeless and not influenced by the national idea of State. Today, Anton Kuh is a long-forgotten writer, even among German and Austrian scholars. Kuh published biting, satirical works, and short pieces of prose, in them he confronted the problems of his days in Fin-de-siècle Vienna and interwar Vienna and Berlin, in a witty, ironic and critical way. In the numerous feuilletons, speeches and essays Kuh wrote, he expressed his growing skepticism in the German concept of the Geist, in the Spirit, and in its political meaning. In 1926, Kuh moved to Berlin, where he wrote for several newspapers and he even participated with Franz Blei in the film *Maria Stuart* from 1927. With Hitler's rise to power, Kuh, who was a Jew and seen by the Nazis as Kulturbolschewist, left for Paris, then Prague and London and finally emigrated to New York, where he died of a heart attack in 1941. In New York, he lived and published, in *Aufbau* and other magazines, under the pseudonym of Yorick and wrote against Nazism.

Robert Felix Lamberg (1929–), b. Liberec, Czech., was trained as a lawyer at Charles Univ. (JUDr., 1952). In 1957 he immigrated to Norway, where he worked as a journalist and, in 1963, he moved to Bonn as an editor-in-chief. In 1969–71, he taught history and sociology in Mexico. In the next six years, he worked as a correspondent for *Neue Zurcher Zeitung* (NZZ) on Wall Street and the United Nations in NYC. During 1977–85, he was based in Latin America, in Rio de Janeiro. He authored a number of books, including *Prag und die dritte Welt* (1966), *Die castristische Guerilla in Lateinamerika* (1977), *Nicaragua, von Somoza zu Ortega* (1985), *Bootspartie am Acheron* (2006).

Otto Leichter (1897–1973), b. Vienna, of Moravian parents, was a left-wing activist, journalist and author. He became editor of the major Austrian socialist newspaper *Die Arbeiter-Zeitung*. Together with his wife Käthe, they played active roles in the socialist underground in Austria after 1934. After the Anschluss in 1938, Leichter and his two sons succeeded escaping to Switzerland and subsequently found refuge in the US. His wife, unfortunately, was arrested, while paying a final visit to her mother, before attempting to flee to Czechoslovakia. She died in the Nazi concentration camp in 1942. He was the author of *Zwischen zwei Diktaturen*.

Oswald Ottendorfer (1826–1900), b. Svitavy, Moravia, educated at Univ. of Prague, was the editor and publisher of the *New York Staats-Zeitung* from 1859 to 1900. His journal, in which he endeavored to reflect the sentiments of German-Americans, became one of the most widely circulated and influential papers in New York.

Frederick Porges (1890–1977), b. Vienna, of Bohemian ancestry, studied philology at the University of Vienna and, apart from that, was interested in journalism. Before World War II, he was a writer at the daily newspaper *Die Zeit*, then at the *Morgen* (1924). He was a playwright for the film company Sascha Messter and Sascha. Later, he worked as a writer at the newspaper *Wiener Sonn- und Montagszeitung*. In 1924, Porges became writer in chief at the theater review *Bühne* and correspondent of the Viennese theater for the Berliner newspaper *Berliner Zeitung am Mittag*. In 1938, he immigrated to England via Switzerland. He worked as a journalist in London until he immigrated to the United States in 1945. He then became the correspondent of many newspapers and radio stations. He published his own newspaper *Allgemeine Theaterzeitung* (1912/13) and the weekly magazine *Mein Film*.

Georg Stefan Troller (1921–), Vienna, of Moravian father, after high school began training as a bookbinder, but Nazi violence forced the teenager to flee Vienna. In 1938 he immigrated – via France and North Africa – to the United States. Troller worked in a bookbindery from 1941 to 1943, when he joined the US. Army. During the last years of World War II, he was stationed in Europe and assigned to a division that questioned prisoners of war. Troller's company remained stationed in Munich until 1946. For several years after completing his military service, Troller studied English literature at the University of California, eventually returning, briefly, to Vienna and then Paris, in 1949, where he settled and began work as a journalist in 1951. Throughout a long career as a writer and journalist, Troller wrote for various radio and television programs broadcast in West Germany, including the radio program *Pariser Journal* which he produced for 10 years, and programs for ZDF. Troller had collaborated with director Axel Corti on several projects, including Young Dr. Freud (1976), before the two men teamed up on 'God Does Not Believe in Us Anymore,' 'Santa Fe,' and 'Welcome in Vienna,' three feature films which became the Where to and Back trilogy. The films, written by Troller and directed by Corti, are loosely based on Troller's experiences between 1938 and 1946.

Adolf Wiesner (orig. Wiener) (1807–1867), b. Prague, Bohemia, of Jewish family, was an Austrian journalist, playwright, author, and revolutionary who fled to the United States after the Revolutions of 1848. Although trained as a lawyer, he was primarily involved as a journalist and author. In 1852, he settled in New York, and it was due to his activity that the Schiller monument was erected in New York in 1859. In 1860, he edited the periodical *Geist der Weltliteratur*, which enjoyed but a brief existence. He afterward moved to Baltimore, where he edited the *Turn-Zeitung*. Early in 1866, he became editor of the *Illinois-Staatszeitung*.

5. Yiddish-Language Journalists

Sender Deutsch (1922–1998), b. Veľké Berezné, Czech., Rabbi, was leader of one of the largest Hasidic Jewish groups in the US, and the longtime chief editor of *Der Yid*, a Yiddish-language weekly newspaper. Rabbi Deutsch also founded another Yiddish-language newspaper, *Yiddische Zeitung*. But it ceased publication after a few years. *Der Yid* had a circulation of 50,000, including overseas subscriptions, at the time of his death. Using the pen name Eliezer Epstein, Rabbi Deutsch wrote columns and editorials for the newspaper. Rabbi Deutsch served as senior vice president of the World Council of Orthodox Jewish Communities, which was part of the class-action lawsuit against Swiss banks holding dormant Holocaust-era accounts. He also worked as a close aide to the current Satmar Grand Rabbi, Moses Teitelbaum, and his predecessor, Grand Rabbi Joel Teitelbaum.

6. TV & Radio Journalists

Abilio James 'Jim' Acosta (1971–), b. Washington, DC, of Irish and Czech ancestry on his mother's side, is an American broadcast journalist, who is an anchor and the chief domestic correspondent for CNN. Previously, Acosta served as the network's chief White House correspondent during the Trump administration, in which he gained national attention for President Donald Trump's clashes with him at press briefings. Acosta also covered the Obama administration as CNN's senior White House correspondent. As Trump was about to leave office, it was announced on January 11, 2021, that Acosta had been appointed CNN's Chief Domestic Correspondent.

Margot Susanna Adler (1946–2014), b. Little Rock, AR, of Bohemian ancestry, was an American author, journalist, lecturer, Wiccan priestess, and New York correspondent for National Public Radio (NPR). Adler received a Bachelor of arts in political science from the University of California, Berkeley and a Master's degree from the Columbia University Graduate School of Journalism in New York in 1970. She was a Nieman Fellow at Harvard University in 1982. Adler joined NPR in 1979 as a general assignment reporter, after spending a year as an NPR freelance reporter covering New York City, and subsequently worked on a great many pieces dealing with subjects as diverse as the death penalty, the right to die movement, the response to the war in Kosovo, computer gaming, the drug ecstasy, geek culture, children and technology and Pokémon. Since 9/11, she focused much of her work on stories exploring the human factors in New York City, from the loss of loved ones, homes and jobs, to work in the relief effort. She was the host of *Justice Talking* up until the show ceased production on July 3, 2008. She was a regular voice on *Morning Edition* and *All Things Considered*. She was also co-producer of an award-winning radio drama, *War Day*. Adler authored *Drawing Down the Moon* (1979), a book about Neopaganism, which is considered a watershed in American Neopagan circles, as it provided the first comprehensive look at modern nature-based religions in the US. Her second book was *Heretic's Heart: A Journey Through Spirit and Revolution* (1997). Adler was a Wiccan priestess in the Gardnerian tradition, an elder in the Covenant of the Goddess, and she also participated in the Unitarian Universalist faith community.

Tom Becka, b. Cleveland, OH, of Czech ancestry, is an American talk radio personality and was the host of the Tom Becka Show on 1290 KOIL in Omaha. He is known for his gravelly voice, and libertarian political views. For a number of years, he was heard on KFAB in Omaha. He left KFAB on October 26, 2011. His departure was due to Clear Channel Radio making cutbacks across the country. Becka has started blogging and podcasting at tombecka.com. While living in Albuquerque, he went to an open mike night at Laffs comedy club and figured he could do just as well as some of the people he was seeing there. The host of the open mike night was Marc Maron. He went on stage and got some good laughs and was soon spending all the time he could at the club and fighting for stage time. Becka spent a number of years on the road as a standup comic, working with acts including Jerry Seinfeld, Sam Kinnison and Lewis Black. Becka has hosted shows on KMBZ in Kansas City. He has written a book called *There's No Business without the Show: Using Showbiz Skills to Get Blockbuster Sales*.

Craig Bolerjack (1958–), b. Willow Springs, MO, of Moravian ancestry, is an American sportscaster. He is currently an announcer for FOX Sports and for Root Sports for Utah Jazz telecasts with Matt Harpring, working mostly college football and college basketball games. He has called college football and college basketball games for Fox Sports Net, FX, FOX, CBS, ESPN, and CBS College Sports. He called arena football games for ESPN as well as Miami Dolphins preseason games. He called regional NFL games for CBS until 2011. He is also the TV voice of the Utah Jazz. He filled in for Dick Stockton on the *NFL on Fox* on week four of the 2011 season between the Atlanta Falcons and the Seattle Seahawks.

Mike Cejka (1959–), b. New Bedford, MA, has been a broadcast meteorologist for WIVB since January 1983, making him the longest standing on-air meteorologist in the Buffalo television market.

Tony Dokoupil (1980–), b. CT, of Czech descent, is an American broadcast journalist, known for his work as a co-anchor of *CBS Mornings*. He was also a news correspondent for CBS News and MSNBC. He studied business at George Washington University, graduating first in his class, and pursued media studies at Columbia University. From 2007 to 2013, Dokoupil was a senior writer at *Newsweek* magazine and the website *The Daily Beast*. In September 2013, he joined NBC News as a senior writer. He released a memoir titled *The Last Pirate: A Father, His Son, and the Golden Age of Marijuana* in April 2014. He later became a reporter on MSNBC. Following his departure from NBC News and MSNBC, Dokoupil joined CBS News as a New York-based correspondent in August 2016. In May 2019, Dokoupil was named the new co-anchor of the morning program CBS *This Morning*; he made his debut on May 20. The program was renamed *CBS Mornings* in September 2021.

John C. Dvorak (1952–), b. Los Angeles, CA, of Czech ancestry, is a columnist and broadcaster in the areas of technology and computing.

Hana Gartner (1948–), b. Prague, Czech., is a Canadian television journalist, who has hosted a variety of programs for the Canadian Broadcasting Corp. Gartner won the Gordon Sinclair Award for excellence in broadcast journalism in 1985. She has also won three Gemini Awards.

Donna Hanover (née Donna Ann Kofnovec) (1950–), b. Oakland, CA, of Czech ancestry, is an American journalist, radio and television personality, television producer, and actress, who appears on WOR radio in New York City and the Food Network. From 1994 through 2001, she was First Lady of New York City, as the then-wife of Rudy Giuliani. She and Giuliani were married for 18 years and had two children, Andrew and Caroline.

John Honner (1968–), b. Brno, Czech., is a producer of Czech-American TV Herald broadcasting weekly to Czech-American community.

Anna C. Hridel (1913–1996), b. Cleveland, OH, of Czech ancestry, was a radio music journalist who had a long career in broadcasting ethnic music on Cleveland RADIO.

Eva Jinek (1978–), b. Tulsa, OK, of Czech parents, is a journalist and television presenter. Her Czech parents decided to move to the Netherlands when she was eleven. After studying American history at the University of Leiden in 2004, she became foreign editor of the Dutch public network news NOS Journaal, where she covered the United States. In addition, since the end of 2007 she anchored the news show *NOS op 3*. Since the autumn of 2008, Jinek presented the morning and afternoon news bulletins of the NOS. She is well known as a co-host of the show *Amerika Kiest* (America Votes) of the NOS on the U.S. presidential elections, seen from the Netherlands on November 4 and 5th, 2008. On January 20, 2009, she was the host of the live broadcast on Nederland 1 of the inauguration of Barack Obama as 44th President of the United States. She debuted as radio show host on June 4, 2010, for the program *Met het Oog op Morgen* (A Glance at Tomorrow).

Harry Norbert Kalas (1936–2009), b. Chicago, IL, of Czech ancestry, Kalas graduated from the University of Iowa in 1959. Upon graduation, he was immediately drafted into the United States Army and stationed in Hawaii. After his discharge in 1961, Kalas began calling minor-league baseball games for the Hawaii Islanders. As a sportscaster, best known for his Ford C. Frick Award-winning role as lead play-by-play announcer for Major League Baseball's Philadelphia Phillies, a position he held from 1971 until his death in 2009. Kalas was also closely identified with the National Football League, serving as a voice-over narrator for NFL Films productions (a regular feature on *Inside the NFL*) and calling football games nationally for Westwood One radio. Kalas made his major-league debut in 1965 with the Houston Astros, replacing Al Helfer and working alongside Gene Elston and Loel Passe. He called the first game at Houston's Astrodome, on April 12, 1965. He was hired by the Phillies in 1971 to succeed Bill Campbell, and was the master of ceremonies at the 1971 opening of Veterans Stadium. After the retirement of By Saam, Kalas was paired with Andy Musser and Hall of Fame player Richie Ashburn. Nicknamed 'Harry the K', a nickname quickly adopted by Phillies fans, Kalas received the Ford C. Frick Award from the National Baseball Hall of Fame in 2002. In 2004, he was named Person of the Year by the Broadcast Pioneers of Philadelphia. That year, he was also inducted into the Philadelphia Sports Hall of Fame, as a member of the charter class (21 members). He was named Pennsylvania Sportscaster of the Year 18 times.

Todd Harry Kalas (1965–), b. US, of Czech ancestry (the son of the late longtime Philadelphia Phillies Hall of Fame broadcaster Harry Kalas), graduated from Syracuse University with a degree in broadcast journalism. He moved to Tampa Bay as sports director at Vision Cable in Clearwater. He began his baseball career in 1991 with the Louisville Redbirds. He is a television broadcaster for the Tampa Bay Rays. Before joining the Rays, he was on the radio broadcast team of the New York Mets for two years, and the television broadcast team of the Philadelphia Phillies for three years. Kalas has been with the Rays since their inaugural season in 1998. He works on Fox Sports Florida and Sun Sports in his primary role as pregame and postgame host and in-game reporter, and also substitutes as color commentator when needed. He has also filled in with play-by-play on both the Rays' television and radio networks.

Edward V. Klauber (1887–1954), b. Louisville, KY, of Bohemian ancestry, was a reporter, editor and ultimately executive vice president of Columbia Broadcasting System (CBS). He was considered by many the father of CBS News which was the model for all subsequent news programs. He began work for CBS in 1930, becoming executive vice president in 1931. He became director at CBS in 1937 and chairman of the executive committee in 1942, retiring in 1945.

Elizabeth 'Liz' Kotalik (ca. 1990–), b. Phoenix, AZ, of Czech ancestry, attended Saint Monica Coll. (A.A., 2010) and Walter Cronkite School of Journalism at Arizona State Univ. (B.A., 2012). She was a multimedia journalism intern with Superior Court of Maricopa County

(2011-12) and intern with Arizona Republic (2012) and with CNN (2012). She worked for Cronkite News Watch as anchor/reporter (2012) and then joined KGUN9, Tucson, AZ, as multimedia journalist (2013), as news reporter (2013-14) and currently as morning news anchor (s. 2014).

Mark Knoller (ca. 1952–), Brooklyn, NY, of Czech ancestry, is an award-winning White House correspondent for CBS News. He reports for CBS Radio News, as well as *The Saturday Early Show*. He also contributes to the weekend editions of the *CBS Evening News* and *Up to the Minute*. During his career as a reporter, he has covered every President since Gerald Ford. Knoller came to CBS News in 1988 after 13 years as a correspondent with the Associated Press Radio Network, where he was on the front lines of national news coverage — everything from Presidential campaigns and hurricanes to the death and funeral of Elvis Presley. After serving three years as Assignment Manager in the CBS News Washington bureau, Knoller was assigned to the White House, where he covered the last year of the George Bush Presidency and every day of Bill Clinton's. In fact, he has logged more miles covering President Clinton that any other member of the White House press corps. He is now covering the presidency of George W. Bush. He has earned a reputation as one of the leading reporters on the White House beat. He has been honored with a number of AP Awards and with the Merriman Smith Award for Deadline Reporting on the Presidency, bestowed by the White House Correspondents' Association.

Terry Kovarik (ca. 1960–). b. nr. Detroit, MI, probably of Czech ancestry, a graduate of Central Michigan Univ., is a TV reporter. He joined CBS 5 in July 1990 as a general assignment reporter. For most of that time, he also served as his own photographer. From 1981 to 1990, he worked as a reporter/photographer and weekend anchor for WLUC-TV in Marquette, Michigan. He learned a lot about reporting, shooting and producing news magazine segments. He also took home an AP award for best use of natural sound in a segment on an Escanaba Police officer. During his tenure with Channel 5, he won honors from the Milwaukee Press Club and Wisconsin AP.

William John Kucera, 3rd (1948-2010), b. Minneapolis, MN, of Czech ancestry, was a local media and public relations personality. As a child, he moved with his family to Santa Barbara, CA. He enrolled in the motion picture program at UCLA graduating in 1970 with a bachelor's of fine arts. In 1973, Bill took his first media position as a weekend and evening drive time announcer in Santa Barbara. From there, he worked as news anchor and reporter in Twin Falls and Boise Idaho, Cedar Rapids, Iowa and Oklahoma City. In 1979, Bill moved to Salt Lake City, Utah to accept a position with KUTV. In 1983, joined the news team at KSL moving in 1989 to KUED in community relations where he produced and hosted *CONTACT* a nightly community service program. In 1993, Bill became the manager of public communications and information for the Utah Education Network where he remained the rest of his career.

Otto Lowy (1921–2002), b. Prague, Czech., came to Vancouver from Czechoslovakia in 1948, and began his CBC career as a foreign-accented bit player in a series called *Adventures in Europe*. He was best known as the host of *The Transcontinental*, a weekly musical journey through Europe with a railway motif. The show ran for 22 years. He also wrote radio plays and television scripts, produced documentaries and acted in dramas and comedies.

Deb Matejicka, b. Winnipeg, Manitoba, of Czech ancestry, is a sports journalist formerly working for The Score, a Canadian sports television network. After launching her journalism career in Brandon, Manitoba, she worked for the CTV network in Saskatoon and Regina, Saskatchewan, A-Channel in Calgary, and CKVU in Vancouver. Matejicka began working for The Score on October of 2001 as the Calgary Bureau Reporter.

Rudolph 'Rudy' Joseph Maxa, Jr. (1949–), born in Cleveland, OH, of Czech ancestry, is an American consumer travel expert. He's the host and executive producer of 85 half-hour travel shows on the world's great destinations that are broadcast on public television in the US. In addition, Maxa hosts America's most widely syndicated radio travel show, a two-hour weekend show also called *Rudy Maxa's World*.

Donald 'Don' McNeill (1907–1996), b. Galena, IL, of Bohemian ancestry on his mother's side (he was first cousin of Casper Weinberger), began his radio career in Milwaukee in 1928, first as a script editor and announcer at station WISN, and later working for the station owned by *The Milwaukee Journal*. McNeill moved on to Kentucky, working for the Louisville Courier-Journal's station, WHAS. This was followed by working in San Francisco as a comedy act with singer Van Fleming, called 'The Two Professors,' following a failed career move to New York City, McNeill returned to Illinois in 1933. McNeill applied for a job at NBC and was sent to Chicago to audition. He was assigned to host an unsponsored early morning variety show called *The Pepper Pot*, which had an 8 AM time slot on the NBC Blue Network (later to become ABC radio). McNeill re-organized the hour show as *The Breakfast Club*, dividing it into four segments he called 'the four calls to breakfast'. The show premiered on June 23, 1933, with informal talk and jokes based on topical events, and often included audience interviews. In its final form, the show featured piano music and vocal groups and soloists, with recurring comedy performers. McNeil gained a sponsor, Swift and Company. He is credited as the first performer to make morning talk and variety a viable format in radio. McNeill attempted to transfer the show to television as *Don McNeill's TV Club* (1950–1951). *The Breakfast Club* was simulcast on television in 1954–1955. McNeill appeared occasionally on game shows, and in 1963 hosted a short-lived game show *Take Two*, built around photo comparisons. McNeill's radio series finally ended in 1968, when McNeill retired from entertainment and public life.

Monica Novotny (1972–), of Czech ancestry, is a former news anchor for MSNBC. Novotny joined MSNBC as an Internet reporter for *HomePage* after four years working at the Channel One network as a reporter and anchor, where her work was seen daily by some 8 million teenagers and their teachers. She is now a news anchor for *Wake Up with Al* on the Weather Channel, provides news updates for CNBC, and substitute anchors MSNBC Live.

Burton Paulu (1910–2003), b. Pewaukee, WI, of Czech ancestry, was a pioneer in American educational radio and television, an internationally recognized scholar of comparative broadcasting. Paulu became manager of University of Minnesota radio station KUOM in 1928, in the early years of broadcasting, and participated in the development of public radio and television in the US, presiding as the University of Minnesota expanded its broadcasting activities to include short-lived innovations such as the use of closed circuit television to teach college courses and permanent changes to the American broadcasting landscape such as the introduction of educational television to the general public. He taught classes on American and international broadcasting until he retired with the title of professor and director of the University's Media Resources Department in 1978.

Walter Rudolf Porges (1931–1999), b. Vienna, of Bohemian ancestry, during his US Army service, Porges was editor of the newspaper at his Army post. He later worked for several New York radio stations, before landing in 1958 at ABC News as a radio news writer and editor. Over the course of his 35 years with ABC, Porges held numerous positions, including associate producer, assistant assignment manager and director of foreign news coverage.

Russ Ptacek (1963–), b. Great Bend, KS, of Czech ancestry, is a graduate of the University of Kansas. Russ began his career in Lawrence as a student reporter on University of Kansas radio station KJHK where he was news director and the host of a news talk show. Topeka CBS affiliate WIBW hired Russ as a part-time reporter, while he was still a student at KU. WIBW then offered Russ a full-time spot as the morning and noon anchor (1988–93). While at WIBW, Russ won regional and national awards for his reporting and was a contributor to network newscasts. He left WIBW to found an internationally recognized news agency, News TV Corporation (1992–2002). He sold the firm in 2001 and returned to the University of Kansas to finish his degree. After graduating from KU, Russ studied and lived in Germany prior to returning to Kansas City to report for NBC Action News. He returned to the Washington area to lead WUSA 9's Wants to Know investigative unit (s. 2012). Since arriving at WUSA 9 in 2012, Russ has sparked debate in three separate Congressional hearings, exposed Pepco and BGE continuing to bill electrical consumer services while they were disconnected during storms, and uncovered serious health risks at dozens of DMV restaurants. He also sparked reform at State and Federal agencies. He's also reported on millions of dollars in unreported government bonuses, race biased taxis, and restaurant health risks. His web analyses have identified Smartphone privacy risks and exposed a politician who stalked teens online.

Mika (Emilie Leonia) Brzezinski Scarborough (1967–), b. New York, NY, the daughter of Emilie Anna Benešová (1932–), of Czech descent and former National Security Advisor Zbigniew Brzezinski, is an American journalist, talk show host, liberal political commentator, and author who currently co-hosts MSNBC's weekday morning broadcast show *Morning Joe*. She was formerly a CBS News correspondent and was their principal 'Ground Zero' reporter during the morning of the September 11 attacks. In 2007, she joined MSNBC as an occasional anchor, and was subsequently chosen as co-host of *Morning Joe*, alongside Joe Scarborough, whom she later married.

Cornelia Ludmila Schacht (ca. 1944–), b. Prague, grew up in Munich, Germany. She received her Ph.D. (1970) in Slavic philology from the University of Munich. After coming to the USA, she taught college, and worked as managing editor and radio producer of biweekly German and Russian radio programs for the Christian Science Publishing Society in Boston, MA. Since 1994, she has been involved with real estate as an investor, developer and manager of her own properties in Boston, later also in Newport and in Providence.

Joe Schlesinger (1928–2011) b. Vienna, of Czech ancestry, raised in Prague, is a Canadian television journalist and author. After studying at the University of British Columbia in Vancouver, he reported for *The Province* and the *Toronto Daily Star*, and edited for UPI in London and the *International Herald Tribune* in Paris. In 1966, he joined the Canadian Broadcasting Corporation and retired from full-time employment in 1994, but continues to produce essays and special reports for CBC News. He was a host on CBC Newsworld and producer of commentaries and documentaries for *CBC Prime Time News*. He was nominated for 18 Gemini Awards and won three awards, for 'Best Reportage' (1987 and 1992) and 'Best News Magazine Segment' (2004).

Walter Schmolka (1909–1976), b. Prague, Bohemia, was trained as a lawyer at Charles Univ. (JUDr., 1932). After coming to Canada, he became head of the Czechoslovak section of the Canadian Broadcasting Corp., Montreal.

Markéta Slepčíková-Resovská (née Maresová) (1968–), b. Pardubice, Czech., completed her Master degree at Charles University in Prague in the department of Television and Film Journalism. She briefly worked in Czech Television in Prague as a reporter and a host, and later produced her own documentaries and TV series. In 2001, she came, with her husband

and son to Canada. After 3 years of various odd jobs, she founded a Czech TV program in Ontario, entitled *Nová Vize*, presumably one of the first Czech production in the world. As of now (2014), some 550 programs, of 30 min length, have been prepared, covering social, cultural and political events bearing on the life of Czech Canadian community. Together with her second husband, the filmmaker Igor Resovský, and with her son Sebastian, she also produced two important 60 min. documentaries about the Czech Canadians, for the general public. For her efforts, she received in 2001 Masaryk Award for promoting Czech culture in Canada, from the Czech and Slovak Association of Canada.

Wilma Smith (née Pokorny) (1946–), b. Garfield Heights, OH, of Czech ancestry, graduated from Garfield Heights High School in 1964 and then earned a Bachelor's degree in speech and English from Bowling Green State University. She also holds a Master's degree in broadcast journalism. She was an American local television news anchor from 1977 to 2013 in Cleveland, Ohio. She was with Fox affiliate WJW-TV from 1994 to 2013, following 17 years at ABC affiliate WEWS-TV. She was 10-time Lower Great Lakes Emmy Award winner. In 1999, she was Silver Circle Award winner (Lower Great Lakes Emmy Awards).

Karl Štefan (1884–1951), b. Žebrákov, Bohemia, apart from his political activities, was a successful editor, radio commentator and publisher. In 1885, he moved with his parents to Omaha, Nebraska. He was taught in the public schools and later Y.M.C.A. night school. He joined the United States National Guard, being first a private in the Illinois National Guard and then a lieutenant in the Nebraska National Guard. He was an inspector of telegraphs in the Philippine Constabulary from 1904 to 1906. He moved to Norfolk, Nebraska in 1909 to serve as a telegrapher. He became an editor of the *Norfolk Daily News* until 1924 and a radio commentator and contributor to newspapers and magazines until 1934. He was president of the Stefan Co. and publishers' agent for magazines and newspapers. During his years as WJAG's first announcer, Stefan is credited with developing much of WJAG's programming, including a noontime show. Stefan was not only an announcer and newscaster but also the creator and producer of station programming. In 1922, he originated the 'radio family,' whose members gathered around a mythical dinner table each noon hour.

Michael 'Mike' Straka (1969–), b. Newark, NJ, of Czech ancestry, is an American television host, author and producer. He was co-host and producer on Spike TV's primetime MMA news magazine show, *MMA Uncensored Live* and he was the creator and the host of 'TapouT Radio' on Sirius XM Sports. He serves as the in-cage post-fight interview correspondent for World Series of Fighting and as UFC correspondent for Fight Now TV. WSOF 1 aired live on NBC Sports Network on November 3, 2012 from Planet Hollywood in Las Vegas, Nevada. Straka hosted *Fighting Words with Mike Straka* on HDNet which featured interviews with mixed martial arts athletes. He is a regular contributor to *FIGHT! Magazine*, and wrote a book on MMA, based on interviews from his television show, *Fighting Words*, which was published by Triumph Books. Straka is also a producer at Fuse TV and has interviewed and produced several television pieces on well-known artists, including Sinead O'Connor, Zedd, Sam Smith, Naughty Boy, Wiz Khalifa, R Kelly, Lou Reed, Armin Van Buuren, Jeff Bhasker and more. Straka was a vice president and executive producer at FOX News Digital, and also served as an on-air commentator on Hollywood and celebrity topics, as well as sports, for the cable net and on FOXNews.com. He created and produced *Strategy Room*. Straka hosted and was executive producer of FOX Fight Game, mixed martial arts (MMA) features and news program, and was a columnist on FOXNews.com.

Jim Svejda (1974-), b. Chicago, IL, of Czech descent, is a former announcer for KUSC radio in Los Angeles, a nationally known classical music station. He hosted the station's local week-nightly classical series *The Evening Program*, until retiring on February 18, 2022. From 1983, he hosted the Sunday night syndicated classical music program *The Record Shelf*. He also hosted the now-cancelled series *The Opera Box*.

Frederick C. Wolf (1902-1972), b. Prague, Czech., became noted in Cleveland Radio as a pioneer in nationality and classical music programming. After attending the Prague Commercial Academy, he worked for the Krupp Munition Works before immigrating to Cleveland in 1927. He became an editor for the Czech daily *America*. He began broadcasting a Czech program in 1929 over WHK, moving it to WJAY the following year and to WGAR in 1936. In 1934, he founded the Cleveland Recording Co. for the production of spot commercials, nationality music, and auditions. He also formed the Nationalities Broadcasting Assn., an organization for all foreign radio programs, the same year. On 30 April 1950, Wolf and several partners started their own station, WDOK. By 1957, it was the radio home for 18 different nationality programs, most of them broadcast on Sundays. It also bucked contemporary music trends by broadcasting 2 hours of classical music each night. Wolf sold WDOK to Transcontinent Television Corp. of New York in 1962. He also sold Cleveland Recording Co., though he was continuing as a director. Because of his influence in ethnic affairs, Wolf was an important voice in local Republican politics.

Jeff Zeleny (ca. 1974-), b. Exeter, NE, of Czech ancestry, was named ABC News Senior Washington Correspondent in February 2013. In this role, he covers Congress and national politics for the network, reporting for all broadcasts and platforms. Prior to joining ABC News, Mr. Zeleny was the national political correspondent for *The New York Times*, where he was the lead reporter on the 2012 presidential campaign. Before his tenure at the *Times*, Mr. Zeleny was the national political correspondent for the *Chicago Tribune*.

D. Publishing

1. Czech-Language Publishers

Václav Bureš (1859-d.), b. Voseček, Bohemia, came to US in 1863 and until 1886 lived in Iowa. At the age of nineteen, he attended Western College, then an academy in Iowa City, and later for two years the Iowa State University. In August 1886, Bures and family moved to Omaha, where at first he engaged in business, then was deputy in the office of county and city treasurers. In 1900, he helped to form the company Pokrok Publishing Co., of which he became secretary, which took over the publishing of the periodical *Pokrok Západu*. Within a short time, he began publishing local editions for various Czech localities, i.e., *Cretský Pokrok, Wilberský Týdeník, Dakotský Pokrok, Iowský Pokrok, Kansaský Pokrok, Minnesotský Pokrok*. After 1902, he became the owner of the company and remained in business until 1921.

August Geringer (1842-1930), b. Březnice, Bohemia, originally a teacher, became Czech-American publisher in Chicago. Despite the earlier failures of others in publishing, he succeeded in launching highly successful *Svornost* (1875), the first Czech daily in US. For immigrant farmers, he published bi-weekly *Amerikán* (1878) and later for the various local American editions with local news.

Jiří Hlubůček (1906-1984), b. Klokoč, Czech., owned an advertising agency in Prague and later became a publisher of magazines. In 1951, he emigrated to Canada, where he co-founded the Litera Printing Co. publishing firm in Toronto. In 1955, he began publishing the periodical *Naše Hlasy* (Our voices). He also published a number of books.

John A. Hospodský (1858-1929), b. Tábor, Bohemia, in 1879, worked on the *Volnost* in Cleveland, later on the *Nová Vlast* in North Bend, NE. He then brought the paper to Omaha and renamed it *Národní Listy*. Subsequently, he edited the populist weekly *Přítel Lidu* in Wahoo, and after acquiring its ownership, he moved it to Wilbur, NE.

Mirko Janeček (1927-2017), b. Bratislava, Czech., of Czech parents, returned with his parents to Pardubice, when he was three years old. He attended the University of Agriculture in Prague (1946-48) and in February 1948 participated in the student demonstration and their march to Prague Castle. He was expelled and subsequently escaped to Germany. He then went to Sweden, where he continued in his studies at Univ. of Uppsala (1949-51). In 1951, he immigrated to Canada where he completed his studies. In Canada, he was employed as an employment counselor with Federal Dept. of Employment and Immigration, from which he retired in 1988. His interests have been in integration of immigration in Canada, social work, photography, and above all, journalism. In 1968, he began publishing a monthly, *Hlas nových* (Voice of the New), which he renamed to *Kanadské Listy* in 1973, from the basement of his Mississauga home, Canada for 42 years.

Frank Kořízek (1820-1899), b. Letovice, Moravia, after settling in Racine, WI, began publishing, in 1860, Czech newspaper *Slowan Amerikánský*, the first Czech newspapers in the US. Within a short time, the newspaper combined with *Národní Noviny*, under the new title *Slavie*. In 1877, Kořízek also began publishing *Dennice Novověku*, a weekly devoted to the development of free thought.

Stanley L. Kostoryz (1866-1924), b. Jemnice near Strakonice, Bohemia, was a newspaper publisher and land developer. He bought an English-language newspaper in 1898, purchased a Czech-type font, and founded *Osvěta* (Enlightenment). *Osvěta* began publication as a semiweekly; later it became a daily. He established the first Czech daily newspaper in Nebraska and was the first to start publishing editions for Czech localities in the state. *The Wilberské Listy* (Wilber News) was established as a weekly in July 1893.

Jan Bárta Letovský (1821-1898), b. Letovice, Moravia, assisted Frank Kořízek with publication of *Slowan Amerikánský*, in the capacity as editor. After the two parted ways, he established his own periodical in 1869 in Iowa City, bearing similar title *Slovan Americký*. The paper was later moved to Cedar Rapids, IA. It was at his specific invitation that L. Klácel came to America to assume editorship of this periodical. He was sent, together with Mráček, as emissaries to Russia to ascertain and explore possibility of establishing a Czech settlement there.

Jan Milostín Bárta Letovský (1845-1931), b. Letovice, Moravia, came to America with his parents and landed in Boston in 1853, thence to Racine, WI and in the spring of 1853 moved with his parents to Jefferson Township, Johnson Co, IA. In 1859, he went to Racine, and in 1869, came to Iowa City and worked on the Bohemian paper, started by his father and Joseph Pisha, and finally bought an interest in the paper that he had successfully edited. He held several functions in the city. He was a member of the Iowa City School Board and a member of the city council for six years. His paper was one of the official organs of Johnson County and the only Czech paper in the state of Iowa.

Procopius Neužil (1937-1946), b. Bechyně, Bohemia, R.C. priest, was the founder of the Benedictine Press. Their most popular publication was *Přítel Dítek* (Children's Friend) which ran for 58 years (1889-1947). Father Neužil founded the magazine and served as the first editor.

Anton Novák (1845-d.), b. Březovice, Bohemia, a printer by trade, after settling in Milwaukee, WI, started publishing (1882) *Domácnost* (8000 copies) and in 1904, the *Orgán*

Bratrstva (17,000 copies). He also published other periodicals, including *Hospodář Americký, Besídka Dětská, Hospodyně, Čas, Vlastimil* and a very popular annual the *Naše Vlast*. In addition, he also published books, among them Klácel's brochures and monographs.

Dagobert Novák (1874-d.), b. Prague, Bohemia, was an owner of prosperous printing shop in Chicago and publisher of periodical *Šotek, Předměstské Listy* and English written weekly *Cicero Times*. He also had interest in the Milwaukee's *Čechoslovák* and *St. Louiské Listy* and was founder of periodical *Texan*, published originally in Galveston.

Frank J. Riha (1885-d.), b. Chamberlain, SD, of Czech ancestry, came with parents to Omaha, NE in 1890. He was employed by Redfield Printing Co. (s. 1890); later became printer and type setter for Eggerss & O'Flyng; printer for A. I. Medlar; and publisher Omaha Hotel Reporter. Prior to 1907, he worked for various newspapers in Nebraska and Iowa. Subsequently, he co-established a commercial printing firm, Comstock & Riha, Omaha (1907-17) and later became an owner and operator of Riha Printing & Publishing Co., Omaha (s. 1917). He became owner of *The Progress of the West*, a weekly Czech paper (1921) and changed its name to *Národní Pokrok*. He was elected a member of the NE House of Representatives (1911); and became chairman of the Board of County Commissioners (1931-34). He was an active member of Sokol and in 1907, he was a member of the American team representing US at gymnastic tournament in Prague. He was a gymnastic teacher in Omaha for 16 years. Also, he held the office of State president of Czech-American Society.

Edward Rosewater (1841-1906), b. Bukovany Bohemia, apart from his English paper *The Daily Omaha Bee*, he also published a Czech weekly *Pokorok západu* (The Progress of the West).

Edward Rosewater (1841-1906), b. Bukovany, Bohemia, was the founder of the daily *The Omaha Daily Bee* which developed into the largest and most influential newspaper in the mid-west. He also published the *Beobachter Missouri* for German readers and Czech weekly *Pokrok Západu* (Progress of the West).

John Rosický (1845-1910), b. Humpolec, Bohemia, in 1877, took over from Edward Rosewater the weekly *Pokrok Západu* (Progress of the West) and raised it from a small sheet to the front of Czech weeklies. In 1884, he attempted to publish a Czech literary periodical *Květy Americké* which had a short life and was substituted in 1903 by *Osvěta Americká* (American Culture). The most profitable Rosicky's venture proved to be an agricultural paper, *Hospodář*, which commenced publication in 1891, was issued twice a month and which claimed the largest circulation of all agriculture related Czech periodicals.

Zdena Josefa Salivarová (1933-), b. Prague, Czech., together with her husband, Jiří Škvorecký, founded the '68 Publishers,' in Toronto, of which she became the manager.

She did most of the work herself, including the technical editing. She was also a writer in her own right and many of her essays appeared in the magazine *Západ*.

František Škarda (1848-1900), b. nr. Strakonice, Bohemia, after a short stay in NYC, went to Cleveland, where with the help of socialist Lev Palda in 1875, he established the first Czech workingmen paper in America, *Dělnické Listy*. In 1877, it was transferred to NYC where it was combined with *New Yorské Listy*.

Louis J. Sulak (1885-1967), b. Carmine, TX, of Czech ancestry, was an editor and publisher. He was dir. of West News (Novinv) (1906-12) and later founded Texas Leader in Waco. He was also an owner and editor of *Fayette County Record* (s. 1922) and *Svoboda* (s. 1927), the oldest Czech newspaper in Southwest.

Frank Švehla (1917-1990), b. Prague, Czech., a graphic artist by trade, worked for 17 years for Orbis Printing Co. in Prague and for 12 years for New York Herald in NYC. In 1956, he established his own typographic company and in 1958, publishing house Universum Press Co. He published a number of important books by Czech exiles, including those of F. Peroutka, Egon Hostovský, M. Rašín, L.F. Feierabend, etc. In 1962, he began publication of weekly *Americké Listy* and in 1966, the *New Yorské Listy* and *New Yorský Deník*.

F. H. Svoboda (1871-d.), b. Kynice, Moravia, was a publisher, who at one time published the first and only Czech juvenile magazine in Nebraska – *Zlatá Hvězda* (The Golden Star). With his parents, he immigrated to Saunders County, NE, in 1872. He attended public school, then prepared himself for the teaching profession in Fremont, where he also studied Czech. He became a teacher, moved to Prague, Saunders County, where he taught school five years, during four of which he was principal. He taught Czech on Fridays. Then he moved to Schuyler, where he began to publish *The Golden Star*, thus realizing a dream of many years, but was unsuccessful after all, from the financial view. He again taught school, then engaged in photography and in 1909 began to publish *The Schuyler Messenger*. In 1920, he was succeeded by his son, Amos, whereupon he resumed photography.

Frank J. Svoboda (1873-1965), b. Bohemia, was a newspaper publisher in Ohio (1899-1939). In 1894, he opened his own printing office, and in 1899, began publishing a Czech daily newspaper, the *Američan*, especially popular among Czech Catholics. In 1908, the *Američan* absorbed the weekly *Volnost* (Freedom).

Jan Vaculík (1945-), b. Czech., is publisher and editor of *Hospodář*, based in West, Texas. He has been in business since the 1970s and now publishes the newspaper from his home. The newspaper was originally founded in 1890 in Omaha, NE by Jan Rosický.

2. Slovak-Language Publishers

John Denďúr (1898–)1988), b. Petrovec, Yugoslavia; printer, teacher, journalist, publisher, editor of *Náš Svet*, a Slovak weekly, dramatic director of the Slovak Worker's Society.

Stephen Furdek (1855–1915), b. Trstená, Slovakia, R.C. priest, was the founder and publisher of *Jednota,* the journal of the First Catholic Slovak Union.

Milan Alexander Getting (1878–1951), b. Bytča, Slovakia, was the publisher of *Slovenský Sokol.* He was a signatory of 'Pittsburgh Agreement.'

John J. Lach (1894–1960), b. Hibernia, NJ, of Slovak descent, R.C. priest, pastor of Immaculate Conception Church, Whiting, IN, was the owner of *Slovák v Amerike*, the oldest Slovak newspaper in US (s. 1951).

John Matlocha (1879–1944), b. Zvolen, Slovakia; editor and publisher, editor of *Tatran*, a monthly journal, owner of the Mally Press, Printers and Binders Co., residing in Chicago.

Ján Pankúch (1869–1952), b. Prešov, Slovakia; newspaper editor and publisher, long-time editor, and publisher of *Hlas* (The Voice), Cleveland's only Slovak newspaper.

Joseph Paučo (1914–1974), b. Slovakia; journalist, publicist, publisher of *Slovák in America*, Middletown, PA.

Karol Salva (1849–1913), b. Liptovská Sielnica, Slovakia, was one of the most influential publishers of Slovak literature, while, at the same time being an activist, teacher, evangelical priest, writer, and book printer. In 1909 he emigrated to the USA.

Edward Schwartz-Markovič (1850–1933), b. Ťepla, Slovakia, was a pioneer journalist in Streator, IL, and publisher of *Nova Vlast* (New Home).

John Spevak (1866–1887), was an editor and publisher of *Slovák v Amerike* (Slovak American), published in NYC.

Július Wolf (1860–1930), b. Krompachy, Slovakia; journalist, together with Ján Slovenský, was publisher of *Amerikanszko-Szlovenszke Noviny* (American-Slovak News). Written in eastern dialect with Magyar orthography with pro-Hungarian political leaning.

3. English-Language Publishers

James Nathan Beck, son of Johanna Augusta Reinke (1795–1877) of Moravian ancestry, and John Beck, was the owner of a small publishing company. He married to Margaretta C. Darling and had six children.

I. INFORMATION RESOURCES

Charles Edward Bloch (1861–1940), b. Cincinnati, OH, of Bohemian ancestry, was American Jewish publisher. Affectionately called 'dean of the Jewish publishers,' he was the founder of Reform Advocate, Chicago (1891). After coming to NYC, he established Bloch Publishing Co. (1901).

Edward Bloch (1816–1881), b. Bohemia, established Cincinnati Bloch & Co. (1854), the first Jewish publishing house in US.

Ladislaus Joseph Bolchazy (1937–2012), b. Michalovce, Czech., was a publisher. He was co-owner and president of Bolchazy-Carducci Publishers, Mundelein, IL, a company devoted to the ancient world, classics, and textbooks.

Jonas (ben Abraham) Bondi (1804–1874), b. Dresden, Germany, of Bohemian ancestry, after a short career as a preacher in NY, began publishing articles promoting Orthodox Judaism in Philadelphia's Jewish journal, *The Occident*. He was subsequently offered the position of associate editor. From 1860 to end of his life, he was proprietor and editor of Jewish paper *The Hebrew Leader*, published in English and German.

David Tennant Bryan (1906–1998), b. Richmond City, VA, desc. from Augustine Heřman, was a publisher of *Richmond Times-Dispatch* and *Richmond News Leader* (to 1978). He was the leader of the Richmond press for more than fifty years. In addition to publishing two papers, he was president of the American Newspaper Publishers Association, a director of the Associated Press, head of the Virginia Associated Press Newspapers, a director of the Southern Newspaper Publishers Association and a trustee of the Washington Journalism Association. He formed and was chairman of Media General and expanded into cable television and other businesses. He was elected to the Virginia Communications Hall of Fame and the Virginia Business Hall of Fame.

John Stewart Bryan (1871–1944), b. Henrico Co., VA, desc. f. Augustine Heřman, was a Richmond newspaper publisher. In 1900, he began work as a reporter at the *Richmond Dispatch*, owned by his father, Joseph Bryan, and within a year was vice president of the holding company. Upon his father's death in 1908, he became president of the company and owner and publisher of the *Richmond News Leader*. There he hired as editor Douglas Southall Freeman, who went on to win two Pulitzer Prizes for his historical writing.

John Steuart Bryan, 3rd (1938–2016), b. Richmond, VA, desc. f. Augustine Heřman, was educated at the University of Virginia. Bryan worked in the circulation department of *The Richmond News Leader*, in the advertising and production departments of *The Burlington (VT) Free Press* and as a reporter for *The Tampa Times* and the *Richmond Times-Dispatch*. He became vice president of The Tribune Company in 1968, executive vice president in December 1971 and publisher in June 1976. He was named president and publisher of the *Times-Dispatch* and *The News Leader* in 1978, and was elected chairman, president and CEO of Media General, Inc., on May 15, 1990. He stepped down as CEO on July 1, 2005 and continued to serve as chairman of the Board.

William Cepak (1896–ca. 1979), b. Chicago, IL of Czech ancestry, was a publisher of *The Suburban Leader, Cicero Life* and *Berwyn Life*. He was also co-owner of the *Illinois Tavern News, The Missouri Tavern News* and *Wisconsin Tavern News*.

Winslow Cipra (1873–1939), b. Teskov, Bohemia, was a publisher. He came to America with his parents in 1881 and settled in Kansas. In 1900, he graduated from the Salina Normal University with a teacher's certificate and the degree of A.B. In 1896, at the age of twenty-three, he had begun teaching, first in Ellsworth County, and then in Palacky Township, and for one year was principal of the Holyrood Schools. It was through his earnings as a teacher that he paid for his higher education at Salina. After giving up teaching, Mr. Cipra clerked in a general merchandise store at Holyrood until 1907, and then entered the newspaper business. At that time, he bought the *Holyrood Banner*, but sold it in 1911 and, coming to Lincoln, became proprietor of the *Lincoln Sentinel*. The *Sentinel*, which was the Democratic paper, was the official county paper of Lincoln County and was a prosperous, thriving business with a large circulation and with an increasing influence as an organ of opinion. At the invitation of President Wilson, he took the office of postmaster of Lincoln in 1914.

Steven Cohn (1949–), b. US, of Bohemian ancestry on his mother's side (Zucker), held the position of director of Duke University Press (s. 1993). As director, Cohn oversees all operations of the Press. He has guided the Press through a period of great change in the publishing industry and academic publishing in particular. He has developed a flexible business model and launched initiatives into electronic publishing while building the Press' strengths in both books and journals. Before he was director of the press, Cohn worked at Duke as the Press's journals manager and as the managing editor of a journal of health policy. He also has taught English at Stanford University, George Peabody College for Teachers, and Durham Technical Institute and has worked in a variety of fields from construction to teaching and counseling problematic children.

Robert C. Dvorak (1915–), b. Tabor, SD, of Czech parents, was publisher of *Milligan Review*, Milligan, NE (s. 1936). Prior to that he was a linotype operator in Aberdeen, ID and then was involved in newspaper work in Arcadia, NE. He was a member of Czech National Alliance.

Henry Clarence Dworshak (1894–1962), b. Duluth, MN, of Bohemian ancestry, attended its local public schools and learned the printer's trade. During the First World War, he served as a Sergeant in the US Army Fourth Antiaircraft Machine Gun Battalion in the American Expeditionary Forces. After the war, Dworshak managed a printing supply business in Duluth. He moved west in 1924 to Burley, Idaho, to become the publisher and editor of the *Burley Bulletin*, a semi-weekly newspaper in Cassia County for 20 years (1924-44). Dworshak became a public figure when he was elected president of the Idaho Editorial Association in 1931, and he was a prominent member of the American Legion and Rotary International. He was also a member of the Elks and a Freemason. He served over 22 years in the House (1939-46) and Senate (1949-62).

Peter F. Fleischmann (1922-1993), b. NYC, of Moravian ancestry, for 32 years, he served as an officer of *The New Yorker*. His father, Raoul H. Fleischmann, was the financial backer who co-founded the magazine in 1925 with the editor Harold Ross, and was its first president, chairman and publisher. Fleischmann joined the company as a director in 1953. He became treasurer of the Board in 1955, while still in his early 30s; executive vice president in 1965, and president in 1968. After his father's death in 1969, he succeeded as the chairman. For many years the magazine flourished, both as a literary journal and a business. At its peak, *The New Yorker* was forced to turn down some advertising for lack of space. Mr. Fleischmann upheld his father's tradition of strict separation of the magazine's business side from its editorial functions under Mr. Ross and his successor as editor, William Shawn.

Washington Flexner (1869-1942), b. Louisville, KY, of Bohemian father, as a young man was associated for a number of years with the printing dept. of the *Louisville Courier Journal*. He was also the owner of a book store and a printing office. He established the first printing plant in Louisville. In 1915, he moved to Chicago and organized the Lincoln Printing Co. and in 1927, he extended the business to New York City, incorporating the Lincoln Engraving & Printing Corp. In 1928, he formed the Lincoln Printing Co., a Delaware corporation, which acquired all the stock of the Chicago and New York companies and continued to operate the plants in those cities. From the time he moved to Chicago, Flexner specialized in financial printing and the concern he founded became the largest in the field. He was president of the three Lincoln corporations from their organization until his death.

Eugene Fodor (1905-1991), a native of Letice, Slovakia, who immigrated to the US in 1938, was the founder of popular tourist guidebooks which provided reliable and practical information, written in a readable style to help the inexperienced tourist.

Harold Kleinert Guinzburg (1899-1961), b. New York City, of Bohemian ancestry, was a co-founder of the publishing firm Viking Press, Inc. (1925). In the early 30s, the Viking Press expanded its publications by adding a juvenile dept. which produced a distinguished list of children's literature. He was also responsible for establishing Viking's Portable Library, a series of compact anthologies for servicemen and the Compass Books, paperback reprints of important works.

Ruth Sulzberger Holmberg (1921–2017), a native of New York, of Bohemian ancestry, a great-granddaughter of Rabbi Isaac Mayer Wise, is one of the nation's most prominent newspaper women, having been publisher of *The Chattanooga Times* since 1964. Under Mrs. Holmberg, *The Chattanooga Times* has attained a reputation for aggressive reporting and sometimes unpopular editorial opinion, urging support for civil rights legislation during the years of segregation and supporting tightened environmental controls that have been unpopular among many in Chattanooga, a city of heavy industry. In 1987, Mrs. Holmberg was elected a director of *The Associated Press*. She is also a director of The New York Times Company. Mrs. Holmberg's father, Arthur Hays Sulzberger, was publisher of *The New York Times* from 1935 until 1961 and was also publisher of *The Chattanooga Times* from 1955 to 1957.

Benjamin Huebsch (1875–1964), b. New York, NY, of Slovak descent, (the son of a prominent American Rabbi and scholar from Liptovský Svätý Mikuláš,) was a pioneer publisher. From a small print shop, he built the large publishing house, B. W. Huebsch Co., which in 1925, combined with the famous American firm Viking Press and subsequently became the vice president and the chief editor of the new corporation.

Jonathan Marshall (1924–2008), the son of Lenore K. Guinzburg (1897–1971), of Bohemian ancestry, and the journalist James Marshall, was the publisher of the *Scottsdale Daily Progress*. Marshall was dyslexic but earned a Bachelor of Science degree in economics and political science from the University of Colorado in 1946. He earned a Master's degree in journalism from the University of Oregon in 1962. Marshall bought a bankrupt fine art magazine called *Art Digest* in 1953 in partnership with James N. Rosenberg. After changing the format and changing the name to *ARTS*, Marshall sold the magazine in 1958 to join the Ford Foundation's Humanities and Arts program. *ARTS* would later become *Arts Magazine*. In 1963, Marshall purchased *the Scottsdale Daily Progress* newspaper, and published it for 24 years. He took a brief hiatus in 1974 to run unsuccessfully for US Senate against Barry Goldwater. In 2003, Ruder-Finn Press published Marshall's novel *Reunion in Norway*. The novel was inspired by Marshall's visit to a museum in Bergen which documented the Norwegian resistance movement against the German occupation of Norway during World War I. Twice he was nominated for a Pulitzer Prize; and was granted the Arizona Press Club's Distinguished Service Award, the Arizona Newspaper Association's Master Editor Publisher Award, and the Society of Professional Journalists National First Amendment Award. He served as president of the Arizona Newspaper Association and chairman of the National Newspaper

Association's Freedom of Information Committee. Marshall was inducted into the Arizona Newspapers Association Hall of Fame in 1996, the same year as Don Bolles and Charles E. Thornton. Induction was previously a posthumous honor; Marshall was among the first journalists to be inducted during his lifetime. In 1955, he married Maxine Sue Besser (1926-2015) of St Louis, with whom he had 4 children.

Joseph Pulitzer (1847-1911), b. Mako, Hung., of Moravian ancestry, was an American newspaper publisher of the *St. Louis Post Dispatch* and the *New York World*. In the 1890s, the fierce competition between his *World* and William R. Hearst's *New York Journal* introduced yellow journalism and opened the way to mass circulation newspapers that depended on advertising revenue and appealed to the reader with multiple forms of news, entertainment, and advertising.

Joseph Pulitzer, Jr. (1885-1955), b. New York, NY, of Moravian ancestry, was an editor and publisher of *St. Louis Post-Dispatch*. A communication pioneer, the second child of Joseph Pulitzer, he attended Harvard Univ., but a poor academic record prompted his father to insist that he withdraw from the university during his sophomore year to begin an apprenticeship at the *New York World*, a New York newspaper owned by the family. Subsequently, the elder Pulitzer sent his son to St. Louis in 1906 with a note to the editor of the *Post-Dispatch* 'This is my son Joseph. Will you try to knock some newspaper sense into his head?' From 1906 to 1911, Pulitzer served as an apprenticeship at the *Post-Dispatch*. Although the apprentice often antagonized the elder Pulitzer, he won father's approval by punching Randolph Hurst in the stomach because the renowned publisher had been critical of the 'Old J.P.' In 1912, following the death of his father, Joseph Pulitzer became president of the Pulitzer Publishing Co. and he remained in St. Louis to publish the *Post-Dispatch* for the next 43 years. The *Post-Dispatch* became one of the nation's most highly respected newspapers.

Joseph Pulitzer, 3rd (1913-1993), b. St. Louis, MO, of Moravian ancestry (a grandson of the famous newsman Joseph Pulitzer), was himself publisher of the *St. Louis Post-Dispatch* for 38 years and one of the most famous newsmen of the day. For 31 years, he chaired the Board which was responsible for awarding the Pulitzer Prize, and from 1955-1993, he was chairman of the Pulitzer Publishing Company.

Ralph Pulitzer (1879-1939), b. St. Louis, MO, of Moravian ancestry, the son of newspaper magnate Joseph Pulitzer, was an influential publisher and socialite. Upon Joseph Pulitzer's death, he acquired control of the *New York World*, an influential American newspaper. For decades, Ralph Pulitzer was one of the most influential men in American journalism.

Charles Coleman Rosewater (1874-1946), b. Omaha, NE, of Bohemian ancestry, was a manager, organizer and publisher of newspapers and magazines in Omaha, NE, Los Angeles, CA, Kansas City, KS, Seattle, WA and New York City. This included *The Twentieth Century Farmer, Los Angeles Express* (1917), *Los Angeles Times* (1918), *Kansas City Journal* (1919-21), *Seattle Post-Intelligencer* (1922-24) and *Success Magazine* (1924-27).

Edward Rosewater (1841 1906), b. Bukovany, Bohemia, was the founder of the daily *The Omaha Daily Bee* which developed into the largest and most influential newspaper in the mid-west. He also published the *Beobachter Missouri* for German readers and Czech weekly *Pokrok Západu* (Progress of the West).

Rosa Sonneschein (1847-1932), b. Prostějov, Moravia, was a pioneer Jewish publisher and editor. She was the founder and editor of *The American Jewess* magazine. It was the first English-language periodical targeted to American Jewish women. At first, she also published and managed the business affairs of the magazine but later she sold it, though she retained editorship.

Louis J. Sulak (1885-1967), b. Carmine, TX, of Czech ancestry, was an editor and publisher. He was dir. of *West News (Novinv)* (1906-1912) and later founded *Texas Leader* in Waco. He was also an owner and editor of *Fayette County Record* (s. 1922) and *Svoboda* (s. 1927), the oldest Czech newspaper in Southwest.

Arthur Hays Sulzberger (1891-1968), b. New York, NY, of Bohemian ancestry, was the publisher of *The New York Times* from 1935 to 1961. During that time, daily circulation rose from 465,000 to 713,000 and Sunday circulation from 745,000 to 1.4 million; the staff more than doubled, reaching 5,200; advertising linage grew from 19 million to 62 million column inches per year; and gross income increased almost sevenfold, reaching 117 million dollars.

Arthur Ochs 'Punch' Sulzberger (1926-2012), b. NYC, of Bohemian ancestry, succeeded his father as publisher and chairman of *The New York Times* in 1963. In the 1960s, Sulzberger built a large news-gathering staff at *The Times*, and was publisher when the newspaper won a Pulitzer Prize in 1972 for publishing *The Pentagon Papers*.

Arthur Ochs Sulzberger, Jr. (1951-), b. Mount Kisco, NY, of Bohemian ancestry, became the publisher of *The New York Times* in 1992 and chairman of The New York Times Co. in 1997.

Iphigene Ochs Sulzberger (1892-1990), b, Chatanooga, TN, of Bohemian ancestry, desc. f. Rabbi Isaac M. Wise, was a newspaper executive. She was a director of special activities, *New York Times* (s. 1949), The New York Times Co. (s. 1917); with Times Printing Co., Chattanooga, TN (s. 1919). She once inspired a series of articles that demonstrated the public's low interest and competence in history, a series that won *The Times* a Pulitzer Prize for public service in 1944 and provoked curriculum changes in many states. She also encouraged the paper to develop its potential as a classroom aid to teachers, which helped to make it the most widely circulated daily newspaper in schools and colleges.

Francis Brewster Taussig (1900–1970), b. Yonkers, NY, of Bohemian ancestry, was a publisher (s. 1922). He was vice president, Americana Corp. (1948–70); exec. vice president, director, Grolier Soc. Inc. (1949–70), publishers of the *Book of Knowledge*; president, Grolier International (1966–70), chair and director, Richards Co. (until 1970). He served as chairman of Nat. Postal Com. for Books (1954) and as chair of the Joint Foreign Trade Com., Am. Book Pub. Council.

Jan Vaculík (1945–), b. Czech., is publisher and editor of *Hospodář*, based in West, Texas. He has been in business since 1970s and now publishes the newspaper from his home. The newspaper was originally founded in 1890 in Omaha, NE by Jan Rosický.

Maurice Weidenthal (1856–1917), b. Hostice, Bohemia, was a journalist whose jobs included reporter for the *Herald* (later the *News*), drama critic and editorial writer for the *Cleveland Press*, and city editor for the *Plain Dealer*. In 1906, he founded the *Jewish Independent* and became its publisher and editor, positions he held until his death.

Leo Wise (1849–1933), b. Albany, NY, son of Isaac Mayer Wise, was first associated with the periodicals *Deborah* and *The American Israelite*, founded by his father. He was publisher of the *Deborah* and managing editor and publisher of *The American Israelite* from 1900–1928. At same time was publisher of the *American Jewish Annual* for eight years, a yearly publication devoted to literature from 1884–92. In 1885, he established the *Chicago Israelite*. Since 1908, he was connected with the National Printing and Publishing Co. which was organized by his father in 1891 and since 1920, was president of company employing over two hundred men and women.

4. German-Language Publishers

Oswald Ottendorfer (1826–1900), b. Svitavy, Moravia, educated at Univ. of Prague, was the editor and publisher of the *New York Staats-Zeitung* from 1859 to 1900. His journal, in which he endeavored to reflect the sentiments of German Americans, became one of the most widely circulated and influential papers in New York.

II. The Mythical New World

Martin Behaim (1459–1507), b. Nuremberg, of Bohemian ancestry, according to some historians, had discovered America before Columbus. Other authors say that Behaim at least gave Columbus the idea of sailing west. Behaim was known to take part in the expedition of Diogo Cão (1452–1486) which followed the coast of Africa to Cape Cross. His most important work, which places him among the greatest geographers of the Renaissance, was his terrestrial globe, the earliest extant known, which has been preserved in Nuremberg. What role this globe played in the actual discovery of the New World is not known.

Be that as it may, the news of the discovery of the New World reached the Kingdom of Bohemia as early as the first decade of the 16th century, during the reign of Vladislav the Jagellonian (1471–1516). Definite proof of this is given by the existence of an early print in the Czech language, *Spis o nowých zemiech a o nowém swietie o niemžto jsm prwe žádné známosti neměli ani kdy tzo slýchali* (Description of New World), the origin of which was placed between 1505 and 1508. It is an adaptation of the renowned letter of Amerigo Vespucci addressed to the Medici family, appended with other texts. The Czech version apparently preceded the other European nations in this regard since only the Latin original exists from that period. The printer and publisher of this rare print is purported to be Mikuláš Bakalář, originally Štětina, of Pilsen, Bohemia.

It is, in fact, a paraphrase of the letter by Amerigo Vespucci, generally known as *Mundus Novus,* which is, however, here expanded to include additional facts. The publication shows that the author was acquainted with Columbus's travels, despite the fact that his name is not mentioned there. He writes about five large islands in the Caribbean and that the local population "is peaceable and kind. Women and men all walk around naked, not covering any parts of their bodies, but just the way that they were born—that is how they walk about till the day they die. Their bodies are large and well-proportioned and they are of a reddish color and that, I imagine, is due to the fact that since they walk around without any clothes they are burnt by the sun and so appear to be red. Their hair is black and long. They walk rapidly and freely and with joyful expressions. But they disfigure their own faces by perforating their cheeks, lips, noses and ears." About the women, he speaks with disdain, criticizing them for being "too sensuous; however their bodies are noble and clean."

We further learn that "those people have no private possessions but hold everything in common. They live without any king, each being his own master. They have as many women as they wish and as often as they like they divorce their wives, not abiding by any law" And, furthermore, "there is no metal there except for gold. And they told us that in the midst of these lands there is much gold. They also have plenty of pearls."

The book ends with a paean of praise to the King of Spain, who is said to have sent "a large quantity of cloth and canvas on many ships into these countries, in order to clothe these naked folk. He also sent various artisans there, as well as many wise men, in order that they should teach this brutish folk human customs and morals...."

Václav Šašek of Biřkov, Bohemia (born in the first half of the 15th century), long before Columbus, in his fictive travelogue, describes the journey of Leo of Rožmitál through the Pyrenean Peninsula in 1466, preparing the Czechs for the discovery of the New World. There we can read how, setting out from the city of St. James, Leo of Rožmitál, with his companions, visited the hill *Stella Obscura*, which has a large settlement extending beneath it, known as *Finis Terrae* (the end of the world), since "beyond it there is nothing but an immense ocean, whose limits are known only to God. The eye sees nothing more than the sky and water. The sea is said to be so stormy that it is impossible to sail across it, and therefore no one knows what might be beyond it. They told us that some people wished to learn what was there on the other side and they ventured out on galleys and on ships. But not a single one of them is said to have come back."

In the same travelogue, Václav Šašek refers to legends about a land beyond the sea, which is said to be mentioned in chronicles. One Portuguese King sent out four ships for four years. After two years' sailing, the ships were enveloped in darkness, in which the sailors sailed for two weeks. Then they landed on an island, where they found houses built underground, on top of which were gardens and vineyards. When they sailed away from there, they found terrifying waves and they resolved that two of their ships would explore them. The third stayed behind and waited until the others came back. For 16 days, the sailors waited in vain for their companions and two years later returned to Lisbon.

III. Pioneers

A. Early Colonists

Móric Benyovszky (Benovský) (1746–1786), b. Vrbové, Slovakia; Count, soldier of fortune, globetrotter. He began his career as an officer in the Seven Years' War, after which he fought for Poland against Russia. He was promoted to general and named a Count, was a prisoner in Siberia where he led a revolt and captured the governor's palace (and the governor's lovely daughter). After all that, he managed to capture a Russian battleship and explore the Pacific! He visited several Pacific islands, helped resolve political tensions in Formosa (now Taiwan) and then checked out Madagascar. Landing in France, the smooth-talking Count finagled Louis XV into appointing him a French general and naming him a count. He then made his way to the United States and, with a recommendation from Benjamin Franklin, whom he had met in Paris, attempted to persuade George Washington to fund a militia under Benyovszky's leadership, to fight in the American War of Independence, but was turned down. He sailed back to Madagascar and, after defeating several tribes of natives with the help of other tribes, he was proclaimed Emperor of Madagascar, where he ruled for three years. Restless again, he eventually returned to Hungary where he talked Queen Maria Theresa into making him a count and appointing him a general.

Johann Berger (ca. 1502–), b. Osoblaha (Hotzenplotz), Moravia, in 1519, took part as a soldier in the expedition of Hernán Cortés (1485–1547) against Aztecs.

Jacob Boehm (1668–1759), whose descendants claim that he was of Bohemian origin, settled near Lancaster, PA in 1715. They later changed their surname to Beam.

Mathias Bush (1722–1790), b. Prague, Bohemia arrived in New York City in the early 1740s and around 1742 moved to Philadelphia where he became a pioneer merchant.

Jacobus Fabritius (1618–1890), a Lutheran pastor from Silesia, was given permission to become pastor in New York in 1669. In 1670, he became pastor of the Swedes on the Delaware.

Juriaen Fradel, from Moravia, was listed, in 1645, in the archives of the Reformed Dutch Church of New Amsterdam, as marrying Tryn Hersker.

Joachim Gans (fl. 1581–1589), from Prague, metallurgist, member of the first English colonization effort in America (Roanoke, 1585).

Bernard Gratz (1738-1801), b. Langendorf, Silesia, immigrated via London to America, settling in Philadelphia, PA in 1754. Together with his brother Michael, he became a prominent merchant.

Michael Gratz (1740-1811), b. Langendorf, Silesia, immigrated to America, settling in Pennsylvania in 1758.

Henry George Hauptmann (ca. 1692-d.), b. Prague, Bohemia, immigrated in 1723 to St. Charles, Louisiana, where he was married that year. His son Antoine Henry changed his name to Hoffman (1728-1792) and left numerous descendants.

Augustine Heřman (1621-1686), b. Prague, Bohemia, was one of the earliest immigrants in America from Bohemia. He was a surveyor and skilled draftsman, successful planter and developer of new lands, a shrewd and enterprising merchant, a bold politician and effective diplomat, fluent in several languages – clearly one of the most conspicuous and colorful personalities of the seventeenth century colonial America. After coming to New Amsterdam (present New York), he became one of the most influential people in the Dutch Province which led to his appointment to the Council of Nine to advise the New Amsterdam Governor. One of his greatest achievements was his celebrated map of Maryland and Virginia commissioned by Lord Baltimore on which he began working in earnest after moving to the English Province of Maryland. Lord Baltimore was so pleased with the map that he rewarded Heřman with a large estate, named by Heřman "Bohemia Manor", and the hereditary title, Lord.

Martin Hermanzen Hoffman (1625-1712), b. Revel, Estonia, presumably of Bohemian ancestry, is said to have been Rittmaster in the Army of King Gustavus Adolphus. Prior to his departure for America, he lived a short time in Holland. He came to New Netherlands in 1657, and settled first in Esopus (1658), and two years afterwards in New Amsterdam. He must have brought over considerable wealth with him, as in 1661 he resided on Lower Broadway, and was a large taxpayer. Life on Manhattan does not seem to have agreed with him, because after a few years he moved to Albany, then known as Fort Orange, where he resided for nine or ten years. Again, he changed his residence and settled in Esopus, or Kingston, where he passed the remainder of his life. He was a man of great energy. Besides managing his property and opening up new territory in Ulster County, he had a large saddlery and leather business, which he conducted for several years.

Andrew Jelik (ca. 1730-1783), b. Baja, Slovakia, was a traveler and adventurer of note. As a tailoring journeyman, he visited many places: Vienna, Prague, Germany, England and France. He had many exciting experiences, for he seemed fated to come into a town or village just when men were being recruited into the army. Naturally, he had to do his utmost to avoid getting involved. Often, he had to use his wits very speedily to escape conscription officers. Once, he escaped by boat only to be shipwrecked at sea. He saved himself by clinging to some debris and then found himself stranded, but alive, on the shore of England. After this terrifying episode, he decided to leave Europe by joining a Dutch ship bound for the West Indies and America. It was on this voyage that he came to the United States but for only a very brief period. On concluding the business of the expedition, the captain and crew returned to Europe. As a member of the crew, Jelik also returned. In 1778, after more exciting adventures, Jelik finally extinguished the flames of his somewhat enforced wanderlust and returned to his native Slovakia where he died in 1783.

Burger Jorissen (Citizen Jorissen) (1612-1671), native of Silesia, in 1637, settled at Renssalaerswyck on Hudson River, New Amsterdam. He was a blacksmith by trade, who bought and conducted business on Hudson River.

Jiří Kryštof Kaplíř ze Sulevic (ca. 1600-1649), b. Bohemia, is thought of being one of the first Czechs to enter Brazil in 1647.

Šimon Kohout z Lichtenfeldu (?-1648), b. Bohemia, was a Prague physician who came to Brazil in 1647 where he soon died from swamp fever.

Matthias Kreisler (later Crisler) (1678-d.), from Silesia, landed with his three sons (Theobolt, David and Michael) in Philadelphia in late December 1709. The family first settled in Germantown, 12 miles from the port of Philadelphia. Later Matthias and his two youngest sons moved to their land patent at Madison, VA, leaving Thebolt behind in Philadelphia.

Andrés Morav (Morales) or Andrés Aleman, possibly born in Brno, Moravia, in 1536, was accused of heresy by the inquisition in Mexico.

Philip Ott (fl. 1732-), b. Bohemia, landed in Philadelphia in 1732 and after a few years of residence in Pennsylvania, moved to South Carolina. His descendants spelled their name Otts.

Frederick Philipse (1626-1702), was a Dutch immigrant to North America of Bohemian heritage, who arrived in America as early as 1653. Starting as a carpenter for the Dutch West Indies co., he soon became to be known as Governor Peter Stuyvesant's 'architect-builder,' He soon extended his activities into trade. Through a fortuitous 1662 marriage to a wealthy and driven widow, Margaret Hardenbrook de Vries, the couple combined their industry to amass a fortune. By exporting furs and tobacco, importing goods to Europe, and speculating with 'wampum,' Philipse became one of the wealthiest men in the Province by 1674. In later years, he also shipped grains and foodstuffs to the West Indies and to import slaves from Africa. By 1690s, he was heavily invested in the Madagascar slave trade. He used profits from his commercial ventures to buy land in Manhattan, New Jersey and the Hudson Valley. In 1690s, Philipse's holdings extended for 22 miles along the banks of the Hudson River, and the British Government recognized him as lord of the Manor of Philipseborough.

John L. Polerecký (1748-1830), b. France, of Slovak father, was Major of Lauzun's Polish Lancers, veteran of the American Revolutionary War. As a civilian, Polerecký chose to stay in America permanently. He bought a farm in Dresden, Maine. Over the years, he held a number of public positions: Deputy Marshall, census commissioner, town clerk of Dresden, and lighthouse keeper.

Juriaen Probasco (1627-1664) of Silesia immigrated to New Amsterdam in 1654.

Isaac Ferdinand Šarošy (aka Izák Šároši, Isaacus Sharoshi) (bf. 1695-), b. Slovakia, was a Protestant preacher who journeyed in 1695 to what is today Germantown and Philadelphia and there he became preacher and teacher to the pioneers in the Francis Daniel Pistorius' colony. After spending two years in their service, he found that the blessings of this colony were at least matched if not outweighed, by the sacrifices that were demanded of the colonists. He found it difficult to adjust to the rigors of this environment, so that in 1679, he decided to go to Maryland either to improve his position or to leave from Baltimore on a return trip to Europe.

Ezekiel Solomon(s) (1735-1808), b. Berlin, Germany, of Bohemian ancestry, who served with the British Army, arrived at Michilimackinac, Mackinaw City, Michigan, in the summer of 1761. He is Michigan's first known resident of the Jewish faith. Solomon was one of the most active Mackinac fur traders until his death in 1808. He was one of those who narrowly escaped death in the massacre of 1763. During the Revolutionary War, he and other hard-pressed traders pooled their resources to form a general store. In 1784, he was a member of a committee of eight, formed to regulate the Mackinac area trade. Ezekiel Solomon's business often took him to Montreal, where he is believed to have been buried and where he was a member of Canada's first Jewish congregation Shearith Israel.

John Stephen Steiger (1688-1736), of Bohemia, in 1712-14, settled in Germantown, PA, where he lived until 1727. His descendants later changed their name to Styer.

Marcus Thiel of Burkvíz, Moravia was listed in the 1724 Louisiana Census; he was a shoemaker by trade.

Jaques Touchet (orig. Tutzek or Tuček) (ca. 1721–ca. 1763), b. Prague, Bohemia, in 1730, came to Louisiana.

Hans Trumpel (aft.1500–d.) was one of the minors from Jáchymov, Bohemia, who left for America in July 1528, via Antwerp and Seville, sailing off for San Domingo on the island of Haiti.

Johann Peter Varn (1718–1774), b. Varnsdorf, Bohemia, settled in Orangeburg, Berkeley Co., SC in 1735.

Johannes Wildfang (1695–1769) and his wife Elizabeth (Gruber) Wildfang (1700–1763) arrived from Bohemia with their two children in Philadelphia in 1734 and took the oath of Allegiance at the court house on the same day as arrival.

B. Jesuit Missionaries

Stanislaus (Stanislav) Arlet (1652–1717), b. Opole, Silesia, a Bohemian Jesuit, joined the S.J. Order in 1679. He studied philosophy in Prague and theology in Olomouc, Moravia. He left for mission work in Peru in 1693. Just like F. Boryně, he worked on the territory of the Moxos Indians. He established his own reduction which he named San Pedro. Later, he worked as a rector of the Jesuit College in La Plata.

Juan Xavier Bischoff (1710–1786), b. Kladsko, a Bohemian Jesuit, entered the S. J. Order in 1729. In 1746, came to Lower California. He initiated a broad campaign to reduce the incidence of undesirable conduct, such as excessive drinking, loitering and gossiping. He served in the following missions: San Luis Gonzaga (1746–50), Santa Rosa (1751–52), Loreto (1753–57), La Purísima (1758–66), and Todos Santos (1767–68). He was expelled to homeland in 1768. He died in Prague.

Franciscus Borinie (František Boryně) (1663–1721), b. Malonice, Bohemia, a Bohemian missionary, studied philosophy in Olomouc and theology in Prague. In 1695, he was sent with other missionaries to Peru, where he remained until he died in 1722. He worked among the Indians of Moxos tribe in Bolivia. The first 7 years he spent in St. Francisco de Borja Mission, Bolivia. He then founded San Pablo Mission in Beni, North Bolivia, where he arrived in 1703. He was one of the best missionaries who christened hundreds of unknown Indian tribes, according to his contemporaries. On two occasions he was wounded by Indian arrows, and to illustrate the remoteness of his station, he complained to a friend in Prague that during 23 years he had been away, he had received no news from Bohemia. He died on July 26, 1721 in the mission.

III. PIONEERS

Šimon Boruhradský (1650–1697), b. Polná, Bohemia, a Bohemian Jesuit joined the S.J. Order in 1670. Brother Boruhradský was sent as a missionary to Mexico, where he changed his name to Simón de Castro. He started as a treasurer of Jesuit College but is best known as an architect and builder. He died on his way to Marian Islands.

Jiří Brand (1654–1690), b. Wartemberg, Silesia, entered the S.J. in 1670. He studied philosophy in Prague and theology in Olomouc. In 1684, he left together with other missionaries, for Peru. He worked among the Moxos Indians in the reduction of St. Jacob. He died in Santiago, Chile.

Jiří Burger (1654–1720), b. Vyškov, Moravia, a Bohemian Jesuit missionary, entered S.J. in 1669. He was sent to South America in 1684 and served in the Chilean province and also in Peru. His Spanish far exceeded that of most native speakers. In 1700, he was put in charge of a college in Chillan.

Václav Christman (Chrisman) (1647–1723), b. Prague, Bohemia, entered the S.J. Order in 1664. He was one of the earliest Jesuit missionaries in Latin America. He worked in Paraguay in the reduction of San Loreto among Guarani Indians. Later, he worked as a director of a school at Santa Fé.

Matthias Cuculinus (Kukulín) (1641–1696), b. Mohelnice, Moravia, a Bohemian Jesuit Father, in 1678 was one of the first Bohemian Jesuits to be sent to America. But he never made it to Mexico and instead went to Philippines and eventually, together with Strobach, sailed to Marianas Islands. There he attained the rank of a provincial. In Aganda, he witnessed an uprising against the Spanish rule about which he left an important account.

Juan de Esteyneffer (orig. Jan Steinhöffer) (1664–1716), b. Jihlava, Moravia, was a lay Bohemian Jesuit, having joined the S.J. Order in 1684. He studied pharmacy in Brno, Moravia. He was sent to the Jesuit College at Chihuahua to help care for elderly and ill missionaries. While there, he compiled the *Florilegio Medicinal*, completing it in 1711, with the first publication in 1712. The work combined traditional European material medica and the New World medical lore with what was then modern medical science, and anthropologist Margarita Artschwager Kay posits that it served to standardize herbal therapy in Northern Mexico and the Southwestern United States. Esteyneffer died in 1716, while visiting Sonora.

Martin Dobrizhoffer (1718–1791), a Jesuit from Bohemia, joined the Austrian Province of the Society of Jesus in 1736. He was sent to Paraguay in 1749 and spent 18 years working principally among the Abipon Indians who were incorporated into the mission system of the Guarani Indians. He was a keen observer of native customs and rituals and became fluent in their languages. Before the expulsion of the Jesuits in 1767, he worked in the reduction (Indians' settlement organized by the missionaries) of San Joaquin in the Gran Chaco, north of Ascunción. Between 1777 and 1782, he composed a three-volume history of the Abipones in Latin, which is considered one of the key sources for the history of Paraguay missions, as well as a pioneering work in the field of ethnology.

Wenceslao (Václav) Eymer (1661–1709), b. Mělník, Bohemia, a Bohemian Jesuit Father, entered the S. J. Order in 1768. In 1692, traveled to Tarahumara, Mexico, where he served as missionary for over thirty years. He took up work in Arisiachi mission, a little west from Papigochi. In spite of his busy schedule, he found time to explore the surrounding regions. Through his observations of natural phenomena, he concluded that California was a peninsula and not, as was claimed, an island. Challenging that huge myth, Eymer proclaimed: "Away now with British temerity, with her English Drake and let him keep silent who boasts that he has circumnavigated California, as if, by a foolish fiction, California were the Atlantis of the West." He died in Papigochi in 1709.

Samuel Fritz (1654–1725), b. Trutnov, Bohemia, a Bohemian Jesuit, in 1684, was sent to Quito. He is noted for his exploration of the Amazon River and its basin. Fritz succeeded in converting, among others, the powerful tribe of Omaguas and in concentrating into civilized settlements the savages of forty different localities. Adept in technical arts and handicraft, he also was endowed with extraordinary linguistic abilities, supplemented by the rare gift of knowing intuitively how to treat the Indians. In 1689, he undertook, in primitive Parakou, a daring expedition down the Amazon to Para, where he was captured and imprisoned for two years on the suspicion of being a Spanish spy. Although only imperfectly equipped with the necessary instruments, he completed a relatively accurate chart of the river's course. This was the first such attempt to chart the Maranon territory.

Adam Gilg (1653–ca. 1710), b. Rýmařov, Moravia, a Bohemian Jesuit, entered the S. J. Order in 1670. He was sent to assist Father Francisco Eusebio Kino, soon after his arrival in Mexico. He started his work in Guaymas on the coast but in 1688, he moved into the interior, to the region of the Indian tribe Seris. He also worked in the mission of Santa Maria del Populo on the River Sonora. In 1699, he accompanied Kino on the expedition toward the rivers Gile and Colorado (present Arizona). In 1700 and 1701, he was Superior of the San Francisco mission, south of his original station. In 1704, he consecrated the newly built churches of Nuestra Señora de los Remedios and Nuestra Señora del Pilar in central Pimeria, south of border which now divides Arizona from Sonora. In 1706, he was a rector in Mátape. He compiled a dictionary of the dialects of Pinas and Eudeve tribes.

III. PIONEERS

Jan Gintzel (1660–1743), b. Chomutov, Bohemia, a Bohemian Jesuit, entered S.J. in 1676 and studied theology in Prague (1687–90). He went by Lisbon to Brazil, arriving in Bahia in 1694. He was active in many places, also among Tupuyos Indians at Rio San Francisco. In one of his letters, he complained: "The more you do for them, the worse they are. They value horse or cow more than God. To church, you get them only by beating or by threats."

Francisco Hlava (1725–1768), b. Prague, Bohemia, a Bohemian Jesuit Father, entered the S.J. Order in 1740. In 1756, arrived in Veracruz, Mexico as a missionary. He went north to serve at Suamca, Cocóspera, and San Ignacio. He was not in the Pimería Alta long, however, and was at Mocorito, Sinaloa at the time of the expulsion. Of the seven priests whose names appear in the Guevavi and Suamca mission records, who died on the forced march through the coastal jungles between Tepic, Nayarit, and Guadalajara, Jalisco during the Expulsion Padre Hlava, the third to die, passed away on September 7, 1768. He was the second youngest of the seven priests at forty-three years, eight months, and seven days of age when he died at Ixtlán, Nayarit, Mexico.

Jiří Hostinský (1652–1726), b. Valašské Klobouky u Brna, Moravia, a Bohemian Jesuit, was sent as a missionary to Mexico in 1686, arriving in Veracruz. His center of activities was Tarahumara in the Cajurichi settlement. In 1690, his life was saved only through receiving a timely warning when a storm broke out in the region. He then moved to the region further northwest, called Pimeria Alta. In 1693, he was director of the mission at San Ignacio on Rio Magdalena. In 1694, he participated at consecration ceremony of the church of Nuestra Senora de los Dolores, located in southern Arizona. In 1697, in another rebellion, he again escaped in time. Subsequently, he worked in the region of Chínipas, surrounded by high mountains on all sides, where he held the office of superior of the mission. Later he returned to Tarahumara and became Superior of the mission of Santa Tomás, near Papigochi (1721-26). Hostinsky wrote four accounts dealing with the missions and a monograph entitled *Ophirium*. He died in Papigochi in November 1726.

Daniel Januschke (Januška) (1661–1724), b. Silesia, a Bohemian Jesuit missionary, entered the S. J. Order in Breslau in 1676. He was sent to Mexico in 1692. He was located at mission of San Pedro Tubutama, west of the mission of Nuestra Senora de los Dolores, in today's southern Arizona. He was first assigned to the Tarahumara, but after the rebellion of 1690, he came to Tubutama in the spring of 1693. He left there after the revolt of 1695 and was at Teópare in the Sierra in 1697 and 1698. By 1702, he had moved to Oposura where he remained until at least 1721 and probably until his death in March 1724.

Jan John (1655-1702), b. Jaroměř, Bohemia, a Bohemian Jesuit, entered S. J. in 1672. In 1691, he sailed from Cardiz, arriving at Buenos Aires in April. He first worked at the mission of St. Thomas and then at the mission of St. Anna. He died in Sandiego.

Adamus Kall (Kaller) (1657-1702), b. Cheb, Bohemia, a Bohemian Jesuit, studied philosophy in Olomouc and theology in Prague. In 1687, he was sent as a missionary to Mariana Islands, by way of Mexico. In one of his letters, he described in detail his long, perilous journey from Cadiz to Puerto Rico and from there to Veracruz, Mexico. In Mexico, he also visited Puebla. Later he wrote at great length about his impressions and experiences there. He gave a detailed account of the life of Catalina, a young woman who died shortly before his arrival there, with the reputation of being a saint. When she saw Bohemian Jesuit Strobach and his four companions, with whom he was to leave for the Marianas Islands, she declared the stars shone above their heads, auguring a martyr's death. When Kaller was in Puebla, he often recalled the maid Catalina's vision for the prophecy proved true. In 1684, Strobach and his four companions were killed by savages on the island of Rota.

Ignacius Xavier Keller (1702-1759), b. Olomouc, Moravia, a Bohemian Jesuit, joined the S.J. Order in 1717 and studied theology in Olomouc. He left for South America as a missionary in 1730, arriving in Havana Harbor in February 1731; in April, he crossed over Vera Cruz and from there he went on mule back to Mexico and mid-June left for duty in the Pimeria Alta. In 1732, he was assigned to Santa Maria Suamca Mission, located in southern Arizona, where he remained for 27 years. Father Keller had become lord and master to the Indians and as long as he lived, they would accept no other. He also explored along the Gila River in 1736-37 but in the following year was prevented by the Apache from reaching the Hopi country. One of his accomplishments was the preparation of a map of Upper Pimeria (1744), encompassing rivers, villages, missions and names of Indian tribes. He died at Santa María Suamca in 1759.

Jindřich Kordule (1658-1727), b. Běstviny, Bohemia, entered the S.J. in 1675. He studied philosophy in Olomouc and theology in Prague and was ordained priest in 1687. In 1689, he left Bohemia for missionary work in Latin America. Later he worked in Paraguay in the Chiantitoc mission, together with another Bohemian Jesuit, Jan Neumann. Since 1714, he worked in the reduction of San Ignacio. In 1724, he became consultant of the Parana mission.

Wenceslao Linck (Link) (1736-1797), b. Nejdek, Bohemia, a Bohemian Jesuit, joined the S.J. Order in 1754 and studied in Brno and in Prague, and later in Mexico City and Puebla (1756-61). In 1762, he was sent to Baja California, initially to Santa Gertruidis and then he moved north to found the Mission of San Francisco de Borja (1762-68), in the center of the San Borja Desert at the watering hole of Adac. Over the next five years, Linck undertook a series of exploring expeditions to scout future missions and resolve geographical puzzles. In 1766, he was ordered to proceed over land to the Colorado River. He proceeded as far as the region of San Bonaventura, located in Ventura, California. He returned to Bohemia, when the Jesuits were expelled in 1768. He died in Olomouc in February 1797.

Joseph Neumann (1648–1732), b. Brussels, Belgium, became member of the Bohemian Province of Jesuits in 1663 and studied philosophy in Prague and theology in Olomouc, Moravia. At the age of 33, he took up missionary work and his activities spread over more than 50 years in Mexico. He worked for 12 years at the Sisoguichi mission. In 1693, he arrived at Carichi mission, where he remained until his death in 1732. During his long work, Neumann was several times Mission Superior and visitor. He founded new centers and initiated younger priests into the work. Neumann was considered a model of the permanent missionaries and one of the pillars upon which the missions in Tarahumara rested. In 1724, University of Prague published his history dealing with the uprisings of Tarahumera tribes, under the title *Historia Seditionum*.

Florián Paucke (Baucke) (1719–1780), b. Winzig, Silesia, a Bohemian Jesuit, entered the S.J. Order in 1736. He studied philosophy in Prague and theology in Breslau. In 1748, he was sent through Lisbon to South America as a missionary. He worked mostly in Gran Chaco, Rio de Plata, Paraguay. He became a teacher and modernizer. He introduced the Indians to the advantages of a settled lifestyle, stone houses, planted fields and cultivated yerba malé (special herb tea in the region). A careful observer, he wrote an illustrated report, first published in 1829 as *Reise in die Missiones* (Journey to the Missions), a humorous description, full of anecdotal material and the ethnographic details. Well educated in music, he left rich documentation about his music activity. He was expelled, together with the S.J. Order, after 1767 and returned to Bohemia.

Francisco Xavier Pauer (František Bauer) (1721–1770), b. Brno, Moravia, a Bohemian Jesuit Father, entered the S. J. Order in 1737. After a nearly a dozen years of study in Olomouc, in May 1749, he set out for Cádiz, Spain and from there by ship to Veracruz, Mexico, where he disembarked in August 1750. In the fall, he set out for the northwest, and together with other Jesuits, rode mules from Quadalajara over primitive roads, reaching San Ignacio in May 1751 and soon after proceeded to San Xavier de Bloc, located in today's Arizona, where he was to work as a missionary. Father Pauer arrived at Guavavi after the worst revolt in the history of Pimeria Alta. He labored at reconstruction for 6 years. He managed to endure among the Indians who at first did not want him. He had baptized more of them than any other priest. He built churches at Tumacácori and Sonoita. After being named

Father Rector of Pimeria Alta, Pauer was reassigned to San Ignacio in mid-January 1760. After expulsion of Jesuits in 1767, he survived the death march across Mexico to Veracruz, dying in Cádiz' prison on January 6, 1770.

Henricus (Jindřich Václav) Richter (1653–1696), b. Prostějov, Moravia, studied at Univ. of Prague, entered the Society of Jesus in 1670 and was sent in 1684 to work in the Peruvian mission territory, known as Minas. He arrived together with Samuel Fritz, a fellow Bohemian Jesuit, and the two together became the most outstanding mission builders in the Peruvian Amazon basin in the 17th century. Richter was sent to work along the Ucayali River which is a major north-south tributary of the Marañón and Amazon Rivers. Based in Laguna, he worked especially among Conibos, but also had contact with the Piros and the Campas. In 12 years, he founded nine reductions (a mission town), along the Ucayali River. Richter was killed by Piro Indians, who were incited by a Canibo whose wife had been stolen by a Spanish soldier. Richter, was considered the Apostle of the Ucayli, wrote catechisms and vocabularies in the languages of Conibo, Piro, Campa and Cocama Indians.

Jan Röhr (Rehr) (1692–1762), joined the S.J. in 1709. He studied philosophy in Olomouc and theology in Prague. He left for missionary work in South America in 1723. Since 1724, he worked as a missionary in Peru among the Moxos Indians. He was a noted mathematician and architect in Lima, Peru. He wrote also a meteorological treatise in Spanish, entitled *El Conocimiento de los Tiempos*.

Valentin Stansel (1621–1705) was apparently the first Jesuit who worked in Latin America. After joining the Jesuit Order, he became a professor of rhetoric and mathematics in Olomouc, Moravia and, later, in Prague. After ordination, he opted for missionary work in India and left for Portugal where he awaited the arrival of a ship. In the meantime, he taught astronomy at the University in Evora. When his trip to India did not materialize, he was sent in 1657 to Brazil and taught at the Jesuit College and Seminary in Bahia (present Salvador). First, he held the position of a professor of moral theology and later was promoted to a Chancellor. In addition to his teaching career, he also conducted research in astronomy and made a number of important discoveries, especially of comets. Some of his observations were subsequently published in Prague, under the title *Observationes Americanae Cometae*.

Mathias Steffel (1734–1806), b. Jihlava, a Bohemian Jesuit, joined the S.J. Order in 1754. In 1755, he left for New Spain, specifically for Mexico. He worked among the Tarahumara Indians. He compiled a dictionary of their languages, as well as their grammar. He returned to Brno in 1768, having been evicted, together with the other Jesuits. He died in Brno in 1806.

Andreas (Ondřej) Suppetius (1654-1712), b. Ratibuř, Silesia, a Bohemian missionary, was sent to South America where he remained from 1684 to 1712. He held the position of a Chancellor at the Jesuit College in Santiago, Chile.

Ignác Tirsch (1733-1781), a Bohemian Jesuit of Chomutov, Bohemia, joined the S.J. Order in 1754. He studied philosophy in Brno and in 1755, he left for Mexico. In 1762, he was a missionary assistant to Padre Procurador Lucas Ventura at Loreto and in 1763-68, he served as missionary at Santiago. He had a keen interest in natural history and created a valuable series of Lower California plants, animals, Indians and - rarest of all - gente de razón. He returned to Europe after the expulsion of Jesuits from South America. He died in Chomutov in 1781.

Johann Nepomuk Walter (1713-1773), b. Hlohov, entered the Bohemian Province of the Jesuits in 1731. Between 1746 and 1748, he traveled to Chile where he worked initially as a pastor in Santiago. From 1750 to 1755, he was a missionary to the Indians and superior of Arauco. In 1755, he was named procurator general of the province. Walter rendered great service in the mission to the Indians of southern Chile. He died in Pulice, Moravia in 1773.

C. Moravian Brethren

John Beck (1706-1777), b. Holašovice, Silesia, Moravia, a Moravian Brother, came to Herrnhut in 1732. In 1734, went with Frederick Boehnisch to Greenland as missionary. In 1746, he was ordained deacon and in 1747, presbyter. After forty-three years of service in Greenland, he died in 1777. He translated large parts of the Bible and many hymns into Eskimo. He was the ancestor of long line of Moravian missionaries.

Christian David (1691-1751) from Ženklava, near Fulnek, where Comenius used to preach. His admirers called him 'the Godly Carpenter,' 'the Moravian Carpenter,' 'the Apostle,' 'the Wandering Apostle,' 'Builder of Herrnhut,' 'the Indefatigable Evangelist' or 'the Servant of the Lord.' He was a devout Catholic in his youth and a flaming evangelist after his conversion to Hus' teachings. Although he was entirely uneducated and till his conversion illiterate, even the scholarly John Wesley was deeply impressed by his sermons. Before coming to exile, he used to travel through Bohemia and Moravia, seeking 'the hidden seed' among the descendants of Bohemian Brethren. He led the first refugees from Bohemia to Moravia in 1722. He kept a week's services at Halle, preached in Holland, the Baltic Provinces and had much to do with the founding of the Diaspora work. He went to Greenland in 1733 to build the house for the missionaries and in 1747, he built a church there. He came to Bethlehem on the 'Irene' in 1749 with the 'Third Sea Congregation.'

Christoph Demuth (1738-1818), b. Germantown, PA, of Bohemian ancestry, in 1770, founded a tobacco shop in Lancaster, PA which has passed from generation to generation and remained in the Demuth family to date.

Gotthard Demuth (1694-1744), b. Karlov, Bohemia, arrived in Savannah, GA with the first group of the Moravian Brethren in 1735. He was a cabinet maker and watchmaker by vocation, and died at a young age in Germantown, PA.

Gottlieb Demuth (1716-1776), b. Karlov, Bohemia, joined the Moravian group for Savannah, GA, arriving there in February 1736. At the end of 1738, he left for Pennsylvania. He was an ancestor of the US First Lady Barbara Bush.

Charles Christian Dober (1792-1840), b. Herrnhut Saxony, of Bohemian ancestry, was a Moravian clergyman educated at Moravian Theological Coll. and Sem. in Germany. He came to US in 1831 and taught for a year at the Theological Sem. at Nazareth, before becoming pastor of the Church at York and later at Schoeneck. In 1837, he again taught at the Seminary and a year later at Bethlehem.

John Leonard Dober (1706-1766), b. Muenschrode, Swabia, of Bohemian ancestry, a potter by trade, came to Herrnhut in 1730. He became the first Moravian missionary on St. Thomas, with David Nitschmann. In 1734, he was called back to Herrnhut to become chief elder of the renewed Unity of the Brethren. In this capacity he traveled a great deal, visiting the congregations. In 1741, he was consecrated bishop of the Moravian Church. Was active in Livonia, London and Herrnhut. After Zinzendorf's death, was member of the Enge Conference. In 1762, he became head of entire Unity. From 1765 to his end, he was charged with the revision of the Unity archives. During this time, he alone visited numerous congregations and for a time lived in Gnadenfrei. In 1766, returned to Herrnhut where he died.

Gottlieb Haberecht (1700-1767), b. Lower Silesia, a tailor, came to Georgia in 1737 and soon after, he moved to Pennsylvania. In 1743, returned to Europe with Count Zinzendorf. In 1747, he went to Algiers for 10 months. In 1749, he was in London and in 1754, he was one of the first missionaries to be sent to Jamaica, West Indies. Later he went to Christianspring as superintendent of the weavers' shop, where he died.

Christian Renatus Heckewalder (1750-1803), b. Misfield, England, a son of Rev. David Heckewelder, came to America in April 1754, arriving in New York. In 1766, he walked with a group of other Moravians from Pennsylvania to the Moravian community in North Carolina, which he joined. He was a storekeeper, and made frequent trips to Cross Creek, NC (now Fayetteville) and to Charleston, SC to buy goods and supplies for the community.

In 1780, he became the teacher of the older boys. He seems to have left the community sometime in the 1780s.

John E. G. Heckewelder (1743–1823), b. Bedford, England, of Moravian parents, was a famed Moravian missionary among Indians. He came to America in 1754 and attended the Moravian boys' school in Bethlehem. He was dispatched as a messenger to Indian settlements in which work he showed unusual ability to understand the language and customs of the Indians. Beginning in 1771, he became an able assistant to David Zeisberger for fifteen years. In 1792, Secretary of War General Knox appointed him to accompany General Putnam on a mission to arrange the peace treaty at Vincennes, IN. Next year, he served on a similar mission going by way of the Iroquois country to Detroit. In 1801, he returned to Gnadenhutten where he administered for nine years the Indian 'estate' on the Muskingum. Last years of his life were spent, at the request of the American Philosophical Society, in recording some of the knowledge of Indian life that he had acquired. This led to several important publications, i.e., *Account of the History, Manners and Customs of the Indian Nations Who Once Inhabited Pennsylvania and the Neighboring States* (1819).

Juliana Jaeschke (1724–1766), Žilina, Moravia, a seamstress, immigrated to Savannah, GA in February 1736. Soon after her arrival, it was suggested that she marry Peter Rosa, but the lot forbade it. George Waschke, a carpenter from Kunín, Moravia, thought he would like to marry Juliana, but she refused, even though Bishop Nitschmann, and Mr. and Mrs. Toeltschig pleaded with her. Her preference was for George Haberland, and the result was an uncomfortable state of affairs, which disturbed the leaders of the 'Society' not a little, for living as they did as one large family which meant constant friction on all sides. They did not know whether to force Juliana to submit to their authority, (as a member of the 'Society' she had pledged herself to obedience to the duly elected officers), or whether they should wait and hope for a better frame of mind. At last, they referred it to the lot, which read 'Juliana shall not marry any one yet.' This settled the question for the time being. On the 10th of June, the matrimonial troubles of George Waschke and Juliana were resolved by their marriage. They lived happy lives together.

Andreas Anton Lawatsch (1712–1771), b. Kreisendorf, Silesia, joined the Moravians (1736) and married Anna Maria Demuth (1738). He became a Moravian minister, and together with his wife, came to America in June 1752, initially settling in Bethlehem. He must also concerned himself with commercial matters, because he represented the town in the Commercial Society. In 1752–64, they resided in Nazareth. His wife died in 1760. In 1764, he was sent as missionary to Surinam, where he remarried twice, i.e., Rosina Gartmann in 1768 and Anna Elisabeth Paul in 1770. He died in Paramaribo in Surinam.

Augustine Neisser (1717–1780), b. Žilina, Moravia, cutler and clock-maker, arrived in Georgia with his brother George in February 1736. In 1738, he left for Philadelphia where he made the first town clock for Bethlehem, which was placed in the turret of the Bell House. He was one of 15 who were present at the laying of the cornerstone of the Gemein Haus in Bethlehem in September 1741. He returned to live in Germantown, PA.

George Neisser (1715–1784), b. Žilina, Moravia, who initially immigrated to Savannah, GA, became the first school-master of Bethlehem, when the school was opened in 1742. He was also the first Moravian diarist and the postmaster. He was ordained deacon in 1748 and presbyter in 1755. He was very active as pastor and vice elder, serving in Bethlehem, Nazareth, Heidelberg, Lancaster, Lebanon, Bethlehem, Warwick (Lititz) and York in PA; New York, Piles Grove, NJ and Monocacy in MD. He wrote a number of hymns and chronicle "Moravian History in America." Among his publications is *A List of the Bohemian and Moravian Emigrants to Saxony*, written in German and translated into English in 1911 by A G. Rau.

Anna Caritas Nitschmann (1715–1769) of Kunín, Moravia, who exerted a remarkable spiritual influence on high and low alike in the early days of the Renewed Unity. She was generally known as 'The Blessed Disciple.' She was a close collaborator of Zinzendorf who held the office of Moravian Bishop and accompanied him on his trips to various missions. When she was only fifteen years old, in 1730, the lot designated Anna as the Eldress of all the women of Herrnhut. In the same year, she formed the Choir of Unmarried Women. Although she initially declined all offers of marriage, she married Zinzendorf as his second wife, when his first wife died. It should be noted that Count Zinzendorf then resigned as Count of the Realm and devoted himself exclusively to religious work.

David Nitschmann (1696-1772), b. Suchdol, Moravia, who was consecrated the first Bishop of the Renewed Brethren's Unity in 1735, by Bishop Jablonsky, a grandson of John A. Komenský (Comenius). The following year, he accompanied the second group of Moravian missionaries to Savannah, GA. He was dispatched to establish a Brethren settlement in Northern America which led to his founding of Bethlehem, PA. Much of his life was spent in travel. Towards the end of his life, he resided in Bethlehem.

David the 'Syndic' Nitschmann (1705–1779), b. Suchdol, Moravia, a weaver, was one of the 'Five Churchmen' who arrived in Herrnhut in 1724 for the purpose of renewing the *Unitas Fratrum*. In 1735, he made an exploratory journey to St. Petersburg and following year was missionary in Ceylon. In 1741, was Zinzendorf's assistant in dealing with governments and received the title 'Syndic.' In 1746, he was consecrated Bishop of the Moravian Church. In 1764-65, he visited Bethlehem and other congregations.

Peter Rosa (?-1740), a native of Bohemia, was one of the first group of missionaries in Savannah, GA in March 1735. There he married the widow of Frederick Riedel, Catherine Pudmensky, orig. of Moravia. They moved into the schoolhouse at Irene, several miles from Savannah, where they both served as teachers to Creek Indians, who loved them. After the school was closed, they moved to Germantown, where Peter Rosa died.

Anna Johanna Seidel (née Piesch) (1726-1788), b. Berthelsdorf, of Moravian parents (a daughter of George and Rosina Piesch), was one of the most influential women in the 18th century Moravian Church. At the age of nineteen, she was made General Eldress of all Single Sisters Choirs, in which capacity she traveled extensively across Europe and America with Zinzendorf and her aunt Anna Nitschmann. At the age of 35 (1760), the marriage to Bishop Nathaniel Seidel was proposed to her, which she accepted with great difficulty but recognized the administrative necessity of such a move, with the departure of Zinzendorf and Anna Nitschmann. After all, she and Bishop Seidel were two of the best-known members of the Moravian Church in Europe and America. She resided in Bethlehem since 1761. She died at Nazareth where she is also buried.

Nathaniel Seidel (1718-1782), b. Laubau, Silesia, of Bohemian parents, in 1718, was consecrated Bishop of Moravian Church. He served for twenty years as President of the American Provincial Board of the Elders. He came originally to Bethlehem in 1742 as a missionary among Indians. In 1748, became Presbyter and five years later, was sent to the mission in Surinam, South America.

Gottlieb Shober (1756-1838), b. Bethlehem, PA, of Moravian ancestry, resided with his parents in Bethabara, a Moravian settlement in the south, where he received a common-school education. He taught for a few years, then learned the trade of a tinsmith, and began business in Salem, South Carolina, where he soon combined a bookstore with his tin-shop, became postmaster, and built the first paper-mill south of the Potomac. While an apprentice, he had studied law, was admitted to the bar, and soon acquired an extensive practice among the German settlers. Later he became a large landowner, had numerous slaves, and was frequently elected to the legislature. After his fiftieth year, he desired to enter the ministry, but, finding it impossible to take the long theological course that was required by the Moravian church, he induced the village authorities to make a change in their laws, which, being confirmed by the legislature, permitted another denomination within their borough. He then took a course of reading, and in 1811, was appointed by the Lutheran Synod Pastor at Salem. The indignant Moravians tried to compel him to leave the town, but he proved his right to remain by their own recent enactment and labored there gratuitously till a few years before his death. He was a founder of the general synod of the Lutheran church, of which he was president in 1825, and one of the committee to prepare a Lutheran hymnbook, and to publish the translation of Luther's catechism. In 1825, he was a director of the theological institution which adopted measures for the formation of the seminary at Gettysburg, Pennsylvania, to which he left three thousand acres of land.

Anton Seifert (1712–1785), b. Lipka, Bohemia, a carpenter, arrived with the first group of Moravians in Savannah, GA in March 1735. In 1736, he was ordained by Bishop Nitschmann to ministry of the Moravian Church, who put him in charge of the congregation in Savannah, GA. In 1740, he removed to Pennsylvania, where he served in the church schools and in the ministry till April 1745, when he returned to Europe. He is considered to be the first Moravian minister in America.

Matthew Stach (1711–1787), b. Mankovice, Moravia, Moravian missionary, wool spinner by trade, in 1733, together with his brother Christian, accompanied Christian David to Greenland as a missionary. He baptized the first Eskimo convert Kajarnak in 1740. He was ordained presbyter in 1741 and following year returned to Greenland. In 1747, he visited Europe and in 1748 sailed, to NY with Bishop David Nitschmann, visiting Bethlehem and Gnadenhutten in PA. Subsequently, he went back to Greenland, staying there till 1751 and returned to Herrnhut. In 1758, was called to start a new mission in the Fischer-Fiorde in Greenland and when Frederick Boehnisch died in 1763, he took charge of the mission in New Herrnhut. In 1771, he retired at Barby. In 1772, he moved to Bethabara, NC taking charge of the congregation there and of the boys' school. He also became member of Committee of Oversight. He died in Bethabara.

David Tanneberger (Tannenberg) (1728–1804) of Moravian parentage, born on Count Zinzendorf's estate in Berthelsdorf, was a noted organ builder. He was a skillful joiner, a notably good tenor, and played the violin. He learned the organ-building craft and soon became well-known for his unique technical skills. Organs of his manufacture were in high repute and were shipped from his Lititz shop all over eastern Pennsylvania, even to such distant places as Albany, NY.

David Zeisberger Jr., whose parents forsook their considerable estate in Moravia and fled for conscience sake to Herrnhut, after coming to America in 1738, embarked on an intensive study of Indian languages which provided a foundation for his illustrious career among American Indians, lasting more than sixty years. Zeisberger's able assistant, John Heckewelder, of Moravian ancestry, also attained prominence as a missionary among the Indians. Besides his missionary labors, he was a postmaster, Justice of Peace, as well as Justice of the Court of Common Pleas. In the last years of his life, he engaged in literary pursuits which led to his election in the prestigious American Philosophical Society of

Philadelphia. Thanks to Zeisberger's and Heckewelder's writings, we have preserved accurate documentation of the life and the customs of American Indians.

Count Nicholaus Ludwig Zinzendorf (1700-1760), b. Dresden, Saxony, a descendant of Bohemian aristocracy, a theologian, became a leader of the Protestant Reformation and the founder of the Renewed Moravian Church. Zinzendorf built the Moravian Church upon the foundation of Comenius's Revision of *The Order of Discipline of the Church of the Brethren*. Zinzendorf wrote the *Brotherly Agreement of 1727* for the Protestant refugees who had taken refuge on his estate. He soon became the leading theologian of the Moravian Church.

Countess Benigna Zinzendorf (aka Henrietta Benigna Justine Zinzendorf von Watteville) (1725-1789), b. Berthelsdorf, Saxony, was of Bohemian ancestry, being the daughter of Count Nicolaus Zinzendorf and Countess Erdmuthe Dorothea of Reuss-Ebersdorf, the latter a descendant of the Bohemian King George of Podiebrad. She was as the founder of the first boarding school for girls in the British American colonies, which became Moravian College. She was a missionary among Native Americans and assisted her father, Count Nicolaus Zinzendorf, in his religious activities in Europe and America. She enjoyed music and was an Eldress to girl's choirs beginning at the age of 14 and was a leader in an adult choir after she was married.

1. The Forty-Eighters

Johann R. Adam (some refer to him as Gustav) (1815-1866). b. Příbram, Bohemia, a Czech patriot who had participated in the insurrection against Austria in 1848, had to escape to the US to save himself from being jailed and possible death. He was probably the first Czech to reach Cleveland, OH. He was a good musician and became an orchestra leader in Cleveland's theater, the Athenaeum. He later moved to Tennessee.

Leopold Adler (1828-d.), b. Prachatice, Bohemia, a physician, who immigrated to Milwaukee, WI, where he opened his practice. He was the first Czech physician in Milwaukee. He served as a surgeon in the Austrian army and during the revolutionary events of 1848, he had to leave the country.

Hans (Jan) Balatka (1827-1899), b. Doly u Bouzova, Moravia, a musician, joined the Viennese Academic Legion during the Revolutions in 1848 and because of his involvement, he had to escape to America. In 1849, he reached Wisconsin and, following a romantic impulse, tried rural life for a spell, but soon settled in Milwaukee, where he conducted the Musical Society (German: Musikverein), founded in 1850. He produced several oratorios and operas, and conducted musical festivals in Cleveland, Cincinnati, Detroit, Chicago, and Pittsburgh. His efforts contributed much to the great increase in popularity of European classical music in the United States during the late 19th century.

August Bondi (1833-1907), a native of Vienna, of Bohemian parents, was one of the youngest members of the Students' Corps in Vienna, in the unit led by Capt. Zach, when the Revolution erupted there. He succeeded to escape with his parents to the US, initially settling in St. Louis, MO. In 1860, Bondi enlisted in an expedition to liberate Cuba from the Spanish yoke. When this came to naught, after spending part of 1851 in Texas, he returned to St. Louis. He soon became restless and moved, together with another Bohemian, by name Jacob Benjamin, they moved to Kansas, where they established a trading post. Besides the usual hardships of pioneer life, they were subjected to threats from active pro-slavery groups. He joined the John Brown's group and took part in many scuffles and skirmishes with the slaver followers. He describes his experience in his autobiography. About his student years in Vienna, he wrote that he was full of hatred against the moral and government tyranny and how he was heartfelt with humanitarian ideals and how he fully sympathized with all the oppressed people in Austria. When the Civil War broke out, he was among the first to enlist. After the war, he became a successful lawyer in Kansas.

Adolph Brandeis (1824-1906), b. Prague, Bohemia, in anticipation of the Revolution of 1848, was sent to America as an emissary, by the two prominent Prague Jewish families of Wehle and Brandeis, to scout the territory of the 'Promised Land.' He left in August 1848. He had preceded the Brandeis-Wehle group of twenty-six persons who arrived in 1849. His experiences had convinced him that farming was out of question for his family and their best chance lay in the opportunities afforded by the great river traffic of the Ohio Valley. After a start in Madison, IN, Brandeis formed the partnership of Brandeis & Crawford in Louisville, KY, a wholesale grain and produce business. During the Civil War, Brandeis & Crawford were important purveyors of grain and food for the Union Army. Adolph Brandeis was the father of the US Supreme Court Justice Louis D. Brandeis.

Isidor Bush (orig. Busch) (1822-1898), b. Prague, was an editor and publisher of several revolutionary papers in Vienna in which he encouraged the Jews to immigrate to America. When the Revolution of 1848 failed, he had to flee to New York, where he arrived in January 1849. There, Bush opened a store for the sale of newspapers and stationery, and on March 30, 1849, published the initial number of *Israel's Herald*, the first Jewish weekly in the United States. In the summer of 1849, Bush went to St. Louis where he managed a general store for six years. In 1857, Bush was made president of the People's Savings Bank. When the Missouri Convention was called to determine whether the State should join in the secession movement, Bush was chosen a member on the Unconditional Union ticket and was made a member of the Committee of Nine, to which most important matters were referred. When

Fremont took command in 1861, with headquarters in St. Louis, Bush was made his aide-de-camp, with the rank of captain. Bush was chosen member of the state convention called to abolish slavery and to form a new constitution. He was elected a member of the Missouri State Board of immigration to repair losses in population resulting from the war, which post he retained for twelve years. Later in life, Bush became interested in viticulture. He purchased a tract of land (named by him 'Bushberg') outside the city, which became noted for its products; and he even sent large quantities of cuttings from his vineyards to France to replace ravages by phylloxera. Bush, after years of preparation, published a catalogue of grapes, *The Bushberg Catalogue*, which has gone through several editions and has been translated into several languages.

Fredericka Dembitz (1826–1901), b. Poland, of Bohemian mother; future wife of Adolph Brandeis, and mother of Louis D. Brandeis.

Péter Pál Dobozy (1832–1919), location of his birth uncertain but could be of Slovak ancestry. He was a soldier in Hungarian revolution of 1848. He resided in US s. 1861. He was a Civil War veteran. After the Civil War, he resided in Missouri as a farmer.

Alexander Eisenschiml (1832–1888), b. Měčín, nr Přeštice, Bohemia, immigrated to America, when revolutionary sentiments grew rife in Austria. Upon landing in New York, news reached the boat that gold had been discovered in California. Crew and passengers decided to make for San Francisco. After adventurous career in California and Nevada, he gave up prospecting and turned soldier. In 1861, he joined the Illinois regiment and saw action at Shiloh, the crucial battle between the Union soldiers and the Confederates. The reality of war quickly induced him to resign the commission and thereafter, during the remainder of the war, he became an Indian Scout. After a dreadful witnessing how his comrades were captured by a bloodthirsty Indian tribe and tortured to death, he quit the Indian Service also. Taking out his citizenship papers in Nevada, he turned to a peaceful occupation of running a meat market in Chicago.

Kornél (Cornelius) Fornét (1818–1894), b. Stráže pod Tatrami, Slovakia, an engineer, was a soldier in Hungarian war of 1848. He immigrated to the US in 1849 and participated in Civil War with the rank of Major of Engineers. Due to injuries, he then returned to Hungary, where he became government official.

František Samuel Figuli (1825–1880), b. Klenovec, Slovakia, was an adventurer, traveler, writer, and participant in the 1848 Revolution. He fought in the Civil War, owned a plantation in Virginia, later joined an exploratory expedition to the North Pole.

Andrew Gálfy-Gállik (1818-1883), b. Brzotín, Slovakia, merchant in Košice, was an officer during the 1848 revolution. He came to America, settling in Cincinnati, OH; in 1862, enlisted in the 58th Ohio Infantry Regiment, in which he was appointed Major. After being captured, he was exchanged and then served on the gunboat Mound City. After the war, he studied medicine and then practiced in Boston, then in Cincinnati and finally in Kansas City. In 1881, he returned to Košice.

Anthony (Antal) Gerster (1825-1897), b. Košice, Slovakia, uncle of Dr. Arpad G. Gerster, was a civil engineer and a military officer in the 1848 Revolution in Hungary. He immigrated to the US in 1852. He served in the Civil War as an officer of the engineer corps under General John C. Frémont, with General Alexander Asboth and later served under the Generals Rosecrans and Grant. He died in California in 1897.

Regina Goldmark (née Wehle) (1835-1924), b. Prague, Bohemia, in US s. 1849; wife of Dr. Joseph J. Goldmark; mother of Alice Goldmark Brandeis, the wife of Justice Louis D. Brandeis.

Friedrich Hassaurek (1831-1885), b, Vienna, attended the Piaristen gymnasium. In the Revolution of 1848, he served in the Student Legion, and was twice wounded. After the failure of the Vienna Rebellion in 1848, he came to the United States, settled in Cincinnati, Ohio, and engaged in journalism, politics, and the practice of law. He was Ohio's delegate to the new Republican Party's National Convention in 1860 and 1868. He was appointed by President Abraham Lincoln as the U.S. Minister to Ecuador and served in that role from 1861 to 1866. He then became the editor of the *Cincinnati Volksblatt*.

John Heřman (1812-1888), b. Nebužely, nr Mělník, Bohemia, was a very wealthy and prominent man, a member of Austrian parliament and of a delegation sent to interview the Emperor. He took part in the Revolution of 1848 and being persecuted, was obliged to flee his country in 1853. He immigrated to Wisconsin, but then moved to Nebraska, settling in Arago in 1864. Then for a while, he lived in Aspinwall and about 1868, he came to Wilber where he died. He was considered the richest immigrant that ever came to America, for he brought with him 80,000 Austrian gold to Wisconsin, but lost it all through unfortunate ventures.

Prokop Hudek (1843-1886), b. Staňovice, Bohemia, was one of the Forty-Eighters, who left for US in 1854. He was one of the organizers of Czech national life in Chicago. He was one of the "Slavonic Artillerymen" of the 24th Illinois Infantry Regiment, and one of the co-founders of the Workingmen's Party of Illinois. He was an unsuccessful candidate for the Illinois Senate.

Adolph Huebsch (1830–1884), b. Liptovský Svatý Mikuláš, participated as a soldier and officer in the Hungarian revolutionary army in the uprising of 1848, and barely escaped alive. Later, he served as rabbi in Myjava, Moravia and in the New Synagogue in Prague. In 1866, he received a call as rabbi and preacher to the congregation Ahabath Hesed of New York City, then composed almost entirely of Bohemian Jews.

Charles (Karel) Jonáš (1840–1896), b. Malešov, Bohemia, studied at Polytechnic Institute in Prague, as well as attending lectures at Charles University in Prague. A strong Czech nationalist and friend of Vojtěch Náprstek, he fled Bohemia in 1860 after clashes with the authorities, moving via Bremen to London, where he continued to work as a journalist. In March 1863, he immigrated to Racine, Wisconsin, just south of Milwaukee, where Náprstek had been the first Czech to publish a periodical in the United States. There he edited and published the Czech language newspaper *Slavie*. In November 1886, Jonáš was appointed US Consul in Prague by President Grover Cleveland, which position he held until July 16, 1889. In 1890, he was elected 16th Lieutenant Governor of Wisconsin. He would serve in that office from 1891 until 1894, when he resigned to become the US Consul in St. Petersburg, Russia; in 1896, he was transferred to Crefeld, Germany, where he died that same year.

Francis (František) J. Korbel (1830–1920), b. Bechyně, Bohemia, was one of the most famous Forty-Eighters from Bohemia to come to America, where he arrived in 1850. During the Prague disturbances of 1848, he was arrested and interned in military barracks, from where he succeeded to flee to Saxony and from there to New York. For a while, he worked as a technician in surveying the route of the Panama railway and then came to New York where he started a cigar manufacturing business. Following the amnesty, he returned to Bohemia, but soon we see him with his two brothers, Antonín and Josef, on their way back to New York. Later, all three of them moved to San Francisco, where he established a factory manufacturing cigar boxes. At the same time, he went into business with cedar, which he exported on his own ship named *Bohemia*. From the proceeds, he purchased forests and exported sequoia wood as far as Australia, South America, Europe and China. Korbel used the soil of the forests he cut down for the planting of extensive vineyards. In time, he established one of the largest lumber and wine-growing industries in the US. His financial contribution to his Czech countrymen made possible the founding of the Czech American Press Agency in 1909.

Philip Korn, bookseller from Bratislava; Captain in the Hungarian Revolutionary Army, managed to escape to US.

Lajos Kossuth (in Slovak: Ludevít Košút), (1802-1894), b. Monok, of Slovak descent, was a Hungarian nobleman, lawyer, politician, statesman, a revolutionary. He immigrated to the US in 1851. He later returned to Europe.

Anton Krásný (ca. 1812-1870), a R. C. priest, a sincere patriot and political offender, was imprisoned in Prague in St. George Monastery that was converted into a prison after the 1848 Prague disturbance. Many of the Forty-Eighters were thrown into the new prison to frighten the Czech nation and to make them confess that broad conspiracy had been prepared in Bohemia. He arrived in New York, after being incarcerated from 1849 to 1857. He then removed to Cleveland, OH, where he became the first Czech Catholic priest.

Joseph Křikava (1821-1888), b. Ouboč, nr. Nová Kdyně, student at Prague Polytechnic, after participating in 1848 Revolution, immigrated to America, arriving in New York in 1849. After various unsuccessful ventures, he opened a wine-shop at 50 Avenue B, which was patronized by the best people in town. The patriarchal looking proprietor was affectionately called 'Grandfather.'

Antonín Kroupa (1816-1900), b. Vlašim, Bohemia, a political refugee, was the first Czech to reach Racine. He arrived in America shortly after the 1848 uprising, settling for a while in Cleveland, while working for twelve dollars a month. After sixteen weeks, desolate, he left Cleveland for Racine. He eventually found employment at J. Conroy's hardware store, where he worked for 16 years and after Mr. Conroy's death in 1865, he ran the store himself.

Hans Kudlich (1823-1917), a native of Úvalno, Silesia, studied law in Vienna. Early in 1848, at the age of 25, he participated in the student rebellion in Vienna and later was elected by the constituency of his region to the Reichstag (Parliament), having been the youngest ever to serve. Hans Kudlich introduced a bill to abolish all forms of servitude of farmers (Bauernbefreiung) which was unanimously approved. In October of 1848, a Revolution broke out and Vienna was taken by the rebels. During this rebellion, the War Minister of Austria, Graf Latour, was assassinated and Hans Kudlich was unjustly implicated. The Austrian Army crushed the rebellion and the revolutionaries fled or were arrested, tried and severely punished. Hans Kudlich fled via Sachsen, Stuttgart to Baden, participated in the respective rebellion and later went to Switzerland. There he studied medicine, married the daughter of his professor and then immigrated to the United States where he established a medical practice in Hoboken, New Jersey. In 1854, Hans Kudlich was tried in absence by the Austrian court as a conspirator to the assassination of Graf Latour and sentenced to death. Emperor Franz Joseph of Habsburg in 1867 pardoned Hans Kudlich and permitted him to return to his homeland.

III. PIONEERS

Josef Lewi (1820–1897), b. Radnice, Bohemia, Prague-trained physician, belonged to a close circle of intellectuals who inspired the Revolution of 1848. When he realized that the Revolution cannot succeed, he did not wait for its defeat in Vienna and immigrated to America. He settled in Albany, the capital of New York, where he became one of the most popular physicians. He held the post of chairman of the medical society and was also the main supervisor of the Medical Society of the State of New York. During the Civil War, he served as district medical examiner.

Joseph Majthenyi, b. Nitra, Slovakia; member of the landed gentry and prominent politician, was a member of upper chamber of Hungarian parliament. Having taken part in the War of Independence, he was forced to flee to America. He and his family settled in New Buda, Iowa, but soon moved to Davenport.

Max Maretzek (1821–1897), b. Brno, Moravia, a composer and conductor, and future impresario, was one of the revolutionaries who had to leave his country for political reasons. Upon arrival in New York in 1848, he was appointed conductor of the Astor Place Opera House, of which he later became director.

Vojta Mašek (1839–1907), b. Pohořovice, Bohemia, a student at Technical Univ. in Prague, was jailed during the Prague riots, together with Karel Jonáš. After an interrogation by the police, he was 'interned' to his home. He came to America in 1860, settling in Racine, WI, where, before the arrival of Jonáš, the future editor of *Slavie*, served as editor-in-chief of *Slavie*. He soon gave up journalism and became a successful businessman.

Wilhelm Meyerhoefer (1814–1880), b. Prague, Bohemia, already in 1848, immigrated to America as a political refugee. After completing his law studies, he became a librarian at the Royal Library in Prague. However, his life-long passion was music, and this eventually led him to a change of profession. Due to his close friendship with Mendelssohn, he was named professor and organist at the conservatory in Leipzig. After coming to US, he became an organist and music teacher in New York. In 1877, he was named professor of music at the conservatory in Louisville, KY.

Franta Rostislav Mráček (1828–1895), a native of Nenakonice, Moravia, attended the Prague Technical School. For political agitation, he was sentenced to 20 years to Kufstein Prison and served until 1857. He was amnestied and came to New York in 1857. In New York, he made his livelihood by making cigars. He then went to St. Louis in 1861 to edit the newspaper *Národní Noviny* there. He traveled with J. Bárta Letovský to Russia to see whether New Bohemia could be located there. He died there.

Vojtěch 'Vojta' Náprstek (1826–1894), b. Prague, Bohemia, was among the most famous Czech Forty-Eighters, who holds a foremost position in the cultural life of the age that saw the rebirth of the Czech nation. In 1840, he went to pursue his studies in Vienna, where he also developed political activity, particularly in the Czech-Moravian-Silesian Association. On March 13th 1848 at the Estates House (Stavovské divadlo), he made a speech to the people on the equal rights of all nations in the Austrian Empire, which was loudly acclaimed. Already then, he also spoke before the Association on the emancipation of women and devoted attention to this question for the rest of his life. Immediately after the October Revolution, he decided to travel to America because a warrant for his arrest had been issued. Following a brief stay in New York, where he organized the Bohemian Association – the first Czech Society in America – he left for Milwaukee. Here, he opened a bookstore and a print shop and soon began to publish in German a weekly paper entitled *Milwaukee Flug-Blätter*, in which he promoted his liberal ideas. On Náprstek's initiative and in accordance with his plans, the first Czech newspaper was published in St. Louis in 1860 under the title of *Národní Noviny* (National Newspaper). He himself, however, returned to his native land already in 1858 and performed a huge piece of work here in the field of culture. His guesthouse "U Halánků" became a favorite centre of the Czech intelligentsia and a sought-after refuge for all Czechs living abroad.

Joseph Nemeth (1816–1889), b. Lošonec, Slovakia; professional soldier in the 4th Cavalry Regiment in the Imperial Army with the rank of 1st Lieutenant. At the outbreak of the Hungarian War of Independence, deserted with some 500 hussars and returned to Hungary. He volunteered in one militia regiments and was mustered as 1st Lieutenant, later elevated to a Captain in the 62nd Honved Battalion. He participated in more than two dozen engagements and was wounded several times, until he was discharged in July 1849. After the surrender of the Hungarian revolutionary forces, he fled to Turkey. In 1851 arrived in the US.

Isaac Neustadtl (1801–1877), b. Bohemia, a grocer, was among the earliest Jewish immigrants to settle in Milwaukee in 1844. Although not strictly a Forty-Eighter, Neustadtl sympathized with the European revolutionary movement of 1848 and headed an association in Milwaukee for aiding political refugees from Europe.

Oswald Ottendorfer (1826–1900), a native of Svitavy in Moravia, urged, as a twenty-two-year-old student, the overthrow of the reactionary regime in Austria. He was among the first to join the Student Legions in Vienna, he fought in Schleswig-Holstein, then joined the battalion of Robert Blum, fought on the barricades in Dresden and took part in renewed attempts at a revolution in Prague. Many of his fellow revolutionaries were captured or killed. He managed to escape. He was concealed by a friendly porter in a bookstore until the excitement subsided, and then fled to the Bohemian frontier and from there to Saxony. He subsequently became involved in the 1849 uprisings in Saxony and Baden, after the failure of which, he fled to Switzerland. He briefly considered giving himself up to the government in Vienna but was informed that would cost him his life. He fled to Switzerland, from where, after two years of an adventurous life, he left for New York in 1850. Here he found employment at the *Staatszeitung* newspaper and over time became its co-publisher. Under Ottendorfer's direction, the newspaper became the most widely read German-language daily in the entire United States. He was a supporter of the Democrats, however, in 1860 he resigned from his position of presidential elector, when the Democratic Convention in Charleston nominated Breckenridge as its presidential candidate. His newspaper began to support the interests of the Union.

Franz Josef Pabisch (1825–1879), a native of Slavonice in Moravia, studied law in Vienna. When the revolution broke out, he joined the Academic Legion and fought on the barricades. In spite of this, he was permitted to complete his studies and after switching to theology, was ordained in 1850. Due to disagreements with his superiors, he decided in 1851 to emigrate to the USA. Initially, he worked in small parishes and after further studies in Rome, accepted the position of professor of church history at St. Mary's Seminary of the West in Cincinnati, Ohio.

Vilém Pflanzer (1825–1908) of Horažďovice, Bohemia, a close friend and a classmate of Vojta Náprstek, greatly dissatisfied with the political situation and oppression in Austria, for months, secretly planned to leave for the US to see how the free, democratic Americans live. He might have even contemplated to remain in America for some time, if not permanently. Barely, a twenty-year old, he dared to undertake the voyage across the ocean without his parents' knowledge, arriving in Baltimore on September 28, 1847. He visited main cities in the Midwest and the northeast and even ventured into American jungles, one of the first Czechs to do so. He only learned about the second day of the Revolution in Prague on his way back to Europe on June 24, 1848 in La Havre Harbor.

Václav Pohl (1817–1893). b. Plasy, Bohemia, claimed to have fought in 1848 behind the barricades in the short-lived revolution in Prague. After coming to America, he settled in New York, where he became president of the Czech Society, the first Czech fraternal organization, organized in 1850. A radical, Pohl converted many a pioneer to his way of thinking. He remained in New York till 1852. He frequently changed occupations and residences. He was an expert cabinet maker and wood-carver from home, milkman, grocer, saloon keeper, etc. In St. Louis, he established an herbalist store and then went to farming. In Kewaunee, WI, he had a bar and a hotel.

Eduard Preiss (1823-1883), b. Prague, Bohemia, graduated from the artillery school in Vienna. During the Revolution of 1848, he fought on the side of Hungary. He fled to Turkey, where he converted to Islam. In 1851, he travelled to London and from there to New York. The same year he landed in China. In Siam, he was asked by the King to reorganize the school of artillery. Afterwards he sailed to Australia, where he remained ten years, of which he spent three years living the primitive life of an aborigine. In 1863, he sailed to the United States for the second time and, after a brief stay among the Mormons, wandered off to Mexico, which was at that time under the sway of Emperor Maximilian. From there he returned to San Francisco, where he met Count Thun, with whom he then embarked on a journey to South America. His life ended tragically. On the Texas prairie he was willfully murdered, while distributing Gering's calendar among his Czech countrymen.

Emeric (Imre) Radnich (1824-1903); b. Selice, Slovakia; railroad engineer. When the Hungarian War for independence started, he enlisted as lieutenant, first at the 3rd, then at the 2nd Sapper Battalion. In July, he was promoted to 1st Lieutenant and in August, he was, not only, transferred to the Sapper Battalion in Komárno, but further elevated to the rank of Captain. After the collapse of the Hungarian cause, the Austrian government granted him a safe conduct and he escaped first to Hamburg, then to Britain. Along with the Újhazy family, he soon set sail for America, arriving in NYC in December 1849. He then was farming in Prairie, AR. Soon after, he then joined Narciso Lopez's expedition to Cuba, but the enterprise turned out to be a huge fiasco. The Spanish defeated the small army, and Radnich was sentenced to hard labor in Ceuta, North Africa. At the intervention of his brother John, at the legation of the US in Madrid, the Queen of Spain granted him a pardon. After his return to the US, he settled down in New Buda, Iowa, working as an engineer. After the Compromise of 1867, he returned to Hungary, where he had prominent career. He became inspector of the Hungarian State Railways and then director of the Railway Gyor-Sopron-Ebenfurt.

Stephen Radnich (aka István Radnich) (1828-1912), b. Egreš, Slovakia; took part in the Hungarian War of Independence, as an officer. Some sources claim that he served in a cavalry unit under General Bem, whereas others refer to him as an artillery lieutenant. After the surrender of the revolutionary army, he left the country, first he moved to Britain and finally immigrated to the US in 1850.

Johann Theodore (Tivadar) Rombauer (1803-1855), b. Levoča, Slovakia; metallurgical engineer and entrepreneur who played significant role in the development of metal industry in Hungary; the founder of the iron works at Rimamurány-Salgótarján (near Slovak border); and the leading personality of arms supply in the Revolution. After the capitulation at Vilagos in 1848, Rombauer had to flee disguised as a poor journeyman. He traveled to

Hamburg through Austria, to England, finally immigrating to America. He got involved there with mining and foundry. He even made a proposal for President Washington regarding gold mining in California but was refused. After his tour to South America, where he met many of his countrymen, he returned and settled in Iowa, near Davenport. He became co-editor of the German-language newspaper *Der Demokrat,* but a few years later died; he was only fifty-two years old. His wife, Bertha, who also participated in the War of Independence, as a nurse, followed him to the US in 1850. They had eleven children, many of whom excelled professionally. Upon his death in 1855, the family moved to St. Louis, Missouri, a burgeoning city offering plenty of opportunities to immigrants. Several of his sons participated in the Hungarian Revolution and, in the US, they took part in the Civil War.

Richard Rombauer (1831–1848), b. Szeleszto, of Slovak-born father; doing battle for liberation, as the 2nd oldest son, a soldier in the Hungarian revolutionary army of 1848, severely wounded at the disastrous battle of Vizakna, died of his wounds, and rests in an unknown grave. He was only eighteen years old.

Robert Julius Rombauer (1830–1925), b. Mukačevo, of Slovak father (from Levoča). After finishing the Lutheran HS in Bratislava, moved to Vienna in 1848 and as a freshman in the Polytechnic, joined the Legion of the Academy and later entered the army as a Lieutenant in artillery. After the fall of the Revolution, enlisted in the Austrian army as a private, but in 1850, freed by ransom, immigrated to America with his mother.

Roderick Rombauer (1833–1924), b. Szeleszto, of Slovak father; fought in the Hungarian War of Independence with his three brothers. He immigrated with his mother and six siblings from Hamburg to New York in September 1851.

Johann Rittig (1829–1885), born in Prague, studied law and was jailed during the Revolution of 1848. He succeeded to flee abroad, however, and in 1851, held the position of secretary with the well-known German liberal in exile, Karl Vogt. The Austrian government, in the meantime, condemned him to death *par contumace*. After Napoleon's putsch, he left for America and settled in Cincinnati. Here he founded an anti-slavery newspaper, which, however, lasted only a short period of time. After that, he became an actor, performing in various places such as Cincinnati, Milwaukee, Chicago, St. Louis and Louisville. From 1857–1861, he held the position of co-editor of the New York paper *Staatszeitung* and afterwards founded his own New York journal. In 1874, he became editor of the Sunday edition of *Staatszeitung.*

Joseph Rudolph (1825–1912), b. Teplice, Bohemia, during his university studies in Vienna, joined the Viennese Academic Legion. After emigration to US in 1849, he settled in Cincinnati, where, together with Hassaurek, founded the organization Verein freier

Männer, of which he became secretary. After a short stay in St. Louis and in Dubuque, he opened a jewelry store in Chicago. After the disastrous Chicago fire, in which he lost all his property, he entered the furniture business.

Matthias Ernest Rozsafy (orig. Ruzicska) (1828–1893), b. Komárno, Slovakia, presumably of Czech origin; was a pioneer journalist. As a twenty-year old, he took part in the 1848 revolution, during which he almost lost his life. When the Revolution failed, he got involved in planning a new insurrection, during which he was captured, and sentenced to death. Fortunately, he succeeded to escape, garbed in woman's clothing. Eventually, he got to London, and in 1850, moved to America. There he took part in the Civil Artillery Regiment; was mustered out as a Major by brevet. After the War, he lived in New York, and later moved to Washington, DC, where he had a government position and later had his own patent bureau. He died in Washington and was buried in Arlington National Cemetery.

Károly Semsey (1830–1911); b. Kračúnovce, Slovakia; officer in revolution of 1848, with the rank of captain in US s. 1859; veteran of Civil War with the rank Major of the 45th New York Volunteer Infantry Regiment. After the war, worked in the Customs Office and then in the immigration service.

Libor Alois Schlesinger (orig. Šlesinger) (1806–1893), a native of Řepka, nr. Ústí nad Orlicí, Bohemia, a merchant, although taking part in 1848 Revolution, did not get to the US until 1857. In the famous meeting in Prague on March 11, 1848, he was elected one of the national delegates to meet with the Austrian Emperor but hardly any success was achieved at the meeting with him. On Pentecost Sunday, he fought along with the members of the *Svornost* (Solidarity) group, on barricades in the streets of Prague. His Captain Kajetán Tyl sent him to the country on the next day to stir the notion of liberty among the people. Having returned to Prague, he was arrested and then kept in prison with others for several months. After his release, he was elected Delegate to the Regional Assembly. When the conditions in the country became intolerable under Bach's absolutism, Šlesinger decided to emigrate to America. In the 1856, he left his native country and in January 1865, arrived in Cedar Rapids. He settled in Nebraska and transported good between Omaha and Colorado. He later moved to Denver, CO, where he died.

Josef Sosel (1818–1887), a native Benešov nad Ploužnicí, Bohemia, succeeded in escaping from his native country, where he was persecuted for his involvement in the revolution of 1848. He emigrated in adventurous way, by hiding in a beer barrel and having been smuggled across the border. He arrived in New York in 1848 but did not do well there. He then moved to Iowa where he worked on a farm. He settled in Iowa City, from where he departed for Cedar Rapids in 1864 and became a lawyer.

III. PIONEERS

Jakob Sternberger (1823–d.), b. Kadaň, Bohemia, into a prominent family (his grandfather was the first mayor of the city), immigrated in 1850 to Wisconsin, one of the many 'Forty-Eighters' – people who left Europe after the failed revolutions of 1848/49. He studied law and mining at the University of Prague. There, he was a member of a political engaged student group, fighting for democracy and equality in the Kingdom of Bohemia. In Wisconsin, Sternberger purchased land near Portage, Columbia County, and tried his hand (and eventually failed) at farming, one of many so called 'Latin Farmers' – well-educated immigrants who knew Latin but not much about farming. He also tried to establish the nucleus of an ideal world by founding 'Marienstern,' a communitarian society in which, among other things, all property belonged to everyone, every member had an equal voice in decision making and women were regarded as equals in every respect. In April 1861, Jacob Sternberger (then 39 years old) enlisted in the Union army, the day after Governor Alexander Randall had asked for Wisconsin volunteers, and two days after President Lincoln's call for 75,000 volunteers. Sternberger served as a private in the 1st Wisconsin Infantry regiment, Company E. He mustered out on August 21, 1861. At this time, he was still a 'subject of the Austrian Emperor,' becoming an American citizen on June 7, 1865.

Edward R. Strážnický (1820–1876), b. Moravia, was educated at the University of Vienna, receiving degrees in the departments of medicine and philosophy, and acquired by travel a familiar knowledge of modern languages. During the Hungarian Revolution of 1848, he served as an officer in the Hungarian Revolutionary Army. After the defeat of the nationalists, he was exiled, and his property was confiscated. After a brief residence in England, Strážnický went to the United States, and found employment as a merchant in Philadelphia. In 1859, he became an assistant librarian in the Astor Library in New York City, and in 1872, he was elected superintendent, an office he held until he died. Strážnický was also secretary of the American Geographical Society.

Benjamin Szold (1829–1902); b. Zemianske Sady, Slovakia; future rabbi; for his participation in the Revolution of 1848 was expelled from Vienna where he studied.

James Taussig (1827–1916), b. Prague, Bohemia, left Prague University in 1848 and joined the student revolutionary bands. He served in them without interruption for the entire duration of the siege, until the occupation of Prague by Austrian troops. He had to flee, immigrated the same year to the United States and settled in St. Louis. Here, he enrolled in law school and in 1851, received his license to practice law. He was a supporter of the Republican Party. In 1862, he was sent by a group of radical Republicans to request from President Lincoln the immediate release of all black slaves. As was characteristic for the rapid sequence of events of that time, Lincoln answered him that such an action would be suicidal, nevertheless, only three months later, issued his landmark Emancipation

Proclamation. Despite a number of offers, Taussig rejected all political positions and fully devoted himself to his legal practice.

Laszlo Újházy (1795–1870), b. Budimír, Slovakia; son of a landowner of the lesser nobility; one of the defenders of Komárno fortress, the last stronghold of the Hungarian army in the fall of 1849. In exchange for the fortress, soldiers were granted amnesty and they wished also a passport for emigration. Újházy belonged to the first group of Hungarian refugees who arrived in New York in December 1849.

Charles Wehle (1827–1900), b. Hungary, of Bohemian ancestry, was Kossuth's staff officer during the Revolution of 1848, who by miracle saved his life and escaped to the US. He became a successful lawyer.

Gottlieb Wehle (1802–1881), b. Prague, Bohemia, around June 1849, brought his extended family, some 26 people, to the US, settling in Madison, IN, after their temporary stay in Cincinnati, OH. They were all Forty-Eighters and an excellent book about them was written by Wehle's granddaughter Josephine Goldmark, under the title *Pilgrims of '48: One Man's Part in the Austrian Revolution of 1848* and *A Family Migration to America*. They decided on Madison, a town of ten thousand inhabitants, destined in the belief of its inhabitants to rival the already large Ohio Valley cities of Louisville and Cincinnati. Gottlieb Wehle became one of the leaders of Jewish community in Madison and in 1853, he was chosen as president of the newly found congregation. The family stayed in Madison, IN for about 7 years and in 1856 they removed to New York.

IV. Wanderers

A. Explorers

Bedřich Všemír Berchtold (1781-1876), b. Stráž nad Nežárkou, Moravia, was notable botanist and traveler. In 1835-55, he traveled throughout Western Europe, Asia Minor, Palestine, Egypt and other countries. In 1846-47, accompanied noted Viennese traveler, Ida Pfeifer to Brazil on her first trip around the world.

František Boryně ze Lhoty (1663-1722), was a Bohemian missionary who was sent to Peru in 1695. He was one of the best missionaries who christened hundreds of unknown Indian tribes. He founded a settlement of San Pablo (1704) and, together with another Bohemian Jesuit S. Arlet, a new settlement of San Pedro. He brought thousands of Indians into the settlements, established a number of new posts, built beautiful churches, introduced new agricultural practices and new trades, taught native women how to spin flax and men how to weave, raise cattle, and even play music.

Jiří Daneš (1880-1928), b. Nový Dvůr, nr. Pavlov, Bohemia, was a noted Czech geographer and traveler, professor at Charles University, who was killed in an auto accident in Los Angeles, CA. In 1904, he attended the Geographical Congress in Washington as the only Czech representative. He combined the visit with several other expeditions on American continent during which he managed to cover a large part of the US and Mexico. Two years later, he returned to America for the International Geological Congress in Mexico. This time, the karst terrain of Cuba and Jamaica interested him most.

Anthony Fiala (1869-1950), Jersey City Heights, NJ, of Czech parents, was educated at Cooper Union and the National Academy of Design, New York City. In early life, he was engaged in various employments - as lithographic designer, chemist, cartoonist, head of the art and engraving department of the *Brooklyn Daily Eagle* (1894-99), and correspondent for that paper while serving as a trooper in the Spanish-American War. In 1901 and 1902, he accompanied the Baldwin-Ziegler polar expedition as photographer. From 1903 to 1905, he was in command of the Ziegler Polar Expedition, reaching 82°4' north, discovered and mapped new islands and greater part of Franz Jozef Archipelago. In 1914, Fiala accompanied Theodore Roosevelt on the Roosevelt-Rondon Scientific Expedition into hitherto unexplored parts of Brazil; he explored Papagaio River and descended Jurnena and Tapajos Rivers of Brazil.

Alberto Vojtěch Fric (1882-1944), b. Prague, Bohemia, was a famous Czech botanist, ethnographer, writer and explorer. He undertook 8 voyages in America and discovered and catalogued many species of cactuses. South American Indians called him 'Karaí Pukú' (in English Long Hunter), in Europe he was called 'Hunter of Cactuses.'

Emanuel von Friedrichsthal (1809–1842), b. Brno, Moravia, was a traveler, daguerreotypist, botanist, and amateur archaeologist, who traveled through the Balkans and in Central America and documented his findings. He was educated in Vienna at the Theresian Military Academy and entered Austrian government service, but soon left to pursue scientific travels. He traveled through Rumelia (the Balkans) in the 1830s, publishing his findings in two books: *Reise in die südlichen Theile von Griechenland* (Journey to the Southern Parts of Greece, 1838) and *Serbiens Neuzeit in geschichtlicher, politischer, topographischer, statistischer und naturhistorischer Hinsicht* (Modern Serbia in Historical, Political, Topographical, Statistical, and Natural-Historical Respects, 1840). These publications acquired for him in particular a reputation in botany for their descriptions of the flora of Greece and Serbia. In 1840, he was posted as first secretary of the Austrian Legation to Mexico, where he became interested exploring the ruins of Maya civilization after reading the writings of John Lloyd Stephens and Frederick Catherwood. He discussed his plans with historian William H. Prescott during a trip to Boston and bought a daguerreotype apparatus in New York City. He went to the Yucatán in mid-1840, and traveled throughout the Yucatán and Chiapas, becoming the first person to take daguerreotypes of the Mayan ruins, and the first European in the 19th century to visit the ruins of Chichen Itza. He fell ill during his travels, probably with malaria, which necessitated his return to Europe in 1841, where he died in Vienna in 1842. This early death prevented him from publishing the results of his Central-American travels, but he had put on an exhibition of twenty-five daguerreotypes in New York, in the British Museum in London and in Paris, for which he was honored by the Académie des Inscriptions et Belles-Lettres.

Samuel Fritz (1653–1728), b. Trutnov, Bohemia, was a Bohemian Jesuit missionary noted for his exploration of the Amazon River and its basin. In 1689, he undertook a daring expedition down the Amazon to Pará, where he was captured and imprisoned for two years on the suspicion of being a Spanish spy. Although imperfectly equipped with the necessary instruments, he completed a comparatively accurate chart of the River's course. This was the first approximately correct chart of the Marañón territory.

Jan Havlasa (orig. Klecanda) (1883–1964), b. Teplice, Bohemia, was a writer and traveler who came to the US in 1904 to see the World's Fair in St. Louis. Until 1910, he lived in Los Angeles and then got married to an American girl of Czech origin. He then lived 2 years in Tahiti, and Japan. After his extensive travels in China, Malaya and India, he returned to Prague where he then lectured about his long-time experiences. His experiences from various trips are reflected in his novels, most of which are placed in exotic settings. He also served in the

Czechoslovak diplomatic service, holding the post of the first Czechoslovak Ambassador to Brazil (1920-24) and Czechoslovak Ambassador in Chile (1945-47).

Thaddeus (Tadeáš) Haenke (1761-1817), b. Chřibská, Bohemia, a noted Czech naturalist, in 1789, entered the service of the Spanish Government as botanist, in order to accompany Malaspina in his tour around the world. Having reached Spain too late, he embarked at Cadiz for Montevideo, and, after suffering shipwreck, finally joined Malaspina in Chile, accompanying him in his voyage to the north, along the American coast as far as Nootka Sound in Vancouver Island, Can.

John G. E. Heckewelder (1743-1823), b. Bedford, England, of Moravian ancestry, a pioneer Moravian missionary among American Indians, was a most observant early traveler through the eastern woods as he recorded invaluable observations on the Indian life and pioneer history of the early frontier. From 1754 to 1813, Heckewelder crossed the Allegheny Mountains 30 times and his adventures along the Indian trails of Western Pennsylvania into the 'Ohio Country' are interwoven with the movements of the Moravian Indian missions. He lived among the Indians for almost sixty years, learning their language, sharing their activities, recording clearly and vividly what he saw and heard, being most at home with the Ohio Country Indians. His travels have been described in Paul A. W. Wallace's monograph *Thirty-Thousand Miles* with John Heckewelder, published in 1958.

Bohumil Houda (1855-1916), b. Panenský Týnec, Bohemia, was a gardener by training. He was a nephew of Bohumil Roezl, whom he accompanied in 1874 on his study tours of America. He later permanently settled in California where he died.

Eduard Ingriš (1905-1991), b. Zlonice, Bohemia, was an American composer, photographer and adventurer. In 1947, left Czechoslovakia for South America, lived in Brazil and Peru. In 1954 and 1959, he organized Kantuta and Kantuta II raft voyage, in similar style as Thor Heyerdahl Kon-tiki and sailed across the Pacific. Ingriš was born with many talents and has made use of them zestfully throughout his life. They have taken him from his native Prague to several continents as a composer, conductor, film cameraman and explorer. He has traveled in Europe, Africa, South America, and the South Seas Islands.

Miroslav Jakeš (1951-), b. Havlíčkův Brod, Czech, is a Czech polar explorer and a guide. In 1986, he was the first Czech to undertake a winter ascent of Aconcague. He suffered frostbite to his feet, causing him to lose five toes. He also participated in expeditions to Arctic shores and helped build the Czechoslovak Arctic Station on Nelson Island. In 1993, he was accepted to a Sports Expedition to the North Pole, where he stood as the first native Czech on May 10. He returned to North Pole in 1996, when he crossed Greenland alone. In 1997, he stood on top of the highest peak in Spitsbergen, Newtontoppen, with the altitude of 1,713 meters above the sea level.

Heinrich Wenzel Klutschak (1848-1890), b. Prague, Bohemia, was an American engineer, artist, naturalist, author, and explorer. He travelled to the Arctic and Southern Atlantic, visiting Repulse Bay, Nunavut in 1871 and South Georgia in 1877. He served as a part of Frederick Schwatka's 1878-1880 Arctic expedition to uncover information about the lost 1845 Franklin Expedition. He wrote and provided illustrations of his voyages and provided one of the earliest reliable Western accounts of the Aivilingmiut, Utkuhikhalingmiut, and Netsilingmiut Inuit.

Věra Komárková (1942-2005), b. Písek, Czech., a botanist and mountain climber, who was among the first women to scale some of the world's highest peaks. In the fall of 1978, the American Women's Himalayan Expedition left the United States for Annapurna in Nepal, the 10th highest mountain in the world. Dr. Komárková and her climbing partner Irene Miller, with the help of two Sherpa guides, became the first women and the first Americans to reach the summit. At the time, it was only the fourth expedition to reach the top, and Annapurna is now thought to be one of the most dangerous of the world's 8,000-meter mountains, a class that includes Everest. Two other members of the team fell to their deaths in the attempt. It was then generally believed that women were not physically and emotionally strong enough to endure such demanding climbs, and women had problems getting climbing permits or joining men's teams. In 1984, Komárková led another successful Himalayan expedition, to Cho Oyu in Tibet, the world's sixth highest peak. She and her partner were the first women to reach that summit, and it was her last major climb.

Richard Konkolski (1943-), b. Bohumín, Czech., developed reputation as a world class sailor, earning honor upon honor. With his family, he crossed the border between Czechoslovakia and Poland and managed to set sail from Szczecin, Poland, bound for Newport, RI. He is the winner of over forty different sailing races and holder of many championship titles. Four times the best sailor of the year in three different countries, he has made and broken six world speed records in sailing and has sailed over 120,000 miles single-handedly. First person to sail around the world three times solo by real circumnavigation route (passing antipodes). He did his first solo circumnavigation on a twenty-four-foot boat NIKE, second smallest vessel to circumnavigate globe at that time.

George F. Kosco (1908-2008), Harrisburg, PA, of Slovak descent, Captain, US Navy, was chief aerologist and chief scientist of US Navy Operation Highjump (1946-47). He visited North and South Pole with Admiral R. E. Byrd. Kosco Glacier is named in his honor.

IV. WANDERERS

Bohuslav Kroupa (1838–1912), b. Bohemia, was an illustrator who lived in Scotland. During his trip in 1872, he became very well acquainted with America and Canada. He made drawing, wherever he went, in connection with his job for Sanford Fleming's expedition and which were later published in the book *From Ocean to Ocean*. Two years later, he made another study tour through the US, Canada and Mexico. He went as far as Hawaiian Island and returned by way of Panama to New York. He described this trip in an extensive book, which was published under the title *An Artist's Tour: Gleaning of Travel in North and Central America and the Sandwich Islands. With Illustrations by the Author* (1890). He taught art drawing at the Edinburgh College in Scotland.

Wenceslao Linck (Link) (1736–1790), b. Jáchymov, Bohemia, was a Bohemian Jesuit missionary, and intrepid explorer, who had learned the Comichí language, founded in 1762 the Mission of San Francisco de Borja in a broad arroyo, surrounded by forbidding mountains and lying thirty leagues northwest of Santa Gertrudis. He was the first person to reach San Felipe by land.

Alexander Liška (1883–1941), b. Yugoslavia, of Czech father and Slovak mother, raised in Zamarovce, Slovakia, was an explorer, physician, geologist, and a gold-digger.

Frederic August Lotter (1741–1806), b. Malá Úpa, Moravia, was attached as botanist to the expedition that was sent by the Spanish government around the world under command of Captain Malaspina. He explored the interior of Mexico as far as Lower California. Afterward he visited Peru, Chile and the Argentine provinces.

Vilém Pflanzer (1825–1908), b. Krimice u Plzně, Bohemia, was one of the first Czechs in the 19th century who had courage to enter jungles in the US. He studied philosophy at the University of Prague and was a close friend of Vojta Náprstek with whom he dreamed about idealized hypothetical state 'New Čechie' somewhere on Amur. During his law studies in Vienna, he decided to go to America to check the conditions there for the idealized state. He left Prague in 1847 and without knowledge of his mother, he crossed the ocean. He visited various places and cities, including Pittsburgh, Cincinnati, New Orleans, St. Louis, Chicago, Buffalo, New York. He kept a detailed diary of his experiences in the *Czech Kurrent* which has been preserved. After a year, disappointed, he returned to Bohemia.

Johann Baptist Emanuel Pohl (1782–1834), b. Česká Kamenice, Bohemia, was a botanist, entomologist, geologist, and physician. He studied in Prague and graduated as Doctor of Medicine in 1808. In 1817, he accompanied the Archduchess Leopoldine to Brazil on the occasion of her marriage to Dom Pedro I, and then was chosen by his government to participate in the Austrian Brazil Expedition in charge of mineralogy and geology. After the return of Dr. Mikan to Europe, he was responsible for the botany collections as well.

Pohl spent four years between 1817 and 1821 in Brazil, during which time he explored mainly the provinces of Minas Gerais, Goias, Bahia as well as the province of Rio de Janeiro as far as the District of Itha Grande. His voluminous collections, among them some 4000 specimens of plants, were housed with the rest of the expedition collections in the Brazil Museum of Vienna, which included also two live specimens, a pair of Botocudo tribe people. The woman died soon after and the man was eventually returned to his native land. After his return, Pohl served as a curator at the Vienna Natural History Museum and the Vienna Brazilian Museum until his death.

Benedikt Roezl (1824-1885), b. Horoměřice, Bohemia, was trained as a gardener, in 1854, undertook a study trip to America to learn about tropical plants and did not return until 1871. He traveled throughout Central America and collected less known or unknown plants which he sent in thousands of samples to Europe. On a return trip from Europe, he traveled to Mexico, Panama, Peru and Cuba, a trip, which took one year. He wanted to establish a Czech colony there but because of the difficult climatic conditions, he could not realize his plan. He also traveled extensively in the southeastern US where he discovered a number of new orchids.

Kira Salak (1971-), b. Chicago, IL, likely of Czech ancestry, is a journalist, writer and adventurer. She has traveled solo to almost every continent, visiting the world's remotest places. In 2002, Salak became the first person in the world to kayak solo 600 miles down the Niger River to Timbuktu in Mali. The first woman to cross Papua New Guinea, she also cycled 800 miles across Alaska to the Arctic Ocean. In 2007, Salak became one of a rare few to successfully complete Bhutan's 216-mile Snowman Trek—the hardest high-altitude trek in the Himalayas (more people have reached the top of Mt. Everest than have completed the Snowman). *Book Magazine* has called her "the gutsiest—and some say, craziest—woman adventurer of our day." Says *The New York Times*: "Kira Salak is a tough, real life Lara Croft." Salak was one of five people in the world to receive a 2005 National Geographic Society Emerging Explorer Award, and she has led expeditions to such places as Libya, Iran, and Burma. A contributing editor for *National Geographic Adventure* magazine, her article about the Democratic Republic of Congo's civil war won her the prestigious 2004 PEN Award in Journalism. The United States Library of Congress chose Salak for inclusion in its "Women Who Dare" publications, highlighting the world's top women explorers and leaders.

Tina Sjögren (1959-), b. Prague, Czech., is the first woman to have completed the Three Poles Challenge – climbing Mount Everest and going to the North and South Poles – in 2002. She left Czechoslovakia, when she was 9 years old as a political refugee. She ended up in Sweden, where she married the Swede Tom Sjögren in 1983. The couple immigrated to New York in 1996. In 1999, Tina and Tom Sjögren (known as T&T) climbed Mount Everest, and then broke the record of high-altitude broadcasting. In November 2002, they were the first to broadcast live pictures and sounds from the Antarctic ice cap. On February 2, 2002, they reached the South Pole after 63 days of skiing. On 29 May 2002, just four months after having returned from Antarctica, they reached the North Pole completely autonomously at record speed (118 days), and also transmitted the first ever live broadcast of satellite images and sounds from the Arctic pack ice.

Václav Vojtěch (1901–1932), b. Skřivany u Nového Bydžova, Bohemia, inspired by Admiral Scott, the conqueror of South Pole, and with the help of President Masaryk, he set off on a journey in 1928 to Antarctica, working as an assistant stoker on the ship of Admiral Byrd. On January 27, 1929 he was the first citizen of Czechoslovakia to step onto the Antarctic continent. Later he was sent to the South Alps in New Zealand to train huskies for Byrd's expedition. He was awarded the Gold Medal by the US Congress. In the summer of 1934, he tragically drowned in the Labe River.

Julius von Payer (1842–1915), b. Teplice-Šanov, Bohemia, an American navigator and explorer, noted for the discovery of Franz Joseph Land, received his education in the military academy of Vienna. He entered the Army as Lieutenant in 1859, became professor of history in the military academy in 1865, and, being attached in the following year to the general staff, determined the altitude of most of the Austrian Alps. He accompanied the German expedition to the North Pole, under command of Captain Karl Koldewey, in 1869–70, and discovered in the interior of Greenland a range of mountains with summits 11,000 feet high. The results of the expedition are recorded in *Die zweite deutsche Nordpolarfahrt*, which Payer wrote in association with Koldewey. In 1872, he was given, in conjunction with Herr Weyprecht, the mission to ascertain if an open sea exists east of Spitzbergen, between Europe and America. They sailed from Bremen, 13 June, 1872, on the steamship *Tegetthoff*, but were imprisoned by ice-fields near Nova Zembla, and, after enduring great hardships, landed, in April, 1874, at Franz Joseph Island, where they were compelled to abandon the ship. After performing a remarkable sledge-journey of 300 miles, they embarked in two canoes, and were in a state of great destitution when they met a Russian whaler, which carried them to Lapland, whence they returned by land to Vienna in July, 1874. Payer was retired from the Army the following year, and then lived in Frankfort, devoting his time to scientific researches. He also did several art works in oil of the arctic regions. He published *Die Expedition der Tegetthoff, Reise nach den Eisfeldern des Nordpols* (1876).

Enrique Stanko Vráz (1860–1932), b. Trnovo, Bulgaria, of Czech mother, was an explorer, writer and lecturer. He traveled in Asia Minor with his father who was in Foreign Service. In 1877, as young cadet, he fought against the Turks in battle of Plecno. Inspired by the famous explorer Livingstone, left for Gibraltar for the 'dark continent' in 1880. During 1883–85, he traveled across Sahara to West Africa and then through the countries in Guinea Bay area (1885–87). In 1889, he went to the Caribbean Islands and to Venezuela and during 1892–93, he realized a journey across South America. During his travels, he collected ethnographic material with photographic documentation which he brought to Prague, where he returned in 1894. In 1895, he traveled across North America, Japan, China, New Guinea, Borneo, Ceylon and Suez and back to Bohemia. In 1897, he went to Venezuela, then USA, Mexico and during 1901–04, across South America again. After an extensive lecture tour in Bohemia (1901–04), he moved to Chicago, where he became President of Czech National Council (1911). In 1921, he returned to Prague. He was the author of the whole series of popular travel books.

Jan Eskymo Welzl (1868–1948), b. in Zábřeh, Moravia, was a traveler, adventurer, hunter, gold-digger, Eskimo Chief and Chief Justice in New Siberia and later story-teller and writer. He was known under the pseudonym Eskymo Welzl or the nickname Arctic Bismarck. He traveled through the Balkans and then Siberia, and the Novosibirsk Islands, where he spent some 30 years of his life. He lived among Eskimos in Yukon Territory. He wrote about his experiences in the popular book *Eskymo Welzl* (1928). Subsequently, he left his homeland permanently and settled in Northwestern Canada where he died. The asteroid 15425 Welzl, discovered in 1998, is named in his honor.

David Zeisberger (1721–1808), b. Suchdol, Moravia, had come with his parents to Herrnhut and then followed them to Georgia, and later yet to Bethlehem, PA. In this latter place, he began his acquaintance with the Delaware Tribe, among whom he would minister for so many years. For sixty-three years, he lived among the Indians, learning their ways. He was admitted a member of the Six Nations, received an Indian name, and became a member of an Indian family. He understood the hidden science of belts and strings of wampum; he could un-riddle their mysterious messages and make speeches in their bombastic style; and he spoke in their speech and thought in their thoughts and lived their life in their bark huts. Above all, he loved the red-brown Indians themselves. He established communities of Munsee (Lenape) converts in the valley of Muskingum River in Ohio; and for a time, near modern-day Amhersburg, Ontario.

B. Astronauts

John Blaha (1942–), b. San Antonio, TX, of Czech ancestry, received a Bachelor of Science in engineering science from the United States Air Force Academy in 1965 and a Master of Science in astronautical engineering from Purdue University in 1966. Selected as an astronaut in May 1980, Blaha has logged 161 days in space on five space missions. He served as pilot on STS-33 and STS-29, was spacecraft Commander on STS-58 and STS-43, served on Mir-22 as Board Engineer 2, and was a Mission Specialist on STS-79 and STS-81. In addition to flying five space missions, Blaha has served as the Chairman, NASA Space Flight Safety Panel; Weather Manager, Mission Management Team; lead spacecraft communicator; member, NASA Space Shuttle Improvement Panel. Blaha also led the design, development, and integration of the Orbiter Head Up Display system. Additionally, he led the development of contingency abort procedures which significantly improve crew survivability in the event of multiple main engine failures during ascent. He has logged more than 7,000 hours of flying time in 34 different aircraft and has written numerous technical articles on spacecraft performance and control. John Blaha retired from NASA in September 1997 to return to his hometown of San Antonio, Texas, where he joined the executive management team of the United Services Automobile Association.

Robert J. Cenker (1948–), b. Uniontown, Pa, of Slovak descent, was an American aerospace and electrical engineer, aerospace systems consultant, and former astronaut. In January 1986, Cenker was a crew member on the twenty-fourth mission of NASA's Space Shuttle program, the seventh flight of Space Shuttle Columbia, designated as mission STS-61-C. Cenker served as a Payload Specialist, representing RCA Astro-Electronics. This mission was the final flight before the Challenger disaster, which caused the Space Shuttle program to be suspended until 1988, and impacted NASA's Payload Specialist program for even longer. As a result, Cenker's mission was called "The End of Innocence" for the Shuttle program. Following the completion of his Shuttle mission, Cenker returned to work in the commercial aerospace field.

Eugene Cernan (1934–), b. Chicago, IL, of Czech mother, and Slovak father, He received a Bachelor of Science degree in electrical engineering in 1956 and was commissioned an US Navy officer through the Naval Reserve Officers Training Corps at Purdue. He became a Naval Aviator flying jet interceptors. He received a Master of Science in aeronautical engineering from the Naval Postgraduate School in 1963. Cernan was selected among the third group of NASA astronauts in October 1963 by NASA to participate in projects Gemini and Apollo. Cernan is one of only three humans to voyage to the Moon on two different occasions (the others being Jim Lovell and John Young), one of only twelve people to walk on the Moon and the only person to have descended toward the Moon in the lunar lander twice (the first was Apollo 10's non-landing mission). Apollo 10 holds the world/moon record for the highest speed attained by any manned vehicle at 39,897 km/h (11.08 km/s or 24,791 mph) during its return from the Moon on May 26, 1969. He was last man of Apollo to leave his footprints on the moon. In 1976, Cernan retired both from the Navy (as a Captain) and from NASA and went into private business.

Michael Fincke (1967–), b. Pittsburgh, PA, of Slovak ancestry, is a retired United States Air Force officer and an active NASA astronaut. So far, he has served two tours aboard the International Space Station as a flight engineer and Commander. He flew on one Space Shuttle mission, STS-134 as a Mission Specialist. Fincke logged just under 382 days in space, placing him second among American astronauts for the most time in space, and 20th overall. He completed nine spacewalks in Russian Orlan spacesuits and American EMUs. His total EVA time is 48 hours and 37 minutes placing him 11th all-time on the list of spacewalkers.

James 'Jim' A. Lovell, Jr. (1928–), b. Cleveland, OH, of Czech mother, as a boy, was interested in rocketry, and built flying models. He attended the University of Wisconsin, Madison for two years, joining the Alpha Phi Omega fraternity. He continued on to the US Naval Academy and, after graduating in 1952, entered the US Navy. He is a former NASA astronaut and a retired Captain in the US Navy, most famous as the Commander of the Apollo 13 Mission, which suffered a critical failure en route to the Moon but was brought back safely to Earth by the efforts of the crew and mission control. Lovell was also the command module pilot of Apollo 8, the first Apollo mission to enter lunar orbit. Lovell is a recipient of the Congressional Space Medal of Honor and the Presidential Medal of Freedom. He is one of only 24 people to have flown to the Moon, the first of only three people to fly to the Moon twice, and the only one to have flown there twice without making a landing. Lovell was also the first person to fly in space four times.

George David Low (1956–2008), b. Cleveland, OH, of Czech ancestry. He was an American aerospace executive and a NASA astronaut. He received a Bachelor of Science degree in physics-engineering from Washington and Lee University in 1978, a Bachelor of Science degree in mechanical engineering from Cornell University in 1980, and a Master of Science degree in aeronautics and astronautics from Stanford University in 1983. He also went to Harvard and Johns Hopkins. Low worked in the Spacecraft Systems Engineering Section of the Jet Propulsion Laboratory, California Institute of Technology, from March 1980 until June 1984. During that time, he was involved in the preliminary planning of several planetary missions, an Autonomous Spacecraft Maintenance study, and the systems engineering design of the Galileo spacecraft. Following a one-year leave to pursue graduate studies, Low returned to JPL where he was the principal spacecraft systems engineer for the Mars Geoscience/Climatology Observer Project.

C. Aviators & Navigators

Karl Arnstein (1887–1974) b. Prague, Bohemia, a trained engineer at Univ. of Prague, specialized in the design and construction of airships. Among them was the famous airship *Los Angeles*, which first crossed the Atlantic. In 1924, he piloted it on its first 81-hour flight across the Atlantic Ocean to America.

George John Dufek (1903–1977), b. Rockford, IL, of Czech ancestry, Rear Admiral of US Navy, in the 1940s and 1950s, spent much of his career in the Antarctic and was the first American at geographic South Pole in 1956. In the spring of 1939 Dufek, at that time a Lieutenant, requested and received an assignment with Rear Admiral Richard E. Byrd's third expedition to Antarctica, where he served as navigator of the USS *Bear*, the flagship of the expedition. In recognition of his many hours of exploratory flying over the South Polar continent Dufek, later received the Antarctic Expedition Medal. After a brief post-war stint in Japan, Dufek was assigned as chief staff officer to a US Navy-Coast Guard task force to establish weather bases in the Polar Regions. While there, he participated in Operation Highjump, a Naval expedition to Antarctica under the command of Admiral Byrd, during which he made the first flight over the Thurston Peninsula and later rescued six survivors of another flight over the same area. He returned to Washington, DC briefly, but by 1947 was back in the Antarctic, this time commanding a task force sent to supply existing weather stations and to establish new ones near the Pole. In 1954, Dufek joined a special Antarctic planning group preparing for the Navy's Operation Deep Freeze, a scientific polar research expedition. When planning was complete, Dufek was given command of Task Force 43 which, with more than 80 officers and 1000 enlisted men, three ice-breakers, and three cargo ships, was charged with logistics and support for the expedition. Among other accomplishments, the task force established bases on Ross Island and in Little America, and on October 31, 1956, Admiral Dufek and a crew of six became the first Americans to set foot at the South Pole and to plant the American flag there, and the first men to land on the pole from the air. On November 28, 1957, Dufek was present with a US congressional delegation during a change of command ceremony held at McMurdo Sound. After Admiral Byrd's death, Dufek was appointed to succeed him as supervisor of US programs in the South Polar Regions.

Nadia Marcinko (1986–), b. Košice, Czech., is a 'Global Girl.' She is FAA-certified commercial rated pilot and flight instructor, holding a Single (land & sea) Multi-engine (land) instrument rating and Gulfstream C/G-IV & C/G-1159–type rating certificate.

Mira Slovak (1929–2014), b. Cifer, Slovakia, was a daring pilot, Cold War defector, stunt flyer, and Hydroplane racing champion. A young airline pilot in 1953, he fled Communist Czechoslovakia by hijacking his own commercial flight to West Germany. Mr. Slovak, then in his early 20s, was the captain of a Czechoslovak Airlines DC-3 when, on the night of March 23, 1953, he and a few others on board carried out the hijacking. They had spent months planning it. Shortly after takeoff, with more than 20 passengers aboard, Mr. Slovak locked his co-pilot out of the cockpit. He then took the plane on a sharp dive to help subdue others and to drop the plane to below 1,000 feet, where radar would not detect it. The plane, scheduled to fly from Prague to Brno, Czechoslovakia, landed at a military base in Frankfurt about an hour later. Mr. Slovak said he had navigated the night flight with the help of moonlight above and neon lights from businesses below, electric evidence that he had entered the West. Requesting political asylum, he was questioned in Europe and the United States for several months before being allowed to live freely in the United States. But his status as a Communist initially prevented him from getting a commercial pilot's license. So Mr. Slovak found one way to fly that required few credentials: dusting crops. Before the decade was done, he had flown crop dusters in jobs across the West, doused wildfires from the air and worked as a personal pilot for Bill Boeing Jr., son of the Boeing Company's founder. He was introduced to Mr. Boeing through a connection he had made while spraying fields in Washington State. Mr. Boeing introduced him to hydroplanes. In 1958, Mr. Slovak won a national championship driving *Miss Bardahl*, owned by a Seattle oil company. The next year, he was driving *Miss Wahoo* when he won the President's Cup on the Potomac River in Washington, D.C. He continued racing through 1967, winning another national championship. He took his last lap in a hydroplane at age 81, reaching 140 m.p.h. In 1959, when he went to work for Continental Airlines as a pilot; he settled down, relatively speaking, performing only the occasional stunt in a biplane. Flying under bridges, upside down and arms overhead, was how he relaxed. His daring feats earned him the nickname the 'Flying Czech.'

Apollo Soucek (1897–1955), b. Lamont, of Czech ancestry, was an aviation pioneer in his day. Soucek first gained recognition on May 8, 1929, when flying an open cockpit Wright Apache Plane, he set the world altitude record at 39,140 feet. While the record was beaten less than three weeks later, Soucek set a new one on June 4, 1929 for Class 'C' Seaplanes, when he reached 38,559 feet, a record that remained for 10 years. On the first anniversary of that seaplane record, Lt. Soucek took off from NAS Anacostia, near Washington D.C., in a Wright Apache Land Plane with a 450 horsepower Pratt and Whitney engine and regained the world altitude record at 43,166 feet. The record remained for two years. That accomplishment earned him the Distinguished Flying Cross for his "hazardous high altitude flights and experiments to develop and perfect superchargers, propellers, oxygen breathing equipment and protective clothing." At the time of his records, Soucek was serving as superintendent of the aeronautical engine laboratory at the Naval Aircraft Factory in Philadelphia.

Zeus Soucek (1899–1967), b. Lamont, of Czech ancestry (Apollo Soucek's brother), Lieutenant of US Navy, in a PN-12 powered by two Wright engines, set world marks for Class

C seaplanes with a 1,000-kilogram useful load: speed over 2,000 kilometers at 80.288 M.P.H.; distance at 1,243.20 miles; and duration at 17 hours 55 minutes 13.6 seconds.

Julius von Payer (1842-1915), b. Teplice-Šanov, Bohemia, an American navigator and explorer, noted for the discovery of Franz Joseph Land, received his education in the military academy of Vienna. He entered the Army as Lieutenant in 1859, became professor of history in the military academy in 1865, and, being attached in the following year to the general staff, determined the altitude of most of the Austrian Alps. He accompanied the German expedition to the North Pole, under command of Captain Karl Koldewey, in 1869-70, and discovered in the interior of Greenland a range of mountains with summits 11,000 feet high. The results of the expedition are recorded in *Die zweite deutsche Nordpolarfahrt*, which Payer wrote in association with Koldewey. In 1872, he was given, in conjunction with Herr Weyprecht, the mission to ascertain if an open sea exists east of Spitzberyen, between Europe and America. They sailed from Bremen, 13 June, 1872, on the steamship *Tegetthoff*, but were imprisoned by ice-fields near Nova Zembla, and, after enduring great hardships, landed, in April, 1874, at Franz Joseph Island, where they were compelled to abandon the ship. After performing a remarkable sledge-journey of 300 miles, they embarked in two canoes, and were in a state of great destitution when they met a Russian whaler, which carried them to Lapland, whence they returned by land to Vienna in July, 1874. Payer was retired from the Army the following year, and then lived in Frankfort, devoting his time to scientific researches. He also did several art works in oil of the arctic regions. He published *Die Expedition der Tegetthoff, Reise nach den Eisfeldern des Nordpols* (1876).

D. Adventurers, Globetrotters, Daredevils

Móric Benyovszky (Benovský) (1746-1786), b. Vrbové, Slovakia; Count, soldier of fortune, globetrotter.

August Bondi (1833-1907), b. Vienna, Austria, of Bohemian parentage, immigrated with his parents to St. Louis at an early age. In 1850, he enlisted in an expedition to liberate Cuba from the Spanish yoke. In 1866, he settled in Kansas where he joined John Brown's military company against terrorism of 'Border Ruffians' during Civil War, he was one of the first to enlist, being top sergeant of Company K of the Fifth Kansas Cavalry. In 1861, he participated in every engagement of his regiment, remaining in active service over three years.

Renata Chlumská (1973-), b. Malmö Sweden, of Czech parents, is an adventurer. In 1999, she became the first Swedish and Czech woman to climb Mount Everest. During 2005 and 2006, she performed a challenge called "Around America Adventure" in the lower 48 states of the United States. She paddled a kayak from Seattle to San Diego, bicycled with the kayak on a carriage from San Diego to Brownsville, Texas, continued kayaking around Florida to Eastport, Maine, and then bicycled back to Seattle. She became the first person to circumnavigate 32 states by bicycle and kayak.

Alexander Eisenschiml (1832–1879), b. Měčín, Bohemia; veteran of US Civil War, Indian Scout.

Augustine Heřman (1621–1686), b. Prague, Bohemia, a successful merchant and notable cartographer, was also an adventurer. The following illustrates his adventurous spirit and bravery. According to one version of the story, the Dutch held him prisoner of war in New Amsterdam at one time, under sentence of death. A short time before he was to be executed, he feigned himself to be deranged in mind, and requested his horse be brought to him, and seemed to be in the prison. The horse was brought, finely caparisoned, Heřman mounted him, and seemed to be performing military exercises. On the first opportunity, he bolted through one of the large windows that was some fifteen feet above ground, leaped down, swam the North River, ran his horse through Jersey and alighted on the bank of the Delaware, opposite of New Castle and thus made his escape from death and the Dutch. His brave horse was buried in his grave.

Andrew Jelik (ca. 1730–1783), b. Baja, Bačka region of Serbia, was an adventurer. His anonymous biographer did not document his sources, but based his story on Jelík's own oral account, so facts are difficult to verify. He traveled around Europe, escaped military service, but was finally caught in Rotterdam and impressed on a ship to the Far East. He survived an Atlantic storm and washed ashore to England. Hired as a tailor, he sailed on a Dutch ship to America and returned to Europe via Portugal. On his way to Venice, pirates captured him, and he was sold as a slave to a wealthy Turk. After escaping following a beating, he earned his keep as a tailor and traveled to India and China, where he joined the Dutch military for a short time. Moving to Java, he married an English colonist, but was drafted again and escaped to a desert island. After over a year, he became wealthy in Batavia, but returned to Europe after his wife's passing, left his daughter in England, and died in Budapest.

Frederick Lemsky (bf. 1836–after 1856), b. Bohemia, came to Texas in 1836. He took part in the Texas Revolution, playing the fife in the Texas band at the Battle of San Jacinto. Lemsky, who did not dream that piping that popular love song (some historians say it was "Yankee Doodle") would make him one of the few individual Texans whose performance would be singled out in history, was a newcomer to Texas. He came here in February 1836, just in time to join up with Sam Houston's San Jacinto campaign. He was a musician in three different companies.

Čeněk Paclt (1815-1887), b. Turnov, Bohemia, was trained as a soap maker but decided to be a precious stone cutter. In 1846, he left for the US. On his trip from New York to New Orleans, he volunteered to join US Army at the outbreak of the war with Mexico. After the war, he was sent to Florida. After his release from the Army, he did some farming in Virginia and Georgia and then he left for Rio de Janeiro, in the hope of finding precious stones in Brazil. Without success, he returned to New York and from there in 1857, went to Australia to look for gold. Again, without success, he decided to travel to Calcutta where they had the famous gold mines. He was disappointed in what he saw, and he departed by way of Hong Kong for Adelaide, Australia. He then went toward the river Lachlan where he succeeded in finding some gold. He then left for London via Paris and returned to Bohemia. In 1862, he was again traveling to Australia and to New Zealand. After his return to Bohemia, he had to escape because of his political speeches. He left for Africa where he continued in his quest for precious stones. All the news about him then ceased until it was learned that he died in Keiskamma. Only after his death were his experiences and letters published in the book form under the title *Čeňka Paclta cesty po světě* (Čeněk Paclt's travels around the world) (1888).

John L. Polerecky (1748-1830), b. France, of Slovak father; Major of Lauzun's Polish Lancers, was a veteran of the American Revolutionary War.

Frances Sedlacek (later known as Fannie Quigley) (1870-1944), b. Wahoo, NE, of Czech immigrant parents, in 1897, at the age of twenty-seven, followed the stampede to the Klondike, AL. There she developed the knack of being the first on the scene of a new gold strike. She hiked in dragging her sled laden with a tent, Yukon stove, and supplies, and hanging out her shingle for "Meals." Far from Dawson, her efforts earned top dollar and her nickname, "Fannie the Hike." She also had her own free miner's certificate. Fannie staked a claim in August 1900 on a stampede to Clear Creek, a tributary of the Stewart River, 125 miles from Dawson, where she must have also met the dapper Angus McKenzie. They were married on October 1, 1900, just a few days after her return to Dawson. In January 1903, Fannie left Angus and the Klondike and set off on an 800-mile hike down the Yukon to Rampart. From Rampart, she followed the stampede to the Tanana and was soon in the town of Chena. In August 1906, Fannie struck out for the new Kantishna diggings, recently discovered by Joe Quigley, and others. It was the beginning of Fannie's pursuit of mining, and her hopes for a profit from her years of effort. She staked her share of mining claims, and mined them, and although she never shot an animal until she arrived in Kantishna, her prowess as a hunter became legendary throughout the Alaskan territory. She swore, used foul and gruff language, and wore rough men's clothing. Her drinking habits were legendary. Unable and unwilling to adapt to civilization, she preferred the life in the open. She was there to greet Bradford Washburn when he descended from his successful summit climb on Denali in 1942, just as she had greeted the successful Denali climbing party of Hudson Stuck thirty years before. She died alone in her cabin in the summer of 1944.

E. Spies

John Stephen Bugas (known as Jack Bugas) (1908–1982), b. Rock Springs, WY, of Slovak parents; businessman, cattle rancher, FBI agent. Bugas rose quickly through the ranks of the FBI. By 1938, J. Edgar Hoover appointed him head of the FBI's Detroit office, a strategically very important position as at the time, Michigan counted "heavily in the national defense plans." Bugas established a reputation as a "man with unlimited patience and efficiency" in his work on "notorious kidnapping, espionage, bank robbery and other major cases." At the FBI, he most notably led the quashing of two Nazi spy rings (including German Countess Grace Buchanan-Dineen, whom Bugas 'turned' to a double agent) and personally captured Public Enemy Number One Tom Robinson at gunpoint. Most of all, Bugas made a notable record when he "kept sabotage in war plants at 0." Bugas was known in the bureau as "an 'agent's agent-in-charge,' a man all like to work for" ("the highest compliment in the service"), always leading his men personally on important cases.

Ruth Fischer (orig. Elfriede Eisler) (1898–1962), b. Leipzig, of Bohemian ancestry; co-founder of the Austrian Communist Party; later becoming a staunch anti-Communist activist and served as a key-agent of the American intelligence service, known as 'The Pond.'

Eugene Fodor (1905–1991), b. Levice, Slovakia; writer and publisher of travel literature; secret spy. During the second World War, he served at the Office of Strategic Services (OSS), which was located in Europe. A multilingual and wide-ranging knowledge-based knowledge has taken him to a service in the US Army Intelligence Service. He participated in the liberation of Prague and Pilsen for which he was also decorated. During the Cold War, he served as a CIA agent in Vienna and Budapest. Many of the writers of Fodor guides were secret embassies in favor of the US.

Josef Frolík (1928–1989), born in Libušín, Czechoslovakia, was a Czechoslovak spy who, in 1969, defected to the United States and joined the CIA.

Maria Gulovich (1921–2009), b. Litmanová, Czech.; trained as schoolteacher, a member of the underground resistance during World War II, aiding agents of OSS and British intelligence escape the Nazi-occupied territory.

IV. WANDERERS

John G. E. Heckewelder (1743–1823), b. Bedford, England, of Moravian parents, a famed Moravian Missionary among Indians, at least from 1778 until 1782, at risk of his own life, had also acted as a spy for General Washington in Ohio during the American Revolution. During the Revolutionary War, starting in 1776, perhaps less than officially, but certainly under the highest orders, Heckewelder acted as a spy for General George Washington, keeping his commanders at Ft. Pitt informed of League operations in Ohio. Colonel Daniel Brodhead, Washington's longtime commander at Ft. Pitt, specifically admitted this on January 14, 1799. General Edward Hand, who as Colonel Hand had commanded at Ft. Pitt in 1778, confirmed Brodhead's statement on February 14, 1800. In the late 1950's, historian Paul A. W. Wallace found both of these attestations in the Moravian Church archives at Bethlehem, PA. In his own documents, Heckewelder was coy about admitting the extent of his agency during the Revolution, but it is incontestable that, as historian Wallace put it, "Heckewelder acted as an intelligence agent" who kept the American authorities at Pittsburg informed of enemy (British) activity throughout the Revolutionary War.

Josef L. Hůrka (1925–2005), b. Radnice, Czech., was a Czech resistance fighter whose life was documented in his son Joseph's memoir, *Fields of Light: A Son Remembers His Heroic Father* (2001). After the war, he graduated from the Military Academy of Hranice with an advanced degree in ballistics and military sciences and served as a Lieutenant in the Czech Air Force; he was stationed at the Air Force Academy at Hradec Králové. He was, simultaneously, a member of the Czech National ski team. In February 1949, Hůrka was jailed by the STB on a false charge of espionage: he spent eight months in Communist prisons, including in the Pankrác and Loreta prisons of Prague. Released in August 1949, he immediately joined an underground group and took on the codename 'Vlasta.' After a narrow escape to West Germany, he was recruited for the US Intelligence Services and, undercover, took on a number of identities: he presented himself as a US Air Force Captain, a meteorologist, a Colonel in the Norwegian Army. He was involved in numerous, dangerous missions, including investigations of the Soviet nuclear submarine base in Murmansk; his work took him throughout Europe and frequently into the Soviet bloc. Hůrka left the intelligence services in 1958 and came to America.

Karel Koecher (1934–), b. Bratislava, Czech., who lived in US s. 1965, was a mole known to have penetrated the CIA. Koecher's father was a Vienna-born Czech and his mother Irena was a Slovak Jew. The family moved to Prague when Koecher was four. He attended an English language grammar school. In his late 20s, after years of being courted and sometimes followed by the Czech security agency, StB, he began to work in counterintelligence in Prague, targeting West Germans. Then, in 1965, he was told to go to the United States for an assignment of a lifetime: To penetrate CIA. He and his wife moved to the United States via Austria by posing as defecting dissidents fleeing life under communism. He worked for Radio

Free Europe, where his English language skills made him an easy hire, and eventually picked up a Doctorate in philosophy from Columbia University. His wife was beginning to make a career for herself in the diamond industry. Six years after his arrival, in 1971, he was naturalized as an American citizen. Within a year, he had passed CIA pre-employment screens; a year after that, he was hired full-time as a translator and analyst, handling sensitive documents, lists and transcripts. Everything he saw he sent back home to the StB. Over time, Koecher's relationship with the StB soured, as they grew suspicious that he was operating under American instructions. The agency ordered Koecher to resign from the CIA on pain of death. He was interrogated for a week in Czechoslovakia—on his return to New York, he left the CIA and took a job in academia. But as tensions grew under Ronald Reagan, he was approached by the KGB in early 1982 and asked to return to work for the CIA. The agency took him back seemingly without question but say now they were already beginning to monitor him for unusual activity. Two years later, his career as an American spy was over and he was expected to languish in jail for the rest of his life. Koecher and his wife didn't just live double lives, however. There was another, more sordid aspect to their New York existence which went beyond mere recreation. According to Ronald Kessler, in *The Bureau: The Secret History of the FBI*, "Koecher had an unusual way of obtaining classified information—attending sex parties." He and his wife developed a taste for swinging and spouse-swapping shindigs, where his wife's good looks made her a popular attendee. Because it was against the rules of the spy agencies to attend such parties, agents at the parties were already compromised. Information from the FBI and the Defense Department flowed with the drinks. The CIA has never revealed who alerted them to Koecher's treachery, though he left a trail of destruction in his wake that included the suicide of Aleksandr Dmitrievich Ogorodnik, a Soviet diplomat working undercover for the CIA. Once incarcerated, Koecher faced a miserable future in jail. After a stabbing attempt by a new inmate, who Koecher now believes to have been a CIA mole, he appealed to the KGB in a letter, saying he feared for his life. And so, in February, 1986, Koecher and his wife became part of the final prisoner exchange, held on the frigid Glienicke Bridge, in Berlin. A gold Mercedes was waiting for them, driving them back into their old world and freedom, of sorts. Two months of interrogation followed, before they were able to move back in with his mother, who had believed her son had been a dissenter. Today, the couple live in a quiet village outside Prague: Hana organizes seminars between construction professionals and professors from technical schools, while her husband is retired, and spends his days reading or exercising in a nearby forest. It's a far cry from their former glitzy existences as double agents in New York City – or the seemingly inevitable life behind bars that they managed to escape.

John Leopold (1890–1958), b. Bohemia, came to Canada in 1913. He tried to enlist in the North-West Mounted Police Expeditionary Force to fight the Bolsheviks in Siberia; but he was too small to meet the requirements for the NWMP, and the force was then discriminatory towards most ethnic nationalities. They did recruit him, though, as he spoke five languages, into the Royal Canadian Mounted Police and appointed him to the security intelligence service to spy on labor, socialist, and immigrant organizations. He led a secret life in Regina as Jack Esselwein, a painter, and became active in the Painters' Union, in which he served as secretary from 1922 to 1927. He regularly attended the Regina Trades and Labor Council, and after their formation, Esselwein became the secretary of the Communist Party's Regina branch. He also took up work as an insurance agent and a salesman, which allowed him flexibility to travel to and infiltrate organizations in other cities. In 1927, he was transferred to Toronto, where the stress of his double life led to heavy drinking. The Communist Party exposed him in 1928, and he was transferred to Whitehorse. Leopold resurfaced as a regular member of the RCMP when he stood witness in the trial of the eight jailed leaders of the Communist Party in 1931. He returned to Regina on July 1, 1935, with files that convinced the police to arrest the leaders of the On-to-Ottawa Trek which initiated the Regina Riot. Later, he was involved in the early Cold War defection of Igor Gouzenko. Leopold was ultimately promoted to the rank of Inspector in the Research Section of the Intelligence Service. He retired one year later in 1952 and died in Ottawa in 1958.

Lawrence Martin-Bittman (orig. Ladislav Bittman) (1931–), b Czech., was a Czechoslovak spy in the 1960s, who was originally trained as lawyer and journalist at Charles Univ. He had 14 years of experience as a spy and as deputy commander of the disinformation department of the Communist Party in the former Czechoslovakia. In 1968 he defected to the US.

František Moravec (1895–1966), b. Čáslav, Bohemia, was Czechoslovak military intelligence officer before and during World War II. During 1937–1939, Moravec was head of the service. In March 1939, he and 10 of his fellow intelligence officers secretly managed to fly away with the most valuable intelligence files and archives from Prague Ruzyně Airport to London Croydon Airport with a stopover in Rotterdam on ad hoc chartered KLM Douglas DC-3, as they knew in advance from their secret agents operating in Nazi Germany that the invasion leading to German occupation of Czechoslovakia was to be on March 15, 1939 at 6 a.m. Rescued files and archives were handed over to the British MI6 to be used against Germany. Later in Britain, from 1940 to 1945, Moravec served as the chief of the intelligence service of Czechoslovak Government in Exile. Moravec maintained secret radio contact with the Czech anti-Nazi Resistance group known as Three Kings Group from 1939 until 1942. He coordinated the Czechoslovak co-operation with SOE. He participated in planning and preparation of Operation Anthropoid resulting in the assassination of Reinhard Heydrich. He also planned the assassination of his namesake Emanuel Moravec – a traitor and Nazi collaborator who was also known as the 'Czech Quisling.' František Moravec returned to the liberated Czechoslovakia in 1945, but left it secretly again in 1948, shortly after the communist takeover of power. He settled in the USA where he worked until his death as an intelligence advisor in the Department of Defense.

Barbara Lauewers Podoski (née Božena Hauserová) (1914–2009), b. Brno., Moravia, obtained her Doctorate of law degree from the Law Faculty of Masaryk University in Brno. In spring 1938, she changed from the career of attorney's clerk to editorial work with Baťa firm in Zlín. After a brief stay in Africa, in April 1941 she immigrated to the US and for almost two years worked at the Czechoslovak legation in the press section. On the day she received her American citizenship, she volunteered to join the American Army. She joined the Woman's Army Corps on June 1, 1943. As a fluent speaker of several languages, including German and French, she was selected, after basic training, for the new OSS and sent to Washington. By the start of 1944, she was sent to North Africa and from there to Rome. Barbara Podoski launched one of the most successful psychological operations campaigns in World War II, which resulted in the surrender of more than 600 Czechoslovak soldiers fighting for the Germans. One of the few female operatives in the Office of Strategic Services, the wartime predecessor of the CIA, she found creative ways to undermine German morale. Much of her work remained secret until her OSS personnel records were declassified. The pamphlets she wrote were distributed among German POWs being held in and near Italy whom she helped select and train during 'Operation Sauerkraut,' which sent them behind German lines to litter the countryside with propaganda claiming that the attempt on Adolf Hitler's life in July 1944 sparked a revolution in the Army.

Ota Rambousek (1923–2010), b. Prague, Czech., was an anti-Nazi fighter, anti-communist agent and later Czech-American writer. At the age of 22, he participated in the Prague Uprising in the battle for the Prague Radio. After 1948, he left for exile and joined the anticommunist resistance movement. In 1949, he was sent as an agent to communist Czechoslovakia, where he was caught, jailed and sentenced for life. He was released in 1964 and after the Soviet occupation of Czechoslovakia in 1968, he left for exile again. After emigration to Canada, he founded the Klub 231. He was the author of his reminiscences *Krochnu s sebou* (1990) and the monograph *Jenom ne strach* (1990) about the Mašín brothers. His personal memoir *Paměti lichoběžníka* was published in 1999.

Jan Šejna (1927–1997), born in Radhostice, Czechoslovakia, was, at the time of communist Czechoslovakia, Major General of the Czechoslovak Army. After losing political power and influence at the beginning of the Prague Spring, he sought refuge in the US consulate in Trieste and defected to the United States. He is the highest ranking (Major General) Soviet bloc official to ever defect.

IV. WANDERERS

Kurt D. Singer (orig. Deutsch) (1911-2005), b. Vienna, of Czech parents, was an activist, spy, publisher, and author. Singer was an anti-Nazi activist and spy against Germany during World War II who later became known for his espionage and crime books. After attending the University of Zurich, he started *Mitteilungsblätter*, an underground newspaper strongly against the Nazis, in 1933. This, naturally, put him in danger and he soon had to flee to Sweden. He attended the Labor College in Stockholm and published the titles *Det Kommandet Kriget* (1934), coauthored *Carl von Ossietzky* (1937), and *Goering: Germany's Most Dangerous Man* (1940). The book on Ossietzky was part of an effort to have that anti-Nazi leader released from a concentration camp. With the publication of the Goering biography, the German government demanded that Sweden ban the title. Sweden complied, though it refused to extradite the author as the Nazis also wished. Seeing the situation in Europe spiraling downward, Singer decided to move to the United States. While in Sweden, he had also been involved in counterespionage, and he continued these activities after he moved to America. He worked with the US government, as well as with the secret service in Great Britain and Norway. Meanwhile, he continued to write about the war, focusing on the espionage side with titles such as *Spies and Traitors of World War II* (1945). After the war, Singer, who had changed his original surname from Deutsch, attended the Divinity College of Metaphysics, where he completed a Ph.D. in 1951. In 1955, he founded the news service Singer Communications, Inc., in California. He continued to write and edit books on spying, as well as on crime, including *Spies and Traitors: A Short History of Espionage* (1953), *Crime Omnibus* (1961), and *I Spied and Survived* (1980). He also wrote biographies such as *The Danny Kaye Saga* (1957) and *Mata Hari* (1967), and tales of the supernatural, including *The Unearthly: The World's Greatest Stories of the Occult* (1962) and *Strange Stories of the Unknown* (1980). With his wife, Jane Sherrod, he penned several children's books that also covered espionage, biography, and ghost tales. Among his more recent titles, which again prove his versatility, are *The Complete Guide to Career Achievement* (1994), *Success Secrets* (1995), *The Joy of Practical Parenting* (1995), and *Der deutsche Widerstand gegen Hitlers Krieg—1939-45* (2002). An acknowledged authority on World War II history, Singer was in demand as a lecturer on the war and its espionage efforts.

Henry Strasak (1901-1985), born in Rock Island, IL, of Czech ancestry, was an American Federal Bureau of Investigation (FBI) and Central Intelligence Agency (CIA) officer. In the mid 1930's, he was recruited by J. Edgar Hoover and joined the Federal Bureau of Investigation. His main responsibility was to gather intelligence on Fascist and Nazi sympathizers in the US as well as identify these networks abroad. Later, Strasak was sent to occupied Europe where he worked closely with the Office of Strategic Services (the precursor to the CIA), which had helped to organize guerrilla fighting, sabotage and espionage during World War II. He gathered intelligence on German activities and plans in

Austria and Protectorate Bohemia and Moravia, reporting directly to Allen Dulles, an OSS station chief in Berne, Switzerland. After the war in Europe, Strasak resigned from the FBI and joined the War Department as an intelligence officer, working under Brig. General John Magruder. Later he worked with the Central Intelligence Group (CIG) and together with Jackson, Correa and Souers, Strasak helped to lay the foundation for establishment of the CIA. Henry Strasak remained with the Agency for the rest of his life, working in the Directorate for Plans and acting as an advisor to several CIA directors, including Dulles, McCone and Helms. However, very little is known about his career in the CIA and his later life.

Emanuel Viktor Voska (1875–1960), born in Kutná Hora, Bohemia, was U.S. intelligence agency officer (World War I and World War II) who died in Czechoslovak communist prison. Before World War I, he was intensively working with Tomáš Garrigue Masaryk (1850–1937), first President of Czechoslovakia. His intelligence activities are blamed for the fall of Bagha Jatin. Voska was also instrumental in preventing the efforts of German agent Franz von Rintelen to restore Victoriano Huerta to the Mexican presidency during World War.

V. The Society

A. Education & Learning

Abraham Reinke Beck (1833–1928), b. Lititz, PA, the son of Johanna Augusta Reinke (1798–1877) of Moravian ancestry, and the teacher John Beck, was educated at his father's school, a private institution of considerable size and influence from 1819 to 1865. He was a teacher at Nazareth Hall from 1855-57. In the summer of the latter year, he entered his father's school as teacher, and in the same year began his musical service in the Lititz Moravian church. Upon retirement from school work in 1895, Mr. Beck became archivist of the Lititz Moravian Church in which position he translated and compiled numerous historical works of lasting value, notably his *Moravian Graveyards of Lititz*. He was a botanist, an ornithologist, writer, musician and artist. Mr. Beck was a born teacher and, as a composer, he is best known for his male quartet to the words "Just As I Am," regularly used on Palm Sunday in many Moravian churches. In 1865, he established the Beck Family School for Boys. This was successfully conducted at Audubon Villa, Lititz for 30 years and had as patrons' prominent people of their day. In 1860, he married Joanna Salome Huebener and had five children.

Heinz Erie Bondy (1924–2014), b. Gandersheim, Germany, son of Gertrud Wiener (1889–1977) of Prague, Bohemia, and the reform educator, Max Bondy, became a teacher, who, after his father's death, assumed the headmastership of the school, later known the Windsor Mt. School, which closed in 1975. After the Windsor Mountain School closed due to the recession in the mid-1970s, Heinz became a vice chancellor at the University of Massachusetts, Boston. Subsequently, he helped to find the Elkins Mountain School in Elkins, West Virginia, and later served as Headmaster of the Canterbury School in Accokeek, Maryland and then as Director of the Christian Family Montessori School in Mount Rainier, MD from 1994-98. He retired from his lifetime as an educator at the age of 74 years. He was married to Dr. Carolyn Ann Louks (1945–2016) of New York, NY.

Max Bondy (1892–1951), b. Hamburg, Germany, whose father, Solomon Siegmund Bondy was from Jihlava, Moravia and mother, Marie Lauer from Lovosice, Bohemia, was initially an art historian, later in his career becoming a reform educator. Bondy saw the German public schools of the day as focusing almost exclusively on obedience and stern discipline. Germany had raised a generation of bullies, cruel to anyone weaker than they. The only way to change this, Bondy decided, was to change the way children were educated. He was head of several schools in Germany and Switzerland before he emigrated to the United States in 1939. The following year, he founded the Windsor School in Windsor, Vermont. This progressive, coeducational school was designed to implement Bondy's educational philosophy. The teaching was on a high level, with special emphasis on languages. The pupils were self-governing and had equal voting rights with the teachers on all important matters. They were also trained to take an active part in the activities of the community. In 1943, the school moved to Lenox, Massachusetts. After Bondy's death, the school was directed by his widow, Gertrud.

Peter George Braunfeld (1930–), b. Vienna, of Moravian ancestry, was trained as an educator at Univ. of Chicago. He has been with Univ. of Illinois (s. 1959), as prof. of mathematics and education (s. 1968). He retired in 1997. He has worked in a wide variety of areas in mathematics education and development, including: grades 7–16 curriculum development; pre- and in-service teacher training; and educational technology. His major contributions include his work in the middle sixties as co-creator of PLATO —one of the earliest computer-based teaching systems. He was also chief author of *Stretchers and Shrinkers*, a 7th grade mathematics text that aroused national and international attention, both for its unusual mathematics content, and its pedagogical innovations (1969). From 1994 to 1996, he was a program director for mathematics education at the National Science Foundation (NSF).

Michael Duda (1909–1968), b. Donora, PA, of Slovak descent, held Doctorate in education. He chose coaching as his career; he won his first teaching and coaching jobs in 1935, when he joined the Donora School District. There he learned under legendary coach James K. Russell and coached football, basketball and baseball, while also officiating at WPIAL football and basketball games. During his early teaching and coaching days, Dr. Duda became a mentor and lifelong confidant to many fine scholar-athletes, including eventual Major League Baseball Hall of Fame member Stan Musial. A tireless worker, Dr. Duda served as a teacher, guidance counselor, director of playgrounds and scoutmaster before becoming a principal in the Donora school district from 1942–1951. He then was named superintendent of the Monessen School District, a position he held until becoming president at California. Coincidentally, Dr. Duda was inducted into the Mid-Mon Valley All Sports Hall of Fame in 1956, the same year he began his California presidency. In the Hall of Fame's Biographical Journal, he was labeled "the quintessential scholar-athlete of the Mon Valley."

August Dvorak (1894–1975), born in Glencoe, MN, of Czech ancestry, was an educational psychologist and professor of education at the University of Washington in Seattle, Washington. He is best known for creating the Dvorak Simplified Keyboard layout in the 1930s as a replacement for the QWERTY keyboard layout. In the 1940s, Dvorak designed keyboard layouts for people with the use of one hand.

Květa (Marie) Eakin (née Šimunek) (1956-), b. Karlovy Vary, Czech., is an education specialist and vocation rehabilitation counselor. She studied psychology (B.A., 1994), and education and vocational counseling (M.Ed., 1994), both at Kent University. She has been employed as a vocational rehabilitation case manager, with CMN for 6 years (1996-2004); Director of Independent Vocational Services (IVS) for 8 years (2005-2013). Subsequently, she formed her own company, Eakin Consulting, providing disability management and job placement services to Ohio injured workers as a BWC provider. She was married to Thomas Glenn Eakin (1956-2003).

Abraham Flexner (1866-1959), b. Louisville, KY, of Bohemian ancestry, an educator, is credited with reforming medical education in the United States, as well as founding the Institute for Advanced Study at Princeton. In his now classical *Flexner Report* (1910) he examined the state of American medical education which led to far-reaching reform in the training of doctors. The Flexner report led to the closure of most rural medical schools and all but two African American medical colleges in the United States, given his adherence to germ theory, in which he argued that if not properly trained and treated, African Americans and the poor posed a health threat to middle/upper class whites.

Rebecca Gratz (1781-1869), b. Philadelphia, of Silesian ancestry, was a preeminent Jewish American educator and philanthropist. At the age of 20, she helped establish the Female Association for the Relief of Women and Children in Reduced Circumstances, which helped women whose families were suffering after the American Revolutionary War. She was also a founder of the Female Hebrew Benevolent Society, which provided food and shelter, and an employment bureau for poor Jewish women and children.

Arthur Arton Hamerschlag (1872-1827) a native of New York City, of Bohemian ancestry, was electrical and mechanical engineer who served as the first President of Carnegie Mellon University in Pittsburgh.

Frances Ruml Jordan (1889-1980), b. Cedar Rapids, IA, the daughter of the famed educator and business executive Beardsley Ruml, whose father came from Bohemia, was a famed educator. Graduated from Vassar College in 1921, Jordan received her Master's degree in economics from Radcliffe in 1928 and was appointed tutorial secretary for Radcliffe later that year. Jordan continued to work for Radcliffe, as assistant dean, acting dean and then as dean for academic affairs. She was an extraordinary woman, very strong and with a brilliant mind, The wife of Dr. Wilbur Kitchener Jordan, Frances Jordan ended her work at Radcliffe when her husband was appointed president of Radcliffe in 1943, because she felt she couldn't keep on when Mr. Jordan was made president. Although she ended her work at Radcliffe, Jordan remained active in the Boston community during the years of her husband's presidency, from 1943-60. She held the position of executive secretary to the Commission on Plasma Fractionation and Related Processes at the Medical School and was a member of the executive committee and of the board of trustees of Wheaton College, Abbot Academy, and the School of Nursing of the Massachusetts General Hospital.

Eva Dubská Kushner (1929–), a noted scholar in the fields of comparative and French literature, was named President of Victoria University in 1987.

George Michael Low (orig. George Wilhelm Low) (1926–1984), an engineer and former NASA administrator, in the spring of 1976, accepted Rensselaer Polytechnic Institute's (RPI) offer to become the 14th president of the Institute. During his eight years in office, he developed RPI into a nationally renowned research university, broadened the Institute's programs to include several new areas of technology and, through these programs, established RPI as a setting for the cooperative interface of academia, industry and government. He developed the concept of Rensselaer 2000 as a planning guide for the university, undertook major fund-raising activities, and oversaw the completion of such campus building and renovation projects as the Jonsson Engineering Center and the Voorhees Computing Center.

Louise Herschman Mannheimer (1845–1920), b. Prague, Bohemia, was a Czech-American Jewish author, poet, school founder, and inventor. Mannheimer was the founder of the Cincinnati Jewish Industrial School for Boys. She was educated at St. Teine School, privately, and at Normal School, Prague, and University of Cincinnati. She held patents for several devices. She was the inventor of the "Pureairin" Patent Ventilator. She worked as a director of a private school, in Prague; teacher of a Sabbath School, Congregation Berith Kodesh, in Rochester; and teacher, Mrs. Leopold Weil's School, New York City. She served as president of the German Women's Club, Rochester; was a contralto at the Temple Ahawath Chesed, New York; and Sabbath School teacher, at Temple Shaare Emeth, St. Louis, MO.

Milicent Carey McIntosh (1898–2001), a native of Baltimore, MD, of Moravian ancestry, in 1947, took the office as the 4th President of Barnard College.

Margit Meissner (1922–), b. Innsbruck, Aust., of Bohemian parents, was raised in Prague. She studied at Sorbonne University, Paris, Columbia University Teachers Coll., and Trinity College, Washington, D.C. She started her career as a designer and manufacturer of children's dresses in San Francisco. After getting married, she moved to Maryland, where she became associated with the Montgomery County Public Schools, as a program planner and administrator in the education of children with disabilities (1975–92). She was also a special education consultant to U.S. Department of Education and the Maryland State Department of Education. She was a co-founder of TransCen, a private non-profit agency to promote employment of persons with disabilities nationwide and a co-founder of

Voices vs. Violence, a violence prevention program. After she retired, she became a translator, guide and speaker at the US Holocaust Memorial Museum. In 2004, she was inducted into Montgomery County Human Rights Hall of Fame. She received a number of awards for her work.

Ernst Papanek (1900-1973), b. Vienna, of Moravian ancestry, was a child psychologist and educator known for his work with refugee children during and after World War II and for his involvement in socialist parties in Europe and the United States. He is active in the Verband der Sozialistischen Arbeiterjugend Deutschösterreichs (SAJDÖ) from 1919 and its president 1933-1934; member of the City Council of Vienna 1932-1934; member of the executive committee of the Socialist Youth International (SYI) 1934-1939. He fled to Czechoslovakia 1934, where he supported the illegal Revolutionäre Sozialistische Jugend (RSJ) in Austria; editor of the International Pedagogical Information (IPI) 1936-1938. He fled to France 1938; worked for the Organisation de Santé et de l'Éducation (OSE), which was founded by Russian Jews and smuggled children out of Germany, housing them in castles in France 1938-1940. He fled to the United States 1940; worked for the Children's Aid Society; active in various Austrian emigrant organizations and from 1941, member of the American Socialist Party. In 1945, he was director of the Child and Youth Project Department of the Unitarian Service Committee (USC) and later director of American Youth for World Youth (AYWY); in 1947, head of the Brooklyn Training School for Girls and from 1949, head of the Wiltwyck School for Boys in New York.

Emma Karoline 'Nuschi' Plank (née Spira) (1905-1990), b. Vienna, was the daughter of Emil Spira (1875-1938) and Doris Langbein (1877-1954), both of Czech ancestry, the former being born in Třebíč, Moravia, and the latter in Karlovy Vary, Bohemia. She was an educator, author and specialist on child development. She studied under Maria Montessori and Anna Freud. In 1938, she immigrated to the United States and earned a Master's degree in child development from Mills College in San Francisco. She came to Cleveland in 1951 to direct the school of the Children's House (later Hanna Perkins School) of University Hospital. In 1955, Dr. Frederick C. Robbins asked Plank to come to the Department of Pediatrics of City Hospital (later Metro Health Medical Center) to address the educational, social, and psychological needs of children receiving long-term care. Plank seized this opportunity to find the Child Life and Education Division of the Department of Pediatrics at City Hospital and directed it until 1972. She was a co-founder of the interdisciplinary Association for the Care of Children's Health in 1965. Her 1962 book, *Working with Children in Hospitals*, has been translated into several languages; it endures as both a philosophical guide and a practical manual for those providing healthcare to children worldwide. Plank received an honorary degree from Wheelock College in Boston (1988) and many awards, including the Medal of the City of Vienna

(1970), the Gold Medal from the Montessori Centennial (1970), and the Early Childhood Award from the Ohio Association for the Education of Young Children (1979).

Carrie T. Pollitzer (1881–1974), b. Charleston, SC, of Czech parents, was an innovative teacher. Under her leadership, Carrie introduced features of early education that are now commonplace in South Carolina schools, such as teacher visits to student homes, a Parent-Teacher Association (PTA), and social work consultation for children and their parents. By 1953, Carrie helped established two free kindergartens in Charleston for children. Pollitzer also incorporated health and nutrition into the curriculum and facilitated medical examinations by pediatricians and instigated the first public school lunches in Charleston.

Mabel L. Pollitzer (1885–1879), b. Charleston, SC, of Czech parents, was another innovative Charleston school teacher. She organized the Department of Natural Science at Memminger School and also designed a laboratory. Mabel involved students in environmental conservation efforts and successfully advocated for state legislation to prevent the destruction of wild flowers along state highways. She also established a "No Cheat Club," which was the forerunner of a school Student Council. In the 1920s, she introduced sex education in her biology classes.

Julia Richman (1855–1912), b. New York, NY, of Czech parents, was a polarizing and important social reformer, Julia Richman sought to better manage the massive influx of immigrants in New York by Americanizing the new arrivals as quickly as possible. Richman helped organize the Young Women's Hebrew Association and was active in the Educational Alliance, formed in 1885 by American Jews to handle the wave of new immigrants. Richman used both public schools and the Education Alliance to develop a program to train immigrant children in English, penalizing them for speaking their native languages. In 1903, she was named district superintendent of the Lower East Side schools, creating playgrounds, improving school lunches, and enforcing health examinations for students. She also published articles on education and social reform as well as two textbooks, *Good Citizenship* (1908) and *The Pupil's Arithmetic* (1909). She was the first woman district Superintendent of Schools in the City of New York. Her innovations, leadership and curriculum brought an entire new dimension to public school education at the beginning of the 20th century.

Annemarie Bondy Roeper (1918–2012), Vienna, Austria, daughter of Gertrud Wiener (1889–1977) of Prague, Bohemia, and the reform educator Max Bondy, was co-founder of The Roeper School. She married George Roeper (1910–1992), a man who'd been a student at her parents' school and came to the U.S. with her husband in advance of the Bondys. The

Roepers moved to Detroit where they founded a school dedicated to the education of gifted students. Early civil rights activists, they integrated the student body in 1955. The school became the second elementary school in the country to focus exclusively on gifted education. In 1965, in another ground-breaking endeavor, Annemarie was a consultant on the development of *Sesame Street*. A pioneer in the emerging gifted education community, she retired from Roeper School in 1980 and began a consultation practice, receiving the President's Award from the NAGC in 1989 for a lifetime of distinguished service to the field.

Laura Skandera Trombley (1960–), b. Los Angeles, of Czech ancestry, is the fifth president of Pitzer College and a nationally recognized champion of liberal arts education. Under her leadership, Pitzer has founded several visionary collegiate centers and majors, including the Robert Redford Conservancy for Southern California Sustainability. Since Trombley became president in 2002, she has raised Pitzer's national profile and enhanced its reputation for academic excellence. The College moved up 35 spots in *U.S. News and World Report* rankings—from #70 in 2004 to #35 today. In 2012, Pitzer was named the 20th most selective higher education institution in the country. Nationally, Pitzer has been the leader in Fulbright Fellowships per 1,000 students for 10 of the last 11 years and has been the top producer of Fulbright awardees among all US liberal arts colleges for four consecutive years, from 2010–2013. In 2013, President Barack Obama appointed Trombley to the 12-member J. William Fulbright Foreign Scholarship Board. A passionate proponent of environmental sustainability, President Trombley led the initiative to construct eight mixed-use residential buildings that have earned either LEED Platinum or Gold certification. Over the past dozen years, Pitzer's annual fund has grown by approximately 80 percent and the College's endowment has increased by more than 170 percent. Trombley secured the four largest single donor gifts in Pitzer's history.

Benigna von Watteville (1725–1789), b. Berthelsdorf, Saxony, was a pioneer and innovative educator. She resided in America since 1741. She was the daughter of Count Nicolaus Ludwig von Zinzendorf and Countess Erdmuthe Dorothea von Reuss. Her mother was a descendent of the King of Bohemia, George of Poděbrady. She was a pioneer Moravian educator and a key figure in the beginnings of Moravian Seminary and College for Women. On May 4, 1742, at her father's suggestion, the 16-year-old Countess, with 2 assistants, opened a girls' school in the Ashmead house in Germantown, Pennsylvania. Here 25 pupils were instructed in reading, writing, religion, and the household arts in what was probably the first boarding school for girls in the 13 British American colonies. Seven weeks later, the school moved to Bethlehem; and in 1745, to nearby Nazareth, returning permanently in 1749, to Bethlehem, the center of the Moravian Church in America. Count Zinzendorf's 16-year-old daughter, Benigna, upon meeting the Indian children at the settlement, decided that the girls should have the opportunity to go to school just like white boys. The same year she founded

Moravian Seminary in Germantown, Pennsylvania. Shortly thereafter, it was moved to Bell House in Bethlehem, and Lady Benigna invited all the Indian girls to come. Moravian Seminary was the first boarding school for girls in the New World, and over time it gained a superb reputation – so much, so that 50 years later, while he was President, George Washington personally petitioned for admission of his great-nieces. Eventually, the school's charter was expanded, and it became Moravian College and Moravian Academy, both of which remain to this day. This was the first College that admitted women in America, some 200 years before women were admitted to Ivy League Universities.

Gertrud Wiener (1889-1977), b. Prague, Bohemia, was a medical doctor and psychoanalyst. She and her husband, Max Bondy (1892-1951), founded a series of schools in Germany based on a psychoanalytic understanding of human development. When the Nazi Party ascended to power, the Bondys emigrated to the U.S.

Isaac Mayer Wise (orig. Weiss) (1819-1900), b. Lomnička, Bohemia, an American Reform rabbi, earnest as he was in proclaiming the necessity for union among the congregations, was equally indefatigable in insisting upon the pressing need of a theological seminary for the training of rabbis for American pulpits. He had scarcely arrived in Cincinnati when, with his characteristic energy, he set to work to establish a college in which young men could receive a Jewish education. He enlisted the interest and support of a number of influential Jews of Cincinnati and adjacent towns, and in 1855 founded the Zion Collegiate Association. The venture, however, proved a failure, and the society did not succeed in opening a college. Not daunted, Wise entered upon a literary campaign, and year in and year out, he presented the subject in the columns of *The American Israelite*. His indomitable perseverance was crowned with success when, on 3 October 1875, the Hebrew Union College opened its doors for the reception of students, four of whom were ordained eight years later. It was the first permanent Jewish institution of higher learning in the New World. Isaac Mayer Wise was its first president (1875-1900).

Karen Worth (née Weisskopf) (1942-), b. New York; the daughter of Prof. Victor Frederick Weisskopf (1908-2002) of Bohemian ancestry, and Ellen Margrete Tvede, is an educator, specializing in science education. She studied at Radcliffe Coll. and received her Master's degree from Bank Street College of Education in New York City. She works at the Education Development Center, Inc. (EDC) in Newton, MA. She also holds the Chair of Elementary Education at Wheelock Coll. She teaches courses in elementary education and science education for both pre-service and in-service teachers at the graduate and undergraduate levels. She has done extensive development work in science education. A current focus is developing teacher skills in the use of language in science as a critical tool for scientific reasoning. She has been the principal investigator on a number of National

Science Foundation projects in which she developed and published science curriculum materials for early childhood and elementary classrooms and led large-scale efforts to support the implementation of inquiry-based science programs in schools. She was part of the development team for the National Science Education Standards, chairing the Working Group on Science Teaching Standards. She consults nationally and internationally on the implementations of inquiry-based science programs for children at pre-school and elementary levels and has served as an advisor to several informal science organizations, public television stations, and national science reform projects. She is a recipient of the Exploratorium's Outstanding Educator Award for her work in science education, the international Purkwa Prize for improving the scientific literacy of the children of the planet, and the NSTA Distinguished Service Award. She is married to the poet Douglas Grey Worth (1940–) and they have 2 children.

Jaroslav Zmrhal (1878–1951), b. Chicago, IL, of Czech ancestry, in 1905, at the age of 27, was elected principal of the Edgar Allan Poe School in Pullman, the first Czech in Metropolitan Chicago to attain such position. Later he was made principal of the N. S. Davis School and was commissioned to organize a new school, 'Theodore Herzl' on the West Side which had become one of the largest and most progressive schools in Chicago. Since 1921, he had been District Superintendent of the Chicago Schools.

B. Economy & Business

Solomon Adler (1816–1890), b. Bohemia, came to New York in 1843 and to Milwaukee in 1847. He assisted in conducting the first Jewish service in Wisconsin, was secretary of the first Jewish Cemetery Association, organizer and secretary of the city's first Jewish congregation, and organizer and first president of the consolidated Congregation Emanu-El B'ne Jeshurun. Adler was a retail clothing merchant (1848–1857); he joined his brother David in a wholesale clothing firm from 1860 until he retired to New York in 1874.

Roland E. Arnall (1939–2008), b. Paris, France, of Czech ancestry, a businessman and diplomat, was an owner of ACC Capital Holdings and Ameriquest Mortgage. He was an American billionaire, listed among the 400 richest Americans, as per the Forbes listing; worth $3B in 2006. The son of a tailor. His family relocated to Canada in 1953 and then to the US in 1957. He peddled flowers on streets of LA, began buying and selling commercial buildings. Started Long Beach Savings in 1979; first to use computers to search for prospective borrowers to speed up loan process.

Jan Antonín Baťa (1898-1965), b. Uherské Hradiště, Moravia, was a successful shoe manufacturer, who settled in Brazil, where he founded several towns, including: Bataiporã, Bataguassu, Batatuba, Anaurilândia and Mariaopolis.

Thomas J. Baťa (1914-2008), b. Prague, Bohemia, was a head of the worldwide family shoe empire, with headquarters in Canada. He ran the Bata Shoe Company from the 1940s until the 80s.

James Montgomery Beck, 3rd (1929-2006), b. London, England, the son of James Montgomery Beck, Jr. (1892-1972), of Moravian ancestry, and Clarissa Madeline Georgina Felicite Tennyson, a longtime Princeton resident, was a graduate of the Hun School and Princeton University. Born in London to an American father and British mother, he came to the United States at the age of 10 in 1939 but returned to the United Kingdom after graduation from Princeton. He also lived at times in Newport, R.I., Hollywood, Calif., Savannah, Ga., New York City, Mexico, and Switzerland. He had a varied career. He owned a restaurant in London. He also worked for an advertising agency in New York City, for the U.S. Department of Agriculture in Georgia, and as a college librarian in Newport before retiring to Princeton to devote himself to historical research on his family. Mr. Beck was a former board member of the Princeton branch of the English Speaking Union, and a member of Trinity Episcopal Church, the Nassau Club, the Princeton Club of New York, and the Spouting Rock Beach Association of Newport, RI.

Peter John Gerald Bentley (1930-2021), b. Vienna, of Bohemian ancestry, is a Canadian businessman and the third Chancellor of the University of Northern British Columbia. He is the son of Leopold Bloch-Bauer and Antoinette Ruth Pick. His family fled Vienna in 1938 and settled in British Columbia. His father, who changed his name to Leopold "Poldi" Bentley, founded a furniture and paneling veneer company called Pacific Veneer with his brother-in-law John Prentice, that later became Canfor Corporation, an integrated forest products company. In 1970, he became executive vice-president of Canfor Corporation, becoming president in 1975. He became chairman and CEO in 1985, a position he held until 1995. From July 1997 to January 1998, he was again president and CEO. He is currently chairman of the Board. He was a director and is currently an honorary director of the Bank of Montreal, a member of the Canadian Council of Chief Executives, a chairman of Sierra Mountain Minerals Inc. (produces SierraSil) and a member of the board of directors of the Vancouver General Hospital University of British Columbia Hospital Foundation. In 1983, he was made an Officer of the Order of Canada and was awarded an honorary Law degree from the University of British Columbia. In 2004, he was appointed Chancellor of the University of Northern British Columbia and held that post until mid-2007. In 2005, his family was awarded a portion of US$21.8-million in restitution payments for the theft of the family's sugar refinery in Austria.

Joseph Biederman (1856–1904), b. Bohemia, was a co-founder and co-owner of Printz-Biederman Co., Cleveland, OH, one of the oldest American manufacturers of women's apparel. It was incorporated in 1904.

Ivan Bielek (1886–1942), b. Dohňany, Slovakia; in US s. 1906; vice-president and director of the Czecho-Slovak Commercial Corp. of America, an import company founded in 1918; editor, *Národné noviny;* president, Slovak League of America (1920–1923); signatory of Pittsburgh Agreement.

Henry W. Bloch (1922–), b. Kansas City, MO, of Bohemian ancestry, was a co-founder (with his brother Richard) of H&R Block Co., a tax preparation company in the US, claiming more than 22 million customers worldwide.

Arthur D. Brandeis (1862–1916), b. Manitowoc, WI, of Bohemian ancestry, was president of the J. H. Brandeis Company of Omaha, NE, the biggest department store west of Chicago, and later First Vice President of Stern Brothers. With the expansion of the department store business, Mr. Brandeis became heavily interested in various other enterprises. He organized the Brandeis Realty Company, which became one of the factors of Omaha. He also headed the Boston Store Realty Company and the Arthur Realty Company. Later he branched out as a theatre owner. He became President of the Brandeis Theatre, the American Theatre Company, and the Empress Theatre Company of Omaha. The Fonterille Hotel, a million-dollar Omaha undertaking, was another enterprise that numbered Brandeis among its supporters. He was also a director at the United States National Bank of Omaha.

Leslie Buck (orig. Laszlo Büch) (1922–2010), b. Chust, Czech., was an American business executive and Holocaust survivor. His parents died during the Holocaust during World War II. Buck was imprisoned by the Nazis during the occupation, surviving his captivity at Auschwitz and Buchenwald concentration camps. Buck moved to the United States following World War II, settling in New York City. Buck partnered with his brother, Eugene, and ran an import-export business. The two brothers launched a paper cup maker based in Mount Vernon, New York called Premier Cup sometime in the late 1950s. Buck left the family business to take a position with a start-up paper cup manufacturer called the Sherri Cup Company during the mid-1960s. Buck designed the Anthora paper coffee cup using the blue and white colors of the Greek flag, though he was not trained as an artist. The name of the Anthora coffee cup came from a mispronunciation of the Greek word, amphora, as Buck pronounced it with an Eastern European accent. Buck's Anthora cup was introduced in the mid-1960s and became a huge success throughout New York

City. The cups became a ubiquitous symbol of the city, appearing in New York-themed television shows including *Law & Order*. For decades, hundreds of millions of cups were sold annually. In 1994, the Sherri Cup company sold 500 million Anthora cups.

Arde Bulova (1889-1958), b. NYC, of Bohemian ancestry, started with J. Bulova Co. in 1905, becoming vice president and treasurer in 1911. He established a plant in Providence, RI and two years later the business expanded to include importing, assembling and selling of fine watches and in 1919, a plant was acquired in Switzerland to manufacture watch movements. In the late 20s, a plant was opened in Woodside, NY which in time, enabled manufacturing all watch parts in the US. Later, the company acquired a number of subsidiaries and established additional plants. Bulova himself was responsible for instituting new manufacturing processes that permitted standardization of watch parts and movements. He also invented many improvements that were incorporated in the company's products and designed a considerable number of special tools, gauges and machines used in the production. Later on, the company further diversified and began manufacturing radio receiving sets, portable clock radios, transistor radios, electric razors. By 1957, Bulova watch products were being sold in some 18,000 stores in the US and Canada. In the last year of Bulova's direction of the company, assets were valued at $46 million sales amounted to more than $76 million and net profits were over $7 million.

Sigmund Eisner (1859-1925), from Horažďovice, Bohemia, was a large clothing manufacturer. His Red Bank, New Jersey company, the Sigmund Eisner Co., was a chief supplier of uniforms for the American Army and the exclusive manufacturer of uniforms for the Boy Scouts of America. During First World War, the Eisner Co. produced also uniforms for the British, French, Belgian, Italian armies. The company operated plants in Red Bank, Freehold and South Amboy, NJ.

John L. Ernst (1941-), b of Bohemian ancestry, is the son of Richard C. Ernst and Susan Bloomingdale. He has been chairman and president of Bloomingdale Properties Inc. since September 1984. Mr. Ernst serves as the Director of First Financial Caribbean Corporation. He served as a Director of Griffin Land & Nurseries Inc. from April 1997 to May 16, 2006. Mr. Ernst served as a Director of General Cigar Holdings, Inc. since 1983. He served as a Director of Doral Financial Corp., since 1989 until August 2007. Mr. Ernst served as a Director of Culbro Corp., from 1983 to 1997.

Frederico Figner (1866-1947) or simply Fred Figner, as he was known, was a Czech born Jewish emigrant of humble background, who left his mark in the annals of the history of Brazil. He lived initially in the United States before landing in Belém, Brazil in 1891. Considered a visionary, his entrepreneurial character was responsible for profound transformations in his days, a time when he brought to the country many novelties, among them the phonograph, the gramophone, and music records. At 13, he left the house in search of work. That was the beginning of his long journey, which would include several countries. Possessing a singular commercial adroitness, Figner rapidly made his fortune. In 1902, he founded the famous 'Casa Edison' in downtown Rio de Janeiro, the first commercial recording company in Brazil. The company was considered a pioneer in recording and selling Brazilian popular music. He also created Odeon, the first recording company for Brazilian music.

Charles Louis Fleischmann (1835-1897) from Krnov, Moravia was an innovative manufacturer of yeast in Cincinnati who in the late 1860s, created America's first commercially produced yeast. This revolutionized baking, enabling today's mass production and consumption of bread.

Louis Gans (1840-1904), b. Neustadt, Bohemia, was a merchant, who was educated in Prague, where he was a student of theology. He came to the US when he was nineteen (1858) and began his career by teaching. He went to California and later to Helena, Montana, where he was a clerk in a general store, dealing largely with miners' supplies. In 1860, he went into business for himself and founded a partnership with the firm title Gans & Klein. The firm prospered and Mr. Gans became the resident buyer in New York in 1864. He amassed a huge fortune. Upon his death, he made liberal bequests in many directions, including his native village in Bohemia.

Martin Greenfield (1928-2024), b. Pavlovo, Slovakia, is an American master tailor, based in Brooklyn, NY, specializing in men's suits. He has been described as the best men's tailor in the United States. His list of clients includes six US Presidents, as well as other notable politicians and celebrities. His company, Martin Greenfield Clothiers, has also fashioned men's suits for clothing lines DKNY and Rag & Bone, and the television show *Boardwalk Empire*. Greenfield is a Holocaust survivor, having been imprisoned as a teenager at Auschwitz, where the rest of his immediate family were killed.

Benedict Joseph Greenhut (1870-1932), b. Chicago, IL, of Bohemian father, in 1896 went to NYC, where he was associated with his father in business. He became a secretary and treasurer of Siegel and Cooper Dept. Store, known as 'The Big Store,' while his father was president. In 1907, the Greenhut and Co. Dept. Store was established, of which he later became president. He was also president of the Empire City Safe Deposit Co., vice president of the National Cooperage and Woodenware Co. of Peoria and director of the Trans. Lux Daylight Picture Screen Corp., Murray Envelope Corp., Union Exchange National Bank and

Fidelity Phoenix Insurance Co. He was an outstanding personality in the dept. store field in America.

Joseph Benedict Greenhut (1847–1918), from Horšovský Týn, founded the Great Western Distillery in Peoria, IL, the then largest distillery in the world. In 1887, he organized The Distillery and Cattle Feeding Co., with a cap of $35 million, comprising practically all large distilleries in country.

Jacob Greil (1839–1900), b. Bohemia, was a wholesale grocer. He was educated principally in Bohemia. After coming to the US in 1856, he clerked at West Point, GA., and then in Chambers County. In 1860, he went into the dry goods business at Milltown. During the Civil War, he enlisted in the Army, taking part in a number of battles. After leaving the service at the rank of Captain, he settled at Montgomery, GA, and entered the retail grocery business which he remained in until 1872 when he went into the wholesale grocery business with his brother, Nathan Greil. He served twelve years as alderman of Montgomery, and at one time was commissary of the Second regiment, Alabama State Troops. He was vice-president of the Farley National Bank; president and vice-president of the National Building & Loan Association; director of the Capital City Insurance Company; director of the Bank of Montgomery; president of the Commercial Industrial Association of Montgomery; and president and founder of the People's Cotton Mill. He was a Mason and grand master of the exchequer of the grand lodge of Knights of Pythias of Alabama.

Ralph Kleinert Guinzburg (1891–1957), b. NYC, of Bohemian ancestry, was president and director I. B. Kleinert Rubber Co., manufacturers of rubber ware. Under his leadership, the firm expanded from seasonal manufacture of ear muffs to dress shield manufacturer. Other lines of apparel were gradually introduced and in addition, the company produced many new articles in which rubber was combined with fabrics. He was an advocate of putting notion depts. in department stores and of extensive advertising and merchandising methods. He was also a director of the Federal Employment Service.

Henrietta Hartford (née Pollitzer) (1881–1948), b. Buffton, SC, of Czech ancestry; wife of Edward V. Hartford. She was an heir of the A&P fortune, which in the early 20th century had an estimated 16,000 stores. Her husband died in 1922 and left an estate estimated at 200 million dollars. Fifteen years later, Henrietta married Prince Guido Pignatelli and thus becoming a princess.

Joseph S. Hartmann (1846–d.), b. Břeskovice, Bohemia, a few years after he established his home in Milwaukee, WI, embarked in the trunk business there under the name of Carpeles-Hartmann & Company, and later removed to Chicago, although he established his business in Racine. They manufactured the Hartmann wardrobe trunk and the company had over one hundred patents issued. This trunk received the grand prize at the California exposition. Hartmann eventually offered over 800 models, sizes and colors of steamship trunks and luggage.

Rochus Heinisch (1801–1874), b. Litoměřice, Bohemia, a surgical instrument maker, after immigrating to America, conceived the idea of manufacturing shears of malleable iron faced with steel. Having demonstrated its practicability, he established in the city of Elizabeth a factory for the manufacture of shears. Some years later, he removed to Newark, NJ and engaged in a similar enterprise, with which he was identified until his death. He was the pioneer in this branch of industry, and known as a successful inventor, his most prominent achievement having been the invention of the tailors' shears, which have since found a market in nearly every portion of Europe and America.

Harry Bulova Henshel (1919–2007), b. NYC, son of Emily Bulova (1892–1989) of descent, and Harry Davis Henshel was an American businessman and the last member of the Bulova family to head the Bulova Watch company, as president, chairman, and chief executive officer. He graduated from Brown University (B.A., 1940) and the Harvard School of Business (M.B.A., 1951).

John D. Hertz (1879–1961), b. Sklabiňa, Slovakia, was an American businessman, thoroughbred racehorse owner and breeder, and philanthropist. He founded the Yellow Cab Company in Chicago in 1915, which offered taxicab service at a modest price. The distinctive yellow cabs became popular and were quickly franchised throughout the United States. He then founded the Chicago Motor Coach Company in 1917 to operate bus transport services in Chicago and the Yellow Cab Manufacturing Company in 1920 to manufacture taxicabs for sale. In 1923, he founded the Yellow Coach Manufacturing Company to manufacture coaches and later cars. In 1924, he acquired a rental car business, renaming it Hertz Drive-Ur-Self Corporation.

Henry Horner (1817–1878), b. Čkyně, Bohemia, settled in Chicago, where he founded a grocery store in 1842, two years after he emigrated from Bohemia. Horner's first store, at Randolph and Canal Streets, was one of Chicago's earliest retail groceries. In 1856, he started a wholesale operation. After he died, his wife Hannah and his four sons took charge of the business, which became one of the leading grocery wholesalers in the Midwest. Horner was instrumental in forming the Chicago Board of Trade.

(Carla) Jayne Hrdlicka (ca. 1963–), b. Wichita, KS, of a Czech immigrant father, is an American-born business executive based in Australia. She is currently the chairman and Board President of Tennis Australia, having been appointed in October 2017. In November

2020, she became the chief executive officer (CEO) of Australian airline Virgin Australia, replacing Paul Scurrah.

John Horský (1838-1924), b. Bohemia, was reared and educated in his native land, and in 1855, came with his parents to America. After a variety of jobs, in the spring of 1865, he came to Helena and, in company with George Butz, turned his attention to the brewing business. They built the first brewery in the city, the Helena Brewery. Mr. Horsky continued successfully in the brewing business until 1891 when having secured a competency, he sold out and retired from active life. During his residence here, he has all along been more or less interested in mines and mining, having done much to develop these interests in Montana. He built on Main Street a fine brick block 42 x 110 feet, three stories and basement, which was rented for stores, offices and a commercial college.

Brett Icahn (1979–), New York, NY, is the son of former ballerina Liba Trejbal (ca. 1905) from Czechoslovakia and billionaire investor Carl Icahn, an American businessman, investor, and philanthropist. He graduated from Choate Rosemary Hall and Princeton University. Icahn interned at Goldman Sachs. Shortly after, he directed art films. In 2001, he founded Myelin Media. He joined his father's company, Icahn Enterprises, in 2002. Since June 2004, he has been an investment analyst for Icahn Partners LP, Icahn Master, Icahn Master II, Icahn Master III, and Icahn Partners Master Fund LP. He co-manages a hedge fund with David Schechter, which includes the Sargon portfolio from his father's company. Icahn and Schechter have invested heavily in Apple and Netflix shares. In 2011, his hedge fund had a return of 50 percent. Icahn has played an instrumental role in his father's company's attempted takeover of Lions Gate.

Albert P. Kalabza (1875-1966), b. Liškov, Bohemia, came to America at an early age, settling in Chicago. Within a short time, he became one of the most skilled electrotypers in Chicago, while working for the Chicago Electrolyte & Stereotype Corp. In 1905, he moved to NY and in 1918, became a partner of Stoddard-Bell Electric Co. Within five years, he became its sole owner. Under his guidance, Stoddard-Bell grew and became the foremost electrotype company in the NY Metropolitan area and it remained in the family until 1962.

Travis Kalanick (1976–), b. Los Angeles, CA, of Slovak ancestry, is an American businessman best known as the co-founder and former chief executive officer (CEO) of Uber. Kalanick was CEO of Uber from 2010 to 2017. Previously he worked for Scour, a peer-to-peer file-sharing application company, and was the co-founder of Red Swoosh, a peer-to-peer content delivery network that was sold to Akamai Technologies in 2007. In 2018, Kalanick started a venture fund named 10100, which intended to invest in e-commerce, innovation, and real estate in emerging markets like China and India. That same year, Kalanick announced an investment of $150 million in real estate redevelopment company City Storage Systems; he also announced that he would serve as its CEO. The company operates a ghost kitchen startup under the name Cloud Kitchens, for which Kalanick has invested $300 million.

John Karmazin (1884-1977), b. Tman, Bohemia, was an American engine component inventor and business founder. While working for the Harrison Radiator Division of General Motors, Karmazin obtained patents for major improvements to the automobile radiator cap. With royalties earned from General Motors for his radiator cap patent, he founded the Karmazin Products Corporation in Wyandotte, Michigan in 1946. The company produced radiators, oil coolers and many other heat transfer devices that were primarily used in heavy construction equipment, tractors and trucks. Most of the company's products were based on patents obtained by Karmazin who was awarded more than 50 patents by the U.S. Patent and Trademark Office during his lifetime. During its peak sales in the 1970s, the company had approximately 300 workers and was one of the largest private sector employers in Downriver Detroit.

Tobiáš Kohn (1817-1898), b. Prague, wove the first piece of silk goods produced by a loom in the US and is known as the founder of the silk industry in this country. Kohn devised machinery and methods of his own, which, at first, he did not protect; but between 1865 and 1868 he took out several patents, and his success had great influence in establishing the silk industry in Paterson, N. J., where some of his inventions were used.

Paul Kohner (1900-1965), b. Tachov, Bohemia, had escaped the Nazis from Czechoslovakia, and brought his family to the United States including his brother Frank (10 years his junior) shortly thereafter. In 1941, Paul founded the firm Kohner Bros., a wooden bead company, and made Frank his 50% partner upon his arrival. They made pocketbooks and necklaces out of colored wooden beads (the family business in the old country) that fortunately for them, became the height of fashion during the war years. With the knowledge of wood, their first excursion outside of beads were wooden toys (pull toys, specifically one called Tricycle Tom) and in the mid-forties, Paul obtained the rights to push button puppets from a Swiss inventor. These puppets (the now familiar ones you push from the bottom, and they wiggle on top of a base) proved to be a big success and further propelled the company into the toy business. These same push-button puppets were later to be made of plastic and marketed in every conceivable character license including Disney, Hanna Barbera, King Features, and Marvel to name just a few. These puppets were sold in every discount chain in America from Woolworths to McCrorys. To reminisce, all one has to do is go to eBay and hit 'Kohner push button puppets.' Kohner Brothers was also among the first companies to convert to plastic.

Francis J. Korbel (1831–1920), a native of Bechyně, Bohemia, was the founder of one of the largest lumber and wine-growing industries in the US; he was also a manufacturer of handcrafted brandies while also creating premium champagnes.

Ray Kroc (1902–1984), b. Chicago, IL, of Czech parents, a Multi-Mixer salesman, took note of the McDonald brothers who had purchased 8 of his Multi-Mixers. He became convinced that the setup of this small chain had the potential to explode across the nation. He joined McDonald's in 1954 and built it into the most successful fast food operation in the world. Kroc was included in *Time 100: The Most Important People of the Century* and amassed a fortune during his lifetime.

Robert Kyncl (1970–), b. Czech., is an American business executive. He is the Chief Business Officer at YouTube where he oversees all business functions, partnerships, and operations. Previously, Kyncl was Vice President of Content Acquisitions at Netflix, where he spearheaded the company's content acquisition for streaming TV shows and movies over the Internet. Mr. and Mrs. Kyncl reside with their two daughters in Los Angeles and founded Kyncl Family Foundation focused on supporting the educational needs of underrepresented communities.

Anton Laadt (1873–1960), b. Jindřichův Hradec, Bohemia, came to the US in 1891. He studied business at Northwestern Univ. He became general manager of the most famous Czech brewery in Chicago, the Atlas Brewing Co. Under his management, the company grew into a huge undertaking which did not stop its activities during the Prohibition era but developed its near-beer business in such enormous dimensions that the Atlas Brewery was the greatest commercial venture of this kind in the US. He also served as Director of Peabody & Co. and was founding member of the Chicago World's Fair (1933). Laadt was a member of numerous organizations, including the Bohemian Beseda Club, Bohemian Arts Club, Plzeňský Sokol, Athletic Club, etc.

Francis W. Lassak (orig. František Vlasák) (1793–1889), b. Prague, Bohemia, was a pioneer furrier in NYC, partner to James Astor; he was considered the first Czech millionaire.

Aerin Lauder (Aerin Rebecca Lauder Zinterhofer) (1970–), b. New York, NY, is an American billionaire heiress and businesswoman. Lauder is the daughter of Jo Carole Lauder (née Knopf) and Ronald Lauder; and granddaughter of Estée Lauder and Joseph Lauder, the cofounders of the cosmetics company Estée Lauder Companies. Lauder is the style and image director for The Estée Lauder Companies and has her own cosmetic, perfume, fashion, and furniture line named AERIN. She also has a furniture and accessories collection. She owns 16 million shares in the Estée Lauder Companies making her worth $2.7 billion as of 2019 and ranking her 319 on the Forbes 400 list of richest Americans.

Estée Lauder (née Mentzer) (1908-2004), b. Corona, Queens, NY, of Czech and Slovak ancestry, was an American businesswoman and entrepreneur. She co-founded her eponymous cosmetics company with her husband, Joseph Lauter (later Lauder). Lauder was the only woman on *Time Magazine*'s 1998 list of the 20 most influential business geniuses of the 20th century. In 1953, Lauder introduced her first fragrance, Youth-Dew, a bath oil that doubled as a perfume. Instead of using French perfumes by the drop behind each ear, women began using Youth-Dew by the bottle in their bath water. In the first year, it sold 50,000 bottles; by 1984, the figure had risen to 150 million.

Jane Lauder (Jane Lauder Warsh) (1973-), b. New York, NY, is an American billionaire heiress and businesswoman. Lauder is the daughter of Jo Carole Lauder (née Knopf) and Ronald Lauder; and granddaughter of Estée Lauder and Joseph Lauder, the cofounders of the cosmetics company Estée Lauder Companies. Lauder graduated from Chapin School and Stanford University. Lauder joined the family business in 1996. In 2013, she was promoted to global president and general manager of Estée Lauder's Origins, Darphin, and Ojon brands. She currently runs the company's Clinique unit, a skincare line frequently sold in malls. Lauder owns 20 million shares in the Estée Lauder Companies making her worth $4.2 billion in 2019. In 2018, Lauder joined the board of Eventbrite.

Jonathan Joseph Ledecky (1958-), b. New York City, of Czech immigrant father, came to America eleven years prior to study English at Rutgers University. Growing up in Queens and Brooklyn, he became a New York Yankees fan. After moving in 1972 to Greenwich, Connecticut, Ledecky attended Greenwich High School, with extracurricular journalism work that would have earned Ledecky a scholarship at Vanderbilt University if his father had not insisted on attending an Ivy League school. Thus, Ledecky started studying business administration at Harvard University, continuing his reporter work at *The Harvard Crimson* and college station WHRB. Ledecky earned his Bachelor's degree in 1979 and completed a Master of Business Administration in 1983, which was followed by a series of venture capital-type jobs. After being dismissed from Steelcase in 1994, Ledecky decided to open his own company in the office supplies business. Backed by a number of Harvard alumni, U.S. Office Products was founded in 1994, and had its initial public offering one year later. By the time Ledecky left U.S. Office Products in 1998, his fortune was estimated at $200 million. Currently, he is also a minority owner of the NHL team New York Islanders and their AHL affiliate Bridgeport Sound Tigers. At the end of the two-year transition period (2016), he will acquire majority shares. His niece is Olympic gold medalist swimmer Katie Ledecky.

Ralph Pokorney Levey (1890-1958), b. New Orleans, LA, son of Bella Pokorny (1864-1944) of Czech descent and Moses Edmund Levey, was president of the retail shoe business of M. Pokorny & Sons. He was educated in the city's public schools and entered the Pokorny firm in the first decade of this century. He was the president of the company for the last 30 years. He was active in civic work; he was one of the organizers of the Better Business Bureau and the New Orleans Retail Merchants Credit Bureau and at the time of this death, was an active member of their boards of directors. For more than 30 years, he was a member of the board of directors of the Whitney National Bank and of the St. Charles Betterment Association. He also held membership in the Chamber of Commerce of the New Orleans Area, the Sertoma Club, and the National Retail Shoe Merchants Association.

Sir Frank P. Lowy (1930–), b. Fiľakovo, Czech., an Australian-Israeli businessman of Jewish Slovak origin and the former long-time Chairman of Westfield Corporation, a global shopping centre company with US$29.3 billion of assets under management in the United States, United Kingdom, and Europe.

Robert Alfred Lurie (1929–), b. San Francisco, CA, is a real estate magnate, philanthropist and former owner of the San Francisco Giants franchise of Major League Baseball from March 2, 1976 until January 12, 1993. He took over the real estate company founded in 1922 by his father, Louis Lurie, whose name is synonymous with San Francisco real estate development during the middle part of the 20th century. The company built a number of properties along Montgomery Street over the years, including a building Bank of America bought and tore down for its world headquarters at 555 California St., and it still owns many of them. Other notable local properties owned by Lurie are the Mark Hopkins Hotel and the Curran Theatre. Lurie's real estate company has also upgraded some older properties in San Francisco. For example, Lurie invested $20 million in 901 Market St. and brought in retailers Copeland's Sports and Marshalls, transforming the 200,000-square-foot (19,000 m^2) mid-Market Street eyesore into a winner. Since selling the Giants, Lurie has focused his efforts on his real estate firm, the Lurie Co., buying and selling properties and branching out beyond its core office holdings totaling over 4,000,000 square feet (370,000 m^2), not including two hotels, a theater and a parking facility it owns. He is also involved in various philanthropic activities, which include the $20 million Louis R. Lurie Foundation.

William Lyons (1867–1955), b. Memphis, TN, son of Bertha Lederer (1846–1942) of Czech descent, and Mark Lyons, was a manufacturer of cigars. He was the president of the firm, B. Lyons Co., a large manufacturer of cigars in Appleton, WI. He received early education in public schools and later attended Ryan High School in Appleton, WI, and graduated from the De Land Business College, after which he learned the cigar-making business with the company founded by his father. In 1906, the business was incorporated with William L. Lyons, president, and general manager; B. F. Lyons of Beloit, WI, vice-president; and C. B. Lyons, secretary. William L. Lyons was a member of the Knights of Pythias and of the Blue Lodge and Chapter of the Masonic fraternity.

V. THE SOCIETY

Sigmund S. Mandl (1898–1976), b. Úsov, Moravia, was the founder of the Husky Wrench manufacturing company. He immigrated to the United States from Czechoslovakia, born to a Jewish family. His brother Hugo was born in Úsov. In January 1924, he founded Husky Wrench in Milwaukee, Wisconsin, with two partners, at about the time he filed his first patent. After selling the business, Mandl went to Blackhawk Manufacturing in 1931 and became one of their two chief design engineers. Later, he was General Manager of Die-Mold Corporation, while continuing to hold his position at Blackhawk. Mandl received a number of patents for tool design.

Thomas W. Matey, Sr. (1931–2017), b. Warren, OH, of Slovak descent, was a business executive. He graduated from Warren Harding High School and the University of Notre Dame (B.A., 1953). Tom started his career with Inland Steel in Indianapolis, then Chicago where he spent most of his career as a Steel Executive. In 1979, Tom and his wife Victoria started their second career in Brevard County as developers of the Las Olas Beach Club timeshare resorts in Satellite Beach and Cocoa Beach. They were early leaders in the timeshare industry and affiliated with Resort Condominiums International since 1979. Tom was an NCAA All-American and captain of the ND golf team and won many tournaments including the Ohio High School Championship, the Illinois State Amateur Championship, and numerous Club Championships; was a participant in the USGA Open Championship, the USGA Amateur Championship, and the British executive with Inland Steel, Indianapolis.

Peter Munk (1927–2018), b. Budapest, of Slovak descent (the family came originally from the Nitra District in Slovakia), is a Canadian businessman. He is an industrial tycoon, investor, philanthropist, and one of the richest men in Canada. He is the founder of Barrick Gold (the world's largest gold-mining corporation) and the multi-billion-dollar Canadian construction and development firm Trizec Properties. Munk is known for his philanthropy, as a donor to the Munk School of Global Affairs at the University of Toronto and the Peter Munk Cardiac Centre at the Toronto General Hospital. He is also well known for supporting the Munk Debates.

Edward Andrew Oberwesier (1879–1954), b. Menasha, WI, of Bohemian father, began his career in 1896 as a teller in the Menasha Bank. In 1908, he became manager and secretary of the Whiting-Plover Paper Co., Stevens Point, WI. He continued in those positions until 1930 when he was named president and manager of the company, positions he maintained until 1937 when he left the firm and sold his stock holdings in it. In 1938, he headed a group that purchased the Fox River Paper Corp., Appleton, WI, and he served as president of the firm until 1953 when he became chairman of the Board, the position he maintained until he was close to his death. The firm was originally founded in 1883. By 1953, it had annual sales of $6,000,000 and about 400 employees and produced 15,000 tons of paper yearly. At that time, the firm's principal products were cotton-content writing and technical papers. Aside from his paper manufacturing interests, Oberweiser was president of the Citizens National Bank, Stevens Point, during 1919-42 and chairman of the board from the latter year until 1947. He was also instrumental in obtaining funds for the construction of the Hotel Whiting, Stevens Point.

Steve Obsitnik (1967-), b. Stamford, CT, of Slovak descent, is US Naval Academy and the Wharton School graduate. He is an electrical engineer by training and entrepreneur. He is president, COO & CFO, Calabrio Inc. (2002-05); Venture Advisor, SRI International (2005-08); chairman & CEO, Quintel Technology (2007-12); High Tech CEO, Saugatuck Advisory (s. 2012). He is also an adjunct professor of business and entrepreneurship, at Sacred Heart University (s. 2010). He is also a politician.

Frank S. Pohanka (1891-1959), b. New York, NY, of Moravian ancestry, was the founder of The Pohanka Automotive Group, one of the nation's oldest families that owned car dealership groups. He founded his first Pohanka dealership in 1919, selling and servicing Chevrolets at Ward Place, N.W., in downtown Washington, D.C. The Pohanka Automotive Group now has locations in Marlow Heights, Md., Salisbury, Md., Bowie, MD, Chantilly, VA, and Fredericksburg, VA. Pohanka dealerships sell 14 makes of cars and trucks, including Acura, Cadillac, Chevrolet, Honda, Hyundai, Isuzu, Lexus, Mazda, Mercedes, Nissan, Oldsmobile, Saturn, Subaru, and Toyota.

Alexander Printz (1869-1947), b. Košice, Slovakia, was a merchant. He was educated in public schools in Cleveland and preparatory schools for Columbia School of Mines. At the age of 17, abandoned study, and became connected with D. Black & Co., as a stock boy; then traveling salesman, until 1893, when he organized Printz-Biederman & Co., manufacturers of ladies' coats and suits. The firm was incorporated in 1904 when he became president. Employing over 1,000 people in the main factory in Cleveland; offices in New York, Chicago, and St. Louis; one of the three concerns of its kind whose goods have been trademarked and advertised in the magazines for the benefit of the buyer.

Daniel Pritzker (1959-), b. Marin Co., CA, son of Marian Cindy Friend (1923-) of Bohemian ancestry, and Jay (Arthur) Pritzker, is an American billionaire heir, musician, film director, and member of the Pritzker family. He is a 1981 graduate of Tufts University and earned a Juris Doctor from Northwestern University Law School in 1986. Daniel and his wife Karen are trustees of the Jay Pritzker Foundation, a philanthropic fund that created the Pritzker Challenge at Tufts with gifts of $10 million. Pritzker is ranked 353 in the 2020 list of "The 400 Richest Americans" by Forbes magazine, with a net worth of $2.4 billion.

John A. Pritzker (1953–), b. Chicago, IL, son of Marian Cindy Friend (1923–) of Bohemian ancestry, and Jay (Arthur) Pritzker, is an American billionaire and investor. He runs his own private equity firm Geolo Capital, which focuses on investments in hospitality, entertainment, and health and wellness companies. In 2010, he purchased a majority interest in the Joie de Vivre Hotel chain and later merged it with the Pomeranc family's Thompson Hotel Group.

Thomas Pritzker (1950–), b. Chicago, IL, son of Marian Cindy Friend (1923–) of Bohemian ancestry, and Jay (Arthur) Pritzker is an American billionaire heir and businessman. He holds a JD and an MBA from the University of Chicago, and a BA from Claremont McKenna College. A member of the Pritzker family, he is the chairman and chief executive officer (CEO) of the Pritzker Organization (TPO), which manages the various Pritzker family business assets, and the executive chairman of the Hyatt Hotels Corporation.

Luke Pustejovsky (1977–), b. Channelview, TX, of Czech ancestry, studied at Harvard University (A.L.B., 2002) and at London School of Economics (1999). Early in his career, Luke worked as an analyst at Saturn Capital and as an associate at Echelon Ventures, both Boston-based venture capital funds supporting interdisciplinary innovations like fuel cell/MEMS tech. He is co-founder and EVP, Business Development at lvl Analytics, at San Francisco Area. He is an innovation analyst in resource efficiency sectors like energy, power, water and materials. As an entrepreneur, Luke co-founded the brick and paver businesses at CalStar Products (previously CalStar Cement). Luke's additional experience includes tenure as director of sales & marketing at Calera Corporation, a well-funded carbon mineralization experiment funded by DOE, Khosla Ventures, Peabody Coal and Madrone Capital. In the last three years, he has consulted with founders and CEOs at 15+ greentech companies on new market entry, global partner development and innovation funding strategies. His clients include Cleantech Group, Genan, and Repsol.

Morris Rich (1847–1928) and his brother William, both natives of Košice, Slovakia, moved to the United States in 1860; they became peddlers in Cleveland (Ohio). In 1865, Morris moved to Atlanta (Georgia) where in 1867, he opened a retail store that was the first of a leading chain of department stores in the South. His brothers, Emanuel (1849–1897) and Daniel (1843–1920) who had come to the United States in 1862, and later Walter Henry (1880–1947), joined him in his successful business. Rich's of Atlanta was the first major retail store in the area to introduce liberal credit terms and homespun ways of merchandising, which popularized the store among the large black population. The firm's credit policy was a major factor in its rehabilitation after a disastrous fire swept Atlanta in 1917. The company also simplified internal administration and became famous for its excellent labor relations. Its owners and senior officers were prominent in many local and national civic organizations and charities which included the Rich Foundation, a major endower of Emory University's School of Business Administration.

Richard H. Rich (orig. Rosenheim) (1901–1975), b. Atlanta, GA; of Slovak ancestry, on his mother's side, was a merchant and business executive. His father was a shoe manufacturer in Savannah, his mother the daughter of Morris Rich, founder of Rich's department stores in Atlanta. Richard Rich legally changed his name from Rosenheim to Rich in 1920 at the urging of his grandfather. He graduated from the Wharton School of the University of Pennsylvania in 1923 with a Bachelor of Science degree in economics. His formal schooling ended with post-graduate studies at Harvard University in 1923-1924. He joined M. Rich and Bros. as a full-time employee in 1924. From 1924 to 1933, he worked in the business office and merchandising departments. In 1924, he was elected a member of the Board of Directors of M. Rich and Brothers' real estate holding company and, in 1929, the year the company changed its name from M. Rich and Bros. to Rich's, Inc., he became a Rich's director. From 1933 to 1936, Rich headed the store's buying operation in New York City, then returned to Atlanta to be General Sales Manager and Publicity Director. He continued his rise through management ranks, being elected company vice-president in 1937, treasurer in 1947, and president in 1949. Twelve years later, he became Chairman of the Board, a position he held until 1972 when he entered semi-retirement as Chairman of the Executive Committee. He held that office at the time of his death. As a chief executive of Rich's, 'Mr. Dick,' as employees called him, oversaw the store's tremendous expansions of the mid-twentieth century. Rich's continued to expand in the 1940's and 1950's to become the largest department store in size and volume of sales in the southeast. The 1950's also saw the opening of Rich's first branch stores in Knoxville (a merger with S. H. George's which was sold in 1958) and in Atlanta at Lenox Square Shopping Center (1959). The company opened eight other branches in Atlanta and Birmingham before Rich died in 1975. They also opened several budget convenience stores, Richways, in Georgia and neighboring states.

John M. Romadka (orig. Hromádka) (1838–1898), b. Sedlčany, Bohemia, with his two brothers, Anthony Vincent and Charles, started Romadka Brothers Trunk Store and Factory, later renamed Romadka Brothers Co., manufacturers of trunks and traveling bags, Milwaukee. It was one of the largest enterprises of its kind in the US.

Stephen Boleslav Roman (1921–1988), b. Veľký Ruskov, Slovakia, is a prominent Canadian mining engineer, and mining executive, called the 'Uranium King of Canada.' He emigrated to Canada when he was 16 years old. From 1945, he focused his attention on business opportunities in the mining industry and created an imposing complex mining industrial company limited by capital value in the mid-60s estimated at $70 billion. He began as a poor immigrant and became the most influential figure in Canadian industry – CEO and Chairman of Denison Mines Limited, which owned the largest uranium mine in the world. Since his youth, he was strongly connected to the Greek Catholic Church. He helped to found and organize the Slovak Catholic Eparchy of Saints Cyril and Methodius of Toronto. The monumental Cathedral of the Transfiguration of our Lord in Markham was funded and designed by him, modeling the structure of the church in Veľký Ruskov. Roman was invested in the Order of Canada and the Canadian Mining Hall of Fame.

John Rybovich, Jr. (1913–1993), b. Florida, of Slovak descent, was a boatbuilder. He was a designer and builder of the first modern sportfishing boats and incorporated new technology; inducted into the IGFA Fishing Hall of Fame. An avid angler, he was the driving force behind several major fishing tournaments, such as the prestigious Invitational Masters Angling Tournament. Deeply concerned about marine fisheries conservation, Rybovich tirelessly worked to protect marine resources at the local, state, and federal levels. As president and founder of the Game Fish Research Association, Rybovich was instrumental in getting Florida to enact regulations to protect sailfish and initiating sailfish research. Still, he was best known for the sleek fishing boats crafted at his family's Rybovich and Son's boat yard in West Palm Beach. The boats were as practical as they were beautiful. Designed specifically for fishing, Rybovich boats are still the standard against which all others are judged.

Benedict Schwanda (1915–2006), b. Hlinsko, Bohemia, was the founder of firm B. Schwanda & Sons, which occupied the top-ranking position in the pearl button industry in the US. The family brought their button manufacturing skills with them from Bohemia, when Benedict Schwanda, his family, and two apprentices immigrated to the United States in 1898. They settled in New York City and began cutting and carving ocean pearl buttons by hand out of their home at East 74th Street. In 1902, they moved their operation to Winfield, Long Island, later purchasing a factory in Philadelphia. By 1917, they purchased the United Manufacturing Company of Stafford Springs and, under the management of Benedict Jr. and Joseph Schwanda, began manufacturing ocean pearl buttons on a larger scale. They also opened plants in 1933 in Long Island City and in Denton, Maryland.

Paul Schwarzkopf (1886–1970), b. Prague, Bohemia, was trained at Tech. Univ. of Prague as a powder metallurgist. He was founder of number of metallurgical laboratories and plants throughout Europe. In 1939, with Hans Petschek, established res. lab. and manufacturing plant, Am. Electro Metal Corp., Yonkers, NY, becoming dir. of research and pres. (s. 1946). He held many patents in powder metallurgy.

Martin Mathias Secor (1841–1911), b. Prague, Bohemia, was the founder and proprietor of the Northwestern Trunk and Traveling Bag Manufactory and M. M. Secor Trunk Company, Racine, Wisconsin.

Murray Seeman (1914–2017), b. Ridgewood, Queens, NY, of Czech Jewish descent, was an American lawyer and real estate developer on Long Island, New York. He was known for his contributions to the community as Mayor of Great Neck Estates, as a World War II veteran, and as a Biblical scholar. In 1934, Seeman received a BA from Brooklyn College and was voted "most likely to succeed" in his class. During the Great Depression, he worked two jobs while attending Columbia Law School, where he graduated with a J.D. in 1937. Seeman practiced law for three years before he was drafted to serve in the US Army on June 5, 1941. After the war, Seeman worked as an attorney in private practice and as a real estate developer. He served on the NY State Pension & Retirement Commission under Governor Hugh Carey.

Václav F. Severa (1853–1938), b. Doubravice, Bohemia, a pharmacist by trade, became a pioneer drug manufacturer, the founder of the firm W. F. Severa Co., in Cedar Rapids, which became known throughout the US.

Joseph 'Pep' Simek Sr. (1926–2013), b. Ogema, WI, of Czech. Descent was an American businessman who co-founded, alongside his brother, Tombstone pizza, a widely available American brand of frozen pizza. Pep Simek opened a second pizzeria, Pep's Pizza, in Medford following Tombstone's sale to Kraft. Simek also pursued other business and philanthropic ventures after Tombstone. He purchased the Enerquip company in Medford. He also entered into the travel and leisure industry, acquiring the Paradise Shores Hotel and Resort in Lake Holcombe, Wisconsin, and Captain Morgan's Retreat in Belize. In 1987, Simek purchased the Embassy Suites and Regency Suites Hotel complex in Green Bay, Wisconsin. He sold his Green Bay hotels in 2007 to the Lodge Works corporation. Simek and his wife donated more than one million dollars to Holy Rosary Catholic Church in Medford. The couple also donated $900,000 to fund a new fire station and the Simek Recreation Center. Frances Simek, with the support of her husband, gave one million dollars to construct a new Medford library to halt an ongoing dispute over a source of funding.

Daniela Simpson (1976–), b., of Czech descent, is a marketing executive and an American businesswoman. She is currently the General Manager at Ferrara Candy Company and is a two-time winner of the Most Innovative New Product Award in the non-chocolate category at the National Confectioners Association Sweets & Snacks Expo. Simpson's undergraduate degree is in marketing from the University of Economics, Prague and she received her M.B.A. from UCLA Anderson School of Management.

Ezekiel Solomon (1735–1808), a native of Berlin, of Bohemian ancestry, was among the first Jewish merchants to go to Montreal, Canada, at the time of the British occupation. Solomon was a partner with Chapman Abraham, Gershon Levy, Benjamin Lyon, and Levi Solomons, who were originally army purveyors and who later figured prominently as pioneer fur traders in Michigan. Solomon helped raised funds for the Shearith Israel Congregation in Montreal. It opened in 1760. It was the first Jewish congregation in Canada. In 1761, Solomon went to Fort Michilimackinac, today's Mackinaw City in Michigan. He was captured by the Indians during their 1763 massacre but gained his freedom by being ransomed. He was a partner of the Mackinaw Company enterprise, which was organized in 1779 by some 30 traders and companies, and which is believed to be the first example of a department store operation.

Thomas Spiegel (1946–), b. Košice, Czech., is an American banker and investor. He was the former chief executive of the failed Columbia Savings & Loan. He is currently the chairman and CEO of Linq3, specializing in the lottery industry. His family immigrated to the United States in 1948. His parents, Abraham and Edita Spiegel had been imprisoned in Auschwitz in 1944. Their 2-year-old son, Uziel, was killed in the Holocaust. Spiegel earned a Bachelor's degree in business in 1967 from the University of Southern California. He also attended Loyola Law School for one year. Spiegel worked for both A.G. Becker & Co. and Drexel Burnham as a stock broker through 1973.

Henry Bernard Steele (1863–1909), b. Chicago, IL, son of Sophie Wedeles (1840–1909) of Czech immigrant parents, and Bernard Steele, was president of the wholesale Steele-Wedeles Co., Importers, in Chicago.

Maurice Bernard Steele (1871–1906), the third son of Sophie Wedeles (1840–1909) of Czech immigrant parents and Bernard Steele.

Samuel Bernard Steele (1866–1950), b. Chicago, IL, the second son of Sophie Wedeles (1840–1909) of Czech immigrant parents and Bernard Steele, was also associated with Steele-Wedeles Co., serving as secretary, VP, and eventually president.

John Joseph Taussig (1843–1918), b. Prague, Bohemia, started as a grain merchant, but in 1865, he became senior a partner in the firm of Taussig & Fisher, Bankers, and Brokers, out of which grew the firms of Taussig, Fisher & Co., of New York, and Gempp & Taussig, Frankfort-on-the-Main, all of which were swept away in a panic of 1873. He had since confined operations to St. Louis, and since 1874, as a member in the firm of J. & J. Taussig, Bankers, and Brokers.

Charles William Taussig (1896–1948), a native of New York, was of Bohemian ancestry. He was president of the American Molasses, the firm founded by his grandfather William Taussig and is still owned almost entirely by Taussigs. It had plants in New Orleans, Montreal, Boston, Wilmington, N. C., and a brand-new sugar refinery in Brooklyn. Its subsidiary Sucrest Corp. refined and sold sugar. Its subsidiary Nulomoline Co. sold cane syrup preparations to bakers. Its most famous product was 'Grandma's Old Fashioned Molasses,' which in winter was sledded in huge casks into Maine's lumber camps.

Louis Taussig (1837–1890) founded The Taussig Co. in San Francisco, which became one of the largest wholesale liquor establishments in the west, eventually expanding into Cincinnati, New York City, and Kentucky.

Ralph J. Taussig (1922–2007), b. Elkins Park, PA, of Bohemian ancestry, was an investment banker who specialized in international finance. He worked from his home office since the late 1980s and commuted to New York for 30 years to work for investment companies. He also traveled abroad, advising governments on financial matters. He spoke French, German, and Arabic.

Samuel Taussig (1854–1926), b. Hostouň, Kladno Dist., Bohemia, son of Lazarus Taussig and Eleanor Federer, was in notion business until 1887. He then came to America and engaged, with his brother William, in the leaf tobacco business in Chicago until 1893. Subsequently, he removed to Minneapolis, MN, and conducted the wholesale tobacco house alone (1894–1904). Since then, he resided in St Louis, as president of the St. Louis Leaf Tobacco Co. He was married to Flora Bondy (1861–1914) and they had 4 children: Irma, Blanche, Frances, and Lester.

William Taussig (1847–1922), b. Hostouň, Kladno Dist., Bohemia, son of Lazar Taussig and Henrietta Juditha Flusser, was a tobacco dealer in Chicago. He was liked and generally known as 'Uncle Billy.' He was head of the leaf tobacco house Taussig & Co., Chicago. At one time he was a partner in the firm William Tausig, Emil Wedeles, Importers, Growers, and Packers of Leaf Tobacco, established in 1868. Extensive growers of Florida Havana and Sumatra Tobacco with Plantations in Gadsden Co., FL, and Warehouses in Quincy, FL. He was married to Julia Stein and they had 2 sons: Henry G. and Leo L., and 3 daughters.

Václav Triner (1873–1939), b. Pilsen, Bohemia, was a scale manufacturer. At the age of seven, he came to America with his parents. He studied mechanical engineering in Chicago. He began as a tool and die maker with the E. F. Angel Co., where he rose to the position of a manager. With two partners, they bought out the American Roller Scale Co. and started the manufacturing of scales. In 1904, he organized a scale business of his own known as Triner Scale and Mfg. Co., of which he had been president. In 1912, the US government selected the company out of 22 firms and gave it an order for thousands of scales for the US post offices. In 1915, he devised an automatic scale automatically showing amount of parcel postage, which was immediately installed in all the larger US post offices. His office was on West 21st Street, Chicago.

James 'Jim' R. Trueman (1935-1986), b. Cleveland, OH, of Slovak descent, was the founder of the Red Roof Motel chain as well as one of the nation's leading race car drivers, owners, and sponsors. He was a 1953 graduate of Benedictine High School, where he became an outstanding runner in cross country and track. His engineering studies at Ohio State University were interrupted by service in the U.S. Army. He entered the construction business in Columbus. He also began driving race cars, winning 125 victories including 2 Sports Car of America championships. Traveling the race car circuit demonstrated to Trueman the need for inexpensive lodgings, and he opened his first Red Roof Inn near Columbus in 1973. The chain grew to more than 100 units within a decade, and Trueman began to sponsor his own race cars and promising young drivers. He purchased the Mid-Ohio Sports Car Course in Lexington, OH, and formed the TrueSports Indy Car team with driver Bobby Rahal. It won the first Budweiser Cleveland 500 in 1982 and the Indianapolis 500 in 1986, only 11 days before Trueman's death from cancer in Columbus.

Donald (John) Trump, Jr. (1977-), b. Manhattan, NYC, son of Ivana Zelníčková (1949-) from Zlín, Moravia, and mogul Donald John Trump, is an American businessman. He currently works along with his sister Ivanka Trump and brother Eric Trump in the position of Executive Vice President at The Trump Organization.

Eric (Frederick) Trump (1984-), b. Manhattan, NY C, is of son of Ivana Zelníčková (1949-) from Zlín, Moravia, and mogul Donald John Trump, was a businessman. He is the executive vice president, development and acquisitions, of The Trump Organization, and directs all new project acquisitions and development throughout the world, with his brother, Donald, Jr., and sister, Ivanka. In 2006, he founded the Eric Trump Foundation, which raises money for St. Jude Children's Research Hospital. He is also the owner of Trump Winery.

Ivanka Marie Trump (1981-), b. Washington, DC, daughter of Ivana Zelníčková (1949) from Zlín, Moravia, and mogul Donald John Trump, is a businesswoman and fashion model. She is currently Vice President of Real Estate Development and Acquisitions at the Trump Organization. Before working for her father, Ivanka worked for Forest City Enterprises. Trump joined forces with Dynamic Diamond Corp., a Diamond Trading Company Sightholder, to design and introduce a line of jewelry slated to be unveiled in September

2007 at the opening of the brand's first flagship retail store on Madison Avenue which is called 'Ivanka Trump'.

Sharon K. Valášek (1957–), a native of Ord, NE, of Czech ancestry, graduated from Univ. of Nebraska-Kearney, majoring in business administration (B.A., 1979) and from Avilla College (M.B.A., 1992). Sharon is presently a business continuity consultant and project manager with Hewlett Packard (HP). Her work helps business clients protect their information technology infrastructure and improve productivity and results. In 2003, Sharon was appointed Honorary Consul of the Czech Republic, serving Kansas, Missouri, and Nebraska. As consul, she works to further economic, political, educational, and cultural interests on behalf of the Czech Republic. She is a past president of the Greater Kansas City chapter of People-to-People International (GKCPTP), a past Board member of the International Czech Republic Flag Image Relations Council of Kansas City, and a current Board member of the International Trade Council of Kansas City and the Greater Kansas City Czech & Slovak Club. She is married to Gary Lofstrom (1957–).

John Vanhara (1972–), b. Brno, Czech, is an American-Czech businessman, writer, and blogger. He was born in Czechoslovakia as "Jan Vaňhara", but in 2002 he moved to the United States, where he studied business administration at the California Coast University. His business activities started in Las Vegas, Nevada, where he founded several companies including EastBiz.com, IncParadise, etc. In 2007, he founded the transport company Shipito, which was sold to Tritium Partners in 2015.

Karel Adolf Velan (1918–2017), b. Ostrava, Czech., was trained as a mechanical engineer at Brno Inst. of Technology. He is president of Karel Velan Engineering Companies, Montreal, Canada, one of the world's leading manufacturers of industrial steel valves with eleven specialized manufacturing plants, including four in Canada, two in the U.S., and one each in France, the U.K., Portugal, Korea and Taiwan. They employ some 1,150 employees in North America and 250 overseas. They owe much of their success to quality and innovation, which have been the cornerstone of Velan since its inception in 1950. Velan is the largest manufacturer of steel gate, globe and check valves in North America and the second largest in the world. Their worldwide sales total amounted to $350,000,000.

Ludwig Vogelstein (1871–1934), b. Pilsen, Bohemia, was the founder of the metal firm Ludwig Vogelstein & Co. which was amalgamated in the Am. Metal Co., Ltd. in 1920, becoming its vice pres. and in 1924 chairman of the Board. He was also instrumental in establishing and expanding US Metal Refining Co., copper refinery in Ontario, Canada, the International Nickel Co. and Climax Molybdenum Co., American Zinc and Chemical Co., and Copper Exporters Inc.

Henry Waldes (1876–1941), a native of Prague, was an industrialist, known worldwide by the snap fasteners manufactured in his factories in Prague, Dresden, Long Island and Switzerland. Waldes employed thousands of workers; his factory in Long Island alone had more than fifteen hundred. The New York Company, which first opened its sales office in New York in 1911, was incorporated in New York in 1925 under the name Waldes Kohinoor. The Long Island Company was started in 1919 under the name Waldes & Co. Henry Waldes was senior partner in the New York Company and practically commuted between Prague and New York City during the 1920s. He lived through the Nazi invasion of Prague but eventually succeeded in 1941 to come to US.

Charles Alfred Wyman (orig. Weinmann) (1914–1971), b. Ústí n/L, Bohemia, was trained as a lawyer at Charles Univ. He emigrated to Canada in 1940 and to the US in 1941. In 1944, he became assistant to the president of the Universal Plastic Corp., New Brunswick, NJ, a post he held until 1945 when he was elected president. He left Universal the following year to become executive vice-president of the H. O. Canfield Co., Bridgeport, CT, a manufacturer of mechanical rubber goods, which his father headed. After three years in this capacity, he was appointed to the additional post of vice-president of the Pantasote Co., with headquarters in NYC, which his father also headed. Pantasote Co. manufactured polymers which it converted into semifinished and finished articles such as compounds, films, and packaging material known as Panta-Pak. Upon his father's death in 1960, Wyman was elected chairman of the Boards of both companies, and he continued in those capacities until he died.

C. Religion

1. Catholic Clergy

Rudolph G. Bandas (1896–1969), b. Silver Lake, MN of Czech ancestry, was a Catholic theologian educated at Louvain and Angelico Univ., Rome. He served as prof. of dogmatic theology and catechetics at St. Paul Sem. (s. 1925), prof. of scripture and ethics at St. Catherine's College, St. Paul (s. 1925) and prof. of scripture at the Diocesan Teachers College, St. Paul (1925–32).

George Joseph Biskup (1911–1979), b. Cedar Rapids, IA, of Czech ancestry, was Catholic Bishop of Des Moines, Iowa (1965–1967) and later Archbishop of Indianapolis (1970–1979).

Daniel Černý (1983–), b. Košice, Czech., is R.C. priest and theologian. He received his Ph.D. in 2014 from the Pontifical Oriental Institute in Rome, with a thesis on The History of the Slovak Greek Catholics in Canada before the creation of their own Eparchy. He continues writing in his spare time, focusing on Slovaks and their diaspora, especially those of the

Byzantine rite. His articles have been published by the Slovak Academy of Sciences (Jan Stanislav Institute of Slavistics), and can be found in numerous other publications and on web pages, both home and abroad – most recently in the 2017 *Slovakia*, published annually by the Slovak League in America.

Edward A. Cerny (1890-1915), b. Dubuque, IA, of Bohemian ancestry, R.C. priest, served as a professor of Scripture at St. Mary's Sem.

Michael J. Chaback (1944-), b. Fountain Hill, PA, of Slovak descent, is a R.C. priest, S.T.D., Msgr., and theologian. He grew up in the Bethlehem parish that he then headed as pastor for 16 years. He led SS. Cyril and Methodius in Bethlehem until 2008, when he became director of the diocese's Office of the Permanent Diaconate. That's the office that prepares men to be permanent deacons, people who aren't priests but who assist with Mass and other parish duties. He was professor of theology, St. Charles Borromeo Seminary, Philadelphia (1973-92).

Ján Dolný (1981-), b. Bratislava, Czech., is a R.C. priest, theologian, and monk. He received his formation for the priesthood at St. Charles Borromeo Seminary in Košice (2000-2003) and at the Theological College of the Catholic University of America in Washington, DC (2004-08). Ján was ordained to the priesthood in Košice on June 21, 2008. In 2014, he became a postulant of the Benedictine religious order at the Transfiguration Monastery in Sampor, Slovakia.

Baldwin Dworschak (1906-1996), b. Arcadia, WI, of Bohemian ancestry, professed in Benedictine Order and was ordained to priesthood in 1933. Before and after his ordination, Father Baldwin taught English, religion and metal craft classes at Saint John's. He was a student dormitory prefect for ten years, acted as the faculty advisor of the university's student newspaper and yearbook, served as Dean of Men for a year, and was the superior of monastic priesthood students for three years. In January 1947, he was appointed the new Prior of the St. John's Abbey, Collegeville, MN (1947-51) and in 1950, Father Baldwin was elected the abbey's sixth Abbot. Soon after, he was also named president of St. John's Univ., Collegeville, WI (1951-57), and chancellor (s. 1958).

Leo Ferdinand Dworschak (1900-1976), b. Independence, WI, of Bohemian ancestry, was a Catholic Bishop of Fargo, ND (1960-70).

Petr Esterka (1935-), b. Dolní Bojanovice near Hodonín, Czech., immigrated to Austria in 1957. He began studies at Nepomucenum House in Rome, which led to his ordainment into priesthood in 1963. He was sent to minister to his fellow expatriates in Texas, USA. He returned to Rome in 1966 to undertake doctoral studies. He continued to visit the northern part of the USA, Minnesota, where he took up an academic post in 1967, as prof. of theology, College St. Catherine, St. Paul, MN. In 1974-1995, he served as a military chaplain in reserve in the US Air Force. In 1978, he began working with Czech Catholics in the USA and Canada. He was reunited with his parents and his sister for the first time in Vienna in 1968. In 1987, he received the title of Monsignor, and in July 1999, he was appointed Titular Bishop of Cefala, and Auxiliary Bishop of Brno charged with pastoral care for Czech Catholics abroad. He moved to California in 1992. In 2003, he was made a Bishop Emeritus. He is a specialist on moral theology, ecumenism, Christian marriage.

Edwin Francis Falteisek (1925-1998), b. River Falls, WI, of Bohemian ancestry, S.J., studied theology at Pontif. Gregor Univ. He held the position of prof. of religious studies at Trinity Coll., VT (s. 1980).

Francis Lad Filas (1915-1985), b. Cicero, IL, of Czech ancestry, was a Catholic theologian, who was associated with the Loyola University of Chicago for more than 35 years. He served as a longtime professor of theology, for several years Filas leading studies about the Shroud of Turin, traditionally venerated as the burial cloth of Jesus Christ.

Bernard J. Ganter (1928-1993), b. Galveston, TX, of Czech mother, was the first Catholic Bishop of Tulsa (1973-1977) and then Bishop of Beaumont, TX (1977-1993). He was educated at St. Mary's Sem. and Catholic Univ. of Am.

Rev. Joseph John Gavenda (1902-1980), b. Jessup, PA, of Slovak parents, was a R.C. priest, and theologian, educated at St. Bernard's Sem., St. Vincent's Seminary, Catholic University of America (J.C.L., 1926). Coll. Theol. Studiorum Univ. Rome (S.T.D., 1927), Pontifical Sem., Rome (J.C.D., 1927). He was professor of Latin and psychology, St. Thomas Coll. and Marywood Coll., Scranton, PA, Vice Chancellor, Diocese of Scranton (1928). He was a pastor of St. Joseph's Church. He resided in Hazelton, PA (s. 1934).

Roger Gries (1937-), b. Cleveland, OH, of Czech mother, OSB, attended Loyola University Chicago. He entered the Benedictine Order of Cleveland at Saint Andrew's Abbey and was ordained a priest on May 18, 1963. He became prior of the abbey and was elected the fifth Abbot of the abbey in 1981, a position he held for over 20 years. He was named Auxiliary Bishop of Cleveland by Pope John Paul II on March 25, 2001 and was consecrated with Bishop Martin Amos on June 7, 2001.

Jerome (orig. George) Hanus (1940-), b. Brainard, NE, of Czech ancestry, made his profession as a Benedictine monk in 1961, taking the name Jerome. He studied at Conception Seminary College, where he earned a Bachelor of Arts degree in 1963. He continued his studies at the Pontifical University of St. Anselm in Rome, receiving a Licentiate of Sacred Theology in

1967. He was ordained to the priesthood on July 30, 1966. He taught scholastic theology at Conception Seminary College from 1967 to 1969. He studied moral theology at Princeton University, and there earned a Master of Arts degree in 1972. He then returned to Conception Seminary, where he served as professor of religion from 1973 to 1976. From 1974 to 1976, he was an adjunct professor of moral theology at the Pontifical University of St. Anselm in Rome. Hanus was elected the sixth Abbot of Conception Abbey in January 1977. In addition to his role as Abbot at Conception Abbey, he served as Abbot President of the Swiss-American Congregation, to which the Abbey belonged from 1984 to 1987. In July 1987, Abbot Jerome was appointed the eighth Bishop of Saint Cloud by Pope John Paul II. In August 1994, Pope John Paul II appointed Bishop Hanus as the Coadjutor Archbishop of Dubuque. After one year, Archbishop Kucera decided to retire. When Kucera's request was approved by the Holy See in October 1995, Hanus automatically succeeded him as 11th Bishop and 9th Archbishop of Dubuque.

John Hardon (1914-2000), b. Midland, PA, of Slovak ancestry; Jesuit priest, theologian. He has taught at the Jesuit School of Theology at Loyola University in Chicago and the Institute for Advanced Studies in Catholic Doctrine at St. John's University in New York. A prolific writer, he authored over forty books. In addition, he was actively involved with a number of organizations, such as the Institute on Religious Life, Marian Catechists, Eternal Life and Inter Mirifica, which publishes his catechetical courses.

Edward Joseph Hodous (1898-1984), b. Cleveland, OH, of Czech ancestry, member of S. J., was a Pontifical Bibl. Inst. (Rome) educated theologian. He held the position of prof. of theology and dept. head at John Carroll Univ. (1937-39), prof. of dogmatic theology at West Baden Coll., NC (1939-41) and prof. of Bible, Greek and sacred scripture (1941-55) and, s. 1956, prof. of theology at Univ. of Detroit.

Beda Horsák (1883-1934), b. Moravia, immigrated to West Texas at age four. He was educated at St. Joseph's Seminary, Gessen, LA. He made his vows as Benedictine and was ordained an R.C. priest. He did post graduate studies at Anselmianum, Rome and earned his Doctorate in Cannon law. From 1924-28, he taught at St. Joseph's Seminary, St. Benedict, LA and from 1930-34, at Conception Abbey in MO.

David Matthew Hynous (1932-2016), b. Chicago, IL, of Czech ancestry, joined the Dominican Order (1953) and was ordained R.C. priest (1959). He was a graduate of Loras College, Dubuque, IA. His first assignment was teaching Theology and Philosophy at Dominican College in Racine, WI from 1960-66. From 1966-69, he studied in Rome at the University of St. Thomas, the Angelicum, and earned a Doctorate degree in Canon Law. For the next ten years he taught Canon Law at Aquinas Institute of Theology in Dubuque. From 1979-81, he served as Secretary for the Apostolic Nunciature in Washington, D.C. In 1981, Fr. Hynous was appointed Vicar Provincial for the Dominicans and served for four years. From 1986-95, he served the Archdiocese of Chicago on the Marriage Tribunal and as Vice-Chancellor. In 1995, he was called to Rome as Procurator General for the Dominican Order. In 1997, he returned to the Marriage Tribunal in the Archdiocese of Chicago and for the last few years, has worked for the Tribunal in the Diocese of Joliet until his death.

Charles Nepomucene Jaeger (1844-1924), b. Kutná Hora, Bohemia, R.C. priest, helped to establish the Benedictine monastery in Chicago, becoming its Prior in 1888. In 1894, when the Holy See changed the status of St. Procopius from priory to an abbey, Jaeger became its 1st Abbot. His passing in 1924 was marked by all Chicago dailies which noted among other "the venerable Abbot of the monastery... the little brother of the poor, hero of Chicago labor riots of 1894, hero of the smallpox epidemic... is dead" or "Among the Bohemians of the Westside he was regarded as Saint. Here he fed the hungry and comforted the stricken."

Robert Norman Janacek (1930-), b. Augusta, GA, probably of Czech ancestry, is a clergyman educated at Nazarene Theological Seminary, Winona Lake School of Theology and Princeton Theological Seminary. He was ordained in ministry, Church of Nazarene, and served as pastor, of churches Siloam, KY (1957-58), Timblin, a borough in Jefferson Co., PA (1958-60), and Chadron, NE (1960-61). Subsequently, he was ordained in ministry of the United Methodist Church and served as pastor of churches Arapahoe, NE (1961-65), Reedville, PA (1965-67), Waverly, NE (1967-71), and Edison Good Samaritan Church (1971-73). He became academic dean and director of counseling service, at Transylvania Bible School, Freeport, PA (s. 1971) and then professor of systematic theology, Geneva, at St. Albans Theological College, Knoxville, TN (s. 1973).

Frederick Xavier Katzer (1844-1903), b. Ebensee, of Moravian father, was a Catholic Bishop of Green Bay (1886-91) and Archbishop of Milwaukee in Wisconsin (1891-1903).

Valentine Kohlbeck (1864-1937), b. Bedřichovice, Bohemia, was educated at St. Vincent's Coll. and Sem. He entered Benedictine Order and was ordained R.C. priest. He became pastor, St. Vitus Church, Chicago (1888-93), St. Procopius Church (1892); managing editor of the Bohemian daily *Národ* (Nation), Chicago and the semi-weekly *Katolik* (1896-1919). He was then elected the 2nd Abbot of St. Procopius Abbey, Lisle, IL (s. 1919) and pres., St. Procopius Coll. (s. 1919).

Joseph Andrew Komonchak (1939-), b. Nyack, NY, of Slovak descent, is a R.C. priest, theologian, and church historian. He attended Cathedral College in Brooklyn, and in 1960, received a Bachelor of Arts degree from Saint Joseph's Seminary in Dunwoodie, Yonkers.

He studied at the North American College in Rome, earning a Licentiate of Sacred Theology from the Pontifical Gregorian University in Rome. He received a Doctorate from Union Theological Seminary in New York. Ordained in 1963, he did parish work along with college and seminary teaching, before joining the faculty at Catholic University of America in 1977. Komonchak is a leading interpreter of the Second Vatican Council, co-editor of the English version of the five-volume history of the Council, and the chief editor of *The New Dictionary of Theology*. In June 2015 he received from the Catholic Theological Society of America the John Courtney Murray Award, the highest honor it bestows. He served as a consultant to three committees of the National Conference of Catholic Bishops and published more than 150 articles.

Joseph Maria Koudelka (1852-1921), b. Chlístov, Bohemia, at age 13, immigrated with his parents to US and settled in Manitowoc, WI. He studied theology at St. Francis Sem., Milwaukee and was ordained R.C. priest in 1875. He did pastoral work at St. Procopius Church in Cleveland, OH until 1882; served as editor of Czech Catholic paper *Hlas*, in St. Louis, then returned to Cleveland as pastor of St. Michael's (1883-1907), where he built the parish church and school. In 1907, was appointed an auxiliary bishop in Cleveland to care for the foreign populace, especially the Slavic people; and in 1908, was consecrated Bishop of Germanicopolis. He was the first aux. bishop of special jurisdiction appointed in the US, serving in Cleveland until 1911. Subsequently, he was transferred to Milwaukee as an aux. Bishop and in 1913, was appointed second Bishop of the diocese of Superior. During his 8-year administration, 10 parish churches, 22 missions, 3 hospitals, 8 schools and 1 orphanage were built. He was also literary active, having written readers for Czech schools, a history of the Catholic Church and compiled prayer books. He spoke Czech, German, Polish as well as English and had a command of the Classical languages.

Daniel W. Kucera (1923-2017), b. Chicago, IL, of Czech ancestry, in 1977, was named, by Pope Paul VI, Titular Bishop of Natchesium and Auxiliary Bishop of Joliet. In 1980, Pope John Paul II appointed Kucera as the 8th Bishop of Salina, KS and in 1983, the same Pope appointed Kucera as the 10th Bishop and 8th Archbishop of Dubuque.

Louis Benedict Kucera (1888-1957), b. Rice Co., MN, of Czech ancestry, was a Catholic Bishop of Lincoln, NE from 1930 until his death in 1957.

Emmanuel Boleslaus Ledvina (1868-1952), b. Evansville, IN, of Czech father, was a Catholic Bishop of Corpus Christi from 1921 to 1949.

Radoslav Lojan (1976-), b. Kamenice nad Cirochou, Slovakia, is a R.C. priest and Catholic theologian, with bioethics orientation. In 2002, Lojan graduated from the Comenius University in Bratislava, Theological Institute in Košice. In 2012, he completed his

Doctoral studies at Saint Paul University in Ottawa and University of Ottawa, Canada. Since 2013, Radoslav Lojan is associate professor and a faculty moderator at the Catholic University in Ružomberok, Theological Faculty in Košice. His research interests focus on moral theology, palliative care and bioethics. Radoslav Lojan has experience with the project activities. He is a member of the Council for Research in Values and Philosophy (RVP), Washington DC and also, he was a member of the research team in KEGA 022K-4/2013, which ended in 2015.

Eugene H. Maly (1920–1980), b. Cincinnati, OH, likely of Czech ancestry, is a Catholic theologian, educated at Angelicum Univ. and Pontifical Inst., Rome. He has been associated with the Mt. St. Mary's Sem., Athenaeum of Ohio as a professor (s. 1958), and Dean and Vice Rector (s. 1971). He is the author *The World of David and Solomon* (1966), *The Prophets of Salvation* (1967) and *Sin: Biblical Perspectives* (1973).

Vaclav Michalicka (1894–1982), b. Union City, of Czech ancestry, served as a prof. of dogma at St. Procopius Coll., Lisle, IL.

Alois J. Morkovsky (1899–1990), b. Old Sweet Home, TX, of Czech parents, was educated at St. John's Seminary, San Antonio and St. Meinrad Seminary, IN. He was ordained R.C. priest (1924). He became prof. at St. John's Seminary, San Antonio, serving from 1924 to 1942. Simultaneously he was a pastor of the Sacred Heart Church Hallettsville, TX (s. 1941), dean (s. 1946); and later pastor of the Holy Rosary Church, Hostyn, TX (1967–74).

John Louis Morkovsky (1909–1990), b. Moulton, TX, of Czech ancestry, was a Catholic Bishop of Amarillo (1958–1963) and Bishop of Galveston-Houston (1975–1984).

John Nepomucene Neumann (1811–1869), b. Prachatice, Bohemia, was a Catholic Bishop of Philadelphia (1852–60). He was the first American male Saint.

Procopius Charles Neužil (1861–1946), Bechyně, Bohemia, professed in Order of St. Benedict and was ordained R.C. priest. He became the first principal of St. Procopius HS (1887–94); prior, St. Procopius Abbey, Lisle (1899–1919, 1927–37); rector, St. Procopius Sem., Lisle (1917–19, 1920–24); instructor, St. Procopius Coll. and Sem. (1887–90, 1917–24); and administrator, St. Procopius Abby (1917–19). In 1937, he was elected the 3rd Abbot of the St. Procopius Abbey in Lisle, IL. He was the head of the post War Mission to Czechoslovakia in 1920.

Alfred Novak (1930–2014), b. Dwight, NE, of Czech ancestry, was ordained as R.C. priest in 1956. Novak served as a missionary in Brazil until April 19, 1979 when Pope John Paul II named him Titular Bishop of Vardimissa and Auxiliary Bishop of São Paulo. He served the archdiocese for ten years. On March 15, 1989, John Paul II named Novak as the second Bishop of Paranaguá. He served the diocese as its Bishop for 17 years before Pope Benedict XVI accepted his resignation in August 2006, and he became Bishop Emeritus.

Vincent Michael Novak (1924–2012), b. Jersey City, NJ, of Czech ancestry, entered the Society of Jesus at St. Andrew-on-Hudson, Poughkeepsie, N.Y., in September 1942. Following his novitiate and first vows, he studied both philosophy and theology at Woodstock College, Woodstock, Md., receiving the Licentiate of Sacred Theology in 1956. In his regency, he taught Latin and English at Canisius H.S., Buffalo, N.Y., 1949-52. He was ordained in June 1955 at the Fordham University Church, the Bronx. He received the S.T.D. Diplôme de Lumen Vitae, Brussels, and was a post-doctoral scholar at UCLA, 1971-72. He served almost all of his priestly life at Fordham University's Bronx campus. He taught Latin, English and religion at Fordham Prep, 1958-65. With his interest in religious education, he became editor-in-chief of the *Lord and King High School Religion* textbook series, and authored two student texts: *Jesus Christ, Lord of History*, and *Jesus Christ, Our Life and Worship*. To meet the demand for religious education training for high school religion teachers, he, along with his brother, Father Joseph Novak, S.J., and John Nelson, established a Graduate Institute of Religious Education in 1964. Father Novak served for 40 years as founder, administrator and teacher of what eventually became the Graduate School of Religion and Religious Education (GSRRE).

John Maria Oesterreicher (1904–1993), b. Libava, Moravia, was Roman Catholic theologian and a leading advocate of Jewish-Catholic reconciliation. He was one of the architects of Nostra Aetate or 'In Our Age,' which was issued by the Second Vatican Council in 1965 and which repudiated anti-Semitism. Oesterreicher was born a Jew who converted to Catholicism and became a Roman Catholic priest in 1927.

Ambrose Leo Ondrak (1892–1961), b. Chicago, IL, of Czech ancestry, was educated at St. Procopius Coll. and Univ. of Illinois. He professed in Benedictine order and was ordained R.C. priest. He taught mathematics and physics at St. Procopius Acad. (1918-21) and St. Procopius Coll. (1921-24). He then became a curate at St. Michael's Church, Chicago (1924 46) and in 1947 was blessed as Abbot of St. Procopius Abbey.

Christian Robert Oravec (1937–2014), b. Johnstown, PA, was a R.C. priest and educator. After high school graduation, he entered the Third Order Regular in September 1955 in Loretto. He entered novitiate at Portiuncula Friary, Washington, D.C. in June 1956, and made his first profession of vows on July 1, 1957. Fr. Christian was ordained to the priesthood by the late Bishop J. Carroll McCormick, D.D. of the Diocese of Altoona-Johnstown, at the Cathedral of the Blessed Sacrament, Altoona, in May 1964. Fr. Christian received his Bachelor of Arts degree in Philosophy from St. Francis University, Loretto, 1960; Theological studies, St Francis Seminary, Loretto, 1964; graduate studies, the Catholic University of America, Washington, D.C. He did graduate studies at the University of Paris, France. He received a Baccalaureate, Universite de Louvain, Belgium, 1965; Licentiate Universite de Louvain, Belgium, 1967; Doctorate, Universite de Louvain, Belgium, with the doctoral dissertation *The Ecclesiology of Dietrich Bonhoeffer: Exposition, Evolution, Analysis*, 1969. For over half a century, Fr. Christian was a faithful son of St. Francis, a renowned educator and a respected business and civic leader. He was professor of Dogmatic and Systematic Theology, St. Francis Seminary, Loretto (1969–76); Director of Postulants of the Third Order Regular (1970–76); Executive Vice-President, St. Francis University (1976–77); President of St. Francis University (1977–2004). He was elected to the Provincial Council four times and served sixteen years. He was Minister Provincial for two terms and served eight years.

Franz Joseph Pabisch (1825–1879), Slavonice, Moravia, was a Roman Catholic priest. In 1851, he was ordained priest and became chaplain in Brno, then ceremonial of Prince Archbishop Milde in Vienna. He prepared for a mission and research trip in West Africa through various studies but emigrated to America in 1851 and became a pastor in several German congregations in the area of Cincinnati and later a teacher of church history and modern languages in Cincinnati. From 1856, he studied in Rome (Dr. theol. and Dr. jur.). In 1861, and then became professor in Cincinnati and, in 1862, Rector of Mount St. Mary Seminary of the West, to whom he devoted all his strength. In 1866, he worked as a notary in the Consulate in Baltimore. During his Roman stay, Pabisch was in the district of German painters such as Cornelius, Overbeck and others, was himself a gifted painter in the Nazarene style and created several altarpieces. Rev. Pabisch who spoke about 18 languages, made great contributions through the translation of church history of Alzog into English.

Joseph Papin (1914–1989), b. Parchoviany, Slovakia; professor of religious studies, Villanova University, Villanova, PA (s. 1963), founder and director of the Villanova Theology Institute (s. 1967).

Thomas M. Pucelik (1932–2005), b. Plattsmouth. NE, of Czech ancestry, R.C. priest and theologian, studied at St. Paul Seminary, MN (B.A., 1954), at Pontifical Univ. of St. Thomas, Rome (S.T.L., 1961; S.T.D., 1962). He has been associated with Bradley Univ., Peoria, IL, as asst. professor (1967–68), as assoc. professor of religious studies (s. 1968), as chairman of the dept. (s. 1989), later professor emeritus. He was the author of *Christian Perfection according to John Wesley: a Summary and Evaluation of this Doctrine as Taught by the Founder of Methodism* (1963).

Valentine Skluzacek (1915-2000), b. nr. New Prague, MN, of Czech ancestry, was educated at Catholic University of America. He professed in St. Benedict Order and was ordained R.C. priest. He became Dean of Students, St. Procopius Coll. (1956-63); pastor, St. Joan of Arc, Lisle (1971). He was elected the seventh Abbot of St. Procopius Abbey (1978), who presided over the Abbey's centenary celebrations from 1984 to 1985. He was also a teacher of political science, St. Procopius Coll. (for 20 years); and chancellor, Illinois Benedictine Coll. and Bennet Acad.

Richard Stika (1957-), b. St. Louis, MO, of Czech ancestry on his father's side, is an American Prelate of the Roman Catholic Church. He is the third and current Bishop of Knoxville.

Joseph Supa (1937-), b. Mutenice, Czech., is a theologian, educated at Pontif Lateran Univ. He was with Pontif. Coll. Josephinum (s. 1970). He is a specialist on systematic theology.

Arnold John Tkacik (1919-2003), b. Parchovany, Czech., O.S.B., was a theologian and Biblical scholar. He was a member of Benedictine Monastery. He was associate professor, Kansas School of Religion, University of Kansas (1967-71); associate professor of Biblical literature, Illinois Benedictine College, Chicago, IL (1954-72, 1972-73).

Edward Vacek (1942-), b. Omaha, NE, of Czech ancestry, is a Jesuit Catholic priest. He studied philosophy and Classics (A.B., 1965) and philosophy and letters (A.M., 1967) at Saint Louis Univ.; theology at Weston College School of Theology, Boston College (M.Div., 1973); and philosophy at Northwestern Univ. (Ph.D., 1978). He also holds a License in Sacred Theology from Loyola University of Chicago (S.T.L., 1981). He was associated with Jesuit School of Theology, Chicago (1978-81), prior to joining Weston Jesuit School of Theology, as professor of Christian ethics (1981-2008), which became in 2008 the Boston College School of Theology and Ministry, where he held the position of professor of moral theology (2008-12). Afterwards he was named to Stephen Duffy Chair in Systematic Theology, Loyola Univ., New Orleans (s. 2012). He also held McKeever Chair of Moral Theology at St. John's University, New York (1995-96). He teaches moral theology, with special interests in emotions and ethical theory, as well as sexual, business, and biomedical ethics. His research interests are in foundations of Christian ethics; phenomenology of emotions in Christian life and sexual ethics. He is the author of the book entitled *Love, Human and Divine*. He has given numerous talks to popular and professional audiences.

Joseph A. Valenta (1886-1973), b. Svebohov, Moravia, immigrated to TX in 1892. He studied theology at St. Mary's Sem. La Porte, TX and was ordained R. C. priest in 1911. He became pastor, Immaculate Conception Church, Sealy, TX (1912); professor, St. Mary's

Sem., procurator, vice rector and spiritual director (1912-47); pastor, Holy Cross Church, East Bernard, TX (1951-66).

Robert Francis Vasa (1953-), b. Lincoln, NE, of Czech ancestry, was named the 5th Bishop of Baker, OR, by Pope John Paul II. In 2001, he became Bishop of the Roman Catholic Diocese of Santa Rosa in California.

Leslie J. Vasek (1923-1967), b. Houston, TX, of Czech ancestry, R.C. priest and member of the order C.S.B., served his Order at the Univ. of St. Thomas, Houston, TX, as treasurer and professor in 1951, as bursar from 1952-56 and as treasurer.

John George Vlazny (1937-), b. Chicago, IL, of Czech ancestry, was an Auxiliary Bishop of Chicago (1983-1987), Bishop of Winona (1987-1997) and Archbishop of Portland, OR, serving since 1997.

Raymond James Vonesh (1916-1991), b. Chicago, IL, of Czech ancestry, was Auxiliary Bishop of Joliet, IL and Titular Bishop of Vanariona, retiring in 1991.

John George Vrana (1941-2022), b. Cleveland, OH, of Czech ancestry, was ordained as a priest for the Diocese of Cleveland in 1967. He studied theology at Catholic Univ. of America (S.T.B., 1967), at St. Paul University in Ottawa, Canada (S.T.L., 1970) and at the Katholike Universitet Leuven in Belgium where he earned the degree, Doctor of Sacred Theology (S.T.D., 1976). He was assigned to teach at Saint Mary Seminary in Cleveland, where he advanced from asst. professor to professor of moral theology and spiritual director (1970-1989). He has served as a director for retreats at JRH and elsewhere and continues to serve as a spiritual director for priests, women religious and laity. He has also served in a number of pastoral assignments including pastor of St. Martin of Tours Parish in Maple Heights (1992-99). He served on staff at St. Jude Parish in Elyria, Ohio, as senior parochial vicar (s. 2010).

Emil Aloysius Wcela (1931-2022), b. Bohemia, NY, graduated from Sr. Francis College, Brooklyn, NY (B.A., 1952) was ordained a priest for the Roman Catholic Diocese of Brooklyn in 1956. He then studied classical languages and literatures at Fordham Univ. (M.A., 1963) and continued his studies at Catholic Univ. (STL, 1962; M.S., Semitic Stud., 1963). He also studied at Pontifical Biblical Inst. in Rome (SSL, 1965). In October 1988, Wcela was named titular bishop of 'Filaca' and auxiliary Bishop of the Roman Catholic Diocese of Rockville Centre, NY and was consecrated on December 13, 1988. He retired in 2007.

Cassian Yuhaus (1922-2013), b. Hazleton, PA, of Slovak descent, is R.C. priest, CP (member of the Passionists). He professed his vows as a Passionist religious in August 1944 and was ordained a Passionist priest in February 1951. He was awarded a Doctorate in church history and the Papal Gold Medal for excellence from Gregorian University in Rome in 1962. He engaged in additional studies in Munich, Montreal, New York, Boston, and Paris. He was professor of church history at various Passionist Monasteries in the Eastern US from 1954 until 1968. A research scholar, a noted international lecturer and innovator in Catholic Church Renewal, Father Yuhaus served in leadership positions in Passionist Community, coordinated Program in the Religious Life Program for the Center for Applied Research in the Apostolate 'CARA' in Washington, DC from 1975 until 1980 and was president of CARA in Washington from 1980 until 1984. In the years after the Second Vatican Council, Father Yuhaus became an international recognized consultant for many religious communities of Brothers, Sisters and Priests. He was national director for the Institute for Religious from 1968 until 1980 and was co-founder and director of the Institute for World Concerns at Duquesne University in Pittsburgh from 1984 until 1989. An imagination scholar, Father Yuhaus wrote *Compelled to Speak*, a history of the Passionist Community in the US. He also championed the cause of the poor and victims of injustice, as a member of the Amnesty International, World Futures Society and Bread for the World and Pax Christi USA. Father Yuhaus served as rector of St. Ann's Monastery and Basilica from 1998 until 2002 and resided there until his death.

Francis Zeman (1918-d.), b. Viničné, Slovakia; theologian, archeologist; professor of Holy Scriptures and Oriental Languages, Major Seminary, Nicolet, P.Q., Canada (s. 1952); professor of Near East, Université du Québec à Trois-Riviéres (s. 1969)

Alois Žiškovský (1877–1967), b. Veselí n/L, Bohemia, served as a prof. of Holy Scripture at St. Paul Sem., St. Paul, MN.

George Joseph Žiškovský (1903–1984), b. Veseli, MN, of Czech ancestry, was R. C. theologian, trained in Rome at the Gregorian. He had S.T.D. and LS.S. degrees and was named Msgr. He held the position of prof. of Sacred Scripture, Hebrew and liturgy at St. Paul Theol. Sem., St. Paul, MN (1932–62).

Theodore Joseph Zúbek (1914–1988), b. Malacky, Slovakia; R.C. priest, O.F.M.; theologian, writer; church and literary historian, translator, publicist. He wrote a dissertation "Interventions by Joseph II into the life of Slovak Franciscans." Dean of Franciscans studying at the Faculty of Theology in Bratislava, taught in a Žilina monastery after WWII to 1950; put in a concentration camp after the communist closure of monasteries; escaped to Austria in 1951; to USA in 1952. He worked in parishes; professor of theology at Seton Hall University; editor of *Listy sv. Františeka*. From 1964–1970, he was the Superior of the Slovak

Franciscans in America. Published in Slovak and English in Slovak and American journals. His most important book: *The Church of Silence in Slovakia*, Whiting, IN: J. J. Lach, 1956.

Patrick Zurek (1948–), b. Sealy, TX, of Czech parents, has served as Catholic Bishop of Amarillo since 2008.

2. Protestant Clergy

Igor Vladimir Bella (1933–2015), b. Bridgeport, CT, of Slovak father, being the son of Rev. Julius Igor Bella, was a Lutheran minister. Igor grew up and attended schools in Bridgeport, Conn. He moved to Bratislava, Slovakia before moving to Geneva, Switzerland where he began his academic career while attending the Ecole Internationale and the University of Geneva. Igor went on to seminary at the Hamma Divinity School in Springfield, Ohio. After graduation, he moved to Strasbourg, France to work on his Ph.D. at the University of Strasbourg. He then moved to Toledo, Ohio where he was ordained as a Lutheran minister. Igor received his Doctorate in the Science of Philosophy in 1966 from the University of Strasbourg. He served several parishes throughout Ohio including Clinton, Martins Ferry, and Deshler.

Julius Igor Constantine Bella (1901–d.), b. Slovakia, was a Lutheran minister. He had a Ph.D. degree. He was a professor of religion at Wittenberg University, Springfield, Ohio. He was the pastor of the Slovak Evangelical Lutheran Holy Trinity Church, Bridgeport, Fairfield Co, CT. He also served the Holy Trinity Slovak Lutheran Church in Torrington, Litchfield Co., CT. He was the father of Rev. Igor Vladimir Bella.

Bernard Jean Bettelheim (1811–1870), b. Bratislava, Slovakia, although of Jewish ancestry, became Christian missionary to Okinawa, the first Protestant missionary to be active there. Bettelheim earned a degree in medicine from a school in Padua, Italy in 1836. He traveled much in these years, practicing medicine in a number of Italian cities, aboard an Egyptian naval vessel, and in a Turkish town called Magnesia, where, in 1840, he began studying Christianity. He converted to Christianity, and was baptized a short time later, in Smyrna. During his time in Turkey, he held theological debates with local rabbis and published pamphlets on the matter in French. He was the first Protestant missionary to Japan (1846–54). He translated portions of the Holy Bible into Ryukyuan, the common language of Okinawa, and Japanese. He also compiled a dictionary and grammar of the Ryukyuan language which is now preserved in the British Museum. During Commodore Perry's expedition to open up Japan to Western diplomacy and trade, Bettelheim served as his interpreter to the Okinawa Royal Court at Shuri. His missionary experience was the subject of a Doctoral dissertation written by Dr. Jack Teruya for the faculty of the University of Colorado in 1969. There are monuments to him on Okinawa and the Anglican-Episcopal

Diocese there recently named their headquarters "Bettelheim Hall" in honor of him. His mission was the theme of the 1996 Bible Campaign of the Japan Bible society. A brief account of his life has been published by Professor Konnyu in a book titled *Bettelheim Memorial Album*, but his story is largely unknown in the United States. He served as an Army physician during Civil War.

George Wesley Buchanan (1921–2019), b. Denison, IA, of Czech mother, a Methodist minister, has spent fourteen years as a pastor before teaching thirty-one years in a Theological Seminary in Washington, DC. He was Professor Emeritus of New Testament at the Wesley Theological Seminary. He worked extensively in the Near East, published many sermons, church school materials, poems, seventeen books, and more than sixty articles in academic journals. He was on the Editorial Advisory Board of the *Biblical Archaeology Review*.

Mája V. Čapek (née Oktávec) (1888–1966), b. Chomutov, Bohemia, came to the United States in 1907. She studied library science at Columbia University and in 1914 was put in charge of the Czechoslovak Department of the New York Public Library. There she met Norbert Čapek who was studying for a Ph.D. at City College. They were married in 1917 and moved to Belleville where Čapek became pastor of a small congregation. But in 1919, having come to the conclusion that he could no longer be a Baptist, he resigned his pastorate. At the end of World War I, the Austro-Hungarian Empire fell apart and Czechoslovakia became independent. The Čapeks, like other War refugees, were eager to return to their home country and play a part in its spiritual reawakening. By February 1922, the Čapeks, working as team, had organized the Prague Congregation of Liberal Religious Fellowship. Almost immediately, the services were drawing standing-room-only crowds. In 1926, Mája Čapek was also ordained as a Unitarian minister. On June 24, 1923, the first Flower Festival was celebrated. This ritual now celebrated annually by UU congregations the world over, originated in the Prague Congregation. In 1939, Mája Čapek left for the United States for what was supposed to be a brief lecture tour to raise funds for a joint Unitarian and Society of Friends program to assist endangered refugees and internees. She brought the Flower Festival Service with her and it was celebrated for the first time in the United States at the First Unitarian Church in Cambridge, Massachusetts, in the spring of 1940. Tragically, the Germans took Czechoslovakia, while Mája was still on tour, which prevented her from returning to Prague. She stayed in Massachusetts during the War working at the church in New Bedford. Her husband died in the Dachau concentration camp. Mája Čapek did not learn of Norbert's death until after the War. Leadership of the Prague church passed to the Čapeks' daughter and son-in-law, both ordained Unitarian ministers. Mája Čapek decided to work to help the victims of the War and joined the staff of the United Nations Relief and Rehabilitation Agency. She worked for a number of years as a Displaced Persons Specialist in Egypt and Palestine. Those who knew her described her as possessing tremendous drive and determination combined with a sensitive and loving heart–another fire flower blooming in the burned-out places of the world.

Katherine Cartwright (1961–), b. Marion, IN, of Slovak ancestry; a theologian., a Lutheran pastor. She grew up in Washington, DC, and currently lives in Yardley, PA. She studied journalism, with minor in literature and creative writing, at Indiana University (A.B., 1986) and then theology at the Lutheran Theological Seminary at Gettysburg, PA (M.Div., 1990). She was ordained in 1990 and has been a pastor serving congregations in the Evangelical Lutheran Church in America for 25 years. She specializes in transformational and transitional ministries, assisting congregations and congregational leadership in times of challenge and change working as both an interim pastor, and as a consultant and leadership coach. She is certified in transformational training design, spiritual direction, interim ministry, and coaching. She is a regular contributor to the *Bucks County Courier Times* 'From a Faith Perspective' column, poet, speaker, and workshop leader.

Eva M. Cesnakova (1942–), b. Marshall, TX, of Czech ancestry, graduated from Ohio City Univ. (B.A., 1967) and studied theology at Phillips Theol. Seminary (M.Div., 1997). She held the position of religious educator at the Unitarian Universalist Fellowship of Huntington, NY.

Marianka S. Fousek (1930–), b. Prague, Czech., is a theologian and a church historian. She studied history at Wellesley Coll. (B. A., 1952) and theology at Union Theol. Sem. (B.D., 1955) and church history at Harvard Univ. (Th.D., 1960.) She did postgraduate work at Heidelberg University. Dr. Fousek served as book-editor for *Fortress Press* (*Luther's Works*, American ed.), research editor for Concordia Publishing House and then as Assistant Professor of Church History at Duke University, Durham, NC. She was associated with Rosary Coll., River Forest, IL and Miami Univ., Oxford, where she held the position of Associate Professor. Her specialty was Bohemian reformation. She was the author of *The Eclipse of Lutheranism in the 17th Century Czechoslovakia* (1966), *The Church in a Changing World – Events and Trends from 250 to 600* (1971) and *The Church from Age to Age: From Galilee to Global Christianity* (2011).

Eugenia A. Gamble (1931–), b. Greenville, AL, of Bohemian ancestry on her mother's side (Steiner), graduated cum laude from the University of Alabama with a degree in creative writing. She received her M. Divinity at St. Luke's School of Theology, University of the South, Sewanee, TN and did postgraduate work at Louisville Presbyterian Theological Seminary. She was ordained in 1984. She has supervised seminarians and taught on the continuing education faculties of Louisville Presbyterian Seminary, Columbia Presbyterian Seminary, Pittsburgh Presbyterian Seminary, Iliff Seminary, Beeson Divinity

School, and Princeton Seminary. She is the pastor of Nipomo Community Presbyterian Church, Nipomo, CA, has served as senior pastor of the First Presbyterian Church in Birmingham, Alabama, and Englewood, Colorado, and Director of Spiritual Development at First Presbyterian Church in San Luis Obispo. Rev. Gamble is widely acclaimed as one of the finest speakers in church circles today, serving as keynote speaker at numerous conferences, schools and colleges, retreats, and seminars. Her in-depth Biblical analysis, combined with great wit and humor, keep audiences highly involved. She has spoken at churches and events in 40 states and six foreign countries. In addition, Rev. Gamble has authored books, Bible-study guides, and articles, including "Out of the Whirlwind," a continuing column appearing in *Horizons Magazine* for 17 years. She has also served on the continuing education faculties at Princeton Theological Seminary, Louisville Presbyterian Theological Seminary, Pittsburgh Seminary, and San Francisco Theological Seminary.

Paul Hinlicky (1952–), b. Portchester, NY, of Slovak descent, is a Lutheran minister. Ordained a Lutheran minister in 1978 in a predecessor body of the Evangelical Lutheran Church in America, he has been the pastor of the New River Parish, Blacksburg, Virginia, in partnership with his wife Ellen (2003–2008), and previously assistant to the pastor at St. Mark Lutheran Church, Roanoke, VA and interim pastor at Christ Lutheran Church, Roanoke, VA. He holds the B.A. from Concordia Senior College, Fort Wayne, IN; the M.Div. from Christ Seminary-Seminex, St. Louis, MO; the Ph.D. (1983) from Union Theological Seminary, New York, NY. While still a graduate student at Union, he served as assistant pastor in several New York City parishes, until he became Research Associate for the Department for Church in Society of the Division for Mission in North American of the Lutheran Church in America, a position he held for almost four years. In 1985, he became the pastor of Immanuel Lutheran Church, in Delhi, NY, a post he held until 1993. He was Visiting Professor of Systematic Theology at the Protestant Theological Faculty of Comenius University in Bratislava, Slovakia, from 1993-99, where he earned the title 'Docent' in 1999 on the basis of the successful defense of his habilitation work. He served as editor of *Lutheran Forum*, (1988-93). In 1991, Theophilus Press published his *Mission to the Catskills: A History of Immanuel Lutheran Church of Delhi, New York*. His other books include *The Substance of the Faith: Luther's Doctrinal Theology for Today,* and *Paths Not Taken: Fates of Theology from Luther through Leibniz* (2010), *Luther and the Beloved Community: A Path for Christian Theology after Christendom* (2010) and *Divine Complexity: A Theological Account of the Rise of Creedal Christianity* (2010).

Lewis Hodous (1872–1949), b. Vesec, Bohemia, was a Congregational minister. He migrated to the United States with his parents in 1882. He graduated from Cleveland High School in 1893, from Adelbert College of Western Reserve University in 1897 and Hartford Theological Seminary in 1900 and studied one year at the University of Halle in Germany.

Hodous was ordained as a Congregational preacher in September 1901 at Bethlehem Church in Cleveland, OH and was later sent as a missionary to China, where he served until 1917. He served in Ponasang from 1901 to 1904, teaching at the mission's theological seminary, and was president of Foochow Theological Seminary from 1902 to 1912. After returning home from the mission field, from 1917 to 1945, Hodous was professor of Chinese culture at the Kennedy School of Missions of Hartford Seminary Foundation, and from 1928 to 1941, professor of history and philosophy of religion at the seminary.

Joseph Lukl Hromádka (1889-1969), b. Hodslavice, Czech., was a Czech Evangelical theologian of note. Hromádka studied theology in Vienna, Basel, and Heidelberg, as well as in Aberdeen. He was a supporter of and member from its foundation in 1918 of the unified Evangelical Church of Czech Brethren. In 1939, Hromádka fled the Nazis into exile, taking up a post as guest professor at Princeton Theological Seminary in the United States (1939-47). After the War, he returned to Prague in 1947 to resume his post at the Comenius theological faculty. He was the author of a number of books. He was a founder of the Christian Peace Conference.

Robert 'Bob' Janacek (1930-2017), b. Kalamazoo, MI, of Czech father, was a Protestant minister, a theologian and mental health administrator. He was a very educated man who used his knowledge and experience to help others. Some of his education credentials were a Bachelor's from Eastern Nazarene College in Massachusetts, a Bachelor's from Boston University, a Master's degree from Princeton Seminary, a Master's from Winona Lake Seminary, a Doctorate of Sacred Theology from Geneva College, and a Doctorate of Ministry from Boston University. He attended school while he was working and raising his family. His first charge after graduating seminary was as a Church of the Nazarene Minister, which he held for about 4 years. In 1960, Bob converted to the Methodist Church and became a minister in Arapahoe, Nebraska. His ministerial duties took him many places including becoming pastor of the Meade Chapel and Port Barnett Churches. In 2004, Bob and Patricia moved to Columbus, OH. In 2014, they came back to retire in the Brookville Area, and have been here ever since. In addition to the Methodist Church, Bob was a past member of the Junior Chamber of Commerce in Arapahoe, the Lions Club, and the Sertoma Club. He was Chaplain of the Riverside Methodist Hospital in Columbus, OH, and the Civil Air Patrol in PA. He was also an honorary member of the Nebraska Navy.

Christopher Barina (Bařina) Kaiser (1941-), b. Greenwich, CT, of Moravian ancestry, began his education and professional life as a physicist at Harvard Univ. (B.A., 1963), astrogeophysicist at University of Colorado (M.A., 1968) and later devoted his life to theology at Univ. of Edinburgh (Ph.D., 1974). His teaching and research aim to build bridges (or dig tunnels) between the two academic disciplines. Since 1976, Dr. Kaiser has served as a professor of theology (emeritus since 2012) at Western Theological Seminary in Holland, Michigan, which is associated with the Reformed Church in America. He has also taught at Calvin Theological Seminary, the University of Edinburgh, and the Reformed Theological Academy in Sárospatak, Hungary. He has written five books: *The Doctrine of God* (1982, 2001), *Creation and the History of Science* (1991), *Creational Theology and the History of Physical Science* (1997), *Toward a Theology of Scientific Endeavour* (2007), and *Seeing the Glory of the Lord* (2014). With a deep interest in ecumenical relations, he has served on the Orthodox-Reformed Dialogue and the Oriental Orthodox-Reformed Dialogue—both sponsored by the World Communion of Reformed Churches—and the West Shore (Michigan) Committee for Interfaith Dialogue.

John D. Kovac (1922–2007), b. Hazleton, PA, of Slovak ancestry; a Lutheran minister; pastor at St. John Evangelical Lutheran Church at Tarentum, Penn.; St. Peter and St. Paul Lutheran Church in Central City, Penn.; Immanuel Lutheran Church in Linn, Kan.; St. Peter Lutheran Church in Deshler; St. Paul Lutheran Church in Utica; and he was retired from St. John Lutheran Church in Seward. He was a member of the Lutheran Layman's League, Seward Kiwanis Club and the Kitones. He served as the circuit counselor for four different zones and was Central District (Slovak) secretary.

Tony Kriz (1970–), b. Newberg, OR, of Czech ancestry, received a degree in historical rhetoric from Oregon State University and a Master of Divinity with an intercultural emphasis from Multnomah Biblical Seminary and a Doctorate in Theology from George Fox University. Kriz served with a variety of international organizations, including Campus Crusade for Christ for 12 years, the majority of that time in Eastern Europe: living with Muslims in Albania and serving the war-torn former Yugoslavia. He also chaplained for several years on the campus of Reed College in Portland, some of the exploits of which are described in Donald Miller's best-selling book *Blue Like Jazz*. He has taught at numerous graduate schools and universities (currently 'Author in Residence' at Warner Pacific College from 2011), specializing in the topics of authentic faith, spiritual formation, cultural integration, cross-spiritual communication and sacred friendship. His writing life encompasses numerous articles and several books including *Neighbors and Wise Men* (2012) and *ALOOF: Figuring Out Life with a God Who Hides* (2015).

Wilma Kucharek (1954–), b. Johnson City, NY, of Slovak descent. She graduated from Valparaiso University, Valparaiso, Indiana, and earned her M.Div. and STM degrees at the Lutheran Theological Seminary at Gettysburg, PA. She served as pastor of Holy Emmanuel Lutheran Church, Mahanoy City, Pennsylvania, from 1982 to 1986; St. John Lutheran Church, St. Clair, Pennsylvania, from 1982 to 1986; and St. John Lutheran Church, Nanticoke, Pennsylvania, from 1983 to 1986. In 1986, she accepted the call to serve as pastor of Holy

Trinity Lutheran Church, Torrington, CT. In 2002, Kucharek was elected to a 6-year term as Bishop of the Slovak Zion Synod of the Evangelical Lutheran Church in America and re-elected to a second term in June 2008 and a third term in November 2014. She is the first woman of Slovak descent to become a Bishop and, as of 2016, is the longest serving female bishop currently serving in the ELCA.

Robert C. Kurka (1953–2018), b. Cedar Rapids, IA, of Czech ancestry, was professor of theology and Church in culture (Seminary) at Lincoln Christian University. He also directed LCU's Issachar Institute which promotes Christian worldview thinking through lectureships, seminars, and faculty scholarship. He specialized in biblical theology, systematic theology, historical theology, Stone-Campbell intellectual history, theology of missions, contemporary religious movements, apologetics, and bioethics. He held an undergraduate degree from Crossroads College (MN), a M.Div. (1979) from Lincoln Christian Seminary, and a D. Min. (1984) from Trinity Evangelical Divinity School. He also completed the residency requirements for a Ph.D. from Trinity (1913). He joined the faculty of Lincoln in 1992, first serving in the undergraduate school before assuming his role in the Seminary in 2006. Prior to coming to LCU, he taught at Saint Louis Christian College for seven years. Kurka had published a number of articles in journals and magazines as well as contributed to a number of multiple-author books on a diversity of theologically-oriented topics. He regularly delivered academic papers in professional society meetings as well as presented popularly-oriented venues at conferences such as the North American Christian Convention and the ARS. He had preached and taught around the world, including China, Myanmar, Ghana, South Africa, and Haiti. He was a regular lecturer for the Pasadena, CA-based, 'Perspectives on the World Christian Movement' program.

Enrico Selley Molnar (1913–1999), b. Frankfurt a/Main, of Czech ancestry, was a theologian, educated at Pacific School of Religion and Iliff School of Theology. He served as warden and prof. of liturgics at Bloy House Theological School, Pasadena (s. 1957) and then a dean. He was a specialist on Czech and Anglican history and orthodox theology.

Mark H. Muska (1953–), b. St. Paul, MN, of Czech ancestry, received his Bachelor of Arts degree in Ministries, from the University of Northwestern, St. Paul (1976), his Masters of Theology in Christian Education from Dallas Theological Seminary, Dallas, TX (1984) and his Doctor of Education degree in higher education from St. Mary's Univ. of Minnesota (2000). He has worked at the University of Northwestern, St. Paul, MN, as asst. professor (s. 1985) and as assoc. professor (s. 1988). His specialty areas are in Biblical exposition and theology. His two most recent areas of research are in Satan and the Occult, and Christian Liberty. He was named the Teacher of the Year at Northwestern (1994 and 2010).

David Nitschmann (1696-1772), b. Suchdol, Moravia, who was consecrated the first Bishop of the Renewed Brethren's Unity in 1735, by Bishop Jablonsky, a grandson of John A. Komenský (Comenius). The following year, he accompanied the second group of Moravian missionaries to Savannah, GA. He was dispatched to establish a Brethren settlement in Northern America, which led to his founding of Bethlehem, PA. Much of his life was spent in travel. Toward the end of his life, he resided in Bethlehem.

John Nitschmann (1703-1772), b. Šenov, Moravia, in 1741 was consecrated to the episcopacy, and eight years later, he came to America in order to supply the place of Augustus Spangenberg as presiding Bishop. He returned to Europe in 1751.

Joseph Novotný (1886-1967), b. Prague, Bohemia, was a Baptist minister. He received his education at the Universities of Prague, Vienna and Geneva, Nottingham, England, and received a Doctor of Divinity degree from Acadia University in Nova Scotia. He was ordained in 1909 and served as pastor of the Prague Baptist Church. When Czechoslovak patriots revolted against the domination of Austria by the Bolsheviks during World War I, he was sent by the YMCA to serve as a chaplain to Czech troops aiding the White Russians. For his service, he was awarded the Revolutionary Medal by the Czech government. Returning to Prague, he served as pastor of the Baptist Church and became the founder and first secretary of the Prague Y.M.C.A. In 1928, he came for a second time to the United States (first in 1919) to teach at the International Baptist Seminary in East Orange, NJ. During World War II, he served as pastor to two Baptist churches in Yonkers and one in New York. In 1946, he accepted a posting to Wiesbaden, Germany, where he served as director of the Christian Relief agencies licensed to operate in Germany after World War II. While there, he became a delegate to the first assembly of the World Council of Churches, held in Amsterdam. In 1952-56, he became pastor of the North Congregational Church in New Hartford, CT. Having retired in 1957, he moved to Harwich, MA, where he served as interim at a number of Cape Cod churches. He was the author of more than 50 religious books and children's stories and was a painter in both oil and water colors.

Jaroslav Pelikan (1923-2006), b. Akron, OH, of Slovak ancestry, was an American scholar of the history of Christianity Christian theology and medieval intellectual history. In 1946 when he was 22, he earned both a seminary degree from Concordia Seminary in Saint Louis, Missouri, and a Ph.D. at the University of Chicago. He joined Yale University in 1962 as the Titus Street Professor of Ecclesiastical History and in 1972, was named Sterling Professor of History, a position he held until achieving emeritus status in 1996. He served as acting dean and then dean of the Graduate School from 1973 to 1978 and was the William Clyde DeVane Lecturer 1984-1986 and again in the fall of 1995. Pelikan wrote more than 30 books, including the five-volume *The Christian Tradition: A History of the Development of Doctrine* (1971-

1989). Awards include the Graduate School's 1979 Wilbur Cross Medal and the Medieval Academy of America's 1985 Haskins Medal. He was the president of the American Academy of Arts and Sciences. He was editor of the religion section of *Encyclopædia Britannica*, and in 1980, he founded the Council of Scholars at the Library of Congress. In 2004, having received the John W. Kluge Prize for Lifetime Achievement in the Human Sciences, an honor he shared with the French philosopher Paul Ricoeur, Pelikan donated his award ($500,000) to Saint Vladimir's Orthodox Theological Seminary, of which he was a trustee.

Tom Schwanda (1950-), b. East Stroudsburg, PA, of Czech ancestry, studied theology at New Brunswick Theol. Sem. (M.Div., 1975) and Fuller Theol. Sem. (D.Min., 1992) and historical and practical theology at Columbia Theol. Sem. (Ph.D., 2007). He is a Reformed Church pastor of some 20 years. Since 1992, he has served as an adjunct professor at various colleges and seminaries, including Fuller Theol. Sem. (s. 1998). Subsequently, he held the position of assoc. professor of spiritual formation and biblical studies at Kuyper Coll. (1999-2006) and then became assoc. professor of Christian formation and Ministry at Wheaton Coll. (s. 2006). He has written a number of books, including *The Emergence of Evangelical Spirituality: The Age of Edwards, Newton and Whitefield* (2014), *Soul Recreation: The Contemplative-Mystical Piety of Puritanism* (2012) and *Celebrating God's Presence: The Transforming Power of Public Worship* (1995). He is a specialist on spirituality of worship, Czech reformation, John Hus and the Hussites, and spiritual formation and direction.

Josef Šolc (1943-), b. Prague, Czech., lived in a Communist sphere for 25 years. He moved to the United States as a scholarship tennis player, and he also has played professional ice hockey and professional tennis in both Europe and the United States. He received Master of Divinity degree (1974) and Ph.D. in systematic theology (1978) at Southwestern Baptist Theol. Sem. He was ordained to the ministry by FBC, Tulsa, in 1975. His expertise is in sports evangelism. Šolc served as pastor of the Hulen Street Baptist Church in Forth Worth, Texas, for 17 years and has also worked with the North American Mission Board and Trans World Radio. He has been associated with the Southeastern Baptist Theol. Sem., Wake Forest, NC (s. 1997), where he holds the position of professor of evangelism and missions. He is also a pastor of Mount Hermon Baptist Church, and a passionate evangelist of the Gospel of Jesus Christ. His organization, JSEV organizes evangelism mission trips all around the world with a special emphasis on athletics as a means to engage the culture with the gospel.

Matthew Spinka (1890-1972), b. Štítary, near Kolín, Bohemia, was a Chicago Theol Sem. and Univ. of Chicago educated church historian. He served as assoc. prof. of history of Eastern Christianity at the Chicago Theological Seminary (1926-38), assoc. prof. of church history at Univ. of Chicago (1936-43), prof. of church history at Hartford Theol. Sem.

(1943-58) and prof. of historical theology at Claremont School of Theology and Grad School (s. 1959). He was an authority on Orthodox Eastern and Czech Church history and the author of many books.

Glen Harold Stassen (1936-2014), b. MN, of Bohemian ancestry, a son of Harold Stassen, was a noted Christian theologian and ethicist. He received his BA in Physics from University of Virginia, his B.D. from Union Theological Seminary in the City of New York, and his Ph.D. from Duke University. He was a visiting scholar at Harvard University, Duke University, Columbia University, and the University of Heidelberg in Germany. Stassen held teaching posts at Duke University, Kentucky Southern College, Berea College, and Southern Baptist Theological Seminary (at SBTS for 20 years). He served as the Lewis B. Smedes Professor of Christian Ethics and the Executive Director of the Just Peacemaking Initiative at Fuller Theological Seminary in Pasadena, California. Stassen contributed to *Sojourners Magazine* and frequently appeared in the media, including the *Los Angeles Times* and *The O'Reilly Factor*. Stassen was recognized for his excellence in teaching with Fuller's 1999 All Seminary Council Faculty Award for Outstanding Community Service to Students, as well as the Seabury Award for Excellence in Teaching at Berea College and the Weyerhaeuser Award for Excellence in Teaching. He was named as a 2013 recipient of the Baptist World Alliance Denton and Janice Lotz Human Rights Award and named the 2012 Baptist of the Year by EthicsDaily.com. His book *Kingdom Ethics: Following Jesus in Contemporary Context*, was awarded Best Book of the Year in the Theology/Ethics category by *Christianity Today* in 2004. His last published book, *A Thicker Jesus: Incarnational Discipleship in a Secular Age* (2012), was named a top ten book by *The Christian Century*.

Edward Alfred Steiner (1866-1956), b. Senica, Slov., was raised in Plzeň, Bohemia, and received Ph.D. at Univ. of Heidelberg. After coming to the US, he attended Oberlin Coll., where he received his B.D. in 1891 and in the same year was ordained a minister in Congregational Church. He served as a pastor of churches in Saint Cloud, MN (1893-96), Pacific Avenue Church, Saint Paul, MN (1893-96), First Springfield, OH (1896-99) and churches in Sandusky, OH, thereafter until 1903. In the last year, he was appointed professor of applied Christianity at Grinnell Coll., where he remained until his retirement in 1941. His writing and lecturing established his reputation as an expert on immigration, and he was credited with motivating certain reforms in the administration of immigration centers at Ellis Island and elsewhere.

Miloš Štrupl (1924-1984), b. Prague, Czech., was a Presbyterian minister and theologian. He was raised in the Evangelical Church of the Czech Brethren which was associated with the Presbyterian Church. He attended Charles University in Prague (1945). In the year 1948, Milos Strupl attended and graduated with a Master in Theology, at the Union

Theological Seminary Richmond Virginia (Th.M., 1948). He then went to complete his postgraduate Study as an Ecumenical Fellow, in the program of Advanced Religious Studies, at the Union of Theological Seminary in New York, NY. This he completed in year 1962. During this time, he also started doing translations. Most of the translations were from Czech to English with German essays mixed in. Later, Strupl went to receive his Doctorate in Philosophy at Vanderbilt University (Ph.D., 1964). There he started writing about the Brethren and got deeply involved with the history of the *Unitas Fratrum*. For the next ten years, Strupl worked at several Universities as a Professor in Theology and as a minister at the Universities Presbyterian Churches, including being a pastor at Marshville, NY, Salisbury NC, Lavergne, TN and Melnik, WI. He worked at the University of Illinois till 1965 and then at Defiance College, Ohio, for eight years. He also taught at the Hillsboro Community College and Newberry College, SC (1976–84). He was a specialist on Czech reformation, historical theology and church history.

A. J. Swoboda (1981–), b., Albuquerque, NM, of Czech ancestry, is a professor, author, and pastor of Theophilus in urban Portland, Oregon. He teaches theology, Biblical studies, and Christian history at George Fox Evangelical Seminary and a number of other universities and Bible colleges. Previous to this, he served as a campus pastor at the University of Oregon. His doctoral research at the University of Birmingham (U.K.) explored the never-ending relationship between the Holy Spirit and ecology. He is a member of the American Academy of Religion and the Society for Pentecostal Studies. Rev. Swoboda is the author of *Messy: God Likes It That Way* (Kregel) and *Tongues and Trees: Toward a Pentecostal Ecological Theology* (JPTSup, Deo).

Jarold Knox Zeman (1926–2000), b. Semonice, Czech., after World War II, enrolled in Charles University, first in philosophy and then in theology. In 1948, he received a scholarship to continue his studies at Knox College, University of Toronto. He earned degrees at Charles University (Th.C., 1948) and Knox College (B.D., 1952), and at the University of Zurich (Dr. Theol., 1966). Later on, he also received Honorary Doctorates from McMaster Univ. (D.D., 1985) and Acadia Univ. (D.D., 1994). J. K. Zeman was active both in his church and in academia. He served as a Baptist minister in Toronto to his fellow Czech-speaking compatriots for six years, as well as in a rural church where he continued his contacts with Czech immigrants. He also provided leadership to the Department of Canadian Missions of the Baptist Convention of Ontario and Quebec. After receiving his Doctorate, he assumed the chair of Church History at Acadia Divinity College, Acadia University, Wolfville, Nova Scotia, where he taught for 23 years (1968–91). He was a specialist on reformation history, Czech and East European history, religious liberty, Baptist history and ecumenism.

3. Jewish Clergy

Alexander Altmann (1906-1987), b. Košice, Slovakia, was an Orthodox Jewish scholar and rabbi. He emigrated to England in 1938 and later settled in the United States, working productively for a decade and a half as a professor within the Philosophy Department at Brandeis University.

Leo Baeck (1873-1956), b. Lissa, Poland, of Moravian ancestry, was a rabbi and religious thinker and one of the most profound and creative liberal Jewish theologians of the 20th century. He began his education at the Jewish Theological Seminary of Breslau in 1894, where he received his rabbinic diploma in 1897. Leo Baeck's rabbinic career took him to communities in Silesia, Düsseldorf and, from 1912, Berlin. During World War I, he served as a military chaplain and saw service on both the eastern and western fronts. In addition to ministering to the troops, he tended to the spiritual needs of local Russian Jews. In 1943, Leo Baeck was deported to Theresienstadt concentration camp in Czechoslovakia. There, he was put to hard physical labor on a garbage cart. Baeck was appointed honorary president of the camp's Ältestenrat-the Jewish Council of Elders. He strove to preserve the humanity of those around him and ministered to Jewish and Christian inmates alike. Following the liberation of Theresienstadt in May 1945, Baeck prevented the camp's inmates from killing the guards handed over to them by the Russians, and then stayed on to minister to the sick and the dying. Finally, he traveled on to London where he eventually served as chairman of the World Union for Progressive Judaism. He taught intermittently in the US as prof. of history of religion at Hebrew Union College, Cincinnati. He authored numerous publications, mostly in German. In 1954, the Leo Baeck Inst. for the Study of History of the Jews from the German Speaking Countries was established in NYC in his name and he served as its first president.

Leo Baerwald (1883-1970), b. Žatec, Bohemia, after serving in World War I as a military chaplain, he became a Rabbi for the Jewish community in Munich. In 1940, he succeeded to leave from Germany and immigrated to the US. Baerwald settled in New York City, where he became the rabbi of the Congregation Beth Hillel in Washington Heights. He served as president of the B'nai B'rith Lodge (1947-49).

Solomon Baum (1868-1932), b. Šebeš, Slovakia, was Cantor of congregation Beth Israel Bikur Cholim, NYC (since 1894). He was educated in Budapest. Cantor diploma conferred by Professor Moritz Friedman of the Budapest Conservatory. Officiated as Cantor in Europe, and as Rabbi and Cantor in Congregation Beth Jacob, Brooklyn, NY.

Aaron Albert Siegfried Bettelheim (1830-1890), b. Hlohovec, Slovakia, was Rabbi and Hebraist. At the age of eleven, he entered the yeshibah of Bratislava, and afterward studied in the Talmudical schools at Lipnik, Moravia, and Prague; enjoying the tutelage of S. L. Rapoport, from whom, at the age of eighteen, he obtained his rabbinical diploma. Bettelheim officiated for a short time as rabbi and religious teacher at Mnichovo Hradiště, Bohemia and then returned to Prague to enter the university, whence he graduated with the degree of Ph.D. Bettelheim's progressive political views brought him into trouble with the government, and he emigrated to America in 1867. He served as rabbi in Philadelphia, and on the faculty of the short-lived Maimonides College. He also acquired a medical degree. In 1875, Bettelheim accepted a pulpit in San Francisco. There he organized a society for Hebrew study for Christian clergymen, and was active in civic affairs, especially prison reform. He coedited a weekly, the *Jewish Times* and *Observer*, which represented the traditionalists' views. In 1887, he returned East to a pulpit in Baltimore. A foundation to aid needy scholars in Vienna was established in his memory by his daughter Rebekah, wife of Alexander Kohut. Bettelheim left no complete scholarly work, but he wrote many articles on art, medicine, and other subjects and some of his notes and suggestions were incorporated into Kohut's Arukh. His son, Felix Albert Bettelheim (1861-1890), a physician, also moved to the United States and initiated the establishment of the first hospital in Panama, serving as head physician between 1883 and 1889.

Daniel Block (1802-1853), b. Bohemia, was a Jewish leader who founded the B'nai B'rith synagogue is St. Louis, Missouri.

Jacob Bloch (1846-1916), b. Bohemia, came to US as a young man, and his work as a Rabbi commenced in Pine Bluff (to 1872) and Little Rock, Arkansas (to 1880). He moved thence to Sacramento, California (to 1884) and was then called to take charge of Congregation Beth Israel, in Portland, Oregon (1884-1990) and finally at Congregation Emanu El, Spokane, WA (1900-04), during which time the Congregation was transformed from orthodoxy to reform. Educated in Pilsen and University of Prague (M.A.). Rabbinical diploma conferred by Rabbi Dr. Saul Isaac Kaempf, Rabbi M. Bloch and Rabbi Dr. M. Deutsch. LL.D. Oregon University.

Jonas (ben Abraham) Bondi (1804-1874), b. Dresden, Germany, of Bohemian ancestry, came to US in 1859, in answer to a call to become preacher of Congregation Ansche Chased of NYC. During his brief tenure there, he was instrumental in reshaping the synagogue's prayer book. The revised prayer book was part of a larger effort of revamping the prayer service to promote decorum. Though not an ordained rabbi, Bondi was knowledgeable in the Talmud and occasionally expressed his opinion on matters of Jewish law.

Herman Bories (1819-1901), a pioneer Rabbi from Bohemia, came to America in 1849 and initially lived in Nevada and California during the early mining excitement years. Since 1861, together with his wife Rosa (nèe Freiman), who was also from Bohemia, he resided in Portland, OR, where their son Frederick was born, two years later. According to 1880 census, he was a teacher. He was the first Rabbi who came to Oregon, serving in Portland (1861–63).

Zvi Dershowitz (1928–2023), b. Brno, Czech., is an American rabbi, currently Rabbi Emeritus at Sinai Temple in Los Angeles. In 1938, just 33 days before the Nazis invaded, Dershowitz fled the country with his family. In February 1939, Zvi immigrated to New York City along with his parents. They settled in Brooklyn, in the Williamsburg neighborhood. There, he learned English, attended Mesivta Torah Vodaath, and became ordained as an orthodox rabbi in 1953. In 1949, Dershowitz spent a year studying in Jerusalem, where he helped Jewish refugees from Yemen and elsewhere in the newly established State of Israel. Dershowitz later became rabbi at Temple Beth Shalom in Kansas City, Missouri before moving to St. Paul, Minnesota where he became a rabbi at the Temple of Aaron. He later went on to direct many Jewish summer camps, including Herzl Camp in Wisconsin from 1954–1961, Camp Alonim/Brandeis-Bardin Institute (BCI) in Simi Valley, CA, from 1961–1963, and directed Camp Ramah in California for 10 years (from 1963–1973). In 1973, Dershowitz became associate rabbi at Sinai Temple. He would remain in that role for 25 years before becoming the synagogue's Rabbi Emeritus in 1998. In 1973, Dershowitz became associate rabbi at Sinai Temple. He would remain in that role for 25 years before becoming the synagogue's Rabbi Emeritus in 1998. For many years, Dershowitz also served as the chaplain from the local Board of Rabbis of Southern California to the Los Angeles jail system.

Gotthard Deutsch (1859–1921), b. Dolní Kouice, Moravia, was a Rabbi and American scholar of Jewish history. He was professor of Jewish history and philosophy at Hebrew Union College in Cincinnati. (s. 1891).

Sender Deutsch (1922–1998), b. Veľké Berezné, Czech., was a rabbi, leader of one of the largest Hasidic Jewish groups in the US. He is an editor of *Der Yid*.

Sigmund Drechsler (1845–1908), b. Brezová, Slovakia, had Dr. degree and came to the US in 1887, settling in Cleveland, OH. He was Rabbi of the Hungarian Congregation Bne Jeschurun, Cleveland, OH (since 1886). Educated under Dr. L Hildesheimer at Eisenstadt, Hung. Rabbinical diploma conferred by Dr. L. Hildesheimer and Rabbi Mannheimer from Užhorod. Was Rabbi at Kovago Eors for three years; Nagy Laszony for three years and Peczel for 14 years, all in Hungary.

Shmuel Ehrenfeld (1891–1980), b. Mattersdorf, Austria, of Slovak ancestry, known as the Mattersdorfer Rav, was a pre-eminent Orthodox Jewish rabbi in pre-war Austria and a respected Torah leader and community builder in post-war America. He established

Yeshivas Chasan Sofer in New York City and taught thousands of students who went on to become leaders of American Torah Jewry. He also founded the neighborhood of Kiryat Mattersdorf in Jerusalem, where his son and grandson became prominent Torah educators.

Maurice Faber (1854–1934), b. Široké, Slovakia, was Rabbi of Congregation Beth-El, Tyler, TX. Educated at Talmudical Colleges, Hung. Rabbinical diploma conferred by rabbi Wolf Tannenbaum, Verpelet, Hung. Was Rabbi of Congregation B'nai Zion, Titusville, PA, for ten years and of Congregation B'nai Israel, Keokuk, IA, for two years. He was Professor of German Language and Literature at Titusville High School for nine years.

Samuel Freilich (1902–1993), b. Hungary, was a rabbi educated at Charles Univ. in Prague, before serving as a district rabbi in Czechoslovakia. He helped organize an escape of Jewish men from the Nazis during a forced march to Auschwitz in 1945 and later established a network of schools for Jewish orphans in Hungary. Rabbi Freilich served as Rabbi of Ohave Sholom Synagogue in Gardner, MA for two years and then as Rabbi of Temple Beth Sholom in Lake Worth, FL, from 1958 to 1961. He returned to Ohave Sholom when he was given lifetime tenure as Rabbi there.

Sigmund Frey (1852–1930) b. Nový Rusínov, Moravia, held rabbinical positions in Philadelphia, Chicago, Springfield, IL, Wabash, IN, Altoona, PA and was the 3rd Rabbi of the Montefiore Congregation of Las Vegas, NM (1889–90). Frey also worked as a professor and social worker and was the author of *Homer and the Bible, Comparisons of the World's Literature and Rabbinic Lore, Caveant Consules.* He was educated at Gymnasium, Brno, Moravia. Rabbinical diploma was granted by Dr. Samuel Gruen.

Zachariah Gelley (1933–2018), b. Topoľčany, Slovakia; Holocaust survivor; rav (rabbi), K'hal Adath Jeshurun (KAJ) in the Washington Heights neighborhood of upper Manhattan in New York City. Rav Gelley was a noted talmid chochom and manhig, who guided KAJ, which is comprised of an elementary yeshiva for boys and girls, a Bais Yaakov middle school for girls, a mesivta high school for boys, a bais medrash and kollel, a mikvah, a kashrus supervisory organization, a chevra Kadisha.

David L. Genuth (1901–1974), b. Romania, of Slovak descent, was one of Cleveland's most influential Orthodox rabbis for more than 40 years. He emigrated to the US in 1922. He attended the graduate school of Yeshiva University in New York, the Yeshiva in New Haven, Connecticut, and the Yale University Divinity School. Genuth was ordained in 1926. In 1930, Genuth was appointed as the first Rabbi of Beth Israel Synagogue in Norwalk, CN, he was an active supporter of the Norwalk Hospital. In 1931, he moved to Cleveland and in 1933, he was appointed the first rabbi at the Kinsman Jewish Center. At the Kinsman Jewish Center, whose membership included many members of the radical Labor Movement, Genuth created an important congregation by applying a modern view of Orthodoxy. In 1950, after a disagreement with board members, Genuth left the Kinsman Jewish Center with eight families establishing Temple Beth El which described itself as 'egalitarian/traditional' and was particularly notable for its seating of men and women together. The congregation moved into its building on Chagrin Blvd in 1954 – the first synagogue within the city limits of Shaker Heights. Genuth served as Temple Beth El's sole rabbi until his death in 1974. Throughout the 1930s, Genuth was active with the Orthodox Jewish Children's Home and the Mt. Pleasant Consumptive Ladies Aid Society. Genuth was also active in aiding the United Order of True Sisters, the American Jewish Congress and was an organizer of the Jewish Community Council serving as a representative to its delegate assembly.

Samuel Greenfield (1870–1973), b. Košice, Slovakia, was Rabbi of Mount Zion Congregation, NYC (since 1899). He was educated in Košice, NYC, and Cincinnati, OH; Rabbi, Hebrew Union College; University of Cincinnati (B.L.). He was Rabbi at Peoria, IL (1891–93), Rodeph Shalom Congregation, Pittsburgh, PA (1893–93); and Temple Beth Elohim, Brooklyn, NY (1896–99). He was editor of the *Jewish Criterion* (1895–98).

Moses J. Gries (1868–1918), b. Newark, NJ, of Bohemian mother, served as a rabbi in Chattanooga, TN (1889–92) and at the Cong. Tifereth Israel in Cleveland (1892–1917). Under his leadership, Tifereth Israel became one of the leading congregations in the US. He was advocate of liberal Judaism and his congregation was one of the first to have women on the board of trustees. Services on Sunday took place of the traditional Sabbath service. He was also the first to advocate and conduct 'the open temple,' the forerunner of the later center movement. He was educated at University of Cincinnati (B.L., 1889) and Hebrew Union College (Rabbi, 1889).

Aaron Guinzburg (1813–1873), b. Prague, Bohemia, came to this country in the year 1849, where he officiated as Rabbi in Baltimore, Rochester, and Boston. Dr. Guinzberg was a man of considerable erudition, which he strove to utilize for the moral advancement of his brethren and the vindication of his religion. He was favorably known as a teacher of distinction at various institutes of learning. He was a frequent contributor to the Jewish and general press, and his writings were usually of a polemic character. He belonged to the conservative school.

Aaron Hahn (1846–1932), b. Bohemia, was a Rabbi of Orthodox Rodef Sholom Cong., NY (1869) and since 1874 to 1892 of the Tifereth Israel Reform Cong., in Cleveland. During his rabbinate, the congregation moved to an elegant temple on East 55th and Central. In 1886, the congregation included 145 families and had begun Sunday morning lectures.

Sigmund Hecht (1849-1925), b. Hliník nad Hronom, Slovakia, was Rabbi of Congregation B'nai B'rith, Los Angeles, CA (since 1899). Educated privately by his father at Zsolna, Hung.; at Seminary and university of Vienna. Rabbinical diploma granted by the Rabbi of Bystricka; University of Alabama (D.D.). He was Rabbi at Montgomery, AL (1876-88); of Temple Emanu-El, Milwaukee, WI (1888-99).

James Gutheim Heller (1892-1971), b. New Orleans, of Bohemian father, was a leader of Reform Judaism, Rabbi and the American Zionist. He served as a Rabbi at Little Rock, AR (1919-20) and then as a Rabbi at Isaac M. Wise Temple, Cincinnati (1920-50). He also excelled as a composer.

Maximilian H. Heller (1860-1929), b. Prague, Bohemia, was a leader in Reform Judaism and an early Zionist leader. He served as a Rabbi of Temple Sinai in New Orleans (1887-1927) and as a professor of Hebrew language and literature at Tulane University (1912-28). He was educated at Gymnasium, Prague; Hebrew Union College (Rabbi); and University of Cincinnati (B.L., M.L.).

Adolph Huebsch (1830-1884), b. Sv. Mikuláš, Slovakia, was a Hebrew scholar and Rabbi, who received the degree of Ph.D. from Prague Univ. and preached in that city for a short time. In 1866, he was called to New York as Rabbi of a synagogue, where he preached until his death. Dr. Huebsch was a Talmudic and Semitic scholar of high attainments, a preacher of rare power, with a personality that charmed old and young, he was peculiarly successful in his ministry.

Bernard Illowy (1812-1871), b. Kolín, Bohemia; a leader of Orthodox Judaism in the US, officiated as Rabbi in New York, St. Louis, Syracuse, Baltimore, New Orleans, and Cincinnati. He was a Talmudist of distinction, and well known for his conservative views, an accomplished linguist, and an orator of power. His command of Hebrew was notable.

Leo Jung (1892-1972), b. Uherský Brod, Moravia, was an Orthodox Rabbi and philosopher, who was one of the major architects of American Orthodox Judaism. He was the younger brother of Moses Jung. He attended Cambridge University and he received his Doctorate from the University of London. In 1910, he attended the Yeshiva of Prešov and in 1911, he went to study in Galanta, Hungary. He also attended the Hildesheimer Rabbinical Seminary in Berlin. Jung claimed that he received three rabbinic ordinations, from Rabbi Mordechai Zevi Schwartz, Rabbi Abraham Isaac Kook and Rabbi David Zvi Hoffmann of Berlin. Rabbi Jung's first American pulpit was in Cleveland, where he arrived in January 1920. In Cleveland, he was an, "utterly novel phenomenon, the first English speaking Orthodox rabbi, bearded and a Ph.D." After serving for two and a half years at the Knesset Israel congregation in Cleveland, in 1922 he was asked to become the rabbi at the prestigious Jewish Center Synagogue, in New York. He shaped the congregation into a bastion of modern Orthodoxy based on the philosophy of Torah and Derekh Eretz. Jung emerged as one of the best-known spokesmen of neo-Orthodoxy in America. He helped organize the Rabbinical Council of the Union of Orthodox Congregations, which served English-speaking rabbis, and was its president from 1928 to 1935. He became professor of ethics at Yeshiva University in 1931 and held a similar position at Stern College for Women from 1956. During World War II, he personally collected 1,200 affidavits and helped rescue some 9,000 Jews. A noted writer and editor, Jung started the Jewish Library in 1928 and edited eight volumes. His own writings numbered some 35 books. His *Harvest: Sermons, Addresses, Studies* appeared in 1956.

Moses Jung (1891-1960), b. Uherský Brod, Moravia, the older brother of Leo Jung, was a Rabbi and noted theologian. He was educated in Berlin, Vienna, London (LL.B.) and Cambridge. After coming to the US in 1922, he received his Doctorate at Dropsie College (Ph.D., 1924). He served as prof. of religious education at the Hillel Foundation in Champaign, IL (1924-29); and for next ten years he was prof. of religion at Univ. of Iowa. He was the author of *The Jewish Law of Theft* (1929) and *Guidance of Youth* (1936) and a co-author of *Chronological Tables of Jewish History and Source Book of Jewish History* (1938) and an editor of *Modern Marriage*.

Alois Kaiser (1840-1908), b. Sobotiste, Slovakia, who lived and worked in Prague, became an American chazzan and composer and is considered to be the founder of American cantorate. Kaiser arrived in New York City in June 1866, and in the following month was appointed cantor of the Oheb Shalom congregation in Baltimore, Maryland. He was for several years president of the Society of American Cantors. From 1895, he was honorary member of the Central Conference of American Rabbis, which in 1892, entrusted him and William Sparger with the compilation of the musical portion of a Union Hymnal, published in 1897.

Alexander Kaufman (1886-d.), b. Bardejov, Slovakia, was rabbi, editor, publisher at St. Louis, MO. He came to the US in 1914. He was educated at Etz Chaim Theological Seminary, Prešov (Rabbi, cum laude); Evangelical Lutheran Collegium of Prešov; Inst. of Technology, Biliz; and University of Budapest (M.E., Ph.D.). He was editor and publisher, St. Louis; with *Saddle and Bridle*, and the *Jewish Voice*.

David Klein (1868-1926), b. Lipany, Slovakia, was Rabbi of Congregation B'nai Israel, Columbus, OH. Educated at Talmudical College; a Gymnasium; the Ohio State University (B.Ph., M.A.); and privately by his father. He was previously Rabbi of Congregation Rodef Shalom, Reading, PA (189-92); and of Akron (OH) Hebrew Congregation (1892-96).

Henry Klein (1859-d.), b. Lipany, Slovakia; was Rabbi of the Hebrew Reform Congregation, Altoona, PA (since 1896). Educated at Gymnasium of Miskolc and Talmudic College at Berehovo. Rabbinical diploma granted by Rabbi Moses Margarethen. Was Rabbi at Amsterdam, NY for 3 years, and Canton, OH, one year.

Jacob Klein (1870-d.), b. Veľká Ida, Slovakia, was Rabbi of Congregation Emanuel, Statesville, NC. Educated in Košice. Attended several Talmudical Colleges and was graduated at Teachers' Seminary. Rabbinical diploma conferred by Rabbi Isaac Billitzer. Was Superintendent of Chicago Home for the Jewish Friendless; and Rabbi of Congregations Agudath Achim and Ohave Zedek, Chicago, IL. Contributed articles and poems to *Die Deborah*.

Philip Klein (1849-1926), b. Bardoňovo, Slovakia, was Rabbi of the First Hungarian Congregation Ohab Zedek, NYC. Educated at Talmudical Colleges in Hungary; Gymnasium in Bratislava; Universities of Vienna and Berlin (Ph.D.). Rabbinical diploma conferred by Dr. H. B. Auerbach, Halberstadt. Was Rabbi in Libava.

Eugene Kohn (1887-1977), b. Newark, NJ, of Bohemian ancestry was an American Reconstructionist Rabbi. He earned his B.A. from New York University (1907) and was ordained by the Jewish Theological Seminary in 1912. It was here that he met Rabbi Mordecai Kaplan who taught him homiletics. Between 1912 and 1939, he served as a congregational rabbi in Conservative synagogues in the U.S. states of Maryland, New Jersey, New York, Wisconsin and Ohio. He also served as the president of the Rabbinical assembly 1936-1937. He played a central role in the Reconstructionist movement. He edited its journal *The Reconstructionist* and, alongside Kaplan and Ira Eisenstein, edited *The New Haggadah* (1941), *The Sabbath Prayer Book* (1945) and *The Reconstructionist Prayer Book* (1948). Alongside Jack Cohen, Eisenstein and Milton Steinberg, he was one of Kaplan's main disciples.

Jacob Kohn (1881-1968), b. Newark, NJ, of Bohemian ancestry, was a conservative Rabbi. He became associated with the newly founded Univ. of Judaism (1947), where he was Dean of graduate school and prof. of theology. He had lectured on Judaism at Teachers College, Columbia University and served on the faculty of the University of South Carolina. He had been vice-president of the United Synagogue of America, the association of Conservative congregations, and a member of the executive council of the Rabbinical Assembly, the association of Conservative rabbis. He was the author of *Modern Problems of Jewish Parents* (1932), *Moral Life and Man: Its Philosophical Foundation* (1956) and *Evolution as Revelation* (1963).

Mayer Kopfstein (1866-1934), b. Bratislava, Slovakia, was a rabbi. Rabbinical education in Bratislava, Mattersdorf and Seret; secular education in Vienna under the guidance of Dr. A. Jellinek. Rabbinical diploma granted by Rabbi Samuel Ehrenfeld. Held positions in Elmira,

NY for 2 years; in Congregation Ansche Chesed, NYC for 6 years; in Congregation Hand in Hand, NYC for 2 years; and at Perth Amboy, NJ, less than a year. He resided in NYC.

Joseph Saul Kornfeld (1876-1944), b. Zlaté Moravce, Slovakia, was Rabbi of Congregation Anshe Emeth, Pine Bluff, AR. Educated at the schools of Topoľčany; high school, Cincinnati; University of Cincinnati (B.A., 1898) and Hebrew union college (B.H.L., B.D., and Rabbi).

Marcus Krauskopf (1848-1936), b. Merklin, Bohemia, was educated in Pilsen, Bohemia. Rabbinical diploma was conferred on him by Rabbi Angelus Kafka in Pilsen. He was Rabbi at Congregation Shearith B'nai Israel, NYC (1883-93); at Congregation Atereth Israel, NYC (s. 1893). He was Past Grand Master of Independent Order of Free Sons of Israel.

Moses M. Landau (1907-d.), b. Austria, desc. of Rabbi Ezekiel Landau of Prague, was educated at Univ. of Vienna and Israelische theologische Lehranstatt, Vienna. He came to US in 1938. He was Rabbi, Temple Judea, Chicago (1941-46); Mt. Sinai Cong. Texarkana (1946-59); Temple Beth David, CA (1950-54); Moses Montefiore Cong., Bloomington, IL (1954-57); Adath Israel Cong., Cleveland, MS (s. 1957). In 1957, Adath Israel began to enjoy some rabbinic stability with the arrival of Rabbi Moses Landau, who served the congregation well into the 1990s. Under his leadership, the congregation thrived. In the 1960s, the congregation renovated its sanctuary, built a rabbi's study, and also acquired a parsonage for the rabbi. Rabbi Landau was also a member, teaching staff, Delta State College, Cleveland, MS. He was the author of works in Hebrew language.

David Lefkowitz (1875-1955), b. Prešov, Slovakia, was rabbi. Educated in public schools of NYC; College of the City of New York (B.S.); University of Cincinnati (B.L.); and Hebrew Union College (Rabbi, 1900). He was Rabbi, Cong. Bnai-Yeshurun, Dayton, OH (1900-20), Temple Emanu-El, Dulles, TX (1920-1949). He was a Founding Executive Committee Member of the Dayton Branch of the National Association for the Advancement of Colored People (NAACP).

David Lefkowitz, Jr. (1911-1999), b. Dayton, OH, of Slovak ancestry, was a Rabbi in Shreveport, LA. He attended both the University of Texas and Southern Methodist University before entering the University of Cincinnati, from which he graduated in 1932. He received his rabbinical training from the Hebrew Union College, from which he was ordained in 1937. Rabbi Lefkowitz' first pulpit assignment was as assistant rabbi to his father at Temple Emanu-El in Dallas, the first instance in the American rabbinate where father and son served the same congregation. In 1940, he was called to the pulpit of B'nai Zion congregation in Shreveport, Louisiana to serve as associate rabbi to then Senior Rabbi Abram Brill. Lefkowitz attained the post of senior rabbi upon Brill's retirement in

January 1941 and retained that position until his retirement in 1972. Lefkowitz served as a chaplain in the United States Air Force from 1943 through 1946. During that time, he served both at home and in Europe, where he helped homeless Jews in the various centers for displaced persons.

Joshua Loth Liebman (1907–1948), b. Hamilton, OH, of Bohemian ancestry, in 1931 accepted position of Rabbi in Lafayette, IN and at same time, was appointed instructor at Hebrew Union Coll. In 1934, he was appointed to Kehilath Anshe Maarab Temple in Chicago and in 1939, to Temple Israel in Boston. He was widely known for his regular sermons on Sunday mornings over two Boston radio stations. Phenomenal success of his book *Peace of Mind* (1946) brought him national fame.

Eugene Max Mannheimer (1880–1952), b. Rochester, NY, of Bohemian ancestry, served as a Rabbi in Sioux City, Iowa, and in 1905, he moved to Des Moines, Iowa, to serve the congregation at Temple B'nai Jeshurun. Mannheimer was elected as first vice president of the School of Religion at the State Univ. of Iowa in 1949. He also served as president of the Federated Jewish Charities of Des Moines (s. 1906) and was organizer and member Board of Jewish Community Center (s. 1907) and an organizer and member of the Board of United Jewish Philanthropies (s. 1913).

Leo Mannheimer (1878–1954), b. Rochester, NY, of Bohemian mother, was a Rabbi educated at Univ. of Cincinnati and Hebrew Union Coll. He served as Rabbi of Mizpah Congregation, Chattanooga, TN (s. 1902). He also traveled to Lexington every other Sunday to lead services there. In the mid-1898, he apparently also served in El Paso, TX.

Bernard Dov Marton (1909–1990), b. Velete; rabbi; educated in Czechoslovakia; in US s. 1933; rabbi of Congregation Sharei Zedek, the Sea Gate Sisterhood and Talmud Torah in Brooklyn, NY; rabbi of First Congregation Anshe S'fard of Borough Park, Brooklyn, NY (s. 1941), In 1945, Marton became rabbi of Congregation Kenesseth Israel in San Francisco, CA. He founded and served as dean of the Hebrew Academy of San Francisco, an Orthodox Jewish day school. He also founded, published, and edited the *Jewish Courier*, a monthly newspaper, and was appointed West Coast Chairman of the Rabbinical Alliance. He left San Francisco in 1952 to become Executive Vice-President and Provost of the Yeshiva Torah Vodaath schools in Brooklyn, NY. In the fall of 1952, Marton became rabbi of Congregation Adas Israel and Mishnayes in Newark, NJ. In 1955, Marton left Newark for a 'lifetime position' at Congregation B'nai Reuben in Los Angeles.

Shmuel Mendlowitz (1926–2017), b. Williamsburg; son of the legendary Rav Shraga Feivel Mendlowitz; Rav, founder and menahel of Mesivta Bais Shraga of Monsey, NY.

Shraga Feivel Mendlowitz (1886-1948), b. Svetlice, Slovakia; rabbi; leader of American Orthodoxy and founder of key institutions such as Torah Vodaath, a Yeshiva in Brooklyn, and Torah U'Mesorah, an outreach and educational organization. In the words of rabbi Moshe Feinstein: "Were it not for him, there would be no Torah study and no Fear of Heaven at all in America."

Nathan Michnik (1863-1911), b. Bílsko, at Moravian/Silesian border, was educated in Vienna and Bratislava. He served as Rabbi in Springfield, IL, Helena, MT, Huntsville, AL, Jonesboro, AK, Port Gibson, MS and at Congregation Beth Israel, Woodville, MS. His Rabbinical diploma was conferred by Rabbi Simon Schreiber.

Ignatius Mueller (1857-1925), b. Prešov, Slovakia, was Rabbi of Congregation B'rith Shalom, Louisville, KY. He received his education at Gymnasium and later studied at University of Berlin, where he received his Doctorate. He received his Rabbinical diploma from the Hebrew Union College. He was Rabbi at Kalamazoo, MI and Des Moines IA; teacher at the Hebrew Union College, Cincinnati, OH; Professor of German at Highland Park Normal College.

Baruch Myers (1964-), b. Orange, NJ, is s a Chabad-Lubavitch Hasidic rabbi. Myers married Chana Myers in March 1989 and moved to Bratislava, Slovakia in 1993. He was inaugurated on June 20, 1993 as Bratislava's Chief Rabbi, the Jewish community's first rabbi in 15 years since the last rabbi of Bratislava Izidor Katz died in December 1978 (former rabbi of Galanta). In addition to serving as the community's official Rabbi, he currently has a Chabad house where he hosts programs, activities, and services for the local Jewish community and tourists, a Jewish kindergarten (cheder), in the afternoons, and a summer camp. Myers lives with his wife and 13 children in Bratislava and runs Chabad of Slovakia there. He organized a Chassidic Songs Project with Slovak cello player, Jozef Lupták.

Morris Newfield (1869-1940), b. Humenné, Slovakia, was US Reform rabbi and social worker. After his ordination, Newfield was appointed rabbi of Temple Emanu-El in Birmingham, Alabama, a position he retained throughout his life. He also joined the faculty of Howard College, where he taught Hebrew and Semitics. Newfield founded the local Federation of Jewish Charities, later renamed the United Jewish Fund. He was also instrumental in organizing the Alabama Jewish Religious School Teachers Association, serving as its president for two years. Newfield went on to serve as secretary of the Central Conference of American Rabbis (CCAR) and was ultimately elected to its highest office in 1931. During his two-year term as CCAR president, Newfield steered a non-Zionist course; within a few years, however, in response to the rise of Nazism, he had become a staunch

Zionist. He spent the final years of his life championing the cause of the Jewish homeland in Palestine.

Siegmund Moses Reich (1873–d.), b. Bohemia, was Rabbi of Temple Beth Zion, Bradford, PA. He was educated at college of the City of New York (B.A., 1895); Columbia University (M.A., 1900); and Jewish Theological Seminary of America. Rabbinical diploma conferred by Rabbi Siegmund Richter. Instructor in Bible and Hebrew grammar in Jewish Theological Seminary of America (1897-99); teacher in NY Public schools (1895-97). He was the author *Yemen Textbook for the Instruction of the Jewish Child*.

Samuel Rosenblatt (1902–1983), b. Bratislava, Slovakia; rabbi, Trenton, NJ, and since 1927 onward, served Congregation Beth Tefiloh in Baltimore, MD.; head of the Baltimore Board of Rabbis (1952), Mizrachi (1938-42), and the American Jewish Congress (1942-47).

Bernard Sadler (1854–1917), b. Kostelní Bříza, Bohemia, held rabbinical posts at South Bend, IN (1894-95), Owensboro, KY (1897) and at Montefiore Congregation, Cairo, IL; he organized the latter in 1894. He also served as Rabbi in Easton, PA.

Max Schlesinger (1837–1919), b. Vitschen, Silesia, was a pioneer noted Rabbi educated at Breslau and Univ. of Prague. He served as a Rabbi, Cong. Beth-Emeth, Albany, NY.

Emanuel Schoenbrun (1859–1943), b. Veľké Kapušany, Slovakia, was Rabbi of Congregation Kneset Israel in Cleveland, OH. He was educated at Vacov and Deutsch-Kreutz, Hungary. Rabbinical diploma was conferred by Rabbi Silberstein and Rabbi E. Prossnitz.

Emanuel Schreiber (1852–1932), b. Lipnik, Moravia, was a pioneer American Rabbi, who served successively the rabbinates of Los Angeles, CA, Little Rock, AR, Spokane, WA, Toledo, OH, Youngstown, OH and then became a Rabbi of Congregation Emanu-El, Chicago. Schreiber was editor of the *Jüdische Gemeinde- und Familien-Zeitung* (later *Die Reform*) from 1876 to 1881, and of the *Chicago Occident* from 1893 to 1896.

Morris Sessler (1880–d.), b. Hlohovec Slovakia; rabbi; held positions in Alexandria, VA, Wheeling, VA, Providence, RI, and New Orleans, CA.

Solomon H. Sonneschein (1839–1908), b. Turč. Sv. Martin, received his rabbinical diploma from the Chief Rabbi of Boskovice, Moravia (1863). He was a Rabbi in Prague, New York, St. Louis and of Temple Bnei Yeshurun, Des Moines, IA. He served as vice-pres. of the National Conference of Charities and Corrections (1886-88) and was editor and contributor to German and English Jewish press for many years.

Hugo Stránský (1905-1983), b. Prague, Bohemia, was ordained Rabbi, and also held a doctorate in Oriental languages and philosophy from Univ. of Prague. He served as a Jewish Chief Chaplain of the Czechoslovak Armed Forces and of the Czechoslovak Brigade under Allied Command during World War II. He then became a Chief Minister of the Melbourne Hebrew Congregation, Australia. After coming to US, became Rabbi of Congregation Beth Hillel of Washington Heights, NYC.

Benjamin Szold (1829-1902); b. Zemianske Sady, Slovakia, was an American rabbi and scholar. In 1859, he accepted a call from the Temple Oheb Shalom (Baltimore, Maryland) in whose service he remained until his death, first as rabbi and later (after 1892) as rabbi emeritus. He arrived in the United States in September 1859 and immediately took active charge of the congregation. Under his guidance, it grew rapidly, and actuated by his example, it became widely known for its strict observance of Shabbat. He took a prominent part in communal life, and besides aiding in establishing the charitable institutions of Baltimore, he devoted himself to helping Russian refugees who had emigrated to America on account of the iniquitous May Laws. He was in sympathy with the nationalist (later Zionist) movement, speaking in its favor as early as the winter of 1893-94 before the Zion Society of Baltimore.

Benjamin Abner Tintner (1884-d.), b. Newark, NJ, of Moravian ancestry, held rabbinical posts at Liberal Temple, Schenectady, NY (1907), Cong. B'nai Jeshurun, NYC (1908-11), Temple Mt. Zion (1911-29); Temple of Covenant (1931-37); MA Zion Cong. (s. 1937). He also served as the State chaplain of the American Legion, Department of New York.

Moritz Tintner (1843-1906), b. Slavkov, Moravia, after coming to US, became Rabbi of Congregation Shaare Rachamim, NYC, Cong. Beth Israel, Brooklyn, NY, of Cleveland, OH and Cong. Beth Israel Emanuel, NYC. He was educated in Bratislava, Breslau, Berlin, and Munich (Ph.D.). Rabbinical diploma was conferred by Rabbi W. Sofer of Bratislava, Rabbi A. Platsek of Boskovice, Moravia, and Dr. Aub of Munich.

Hermann Vogelstein (1870-1942), b. Pilsen, Bohemia, a Rabbi, immigrated to US in 1939 and was active as a member of the NY Board of Jewish Ministers and the Assoc. of Reform Rabbis in NYC. In 1940, Hebrew Union Coll. conferred on him the honorary Doctorate of Divinity. He was also a historian of note.

Max Vogelstein (1901-1984), b. Bohemia, son of Hermann Vogelstein, was a Rabbi, who immigrated to the US in 1938.

Morris Wechsler (1849-1919), b. Michalovce, Slovakia, was Rabbi of Congregation Brith Sholem, NYC (since 1895). Educated in Bratislava, Erlau and Lipany. Rabbinical diploma conferred by Rabbi Moses Margarethen, Rabbi F. Tannenbaum and Rabbi Solomon Wechsler. Was Rabbi of Congregation Ohev Zedek, Yonkers, NY; and congregation Kol Israel Achim, New Brunswick, NJ. He was editor of the *New York Jewish Times*.

Norbert Weinberg (1948–), b. Frankfurt, Germany, of Bohemian ancestry, was ordained as Rabbi and received his MA from the Jewish Theological Seminary, and his BA from New York University. He has also studied at the Hebrew University in Jerusalem. He was awarded the degree of Doctor of Divinities, honoris causa, by his alma mater, the Jewish Theological Seminary, in recognition of his services. He returned to serve as Rabbi to Hollywood Temple Beth El in Los Angeles, where he also served from 1990 to 1996, where his main focus was the integration of the new wave of Russian Jewish immigrants into American Jewish life. Prior to that, he directed the Central Institute for Jewish Studies at Beit Berl, Israel, under the auspices of Israel's Federation of Labor. His mandate was to help bridge the gap between the secular and religious Jews within the labor movement and to emphasize Jewish societal values. He has also served as Rabbi in Whittier, California, Newport-News, Virginia, and Houston, Texas. He is currently working on historical research on the Jews of 20th Century Europe, 'The Courage of the Spirit: The story of Europe's Jewry in the 20th Century, from family accounts and documents.'

William (Wilhelm) Weinberg (1901–1976), b. Dolina, Galicia, of Bohemian ancestry, during the outbreak of World War I, he with his parents, Samuel and Bina Weinberg, and his only sibling, Benjamin, fled to Vienna, where they settled. He attended the University of Vienna, where he completed his doctorate in political science in 1928; his diploma was signed by the University's Chancellor, Theodor Kardinal Innitzer. In 1932, he went to Berlin to study for ordination under Rabbi Leo Baeck at the Hochschule für die Wissenschaft des Judentums. During that time, he suffered persecution and imprisonment under the Nazi regime for his attempts to help fellow Jews leave Germany and was forced to return to Austria. He survived World War II in Czechoslovakia, Poland, and in the Soviet Union. In 1948, he was called to serve as the first Landesrabbiner of Hesse in Germany and as chairman of the Union of Rabbis of Germany. He came to the United States of America in 1951, where he served as a Rabbi to several congregations in the northeastern regions of the country and was a member of the Rabbinical Assembly of America. He passed away March 16, 1976.

Alexander Sandor Wiesel (1894–1971), b. Slovakia, was Rabbi in Montgomery AL, Shreveport, LA (s. 1926). He was editor of *Jewish Monitor*. Officer of Zionist Org. of America, B'nai B'rith and Civic Music Association.

Mayer Winkler (1882–1944), b. Vel'polie, Slovakia, was a prominent rabbi, first in Budapest, then in the US. He studied in the seminaries of Budapest and Vienna. He graduated from

Vienna University with Ph.D. degree and also the Jewish Theological Seminary of Vienna. For five years he studied under Rabbi Moses Bloch, a man of eminence. In 1912, he was appointed a Rabbi in Beth Israel Congregation, the largest in Budapest, for nine years. He arrived with his family at the port of New York in April 1921. He was subsequently elected Rabbi of the Homestead Hebrew Congregation Rodef Shalom (HHCRS) at Homestead, PA, where he stayed for about a year. He resigned in September 1922 to accept position of a Rabbi at Temple Sinai Congregation in Los Angeles. He served as Rabbi in Los Angeles two full terms and part of a third before resigning in 1930 seemingly due to his refusal to fundraise. Soon after, he organized a free synagogue in Los Angeles, which he called Community Synagogue of Los Angeles. He was one of the first rabbis in the US to speak regularly over the radio as the founder of the radio program 'Synagogue on the Air,' which he conducted for seven years.

David Wirtschafter (1970–), b. Lexington, KY, of Slovak ancestry; rabbi at Amos Jewish Congregation in IA and then at Temple Adath Israel in Lexington.

Aaron Wise (1844–1896), b. Erlau, Hung., son of Chief Rabbi Joseph Hirsch Weiss of Moravia, in 1874 immigrated to the US, and became Rabbi of Congregation Beth Elohim in Brooklyn. Two years later, he was appointed Rabbi of Temple Rodeph Shalom in New York, which office he held until his death. Wise was the author of *Beth Aharon*, a religious school handbook; and he compiled a prayer-book for the use of his congregation. He was for some time editor of the *Jewish Herald* of New York, and of the *Boston Hebrew Observer*.

Isaac Mayer Wise (orig. Weiss) (1819–1900), b. Lomnička, Bohemia, was an American Reform Rabbi, an outstanding Jew and leading Rabbi during the 19th century. He completed his formal education by attending the University of Prague and the University of Vienna for three years. At the age of 23, in 1842, he appeared before a Beth Din – or a rabbinical court – of three well-known rabbis: Solomon Judah Rappaport, Samuel Freund, and Ephraim Loeb Teweles, who together conferred on him the title of Rabbi. In 1843, he was appointed rabbi at Radnice, near Pilsen, Bohemia, where he remained for about two years. In 1846, Weis emigrated to the United States, where he changed the spelling of his surname to Wise. Wise became the rabbi of Congregation Beth El in Albany, N.Y. He was there four years, initiating new reforms in the religious services. He introduced choral singing, confirmation to replace Bar Mitzvah, and the seating of men and women together in pews for services. His changes resulted in much disapproval. In 1850, on the morning of the beginning of Rosh Hashanah that evening, Wise was dismissed at a rump meeting of the board of directors. The next day havoc, broke loose between his followers and those who opposed him. Soon after, a group broke away from Beth El and, with Rabbi Wise, established a new Reform synagogue called Anshe Emet – "men of truth." In 1854, Wise went to Cincinnati, Ohio, to become rabbi of Beth K.K. B'nai Yeshurun, a Reform congregation (since 1931, the temple has been known as the Isaac M. Wise Temple.) He stayed there the rest of his life. It was from there that he tried creating a national organization of congregations – the union of American Hebrew Congregations. Wise was also an organizer and mover in the establishment of the Central Conference of American Rabbis in 1889 and was elected its president, serving until he died. He was also an organizer and mover of the Hebrew Union College, the first Jewish seminary in the United States that trained rabbis in the Reformed Jewish tradition. Wise served as the college's first president as well as a teacher.

Jonah Bondi Wise (1881-1959), b. Cincinnati, OH, son of Isaac Mayer Wise, was a Reform rabbi. He held rabbinate at Mizpah Temple, Chattanooga, TN, after 1906 at Temple Israel, Portland, OR and in 1925, became Rabbi of the Central Synagogue in New York, serving until his death. While in Portland, he established a weekly Jewish newspaper *The Scribe*. He also served for a while as editor of the *American Israelite*.

Stephen Samuel Wise (orig. Weiss) (1874-1949), b. Budapest, of Slovak and Moravian ancestry, was an American Reform rabbi, Zionist leader, and a theologian. Wise studied at the College of the City of New York, Columbia College (B.A., 1892), and Columbia University (Ph.D., 1901). He served as a rabbi in New York City (1893-1900) and in Portland, OR (1900-1906). Returning to New York, he founded (1907) the Free Synagogue, of which he was rabbi until his death. Wise worked for labor reforms, world peace, alleviation of the problems of the Jewish minorities in Europe, and relief for refugees. He was one of the foremost leaders of Zionism and Reform Judaism. Among the many organizations in which he was active were the American Jewish Congress, the World Jewish Congress, and the Zionist Organization of America. He founded (1922) the Jewish Institute of Religion for the training of a modern rabbinate and of Jewish educators and community workers. His writings include *The Great Betrayal* (with Jacob De Haas, 1930), *As I See It* (1944), and his autobiography, *Challenging Years* (1949).

Samuel Wolfenstein (1841-1921), b. Velké Meziříčí, Moravia, served as rabbi of Congregation B'nai El in Saint Louis (1870-78) and then became a superintendent of Cleveland Jewish Orphan Asylum (1878-1913).

4. Other Religions

William M. Bodiford (1955-), b. Nashville, TN, of Czech ancestry on his mother's side, received his Ph.D. from Yale Univ. in the Department of Religious Studies, where he specialized in Buddhist Studies. He is a professor in the Department of Asian Languages and Cultures at the Univ. of California, Los Angeles, where he teaches courses on religion in the cultures of Japan and East Asia and Buddhist Studies. In addition to UCLA, he also has taught at Davidson Coll., NC, Univ. of Iowa and Meiji Gakuin Univ., Japan. His research spans the medieval, early moder, and contemporary periods of Japanese history.

Francis Penkava (1953–), b. Asheboro, NC, of Czech ancestry, received the Bachelor of Arts degree in religious studies from Univ. of North Carolina (UNC), Charlotte in May 2000, with a focus on religious tradition in China. He received a Master of Arts degree from Arizona State University in December 2004. In this program, he took a varied approach and followed a portfolio route to the degree, with special coursework in Chinese traditions, Southeast Asian Buddhism, the early history of Christian mysticism, religion and the body, the sociology of new religious movements and apocalyptic movements, the early Crusades, and the history of the Protestant Reformations in Europe. Additionally, he pursued independent studies in some of the works of Kierkegaard, the history of Quakers in America, and the phenomenon of non-Trinitarian churches that arose out of the 19th-century Adventist movement in America. He was a Teaching Assistant at Arizona State for four semesters, working in courses on American Religious Traditions, Native American Religious Traditions, and World Religions. Presently he teaches in the dept. of religious studies at Univ. of North Carolina, Charlotte. His areas of interests are: the continuing and evolving role of Confucianism in current-day China; contemporary apocalypticism in America; the influence of religious ideas on the creation of the American republic; and religion and psychology, with particular emphasis on existentialist elements suggested in religious belief and practice.

Reinhard Erich Pummer (1938–), b. Znojmo. Czech., educated at Univ. of Vienna, is an adjunct and emeritus professor of Religious Studies, Department of Classics and Religious Studies at the Univ. Ottawa, with which he has been associated (s. 1970). He specializes in the field of history of religions, including the methods and history of the discipline. For many years now, he has focused on a sister religion of Judaism, that is, Samaritanism. Like Christianity, Samaritanism as it has existed for the last two thousand years developed out of the matrix of the biblical tradition and became an independent religion. Among his publications are the books *Early Christian authors on Samaritans and Samaritanism* (2002) and *The Samaritans: A Profile* (2016).

D. Law

Nina Appel (née Schick) (1936–), b. Prague, Czech., was trained as a lawyer at Columbia Law School. After graduating, she lived in Palo Alto and lectured and designed courses at Stanford University. In 1973, she was hired at Loyola Law School as a law teacher, and she immediately began to teach in torts, administrative law, product liability, and evidence.

In 1976, she was promoted to full professor and then to associate dean by Dean Charles W. Murdock, who she would eventually succeed as Dean. She was the unanimous choice of the search committee in 1983, when she was appointed the Dean of Loyola Law School despite being a woman in a male-dominant field and Jewish at a Jesuit institution. She served as the dean until 2004. As dean, she was given many honors and awards. She was married to Alfred Appel (1934-2009) and they had 2 children.

Nicholas 'Nick' Bala (1952-), b. Montreal, Canada, of Czech immigrant parents, was a legal scholar and educator. He studied economics at the University of Toronto (B.A., 1974) and has law degrees from Queen's University (LL.B., 1977) and Harvard (LL.M., 1980). He joined the Faculty of Law at Queen's University, Kingston, Can. in 1980, where he is now a law professor, specializing in family and children's law. He was also a Visiting Professor at McGill, Duke, and the University of Calgary. In 2006, he was the founding Academic Director for the Osgoode Hall Law School Part-time Family Law LL.M. Program, and he continues to serve in that part-time role. In 2009, he received the Family Law Excellence Award from the Ontario Bar Association, and the Law Society Medal, and in 2013, he was elected a Fellow of the Royal Society of Canada. Nick's research focuses on a range of issues involving families, children and youth, including young offenders, child witnesses and child abuse, spousal abuse and its effects on children, parental rights and responsibilities after divorce, polygamy and the Convention on the Rights of the Child. Much of his research work was interdisciplinary and he has collaborated with psychologists, social workers, criminologists and health professionals, to better understand the impact of the law and involvement in the justice system on children and families. Bala has contributed much to the public discourse about family and children's law in Canada, seeking to improve the way in which the justice system affected families and children; he was involved in a number of law reform efforts, and was frequently interviewed by the media. He published extensively in journals of law, psychology, social work and medicine, writing or co-authoring 18 books and over 150 articles and book chapters. His work has often been cited by all levels of court in Canada, including the Supreme Court of Canada and courts of appeal in several provinces.

Raymond Batla, Jr. (1947-), b. Cameron, TX, of Czech ancestry, majored in Civil Engineering at the University of Texas at Austin, graduating in 1970 with highest honors and ranking first in his civil engineering class. Law school at the University of Texas followed, where he was an officer of the *Texas Law Review* and awarded a Juris Doctor in 1973 with honors, and selected Order of the Coif. He joined the 80 lawyer Washington, D. C. law firm of Hogan & Hartson following graduation and practiced with that firm and its successor, Hogan Lovells, his entire 40-year career in the practice of law, becoming a partner in the firm in 1983. Hogan & Hartson appointed Raymond their European Practice Coordinator in 1997, basing him and his family in London, from where he continued to open new offices throughout Europe and eventually Asia and Latin America. In 2000, Raymond was elected to Hogan & Hartson's five-partner governing Executive Committee, and in 2001, appointed Managing Partner for Hogan & Hartson's International Offices, which he served for six years. In 1990, Raymond was appointed to the election observer delegation organized by the American Endowment for Democracy to monitor the June 1990 parliamentary elections in the Czech and Slovak Federal Republics, which was co-chaired by Madeleine Albright and John McCain. Following that experience, Raymond organized several trips to investigate opportunities to assist with the influx of Western investment and was retained by a number of Czech firms to assist with privatization efforts. This led to the opening of Hogan & Hartson's office in Prague in 1991, with Raymond as the Managing Partner of that office, and the relocation of Raymond's family from Washington to Prague. In these early years, he represented Czech firms in numerous privatizations and financings, leading Western investors and he negotiated some of the first telecommunications licenses in the Czech Republic.

Stan D. Benda (1955-), b. Toronto, Canada, of Czech father, was trained as a lawyer at Univ. of Calgary (LL.B., 1981) and Osgoode Law School, York Univ. (LL.M., 2002; Ph.D., 2009). He served as Counsel for Justice Canada at Whitehorse (1988-90), Edmonton (1990-95), and Toronto (1996-2010). Subsequently, he was associated as a counsel with the firm Sim Lowman & McKay in Toronto (2010-11) and since 2010, has been in solo practice. He has also served as adjunct professor at Univ. of Ontario (2011-12), Osgoode School of Law (s. 2004) and at Ryerson Univ. (s. 2010). His legal interests lie in agricultural biotechnology and the intersection of regulatory law and science.

Alfred Abraham Benesch (1879-1973), b. Cleveland, OH, of Czech parents, received his law degree from Harvard in 1903 and established a practice with Benjamin Star. He was an active community leader and senior partner in one of Cleveland's most prestigious law firms – Benesch, Friedlande, Mendelson & Coplan. Among his clients was the predominantly Jewish Peddlers' Self-Defense Assoc., for whom Benesch obtained better police protection and fair treatment in the courts. Benesch entered politics as a Cleveland city councilman (1912-1915). His next offices included: Ohio Director of Commerce (1935-1939), Rent Control Director for Cuyahoga, Lake and Geauga Counties (1942-1945), and President of the Cleveland Board of Education.

Susan Benesch (1964-), b. New York, N.Y. of Czech ancestry on her father's side, received her legal training at Yale Law School (J.D., 2001) and at Georgetown (LL.M., 2008). She is adjunct assoc. professor at the School of International Service of American Univ. (AU). She is also a Faculty Associate of the Berkman Center for Internet and Society at Harvard University, and Director of the Dangerous Speech Project (voicesthatpoison.org). She founded the Project in 2009, to find methods for preventing collective violence by limiting the catalytic force of inflammatory speech. In 2012-2013, she was the Edith Everett Genocide Prevention Fellow at the United States Holocaust Memorial Museum. She has previously taught human rights and refugee law at AU's Washington College of Law, at Georgetown and Princeton, among other universities, and has lectured at schools including Yale, Duke, and Johns Hopkins. She has also worked at the Center for Justice and Accountability, Amnesty International, and Human Rights First. Her primary interests are in the area of human rights, international criminal law, transitional justice, comparative law, media law, refugee law, international law and has additional interests in constitutional law, immigration law, and national security law.

Alois Bohmer (1911–2008), b. Prague, was trained as a lawyer at Charles Univ. (JUDr., 1935) and in comparative law at George Washington Univ. (M.C.L., 1955). He was associated with US Library Congress, where he held the position of Senior Legal Specialist. He has authored or edited a number of books, including *Legal Sources and Bibliography of Czechoslovakia* (1959), appeared in 8 editions: *Copyright in U.S.S.R. and Other European Countries and Territories under communist government* (1960), etc.

Louis D. Brandeis (1856–1941), b. Louisville, KY, 1856, of Bohemian Jewish parents, was United States jurist. He made an eminent scholastic record for himself at the Harvard Law School and was graduated with honors before the required age of twenty-one (LL.B., 1877). He was admitted to the Bar and practiced a short time while in St. Louis. In 1879, returned to Boston, where he remained a practicing lawyer, with the firm Warren and Brandeis (1879–97), and as partner with his own firm Brandeis, Dunbar and Nutter (1897–1916). Subsequently, he was appointed by President Woodrow Wilson as Associate Justice of the US Supreme Court (1916) and served until his retirement in 1939. He was the first Jew to be named to the Court. As a lawyer, Brandeis was highly successful and he served in many precedent-setting cases. Widely known as "the people's attorney," Brandeis pioneered pro bono work and was a true reformer. Brandeis was also the first to cite law reviews both in his briefs before the court and in his opinions as a justice. In 1907, he pioneered a new type of legal document, the "Brandeis Brief." It included three pages of traditional legal citations and over 100 innovative pages of citations to articles, government reports, and other references. He was not only a great justice, but also a social reformer, legal innovator, and labor champion. Brandeis lived to see many of the ideas that he had championed become the law of the land. Wages and hours legislation were now accepted as constitutional, and the right of labor to organize was protected by law. His spirited, eloquent defense of free speech and the right of privacy have had a continuing, powerful influence upon the Supreme Court and, ultimately, upon the life of the entire nation. *The Economist* magazine has called him "A Robin Hood of the law." An enemy of industrial and financial monopoly, he formulated the economic doctrine of the New Freedom that Woodrow Wilson adopted in his 1912 presidential campaign. After Franklin Delano Roosevelt became (1933) President, Brandeis was one of the few justices who voted to uphold most of Roosevelt's New Deal legislation. He was a great help to future President of Czechoslovakia, Thomas G. Masaryk, in facilitating contact with the White House, which was acknowledged by Masaryk himself in these words: "More than all others (American Jews), Brandeis was helpful as a descendant of Czech Jews and an intimate friend of President Wilson."

Fritz Braunfeld (1892–1971), b. Brno, Moravia, a Holocaust survivor, was a lawyer and legal scholar. He studied at University of Vienna (Dr.Jur., 1919), He was in private practice in Vienna (1928–38). In 1938, he emigrated to Czechoslovakia, and after a harrowing escape, to Great Britain and in 1939, to the US. In 1944, he obtained another law degree from University of Chicago and opened private practice in Chicago. He became law professor at John Marshall Law School in Chicago.

Thomas Buergenthal (1934–2023), b. Lubochňa, Slovakia, of Jewish parents, was a lawyer, jurist, and legal scholar. Thomas Buergenthal is known as one of the youngest holocaust victims to survive places like Auschwitz and Sachsenhausen, which were horrific concentration camps, grew up in the Jewish ghetto of Kielce (Poland) and later in the concentration camps at Auschwitz and Sachsenhausen. After the War, he lived with his mother in Göttingen. On 4 December 1951, he emigrated from Germany to the United States. He studied at Bethany College in West Virginia (graduated 1957) and received his J.D. at New York University Law School in 1960, and his LL.M. and S.J.D. degrees in international law from Harvard Law School. Buergenthal served as a judge on the International Court of Justice at The Hague from 2 March 2000 to his resignation on 6 September 2010. Prior to his election to the International Court of Justice, he was the Lobingier Professor of Comparative Law and Jurisprudence at The George Washington University Law School. He was Dean of Washington College of Law of American University from 1980 to 1985 and held endowed professorships at the University of Texas, Austin (s. 1978) and Emory University. Before that, he was professor of law at SUNY Buffalo (1962–77). Buergenthal served as a judge for many years, including lengthy periods on various specialized international bodies. Between 1979 and 1991, he served as a judge of the Inter-American Court of Human Rights, including a term as that court's president; from 1989 to 1994, he was a judge on the Inter-American Development Bank's Administrative Tribunal; in 1992 and 1993, he served on the United Nations Truth Commission for El Salvador; and from 1995 to 1999, he was a member of the United Nations Human Rights Committee. Buergenthal is the author of more than a dozen books and a large number of articles on international law, human rights and comparative law subjects. He is member of a number of editorial boards of law journals, including the

American Journal of International Law. Judge Buergenthal is the recipient of numerous honorary degrees from American, European and Latin American universities.

Vratislav Bušek (1897-1972), Prague, Bohemia, was a legal scholar. He graduated from Charles University School of Law (JUDr., 1920). He became an instructor of Canonic Law at that university (1921-22), assistant Professor (1922-24), associate Professor (1924-29). He was a Professor of Canonic Law at Komenský University Law School, Bratislava (1929-30). He became Dean of that university, University Law School, Brno (1939-40). Dr. Bušek spent the war years as political prisoner in a German concentration camp, Mauthausen. After the war, he taught Canonic and Roman Law as a Professor of Charles University Law School, Prague (1945-48). He fled Czechoslovakia in April 1948, was research assistant to M. Pierre Caron, Paris, France and did research work at various institutions in Paris, until 1950, when he entered the US. He taught at Seton Hall College, South Orange, NJ (1950) and worked for Radio Free Europe (1950-61). He had since been a freelance writer. He was editor of legal periodicals in Czechoslovakia, wrote chapters on church Law in Czech legal publications, and contributed frequently to scholarly journals in his field. He published a *Manual of History of Canon Law* (1946-7) and was co-editor of *Czechoslovakia* (1956). He was active in the Council of Free Czechoslovakia and in the Czechoslovak National Council of America, where he was vice president since 1962. He was also active in SVU.

David Lee Callies (1943-), b. Chicago, IL, son of Ann Dolores Blazek (1906-2004) of Czech immigrant parents and Gustav E. Callies, is an American lawyer and educator.

John Jay Chapman (1862-1933), b. New York City, desc. f. Frederick Philipse, was an American poet, dramatist, and critic who attacked the get-rich-quick morality of the post-Civil War "Gilded Age" in political action and in his writings. He was educated at St. Paul's School, in Concord, New Hampshire, and at Harvard University. After graduating from Harvard in 1884, he toured Europe before resuming his studies at the Harvard Law School. In 1887, he assaulted a man for his supposed insulting attentions to the woman who later became Chapman's wife. In remorse, Chapman plunged his left hand into a fire and injured it so severely that it had to be amputated. Admitted to the New York bar in 1888, Chapman practiced for 10 years, meanwhile becoming a leading reformer as president of the Good Government Club and editor and publisher of the periodical *The Political Nursery* (1897-1901), taking a leading part in the movement in New York City against the machine politics of Tammany Hall. Out of these activities came two books—*Causes and Consequences* (1898) and *Practical Agitation* (1900). Both stressed his belief that individuals should take a moral stand on issues troubling the nation. On the first anniversary of the lynching of a black man in Coatesville, CA, Chapman hired a hall and held a memorial service with only two other persons present. His memorable speech delivered on that occasion was published in his book *Memories and Milestones* (1915). He was the author of a biography of the Abolitionist leader William L. Garrison (1913).

Jan Paul Charmatz (1909-1984), b. Prague, Bohemia, earned a Doctorate in civil and canon law at Univ. of Prague (JUDr., 1933) and had taught there until shortly after the German takeover of Czechoslovakia in June 1939, when he left to underground for political reasons. When the American Armed Forces liberated his country in spring of 1945, he succeeded in talking his way into membership in the US Army and, from 1945 to 1948, had served in the Office of the US Counsel for the Prosecution of major War Criminals, playing a major role in the prosecution of both Albert Speer and Hermann Goering. After teaching for a couple of years in Cuba and ten in Puerto Rico, he was awarded a sterling fellowship at the Yale Law School and earned a Master of Laws degree there in in 1952. Then, from 1953 to 1955 he taught civil law at the Louisiana State university and in the summers, both took courses and taught at the University of Mississippi Law School. Awarded his LL.B. in 1955, for the next two years, he served as a full professor on the Mississippi Law faculty, before going on to Tulane, ultimately, ending up on the law faculty at Southern Methodist University on Dallas (1958-72). He was an authority on procedure, conflict of laws, comparative recent legal history.

Andrei Hugo Cherny (1975-), b. Los Angeles, CA, of Czech ancestry, graduated with honors from Harvard College and from the University of California Berkeley Law School. He has been called a 'superstar' by CNN, a 'progressive reformer' by Washington Monthly, and one of America's 'top young thinkers' by *The New York Times*. He is a co-founder and CEO of Aspiration, an investment firm with a conscience, dedicated to serving the middle class in a way that marries profit with philanthropic purpose. He brings to this role nearly twenty years of experience as a consultant to some of America's top companies, the co-founder and president of a media start-up, a financial fraud prosecutor, a bestselling author, a senior White House aide, and a nationally recognized economic policy expert. Cherny is the founder and president of *Democracy*, a public policy journal and think tank that seeks to spur new ideas on the major issues facing America and the world. *Democracy*'s ideas, such as the Consumer Financial Protection Bureau at the heart of the 2010 Wall Street reform, have made their way into the national political debate and into legislation in Congress and states across America. Today, in print and online, *Democracy* has over 300,000 readers in every state and more than 150 countries around the world. Cherny worked in the Clinton White House as a senior advisor to Vice President Al Gore, was the lead negotiator and chief drafter of the 2000 Democratic Party platform, and helped develop the winning message for John Kerry in the 2004 Democratic primaries, and served as a part-time advisor to Barack Obama's presidential campaign and co-author of his campaign policy book, *Change We Can Believe In*. As the chair of the Arizona Democratic Party from 2011-12, he worked to build a big-tent, mainstream party that is ready to provide leadership for a stronger economy, safer streets, and better schools. He is a former Senior Fellow at both Harvard University's Kennedy School of Government and the Center for American Progress, and a former Assistant Arizona Attorney General. Cherny has written frequently on global economic policy, politics, and history for newspapers such as *The New York Times, Washington Post, Los Angeles Times, USA Today, Financial Times* and *Investor's Business Daily*. He has appeared as a commentator on television news programs including ABC's *Good Morning America* and *World News Tonight*, CBS's *The Early Show, The Colbert Report*, and *The O'Reilly Factor*. He is the author of the bestselling *The Candy Bombers: The Untold Story of the Berlin Airlift* and *America's Finest Hour*, was described as like 'Stephen Ambrose at his best' by historian Douglas Brinkley and 'everything one could want from a work of history—engrossing, informative and stirring' by the *Washington Post*.

Natasha Dolezal (ca. 1979–), b. of Czech ancestry, graduated from Gonzaga Univ. (B.A., 2001) and received training in law at Lewis & Clark Law School (J.D., 2006). Prior to practicing law, she was involved in wildlife conservation in Kenya, performing conservation genetics research on various species and training, and caring for assistance of dogs at a large nonprofit org. Natasha Dolezal began her legal career in the Oregon Legislature as a senator's legislative assistant. In this capacity, she was instrumental in bringing the Senate Judiciary Committee to Lewis & Clark for public hearings on various animal-related legislation and successfully shepherding a bill recognizing the link between animal abuse and child abuse into law. Ms. Dolezal then transitioned to a position as a Deputy District Attorney where she prosecuted felony and misdemeanor crimes, including animal abuse cases. She then became Associate Director for State Relations at Oregon Health & Science University. Subsequently, she joined the Center for Animal Law Studies (CALS) at Lewis and Clark Law School, Portland, OR. She oversees all aspects of the Animal Law LL.M. program. She also teaches the Animal Law Legislative Drafting and Lobbying course.

Alice M. Dostálová-Busick (1978–), b. Prague, Czech., is practicing as a lawyer. She immigrated to the United States as a young girl and grew up in the San Francisco Bay Area. Alice attended and graduated from Georgetown University (B.S.F.S., 2001) and subsequently received her Juris Doctor from the University of San Diego School of Law (J.D., 2006). Alice moved to Fresno, CA, where she began her legal career at McCormick Barstow (2006–08). She then was associated as an attorney with Wolfe & Wyman LLP (2008–13), and, presently, with Wright & Wright (s. 2016), representing clients in civil and commercial litigation matters. Alice is a member of Wealth Counsel, the Probate Section of the Fresno County Bar Association, the Fresno Estate Planning Council, and the California State Bar. Alice is admitted to practice law in California State Courts, the US District Court for the Eastern and

Northern District, and the Ninth Circuit Court of Appeal. She married the lawyer Mark L. Busick and they have five children.

John Francis Drac (1920–2004), b. Zborov, Czech., was a legal scholar. He received his Doctor of Law degree from the University of Prague, Czechoslovakia, and his Master's degree in Library Science from Columbia University, New York City. He was Professor Emeritus of Law from IIT-Chicago Kent College of Law where he taught since 1957. He was a chief law librarian (s. 1957), associate professor of law (s. 1969), Chicago-Kent College of Law, Chicago, IL.

Richard C. Ernst (1915–1984), b. of Bohemian ancestry, was the son of Bernard M. L. Ernst, who was an attorney for the escape artist and magician, Harry Houdini. He was a graduate of Harvard University and the Columbia University Law School and was associated with the publishing companies of Howell Soskin and Alfred A. Knopf before joining Bloomingdale Properties. During World War II, Mr. Ernst was promoted to Captain while serving in Europe with the Ninth Infantry Regiment of the Second Army Division. He took part in the invasion of Normandy and the Battle of the Bulge and earned five battle stars. He also received the Bronze Star, the French Croix de Guerre, and the Belgian Fourragère. Mr. Ernst was president and later chairman of the Board of Bloomingdale Properties, an investment organization for members of the Bloomingdale family, from the mid-1950s to 1983. At his death, he was chairman of the company's executive committee. In 1959, he was a founding director of and stockholder in Atheneum Publishers. Atheneum merged with Charles Scribner's Sons in 1978 to become the Scribner Book Company, of which Mr. Ernst was also a director. Scribner Book Companies was taken over by Macmillan Inc. Mr. Ernst's wife, Susan Bloomingdale, a granddaughter of the founder of Bloomingdale's department store, died in 1981.

Bernard Flexner (1865–1945), b. Louisville, KY, of Bohemian ancestry, practiced law in Louisville, Chicago, and New York City. Throughout his career, Flexner was much concerned with social welfare and labor problems. He was chairman of the Juvenile Court Board in Louisville and helped establish the first juvenile court in Chicago. He was a co-founder of the American Civil Liberties Union.

Felix Frankfurter (1882–1965), b. Vienna, of Slovak father and Czech mother, both being Jewish, was a lawyer and jurist. In 1900, the family emigrated to the US. After graduating from City College of New York in 1902, Frankfurter entered Harvard Law School. In 1906, Henry Stimson, a New York attorney recruited Frankfurter as his assistant. When President William Howard Taft appointed Stimson as his Secretary of War in 1911, he took Frankfurter along as law officer of the Bureau of Insular Affairs. In 1914, Frankfurter returned to Harvard Law School as professor of administrative law. Over the next few years, he acquired a reputation for holding progressive political views. A founding member of the American civil liberties Union (ACLU), he criticized the Tennessee Anti-Evolution Law and joined the campaign to overturn the death sentence. When Roosevelt became President, he often consulted Frankfurter about the legal implication of his New Deal Legislation. In 1939, Franklin D. Roosevelt appointed Frankfurter as a Supreme Court Justice. He served on the Supreme Court from 1939 to 1962. He was the most open-minded follower of judicial discipline. A noted advocate of judicial restraint in the judgments of the Court, Frankfurter, however, took a strong stand on individual civil rights and this led to his being condemned by some as an 'extreme liberal.' Frankfurter published several books including *A Selection of Cases Under the Interstate Commerce Act* (1922); *The Business of the Supreme Court* (1927); *Justice Holmes and the Supreme Court* (1938); *The Case of Sacco and Vanzetti* (1927) and *Felix Frankfurter Reminisces* (1960).

Paul Abraham Freund (1908–1992), b. St. Louis, MO, of Bohemian ancestry, was a legal scholar. He attended Washington University (A.B., 1928) and Harvard University (LL.B., 1931; S.J.D., 1932). He was associated with Harvard (s. 1939), as prof. of law (1940–76). He was an authority on public law, understanding the Supreme Court.

Charles Fried (1935–2024), b. Prague, Czech., was a lawyer and a jurist. He left Czechoslovakia in 1939, going first to England and coming to New York in 1941. He attended Oxford University, where he earned a Bachelor's and a Master's degree in Law in 1958 and 1960, respectively, and was awarded the Ordronnaux Prize in Law (1958). In 1960, Mr. Fried received the Juris Doctor degree from Columbia University School of Law, where he was a Stone Scholar. Subsequently, he served as law clerk to Associate Justice John Marshall Harlan. He has served on the Harvard Law School faculty since 1961, teaching courses on appellate advocacy, commercial law, constitutional law, contracts, criminal law, federal courts, labor law, torts, legal philosophy, and medical ethics. In October of 1985, Mr. Fried was appointed Solicitor General of the United States, having previously served as Deputy Solicitor General and Acting Solicitor General. During his term of office, he represented the Reagan administration before the Supreme Court in twenty-five cases. At the end of the Reagan Administration, he returned to Harvard Law School, where he held the chair of Carter Professor of General Jurisprudence at the Harvard Law School. From September 1995 until June 1999, Charles Fried was an Associate Justice of the Supreme Judicial Court of Massachusetts, while teaching constitutional law at Harvard Law School as a Distinguished Lecturer. On July 1, 1999, he returned to Harvard Law School as a full-time member of the faculty and Beneficial Professor of Law. He is an authority on legal philosophy and constitutional law.

Lawrence A. Frolik (1944–), b. Lincoln, NE, of Czech ancestry, received his legal training at Harvard Univ. (J.D., 1969; LL.M., 1972). He has been associated with Univ. of Pittsburgh School of Law, where he advanced from asst. professor to associate professor (1978) and then to full professor (s. 1981) and a distinguished faculty scholar (s. 2009). He is a nationally recognized scholar and lecturer on legal issues of aging, including end-of-life planning. His books include: *Everyday Law for Seniors* (with Whitton; 2012), *Residence Options for Older or Disabled Client* (2008), *The Law of Later-Life Health Care and Decision Making* (2006), *Advising the Elderly or Disabled Client* (with Brown, 2nd ed., 1999), *Elder Law in a Nutshell* (with Kaplan; 6th ed., 2014), and the casebooks, *Elder Law: Cases and Materials* (with Barnes; 5th ed., 2011), and *The Law of Employee Pension and Welfare Benefits* (with Moore; 3rd ed., 2012).

Walter Fischel Gellhorn (1906–1995), b. St. Louis, MO, of Bohemian ancestry on his mother's side, was a legal scholar. He was the longtime Columbia University law professor whose writings, teachings and periodic sallies into the public arena helped shape key elements of modern American law. He was awarded the A.B. from Amherst in 1927 and earned his law degree in 1931 from Columbia, where he was an editor of the *Columbia Law Review*. Following his graduation from law school, he clerked from 1931 to 1932 for then Associate Supreme Court Justice Harlan Fiske Stone, a former Columbia law professor and Dean who later became Chief Justice of the United States. In 1933, he returned to Columbia as assistant professor of law, specializing in teaching legislation and administrative law and, in 1937, he also became a member of the political science faculty. In 1938, he was appointed associate professor of law, became professor in 1945, was named Betts Professor of Law in 1957 and University Professor (Columbia's highest academic rank) in 1973. He was the author of 14 books. In 1966, he wrote *When Americans Complain*, which explored means by which citizens might challenge official actions and failures to act. A companion volume, *Ombudsmen and Others*, appraised the effectiveness of grievance procedures other countries had developed for dealing with citizens' complaints. He was also an eloquent defender of civil rights and free speech. His 1950 book *Security, Loyalty, and Science* was a forceful denunciation of McCarthyism. His *Individual Freedom and Governmental Restraints* (1956), *American Rights: The Constitution in Action* (1960) and *The Freedom to Read* (with others, 1961) were other works that bore on public policies he regarded as threatening. For 25 years, beginning in 1944, he was a member of the Board of Directors of the American Civil Liberties Union; he served also as a director of the NAACP Legal Defense and Educational Fund.

George Ernest Glos (1924–ca. 2013), b. Poznan, Poland, of Czech parents, received his legal education at Charles Univ. (JUDr., 1948), Univ. of Melbourne (LL.B., 1956) and Yale University (LL.M., 1959; J.S.D., 1960). He was prof. of law, St. Mary's Univ. (1964-80); afterwards he served as a legal specialist at Library of Congress (s. 1980). He was also

Professor of Law at Georgetown University Law Center, Washington, DC. He was a specialist on international and comparative law, conflict of laws, legal history.

Ariela Gross (1965-), b. CA, of Czech. ancestry, received her J.D. from Stanford Law School (1994), and her Ph.D. in history from Stanford University (1996). She has been with Univ. of Southern California's Gould School of Law (s. 1996), as prof. of law and history (2001-07), as co-dir. of Center of Law, History and Culture (s. 2004), as John B. and Alice R. Sharp Prof. of Law and history (s. 2007). Her research and writing focus on race and slavery in the United States. She teaches contracts, history of American law, and race and gender in the law. She is the author of *What Blood Won't Tell: A History of Race on Trial in America* (2008).

Samuel R. Gross (ca. 1946-), b. of Czech ancestry, earned a J.D. from the University of California at Berkeley. He holds the position of Thomas and Mabel Long Professor of Law at Univ. of Michigan, where he teaches evidence, criminal procedure, and courses on the use of the social sciences in law. He was a visiting lecturer at Yale Law School and came to the University of Michigan from the Stanford Law School faculty. Prior to that, he was a criminal defense attorney in San Francisco for several years and worked as an attorney with the United Farm Workers Union in California and the Wounded Knee Legal Defense Committee in Nebraska and South Dakota. Gross is best known for his work in false convictions and exonerations, notably the Larry Griffin death penalty case. Samuel Gross has been leading a team of lawyers in statistics and in law that determined the likely number of unjust convictions of prisoners on death row. The study determined that at least 4% of people on death row were and are innocent.

Stella Eugenia Hammerschlag Guerrini, b. Panama, of Czech ancestry, studied law and political science at Panama University. She has experience as labor law counselor and litigator (s. 1981), as arbiter for the corporate sector before the Labor Conciliation and Decision Boards (s. 1985). She was professor of labor law and labor procedure, University Santa Maria La Antigua (1997-2005), professor of civil law and labor law, Universidad Latina de Panama (1993-1997), professor of commercial law and civil law, Panama University (1993-1996).

Brian F. Havel (1958-), b. Ireland, of Czech ancestry, holds Master's degrees in law from University College Dublin and Columbia University Law School, as well as a Master's degree in languages and linguistics from Trinity College Dublin and a Doctoral degree in international and comparative law from Columbia. He was the Wien Fellow in International and Comparative Law at Columbia and received the inaugural Outstanding Achievement Award of the Parker School of International and Comparative Law at Columbia for his work on international air transport deregulation. He practiced transnational corporate and antitrust litigation at Paul Weiss Rifkind Wharton & Garrison in New York City, before joining DePaul faculty in 1994. There he holds the position of Distinguished Research Professor of Law, Director of the International & Comparative Law Program, and Director of the International Aviation Law Institute. From 2011 through 2013, Professor Havel is the Keeley Visiting Fellow at the University of Oxford, Wadham College. His publications have an interdisciplinary focus and include *Beyond Open Skies: A New Regime for International Aviation* (2009), a follow-up to his *In Search of Open Skies: Law and Policy for a New Era in International Aviation* (1997).

Richard W. Havel (1946–), b. Fairmont, MN, of Czech ancestry, was a legal scholar. He was a graduate of University of Notre Dame (B.A., 1968) and received his legal training at Univ. of California, Los Angeles (J.D., 1971). He was admitted to CA State Bar in 1972 and to Utah State Bar in 2006. He is one of the senior members of Sidley Austin's bankruptcy and corporate reorganization practice in Los Angeles. Mr. Havel started his practice in the area of Chapter 11, bankruptcy and corporate reorganization, and is nationally recognized in bankruptcy and corporate reorganization matters. Mr. Havel has represented parties in informal workouts and in Chapter 11 proceedings, and has served as counsel to creditors' committees, Chapter 11 trustees, debtors and other parties of interest. He was instructor in law at Loyola Univ. (1975–80) and taught at the Litigation Inst., San Francisco (1988–93). He was a member of Board of Governors for Financial Lawyers Conference (1991–98, 2002–14) and was Chairman of the Board of Directors for Industrial Development Authority for the City of Los Angeles (1993–98). He was note and comment editor, *UCLA Law Review* (1970–71).

Emil J. Hayek (1924–2013), b. Czech., received his legal training at Charles Univ. He was professor of law, Univ. of Ottawa, Canada. He retired in 1990 but continued to teach part-time until 1999. He received the University of Ottawa's Excellence in Teaching Award in 1985. He retired as Professor Emeritus in 1990 but continued to teach part-time until 1999. He then became Visiting Professor, Faculty of Law, James Cook University of North Queensland, Townsville.

Fred Herzog (1907–2008), b. Prague, Bohemia, received his first law degree in 1931 from the University of Graz. After escaping from Nazism, he immigrated to the US where he obtained his second law degree at University of Iowa (1942). He then moved to Chicago and began a new career as an editor-in-chief of legal periodicals and as a lawyer. In 1947, Fred Herzog began a 25-year association with what would become the Chicago-Kent College of Law, first as a professor, then as an Associate Dean (1947–73), and then as Dean of the Law School. Later he became prof. at John Marshall Law School, Chicago (1974–2008) and its Dean (1976–83).

Frank Edward Horack, Jr. (1907-1957), b. Iowa City, IA, of Czech ancestry, was a legal scholar. He attended the State University of Iowa (A.B., 1926; J.D., 1929). Additionally, he received a LL.M. (1930) and a S.J.D. (1931) from Harvard University. He served as Acting Dean of the Indiana University School of Law, during the 1948-49 academic year. Prior to coming to Indiana, he served on the faculty of the University of West Virginia Law School (1931-1933), as well as serving as both Assistant General Counsel of the U. S. Treasury Department and Adviser to the General Counsel of the Federal Securities Agency in 1934. In 1935, he became a member of the Indiana University School of Law faculty, a position he held until his sudden death in 1957. He was the author of *Cases and Materials on Legislation* (1940), *Statutory Construction* (3 vols., 1943). Ed., *Int. Administrative Code* (1941).

Hugo Claude Horack (1877-1958), b. Belle Plains, IA, of Czech ancestry, was a lawyer and Dean of the Duke University Law School. He completed a Bachelor of Philosophy degree at the State University of Iowa in 1899. He obtained Bachelor of Laws degrees at the State University of Iowa and Harvard in 1900 and 1904, respectively. Horack became professor of law at Univ. of Wisconsin (1903-30); prof. of law at Duke University (1930-47) and Dean (s. 1934). He was an authority in the field of equity, trust and agency law; he made significant contributions to raising national standards of legal education and admission to the Bar.

Mark R. Hornak (1956-), b. Homestead, PA, of Slovak descent, was a lawyer. While in law school, he served as editor-in-chief of the *University of Pittsburgh Law Review* and was inducted into the Order of the Coif. He was an associate, then a partner at the Pittsburgh law firm Buchanan, Ingersoll & Rooney, specializing in civil litigation, labor and employment law, media defense and governmental representation. For 15 years, he also was solicitor of the Sports & Exhibition Authority of Pittsburgh and Allegheny County. Recognized as "Best Lawyer in America," as one of the "Top 50 Lawyers" in Pittsburgh, and as Pittsburgh's 2012 Lawyer of the Year in labor law. From 1989 to 1993, he served as an Adjunct Professor of Law at the University of Pittsburgh, teaching employment litigation.

Robert Emil Hudec (1934-2003), b. Cleveland, OH, of Slovak ancestry, was a legal scholar. He attended Kenyon College (B.A., 1965) and Cambridge University (M.A., 1958). After Law School at Yale, where he served as editor-in-chief of the *Yale Law Journal*, he became a clerk for Justice Potter Stewart of the U.S. Supreme Court from 1961 to 1963. He then became asst. gen counsel., Office Sp. Rep. for Trade Negotiations, Executive Offices (1963-65); Assoc. prof. law, Yale U. Law School, (1966-92); prof. law, University of Minnesota Law School, Minneapolis (1972-2000), Melvin C. Steen, prof. of law (1986-2000); prof. of law, Tufts University (2000-03). He was the author of *The GATT Legal System and World Trade*

Diplomacy (1975), *Developing Countries in the GATT Legal system* (1987), *Enforcing International Trade Law* (1999). He was an authority on trade law and the GATT.

Gerhart Husserl (1893-1973), b. Halle, Germany, of Moravian ancestry (son of Edmund Husserl), was a legal scholar and philosopher. Husserl became a Professor of Law at the University of Kiel in 1926. He was dismissed due to the Law for the Restoration of the Professional Civil Service in 1933, and eventually immigrated to the United States. He became prof. of laws at the National Univ., Washington, DC (1940-48). He was a founding member of *Philosophy and Phenomenological Research*.

Ann Janega (c. 1978–), of Slovak parents, was a lawyer. As provincial Vice President of Canadian Manufacturers and Exporters, Ann Janega works with businesses, consumers, and non-governmental organizations to create and sustain economic prosperity for the community. Because of her commitment to helping businesses succeed, she was recognized as a Champion for Women in Business. Ann Janega is a former RCMP constable and the former Director of Public Affairs at Dalhousie University in Halifax.

John Jay (1817-1894), b. New York, NY, desc. Fr. Frederick Philipse, a lawyer by profession, as a student, was a manager of NY Young Men's Anti-Slavery Society. As a lawyer, he was active in seven-years struggle to procure admission of St. Philip's Church (black) to Protestant Episcopal Convention. After enactment of Fugitive-Slave Law (1850), he acted as counsel for many black fugitives.

William Jay (1789-1858), b. New York City, desc. f. Frederick Philipse, served as Judge of the Court of Westchester Co., NY, which office he held until 1843, when he was removed through the influence of pro slavery Democrats. He was active in championing the cause of emancipation, often agitating for the abolition of the slave trade, twenty-two years before Congressional action brought it about. He helped establish the NYC Anti-slavery Society and largely through his efforts, a National Anti-Slavery Convention in Philadelphia inaugurated a campaign. He opposed the plan to colonize the former slaves in Africa, declaring that those who favored that plan were not moved by 'the precepts of the Gospel' but by 'prejudice against an unhappy portion of the human family.'

Charles Raper Jonas (1904-1988), b. Lincolnton, NC, of Czech ancestry, having been the son of the notable Charles Andrew Jonas of Racine, WI. He graduated from Lincolnton High School in 1921; University of North Carolina at Chapel Hill (A.B., 1925), and from the same university Law School (J.D., 1928). He was admitted to the Bar in 1927 and commenced practice in Lincolnton, N.C., in 1928; assistant United States attorney for the western district of North Carolina, 1931-1933; member of the North Carolina National Guard since 1927; entered active duty in the Army of the United States as a captain,

September 21, 1940, and was separated from the service April 20, 1946, as a Lieutenant Colonel in the Judge Advocate General's Corps; president, North Carolina Bar Association, 1946-1947; member, Board of Law Examiners, 1948-1950; resumed the practice of law; delegate to the Republican National Convention in 1952; elected as a Republican to the Eighty-third and to the nine succeeding Congresses (January 3, 1953-January 3, 1973); was not a candidate for reelection in 1972 to the Ninety-third Congress; was a resident of Lincolnton, N.C., until his death there September 28, 1988.

Felix Kaufmann (1895-1949), b. Vienna, of Bohemia ancestry, was a philosopher of law. Kaufmann studied jurisprudence and philosophy in Vienna. From 1922 to 1938, he was a Privatdozent there. During this time, Kaufmann was associated with the Vienna Circle. In 1938, the conditions for Jewish scholars became too hard and he left for the USA. There he taught until his death as a law professor, in the Graduate Faculty of the New York School for Social Research. Kaufmann also aided fellow Austrian emigres in need of assistance during the pre-war years when the situation became dire for Jewish academics and scholars in Germany and Austria. In 1936, he produced a book on the methodology of the social sciences. After moving to the United States, he was invited to write a similar book in English, but what he produced (1944) was significantly different, under the influence of Dewey's *Logic: The Theory of Inquiry*. The original book was translated over 70 years later (2014).

Otto Michael Kaus (1920-1996), b. Vienna, the son of the novelist Gina Weiner (1893-1985) of Czech ancestry and Otto F. Kaus, was an American lawyer and judge from the State of California. He graduated from the University of California at Los Angeles in 1942 with a B.A., and then joined the U.S. Army, where he served until 1945. Following his discharge, he graduated from Loyola Law School in 1949 and was admitted to the State Bar that year. He then joined the law firm of Chase, Rotchford, Downen & Drukker, where he practiced for 11 years and became a partner. Together with his wife, civic activist Peggy A. Huttenback, they had a son.

Hans Kelsen (1881-1973), b. Prague, Bohemia, was a jurist, legal philosopher and political philosopher. Kelsen is most famous for his studies on law and especially for his idea known as the pure theory of the law. He studied at several universities, including Berlin, Heidelberg, and Vienna. He received a Doctor of Laws degree from Vienna in 1906 and began teaching at the school in 1911. He taught public law and jurisprudence at Vienna until 1930, when he moved to Germany to teach at the University of Cologne (1929-33). There he taught international law and jurisprudence and served as Dean for two years. With the rise of the Nazi government, he left Germany and emigrated to Switzerland in 1933. He taught at the Graduate Institute of International Studies of the University of

Geneva until 1940. He accepted a position as lecturer at the Harvard University Law School the same year and relocated to the United States. Later in 1940, he accepted a teaching position at the University of California at Berkeley. He remained at Berkeley until his retirement in 1952. Kelsen received acclaim for authoring many publications, including *General Theory of Law and State* (1945), *The Law of the United Nations* (1950-51), *Principles of International Law* (1952), and *What Is Justice?* (1957).

Guido Kisch (1889-1985), b. Prague, Bohemia, was a jurist and legal historian. He received his legal training at Univ. of Prague. Former prof. of legal history and civil and business law, Univ. of Koenigsberg (1920-22); Univ. of Halle (1922-24); Univ. of Prague (1924-25); and Halle (1925-33), Dean of law fac. (1932-36). After his dismissal by the Nazi regime, he taught history at the Jewish Theological Seminary in Breslau. In 1934, he came to US and became vis. prof. of Jewish history, Hebrew Univ. (1937-50), res. prof. (s. 1950). He was an authority on history of law, legal institutions, legal and social status of Jews.

Karen Knop (1960-2022), b. Halifax, Canada, of Czech ancestry, holds graduate degrees in law from Columbia Univ. (LL.M., 1990) and the Univ. of Toronto (S.J.D., 1999) and degrees in mathematics and law from Dalhousie Univ. (B.Sc., 1982; LL.B., 1986). She became asst. prof. of law at the Univ. of Toronto in 1993, was promoted to assoc. prof. (1999-2005) and full prof. (s. 2006) and served as editor of the *Univ. of Toronto Law Journal* (2007-12). She has been a visiting prof. at Georgetown Univ. (2011) and also taught at the Univ. of Melbourne (2005, 2013). She specializes in international law, and her book *Diversity and Self-Determination in International Law* (Cambridge Univ. Press, 2002) was awarded a Certificate of Merit by the Am. Society of International Law.

Albert Kocourek (1875-1952), b. Louisville, KY, of Czech ancestry, Univ. of Michigan educated lawyer (LL.B., 1897), was associated with Northwestern Univ. (s. 1907), as prof. of jurisprudence (s. 1914). He was an authority on jurisprudence and philosophy of law. He was editor-in-chief of the *Illinois Law Review*.

Thomas Frank Konop (1879-1964), b. Franklin Twp., WI, of Czech ancestry, was a lawyer and US Congressman from Wisconsin. He received his legal education at Univ. of Nebraska (LL.B., 1904). He was admitted to the Bar in 1904 and commenced practice in Kewaunee, Wisconsin. He served as district attorney of Kewaunee County, Wisconsin from 1905 to 1911. He moved to Green Bay, Wisconsin, and practiced law from 1915 to 1917. Konop was elected as a member of the Democratic Party to the Sixty-second, Sixty-third, and Sixty-fourth Congresses (March 4, 1911-March 3, 1917). He then moved to Milwaukee, Wisconsin, and continued the practice of law in 1922 and 1923. He became prof. of law at Univ. of Notre Dame Coll. of Law (1923-50) and Dean (1923-41).

Frank Kopecky (1942-2019), b. Berwyn, IL, of Czech ancestry, attended University of Illinois at Urbana-Champaign (B.A., 1964; J.D., 1967). He was prof. of legal studies, Univ. of Illinois at Springfield (UIS). He was part of a Center for Legal Studies team that trained every new probation officer in every county except Cook. That meant almost 400 people a year come to UIS for 40 hours of training and return home better equipped to work in the criminal justice system. Professor Kopecky helped get this Probation Training Project started in 1975, the same year he joined what was then Sangamon State University. He was also the founding director of the Center for Legal Studies. Professor Kopecky had a joint appointment in the Institute's Center for Legal Studies and the Legal Studies Program.

Rande W. Kostal (1957-), b. Hamilton, Ont., Canada, of Czech ancestry, received his legal training at Univ. Western Ontario (L.L.B., 1981), and additional training in history at McMaster Univ. (M.A., 1983) and in modern legal history at Oxford Univ. (Ph.D., 1990). He has been a member of the Bar of Ontario (s. 1984). He is also associated with the Univ. of Western Ontario (s. 1988), where he holds the position of Professor of Law and History. He is the author of Law *and English Railway Capitalism* (1995); *A Jurisprudence of Power* (2005); *Laying Down the Law: The Legal Reconstruction of Germany and Japan* (2019).

Daniel Jerome Kucera (1939-), b. Hinsdale, IL, of Czech ancestry, graduated from Yale University (B.S., 1961) and studied law at Harvard Univ. (J.D., 1964) and then business administration at DePaul University (M.B.A., 1966). He has been in legal practice in Chicago (s. 1964), being a managing partner at Chapman & Cutler, Chicago (s. 1964). He had an academic appointment as prof. of law, John Marshall Law School (1966-82).

Arthur Lenhoff (orig. Löwy) (1885-1965), b. Teplice-Šanov, Bohemia, was a legal scholar. He was Univ. of Vienna educated lawyer (Dr. Jur., 1908). He was a highly successful lawyer in Austria, a judge of the Austrian Constitutional Court, and a prolific author. He arrived in the US in 1938 after a narrow escape from Austria. In 1939, he started over as a librarian at the Law School in Buffalo while at the same time undertaking to study for the New York Bar examination. He became prof. of law at Buffalo Law School (1939-57). He was an authority on labor law, comparative law, Roman law, conflict of laws.

Nathan Levy, Jr. (1923-1994), b. Vicksburg, MS, of Bohemian ancestry, was an attorney and a legal scholar. He graduated from Mississippi State University in Aeronautical Engineering. He served for two and a half years in the U.S. Army with active duty in the Philippines during World War II. He continued in the Army Reserves for 20 years, retiring with the rank of Major. He graduated from the University of Mississippi (Ole Miss) Law School, where he was a member of the *Law Review*. After graduation he practiced law in

Vicksburg, Miss., for seven years. He received a fellowship from Yale University, where he earned a Doctorate degree in Law. Dr. Levy joined the faculty of the University of Connecticut School of Law in 1956 and retired as Professor Emeritus of Law in 1992. At the time of his death, he was counsel with the law firm of Brown & Welsh, P.C., Meriden. Dr. Levy was the author of *the Bankruptcy Handbook*, published by Little, Brown & Co., and he was also a contributor to many law journals. He was a frequent lecturer for Continuing Legal Education for the State of Connecticut.

Theodore Macejko, Jr. (1938–2011), b. Youngstown, OH, of Slovak descent, was a lawyer. He practiced in Struthers and Youngstown, OH, with his father, in Macejko & Macejko law firm, specializing in the field of general civil trial practice in all courts, insurance products liability, medical legal, corporate, real estate, municipal and probate law, family law, criminal law, insurance subrogation and litigation. He served as assistant Mahoning County prosecutor (1972–76, 1984–88). He was president of the Mahoning County Bar Association and served also as a visiting Judge in the Struthers courts on various occasions.

Maria Lenhoff Marcus (1933–2022), b. Vienna of Bohemian ancestry is a lawyer. In the US in 1938, she graduated from Oberlin College (B.A., 1964) and studied law at Yale University Law School (J.D., 1977). She has been associated with Fordham University (since 1978, and she has held the position of McLaughlin Professor of Law (since 1997). She was married to the lawyer Norman Marcus (1932–2008).

Jaro Mayda (1918–2005), b. Brno, Czech., studied law at Masaryk Univ. (JUDr., 1945) and Univ. of Chicago (J.D., 1957). He became prof. of law and public policy, Univ. of Puerto Rico, Rio Piedras (1958–85), as res. prof. (1985–89). He was an authority on jurisprudence, international law, public policy.

Victor Morawetz (1859–1938), b. Baltimore, MD, of Bohemian ancestry, was a graduate of Harvard Univ. and received the honorary degree of A.M. from Columbia Univ. He was in the practice of law, chiefly as counsel and attorney for railroads and other corporations. He was general counsel and chairman of the executive committee of the Atchison, Topeka and Santa Fe Railway Co. and a director of Norfolk and Western Railway Co. and the National Bank of Commerce of New York. He was one of the best authorities on the trust law and a financial expert. He belonged to a number of Clubs. He was the author of *Law of Private Corporations* (1882), *Banking and Currency Problems in the US* (1909) and *Elements of the Law of Contracts* (1927).

Jiří George Neuspiel (1924–2006), b. Prague, Czech., immigrated to North America at the age of 13. George enlisted in the Canadian Army at the age of 16 and served overseas from 1941-1945. He was a strong supporter of the anti-fascism fight and was a distinguished Officer of

Intelligence de-Nazifying and arresting war criminals throughout his career. Subsequently, he studied law at Univ. of London and Queens University which awarded him his law degree and became an internationally respected and renowned professor of law at Carleton University, Ottawa, Canada. Although he retired in 2004, after 37 years of teaching, as Professor Emeritus he remained an active participant and advisor in the International Legal human rights community. He was a specialist on public law, comparative constitutional law of federal states, international law of treaties and peace-making.

Karen Appel Oshman (née Appel) (1960–), b. NYC, the daughter of English scholar Alfred Appel and Loyola Law School Dean Nina Schick Appel, the latter being a native of Prague, Czech., is a lawyer, with a J.D. degree from Yale University (1985). After completing both college and law school at Yale University, she clerked for Judge Carolyn King on the Fifth Circuit Court of Appeals. She is a member of the Texas State Bar and practices in Houston, where she has resided s. 1985. She is associated with Susman & Godfrey LLP, of which she is a partner. She represents both plaintiffs and defendants in a variety of commercial matters, including securities litigation, breach of contract, fraud, and tortious interference with contract. She is married to the lawyer Gene J. Oshman and they have two children.

Vratislav Pěchota (1928–2005), b. Dobruška, Czech., studied at Charles Univ. (JUDr., 1951; CSc./Ph.D., 1962). After coming to the US, he was associated with Columbia Univ., as senior research scholar and adjunct professor of law and assoc. director of Parker School of Foreign and Comparative Law. His research interests were in the area of international law, comparative law, civil and commercial law. He was the author of *The Quiet Approach: A Study of the Good Offices Exercised by the U.N. Secretary-General in the Cause of Peace* (1972), *The World Arbitration Reporter* (1987), *Central and Eastern European Legal Materials* (1990), *Legal Materials: Russia and the Republics* (1990). He was also editor-in-chief of *American Review of International Arbitration* and the *Journal of East European Law*. According to his peers, his voluminous work on arbitration is unparalleled in breadth and intricacy, and in doing so, Vrat, as he was known among his colleagues, made a monumental contribution to the study of arbitration. He authored some 32 books.

Charles (aka Karel) Pergler (1882–1954), b. Liblin, Bohemia, as a Czech-American lawyer, journalist, diplomat and politician. He was a Czechoslovak First Republic Ambassador to the United States and Japan. He moved to the United States at a young age. When his father died, the family moved back to Bohemia, where Pergler got active in the socialist and nationalist movements supporting Czechoslovak independence from Austria-Hungary. He went back to the United States in 1903, studying law at Kent State, and afterwards practicing law in Iowa till 1917. He served as the secretary of Professor Thomas Garrigue Masaryk from May 1918 in America. He became Ambassador to the United States after Czechoslovak independence in 1918, then becoming ambassador to Japan in 1920. He was dismissed from the foreign service in 1921, with his pension taken away, because of fraud at the Tokyo Embassy. He returned to the United States, obtaining a Master of Laws degree from American University. He would return to Czechoslovakia in 1929, where he worked together with Radola Gajda and Jiří Stříbrný against Edvard Beneš, and got elected to parliament. In February 1931, he had to relinquish his post, because issues were raised over his citizenship. He returned to America and became Prof. of constitutional law and jurisprudence and Dean at the National Univ. School of Law, Washington, DC (1936-46). He was an authority on international law, constitutional law and jurisprudence. He was also a lecturer at Catholic University of America and American University in constitutional law. Charles Pergler wrote a number of books during his lifetime, most of which were on Czechoslovakian history or international law: *The Czechslovak State* (1919), *Towards the National State (1920?), America in the Struggle for Czechoslovak Independence (1926)* and *The American Constitutional System* (1929) all in Prague; and *Judicial Interpretation of International Law in the United States* (1928) in the US. He died in Washington, D.C., in 1954.

Alexandra Perloff-Giles (1989-), b. NYC, the daughter of Carey Perloff (1959-) of Czech ancestry, and the lawyer Anthony Giles, works at the intersection of art and law. She holds a B.A. in History of Art and Architecture from Harvard College, a Master's in Contemporary Art and its Exhibition from the Université de Paris-Sorbonne, and a J.D. from Yale Law School. Perloff-Giles currently serves as a litigation associate at Gibson, Dunn & Crutcher. Previously, she served as the First Amendment Fellow at *The New York Times*. She is also actively involved in the art world and has curated exhibitions at the Goethe Institute in New York, Main's d'Oeuvres in Saint-Ouen, and the Palais de Tokyo in Paris. She also helped develop the database of works subject to national repatriation claims called the Cultural Property Case Resource and organized the conference "The Legal Medium: New Encounters of Art and Law" at Yale Law School.

David Petrasek (1961-2020), b. Toronto, Canada, of Czech father, received his legal training at York Univ. (LL.B., 1987) and at London School of Economics, Univ. of London (LL.M., 1988). David Petrasek is Associate Professor at the Graduate School of Public and International Affairs, University of Ottawa. Formerly Special Adviser to the Secretary-General of Amnesty International, David Petrasek has worked extensively on human rights, humanitarian and conflict resolution issues, including for Amnesty International (1990-96), for the Office of the UN High Commissioner for Human Rights (1997-98), for the International Council on Human Rights Policy (1998-02), and as Director of Policy at the HD Centre (2003-07). He has taught international human rights and/or humanitarian law courses at the Osgoode Hall Law School, the Raoul Wallenberg Institute at Lund University, Sweden, and at Oxford University. David has also worked as a consultant or adviser to several NGOs and UN agencies. His research interests are in the area of human rights and armed conflict, human rights in Canadian foreign policy, strengthening international human rights law, human rights and poverty and conflict mediation in theory and practice.

Michael T. Petrik (1957–), b. Chicago, IL, of Czech ancestry, graduated from Eastern Illinois in 1979 with a BS in management and a BA in economics. Upon receiving a law degree from Duke Law School (J.D., 1983), he joined the law firm of Alston & Bird LLP. He was elected a partner in 1990. He chaired the Alston's State & Local Tax Practice Group from 1998 through 2013. Mike Petrik concentrates his practice on sophisticated, multistate tax planning and disputes for businesses, including income tax, franchise tax, sales/use tax and other state and local taxes. He maintains a national administrative tax dispute and negotiation practice, including audit appeals, the negotiation of special filing or apportionment methods and voluntary disclosure 'amnesty' applications. Mr. Petrik also has extensive experience in developing and implementing new corporate structures designed to achieve multistate tax efficiencies. He has held the position of instructor at Georgia State University where he taught a course on state and local taxation. Previously, he was an instructor at Atlanta Law School where he taught courses on constitutional law and federal income taxation. Mr. Petrik is listed in Who's Who in America, Georgia Super Lawyers, The Best Lawyers in America, and by Chambers USA as one of America's Leading Tax Lawyers. He also serves on the Board of Governors of the Georgia Chamber of Commerce where he chairs the Tax & Finance Policy Committee.

George Petschek (1872–1947), b. Kolín, Bohemia, to a famous Bohemian-Jewish industrial family, was a legal scholar. In 1890, Petschek began studying law at the then Karl Ferdinands University in Prague, from where he graduated in 1894. Petschek received his Doctorate in Prague in 1896 and subsequently took up employment in the Prussian civil service. In parallel to his employment at the Court in Halle an der Saale, he began studying for a habilitation. In 1902, Petschek habilitated on the subject of "Austrian civil court proceedings" in Prague and, in 1904, was appointed an extraordinary titular professor. Since 1907, Petschek worked as an associate professor at the University in Galician Czernowitz. After his habilitation again in 1920, he took over the professorship for civil procedural law at the University of Vienna, where he was a full professor until 1938. After the annexation of Austria by Nazi Germany, Georg Petschek fled to the United States in 1938, where he worked at the Harvard Law School until his death.

Louis Heilprin Pollak (1922–2012), b. New York, NY, of Bohemian ancestry, was an attorney, jurist, educator and legal scholar. He received his A.B. magna cum laude from Harvard College in 1943 and his LL.B. from the Yale Law School in 1948, where he was editor of the *Yale Law Journal*. After completing his undergraduate studies at Harvard,

Pollak entered the United States Army in 1943, during World War II. The war ended before he would be deployed outside of the United States. Pollak served as a law clerk to Justice Wiley Rutledge of the US Supreme Court following graduation from law school. After completing his clerkship, from 1949 to 1951, Pollak worked at the law firm now known as Paul, Weiss, Rifkind, Wharton & Garrison. He then served in the US Department of State as special assistant to Ambassador-at-large Philip C. Jessup until 1953. Thereafter, Pollak worked as assistant counsel for the Amalgamated Clothing Workers of America. In 1955, Pollak joined the faculty of the Yale Law School, where he would remain until 1974. He served as Dean from 1965 to 1970. In 1974, he moved to the Univ. of Pennsylvania Law School, becoming dean the following year. In 1978, he left the University when he was appointed to the bench. Until his death, Pollak remained an adjunct member of the Penn Law faculty and taught there regularly. Beginning in 1950, Pollak provided assistance to the NAACP Legal Defense Fund. He worked actively on Brown v. Board of Education. Because he was then working for the State Department, he was not listed on the briefs in the Supreme Court.

Adolf Procházka (1900–1970), b. Napajedla, Moravia, was a legal scholar and politician. He studied law at Masaryk Univ. (JUDr., 1924). He was a member of the Bar of Czechoslovakia (1929–38). He was appointed private Docent of Civil Law at Masaryk Univ. (1929–34), assoc. professor of civil procedure (1934–45) and full professor (s. 1945). He developed his theory of law and authored several books, including *Fundamentals of Intertemporal Law* (1928), *The Legal Case of Dr. Charles Pergler* (1931), *Cause of Action* (1932), and *The Making of Law and its Finding* (1937). He was active in the Czechoslovak underground movement (P.U.) (1939–40). He then spent the war years in Paris and London, where he served as legal advisor to the Prime Minister of the Czechoslovak Government in Exile and chairman of its Legal Council. He returned to Czechoslovakia with President Beneš and was a member of the Czech National Assembly and Minister of Public Health (1945–48). After the communist takeover in February 1948, he abdicated from government, left Czechoslovakia and, after staying in Germany, France and England, entered the US. He became chairman of the Executive Committee of the Christian Czechoslovak Democratic Union of Central Europe and was active member of the Council of Free Czechoslovakia and General Committee of Assembly of Captive European Nations. He was the husband of Helena Koželuhová.

Ernest Aloysius Raba (1912–2007), b. San Antonio, TX, of Bohemian parents, was a lawyer and a Dean of the St. Mary's University School of Law. He graduated *summa cum laude* from St. Mary's University, Texas in 1934. He then received his law degree from St. Mary's University School of Law in 1937, graduating at the top of his class. After involvement in private practice, Raba taught as an Adjunct Law Professor at St. Mary's University School of Law (s. 1938), as Professor of Constitutional Law (s. 1946), as Dean (s. 1946) and Vice

President (1963–65). In 1942, he was inducted into the Army. Soon after, he was accepted into the first Judge Advocate General's School for service members at the University of Michigan Law School. Following the JAG program, Raba served in the JAGC 8th Service Command Headquarters in Dallas. He later served as Staff Judge Advocate at Fort Polk, Louisiana. He was an authority on constitutional law.

Walter Brandeis Raushenbush (1928–2023), b. Madison, WI, of Bohemian ancestry, is attorney, educator, legal scholar. He received his A.B. magna cum laude from Harvard College (1950) and his law degree with high honors from the University of Wisconsin (1953). He was an Air Force lawyer from 1953 to 1956, and then a general practice lawyer in Madison, Wis., until he joined the University of Wisconsin Law School faculty in 1958. He was emeritus professor there, where he continued to teach full-time each fall semester. He was a visiting professor at the University of San Diego School of Law from 1987 to 1988 and from 1992 to 1994. His primary teaching interests have been property, real estate transactions and, more recently, professional responsibility. Professor Raushenbush has been active for 30 years in the National Law School Admission Council and was president of the council from 1980 to 1982. Since 1986, he has served as a member of the real property question-drafting committee for the Multistate Bar Examination.

Joseph Redlich (1869–1936), b Hodonín, Moravia, was a jurist, politician, educator and legal scholar. He received training at Univ. Vienna (dipl., in 1915). He made a thorough study of American instruction in law, at the request of the Carnegie Foundation for the Advancement of Teaching. In 1929, he was appointed Fairchild Prof. of Comparative Law at Harvard Univ. and made head of Harvard's newly founded Institute of Comparative Law but, in 1931, he returned to Europe.

John (Glover) Roberts, Jr. (1955–), b. Buffalo, NY, the son of Rosemary Podrasky (1929-2019) of Slovak descent, and John Glover 'Jack' Roberts Sr., is an American lawyer and jurist serving as the 17th chief justice of the United States since 2005. He studied history at Harvard University and then attended Harvard Law School, where he was managing editor of the *Harvard Law Review*. He served as a law clerk for Circuit Judge Henry Friendly and then-associate justice William Rehnquist before taking a position in the attorney general's office during the Reagan administration. He went on to serve the Reagan administration and the George H. W. Bush administration in the Department of Justice and the Office of the White House Counsel, during which he was nominated by George H. W. Bush to the U.S. Court of Appeals for the D.C. Circuit, but no vote on his nomination was held. Roberts then spent 14 years in private law practice. Roberts became a federal judge in 2003, when President George W. Bush appointed him to the U.S. Court of Appeals for the D.C. Circuit. In 2005, Bush nominated Roberts to the Supreme Court, initially to be an associate justice to fill the vacancy left by the retirement of Justice Sandra Day O'Connor. Chief Justice William Rehnquist died shortly afterward, however, before Roberts's Senate confirmation hearings had begun. Bush then withdrew Robert's nomination and instead nominated him to become Chief Justice, choosing Samuel Alito to replace O'Connor.

Josef Rohlík (1940-), b. Brno, Czech., received his law degree (JUDr.) in 1966 and CSc./Ph.D. in 1968, both at Charles Univ. He also received LL.M. degree from Columbia Univ. (1969). He has been associated with Saint Louis Univ. School of Law (s. 1971), as professor (s. 1977), as professor emeritus (s. 2013). He was a commercial tribunal administrator with the American Arbitration Association in New York City before joining Saint Louis University. He specializes in international law, private international law, and arbitration. Much of his scholarship concentrates on international trade and economic relations.

James B. Sales (1934–2023), b. Weimer, TX, of Czech ancestry, graduated from Univ. of Texas (B.S., 1956) and received training in law at Univ. of Texas School of Law (LL.B., 1960), where he was associate editor of the *Texas Law Review* and a member of the Order of the Coif. After graduation, he joined Fulbright & Jaworski. In 1979, he took over as head of the firm's Litigation Department and remained in that position for over 20 years until his retirement. Throughout his 52-year career, his practice had concentrated on litigation of all types, with an emphasis on tort-related litigation matters. For the last 20 years, he has devoted his practice to the defense of a variety of complex litigation liability cases. He has handled and tried numerous general liability, product liability, commercial liability and business-related cases in both the state and federal courts. In 1980, Mr. Sales was elected as president of the Houston Bar Association. While serving as president of the Houston Bar Association, he envisioned a program that would provide delivery of legal services to the working poor in the greater Houston area who otherwise would be denied access to the justice system. These were the large group of people whose wages exceeded the federal poverty guidelines, but who could not afford an attorney to gain access to the justice system. With the support of the Houston Bar Association's Board of Directors, he launched the Houston Volunteer Lawyers Program. In 1988, Mr. Sales was elected as president of the State Bar of Texas. As president, he led the State Bar in adopting a mass disaster plan to prohibit improper solicitation and harassment of victims in disaster situations. He also led a drive to restructure and approve a new Texas Disciplinary Rules of Professional Conduct. He also acted to establish and implement the Texas Lawyer Assistance Program which today is a network of lawyer intervention programs designed to assist and help rehabilitate substance-impaired attorneys in the state. In 2004, the Supreme Court of Texas appointed him to Chair the Texas Access to Justice Commission which the Court had established in 2001 to coordinate the delivery of legal services to poor and low-income Texans. As Chair, he was responsible for promoting and coordinating the delivery of legal services to poor and low-income citizens throughout the state of Texas. In addition to authoring numerous law reviews and journal articles, he is co-author of *Texas Tort and Remedies*, a 6-volume treatise, co-author of the treatise *The Law of Strict Tort Liability in Texas* and is the author of the treatise *Product Liability Law in Texas*.

Andrew Schapiro (1963–), b. Chicago, IL, son of Raya Czerner (1934–2007), a native of Prague, Czech., and the physician Soloman Schapiro, is an American attorney and diplomat. He attended Yale University, graduating with a B.A. in history, magna cum laude, in 1985. Schapiro then attended Merton College, Oxford on a Marshall Scholarship, earning an M.A. in philosophy, politics, and economics, with first-class honors, in 1987. He then entered Harvard Law School, where he served on the *Law Review* with Barack Obama. Schapiro was awarded a J.D. degree in 1990. Schapiro served as a law clerk for Judge Richard Posner of the United States Court of Appeals for the Seventh Circuit in Chicago, and then clerked for U.S. Supreme Court Justice Harry Blackmun, in Washington, DC. Following his clerkships, Schapiro spent five years as a public-interest lawyer in the office of the Federal Public Defender in New York City, defending individuals charged with federal crimes but could not afford to hire their own attorney. As a partner at two global law firms—first Mayer Brown and then Quinn Emanuel Urquhart & Sullivan—he specialized in intellectual property and commercial litigation and appeals. He then served as US Ambassador to the Czech Republic from September 30, 2014, to January 20, 2017. He was nominated by President Barack Obama on March 6, 2014, and confirmed by the Senate in July 2014. He was sworn in on August 14, 2014 and presented his credentials to President Miloš Zeman on September 30, 2014. Following diplomatic service, he returned to Quinn Emanuel Urquhart & Sullivan, again as a partner.

Frederick Schenk (1949–), b. Bronx, NY, the son of the Holocaust survivors, Elsa Roth (1917–2012) from Užhorod, Czech. and Sidney Schenk, is a noted trial lawyer. He has been with Casey Gerry for more than 35 years and achieved the largest verdict ever in San Diego against an asbestos manufacturer – Owens Corning Fiberglass – obtaining a $2.4 million verdict in punitive damages as well as economic losses. In addition, he is a specialist in auto collision litigation and coauthor of the LexisNexis California Automobile Litigation Handbook. Over the years, Schenk has received numerous awards and honors for his work – including recognition as an Outstanding Trial Lawyer from the Consumer Attorneys of San Diego, and twice has been recognized by Best Lawyers as San Diego's Trial Lawyer of the Year in the area of mass torts in both 2014 and 2018.

Lynn Schenk (1945–), b. The Bronx, NY, the daughter of the Holocaust survivors, Elsa Roth (1917–2012) from Užhorod, Czech. and Sidney Schenk, is an American politician and lawyer from California. She received her B.A. from U.C.L.A. in 1967 and her J.D. from the

University of San Diego School of Law in 1970. Schenk worked as a White House Fellow, under Vice Presidents Nelson A. Rockefeller and Walter Mondale, as a deputy attorney general in the office of the California Attorney General, and as an attorney for San Diego Gas and Electric. California Governor Jerry Brown appointed her deputy secretary, and later secretary, of the California Business, Transportation and Housing Agency from 1977 until 1983. After Brown decided not to run for a third term, she returned to private practice. In 1992, Schenk won the Democratic nomination to run for Congress from California's 49th congressional district, covering most of San Diego. Schenk won, becoming the first Democrat to represent the area in 40 years. After serving in Congress, Schenk served in various positions in the California state government under California Governor Gray Davis, including Chief of Staff, from 1998 until Davis was recalled in 2003. Currently, Schenk practices corporate law. She sits on the boards of various organizations including The Scripps Research Institute Board of Trustees, and the California High-Speed Rail Authority. Lynn Schenk was nominated and inducted into the Women's Hall of Fame in 2012 for the title of Trailblazer, meaning, women who have paved the way for other women, or were the first in their field.

Randol Schoenberg (1966–), b. Santa Monica, CA, of Czech ancestry (the grandson of the composers Arnold Schoenberg and Eric Zeisl), graduated from Princeton University with a Bachelor of Arts in Mathematics in 1988 and a certificate in European Cultural Studies. In 1991, he received his Juris Doctor degree from the University of Southern California. He was the co-founding partner of Burris, Schoenberg & Alden, LLP, where he handled a number of complex business litigation matters, specializing in cases involving looted art and the recovery of property stolen by the Nazi authorities during the Holocaust. He won the return of five famous Klimt paintings for his client, Maria Altmann. Schoenberg is widely known as one of the central figures of the 2015 film *Woman in Gold*, which depicted the case of Maria Altmann against the government of Austria. Schoenberg is portrayed by Ryan Reynolds. In 2007, Mr. Schoenberg received the California Lawyer Attorney of the Year award for outstanding achievement in the field of litigation. He also received the 2006 Jurisprudence Award from the Anti-Defamation League and the Justice Louis D. Brandeis Award from the American Jewish Congress. Mr. Schoenberg has served as President of the Los Angeles Museum of the Holocaust since 2005, during which time the museum constructed its new building in Pan Pacific Park.

Eva Segert-Tauger (née Segert) (1958–), b. Prague, Czech., was trained as a political scientist at UCLA and later as a lawyer at West Virginia Univ. (J.D., 2002). After initially teaching political science at West Virginia Univ., after receiving her J.D. degree, she was in solo law practice in Virginia (2007–11), with a focus on family law, social security disability and immigration. Since then, she has been engaged as a CLA attorney at Legal Aid of West Virginia. She is married to Mark B. Tauger (1954–).

Michael P. Seng (1942–), b. Cedar Rapids, IA, of Czech ancestry, received his JD degree from the Notre Dame Law School in 1967. He served as a judicial law clerk for Judge John Kilkenny on the United States District Court in Oregon from 1967-68, was an associate attorney at Jenner & Block in Chicago from 1968-72 and was the directing attorney of the Land of Lincoln Legal Assistance Foundation in Cairo, Illinois from 1972-76. He is a professor of law at the John Marshall Law School, a private independent law school in Chicago, Illinois. He is the co-executive director of the Law School Fair Housing Legal Support Center and Clinic, which is a unique law school program that devotes itself exclusively to housing discrimination issues. He is the director of International Programs, where he coordinates the activities of international students at the John Marshall Law School. He is also the director of the John Marshall Law School Czech/Slovak Legal Institute, which has been engaged in exchange programs in the Czech and Slovak Republics since 1993. He has co-authored books on *Eyewitness Testimony and European Community Law.*

Brian Soucek (1976–), b. Plantation, FL, of Czech ancestry, is an Acting Professor of Law at Univ. of California at Davis. He is a graduate of Boston College (B.A., Philosophy and Economics), Columbia University (Ph.D., Philosophy), where he was awarded the Core Preceptor Prize for his teaching and Yale Law School (J.D.), where he was comments editor for the *Yale Law Journal*, a Coker Fellow in Procedure and won the Munson Prize for his work in the school's immigration clinic. Prior to law school, Soucek taught for three years in the Humanities Collegiate Division and Philosophy Department at the University of Chicago, where he was Collegiate assistant professor and co-chair of the Society of Fellows in the Liberal Arts. After law school, he clerked for the late Mark R. Kravitz, US District Judge for the District of Connecticut, and the Hon. Guido Calabresi of the Second Circuit Court of Appeals. In addition to book chapters and articles in the philosophy of art, Soucek's legal publications include work on asylum law, on due process values embodied in contemporary courthouse art, and, most recently, on unpublished appellate opinions and the precedential force they gain by being copied and pasted. He is currently completing articles on a neglected argument for affirmative action and on employment discrimination claims brought by plaintiffs perceived to be gay. Uniting all of these projects is an overarching concern for the role appearances play throughout the law, particularly in two areas that Soucek will be teaching at UC Davis School of Law: antidiscrimination law and civil procedure.

Eric Stein (1913–2011), b. Holice, Bohemia, was an educator and legal scholar. He was Charles Univ. and Univ. of Michigan educated lawyer. He was associated with Univ. of Michigan Law

School (s. 1956). He became prof. of international law and organization (1958-83) and dir. of international legal studies (1976-81). He was an authority on international law and organization, European law, comparative law.

Jeff Strnad (1952-), b. Cleveland, OH, of Czech ancestry, graduated from Harvard University (B.A., 1975) and then studied law at Yale Law School (J.D., 1979) and economics at Yale University Graduate School (Ph.D., 1982). He now holds the position of Charles A. Beardsley Professor of Law at Stanford Law School. Before joining the Stanford Law School faculty in 1997, he was a professor of law and economics at the California Institute of Technology and the John B. Milliken Professor of Taxation at the University of Southern California Law Center. Professor Strnad also holds a courtesy appointment as Professor of Economics with the Stanford University Department of Economics. His research is spread across the fields of taxation, public finance, finance, and empirical analysis. He has published leading works on the taxation of financial instruments. Professor Strnad is an innovative teacher.

Ralph Edward Svoboda (1901-1969), b. Howells, NE, of Czech ancestry, was a lawyer and legal scholar. He studied law at Creighton University and was admitted to Nebraska Bar in 1927. He was a partner of the firm, Kennedy, Holland, DeLacy & Svoboda (1931-69). He became prof. of corps. and damages, Univ. of Omaha Law School (1947-55).

Edward Otto Tabor (1885-1948), b. Oxford Junction, IA, of Bohemian ancestry, a lawyer, he actively involved in Czechoslovak-American activities on behalf of the Republic of Czechoslovakia from 1918 to 1948. His papers, housed in the Library of Congress, contain correspondence, reports, speeches, and other materials reflecting his advocacy efforts. While specific details about his legal career are limited, his contributions to Czechoslovak interests remain significant.

Joseph J. Talafous (1929-2008), b. New York, NY, of Slovak parents, was a lawyer. He was a graduate of Lincoln High and Rutgers University and received his Juris Doctorate from Seton Hall Law School in 1958. He practiced law at Journal Square in Jersey City since 1959. He served the Jersey City and Hudson community as former assistant prosecutor of Hudson County, former assistant corporation counsel for the City of Jersey City and former Jersey City municipal court judge. Mr. Talafous also served as chairman, finance and legal counsel to various church and community organizations and was also the former chairman of the International Law Section of the N.J. State Bar Association. He was honored in 1996 by President Bill Clinton and Vice President Al Gore as a Slovak-American leader. He was a past chairman and vice president of the Slovak League of America and former chairman of the Slovak Catholic Sokol in Passaic. He served as the Slovak member of the Governors Ethnic Advisory Council in New Jersey under former Governor Florio and former Governor Whitman. In 1996, he was the recipient of the prestigious Ellis Island Medal of Honor Award for dedicated service on behalf of Slovak-American citizens. Mr. Talafous was a U.S. Army Korean War veteran, having served in the Military Police Criminal Investigation Detachment; he was post commander and judge advocate of the Lafayette Amvets Post 33, a life member of the Korean War Veterans Association and a member of the American Legion.

Jiří Toman (1938–2020), b. Prague, Czech., studied law at Charles University in Prague (JUDr., 1966) and political science at University of Geneva (Ph.D., 1981). He held the position of professor of law at Univ. of Santa Clara, CA. He has had extensive experience academically and legally in the fields of international and humanitarian law. Prior to joining the Sant Clara University School of Law faculty, Professor Toman taught at the School of Economics and School of Law at Charles University in Prague, the University of Geneva, and was a visiting professor at Santa Clara University, George Washington University, and Université de Franche-Compté in Besançon. From 1969 until June 1998, he was director of the Henry Dunant Institute in Geneva, the research and training center of the International Red Cross. He is the author of *Cultural Property in War* (2010) and co-editor of *The Laws of Armed Conflicts* (4th ed., 2004).

Joseph G. Tomascik (1914–1970), b. Wilkes-Barre, PA, of Slovak descent, was a lawyer. He had A.B. from Cornell University; M.A. from Harvard University; M.S. from Columbia University; LL.B. from Georgetown University and LL.M. from George Washington University. He was an attorney at the United States Department of Agriculture and Civil Aeronautics Administration and a public opinion analyst and translator at the United States Library of Congress. He was Special Deputy Attorney General of the Commonwealth of Pennsylvania; Assistant Professor, government, King's College (1948–1952); and Assistant District Attorney, Luzerne County. He was also a legislator, and has been a Representative from Luzerne County.

Jennifer Trahan (1964–), b. North Adams, MA, daughter of Elisabeth Welt (1924–2009) of Moravian ancestry, and the mathematician Donald Herbert Trahan, is a lawyer. She holds an A.B. (1985) from Amherst College, and a J.D. (1990) from N.Y.U. School of Law, and LL.M. (2002) from Columbia Law School, specializing in international law. Earlier in her career, she spent 10 years in private practice as a litigator at a large New York City law firm. She has also taught at Columbia University, Fordham Law School, Brooklyn Law School, and The New School, and lectured at Salzburg Law School's Institute on International Criminal Law. Currently, she is an associate clinical professor of global affairs at N.Y.U. She teaches international law, human rights in theory & practice, international justice, and transitional justice. She has served as counsel to the International Justice Program of Human Rights Watch; served as Iraq Prosecutions Consultant to the International Center of Transitional Justice; and worked on cases before the Special Court for Sierra Leone and the International Criminal Tribunal for Rwanda. She is the author of *Genocide, War Crimes and Crimes against Humanity: A Digest of the Case Law of the International Criminal Tribunal for Rwanda* (2010), and *Genocide, War Crimes and Crimes against Humanity: A Topical Digest of the Case Law of the International Criminal Tribunal for the former Yugoslavia* (2006). She was married, in 1995, to Barry Wayne Rashkover.

Leslie T. Tupy (1901-1975), b. Chicago, IL, probably of Czech ancestry, was a legal scholar and educator. He received his BS and MS degrees from the University of Illinois and his law degree from the University of Kansas (LL.B., 1933). He also received CPA certification. He then left the university, having been appointed by Kansas Governor Alfred Landon in 1933 to head the State's securities Corporation Code. Subsequently, Professor Tupy returned to the University to teach at the School of Law, as a professor, from 1936 until his retirement in 1972. With 4 other faculty, Professor Tupy established the Law School Book Exchange, which operated until the spring of 2008. Memorial Scholarship was instituted at KU in 1974 in honor of Professor Tupy at his retirement and, after his death in 1975, many former students and friends added to the fund in his memory.

Joseph J. Vacek (1980-), b. Grand Forks, ND, of Czech ancestry, received his legal training at Univ. of North Dakota School of Law (J.D., 2006). He was a commercial pilot before starting his career as an attorney. He was licensed to practice law at Minneapolis Supreme Ct. and at North Dakota Supreme Ct. since 2007. He practiced law in Minneapolis (2007-08) and then in Great Falls, ND (2008-12). He has been associated with the Univ. of Dakota where he has taught aviation law, as asst. professor (2007-13), as assoc. professor (s. 2013); and also as adj. asst. professor of space studies (s. 2010). He specializes in aviation law, both as a professor and in his law practice.

John Wattawa (1859-1904), b. Milwaukee, WI, of Bohemian ancestry, was preeminently a self-made man. At the age of sixteen, he succeeded in acquiring an academic education, at which time he commenced teaching and for several years he was principal of the Ahnapee HS, WI. When twenty years old, he was elected county superintendent of the schools of Kewaunee Co., a position he held for five years, during which time he studied law and in 1887 he was admitted to the Bar, at once commencing the practice of his profession in Kewaunee. His legal business grew steadily, and he enjoyed one of the most lucrative practices in the county. As a Democrat, he entered the politics of both city and county, each of which he had served in various capacities, such as Mayor of Kewaunee (1893-94, 1897-

98), a city attorney, member of the council, and county board. In the Presidential election he was a Presidential elector. All his three sons subsequently took up law.

Joseph Augustus Wickes (1896–1975), b. Chestertown, MD, desc. of Augustine Herman, graduated with honors from Princeton University in 1917. He studied law at Univ. of Texas (LL.B., 1921) and at Harvard Law School (S.J.D., 1928). After serving in the Marine Corps during World War I, he established a private law practice in Dallas, TX (1923–27). He later taught law at the University of Texas in Austin, TX (s. 1928), where he had done postgraduate study, and the University of Wyoming in Laramie, WY. After the War, Wickes moved to Baltimore. He did not actively practice law there but assisted fellow lawyers in preparing cases.

John Wurts (1855–1936), b. Carbondale, PA, desc. f. Frederick Philipse, studied law at Yale Univ. He practiced law in Jacksonville, FL (1884–95). He has also an academic appointment with Yale Univ. (s. 1896), as prof. of law (1897–1920). He was an authority on elementary law and real state property, legal education. He was the author of numerous books, including *The Anti-Slavery Movement with Relation to the Federal Constitution* (1883), *Systems in Legal Education* (1907), *The Law of the Habeas Corpus* (1915), etc.

Hans Zeisel (1905–1992), b. Kadaň, Bohemia, was an educator, sociologist, and legal scholar. He moved with his family to Vienna, Austria, where he grew up. He received his Doctorates in law and political science from the University of Vienna in 1927. After receiving his Doctorates, Zeisel worked with Paul Lazarsfeld and Marie Jahoda on the 1933 celebrated study *Die Arbeitslosen von Marienthal*. Also after graduating from the University of Vienna, he practiced law and engaged in pro-socialism activism until 1938, when he immigrated to New York City in response to the Anschluss Österreichs. In New York, he became influential in the fields of media market research, and his research in these areas led to the 1947 statistics book *Say It with Figures*. In 1953, Zeisel joined the faculty of the University of Chicago Law School to study the American jury system with Harry Kalven. The research Zeisel and Kalven conducted on the jury system produced two books: *Delay in the Court* (1959) and *The American Jury*. He stayed with the University of Chicago from 1953 till 1976. After retiring from the University of Chicago, he continued conducting research, especially on capital punishment (of which he was a firm opponent) and trademark infringement. In 1977, he was elected as Fellow of the American Statistical Association. One of the last works he wrote discussed the limits of using statistical methods to study the legal system. This book was posthumously published in 1997 as *Prove It with Figures*. He was an authority on legal institutions, law enforcement, and sociology. He initiated the use of empirical research techniques for the study of legal systems.

Sigmund Zeisler (1860-1931), b. Bilsko, on Moravian Silesian border, a trained lawyer, in 1886-1887, was co-counsel for the defendants in the Anarchist cases, popularly known as the Haymarket cases. He was prominent as Sound Money Democrat in campaign of 1896. He was speaker at the first anti Imperialist meeting held west of the Alleghenies, Chicago (1899), and a member of the Executive Committee of the American Anti-Imperialist League (1899). He was an acting chair during National Liberty Congress (1900). He stumped the country as an anti Imperialist in favor of Bryan campaign of 1900. He was a member of the Executive committee of Voters' League and Civil Service Reform Assn.

Chad Zenisek (1984-), b. Cedar Rapids, IA, of Czech ancestry, after graduating from Prairie High School in 2002, he went on to attend Coe College, where he received a degree in political science and business administration in 2006. After taking a couple years to work for a credit union and a bank, he was accepted to the University of Iowa College of Law, which was then ranked among the top 30 law schools in the country. During law school, he clerked for the Iowa Attorney General Environmental Division and Farm Division, and for the law firm Klinger, Robinson & Ford, LLP, where he began his practice after passing the Bar in 2011. His philosophy places clients first by using technology to work efficiently, and quickly communicate important information. He maintains a general practice, including but not limited to, business formation, transactions and litigation, consumer and commercial bankruptcy, real estate, landlord-tenant, agricultural law, family law (divorce, custody), trusts and estates/probate, environmental law.

John Adam Zvetina (1898-1984), b. Chicago, IL, of Czech mother, was a lawyer and educator. He attended Loyola University (A.B., 1921; LL.B., 1924; J.D., 1925; M.A., *cum laude*, 1936), with graduate studies at Belgrade University. He was in general law practice s. 1925. He also held the position of prof. of history, St. Ignatius Academy (1921-24); and prof. of law, Loyola Univ. (s. 1925). He was recipient of Medal of Excellence from Loyola School of Law in 1968. For his outstanding work as a Catholic layman, Professor Zvetina was named a Knight of St. Gregory in 1954, by Pope Pius XII.

E. Medicine

Franz Gabriel Alexander (1891-1964), b. Budapest, of Slovak-born grandfather, was a physician and psychoanalyst. He is considered the father of psychosomatic medicine. He was the founder and director of the Chicago Institute of Psychoanalysis (1932-56) and a professor in the department of psychiatry at the University of Illinois Medical School in Chicago (1938-56).

Dr. George O. Baumrucker (1905–1991), b. McHenry, IL, the son of Ottillie Železný (1879–1963) of Dobrapul, Bohemia, and Dr. Otto Baumrucker, was a physician, specializing in urology. He also was a teacher and inventor and past president of the Chicago Urologic Society. He did his residency in urology at Presbyterian Hospital and worked at the Veterans Hospital in Indianapolis. During World War II, he was a major in the Army Medical Corps. After the war, Dr. Baumrucker was chief urological consultant and surgeon at the Hines Veterans Hospital. While there, he invented several devices that enabled paraplegics previously unable to exercise to do so. He subsequently fashioned an instrument for observing and removing damaged tissue from the bladder. He also patented a medical device to help incontinent patients. Dr. Baumrucker practiced for 31 years at the Hinsdale Sanitarium.

Dr. Frank M. Berger (1913–2008), a native of Pilsen, West Bohemia, is best known for his introduction in 1955 of meprobamate, also known as Miltown or Equanil, a prescription drug described as a tranquilizer that would relieve tension, and as such was a forerunner of more potent drugs, such as the benzodiazepines. Berger observed that throughout history, mankind sought relief from tension by means of alcohol, opium, hashish, peyote etc. and that meprobamate was unique in that it offered relief from tension free of the excitation, hallucinations, and addiction of the ancient remedies, which compromised their use in our daily lives. Meprobamate became the most frequently prescribed drug in the United States soon after its release and prevailed into the 1960s.

Kyra J. Bobinet (1970–), a native of Edmond, of Czech ancestry, is a national speaker, author and CEO-founder of Engaged, a neuroscience behavior design firm. She devotes her life to cracking the code of why we engage in our health. Every day, she and her team use neuroscience to make products and communications more. engaging. For this work, she received the 2015 Innovator Award from Harvard where she received her Master's in Public Health (M.P.H., 2008). She earned her medical degree at UCSF School of Medicine. (M.D., 1998). Dr. Bobinet is the author of *Well Designed Life: 10 Lessons in Brain Science* and *Design Thinking for a Mindful, Healthy, and Purposeful Life*. She has founded health start-ups, and created blockbuster products, health apps, big data algorithms, and evidence-based programs in mind-body & metabolic medicine. Dr. Bobinet, co-teaches patient engagement and health design with Dr. Larry Chu at Stanford School of Medicine, and studied in BJ Fogg's behavior design lab. She is married to the lawyer Josh Leichter.

Dr. Radan Čapek (1931–), b. Prague, Czech, is known for his research on the electrophysiological analysis of drug action on synaptic transmission and excitability in the central nervous system, in particular, the mechanisms by which anticonvulsants control the initiation and spread of seizure activity, selective targeting of the drug action on hyperexcitable neurons involved in seizures, and plastic changes in the brain induced by an insult leading to epileptogenesis. He is a core member of the Centre for Medical Education. His research interest is in evaluation of undergraduate medical students and in faculty development. He also collaborates in pharmacoepidemiology research on new methods for population-based studies of effectiveness and safety of medications.

Tomáš Cihlář (1967–), a native of Pilen, Czech., is a biochemist known for his role in the development of remdesivir, originally intended for treatment of Ebola. However, the Ebola epidemic ended before the new drug could be tested. Remdesivir briefly showed considerable promise in treating COVID-19 infection; In April 2020, the company provided 5,000 doses for experimental use in China and four hundred patients in 50 other countries. Remdesivir was used to treat the first confirmed case of coronavirus in the U.S. A specialist in virology, Cihlář holds the positions of Senior Director, Biology, and Vice-President at American pharmaceutical company Gilead Sciences. As a student, Cihlář assisted fellow biochemist Antonín Holý in developing Viread, the primary drug used to fight HIV infection.

Charles William Flexner (1956–), of Czech ancestry, is an American physician and clinical pharmaceutical scientist, known for his work on the basic and clinical pharmacology of drugs or HIV/AIDS and related infections, including tuberculosis and viral hepatitis. He participated in the discovery and clinical development of several new molecules and formulations for immediate-release and long-acting parenteral administration. He founded and directs the Long Acting/Extended Release Antiretroviral Research Resource Program (LEAP). In his studies regarding treatment of HIV, Flexner was an early advocate of use of ritonavir to enhance the pharmacokinetics of other drugs. He was also an early proponent of using the combination of the integrase inhibitor, cabotegravir, and the non-nucleoside reverse transcriptase inhibitor, rilpivirine, in a long-acting injectable form as an antiretroviral treatment option for people with HIV.

Louis Barkhouse Flexner (1902–1996), a native of Louisville, KY, of Bohemian ancestry, was a pioneer in the field of neurochemistry and made notable contributions also to the physiology of the cerebrospinal fluid and meninges, to the function of the placenta, and to the biochemistry of development. Through his organization and direction of the Institute of Neurological Sciences at the University of Pennsylvania, he had a major role in the development of neuroscience in this country. Louis received his undergraduate education at the University of Chicago (B.S., 1923) after which he received his medical education at Johns Hopkins University (M.D., 1927).

Simon Flexner (1867–1946), b. Louisville, KY, of Bohemian ancestry, was a microbial biologist. His groundbreaking research focused on the way viruses and bacterial infections invade and function within hosts. His development of a treatment protocol for meningitis was a major breakthrough, as he determined that antibacterial serum had to be administered directly into the fluid encompassing the brain and spinal column so that it could reach bacteria insulated by the blood-brain barrier. Flexner also conducted studies on poliomyelitis by inoculating monkeys with the virus. He found that the antibodies that formed could be used to counteract the virus, an important step in the development of a vaccine. Flexner was apprenticed to a druggist and then attended the Louisville College of Pharmacy, where he graduated in 1882. He later earned his MD degree from the University of Louisville in 1889 and then studied pathology and bacteriology at the Johns Hopkins Hospital. He served as professor of pathological anatomy at Johns Hopkins University from 1895 to 1898. In 1899, he moved to the University of Pennsylvania and became the professor of pathology. He was appointed the first director of the Rockefeller Institute for Medical Research, serving there from 1901 to 1935.

Erna Furman (née Erna Mary Popper) (1926–2002), b. Vienna, Austria of Czech descent, was an American child psychoanalyst, psychologist, and teacher. When she was twelve years old, her family, having Czech citizenship, fled to Czechoslovakia to escape the Nazis. Unfortunately, this did not save her from being sent to a concentration camp after the Nazis occupied Czechoslovakia. She survived the Holocaust. In 1945, Anna Freud took a small group of Terezín children to England, Erna being one of them, and they were taken care of under Anna Freud's supervision. A graduate of the Child Therapy Training Program offered by Anna Freud in Hampstead following World War II, Erna Furman was a child psychoanalyst, a licensed psychologist, and a teacher. She immigrated to the United States with the help of Anny Katan in the 1950s. Erna Furman specialized in children and how children process grief. Of particular importance was her evidence that children as young as three essentially process grief no differently than adults and her insistence that children are not misled or deceived when a parent dies. She practiced at the Hanna Perkins Center for Child Development and also saw patients in her Cleveland Heights home. She was a prolific writer; over the years she received extensive accolades for her contributions to psychoanalysis. She was made an honorary member of the American Psychoanalytic Association in 1999. She was married to child psychiatrist Dr. Robert A. Furman, and they had 5 children.

Daniel Carleton Gajdusek (1923–2008), b. Yonkers, NY, of Slovak father; physician, pediatrician, virologist, and medical researcher, who was the co-recipient (with Baruch S. Blumberg) of the Nobel Prize in Physiology or Medicine in 1976 for work on an infectious agent which would later be identified as the cause of kuru, the first known human prion disease. He graduated in 1943 from the University of Rochester, where he studied physics, biology, chemistry and mathematics. He obtained an M.D. from Harvard University in 1946 and performed postdoctoral research at Columbia University, the California Institute of Technology, and Harvard. In 1951, Gajdusek was drafted into the U.S. Army and assigned as a research virologist at the Walter Reed Army Medical Service Graduate School. In 1954, after his military discharge, he went to work as a visiting investigator at the Walter and Eliza Hall Institute of Medical Research in Melbourne, Australia. There, he began the work that culminated in the Nobel Prize. He was elected as a member of the American Philosophical Society in 1978.

Peter Ganz (ca. 1949–), b. The US, a Slovak father, is a cardiologist. He received his M.D. from Harvard and completed his residency at the Massachusetts General Hospital. He is the director of the Center of excellence in Vascular Research and a Professor of Medicine at the University of California, Francisco. He spent 25 years directing cardiovascular research in the cardiac catheterization laboratories at the Brigham and Women's Hospital and Harvard Medical School prior to arriving at UCSF in 2008. He was the first to describe vascular endothelial function in health and its dysfunction in atherosclerosis in humans.

Rochus Heinisch (1801–1874), b. Litoměřice, Bohemia, a surgical instrument maker, was a successful inventor, his most prominent achievement having been the invention of the tailors' shears, which have since found a market in nearly every part of Europe and America.

Jan Klein (1936–2023), b. Štemplovec, Opava, Czech., was an immunologist, best known for his work on the major histocompatibility complex (MHC).

Karl Koller (1857–1944), b. Sušice, Bohemia, was an ophthalmologist, He began his medical career as a surgeon at the Vienna General Hospital and a colleague of Sigmund Freud. Prior to this discovery, he had tested solutions such as chloral hydrate and morphine as anaesthetics in the eyes of laboratory animals without success. Freud was fully aware of the pain-killing properties of cocaine, but Koller recognized its tissue-numbing capabilities, and in 1884 demonstrated its potential as a local anaesthetic to the medical community. Koller's findings were a medical breakthrough. Prior to his discovery, performing eye surgery was difficult because the involuntary reflex motions of the eye to respond to the slightest stimuli. Later, cocaine was also used as a local anaesthetic in other medical fields such as dentistry.

Bohdan Pomahač (1971–), b. Ostrava, Czech., is a plastic surgeon, he led the team that performed the first full face transplant in United States and the third overall in the world. He is the division chief of Yale Medicine Plastic & Reconstructive Surgery, and director of the Face Transplant Program, a program that focuses on face transplantation for patients who have severe disfiguration. He also performs a broad variety of plastic and aesthetic procedures on the entire body, and has special expertise in breast reconstruction, aesthetic surgery, head and neck facial reconstruction, and trauma and burn reconstruction.

Nathan Rosewater (1854–1926), b. Buchovany, Bohemia, a pharmacist by training, developed and published many formulae for Vaseline preparations, some of which were exhibited at the Paris Exposition of 1889 and won prizes there. He also perfected mineral oil for general use. As a chief chemist at New York Hospital, he invented the first antiseptic surgical dressings to be used in the US. He later invented and patented a percolator for making extracts from herbs, a device which bears his name and is still used by pharmacists all over the world.

Peter Safar (1924–2003), b. Vienna, of Czech descent, was an Austrian anesthesiologist of Czech descent. He is credited with pioneering cardiopulmonary resuscitation (CPR). Safar's other achievements included the establishment of the United States' first intensive-care unit in 1958, at Baltimore City Hospital. In 1961, he went to the University of Pittsburgh, where he established its notable academic anesthesiology department and the world's first intensive-care medicine training program. He initiated the Freedom House Enterprise Ambulance Service, one of the first prehospital emergency medical services in the United States in 1967 and together with Dr. Nancy Caroline, developed standards for emergency medical technician (EMT) education and training, as well as standards for mobile intensive-care ambulance design and equipment. He was nominated three times for the Nobel Prize in Medicine.

Hans Selye (1907–1982), b. Vienna, of Slovak descent, was raised in Komárno, Slovakia, and educated in Prague. He was a physician, pioneering Canadian physiologist, and endocrinologist. He is acknowledged as the 'Father' of the field of stress research, having gained world-wide recognition for introducing the concept of stress in a medical context.

Helen Brooke Taussig (1898–1986), b. Cambridge, MA, of Bohemian ancestry, is known as the founder of pediatric cardiology for her innovative work on "blue baby" syndrome. In 1944, Taussig, surgeon Alfred Blalock, and surgical technician Vivien Thomas developed an operation to correct the congenital heart defect that causes the syndrome. Since then, their operation has prolonged thousands of lives, and is considered a key step in the development of adult open heart surgery the following decade. Dr. Taussig also helped to avert a thalidomide birth defect crisis in the United States, testifying to the Food and Drug Administration on the terrible effects the drug had caused in Europe. Despite suffering from dyslexia—a reading impairment—Taussig excelled in higher education. She graduated from the Cambridge School for Girls in 1917 and became a champion tennis player during her two years of study at Radcliffe. She earned a B.A. degree from the University of California at Berkeley in 1921, and after studying at Harvard Medical School and Boston University she transferred to Johns Hopkins University School of Medicine to pursue her interest in cardiac research. Taussig graduated from Hopkins in 1927 and served as a fellow in cardiology at Johns Hopkins Hospital for the next year, followed by a two-year pediatrics internship. In 1930, she was appointed head of the Children's Heart Clinic at the Johns Hopkins Hospital pediatric unit, the Harriet Lane Home, where she worked until her retirement in 1963. By the time Taussig graduated from Hopkins, she had lost her hearing and relied on lip-reading and hearing aids for the rest of her career.

Jan Vilček (1933–), a native of Bratislava, Czech., is a Slovak American biomedical scientist, inventor, and philanthropist. To protect him from deportation to a concentration camp in 1942, his parents placed Jan in an orphanage run by Catholic nuns. Vilček received his M.D. degree from Comenius University Medical School in Bratislava in 1957; and his Ph.D. in Virology from the Institute of Virology, Czechoslovak Academy of Sciences, Bratislava, in 1962. He defected from Communist Czechoslovakia during his visit to Vienna in 1965, and then emigrated to the US. In 1959, while still in Czechoslovakia, he started working on interferon, a protein made in response to infection with viruses and other pathogens. At the time, interferon was still a poorly defined protein studied by only a handful of scientists across the world. In 1964, Vilček organized the first international conference on interferon that was attended by many scientists active in the field at the time. Upon emigrating to the United States in 1965, Vilček joined the faculty of NYU School of Medicine as an assistant professor of microbiology. At NYU, Vilček continued research on interferon. He helped to develop methods for the production of human fibroblast (beta) interferon that enabled its clinical utilization and molecular characterization. He and his colleagues showed that human leukocyte (alpha) and beta interferon are antigenically distinct, laying the groundwork for the later demonstration that these interferons are encoded by distinct genes that belong to the same gene family. He and his coworkers also contributed to the characterization of human immune (gamma) interferon. In the 1980s, Vilček became interested in the study of another cytokine, termed tumor necrosis factor (TNF). His work helped to elucidate novel biological actions of TNF, led to the discovery of novel genes and proteins, and helped to identify signaling pathways. Together with Junming Le, Vilcek helped to develop the biologic drug, now known as Remicade. Remicade is a potent anti-inflammatory agent used in the treatment of rheumatoid arthritis, Crohn's disease, ulcerative colitis, ankylosing spondylitis, psoriatic arthritis, plaque psoriasis and other inflammatory diseases. Remicade was the first TNF blocking agent successfully used in patients. The success of Remicade spurred the development and regulatory approval of several other anti-TNF agents (TNF inhibitor), including adalimumab-Humira, etanercept-Enbrel, golimumab-Simponi, and certolizumab pegol-Cimzia, all of which are being used to treat numerous inflammatory autoimmune diseases. It is estimated that close to 3 million patients have been treated with Remicade, and more patients benefited from treatments with other anti-TNF agents. With the royalties from the sales of Remicade, Vilček and his wife Marica established the Vilcek Foundation in 2000, devoted to increasing public awareness of the contribution of immigrants to professional, academic and artistic life in the United States. In 2005, the Vilčeks made a donation to NYU School of Medicine valued at over 100 million dollars, for use towards basic research.

F. Agriculture

Abram Block (1830–1960), b. Švihov, Bohemia, became a resident of San Francisco, where his mercantile firm also engaged extensively in business. In 1873, he established the A. Block Fruit Company, located on the northwestern limits of Santa Clara, which was thought to be at the time the largest deciduous fruit house in the world, packing in different years, according to the size and quality of the crop, from 500 to 900 carloads, all assorted and boxed by experienced hands and shipped to almost every corner of the globe—China, Europe, South America, South Africa. The Blocks made a specialty of quality fruits, the bulk of which was grown in their own orchards.

John Beale Bordley (1727–1804), b. Annapolis, MD, desc. f. Augustine Heřman, Maryland Judge, from 1770 on, was engaged in agricultural experimentation with new machinery, seeds and crop rotation on extensive lands, at the mouth of the Wye River and on Pooles Island, MD. A founder of the Philadelphia Society for Promoting Agriculture in 1785, he also served as the Society's vice president (1785–1804). Bordley wrote the following essays: *A Summary View of Courses of Crops in the Husbandry of England* and *Maryland* (1784) and *Essays and Notes on Husbandry and Rural Affairs* (1801).

Adolph Brandeis (1824–1906), b. Prague, Bohemia, in 1852, came to Louisville, KY where he became a successful grain merchant. He was a member of the pioneer firm Brandeis & Crawford which did extensive business in grain. He was the father of the Supreme Court Justice Louis D. Brandeis.

Alfred F. Brandeis (1854–1928), b. Louisville, of Bohemian father, was twenty-four years old when he was taken into partnership in the firm of A. Brandeis & Son, and for over forty years had been active in the management of the increasing fortunes of that widely known grain firm. The great volume of business transacted by this firm has probably contributed more than anything else toward making Louisville a great grain market. Alfred Brandeis was one of the organizers of the Louisville Board of Trade and has been one of the directors and leading members of that organization for thirty-four consecutive years. On account of his prominence in the grain trade early in America's participation in the World War, he was one of the business men associated with war administration measures, and from 1917 until 1920, gave his time without compensation and defraying his own expenses to the duties of chief of the cereal enforcement division of the US Food Administration in Washington. He was also one of the organizers of the Lincoln Savings Bank & Trust Company, and was a director of that institution until 1918, when he resigned.

Julius Bunzl (1830–1887), b. Prague, Bohemia, was a wholesale tobacco merchant in New York City to where he immigrated in 1884. After the retirement of his partner, Henry Dormitzer, the firm changed its name to J. Bunzl & Sons.

Isidor Bush (orig. Busch) (1822–1898), b. Prague, Bohemia, after moving to St. Louis, in 1851 acquired a hundred acres of land in Jefferson County, MO, at a place, later called Bushberg, where he engaged in growing grapes. He developed a keen interest in viticulture and came to be recognized as a leading authority in the field. In 1868 he published the *Bushberg Catalog*, a grape manual which was translated into many languages and enjoyed international circulation. Bush also established a wine and liquor business.

Joshua Clayton (1829–d.), b. Dover, DE, desc. f. Augustine Heřman, was Princeton Univ. trained lawyer. After several years in the law practice, he became fully engaged in agriculture. He purchased three thousand acres of land, a bulk of which originally belonged to Bohemia Manor. He made improvements to the land and buildings, raised large quantities of grain, raised livestock on a large scale and became one of the most extensive cultivators of peaches in the county of New Castle. At one time, he owned over 21 thousand acres of land, two thousands of which he gave to his ten children.

Anton F. Dobrý (1862–1951), b. Bohemia, was a co-owner with Kroutils of the Yukon Mill and Grain Company in Yukon. From a small milling operation in 1893, they grew tremendously, and by 1915, were shipping flour and feeds throughout the south and even overseas. In 1934, A. F. Dobry withdrew and built the Dobry Mills.

Joseph O. Dostál (1842–1925), b. Říčany, Bohemia, immigrated with his parents to New York in 1856 and moved immediately to a homestead near Iowa City, Iowa. A veteran of the US Civil War, he came to Colorado in 1886 to run a meat market in the mountains and ended up establishing the J.O.D. ranch west of Kit Carson, Colorado. Dostal and his JOD Ranch raised Hereford cattle which, when exhibited, won many prizes. When Cheyenne County was formed in 1889, Dostal was the new county's largest property taxpayer. Dostal was also instrumental in organizing the stockmen's association in the state, for protection against rustlers.

Lumir Dostal (1910–1986), b. Iowa, of Czech ancestry, was a successful farmer in Marion, IA. His corn always looked best and that's why the National Corn Picking Contest was held on his place. He hosted State and National Corn picking championships at his farm in 1958 and in 1985, he hosted the Farm Progress Show. President Dwight D. Eisenhower and Massachusetts Senator John F. Kennedy came to his father's Marion farm for the National Corn Picking Contest on October 17, 1958. On that occasion, President Eisenhower actually opened his presidential campaign. Some 100,000 people or more were in attendance. They wanted Dostal's wife to have lunch with First Lady Mamie Eisenhower in Cedar Rapids, but Dostal said "either the whole family has lunch with the president or none." Lumir Dostal, Sr., the host of the event, got his way and he and wife Libby, and Lumir Dostal, Jr. and his sister Darlene shared box lunches with both the president and Senator John F. Kennedy under a tent surrounded by a sea of onlookers outside.

Lumir E. Dostal, Jr. (1936–2012), of Czech ancestry, graduated from Marion HS and attended Iowa State Univ., graduating in 1961. He was a lifelong farmer and leader in no-till sustainable farming since 1988. He was president and director of Dostal Farm Enterprises, Cedar Rapids. He served as director of State and County Committees for Farm Bureau. He was elected founding director of the United Soybean Board (1991-96). He is credited with the establishing of Established Vocational Agricultural at Lin-Mar's large urban school in 1975. He served for 15 years on the Linn-Mar School board, following in the footsteps of his father. It wasn't until 1994 that he decided to run for Linn County supervisor as a Republican. He wanted to give the rural areas of the county a voice on the Board, a board that seemed to some having become urban centric. He became the first Linn County Republican supervisor in 22 years. He had a big hand in the writing of a new county land-use plan. He also kept a close eye on county roads and the park system. He also served two terms as chair of Bluestem, now the Cedar Rapids/Linn County Solid Waste Agency. In 1997, Lumir Dostal, Jr. was elected a Centennial Honor Roll Member of Alpha Zeta, the oldest fraternal society in agriculture.

Andrew Duda (1873–1958), b. Velčice, Slovakia, was a rancher, philanthropist, and entrepreneurial farmer in Florida, who acquired the nickname 'the Celery King.' His enterprise grew from his family's small farm to an international agricultural corporation in the small Slovak colony of Slavia, Florida. Among those who founded the small Slovak community of Slavia in Central Florida, Duda and his three sons, John, Andrew, Jr., and Ferdinand, harvested their first cash crop of celery in 1926 and established A. Duda & Sons. The three brothers were visionary in building the business, acquiring land, diversifying their operations, relying on others inside and outside of the business for advice, having integrity in their business practices, and–above all else–trusting in God. In the early 1970s, the reins of management were transferred to the third-generation sons of the Three Seniors. A more market-driven business strategy was developed for DUDA's fresh produce operations to satisfy market demands. To offer farm-fresh produce year-round to their growing customer base, the company acquired farmland in California and Texas. Sod was also added to the company's agricultural offerings in the 1970s. In the 1980s, due to the growth of Brevard County, Florida, plans were set in motion to build a master-planned community on DUDA's Cocoa Ranch. The town of Viera, which means "faith" in Slovak, was established in 1989. Eventually, a home building division, commercial sales division, and a championship golf course were all added to the company's fully integrated real estate operations. Now in its fourth generation of leadership, the company is professionally managed by men and women of the third, fourth, and fifth generations of the Duda Family, and a team of experienced managers. The company is governed by a Board of Directors consisting of six members of the Duda family and four non-family members from varying business backgrounds. In 2004, the Duda family established the Duda Family Council to address some of the governance issues that family businesses in their third and subsequent generations must begin to address. Its mission is: One family, growing together, making an eternal difference. Through elected family representatives, the Council develops processes and structures for the family and owners. The importance placed on philanthropy is reflected in DUDA's stated purpose: We multiply and share God's blessings. This philosophy is central to all of DUDA's business operations and actions. The values passed down from Andrew through each generation at DUDA have earned the company its reputation for quality, integrity, and innovation. Its focus on market trends and customer needs has helped the company maintain a competitive edge in all of its business operations. The company has been rewarded by earning recognition for its leadership in business integrity, environmental stewardship, and employee benefits.

Joe Dusek (1866–1943), b. Bohemia, started as a farm lad. In 1892, he began farming. At the time he reached sixty, he owned three farms, totaling eight thousand acres in Sweetwater, Buffalo Co., NE.

Daniel N. Friesleben (1832–1897), b. Mariánské Lázně, Bohemia, came to Oroville, CA in 1857. He was soon engaged in the mercantile business. In 1864, he was one of a joint stock company to build the Union Hotel; and three years later, he bought out all the stock and became the proprietor. His first purchase of real estate was the building later occupied by N. Goldstein; the third purchase was the St. Nicholas Hotel. Mr. Friesleben was also one of the Oroville Water Company's stockholders and vice-president of the Rideout-Smith National Bank. He became very active in the Oroville citrus fairs. Being confident that the climate and soil were favorable for citrus fruits, he was one of the original members of the Oroville Citrus Association, which planted the first forty-acre commercial orange orchard in Northern California. At the mouth of the Honcut, he owned one of the finest ranches in the county, and therefore had a personal knowledge of ranching and ranch products. The Friesleben Ranch comprised about eighteen hundred acres of land, some of the most fertile in the state, which is devoted to farming and cattle-raising, for which it is particularly adapted, lying at the junction of the Feather River and Honcut Creek.

Antone Gatterman (1858–d.), b. Kriesdorf, nr Mladá Boleslav, Bohemia, came to America with parents when he was 13 years old. He traveled throughout the country, before he decided to settle in Kansas. As a farmer, his first important profits were made in cattle and hogs. Contrary to the usual experience, corn proved a fairly safe crop with him, and he fed his corn to the stock, raised and fattened them on his land and sold them at good prices to the local markets. As a land buyer, he paid $1,000 for one quarter and continued buying until the price had risen to $4,000 a quarter section. As a result of his growing prosperity and his continued faith in land as a medium of investment, Mr. Gatterman accumulated sixteen quarter sections, including 823 acres at Felsburg, 960 acres in Gray County, 640 acres in Haskell County and 160 acres in Prowers County, Colorado. Of all this, he has brought under cultivation over 2,400 acres. Besides his extensive holdings of land, Mr. Gatterman was president of the Felsburg State Bank and president of the Equity Farmers Elevator of Felsburg. He had served as Justice of the Peace, as trustee, as member of the School Board, and as treasurer of the United Brethren Church in Felsburg. In 1916, Mr. Gatterman established his residence in Kinsley, where he owned one of the best homes of the town.

Frank Hamáchek (1853–1935), b. Bohemia, machinist, invented so called Hamachek Ideal Pea Harvester, for harvesting green peas, which represented the work of several years. His other inventions included Ideal Viner Feeders, a self-feeder to feed the vines into a pea huller; tailing separators, a machine to save those peas that the viner has hulled out but which are still entangled among the vines; and viner improvements. In 1911, he invented Ideal Chain Adjusters. At his plant in Kewaunee, Wisconsin, he manufactured feed and ensilage cutters, feed mills, horse powers, chain adjusters, tailing separators, viner feeders, and viner improvements, all of which are his own inventions. He was also an inventor of stump puller, the feed cutter and giant feed mill. He was granted over 30 patents.

Adolph Rudolph Hanslik (1917–2007), b. Halletsville, TX, of Czech ancestry, was a Lubbock businessman and philanthropist known as the 'Dean of the West Texas Cotton Producers.' Hanslik was among the first in the US to export cotton to Bangladesh. He entered World War II with the 124th Army Signal Corps radio intelligence unit. Thereafter, he was employed by the Otto Goedecke Cotton Company in Hallettsville as a cotton merchant apprentice. In 1952, he moved to Corpus Christi, the seat of Nueces County on the Texas Gulf Coast and launched his Adolph Hanslik Cotton Company. In 1954, he moved the company to Lubbock, where it became a successful exporter of Texas cotton abroad. He was active as president of his company until his death. Heavily involved in community affairs, Hanslik was a past president of the Texas Cotton Association, Lubbock Cotton Exchange, etc.

Bernhard Heller (1808-1891), b. Křivenice, nr. Citov, Bohemia, was the "father of sausage industry" in Milwaukee, WI. He immigrated with his wife and 5 children to Milwaukee in 1848. The journey by sailboat lasted 6 weeks, and the subsequent travel from Milwaukee across to Erie Canal and Great Lakes lasted just as long. Behind their modest dwelling, Indians camped out in their tents. Heller founded a butcher store in Milwaukee, the first in the city, under the name Milwaukee Sausage Works. According to the Census of 1850, he was then 40 years old, and his wife Sarah was 34. Their children ranged from 1-10. According to 1880 Census, the children, having grown up, did not live in the house anymore. When he died, at age 83, his obituary stated that he was 'father of sausage industry' in Milwaukee. In stature, he was tall, had black beard and a mustache. He always dressed elegantly and wore a vest with a watch chain.

John Horský (1838-1924), b. Bohemia, in the spring of 1865, he came to Helena, MT, and in company with George Butz, he turned his attention to the brewing business. They built the first brewery in the city, the Helena Brewery. Mr. Horsky continued successfully in the brewing business until 1891 when having secured a competency, he sold out and retired from active life.

Otto Jangl (1924-2008), b. Czech., an agricultural engineer, was a pioneer of the golf course industry. He immigrated to Canada, settling in Sherrington, Quebec. He was the founder and owner of O. J. Company, specializing in agricultural products, such as fertilizers, seed, agrochemicals, etc. The company, very small at first, specialized only in seed sales. Today, O. J. Company is a dynamic enterprise that can easily be called the leader in the field of green space management.

Jerry Kane (1947-), b. Prague, Czech., has been with Sam Kane Co., Corpus Christie, TX, (s. 1969); as manager of Sam Kane Beef Processors, Inc. (s. 1973), as vice pres. (s. 1979) and presently president and CEO. He served also as director Nat. Meat Assn. (s. 1974) and director of Southern Meat Packers Assn. (1976-79).

Sam Kane (1919-2010), b. Spišské Podhradie, Czech., overcame the Nazi occupation of Europe, was a World War II resistance fighter and survived the loss of much of his family to the Auschwitz Concentration Camp. He came to America in 1948 to start over, with his wife, Aranka. Kane embodied the American dream, building a tiny meat counter into Sam Kane Beef Processors, Inc., the seventh largest meatpacker in the world. He shook hands with presidents and counted some of the world's most powerful as his friends. He was president, Sam Kane Wholesale Meat Inc., Corpus Christie, TX (s. 1956), Sam Kane Meat Inc., Corpus Christie (s. 1956), and Sam Kane Packing Co. He was also director of Guaranty Nat. Bank, Corpus Christie, and Corpus Christie Bank and Trust. He served as president, Jewish of the Welfare Appeal (1962) and as vice president of the Combined Jewish Appeal (1968).

Herman Koehler (1833–1899), b. Bohemia, was senior partner in the firm Koehler & Co., brewers and malters, New York City. The company existed from 1862–1917. He was an active member of the Brewers Assn.

Charles Kohn (1848–1910), b. Vlachové Březí, Bohemia, was one of the most prominent citizens of the Pacific Coast. He immigrated to California in 1868, entering what was then known as Union College, to complete his education. In 1865, he became connected with the firm of Marcus, Kohn & Co., wholesale and retail clothiers. In 1869, he entered the great commercial house of Wilmerding & Co. as a traveling representative, remaining with that firm for many years. In 1883, he established the wholesale wine and liquor house of Charles Kohn & Co., in Portland, Oregon. His brother Napthally was his partner. They secured suitable offices in the old O.S.N. Co. block, at No. 41 Front Street. Kohn's wholesale house was both successful and long-lived, spanning over 27 years in Portland, OR. The firm would relocate to Third and Pine Street where they were located most of that period. Charles Kohn died suddenly of a heart attack on September 21, 1910, just after returning from a business trip to San Francisco. He had amassed a small fortune from his great business years.

Francis Korbel (1830–1920), b. Bechyně, Bohemia, a famous Forty Eighter, and cigar maker in New York, left the crowded conditions of New York City for the less populated and less settled locale of San Francisco, making his way there through the Isthmus of Panama. He arrived in 1860 and turned his attention to cigar boxes, opening up a repair shop. In order to manufacture his own cigar boxes, he asked his brothers back in Bohemia to join him in San Francisco to assist in his enterprise. In 1862, they formed a partnership, F. Korbel & Bros., and opened the first cigar box factory in San Francisco. It was an immediate success, and it was not long before they owned their own schooner, aptly named 'The Bohemia,' to import veneers from around the world. They acquired more ships and became involved in the export of hardwood. They also bought timber for shipping and opened sawmills to produce lumber for use in San Francisco's booming building industry. It was the timber that first attracted the Korbel brothers to the Russian River Valley of Sonoma County in

1872. When the building boom subsided, however, they found themselves holding a lot of timber for which there was little demand. Forever resourceful, they researched what could be done with the cleared acreage and decided the land was ideal for any number of agricultural purposes. They began to grow alfalfa, beets, corn, prunes, and wheat and used some of the crops to feed cows and start a dairy. The Korbel brothers also began to plant vineyards on their Russian River property. They experimented with different varieties of grapes, including Pinot Noir, the favorite of winemakers in France's Champagne region. They also became winemakers. According to company records, the brothers were producing as much as 30,000 gallons by 1882. The winemaking operation was so promising that over the next two years they devoted all their attention to it, converting their farmland to vineyards and shutting down the dairy. They brought an experienced Prague winemaker named Frank Hasek to become their champagne master in 1884. At the time, it was believed that suitable champagne could not be produced in California. Hasek used the 'methode champenoise' approach to making champagne and spent the next decade blending the results of different grape harvests to produce a distinctive house style for Korbel champagne. By 1894, the Korbel brothers began to sell their champagne, and the people who doubted that California could produce excellent champagne were silenced. By the end of the 1800s, Korbel was an award-winning, internationally recognized label.

John Francis Kroutil (1875–1954), b. Prague, Bohemia, established himself in Yukon, as a farmer and grain trader. He acquired an elevator and eventually a small mill, which he expanded into a multimillion-dollar enterprise. By 1928, 'Yukon Best,' the famed trade name was prominent in the Southwest. John Kroutil became president of both the State Oklahoma Millers Assn. and pres. of the regional Southern Millers Assn. He was also president of the Progress Brewing Co. in Oklahoma City and organizer of the Yukon National Bank.

Max M. Lederer (1860–1926), b. Englishtown, NJ, of Bohemian ancestry, a merchant, was one of New Brunswick's prominent citizens, long identified with the leather, hide and fertilizer business. When he was very young, his parents moved with their family to New Brunswick, New Jersey. He received his education in the schools of New Brunswick, and as a young man, entered the business of his father. For over twenty years, he had the sole management of the business started by his father, and in 1906, he purchased the entire interests of the firm. The business, started under the name Samuel Lederer & Son, bore the original title and enjoyed a well-known reputation in the industrial life of the community under the direction of Max M. Lederer. Mr. Lederer was well known, fraternally, being a member of the Free and Accepted Masons, of the Independent Order of Odd Fellows, and of the Knights of Pythias, and having served as a chancellor in the latter order, Friendship Lodge, No. 30, of New Brunswick.

V. THE SOCIETY

Adolph Levi (1858-1943), b. Dlouhy Újezd, Bohemia, moved to San Diego in 1877. He owned ranches and dairy farms all over San Diego County.

Nathan Levy (1889-1967), b. Vicksburg, MS, of Bohemian ancestry, for one year he was a student at South Business Coll. at New Orleans. He began his career as cotton buyer and bookkeeper in Vicksburg. In 1921, he founded Nathan Levy & Co., a cotton business in Vicksburg. The firm was on Crawford Street. In 1918, he also began a successful life insurance agency. In 1924, he had been named district manager of the Union Central Life Insurance Co. of Cincinnati. He received many citations for his insurance work. He was also associated with his sister, Amelia Levy, in a family and rental business. He was a director of the Vicksburg Chamber of Commerce of which he was one of the co-founders. He also worked for Red Cross and the United Service Organizations for which he received several citations from the President of the US and from the director of the United Service Organizations.

Solomon Levy (1839-d.), b. Karlovy Vary, Bohemia, was the senior member of the firm of S. Levy & Co., general commission merchants and dealers in poultry, eggs, fruit, potatoes, butter, hides, California and Oregon produce of all kinds, 218 and 220 Washington Street, San Francisco. This house was established in 1864 and was one of the representative commission firms of the coast doing a large and profitable business in the northwest, besides having an extensive local trade.

Albert Anthony Manda (1862-1933), b. nr. Prague, Bohemia, was a leading florist in NJ, with gardens and hot houses in South Orange. He began his career as curator of botanical gardens at Harvard Univ. After five years, came to NJ where he opened his business. He had one of the largest distributing depots in the country and kept the largest variety of plants in US. He imported plants from every part of the world, and also shipped to many of the civilized ports. He had in his possession a 'Cycas' plant which was originally owned by George Washington.

Wenzel Medlin (1871-1947), b. Bohemia, was a brewer, the founder (1892) of Pilsener Brewing Co., Cleveland, once located at the southwest corner of Clark Ave. and W. 65th St. The corner site of the Pilsener Brewing Co. was once known as Pilsener Square. The name Pilsener comes from the Czech city of Pilsen (Plzeň), where the light Bohemian lager beer was first made. In 1917, Pilsener produced 4 different brews: P.O.C. (which stood for 'Pilsner of Cleveland'), Gold Top, Extra Pilsener Beer, and Pilsener Dark Lager. Consumers received coupons for the return of empty bottles and exchanged them for premiums in a Pilsener catalog. Brewery operations were interrupted by Prohibition Amendment but bottling resumed on 2 May 1933. The Cleveland-based City Ice & Fuel Co. took control of Pilsener in 1935.

Arthur Nohel (1884-1973), b. nr. Chomutov, Czech., was an outstanding agronomist in Czechoslovakia. He arrived in US in 1938. He raised onion seed for Ferry-Morse Seed Co., San Francisco and sugar beet for Spreckels Sugar Co., tomatoes for California Packing Co., Sacramento. He urged a way to help against hunger in India and other Asian countries. He attracted attention of Senator Robert Dole from Kansas and with the help of the Rockefeller Foundation, courses of instruction were started for young farmers in India.

Gustave M. Pollitzer (1853-1909), b. New York, NY, of Moravian and Bohemian parents, was a cotton exporter. He moved with parents to Beaufort, SC and then to Charleston at age 16 and married Clara Guinzburg of Baltimore, a graduate of New York's Hunter College. Gustave Pollitzer was a successful cotton factor and, like his father, won acceptance to the upper echelons of low country society. He was a member of the Cotton Exchange and took lively interest in the business of the port. He supported Wade Hampton's successful bid for Governor in 1876 which brought an end to carpetbag rule in the State. He was elected to the South Carolina Society in 1891, served as commissioner of the city hospital and the public schools, vice-president of Kahal Kadosh Beth Elohim, president of the Hebrew Benevolent Society, and member of the Board of Health and the Committee of the Fireman's Relief Fund. He was on the Committee on Arrangements for the South Carolina Inter-State and West Indian Exposition of 1901-02, and when President Theodore Roosevelt was feted in Charleston, Gus Pollitzer was among the honored guests.

Moritz Pollitzer (1819-1902), b. Mikulov, Moravia, after initial stay in New York, moved to Beaufort, SC in 1862. He brought his family to Beaufort, SC during the Union occupation at the start of the Civil War. He established himself as a cotton merchant and agent for a cotton gin manufacturer. Though he did not become a planter himself, he accumulated extensive land holdings and personal property, valued at $15,700 in 1870. Technically a carpetbagger, that is, a northerner who came South to profit from the upheavals of war and reconstruction, Pollitzer nevertheless gained respect and authority in his adopted hometown.

Francis Xavier Richter (1837-1910), b. Frýdlant, Bohemia, was a pioneer settler, miner and rancher in 19th century Washington and British Columbia. At the age of 15, he emigrated to Texas, and after a misadventure where he was wounded and captured by Indians, following the lure of the gold rushes westward, he came to Rich Bar, Washington and with the take from his placer claim opened a small store and operated a small riverboat. Hearing of good grazing land northwards in British Columbia, he sold out his holdings in

Oregon and Washington and bought 40 heads of cattle and drove them to the Keremeos area of the Similkameen Country of British Columbia's Southern Interior in October 1864. He pre-empted land six miles (10 km) down the Similkameen from Keremeos and founded the 'R' Ranch. He also worked for a while for the Hudson's Bay Company at Fort Similkameen (Fort Keremeos). With his cattle business thriving, he started a new ranch at what was to become Keremeos Centre, where he also operated a thriving store. In addition to an opulent new residence, Richter planted 30 acres (120,000 m²) of fruit trees on the new property, which was to become the foundation of the Similkameen's still-thriving orchard industry and, alongside the Oblate priests of Okanagan Mission, is reckoned to be the founder of BC's fruit industry. The house and the Richter household became social pillars of British Columbia society and important guests were common at the Richter ranch. Among those hosted by Richter was Earl Grey in 1908. Eventually, the Richter holdings comprised 10,000 acres (40 km²) of land and 1,500 head of cattle. His legacy is maintained by the following geographical names: Richter Pass, Richter Mountain, Richter Creek and Richter Lake, all in the small mountain range at the southeast end of the Thompson Plateau between the lower Similkameen and South Okanagan, named for him. The Richter Ranch, to this day, continues in operation in the same area.

Koerner Rombauer (1934-2018), b. Escondido, CA, of Slovak descent; commercial pilot, the founder of Rombauer Vineyards Valley, CA.

Francis William Ruzicka (1908-1984), b. New Providence, NJ, of Bohemian ancestry, was a wholesale rose grower, trained at Cornell Univ. He was pres. of Ruzicka's Inc, Chatham, NJ (s. 1935), Silver Seald Flowers Corp. President, Chatham Bd. Edu. He also served as president of the National Rose Growers Association.

Joseph F. Růžička (1878-1957), b. Kaňk, Bohemia, was a well-known cultivator of roses. Hardly a flower shop in NYC did not have roses from Ruzicka Inc. The firm's large gardens were located in Florham, NJ.

Maximillian 'Max' Schling (1874-1943), b. Horní Cerekev, Bohemia, a noted horticulturist, began as a retail florist in New York City in 1901. He became owner and president, Max Schling, Inc. and president, Max Schling Seedsman, Inc.

Max Schling, Jr. (1914-1971), b. Yonkers, NY, of Bohemian ancestry, was associated with Max Schling Inc., florists, NYC (1935-71), as chairman of the Board (1969-72); with Max Schling Seedsman (1935-63), as pres. (1942-63); vice pres., Constance Spry Inc., (1949-68).

John A. Semrad (1866–d.), b. Polanka, Bohemia, came to US in 1868. He was president of the Semrad Brothers & Pusch Brewing Company, Highland, WI. The original brewery was founded about 1860 and purchased by John V. Semrad in 1887, who conducted it up to 1893, when he retired, and turned the business over to his sons, John A., Frank F., and Joseph E., who managed it under the firm name of John A. Semrad & Brothers until 1904, when Anton J. Pusch purchased an interest, and the firm was re-established under the name of Semrad Brothers & Pusch Brewing Company. The capacity of the brewery was 20,000 barrels per year, as compared with its start, in 1888, when the output was less than 500 barrels annually.

John H. Shary (1872–1945), b. Wilber, NE, of Czech ancestry, was an American farmer and entrepreneur. By the age of eighteen, he had worked his way through college to become one of the youngest men certified as a pharmacist in that state. When he was twenty-two, he accepted a job as a traveling salesman for a California drug company. His travels took him throughout the United States and Canada. While in Texas, he took notice of the great potential for land development. He first purchased 30,000 acres (120 km^2) of land between Corpus Christi and San Antonio. The sale of this property earned him much profit and inspired him to enter the land development business. In 1912, Shary made his way to the Rio Grande Valley and realized the possibilities of this lush area. At the time, it was largely brush and cactus, but Shary was impressed with citrus crops that were being grown by early citrus experimenters and felt that citrus was the crop of the future for Texas. Citrus crops needed irrigation and in 1914, Shary purchased the First Lift Station which pumped life giving water from the Rio Grande to irrigate 15,000 acres (61 km^2) of surrounding crops. The following year, Shary planted the first commercial citrus orchard. His first crops were seeded white grapefruit. His citrus empire would eventually grow to almost 15,000 acres (60 km^2) of groves. The first commercial shipments of citrus, packed in onion crates, were shipped from the lower Rio Grande Valley in 1920. By 1922, much of the land had been transformed into citrus groves, and cotton, onion, and vegetable fields. Shary took the lead in organizing and building the United Irrigation Company, in order to assure water supplies for future developments. Because of his significant role in the development of the area, Shary was named to the Texas Business Hall of Fame and is remembered as the 'Father of the Texas Citrus Industry.' He greatly assisted in the establishment of citrus as a productive commercial crop in the Rio Grande Valley. Since 1932, the Texas Citrus Fiesta has been held to commemorate the abundant harvest of the Texas citrus industry. To this day, this area is known for producing some of the sweetest and best quality citrus in the world. He purchased 36,000 acres (150 km^2) of land near Mission. This area would later become known as 'Sharyland.'

John A. Sokol (1875–1942), b. Chodov, Bohemia, came to US in 1889, settling in Chicago. He became interested in the importing business and in two years' time, bought a coffee and grocery business. After he got married, he moved to Mexico where he became a manager of coffee plantation. From Mexico, he exported coffee to New York, New Orleans and Chicago, until a revolution broke out in Oaxaca. He returned to Chicago where he founded a wholesale coffee and spice importing business. In 1907, he bought the production plant American Spice Co. Sokol pioneered in the commercial importation of a variety of food products. He became the main importer of sage from Yugoslavia, of mushrooms from Central Europe, as well as of poppy from Czechoslovakia, Poland and Hungary. He was instrumental in founding Czechoslovak American Chamber of Commerce.

Adolf Stein (1853–1919), b. Bohemia, came to Chicago in the year of 1867 where he became employed by an uncle named Joseph Stein, working for his room and board. When he was eighteen years old, he left the employ of his uncle and went into business for himself. For many years he was associated with his brothers in the liquor business. The Stein Brothers built up a large trade and were recognized as one of the leading firms in their line. Apart from being president of Stein Bros., Inc., he was vice-president of Art Wall Paper Mills, vice-president of Calumet Distilling Company, and vice-president of Monarch Brewing Company.

Charles Vincent Svoboda (1859–1953), b. Jaroměřice Moravia, came to America with parents in 1874, settling in Schuyler, NE. He became farmer in Howard Co., NE and owned several thousands of acres of land in Nebraska, New Mexico, Texas and Canada. He was a member of the firm Svoboda & Gruber, brick mfg. & contracting bus., St Paul & Ord. He built Bohemian Catholic Church at Warsaw and St. Paul Business College bldg. He served as Howard Co. clerk (1891–97); as a member of the Nebraska Constitutional Convention (1919–20) and chairman of the Howard Co. Central Committee. He was elected, as Democrat from Howard Co., a member of the NE House of Representatives (1923). He was an organizer and for 15 years, he was secretary of the Farmers Union & Farm Bureau; and also served as president and co-organizer of the Farmers Alliance. He was also a road supervisor and assessor for 6 years and a member of Board of Education. During World War I, he was a member of the Howard Co. Council of Defense. He was also president of the Czech Historical Society of Nebraska and secretary of ZCBJ (s. 1907). He was a frequent contributor of articles to newspapers and served early settlers as interpreter, having knowledge of 6 languages.

Louis Taussig (1837–1890) founded The Taussig Co. in San Francisco, which became one of the largest wholesale liquor establishments in the west, eventually expanding into Cincinnati, New York City and Kentucky.

Samuel Taussig (1854-1926), b. Bohemia, was in notion business until 1887. He then came to America and engaged, with his bother William, in leaf tobacco business in Chicago until 1893. Subsequently, he removed to Minneapolis, MN and conducted the wholesale tobacco house alone (1894-1904). Since then, he resided in St. Louis, as president of the St. Louis Leaf Tobacco Co.

Charles J. Vopička (1857-1935), b. Dolní Hbity, Bohemia, a businessman, in 1891, organized the Atlas Brewing Co. in Chicago, becoming its president and manager.

Jerome Vostrovsky (1836-1901), b. Semily, Bohemia, immigrated to Champaign, IL in 1863 and in the following year, moved to St. Louis. In 1867, he went to Cedar Rapids, IA, and in 1870, to West Point where he opened a dry goods store. In 1875, with his family, he removed to California, but in 1879, returned to West Point. In 1883, he returned to California, where he acquired wealth in grape culture. In St. Louis, he married Mrs. Anna Mudroch (born Vitousek). His daughter Anna married Thomas Čapek of New York, a banker and well-known Czech-American author. The other daughter Clara (Mrs. Winlow) has translated and also written several books. He died in San Jose in May 1901.

Emil Wedeles (1861-1928), b. Pilsen, Bohemia, was a leaf tobacco merchant. He began in leaf tobacco business in Chicago (1878) and advanced to salesman. He was associated with his brother Joseph (1888) and organized firm Wedeles Brothers, dealers and packers of leaf tobacco.

Virgil Orville Wodicka (1915-2005), b. St. Louis, MO, of Czech ancestry, was a food scientist. He was trained as a food scientist at Univ. of Washington St. Louis. He was chief, animal products div., Quarter Master Food and Container Inst., Chicago. Later became Director, Division of Food Chemistry & Technology, Bureau of Foods & Pesticides, FDA, DHEW (1969-72). Subsequently, he was promoted to Director of Bureau of Foods, FDA, DHEW (1973-74).

Emanuel Woodic (1836-d.), b. Bohemia, arrived in America in 1854 at the age of eighteen. His first job was working on a farm in Long Island, NY and later hired out on a wrecking vessel that cruised in Delaware Bay. In 1856, he enlisted in the US Army. After a heroic career in the Civil War, he went to Michigan. He bought a forty-acre farm in McComb Co., where over the next quarter-century, he became one of the foremost farmers in the county. Because of his expertise, as experienced farmer, he was consulted by the Jewish community to improve the agricultural conditions in the newly established Palestine colony near the village, Bad Axe, Michigan. Wodic bought equipment, livestock, groceries, and seed for planting for each family. Becoming the agricultural advisor and leader of the colony, he remained through the summer of 1892 teaching the colonists how to sow, cultivate, and harvest, and he oversaw the installation of a temporary sawmill to cut logs from the continuing clearing of the land. However, living accommodations were so poor that he lived in the village of Bad Axe, making the journey to the settlement every day. Woodic received no compensation for his work.

VI. Public Life

A. Executive Branch Officials

Madeleine Albright (née Korbelová) (1937-2022), b. Prague, Czech., is Columbia Univ. trained political scientist. She has served as a professor of international relations at Georgetown University's Walsh School of Foreign Service. She was appointed by US President Bill Clinton as US Secretary of State, serving from 1997-2001, first such post held by a woman. During her tenure, Albright considerably influenced American foreign policy in Bosnia and Herzegovina and the Middle East. Following Albright's term as Secretary of State, many speculated that she might pursue a career in Czech politics. Czech President, Václav Havel, spoke openly about the possibility of Albright succeeding him. Albright was reportedly flattered but denied ever seriously considering the possibility of running for office in her country of origin. In May 2012, she was awarded the Presidential Medal of Freedom by U.S. President Barack Obama.

Thomas F. Bayard (1828-1898), b. Wilmington, DE, desc. f. Augustine Heřman, was an American lawyer, who became US Secretary of State (1885-89) in President Grover Cleveland's first Administration. He is best known for negotiating the Fishery Treaty, settling fishing rights between the United States and Canada in the North Atlantic.

James Montgomery Beck (1861-1936), b. Philadelphia, PA, of Moravian ancestry, was an American attorney who became US Solicitor General (1921-25) in President Warren G. Harding administration. During his term, he was responsible for more than 800 cases before the US. Supreme Court. He personally and successfully argued more than 100 of those cases.

Francis Beverley Biddle (1886-1968), b. Paris, France, desc. f. Augustine Heřman, was an American lawyer and judge who was US Solicitor General in President Franklin D. Roosevelt's Administration (1940) and US Attorney General (1941-45) in President Roosevelt and President H. Truman's Administrations.

Charles Paul Blahous, 3rd (1963-), b. Alexandria, VA, of Czech ancestry, was Special Assistant to US President George W. Bush for economic policy within the National Economic Council, whose Deputy Director he was in 2007-2008. Currently, he is a Senior Fellow at the Hudson Institute, focusing on social security. He was raised in Pittsburgh, Pennsylvania and received an undergraduate degree in chemistry from Princeton University in 1985, and a Ph.D. in computational quantum chemistry from the University of California, Berkeley in 1989.

Stuart J. Bohacek (1910-1982), b. Nebraska, of Czech ancestry, was chief of the Czechoslovak Service of the Voice of America, the United States Information Agency's radio arm. Bohacek was one time the editor of the *Wilber Republican* in Wilber. He attended Doane College in Crete, later receiving his Bachelor's Degree from Syracuse University. He returned in 1965 from his post with USIA in Prague, Czechoslovakia where he was cultural affairs officer. He has also been stationed in Nagoya and Kobe, Japan. Mr. Bohacek's new assignment puts him in charge of all *Voice of America* programs that are beamed to various Czech speaking areas explaining American Foreign Policy and portraying the hopes, problems and aims of the people of the United States.

Barbara Bush (1925-2018), b. Rye, NY; descendent of the Moravian Brethren family of Demuth, who immigrated to the US in 1736, first settling in Savannah, GA and then moving to Bethlehem, PA. She was the First Lady of the United States, from 1989 to 1993, as the wife of George H. W. Bush, who served as the 41st President of the United States, and founder of the Barbara Bush Foundation for Family Literacy. She previously was Second Lady of the United States from 1981 to 1989. She was one of the most popular First Ladies, noted for her charitable and humanitarian efforts. Among her six children are George W. Bush, the 43rd President of the United States, and Jeb Bush, the 43rd Governor of Florida. In 1982, Barbara Bush received the D.A.R. Medal of Honor from the Daughters of the American Revolution. In 1995, Bush received the Award for Greatest Public Service Benefiting the Disadvantaged, an award given out annually by Jefferson Awards. In 1997, she was the recipient of The Miss America Woman of Achievement Award for her work with literacy programs. In 2016, she received honorary membership in Phi Beta Kappa from the University of Houston chapter. Barbara Bush Elementary School in the Parkway Villages neighborhood in Houston, operated by the Houston Independent School District, is named after her.

George W. Bush (1946-), b. New Haven, CT, of Czech ancestry on his mother's side, was the 43rd US President, serving for 2 terms from 2001 to 2009.

Robert Williams Daniel, Jr. (1936-2012), b. Richmond, VA, desc. f. Augustine Heřman, US Congressman, served as Deputy Assistant to Secretary of Defense, Caspar Weinberger, from 1984 to 1986; and Director of Intelligence for the Department of Energy from 1990 to 1993. He was a recipient of the National Intelligence Distinguished Service Medal.

Charles Fried (1935-2024), b. Prague, Czech., is an American jurist and lawyer, who served as US Solicitor General under President Ronald Reagan from 1985 to 1989. He was a professor at Harvard Law School and a visiting professor at Columbia Law School. He also served on the board of the nonpartisan group, the Campaign Legal Center. Fried was the author of more than ten books and over 30 journal articles, and his work appeared in over a dozen collections.

Rayburn D. Hanzlik (1938–), b. Los Angeles, CA, of Czech ancestry, a lawyer, served on the staff of Presidents Nixon and Ford during (1970-76), holding the position of Associate Director, White House Domestic Council (1975-77). Following his unsuccessful Senate campaign, he joined the 1980 Presidential campaign of Ronald Reagan and then returned to Washington with the Presidential appointment of Administrator of the Economic Regulatory Administration in the US Dept. of Energy (1981-85). Subsequently, he returned to his law practice.

Eliška Hašek (1941–), b. Prague, Czech.; in US s. 1980. After graduating from the Georgetown University School of Foreign Service 1963, she served for 18 years (1963-81) as Director of the Office of Presidential Messages and Special Assistant to the President. From 1981 to 1990, she served in the Department of State on the personal Staff of Secretary of State Alexander Haig and later under Secretary of State George Shultz as Congressional Liaison Officer for the Inter-American Bureau, Assistant Chief of Protocol of the U.S. and as Alternate Delegate to the Organization of American States. She took early retirement from the government in 1990 to be free to travel to the Czech Republic where she founded Coolidge Consulting Services.

Charles A. Horsky (1910-1997), b. Helena, MT, of Czech ancestry, was a lawyer and former Government official who helped redevelop the Nation's Capital during the Kennedy and Johnson Administrations. Mr. Horsky argued many cases and held many important positions in a law career that began in 1934, but it was his work as Adviser to the President for National Capital Affairs from 1962 to 1967 that had the greatest impact on those who live in or visit Washington, an impact that will be felt for years to come. President John F. Kennedy appointed him to the White House job and Lyndon B. Johnson carried him over when Johnson succeeded to the Presidency in 1963. During Mr. Horsky's time at the White House, he pressed for switching money from a highway project to the construction of a subway system, and the resulting Metro is now regarded as one of the best in the world. He worked on the redevelopment of Pennsylvania Avenue, a project that was begun after the 1961 inaugural parade and Kennedy determined that America's Main Street had become seedy and unworthy of a great nation. That project is just being completed with the opening soon of the Ronald Reagan Building. Another of Mr. Horsky's accomplishments is enduring a melancholy chapter. For years, Washington was run as a virtual fiefdom of Congress, with residents having no say in its Government. During the Johnson Administration, a push was made to establish home rule for Washington, and it was Mr. Horsky who played the pivotal role in getting legislation for it through Congress.

John Jay (1745-1829), b. New York, NY, grandson of Frederick Philipse's stepdaughter, was an American statesman, patriot, and a Founding Father of the US, who served as 2nd US Secretary of Foreign Affairs July 1784, which position he held until the establishment of the Federal Government in 1789, when Congress passed a law giving certain additional domestic responsibilities to the new Department and changing its name to the Department of State.

John R. Karlik (1938-), b. White Plains, NY of Czech ancestry, served as Deputy Assistant Secretary, US Dept. of Treasury (1977-81).

John T. Kmetz (1893-1968), b. Lepuhov, Slovakia; labor union official; Assistant Secretary of Labor, having been appointed by President Truman (1947).

Frances Gladys Knight (1905-1999), b. Newport, RI of Czech ancestry, was Director of the US Passport Office (1955-77), serving under five different Presidents. She ran the US Passport Office for 22 years with efficiency and conservative zeal, denying passports and entrance visas to those she regarded as enemies of the nation and surviving efforts to remove her. Her widely publicized improvements in the Passport Office, including her frequent boast of being one of the few Federal agencies to actually earn a profit, gained her many supporters on both sides of the aisle in Congress.

Thomas C. Komarek (1940-), b. NE, of Czech ancestry, served as Assistant Secretary for Administrative Management, US Dept. of Labor (1984-85, 1989-93).

Jo Ann Krukar (1948-), b. Ford City, PA, of Slovak descent, was healthcare lobbyist and senior director of federal relations and policy for the American Organization of Nurse Executives. She was the highest-ranking woman in the Department of Veterans Affairs (VA) upon her appointment as Under Secretary of Veterans Affairs for Memorial Affairs, director of the National Cemetery System (NCS) by President George H.W. Bush on October 10, 1989. She moved on in November 1991 to become VA's Assistant Secretary for Policy and Planning.

Gerhard F. Kuska (1966-), b. Passaic, NJ, of Czech ancestry, with Ph.D. in marine studies (2005), has served over the past several decades in a variety of positions and organizations in the US, Europe, and the Middle East, and continues to serve in advisory board capacities around the world. From 2006 to 2008, Dr. Kuska served as Associate Director of the White House Council on Environmental Quality and Director of Ocean and Coastal Policy in the Executive Office of the President, where he advised the President of the United States on a broad array of ocean, coastal, and maritime issues, and oversaw the implementation of the President's Ocean Action Plan and several high-profile initiatives.

Lucius Quintus Cincinnatus Lamar, 2nd (1825–1893), b. Eatonton, GA, desc. f. Augustine Heřman, was an American lawyer and politician, who served as US Secretary of Interior (1885–88) in the first administration of President Grover Cleveland.

Ronald Stephen Lauder (1944–), b. New York, NY of Slovak ancestry, served as Deputy Assistant Secretary, US Dept. of Defense (1983–85).

Richard A. Lidinsky, Jr. (ca. 1946–2022), b. Baltimore, MD, of Czech ancestry, studied at School of Government and Public Administration of American University (B.A., 1968), and law at the University of Maryland (J.D., 1972). He is a 37-year veteran in the maritime trade industry from positions held in both business and government. After serving as a Congressional aide on the US House of Representatives Merchant Marine and Fisheries Committee, he began his professional legal career in the FMC's Office of General Counsel as Legislative Counsel from 1973–75. In 1975, the Maryland Port Administration appointed him to be Director of Tariffs and National Port Affairs, as well as counsel. Most recently, Lidinsky worked as an attorney and international trade consultant in private practice. In 2009, he was sworn in as Federal Maritime Commissioner for a term to expire on June 30, 2012. He was nominated by President Barack Obama on June 18, 2009 and confirmed by the Senate on July 24, 2009. On September 11, 2009, he was designated Chairman. He served until 2013.

David Eli Lilienthal (1899–1981), b. Morton, IL, of Slovak ancestry; American attorney, chairman of Tennessee Valley Authority (TVA) and of the Atomic Energy commission.

George Michael Low (orig. George Wilhelm Low) (1926–1984), b. Vienna, of Czech ancestry, served as NASA Deputy Administrator, from December 1969 to June 1976. As such, he became one of the leading figures in the early development of the Space Shuttle, the Skylab program, and the Apollo-Soyuz Test Project.

Frederic Vincent Malek (1936–2019), b. Berwyn, IL, of Czech ancestry, a successful businessman, served under US Presidents Richard Nixon and George H.W. Bush. He was appointed served as Deputy Under Secretary, US Dept. of Health, Education and Welfare (1969–70), as Special Assistant to the President (1970–73), as Deputy Director, US Office of Management and Budget (1973–75). Malek served as a National Finance Committee co-chair of John McCain's 2008 Presidential campaign and has played a role in every Republican nominee for President over the past four decades. In 2011, he received the Horatio Alger Award.

Jan W. Mares (1936-), b. St. Louis, MO, of Czech ancestry, served as Assistant Secretary (Fossil Fuels), US Dept. of Energy (1983-84); as Assistant Secretary for International Affairs, Policy, Safety and Environment, US Dept. of Energy (1985-86).

Joseph Anthony Panuch (1900-1975), b. Prague, Bohemia, served as Deputy Assistant Secretary for Administration, US Department of State (1945-47). Panuch was brought into the Department by Byrnes, in October 1945, to supervise the 'coordination and integration' of the OSS, the OWI, the Foreign Economic Administration, the Office of Inter-American Affairs and the Office of Foreign Liquidation, all of which had been transferred to the department under a reorganization scheme devised by the Budget Bureau. Panuch had the job of setting up a security system to screen more than four thousand new employees who were scheduled for permanent integration into the department.

Harry Franklin Payer (1875-1952), b. Cleveland, OH, of Czech ancestry, served as Assistant Secretary, US Dept. of State (1933).

Kenneth G. Picha, Jr. (ca. 1952-), b. US, of Czech ancestry, is currently the Acting Deputy Assistant Secretary for Tank Waste and Nuclear Materials Management in the Office of Environmental Management (EM). Mr. Picha has over thirty years of experience in engineering, operations, and project management for the government and the private sector.

Edmund Jennings Randolph (1753-1813), b. Williamsburg, VA, desc. of Augustine Heřman, was an American lawyer, who became the first US Attorney General (1789-1794) and the second US Secretary of State (1794-95) in President George Washington's Administration.

Miloslav 'Mila' Rechcigl (1930-), b. Mladá Boleslav, Czech., a trained biochemist, was appointed Special Assistant for Nutrition and Health, in HSMHA, DHEW (1969-70). Subsequently, he served as Sr. Nutrition Advisor (1970-71) and then headed research grants and institutional grants program in AID, US Department of State (since 1975). Subsequently, he was appointed director of Research Review in the AID Office of the Science Advisor (since 1982).

Pete Rouse (1946-), b. New Haven, CT, of Czech ancestry, is an American political consultant who served as interim White House Chief of Staff to US President Barack Obama. Rouse has spent years on Capitol Hill, becoming known as the '101st Senator' during his tenure as Chief of Staff to Senate Democratic leader Tom Daschle. When Daschle lost his seat in 2004, Rouse was persuaded to stay in Congress as Chief of Staff to then-freshman Senator Barack Obama. Rouse followed Obama to the White House as a senior advisor in 2008 and became interim

Chief of Staff there for several months upon the departure of Rahm Emanuel in October 2010.

Richard Francis Schubert (1936–), b. Trenton, NJ, of Czech ancestry, graduated from Eastern Nazarene Coll. (B.A., 1958) and received training in law at Yale Univ. (LL.B., 1961). He was appointed Undersecretary, U.S. Dept. of Labor (1973-75) in President Nixon's and Ford's administrations. Later he became President of the American Red Cross.

John Slezák (1896-1986), b. Stará Tura, Slovakia; Colonel, mechanical engineer, businessman, Under Secretary of the Army (1954-55).

Harold Stassen (1907-2001), b. West St. Paul, MN, of Czech ancestry, was an American lawyer and a politician, who served in the Eisenhower Administration, filling posts including director of the Mutual Security Administration (Foreign Aid) and Special Assistant to the President for Disarmament. During this period, he held cabinet rank.

John K. Tabor (1921-1999), b. Uniontown, PA, of Czech ancestry, a lawyer, who was prominent in Republican Party politics in Pennsylvania in the 1960's, became Under Secretary of Commerce in the Nixon Administration. From 1973, when President Richard M. Nixon named him to the commerce post, to 1975, when he returned to his law practice, Mr. Tabor pursued policies intended to promote American exports and stimulate minority business enterprise. He first gained experience in this field in 1963, when Gov. William W. Scranton of Pennsylvania appointed him to lead the State's Commerce Department.

Charles William Taussig (1871-1957), b. of Bohemian ancestry, was president of American Molasses Company (Grandma's Molasses) and early Brain Trust advisor to Franklin Delano Roosevelt. From 1934 to 1935, he served as chair of the National Advisory Committee of the National Youth Administration. He served on the Anglo-American Caribbean Commission, as co-chairman in 1942 and as chairman of the American Delegation for 1946 until 1948. He also served as a member of the President's council for Virgin Islands. Chairman of the US commission to study social and economic conditions in the British East Indies and on the United Nations Conference on International Organizations.

Frank William Taussig (1859-1940), b. St. Louis, MO, of Bohemian ancestry, an industrialist, served as Chairman, U.S. Tariff Commission (1917 19) in President Woodrow Wilson's administration.

Joseph K. Taussig, Jr. (1920-1999), b. Newport, RI, of Bohemian ancestry, served as Deputy Assistant Secretary (1981-85), as Assistant Deputy Under Secretary of the Navy (1985 1993), Dept. of the Navy.

Ivanka Marie Trump (1981-), b. New York, NY, is an American businesswoman, writer, and former model and politician. She is the daughter of President Donald Trump and Donald's first wife Ivana. She is the first Jewish member of a First Family, having converted, before marrying her Jewish husband, Jared Kushner. Trump is a fourth-generation businessperson who followed in the footsteps of her great-grandmother Elizabeth, grandfather Fred, and father, serving for a time as an executive vice president of the family-owned Trump Organization. She was also a boardroom judge on her father's TV show *The Apprentice*. Starting in March 2017, she left the Trump Organization and began serving in her father's Presidential administration as an adviser alongside her husband. She assumed this official, unpaid position after ethics concerns were raised about her having access to classified material while not being held to the same restrictions as a federal employee. She was considered part of the president's inner circle even before becoming an official employee in his administration.

Sanford 'Sandy' J. Ungar (1945-), b. Slovak ancestry; journalist, director of *Voice of America*.

Caspar Willard Weinberger (1917-2006), b. San Francisco, CA, of Bohemian ancestry on his father's side, was an American lawyer, who served as US Secretary of Health, Education, and Welfare (1973-1975) in President Richard Nixon's Administration and US Secretary of Defense (1981-87) in President Ronald Reagan's Administration.

Jonathan Mayhew Wainwright (1864-1945), b. New York, NY, desc. f. Frederic Philipse, served as Assistant Secretary of War (1921-23) in President Warren C. Harding's administration.

John Skelton Williams (1865-1926), b. Powhatan Co., VA, desc. f. Augustine Heřman, was the first Assistant Secretary of US Dept. of Treasury (1913) and Comptroller of the Currency (1914, 1919), appointed by President Wilson.

Thomas G. Wyman (1923-2020), b. Ústí n/L., served as Assistant Secretary, US Dept. of Commerce (1964-65) in President Lyndon B. Johnson's administration.

B. Diplomats

Madeleine Albright (née Korbelová) (1937-2022), b. Prague, Czech., graduated from Wellesley College in 1959 and earned a Ph.D. from Columbia University in 1975, writing her thesis on the Prague Spring. She worked as an aide to Senator Edmund Muskie before taking a position under Zbigniew Brzezinski on the National Security Council. She served in that position until the end of President Jimmy Carter's singular term in 1981. After leaving the National Security Council, Albright joined the academic faculty of Georgetown University and advised Democratic candidates regarding foreign policy. After Clinton's victory in the 1992 presidential election, she helped assemble his National Security Council. In 1993, Clinton appointed her to the position of U.S. Ambassador to the United Nations, first such office, held by a woman. She held that position until 1997, when she succeeded Warren Christopher as Secretary of State.

Roland E. Arnall (1939-2008), b. Paris, France, of Czech ancestry, served as US Ambassador to the Netherlands (2006-08).

John L. Baikal (1888-d.), b. Wilbur, NE, of Czech ancestry, served as Vice Consul de Carriere (1920), Consul, Prague (1922-23) and Consul, Port Said, Egypt (1923).

Richard Henry Bayard (1796-1868), b. Wilmington, DE, desc. f. Augustine Heřman, was an American lawyer and politician, who served as Chargé d'affaires to Belgium (1850-53), having been appointed by President Millard Filmore.

Thomas Francis Bayard (1828-1898), b. Wilmington, DE, desc. f. Augustine Heřman, was an American lawyer and politician, who was appointed US Ambassador to Great Britain (1893-97), during President Cleveland's second administration, the first U.S. diplomatic minister to hold Ambassadorial rank. Bayard is sometimes credited for building the first strong links between the United States and the United Kingdom.

John L. Bouchal (1888-1970), b. Wilber, NE, of Czech ancestry, started as a teacher in country schools and after saving some money entered the State University. He obtained a position as clerk to the Consul in Prague, Bohemia, where he went in July, 1912. In May 1920, he was made Vice-Consul de Carriere and in June 1922, Consul in Prague. In November 1923, he was appointed Consul in Port Said, Egypt.

Lloyd S. Bryce (1851-1917), b. Flushing, NY, desc. f. Augustine Heřman, was a magazine editor and politician, who was appointed US Minister to the Netherlands and Luxemburg (1911-13).

James E. Brice (1784-1827), b. Baltimore, MD, desc. f. Augustine Heřman, served as US Consul and commercial attaché to Haiti (1822-27).

Mark Francis Brzezinski (1965-), b. New York, NY, of Czech mother, is an American lawyer and political scientist, who was appointed by President Obama US Ambassador to Sweden (2011-2015).

VI. PUBLIC LIFE

Victor Hugo Duras (1880–1943), b. Crete, NE, of Czech ancestry, served as an US Vice Consul to Leige, Belgium (1913 14) and then as Vice Consul to Petrograd, Russia (1914–15).

Norman L. Eisen (1960–), b. Los Angeles, CA, of Slovak descent; lawyer, US Ambassador to the Czech Republic (2011–2014).

Roger Ernst (1924-2014), b. New York, NY, of Bohemian ancestry, was educated at Williams Coll. and the National War College. He served in the US Army in Berlin, was Officer in Charge of the Marshall plan for Austria and Assistant Director for NATO and Assistant Director for Planning, Office of Secretary of Defense. He started the Peace Corps in India, served as Deputy Director of the US Economic Assistance Mission in Taiwan and Korea, then was Director of USAID in Ethiopia and Thailand. He also was a Fellow at the East-West Center in Hawaii and taught at the University of South Florida.

Clayland Boyden Gray (1943-2023), b. Winston-Salem, NC, of Moravian ancestry, is an American lawyer, who became US Ambassador to the European Union (2006–07), having been appointed by President George W. Bush.

Vladimir A. Geringer (1872-1968), b. Chicago, IL, of Czech ancestry, served as US Trade Commissioner to Czechoslovakia (1918–23), having been appointed by President Wilson.

Francis Joseph Grund (1805-1863), b. Prague, Bohemia, a journalist, served as US Consul in Bremen (1841–42), in Antwerp (1854–60), at the Consulate Havre (1860–61), and as diplomatic agent to the South German States (1862).

Theodore Joseph Hadraba (1907–2001), b. Omaha, NE, of Czech ancestry, served as Consul General, Stuttgart, Germany (1955–57), as Economic Counselor, US Embassy, Vienna (1957-59), as Deputy Assistant Secretary of State (1961–63), as Commercial Counselor, American Embassy Rome (s. 1963).

Robert G. Houdek (1940–), b. Chicago, IL, of Bohemian ancestry, is a career diplomat, who served as US Ambassador to Uganda (1985–88) and Chargé d'affaires to Ethiopia (1988–91).

Felix Bohumil Janovsky (1880–1953), b. Blatná, Bohemia, a notary and a journalist, became Czechoslovak Consul in Los Angeles for 20 years, following Josef T. Triska.

John Jay (1745–1829), b. New York, NY, grandson of Frederick Philipse' s stepdaughter, was an American statesman, patriot, and a Founding Father of the US, who became Minister Plenipotentiary to Spain (1779–1782). He was appointed one of the ministers to negotiate peace with Great Britain June 14, 1781 and signed the Treaty of Paris. He was also appointed one of the ministers to negotiate treaties with the European powers on May 1, 1783.

Peter Augustus Jay (1877-1933), b. Newport, RI, desc. f. Frederick Philipse, was an American lawyer, and career diplomat, who served as US Minister to El Salvador from 1920 to 1921. From 1921 to 1925, he was Minister to Romania where he assisted in negotiating that country's repayment terms for wartime and post-World War I development loans. In 1925, he was appointed US Ambassador to Argentina, serving through 1927.

Charles (Karel) Jonáš (1840-1896), b. Malešov, Bohemia, was a journalist, who became US Consul to Prague (1886-89), appointed by President Cleveland. Later he was appointed US Consul to St. Petersburg (1894), and then US Consul to Krefeld, Germany (1896).

John C. Karel (1851-1914), b. Německá Bříza u Plzně, Bohemia, was a lawyer and banker, who served as US Consul to Prague (1893), appointed by President Cleveland; he then moved to Consulate in St. Petersburg (1897).

John Karch (1923-2010), b. Velká Domaša, Czech.; in US. s. 1934; US Navy veteran; US diplomat; Chief of the European Division at the *Voice of America* from (1960-68); professor at the National War College, Washington (1979-82); Counselor with the US Mission to International Organizations, Vienna (till 1996).

John F. Keane (1944-), b. New York, of Czech ancestry, is a career diplomat, who served as US Ambassador to the Republic of Paraguay (2003-2005).

Richard John Kerry (1915-2000), Boston, MA, of Moravian parents, was trained as a lawyer at Harvard Univ. Kerry entered the American Foreign Service and served as a diplomat in positions both in the United States and at Embassies in other nations, including Germany and Norway. He also served as a lawyer in the Bureau of United Nations Affairs. He was the father of US. Senator John Kerry.

Joseph J. Langer (1860-1927), b. Roudnice nad Labem, Bohemia, while living in Wilber, NE, in 1901, was appointed by President McKinley Consul to Solingen, Germany.

Ronald Stephen Lauder (1944-), b. New York, NY of Czechoslovak ancestry, is a businessman and philanthropist, who became US Ambassador to Austria (1986-87), appointed by President Ronald Reagan.

Henry Brockhorst Ledyard (1812-1980), b. New York, NY desc. f. Frederic Philipse, served as Secretary of US Legation, Paris (1839), as Chargé d'affaires of Legation (1842-44).

Deborah R. Malac (1955-), b. of Czech immigrant father, is a career member of the Senior Foreign Service. She is an American diplomat and served as the United States Ambassador to Uganda (2016-20), having been nominated by President Barack Obama. She previously served as United States Ambassador to Liberia (2012-15). Before that, she served as the Director of the Office of East African Affairs at the State Department in Washington, D.C. In 1977, Malac earned a B.A. in international studies magna cum laude and Phi Beta Kappa from Furman University. She also received an M.A. in foreign affairs from the University of Virginia in 1981. She later studied at the Industrial College of the Armed Forces (now Dwight D. Eisenhower School for National Security and Resource Strategy) and received an M.S. in national resources strategy there in 2002.

J. Pierrepoint Moffat (1896-1943), b. Rye, NY, desc. F. Frederic Philipse, served as First Secretary of Legation, Berne, Switzerland (1927-31), as Consul General, Sydney, Australia (1935-37), as US Minister to Canada (s. 1940).

Albert Richard Morawetz (1856-d.), b. Baltimore, MD, of Bohemian ancestry, was educated in private schools in Baltimore, Germany, and Switzerland. He was a career diplomat, who served as Vice and Deputy Consul at Nogales, Mexico (1898-1902); as Consul at Nogales (1902-6), as consul at Bahia, Brazil (1906-7); as Consul General-at-large (1907-10); as consul in Leipzig,

Robert G. Neumann (1916-1999), b. Vienna, of Moravian mother, was a political scientist and a diplomat, who became US Ambassador to Afghanistan (1966-1973), named by President Lyndon B. Johnson; he then became US Ambassador to Morocco (1973-1976) and US Ambassador to Saudi Arabia (1981).

Ronald E. Neumann (1945-), b. Washington, DC, of Bohemian ancestry, is an American diplomat who served as the United States Ambassador to Afghanistan (2005-2007), Bahrain (2001-2004) and Algeria (1994-1997). He is the son of former Ambassador Robert G. Neumann and traveled extensively after college in Afghanistan while his father was Ambassador there.

Vincent Obsitnik (1938-), b. Moravany, Czech.; Ambassador of the US of America to the Slovak Republic (2007-09).

Rudolf V. Peřina (1945-2018), b. Tábor, Czech., was trained as a historian at Columbia Univ. In a 32-year Foreign Service career, Peřina specialized in Russian, East European, German and NATO affairs. He served at the US Embassy in Ottawa, the NATO desk of the State Department, the US Embassy in Moscow, the US Mission in Berlin, the US Mission to NATO in Brussels, and as Director for European and Soviet Affairs on the National Security Council staff. He also served as Senior Deputy Assistant Secretary of State for European and Canadian Affairs, Chief of Mission at the US Embassy in Belgrade, and Deputy Chairman of the US Delegation to the Vienna Negotiations on Confidence and Security-

Building Measures in Europe. Most recently, he served as the Chargé d'Affaires at the US Embassies in Prague (2013), Reykjavik (May–June 2010), Yerevan (July–October 2007) and Chisinau (June–August 2006) and as a senior State Department inspector (2008). From 2004 to 2006 he served as the Deputy Director of the State Department's Policy Planning Staff. Previously, he was the US Special Negotiator for Nagorno-Karabakh and Eurasian Conflicts (2001–2004) and Ambassador to the Republic of Moldova (1998–2001). He has also most recently been President of the CEELI Institute in Prague.

Andrew Schapiro (1963–), b. Chicago, IL, of Bohemian ancestry, on his mother's side, was appointed US Ambassador to the Czech Republic in September 2014.

Michael J. Senko (1950–), b. Washington, DC, of Slovak parents; career foreign service officer. Served as U.S. Ambassador to the Republic of the Marshall Islands and the Republic of Kiribati (s. 2001), having been nominated by President William Jefferson Clinton. He entered the Foreign Service in 1977 and served in a variety of consular, administrative, political and management positions in the Dominican Republic, Uruguay, El Salvador, Mongolia, Belize, Bosnia and Herzegovina, and Washington. He also served in the Marshall Islands, where he opened the U.S. Status Liaison Office in 1984. Ambassador Senko last served as Policy Planning Director in the Bureau of International Narcotics and Law Enforcement Affairs.

Charles G. Stefan (1920–2003), b. Omaha, NE, of Czech ancestry, held a degree from the University of California at Berkeley and was a graduate of the Russian Institute at Columbia University and the National War College. He spent thirty years (1947–77) in the US Foreign Service, specializing in Soviet affairs. He had assignments in the Soviet Union and several East European countries, as well as the Department of State. Since retirement in Gainesville, Florida, he had written extensively on US-Soviet relations.

László Újházy (1795–1870), b. Budimir, Slovakia; son of a landowner of the lesser nobility; in US s. 1849, arriving in NYC with the first group of Hungarian refugees; after the unsuccessful Hungarian revolution; lawyer by training; Kossuth's representative with the US government; founder of a Hungarian colony, New Buda in Iowa. Ujhazy and his family settled near San Antonio, TX, where he farmed and ranched. He served as Abraham Lincoln's consul at Ancona, Italy (1862–64).

Charles J. Vopička (1857–1935), b. Dolní Hbity, Bohemia, was a businessman, who became US Envoy Extraordinary and Minister Plenipotentiary to Romania, Serbia and Bulgaria (1913–20), having been appointed by President Wilson.

Louis Brandeis Wehle (1880–1959), b. Louisville, KY, of Bohemian ancestry, during the World War II, was appointed chief of the US Foreign Economic Administration's Mission to the Netherlands. Wehle was invested with US Ambassadorial status and also with the assimilated rank of Brigadier General. On the day the Germans withdrew from the Netherlands, he established headquarters in The Hague and immediately set into motion machinery for the distribution of food supplies and for dealing with other emergency functions. It was later revealed that he served as unpublicized advisor to President F. D. Roosevelt throughout the latter's political career.

Murat Willis Williams (1914-1994), b. Richmond, VA, desc. f. Augustine Heřman, was a career diplomat, who was appointed Ambassador to El Salvador (1961-64).

Andrew Jan Winter (1946-), b. US, of Czech parents, was appointed US Ambassador to Gambia (1993-95).

C. US Legislators

John Joseph Babka (1884-1937), b. Cleveland, OH, of Czech immigrant parents, was an American lawyer and politician who served as a Democratic U.S. Representative from Ohio for one term from 1919 to 1921. In 1908, he graduated from the Cleveland Law School. Babka was admitted to the bar the same year and commenced practice in Cleveland. He served as special counsel to the attorney general of Ohio in 1911 and 1912, and as assistant prosecuting attorney of Cuyahoga County from 1912 to 1919. Being an unsuccessful candidate for election in 1920 to the 67th Congress, he resumed the practice of law and served as a delegate to the Democratic National Conventions in 1920 and 1932.

Walter Stephan Baring, Jr. (1911-1975), b. Goldfield, NV, was of Czech ancestry, his maternal grandfather being from Bohemia. Baring graduated from the University of Nevada in 1934 with two bachelor's degrees. After graduating, he worked as a collector for the U.S. Internal Revenue Service. Baring served as a Member of the Nevada Assembly in 1936. He was subsequently reelected but resigned in 1943 so that he could serve in the United States Navy during World War II. After the war, he was elected to the Reno City Council. Baring was first elected to Nevada's sole seat in the House of Representatives in 1948, unseating first-term Republican incumbent Charles H. Russell by 761 votes. He was reelected in 1950. After several losses, Baring ran for Congress again, defeating Las Vegas City Attorney Howard Cannon in the Democratic primary before winning the general. Baring was reelected in a landslide in 1958, while Cannon was elected to the U.S. Senate.

Richard Bassett (1745-1815), b. Cecil Co., MD, desc. f. Augustine Heřman, was a delegate to the Constitutional Convention of 1787 and is considered one of the Founding Fathers of the US. He became US Senator from Delaware (1780-93), elected as a Federalist.

James Asheton Bayard, Jr. (1799-1880), b. Wilmington, DE, desc. f. Augustine Heřman, was an American lawyer, who was elected as a Democrat to the US Senate from Delaware in 1851, reelected in 1857 and 1867, serving from 1851 to 1864.

Richard Henry Bayard (1796-1868), b. Wilmington, DE, desc. f. Augustine Heřman, was an American lawyer, elected as an Anti-Jacksonian to the US Senate to fill the vacancy caused by the resignation of Arnold Naudain and served from 1836-39, when he resigned to become Chief Justice of Delaware. He was elected again to the US Senate, as a Whig, to fill the vacancy which had existed since his own resignation in 1839 and served from January 1841 to March 1845.

Thomas Francis Bayard (1828-1898), b. Wilmington, DE, desc. f. Augustine Heřman, was an American lawyer, who, at the expiration of his father's Senate term in 1869, was elected as a Democrat to the US Senate. He was reelected in 1875 and 1881, serving from 1869 to 1885, when he resigned to become Secretary of State. He served as President pro tempore of the Senate during the 47th Congress.

Thomas Francis Bayard, Jr. (1868-1942), b. Wilmington, DE, desc. f Augustine Heřman, was an American lawyer, who was elected in 1922, as a Democrat to the US Senate to fill the vacancy caused by the resignation of Josiah O. Wolcott; on the same day was also elected for the full-term commencing March 1923, and served from 1922 to 1929.

James M. Beck (1861-1936), b. Philadelphia, PA, of Moravian ancestry, was an American lawyer who was elected as a Republican from Pennsylvania to the 70th Congress to fill the vacancy caused by the resignation of James M. Hazlett; reelected to the 71st, 72nd, and 73rd Congresses and served from November 1927, until his resignation on September 30, 1934.

Mark Peter Begich (1962-), b. Anchorage, AL, of Bohemian ancestry on his mother's side, is the junior United States Senator from Alaska and a member of the Democratic Party. A former Mayor of Anchorage, he served on the Anchorage Assembly for almost ten years prior to being elected Mayor in 2003. In the 2008 Senate election, Begich defeated incumbent Ted Stevens, the longest-serving Republican member of the Senate of all time. After being elected, Begich became a member of the moderate Democratic caucus in the Senate. Begich became the Chairman of the Democratic Steering and Outreach Committee in 2011.

George Harrison Bender (1896-1961), b. Cleveland, OH, of Bohemian ancestry, was editor and publisher, who was elected as a Republican from Ohio to the 76th and to the four succeeding Congresses (1939-1949). He was elected again to the 82nd and 83rd Congresses and served from 1951, until his resignation effective December 15, 1954. He was then elected as a Republican to the US Senate to fill the vacancy in the term ending January 1957, caused by the death of Robert A. Taft, and served from December 1954 to January 1957.

Dan Benishek (1952-2021), b. Iron River, MI, of Czech father, is a physician, who was elected as a Republican from Michigan to the 112th and to the succeeding Congress (s. 2011).

Victor L. Berger (1860-1929), b. Nieder Rebbach, Austria, of Slovak parents, was an American journalist, and socialist politician, who was a founding member of the Social Democratic Party and its successor, the Socialist Party of America. As a politician, in 1910, he was elected as the first Socialist to the U.S. House of Representatives, representing a district in Milwaukee, Wisconsin.

James Wood Bouldin (1792-1854), b. Charlotte Co., VA, desc. f. Augustine Heřman, was American lawyer, who was elected as a Jacksonian to the 23rd Congress to fill the vacancy caused by the death of Thomas T. Bouldin; reelected as a Jacksonian to the 24th Congress; reelected as a Democrat to the 25th Congress; and served from March 1834 to March 1839.

Thomas Tyler Bouldin (1781-1834), b. Charlotte Co., VA, desc. f. Augustine Heřman, was an American lawyer, who was elected as a Jacksonian to the 21st and 22nd Congresses (1829-1833). Subsequently, he was elected again to the 23rd Congress to fill the vacancy caused by the death of John Randolph and served from August 1833, until his death in Washington, D.C., February 11, 1834.

John Bayne Breckinridge (1913-1979), b. Washington, D.C., desc. f. Augustine Heřman. was an American lawyer, who was elected as a Democrat from Kentucky to the 93rd and to the two succeeding Congresses (1973-1979).

David Baugh Brewster (1923-1969), b. Baltimore, MD, desc. f. Augustine Heřman, was an American lawyer, who was elected as a Democrat from Maryland to the 86th and 87th Congresses (1959-1963). In 1962 he was elected as a Democrat from Maryland to the US Senate in 1962, serving from 1963 to 1969.

Lloyd Stephens Bryce (1851-1917), b. Flushing, NY, desc. f Augustine Heřman, was an American lawyer, was elected as a Democrat from New York to the 50th Congress, serving from 1887 to 1889.

Ezekiel Forman Chambers (1788-1867), b. Chestertown, Kent Co., MD, desc. f. Augustine Heřman, was an American lawyer, who was elected as Democrat from Maryland to the US Senate to fill the vacancy caused by the resignation of Edward Lloyd; reelected in 1831 and served from 1826, until his resignation in December 1834.

Thomas Clayton (1778-1859), b. Massey's Cross Roads, MD, desc. f. Augustine Heřman, was an American lawyer, who was elected as a Federalist from Delaware to the 14th Congress (1815-1817). Subsequently, he was elected as an Adams-Clay Federalist (later Adams) to the US Senate to fill the vacancy caused by the resignation of Caesar A. Rodney and served from 1824 to 1827. He was elected again as an Anti-Jacksonian (later Whig) to the US Senate to fill the vacancy caused by the resignation of John M. Clayton; reelected in 1841 and served from 1837 to 1847.

Albert Constable (1805-1855), b. Charlestown, MD, desc. f. Augustine Heřman, was an American lawyer, who was elected as a Democrat from Maryland to the 29th Congress (1845-1847).

Mark Critz (1962-), b. Irwin, PA, of Slovak ancestry; former US Representative for Pennsylvania's 12th Congressional district.

Robert Williams Daniel, Jr. (1936-2012), b. Richmond, VA, desc. f. Augustine Heřman, a farmer and businessman, who was elected as a Republican from Virginia to the 93rd and to the four succeeding Congresses (1973-1983).

Henry Clarence Dworshak (1894-1962), b. Duluth, Minn., of Bohemian ancestry, editor and publisher, was elected as a Republican from Idaho to the 76th and to the three succeeding Congresses and served from 1939 to 1946. He was elected then in a special election held on November 5, 1946, to fill the vacancy caused by the death of John Thomas; served from November 1946 to January 1949. He was appointed on October 14, 1949, to the US Senate and subsequently elected on November 7, 1950, as a Republican to fill the vacancy caused by the death of Bert H. Miller; reelected in 1954 and again in 1960 and served from October 1949, until his death in Washington, D.C., July 23, 1962.

Renee Ellmers (née Jacisin) (1964-), b. Ironwood, MI, of Czech ancestry, is an American politician who was the U.S. Representative for North Carolina's 2nd congressional district from 2011 to 2017. She is a member of the Republican Party. She moved to Madison Heights as a child, when her father got a job in the automobile industry. She graduated from Madison High School and paid her way through Oakland University by working various jobs, training as a medical assistant. In 1990, she graduated with a Bachelor of Science in Nursing. Ellmers worked as a nurse in Beaumont Hospital's surgical intensive care unit. In North Carolina, she was clinical director of the Trinity Wound Care Center in Dunn. Ellmers met her husband Brent Ellmers, a surgeon, while working at Beaumont Hospital. After the birth of their son Ben, the family moved to Dunn, North Carolina, where she and her husband ran a practice. Elmers became involved in politics after the passage of the Patient Protection and Affordable Care Act, which she opposed. She became involved in local Republican politics and joined Americans for Prosperity, a free-market political advocacy group. In November 2011, she was elected the US Congressman from North Carolina's 2nd Congressional district.

Joseph M. Gaydos (1926–2015), b. Braddock, PA, of Slovak ancestry; Democratic member of the U.S. House of Representatives from Pennsylvania.

Otis Ferguson Glenn (1879–1959), b. Mattoon, Coles Co., IL, desc. f. Augustine Heřman, was an American lawyer, who was elected as a Republican from Illinois to the US Senate to fill the vacancy caused by the resignation of Frank L. Smith and served from December 1928 to March 1933.

Julius Goldzier (1854–1925), b. born in Vienna, of Bohemian ancestry on his mother's side, was a Chicago lawyer, who was elected as a Democrat from Illinois to the Fifty-third Congress (1893–95).

Roman Lee Hruska (1904–1999), b. David City, NE, of Czech ancestry, was an American lawyer, who was elected as a Republican from Nebraska to the 83rd Congress and served from 1953, until his resignation November 8, 1954, having been elected to the US Senate. He was reelected in 1958, 1964, and again in 1970 and served from November 1954, until his resignation in December 1976.

Darrell Edward Issa (1953–), b. Cleveland, OH, of Bohemian descent on his mother's side, a businessman, was elected as a Republican from California to the 107th and to the six succeeding Congresses (s. 2001). He was formerly a CEO of Directed Electronics, a Vista, California-based manufacturer of automobile security and convenience products. Since January 2011, he has served as Chairman of the House Oversight and Government Reform Committee. As of 2013, Issa is a multi-millionaire with a net worth estimated at as much as $450 million, which, if accurate, makes him the wealthiest currently serving member of Congress.

John Jay (1745–1829), b. New York, NY, grandson of Frederick Philipse's stepdaughter, became President of the Continental Congress and served in that capacity from December 10, 1778 to September 28, 1779.

Benjamin Franklin Jonas (1834–1911), b. Williamsport, KY, of Bohemian ancestry on his mother's side, was an American lawyer, who was elected as a Democrat from Louisiana to the US Senate and served from 1879 to 1885.

John Richard Kasich (1952–), b. McKees Rocks, Allegheny Co., PA, of Czech ancestry, was elected as a Republican from Ohio to the 98th and to the eight succeeding Congresses (1983–2001).

John Katko (1962–), b. Syracuse, NY, of Slovak ancestry; attorney and politician, attorney and politician, Republican member of the US House of Representatives from New York's 24th district, based in Syracuse, since 2015. A member of the Republican Party, he previously was an Assistant United States Attorney who led the organized crime division at the U.S. Attorney's Office in Syracuse.

John Forbes Kerry (1943–), b. Aurora, CO, of Moravian ancestry on his father's side, is an American lawyer, who was elected as a Democrat from Massachusetts to the US Senate in 1984; subsequently appointed to the remainder of the term left vacant by the resignation of Paul Tsongas, and took the oath of office on January 2, 1985; reelected in 1990, 1996, 2002, and again in 2008, and served from 1985, until his resignation on February 1, 2013, to accept a Cabinet position, as US Secretary of State.

Thomas F. Konop (1879–1964), b. Franklin, WI, of Czech descent, was U.S. Representative of Wisconsin. He graduated from the University of Nebraska–Lincoln College of Law in 1904. He was admitted to the bar in 1904 and commenced practice in Kewaunee, Wisconsin. He served as district attorney of Kewaunee County, Wisconsin from 1905 to 1911. He moved to Green Bay, Wisconsin, and practiced law from 1915 to 1917. Konop was elected as a member of the Democratic Party to the Sixty-second, Sixty-third, and Sixty-fourth Congresses (March 4, 1911–March 3, 1917). He represented Wisconsin's 9th congressional district. Konop served as dean of the College of Law of the University of Notre Dame from 1923 to 1941. He then resumed the practice of law in Madison, WI.

Milton Kraus (1866–1942), b. Kokomo, Indiana, of Bohemian father, was a U.S. Representative from Indiana. He graduated from the law department of the University of Michigan at Ann Arbor in 1886. He was admitted to the bar in 1887 and commenced practice in Peru, Indiana. He organized a company of volunteers for the Spanish American War. Kraus was elected as a Republican to the Sixty-fifth, Sixty-sixth, and Sixty-seventh Congresses (1917–1923). He then resumed manufacturing activities. He died in Wabash, Indiana, November 18, 1942.

Lucius Quintus Cincinnatus Lamar (1825–1893), b. Eatonton, GA, desc. f. Augustine Heřman, an American lawyer, was US Representative from Mississippi (1857–60), having been elected as a Democrat. He was elected again in 1873–1877, the first Democrat from Mississippi to sit in the US House of Representatives since the Civil War. In 1876, he was elected as a Democrat from Mississippi to US Senate; reelected in 1883 and served from 1877 until 1885, when he resigned to accept a Cabinet post.

William Bailey Lamar (1853-1928), b. Monticello, FL, desc. f. Augustine Heřman, was US Representative from Florida (1903-1910), having been elected as a Democrat to the 58th, 59th and 60th Congresses.

William Langer (1886-1959), b. nr. Casselton, ND, of Bohemian ancestry, was an American lawyer, who was elected, as a Republican from North Dakota to the US Senate in 1940; reelected in 1946, 1952, and again in 1958, and served from January 1941, until his death in Washington, D.C.

Arthur Albert Link (1914-2010), b. Alexander, ND, of Bohemian father, a successful North Dakota State legislator, in 1970, was persuaded to run for US Congress from the western district of North Dakota to succeed Republican incumbent Thomas S. Kleppe, who ran unsuccessfully for the U.S. Senate. He was narrowly elected as a Dem-NPLer to the Ninety-second Congress (1971-73) as a mild surprise. He was not a candidate for reelection in 1972 because he decided to run for Governor of North Dakota in 1959.

Joe Manchin (1947-), b. Farmington, WV, of Czech ancestry, s an American politician serving as the senior United States senator from West Virginia, a seat he has held since 2010. A member of the Democratic Party, he was the 34th Governor of West Virginia from 2005 to 2010 and the 27th Secretary of State of West Virginia from 2001 to 2005.

Daniel Mica (1944-), b. Binghamton, NY, of Slovak descent; Republican US Representative from Michigan.

John L. Mica (1943-), b. Binghamton, NY, of Slovak ancestry; Republican US Representative from Florida's 7th Congressional district (1993-2017).

Anthony Michálek (1878-1916), b. Radvanov, Bohemia, was US Representative from Chicago (1905-1907), having been elected as a Republican from Illinois to the 59th Congress.

George Edward Mitchell (1781-1832), b. Head of Elk, MD, desc. f. Augustine Heřman, a physician, who was elected as an Adams-Clay Republican from Maryland to the 18th Congress and reelected as a Jacksonian to the 19th Congress (1823-1827). He was elected again as a Jacksonian to the 21st and 22nd Congresses and served from December 1829 until his death in Washington, D.C., June 28, 1832.

Ronald M. Mottl (1934-2023), b. Cleveland, OH, of Czech descent, was US Representative from Ohio (1974-83), having been elected as a Democrat to the 94th through 97th Congresses.

Robert J. Mrazek (1945-), b. Newport, RI, of Czech ancestry, a businessman, who was elected as a Democrat from New York to the 98th and to the four succeeding Congresses (1983-1993).

Francis Swaine Muhlenberg (1795-1831), b. Philadelphia, PA., was a realtor, who was elected as an Adams candidate from Pennsylvania to the 20th Congress to fill the vacancy caused by the resignation of William Creighton, Jr., and served from December 1828 to March 1829.

Frederick Augustus Muhlenberg (1887-1980), b. Reading, Berks Co., PA, was an architect and a politician, who was elected as a Republican to the 80th Congress (1947-1949).

Frederick Augustus Conrad Muhlenberg (1750-1801), b. Trappe, PA, of Bohemian ancestry, a Lutheran Pastor and politician, who was elected as a Pro-Administration candidate to the 1st Congress, reelected as an Anti-Administration candidate to the 2nd and 3rd Congresses, and elected as a Republican to the 4th Congress, serving from March 1789 to March 1797. He was a Speaker of the House of Representatives (1st and 3rd Congresses).

Henry Augustus Philip Muhlenberg (1782-1844), b. Lancaster, PA., May 13, 1782, was a Lutheran pastor, who was elected as a Jacksonian to the 21st Congress; reelected as a Jacksonian to the 22nd through 24th Congresses and reelected as a Democrat to the 25th Congress and served from 1829, until his resignation on February 9, 1838.

John Peter Gabriel Muhlenberg (1746-1807), b. Trappe, PA, was a Lutheran pastor, then an Anglican priest, soldier and politician, who was elected to the 1st Congress (1789-1791), the 3rd Congress (1793-1795), and the 6th Congress (1799-1801). Subsequently, he was elected to the US Senate from Pennsylvania and served from March 1801, until his resignation on June 30, 1801 to accept government job.

Henry Myer Phillips (1811-1884), b. Philadelphia, PA of Bohemian ancestry, was an American lawyer, who was elected as a Democrat to the 35th Congress (1857-1859).

Joseph Pulitzer (1847-1911), b. Mako, Hung, of Moravian ancestry, was a lawyer and journalist, who was elected as a Democrat from New York to the 49th Congress and served from March 4, 1885, until April 10, 1886, when he resigned.

Edmund Jennings Randolph (1753-1813), b. Williamsburg, VA, desc. f. Augustine Heřman, an American lawyer, was a Member of the Continental Congress in 1779, 1781, and 1782.

Tom Ridge (1945-), b. Munhall, PA, of Slovak ancestry; politician, former Republican US Representative from Pennsylvania's 21st district.

David Ross (1755-1800), b. Prince Georges Co., MD, desc. f. Augustine Heřman, a lawyer, was a member of the Continental Congress (1787-1789).

Philip Ruppe (1926-), b. Laurium, MI, of Slovak ancestry, is a politician. And a member of the Republican Party. He served in the U.S. House of Representatives from Michigan's 11th district from 1967 to 1979, before running, unsuccessfully for the United States Senate in 1982. He is a Korean War veteran, having served as a lieutenant in the U.S. Navy. After leaving the U.S. House, Ruppe became active in the business. He served as president of Woodlake Co. in 1986.

Adolph Joachim Sabath (1866-1952), b. Záboří, Bohemia, was a lawyer, who was elected as a Democrat from Illinois to the 60th and to the twenty-three succeeding Congresses, but died before the convening of the 83rd, serving from March 4, 1907, until his death in Bethesda, MD, November 6, 1952.

Lynn Schenk (1945-), b. Bronx, NY, of Czech ancestry on her mother's side, is an American lawyer, who was elected as a Democrat from California to the 103rd Congress (1993-1995).

Claudine Schneider (née Cmarada) (1947-), b. Clairton, PA, of Slovak ancestry; former US Representative from Rhode Island. She was the first, and to date only, woman elected to Congress from Rhode Island. She was elected as a Republican to the 97th Congress and was re-elected to the four succeeding Congresses, serving from January 3, 1981 to January 3, 1991 for Rhode Island's 2nd Congressional district. After leaving Congress, she served as a member of the faculty of the John F. Kennedy School of Government of Harvard University.

Shelley Sekula-Gibbs (1953-), b. Floresville, TX, of Czech ancestry, is a physician who was elected as a Republican from Texas to the 109th Congress, by special election to fill the vacancy caused by the resignation of US Representative Thomas DeLay (November 13, 2006-January 3, 2007). A Republican, she has also served as a city councilwoman in Houston, Texas for three terms, from 2002 to 2006.

Joe Sestak (1951-), b. Secane, PA, of Slovak ancestry; former Democratic US Representative from Pennsylvania's 7th district. A three-star vice admiral, he was the highest-ranking military official ever elected to the United States Congress at the time of his election.

Francis Edwin Shober (1831-1896), b. Salem, NC, of Moravian ancestry, was an American lawyer, who was elected as a Democrat from North Carolina to the 41st and 42nd Congresses (1869-1873). He was appointed Chief Clerk of the US Senate in the 45th Congress; upon the death of Secretary John C. Burch in the 47th Congress, he was appointed Acting Secretary of the Senate and served from October 1881 to March 1883.

Francis Emanuel Shober (1860-1919), b. Salisbury, NC, of Moravian ancestry, was a reporter and editor, who was elected as a Democrat from New York to the 58th Congress (1903-1905).

Karl Štefan (1884-1951), b. Žebrákov, Bohemia, was an editor, radio commentator and publisher. In 1934, he was elected to US Congress and later became a member of Congressional committee aiding inauguration of the Philippine Commonwealth Government in Manila in 1935. He was a delegate to the Interparliamentary Union in Oslo, Norway in 1939. He was also an official adviser at the 1945 United Nations Conference in San Francisco, California. He ran and won to represent Nebraska's 3rd district in 1935 and was reelected eight times. He died while in office on October 2, 1951 in Washington, D.C. He was buried in Prospect Hill Cemetery in Norfolk. Norfolk's Karl Stefan Memorial Airport is named in his honor.

James Traficant (1941-2014), b. Youngstown, OH, of Slovak descent; politician, member of the US House of Representatives from Ohio (1985-2002). He represented the 17th Congressional District, which centered on his hometown of Youngstown and included parts of three counties in northeast Ohio's Mahoning Valley.

Joseph Davies Tydings (1928-2018), b. Asheville, Buncombe Co., NC, desc. f. Augustine Heřman, was an American lawyer, who was elected as a Democrat from Maryland to the US Senate in 1964 and served from 1965 to 1971.

Charles Albert Vanik (1913-2007), b. Cleveland, OH, of Czech ancestry, was an American lawyer, who was elected as a Democrat from Ohio to the 84th and to twelve succeeding Congresses (1955-1981).

Peter John Visclosky (1949-), b. Gary, IN, of Slovak ancestry; Democratic US Representative from Indiana's 1st district. He is a member of the Democratic Party and was the dean of the Indiana congressional delegation before his retirement in 2021. He called himself the "Slovak Kid" and gained votes with hot dog dinners.

Jonathan Mayhew Wainwright (1864-1945), b. New York, NY, desc. f. Frederick Philipse, was an American lawyer, who as a Republican from New York was elected to the 68th and to the three succeeding Congresses (1923-1931).

Frank Hinman Waskey (1875-1964), b. Lake City, MN, of Moravian ancestry, was a mineral prospector and banker, who was elected, as a Democrat, to the 59th Congress, as the first Delegate from Alaska and served from August 1906 to March 1907.

John Matthew Zwach, Sr. (1907-1990), b. Gales Township, Redwood County, MN, of Czech ancestry, attended the public schools and graduated from Milroy High School in 1926. He then received a teaching certificate from Mankato State College in 1927 and graduated from the University of Minnesota in 1933. He worked as a school teacher and superintendent for fourteen years and was also an active farmer. Zwach served in the Minnesota House of Representatives from 1934 to 1946 and in the Minnesota Senate from 1946 to 1966. He was elected as a Republican to the 90th, 91st, 92nd and 93rd Congresses (January 3, 1967-January 3, 1975). He was not a candidate for reelection in 1974. He was a resident of Lucan, Minnesota until his death on November 11, 1990. He was buried at St. Michael's Cemetery.

D. Federal Judges

Samuel Alschuler (1859-1939), b. Chicago, IL, of Czech ancestry, was a Federal Judge, US Court of Appeals for the 7th District. He was appointed by President Woodrow Wilson and served from August 1915 to May 1936.

Richard Bassett (1745-1815), b. Cecil Co., MD, desc. f. Augustine Heřman, an American lawyer and politician, served Chief Justice, Delaware Court of Common Pleas (1793-99). He was appointed Justice of US Circuit Court by President J. Adams in 1801.

Francis Biddle (1886-1968), b. Paris, France, desc. f. Augustine Heřman, studied law at Harvard Univ. After practicing law in Philadelphia for 27 years, President Roosevelt appointed him in 1939 to the US Court of Appeals for the Third Circuit. He served only one year to accept the nomination to the US Solicitor General. In 1941, he became Attorney General of the US. After the World War II, he became the primary American Judge during the Tribunal at Nuremberg.

William Bondy (1870-1964), b. New York, NY of Bohemian ancestry, served as Judge of the US District Court, Southern District of NY (1923-56), having been appointed by President Harding. In 1955, he became Chief Judge.

Louis D. Brandeis (1856-1941), b. Louisville, KY, of Bohemian ancestry, an American lawyer, was appointed Associate Justice of the US Supreme Court (1916-1939) by President Wilson. He was not only a great justice, but also a social reformer, legal innovator, and labor champion.

Victor Hugo Duras (1880-1943), b. Wilber, NE, of Czech ancestry, an American lawyer, served as Judge of US Court Canal Zone in Cristobal, Panama, named when twenty-eight years old, the youngest US Judge ever appointed.

George W. Folta (1893-1955), b. Braddock, PA, of Slovak immigrant parents; bear hunter in Alaska, lawyer, prosecutor, solicitor, presiding judge of the first Federal Judicial District of Alaska, appointed by President Truman.

Morgan Ford (1911-1992), b. near Wheatland, Cass County, ND, of Bohemian ancestry on his mother's side (grandson of Frank J. Langer and nephew of William Langer), graduated from Univ. of North Dakota (B.A., 1935) and studied law at Georgetown Univ. Law Center (LL.B., 1938). He was in private practice, Fargo, North Dakota (1939-49). He served as City attorney, Casselton, North Dakota (1942-1948) and a member, Selective Service Advisory Board (1942-45). He served as Judge, US Customs Court (1949-80); reassigned November 1, 1980; Judge, U. S. Court of International Trade (1980-92); his service terminated on January 2, 1992, due to death.

Felix Frankfurter (1882-1965), b. Vienna, of Moravian mother and Slovak father, was an attorney, professor, jurist, Associate Justice of the US (1939-62), having been appointed by President Franklin D. Roosevelt.

Mark R. Hornak (1956-), b. Homestead, PA, of Slovak descent; lawyer, appointed US District Judge by President Barack Obama on October 19, 2011.

John Jay (1745-1829), b. New York, NY, grandson of Frederick Philipse's stepdaughter, served as Chief Justice of the State of New York (1777-78). Later became First Chief Justice of the U.S. Supreme Court (1789-95), having been appointed by President Washington.

Olga Jurco (1916-2004), b. Illinois, of Slovak descent, a lawyer, was Federal Magistrate judge. She was the first woman to occupy judicial position in the Northern District of Illinois as US Magistrate (for 14 years).

Otto Kerner, Sr. (1884-1952), b. Chicago, IL, of Czech parents, an American lawyer, served as Judge of the US Court of Appeals, 7th Circuit (1939-52), having been appointed by President F. D. Roosevelt.

Otto Kerner, Jr. (1908-1976), b. Chicago, IL of Czech descent, an American lawyer, served as US Circuit Judge, US Court of Appeals 7th Circuit (1968-74), having been appointed by President L. B. Johnson.

VI. PUBLIC LIFE

Lucius Quintus Cincinnatus Lamar (1825-1894), b. Putnam City, GA, desc. of Augustine Heřman, an American lawyer, served as Associate Justice U.S. Supreme Court (1888-93), having been appointed by President Cleveland.

Henry Brockholst Livingston (1757-1823), b. New York, NY, desc. f. Frederick Philipse, an American lawyer, served as Judge of New York Supreme Court (1802-07). Later became Associate Justice of US Supreme Court (1806-23), having been appointed by President Thomas Jefferson.

Coral Wong Pietsch (1947-), b. Waterloo, IA, of Czech immigrant mother and Chinese immigrant father. Brigadier General in US Army Reserve. Presently holds the position of US Judge for the US Court of Appeals for Veterans Claims.

Louis Heilprin Pollak (1922-2012), b. New York, of Moravian ancestry, was a district Judge on the US District Court for the Eastern District of Pennsylvania. He was nominated to the US District Court for the Eastern District of Pennsylvania by President Jimmy Carter in June 1978. He was confirmed by the US Senate on July 10, and began serving on July 12, 1978, occupying the seat vacated by Judge A. Leon Higginbotham, Jr. Judge Pollak assumed senior status in 1991, and continued as an active member of the court. In addition to his district court duties, Pollak sat by designation regularly with the US Court of Appeals for the Third Circuit and was often invited to sit by designation with the Ninth Circuit. A number of Pollak's former law clerks have gone on to clerk on the Supreme Court of the United States. They have worked for Chief Justices Burger and Rehnquist as well as Justices Brennan, Blackmun, Breyer, Stevens, Powell, Ginsburg, O'Connor, and Scalia.

Stephen Roy Reinhardt (1931-2018), b. New York, NY, of Moravian ancestry, enrolled in Pomona College and graduated three years later with a B.A. in Government in 1951. In 1954, he received an LL.B. from Yale Law School. After law school, Reinhardt worked at the legal counsel's office for the United States Air Force as a lieutenant in Washington, DC. Two years later, he clerked for district judge Luther Youngdahl, a former governor of Minnesota, in the United States District Court for the District of Columbia. He then entered private practice, working for the law firm O'Melveny & Myers from 1958 to 1959 practicing entertainment law. After two years at O'Melveny, he began working at a small firm in Los Angeles that became Fogel, Julber, Reinhardt, Rothschild & Feldman specializing in labor law. In 1980, President Jimmy Carter appointed him a Circuit Judge on the United States Court of Appeals for the Ninth Circuit, with chambers in Los Angeles, California.

John Glover Roberts, Jr. (1955-), b. Buffalo, NY, of Slovak ancestry on his mother's side, is an American lawyer, who has served as Chief Justice of the US Supreme Court (s. 2005), having been appointed by President George W. Bush. He was previously a Judge of the United States Court of Appeals for the District of Columbia Circuit (2003-05).

Frank (František) E. Schwelb (1932-2014), b. Prague, Czech., in August 1939, escaped from Nazis and emigrated with his parents to England. After the war, the family moved to New York. Frank attended Yale University where he played soccer and joined the NAACP. He began Harvard Law School in 1954 but volunteered to serve in the U.S. Army in 1955 to gain military naturalization. He served for two years before returning to Harvard and graduating in 1958. Eager to participate in President John F. Kennedy's 'New Frontier,' Frank began working as a lawyer for the Civil Rights Division of the U.S. Department of Justice in October 1962; his work with voter registration discrimination exposed him to the segregated South. He was named to the Superior Court of the District of Columbia by President Jimmy Carter in 1979 and was later appointed by President Reagan to the District of Columbia Court of Appeals, where he was a Senior Judge. He is involved in the Czech and Slovak legal community, meeting with visiting lawyers, judges, and students, and he presented the inaugural Rosa Parks Memorial Lecture (in Czech) at Charles University in Prague.

John Smietanka (1941-), b. Chicago, IL, of Slovak descent; lawyer, prosecutor for Berrien Co., MI; US attorney in Western Michigan, appointed by President Reagan (1981-1994).

Jacob Weinberger (1882-1974), b. Slovakia; lawyer, in private practice, Denver, CO (1904) and Gila County, AZ (1905-11), in San Diego, CA (1911-41); city attorney for San Diego (1941-43); judge of the Superior Court of San Diego County (1943-45); appointed, by President Truman, Federal Judge, to the seat on the US District Court for the Southern California, first in Los Angeles (1946-49), then San Diego (1949-74).

Edward Weinfeld (1901-1988), b. Manhattan, NY, of Slovak descent; lawyer, Federal Judge of the US District Court for the Southern District of New York.

Victor Baynard Woolley (1867-1945), b. Wilmington, DE, desc. f. Augustine Heřman, studied law at Harvard Law School. He was an associate Judge, Supreme Court of Delaware (1903-14); Judge, US Circuit Court of Appeals for the 3rd Circuit (1914-38) by appointment of President Wilson.

E. Governors

Richard Bassett (1745-1815), b. Cecil Co., MD, desc. f. Augustine Heřman, was an American lawyer, who was elected, as Federalist, Governor of Delaware (1799-1801).

Alexis I. du Pont Bayard (1918-1985), b. Wilmington, DE, des, f. Augustine Herman, was an American lawyer and politician from Rockland, near Greenville, in New Castle County,

Delaware. He was a veteran of World War II, and a member of the Democratic Party, who served as the 13th Lieutenant Governor of Delaware (1949-53).

James Brice (1746-1801), b. Anne Arundel County, MD, desc. f. Augustine Heřman, was a planter and lawyer, who was elected Governor of Maryland in 1792.

George W. Bush (1946-), b. New Haven, CT, of Czech ancestry on his mother's side, was elected as a Governor of Texas, having served from 1995 to 2000. He became the first governor in Texas history to be elected to two consecutive four-year terms. He resigned in December 2000 to assume Presidency of the US.

John Ellis 'Jeb' Bush (1953-), b. Midland, Texas, of Czech ancestry on his mother's side, was elected as the 43rd Governor of Florida, having served from 1999 to 2007.

Henry Watkins Collier (1801-1855), b. Lunenburg Co., VA, desc. f. Augustine Heřman, was Governor of Alabama (1849-53).

Harold Giles Hoffman (1896-1954), b. South Amboy, NJ, of Czech ancestry, was an American politician, a Republican who served as the 41st Governor of New Jersey, from 1935 to 1938. He worked with a local newspaper until enlisting on July 25, 1917 as a private in the Third Regiment of the New Jersey Infantry. He served overseas in WWI as a captain and advanced to the rank of lieutenant colonel until he was discharged with the rank of colonel in 1946. After World War I, Hoffman returned to South Amboy and became an executive with the South Amboy Trust Company. He became the bank's president, a position he held until 1942. As governor, Harold Hoffman got into at least two separate fist-fights with reporters. Hoffman's advocacy of a state sales tax cost him the support of his own party, and he was not renominated for a third term as governor. Due to World War II, Hoffman was granted military leave as director of the Unemployment Compensation Commission on June 15, 1942. He reentered the army as a major in the Transportation Corps and served until June 24, 1946 when he was discharged with the rank of Colonel. Upon discharge, Hoffman resumed his position as director of the Unemployment Commission.

Henry Horner (1878-1940), b. Chicago, IL, of Bohemian descent, was the 28th Governor of Illinois, serving two terms from 1933 to 1940, when he died in office. Horner was the first Jewish governor of Illinois.

John Jay (1745-1829), b. New York, NY, grandson of Frederick Philipse's stepdaughter, was an American lawyer, who was elected Governor of New York (1795-1801).

Charles (Karel) Jonáš (1840-1896), b. Malešov, Bohemia, was a Czech journalist, linguist and political activist, who became a Wisconsin journalist and politician. In 1890, he was elected 16th Lieutenant Governor of Wisconsin with a plurality of 34,974 in a four-way race, well ahead of his running mate, Milwaukee mayor George Wilbur Peck. He would serve in that office from 1891 until 1894, when he resigned to become the U.S. consul in St. Petersburg, Russia.

John Richard Kasich (1952-), b. McKees Rocks, PA, of Czechoslovak descent, was elected the 69th and current Governor of Ohio (s. 2011).

Otto Kerner, Jr. (1908-1976), b. Chicago, IL, of Bohemian ancestry, was an American lawyer, who was elected as Democrat the 33rd Governor of Illinois, serving from 1961 to 1968. He is best known for chairing the National Advisory Commission on Civil Disorders (the Kerner Commission).

William Langer (1886-1959), b. nr. Casselton, ND, of Bohemian ancestry, was an American lawyer, who was elected as the 17th and 21st Governor of North Dakota, serving from 1933 to 1934 and from 1937 to 1939.

Arthur Albert Link (1914-2010), b. Alexander, ND, of Bohemian father, a successful ND State legislator and one-term US Congressman, was a successful candidate for Governor of North Dakota. He was reelected in 1976 and served from January 2, 1973, until January 6, 1981. Link was well liked and well respected as a governor. Those of all political persuasions found common ground with him. Some considered him a social conservative who was staunchly pro-life, deeply religious and willing to stand for principles even when political wisdom dictated otherwise, vetoing a bill to lower the state drinking age to 19 years and providing leadership against legalizing gambling in the state. Others viewed him as a moderate as he was also astute fiscally, managing to avoid raising taxes of one of the poorer states in the nation. Still, others saw him as a progressive, since he was still able to maintain and grow an excellent education system with affordable universities and students who consistently achieve some of the top test scores in the US. He was also a leader among governors from neighboring states. When the western United States suffered a severe drought in the mid-1970s, and other western governors called for Federal Aid, Link called for a day of fasting and prayer instead.

Joseph Manchin, 3rd (1947-), b. Farmington, WV, of Czech ancestry, is an American politician. A member of the Democratic Part, he was the 34th Governor of West Virginia from 2005 to 2010 and the 27th Secretary of State of West Virginia from 2001 to 2005.

Edmund Jennings Randolph (1753-1813), b. Williamsburg, VA, desc. f. Augustine Heřman, was an American attorney, who was elected the 7th Governor of Virginia (1786-1788).

Payton Randolph (1779–1828), b. Williamsburg, VA, desc. f. Augustine Heřman, was an American attorney, who, following the death of Governor George William Smith, served as the Acting Governor of Virginia, from December 26, 1811 until January 3, 1812.

Tom Ridge (1945–), b. Munhall, PA, of Slovak ancestry; politician, 43rd Governor of Pennsylvania.

Arnold Alois Schwarzenegger (1947–), b. Thal, Aust., of Czech ancestry on his mother's side (Aurelia Jadrny), a former professional bodybuilder and actor, served two terms as the 38th Governor of California from 2003 until 2011.

John Andrew Shulze (1774–1852), b. Tulpehocken Township, Berks, PA, of Bohemian ancestry, was a Pennsylvania political leader and the sixth Governor of Pennsylvania. He was reelected in 1826 over John Sergeant in one of the most lopsided victories in Pennsylvania political history. He was a member of the Muhlenberg family political dynasty.

Steve Sisolak (1953–), b. Milwaukee, WI, of Slovak descent, is an American businessman and politician serving as the 30th and current Governor of Nevada since 2019. A member of the Democratic Party, he previously chaired the Clark County Commission from 2013 to 2019.

Harold Stassen (1907–2001), b. West St. Paul, MN, of Czech ancestry, was an American lawyer, who was elected as the 25th Governor of Minnesota, serving from 1939 to 1943. In popular culture, his name has become most identified with his fame as a perennial candidate for other offices, most notably and frequently President of the US.

Jesse Ventura (orig. James George Janos) (1951–), b. Minneapolis, MN, of Slovak ancestry; former professional wrestler, 38th Governor of Minnesota.

Scott Kevin Walker (1967–), b. Colorado Springs, CO, is an American Republican politician who is the 45th Governor of Wisconsin. He is a two-term Governor, elected in 2010 and 2014, who also defeated an effort to recall him in 2012. Walker was elected governor of Wisconsin in 2010, defeating the Democratic nominee, Milwaukee Mayor Tom Barrett. After being sworn into office in 2011, Walker introduced a budget repair plan which limited many collective bargaining powers for most public employees. The legislation led to significant protests at the Wisconsin State Capitol and an effort to recall Walker. In June 2012, Walker faced Barrett in Wisconsin's only gubernatorial recall election. After emerging as the winner, Walker became the only governor in the U.S. to date to win a gubernatorial recall election. Walker is seen by many as a potential candidate for the GOP's nomination in the 2016 presidential election, having formed a 527 organization in January of 2015.

F. Mayors

Richard Henry Bayard (1795-1853), b. Wilmington, DE, desc. f. Augustine Heřman, was an American lawyer and a politician, a member of the Whig Party, who served as the first Mayor of Wilmington, the newly incorporated city in 1832.

William Bercik (1876-1957), b. Whiting, IN, of Slovak descent; Mayor of Whiting, IN (1956-1957). He was extremely active in church, fraternal and civic affairs throughout the community. In 1957, William Bercik was serving his second year of a four-year mayoral term when he succumbed to a heart attack.

J. W. Blezek (1877-1956), b. Baldwin, IA, of Czech ancestry, a Nebraska lawyer, served as Mayor of Plainview, NE for three terms. He also served on the School Board, City Council, and was a member of the Chamber of Commerce.

James Brice (1746-1801), b. Anne Arundel County, MD, desc. f. Augustine Heřman, was a planter, lawyer and politician, who was elected Mayor of Annapolis in 1782-1783 and again in 1787-1788.

John Brice, 3rd (1738-1820), born in Annapolis, desc. f. Augustine Heřman, was a lawyer and businessman, who was elected Mayor of Annapolis, MD (1780-81).

John Frank Brůžek (1877-1965), b. Heidelberg, MN, New Prague, MN, of Czech ancestry, was elected Mayor, New Prague, MN.

William Carl Buchta (1866-1948), b. Edwardsville, IL, of Bohemian ancestry, owner of jewelry store in David City, NE, was elected Mayor of David City (1934). He also served as a member of Coty Council for 2 terms.

Anton Joseph Čermák (1873-1933), b. Kladno, Bohemia, was an American politician who served as the Mayor of the City of Chicago, from April 7, 1931 until his death on March 6, 1933. He was killed by an assassin whose likely target was President Franklin Roosevelt, but the assassin shot Cermak instead. He immigrated to America with his parents in 1874, when he was one year old, settling in Chicago. He followed his father into coal mining and labored at mines in Will and Grundy counties. After moving to Chicago at age 16, Cermak worked as a tow boy for the horse-drawn streetcar line and then tended horses in the stables of Chicago's Pilsen neighborhood. During the early years of his working life, Cermak supplemented his education with evening high school and business college classes. After saving enough money to buy his own horse and cart, he went into business selling firewood, and he subsequently expanded his venture into a haulage business. As he became more active politically, Cermak served in municipal government jobs including clerk in the city police court. As his political fortunes began to rise, Cermak was able to avail himself of other business opportunities, including interests in real estate, insurance, and banking. He began his political career as a Democratic Party precinct captain and in 1902, he was elected to the Illinois House of Representatives. Seven years later, he became alderman of the 12th Ward (serving two terms, one from 1909 through 1912 and another from 1919 through 1922). Cermak was elected President of the Cook County Board of Commissioners in 1922, chairman of the Cook County Democratic Party in 1928, and Mayor of Chicago in 1931. Cermak had also, in the 1910s, been elected, and served, as bailiff for the Municipal Court of Chicago.

Joseph G. Cerny (1897–d.), b. Chicago, IL, of Czech ancestry, was elected president (Mayor) of Cicero, IL (1932).

William R. Cervenik (1976–), of Slovak descent; certified public accountant, Mayor, City of Euclid, OH.

Edward A. Coufal (1881–d.), b. nr. Brainard, NE, of Czech ancestry, served as Mayor, David City (1919–23).

Oliver J. Demuth (1860–1946), b. Tuscarawas Co., OH, of Bohemian ancestry, was elected Mayor of New Philadelphia in 1923, his two-year term beginning January 1924.

George E. Dolezal (1919–1990), b. Chicago, IL, of Czech ancestry, was a lawyer who was elected in 1964 as the first Republican Mayor of Berwyn since 1929. As Mayor (1965–68), his accomplishments included revamping the zoning regulations and redrawing district lines.

Anthony V. Dufek (1921–2004), b. Manitowoc, WI, of Czech parents, was elected Mayor of Manitowoc, WI, serving from 1973–89. During his administration he acquired the Manitowoc Transit system, completed construction of 21st Street Bridge in Manitowoc Rapids, developed first industrial park, established I-43 corridor, developed marina, expanded public utilities, made recreational facility improvements and completed senior center construction.

James Joseph Dworak (1925–2002), b. Omaha, NE, of Czech ancestry, a former mortician, was elected Mayor of Omaha, NE, serving from 1961–65. As Mayor, James was responsible for the development of housing for the aged; he was instrumental in major golf course construction in Omaha and, he revamped the Omaha Police Communications System.

Julius Fleischmann (1871–1925), b. Cincinnati, OH, of Moravian father, became Cincinnati's youngest Mayor in 1900 and served until 1905.

Albert Joseph Fousek (1869-1958), b. Bohemia, a cigar maker, was elected Mayor of Great Falls, MT in 1915, serving from 1915-19, 1929-33, and 1935-37.

Frank R. Franko (1920-fl. 1961), b. of Slovak descent; a Democrat; Mayor of Youngstown, OH (1960-1961).

Joseph Grenchik (1926-2020), b. Whiting, IN, of Slovak descent; Mayor of Whiting, IN (1964-68) and (1976-88). He enlisted in the US Air Force for two years. In 1947, he was employed by the American Trust and Savings Bank of Whiting. Since 1962, he became active in his travel agency.

August Haidušek (1845-1929), b. Myší, nr Frenštát, Moravia, was elected Mayor of La Grange, TX in 1876, and served two terms.

Martin Victor Havel (1874-1947), b. České Budějovice, Bohemia, became Mayor of Montgomery, MN, serving from 1903 to 1905.

Matthew 'Matt' J. Hayek (1969-), b. Iowa City, IA, of Czech ancestry, was elected Mayor of Iowa City (2008-2012) and 2nd term (2012-2016). He is also an attorney and has his own firm, under the name Hayek, Brown, Moreland & Smith, L.L.P. in Iowa City.

Harold Giles Hoffman (1896-1954), b. South Amboy, NJ, of Czech ancestry, an American politician, Republican served as Mayor of South Amboy, NJ (1925-26).

Robert 'Bill' Homolka (1939-2012), b. Ellsworth, KS, a farmer and stockman, and co-owner of Homolka Grain & Supply, Ellsworth, served as Mayor of Ellsworth, KS for 27 years (1983-2009).

Edward Horsky (1873-1948), b. Helena, MT, of Czech ancestry, a lawyer, became Mayor of Helena, MT (1911).

Frank Janda (1898-1963), b. Chicago, IL, became the first Czech Mayor of Berwyn, IL. He served from 1925-29. During his two Mayoral terms, Berwyn became a town of paved thoroughfares and alleys.

Anton Janura (1878-1943), b. Hartvíkov, Bohemia, came to US in 1890s, settling in the Česká Kalifornie neighborhood of Chicago. In 1931, the family moved to Berwyn, IL, where Anton Janura made living as a real estate salesman. He was elected Mayor, Berwyn, IL and served from 1935 to 1942.

Stephen H. Jelinek (1887-d.), b. Wilber, NE, of Czech ancestry, a dentist by training, was elected Mayor of Brainard, NE. He was a member of School Board for almost twenty years.

Alan Jilka (1962–), b. Salina, KS, of Czech ancestry, a businessman and political columnist, was elected Mayor of Salina, KS, serving for 3 terms, from 1997 to 2009. He graduated from the University of Notre Dame with a degree in History, and also has an M.A. in Comparative Literature from the University of South Carolina. Alan began his political career as a legislative aide to Congressman Dan Glickman (D-KS). Jilka finished the coursework towards a Ph.D. in Spanish and Portuguese from Vanderbilt University, and has lived four years in Guadalajara, Mexico and Rio De Janeiro, Brazil. He is a writer on various blogs and newspaper sites such as the Kansas Free Press, on issues of business and politics.

Timothy 'Tim' Kabat (1966–), b. La Crosse, WI, of Czech ancestry, a city planner, became the 42nd Mayor of the City of La Crosse, WI (s. 2012).

Alois Kalina (1880–1967), b. Prague, Bohemia, a merchant, became the first Mayor of Malin, OR, serving 10 terms, for 27 years.

Joseph Z. Klenha (1877–1936), b. Chicago, IL, was a lawyer and politician who was elected president (Mayor) of Cicero, IL from 1924 to 1932.

Frederick Kohler (1864–1934), b. Cleveland, OH, of Bohemian ancestry, was a former police captain and a politician of the Republican Party who served as the 40th Mayor of Cleveland, OH from 1922 to 1923.

Frank Koutsky (1871–1944), b. Saunders Co., NE, of Czech ancestry, was elected Mayor of South Omaha, NE (1902–06) and again in 1908–10.

Andrew S. Kovacik (1916–1988), b. of Slovak immigrant parents; Mayor of Whiting, IN (1948–1954). In 1942, he joined the US Army, where he served as a member of the Counter Intelligence Corps for two years.

Robert L. Kriz (1916–1996), b. NE, of Czech ancestry, after completion of his military service in 1945, entered private business and established himself in five states. After his retirement, Kriz was elected Mayor of Grand Island (s. 1978). Mr. Kriz played a significant role in the recovery efforts after the tornadoes of June 3, 1980, and in the establishment of Grand Island as an All-American City for the third time.

Frank X. Kryzan (1914–2010), b. Youngstown, OH; lawyer, practiced law with his brother Anthony in Youngstown, OH; president of City Council; Mayor of Youngstown, OH (1954–60); one of the first politicians in Ohio to support the bid of then Senator John F. Kennedy for Presidency of the US.

Bedrich 'Ben' Fred Kucera (1904-1990), b. Dillonvale, OH, of Czech parents, served as Mayor of Silverhill, AL (1958-72). Previously, he held the position of chief of police in Robertsdale, AL, a small town near Silverhill (s. 1945).

Henry Brockhorst Ledyard (1812-1880), b. NYC, of Bohemian ancestry, desc. f. Frederick Philipse, was the Mayor of Detroit, Michigan and a State Senator. He briefly served as Assistant Secretary under Secretary of State Lewis Cass and was the president of the Newport Hospital and the Redwood Library in Newport, Rhode Island. Henry Ledyard graduated from Columbia College in 1830 and began practicing law in New York. When Lewis Cass was appointed Minister to France, Ledyard accompanied him to Paris, eventually becoming Chargé d'affaires of the Embassy.

William Loeffler (1893-1965), b. Chicago, IL, of Czech ancestry, served as Mayor of the Village of Stickney, IL. By trade, he was a wholesale dealer for more than 25 years.

Edward J. Lukes (1888-1967), b. Protivin, IA, a merchant, was elected Mayor of Protivin, IA (1920-24).

Charles Lutovsky (1875-1935), b. of Czech ancestry, was elected Mayor of Watertown, WI in 1930-34 and 1934-35, the latter date to fill another man's term.

Frank Novotny (1881-1934), b. Chicago, IL, of Bohemian immigrant parents, was elected Mayor of Berwyn, IL, by a large majority (1931-1934), in which capacity he remained until his death in an automobile accident.

George Pankratz (1837-1894), b. Bohemia, a lumberyard owner, who was elected Mayor of Manitowoc, WI, serving from 1884-86.

Robert A. Pastrick (1930-2018), of Slovak descent; Mayor of East Chicago, IN (1973-2004). He was also on the city council for 12 years and controller for seven years.

Emil Frank Pechacek (1910-1983), b. Flatonia TX, studied engineering at Texas A&M University before joining The Texas Company (now Texaco) as an assistant seismograph operator in 1929. He developed and improved the seismograph methods based upon seismic reading of underground explosions and was involved in gas and oil explorations all over Texas and the Southwestern states. Eventually he became the manager of the Texaco Geophysics Western Division and was involved in selecting sites for oil drilling in Montana, Wyoming, Colorado, and New Mexico. After being brought in from the field in a corporate role in Houston TX, he retired in 1976. Returning to hometown Flatonia TX, he became involved in local politics and was elected Mayor of Flatonia for two terms.

VI. PUBLIC LIFE

Richard Perchlik (1928-1988), b. Cleveland, OH, of Czech ancestry, trained as a political scientist, was an active political leader in Greeley, Colorado. Though he ran as a Democrat in a heavily Republican area he was elected Mayor of Greeley twice, in 1969 and 1971. As Mayor, he initiated several public works projects and, in order to make government more accessible, began broadcasting City Council meetings on local radio.

Ralph Perk (1914-1999), b. Cleveland, OH, of Bohemian ancestry, was elected 52nd Mayor of Cleveland, as the first Republican in thirty years and was re-elected in 1973 and 1975, serving until 1977.

Emil Edwin Placek (1877-1972), b. Milligan, NE, of Czech ancestry, a Wahoo banker, was elected Mayor of Wahoo, NE and served from 1918 to 1921.

Henry A. Pokorny (1924-2010), b. Hopkins, MN, of Bohemian ancestry, was elected Mayor of Hopkins, MN, serving from 1969-75.

Ann Pomykal (fl. 2014); b. Texas, likely of Czech ancestry; Mayor of Lewisville, TX (1985-1987), first female Mayor of the City. Other service has included president of Greater Lewisville United Way, director of the TI Foundation, and many other civic roles. Pomykal worked in TI philanthropy for more than 16 years before retiring from the company in 2003 and becoming the executive director of the TI Foundation. In her new role, she will continue her work with many education grants such as AP Strategies, Educate Texas Lancaster ISD initiative, Teach for America, UTeach and the Innovation in STEM Teaching Awards.

Edward Racek (1846-1912), b. Polná, Bohemia, came with his parents to this country in 1851 and settled in Watertown, WI, where he has since resided. Received his education in the schools of Watertown and Bryant & Stratton's Commercial College, Milwaukee; clerked in a mercantile store during the rebellion; served three years as teller in Wisconsin National Bank of Watertown when first organized; and had been engaged in a general mercantile business since 1871. He was also engaged in cement stone construction and production of crushed and building stone for the market from a quarry located at Richwood, WI. In political life, has served nine terms as alderman, representing the 3rd ward, and two terms as Mayor (1896, 1897); and was also elected member of Assembly in 1904.

Edmund Jennings Randolph (1753-1813), b. Williamsburg, VA, desc. f. Augustine Heřman, served as Mayor of Williamsburg, VA. (1776-77).

J. J. Remes (1869-d.), b. MN, of Bohemian parents, a merchant, served as Mayor and city clerk of New Prague, MN and also held other public offices. In the early years, he was a force in the city's metamorphosis which converted it from a sprawling country town with a black ribbon of mud for its main street and business enterprise retarded by inaccessible roads. Remes led the grading and graveling of local roads in the village.

Joseph Herman Romig (1872–1951), b. Edwards Co., IL, a descendant of Moravian immigrants who had settled in Tuscarawas County, Ohio, a Moravian missionary and a physician, was elected Mayor of Anchorage, Alaska in 1937, serving a single term.

Sebastian Ruta (1904–1999), b. NJ, of Czech ancestry, became Mayor of South Hackensack, NJ in 1936 and served for two decades through 1956. A flamboyant mayor, almost single-handedly pulled the township out of bankruptcy during the 1930s.

Raymond Thomas 'R. T.' Rybak, Jr. (1955–), b. Minneapolis, of Czech ancestry, became the 46th Mayor of the city of Minneapolis, MN in January 2002. He won a second term in November 2005 and a third in November 2009.

Frank A. Rybka (1910–1997), b. Elwood, IN, was elected Mayor, Weirton, WV (1963–71).

Mathias M. Secor (orig. Zika) (1841–1911), b. Strakonice, Bohemia, a trunk manufacturer, was elected Mayor of Racine, WI, serving 2 terms (1884–88).

Edmund Premysl Sedivy (1911–1995), b. Verdigre, NE, of Czech ancestry, was elected Mayor of Bozeman, MT, serving from 1966–67, 1974–75 and 1977–79.

Milo J. Sedlacek (1898–1955), b. Cedar Rapids, IA, of Czech ancestry, served as Mayor of Cedar Rapids, IA (1953–54).

F.J. Sokol (1841–d.), b. Bohemia, immigrated to US in 1854 and resided in the village of Onslow, IA. He was a prosperous farmer and merchant. In politics, Mr. Sokol was a Republican and in 1892 was appointed supervisor of Jones County to fill out an unexpired term, after which he was twice regularly elected to the office, serving on the Board for a period of seven years. He was twice elected to the Iowa State legislature. He was the first Mayor of the village of Onslow, serving for four terms as chief executive of the town. He held all of the minor offices of the village and township except that of justice of the peace and refused to serve in that capacity.

Arnold A. Spacek (1886–1952), b. Fayetteville, TX, of Moravian ancestry, served as Mayor of Granger, TX in Williamson County. He was paternal grandfather of the actress Sissy Spacek.

Paul S. Šrámek (1894-1966), b. Ostrava, Moravia, was a farm implement dealer in Meadowlands, MN. He served for 25 years as Mayor of Meadowlands and was 35 years on the village Board. For many years, he was president of the Meadowlands Fair Association, president of the So. St. Louis Co. Fair Association, president and secretary of the Meadowlands Commerce Association etc.

Joseph Stahura (1956-), b. Whiting, IN, of Slovak descent; a Democrat; Whiting City Councilman (served 20 years), Mayor of Whitney, IN (s. 2004; in 2018 in his 4th term.). He was the 7th mayor of Slovak decent.

William A. Stassen (1873-1962), b. St. Paul, MN of Bohemian mother, a farmer and a merchant, was elected Mayor of West St. Paul, serving for three terms s. 1921.

George Stedronsky (1892-ca. 1971), b. Chicago, IL, of Czech ancestry, an attorney, was elected Mayor of Cicero, IL, serving from 1937 to 1942.

William Henry Stepanek (1868 d.), b. Swisher, IA, of Czech ancestry, was Mayor of Cedar Rapids, IA (1932-34).

William J. Swoboda (1898-1955), b. Racine, WI, of Bohemian ancestry, a businessman, at the age of 32, was elected Mayor of Racine (1931-37).

Isaac William Taussig (1850-1917), b. New York City, of Bohemian ancestry, a sugar refiner, was the 22nd Mayor of Jersey City, NJ. He would go on to serve two terms as Mayor (from May 1880 to May 1884).

Walter M. Taussig (1862-1923), b. St. Louis, MO, of Bohemian ancestry, a businessman, became Mayor of Yonkers, NY, serving from 1922-1923.

William Taussig (1826-1913), b. Prague, Bohemia, was a physician who was elected Mayor of Carondelet, MO (1852).

Joseph F. Tobias (1867-1919), b. Elysian, MN, of Czech ancestry, served as Mayor of Wilson, KS for 4 years.

George John Urban (1906-1978), b. Cleveland, OH, of Czech ancestry, was elected Mayor of South Euclid, Cuyahoga Co., OH. After his few terms in the office, opponents quit running against him. He served 24 years as Mayor.

Emil Vacin (1905-1989), served as Mayor of Berwyn, IL from 1969 to 1977.

Joseph John Verchota (1872-1949), b. La Crosse, WI, of Bohemian ancestry, was elected Mayor of La Crosse, WI. He served several terms, from 1923 to 1929, 1931 to 1935 and 1939 to 1947. He led the way for the construction of Logan High School and, as a strong backer of industrial development, was instrumental in the creation of the La Crosse Municipal Airport.

Frank Veselý (1877-1959), b. Bohemia, became Mayor of Silver City, NM in 1924 and served until 1934.

Anton James Vlach (1884-1982), b. Czech., a businessman, was elected Mayor of Clarkson, NE, serving from 1922 to 1926.

Nick Wasicsko (1958-1993), b. Yonkers, NY, of Slovak descent; lawyer, politician; Mayor of Yonkers, NY (s. 1987), the youngest Mayor of Yonkers. As mayor, he fought for the desegregation of public housing. Once out of office, Wasicsko practiced law, taught at John Jay College of Criminal Justice, and hosted a local radio talk show.

John Wattawa (1859-1904), b. Milwaukee, WI, of Bohemian ancestry, a lawyer, became Mayor of Kewaunee, WI (1893-94, 1897-98).

Don Wesely (1954-), b. David City, NE, of Czech ancestry, was elected in 1949 the City of Lincoln's 49th Mayor. As Mayor (1999-2003), Don Wesely presided over the city during troubled economic times, but managed to leave the city on solid financial footing for his successors.

Joseph Zabransky, b. Little Ferry, NJ, of Bohemian ancestry, was elected Mayor, Little Ferry, NJ, serving from 1936 to 1940. During his administration all streets were repaired, new disposal built and extension to library, even in the Depression.

Joseph John Zahorec (1920-1984), b. Lorain, OH, of Slovak descent; owner of Zahorec Realty for 24 years; Mayor of Lorain, OH (1972-79, 1983-84).

Stephen A. Zona (1899-1969), politician, Mayor of Parma, OH (1952-1957).

G. Military

Ján Ambruš, OBE (1899-1994), b. Gorna Mitropolia, Bulgaria, of Slovak parents, was a Slovak aerobatics and fighter pilot. He flew with the French Air Force in the Battle of France and the Royal Air Force in the Battle of Britain. After the Communist takeover of Czechoslovakia, he escaped and settled in the US, where he worked as a design engineer.

Richard Bassett (1745-1815), b. Cecil Co., MD, whose mother was a great grand-daughter of Augustine Heřman, was a veteran of the American Revolution and delegate to the Constitutional Convention of 1787. His most notable contributions during the American Revolution were his efforts to mobilize the state's military. Some sources credit him with developing the plans for raising and staffing the 1st Delaware Regiment, with his neighbor, John Haslet at its command. Known as the 'Delaware Continentals' or 'Delaware Blues,' they were from the smallest state, but as some 800 men, were the largest battalion in the army. David McCullough in 1776 describes them "turned out in handsome red trimmed blue coats, white waistcoats, buckskin breeches, white woolen stockings, and carrying fine, 'lately imported' English muskets" Raised in early 1776, they went into service in July and August 1776. Bassett also participated in the recruitment of the reserve militia that served in the 'Flying Camp' of 1776, and the Dover Light Infantry, led by another neighbor, Thomas Rodney. When the British Army marched through northern New Castle County, on the way to the Battle of Brandywine and the capture of Philadelphia, Bassett "appears to have joined his friend Rodney in the field as a volunteer." Once the Delaware militia returned home after the British retired from the area, Bassett continued as a part-time soldier, assuming command of the Dover Light Horse, Kent County's militia cavalry unit.

Gustavus Becher (1844-1913), b. Plzeň, Bohemia, was Scouts officer. He was brought by his parents to America in 1847 and by 1856 had settled at Columbus, NE. Becher came to know the Pawnees, for he was named Lieutenant, under Luther North as Captain, of a company of Pawnee Scouts in 1867 which were of the battalion of scouts commanded by Frank North. The next year, Becker served under Fred Mathews of another company of Scouts, this time protecting Union Pacific Railroad construction. Becker apparently was at the decisive victory over the Cheyennes at Summit Spring July 11, 1869. He later became a broker and was elected to the state legislature in 1895 and died at Columbus, NE.

Jan Bervida (1893-1962), b. Radkov, Bohemia, during the 1st World War, was sent to Eastern Front and in 1915, he was taken prisoner by Russians, and later as a private of the Czechoslovak Legion, he took part in a march to the United States via Vladivostok. Upon returning to his home country, he graduated from the University of Technology, receiving an M.A. (Ing.) in Aeronautic Engineering. From 1927-29, he worked at the Public Works Ministry in Prague, where he became Head of the Aviation Department in 1929. During the Nazi Occupation of Czechoslovakia from 1939 to 1945, Bervida, as a former member of the Czechoslovak Legion, was fired in 1939 and became a teacher. He taught at a secondary school specializing in engineering. Later he was arrested and interrogated. Because he collaborated with the Czechoslovak government-in-exile in London, he was sentenced to death. He was saved by the end of World War II in May 1945. 1945-47, Bervida became Department Head at the Ministry of Transport (Civilian Airways) and Czechoslovak Airlines

(ČSA) Director. In 1946, was Bervida elected vice president of the FAI and one year later, 1947, was he elected vice president of the International Civil Aviation Organization (ICAO). During the Communist takeover in 1948, he was in France, where he applied for citizenship. In Paris, he was involved with Czechoslovak exile authorities (Council of Free Czechoslovakia). Shortly thereafter, he emigrated to the United States, where he worked with the ICAO in New York and in Montreal.

Claude Charles Bloch (1878–1967), b. Woodbury, KY, of Bohemian ancestry, entered the US Naval Academy in 1895. He volunteered for active duty in the Spanish-American War, serving aboard the USS *Iowa* before he graduated in 1899. During the Boxer Rebellion in 1900, he was a member of the China Relief Expedition. In World War I, Bloch served as navigator on the USS *Arizona*, and he was in command of the USS *Plattsburg*, transporting troops to France. He received the Navy Cross in 1918. From 1923 to 1927, Bloch was chief of the Bureau of Ordnance at the gun factory of the Washington naval yard. He was promoted to Rear Admiral and from 1927 to 1929, he was at sea commanding the USS *California*. In 1930–31, Bloch was stationed at the Newport, RI torpedo station. In 1933, Bloch was judge advocate of the Navy. From 1927 to 1930, he was Commander-in-chief of the US fleet and was promoted to admiral. Bloch was commandant of the Hawaiian Sea frontier, 14th Naval District, at Pearl Harbor when the Japanese attacked in December 1941. In investigating the Japanese attack, the Roberts committee cleared him of any dereliction of duty. He remained in command until April 1942. He retired in 1945 with the rank of Four-Star Admiral.

Abraham Block (1780–1857), b. Bohemia, was the 1812 veteran and pioneer merchant in Washington, AR. He immigrated to this country at an early age. During the War of 1812, he fought with courage and distinction. With his wife, Fannie, he journeyed to Arkansas in the early 1820's, traveling along the old Southwest Trail to claim the bounty land he was entitled to as a veteran. The Blocks arrived in Washington in 1823 and soon established the mercantile business that was to become one of the most prosperous in the state. By all accounts, he was one of the wealthiest men in Hempstead County.

August Bondi (1833–1907), Vienna, of Bohemian parents, was a soldier and patriot, and one of John Brown's men. When only fourteen years of age, he became a member of the Academic League and fought under Kossuth during the Hungarian War for Liberty. For this, he was exiled and in 1848, the family came to America. In 1855, he came to Kansas at a time when the opposition to slavery was crystallizing and became an intense anti-slavery partisan. After remaining two weeks at Lawrence, he went down the Missouri River and back by land to acquaint himself with affairs on the border. With a partner, he 'squatted' on a claim on the Mosquito branch of the Pottawatomie, in Franklin County. In the fall of 1855, he became acquainted with John Brown, and after the burning of Lawrence, he joined the company of John Brown, Jr. When this force disbanded, he did not return to his claim, but joined John Brown, Sr., and took part in the engagement at Black Jack. He was then with Brown in different raids along the border and at the battle of Osawatomie. In Feb., 1857, he laid out the town of Greeley, Anderson County, and was appointed postmaster there. From that time to the outbreak of the Civil War, he kept the 'underground railway' station at Greeley. In Oct., 1861, he enlisted in the Fifth Kansas regiment and was present in nearly all the actions in which the regiment was engaged. On Sept. 14, 1864, he was seriously wounded and made prisoner by the Confederates near Pine Bluff, Ark., but was left on the field. He was discharged in Dec., 1864, and in 1866, he located in Salina. Mr. Bondi held many offices in Saline County, such as probate judge, district clerk and postmaster, and was appointed a member of the State Board of Charities.

Oliver C. Bosbyshell (1839–1921), b. Vicksburg, MS, of Bohemian ancestry, first enlisted in April, 1861, and then re-enlisted again in September, as Second Lieutenant, Forty-eighth Regiment, Pennsylvania Infantry. He embarked with his regiment on the 11th of November, 1861, for Hatteras, North Carolina. When the attack was made on New Berne, General Burnside detailed six companies of the Forty-eighth to accompany his forces, in which expedition Bosbyshell served as acting quartermaster of his regiment. Afterwards he was made acting Adjutant of the Forty-eighth. Next, he was promoted to First Lieutenancy, and afterwards to the Captaincy, of Company G. Captain Bosbyshell was engaged at Bull Run, at Chantilly, at South Mountain, at Antietam, and at Fredericksburg. In the spring of 1863, the Ninth Corps was ordered west, and Bosbyshell was made Provost-Marshal at Lexington, KY. He took part in all the fights in East Tennessee: was in the battles of Blue Springs, Campbell's Station, and the siege of Knoxville. Returning on veteran furlough to Schuylkill County in January 1864, he helped recruit the ranks of the decimated command. The Ninth Corps, after re-organization, moved into Virginia by way of Washington. Bosbyshell was detailed by Colonel Sigfried as acting Assistant Adjutant General, First Brigade, Fourth Division, and Ninth Army Corps. In this capacity, Colonel Bosbyshell served through Grant's campaign, beginning at the Wilderness and ending at Petersburg. During his service, he was commissioned Major of his regiment. He was mustered out of service Oct. 1, 1864.

George Douglas Brewerton (1820–1901), desc. f. Augustine Heřman, was a soldier, writer and artist. He joined Stephenson's regiment of 'California volunteers,' in 1846, as Second Lieutenant, 1st United States Infantry, 22 May, 1847, and First Lieutenant in June, 1850. He is the author of *The War in Kansas: A Rough Trip to the Border among New Homes and a Strange People* (1856); *Fitzpoodle at Newport* (1869); and *Ida Lewis, the Heroine of Lime Rock* (1869). He also published, through a New York firm, *The Automaton Regiment* (1862), *The Automaton Company*, and *The Automaton Battery* (1863). These devices for the instruction of military recruits were brought out when hundreds of thousands of untrained soldiers were eagerly studying the rudiments of the art of war and were extensively used in connection with the regular books of tactics.

Joseph John Broshek (1886–1957), b. New Bedford, MA, of Czech ancestry, was a graduate of US Naval Academy in 1908 and Columbia Univ. in 1915. He was commissioned ensign in 1910, advancing through grades to rear admiral in 1942 and retired in 1946. He served on USS *George Washington* in WWI and was head of maintenance, Bureau of Ships, Navy Dept. to retirement in 1946. He was a Free Mason.

John Marshall Brown (1838–1907), b. Portland, ME, desc. f. Frederick Philipse, was appointed by Pres. Lincoln, Captain and Assistant Adjunct General of ME volunteers and served in SC and FL. He commanded regiment at Totopotomy and Cold Harbor and preliminary movements at Petersburg, where he was severely wounded. At discharge, he was brevetted Colonel and Brigadier General.

Henry Bryan (1835–1879), b. Savannah, GA, desc. f. Augustine Heřman, prior to the Civil War, was employed as a broker. During the Civil War, Bryan served as a staff officer. In July and August of 1861, Bryan was a volunteer aide-de-camp for Brigadier General John B. Magruder. On September 4, 1861, he became a Captain and Brigadier General Magruder's aide-de-camp. He became Major General Magruder's Assistant Adjutant General on January 14, 1862. After briefly serving on the staff of Major General David R. Jones in May of 1862, Bryan rejoined Major General Magruder's staff as a Major and an Assistant Adjutant General. Bryan's left arm was wounded at the battle of Malvern Hill on July 1, 1862. By late 1862, Bryan had joined the staff of General P. G. T. Beauregard as an Assistant Adjutant and Inspector General, a position that he would hold in Charleston, South Carolina – albeit not necessarily with General Beauregard – until he was paroled on April 26, 1865. Following the war, Bryan was employed as a broker and banker.

Lewis Bush (1753–1777), b. Philadelphia. PA, of Bohemian father, was Solomon Bush's brother. He was an American Revolutionary soldier. He received the commission of First Lieutenant of the Sixth Pennsylvania Battalion (June 1776) and was made Captain in the same month. He was transferred in 1777 to Col. Thomas Hartley's additional continental regiment and of this troop, Bush was commissioned Major March 12, 1777. He was a brave soldier, serving with distinction during many engagements. At the battle of Brandywine, Sept. 11, 1777, he received a fatal wound and died shortly after.

Solomon Bush (1753–1795), b. Philadelphia, PA, of Bohemian father (son of Mathias Bush from Prague), was an officer in the Pennsylvania militia (1777–87). On July 5, 1777, he was appointed Deputy Adjutant-General of the state militia by the Supreme Council of

Pennsylvania. In September 1777, he was dangerously wounded in the thigh during a skirmish and had to be taken to Philadelphia. When the British captured the city in December 1777, he was taken prisoner, but released on parole. As he could not earn his living, being kept on account of his wound at his father's home (Chestnut Hill, Philadelphia), the Council passed a series of resolutions, October 20, 1779, respecting him, and on October 27 of that year, he was promoted to Lieutenant-Colonel, with pay in accordance with the rank. Bush was in destitute circumstances in later years, and on November 5, 1785, the Council of Pennsylvania, under the presidency of Benjamin Franklin, ordered that a pension be paid him for his meritorious services. His brother, Jonas Bush, was on the roll of Revolutionary soldiers.

Jerry George Capka (1922–1978), b. Middletown, PA, of Slovak descent, was US Army Lieutenant Colonel, recipient of Legion of Merit for action during the Vietnam War (1965).

Samuel Sprigg Carroll (1832–1893), b. Takoma Park, MD; desc. f. Frederick Philipse, was a career officer in the United States Army who rose to the rank of Brigadier General during the American Civil War. He was most known for his service as the commander of the famed 'Gibraltar Brigade,' an infantry brigade in the Army of the Potomac that played a key role during the defense of Cemetery Hill during the Battle of Gettysburg, as well as in repulsing a portion of Pickett's Charge. He was appointed Brigadier General of volunteers and retired at regular rank of Major General.

Ezekiel Forman Chambers (1788–1867), Augustine Heřman's descendant, was a native of Chestertown, Kent Co., MD. In 1809, he was admitted to the Bar and soon acquired a great reputation as a lawyer. During the War of 1812, he raised a volunteer company, of which he was Captain. With this company, he participated in the battle of Caulk's Field in the summer of 1814, and his bravery was especially mentioned in the official report of the battle. He attained the rank of Brigadier General of militia after the war. In 1826, the legislature of Maryland elected him to the Senate. He was later appointed a Judge of the Court of Appeals of Maryland.

John Rozier Clagett (1852–1902), b. Washington, DC, desc. f. Augustine Heřman, was Major in the US Army. He served on Crook's campaigns against Northern Cheyenne Indians (1876-77); on duty at St. Louis during riots (1877); on campaign against northern Cheyenne Indians (1878); in campaigns against Ute Indians, CO (1880); Apache Indians, AZ (1892). He served on the second Philippine expedition (1898); engaged in assault and capture of Manila (1898); in defense of Manila against Tagalog Insurrection (1899); expedition to Sulu Islands (1899); commander of Home Battalion 25th Infantry after returning to US.

Matthew Clarkson (1758–1825) was born in New York, NY. He was a great-great-grandson of Frederick Philipse. He was an American Revolutionary War soldier and a politician in New York State. The town of Clarkson in Western New York was named after him. He was a great uncle of Thomas S. Clarkson, a member of the family who founded Clarkson University. He served in the Revolutionary War, first on Long Island, subsequently under Benedict Arnold. He was at Saratoga and, later, on the staff of General Benjamin Lincoln, was present at the surrender of Burgoyne at Savannah (1779) and at the defense of Charleston (1780). He was also present at the surrender of Cornwallis. After the War, Clarkson was commissioned Brigadier General of militia of Kings and Queens Counties in June 1786 and Major General of the Southern District of New York in March 1798.

Edmund Ross Colhoun (1821–1897), b. Chambersburg, PA, desc. f. Augustine Heřman, was US Naval officer. He was a Rear Admiral of the United States Navy, who served during the Mexican-American War and the American Civil War. He was appointed a midshipman on 1 April 1839. He served during the Mexican War with Commodores David Conner and Matthew Perry at Alvarado and Tabasco. During the Civil War, he served on both the North and South Atlantic Blockading Squadrons, had command of the monitor Weehawken, and was commended for his participation in the bombardment and capture of Fort Fisher, North Carolina, from December 1864 to January 1865. He commanded the South Pacific Squadron (1874–5), Mare Island Navy Yard (1877–81), and retired from the Navy on 5 May 1883. Two destroyers were named USS *Colhoun* in his honor.

Samuel Reed Colhoun (1846–1920), b. Philadelphia, PA, desc. f. Augustine Heřman (son of Edmund Ross Colhoun), was Capt. S.C., US Navy, on duty (1869–1908). He served on the Marion when she rescued the shipwrecked crew of the *Trinity* from Heard Island in the Antarctic. He served on the Oregon when she made her world-famous run from Bremerton, WA to Cuba and in all her fighting in the Spanish-American War. He became paymaster in the US Navy.

John Watts de Peyster (1821–1907), b. New York City; desc. f. Frederick Philipse, was a student and author of war, an indirect participant in the Civil War, rising to the rank of Major General. In his later years, he became a philanthropist, leaving his name on a number of buildings and institutions. He was well educated, having received M.A. and Ph.D. degrees. He was one of the organizers of the New York City Police and Fire Departments and was active as a volunteer fireman himself. He was also active in the New York State Militia and was promoted to Brigadier General in 1851. At the State level, he also served as Judge Advocate General, and later Adjutant General, before he resigned over a conflict with New York Governor Myron Clark in 1855. At the start of the Civil War, de Peyster was already in his forties. He did offer his services to the Union Army, but was rebuffed, probably for younger candidates. His three sons did serve in the Union Army during the war, and his namesake, John Watts de Peyster, Jr., actually rose to the level of Brevet Brigadier General. During the Civil War, de Peyster wrote a series of articles on war tactics, and some of these tactics were adopted and proved to be practical in the field of battle. For his indirect contributions to the Civil War, the State of New York later elevated de Peyster to brevet major general.

Frederick de Peyster, Jr. (1843–1874), b. NYC, desc. f. Frederick Philipse, was a soldier who did duty both in the line and staff during the Civil War. He was with Gen. B. F. Butler when with some 800 men of the 8th NY and 6th MA Militia, he accomplished his celebrated occupation of Baltimore. He also performed outstanding service at the first battle of Bull Run and in the 4th corps on the Peninsula. For his conduct at Bull Run, he was brevetted Major U.S.V. and Colonel.

John Watts de Peyster, Jr. (1841–1873), b. NYC, desc. f. Frederick Philipse, was a soldier. He joined the staff of Gen. Philip Kearny and participated in the Battle of Williamsburg. He was a Major in the first NY artillery and later served on the staff of Gen. Peck.

Johnston Livingston de Peyster (1846–1903), b. Tivoli-on-the-Hudson, NY, desc. f. Frederick Philipse, was Brevetted Major and Lt. Col., U.S.V. and Colonel, N.Y.V. by the State of NY in 1867 for hoisting the first real American flag over Richmond, the Confederate Capital.

Anthony Michael Dignowity (1810–1875), b. Kaňk, nr. Kutná Hora, Bohemia, was trained as a mechanic. Somehow, he got involved in the Polish revolution in 1831 and later immigrated to America. After his arrival in New York in 1832, he traveled southward and worked at a variety of occupations in various states. During an extended residence in Natchez, MS, he traveled to Texas as far as San Antonio. He studied medicine under doctors Stone and Carrothers in Natchez and at the Eclectic Medical College of Cincinnati, after which he practiced medicine in Mississippi and at Tahlequah in the Cherokee Indian Territory of present-day Oklahoma. When the Mexican War broke out in spring of 1846, he hurried back to San Antonio with a group of Arkansas volunteers. He later became a successful doctor and businessman there, but in the 1850s, his outspoken abolitionist views made him controversial. In 1859, he published an autobiography in English, *Bohemia under Austrian Despotism* to clear his name. He was one of the first Czech-born writers to publish in America. In his book, Dignowity rails against the 'tyranny' of American public opinion and criticizes the American legal system. Dignowity's reputation as a Unionist and abolitionist continued to plague him, and in 1861, he narrowly escaped hanging in the San Antonio Plaza. He traveled by horseback to Washington, D.C., where he was employed by the Federal Government. His property was confiscated, and two of his sons were conscripted into the Confederate Army. The sons later escaped to Mexico, however, and joined the Union Army.

Dignowity returned to San Antonio after the war and managed to recover his properties, but his health had been destroyed. He died in San Antonio on April 22, 1875.

Péter Pál Dobozy (1832-1919), location of his birth uncertain but could be Slovak ancestry; soldier in Hungarian revolution of 1848; in US s. 1861; Civil War veteran; adjutant of General Asboth; commander of the 4th Colored Heavy Artillery Regiment which he organized; mustered in 1866 at Pine Bluffs, AR. After the Civil War, resided in Missouri as a farmer.

James Chatham Duane (1824-1897), b. Schenectady, NY, desc. f. Augustine Heřman, a military engineer, was with McClellan's Army on Potomac during Civil War, who made important contributions with his organization of engineer battalion and engineer equipage. He was chief engineer of the Army of the Potomac. He was Brevetted Colonel of US Army for distinguished service and later made chief of engineers of US Army with the rank of Brigadier General.

George John Dufek (1903-1977), b. Rockford, IL, of Czech ancestry, US Naval officer, in 1925, served aboard the battleship Maryland and was later assigned to submarine duty. During World War II, he helped organize US amphibious assaults on Africa, Sicily and southern France and commanded an anti-submarine task force in the Atlantic that was credited with sinking the last German submarine in that war. In the Korean War, he commanded the aircraft carrier *Antietam*. After retiring in 1959, he became director of the Mariners' Museum in Newport News, Virginia.

Joseph E. Durik (1922-1942), b. Pennsylvania, of Slovak descent, was an apprentice seaman, killed in action following the accidental firing of a torpedo aboard the destroyer Meredith. For his selfless conduct in giving first aid to an injured shipmate although wounded himself, Apprentice Seaman Durik was posthumously commended by Admiral Chester W. Nimitz. The destroyer escort *Durick* was named in his honor.

Herman Ehrenberg (1816-1866), b. Steuben, Prussia, possibly of Bohemian ancestry, came to Nacogdoches, TX and fought in the siege of Bexar, the first major campaign of the Texas Revolution. He was one of a few men who escaped the Goliad Massacre. According to Ehrenberg's own account, after the command to kneel at the start of the shooting, he jumped up and, hidden by the gun smoke, dashed for the San Antonio River. On the way, a Mexican soldier slashed him in the head with his saber, but Ehrenberg managed to get by him and jumped in the river crying, "The Republic of Texas forever!" When he was discharged from the Texas Army on June 2, 1836, he received a certificate for part of a league of land but never personally claimed it. Since it was later (1880) awarded to his heirs from Teplice, Bohemia, he may have been of Bohemian origin.

VI. PUBLIC LIFE

Alexander Eisenschiml (1832–1888), a native of Měčín, near Plzeň, immigrated to America in 1848, when revolutionary sentiments grew rife in Austria. Upon landing in New York, news reached the boat that gold had been discovered in California, crew and passengers alike immediately decided to head for San Francisco. After an adventurous career in California and Nevada, he gave up prospecting and turned soldier. In 1861, he joined the Illinois regiment and saw action at Shiloh, the crucial battle fought between the Union soldiers under Grant and the Confederates under Johnston and Beauregard. But the reality of war quickly induced him to resign his commission. Thereafter during the remainder of the war, he became an Indian Scout. After witnessing what happened to his comrades in capture by the 'bloodthirsty' Indian tribe, he also quit the Indian Service. Taking out his citizenship papers in Nevada, he left the west and turned to the peaceful occupation of running a meat market in Chicago.

Michael J. Estocin (1931–1967), b. Turtle Creek, PA, of Slovak descent, was a US Navy officer and a recipient of the United States military's highest decoration—the Medal of Honor—for his actions in the Vietnam War. He was presumably lost during action. The US Navy named the guided-missile frigate USS *Estocin* (FFG-15), launched in 1979, in his honor.

Ján Fiala (1822–1871), b. Slovakia; emigrated to America; surveyor building railroads and mapping Missouri; a colonel in the Civil War, prepared plans to defend St. Louis and organize German recruits; wounded.

Gustav Joseph Fiebeger (1858–1939), b. Akron, OH, of Bohemian parents, was US Army military officer and civil engineer trained at US Military Academy. He served in the US Army from entering West Point in 1875 until his retirement. He was prof. of civil and military engineering, US Military Academy (1896–1922). He was the author of text books for use in courses at West Point, including Civil Engineering, Field Fortifications, etc. President of the US presented him the Army Distinguished Service for exceptionally meritorious and distinguished services to the Government of the US, in a duty of great responsibility during WWI, as Professor of Civil and Military Engineering at the US Military Academy. As head of the Dept of Civil and Military Engineering, Colonel Fiebeger, for 26 yrs., instructed, both personally and by textbook, the officers of the Army in the principles of warfare, principles later fruitfully applied by many of these officers as commanders in the World War.

Jaroslav Thayer Folda, Jr. (1914–1970), b. Schuyler, NE, was commissioned as 2nd Lieutenant at United States Military Academy (1938). He received additional training in international relations at Georgetown University (M.A., 1948) and National War College (Cert, 1957). He was Headquarters Battery Commander of the 64th Field Artillery Battalion, Schofield

Barracks, Hawaii, at the time of the Japanese attack on Pearl Harbor, 1941, and served with the 25th Infantry Division in the Pacific (1941-45). He was Commander (Brigadier General), 1st Infantry Division Artillery, Fort Riley KS, 1961-1962; Commander (Brigadier General), 25th Infantry Division Artillery, Schofield Barracks, Hawaii, 1962-1963; Commander (Major General), U.S. Army Alaska, 1966-1968. He served as Deputy Secretary and Secretary of Staff for General Alfred Gruenther, Supreme Headquarters Allied Powers Europe (SHAPE), Paris (1954-56); Executive Officer, Office of Assistant Secretary of Defense, International Security Affairs, Washington, D.C. (1961-62); and Director of Management, Office of the Comptroller of the Army, Dept. of the Army (1968-69).

George William Folta (1919-2003), b. Juneau. AK, of Slovak descent; submarine sailor, Capt., US Navy, serving long career, spanning World War II, Korea and Viet Nam.

Gen. Thomas Marsh Forman (1758-1845), Augustine Heřman's descendant, was a native of Rose Hill, Cecil Co., MD. He joined Smallwood's Regiment as a cadet shortly before the Battle of Long Island, the following winter was commissioned First Lieutenant in the Eleventh PA Regiment. Subsequently became Captain in his Uncle David's Continental Regiment, and in 1779, succeeded James Monroe as staff officer to Maj. Gen. Lord Sterling. He served in the Legislature in 1790-1800, and during the bombardment of Fort McHenry in the War of 1812, commanded a brigade of militia. During Lafayette's visit to this country in 1824, Gen. Thomas Marsh Forman went with his carriage with four horses and two servants in livery to meet Marquis and took him in his carriage to Frenchtown where he took the steamboat to Baltimore. Gen. Thomas Marsh Forman had a brother Joseph Forman (1761-1805) who was a Colonel and who was later appointed US Consul to Amsterdam. His son Ezekiel, who was also in the military, became a Major.

Cornelius Fornet (1818-1894), b. Stráže pod Tatrami, Slovakia; engineer; soldier in Hungarian war of 1848; in US s. 1849; in 1852 went back to Europe to get married and returned to US with his wife; in Civil War served under General John C. Frémont, as a Major of engineers; after recovery from a serious accident, he was sent to New Jersey by General Hall to organize the 22nd Volunteer Infantry Regiment of NJ. He was appointed first colonel of the Regiment but, due to injuries, he returned to Hungary, where he became government official.

Andrew Gálfy-Gállik (1818-1883), b. Brzotín, Slovakia; merchant in Košice; Hungarian army officer; came to America, settling in Cincinnati, OH; in 1862, enlisted in the 58th Ohio Infantry Regiment, in which he was appointed major. After being captured, he was exchanged and then served on the gunboat *Mound City*. After the War, he studied medicine and then practiced in Boston, then in Cincinnati and finally in Kansas City. In 1881, he returned to Košice.

Anthony (Antal) Gerster (1825–1897), b. Košice, Slovakia; uncle of Dr. Arpad G. Gerster; civil engineer, military officer in the 1848 Hungarian Revolution; in US s. 1852; served in the Civil War as a Captain of the engineer corps under General John C. Frémont with General Alexander Asboth and later served under the Generals Rosecrans and Grant; with the 5th Missouri Infantry, then the 27th Missouri Infantry. After the War, he organized Gerster's Independent Company of Pioneers, an independent company of military engineers, responsible for building, repairing, or destroying fortifications and bridges. He died in California in 1897.

Otto Herman Goldstein (1883–1937), b. Rokycany, Bohemia, during WWI Capt., served in the US Army. He was promoted to Major Ltd. Colonel, then Colonel Q.M.C.; Col. Q.M.R.C. (s. 1928). He was awarded Order of Purple Heart by Gen. Pershing (1918).

Joseph Benedict Greenhut (1843–1918), b. Prague, Bohemia, came with parents to Chicago in 1852. After working in the south in the tinsmith and coppersmith trade, he came north in 1861 and on April 17, in response to President Lincoln's first call for troops to aid in the preservation of the Union, he enlisted as a private in the Twelfth Illinois Infantry, the first Chicago regiment to respond to the call to arms. Greenhut was the second to enlist from the city of Chicago. Within two months, he was promoted to Sergeant and served until seriously wounded in the Battle of Fort Donelson. When his wound had healed, he recruited a company of infantry of which he was elected Captain. The company was assigned to the Eighty-second Illinois Regiment and subsequently, he was made chief of staff of the brigade. He served in some of the most important battles of the Civil War, including the battles of Fredericksburg, Chancellorsville and Gettysburg. He was made Adjutant General and chief of staff of 3rd Brigade, 3rd Div. of the 11th Army Corps and took part in the campaign and battles of his brigade in Tennessee, continuing in active duty until 1864 when his health failed, and he was allowed to resign. Upon recovery, Greenhut devoted himself to mechanical pursuits and later started in the distillery business in Peoria, IL from which he realized a magnificent fortune. When President McKinley and his entire cabinet visited Peoria in 1899, they were all guests of the Greenhuts.

Jacob Greil (1839–1900), b. Bohemia, came to America in 1856, dry business merchant at Milltown, at the outbreak of the War of Secession, he enlisted in the US Army, becoming fourth sergeant of Co. D, Fourteenth Alabama Infantry Regiment, then commanded by Col. Thomas Judge, and afterward by Col. Bayne. After two years' service, he was made Commissary Sergeant, serving as such until February 1864, and taking part in the battles of Williamsburg, VA, Seven Pines, seven days' fight around Richmond, second Bull Run, Antietam, Frazier's Farm and many minor skirmishes. At the end of the war, he was acting commissary with the rank of Captain. After leaving the service, he settled at Montgomery; entered the retail grocery business in which he remained until 1872.

John Joseph Greytak (1902-1973), b. PA, of Slovak descent, was an American Admiral, US Navy. He commanded USS *Kane* (1942-43) and USS *McKee* (1943-44) during the World War II.

Arthur Hanket (1924-2007), b. Cleveland, OH, of Czech ancestry, was US Army Brigadier General who served in Korea and Vietnam. He was West Point graduate and served in Italy and Trieste after World War II. He was with a combat engineer group in Korea in 1954, commanded a battalion of the 101st Airborne Division and was the Deputy Brigade Commander of the Division's 2nd Brigade. General Hanket received two Master's Degrees, one in engineering from Harvard University and one in international affairs from George Washington University. He also graduated from the US Army War College.

John Henry George Hašek (1938-1994), b. Prague, Czech., was a Canadian soldier, journalist and author. After fleeing post-war communist Czechoslovakia, he and his family emigrated to the United Kingdom, South America and eventually Canada where Hašek joined the Canadian Armed Forces in 1957. Major Hašek graduated from the University of Ottawa and later, the University of New Brunswick with a Master of Arts in Psychology. As a member of the Canadian Forces, he studied and worked as an instructor at the Royal Military College in Kingston, Ontario. Hašek served in the Black Watch (Royal Highland Regiment) of Canada, the Royal Canadian Regiment and later, the Queen's Own Rifles of Canada. While with the Canadian Forces, Hašek served in Ghana, Vietnam and Cyprus and as the first commander of the SkyHawks Parachute Team, which is the Demonstration Parachute Team of the Canadian Forces. An accomplished skydiver, Hašek had several thousand descents to his credit, and served as a member of the Parachute Testing Wing/Trials and Evaluations Centre of the Airborne Centre in Edmonton, Alberta.

Rochus Heinisch (1835-1914), b. Newark, NJ, of Bohemian father, was educated in private schools, and was brought up in manufacturing and business pursuits, following the cutlery business in his father's factory. At the age of seventeen, he joined the Putnam Horse Guards, a famous battalion of mounted men, commanded by Major Heinisch, the father of Rochus. Subsequently, he joined Company B, Newark City Battalion, and during the war, enlisted as a private soldier in Company A, Twenty-sixth New Jersey Volunteers. He was afterward elected Second Lieutenant and was promoted First Lieutenant in the field. He participated in several engagements of his regiment and was a faithful and a brave soldier. At the advance of the Twenty-sixth across the Rappahannock on June 5th, Lieutenant Heinisch was one of the very first to enter the rebel earth works. At the expiration of his term of service, he reentered business life and served two terms in the House of Assembly of the New Jersey Legislature.

Mark Helms (1964–1983), b. Dwight, NE, of Czech ancestry, entered Marine Corps in 1982. On duty in Lebanon, he was killed in blast on the Marine Compound on Oct. 23, 1983.

Frank A. Herda (1947–1968), b. Cleveland, OH, of Czech ancestry, a Specialist Fourth Class, US Army, was awarded Medal of Honor for conspicuous gallantry and intrepidity in action at the risk of his life in Quang Trang Province, Republic of Vietnam, June 29, 1968. Herda joined the Army from his birth city of Cleveland and by June 29, 1968, was serving as a private first class in Company A, 1st Battalion (Airborne), 506th Infantry Regiment, 101st Airborne Division (Airmobile). During an enemy attack on that day, near Dak To in Quang Trang Province, Republic of Vietnam, Herda smothered the blast of an enemy-thrown hand grenade with his body to protect those around him. He survived the blast, although severely wounded, and was subsequently promoted to specialist fourth class and awarded the Medal of Honor for his actions. Herda published the juvenile sword and sorcery novel, *The Cup of Death: Chronicles of the Dragons of the Magi* in 2007.

William Jay (1841–1894), b. New York City, desc. f. Frederick Philipse., was an Aide-de-camp on the staff of Maj. Gen. John E. Wool, Gen. George Morrell, Gen. George G. Meade and Gen. George Sykes. He participated in the battles of Chancellorsville and Gettysburg, in the Wilderness Campaign, in the siege of Petersburg and at the surrender of Gen. Lee's army. He was twice brevetted for gallant and meritorious conduct.

William R. Jecelin (1930–1950), b. Baltimore, of Czech ancestry, as a soldier in the United States Army, who posthumously received the United States military's highest decoration for bravery, the Medal of Honor, for his actions during the Korean War. He was born in and joined the Army from Baltimore, Maryland and was sent as a Sergeant to fight in the Korean War. While there, he was fighting with Company C, 35th Infantry Regiment during the Pusan Perimeter Offensive when a grenade was thrown at them, Jecelin sacrificed himself to save the other soldiers in his unit. He covered the grenade with his body and was killed.

Joseph R. Jelinek (1919–1978), b. Omaha, NE, of Czech ancestry, was US Army General. He was a student at Creighton University when he joined Company L, 134th Infantry Regiment, Nebraska National Guard in 1939. He was a Corporal in 1940 when he was ordered to active duty with his unit for training in anticipation of US entry into World War II. In 1943, he received his commission after graduation from Officer Candidate

School. He served in the Pacific Theater with the 32nd Infantry Division, and received the Bronze Star Medal, Purple Heart and Combat Infantryman Badge. He remained in the National Guard following the war, primarily in command and staff positions with the 34th Infantry Division. He served at the National Guard Bureau as Chief of the Army National Guard's Office of Plans, Policy and Programs from 1967 to 1969, and as the Executive Officer to the Chief of the National Guard Bureau from 1969 to 1971. He then served on the staff in the Office of the Secretary of Defense from 1971 to 1973. As a Brigadier General, he served as Deputy Director of the Army National Guard from 1973 to 1976. He died following an extended illness. In addition to his World War II awards, Jelinek was a recipient of the Legion of Merit and the Meritorious Service Medal.

Benjamin Franklin Jonas (1834-1911), b. Williamsport, KY, of Bohemian ancestry, as a boy, moved with his parents to Quincy, Illinois, where his father became a Republican state legislator and postmaster, and was acquainted with Abraham Lincoln. Despite his family's strong connections with the Republican Party, Benjamin Jonas cast his lot with the South in the Civil War. In 1862, he enlisted in the Confederate Army and served in the Washington Armillary until 1863; appointed Sergeant Major and later Adjutant of the Armillary Regiment commanded by Col. Beckham and served throughout the Civil War. After the war, he returned to New Orleans and became active in state politics as a Democrat. In 1865, he was elected to the state House of Representatives, serving until 1868, and in 1872, he was elected to the State Senate. In 1879, he was elected to the US Senate, and served from 4 March 1879 to 3 March 1885. His four brothers also served in the Confederate Army, all becoming officers just as he was.

Charles H. Jonas (1834-d.) served in the 12th Arkansas Infantry of Confederate Army as Captain. In July 1863, he was captured at Port Hudson in Louisville and imprisoned in New Orleans, and eventually sent to Johnson's Island, where he was kept as prisoner of war, at the time when his father was dying. President Lincoln, who was a good friend of Jonas' family, issued conditionally a personal order in May 1864, allowing "Charles H. Jonas... a parole of three weeks to visit dying father, Abraham Jonas, at Quince, Illinois. June 2, 1864." He arrived in time to say good bye to his father before he died. Captain Jonas honored his parole and remained prisoner of war until his exchange in March 1865.

Emil Joseph Kapaun (1916-1951). was a Roman Catholic priest and United States Army captain who served as a United States Army chaplain during World War II and the Korean War. Kapaun was a chaplain in the Burma Theater of World War II, then served again as a chaplain with the U.S. Army in Korea, where he was captured. He died in a prisoner of war camp. In 1993, Pope John Paul II declared him a Servant of God, the first stage on the path to canonization. In 2013, Kapaun posthumously received the Medal of Honor for his actions in Korea. He is the ninth American military chaplain Medal of Honor recipient.

Timothy J. Kadavy (1963–), b. Lincoln, NE, of Czech ancestry, is a United States Army Lieutenant General who serves as Director of the Army National Guard. He previously served as Special Assistant to the Vice Chief of the National Guard Bureau. His other assignments include Adjutant General of the Nebraska National Guard, Deputy Director of the Army National Guard, and Commander of Combined Joint Inter Agency Task Force-Afghanistan (CJIATF-A), part of the NATO International Security Assistance Force mission in that country.

Leopold Karpeles (1838–1909), b. Prague, Bohemia, entered military service, US Army in Springfield, MA. In 1870, he earned the Medal of Honor during the Civil War for heroism, "May 6, 1864 at the Wilderness Campaign, VA. Color Sergeant Leopold Karpeles was instrumental in turning the tide of the May 1864 Wilderness Campaign, that saw his 57th Massachusetts Regiment suffer the highest casualties." Some historians consider this Civil War battle as the turning point, when the North began its slow march toward victory. In 1870, he was awarded the Medal of Honor for his actions that day. He fought at Spotsylvania Courthouse on May 10, 12, and 18, 1864. At the Battle of the North Anna, on May 24, Karpeles was badly wounded. He refused to relinquish the flag and be evacuated until he fainted from loss of blood. Karpeles spent most of the next year in military hospitals and was discharged in May of 1865. He settled in Washington after the war and was rewarded, for his military service, with a job in the post office, which he held until his death in 1909.

Bradley Kasal (1966–), b. Marengo, IA, of Czech ancestry, a United States Marine who received the Navy Cross for heroic actions performed as the first sergeant of Weapons Company, 3rd Battalion, 1st Marines during a firefight in Operation Phantom Fury in Fallujah, Iraq on November 13, 2004. He received the decoration in May 2006 during a ceremony at Camp Pendleton, followed by his promotion to sergeant major and reenlistment in the U.S. Marine Corps.

Herman Willard Kiihnl (1922–2007), b. Teasdale, MS, of Bohemian ancestry, was a soldier during WWII. He was a member of the U. S. Army Rangers' 2nd Battalion which scaled 100-meter cliffs at Pointe du Hoc between Utah and Omaha Beaches on D-Day in France to knock out heavy artillery pieces defending the beaches. He received the Purple Heart, Combat Infantryman Badge, E.A.M.E. Camp Medal and two Bronze Stars.

Matej Kocak (1882–1918), b. Gbely, Slovakia; US Marine Corps sergeant, posthumous recipient of the Army and Navy Medals of Honor.

Ernest Richard Kouma (1919-1993), b. Dwight, NE, of Czech ancestry, was a soldier in the United States Army during World War II and the Korean War. He rose to the rank of master sergeant and received the Medal of Honor for his actions on August 31 and September 1, 1950, during the Second Battle of Naktong Bulge in South Korea. On the outbreak of the Korean War, Kouma commanded an M26 Pershing tank in the 2nd Infantry Division. While fighting during the Battle of Pusan Perimeter along the Naktong River, Kouma commanded his tank as it single-handedly fended off repeated North Korean attempts to cross the river after units around it had withdrawn. Wounded twice, Kouma killed 250 North Korean troops in this action.

Eugene Arthur Kozlay (1826-1883), b. Slovakia; civil engineer; Brigadier General (USA), officer in the Union Army during the Civil War; recruited by President Lincoln to organize a volunteer regiment, designated the 54th New York Voluntary Infantry in 1861. As Colonel in command, his regiment participated in actions at Shenandoah, the Battle of Cross Keys, the Battle of Chancellorsville and the first day of the Battle of Gettysburg on July 1, 1863. In 1864, the regiment took part in various engagements at Seabrook, John's Island, James' Island and at Santee River in the South Carolina campaign. In March 1865, the 54th entered Charleston, South Carolina where it remained until it was ordered to Hart's Island, New York Harbor, and there, mustered out of the service of the United States, on April 14, 1866. After the war, as a civil engineer, he helped construct the first elevated railroad in Brooklyn, NY.

Matt Konop (1906-1983), b. Stangelville, WI, of Czech immigrant grandparents, was a United States Army officer during World War II, noted for his fighting in the Battle of the Bulge and celebrated in the Czech Republic for his role in the liberation of the cities of Domažlice and Pilsen in Czechoslovakia near the end of the war.

John C. Kubinec (1970-), b. Greensburg, PA, of Slovak descent; trained in military history and organizational management; graduate of Air Command and Staff College, Maxwell Air Force Base, AL and of Air University, AL, and of the National War College. Washington, DC. He holds the rank of Brigadier General, US Air Force and is the Commander, Warner Robins Air Logistics Complex, Robins Air Force Base, Georgia. As the commander, he serves a world-class workforce of over 7,200 military and civilian personnel.

Lucius Quintus Cincinnatus Lamar (1825-1894), b. nr Eatonton, Putnam County, Georgia, desc. f Augustine Heřman, graduated from Emory College and then practiced law and served as state legislator in Georgia and Mississippi. When Mississippi seceded from the Union, he joined the Confederacy on January 9, 1861, and raised, and funded out of his own pocket, the 19th Mississippi Volunteer Infantry and was elected Lieutenant Colonel. In May 1862, Colonel Lamar, while reviewing his regiment, fell with an attack of vertigo, which had previously disabled him, and his service as a soldier was ended. After this, he served as a judge advocate and aide to his cousin, Lt. Gen. James Longstreet. Later in 1862, Confederate States President Jefferson Davis appointed Lamar as Confederate minister to Russia and special envoy to England and France. When the Civil War was over, he returned to the University of Mississippi where he was a professor of metaphysics, social science and law. After having his civil rights restored, following the war, Lamar returned to the House in 1873, the first Democrat from Mississippi to sit in the U.S. House of Representatives since the Civil War. He served there until 1877. Lamar would go on to represent Mississippi in the US Senate from 1877 to 1885.

Henry B. Lederer (1920–2013), b. Bridgeport, CT, of Bohemian ancestry, attended New York University and joined the Army Air Corps in 1942 as an Aviation Cadet. His training was on P-47 Thunderbolts. Afterwards, he was assigned to the 361st Fighter Group, 376 Fighter Squadron. After transfer to 374 Fighter Squadron, he was in Bottisham, England, flying escort to B-17's and B-24's, plus ground support missions. In January of 1944, he was involved in the 361st first combat encounter, which was a fight with about 40 Me-109's. He shared a victory in this battle. Lederer flew 305 hours of combat and received the DFC with two OLC's and the Air Medal with two OLC's. He was an 'Eager Beaver' and the first to finish his tour of duty and be rotated home. He had completed 92 missions. After the war, he taught aerial gunnery at the Suffolk Army Base in Westhampton NY. He also held several US mechanical and design patents and then he opened his own jewelry manufacturing business in 1946 and was the founder of the jewelry firm that made jewelry with the Lady Ellen hang tags.

Frederick Lemský (?–1844) appeared in Texas in February 1836. Not much is known about him except that he came from the Czech Lands and that he was a fifer in the four-piece Texas Army 'band' at the battle of San Jacinto. He enlisted in the Texas Army on March 13, 1836 and served in the company of William E. Howth and Nicholas Lynch. He was a musician in the army until December 31, 1836. He is said to have played "Come to the Bower" on the flute at the battle of San Jacinto. He then settled in Houston. On January 27, 1838, Lemský advertised in the *Telegraph and Texas Register*, offering his services as a music teacher and teacher of German and French. He was a charter member of the German Union of Texas, incorporated on January 21, 1841. In March 1842, the Brazos and San Luis Canal was being dug near the site of what is now the town of Oyster Creek in Brazoria County. Lemský was the employer of thirty men digging there. In January or February 1844, Lemský drowned when a 'hard norther' capsized the barge on which they were hauling corn. Lemský's body was recovered near Virginia Point, on the mainland side of Galveston Bay. According to the probate records in Brazoria County, "one octave flute" and "one keyed flute" were included in the inventory of his property. They were sold for $2.25 at auction in June 1844.

Henry Brockholst Livingston (1757–1823), b. NYC, desc. f. Frederick Philipse, was an American Revolutionary War officer, a Justice of the Supreme Court of New York and eventually an Associate Justice of the Supreme Court of the United States. At the outbreak of the Revolutionary War, he was commissioned Captain in the Continental Army and served as Aide-de-camp to Gen. Philip Schuyler, being attached to the northern dept. and ranking as a Major. He was aide to Gen. Arthur St. Clair and participated in the siege of Ft. Ticonderoga and was present at the surrender of Gen. Burgoyne's army at Saratoga. He returned to Gen. Schuyler's army and was promoted Lt. Colonel.

William N. Lukash (1931–1998), a physician in the US Navy, with the rank of Rear Admiral, served as a White House physician for four presidents. At 34, Lukash was believed to be the youngest doctor ever to receive a White House appointment when he was named assistant physician for President Lyndon B. Johnson in 1966. He was personal physician for President Jimmy Carter the entire four years of his administration. He had been on White House assignment since 1966, first as deputy White House physician, then elevated to personal physician under President Gerald Ford. From 1966 to 1981, he served at the Naval Medical Center in Bethesda, MD as chair of gastroenterology. He was also a professor of medicine at George Washington University. He retired from the Navy in June 1981 and moved to Scripps as a gastroenterologist and chief of its new Preventive Medicine Center.

William F. Lukeš (1847–1923), b. Dolní Pertoltice, Bohemia, was a United States Navy sailor and a recipient of America's highest military decoration—the Medal of Honor—for his actions in the 1871 Korean Expedition. William F. Lukeš enlisted in the US Navy from Tianjin, China and served as a Landsman on board USS *Colorado* in Company D as part of the Korean Expedition. On June 11, 1871, during the capture of the Han River forts on Ganghwa Island, the leader of the American attack, Lieutenant Hugh McKee, was mortally wounded. Landsman Lukeš and two other sailors, Seth Allen and Thomas Murphy, attempted to rescue Lt. McKee but encountered heavy resistance. In the course of the ensuing hand-to-hand fight, Allen and Murphy were killed. Lukes suffered a severe cut to the head but continued to fight; he survived the engagement. For his actions on that occasion, Lukeš was awarded the Medal of Honor. Before leaving the Navy, William Lukeš obtained the rank of Seaman. He died at the age of 76 and is buried in Los Angeles National Cemetery, Los Angeles, California.

Ronald Slidell Mackenzie (1840–1885), b. New York, NY, desc. f. Frederick Philipse, was a Civil War Union Brigadier General. He was 1862 graduate of the United States Military Academy, where he was first in his class. Posted with the Engineers, he served through most of the campaigns of the Army of the Potomac, in July 1864 he was commissioned Colonel of the 2nd Connecticut Volunteer Heavy Artillery. During Major General Philip Sheridan's 1864 'Valley' campaign, he commanded a brigade in the 6th Corps and was wounded at the Battle of Cedar Creek. After his recovery, he was commissioned a Brigadier General of Volunteers and given a division of cavalry under Sheridan, serving with great distinction. General Ulysses S. Grant later said, "I regarded Mackenzie as the most promising young officer in the army." At the end of the Civil War, he was brevetted Major General of Volunteers and brevetted Brigadier General in the Regular Army. On March 6, 1867, he was commissioned Colonel of the 41st United States Infantry and on December 15, 1870, was given command of the 4th United States Cavalry. Post Civil War, he had a distinguished career as an Indian fighter in the west. Wounded in 1871 during an engagement with Indians, it was his seventh wound while in the service. He retired on disability in 1884.

Alexander Slidell Mackenzie, Jr. (1842–1867), b. New York, NY, a desc. f. Frederick Philipse, was appointed to the U.S. Naval Academy in 1855, graduated in June 1859 and was assigned to the newly-completed steam sloop-of-war *Hartford*. During the next two years, Midshipman Mackenzie served in that ship with the East India Squadron. Promoted to Lieutenant in August 1861, he was an officer of the gunboat *Kineo* during the conquest of the lower Mississippi River in 1862. Later transferred to the South Atlantic Blockading Squadron, Mackenzie served off Charleston, South Carolina, in the steam frigate *Wabash* and monitor *Patapsco*, taking part in combat operations against Fort Sumter and Morris Island. Later in the Civil War he commanded the gunboat *Winona*, also in the waters off South Carolina. In July 1865, Mackenzie received the rank of Lieutenant Commander and soon began a second Far Eastern deployment in Hartford. He was killed in action on 13 June 1867, during a punitive expedition ashore in southern Formosa. The Navy has named three ships in honor of Lieutenant Commander Alexander Slidell Mackenzie.

Morris Robinson Slidell Mackenzie (1848–1915), b. NYC, desc. f Frederick Philipse, a graduate of US Naval Academy, was promoted through grades from Ensign in 1868 to Rear Admiral, US Navy (1906). He served on various stations and duties, including being Commander of Prairie (1898–1900), USS *New York* (1901); Navy Yard, Portsmouth, NH (1903) and inspector-in-charge of 3rd lighthouse district (1905).

Theodore Majthenyi (1838–1909), b. Nitra, Slovakia; a Baron, was son of Baron Joseph Majthenyi, member of the landed gentry and prominent politician, a member of upper chamber of Hungarian parliament. Having taken part in the War of Independence, the father was forced to flee. Theodore was only 13 years old when he had to follow his father to exile. They settled in New Buda, Iowa, but soon moved to Davenport. When the Civil War came, Theodore volunteered in the 2nd Iowa Infantry regiment as a Sargent. In St. Louis, he was transferred to the Frémont Body Guard. He was promoted to a 2nd Lieutenant and adjutant within a month. When Frémont was removed, Majthenyi obtained commission as a Captain in Company K of 1st Indiana Cavalry Regiment in 1862, serving until December 1864. He was appointed 2nd Lieutenant of the 5th US Cavalry in February 1866 and elevated to 1st Lieutenant in October. He resigned from the service in December 1868.

Winslow Malý (1843–d.), b. Bohemia, at the outbreak of the war, enlisted in Company E, Independent Battalion, Minnesota Cavalry, August 24, 1864. He was in the western department, and served in the northwestern frontier against the Indians and guarding frontier settlements. He was at Fort Ripley, near the head-waters of the Mississippi River, and in November, 1865, with the whole command, was caught in one of the great blizzards of that section of the country. He was badly frozen, and his eyesight nearly destroyed, and the whole command came near being lost. He was honorably discharged from service May 1, 1866. Malý then followed his trade of shoe-maker at Los Angeles, CA, and was a member of Gelcich Post, No. 106, G. A. R., of the same place and was adjutant of his post.

Matěj Mašek (1857–d.), b. Pohorovice, Bohemia, studied philosophy at Univ. of Prague and then entered seminary at České Budějovice. Before being ordained, he left for America. At first, he worked as a laborer and then joined the Federal Army for eight years. He fought in Arizona and New Mexico in a war against the savage Apache commanded by Geronimo. After he withdrew, he led a very adventurous life. He then settled in Chicago and was a contributor to periodical *Svornost*.

Jerry Vrchlický Matejka (1894–1980), b. Nelsonville, TX, of Czech ancestry, graduated from the University of Texas in 1916 and received a regular commission as a Second Lieutenant in the Coast Artillery Corps. He was detailed to the Signal Corps in 1920, served in the Panama Canal Department, and then graduated from the Signal School in 1930. In August 1940, General Matejka was assigned to General Headquarters of the United States Army, and in May 1941, as a member of the Special Observers Group, was transferred to the United Kingdom. After returning to the States, in July 1943, Matejka had a tour of duty in the Office of the Chief Signal Officer. In December 1945, he came to Fort Monmouth as Commanding General of the Eastern Signal Corps Training Center. Upon deactivation of the Center, Matejka became the fourteenth Commanding Officer of this post and served in that capacity until June 1947. He subsequently (1947–50) was named Chief Signal Officer of the European Theater of Operations and deputy Chief of Staff, Allied Forces Central Europe (1953–55).

VI. PUBLIC LIFE

General Matejka retired as a Major General on 31 October 1955 after more than thirty-eight active years of Army service.

Edward C. Meyer (1928–2020), b. St. Marys, PA, of Slovak ancestry, was US Army General who served as the 29th chief of Staff of the US Army. Meyer's first assignment was as a platoon leader in Company C, 25th Armored Infantry Battalion in the Korean War from 1951 to 1952. After promotion to first lieutenant in July 1952, he served as a platoon leader, company commander, and battalion staff officer with the 2nd Battalion, 24th Infantry Regiment, also in Korea, until 1953. He returned to combat as deputy commander of the 3rd Brigade, 1st Cavalry Division (Airmobile) in Vietnam, later taking command of the 2nd Battalion, 5th Cavalry from 1965 to 1966. Returning stateside, he graduated from the National War College in 1967, then served in the Plans and Operations Division, Office of the Joint Chiefs of Staff until 1969, promoted to temporary colonel in November 1968. He returned to Vietnam to command the 2nd Brigade, 1st Cavalry Division (Airmobile), and then served as division chief of staff, leaving Vietnam in 1970.

Gejza Mihalotzy-Mikulas (aka Géza Mihalótzy/Michalovič) (1825–1864), b. Zemplín region, Slovakia; moved to Chicago. On Feb. 4, 1861, he sent Abraham Lincoln a letter requesting recognition a group of volunteers from Upper Hungary, Poland, and from Bohemia; they became the Lincoln's shooters of Slavic origin and joined the Union's 24th Volunteer Illinois Regiment. He fought at Perryville on October 8, 1862 during Kentucky campaign, and in Jan. 1862–63, at the bloody battle of Stones Rive. Mihalotzy died in 1864 after sustaining injuries at the Battle of Buzzard's Roost Gap in Georgia.

George Edward Mitchell (1781–1832) was born in Elkton, MD. He was a descendant of Augustine Heřman. An 1805 graduate of the University of Pennsylvania, he practiced medicine with his father in Elkton, Maryland from 1806 to 1812. He served in the Maryland House of Delegates from 1808 to 1809 and was president of the State Executive Council from 1809 to 1812. During the War of 1812, Mitchell was commissioned with the Third Maryland Artillery and saw action at York, Fort George, Fort Niagara and Fort Oswego; for his actions in defending the latter, he was brevetted Colonel and presented a sword by the Maryland General Assembly. He resigned his commission on June 1, 1821. Mitchell served two consecutive terms in the US House of Representatives (March 4, 1823 to March 3, 1827) but chose not to run in the 1826 election. He was instrumental in inviting Lafayette to the US in 1824.

Emile Phillips Moses (1880–1965), b. Sumter, SC, of Czech ancestry, attended Sumter schools, South Carolina College and the Georgia School of Technology, and in 1903, took the examination for admittance to the US Marine Corps. He was sent to the training camp for officers at Annapolis and received his commission in early 1904. He was a member of this famous military school in the Nicaraguan campaign and has seen extensive service on both sides of the Pacific and along the Atlantic seaboard. He was entrained for port of embarkation for France when the armistice caused the order to be countermanded. He was commissioned a Major in Marines in 1918. Advanced through the grades to Major General (1942). Commander, Marine Barracks, Parris Island, SC (1941–44). He contributed largely to development and adaptation to military use of the amphibian tractor and to design and use of ramp on landing boats.

Joseph Nemeth (1816–1881), b. Lošonec, Slovakia; officer in the Hungarian revolutionary forces. After the surrender of the of the revolutionary forces, he eventually arrived in the US in November 1851, settling initially in New York. In 1853, he settled in St. Louis. He made excellent use of his experience with horses and started a practice as surgeon and horse doctor. At the start of the Civil War, he enlisted in the 5th Missouri Infantry Regiment as 1st lieutenant and adjutant and was mustered out in August 1861. He reenlisted as a Major in the battalion Benton Hussars and served as its commander until the unit was incorporated into 5th Missouri Cavalry in February 1862. He was then appointed Colonel and the commander of the entire regiment. He was discharged in November 1862. Subsequently, he settled down in Chicago and continued his practice as a veterinary surgeon.

George P. Novotny (1921–2018), b. Toledo, OH, of Slovak descent, enlisted in the US Army Air Corps soon after the bombing of Pearl Harbor; he was assigned to the 325th Fighter Group in May 1943. He left the states and spent the next 13 months in North Africa and Italy flying the P-40 Warhawk, the P-47 Thunderbolt and the P-51 Mustang. He was a celebrated World War II P-47 Ace, was known as 'Toledo's War Ace' and participated in 57 missions. (To receive the title of 'Ace,' a fighter pilot must have shot down five or more enemy aircraft in 'air-to-air' combat.) He was credited with a ninth aerial victory over Budapest on April 13, 1944.

Čeněk Paclt (1815–1887), b. Turnov, Bohemia, an adventurer and globetrotter, came through Texas, while taking part in the Mexican War of 1846. He came to New York that year, and on his way to New Orleans he enlisted in the Army of the United States which had just (May 13) declared war on Mexico, his commitment being for five years. According to his own account, he served in the Army of General Winfield Scott (1786–1860). After the war, he was sent to join the garrisons in Florida and in 1853, he was discharged, and he then returned to Bohemia.

John J. Philipi (1856–1928), b. Prague, Bohemia, a Lewiston, ID, pioneer, served conspicuously through the Nez Perce Indian War. He came to America, locating at Portland,

Oregon. He enlisted in the cavalry of the United States Army, and shortly afterward the troop was ordered to Fort Lapwai to take part in the Indian War of 1877. Philipi was in the battle of White Bird. After his enlistment period was over, he came to Lewiston, ID with his family in 1886, and took up his residence there, remaining until his death.

Coral Wong Pietsch (1947–), b. Waterloo, IA, of a Chinese immigrant father and a Czech American mother, was a Brigadier General in the United States Army Reserve and also the first 'Asian' American woman to reach the rank of Brigadier General in the United States Army. Initially earning a Bachelor's degree in theatre, and later a Master's degree in drama, she went on to attend the Catholic University of America to attend law school. There she would meet her future husband, an Army officer who was also attending to become a lawyer. Commissioned into the Judge Advocate General Corps in 1974, she was assigned to Eighth Army in Korea then to Fort Shafter, Hawaii, completing her active duty requirement, and transferring to the Army Reserves. After active duty, she settled down and began to reside in Hawaii with her husband and became a civilian attorney for US Army Pacific. While a reservist, she had been deployed to Johnston Atoll, Japan, the Philippines, Washington D.C. and Iraq. She was a chair commissioner of the Hawaii Civil Rights Commission, with her term expiring while deployed.

Barbara Hauserová Podoski (1914–2009), b. Brno, Czech., in US s. 1941. She became a lawyer and just before the breakout of war, she also became a journalist. She got married and she and her husband moved to Belgian Congo in 1939 when events started to escalate in Europe. In 1941, they moved to United States. After the bombing of Pearl Harbor, her husband joined the Army and she went to work at the Czech Embassy in Washington, D.C. before joining the WAC herself. She was sent to Algeria and then Rome, Italy. She was a Corporal in the Women's Army Corps (WAC) and won the Bronze Star after one of her operations led to the defection of 600 soldiers from behind Italian lines and the withdrawal of their support from the Germans. She was stationed at the Office of Strategic Services (OSS) Morale Operations (MO) headquarters in Rome, Italy.

John L. Polerecký (1748–1830), b. France, of Slovak father, was a nobleman and soldier who joined the French-Hussar Cavalry unit under the Duke de Lauzun, where he gained the rank of Major. As an auxiliary French army under the leadership of General Rochambeau, these Hussars had come to help Washington conquer the British in the Revolutionary War. He took part in the ten-day crucial bloody battle at Yorktown which ended on October 17. As a civilian, Polerecký chose to stay in America permanently. He bought a farm in Dresden, Maine. Over the years, he held a number of public positions: deputy marshal, census commissioner, town clerk of Dresden, and lighthouse keeper.

Major Frank Fred Pechacek, Jr. (1922–2014), b. Flatonia TX, graduated from Schreiner Military Institute in May 1942 and enlisted in the US Army Air Corp in 1942. He attended the University of Texas at Austin, studying mechanical engineering until called to active duty in January 1944. After completing pilot training through Advanced Twin Engine Flight Training, he was diagnosed with a rare and transient vertigo and rather than take an assignment as Co-Pilot, elected to take a transfer to Navigator Training, receiving his commission as 2nd Lieutenant on 25 Sept 1944. After Air Combat Training as Navigator on a B-24 crew, he was assigned to the 44th Bomb Group at Shipdham Field UK on 7 Feb 1945. Following outstanding navigational performance on his first combat mission successfully guiding his B-24 home to England solo after it was separated from the Bomb Group deep in Germany, he was assigned to the 482nd Bomb Group (Pathfinder Force) for advanced training in radar navigational bombing (H2X) in early March 1945. His initial bombing accuracy on early missions using his revised H2X procedure was so superior (bombs dropped within the pickle barrel's accuracy) that General Dwight Eisenhower personally visited him and asked him to fly daily missions until the end of the war as lead H2X radar navigator on the highest priority 8th Air Force missions targeting jet aircraft factories, synthetic oil refineries, and other critical war production sites. His technical methods and outstanding bombing performance was kept secret even after WWII, and his name was not listed on flight logs or dispatches to keep his identify secret. The US Air Force encouraged him to enter active reserve flying status again, as the 433rd Airlift Wing was re-activated in May 1955 in San Antonio TX. Over time, he assumed more leadership roles, becoming Wing Operations Officer, which was notable since such leadership positions were typically held only by pilots. During the Cuban Missile Crisis in 1962, the 433rd Airlift Wing was selected to be among the lead elements to drop paratroop units into Cuba if the crisis escalated. Major Pechacek held the unit title for best individual performance on accuracy in equipment drop exercises for many years after his retirement in 1966. At retirement, he refused offers from the US Air Force to enter active duty with a promotion to Lt. Colonel and expectations of further advancement.

Edmund Jennings Randolph (1753–1813), b. Williamsburg, VA, was a great great-grandson of Augustine Heřman. He was an American attorney, the seventh Governor of Virginia, the second US Secretary of State, and the first United States Attorney General. He was born to the influential Randolph family in Williamsburg, Virginia and educated at the College of William and Mary. After graduation, he began reading law with his father John Randolph and uncle, Peyton Randolph. Whereas his father reacted to the American Revolution by returning to Great Britain, Randolph joined the Continental Army and served as an Aide-de-camp to General George Washington in 1775.

John J. Remetta (1920-1992), b. Czechoslovakia, KI, resided in Scranton PA. He began his military career in 1942 when he enlisted in the US Army as a private. Six months later, he attended the Officer Candidate School at Fort Belvoir, VA and was commissioned as a second lieutenant in the Corps of Engineers in October 1942. He served throughout Europe during World War II with the US 25th Armored Engineer Battalion, 6th Armored division. He was promoted to First Lieutenant in 1943 and to Captain in 1944. Upon his release from active service in December 1945, he continued military service as a member of the Army Reserve. He was recalled into federal service in September 1950 for the Korean conflict. He held a number of assignments and promotions, being recognized as brigadier general in December 1967. In May 1971, he was as Director, Area Group East, in State Headquarters. In May 1972, he was promoted to Major General.

Sir Frederick Philipse Robinson (1763-1852), b. Highlands, near New York, NY, of Bohemian ancestry, desc. f. Frederick Philipse, came from an illustrious Virginian family; his grandfather was at one time, President of the Council at Virginia. Robinson initially served in his father's, Colonel Beverley Robinson's regiment (The Loyal American Regiment), before acquiring a commission in the 17th (Royal Leicestershire) Regiment of Foot. He saw service in the American War of Independence (serving for a period of time as a prisoner-of-war). The cessation of hostilities brought sad tidings to the Robinson family, as their property was duly confiscated by the fledgling US government because of their unswerving loyalty to the British Crown. Robinson, having in the interim transferred to the 38th (South Staffordshire) Regiment of Foot, then served in England and Ireland before taking part in the expedition to the West Indies (1793), where he was present at the capture of Martinique, St. Lucia and Guadeloupe, but returned to England due to ill-health. Robinson subsequently spent the next few years stationed in England, and by 1807 was a Colonel, having commanded the London Recruiting District. Robinson later saw service in the Peninsular War (from 1812-1813), and as a Major-General commanded a brigade during the Battle of Vitoria, and it was Robinson's brigade that took the village of Gamarra-Mayor at the point of the bayonet, under a heavy curtain of French artillery and musketry fire. This redoubtable old soldier was to further distinguish himself at the Battles of San Sebastian, Bidassoa, Sicoa, the Heights of Cibour and at the Battle of the Nive, later taking over command of the 5th Division. His fighting days, far from over, Robinson then served in Canada during the War of 1812 (1812-1815), being appointed Commander-in-Chief and Governor of Upper Canada, whereupon he became Governor and Commander-in-Chief of the Island of Tobago (1816-1828). Robinson was promoted to rank of full General in 1841, and died at Brighton, Sussex, in January, 1852.

Raphael Guido Rombauer (1838-1912), b. Mukačevo, of Slovak father (from Levoča); the youngest of the Rombauer brothers. He was taken to America by his family, and he followed his older brothers' footsteps when he volunteered in the Civil War. Similarly, to them, he sought service at the 1st Missouri Infantry Regiment, in which he served as sergeant. After three months, he became a lieutenant and adjutant to Colonel Gustav Wagner, chief of Artillery at Cairo, IL. They belonged under the supervision of General Ulysses Grant. Because of secrecy, much of the communication was conducted in Hungarian and it was Raphael's responsibility to do the translation from Hungarian to English for Grant. Later, he became Captain of the 1st Illinois Light Artillery Regiment. In October 1864, he was elevated to Major and in February 1865, he became chief of artillery at Memphis. After the War, he was involved with the expanding railroad business and later established his own enterprise, Rombauer Coal Co. in Missouri.

Robert Julius Rombauer (1830-1925), b. Mukačevo, of Slovak father (from Levoča); 1850, he immigrated to America with his mother, settling down first in Iowa, then in St. Louis, MO. In 1861, he played a major role in rallying the pro-Union elements in St. Louis and became Lieutenant Colonel in the 1st Regiment of US Reserve Corps in Missouri, later as Colonel in command of the 1st Missouri Infantry. Towards the end of the Civil War, he was the commander of the 5th Regiment City Guard in St. Louis, organized in 1864 to protect the city during Major General Sterling Price's invasion of Missouri. At the end of the Civil War, he returned to civil life in St. Louis, and worked as an editor of the local paper, the *New World*. He was much interested in education and was one of the most devoted proponents of the founding the St. Louis Public Library. He even became president of the library for some time, as well as president of the Board of Assessors and Board of Education. He is the author of one of the best histories of the Union movement in St. Louis.

Roderick E. Rombauer (1833-1924), b. Szeleszto, of Slovak father; fought in the Hungarian War of Independence with his three brothers. In 1851, he immigrated with mother and six siblings from Hamburg to New York, settling, in Iowa. He was probably the most successful of Tivadar's children. He studied law in Quincy, IL at the office of Williams and Lawrence and later attended the Harvard University Law School. He then practiced the law in St. Louis. During the Civil War, Roderick served with the 1st Regiment of the US Reserve Corps in Missouri, as a Captain. He took part in organizing a home guard unit and was involved in battles in southeast Missouri. Having overcome typhoid fever, he then joined General Frémont on his staff. After the War, he continued his legal practice. He became judge of the Circuit Court of St. Louis County (1867-70) and then served on the bench of the St. Louis Court of Appeals (1884-96), nine years as presiding judge. He was still practicing law in 1913, at the age of 80.

Roland Rombauer (1837-1898), b. Mukačevo, of Slovak father. He was still a young child when the Hungarian War of Liberation was raging and was taken to the US by his mother, following the head of the family, Tivadar Rombauer. He was only 14 years old. Similarly, to his brothers, he enlisted at Company A of the 1st Missouri Infantry Regiment as a Private. After 3 months, he served as Sergeant in the Company of the 1st Missouri Light Artillery Regiment. He later joined the 1st Florida Cavalry, as Captain, first becoming assistant provost marshal of the District of West Florida, under the command of Brig. General Alexander Asboth and later provost marshal. He was mustered out on November 15, 1865. Subsequently, he settled down in St. Louis and worked as a cashier in a bank. Later, he moved to the West and set off a mining enterprise in Montana, and later was official in the forestry service. He died suddenly of a heart attack in November 1898.

Matthias Ernest Rozsafy (orig. Ruzicska) (1828-1893), b. Komárno, Slovakia, presumably of Czech origin; a pioneer journalist. As a twenty-year old, took part in the 1848 Revolution, during which he almost lost his life. In 1850, he succeeded to come to America and for a time, lived in New York and then did some farming in North Carolina on the Fair Oaks plantation; later he operated a farm in Peekskill, NY. In the Civil War, he served under General Pope as a Captain of the 1st West Virginia Light Artillery Regiment; was mustered out as a Major by brevet. After the War, he lived in New York, and later moved to Washington, DC, where he had a government position and later had his own patent bureau. He died in Washington and was buried in Arlington National Cemetery.

David Ross (1755-1800), b. Prince Georges Co., MD, desc. f. Augustine Heřman, was appointed by Gen. Washington Major of Grayson's additional continental regiment in Jan. and served until Dec. 1777. After the war, he practiced law and managed his family's extensive estates in Frederick, MD. From 1786 to 1788, he was a delegate to the Continental Congress from Maryland.

Francis B. Schaeffer (1819-1900), b. Baltimore, MD, desc. f. Augustine Heřman, served in the US Army before the Civil War. He served with distinction in the Mexican War and was honored by President Lincoln with the captaincy of the select National Riflemen, stationed in Washington at commencement of the Civil War. He subsequently, however, joined the Confederate Army. He was commissioned Second Lieutenant in the regular forces of the Confederate Army in 1861. He later transferred to the Trans-Mississippi Department. In September 1862, he was attached to the staff of Brig. Gen. Albert Pike. Promoted to Major, Schaefer became the chief of artillery of defenses at Galveston, Texas. He received parole on June 22, 1865.

Károly Semsey (1830-1911); b. Kračúnovce, Slovakia; officer in Hungarian army with the rank Captain; in US s. 1859; veteran of Civil War with the rank Major of the 45th New York

Volunteer Infantry Regiment. After the War, worked in the Customs Office and then in the immigration service.

Thomas W. Sima (1932–), b. Hannastown, PA, of Slovak descent; Lieutenant Colonel, US Air Force; Vietnam War (1964–74), POW, recipient of Distinguished Cross w/ Valor.

Robert Ernest Simanek (1930–), b. Detroit, MI, of Czech ancestry, who threw himself on an enemy grenade to save his comrades, was the 36th Marine to receive the Medal of Honor for heroism in the Korean War. The United States' highest military decoration was presented to him by President Dwight D. Eisenhower in a White House ceremony on October 27, 1953. Simanek, who was so badly wounded by the grenade that he later retired, was serving with Company F, 2nd Battalion 5th Marines, 1st Marine Division, when the action occurred on August 18, 1952. His patrol had gone well forward of friendly lines to occupy an outpost when the Marines ran into a trap. He had earned two battle stars by the time he was wounded. In addition to the Medal of Honor and Purple Heart, he was also awarded the Korean Service Medal with two bronze stars; the United Nations Service Medal; and the National Defense Service Medal.

Alexander Rives Skinker (1883–1918), b. St. Louis, MO, desc. f. Augustine Heřman, was a Medal of Honor recipient during World War I. He graduated from Washington University in St. Louis in 1905 before becoming commissioned as an officer in the United States Army. He was awarded the medal while leading an attack on German pill boxes in the Hindenburg Line in which he was subsequently killed. His Medal citation read: "Unwilling to sacrifice his men when his company was held up by terrific machinegun fire from iron pill boxes in the Hindenburg Line, Capt. Skinker personally led an automatic rifleman and a carrier in an attack on the machine-guns. The carrier was killed instantly, but Capt. Skinker seized the ammunition and continued through an opening in the barbed wire, feeding the automatic rifle until he, too, was killed. Place and date of his action: Cheppy, France, September 26, 1918."

Richard Smykal (1900–1958), b. Chicago, IL, of Czech ancestry, an Army officer, advanced through ranks to Major General. He served in China, Burma, India Theater and in Europe during World War II. As assistant chief of staff to the late Lt. Gen. Joseph Stilwell in Burma, General Smykal won the Legion of Merit for organizing supply and transportation for Stilwell's fighting forces. During 26 months in the China-Burma-India Theater, General Smykal served as deputy chief of staff for the Chinese combat command and later as Commander of a joint Army-Navy task force in south China. Following reorganization of the Illinois National Guard after the war, General Smykal was appointed assistant commander of the 33rd Division. Later he rose to command the division and the entire guard, retiring in March 1951, with the rank of Lieutenant General. Chicago Mayor Daley called General Smykal an 'outstanding public servant.' Head of his own home building firm, General Smykal had served as acting Illinois state architect, acting city building commissioner, and chairman of the community conservation board from' its creation Jan. I, 1956, until ill health forced his retirement.

William Solomon (1777–1857), b. Montreal, Upper Canada, of Bohemian ancestry, was the fourth child of a German Jewish merchant who had come to New France from Berlin during the Seven Years' War and acted as a supplier to the British Army. By the mid-1790s, William was working in the interior as an employee of the North West Company, and he evidently lived for some time with his parents on Mackinac Island, Michigan. Solomon supported his growing family by working at Michilimackinac, on Mackinac Island, as a clerk for the merchant Joseph Guy and occasionally by doing some interpreting, since he had learned several Indian languages. After war broke out between the United States and Great Britain in 1812, a force assembled by Captain Charles Roberts swiftly descended upon Mackinac Island and captured the fort and town for the British on 17 July, the first military action of the war and a source of some satisfaction to Solomon. By February 1814, he had secured a position with the Indian Department as an interpreter at 4s. 6d. per day. Along with Jean-Baptiste Assiginack and a few others, Solomon was one of the interpreters kept on at Drummond Island as part of the peace-time garrison, which included the Indian Department establishment under the superintendence of William McKay.

Apollo Soucek (1897–1955), b. Lamont, of Czech ancestry, a Naval officer, advanced to Captain and commanding officer to flag rank, and eventually to Rear Admiral. Qualified as naval navigator, he was a crack Navy test pilot and onetime holder of altitude records for sea and land planes. 'Annapolis-man' Soucek, member of a famed Navy flying team (brother Zeus was a retired lieutenant commander turned aircraft-industry executive), was air officer of the carrier *Hornet* when it launched the Doolittle B-25 raid on Tokyo in 1942, later commanded Task Force 77 in Korean waters. He established world's aircraft altitude record at 39,140 ft (1929); seaplane 38,800 ft. (1929), reestablished world altitude record, any type aircraft 43,166 ft (1930). He was Commandant of aircraft carrier USS *Franklin D. Roosevelt* as a Captain (1945) and Commander, Fleet Air Wing One (1946–47). He was appointed assistant chief naval operations for aviation planes (1949–51), chief of the Navy Bureau of Aeronautics (1953–55).

Leo Eugene Soucek (1928–2013), b. Red Cloud, NE, of Czech immigrant father, grew up on a farm near Disputanta, VA. He graduated from the Virginia Military Institute (WDWDR) in 1949. He received a Master's degree in civil engineering from Texas A&M University in 1957 and another Master's degree in international affairs from George Washington University in

1968. He joined the US army, advancing to the rank of Brigadier General. Soucek commanded aviation combat nits in Vietnam and also directed the Army's Primary Helicopter Center at Fort Wolters, TX. As an Army helicopter pilot, he flew more than 3,000 hours in combat operations in Vietnam. His decorations included the Silver Star, four awards of the Legion of Merit, six awards of the Distinguished Flying Cross and two Bronze Star Medals. Gen. Soucek retired from the Army in 1974 after having served as commander of the Army section of a military advisory group in Iran. He then served in a civilian capacity in Iran as Middle East director of operations for Martin Marietta. He settled in Potomac in about 1980 and worked as a consultant for Martin Marietta and later for Lockheed Martin. He retired in 1996.

John Sopko (1930–), b. Tahanovce, Slovakia; a Rusyn-Slovak American; soldier for America during the Korean War. He was highly decorated with several silver and bronze stars for his service and was nominated for the Medal of Honor.

Otto Špaček (1918–2007), b. Brzice, Bohemia, was a Czechoslovakian World War II fighter pilot who fought against Nazi Germany in Great Britain and France. After flying school, he joined the Czechoslovak Air Force in the 1930s. He fled to Poland after the Nazi invasion in June 1939, and then escaped to France, where he served with French Air Force in 1940. After the fall of France, he moved to Britain and joined the Royal Air Force as a fighter pilot in June 1940. Špaček was injured in 1940 and survived three air crashes during World War II. Špaček took part in close air support for the D-Day invasion of Normandy in 1944. He was credited with shooting down 3 German aircraft during the war, and won 5 Czechoslovak War Crosses, the Czechoslovak Bravery Medal and the French Croix de Guerre.

Robert Eugene Steiner (1862–1955), b. Greenville, AL, of Bohemian ancestry, served as Captain, Greenville Guards and Major, 2nd Regiment of Alabama National Guard. He raised a regiment of cavalry (1916) and was appointed Colonel and served with it on Mexican border. Promoted to Brigadier General, National Guards (1917) and Brigadier General of US Army (1917), and Commander, 62nd Infantry Brigade. During the war, returned in command of the 31st div. He was also Brigadier General on reserve by President (1919).

Joseph Edward Stika (1889–1976), b. Milwaukee, WI, of Czech ancestry, was a Vice Admiral in the United States Coast Guard. He graduated from the United States Coast Guard Academy in 1911 and held various commands until he retired in 1951, including the USCGC *Bibb* (WPG-31). In 1934, while commanding the USS *Seneca*, he received a commendation from the government of Sweden for his service during a rescue mission involving the Swedish vessel *af Chapman*. Stika received the Navy Cross for his actions during the T.A. Gillespie Company Shell Loading Plant explosion.

VI. PUBLIC LIFE

Michael Strank (1919–1945), b. Jarabina, Czech., was US Marine Corps sergeant who was killed in action during the battle of Iwo Jima in World War II. Ethnically, he was a Slovak Ruthenian. He was one of the Marines who raised the second U.S. flag on Mount Suribachi on February 23, 1945, as shown in the iconic photograph Raising the Flag on Iwo Jima by photographer Joe Rosenthal. Of border war the six Marines depicted in the photo, Strank was the only one to be correctly identified from the beginning; the other five were either assigned the wrong locations (Ira Hayes and Franklin Sousley), or, were given the names of Marines who were not actually in that particular photo. Before Iwo Jima, Strank served with the Marine Raiders in the Battle of Bougainville. The Marine Corps War Memorial in Arlington, Virginia, was modeled after Rosenthal's photograph of six Marines raising the second flag on Iwo Jima.

Ladislav 'Laddie' Stupka (1878–1946), b. Cleveland, OH, of Czech immigrant parents, was a peacetime recipient of the Congressional Medal of Honor for service in the United States Navy. He was a native of Cleveland, but originally enlisting in the U.S. Navy in 1899 in New York. Stupka was serving as a Fireman, 1st Class aboard the USS *Leyden* when the Civil War-vintage vessel foundered in a heavy fog off the coast of Rhode Island and sank 21 Jan. 1903. Stupka survived and received the Medal of Honor for "seaman-like" qualities in times of emergency on 26 Dec. 1903. He was buried in the Baltimore National Cemetery, MD.

Henry Delp Styer (1862–1944), scion of one of the first Czech families to settle in Colonial Pennsylvania, was a member of the West Point class of 1884. His first military posts were in the west, including Utah, where he was assigned to Indian duty part of the time, and to service as the professor of military tactics at Utah Agricultural College in Logan for part of the time. He served in the Philippines during the Spanish American War, and again several years later. He commanded Fort Niagara for a time and served on the Mexican border during the tense years of the Mexican Revolution. Other duty posts included Trenton, New Jersey, and Camp Lewis, near Tacoma, Washington. Perhaps his most exotic assignment came in 1918, during the Russian Revolution. The Russian Bolshevik faction had signed a separate peace with Germany; the German Army withdrew from the Russian front, and the Russians turned full time to their internal battles. Because the Russians had been allies of the Western Powers contra the Germans, huge stocks of weapons and other supplies had been shipped to Russia, largely from Russia's east coast at Vladivostok where the supplies could be ferried across Asia via the Trans-Siberian railroad. Now the Western Powers became worried that those supplies would fall into the hands of warring Russian factions that would turn them over to the Germans. The US Army's 27th Infantry Regiment, commanded by Col. Styer, was already in Siberia, and was rushed to Vladivostok to take charge of those supplies, in the midst of an international military and diplomatic stew of various Russian factions, and troops from Britain, Canada, Czechoslovakia, China, Italy, France, and Japan. It is of interest that he was later awarded the Czechoslovak Military Cross.

Wilhelm D. Styer (1893-1975), b. Salt Lake City, UT, of Bohemian ancestry (son of Brig. Gen. Henry Delp Styer), graduated from the United States Military Academy at West Point in 1916. He was commissioned as a Second Lieutenant of engineers and served in the Pancho Villa Expedition from 1916 to 1917. Styer also served in France during World War I. From 1919 to 1920, he served on the staff of the Office of the Chief of Engineers in Washington, DC. During the 1920s, Styer served in New York City as executive officer of the Army Corps of Engineers' First New York District, as the district's chief engineer, and as an engineer in Europe for the American Battle Monuments Commission. In 1931, Styer was appointed district engineer for the Corps of Engineers District headquartered in Pittsburgh, Pennsylvania. He was assigned as assistant engineer for maintenance at the Panama Canal in 1936, and in 1938, he was assigned to the Construction Office of the Army's Office of the Quartermaster General. From 1940 to 1942, Styer was deputy chief of construction for the War Department, receiving promotion to Brigadier General. General Styer was Deputy Commander in Chief and Chief of Staff of Army Service Forces from 1940 to 1942 and was promoted to Major General in 1942. From 1942 to 1945, Styer was a member of the Military Policy Committee, a group that included Admiral William Henry Purnell Blandy (1890-1954) and Brigadier General Leslie Groves (1896-1970). The MPC oversaw Development of Substitute Materials (DSM), the project that studied atomic energy during World War II and was later renamed the Manhattan Project.

Styer was promoted to Lieutenant General in 1944. In 1945, Styer was named Commander in Chief of US Army Forces—Western Pacific, based in Manila, Philippines. In this assignment, he chaired the tribunal that tried and convicted General Tomoyuki Yamashita (1885-1946) for war crimes, and he signed Yamashita's execution order. General Styer also chaired the tribunal that tried General Masaharu Homma (1887-1946), the Japanese conqueror of Bataan and Corregidor, for war crimes, and ordered Homma's execution. General Styer retired from the Army in 1947. General Styer's medals and decorations included two awards of the Distinguished Service Medal.

Henry Svehla (1932-1952), Newark, NJ, son of Czech immigrant father, was a soldier in Korean War, whose heroism was recognized belatedly, almost 60 years after his death. By June 12, 1952, Svehla was a Private First Class serving in Korea as a rifleman with Company F, 32nd Infantry Regiment, 7th Infantry Division. On that day, his platoon came under heavy fire, and he charged forward to attack the enemy. When a grenade landed amidst his group, he smothered the blast with his body in order to protect those around him. He was killed in the explosion. His remains have never been recovered. For these actions, Svehla was awarded posthumously the Medal of Honor by President Barack Obama on May 2, 2011, during a White House ceremony.

Edward David Taussig (1847–1921), b. St. Louis, MO, of Czech ancestry (his father Charles immigrated to St. Louis from Prague), was a decorated Rear Admiral in the United States Navy. He is best remembered for being the officer to claim Wake Island after the Spanish-American War, as well as accepting the physical relinquishment of Guam by its Spanish governor following the Treaty of Paris in which Spain ceded Guam to the United States following nearly 300 years of colonial rule. Taussig briefly served as Governor of Guam. He was the first of a four-generational family of United States Naval Academy graduates including his son, Vice Admiral Joseph K. Taussig (1877–1947), grandson Captain Joseph K. Taussig Jr. (1920–1999), and great-grandson, Captain Joseph K. Taussig USMC (1945–). The destroyer USS *Taussig* of 1944–1974, was named in honor of Rear Admiral Taussig.

Joseph Knefler Taussig (1877–1947), b. Dresden, Germany, of Czech ancestry, was a United States Navy officer during and after World War II, and a Navy civilian official in the 1980s. He was the son of Vice Admiral Joseph Taussig, and the grandson of Rear Admiral Edward David Taussig. Taussig was the officer of the deck of USS *Nevada* and senior officer in charge of her anti-aircraft batteries during the Attack on Pearl Harbor on December 7, 1941. Taussig was severely wounded but refused to leave his station until the crew forcibly carried him away. He ended up having his leg amputated, then returned to duty three days later. He received the Navy Cross for his actions that day.

John Dockery Thompson (1743–1826) was born in North Sassafras Parish, Cecil Co., MD. He was a descendant of Augustine Heřman. He was a Lieutenant Colonel, Bohemian Battalion, Cecil Co. Militia, commissioned July 6, 1776. He was a planter and served in MD legislature and was also as Justice.

Walter Robert Tkach (1917–1989), b. La Belle, PA, of Slovak descent, was a command surgeon of Air Force Systems Command, Andrews Air Force Base, MD. He served as White House physician, for 3 presidents.

John Totushek (1944–), b. Minneapolis, MN, of Czech ancestry, is a retired vice admiral in the United States Navy. He was Chief of the United States Naval Reserve from October 1998 until October 2003. After retirement, he served as president and CEO of the United States Navy Memorial Foundation from November 2011 to July 2016. He served as fighter pilot in F-4 Phantom fighter squadrons based in Florida and Virginia.

Stanley 'Swede' Vejtasa (1911–2013), b. Fairdale, ND, of Czech ancestry, had joined the Navy in 1938 and earned his gold wings and ensign bars on 13 July 1939. When the Japanese attacked Pearl Harbor on 7 December 1941, he was part of Scouting Squadron (VS) 5, flying SBD-3s aboard USS *Yorktown* (CV 5). A fine, aggressive aviator, Swede saw action in the Battle of the Coral Sea in May 1942, using his tough little dive-bomber as a fighter against a swarm of seven Zeros, shooting down three of the dangerous fighters just before noon on 8 May. The previous day, he had participated in the attack on the Japanese light carrier *Shōhō*, helping to sink it in less than seven minutes. He received two Navy Crosses for these actions.

Joseph Svojger, Jr. (1919–1945), b. Fort Worth, TX, served in Europe during World War II and fought in Normandy, France, Germany and Belgium. He was wounded in action in 1944. He received the Silver Star for gallantry in action and Purple Heart Medal. He was killed in action in Belgium, January 19, 1945.

Jonathan Mayhew Wainwright (1864–1945), b. New York City, desc. f. Frederick Philipse, served in the 12th Infantry of the NY National Guard, attaining rank of Lieutenant Colonel (1889–1903); also served in the war with Spain as Captain of the 12th Regiment of NY Volunteers. During the First World War, he served in the 27th Div. throughout its entire service (1917–19) and was awarded the Distinguished Service Medal for his bravery.

Philip Van Horn Weems (1889–1979), b. Tennessee, desc. f. Frederick Philipse, received an appointment to the US Naval Academy at Annapolis in 1908. He graduated in the class of 1912 and was commissioned an Ensign. He specialized in navigation and taught at the Academy. In 1927, Weems was sent to the Aircraft Squadron Battle Fleet, before being assigned to the tanker USS *Cuyama* as its executive officer from 1928 to 1930. He retired for the first time in 1933 with the rank of Lieutenant Commander. Weems returned to active service in 1942, serving in World War II as a Convoy Commander, for which he was awarded Bronze Star. He was promoted to Captain in 1945 and retired the following year. With the dawn of the space age, he was called upon to teach space navigation at the Naval Academy from 1961 to 1962. Before the invention of the GPS, Capt. Weems modernized the art of celestial navigation by simplifying techniques and inventing time saving methods.

Emanuel Woodic (1836–d.), b. Bohemia, arrived in America in 1854, landing in New York. In 1856, he enlisted in the US Army. He participated in the Mountain Meadows Massacre and managed to be one of its few survivors. He served throughout the Civil War. He fought in several battles, including the battle of Bull River, Chancellorsville, Gettysburg, the Wilderness, Spotsylvania, Cold Harbor and Petersburg. After being honorably discharged, he moved to Michigan.

VII. Advocacy & Activism

A. Loyalists

Ariana Margaretta Jekyll Chalmers (1768–1845), b. Maryland, of Bohemian ancestry; desc. f. Augustine Heřman; daughter of the wealthy Loyalist, Lt. Col. James Chalmers (1727–1806). She married John Saunders (1754–1834), British soldier, lawyer and Chief Justice of the Colonial Province of New Brunswick.

Susannah Beverley Grymes (née Randolph) (1755–1791), b. Williamsburg, VA, of Bohemian ancestry; desc. of Augustine Heřman. Susannah likely learned to read at a local Williamsburg school. She was accomplished on the harpsichord and guitar, suggesting typical education of a genteel young lady of colonial Virginia. She resided in Williamsburg until 1775 when her Loyalist father arranged passage across the Atlantic for the family. Susannah married her cousin, John Randolph Grymes. Because of their former social standing, Ariana and her husband received some of the largest annual allowances and awards granted the Williamsburg loyalists. Still, they would remain exiled in England living in genteel poverty. Ariana resided in England until her death on October 16, 1791. Her brother Edmund Jennings remained faithful to the US.

Ariana Margaretta Jekyll (1741–1821), b. Boston, MS, of Bohemian ancestry; desc. f. Augustine Heřman. She was a daughter of John Jekyll (1695–1741) and Margaret Shippen. She was a Loyalist and wife of Lt. Col. James Chalmers (1734–1806), commander of First Battalion of Maryland Loyalists and the author of a pamphlet entitled *Plain Truth* in 1776. The pamphlet was written to oppose the work of American Rebel supporter Thomas Paine, *Common Sense* which argued that Great Britain did not have the right to govern America. Chalmers wrote under the pseudonym 'Candidus,' so he wouldn't be found out.

Frederick Philipse, 3rd (1720–1786), desc. f. Frederick Philipse, was the son of Frederick Philipse 2nd, third Lord of Philipsburg Manor. Upon the passing of his father in 1751, he inherited Philipsburg Manor, a 52,000-acre estate comprising much of southern Westchester County, the accompanying title, and commercial interests, including the share of family holdings his father had received from Adolphus Philipse, a bachelor uncle and son of Frederick I, the first Lord of Philipsborough. He did not receive his uncle's 250 square mile Highland Patent, a tract later known as the Philipse Patent, which became today's Putnam County, New York. It was divided among three of his siblings. Like the rest of his family, Philipse was a Loyalist during the American Revolution. At the onset, he leased his lands and left for England, never to return. All lands and commercial interests were lost during the American Revolution when Philipse was attained in absentia, seized by the then-still Colony of New York, then auctioned off by the Commissioners of Forfeiture. He died three years after the Treaty of Paris in 1783, at 65, in Chester.

Mary Philipse (1730–1782), b. Philipse Manor House, on Hudson River, New York, desc. f. Frederick Philipse, was carefully educated and enjoyed all of the advantages that society offered. She was described as having great personal beauty, with dark eyes and hair, strong-willed yet of a kindly disposition. She received notoriety as George Washington's first love, then a Virginia Colonel, 24 years of age, who had just won his first laurels on the field of battle. On his way to Boston to meet General Shirley, Washington stopped at the house of Colonel Beverley Robinson in New York. There he met Miss Mary who was visiting her brother-in-law during the winter months. George was apparently touched by her charm and beauty. He left reluctantly, continuing on to Boston. On his return he was again the willing guest of Colonel Robinson. He remained there, in Mary's company, as long as duty would allow. Speculation is that he offered her his hand but was refused. Shortly thereafter, he heard that Colonel Roger Morris, his companion-in-arms and confidante on the bloody field of Monongahela, won Mary's hand. The couple was married in 1758. They built a mansion on the outskirts of New York where they lived happily, until the Revolution. Then, after Colonel Morris affirmed his allegiance to England and the King, their house was confiscated and, ironically, became Washington's headquarters in the autumn of 1776. Mary, her sister and the wife of Rev. Charles Inglis were the only women accused of treason during the Revolution. Mary went with her husband to England where he died in 1794. Mary lived for another 31 years. She died at the age of 96 and was buried by her husband's side near Saviourgate Church in York, UK.

Susannah Philipse (1727–1822), Mary Philipse's sister, desc. f. Frederick Philipse, was the wife of Beverley Robinson of New York. There is some ground for the belief that "she actually exercised over her husband's mind some portion of the influence said to have been possessed by her sister; for it appears that he was at first disinclined to take any active part in the contest between the Colonies and Great Britain." He was so much opposed to the measures of the ministry, that he would not use imported merchandise; but he was, at length, prevailed on by his friends to enter the Royal service. He and George Washington were intimate friends before they were separated by difference of political opinion. The 'Robinson house,' which had been confiscated with the lands, was occupied by Benedict Arnold as his headquarters, and by Washington at the time of Arnold's treason. When Colonel Robinson gave up the quiet enjoyment of country life, his wife took her share of the outlawry that awaited him, she, as well as her sister, being included in the act of confiscation. After their removal to England, they lived in retirement. She died near Bath, at the age of ninety-four, in 1822.

Ariana Jennings Randolph (1730–1801), b. Anne Arundel County, MD, of Bohemian ancestry; desc. f. Augustine Heřman. She was an urban housewife in Williamsburg until Sept. 1775 when her Loyalist husband, John Randolph arranged passage across the Atlantic for himself, Ariana, and their two daughters, Susannah and Ariana. Their son, Edmund Jennings Randolph stayed behind. Because of their former social standing, Ariana and John received some of the largest annual allowances and awards granted the Williamsburg loyalists. Still, they would remain exiled in England living in genteel poverty. Following the death of her husband, John in 1784, Ariana remained in London. Even though John's body was later brought back to Virginia for burial, Ariana never returned to North America. She is buried in England.

Lt. Col. Beverley Robinson (1754–1816), b. Albany, NY, was the eldest son of Col. Beverley Robinson and Susannah Philipse. He married Anna Dorothea ("Nancy") Barclay, daughter of the Rev. Henry Barclay, rector of Trinity Church in New York and sister of Col. Thomas Barclay, a well-known Loyalist. He settled at Nashwaaksis (Fredericton), New Brunswick, and held the appointments of clerk of the peace, clerk of the Court of Common Pleas, and puisne judge, York County, in 1785. There were six children: Beverley of New York; Morris, the founder of life insurance in North America; a daughter who married Alexander Slidell McKenzie of the United States Navy; Frederick Philipse, who became auditor general of New Brunswick; John, who was a lieutenant in the British army; William Henry, who became a major in the British Army; and Susan, who married George Lee of the British Army.

Sir Frederick Philipse Robinson (1763–1852), b. Highlands, NY, desc. f. Frederick Philipse, was a soldier, who fought for Britain during the American War of Independence. His father was a Virginian who moved to New York, marrying a wealthy heiress of the Philipse family of Bohemian ancestry. On the conclusion of peace, he went to England. He subsequently took part in the War of 1812 and commanded a brigade at the unsuccessful Battle of Plattsburgh. In 1813 and 1814, he commanded a brigade under Wellington in Spain. He was a provisional Lieutenant-Governor of Upper Canada in 1815. Afterwards, he was governor of Tobago, and he became a general in 1841. He died at Brighton, England.

Frederick Philipse Robinson of Nashwaaksis (1785–1877) became Auditor General of New Brunswick. He married Jane, the daughter of Dr. Adino Paddock, Surgeon to the Ordnance in this province. They had five sons and one daughter.

John Robinson (1762–1828), b. Highlands (Hudson Hills), near New York City, third son of Beverley Robinson and Susanna Philipse, and grandson of John Robinson, former president of the Council and administrator of Virginia, was a descendant of Frederick

Philipse. He was a merchant and political figure in the pre-Confederation Province of New Brunswick, Canada. He represented the City of Saint John in the Legislative Assembly of New Brunswick from 1802 to 1809 and from 1810 to 1816. At the start of the American Revolution, he enlisted in the Loyal American Regiment, a loyalist regiment organized by his father. Around 1786, he settled in the valley of the Saint John River. Robinson was named sheriff for Queens County. In 1787, he married Elizabeth, the daughter of George Duncan Ludlow. A few years later, he established himself as a merchant in Saint John. Robinson did not run for reelection in 1809 but was elected to the legislative assembly in an 1810 by-election. He served as acting deputy paymaster general during the War of 1812. He was chosen as Speaker for the Assembly in 1813 following the death of Amos Botsford and served until 1816 when he was named provincial treasurer. In the same year, he was named mayor of Saint John. In 1818, he was named to the New Brunswick Council. In 1820, he was named to the board of directors for the new Bank of New Brunswick and became president. Robinson resigned from the Council in 1826 but continued as mayor and province treasurer until his death in Saint John in 1828.

John Robinson, held the rank of Lieutenant Colonel with the 10th Regiment of Foot, married Eliza Maria Allaire.

John Simcoe Saunders (1795–1878), a native of Fredericton, N.B., was a descendant on the legendary Augustine Heřman from Prague, his mother being Arianna Margaretta Jekyll Chalmers. He was lawyer, legislator, and public servant and a judge of the Supreme Court and later chief justice of New Brunswick. John Simcoe Saunders' father had distinguished himself in the American Revolution as an officer of the Queen's American Rangers under the command of Colonel John Graves Simcoe; he consequently enjoyed the benefit of high official connections in England. Young Saunders was sent to school in England under the supervision of his maternal grandfather, James Chalmers, who had commanded the Maryland loyalists during the American Revolution. After a higher education at Oxford and Lincoln's Inn, Saunders returned to Fredericton where he was called to the bar in 1817. Finding his profession unrewarding, he returned to London and studied law with the eminent pleader, Joseph Chitty. In 1828, he published *The law of pleadings and evidence in civil actions*, a work that enjoyed rapid sale and was reprinted several times in the United States. In New Brunswick there was a rumor, probably caused by envy, that the work was really Chitty's, that for some unknown reason the teacher preferred to publish the book under the pupil's name. Sometime during this period, Saunders married his first cousin, Elizabeth Sophia Storie of Camberwell, Surrey; they had a son and a daughter.

Hon. William Henry Robinson (1793–1848), married Lousia Millidge of Saint John.

B. Abolitionists

August Bondi (1832-1907), b. Vienna, Aust., of Bohemian parents, was bitterly opposed to slavery. In 1856, joined military company organized by son of John Brown and subsequently served as volunteer soldier under John Brown himself. He took part in Battle of Black Jack, KS and in Battle of Osawatomie in 1856. After Brown left Kansas, Bondi continued earnest support of the antislavery cause. He campaigned on behalf of Topeka Constitution promulgated the Free State Party and participated in later clashes between proslavery and antislavery forces in Kansas.

Isidor Bush (orig. Busch) (1822-1898), b. Prague, Bohemia, a journalist and successful merchant, was a political liberal. He served as an aide on General Fremont's staff in 1861. He became one of the St. Louis Delegates to the Missouri Constitutional Convention, MO. When the Union Party was formed in St. Louis, he became one of its Delegates at the State Convention. He supported the cause of the Union and delivered the outstanding unconditional Union speech of the convention. He participated in the deliberations during the meetings and played an important role when the convention concerned itself in 1863 with the problem of slave emancipation. When the committee submitted its resolutions, Bush as the sole dissenter submitted a minority report. His resolution was not accepted, and the convention postponed complete emancipation until 1870. In 1865, after Lincoln's re-election, Bush again was elected a member of the State Convention for drafting a new State Constitution. Bush voted against the proposed Constitution, which he considered too narrow in spirit, and which disfranchised countless citizen because of their sympathy for the Southern cause. The document, which was rejected by the State a decade later, was a complete vindication of the position he had taken.

Lewis Naphtali Dembitz (1833-1907), b. Zirke, Prussia, of Slovak father and Bohemian mother; lawyer, a staunch unionist, frequent antislavery agitator, member of the new Republican Party, member of the Republican Convention that nominated Abraham Lincoln for the President. He practiced law in Louisville, KY where he remained for the rest of his career.

Anthony Michael Dignowity (1810-1875), b. Kutná Hora, Bohemia, immigrated to the United States to flee the Austrian conscription laws. He sailed from Hamburg for New York in 1832. In the United States he traveled from State to State, working at many different jobs. He invented a machine to clean cotton, worked on a plantation, lived with the Creek Indians and studied their culture; studied medicine at Cincinnati College; became a manufacturer, and land agent. After arriving in San Antonio with a group of Arkansas volunteers for the Mexican War, he became a successful doctor and businessman, but in the 1850s, his outspoken abolitionist views made him controversial. Dignowity's reputation as a Unionist and abolitionist continued to plague him, and in 1861, he narrowly escaped hanging in the San Antonio Plaza. He traveled by horseback to Washington, D.C., where he was employed by the Federal Government. His property was confiscated, and two of his sons were conscripted into the Confederate Army. The sons later escaped to Mexico, however, and joined the Union Army.

John Jay (1817–1894), b. New York, NY, desc. Fr. Frederick Philipse, a lawyer by profession, as a student, was a manager of NY Young Men's Anti-Slavery Society. As a lawyer, he was active in seven-years struggle to procure admission of St. Philip's Church (black) to Protestant Episcopal Convention. After enactment of Fugitive-Slave Law (1850), he acted as counsel for many black fugitives.

William Jay (1789–1858), b. New York City, desc. f. Frederick Philipse, served as Judge of the Court of Westchester Co., NY, which office he held until 1843, when he was removed through the influence of pro slavery Democrats. He was active in championing the cause of emancipation, often agitating. He helped establish the NYC Anti-Slavery Society and largely through his efforts, a National Anti-Slavery Convention in Philadelphia inaugurated a campaign. He opposed the plan to colonize the former slaves in Africa, declaring that those who favored that plan were not moved by 'the precepts of the Gospel' but by 'prejudice against an unhappy portion of the human family.'

Johann Rittig (1829–1885), born in Prague, studied law and was jailed during the Revolution of 1848. He succeeded to flee abroad, however, and in 1851, held the position of secretary with the well-known German liberal in exile, Karl Vogt. The Austrian government, in the meantime, condemned him to death par contumace. After Napoleon's putsch, he left for America and settled in Cincinnati. Here he founded an anti-slavery newspaper, which, however, lasted only a short period of time. After that, he became an actor, performing in various places such as Cincinnati, Milwaukee, Chicago, St. Louis and Louisville. From 1857–1861, he held the position of co-editor of the New York paper *Staatszeitung* and afterwards founded his own New York journal. In 1874, he became editor of the Sunday edition of *Staatszeitung* for the abolition of the slave trade, twenty-two years before Congressional action brought it about.

James Taussig (1827–1916), b. Prague, Bohemia, left Prague University in 1848 and joined the student revolutionary bands. He served in them without interruption for the entire duration of the siege, until the occupation of Prague by Austrian troops. He had to flee, immigrated the same year to the United States and settled in St. Louis. Here he enrolled in law school and in 1851 received his license to practice law. He was a supporter of the

Republican Party. In 1862, he was sent by a group of radical Republicans to request from President Lincoln the immediate release of all black slaves. As was characteristic for the rapid sequence of events of that time, Lincoln answered him that such an action would be suicidal, nevertheless, only three months later, issued his landmark Emancipation Proclamation. Despite a number of offers, Taussig rejected all political positions and fully devoted himself to his legal practice.

C. Freethinkers

Bartoš Bittner (1861-1912), b. Milavče, Bohemia, took a course in Catholic theological seminary rebelling at the end. He ran away and came, in 1884, to the US. Soon after arriving, he secured a position as a teacher in a language school in Cedar Rapids. Journalism however, attracted him. He served as editor of *Svornost* in Chicago. He then moved to New York, where he became editor of *Duch Času* in 1890 and in 1893, he began publishing his satirical weekly, the *Šotek* (Imp) which soon achieved marked success. He reached the height of popularity about 1894, when the Chicago Benedictines, angered his philippics, brought a suit for criminal libel against him. Though as poor as the proverbial church mouse, Bittner was able promptly to raise among his admirers $20,000 bail. The winning of the suit still more enhanced his reputation.

August Geringer (1842-1930), Březnice, Bohemia was one of the most prominent people in early Czech Chicago. He was the best known, at least by name, in all of Czech America, as the publisher of Czech books and publisher of the oldest daily newspaper, *Spravedlnost*, beyond the borders of Bohemia. He was a committed Freethinker whose press published numerous works of Freethought literature.

Frank (František) Iška (1863-1921), b. Velešín, Bohemia, started his career as a priest. Unable to believe what he preached, he went over to the Old Catholic Church. In 1902, he arrived in the US with the idea, of organizing in Chicago a congregation of Old Catholics. Failing in this, he returned to his native country, but the following year, came back establishing permanent residence in Chicago. Casting aside Old Catholicism, he avowed his adhesion to the principles for which Klácel and Zdrůbek fought all their lives - freedom of religious expression. He later became editor of an antireligious *Vesmir* (The Universe), which, regretfully, pursued pro-Austrian policy. Dr. Iška thus brought on his name the obloquy which unfavorably belittled the rationalist movement, of which he was, until the war, one of the strongest advocates.

Charles (Karel) Jonáš (1840-1896), b. Malešov, Bohemia, frequently referred to as 'the first Čech in America,' at invitation of publisher Frank Kořízek, came to Racine, WI to take over editorship of his paper *Slavie*, even though he was barely twenty-three. He soon assumed the responsibilities of editor, which position he held for thirty-two years. Among his colleagues, he attained an exceptional position; they looked up to him as an authority, and his views on matters relating to the national life of Czechs in America were regarded as final. Being a politician, he was not as radical freethinker as his countrymen.

Ladimír Klácel (orig. František Matouš) (1808–1882), b. Česká Třebová, Bohemia, originally educated for the priesthood, became the spiritual leader of the rationalistic movement among the American Czechs and, as an advocate of new society, he urged his followers to establish congregations which in 1870, formed the Alliance of Free Thinkers. He established newspaper *Hlas Jednoty Svobodomyslných* (Voice of the Alliance of Free Thinkers) and for the Bohemian Freethinkers in Chicago he founded bimonthly *Svojan*.

Vojtěch 'Vojta' Náprstek (1826–1894), b. Prague, Bohemia, was the first to disseminate rationalism among American Czechs. Náprstek, who was admirer and personal friend of Havlíček's, published in Milwaukee a liberal weekly, the *Flug Blätter*. Though a German-language paper, the *Flug Blättter* was read largely by Náprstek's fellow countrymen. In 1854, the *Flug Blätter* was the subject of some heated debates in both houses of the Wisconsin legislature, the offered resolutions prohibiting the legislative postmasters from distributing this publication to the members, these resolutions were not adopted. Náprstek came to New York as political refugee. After wandering around, he finally settled in Milwaukee, starting his publication in 1852.

Joseph Pastor (1841–1899), b. Hostokrejse u Rakovníka, Bohemia, served as novitiate with the friars of Želiv Abbey. Few journalists waged a more relentless warfare against the clergy than he did, as editor of the weekly *Pokrok*, which appeared in Chicago in 1867.

Václav Šnajdr (1847–1920), b. České Budějovice, Bohemia, came to America in 1869, where he became journalist. He first worked for *Slavie* in Racine, WI, then for *Pokrok Západu* in Omaha, NE and then in Cleveland, OH. In 1873, he founded in Cleveland a radical paper *Dennice Novověku* (Morning Star of the New Era), written in rationalistic style, which he edited until 1910. Under his editorship, the *Dennice Novověku* clearly became the most literate of all Czech language papers published in US at that time. Later, he also published a Sunday paper, *Jednota Osvojených* (1883–86) and from 1891 to 1896, he published *Orgán Bratrstva*. Drawn to free thinkers/rationalists, Šnajdr wrote *For a Better Understanding of Robert Ingersoll* in 1904 and *Ladislav Klacel, His Life and Teachings* in 1908. He also wrote poetry. With the exception of Jonáš, Šnajdr was clearly the most influential Czech American journalist.

František Boleslav Zdrůbek (1842-1911), b. Bozděnice, nr. Hostomice, Bohemia, the 'arch-propagandist of atheism,' was initially sent to a Catholic seminary to be educated for the priesthood. Having experienced a change in religious faith, he left the Catholic for Protestant seminary, from which he graduated. Settling in Chicago and taking up journalism as a profession, he began "to combat the menace of bigotry and superstition among his countrymen." Apart from his journalistic activities, was a faithful follower and promoter of L. Klácel's ideas and succeeded Klácel as the head of the Unity of Freethinkers and became a preacher of their Chicago community. He was more practical than his predecessor and good organizer who inspired great following. He compiled the curriculum for the progressive Czech schools and wrote elementary readers and texts.

D. Suffragists

Ernesta Drinker Ballard (1920-2005), b. Philadelphia, PA, of Moravian ancestry, was a founding member of the National Organization for Women. Ballard marched on Washington, lobbied for the Equal Rights Amendment, and raised money for female political candidates. She also was a founding member of the National Abortion and Reproductive Rights Action League (NARAL) and served as chairwoman of the organization from 1989 to 1991.

Henrietta Bruckman (née Kahn) (1810-1888), b. Prague, Bohemia, was the founder of the United Order of True Sisters (UOTS) - a female counterpart to the B'nai B'rith, open exclusively to women. At its founding, it was the only fraternal organization in America open exclusively to women.

Jean Kane Foulke du Pont (1891-1985), b. Lenape, PA, of Bohemian ancestry, having descended from Augustine Herman from Prague. She was a noted an American suffragette, prison reform activist and philanthropist. She was a progressive woman for her era, and her passion was prison reform; in 1919, she helped found The Prisoners' Aid Society of Delaware as well as Bridge House, a detention home for juvenile offenders in Browntown section of Wilmington. Foulke du Pont was exceedingly active in the women's suffrage movement; in 1916, she picketed the White House with a troop of Delaware women in an effort to persuade President Woodrow Wilson to become active in the cause. She married industrialist Éleuthère Paul du Pont in 1910. Her husband was a member of the prominent Du Pont family and the founder of Du Pont Motors. They had six sons: Éleuthère Paul, Jr. (1911-1963); Francis George (1913-1987); Stephen (1915-2012); Robert Jacques (1923-1989); Benjamin Bonneau (1919-1999), and Alexis Irénée (1928-2016). Their son Stephen, an aviation enthusiast, was inducted into the Soaring Hall of Fame in 1987.

Ernestine Fürth (née Kisch) (1877–1946), b. Prague, Bohemia, was an Austrian-Jewish women's activist, the founder and leader of the women's suffrage movement in Austria. After Austria's annexation to Germany, she resided in the US. Her son was the economist J. Herbert Furth.

Edna Fischel Gellhorn (1878–1970), b. St. Louis, MO, of Bohemian ancestry, was active in the women's suffrage movement. She became the founder and first vice-president of the League of Women Voters in 1920 and President of the St. Louis & Missouri Leagues. Gellhorn was an officer in both the St. Louis and Missouri State Equal Suffrage Leagues from 1910 until the Nineteenth Amendment was passed in 1919. In 1920, Gellhorn became one of the founders, and vice president, of the National League of Women Voters. Gellhorn was asked to be the president of the National League by Carrie Chapman Catt, but declined. Gellhorn also was on the National League's board, was president of the St. Louis League for three terms, and was the first president of the Missouri League of Women Voters. She was elected to the League's state and national Rolls of Honor.

Pauline Dorothea Goldmark (1886–1962), b. Brooklyn, NY, of Bohemian ancestry, was a social worker and activist, a part of a group of women seeking the vote and reforms of the urban and industrial excesses of the early twentieth century. Goldmark pioneered in methods of social research central to these reform efforts.

Florence Bayard Hilles (1885–1954), b. Wilmington, DE, desc. f. Augustine Heřman, was an early worker on behalf of the women's suffrage movement and within that movement became known as a fighter and leader and for her abilities as a speaker. In 1917, leading a group of suffrages she picketed the White House and was jailed for her efforts.

Lilli Hornig (née Schwenk) (1921–2017), b. Ústí nad Labem, Czech., a Czech-American scientist who worked on the Manhattan project, was also a feminist, she was the founding director of HERS (Higher Education Resource Services) under the auspices of the Committee for the Concerns of Women in New England Colleges and Universities first organized by Sheila Tobias. Hornig also served on equal opportunity committees for the National Science Foundation, the National Cancer Institute, and the American Association for the Advancement of Science. She also was the research chair of the Committee for the Equality of Women at Harvard and consulted with and participated in many studies of women's science education and careers. She is the author of three books: *Climbing the Academic Ladder: Doctoral Women Scientists in Academe* (1979), *Equal Rites, Unequal Outcomes: Women in American Research Universities* (2003), and *Women Scientists in Industry and Government: How Much Progress in the 1970s* (1980).

VII. ADVOCACY & ACTIVISM

Chaviva Milada Hošek (1946–), b. Bohemia, is a Canadian academic, feminist and former politician. An active feminist, she served as president of the National Action Committee on the Status of Women from 1984 to 1986. A long-time champion of Canadian education and human rights, Dr. Hošek has served as president and executive member of the National Action Committee on the Status of Women and has held senior governance positions at the Univ. of Toronto and the Univ. of British Columbia.

Fran Hosken (1919–2006), b. Vienna, of Bohemian ancestry, was an American writer, feminist, and social activist. She founded the Women's International Network in 1975 and published a quarterly journal on women's health issues that became known, in particular, for its research into female genital mutilation.

Josephine Humpal-Zeman (1870–1906), b. Sušice, Bohemia, a newspaper writer, was an advocate of woman suffrage. An unfortunate marriage forced her to earn her own living. Through the generosity of Mary Ingersoll in Chicago, she was able to acquire a college education. While studying at Western Reserve Univ., she became chief editor of college paper *College Folio* which she helped establish. Later, she put herself at the head of the Czech woman suffrage movement and in 1894, she founded a weekly paper the *Ženské Listy* (Woman's Gazette). She was also active as lecturer, speaking to both English and Czech audiences. Some journalists referred her ungallantly as 'Mrs. General.' In 1894, she was engaged in the social settlements Hull House where she acquired invaluable social work experience. Subsequently, she was appointed by the city of Chicago a Truant Officer in which position she remained for four years. It was largely through her efforts that the American Czechs participated successfully in the Ethnographic Exposition in Prague in 1895. In 1897 at the Congress of Slavic journalists, she was elected executive secretary. In 1904, she accepted a position of executive secretary of the Woman's Club in Prague. She was the author of *Amerika v pravém světle* (America in its True Light) published in Prague in 1903.

Anna R. Kovanda (1873–1957), b. Table Rock, NE, of Czech immigrant parents, received her education in high school with two additional years of academic work, and special training in dramatics. She has lived in Nebraska all her life and has always been interested in church and club affairs. For several years, she was vice-president of the National American Woman Suffrage Association for Nebraska and in 1915 was elected president. For her loyal and energetic service, she received a diploma entitling her to the Honor Roll of the brave army of men and women who have rendered distinguished service to the cause of woman suffrage in America. During the World War, Mrs. Kovanda was president of the local Red Cross and took part in every drive for funds. She is a member of the Order of Eastern Star. She was assistant postmistress at Table Rock for nine years.

Margaret Millicent Carey McIntosh (1888-2001), b. Baltimore, MD, of Moravian ancestry; daughter of Anthony Morris Carey and Margaret Cheston Thomas. She was an outspoken feminist in the 1940s and 50s before feminism became popular. Mrs. McIntosh was the first married woman to head one of the seven top women's colleges known as the Seven Sisters and became a national icon.

Anita Pollitzer (1894-1975) b. Charleston, SC, of, Czech ancestry, devoted her public life to feminist politics and artistic patronage. Pollitzer's most prominent contribution to feminism came in 1945, when she became Alice Paul's hand-picked successor for the chairmanship of the National Woman's Party. As a party organizer traveling through the states for the NWP, she helped ratify the Nineteenth Amendment to the Constitution. Pollitzer demonstrated her commitment to woman suffrage in 1917 by being arrested as a Silent Sentinel picketing the Woodrow Wilson White House. In August 1920, Pollitzer used her considerable charm to convince legislator Harry T. Burn of Tennessee to cast the deciding vote for the Amendment.

E. Civil and Human Rights Activists

Iris Akahoshi (1929-1987), b. Czech., an engineer by training, was an American human rights activist who became known for her persistent support of a jailed Ukrainian political prisoner.

William Bila (1969–), b. New York, NY, of Slovak Romani descent, is living in New York. He studied business management and organizational behavior and has worked for auditing companies. He has long been involved in commemorating the annihilation of the Romani people by the Nazis. He is a member of the board of the French NGO La Voix des Rroms responsible for international communication, a member of the board of Roma Education Support Trust in the UK, and he serves on the board of the Roma Education Fund.

Alice Goldmark Brandeis (1866-1945), b. Brooklyn, NY, of Bohemian ancestry on her mother's side, a champion of progressive causes, was outspoken on behalf of woman suffrage, industrial reform, organized labor, the legal rights of children, and the fledgling American Zionist movement. She and her three sisters and one brother were raised in New York City. She married attorney Louis D. Brandeis. Alice Brandeis was not one to shy away from a controversial cause: She assisted in the campaign on behalf of anarchists Nicola Sacco and Bartolomeo Vanzetti and embraced the third-party presidential campaign of Robert La Follette (1924). During World War II, Brandeis stirred some controversy by associating herself with militant critics of American policy toward European Jewry and Palestine.

VII. ADVOCACY & ACTIVISM

Alison L. Des Forges (1942–2009), b. Schenectady, NY, of Moravian ancestry (a daughter of Herman A. Liebhafsky), was a human rights activist and historian who tried to call the world's attention to the looming genocide in Rwanda in 1994 and who later wrote what is considered the definitive account of the eventual slaughter of more than 500,000 Rwandans, was among the passengers when Continental Airlines Flight 3407 crashed near Buffalo on Feb. 12, 2009, killing all 49 people on board.

Julia Indichova (1949–), b. Košice, Czech.; American reproductive healthcare activist and author. She is best known for her book *Inconceivable: A Woman's Triumph Over Despair and Statistics* (2001), which was hailed by Library Journal as "an important consumer health resource...the first such book written from the patient's point of view." In 1997, Indichova founded FertileHeart.com, a global, patient driven community, focused on health enhancing approaches to reproductive health.

Eva Kollisch (1925–2023), b. Vienna, of Bohemian ancestry, in 1939, as a 14-year-old Jewish refugee, was rescued by a Kindertransport and brought to England. Some nine months later, she together with her two brothers, came to the US, where there were reunited with their parents. She taught German, comparative literature and women's studies at Sarah Lawrence College for over 30 years. She is the author of *Girl in Movement* a memoir of her early years inside a small American Trockyist party. She also published a number of stories and personal essays. Eva Kollisch has been active in anti-war feminist and human rights causes. In recent years, she became a member of One by One, a small international group that practices dialogue with the enemy. Eva Kollisch went to great lengths to review and preserve her mother's work (Margarete Kollisch). She lived in NYC with her long-time companion, the poet Naomi Replansky.

Victor Kugler (1900–1981), b. Vrchlabí, Bohemia, was one of the people who helped hide Anne Frank and her family and friends during the Nazi occupation of the Netherlands. In Anne Frank's posthumously published diary, *The Diary of a Young Girl*, he was referred to under the name Mr. Kraler. He was arrested by the Gestapo in 1944 and jailed by Nazis until the end of the War. In 1973, he received the Yad Vashem Medal of the Righteous among the Nations and in 1977, the Canadian Anti-Defamation League awarded him a 10,000-dollar prize in recognition for his assistance in the hiding of the Frank and van Pels families.

Josefina Napravilová (1914–2014), b. Plzeň, Bohemia, was a Czech who worked with child refugees after the Second World War. She started her most remarkable work after the Second World War when she began reuniting Czech children with their families after they had been separated by actions in the war. She would wander into camps and call out the

Czech words for Mum and Dad to find out who answered. She reunited between thirty and forty children. Amongst these was Vaclav Hanf who had the dubious claim of being one of the few children to survive the extermination of the village of Lidice in June 1942. He had been taken to Germany to be adopted by a German family at the age of eleven. He returned to find his village razed to the ground, his parents murdered but his sisters were miraculously alive. Other children had been moved to Germany after their parents had either been executed for involvement with the resistance or sent to concentration camps. In 1947, she moved to Vienna where her husband had been given back his stolen property. He only lived a short time and she worked for the International Refugee Organization where she was again assisting refugees but this time from communism. She moved to Canada in 1947 and after a career in banking, she returned to her home country after the fall of the Soviet empire, and she went to live in Bechyně. Her wartime exploits only came to notice because Vaclav Hanf remembered her pivotal role in his life. She was awarded the Order of Tomáš Garrigue Masaryk in 2009.

Julia Lorillard Wampage Pell (1953–2006), b. Washington, DC, of Bohemian ancestry, was the youngest child of Nuala Pell and Claiborne Pell, a six-term United States Senator from Rhode Island. Her name 'Wampage' was derived from her ancestor, the Chief of the Siwanois Indians in Westchester County. She was educated at the Potomac and Madeira Schools in Virginia and graduated from Montesano, Gstaad, Switzerland, she received her Bachelor of Arts from the University of Rhode Island. She was an advocate for the rights of same-sex couples and president of the Rhode Island Alliance for Lesbian and Gay Civil Rights. She served on the Boards of the Newport Art Museum, the National Gay and Lesbian Task Force, and the Potter League for Animals. She was president of the Board and the lobbyist for the Rhode Island Alliance for Lesbian and Gay Civil Rights, and a founding member of Equity Action, a Field of Interest Fund at the Rhode Island Foundation. Julie was a civil rights advocate and passionate about improving the lives of the disenfranchised, the oppressed, and those less-fortunate.

William R. Perl (1906–1998), b. Prague, Bohemia, a retired Army lieutenant colonel and Holocaust survivor and scholar, was the founder of the Washington branch of the Jewish Defense League who organized a little-known rescue effort that smuggled thousands of Jews out of Nazi-occupied Europe and into Palestine in the late 1930s and 40s. Although Dr. Perl's exploits in wartime Europe were frequently honored abroad, he was better known in the United States as a spokesman for militant Jewish causes and a leader of protests and demonstrations at the old Soviet Embassy in Washington. The militant Jewish Defense League targeted the Soviet Embassy to symbolize its fight for the emigration rights of Russian Jews. He won citations from President Ronald Reagan and Congress and numerous humanitarian service awards. In 1990, he was honored in Israel during a 50th anniversary

VII. ADVOCACY & ACTIVISM

reunion of the passengers of the *Sakarya*, a ship he chartered that carried 2,175 Jewish refugees from Constanta, Romania, to Palestine. He had been a militant Zionist since his school days. In the 1930s, Dr. Perl, a follower of militant Zionist Revisionist Vladimir Ze'ev Jabotinsky, was a young Jewish lawyer and teacher in Vienna. Realizing what Adolf Hitler's rise to power meant, he began organizing the voyages to Palestine in the 1930s. Despite being questioned and threatened by German officers, he continued with the clandestine voyages, using cattle boats and ramshackle freighters. In other cases, bribes were paid, and forged documents were used because Britain stopped the legal immigration of Jews into Palestine in 1939. In 1971, Dr. Perl formed the Washington branch of the Jewish Defense League and became enmeshed in a number of controversial incidents. He was arrested and convicted on charges of conspiring to shoot into the Prince George's County apartments of two Soviet Embassy officials in 1976. The conspiracy conviction was later overturned on appeal, but he was sentenced to three years' probation for illegal receipt of a firearm and attempting to damage property.

Ruth Freedom Pojman (1964–), b. New York City, of Bohemian ancestry, is the daughter of Dr. Louis Paul Pojman and Gertrude Burggraaff, who named her after the Civil Rights Act of 1964. She grew up as a third culture kid living in Denmark, England, France, and the US. She graduated from Univ. of Mississippi, majoring in history (B.A., 1988) and international relations and international communications at The American University, School of International Studies (M.A., 1993); later she earned a certificate in documentary film from GWU (2008), and contributed to PSAs and documentary films, especially on human trafficking, organized crime and migration in the E&E region. She became involved in US-USSR citizen diplomacy exchanges in the '80s and early '90s, and when the iron curtain came down, she worked on civil society and democratization issues throughout the former Soviet Union in the mid-1990s. She worked in Eurasia, developing technical assistance and democracy/human rights programs: for the International Organization for Migration (IOM) on programs supporting the development of migration policy, border control, and anti-trafficking; on raising awareness of issues relating to refugees, political asylum and tolerance for the United Nations High Commissioner for Refugees (UNHCR), in the Kyrgyz Republic; and on media relations for Mobil Oil in Kazakhstan. Upon return to the US, she worked at the USAID Europe and Eurasia Bureau, as the first anti-trafficking advisor, assisting missions in the design of anti-trafficking programs, conducting assessments and research throughout the CIS and SEE. She is currently the deputy coordinator at the Organization for Security and Cooperation in Europe's Office of the Special Representative and coordinator for Combating Trafficking in Human Beings, based in Vienna, Austria. She is one of the leading anti-trafficking experts in the world, having worked on these issues since 1997 and working for the highest-level political personality on the issue working full time on the issue.

Eric S. Tachau (1924–2002), b. Louisville, KY, of Bohemian ancestry, trained as a lawyer, was a civil rights activist. In the 1960s, Eric was treasurer of the Allied Organizations for Civil Rights of Kentucky and helped organize the march on Frankfort in 1964 that spurred passage of Kentucky's Civil Rights Act. The principal author of Kentucky's no-fault automobile insurance law in 1974, Eric also oversaw the creation and operation of the Louisville Area Governmental Insurance Trust, a program that saved taxpayers money by reducing insurance premiums.

Judy Baar Topinka (1944–2014), b. Riverside IL, of Czech ancestry, was an American politician and member of the Republican Party from the U.S. State of Illinois. She was supporting the LGBTQ (lesbian, gay, bisexual, transgender and queer) community since the beginning stages of the movement. She supported the LGBTQ causes when it was politically risky for anyone, Democrat or Republican, to be associated with the movement. The fact that she did so as a Republican showed an incredible amount of political courage. Judy Baar Topinka was not only supportive in words, she was supportive in her actions. She supported the Illinois' Marriage Equality Bill and during the November 20, 2013 ceremony at the University of Illinois at Chicago when the state's marriage equality bill was signed into law, Judy Baar Topinka was the only Republican speaker at the event. She opened her office to Equality Illinois' delegation on the group's annual Springfield lobbying days. Still another example was her perennial attendance at Chicago's Pride Parade and Equality Illinois' annual galas.

F. Social Activists & Reformers

Sharifa Alkhateeb (1946–2004), b. Philadelphia, PA, of Czech mother and Yemeni father. She was an American writer, researcher and teacher on cultural communication and community building for Islam and Muslims in the United States. She was involved in feminist causes, domestic violence prevention, as well as interfaith and educational organizations. She founded the first nationwide organization for Muslim women in the US and was the first woman to receive the Community Service Award from the Islamic Society of North America.

Alice Goldmark Brandeis (1866–1945), b. Brooklyn, NY, of Bohemian ancestry; advocate of industrial reform, organized labor and legal rights of children.

Mathias Bush (1722–1790), b. Prague, Bohemia, a prosperous merchant in Philadelphia, on Oct. 25, 1765 signed the Philadelphia Merchants Non Importation Resolution, the first American document of civic rights on record.

John Jay Chapman (1862–1933), b. New York City, desc. f. Frederick Philipse, Harvard Univ. trained lawyer and writer, was leading reformer as president of the Good Government Club and publisher and editor of the periodical *The Political Nursery*, taking lead in the movement against the political machine of Tammany Hall in New York City. Two of his books, *Causes and Consequences* (1898) and *Practical Agitation* (1900) stress his conviction that individuals should take a moral stand on issues of importance to the nation. On the first anniversary of the lynching of a black man in Coatesville, CA, Chapman hired a hall and held a memorial service with only two other persons present. His memorable speech delivered on that occasion was published in his book *Memories and Milestones* (1915). He was the author of a biography of the Abolitionist leader William L. Garrison (1913). John Jay Chapman's grandfather was the son of William Jay and a grandson of Chief Justice John Jay of the United States Supreme Court.

Andrei Hugo Cherny (1975–), b. Los Angeles, CA, of Czech ancestry, graduated with honors from Harvard College and from the University of California Berkeley Law School. He has been called a 'superstar' by CNN, a 'progressive reformer' by *Washington Monthly*, and one of America's 'top young thinkers' by *The New York Times*. He is a co-founder and CEO of Aspiration, an investment firm with a conscience, dedicated to serving the middle class in a way that marries profit with philanthropic purpose. He brings to this role nearly twenty years of experience as a consultant to some of America's top companies, the co-founder and president of a media start-up, a financial fraud prosecutor, a bestselling author, a senior White House aide, and a nationally-recognized economic policy expert. Cherny is the founder and president of *Democracy*, a public policy journal and think tank that seeks to spur new ideas on the major issues facing America and the world. *Democracy*'s ideas, such as the Consumer Financial Protection Bureau at the heart of the 2010 Wall Street reform, have made their way into the national political debate and into legislation in Congress and states across America. Today, in print and online, *Democracy* has over 300,000 readers in every state and more than 150 countries around the world. Cherny worked in the Clinton White House as a senior advisor to Vice President Al Gore, was the lead negotiator and chief drafter of the 2000 Democratic Party platform, and helped develop the winning message for John Kerry in the 2004 Democratic primaries, and served as a part-time advisor to Barack Obama's presidential campaign and co-author of his campaign policy book, *Change We Can Believe In*. As the chair of the Arizona Democratic Party from 2011–12, he worked to build a big-tent, mainstream party that is ready to provide leadership for a stronger economy, safer streets, and better schools. He is a former Senior Fellow at both Harvard University's

Kennedy School of Government and the Center for American Progress, and a former Assistant Arizona Attorney General. Cherny has written frequently on global economic policy, politics, and history for newspapers such as *The New York Times, Washington Post, Los Angeles Times, USA Today, Financial Times* and *Investor's Business Daily*. He has appeared as a commentator on television news programs including ABC's Good Morning America and World News Tonight, CBS's The Early Show, The Colbert Report, and The O'Reilly Factor. He is the author of the bestselling *The Candy Bombers: The Untold Story of the Berlin Airlift and America's Finest Hour*, was described as like 'Stephen Ambrose at his best' by historian Douglas Brinkley and 'everything one could want from a work of history—engrossing, informative and stirring' by the Washington Post.

Ruth Davis (née Hochwald) (1938–), b. Brno, Moravia, as a refugee, was brought to England in 1939. She studied English literature at Somerville Coll., Oxford (M.A., 1961). She started her career as journalist, Yorkshire, England and then served as a correspondent for *The Yorkshire Post* in France (1966–68). She has lived in Jamaica, Queens, NY since 1969. She has been an activist, working for civil rights and disability rights. She served as an assistant editor for *Matilda Ziegler Magazine for the Blind* (2002–07). She founded 'Czechoslovak Jewish Communities Archive' to tape-record memories of vanished Jewish communities in Czechoslovakia. She edited and published *Phoenix: Journal of Czech and Slovak Jewish Family and Community History*. She has done research on topics of nonviolent change and human rights in the Czech Jewish past from the 17th century to the post-Holocaust period.

Josephine Clara Goldmark (1877–1950), b. Brooklyn, NY, of Bohemian ancestry, was a social reformer. She was an advocate of labor law reform in the United States during the early 20th century. Her work against child labor and for wages-and-hours legislation (the 8-hour day, minimum wage) was influential in the passage of the Keating–Owen Act in 1916 and the later Fair Labor Standards Act of 1937. Goldmark was an aggressive investigator of labor conditions and wrote prolifically about her findings. Her research about the effects of industrial work, low wages, and long hours on workers, particularly women and child labor, had a major effect on United States labor law. Goldmark worked for many years as a researcher of labor conditions and their effects in different working environments. She served as a consulting expert for a number of companies, philanthropies, and government commissions, and she was vice chair of the New York City Child Labor Commission.

Pauline Dorothea Goldmark (1874–1962), b. Brooklyn, NY, of Bohemian ancestry, was American social reformer, focused on equal pay and the health aspects of women's work. Goldmark was an executive of the Consumers' League of New York and served on the National Consumers League's boar d for forty years. She was associate director of the New York School of Philanthropy, and served on the New York State Industrial Board, the New

York State Factory Investigating Commission. During World War I, she was secretary of the United States Department of Labor's Commission on Women in Industry. She was manager of the Women's Service Section, United States Railway Administration. She was assistant director of research at the Russell Sage Foundation and consulted on women's working conditions for AT&T after 1919.

Charles Kernaghan (1948-2022), b. Brooklyn, NY, of Czech descent, is the executive director of the Institute for Global Labor and Human Rights, currently headquartered in Pittsburgh. He is known for speaking out against sweatshops, corporate greed and the appalling living and working conditions of impoverished workers around the world.

Ladimír Klácel (orig. František Matouš) (1808-1882), b. Česká Třebová, Bohemia, formerly a member of the Augustinian order and professor of philosophy at the Bishop's Inst. in Brno, because of his liberal views and acceptance of Hegel's thoughts, was removed from his professorship. In the revolutionary year of 1848, he left the order and became editor of *Moravské Noviny* in Brno but was deposed again. Disenchanted, in 1869 he decided to accept John Barta Letovsky's invitation to come to America and edit his paper *Slovan Amerikánský* published in Iowa City. As a respected literary figure and with ties with leading literary figures in the Czech Lands, he was received in US with great enthusiasm and expectations. He became the spiritual leader of the rationalistic movement among the American Czechs and as an advocate of new society, he urged his followers to establish congregations which in 1870 formed the Alliance of Free Thinkers. He established newspaper *Hlas Jednoty svobodomyslných* (Voice of the Alliance of Free Thinkers) and for the Bohemian Freethinkers in Chicago he founded a bimonthly *Svojan*. 'Let us dare to grow intelligent' was his slogan. He strove to found a communal society where the individual (rid of tradition and human failings) would attain a sense of personal dignity and social responsibility and conduct his life in the path of harmony, beauty and universality. The spiritual and social doctrine founded by Klácel was embodied in the principle of his spiritual creed. His philosophy held that a universal law governed the world and that all creation was interdependent. Man was nature's most perfect and yet most dependent being. He was endowed with a will and mind which formed his ego, but he was not free or self-sufficient since he too was subject to the universal law of interrelation with others. Human community existed only as a segment of a greater whole such as a nation, continent or the world. Yet, even the world was interdependent on a greater unity, the universe. Universality necessarily encompassed all natural and human phenomena manifested to or conceived of by man. In spite of his advanced age, he developed enormous activity as a writer, translator and teacher and in a period of eleven years, he produced over eighty publications. Toward the end of his life, he turned to mysticism and in 1882, died destitute.

Oliver Hazard Perry La Farge (1901–1963), b. NYC, desc. f. Frederick Philipse, was an anthropologist and writer of note with lifelong interest in American Indian. He became president of the Eastern Assn. of Indian Affairs (1933–37), increased its membership and changed its name to the National Assn. on Indian Affairs. In 1937, the Association merged with the American Defense Assn. into the Assn. on American Indian Affairs, with La Farge as president. He spent much of his adult life championing American Indian rights. He opposed Pres. Eisenhower's 'termination policy,' an attempt to end all special rights to Indians. He became a genuine 'Indian Man,' as he was called in his childhood.

Lenore Guinzburg Marshall (1897–1971), b. NYC, of Bohemian ancestry, a professional writer, was a member of the Society of Friends. In 1956, she joined with Clarence Pickett and Norman Cousins to found the National Committee for a Sane Nuclear Policy. As one of its directors, she worked with a former US Representative at the UN James J. Wadsworth for the limited test ban treaty. She was closely associated with the Socialist leader Norman Thomas and in 1960, joined him in leading a march in New York City to UN to urge cessation of recrimination in the interest of preserving peace in a nuclear age. In 1971, she was cofounder and cochairman of the Committee for Nuclear Responsibility.

Ambrose Ondrák (1892–1961), b. Chicago, IL, of Czech parents, R.C. priest, helped organize the Back of the Yards Council in Chicago, and later served as its president. Labor leaders called Father Ondrák the 'picket line priest' and credited him with helping to repel efforts by communists to stir up the packing house workers' 1946 strike.

Lev J. Palda (1847–1912), b. Vodňany, Bohemia, is often called the father of Czech socialism in the US. He arrived in New York in 1867 as a journeyman weaver. In spite of his meager formal education, he was a cultured man and soon decided to become a journalist. While in New York, he edited the first attempted Czech newspaper that was called *Lucerna*. Subsequently, he assumed in Chicago the editorship of *Národní Listy* and proclaimed that it will be an 'official spokesman of the working class.' In 1875, together with Frank Škarda, he founded in Cleveland *Dělnické Listy* (The Workmen's News), the motto of the paper being 'Equal duties equal rights' and announced that the paper is being published as the organ of Socialist Workingmen's Party in the US. What Socialist Party it referred to or who the members of the party were was not made clear. In 1877, the *Dělnické Listy* was moved to NYC with the hope that the metropolis would offer to a Socialist paper a wider influence than Cleveland. Palda was an eloquent speaker, an independent thinker and indefatigable organizer. Back in New York, he started organizing Socialist clubs among the Czech Slavic International Workingmen's Assn. of NY. However, he was neither a communist nor a revolutionary. He believed that the social and economic order was unjust. Yet he held the view that society had its power to purge itself no revolution but by evolution. More radical element repudiated him, and some called him a reactionary. He was an idealist and humanist. In 1902, he wrote a remarkable booklet *Myšlenkv o novém náboženství* (Thoughts on a New Religion) in which the thinking man sets out to analyze his creed and not satisfied with evasion, he demands solution of the perplexing problem of religion. He arrives at the conclusion that mere non-belief negativity is not enough. 'I learned by the exposition of my faith, partly to ease my troubled mind, partly, if possible, to assist in approaching regeneration of our liberal party. I see this possible only in a new religion which shall embrace all our desires, all our ideals, our teachings, our views.' His New Religion pleased neither the rationalists nor the old-fashioned believers. Palda's last years were spent in Cedar Rapids, IA, where he operated a small cigar factory.

Ernst Papanek (1900–1973), b. Vienna, of Moravian ancestry, was a child psychologist and educator known for his work with refugee children during and after World War II and for his involvement in socialist parties in Europe and the United States. He was active in the Verband der Sozialistischen Arbeiterjugend Deutschösterreichs (SAJDÖ) from 1919 and its president 1933–1934; member of the City Council of Vienna 1932–1934; member of the executive committee of the Socialist Youth International (SYI) 1934–1939. He fled to Czechoslovakia 1934, where he supported the illegal Revolutionäre Sozialistische Jugend (RSJ) in Austria; editor of the International Pedagogical Information (IPI) 1936–1938. He fled to France 1938; worked for the Organisation de Santé et de l'Éducation (OSE), which was founded by Russian Jews and smuggled children out of Germany, housing them in castles in France 1938–1940. He fled to the United States 1940; worked for the Children's Aid Society; active in various Austrian emigrant organizations and from 1941, member of the American Socialist Party. In 1945, he was director of the Child and Youth Project Department of the Unitarian Service Committee (USC) and later director of American Youth for World Youth (AYWY); in 1947, head of the Brooklyn Training School for Girls and from 1949, head of the Wiltwyck School for Boys in New York.

Elizabeth Brandeis Raushenbush (1896–1984), b. Boston, NA, daughter of US Supreme Court Justice Louis Brandeis, a labor economist and social researcher, together with her husband Paul, did research that led to the signing of the nation's first unemployment compensation law in 1932. This led them to be known in as 'Mr. and Mrs. Unemployment Compensation.' Later she developed interest in the plight of the migrant worker and served as chairperson from 1960 to 1967 on the Governor's Committee on Migratory Labor. She fought for improved conditions for migratory workers and their families and succeeded in bringing them under the protection of the workmen's compensation act. She also was instrumental in establishing summer schools for the migrant workers' children. An account of her involvement in the unemployment compensation movement in Wisconsin can be found in the book *Our U.C. Story* (1930-1967) which she wrote with her husband.

Jean Brandeis Tachau (1894-1978), b. Louisville, KY, of Bohemian ancestry (a niece of Justice Louis D. Brandeis), was a social activist. Her activities led to a number of reforms in Kentucky, including the establishment of the new Kentucky Department of Child Welfare in 1960.

Sigmund Zeisler (1860-1931), b. Bilsko, on Moravian Silesian border, a trained lawyer, in 1886-1887, was co-counsel for the defendants in the Anarchist cases, popularly known as the Haymarket cases. He was prominent as Sound Money Democrat in campaign of 1896. He was speaker at the first anti-Imperialist meeting held west of the Alleghenies, Chicago (1899), and a member of the Executive Committee of the American Anti-Imperialist League (1899). He was an acting chair during National Liberty Congress (1900). He stumped country as an anti-Imperialist in favor of Bryan campaign of 1900. He was a member of the Executive committee of Voters' League and Civil Service Reform Assn.

G. Political Activists

Manfred Ackermann (1898-1991), b. Mikulov, Moravia, was an Austrian Social Democrat politician and trade union official in Austria and the United States. Ackermann served in the Austrian armed forces during World War I. After returning to civilian life, he became involved in trade union activities and the Sozialdemokratische Arbeiterpartei (SDAP). The SDAP was banned in the 1930s and Ackermann was arrested in March 1934, after the Austrian Civil War, and held until summer, 1935 in Wöllersdorf detention camp. He was re-arrested in November 1937 as a result of working illegally and held until Schuschnigg's general amnesty in March 1938. After the Anschluss of Austria by Germany in 1938, Ackermann was, as a Socialist and a Jew, obliged to flee the Nazis. After passing through Italy, Switzerland and Belgium, he lived in Paris, but in 1939, he was imprisoned by the French in Colombes and Montargis. He was subsequently able to go, via Spain and Portugal, to the United States where he worked and was again active in trades unions. Ackermann retired in 1964 and returned to Austria. He lectured there until his death in 1991 and was one of the initiators of the Contact Committee of the Federation of Socialist Youth freedom fighters. He was married to Paula Popp.

Jiřina Adamová (1922-1993), b. Říčany u Prahy, Czech., was a political activist, residing in Hot Springs, AR.

Friedrich Adler (1879-1960), b. Vienna, of Bohemian ancestry, the son of Social Democratic politician Victor Adler, is perhaps best known for his assassination of Count

Karl von Stürgkh in 1916. He studied chemistry, physics and mathematics in Zurich. In 1897, he became a member of the Social Democratic Party of Austria (SPÖ) and from 1907 was editor of the magazine *Der Kampf*. He was a good friend of Albert Einstein. Adler was engaged in the international trade union movement and in 1911, he gave up his scientific activities to become the secretary-general of the SPÖ in Vienna, an office he held until 1914. He became the spokesperson of the left wing of the party and after the start of the First World War, he agitated particularly against the SPÖ's policy of supporting the war. In his fight against the war policy of Austria-Hungary, Adler turned to drastic means. On October 21, 1916, in the dining room of the Viennese hotel Meißl und Schadn, he shot the Minister-President of Austria Count Karl von Stürgkh with a pistol three times, killing him. For this act, Adler was sentenced to death, a sentence which was commuted to 18 years imprisonment. After the outbreak of the revolution of 1918, he was released, and he played a significant role as leader of the Arbeiterräte (Workers' councils) and as a member of the National Council of Austria. From the mid-1920s, he was mainly active in the Socialist International, whose secretary-general he was to remain for over 15 years. After the outbreak of the Second World War, Adler fled to the United States. In 1946, he retired from politics and edited his father Victor's exchange of letters with August Bebel and Karl Kautsky.

Michael Badnarik (1954–), b. Hammond, IN, of Slovak ancestry; software engineer, political figure, radio talk show host, former Libertarian Party nominee for US President.

Alice Goldmark Brandeis (1866–1945), b. Brooklyn, NY, of Bohemian ancestry on her mother's side, a champion of progressive causes, was outspoken on behalf of woman suffrage, industrial reform, organized labor, the legal rights of children, and the fledgling American Zionist movement. She and her three sisters and one brother were raised in New York City. She married attorney Louis D. Brandeis. Alice Brandeis was not one to shy away from a controversial cause: She assisted in the campaign on behalf of anarchists Nicola Sacco and Bartolomeo Vanzetti and embraced the third-party presidential campaign of Robert La Follette (1924). During World War II, Brandeis stirred some controversy by associating herself with militant critics of American policy toward European Jewry and Palestine.

Isidor Bush (orig. Busch) (1822–1898), b. Prague, Bohemia, a journalist and successful merchant, was a political liberal. He served as an aide on General Fremont's staff in 1861. He became one of the St. Louis Delegates to the Missouri Constitutional Convention, MO. When the Union Party was formed in St. Louis, he became one of its Delegates at the State Convention. He supported the cause of the Union and delivered the outstanding unconditional Union speech of the convention. He participated in the deliberations during the meetings and played an important role when the convention concerned itself in 1863 with the problem of slave emancipation. When the committee submitted its resolutions, Bush as the sole dissenter submitted a minority report. His resolution was not accepted and the convention postponed complete emancipation until 1870. In 1865, after Lincoln's re-election, Bush again was elected a member of the State Convention for drafting a new State Constitution. Bush voted against the proposed Constitution, which he considered too narrow in spirit and which disfranchised countless citizen because of their sympathy for the Southern cause. The document which was rejected by the State a decade later, was a complete vindication of the position he had taken.

Ruth Fischer (orig. Elfriede Eisler) (1895–1961), b. Leipzig, of Bohemian ancestry; co-founder of the Austrian Communist Party; later becoming a staunch anti-Communist activist and served as a key-agent of the American intelligence service, known as 'The Pond.'

Albina Rose Čermák (1904–1978), b. Cleveland, Ohio, of Czech ancestry, was apparently one of the few women who became politically active in the early and mid-20th century. She was a lifelong Republican and the first woman to run for mayor of Cleveland. She dropped out of nursing school to become bookkeeper-secretary-buyer in the family Čermák Dry Goods Co. In 1933, she became a bookkeeper for the city public utilities department and within two years, was supervisor. Active as a Republican precinct committeewoman from 1925–53, Čermák served as vice-chairman and secretary of the Cuyahoga County Republican Central & Executive Committee and chairman of the Republican Women's Organization of Cuyahoga County from 1939–53. From 1946–53, she was a member of the Board of Elections and was a delegate to the Republican National Conventions in 1940, 1944, and 1952. In 1953, Čermák resigned from many offices to become US collector of customs, stepping down to run against Anthony Celebrezze in 1961 as the first woman to run for Mayor. She predicted that Celebrezze, if elected, would abandon Cleveland for a cabinet post. As expected, she lost, while Celebrezze became secretary of HEW in 1962. Čermák was rewarded for party loyalty with choice and historic appointments. She was the first woman appointed bailiff to the common pleas court in 1964. In 1965, State Auditor Roger Cloud selected her as an administrative specialist, while Governor James Rhodes named her vice-chairwoman of the Ohio Status of Women Committee in 1966. Single by choice, she was considered among Cleveland's top career women and was a sought-after speaker.

Anton Čermák (1873–1933), b. Kladno, Bohemia, after establishing a successful business, entered politics through Chicago Democratic Party. Starting as a clerk, he advanced to precinct captain and in 1902, won a seat in the State Legislature. In 1909, he became alderman in the City Council. In 1922, he was elected chairman of the Cook County Board of Commissioners and by 1928, he was undisputed leader of the local Democratic Party which brought him the Mayoralty in 1931. Through his influence, Illinois was brought into Roosevelt camp in the 1932 Democratic National Convention. He was mortally wounded by an assassin's bullet intended for Pres. Franklin D. Roosevelt while riding in the president's open touring car and died three weeks later.

Andrei Cherny (1975–), born in Los Angeles, CA, of Czech ancestry, a business consultant, is a current Democratic candidate for Arizona's 9th Congressional district. He served as Chair of the Arizona Democratic Party, Arizona's Assistant Attorney General under Terry Goddard from 2006 to 2009, and a White House aide and advisor to Presidents Bill Clinton and Barack Obama. He is also a business consultant, author, and the founder and president of *Democracy: A Journal of Ideas*.

Lewis N. Dembitz (1833–1907), b. Zirke, Posen, Prussia, of Bohemian mother, a lawyer and staunch unionist, and frequent antislavery agitator, was a member of new Republican Party. He came in personal contact with future President Abraham Lincoln, and in 1860, Lewis Dembitz was one of the twenty-three delegates from Kentucky to the National Republican Convention in Chicago that nominated Abraham Lincoln for the Presidency.

Henry Aaron Guinzburg (1856–1928), b. Baltimore, MD of Bohemian ancestry, a business executive, philanthropist and welfare worker, played an important role in the Democratic Party of St. Louis. He managed the campaign of Sen. William T. Stone for Governor and after Stone's election, was appointed chief of staff, aide-de-camp and Colonel of Cavalry. Later he was appointed chief-of-staff of Gov. McIntyre of Ohio. In 1896, he declined the Democratic nomination of Mayor of St. Louis and Lt. Gov. of Missouri and during Pres. Harrison's Administration, refused the offer of a post as Minister to Mexico. In 1925, he was chairman of the citizen's committee which brought about the nomination of James J. Walker for Mayor of New York City. He was subsequently appointed a member of New York City planning and survey committee.

Carl Newton Gunter, Jr. (1938–1999), b. Alexandria, LA, of Czech ancestry, was a Democratic member of the Louisiana House of Representatives from 1972–1992, known for his support of organized labor and his opposition to abortion and the Equal Rights Amendment.

Augustin Haidušek (1845–1929), b. Moravia, apart from his other virtues, he was a politician and political activist. In fact, it was politics which made him found his own periodic, *Svoboda*, in order that he could affect public opinion. After becoming a lawyer, he was elected chairman of the Fayette County Democratic Executive Committee in 1874. The next year, he was elected Mayor of La Grange, thus becoming one of the first American Mayor of Czech descent. He became a member of the state legislature in 1880, representing Lee and Fayette Counties, and served two terms. He became county judge of

Fayette County in 1884 and was reelected in 1886 and 1888. Haidušek's duties as county judge included serving as ex officio superintendent of public schools. In this role, he vigorously enforced the state law that required English as the principal medium of instruction in the classroom. As a newspaper editor, he wielded his greatest influence. Although *Svoboda* steered clear of religious issues, unlike many other Czech-American publications of the time, its political position was decidedly Democratic, and Haidušek constantly urged his readers toward increased political consciousness and involvement in local and state government. Twice, he was elected chairman of County Democratic Executive Committee and twice a delegate to Democratic National Convention.

Charles (Karel) Jonáš (1840–1896), Malešov, b Bohemia, was a Czech journalist, linguist, and political activist, who became a Wisconsin journalist and politician. He studied at the School of Science and Polytechnic Institute in Prague, as well as attending lectures at Charles University in Prague. A strong Czech nationalist and friend of Vojtěch Náprstek, he fled Bohemia in 1860 after clashes with the authorities, moving via Bremen to London, where he continued to work as a journalist. In March 1863, he emigrated to Racine, Wisconsin, just south of Milwaukee (where Náprstek had been the first Czech to publish a periodical in the United States); there he edited and published the Czech language newspaper *Slavie*. Jonas was skeptical of Abraham Lincoln and the policies of the Republican Party (which he saw as too centralist), and he gradually came to be affiliated with the Democrats. He was appointed to the Board of Managers of the Wisconsin Industrial School for Boys (a reform school) for 1874–1877, serving only through 1875. He was elected an alderman for the City of Racine, serving from 1876 to 1883, and would serve as president of the Common Council of Racine for 1878–79. He was elected as a Democratic member of the Wisconsin State Assembly in 1877 to represent the 1st Racine County district (the City of Racine) (incumbent Republican Norton J. Field was not a candidate for re-election), with 1229 votes to 760 for Republican Edward Gillen; he was assigned to the standing committees on the judiciary and on education. He was not a candidate for re-election in 1878, choosing instead to run on the Greenback Party ticket for the Wisconsin Senate's Third District (Racine County), losing to Republican William Everett Chipman by 3206 to 2177 (there was no Democratic candidate in the race, and some candidates that year ran as Democrats and Greenbackers simultaneously). He was succeeded in the Assembly by Field. He ran again for the Senate in 1882 as a Democrat (to succeed Republican Albert L. Phillips, who was not a candidate for re-election), winning this time with 3213 votes to 2494 for Republican William T. Lewis; and was assigned to the committees on education and on enrolled bills. He did not run for re-election in 1886 and was succeeded by Republican Henry Allen Cooper. In November 1886, Jonas was appointed U. S. Consul at Prague by President Grover Cleveland, which position he held until July 16, 1889. In 1890, he was elected 16th Lieutenant Governor of Wisconsin with a plurality of 34,974 in a four-way race, well ahead of his running mate, Milwaukee mayor George Wilbur Peck. He would serve in that office from 1891 until 1894, when he resigned to become the U.S. consul in St. Petersburg, Russia; in 1896, he was transferred to Crefeld, Germany, where he died that same year. Although in 1919, the Department of State announced that Jonas died of heart failure, recent scholarship has determined that Jonas shot himself. After his death, Jonas was buried in Prague's Olšany Cemetery.

Arthur Kahn (1875-1930), b. Bohemia, a baker by trade, was a trade union activist and organizer from Milwaukee, Wisconsin who served one term as a Socialist member of the Wisconsin State Assembly. He served as a business agent for the Milwaukee Bakers Union, as an organizer for the Bakery and Confectionery Workers Union in the U.S. and Canada, and as a delegate to various conventions of the Wisconsin State Federation of Labor and the American Federation of Labor, as well as representing Philadelphia's Central Labor Union at the Second American Peace Congress in Chicago in 1909.

Ľudovít Kandra (pseud: Peter Klas) (1904-1993), b. Banská Štiavnica, Slovakia; poet, essayist, novelist, freelance writer, lobbyist, political activist.

Jane Lobman Katz (1931-1986), b. Montgomery, AL, of Bohemian ancestry, was a political activist who waged a twenty-two-year war against poor government in Alabama. As the State Legislative Chairperson for the Alabama League of Women Voters, Jane Katz fought for the support for education, equalization of property taxes and stronger consumer protection laws. She supported election law reform and campaign finance reform, and regulation for political action committees. Katz felt there was a need for stronger ethics laws and consumer protection laws. She advocated background checks of providers of childcare. She promoted a constitution reform convention, and the Equal Rights Amendment. Katz created the *Capitol Newsletter*, a newsletter about legislation. Her *Voting Record* reported on how Alabama legislators voted on issues pertinent to the League of Women Voters, the first magazine to do so.

August Klecka (1878-1946), b. Baltimore, MD, of Bohemian ancestry, was a prominent leader among Bohemian-American Democrats in the city, he served as Councilman for the second district from 1915 to 1933, during which time he became Democratic floor leader and vice president of the Council. In 1933, he was appointed US Marshal for the District of Maryland by President Franklin D. Roosevelt and served in that position until his death.

Eva-Maria Kollisch (1925-2023), b. Vienna, of Bohemian and Moravian ancestry on her mother's side; in 1939, as a 14-year-old Jewish refugee, was rescued by a Kindertransport and brought to England. Some nine months later, she together with her two brothers, came to the US, where they were reunited with their parents. She taught German, comparative literature and women's studies at Sarah Lawrence College for over 30 years. She is the author of *Girl in Movement* a memoir of her early years inside a small American Trockyist party. She also published a number of stories and personal essays. Eva Kollisch has been active in anti-war feminist and human rights causes. In recent years, she has become a member of One by One, a small international group that practices dialogue with the enemy. Eva Kollisch went to great lengths to review and preserve her mother's work (Margarete Kollisch). She lives in NYC with her long-time companion, the poet Naomi Replansky.

Rosi Kuerti (née Jahoda) (1905-2004), b. Vienna, of Moravian ancestry, biologist and peace activist, Cleveland. She received her education in biology at Univ. of Vienna (RNDr., 1928). Her career includes being a teacher at Univ. of Istanbul, Turkey (1937-38), Buckingham School, Cambridge (1938-39); professor at Hathaway Brown School, Cleveland (1939-40), before joining Case Western Reserve Univ., Cleveland. She ended her career as professor emeritus of biology at CWRU. She was also a longtime activist in the Cleveland area, with years of involvement in Women Speak Out for Peace and Justice. She volunteered for a number of years, at the Free Medical Clinic and in tutoring inmates at the Cleveland Workhouse. Her love of music was passed on to her son, the famed pianist Anton Kuerti.

John Kulhan (1923-2014); b. Vinodol, Czech.; engineer, Slovak patriot, Czechoslovak Army officer, POW; in US s. 1950; political activist. Founder and first VP of the Slovak Cultural Center of New York; president of the Slovak Catholic Sokol; secretary of the Slovak World Congress.

Ronald Lauder (1944-), b. New York, NY, of Czech. descent, American businessman, heir to the Estée Lauder Corporation, political activist, president of the World Jewish Congress.

Joseph J. 'Joe' Lhota (1954-), b, Bronx, NY, of Czech ancestry, is an American politician, former chairman of the New York City Metropolitan Transportation Authority and former deputy Mayor under Rudy Giuliani. He was the Republican nominee in his unsuccessful bid for the 2013 election for Mayor of New York City. Upon graduating from Harvard, Lhota returned to New York City and began a fourteen-year career as an investment banker at First Boston and Paine Webber. He specialized in public finance, serving state and local governments throughout the US. In 1994, Lhota joined the administration of Mayor Rudy Giuliani, where he held several positions over Giuliani's two terms. He first served as chief of staff to the Deputy Mayor for finance and economic development and that year, was quickly was promoted to New York City finance commissioner. In 1995, he was selected director of the office of management and budget. In 1998, Giuliani appointed Lhota to Deputy Mayor for operations. In October 2011, New York State Governor Andrew Cuomo nominated Lhota to serve as chairman of the Metropolitan Transportation Authority (MTA), the largest mass transit provider in the United States (servicing 8.5 million customers daily). While awaiting confirmation by the New York State Senate, Lhota began serving as interim CEO. He was unanimously confirmed on Jan 9, 2012. Lhota resigned as head of the MTA on December 31, 2012, to explore running for Mayor of New York City.

Michael Lucas (1926-2020), b. Slovakia; an artist, designer and political activist residing in Toronto, Ont., Canada. He is the Chair of the Executive Committee of the Canadian Friends of Soviet People, founded in 1991, and was formerly the chair of the USSR-Canada Friendship Association from 1972 until 1991. He is also the chair of the International Council of Friendship and Solidarity with Soviet People, operating out of Toronto.

Lenore Guinzburg Marshall (1897-1971), b. NYC, of Bohemian ancestry, a professional writer, was a member of the Society of Friends. In 1956, she joined with Clarence Pickett and Norman Cousins to found the National Committee for a Sane Nuclear Policy. As one of its directors, she worked with a former US Representative at the UN James J. Wadsworth for the limited test ban treaty. She was closely associated with the Socialist leader Norman Thomas and in 1960, joined him in leading a march in New York City to UN to urge cessation of recrimination in the interest of preserving peace in a nuclear age. In 1971, she was cofounder and cochairman of the Committee for Nuclear Responsibility.

Hanna (Hammerschlag) Newcombe (1922-2011), b. Prague, Czech., was the recipient of the 1997 Pearson Medal of Peace and was elected a member of the Order of Canada in 2007 for her work in peace research and international relations. She was 17, when the Nazis marched into Prague, prompting her Jewish parents to immigrate with her to Canada in 1939. Newcombe earned a B.Sc. from McMaster University in 1945. She met her husband Alan George Newcombe at McMaster, and they then both went on to earn Doctorates in chemistry from the University of Toronto. After receiving her Ph.D. in 1950, Newcombe never worked full-time as a chemist, due in large part to the fact that, at that time, married women with children were not expected to work. In 1955, the Newcombes moved to the Hamilton area of southern Ontario, where Alan took a job as Director of Research and Development for Porritts & Spencer, a manufacturer of felts for paper making. She also took advantage of her knowledge of several languages, including Czech, German and English, to translate scientific articles. In 1962, she briefly tried teaching high school chemistry, but was dismayed by her students' lack of interest in her subject. The Newcombes founded the Peace Research Institute in Dundas, Ontario in the late 1970s. The Canadian Peace Research and Education Association was also their initiative. They founded and published for many years two scholarly journals: *Peace Research Abstracts* and *Peace Research Reviews*. They also organized summer institutes on peace research at Grindstone Island, located in the Rideau Lakes, which was a center for peace education managed by the Canadian Friends Service

Committee. Hanna was prominent for many decades in the World Federalist Movement, the Canadian Voice of Women, and the Canadian Religious Society of Friends (Quakers). She was also an advocate of mundialization and of twinning. Her writing ranged over many topics, including ruminations on philosophy, religion and the history of science.

George Edward Nowotny, Jr. (1932–), b. Tulsa,, is a retired businessman and politician, who was a three-term Republican State Representative from Fort Smith, Arkansas. Initially elected in 1966 with Winthrop Rockefeller, the first Republican governor of Arkansas since the Reconstruction era, Nowotny left politics in 1972, when he declined to seek a fourth term as a legislator. In 1967, Speaker of the Arkansas House of Representatives Sterling R. Cockrill of Little Rock appointed Nowotny the first ever Minority Leader of the State House. In addition, Rockefeller chose Nowotny as the 'Governor's Representative' on the Arkansas Legislative Council. Nowotny described his political agenda as 'simply good government'. Nowotny led efforts to establish what subsequently became the Booneville Human Development Center, a facility for disabled adults located in Booneville in Logan County. In 1970, Nowotny announced his candidacy for governor but soon withdrew when Rockefeller declared his intention to run again. Nowotny was a delegate to the 1972 Republican National Convention and then managed the Arkansas campaign for President Richard M. Nixon, the first Republican to win the State's electoral votes since 1876.

Oliver Robert Ocasek (1925–1999), born in Bedford, OH, of Czech ancestry, was an American politician of the Democratic Party who served as president of the Ohio State Senate from 1979-81 and serving as Senator from Summit County and the Twenty Seventh District from 1959 until 1986. A former high school principal, he won election over the incumbent Senator Fred Danner in 1958, and again defeated Danner to hold his seat in 1960. In 1962, Ocasek opted to run for Congress against Congressman William H. Ayres, but lost. When Democrats took the majority in the Senate in 1974, Ocasek was elected president pro tempore after serving in lesser leadership roles for a number of years. In 1979, with the Ohio Constitution revised to allow for the majority leader of the Senate to now preside, Ocasek was sworn in as the first president of the Ohio Senate to also be a sitting Senator.

Mildred Otenášek (1914–2012), b. Baltimore, Maryland, of Czech ancestry, an economist, was also a politician. Her name had been synonymous with Women in Democratic politics in Maryland for over 30 years, ever since her selection in 1948 as vice-chairman of the Maryland Democratic Central Committee. For over 20 years, she had served as Democratic National Committeewoman for Maryland, a position she assumed in 1956. She had been a delegate to the five Democratic National Conventions (s. 1968) and a number of committees for these conventions. She was also president of the Central Democratic Club of Maryland (1955–57).

Ralph Perk (1914-1999), b. Cleveland, OH of Bohemian ancestry, was a politician. He was elected to the first of five terms on the Cleveland City Council in 1953; elected County auditor (1962), elected Mayor of Cleveland (1971) as a first Republican in thirty years and was re-elected in 1973 and 1975. He was a three-time chairman of the National Republican Mayors. He served as vice chairman of the platform committee of the Republican National Convention and wrote the Urban Plank in 1976. He served as Presidential Elector for Ohio (1968, 1972, 1980, 1984, 1986) and chairman of Ohio Presidential Electors (1968, 72). He was a member of the Republican National Committee (1976-77) and for eight terms on the Republican State Central and Executive Committee of Ohio. He was a member of the policy board of the advisory council on government for the Republican National Committee (1976-80); National chairman of Czech-Americans for Reagan, Bush 1980 and co-chairman 1984; Ohio chairman of Reagan-Bush (1984); ethnic votes campaign, etc.

Michael Anthony Peroutka (1952-), b. Baltimore, MD, of Czech ancestry. He is a Maryland lawyer, the founder of the Institute on the Constitution. He is a graduate of Loyola College of Maryland and the University of Baltimore School of Law. He has been the chairman of the Constitutional Party and ran for President in the 2004 presidential election. He ran on a platform of 'God, Family, Republic,' emphasizing the Bible, the traditional family, and the need for a more constitutional government in his campaign. He has been a co-host of *The American View* radio program.

Josef Peukert (1855-1910), Albrechtice, Bohemia, was a Bohemian anarchist, known for his autobiographical book *Memoirs from the proletarian revolutionary labor movement*. From the age of six, he worked for his father's company and, by the age of eleven, he was taken out of school. At the age of 16, he left home and worked odd jobs in Germany. Peukert contributed to social democratic workers' associations later becoming an Anarchist communist. In exile in London, Peukert became involved in distributing *Freiheit* published by Johann Most but became increasingly critical of Most as social-revolutionist as opposed to an anarchist. During this time, he became even more radicalized and upon his return in the 1880s, he became the leader of the radical Fraktion, who were believers in the concept of Propaganda of the deed, which calls for the use of terror against society civil rights. In 1881, Peukert became the editor of *Die Zukunft* (The Future), published by Der Rebell, from 1886 to 1893, he was the editor of *Die Autonomie* and co-editor after 1889 of *Der Anarchist*. From 1890, he worked with Emma Goldman for several years in New York City.

Ruth Freedom Pojman (1964-), b. New York City, of Bohemian ancestry, is the daughter of Dr. Louis Paul Pojman and Gertrude Burggraaf, who named her after the Civil Rights Act of 1964. She grew up as a third culture kid living in Denmark, England, France, and the US. She graduated from Univ. of Mississippi, majoring in history (B.A., 1988) and international relations and international communications at The American University, School of International Studies (M.A., 1993); later she earned a certificate in documentary film from GWU (2008), and contributed to PSAs and documentary films, especially on human trafficking, organized crime and migration in the E&E region. She became involved in US-USSR citizen diplomacy exchanges in the '80s and early '90s, and when the iron curtain came down, she worked on civil society and democratization issues throughout the former Soviet Union in the mid-1990s. She worked in Eurasia, developing technical assistance and democracy/human rights programs: for the International Organization for Migration (IOM) on programs supporting the development of migration policy, border control, and anti-trafficking; on raising awareness of issues relating to refugees, political asylum and tolerance for the United Nations High Commissioner for Refugees (UNHCR), in the Kyrgyz Republic; and on media relations for Mobil Oil in Kazakhstan. Upon return to the US, she worked at the USAID Europe and Eurasia Bureau, as the first anti-trafficking advisor, assisting missions in the design of anti-trafficking programs, conducting assessments and research throughout the CIS and SEE. She is currently the deputy coordinator at the Organization for Security and Cooperation in Europe's Office of the Special Representative and coordinator for Combating Trafficking in Human Beings, based in Vienna, Austria. She is one of the leading anti-trafficking experts in the world, having worked on these issues since 1997 and working for the highest-level political personality on the issue working full time on the issue.

Francis Xavier (Frank) Richter, Jr. (1910–1977), b. Keremeos, British Columbia, Canada, of Bohemian father, was a Canadian politician, who served as a member of the Legislative Assembly and Minister of Agriculture and Minister of Mines in the Social Credit government of W.A.C. Bennett in the province of British Columbia. He represented the riding of Similkameen from 1953 to 1966 and its successor riding Boundary-Similkameen from 1966 to 1975.

Victor Rosewater (1871–1940), b. Omaha, NE, of Bohemian parents, a journalist by profession, was also very active politically in the Republican Party. In 1908, he was a delegate-at-large at the Republican National Convention and during 1908 through 1912, a member of the Republican National Committee. In 1912, he was chairman of the National Convention in Chicago. In 1916, he was a member of advisory committee of the Republican National Committee and in 1920, a member of the advisory committee on policies and platform. During WWI, he served on the advisory labor committee of the National Council of Defense and in 1919, he was chairman of the Nebraska Constitutional Convention.

Maria Ruzicka (1976–2005), b. Lakeport, CA, probably of Czech ancestry, was an activist-turned-aid worker. Ruzicka attended Long Island University's Friends World Program, and spent four years traveling throughout Costa Rica, Kenya, Cuba, Israel/Palestine, and Zimbabwe. After graduating in 1999, Ruzicka volunteered for the San Francisco-based organizations Rainforest Action Network and Global Exchange. She developed a unique approach to advocacy for civilian victims of war: she insisted that combatant governments had a legal and moral responsibility to compensate the families of civilians killed or injured in military conflicts. She and her Iraqi translator, Faiz Ali Salim, were killed by a suicide car bombing on Airport Road in Baghdad on April 16, 2005. In 2003, Ruzicka founded the Campaign for Innocent Victims in Conflict (CIVIC), an organization that counted civilian casualties and assisted Iraqi victims of the 2003 US invasion of Iraq. Her organization produced tangible benefits for families of civilian war victims, raised antiwar consciousness, and demonstrated the high cost of modern war (often referred to as 'collateral damage').

Edward H. Sebesta, b. MN, of Czech ancestry, is an anti-neo-Confederate activist and researcher from Dallas, Texas. He has written for a variety of publications, spoken in person, and been quoted as an expert on the movement by several media sources, such as Pacifica Radio and Salon.com. Sebesta's activism includes campaigns to remove historical monuments and statues featuring Confederate generals as well as buildings and parks named after Confederate and southern historical figures. He began his campaign in 1992 when he petitioned the City of Dallas, where he lives, for the removal of a Robert E. Lee statue from a city park. On August 6, 1992 the Dallas City Parks board voted against Sebesta's request by 13 to 0. After this defeat, Sebesta created his website at www.templeofdemocracy.org and began campaigning against Confederate-themed issues. Sebesta's profile increased in the late 1990s when various political personalities began interviewing him on Confederate flag controversies. He was interviewed on Pacifica and the Alan Colmes radio show in 1999 and helped historian James Loewen with research for his book *Lies Across America*. In the early 2000s, he gave more anti-Confederate interviews to groups such as the Southern Poverty Law Center and the Institute for Southern Studies.

John Stafford (1940–2011), b. Parris Island, SC, of Bohemian ancestry on his mother's side, was an American politician and member of the Republican Party from Maryland. He was the Chief Administrative Law Judge for the U.S. Department of the Interior in the first Reagan administration and was a candidate for Senate District 21 in the Maryland Congressional elections, 2006.

Richard W. Stanek (1962–), b. Minneapolis, of Czech ancestry, is a Minnesota Republican politician. He became the 27th Hennepin Co. Sheriff on January 1, 2007. Stanek served from 1986 to 2006 as a police officer in Minneapolis, served from 1995 to 2003 in the Minnesota House of Representatives, and served from 2003 to 2004 as Commissioner of Public Safety under Minnesota Governor Tim Pawlenty.

Harlod Edward Stassen (1907-2001), b. West St. Paul, MN, of Bohemian ancestry, a lawyer and the 25th Governor of Minnesota (1939-43), was a later perennial candidate for other offices, most notably and frequently President of the United States. He was seen as an 'up and comer,' after delivering the keynote address at the 1940 Republican National Convention. At that convention, he helped secure the GOP nomination for Wendell Willkie. Stassen was later best known for being a perennial candidate for the Republican Party nomination for President, seeking it nine times between 1948 and 1992 but never winning it or, after 1952, even coming close. He did receive votes at the Republican National Convention as late as 1968 when he won two votes for president (one from Minnesota and the other from Ohio).

James Taussig (1827-1916), b. Prague, Bohemia, a successful lawyer in St. Louis, was also a politician. Prior to the Civil War, Taussig took an active interest in the political issues and was one of the most ardent supporters of the newly found Republican Party, voting for Fremont in 1850. At the beginning of Pres. Lincoln's administration, he was sent to Washington by the radical Republicans of St. Louis to present to the President resolutions favoring the abolition of slavery. Lincoln, in his session with Taussig, declared the immediate and unconditional emancipation of the slaves to be a suicidal policy, but nevertheless issued his proclamation of emancipation three months later. He was tendered a nomination for Congress in 1862 in district in which nomination was equivalent to election, but he declined in favor of Henry Taylor Blow. He also declined a seat on the bench of the Missouri Supreme Court believing that the post of honor is the private station. Absolute integrity and loyalty to his moral principles and ideals were the essence of his nature.

Jetta Marie Vašák (1927-), b. Chicago, of Czech ancestry, a political and social activist. She attended Morton High School and participated in the band and orchestra there under the direction of Louis M. Blaha and was an excellent French horn player. She played French horn in the Chicago Civic Orchestra for one season while attending Junior College, then graduated with a B.A. from Grinnell College in Iowa in 1950. She was employed as a social worker in California with the Bureau of Public Assistance, in the Aged and the Aid to Dependent Children programs. She also taught 5th to 8th grades and worked a short time at Stanford Research Institute in Palo Alto, California. While married to Alan LeFevre, Jetta was a committed political and social activist: she marched in the Civil Rights Movement in California when the Black Panthers were militant, was active in the anti-Vietnam war movement, active in political demonstrations, worked for justice for the farm workers when Caesar Chavez was trying to unionize, was active in the League of Women Voters, and helped start, then worked for, the Women's and Children's Crisis Shelter in Whittier, California. In addition, Jetta was an original member of the Shelter's Right Hand and spoke to groups to educate them about spousal battering. She has been a one-woman committee to get donations of goods and money for fundraisers, helped run a thrift shop to fund the Shelter, and participated in humorous fashion shows (using clothes from the thrift shop) to support the Shelter. As a political activist, she's worked in party headquarters, working phone banks, walking precincts, explaining propositions, and openly expressing her opinions. She's been a member of the local ACLU board, on the Family Service Board (mental health), on a Mental Health Committee that measured and evaluated the mental health needs of the community (for many years), as well as a Committee on Aging. An ever-selfless daughter and wife, Jetta took care of her mother Zdenka for many years before her death at age 102, and then cared for her husband before his death from Alzheimer's disease. She is widely known to have a quick and informed wit, and spins a bit of thought on diverse topics, mixed with a little humor, wherever she goes.

Anton Bernard Weselak (1918–1989), b. Beausejour, Manitoba, of Czech ancestry, was a Liberal Party member of the Canadian House of Commons. He became a lawyer after studies at the Manitoba Law School. Weselak began a legal practice in Beausejour after his call to the Bar in 1948. He was first elected to Parliament at the Springfield riding in the 1953 general election. After serving only one term, the 22nd Canadian Parliament, he was defeated by Jake Schulz of the Co-operative Commonwealth Federation in the 1957 election. Weselak made a further attempt to win back the seat in the 1958 election but lost to Val Yacula who unseated Schulz. During the 1956 Suez Crisis, Weselak was part of Lester B. Pearson's delegation to the United Nations. Pearson was then External Affairs Minister under the Louis St. Laurent government, and his efforts led to the formation of United Nations peacekeeping force which defused a full-scale Middle Eastern War. In the years before his retirement in 1985, Weselak was a Toronto-based immigration appeal court judge.

Louis W. "Lou" Zaeske, Jr. (1941–2011), b. St. Antonio, TX, of Czech descent, was a mechanical engineer and a political activist in Bryan, Texas. Zaeske was heavily involved in the promotion of Czech heritage groups. He frequently made public presentations on the migration of the Czech peoples from Eastern Europe. Zaeske helped found the Texas Polka Music Museum in Schulenburg. In 1988, he founded the interest group, the American Ethnic Coalition, which lobbied for English as the official language of the United States. The American Ethnic Coalition claimed that twenty-three members of the Texas State Legislature and four U.S. representatives from Texas, all of whom were elected with coalition backing and took office in 1989, were committed to Official English. Zaeske's organization called for abolition of the printing of literature in Spanish by the Texas Workforce Commission and allowing public school districts to reject bilingual education programs. Zaeske urged that Texas Comptroller Bob Bullock be required to report to the legislature on taxpayer costs of bilingual programs and that Attorney General Jim Mattox rule on the constitutionality of such measures. Zaeske's coalition proposed that foreign instructors in Texas public colleges, many of whom teach basic courses at universities, be required to pass an English proficiency test.

H. Zionists

Samuel Bettelheim (1872–1942), b. Bratislava, Slovakia, was an Orthodox journalist and Zionist. He studied at the renowned yeshiva in his native city. In 1897, he was among the founders and the president of the first legally recognized Zionist society in Hungary, the Yagdil Torah Society, renamed Ahavat Tsiyon in 1899. Although its members were hesitant to call themselves Zionists, Rabbi Simḥah Bunem Sofer permitted students from the yeshiva to join and thus eased their way. Bettelheim was the official representative of Hungarian Jewry at the third Zionist Congress in 1899. Subsequently, he assembled the first temporary Hungarian Zionist Committee (with Theodor Herzl as president), which worked until 1904, and later the first Hungarian Zionist Congress, held in Pozsony in 1902. Bettelheim actively participated in the Hungarian Zionist Society of Budapest in 1902–1903 and the First Hungarian Zionist Congress in 1903 in Bratislava. In 1904, Rabbi Yitsḥak Ya'akov Reines commissioned him to be one of the organizers of the First World Congress of the Mizraḥi movement. Between 1904 and 1907, Bettelheim led the Association of Hungarian Zionists (known as the Hungarian Zionist Organization after 1906). In 1908, he founded the *Pressburger jüdische Zeitung* and later the weekly *Ungarländische Jüdische Zeitung*, published in Budapest, which he also edited until 1915; these periodicals advocated Jewish nationalism. In 1915, the government commissioned Bettelheim to lecture in America about the federal system of the Austro-Hungarian monarchy, in support of the Central Powers. He returned to Hungary in 1917 and enlisted in the army; later, he worked in the government's press office. By that time, Bettelheim had distanced himself from Zionism and had come close to the viewpoint of Agudas Yisroel. In 1920, he founded Aguda's central periodical *Die jüdische Presse* in Bratislava and served as its editor. Later, he returned to the United States and published the *Jewish Weekly Bulletin*. Between 1934 and 1937, Bettelheim published the literary and scholarly periodical *Judaica* in Bratislava.

Sara (Abeles) Blum (1910–1986), b. Newark, New Jersey, of Bohemian ancestry, became active in the Conference of Christians and Jews of Essex County to better fight anti-Semitism. She also joined the Black Urban League to improve race relations. A staunch Zionist, Blum founded the South Orange-Maplewood Chapter of Hadassah and committed herself to getting European Jewish children to Palestine. Moving on to become regional president of the Northern New Jersey Region of Hadassah, she was responsible for membership doubling in one year and raising $35,000 at the first donor luncheon. By the early 1940s, Blum was a leader in the United Jewish Appeal (UJA) in Essex County, one of the largest giving regions in the nation. She had also become a partner in Camp Nawita, a girls' camp on Paradox Lake in New York. In 1946, she ascended to the presidency of the Essex County UJA's Women's Division. It had 15,000 members, but Blum sought still more. Women's Division members responded magnificently to her call. Records indicate they contributed more than three times as much to UJA as they had the year before. Blum went on to become a national vice chairman of the UJA Women's Division, her faithful service interrupted only slightly when she left Nawita and purchased Navarac in 1952. She was elected chairman of the Women's Service Group of the Jewish Community Council of Essex County in 1956 and ultimately became vice president of the entire Council. A year later she was named to the National Council of the Joint Distribution Committee, and in 1957, co-chaired the program committee for the 26th General Assembly of the Council of Jewish Federations in New Orleans. In 1958, she was named 'Woman of the Year' by the Betty Chodokowsky Memorial for Crippling Diseases.

Rabbi Louis D. Brandeis (1856–1941), b. Louisville, KY, of Bohemian parents, was an American lawyer and Associate Justice of the Supreme Court of the US. (1916–39). Louis Brandeis was not active in the Zionist movement until he was in his late fifties. He was elected Chair of the Provisional Committee for General Zionist Affairs in 1914 and opened the New England Zionist Office with his own money. While he was a Justice of the Supreme Court, he continued to support the Zionist movement, but as a Supreme Court justice, he was restricted from maintaining his other leadership roles. However, he advised President Franklin D. Roosevelt on Jewish issues and helped establish Ein Hashofet ("well of the judge"), the first American-established Kibbutz in Palestine in 1937. Throughout his life and in his will, many of his charitable donations supported Zionist causes.

Rabbi James G. Heller (1892–1971), b. New Orleans, of Bohemian father, was a leader of Reform Judaism, Rabbi and the American Zionist. He served as a Rabbi at Little Rock, AR (1919–20) and then as a Rabbi at Isaac M. Wise Temple, Cincinnati (1920–50). He also excelled as a composer.

Rabbi Maximilian H. Heller (1860–1929), b. Prague, Bohemia, was a leader in Reform Judaism and an early Zionist leader. He served as a Rabbi of Temple Sinai in New Orleans (1887–1927) and as a professor of Hebrew language and literature at Tulane University (1912–28).

Emil Jacoby (orig. Jakubovics) (1923–), b. Čop, Slovakia; activist with Bnei Akiva, illegal Zionist organization in Europe; eventually immigrated to US where he got his training in education; appointed director of education at Valley Jewish Community Center (later becoming Adat Ari El) (1953–76), executive director of the Bureau of Jewish Education of Greater Los Angeles (1976–1993).

Sarah Kussy (1869-1956), b. Newark, NJ, of Bohemian ancestry, was an educator and community worker, was raised in one of the most established Jewish families in Newark, NJ. She attended public school, and then went on to New York University's Extension School, and the Jewish Theological Seminary's Teachers' Institute. Kussy taught for over thirty-five years in both public and Hebrew schools in the Newark area. She was also part of an early twentieth-century network of influential American Jewish women committed to advancing Judaism, women's roles in Jewish life, and Zionism. With other members of this group, she helped to found Hadassah and the National Women's League of the United Synagogue of America (now the Women's League of Conservative Judaism). She remained active in both of these organizations throughout her life, filling many local, regional and national positions. Kussy's commitment to Zionism also led her to help create the American Jewish Congress and Young Judea. She served as a delegate to the Jewish Agency for Palestine and to five World Zionist Congresses. One recognition, she received was for her work in the Jewish state was the Sarah Kussy Forest, planted by Hadassah in 1950, containing ten thousand trees.

Ruth Goldsmith Kunzer (1915-2005), b. Prague, Bohemia, but raised in Germany. When Hitler came to power, she escaped with her family to England. In 1937, Ruth's Zionist affiliation began when she joined the staff of the Jewish Agency for Palestine in London where she worked with the leaders of the Palestine Jewish community, including David Ben Gurion and Moshe Sharett. In 1945, Ruth made her home in Israel as a Public Relations Officer of the Weizmann Institute of Science. In Israel's War of Liberation in 1948, she was a war correspondent attached to the Israeli Army, and later appointed press officer of the Government of Israel. In 1950, as the Director of Public Affairs of Israel's Consulate General in New York, Ruth was heard weekly over New York radio on "Life in Israel." In Los Angeles, Ruth completed her formal education which had been disrupted by Hitler, graduating summa cum laude from California State University, Northridge. She was professor of Jewish literature and history at Hebrew Union Coll., Los Angeles, CA.

Rabbi Morris Mandel (1875-d.), b. Biel, Slovakia; rabbi; rabbi of Congregation Adas Israel, Washington, DC (1898-1901); Beth Israel Congregation, Atlantic City, NJ (1901-03); vice president, Federation of American Zionists (1899-1900); resided in Allentown, PA.

William R. Perl (1906-1998), b. Prague, Bohemia, a retired Army Lieutenant Colonel and Holocaust survivor and scholar, was the founder of the Washington branch of the Jewish Defense League who organized a little-known rescue effort that smuggled thousands of Jews out of Nazi-occupied Europe and into Palestine in the late 1930s and 40s. Although Dr. Perl's exploits in wartime Europe were frequently honored abroad, he was better known in the United States as a spokesman for militant Jewish causes and a leader of protests and demonstrations at the old Soviet Embassy in Washington. The militant Jewish Defense League targeted the Soviet Embassy to symbolize its fight for the emigration rights of Russian Jews. He won citations from President Ronald Reagan and Congress and numerous humanitarian service awards. In 1990, he was honored in Israel during a 50th anniversary reunion of the passengers of the *Sakarya*, a ship he chartered that carried 2,175 Jewish refugees from Constanta, Romania, to Palestine. He had been a militant Zionist since his school days. In the 1930s, Dr. Perl, a follower of militant Zionist Revisionist Vladimir Ze'ev Jabotinsky, was a young Jewish lawyer and teacher in Vienna. Realizing what Adolf Hitler's rise to power meant, he began organizing the voyages to Palestine in the 1930s. Despite being questioned and threatened by German officers, he continued with the clandestine voyages, using cattle boats and ramshackle freighters. In other cases, bribes were paid, and forged documents were used because Britain stopped the legal immigration of Jews into Palestine in 1939. In 1971, Dr. Perl formed the Washington branch of the Jewish Defense League and became enmeshed in a number of controversial incidents. He was arrested and convicted on charges of conspiring to shoot into the Prince George's County apartments of two Soviet Embassy officials in 1976. The conspiracy conviction was later overturned on appeal, but he was sentenced to three years' probation for illegal receipt of a firearm and attempting to damage property.

Oskar K. Rabinowicz (1902–1969), b. Vienna, of Bohemian ancestry, was a Zionist historian, lecturer and author of many books. Rabinowicz attended the nearby University of Brno and then Charles University in Prague, where he received a Doctorate in philosophy in 1924. As a student, he became involved with the Zionist movement, having attended the Twelfth Zionist Congress in 1921 as an aide to Naḥum Sokolow. In 1924, Rabinowicz moved to Brno, where he became a correspondent for the *Jüdische Volkstimme*, edited by Max Hickl; he wrote regular columns on Zionist and cultural issues until the newspaper's demise in 1932. He also wrote for *Selbstwehr, Židovské zpravy*, and *Tagesbote aus Böhmen*. One of the longer articles on Zionist Revisionism indicated the direction of his interest in Jewish nationalism. When Vladimir Jabotinsky organized a new party, the Union of Zionist Revisionists, Rabinowicz became one of his most ardent disciples after 1923. Rabinowicz established the Czechoslovak branch of the Revisionist Party, and in 1929 was sent by Jabotinsky to London to work for the party's central executive. He remained there for two years. At his father's request, he then went to Berlin to study for the rabbinate at the Hochschule für die Wissenschaft des Judentums. He was ordained in 1933 but never practiced as a rabbi, although he gave occasional sermons at the Pinkas synagogue in Prague. Throughout the 1930s, Rabinowicz lectured widely in central and Eastern Europe on behalf of Revisionist Zionism. In addition to serving on the executive of Jabotinsky's New Zionist Organization, he was a member of the Zionist Actions Committee of the Jewish Agency and was chairman of the Committee to Boycott Nazi Germany. Rabinowicz helped organize emigration to Palestine and continued to write, publishing three books in the 1930s. In 1934, he founded the weekly *Medina Iwrit-Judenstaat* (The Jewish State), which he edited until it ceased publication in 1939. After 1939, he and his family fled to London. His activism, however, declined, especially after the founding of Israel, to be replaced by efforts on behalf of Jewish and Israeli charities and causes. In 1956, he moved to the United States, where he died in 1969.

Imrich Vitzak Rosenberg (1913-1986), b. Nové Mesto and Váhom, Slovakia; lawyer, activist, Zionist, realtor, in exile he resided in Ottawa, Canada. r. Imrich Yitzhak Rosenberg. From the book, *A Jew In Deed*, "he called three quite different parts of the world home: Central Europe, Israel, and Canada. Born in Austria-Hungary, he grew up in the newly created Czechoslovakia. From his youth, he was a busy participant in the growing Zionist movement and in the protection of the Jews in Europe. Rosenberg's fruitful labor on behalf of Jews during and shortly after the Second World War in Europe is the subject of this book. The story is told by Dr. Rosenberg himself, who in 1971 used both primary documentation and his own memory of the Soviet Jewish Anti-Fascist Committee, to which he was a delegate on behalf of the government of Czechoslovakia and the World Jewish Congress, 1944-45, for a Political Science thesis at Carleton University. In the second part, Corey Goldman, a graduate of the Journalism program at Carleton, chronicles, Rosenberg's achievement in connection with the rescue of 301 orphaned children from the Theresienstadt concentration camp in 1945. The extent of Rosenberg's continued dedication to the protection and rehabilitation of the lives and heritage of Jews in Slovakia and elsewhere during his later years in Israel and Canada, is revealed in the Biographical Survey provided by his long-time wife, partner, and friend, Dr. Truda Rosenberg."

Edward R. Rubovits (1840-1905), b. Šebastovce (Sebes), Slovakia, was son of Isaac Rubovits and Salie Klein, a Jewish communal worker and a Zionist. He was educated at Sebes and Prešov public and private schools. While still in Hungary, he was a teacher (1860-66). After coming to America, he was in book, stationery, and printing business, Chicago (1867-96). He became Superintendent of the United Hebrew Charities. He was Director of Cleveland Jewish Orphan Asylum; member Executive Committee, National Conference of Charities and Corrections, 1904. Member Executive Committee, Independent Order of B'nai B'rith (1885-1900); was vice-president Zion Congregation and Isaiah Temple: past master Chicago Lodge, No. 437, Ancient Free and Accepted Masons; member Committee on Russian Refugees (1881-1882). He resided in Chicago.

Rosa Sonneschein (1847-1932), b. Prostějov, Moravia, a rebbetzin and journalist, as one of the best-known society women in St. Louis, a prominent figure in literary circles, and an active worker in the field of charity, independent of creed or nationality. In 1879, she founded the Pioneers, a Jewish women's literary society. Modeled on similar Christian women's clubs, the Pioneers devoted themselves not to studying Jewish literature but to cultivating general literary taste and knowledge. In 1895 (through 1899), she founded the *American Jewess*, the first English-language magazine for Jewish women in the US, to be voice and forum for American Jewish women. Throughout the run of the magazine, Sonneschein was an advocate for the expansion of women's role in the synagogue and the Jewish community. She pushed Temple Isaiah, Chicago to become the world's first synagogue to admit women to full membership without restrictions. She was also among the US first Zionists and advocated for Zionism in the *American Jewess* pages. She viewed Zionism as a potential source of relief for oppressed Jews in Eastern Europe and a source of pride and countermeasure to assimilation for Jews in America and Eastern Europe.

Henrietta Szold (1860-1945), b. Baltimore, MD, of Slovak ancestry; Jewish Zionist leader and founder of Hadassah, the Women's Zionist organization of America. After studying at the Jewish Theological Seminary, she served as executive secretary of the Jewish Publication Society's publications committee, editing and publishing many important works of Jewish history. But her greatest accomplishment was the creation of Hadassah, the women's Zionist organization of the United States. Under her direction, Hadassah became the largest and most powerful Zionist group in the United States, fundraising and setting up hospitals, food banks, nursing schools, and social work programs. Szold's work helped create the medical, educational, and social service infrastructure that helped turn the dream of a Jewish state into a workable reality. During the 1930s, she spearheaded Youth Aliyah, helping Jewish children leave Nazi Germany for Palestine.

Zvi Weinberg (1935-2006), b. Brekov, Czech, was a politician, Zionist, advocate for peace in Middle East, and educator. Weinberg emigrated to Canada and developed there his academic career. He held a Ph.D. in French Literature, chaired academic seminars on Zionist thought and served as deputy chairman of the "Canadian Professors for Peace in the Middle East" organization. Weinberg made Aliyah to Israel in 1992 and joined public actions to encourage immigration of the Soviet Jewry to the State of Israel. He was a founding member of the political party "Yisrael BaAliyah" and was placed on its list of candidates for the 1996 Knesset elections. He served as a member of the Knesset for Yisrael BaAliyah between 1996 and 1999.

Stephen S. Wise (1874-1949), b. Budapest, of Slovak ancestry, was a Reform rabbi and Zionist leader. Wise founded the American Jewish Congress in 1920, became president of the Zionist Organization of America in 1936, and continued to play a key role in the US Jewish community for the rest of his life.

I. Socialists & Radicals

František Choura (1852–1921), b. Bohutin, Bohemia. As a twenty-four-year-old, he delivered speeches and agitated for the Party among the miners. He was chased out from one place to another and was frequently jailed. He came to America in in 1887, settling in Cleveland and later in Woodville, PA, where he found work in his field – mining. The last years he devoted his time to the development of the Czech-Slovak Protective Society in Pennsylvania. He died in Boyerton, PA. He was one of the witnesses and participants in the Pačes drama. After the arrest of Josef Pačes, Josef Rampas and Kryštof Černý, he escaped to America. On him rested a terrible suspicion of having informed on his comrades. The events of the last years, however, fully exonerated Choura. Choura was a member of the National Bohemian Committee which published the periodical *Bohemian Voice*.

Gustav Haberman (1864–1932), b. Česká Třebová, Bohemia, leader of the Czech Social Democrats. Sentenced to three years in prison in Vienna for secret society, he then went to Paris and later to Spain, where he earned his living as a photographer. From 1901, he lived in Pilsen, where he led the Social Democratic Party and was editor-in-chief of the "Nové Doby". From 1907, he was a member of the Reichsrat. At the beginning of the First World War, he fled to Switzerland and helped Masaryk organize the national resistance. After the founding of the Czechoslovak Republic, he was elected to parliament and was Minister of Education and Social Affairs several times.

Bernard Herc (1858–d.), b. Maččice, Bohemia, was Leo Kochmann's comrade and collaborator. He received training in Austria as an organ player. He left for Italy to gain experience and remained there for 3 years. He landed in New York in 1878. He worked in factories manufacturing pianos. He soon left his trade and became a business spokesman for newspapers. Ha became active as a journalist and also literary editor. Together with Kochmann, they founded the weekly periodical *Proletář* (Proletarian) in New York. Because of the weekly's low effectiveness, they established a corporation to publish *Hlas Lidu*. Habenicht referred to Herc, whom he considered a key player, as a Bohemian Jew and anarchist. In 1893, the Czech social socialist party was split, the break apparently caused by Herc and Kochmann. They renounced anarchism and declared the *Hlas Lidu* to be a social democratic paper. The Czech anarchism was on the decline since that time. Later in life, Herc apparently abandoned his radical activities entirely and devoted his energies to more conventional work. For a number of years, he was on the staff of political court in New York where he started as an interpreter of Slavic languages, German and Italian.

Frank Hlaváček (1853–1921), b. Řenčov, Bohemia, on the editorial staff of the Chicago daily *Svornost* (Justice), began life as a miner. Having had a certain degree of newspaper training at home, Hlavacek from the outset (he came to New York about 1887) gave himself wholly to journalism. With several friends, he set up in New York in 1893 the *Dělnické Listy*, the publisher of which was nominally the International Workingmen's Union. By common consent, the *Dělnické Listy* was regarded as the organ of revolutionary socialists. For want of support, the paper was forced to give up its existence in New York. It was removed to Cleveland, where under the editorship of V. Kudlata, it finally went under. Disillusioned, Hlaváček quit New York and went to Chicago. There he returned to his old allegiance - social democracy. With the downfall of the *Dělnické Listy*, the radical wing of social democrats lost its greatest support. Thereafter the decline, of this faction in New York was raid and its ultimate break-up inevitable. Among other small things, Hlaváček published a collection of workingmen's songs in Czech, *The Torch* (214 p.) and a rhymed narrative of the Creation, "accurately according to the version of the Bible."

Frank Janota, a tailor, became, in the eyes of the law, Pačes' accomplice, after the fact, because he had a guilty knowledge of the existence of Pačes' unlicensed printing shop and had omitted to inform the police. Janota saved himself from arrest by a hurried flight to Switzerland. From the Swiss Republic, he went to London and there, he published sheets which he called *Pomsta* (Revenge) and *Revoluce* (Revolution). Reaching New York some time in 1894, he became associated with the *Volné Listy*, remaining at the head of this paper for about five years. Janota signed his articles with the pseudonym 'Rebel.'

Ladimír Klácel (orig. František Matouš) (1808-1882), b. Česká Trebová, Bohemia, a Czech patriot, philosopher, and journalist, is usually grouped with Freethinkers. However, he was also a devoted, although unrealistic socialist, bordering on communism. Toward the close of his life, he turned mystic and visionary. Klácel's pet scheme was the organization in the Middle West, i.e., Black Hills country in South Dakota, of Svojanov communities composed of his followers, who should work the land on the cooperative basis. Fortunately, none of his communities of which he dreamed were realized. Svojanovy were to be built on the basis of science and general love. Klácel's conception of Svojanovy was rather unrealistic and romantic. Among other, children up to one year of age were to be put into common asylum, school and teaching. Canteen, kitchen, laundry, etc., were to be joint. The village should not have any churches and none of the members, whom Klacel called 'Osvojenci' were to belong to any superstitious group which would not be in agreement with the spirit of the Osvojenci. Everybody in the village had a guaranteed sustenance from his assigned task and according to desserts.

Leo Kochmann (1847-1919), b. Nový Strašec, Bohemia, was one of the first fugitive socialists to arrive in America, who escaped on the eve of going to jail to serve a sentence for active participation in the St. Margaret's Congress. Frank Škarda, who at that time

(1882) was looking about for an editor, promptly gave Kochmann employment on the *Dělnické Listy*. From this time on until he retired from journalism (1913), Kochmann resided in New York uninterruptedly, and colony of social democrats in that city came to regard him as one of its strong men. Possessing but an elementary education, diffident as a speaker, upright, but in his earlier years inclined to be fanatical, Kochmann was tolerably well posted on the aums and literature of social democracy.

William (Vilém) Kroužilka (1878–d.), a student from Prague, was the youngest refugee among the young. When, in 1895, he became a member of *Pokrok* in New York, this student was only 17 or 18 years old. He was considered a ready debater and clever newspaper reporter. The party has never had a fiery orator like him. Despite his youth, he rose quickly to prominence in the party. In Chicago, whether he went from New York, he published creditable pamphlets, one of which was *Life of Darwin*. He also wrote *Dozvuky nedavnych dob* (Reviberations of Recent Past) (96p.), from the times of the Spanish-American War, and *Trním života* (Thru thornts of life), episodes from American life (81p.). He died in Chicago.

Václav Kudlata (1871–d.), a student of theology in Bohemia, arrived in the US in 1893. He became a member the *Pokrok* newspaper and in 1896 he became editor of *Dělnické Listy*. He then moved with his paper to Cleveland in 1898, where, with its 5th annual volume, the periodical became extinct. In a public disputation with Rev. Prout, he proved to be a bold orator with excellent knowledge of Bible. By some, he was considered an anarchist. For a short time, he a was a business director of Národní budova (National Hall) in New York. He delivered in 1897 a lecture on the occasion of the tenth anniversary of the death of the "Chicago Martyrs," which was that year published by *Dělnické Listy* printed in pamphlet form, under the heading *After Ten Years*. Another brochure by Kudlata was entitled *Half-hearted and Whole Liberalism* (1897). Kudlata died in 1917, at Elizabeth, New Jersey. He also authored *Komunistický anarchismus a marxistický socialismu*s.

Joseph Martínek (1889–1980), b. Poděbrady, Bohemia, immigrated to the US in 1912. In 1912, Martinek became editor of one of Cleveland's Czech-language newspapers, *Americké Dělnické Listy*. Martínek also became actively involved in Cleveland's social and political spheres. He became a leader of the Workers Gymnastic Union, a Czech-American social and political organization. Martínek also ran for political office, including Cuyahoga County Commissioner in 1926, for the Ohio General Assembly in 1928, and the Cleveland City Council in 1929 and 1933. Campaigning on a socialist platform, Martínek lost all of these elections. During World War I, he enlisted in the Czechoslovakian Foreign Legion. In 1934, he returned to Czechoslovakia to publish another daily paper, *Právo Lidu*. Martínek fled from Czechoslovakia, following the German takeover of the Sudetenland in 1938. Upon returning to the United States in 1938, Martínek remained active in Czech-

American organizations. From 1939 to 1945, he served as executive secretary of the Czechoslovak National Council in Chicago.

Leo Meilbek (1850–1883), b. Čejč, Moravia, a cabinet-maker by trade, was a leading novice of socialism in Chicago. He was a self-made man. Through self-education, he attained a position of subordinated official in Chicago Public Library. In 1878, he was nominated and elected to the Legislature of the State of Illinois, presumably the first of his nationality. He ran on the Workingmen's Socialist ticket. Suffering from incurable diseases, he ended his life by killing himself.

Jacob Mikolanda (1851–1907), b. Tabor, Bohemia, a baker, joined the labor movement in Vienna. He immigrated to the US in 1882 or 1883. Since 1883, he became one of the leaders in Chicago. He became connected with the Chicago *Budoucnost,* and when this radical paper was forced to the wall, he wrote for the *Právo Lidu* (People's Rights), a weekly of more moderate tone than the *Budoucnost.* After the events on the Haymarket Square, he got into the conflict with the authority. For alleged complicity in the Haymarket affair, Mikolanda was sent to the workhouse for six months. His death occurred in Cleveland, where he moved with his family. By that time, he was not active at all in the labor movement. He was dissatisfied with the peaceful socialism in which he saw a compromise. He was a person of simple mind, of simple, who when inspired by an idea, devoted all his energy to it, but in its previous purity.

Edward Milý (1858–1923), b. Bohemia, was a typesetter. From his earliest age, he was infected with the idea of the fighting proletariat. He wrote and printed proclamations and pamphlets which he secretly disseminated. He edited the paper *Proletář* (Proletarian). He was expelled from Bohemia and later from Vienna as a political undesirable. He moved to Budapest, removing in 1854 to London. Later he came to New York. He as the founder and zealous member of the group of 'Bezvládí' (Anarchy) and of the periodical *Volné Listy* (Free News), to which he sent his contributions (1890–93). He wrote under various pseudonyms i.e., Emily, Emil, Nemilý, and Y. He had also written several pamphlets. He died in New York at the age of 52.

Anthony 'Tony" Novotný (1886–1932), b. Královský Městec, Bohemia, occupied a responsible function in the party. After coming to the US in 1906, he settled in Chicago, where he was elected a secretary of the Czech branch of Social Democratic Party. After the comrade Huettler got sick, he was called in in his place as an editor of *Americké Dělnické Listy.* He also worked for the Chicago *Spravedlnos,* dedicated to the cause of workingmen. In New York, where he then moved, he edited the periodical *Práce,* the Czech organ of

Amalgamated Clothing Workers in America. During the War, he was an ardent worker in the liberation movement of Czechoslovakia.

Joseph (Josef) Pačes (1856-1909), b. Horni Stromka u Starych Strasnic, Prague, was a Czech bricklayer, journalist, socialist, anarchist and activist. He was a simple workman, whom social and national wrongs had made a rebel - rebel against society and state. He was a member of the socialist and workers' movement in Prague, later arrested and convicted of left-wing activities, and imprisoned for a total of 17 years. He was one of the first, most prominent and also the longest imprisoned Czech anarchists. T. Capek referred to him as the 'Czech Jean Valjean.' While Jean Valjean stole a loaf of bread and for this was sent to the galleys, Pačes did not steal, cheat or rob. He was a political criminal, though a desperate one, according to the Austrian police. At the beginning of 1882, he was first arrested and imprisoned for banned left-wing association activity for 14 months in prison. After his release, he and his family were deported from Prague. However, he did not slowdown in socialist activities, moved to Liberec to set up a secret printing press for newspapers and leaflets. He came into contact with local left-wing workers' associations, mostly from local textile factories, and from socialism, he gradually radicalized to anarchism. In this form of periodicals or leaflets, Pačes printed a number of texts concerning working conditions and exploitation by their employers. He bought a cottage in the village of Hluboká near Liberec, where he made a living as a shoemaker and where he moved the printer. Later, he was helped by two other men, Kryštof Černý and Josef Rampas. In 1885, Josef Pačes and the anarchist Kryštof Černý were arrested in Pačes' house directly during the crime. Later, Rampas was also detained. During the house search, a number of publications were seized, including the magazine *Budoucnost* published by Czech anarchists in Chicago. In a subsequent trial held in November 1885 in Prague, Pačes, as the main organizer of the press group, was sentenced to 16 years in prison for anti-state activities and violations of the press law with an order every 3 months of the year in solitary confinement. Black and Rampas were sentenced to 15 and 10 years in prison. His mental state subsequently began to deteriorate, he went mad, and he became obsessed with the paranoia that the guards were trying to poison him. In September 1899, less than a year before his release, he attacked the warden, who entered his cell, with a stick with a shoemaker's nail inserted, for which he was sentenced the following year to another three years in prison. After beating the guards, his deformed face remained on the left side of his face, apparently, he could not see with his left eye afterwards. Pačes left the prison in 1902. He eventually left for the US. He first reached Cleveland, where he was supported by the local Czech anarchist community, but then became independent. He was employed in various parts of the American Midwest for wage construction and excavation activities, mostly in a tent camp. He died in Mitchell, Nebraska, at the age of 52.

Leo (Lev) J. Palda (1847–1913), b. Vodňany, Bohemia, is often called the father of Czech socialism in the US. He arrived in New York in 1867 as a journeyman weaver. In spite of his meager formal education, he was a cultured man and soon decided to become a journalist. While in New York, he edited the first attempted Czech newspaper that was called *Lucerna*. Subsequently, he assumed in Chicago the editorship of *Národní Listy* and proclaimed that it will be an 'official spokesman of the working class.' In 1875, together with Frank Škarda, he founded in Cleveland *Dělnické Listy* (The Workmen's News), the motto of the paper being 'Equal duties equal rights' and announced that the paper is being published as the organ of Socialist Workingmen's Party in the US. What Socialist Party it referred to or who the members of the party were was not made clear. In 1877, the *Dělnické Listy* was moved to NYC with the hope that the metropolis would offer to a Socialist paper a wider influence than Cleveland. Palda was an eloquent speaker, an independent thinker and indefatigable organizer. Back in New York, he started organizing Socialist clubs among the Czech-Slavic International Workingmen's Assn. of NY. However, he was neither a communist nor a revolutionary. He believed that the social and economic order was unjust. Yet he held the view that society had its power to purge itself no revolution but by evolution. More radical element repudiated him, and some called him a reactionary. He was an idealist and humanist. In 1902, he wrote a remarkable booklet *Myšlenkv o novém náboženství* (Thoughts on a New Religion) in which the thinking man sets out to analyze his creed and not satisfied with evasion, he demands solution of the perplexing problem of religion. He arrives at the conclusion that mere non-belief negativity is not enough. 'I learned by the exposition of my faith, partly to ease my troubled mind, partly, if possible, to assist in approaching regeneration of our liberal party. I see this possible only in a new religion which shall embrace all our desires, all our ideals, our teachings, our views.' His New Religion pleased neither the rationalists nor the old-fashioned believers. Palda's last years were spent in Cedar Rapids, IA, where he operated a small cigar factory.

Joseph Boleslav Pecka (1849–1897), a moulder by trade, as a young man, took part in the workers' movement, then still national. In the beginnings of the 1870s, Pecka was one of those Czech workers who established a small socialist group in Bohemia, and later on, the Czechoslovak Social-Democratic Party. This young movement was persecuted by the government and Pecka was often imprisoned. In 1882, he became an editor of *Dělnické Listy* in Vienna, but at the beginning of 1884, upon the proclamation of a state emergency, he was expelled from Vienna. In April of that year, he and František Hlaváček established the social-democratic paper *Duch Času*. He made his appearance in Chicago in 1884 and took up the editorship of *Budoucnost*. He stayed at this paper until extinction in 1886. Subsequently, he became editor of the Chicago paper *Práce* (Work) and the local *Dělnické Listy*. Later on, he worked at Matejka's *Chicažské Listy* and the *Právo Lidu* and then the *Hlas*

Svobody and finally he wrote for Geringer's *Duch Času*. Pecka, for more than a quarter of century, worked in the interest of working people who then left him alone in poverty. He was also active in literature.

Frank (František) Škarda (1848–d.), nr. Strakonice, Bohemia, was a publisher of De*lnicke Listy* (Workingmen's News) which he founded, together with Palda in Cleveland in 1875. After finishing several years of Real School, his stepfather made him get training in trade. He arrived in New York in 1868/69, where he learned cigarmaking. In Cleveland, he got acquainted with Palda, where he went to find work. In 1875, together with Palda, he founded the first workingsmen's paper in America - *Dělnické Listy*. He put all of his savings in it. In 1877, they moved the paper to New York where it became extinct. Škarda lost everything. Impoverished, he moved to La Grange, TX, where he remained until he died, making living with cigar making. He was hated by his fellow-tradesmen in New York, but they were afraid of him. When his paper went bankrupt, his enemies rejoiced. He was capable of debating with unusual keenness and conviction. However, he never acquired the journalistic skills, the area in which his wife, Anna Landova from Cleveland, the first Czech-American female editor, got ahead of him. The Socialists nominated Škarda for the position of Lt. Governor but failed to elect him. Generally speaking, it could be said that Škarda was a man of solid principles, which in those days was a rarity.

Norbert Zoula (1854–1886), b. Štýrský Hradec, was a silversmith from Prague. He spent a year and a half in an Austrian prison awaiting trial. After finishing sentence of the months, he repaired to Switzerland, from which country he immigrated to the US. After a comparatively short stay in New York, he proceeded to Chicago to edit in that city the *Budoucnost* (Future), organ of anarchists in the Czech language. The vigorous police censorship which followed the Chicago Haymarket outbreak forced this journal, like many other anarchist papers, to suspend. In the same year, Zoula died in California of tuberculosis, the common malady of the proletariat.

J. Environmentalists & Conservationists

Marion Rombauer Becker (1903–1976), b. St. Louis, MO, of Slovak descent; author and illustrator. She was the co-author with her mother, Irma von Starkloff Rombauer, of the *Joy of Cooking*, first published in 1931, elected by the New York Public Library as one of the 150 most important and influential books of the 20th century. Published by her mother, Marion is best known for the cookbook's illustrations. The friendly, chatty style cookbook is considered as the best-selling cookbook of all time. A prominent Cincinnatian, Becker also worked as an art teacher and later at *Women's Wear Daily*. She was one of the founders of Cincinnati's Modern Art Society and became the Society's first professional director.

Also, a gardener and an environmentalist, she was a pioneer in natural gardening and wrote *Wild Wealth* which chronicled her woodland garden at the family's estate. Becker received the Oak Leaf Award from the Nature Conservancy and the prestigious Medal of Merit from the Garden Club of America. Before her death in 1976, she was recipient of the Greatest Living Cincinnatian Award.

Marian Sulzberger Dryfoos Heiskell (1918-2019), b. New York, NY, of Bohemian ancestry, was a newspaper executive and civic worker. She is a lifelong conservationist, and a leader in numerous public and philanthropic activities. She was a member of the Board of Directors of The New York Times Company from (1963-97), and also served as its director of special activities from 1963 to 1977. She was a citizen founder of Gateway National Recreation Area and is chairman of the National Parks of New York Harbor Conservancy. She is a former trustee of Consolidated Edison Company of New York, Inc. and a former director of Ford Motor Company and Merck & Co., Inc. Mrs. Heiskell and her late husband, Andrew Heiskell, a former chairman of Time Inc., hold many honors, including being recognized in November of 1999 as 'Living Landmarks' by The New York Landmarks Conservancy for their efforts towards preserving New York City. In recognition of her years of service to the city and her efforts to make its neighborhoods green, vital and more humane, the Marian S. Heiskell Garden was opened in September 1997.

Ed Komarek (1948-), b. nr. Thomasville, GA, of Czech ancestry, was born into a family of early ecologists and associates who understood the important role fire played in global ecosystems. He is a longtime UFO/ET investigator and activist having been involved in the field for forty years. In 2012, he published *UFOs Exopolitics and the New World Disorder* that is free on its website. He also was mentored by the best ecologists in the world in his youth as to the importance of light fire in nature's light fire ecosystems. He has just launched his second book *Fire in Nature - A Fire Activists Guide* (2014). This book is the second in a series of books being written on diverse topics of national and international importance.

Elinor 'Nell' Teresa Newman (1959-), b. New York, NY, of Slovak ancestry; the eldest child of actress Joanne Woodward and the late actor, businessman, and philanthropist Paul Newman. She is child actress, who performed under the name of Nell Potts. She is also an environmentalist, biologist, and a prominent supporter of sustainable agriculture, who became an entrepreneur when she founded an organic food and pet food production company, Newman's Own Organics.

Margaret Rockefeller (née McGrath) (1915-1996), b. Mt. Kisco, NY, of Bohemian ancestry; desc. f. Augustine Herman. The wife of David Rockefeller (1915-2017), an eminent banker of New York. As a philanthropist, she worked on behalf of farmland conservation, the

American Farmland Trust, the New York Botanical Garden and the New York Philharmonic. Although she served on numerous Boards and was involved in fund raising for a number of projects, Mrs. Rockefeller, who was known as Peggy, maintained a low profile, preferring to remain in the background and devoting much of her time to causes that were more worthy than fashionable. Particularly concerned with agricultural issues and the environment, she was a founding Board member of the American Farmland Trust and the Maine Coast Heritage Trust, serving as chairman for many years. She was also a member of the Nature Conservancy and the National Historic Trust. In the mid-1970's, Mrs. Rockefeller began to buy and raise cattle, first on Bartlett Island in Maine, near the Rockefeller summer home in Seal Harbor. Mrs. Rockefeller was also a member of the Board of Managers of the New York Botanical Garden. She came up with the idea for and helped finance the garden's series of six illustrated books on America's wildflowers. She organized the National Committee for the Wild Flowers of the United States, which raised some $500,000 for the project. In 1988, Mrs. Rockefeller opened the Peggy Rockefeller Rose Garden at the New York Botanical Garden, a two-acre enclave of some 2,700 roses. The restoration of the original 1915 garden designed by Beatrix Jones Farrand was supported by a $1 million gift from Mr. Rockefeller. Mr. and Mrs. Rockefeller received the Pillar of New York Award, given by the Preservation League of New York State.

Iphigene Ochs Sulzberger (1892–1990), b. Chatanooga, TN, of Bohemian ancestry, who shaped the history of *The New York Times* throughout a long and active life, pursued a variety of other interests, notably those devoted to parks and the environment, and to the welfare of animals. In 1928, she joined the Park Association, a volunteer group devoted to improving the city's parks. She became its president in 1934 and held the office until 1950, when she was elected chairman. She gave up that post in 1957 but kept her active membership. Two results of her work for the parks particularly pleased her: getting the financier Bernard M. Baruch to contribute a chess and checkers house to Central Park and helping to restore Joseph Rodman Drake Park in the Bronx. In 1976, Mrs. Sulzberger received the annual award of the Parks Council - a citizens' group into which the Park Association had merged - for her continuing work on environmental issues. In particular, the award cited a work-study program she had founded in Central Park several years earlier, which was duplicated in other parks. Four years later, Mrs. Sulzberger was named honorary chairman of the newly formed Central Park Conservancy, a group of private citizens who raise funds for Central Park. Another of Mrs. Sulzberger's avocations involved the New York Botanical Garden in the Bronx. Her zeal reflected the delight she took in gardening and in flowers. She was a keen supporter of the institution's program to train student gardeners in cooperation with nearby Christopher Columbus High School. The garden honored her in 1965 with its distinguished service award.

K. Anarchists

Patrick K. Kroupa (aka Lord Digital) (1969–), b. Los Angeles, of Czech parents, was an activist, writer, hacker and cyberculture icon. He was a member of the legendary Legion of Doom hacker group and co-founded MindVox in 1991, with Bruce Fancher. As of 2006, Kroupa is High Priest in the Eastern European based and European Union recognized religion: Sacrament of Transition (a religious organization whose initiation rituals involve the sacramental use of ibogaine), and a member of Cult of the Dead Cow. He was a heroin addict from age 14 to 30 and got clean through the use of the hallucinogenic drug ibogaine.

Hippolyte Havel (1871–1950), b. Tábor, Bohemia, was a Czech-American anarchist. He had been imprisoned as a young man in Austria-Hungary because of his political activities but made his way to London. There, he met anarchist Emma Goldman on a lecture tour from the United States. She befriended him and he immigrated to the US. He was close friends with Emma Goldman, and also became friends with playwright Eugene O'Neill, and various others in the artistic circles, who lived in Greenwich Village, New York, which he declared to be 'a spiritual zone of mind.' For a time, he and his wife ran a restaurant in the village. He also edited radical journals.

Fredy Perlman (1934–1985), b. Brno, Moravia, was an author, publisher and activist. He is one of the founders of the periodical and subsequently the publishing house Black & Red. He is the author, translator and publisher of many radical books and pamphlets; and lifelong anti-authoritarian. Though Perlman detested ideology, his work as an author and publisher has been influential on modern anarchist thought. His published books include: a play entitled *Plunder*, *Worker-Student Action Committees, May '68*, *The Incoherence of the Intellectual*, the satirical *Manual for Revolutionary Leaders*, *Letters of Insurgents*, and *Against History, Against Levithan!* His translations include I.I. Rubin's *Essay on Marx's Theory of Value* (with Milos Samardzija), Guy Debord's *Society of the Spectacle* (with others), Arhsinov's *History of the Makhnovist Movement*, parts of Voline's *The Unknown Revolution*, and Camatte's *The Wander of Humanity*. He died before completing the manuscript of a comprehensive history of *The Strait* (Detroit and surroundings). His most popular work, the book *Against His-Story, Against Leviathan!*, details the rise of state domination with a retelling of history through the Hobbesian metaphor of the Leviathan. The book remains a major source of inspiration for anti-civilization perspectives.

Josef Peukert (1855–1910), Albrechtice nad Orlicí, Bohemia, was a Bohemian anarchist, known for his autobiographical book *Memoirs* from the proletarian revolutionary labor movement. From the age of six, he worked for his father's company and, by the age of eleven, he was taken out of school. At the age of 16, he left home and worked odd jobs in

Germany. Peukert contributed to social democratic workers' associations later becoming an Anarchist communist. In exile in London, Peukert became involved in distributing *Freiheit* published by Johann Most, but became increasingly critical of Most as social-revolutionist as opposed to an anarchist. During this time, he became even more radicalized and upon his return in the 1880s, he became the leader of the radical Fraktion, who were believers in the concept of Propaganda of the deed, which calls for the use of terror against society civil rights. In 1881, Peukert became the editor of *Die Zukunft* (The Future), published by Der Rebell, from 1886 to 1893, he was the editor of *Die Autonomie* and co-editor after 1889 of *Der Anarchist*. From 1890, he worked with Emma Goldman for several years in New York City.

John Zerzan (1943–), b. Salem, OR, to immigrants of Bohemian heritage, trained historian and Ph.D. dropout, is an anarchist and primitive philosopher and writer. His works criticize agricultural production as inherently oppressive and advocate drawing upon the ways of life of prehistoric humans as an inspiration for what a free society should look like. Some of his criticism has extended as far as challenging domestication, language, symbolic thought (such as mathematics and art) and the concept of time. His four major books are *Elements of Refusal* (1988), *Future Primitive* (1994), *Against Civilization: A Reader* (1998) and *Running on Emptiness* (2002). After gaining public notoriety, John Zerzan began accepting speaking engagements and giving interviews around the world explaining anarcho-primitivism and the more general Global Justice Movement. Recently, Zerzan has been involved, however tempestuously, with the Post-left anarchist trend, which argues that anarchists should break with the Left, which they believe is mired in ideology and mostly concerned with seizing state power and crushing individual freedom. Zerzan is currently one of the editors of *Green Anarchy*, the leading journal of anarcho-primitivist and insurrectionary anarchist thought. He is also the host of Anarchy Radio in Eugene on the University of Oregon's radio station.

L. Futurists

Robert Jungk (orig. Baum) (1923–1994), b. Berlin, Germany, of Bohemian ancestry, as a writer, journalist, historian and peace campaigner who wrote mostly on issues relating to nuclear weapons. When Adolf Hitler came to power, Jungk was arrested and released, moved to Paris, then back to Nazi Germany to work in a subversive press service. These activities forced him to move through various cities, such as Prague, Paris, and Zurich, during World War II. Since 1947, he was reporter for German and Swiss newspapers in US. He continued journalism after the war. He is also well known as the inventor of the future workshop, which is a method for social innovation, participation by the concerned, and visionary future planning 'from below,' In chapter six of his book *The Big Machine*, Jungk described CERN as the place to find the "first Planetarians, earth dwellers who no longer feel loyalty to a single nation, a single continent, or a single political creed, but to common knowledge that they advance together." There is an international library in Salzburg called Robert-Jungk-Bibliothek für Zukunftsfragen (Robert Jungk Library for Questions about the Future).

George Jiří Kukla (1930-2014), b. Prague, Czech., was a climate scientist who was among the first to warn of the power of global climate change and inspire government study. A keen interest in the outdoors, especially caves, led Kukla to study geology at Prague's Charles University, where he earned his Ph.D. in 1953. In a career spanning more than five decades, much of it spent at Columbia University's Lamont-Doherty Earth Observatory. Kukla helped pioneer the modern understanding of how natural climate cycles work, and publicly warned that changing climate could affect humanity—though not in the sense that most scientists believe today. Synching climate records on land and at sea, he showed that ice ages in the last few million years were far more common than previously thought. Working from China and eastern Europe to Antarctica and Chile, he also helped to clarify the role that snow and ice, air pollutants, and other factors play in cooling earth's climate. Kukla helped champion the theory that ice ages come and go as the amount of sunlight falling on earth changes due to variations in earth's orbit around the sun—an idea first proposed by Serbian mathematician Milutin Milanković in the 1920s and 1930s, and now well accepted. Kukla also saw evidence that earth was now moving rapidly toward another ice age. Shortly after coming to Lamont, he organized a conference with Brown University geologist Robert Matthews on this idea. They summarized their findings in a 1972 paper in the journal Science, "When Will the Present Interglacial End?" They also wrote to President Richard Nixon of the potential for floods, snowstorms and deadly frosts, as well as "substantially lowered" food production; they warned that the Soviet Union was probably already considering a response. The White House reacted quickly. By 1973, the State Department formed a Panel on the Present Interglacial, and Congress held a series of hearings on the state of climate research and U.S. preparedness. A series of bills to create a national climate program were introduced; in 1979, President Carter signed the National Climate Program Act into law.

Raymond 'Ray' Kurzweil (1948-), b. Queens, NYC, of Moravian ancestry, is a computer scientist, inventor, and futurist. Kurzweil is a public advocate for the futurist and transhumanist movements and gives public talks to share his optimistic outlook on life extension technologies and the future of nanotechnology, robotics, and biotechnology. Kurzweil received the 1999 National Medal of Technology and Innovation, the United States' highest honor in technology, from President Clinton in a White House ceremony. He was the recipient of the $500,000 Lemelson-MIT Prize for 2001. He was elected a member of the National Academy of Engineering in 2001 for the application of technology to improve human-machine communication. In 2002, he was inducted into the National Inventors Hall of Fame, established by the U.S. Patent Office. He has received 21 honorary doctorates, and honors from three U.S. presidents. The Public Broadcasting Service (PBS) included Kurzweil as one of 16 "revolutionaries who made America" along with other inventors of the past two centuries. *Inc.* magazine ranked him #8 among the "most fascinating" entrepreneurs in the United States and called him "Edison's rightful heir."

Václav Smil (1943–), b. Plzeň, Czech., is a Czech-Canadian scientist, policy analyst and futurist. He received a Doctorate in natural sciences from Charles Univ. and another Ph.D. from Penn State Univ. Since that time, Smil has been on the faculty of the University of Manitoba, where he is now a Distinguished Professor of Geography and Environment. He has published more than 30 books and some 400 papers on various global issues, dealing with interactions of energy, environment, food, economy, population, and technical advances. He is the first non-American to receive the American Association for the Advancement of Science Award for Public Understanding of Science and Technology, and in 2010, he was listed by Foreign Policy among the top 100 global thinkers.

Tom Stonier (1927–1999), b. Hamburg, Germany, of Moravian ancestry, was a biologist, philosopher, information theoretic and pacifist. His scientific studies centered on information provide a plausible explanation to evolutionist concepts of Pierre Teilhard de Chardin. He was frequently called 'professor of futurology.' Being Jewish, he fled with his family to New York in 1939. He studied biology at Drew University and received his Ph.D. from Yale University in 1955. He began his academic career at Rockefeller University. Stonier taught biology at Manhattan College from 1962. His book *Nuclear Disaster*, a study of the effects of a hypothetical nuclear strike on New York City, was published in 1964. He was appointed to a position as a visiting professor in the University of Bradford's Department of Peace Studies by Professor Adam Curle soon after the Department's founding in 1973. Stonier would later become head of Bradford's School of Science and Society, another new department. In the 1970s, he also campaigned for the increased use of computers in the classroom. In 1985, he co-founded, with Dave Catlin, Valiant Technology, a London-based company which designed LOGO Programming Language based Turtle robots the Valiant Turtle and the Roamer educational robot.

VIII. Culture: Arts & Letters

A. Creative Writing

1. Czech Language Writers

Pavel Albieri (orig. Jan Mucek) (1861–1901), b. Jaroměř, Bohemia, who lived in US, was a popular Czech short story teller and novelist. His stories and novels, based on army life, were in demand.

Jan Beneš (1936–2007), b. Prague, Czech., was a Czech writer, translator, publicist, and screenwriter. He is an author of many novels and several historical books. He was a political prisoner of Czechoslovak communist regime, and a Green Beret volunteer. In 1969 after the Soviet occupation of Czechoslovakia, Beneš emigrated to United States. He served 20 years at the US Department of Defense. He returned to Czech Republic in 1992 after the change of regime.

Hugo Chotek (1851–1911), b. Jindřichův Hradec, Bohemia, was editor of the *Nova Doba* in Schuyler, NE and worked on papers in New York, NY, La Grange, Texas, Chicago, Detroit and Cleveland. He was a very prolific writer and translator of stories and articles, most of which were published in the almanac *Amerikán*, and *Domácnost* of Milwaukee.

Hannah Margaret Mary Closs (née Priebsch) (1905–1953), b. London, UK, of Bohemian father, was an art critic and novelist. She was the daughter of the scholar Robert Priebsch (1866–1935), a native of Tanvald, Bohemia. Her *Art and Life* (1936), on aesthetics, won an award from the Eugene Field Society in the United States, and her re-working of the *Tristan Story* (1940) also won plaudits. She wrote a trilogy of novels involving the *Albigensians, High are the Mountains* (1945), and *Sombre are the Valleys* (1949, reissued in 1960 as *Deep are the Valleys*), and the posthumously published *The Silent Tarn* (1955). She was described by W. E. Collinson, a student of her father, as 'singularly gifted and charming.' She died of toxemia at Bristol General Hospital on 8 October 1953. Her three novels were re published as the *Tarn Trilogy* in 1978.

Grace Stone Coates (née Stone) (1881–1976), b. outside Ruby, KS, on a wheat farm, the daughter of Heinrich and Olive Sabrina Stone, the latter being of Bohemian ancestry. She wrote short stories, poetry, and news articles. She did most of her writing out of her home in Martinsdale, Montana. Coates published her first poem, "The Intruder," in 1921 and her first series of linked stories, *Black Cherries*, in 1931. She co-edited and wrote for *Frontier*, a literary magazine edited by Harold G. Merriam, a creative writing professor at the University of Montana.

Petr Den (orig. Ladislav Radimský) (1898-1970), b. Kolín, Bohemia, trained as a lawyer and diplomat, was a Czech exile, essayist and publicist. He also served as editor of *Proměny* (Metamorphoses), published by SVU.

Jan Havlasa (orig. Klecanda) (1883-1964), b. Teplice, Bohemia, was a writer, journalist, and traveler. He travelled throughout the world and wrote memorable novels, essays, feuilletons, based on his observations and insights. He was a recognized expert on the Far East.

Egon Hostovský (1908-1973), from Hronov, Bohemia, was a popular Czech novelist who first came to the US in 1940 and permanently settled here in 1948. His works, written in Czech, have been translated into English and other languages.

Arnošt Lustig (1926-2011), from Prague, Czech., the Holocaust survivor, in 1970, moved to the US. He was a popular author of novels, short stories, plays, and screenplays whose works have often involved the Holocaust. His most renowned books are *A Prayer For Katerina Horowitzowa* (published and nominated for a National Book Award in 1974), *Dita Saxová* (1962), *Night and Hope* (1957) and *Lovely Green Eyes* (2004). *Dita Saxová* and *Night and Hope* were filmed in Czechoslovakia.

Václav J. Miniberger (1883-1969), b. Písek, Bohemia, a Presbyterian minister, was a journalist. publicist and writer, who immigrated to America in 1902. Apart from his journalistic career, he was the author of a number of novels.

Bedřich Moravec (1859-1936), b. Prague, Bohemia, was a Czech-American author of a great number of books, which were published in Chicago by A. Geringer. It includes such titles as *Bloudění, Dva legionáři* (1923), *Dvojí duše, Hřích obětí, Muka, naa Cejkově, Na jaře a v podzimu, Perlet*, etc.

Zdeněk Němeček (1894-1957), b. Josefov, Bohemia, was a writer and playwright. He wrote *New York zamlženo* (1932), *Dábel mluví španělsky* (1939), *Tvrdá země* (1954), *Na počátku bvlo slovo* (1956), *Stín a jiné povídky* (1957), *Bloudění v exilu* (1958), *Xenia* (1975).

Iva Pekárková (1963-), b. Prague, Czech., is a writer, who started writing and publishing novels after moving to New York City, where she defected in 1958. Her novels are inspired by her various life experiences, and she writes openly about sexuality, making her controversial in her native country. Most of her novels are originally written in Czech. He first novel *Pera a perutě* (1989) was published in English under the title *Truck Stops Rainbows* (1992). Her second novel, *Kulaty svět* (1994) was translated into English as *The World is Round* (1994). The third novel, *Dej mi prachy* (1996), she translated into English herself, as *Gimme the*

Money (2000). She travelled to Thailand in 1988 which gave her inspiration for her novel *Třicet dva chwanů* (Thirty-two Kwan, 2000). She published *Six Billion Americas* in 2005.

Rudolf Jaromír Pšenka (orig. Pšenička) (1875–1939), b. Jindřichův Hradec, Bohemia, was a Czech-American writer, journalist, and playwright. He was a cofounder and secretary of the Czech-American Press Bureau and played a significant role in the struggle for the Czech independence.

Josef Škvorecký (1924–2012), a native of Nachod, Czech, was a popular Czech writer and publisher who spent much of his life in Canada. He wrote more than 40 books, including his masterpiece, *The Engineer of Human Souls*, which won the Canadian governor general's award for fiction in 1984.

Robert Vlach (1917–1966), b. Prague, Bohemia, was a poet, essayist. and translator. He studied at Charles University. He emigrated to the US in 1958 and, until 1959, taught at Bennet College, Greensboro, NC. Since 1959, he was associated with the University of Oklahoma, Norman, where he held the position of associate professor of Slavic Languages and literatures. Since 1961 he was editor of the *Books Abroad* monthly. He also established the Czech Cultural Council Abroad (1956) and was the founder and editor-in-chief of the literary series *Sklizeň svobodné tvorby* (Harvest of Free Art). He wrote poems, humorous short stories, essays, and articles dealing with the literary life of Czech emigration.

Bronislava Volková (1946–), b. Děčín, Bohemia, is a poet and literary scholar. She has published ten books of existential and metaphysical poetry in Czech and several in English, two books on linguistic and literary semiotics, a large anthology of Czech poetry translations *Up The Devil's Back: A Bilingual Anthology of 20th Century Czech Poetry* (with Clarice Cloutier) and recently her collected poems were published in Czech in the Czech Republic under the title *Vzpomínky moře* (The Sea Recalls).

2. Slovak-Language Writers

Andrej Brázda-Jankovský (1915–2008), b. Slovakia, resided in Canada since 1968. He was a Canadian-based writer who wrote in the Slovak language. These included *Vzbúrenec* (The Rebel), *Svedok Antónia* (The Witness Antonia) and *Kanadský Slovák* (The Canadian Slovak).

Jozef Cíger-Hronský (orig. Jozef Cíger) (1896–1960), b. Zvolen, Slovakia, was a Slovak writer, teacher, publicist. After the World War II, settled in Argentina. There, he established the Matica slovenská Abroad (*Zahraničná Matica slovenská*) and was a chairman of the Slovak National Council abroad and an honorary chairman of the Association of Slovak Writers and Artists Abroad. In his works, he often describes ordinary Slovak people, he often returns to the memories of childhood, so some of his works are strongly autobiographical.

Rudolf Dilong (1905–1986), b. Trstená, Slovakia, a R.C. priest, O.F.M., was a poet, playwright, novelist, author of some 100 books. He first settled in Rome, in 1947 he left for Argentina, and from 1965 he lived in a monastery in Pittsburgh. Dilong is one of the most important and prolific authors of Catholic modernism. He devoted himself mainly to writing poetry, but also to drama. He was also the founder of *Postup* magazine.

Rudolf Kalenčík (1894–1985), b. Nové Mesto nad Váhom, Slovakia, was a writer of short satirical novels. He wrote a satirical novel, *Doktor Šaša* (1965), *The Devil and the Soldier* (1972).

Ľudovít Kandra (pseud: Peter Klas) (1904–1993), b. Banská Štiavnica, Slovakia, was an essayist, novelist, freelance writer, poet, lobbyist, political activist. Since 1949, he has lived in Canada. He was one of the most productive Slovak prose writers in exile. He authored the novels *Svetlo pod halenou* (1974), and *Satan proti Bohu* (1983).

Martin Kukučín (pseud. of Matej Bencúr) (1860–1928), b. Jasenová, Slovakia; physician, who practiced in Buenos Aires and on Punta Arenas, the southernmost town in Chile. He is best-known as a prosaist, novelist, playwright, and publicist. He was a representative of Slovak literary realism, a founder of modern Slovak prose. He was a member of the Czech Academy of Sciences and Arts.

Gustáv Maršall-Petrovský (1862–1916), b. Báčsky Petrovec, Serbia, initially studied law and medicine. He was a Slovak prose writer, journalist, and activist. He immigrated to the USA in 1880. Most of his realistic literary works take place in his native Vojvodina. He also wrote the historical novel *Jánošík* (1894) and a book of short stories, *Under the American Snowdrifts* (1906).

Clement K. Mlynarovich (1887–1971), b. Hasprunka, Slovakia, R.C. priest lived in the US s. 1914. He was a pastor in Indiana, and author, novelist, and poet. He was a co-founder of Slovak Writers and Artists abroad.

Mikuláš Šprinc (1914–1986), b. Krompachy, Slovakia, a R.C. priest and pedagogue, was a poet, prosaist, essayist, and translator. In 1945, after the end of World War II, he emigrated abroad. He first worked in Rome, then in 1946 he left for the USA, where he was secretary of the Association of Slovak Writers and Artists. In 1957 became a professor of languages and philosophy of art at Wickliffe, where he lived until his death. He published his first exile collection of poems, *Traveling Songs* (1950), together with K. Strmeň, and gradually added books of verses *On Florida Alone*, *Face Against the Sun* (both 1953), *From Noon and Midnight* (1960), The *Eagle's Youth* (1962), *My Eyes Pilgrims* (1965).

Karol Strmeň (1921–1994), b. Palárikovo, Czech., was a poet, and translator, residing in Cleveland, OH. He is the author of collections of poems *Silver Legend* (1950), *Waiting for the Floodplains, Spring* (1963), *The Sign of the Fish* (1969), *Preblahoslavená* (1977) and others.

Andrej Žarnov (1903–1982), b. Kuklov, Slovakia, trained as physician, after 1952 moved to Austria, Italy and finally to America. He was a poet, a Slovak Catholic modernist. He was an author of socio-political, patriotic, and reflective poems. He was also a popularizer and translator of Polish poetry works. He was president of the Association of Slovak Writers and Artists Abroad.

Gorazd Zvonický (orig. Andrej Šándor) (1913–1995), b. Michalovce, Slovakia, a R. C. priest, Salesian, was a Slovak poet of Catholic modernism, translator, and pedagogue. After escaping from insulation camp, he went to Argentina. Here he actively participated in the work of the Association of Slovak Writers and the Foreign Matica slovenská. When, in 1963, the Slovak Institute of St. Cyril and Methodius was founded in Rome, he returned to Europe and joined the work of the institute. He became the editor of the poetry edition of *Lyra*. In exile, he published poetry collections: *S ukazovákom na mraku* (1958), *Prebúdza sa zem* (1964), *Na jubilejné víno* (1965), *Slnko ma miluje* (1967), *Na Igricovom kare* (1973), *Napárať čím viac lyka* (1978), *Obolus* (1985), *Smer Mariánska hora* (1988) and the anthology *Si krajšia, moja vlas* (1993).

3. English-Language Writers

Marion Rombauer Becker (1903–1976), b. St. Louis, MO, of Slovak descent, was an author and illustrator. She was the co-author with her mother, Irma von Starkloff Rombauer, of the *Joy of Cooking*, first published in 1931. Elected by the New York Public Library as one of the 150 most important and influential books of the 20th century. Published by her mother, Marion is best known for the cookbook's illustrations. The friendly, chatty-style cookbook is considered the bestselling cookbook of all time. A prominent Cincinnatian, Becker also worked as an art teacher and for *Women's Wear Daily*. She was one of the founders of Cincinnati's Modern Art Society and became the Society's first professional director. Also, a gardener and an environmentalist, she was a pioneer in natural gardening and wrote Wild Wealth which chronicled her woodland garden at the family's estate. Becker received the Oak Leaf Award from the Nature Conservancy and the prestigious Medal of Merit from the Garden Club of America. Before her death in 1976, she was a recipient of the Greatest Living Cincinnatian Award.

Thomas Bell (orig. Adalbert Thomas Belejcak) (1903–1961), b. Braddock, PA, of immigrant Lemko Rusyn parents from Slovakia, was a novelist. He worked in the steel mills in Pennsylvania, beginning at the age of fifteen as an apprentice electrician. In 1922, Bell moved to New York City and worked variously as a mechanic, a merchant seaman, and a bookstore clerk. His first novel, *The Breed of Basil*, was published in 1930. From 1933 he devoted all of his time to writing, completing five more novels: *The Second Prince* (1935), *All Brides Are Beautiful* (1936) (produced as a 1946 film called *From This Day Forward*), *Out of This Furnace* (1941), *Till I Come Back to You* (1943) (which had a life on Broadway as *The World's Full of Girls*), and *There Comes a Time* (1946). Bell's reputation as a writer increased dramatically in 1976 when the University of Pittsburgh Press reissued *Out of This Furnace* to wide acclaim.

Anne Bernays (1930–), b. New York City, the daughter of Edward L. Bernays (1891–1895), of Moravian ancestry on his mother's side, and Doris E. Fleischman, is an American novelist, editor and teacher. Bernays attended the Brearley School on New York City's Upper East Side, graduating in 1948. A 1952 graduate of Barnard College, she was managing editor of *Discovery*, a literary magazine, before moving from New York City to Cambridge, Massachusetts, in 1959 when she began her career as a novelist. Bernays has been published widely in national magazines and journals and is a long-time teacher of writing at Boston University, Boston College, Holy Cross, Harvard Extension, Nieman Foundation for Journalism at Harvard, and the MFA Program at Lesley University. She is a founder of PEN/New England and a member of the Writer's Union. She serves as chairman of the board of Fine Arts Work Center in Provincetown and co-president of Truro Center for the Arts at Castle Hill.

Miles J. Breuer (1889–1945), b. Chicago, of Czech immigrant parents, trained as physician, was an early science fiction writer. He was part of the first generation of writers to appear regularly in the pulp science fiction magazines, publishing his first story, "The Man with the Strange Head", in the January 1927 issue of *Amazing Stories*. His best-known works are "The Gostak and the Doshes" (1930) and two stories written jointly with Jack Williamson, "The Girl from Mars" (1929) and "The Birth of a New Republic" (1931).

Joseph Bruchac (1942–), b. Saratoga Springs, NY, of Abenaki and Slovak ethnicity, is a writer of books relating to the Indigenous peoples of the Americas, with a particular focus on northeastern Native American and Anglo-American lives and folklore. He has published poetry, novels, and short stories. Bruchac is best known for his work as a Native writer and storyteller, with more than 120 books and numerous awards to his credit. Among his works are the novel *Dawn Land* (1993) and its sequel, *Long River* (1995), which feature a young Abenaki man before European contact. Bruchac's poems, articles and stories have appeared in over 500 publications.

Benjamin Cheever (1948–), son of Mary Watson Winternitz (1918–2014) of Bohemian ancestry and writer John Williams Cheever, is an American writer. To date, he has written four adult fiction novels, one children's book, and two nonfiction books.

Mary (Watson) Cheever (née Winternitz) (1918–2014), b. New Have, CT, the daughter Dr. Milton Winternitz, Dean of the Yale School of Medicine, of Czech descent, was an author and poet, best known as the enduring spouse and widow of John Cheever. John Cheever was the least contented of men, an alcoholic who carried on desperate affairs with men and women, including the actress Hope Lange. Yet the Cheevers remained married, long after they stopped sleeping in the same bed or speaking on a daily basis. She nursed him through his cancer and was at his bedside when he died in 1982, several years after he won the Pulitzer Prize for his collected short stories. She was a teacher, fiction editor of *Westchester Magazine*, author of *The Changing Landscape: A History of Briarcliff Manor-Scarborough* and writer of *The Need for Chocolate and Other Poems*, which included the poem "Gorgon" and its note of "life-denying husbandry."

Susan Cheever (1943–), born in New York City, of Bohemian ancestry on her mother's side, is a writer. She is a prize-winning best-selling writer well known for her memoir, her writing about alcoholism, and her intimate understanding of American history. She is a recipient of the PEN New England Award. She authored *My Name is Bill - Bill Wilson: His Life and the Creation of Alcoholics Anonymous*, *Home Before Dark*, *Note Found in a Bottle*, *Treetops: A Memoir* and five other novels.

Hilda Doolittle (1886–1961), b. Bethlehem PA, of Moravian ancestry on her mother's side, was an American poet, novelist, and memoirist, associated with the early 20th-century avant-garde Imagist group of poets, including Ezra Pound and Richard Aldington. She published under the pen name H.D.

Theodore Dreiser (1871–1945), b. Terre Haute, IN, of Moravian mother, ranks as the foremost American writer in the naturalism movement.

Max Eisen (1929–2022), b. Moldava nad Bodvou, Czech., of an Orthodox Jewish family, is an author, public speaker and Holocaust educator. He travels throughout Canada giving talks about his experiences as a concentration camp survivor, to students, teachers, universities, law enforcement personnel, and the community at large. Eisen would live through a 13-day death march from Auschwitz to Loslau and there he was loaded onto metal boxcars made for transporting coal and sent to Mauthausen. Then from Melk, he participated in a three-day march in the mountains to Ebensee. He was liberated on May 6, 1945. From Max's large extended family, only two cousins returned. Max arrived in Quebec City in October 1949 and was sent to Toronto by the Canadian Jewish community.

Eisen had his memoirs published in a book titled *By Chance Alone: A Remarkable True Story of Courage and Survival at Auschwitz*, which was shortlisted for the RBC Taylor Prize in 2017.

James Thomas Flexner (1908–2003), b. New York City, of Bohemian ancestry, was one of American foremost men of letters who wrote with distinction in the fields of American history, biography, and art. His 4 vol. *Biography of George Washington* was awarded a rarely given special Pulitzer Prize citation and a National Book Award.

Arthur Golden (1956–), b. Chattanooga, TN, of Bohemian ancestry, is the writer of the bestselling novel *Memoirs of a Geisha*. After its release in 1997, *Memoirs of a Geisha* stayed two years on *The New York Times* bestseller list. It has sold more than four million copies in English and has been translated into thirty-two languages around the world. In 2005, *Memoirs of a Geisha* was made into a feature film.

James Grippando (1958–), b. Waukegan, IL, of Bohemian mother, is a lawyer and a novelist. He writes novels of suspense in the genre of crime fiction, including psychological thrillers and legal thrillers, many of which draw upon his experiences as a trial lawyer.

Patricia Hampl (1946–), b. St. Paul, MN, of Czech ancestry, is a prosaic poet. She teaches in the MFA program at the University of Minnesota at Minneapolis and is one of the founding members of the Loft Literary Center.

Milton Leon 'Mickey' Herskowitz (1933–), b. Houston, TX, of Czech Jewish immigrant parents, is an American journalist and biographer. He has written more than 50 books and has published autobiographies with several athletes. He was a sportswriter and columnist for the *Houston Post* and the *Houston Chronicle*, and a former ghostwriter for George W. Bush.

Greg Hrbek (1969–), b. Long Island, NY, of Czech ancestry, is a graduate of the Iowa Writers' Workshop. He taught fiction writing at Vassar College and Butler University and was Distinguished Visiting Writer at Boise State University in 2002. Since 2001, he has been Writer-in-Residence at Skidmore College in Saratoga Springs, New York. He is the author of a novel, *The Hindenburg Crashes Nightly* (1999) which was awarded the James Jones First Novel Award by the James Jones Literary Society, and of a collection of stories, *Destroy All Monsters* (2011), winner of the Prairie Schooner Prize in Fiction.

Sonya Jason (1927–), born of Carpatho-Rusyn immigrants, is a writer of novels and stories and freelance journalist. She grew up in Jefferson, PA, a tiny coal patch of company-owned houses in Washington county. She authored: *Concomitant Soldier* (1974); *Helper* (1994); *Icon of Spring*, (1994); *Professional Angel* (2001).

VIII. CULTURE: ARTS & LETTERS

Kathy Kacer (1954-), b. Toronto, Ont., Canada, of Slovak parents was trained as a psychologist. She was a Canadian author of fiction and non-fiction for children about The Holocaust. A winner of the Silver Birch, Red Maple, Hackmatack and Jewish Book Awards, and a finalist for the Geoffrey Bilson and Norma Fleck Awards.

Regina 'Gina' Kaus (1893-1985), b. Vienna, Austria, Austria, of money broker Max Weiner of Czech ancestry, is a noted American novelist and screenwriter. In the twenties, Gina Kaus published her first novel *The Rise,* which won the Theodor Fontane Prize, and was very active in the circle of literary intellectuals in Berlin and Vienna. In March 1938, Kaus moved from Vienna via Zurich to Paris. At the outbreak of World War II in September 1939, Gina Kaus emigrated to the United States. After a few months in New York, she settled in Hollywood in November 1939. She wrote many scripts there and would not return to Vienna until 1948 and visit Berlin until 1951. In 1956, Kaus' 1940 novel *Devil Next Door* was made into the film *Devil in Silk* by director Rolf Hansen, starring Lilli Palmer and Curt Jürgens.

Frederick Kohner (1905-1986), b. Teplice, Bohemia, was an American novelist and screenwriter. He is best-known for having created the *'Gidget'* novels, which inspired a series of movies, two television series, three telemovies and a feature length animated film. He based the title character on his own daughter, Kathy Kohner-Zuckerman.

Andrew Krivak (1963-), b. Wilkes-Barre, PA, of Slovak descent, was an American novelist. His debut novel, *The Sojourn* (2011) was nominated for the National Book Award for Fiction, won the Dayton Literary Peace Prize, and was well received critically. He also wrote a memoir about his time in the Jesuit order, *A Long Retreat: In Search of a Religious Life* (2008). He grew up in Pennsylvania, has lived in London, and has taught at Harvard, Boston College, and the College of the Holy Cross.

Maxine Kumin (née Winokur) (1925-2014), b. Philadelphia, PA, was of Bohemian ancestry. Maxim Winokur Kumin was a notable poet and writer. She received her B.A. in history and literature from Radcliffe College in 1946 and her a Master's degree in 1948. Kumin's first book of poetry *Halfway* was published in 1961. Since then, she has published thirteen additional books of poetry; taught poetry writing at Tufts, Washington, Columbia, Brandeis, and Princeton Universities; received the Pulitzer Prize (1973) and the American Academy and Institute of Arts and Letters Award (1980); served as a consultant in poetry to the Library of Congress (1981-1982); and was elected chancellor in the Academy of American Poets (1996). Kumin has also published four novels, three collections of essays, two books of short stories, and numerous children's books (four with Anne Sexton).

Lenore Guinzburg Marshall (1897–1971), b. New York, NY, of Bohemian ancestry, was an American poet, novelist, and activist. She studied at Barnard College, class of 1919, where she was an editor of the monthly literary magazine *The Bear*, and a member of the Intercollegiate Socialist Society. From 1929 to 1932, Marshall worked as an editor at the publishing firm of Cape and Smith, where she convinced her company to take a chance on William Faulkner's *The Sound and the Fury,* which had been rejected by twelve other publishers. She served as the poetry editor of *American Mercury* in 1938 and during World War II was active in the founding of children's writing clubs in the New York City public schools. Throughout her career, she contributed articles and reviews to New York literary magazines. A poet in her own right, Marshall published *No Boundary* (1943), *Other Knowledge* (1957), and *Latest Will* (1969). She wrote the novels *Only the Fear* (1955), *Hall of Mirrors* (1937), and *The Hill Is Level* (1959). *Unknown Artists* was published in 1947; *The Confrontation and Other Stories* appeared in 1972, shortly after Marshall's death; and *Invented a Person: The Personal Record of a Life* was published in 1979.

Anne S. Perlman (1919–2002), b. San Francisco, CA, the daughter of Ansley Kullman Salz (1880–1957) of Czech ancestry, and Helen Arnstein, was a San Francisco poet and former newspaper reporter. She did not begin writing poems seriously until middle age. Her work was soon being published by some of the major literary magazines in the country, including the *Hudson Review*, the *Paris Review, The Nation, Ploughshares* and *The Southern Review.* Although her poetry explored a variety of human emotions, many were inspired by the natural world and often by the sciences as a result of travels and conversations during her long marriage to David Perlman, *The Chronicle*'s science editor.

Darryl Ponicsan (1938–), b. Shenandoah, PA, of Slovak descent, is an American writer. He is best known as the author of the 1970 novel *The Last Detail*, which was adapted into a 1973 film starring Jack Nicholson. A sequel, *Last Flag Flying*, based on his 2005 novel of the same name, was released in 2017 and he also co-wrote the screenplay with Richard Linklater. He also wrote the 1973 novel and screenplay *Cinderella Liberty*, starring James Caan. Ponicsan has written mystery novels under the pen name Anne Argula.

Jana Přikryl (1975–), b. Ostrava, Czech., is a poet, critic and editor. Her family escaped from Czechoslovakia in 1980 and eventually settled in Hamilton, Ont., Canada. She graduated with a BA in English from the University of Toronto. After time living in Dublin, Prikryl moved to New York in 2003 to study for an MA in cultural reporting and criticism from New York University. Following graduation, Prikryl worked at the *New York Review of Books*, where she was named executive editor. As an essayist, her writings on photography and film have been published in the *Nation* and *The New York Review.* Her poetry and criticism have been published in the *New Yorker*, the *London Review of Books*, the *New York*

Review of Books, the *Paris Review,* the *Nation,* and the *Baffler,* in two collections - *The After Party* and *No Matter,* and three anthologies, Best American Poetry 2020, Best Canadian poetry 2020, and *The Unprofessionals: new American writing from the Paris Review* (2015). *No Matter* was named one of the best poetry books of the year by *The New York Times* and was chosen as one of the best books of the year 2019 in the *New Statesman.*

Frederic Prokosch (1901–1989), b. Madison, WI, of Bohemian ancestry, was a novelist and poet. His first novel *The Asiatics* (1935) was immensely popular and was translated into 17 languages. He also published several books of verse.

Kathryn Ptacek (1942–), b. Omaha, NE, of Czech ancestry, is an American writer and editor. She was raised in New Mexico and studied journalism, with a minor in history, with honors, at University of New Mexico (B.A., 1974). Since 1981, she has published science fiction, fantasy, horror, suspense, and romance short stories and novels. She is the editor and publisher of the writers-market magazine, *The Gila Queen's Guide to Markets.* She has also edited several anthologies of short stories. Her short story "Each Night, Each Year" was nominated for the 1989 Bram Stoker Award for Best Short Fiction. She was married to the novelist Charles Lewis Grant (1942–2006).

James Ragan (1944–), b. Duquesne, PA, of Slovak parents, is a poet, playwright and essayist. He is the author of 8 books and translated into 15 languages, he has read at the UN, Carnegie Hall, and for 7 heads of state including Czech President Vaclav Havel, Korean Prime Minister Young-Hoon Kang and for Mikhail Gorbachev at Moscow's Int. Poetry Festival. He has appeared on CNN, C-SPAN, NPR, PBS and in 30 Anthologies. He has a Ph.D. and has served for 25 years as Director of USC's Professional Writing Program and for 23 summers as Distinguished Professor at Charles University in Prague. He is the author of the poetry collections *In the Talking Hours* (1979), *Womb-Weary* (1990), *The Hunger Wall* (1995), *Lusions* (1997), and *Too Long a Solitude* (2009), etc.

Gregory A. Rucka (1969–), b. San Francisco, CA, of Slovak descent, is an American comic book writer and novelist. He is known for his work on such comics as *Action Comics, Batwoman, Detective Comics,* and the miniseries *Superman: World of New Krypton for DC Comics,* and for novels such as his *Atticus Kodiak* series.

Adam Ehrlich Sachs, b. Boston, MA, the son of the pediatrician Sonia Ehrlich (1954–) from Prague, Czech, and the economist Jeffrey David Sachs, is a writer, living in Pittsburgh. His fiction has appeared in The New Yorker, and Harper's, among other places. For his first book, *Inherited Disorders,* he was named a finalist for the 2017 Sami Rohr Prize for Jewish Literature and received a 2018 NEA Literature Fellowship. In 2019, he received a Berlin Prize. He is also the author of *The Organs of Sense* and *Gretel and the Great War.*

Katherine Schwarzenegger (Katherine Eunice Schwarzenegger Pratt) (née Schwarzenegger) (1989–), b. Los Angeles, CA, of Czech ancestry, is an American writer. She has written three self-help books, on subjects like self-image, forgiveness, and finding direction after college; she has also written a children's book about adopting her dog. Schwarzenegger is the oldest child of Arnold Schwarzenegger and Maria Shriver.

Aranka Siegal (née Meizlik) (1930–), b. Berehovo, Czech., is a writer, Holocaust survivor, and recipient of the Newbery Honor and Boston Globe Horn Book Award, both awarded to her in 1982. She is the author of three books, the best known of which is *Upon the Head of the Goat: A Childhood in Hungary 1930-1944*, a memoir of her childhood in Hungary before her 12-month imprisonment in the Nazi concentration camps, Auschwitz-Birkenau and Bergen-Belsen. Other works include *Grace in the Wilderness: After the Liberation 1945-1948* and *Memories of Babi*. Her novels are sold worldwide and have been translated into several different languages including, but not limited to, English, French, Hungarian, Italian, Japanese, Dutch, and German. She speaks six languages.

Clifford D. Simak (1905–1988), b. Millville, Wisconsin, of Bohemian ancestry, was a newspaperman and award-winning writer of science fiction. He studied journalism at the University of Wisconsin. During the 1930s, he edited newspapers in Michigan, Iowa, North Dakota, and Missouri. Simak worked for the *Minneapolis Star* and the *Minneapolis Tribune* from 1939–76, and he became news editor of the *Star* in 1949. Beginning in 1961, he was the coordinator of the *Minneapolis Tribune*'s Science Reading Series. Simak won many awards for his writing, including the 1953 International Fantasy Award for his book, *City* (1952), the 1959 Hugo Best Novelette for *The Big Front Yard* (1958), the 1964 Hugo Best Novel for Way *Station* (1963), the Grand Master Award from the Science Fiction Writers of America in 1977, and his "Grotto of the Dancing Deer" (1980) won the Hugo Best Short Story and the Nebula Best Short Story in 1981. Simak was inducted into the Science Fiction Hall of Fame in 1973.

Nicholas (Charles) Sparks (1965–), b. Omaha, NE, the grandson of Glenora Frances Kollars (1920-d.) of Czech ancestry and Charles Anthony Thoene, is an eminent American novelist, screenwriter and producer and philanthropist. He has published twenty-two novels and two nonfiction books, all of which have been New York Times bestsellers, with over 115 million copies sold worldwide in more than 50 languages. Eleven of his novels have been adapted to film, including *The Choice, The Longest Ride, The Best of Me, Safe Haven* (on all of which he served as a producer), *The Lucky One, Message in a Bottle, A Walk to Remember, Nights in Rodanthe, Dear John, The Last Song,* and *The Notebook*. Sparks lives in North Carolina, where he contributes to a variety of local and national charities. In 2011, he launched the Nicholas Sparks Foundation, a 501(c) nonprofit committed to improving cultural and international understanding through global education experiences for students of all age.

Joseph Wechsberg (1907-1983), b. Ostrava, Czech., was a writer, journalist, musician, and gourmet. He and his wife requested and received asylum in the United States in 1939 when Germany invaded Czechoslovakia. His mother was among the Czech Jews interned by the Nazis and later was murdered at Auschwitz. Over his career, he was a prolific writer who wrote over two dozen works of nonfiction, including books on music and musicians, and contributed numerous articles to publications such as *The New Yorker*.

Paul Wilkes (orig. Vlk) (1938-), b. Cleveland, OH, of Slovak heritage, was a journalist, writer and documentarian who has written extensively about individual spirituality as well as the role of religion in public and personal lives. In addition to the *New Yorker*, *The New York Times Magazine* and *The Atlantic*, he has written for numerous other publications. He has written over twenty books.

Ben H. Winters (Benjamin Allen H. Winters) (1976-), b. Maryland, of Czech Jewish descent, is an American author. He is the author most recently of the novel *The Quiet Boy* (2021). He is also the author of the novel *Golden State*; *The New York Times* bestselling *Underground Airlines*; *The Last Policeman* and its two sequels; the horror novel *Bedbugs*; and several works for young readers. His first novel, *Sense and Sensibility and Sea Monsters*, was also a *Times* bestseller. Ben has won the Edgar Award for mystery writing, the Philip K. Dick award in science fiction, the Sidewise Award for alternate history, and France's Grand Prix de L'Imaginaire.

Martha Wolfenstein (1869-1906), b. Insterburg, Germany, of Moravian ancestry, was hailed as "the best Jewish sketch writer in America." From the age of nine until her death, Wolfenstein lived in the Cleveland Jewish Orphan Asylum where her father, a rabbi, served as superintendent. She began not as a writer but a translator, bringing German writer Leopold Kompert's stories of the Judengasse (Jewish Street) to American audiences. In the 1890s, she began publishing her own stories of "the Gass," in both Jewish and mainstream literary journals. The stories led to her 1901 novel, *Idylls of the Gass*, which featured strong female characters and a balance between portraying ghetto Jews in a positive light and recognizing the massive cultural shifts underway. After Wolfenstein's untimely death from tuberculosis, Cleveland's Martha House for wayward girls was named in her memory.

Dorothy Woolfolk (née Dorothy Roubicek) (1913-2000), b. New York, NY, of Czech ancestry, was one of the first women in the American comic-book industry. As an editor at *DC Comics*, one of the two largest companies in the field, during the 1940s period historians and fans call the Golden Age of Comic Books, she is credited with helping to create the fictional metal Kryptonite in the Superman mythos.

Elsie Mary 'Peggy' Ziegler (née Reif) (1910–2008), b. Chicago, who had ancestors in Bohemia, was a writer of several prize-winning children's novels. She has written and illustrated short children stories, other short stories, and has been writing throughout her whole life. She received numerous awards for her writing and published stories in *Everywoman*, *Judy's*, *Extension Magazine the Toronto Star*, *The Chicago Daily News Sunday Supplement*, the *Writer's Digest* as well as *Farm Journal Magazine*. Her historically based books for young adults are available in most libraries in the US and the internet, and deal with trades that immigrants brought to this country in the 19th century.

4. German-Language Writers

Vicki Baum (orig. Hedwig Baum) (1888–1960), b. Vienna, Austria, daughter of Mathilde Donath (1865–1908), a native of Buchlovice, Moravia, and Hermann Baum, was a famous novelist. She had a tyrannical, hypochondriac father, a bank clerk, who was killed in 1942 in Novi Sad by soldiers of the Hungarian occupation. She attended Vienna Conservatory to study the harp, later playing the harp professionally and teaching music for several years in Darmstadt. After a number of novels in German, a breakthrough novel, *Menschen im Hotel*, was turned into a play and then at the instigation of producer Irving Thalberg into the highly successful film *Grand Hotel* directed by Edmund Goulding. The story details one weekend in a posh hotel in minute detail – Baum had taken a job as maid to yield realism. The film won the Best Picture Oscar. Her time in the US made her realize it was time to leave Germany, emigrating in 1932. From that point, Baum wrote many of her novels in English and took citizenship in 1938. Residing in California, she lived in Pacific Palisades, Pasadena, and then Hollywood, where she died of leukemia in 1960. Her memoir, *It Was All Quite Different*, was published posthumously in 1964. She wrote more than 50 novels, and at least ten were adapted as motion pictures in Hollywood. Vicki Baum is considered one of the first modern bestselling authors, and her books are reputed to be among the first examples of contemporary mainstream literature.

Oskar Jellinek (1886–1949), b. Brno, Moravia, although trained as lawyer, since 1924, was a freelance writer. In 1939, emigrated to the US and in 1940, to New York and s. 1943 resided in Los Angeles, CA. He was an author of novellas, essays, and short stories. His books were banned in Nazi Germany. Author of *Die Mutter der Neun* (novella, 1936), *Der Sohn* (novella, 1938), *Das ganze Dorf war in Aufruhr* (1930), *Die Seherin von Doroschitz* (1933), *Die Geisten und Lebenstragodie der Enkel Goethes* (1938), *Gesammelte Novellen* (1950), *Gedichte und kleine Erzaehlungen* (1952).

Ernst Lothar (orig. Mueller) (1890-1974), b. Brno, Moravia, was trained as a lawyer, however, he devoted his career mostly to writing. In US, he wrote novels and taught dramatic arts. He was the author of several volumes of poetry and a number of novels. His novel *A Woman is Witness* dealt with the experiences of a woman in the Nazi world. His other books were *Beneath Another Sun* (1943), *The Prisoner* (1945), *Hildenplatz* (1945), *The Angel with the Trumpet* (1944), *The Door Opens* (1945), *Return to Vienna* (1949), *Ausgewählte Werke: Unter anderer Sonne; Roman des Südtiroler Schicksals* (1961).

Hans Natonek (1892-1963), b. Prague, Bohemia, was a novelist, poet, and publicist, as well as journalist. The author of many novels and short stories, Natonek attained official recognition in 1932 when he received the prestigious Goethe Award from the city of Leipzig for his novel *Kinder Einer Stadt*. In addition, Natonek was a theater critic and contributor to many magazines and journals. With the advent of the Nazi Regime in 1933, Natonek fled Germany and returned to Prague. After Czechoslovakia collapsed in 1938, Natonek was compelled to emigrate to France, spending the next few years hiding from the Nazis. In 1941, he reached New York City. He contributed to a variety of newspapers and journals, including *National Zeitung*, Basel (1933-40), *Neue Zuricher Zeitung* (1933-40), *Das neue Tage-Buch* (1938-40), *Die neue Weltbuehnem Prager Tagblatt, Prager Presse, The Free Man, Christian Herald*, NY (1938-40). He was the author of plays, stories, and novels., including *Schminke und Alltag: Bunte Prosa* (1927), *Der Mann, der die nie genug hat* (1929), *Kinder einer Stadt* (1932), *Der Schlemihl* (1936), and autobiography *In Search of Myself* (1943).

Charles Sealsfield (1793-1864), a native of Popovice, Moravia, was one of the first American writers who made his mark in the first half of the 19th century. While he was alive, little was known about his identity. Only after his death, it became known that he originated in Moravia and that his real name was Karl Postl.

Friedrich Torberg (orig. Kantor-Berg) (1908-1979), b. Vienna, of Bohemian ancestry, was a novelist, essayist, and translator. He was a Czech citizen, who also served in the Free Czechoslovak Army, and a close friend of Max Brod and Franz Werfel. During the war years he lived in California and New York, where he wrote a novella *Mein ist die Rache* (1943) and novel *Hier bin ich, mein Vater* (1948). His novel *Die Zweite Begegnung* (1950) takes place in post-war Prague.

Johannes Urzidil (1896-1970), b. Prague, Bohemia, was a Czech-German writer, poet, historian, and journalist. Urzidil was educated in Prague, studying German, art history, and Slavic languages before turning to journalism and writing. His initial efforts in poetry were influenced by Expressionism and were published under the pseudonym Hans Elmar. He also worked as a writer and editor of the monthly journal *Der Mensch*. In 1941, he and his wife, the poet Gertrude Urzidil, came to the United States. Although he published poetry, he is best known for his prose which, though written in exile, reflects his Bohemian heritage just as well as his new American environment.

Franz Carl Weiskopf (1900-1955), b. Prague, Bohemia, studied German and history at Univ. of Prague (Dr. Phil., 1923). He was a prolific novelist, poet, journalist, and translator. He served as cultural attaché at the Czechoslovak Embassy in Washington. Some of his works appeared in English translations, including *The Untamed Balkans* (1941), *Dawn Breaks* (1942), *The Firing Squad* (1944), *Twilight on the Danube* (1946), *Children of their Time* (1948). He also published an anthology of Czech writings under the title *Hundred Towers* (1945) and history of exile literature *Unter fremden Himmeln* (1948).

Franz Werfel (1890-1945), a native of Prague, Bohemia, was a prominent novelist, playwright, and, a poet. An identified Jew, Werfel narrowly escaped the Nazi regime and immigrated to the US. Here, in 1941, he wrote his famous *The Song of Bernadette*.

Stefan Zweig (1881-1942), b. Vienna, of Bohemian ancestry, studied German and Romance languages and law at Univs. of Vienna and Berlin. He published essays and became a member of young Vienna lit. group. In 1917, he went to Switzerland to protest against the war. In 1934, he immigrated to UK and in 1941, to Brazil. He was a biographer, essayist, short story writer, and cosmopolitan, who advocated the idea of a united Europe under one government. Zweig achieved fame with his vivid and psychoanalytically oriented biographies of historical characters. Among his best-known works is *Baumeister der Welt* (1936, translated as *Master Builders*), a collection of his biographical studies. Zweig was a prolific writer. In the 1930s, he was one of the most widely translated authors in the world. His extensive travels led him to India, Africa, North and Central America, and Russia. Among his friends were Maxim Gorky, Rainer Maria Rilke, Auguste Rodin, and Arturo Toscanini.

Hanička Smithin (née Heřmanská, formerly Ciprisová) (1934-2017), b. Brno, Czech., was a writer, translator, interpreter and linguist. She studied at Masaryk University and after coming to America, she continued her studies at McMaster University, first in philosophy (B.A., 1976) and then philology and Russian (B.A., 1980). The name Hanička which is usually a nickname or term of endearment for Hana, was actually her given name, chosen for her by her grandmother in 1934. In later years, it has once again been used, almost exclusively. In 1980, she married economist John Nicholas Smithin (1951-).

B. Music

1. Composures & Conductors & Bandleaders

Gustav Adam (1815–1866), b. Příbram, Bohemia, succeeded in escaping after the Revolution of 1848 and immigrated to the US, settling in Cleveland. He was a good musician and became an orchestra leader in Cleveland's theater, the Athenaeum. After 1853, he moved to Tennessee. Known generally as Professor Adam, he also wrote and taught music. He wrote several pieces (mostly waltzes) in Cleveland and a few pieces in Nashville later in his life. One of his Nashville pieces sang quite the praises of the Confederate cause. He died in Nashville, TN.

Kurt Adler (1907–1977), b. Jindřichův Hradec, Bohemia, was a classical music chorus master, music conductor, author, and pianist. He was best known as the chorus master and lead conductor of the Metropolitan Opera in New York City from 1943 to 1973. He conducted in Austria, Germany, Russia, Czechoslovakia, Ukraine, United States, Canada, Mexico, Yugoslavia, Romania, Bulgaria, and Hungary. In addition to conducting more than 20 different operas and preparing the Met's chorus for 30 years, Adler edited many volumes of music and published the authoritative book *The Art of Accompanying and Coaching* (1965, reprinted 1980). In October 1938, Adler, a Jew, fled Nazi persecution, while his parents were murdered in concentration camp.

Kurt Herbert Adler (1905–1988), b. Vienna, of Slovak ancestry; conductor and opera house director. His work in the field of music led him to become the assistant to Arturo Toscanini at the Salzburg Festival in 1936 and he also worked in Italy. Following the Nazi occupation of Austria in 1938, as a Jew, he was forced to leave and went to the Chicago City Opera Company as assistant chorus director where he worked for five years.

Peter Herman Adler (1899–1990), b. Jablonec nad Nisou, Bohemia, was an American conductor. He was music and artistic director of the NBC Opera Theatre (1950-1964) and the National Educational Television.

Franz Allers (1905–1995), b. Karlovy Vary, Bohemia, was a conductor of ballet, opera, Broadway musicals, film scores, and symphony orchestras. He started playing the violin at the age of 7. In 1920, he moved to Berlin, where he became a violinist in the Berlin Philharmonic. He had a distinguished career in Europe as an opera and symphonic conductor. In 1947, Allers conducted the original Broadway production of *Brigadoon*. He conducted the original 1951 Broadway production of *Paint Your Wagon*. He was the music director for *My Darlin' Aida* the following year, and in 1954 he conducted the score for the animated film, *Hansel & Gretel*. Allers conducted the score to the original Broadway production of *My Fair Lady* in 1957 and would go on to win the Tony Award for Best Conductor and Musical Director. In 1961, Allers conducted the original Broadway production of *Camelot*, which won him a second Tony Award for Best Conductor and Musical Director.

Karel Ančerl (1908-1973), b. Tučapy, Bohemia, of a prosperous Jewish family, was a conductor and a composer. After graduating from the Prague Conservatory, he pursued his conducting studies under Hermann Scherchen and Václav Talich. He later worked with Václav Talich. From 1933 to 1939 and again from 1947 to 1950, he conducted for Prague radio. From 1950 to 1968, he was conductor of the Czech Philharmonic Orchestra. Since 1945, he lived in the US and made his debut at the Metropolitan Opera in 1963. Since that time to his death, conducted the Toronto Orchestra. He was particularly noted for his interpretation of music by Czech composers.

Leo Ascher (1880-1942), b. Vienna, of Moravian parents, was a composer of operettas, popular songs and film scores. He studied law at the University of Vienna where he received his Doctorate in 1904. He also attended the Vienna Conservatory since 1898. He was briefly arrested during the pogrom known as Kristallnacht in 1938; once released, he left Austria forever. Via France and England, he emigrated to the USA where he lived since December 1939 until his death in New York City. Ascher began his career as a composer with the opera *Mamzell Courage*. His first operetta, *Vergeltsgott* to a libretto by Victor Léon, premiered on 14 October 1905 at the Theater an der Wien. He wrote another 30 stage works, among them *Vindobona, du herrliche Stadt* (1910) and *Bruder Leichtsinn* (1917). His most famous work was *Hoheit tanzt Walzer*; its premiere on 24 February 1912 at the Raimund Theater was followed by a run of 500 performances. His operetta *Der Soldat der Marie* (1916) enjoyed 800 performances in Berlin.

Frank J. Bača (1860-1907), b. Bordovice, Moravia, a bandleader, was brought to America with his parents in 1860. He taught himself to play clarinet, alto sax, and slide trombone, beginning his career with the Fayetteville Brass Band. He taught all 13 children to play musical instruments. In 1892, he formed the Baca Family Orchestra, believed to be the first Czech Orchestra in Texas, comprised entirely of his children. His daughters made up the first Texas 'all girls' band to play for dances. Eventually, he added other musicians to the band, which became known as Baca's Band & Orchestra. Frank wrote and composed much of his music, which is still played today. He became known as 'Professor' Frank Baca.

Hans (Jan) Balatka (1827-1899), b. Doly u Bouzova, Moravia, a conductor came to US in 1849, locating in Milwaukee but removed to Chicago in 1860. He organized the string quartet that performed in Milwaukee and in 1851, he founded the famous Musical Verein of Milwaukee which under his leadership, gained great renown. In 1960, he became leader of the newly founded Philharmonic Soc. of Chicago. In 1862, he became conductor of the Musical Union and later of the Oratorio Soc. In 1867, Balatka conducted a musical festival at Indianapolis and in 1868, another at Chicago, which were pronounced the grandest that had ever been held in this country. He became director of the musical society known as Arion dest Westens which entered numerous concerts and oratorios with great success. In 1879, he founded the Balatka Academy of Musical Art.

Béla Bartók (1881-1945), b. Romania, of Slovak mother, is a composer, pianist and ethnomusicologist. He is considered one of the most important composers of the 20th century. Through his collection and analytical study of folk music, he was one of the founders of comparative musicology, which later became ethnomusicology.

Jan Behr (1911-1996), b. Krnov, Moravia, was a conductor and concert pianist, educated at the Academy of Music in Prague and at the Univ. of Prague. He was a resident conductor with the Metropolitan Opera in NY (s. 1951). He made recordings on Columbia and Urania labels.

Ralph Benatzky (1887-1957), b. Moravské Budějovice, Moravia, was composer of operas and operettas, such as *Casanova* (1928), *Die drei Musketiere* (1929), *Im weißen Rössl* (1930), and *Meine Schwester und ich* (1930). He came to the US in 1938.

Louis M. Bláha (?-1953), b. Vienna, of Czech ancestry, received his music education in Vienna and came to the US in the 1920s. As director of the marching band, concert band, symphony orchestra and dance orchestra in J. Sterling Morton High School and College in Cicero, Illinois, Blaha inspired his students as he introduced them to the music of the world's great masters. In addition, he guided them in future pursuits.

Arthur Bodanzky (1852-1921), a native of Vienna, of Moravian ancestry, on his mother's side, once a conducting assistant to Gustav Mahler, was an American conductor at Metropolitan opera, particularly associated with the operas of Wagner. He conducted Enrico Caruso's last performance at the Metropolitan Opera House on Christmas Eve 1920.

Karl August Leopold Böhm (1894-1981), b. Graz, of Bohemian ancestry, was a conductor. He was best known for his performances of the music of Mozart, Wagner, and Richard Strauss. He originally studied law before entering the music conservatory in Graz. He started his career by helping singers at the Graz Opera to learn their roles. Eventually he became conductor at the opera house in Dresden when Fritz Busch lost that job because he said he did not like the Nazis. Böhm worked there for nine years. He became a great friend of the composer Richard Strauss and conducted the first performances of two of his operas there: *Die schweigsame Frau* and *Daphne*. In 1943, got the very important job of conductor at the Vienna State Opera eventually becoming music director. He was invited to conduct many of the leading world orchestras. He often performed at Salzburg, Bayreuth, Vienna, Berlin, Munich, Hamburg, Milan, Paris and New York. In 1957, he made his first appearance at the Metropolitan Opera in New York, conducting Don Giovanni and quickly became one of the favorite conductors of the Rudolf Bing era, leading, all told, 262 performances. He was very popular there and conducted many operas, especially those by Mozart, Wagner and Richard Strauss. Late in life, he was a regular guest conductor with the London Symphony Orchestra.

William Emanuel Bolech (orig. Boleska), was a bandmaster at Brooklyn Navy Yard. He served with the Navy since 1874. During the Civil War, he was bandmaster of the Sixth Regiment of the US Infantry.

Peter Breiner (1957-), b. Humenné, Czech., is a pianist, conductor, and composer. Breiner began to play and study the piano at age four. At age nine, he started to study at the Conservatory in Košice, Slovakia, where he studied piano, percussion, composition, and conducting. He subsequently moved to Bratislava, Slovakia where he attended the Academy of Performing Arts continuing his composition studies under the tuition of Alexander Moyzes; he was graduated from the Academy in 1982. Breiner has recorded over 150 albums as conductor or pianist. He is well known for his arrangements, such as Baroque versions of the Beatles and a similar adaptation of Elvis Presley, as well as arrangements of popular Christmas music. His 2004 release of all the national anthems of the world was used by the Athens Olympic Committee as the music for medal ceremonies at the Games. Breiner lived in Toronto, Canada from March 1992 to June 2007, from June 2007 to June 2020 in New York, United States, since July 2020, he has been residing in London, United Kingdom.

Jimmy Brosch (1924-2013), b. Praha, TX, of Czech ancestry, a popular Texas bandmaster, learned to play the fiddle at a young age. He emulated country music he heard on the radio as a child. He later learned to play the saxophone. When he started playing in polka bands, Brosch incorporated elements of country into his playing. One of his bands even featured a steel guitar. One of his most famous compositions was the *Corn Cockle Polka*, which is now a standard among central Texas Czech bands. Over the years Brosch traveled throughout Texas and across the country. He was in many ways a great ambassador of polka music. Later in life, Brosch worked to preserve polka music's rich history in central Texas. He teamed with author Laura Cernoch Parker to document some of the great Texas polka bands in the book *Jimmy Brosch Remembers Twenty Legendary Texas Czech Polka Bands*.

Joseph Buchar, among the better-known bandleaders, holds the primacy. He was a veteran of the Civil and the Spanish-American Wars, as well as in the War with Indians. He was a bandmaster at West Point.

Edward Cepuran (1898-1952), b. Omaha, NE, of Czech ancestry, a pastor of the Wenceslaus parish in Omaha, became known as the 'Nebraska March King. 'Already at the age of eleven, he was a member of Franek's Czech Band. During his college days at St. Procopius Coll. Lisle, IL, he organized and directed the first band in that institution. His parish in Omaha became known as the 'Notre Dame of Music.' The St. Wenceslaus Czech Band of Omaha had gained national recognition when it won the highest honors at the Century of Progress Exposition in Chicago in 1933 and won honors again in 1936 at the Texas Centennial at Dallas, TX. Father Cepuran received the title of Honorary Doctor of Music from the Charles University in Prague in the year 1929 as a mark of distinction for his ability and fervor for the Czech people here; the honor was conferred upon him by President Tomáš Masaryk.

Vaclav Divina (1896-1961), of Czech extraction, was a music arranger and composer who studied with Foerster and Talich. He was in New York since 1922 and published his *Songs of an Exile* with Carl Fischer. He was for many years with Columbia Broadcasting System and later with the leading Hollywood film studios. He appeared frequently in public recitals as accompanist.

Paul (Deutsch) Dorian (1895-1988), b. Vienna, Aust., of Bohemian ancestry, brother of Max Deutsch, was a French composer, teacher, and conductor who studied with Schoenberg (1913-1920). Deutsch gave the French premieres of some of Schoenberg's works. In 1938, he emigrated to US. He became piano teacher in Los Gatos, CA.

Luděk Drizhal (1966-), b. Prague, Czech., is a composer and record producer. He studied violin starting at age five at the Prague Conservatory. He began performing by the age of nine and won awards at national and international competitions. He received degrees from the University of Texas at Austin Butler School of Music and the USC Thornton School of Music where he taught music composition, orchestration, music history and music theory for six years. He is an award-winning Los Angeles-based composer and music producer, who has written a long list of stylistically wide-ranging film scores, such as comedy/drama *Rounding First* for which he received an award from the Park City Film Music Festival 2006 (Original Music in Independent Film): Silver Medal for Excellence - Audience Choice for Best Impact of Music in a Feature Film.

Tomas (John George) Dusatko (1952-), b. Toronto, of Czech ancestry, is a Can. composer, teacher, guitarist, and pianist. Dusatko's works, ranging from solo and chamber to live electronic and orchestral, have been performed across Canada and in Europe including the International Guitar Festival and the Victoria International Festival of the Arts, while his compositions have received frequent national broadcasts on the CBC and been given several awards.

Frederick R. Dvonch (1912–1976), b. Chicago, IL, of Slovak descent, was a violinist, music director for many productions and a conductor for Broadway shows. he led the orchestra for the Rodgers and Hammerstein musicals *The King and I* and *Carousel* on Broadway, on tour and in London. He was a graduate of the Chicago Musical College, where he won the Gold Medal, the Ditson Award and the Max Fischel Scholarship. He was also a graduate of the Juilliard School of Music in New York, where he won two fellowships, one in violin and the other in conducting. He also received a doctorate in music from the New York College of Music. He had been music director of the New York City Center Light Opera Company. He also conducted the Stadium Symphony Orchestra at Lewisohn Stadium, the Juillard Orchestra, a series of concerts in Carnegie Hall and, concerts broadcast by the Mutual Broadcasting System.

Antonín Dvořák (1841–1904), b. Nelahozoves, Bohemia, a foremost Czech composer, who was invited to the US to head the National Conservatory of Music in New York City. He stayed for 3 years (1892–95) and then returned to his native Bohemia. While in the US, he wrote his well-known symphony *From the New World* which had its glorious premiere in Carnegie Hall in December 1893. While in America, he also wrote the remarkable Cello Concerto and two string quartets.

Raymond Francis Dvorak (1900–1982), b. Algonquin, IL, of Czech ancestry, was trained as a piano-bassoonist at the University of Illinois, where he also served as assistant director of the bands and director of the Glee Club from 1926 to 1934. From 1934–1968, he served as director of the University of Wisconsin bands. Dvorak was elected to the American Bandmasters Association (ABA) in 1933 and served as President in 1959. Though he retired in 1968, he remained active as a guest conductor and worked on efforts to memorialize John Philip Sousa, helping to establish *Stars and Stripes Forever* as the official march of the United States and to have Sousa enshrined in the Hall of Fame for Great Americans.

Hanns Eisler (1898–1962), b. Leipzig, Saxony, of Bohemian ancestry, was a composer. He is best known for composing the national anthem of East Germany, for his long artistic association with Bertolt Brecht, and for the scores he wrote for films. The Hochschule für Musik "Hanns Eisler" is named after him.

Max Vernon Exner (1910–2004), b. Shanghai, of Bohemian ancestry, was a choral music leader and composer. He earned an A.B. in English literature and modern languages from the College and in 1947 earned an M.A. in musicology, composition, conducting and organ from GSAS. After graduation, the Joseph E. Bearnes national composition award allowed Exner to study for a year at the Neues Wiener Konservatorium in Vienna; he received a certificate in conducting and organ in 1937. During WWII, Exner served as field radio operator in the Tunisian campaign and was wounded in action. In Florence, Italy, in 1945, Exner sang weekly in the mass in a choir of Jesuit monks, standing in his brown uniform among their black cowls. After the war, he composed a full mass in the brothers' honor, which they performed. After getting married, the couple moved to Ames, where Exner served in the Extension Service as the State music specialist (1947-80). His choral music has been printed by seven publishers, and his anthem, *I Have a Dream* was approved by the Martin Luther King Foundation and has been performed widely.

Richard Fall (1882-1943), b. Jevíčko, Moravia, was a composer of operettas and popular songs. Fall worked as an operetta conductor in Berlin and Vienna and as film composer in Hollywood. In 1928, he immigrated to France from Vienna. In 1943, he was arrested by Nazis and deported presumably to Auschwitz where he died.

Joseph Aloysius Ferko (1895-1964), b. Philadelphia, PA, of Slovak descent, a pharmacist, who ran drug store in North Philadelphia. He was the founder of the famous Ferko String Band (1922) with rosters. He was a perennial performer in Philadelphia's Mummers Parade. The band gained national popularity through their hit recordings in the 1940s and 1950s. They played for Franklin D. Roosevelt's 1933 Presidential inauguration.

Miloslav Francisci (1854-1926), b. Debrecen, Hungary, of Slovak father, was a physician and composer. He studied medicine in Vienna. After graduating, he emigrated to the US. Miloslav Francisci is the founder of the Kriváň choir. He collected, harmonized, and edited folk songs. He is the author of the first Slovak operettas: *The Rich Men of the Merry Party, Astra, In the Gypsy Camp, The Female Bull, Rhea Sylvia* operas and piano compositions, "Slovak Rhapsody."

Rudolf Friml (1879-1972), b. Prague, Bohemia, is best known as the composer of romantic 1920s operettas. Friml also composed music for films, often based on his popular musicals, such as *Rose Marie* and the *Vagabond King*. He also wrote numerous piano pieces. As concert pianist, he toured Europe with violinist Jan Kubelík.

Herschel Garfein (1958-) b. New York, NY, of Czech ancestry, is a Grammy Award-winning American composer, librettist, stage director, and faculty member of the Steinhardt School of Music at New York University. Garfein is widely known for his Libretto written for Robert Aldridge's *Elmer Gantry*, which won two 2012. Grammy Awards including 'Best Contemporary Classical Composition' won by Garfein and Aldridge. He also collaborated with Aldridge on the oratorio *Parables*. Garfein also composed the music and libretto for an opera based on the Tom Stoppard play *Rosencrantz and Guildenstern are Dead*.

Anselm Goetzl (1878-1923), b. Karlín, Bohemia, was a composer who studied with Winkler, Fibich and Dvořák and later in Vienna. He went to the US and conducted Andreas Dippel's Light Opera Co.

Roman 'Romy' Louis Gosz (1911-1955), b. Grimms, WI, of Czech ancestry, known as 'Polka King,' was a popular and commercially successful polka musician in the upper Midwest. He took over his father's band in 1928. Gosz's music featured the Bohemian brass style and appealed to the many ethnic groups found throughout the region. Between 1931 and his death, Gosz recorded roughly 170 tunes for eleven labels—including Columbia, Decca, King, Mercury—that established a 'Bohemian' polka instrumentation and sound scarcely diminished in eastern Wisconsin. The overall Gosz style favored a slow tempo and heavy feel, anchored by stolid tuba and trap drums. A piano or piano accordion contributed rhythm and fills. Gosz's penetrating trumpet, often in chorus with a second trumpet and saxophones, introduced the melody, with clarinets frequently answering a phrase or chiming in with a countermelody.

Jan Hammer (1948-), b. Prague, Czech., is a musician, composer, and record producer. He rose to prominence while playing keyboards with the Mahavishnu Orchestra during the early 1970s, as well as with his film scores for television and film including "Miami Vice Theme" and "Crockett's Theme", from the 1980s television program *Miami Vice*. He has continued to work as both a musical performer and producer. In 1968, Hammer moved to the United States and resolved to become a citizen after receiving a scholarship at Berklee School of Music in Boston. He performed at various venues in Boston area (1968-70); was an arranger and piano accompanist for vocalist Sarah Vaughan (1970-71); member of Mahavishnu Orchestra, (1971-73); and leader of Jan Hammer Group (1973-76). Then, he was involved in numerous performing and recording projects as composer and/or keyboardist (since 1976); and was composer of musical scores for many motion pictures and television shows (since 1978).

Lumir C. Havlicek (1895-1969), b. Crete, NE, of Czech ancestry, received his music education at Doane College, Vandercook School of Music in Chicago and the University of Nebraska. During the years he spent in Crete as a teacher (s. 1943), he also directed the American Legion Juvenile Band and the Crete Municipal Band. In 1944-1945, he was director of the Navy Band when it was stationed at Doane College. He was also director of the 110th Medical Regiment Band, the first National Guard band west of the Mississippi River, for nine years. Havlicek was also a composer of many band selections and arrangements. He was also piano accompanist for various choral groups, and he played violin in Doane Symphony concerts and trumpet with the Doane Crete Choral Society.

Anthony Philip Heinrich (1781-1861), b. Krásný Buk, Bohemia, was the first 'full-time' American composer, and the most prominent before the American Civil War. He did not start composing until he was 36, after losing his business fortune in the Napoleonic Wars. He was the first composer in US to use American Indian themes in modern music. Critics in his time spoke of him as the 'Beethoven in America.'

James Gutheim Heller (1892-1971), b. New Orleans, LA, of Bohemian ancestry, a rabbi, who was also a talented musician and composer. He wrote the program notes for the Cincinnati Symphony Quartet and composed *Elegy and Pastorale* (1934). Among his works were String Quartet; Violin Sonata; and Jewish services (New Union Hymnal, 1930-32).

Frank W. Hodek (1895-1950), b. Baltimore, MD, of Czech ancestry, was a concert pianist, composer and choral and orchestral director, residing in Omaha, NE. He studied in Prague Conservatory of Music, specializing in piano, harmony and orchestration. He was engaged as conductor of the Nightingale Orchestra in Omaha. NE which made tours throughout Nebraska and neighboring states. Later he was with the NBC orchestra in Hollywood.

Joseph Holik (aka Holick) (1868-1971), b. Moravia, was a clarinetist, bugler and band leader, and a cobbler and boot maker supreme. Only 16 years old, he stowed away on a steamer headed for America and the romanticized life of a rugged cowboy. After several failed attempts at bronc busting and tired of cleaning stalls, he hopped a freight train headed for Orange Texas and the salt grass trail. He fell asleep while the train was sidetracked and disconnected in Bryan and woke up stranded and penniless. Within a few days, he had a part time job as a shoemaker in Bryan and another job as a shoemaker and bugler working in his dorm room at Texas A&M College. His interest and talent as a musician attracted other musicians to gather in his room. After a few months, he approached the military college with the idea of a military band which was established and funded by the Texas State Guard and all 12 members wore the Texas Guard uniform. Joseph was the first Aggie band master and served intermittently for many years. He served the band from its founding until his death. He is recognized for having designed the 'Corp' boot. Holík is credited of having made 30,000 pairs of the Aggie Boots.

James Roy Horner (1953-2015), b. Los Angeles, CA, of Bohemian ancestry (son of Harry Horner), is an American composer of orchestral and film music. He is noted for the integration of choral and electronic elements in many of his film scores, and for frequent use of Celtic musical elements. Horner won two Academy Awards for his score and song compositions for the film *Titanic* in 1997. His score for James Cameron's *Titanic* is the bestselling orchestral film soundtrack of all time. He also wrote the score for the highest-grossing film of all time, Cameron's *Avatar*.

Karl Hoschna (1876–1911), b. Stražný, Bohemia, was an oboist and a composer noted for his songs "Cuddle up a Little Closer, Lovey Mine", "Every Little Movement" and "Yama Yama Man," and for a string of successful Broadway musicals.

Frank Hruby, Sr. (1856–1912), b. Cehnice, Bohemia, became one of Cleveland's foremost band leaders and patriarch of one of America's most renowned musical families. He obtained his first musical job with the Hagenbeck Circus, beginning at the age of 9 and finishing as director of its 3 bands. For several years he then played in a band at Brighton Beach, Eng., before returning to Bohemia to organize a band that toured through parts of Europe. Hruby came to America in 1883, advised by Czech-born band leader Joseph Zamecnik of a need for experienced musicians in Cleveland. In 1889, Hruby reorganized the Great Western Band, leading it in appearances in city parks, at the dedication of the Soldiers' and Sailors' Monument in 1894, and at the Republican Natl. Convention in St. Louis in 1896. As a total of 8 children arrived, he taught them all to play various instruments and organized them into a family band. In 1912, he took them to Europe for a 5-month tour in which they played a repertoire of Sousa marches and the new American novelty, ragtime.

Karel Husa (1921–2016), b. Prague, Czech., was composer and conductor educated in Prague Cons. of Music. He was a professor of composition and conductor of the student orchestra at Cornell Univ. (s. 1954). He composed a large number of works for orchestra as well as chamber music. For his '3rd String Quartet' he received the Pulitzer Prize in Music (1969).

Eduard Ingriš (1905–1991), b. Zlonice, Bohemia, was an American composer educated at Charles Univ. in Prague and the Prague Conservatory. He had many talents, but his first love has always been music. It was he who wrote the first arrangement of the famous "Beer Barrel Polka", after Jaromír Vejvoda came upon the melody and sought Ingriš' help in refining it. The piece was brought to England by Czech pilots flying for the Royal Air Force, and it became an overnight hit there, and subsequently was popularized in America. His compositions number about 1,000, including forty-eight operettas and musical comedies, full opera and symphonies. When nineteen he composed the operetta *The Capricious Mirror*, which played five years in Prague – a record of 1,600 performances (unheard of even on New York's Broadway!) He directed the Symphony Orchestra of Prague and scored 11 European movies.

Jaroslav Ježek (1906–1942), b. Prague, Bohemia, was a Czech composer, pianist and conductor, author of jazz, classical, incidental, and film music. He was almost blind from a young age. He attended a special school for the blind, where he learned to play piano, cello, clarinet and guitar. He studied composition at the Prague Conservatory as a pupil of Karel Boleslav Jirák (1924-1927), at the master school of composition with Josef Suk (1927-1930), and shortly also with Alois Hába (1927-1928). Ježek met the playwrights/comedians Jan Werich and Jiří Voskovec (aka George Voskovec), leaders of the Osvobozené divadlo (Prague Liberated Theatre) in Prague and took up the post of main composer and conductor for their theatre. During the next decade (from 1928 to 1939), he composed incidental music, songs, dances, and ballets for the comic and satirical plays of Voskovec and Werich. In 1934, he became a member of Czech Group of Surrealists. Forced to leave Czechoslovakia following the Nazi occupation, Ježek, Voskovec and Werich went into exile in New York City. He worked as a piano teacher and choirmaster there and continued to work with Voskovec and Werich. In 1942, the long-ill Ježek died of chronic kidney disease in New York. Like Gershwin, Ježek became one of the few composers, who had double careers as composers in both 'jazz' and 'classical' worlds. But his greatest fame he acquired is in the Czech jazz and modern dance with "Tmavomodrý svět," "Hej rup," "Nebe after zemi," "Píseň strašlivá o Golemovi", "Šaty dělaj člověka," "Klobouk ve křoví," "Život je jen náhoda," "Babička Mary" and especially his "Bugatti Step." He wrote between 1928 and 1938 around 30 plays for the Liberated Theatre (Divadlo Osvobozené) for which he was a composer, arranger, music director, pianist all in one.

Karel Boleslav Jirák (1891-1972), b. Prague, Bohemia, was a Czech composer, conductor and musicologist. Jirák became a pupil of Josef Bohuslav Foerster and Vítězslav Novák at Charles University and at Music Academy in Prague. From 1915-18, he was the Kapellmeister at the Hamburg Opera and worked from 1918 to 1919 as a conductor at the National Theatre in Brno and Ostrava. From 1920-30, he was a composition teacher at the Prague Conservatory, and principal conductor of the Czechoslovak Radio Orchestra until 1945. In 1947, he emigrated to the United States, where from 1948 to 1967, a professor at Roosevelt University, Chicago, and, in 1967, a composition teacher at the Conservatory College in Chicago. He remained in this position until 1971. In addition to the opera, *Apollonius of Thyane*, Mr. Jirák was the author of a great many symphonies, serenades, sonatas, sonatinas and other composition and songs. He was a chevalier of the Légion d'Honneur (France), officer of the Order of the Roumanian Star, officer of the Yugoslav Order of St. Sava. He won many prizes, including the Czechoslovak State Prize for Composition (three times), Smetana Prize, prizes of the Czech Academy of Sciences and Arts, and the International Prize in Edinburgh (1951) for his 5th Symphony.

Rafael Joseffy (1852-1915), b. Huncovce, Slovakia, was a Jewish pianist, composer, and teacher. He studied in Budapest with Friedrich Brauer, the teacher of Stephen Heller. In 1866, he went to Leipzig, where his teachers were Ignaz Moscheles and Ernst Ferdinand

Wenzel. In 1868, he became a pupil of Carl Tausig in Berlin, remaining with him for two years. Later he spent two summers with Franz Liszt in Weimar. He made his debut in Berlin in 1872 and was immediately acclaimed as a master pianist of great brilliance. Joseffy made his American debut in New York in 1879, with an orchestra under Leopold Damrosch. He soon after played with the New York Philharmonic Orchestra, and subsequently made many appearances in New York and other American cities with Theodore Thomas and the Theodore Thomas Orchestra.

Milan Kaderavek (1924–2014), b. Oak Park, IL, of Czech ancestry, was a composer, arranger, and instrumentalist. He received Baccalaureate degrees in composition and clarinet, and a Master's degree in composition, from the American Conservatory of Music (Chicago). Thereafter he earned a Doctorate in composition and theory at the University of Illinois at Urbana-Champaign. His awards have included the Tamiment Award (1956) for his String Quartet; first prize in the 1956 National Composition Competition of the Albuquerque Civic Symphony for his Sinfonietta; and the 1961 Pi Kappa Lambda performing award. In 1980, he held a composition residency at the Ossabaw Foundation. His collegiate teaching and administrative positions have included service as chairman of the music department of the University of Illinois (Chicago Circle), and professor of theory and composition at Drake University (Des Moines, Iowa).

Michael (Arnold) Kamen (1948–2003), b. New York, NY, of Czech descent, was an American composer (especially of film scores), orchestral arranger, orchestral conductor, songwriter, and session musician. Kamen attended the Juilliard School, in Manhattan, New York City. Kamen's early work concentrated on ballets before extending to Hollywood with the score for *The Next Man* in 1976, and then to pop and rock arranging, collaborating with Pink Floyd on their album *The Wall*.

Hugo Kauder (1888–1972), b. Tovačov, Moravia, was a composer, violin teacher and conductor. As a boy, had violin lessons with the local teacher, who eventually dismissed him when he had "taught him everything he knew." These lessons were his only formal training in music. He came to US in 1940 and settled in New York. Kauder was self-employed as a composer and teacher of violin, music theory, and composition. As part of his efforts to bring his music to life, he conducted a chorus and a chamber ensemble of students and friends (including his son Otto) who studied and performed the classics as well as his own compositions. He composed 4 symphonies, a cello concerto and a large number of works for chamber music. He defied the atonal trend of his generation with his uniquely harmonic, contrapuntal style.

Walter Kaufmann (1907-1984), b. Karlovy Vary, Bohemia, was a composer, conductor, ethnomusicologist, and teacher. Kaufmann studied composition in Berlin with Franz Schreker before working as an assistant to the conductor Bruno Walter at the Charlottenburg Opera in Berlin and for Radio Prague. His early works were played in Karlovy Vary, Berlin, Wroclaw, Prague and Vienna. Being Jewish, he escaped Europe for Bombay (now Mumbai) in 1934 and researched Indian, Chinese and Tibetan music, before moving to Canada and the USA where he enjoyed a career as a conductor and teacher. Kaufmann was a prolific composer of operas, orchestral music, and chamber music. He taught in Canada from 1947 until 1957, when he moved permanently to the US where he joined the School of Music faculty at Indiana University in Bloomington, as Professor of Music in the department of musicology. He was a specialist on musicology and Oriental studies, and ethnomusicology.

Sammy Kaye (1910-1987), b. Lakewood, OH, of Slovak parents, was an American bandleader and songwriter, whose tag line, "Swing and Sway with Sammy Kaye", became one of the most famous of the Big Band Era. A leader of one of the so-called 'Swee' bands of the Big Band Era, he made a large number of records for Vocalion Records, RCA Victor, Columbia Records, Bell Records, and the American Decca record label. He was also a hit on radio.

Jerome David Kern (1885-1945), b. New York, NY, son of and Fannie Kakeles (1856-1907), of Bohemia immigrant parents, and Henry Kern, was an American composer of popular music. He wrote around 700 songs, including such classics as "Ol' Man River", "Can't Help Lovin' Dat Man", "A Fine Romance", "Smoke Gets in Your Eyes", "All the Things You Are", "The Way You Look Tonight", "Long Ago (and Far Away)" and "Who?", a 6-week number 1 hit for George Olsen & his Orchestra in 1925. His career spanned dozens of Broadway musicals and Hollywood films from 1902 until his death. Although Kern wrote almost exclusively for musical theatre and musical film, the harmonic richness of his compositions lends them well to the jazz idiom (which typically emphasizes improvisation based on a harmonic structure) and many Kern melodies have been adopted by jazz musicians to become standard tunes.

Věra Polenová Kistler (1929-2006), b. Volyně, Czechoslovakia, studied music education at Coker College (B.A., 1968), and music (M.A., 1973) and music composition (D.M.A., 1987) at Univ. of South Carolina. She was an accomplished author, composer, and musician, having received numerous awards in all venues, including Darlington's Citizen of the Year as well as The Order of the Palmetto by the Governor of South Carolina. She was the author of *Hluché fialky* (1982), *Sladké povidones* (1985), *Ptáci jednoho peří* (1986), *Song of Myself* (1986). She also wrote thirteen choral compositions.

Rudolf Komorous (1931-), b. Prague, is a Canadian composer, bassoonist and teacher. Komorous studied bassoon in Prague, at the State Conservatory (1952-56) and with Karel

Pivonka at the Academy of Musical Arts (1952-56). He also studied composition with Pavel Borkovec while at the Academy. As a bassoonist, he won the 1957 International Competition for Musical Performers (Geneva). He subsequently spent 1959-61 teaching bassoon at the Peking (Beijing) Conservatory, and then returned to Prague (State Opera House, first bassoon), and was co-founder of Musica Viva Pragensis, one of the leading contemporary music ensembles. He moved to Canada in 1969. In 1971, he joined the faculty at the University of Victoria, teaching composition, advanced theory and bassoon and developing the electronic studio there, continuing an interest first explored in Warsaw some 12 years earlier. Komorous went on to become acting chairman of the department and director of what is now the School of Music; he then moved to Simon Fraser University in 1989 to act as director of the School of Contemporary Arts, leaving that post for retirement in 1996. Komorous has an extensive list of compositions, including 2 operas, works for orchestra, chamber music and a number of electronic works. His opera *Lady Blancarosa* received its late Canadian premiere in 1998. He sees himself as an avant-garde composer, and believes that his work "must always come from life, not from art."

Leslie Kondorossy (1915-1989), b. Bratislava, Slovakia, was a composer, and conductor. After World War II, he settled in Cleveland. He continued his studies at Western Reserve Univ., and later studied Japanese music and theater at Tokyo's Sophia Univ. Kondorossy was especially proficient in producing short operas. He established the American New Opera Theatre Society in 1954 to encourage the production of one-act operas by contemporary composers, and in 1955, he founded the series 'Opera of the Air' for the Cleveland radio station WSRS.

Erich Wolfgang Korngold (1897-1957), b. Brno, Moravia, was a composer and conductor. A child prodigy at seven, who composed his first work, a ballet *Der Schneemann* (The Snowman), which Emperor Franz Josef ordered performed. He was a composer of operas, symphony works, chamber music and songs; winner of two Academy Oscars for musical scores.

Zdeněk Košler (1928-1995), b. Prague, Czech., was a Czech conductor, who played an important role in Czech musical life of the second half of 20th century, notably during the sixties and the eighties. He was particularly well known as an opera conductor. In 1963, he won the respected Mitropoulos conducting competition in New York, together with Claudio Abbado and the Argentinian Pedro Ignacio Calderón, after which he became assistant conductor to Leonard Bernstein at the New York Philharmonic for one year.

Irwin Kostal (1911-1994), b. Chicago, IL, of Czech parents, was a musical arranger of films and orchestrator of Broadway musicals, as well as conductor. He was essentially self-taught: eschewing college, he picked up the art of music arranging from his local library, studying symphonic scores of the great composers. He started as arranger for the Chicago-based NBC radio show *Design for Listening*, followed by Sid Caesar's *Your Show of Shows* on television. From 1957, he worked on Broadway, notably as orchestrator of the original stage version of *West Side Story*. He followed this with *The Music Man* and *A Funny Thing Happened on the Way to the Forum*. Becoming one of the preeminent Broadway conductors, led, in turn, to a contract with Disney in Hollywood. He was named a Disney Legend. He is known for his work on *The Sound of Music* (1965), *Mary Poppins* (1964) and *West Side Story* (1961). In 1982, the soundtrack for Disney's *Fantasia* (1940) was famously re-orchestrated and re-released in digital stereo, conducted by Irwin Kostal. At the time of his death, he served as president of the American Society of Music Arrangers and Composers.

Vlastimil Kovanda (1925–2009), b. Czech., was the founder of the Kovanda Czech Band in Houston, TX in 1984. The band made its first appearance performing with a Czech play on April 15, 1984. Kovanda wrote most of the arrangements in the band book, all true to the Czech brass band idiom. His vision was to re-create the style of music known in the Czech Republic as 'dechovka.' Texans would recognize this as the style of the original Baca Brass Band of Fayetteville. Years ago, this style of band music was very popular in Texas, but today only small groups can afford to make a living playing live music and most larger groups have vanished.

Ivan Král (1948–2020), b. Prague, Czech., was a Czech-born American composer, filmmaker, guitarist, record producer, bassist, and singer-songwriter. He worked across genres including pop music, punk rock, garage rock, rock, jazz, soul, country and film scores.

Jan Krejcar (1980–), b. Czech., is a pianist, organist, conductor, researcher, and composer based in Montreal, Quebec. Raised in rural Alberta, he returned to the Czech Republic where he graduated from the České Budějovice Music Conservatory in 2002 with an Artist diploma. After touring Germany and Austria with the Tschechische Filharmoniker orchestra, he came to Montreal with his wife, opera singer Marina Krejcarová-Černichovská and earned his Doctorate degree in music at McGill University (D.Mus.). As part of his performing career, he has received numerous prizes and performed in venues in North America, Europe, the Caribbean, and the Middle East. Currently, aside from actively performing as a pianist, he is music and choir director at St. John's United Church in Pointe-Claire, Quebec; as well as being involved in the world music scene in which he founded several groups using Eastern European and Jazz elements in a unique blend. He is also actively involved in research – particularly in Czech music of the first half of the 20th century and in Ukrainian piano music.

Ernst Křenek (1900-1991), b. Vienna, of Czech father, was a composer who explored atonality and other modern styles. He was one of the most prolific musical figures of his time. Born with the century in 1900, he lived until 1991 and was active as a composer for more than seven decades. During that time, he played a part in many of the century's significant artistic movements, from atonality to neoclassicism and from jazz-influenced writing to total serialism, with turns to Schubertian lyricism and avant-garde electronic music at various points. In addition to his astonishing productivity as a composer (his work list includes 242 compositions), he was also a prolific writer and critic as well as an avid educator. He lived in the US since 1938.

Arthur R. Kreutz (1906-1991), b. La Crosse, WI, of paternal Czech grandparents, was an American composer. Kreutz composed the *Paul Bunyan Suite*, the *Dixie Concerto*, the score to Martha Graham's 1942 ballet *Land Be Bright* and *Symphonic Blues* (for orchestra) (1947); some of his orchestral pieces were played by the New York Philharmonic, with whom he appeared at times as a guest conductor. Among his other works is a 1954 opera about the University Greys of the University of Mississippi. Kreutz taught from 1954 until 1961 at the University of Mississippi.

Robert Edward Kreutz (1922-1996), b. La Crosse, WI, of paternal Czech grandfather, was an American composer of Roman Catholic liturgical worship music. Kreutz graduated from Aquinas High School in 1940. Robert Kreutz studied music at the American Conservatory of Music in Chicago, Illinois and at the University of California-Los Angeles. He was best known for the Eucharistic hymn: *Gift of Finest Wheat* which was first performed at the International Eucharistic Congress in 1976, in Philadelphia, Pennsylvania. Kreutz also wrote many other hymns including "Bread of Love", "Rise, O Lord" and others. He was an accomplished choir director at St. Bernadette Catholic Church in Lakewood, Colorado for more than 30 years.

Bohumír Kryl (1875-1961), b. ořice, Bohemia, was most famous as a cornetist, bandleader, and pioneer recording artist, for both his solo work and as a leader of popular and Bohemian bands. He was one of the major creative figures in the era of American music known as the 'Golden Age of the Bands.' He immigrated to the United States in 1889, paying the fare in part by performing with the ship's orchestra. Ten years later, he had established himself as a fine soloist, initially based in Indianapolis playing with the When Clothing Company Band and latterly with the famous Sousa Band. After two years with the Chicago Marine Band, he accepted the solo cornet seat with the Duss Band located at Madison Square Garden. He was paid $800 a month, enjoyed thrilling the crowds often playing two solos per concert and was given the role of assistant conductor in 1903. His departure to form his own band (Kryl Bohemian Band) in 1906, which flourished through to 1931, was reluctantly accepted. It was during this later period that he made numerous recordings. His wonderful range, including the use of pedal-notes in the lower register, crisp articulation, pure tone, and individual phrasing gave his recordings their great attraction.

Rafael Kubelik (1914–1996), a native of Bychory, Bohemia, was the foremost Czech conductor. In 1950 he was appointed music director of the Chicago Symphony Orchestra. In 1973 he was made the first music director of the Metropolitan Opera in NY. He also composed several operas, symphonies, and choral works.

Gail Thompson Kubik (1914–1984), b. South Coffeyville, OK, of Czech ancestry, was an American composer, music director, violinist, and teacher. Kubik studied at the Eastman School of Music, the American Conservatory of Music in Chicago with Leo Sowerby, and Harvard University with Walter Piston and Nadia Boulanger. He taught violin and composition at Monmouth College and composition and music history at Columbia University (1937), Teachers College and Scripps College. Joining NBC Radio as staff composer in New York in 1940, he was music director for the Motion Picture Bureau at the Office of War Information, where, during World War II, he composed and conducted the music scores of motion pictures. He won the 1952 Pulitzer Prize for Music for Symphony Concertante. He was a National Patron of Delta Omicron, an international professional music fraternity.

Ladislav Kubík (1946–2017), b. Prague, Czech. is a contemporary Czech American composer who studied composition and music theory at the Prague Academy of Music. He previously taught at the Prague Conservatory, Charles University in Prague, and the University of South Florida. He has held the current position of Professor of Composition at the Florida State University College of Music in Tallahassee (s. 1900). His compositional career has achieved prominence through 15 international and national awards. With the support of the Florida State University, he sponsors his own contest, The Ladislav Kubík International Prize in Composition, which, since 1995, has rapidly developed as one of the major composition contests worldwide, attracting young composers from more than 30 countries.

Ernie Kucera (1919–2007), b. Linwood, NE, of Bohemian ancestry, was a popular bandleader. With the unique sound of an accordion and the 'oom pah pah' of the tuba, Abie, Nebraska's Ernie Kucera and his band has been entertaining people with polka music for the past fifty years. Kucera first started playing drums in his brother's band, The Kucera Accordion Band in 1938. When war broke out, many of the musicians were drafted, and Kucera reorganized the band in 1942. As he reorganized the band, he started out with a six-piece group. He later went to eight pieces and at the end, he had a seven-piece band. Over the fifty years, the band has continued to play mainly polkas and waltzes with some popular music. By the early

1950's, Kucera's band was becoming a household name to polka lovers, and he created his first record. Along with being named the top polka band in the state, Kucera was named Polka King in 1979 at Peony Park in Omaha and was named to the Sokol Hall of Fame in 1976.

Robert Kurka (1921-1957), b. Cicero, IL of Czech ancestry, was a composer, educated at Columbia Univ. and the Berkshire Music Center. Just before his death, he completed a satirical opera *The Good Soldier Schweik* which had a successful opening in 1958 at New York City Center. He taught at City College, Queens Coll. NY and at Dartmouth Coll. He was a recipient of several awards.

Milan Kymlička (1936-2008), b. Louny, Czech., was a composer, arranger, and conductor. He was a naturalized Canadian. Prior to his arrival in Toronto in 1968, Kymlička had studied with Emil Hlobil at the Prague Cons. and the Academy of Musical Arts and completed a ballet, piano and string quartets, a cello concerto, and some 20 film scores. He was best known for his composition of film and television scores, including those for the animated television series *Rupert and Babar* and the live-action television series *Lassie* and *Little Men*. He received numerous awards for his work, including a Genie Award in 1996 for his work on *Margaret's Museum*.

Wilhelm Labitzky (1829-1871), b. Bečov, Bohemia, son of Joseph Labitzky ('The waltz king of Bohemia'), was a violinist, conductor and composer. The young Labitzky, who had been trained at the Prague Cons., performed in Toronto in 1858 and settled there shortly afterwards.

Franz Lehár (1870-1948), b. Komárno, Slovakia, is one of the most significant composers of operetta in the history of classical music. His lighthearted, comic works like *The Merry Widow* continue to delight audiences today, as do his stand-alone orchestral pieces such as the ever-popular *Gold and Silver* waltz. Franz studied violin at the Prague Conservatory, where his violin teacher was Antonín Bennewitz, but was advised by Antonín Dvořák to focus on composition. Aside from a few clandestine lessons with Zdeněk Fibich, he was self-taught as a composer. After graduation in 1888, he joined his father's band in Vienna as assistant bandmaster. Two years later, he became bandmaster at Lučenec, Slovakia, making him the youngest bandmaster in the Austro-Hungarian Army at that time, but he left the army and joined the navy. With the navy, he was first Kapellmeister at Pola (Pula) from 1894 to 1896, resigning in the later year when his first opera, *Kukuschka* (reworked as *Tatjana* in 1906), premiered in Leipzig. In 1902, he became conductor at the historic Vienna Theater an der Wien, where his operetta *Wiener Frauen*, was performed in November of that year. He is most famous for his operettas – he wrote nearly 40 of them, the most successful of which is *The*

Merry Widow (Die lustige Witwe) – but he also wrote sonatas, symphonic poems and marches. He also composed a number of waltzes.

Stanislav Jan Letovsky (1890-1965), b. Omaha, NE, of Czech ancestry, was a concert pianist and a composer. Letovsky received his first lessons from his father, the cellist and composer Stanislav Barta Letovsky. He later studied with Richard Burmester. At the age of 18, he became second Kapellmeister in Kiel. He went on concert tours as a pianist and had positions in Posen and Schwerin. In Vienna, he received a scholarship. In 1930, Letovsky returned to his homeland, Omaha, for health reasons and worked as a teacher and conductor, occasionally also in Kansas City and Denver. After the death of his wife, he made one last trip to Europe in 1965. He died while visiting Berlin. Among his works, the three act opera *Frau Anne* and various compositions for violin, piano and voice should be mentioned.

Zdeněk Mácal (1936-2023), Brno, Moravia, a respected conductor, is renowned in the world of classical music. Since his American debut with the Chicago Symphony Orchestra over 25 years ago, he has conducted widely throughout North America, regularly leading the New York Philharmonic, the Philadelphia Orchestra, the National Symphony, the St. Louis Symphony, the Pittsburgh Symphony, the Minnesota Orchestra, the Houston Symphony, the New World Symphony and the symphony orchestras of Montreal and Toronto.

Benjamin A. Machan (1894-1966), b. Cleveland, OH, of Czech ancestry, was a pianist and composer. He made his debut as a piano soloist with the Cleveland Symphony Orch. at age seven and composed his first album of piano pieces at age ten. Toured as concert pianist, played viola in a string quartet and French horn in an ensemble; conducted the Machann Concert Jazz Ensemble at Eastman Theater in Rochester. He was a member Ensemble at Eastman Theater in Rochester, as well as member of Rochester Philharmonic Orch. He was a pianist and composer for radio station WHAM (1925-29); on music staff of the Paramount Theatre in NYC (1930-32), and composer for radio and movies and conductor of orchestras in NYC (1932-43). After the War, he devoted his time to composition and teaching.

Gustav Mahler (1860-1941), a native of Kaliště, Bohemia, an eminent composer, is considered one of the leading conductors of his generation. He held a succession of conducting posts of rising importance in the opera houses of Europe, culminating in his appointment in 1897 as director of the Vienna Court Opera. Late in his life, he was director of New York's Metropolitan Opera and the New York Philharmonic. He was noted for his 10 symphonies and various songs with orchestra, which drew together many different strands of Romanticism. Although his music was largely ignored for 50 years after his death, Mahler was later regarded as an important forerunner of 20th century techniques of composition and an acknowledged influence on such composers as Arnold Schoenberg, Dmitry Shostakovich, and Benjamin Britten.

Bohumil 'Boh' Makovsky (1878–1950), b. Františky, Bohemia, was a band director and head of the Department of Music at Oklahoma A&M College from 1915 to 1945, and director of Municipal Band at Cedar Rapids Falls, IA. He is considered "the Guiding Spirit" of Kappa Kappa Psi, a national fraternity for college band members. He had little formal education and was trained in clarinet and violin by his uncle, Tomas Makovsky, who had once taught a royal family in Russia. He got a job rolling cigars in a local shop. A short time later, he joined a travelling wagon show that needed a clarinet player and began his work as a professional musician. A few years later, Boh formed his own band that entertained all across the midlands. He had soon started organizing and directing bands in nearby settlements (Woodward, Mustang, Yukon, Prague) which he would then turn over to local directors. In 1910, Boh also started directing the Oklahoma City Metropolitan Band and had a long-standing association with the Oklahoma State Fairs. In 1915, he was invited by the President of Oklahoma A&M College in Stillwater to become band director and department head. Boh started his work here with bands with about 40–50 members who had never had any experience playing in a college setting.

Max Maretzek (1821–1897), b. Brno, Moravia, was a composer, conductor, and impresario. Between 1849–78, he managed several opera companies at the Academy of Music, NY and touring the US, Canada, and Mexico. He was one of the pioneers in popularizing grand opera in the US. He was responsible for introducing such classics as *Rigoletto*, *Il Travatore*, *La Traviata*, *Romeo and Juliette*, etc.

Bohuslav Martinů (1890–1959), b. Polička, Bohemia, was a prolific Czech composer of modern classical music. He wrote 6 symphonies, 15 operas, 14 ballet scores and a large body of orchestral, chamber, vocal and instrumental works. His symphonic career began when he emigrated to the United States in 1941, fleeing the German invasion of France. His six symphonies were performed by all the major US orchestras.

Jerry Mazanec (1919–1977), b. Cleveland, OH, of Czech descent, was a band leader and a composer. He was the founder of Jerry Mazanec Band. He played Czech pieces exclusively, but in a highly original and distinctive manner. In about 1933, he joined the music department of the Ptak Furniture Co. on Broadway Avenue and remained there for almost forty years. In about 1934, he organized a band which grew to be enormously successful, playing first on Sundays at Czech picnics, regularly for eight years in Fred Wolf's Czech radio-hour into the early 1940s and in person six nights a week at a nightclub, the Golden Goose tavern, near Miles Avenue and East 131st Street. Mazanec made more than sixty records with major label, first with Columbia in 1941 and 1942 and later with Continental and the ensemble became so much in demand that at the height of its popularity, the advance bookings were several years in length.

John Mokrejs (1875-1968), b. Cedar Rapids, IA, of Czech ancestry, was a pianist and composer. He was a piano teacher in NYC and Los Angeles. He also composed, e.g. opera *Sohrab ale rustum* and operetta *Mayflower*.

Victor Joseph Molzer (1919-2003), b. Lincoln, NE, of Czech ancestry (son of August Molzer), was an oboist and bandleader educated at Curtis Institute, Eastman Univ. of Nebraska and the Catholic University. Maj. Molzer was asst. chief and exec. officer of the Air Force bands at the Pentagon. Before his assignment to NORAD, he was director of Air Force Band of the Pacific and command director of Pacific Air Force Bands. He was also instrumental music teacher in, Tacoma, WA, schools.

Paul Moravec (1957-), b. Buffalo, NY, of Czech ancestry, is the composer of over seventy published orchestral, chamber, choral, and lyric compositions, as well as several film scores and electro-acoustic pieces. An honor graduate of Harvard University and Columbia University graduate school, his music has earned numerous distinctions, and he has taught at Harvard, Columbia, Dartmouth, Hunter College (CUNY), and Adelphi University. His recorded collections include: *Songs of Love and War*, his Sonata for Violin and Piano, the orchestral work *Spiritdance*, and an album of his chamber compositions titled *Circular Dreams*. He was a recipient of Pulitzer Prize in 2004.

Oskar Morawetz (1917-2007), b. Světlá nad Sazavou, Bohemia, was a Canadian composer, pianist and teacher. He came to Canada in 1940 to become one of Canada's most frequently performed composers.

Frank Nedela (1842-1924), b. Mšeno, Bohemia, was a bandleader. He was a member of his father Jan Nedela's band in Chicago, which also included Thomas Aron, Joseph Chyba and John M. Svoboda. He moved to Crete, NE which made this community famous. At the time, it was the only band west of the Missouri River and played for Governor David Butler's inauguration. Before the railroad reached Crete, these musicians rode by wagon to Lincoln, and considered themselves well paid, for each man received $8.00 for his playing and the driver (owner of the team) $16.00, half for the team and half for his playing. For more than fifty years Nedela's bands - the old and young - were known far and wide. They played for every occasion requiring music, political rallies, funerals, church, etc.

Václav Nelhýbel (1919-1996), b. Polanka, Czech., was a Czech-American composer. He was educated at Prague Cons. and at the Univ. of Prague. He settled in the US in 1957. He composed mostly for instrumental groups, especially wind ensembles. He also wrote orchestral and choral works, as well as several operas and ballets.

Ottokar Eugen Nováček (1866-1900), b. Bela Cerka, Serb., was a violinist and composer of Czech descent. Nováček studied successfully with his father Martin Joseph Nováček, with Jakob Dont in Vienna (1880-83), and with Henry Schradieck and Brodsky at the Leipzig Conservatory, where he won the Mendelssohn Prize in 1885. He played in the Leipzig Gewandhaus Orchestra and in the Brodsky Quartet, originally as second violin and later as viola. He subsequently immigrated to the United States, where he was a member of the Boston Symphony Orchestra under Arthur Nikisch (1891-92) and was appointed principal viola in the Damrosch Orchestra, New York (1892-93). He also played in the re-formed Brodsky Quartet. As a composer, he is best known for his work *Perpetum Mobile*, written in 1895.

John Novak (1896-1967), b. Maribel, WI, of Czech parents, learned to play the drums by listening to and watching local drummers. He played a variety of instruments with the Denmark (Wisconsin) band, and he served as a bugler for Company C, 340th Infantry in World War I. Over time, he acquired formal training in music and music education, earning the State of Mississippi's lifetime certification as Band and Orchestra Master, in about 1930. Known by many as the 'Father of Music in Baldwin County,' he started school marching bands throughout the area, teaching band classes in the high schools in Bay Minette, Robertsdale, Foley, and Fairhope.

Joseph Pache (1861-1926), b. Frydlant, Bohemia, was a composer, teacher, and director of the Baltimore Oratorio Society from 1892 to 1924 when the society disbanded. Pache spent 32 years directing the Baltimore Oratorio Society and to supplement, also organized the Women's Philharmonic Society and the Oratorio Society of York, PA. He directed the latter for 7 years, simultaneously to his work with the Baltimore Oratorio Society. After the Baltimore Oratorio Society disbanded in 1924, Joseph Pache worked chiefly with the "Choir Invisible," a choir of approximately forty members in Washington D.C. He continued to teach voice and maintain studios in Baltimore, Washington, and Annapolis.

Thomas Pašek (1849-1939), b. Přestice, Bohemia, was a bandmaster. He studied music while going to school and at the age of twelve already took his part in the band. In 1866, he came to St. Louis. MO and was active as a musician. In 1873, he came to Saline County, NE, settling on a farm nine miles northwest of Wilber. During the first year, he and John Vesely constituted the band that played at farm dances. Pašek played the cornet and Vesely the clarinet, and the young folks danced on the grass. Soon thereafter, Pašek was able to get together a very good, full band, which became known not only in the county, but in many other Czech settlements. At first, these men walked to their destination, each carrying his instrument. They played from evening until dawn, for $3.00 each, and in the morning, returned home the way they came. Thomas Pašek has taught many pupils and made them into good musicians.

John Patek (1869–1953), b. Bohemia, was a pioneer Czech-American bandleader. His band, one of the best-known Texas Czech polka bands, had its origins in the 1920s. When he was a boy in Czechoslovakia, John became an accomplished musician. In 1889, at the age of twenty, he immigrated to America and played in community bands. In 1920, he formed the Patek Band of Shiner. As the years went by, his sons took music lessons and joined the band.

Joseph Patek (1907–1987), b. Shiner, TX, son of John Patek, in the early 1940s took over his father's band, which he later renamed the Joe Patek Orchestra. From the time Joe Patek took over the band, it recorded more than twenty-four 78-RPMs, more than twenty-four 45-RPMs, and several tapes and LPs. One of the Patek's most successful records was the "Beer Barrel Polka", which sold more than a million copies. The success of his recordings helped make Patek one of the most popular Czech polka bandleaders in Texas. The band played in rural towns throughout Texas and in larger cities, such as San Antonio, Corpus Christi, Houston, Dallas, Fort Worth, and San Angelo, or wherever a dance or social function was held. Patek is credited for establishing a different style of Texas polka with its harder sound and emphasis on swing.

Karel Paukert (1935–), b. Skuteč, Czech, is an organist, harpsichordist and conductor, and a curator. He graduated from the Prague Conservatory, and the Ghent Conservatory, Belgium. He studied under organists Jan Bedřich Krajs and Gabriel Verschraegen. Paukert immigrated to the United States and gained citizenship in 1972. He taught at several universities and became curator of the music department at the Cleveland Museum of Art in Cleveland, Ohio. During his tenure at Northwestern in the 1960s and 70's, Paukert was Organist Choirmaster of Saint Luke's Episcopal Church in Evanston, Illinois, and conducted the famed men and boys' choir of the church. He founded Bach Week, the annual music festival dedicated to the music of Bach and his contemporaries that has featured leading international performers to this day. Later became organist and choirmaster at St. Paul's Episcopal Church in Cleveland Heights, Ohio. He made recordings for Azica Records. He won the 1995 Cleveland Artist Award.

Thomas Pavlechko (1962–), b. Ohio into a Slovak-Ukrainian family of musicians, was an organist, choirmaster and composer-in-residence, at St. Martin's Lutheran church in Austin, TX. Named the Emerging Hymn Tune Composer by the Hymn Society in 2002, Pavlechko's hymn tunes and liturgical music are in print in denominational hymnals and hymn collections on four continents. He is the co-author of the principal worship planning reference book of the Episcopal Church U.S.A., *Liturgical Music for the Revised Common Lectionary*, released in three volumes by Church Publishing, New York. *St. Martin's Psalter*, his collection of over 600 Psalm settings, is published in two editions by St. James Music Press and Augsburg Fortress. Pavlechko's commissioned compositions for orchestra, concert band, organ, chamber and choral ensembles have received premiere performances throughout the United States.

Adolf Pick (1870-d.) b. Mirovice, Czech., was a violinist and conductor. He studied violin at the Prague Conservatory between 1882 and 1888. In the 1890s, he was concertmaster of the National Theater Orchestra in Zagreb, where he was also active as a chamber musician. In 1902, he performed a piano trio together with O. Schulz and H. Geiger. Later, he was a conductor of the Opera in Bern and emigrated to the United States, where he became head of the violin department at the College of Music in Ithaca, NY (s. 1929), and a member of the Chicago Conservatory of Music.

Paul Amadeus Pisk (1893–1990), b. Vienna, of Moravian ancestry, was a pianist, musicologist, and composer, educated at Univ. of Vienna. Emigrated to US in 1936. He became prof. of music, Univ. of Redlands (1937–51); dir. of School of Music, Univ. of Texas, Austin (1951-63); prof. of music, Washington Univ., St. Louis (1963-72). He composed more than 100 opus numbers, including 'Bucolic Suite' for string orchestra (1946), 'Rococo Suite' for viola and orchestra (1953), 'Baroque Chamber Concerto' for violin and orchestra (1953) plus many chamber music pieces, piano and other solo pieces, sonatas, cantatas, song and choral works.

Roman Placzek (1972-), b. Jeseník, Czech, is a graduate of Janáček State Conservatory, Ostrava (dipl., with Honors, (1993) and studied cello at Ostrava Conservatory (1996–92), Univ. Mozarteum Salzburg (1995–96), Boston Conservatory (GPC, 1998) and at Univ. of Massachusetts, Amherst (M.M., 2000); and cello performance, cognate in music history and literature at Univ. of North Carolina, Greensboro (D.M.A., 2014). Placzek is an independent performing artist, published composer, music educator, and member of The Chamber Orchestra of the Triangle in the Research Triangle Raleigh-Durham-Chapel Hill, NC, USA. He was the founder and executive director of Music without Borders Inc., Zlaté Hory in Moravia, Czech. He specializes in promoting Czech musical heritage and a presentation of original composition. He is a published author of compositions for smaller chamber music ensembles and solo instruments in neo-romantic style promoting the infinite potential of melodic and harmonic principles, organicism and the value of the esthetic impact in musical compositions.

Jan Popper (1907–1987), b. Liberec, Bohemia, was a noted Czech conductor, who fled Hitler's takeover of Czechoslovakia and went on to establish opera workshops at leading CA universities. He taught for 26 years at UCLA until his retirement in 1975. He received a Peabody Award in 1955 for a series of public broadcasting TV shows called *Spotlight on Opera*.

Josef Povolný (1873–1958), b. Poděbrady, Bohemia, was a musician, band leader and composer. He played in an army band, and after being discharged, he enrolled in the Prague Conservatory of Music. After completing his musical education, Povolny traveled with bands in several countries in Europe before moving to Chicago in 1906 with his wife and daughter. The couple would have two sons after arriving in America. Povolny taught his children to play and organized a number of bands, which later broke up and formed new bands. Josef Povolny and his children would team up to play together, as Povolny's Band, which played parades, picnics, dances, concerts and other programs. Josef was a member of the Flint Symphony Orchestra, and he could play every instrument except the accordion and piano. He had over 65 years of playing experience before passing away in 1958 at the age of 85. He was inducted into Michigan State Polka music Hall of Fame posthumously in 1972.

Váša Příhoda (1900–1960), b. Vodňany, Bohemia, was a famous violinist, composer, and child prodigy. He was active mostly abroad, including US. He was considered a Paganini specialist and also known for his interpretation of the works of Bach and Tartini. His recording of the Violin Concerto in A minor by Dvořák is still being praised.

Paul Reif (1910–1978), b. Prague, Bohemia, was a composer. He was educated at Music Academy of Vienna and Sorbonne. He came to US in 1940. He was the composer of song cycle *Five Finger Exercises* (1958), and *Be My Love* (1962), opera *Mad Hamlet* (1962); chamber works: *Reverence for Life* (1960), *Monsieur le Pelican* (1960); cantata: *Requiem to War* (1963); score of life and electronic music *Murderer among Us* (1964); songs, etc.

Alois Reiser (1887–1977), b. Prague, Czech., was a composer. He came to the US in 1905 and played cello with Pittsburgh Symphony and NY Symphony. From 1918–29, he was engaged as theater conductor in NY. Later he settled in Hollywood where he worked as composer and conductor at film studios. He composed a number of works for orchestra, including two tone poems and two cello concertos; he also wrote chamber music, including string quartets, and the opera *Gobi*.

John Michael Robel (aka Jolly Jack Robel) (1903–1968), b. Austria, of Slovak parents, was a musician, bandleader, and polka pioneer. He helped polka music part of the US national culture in the 1930s and 1940s. His parents settled in Bethlehem, PA. He took his first music lessons on a clarinet from Tommy Dorsey, Sr. Later, John played with Jimmy and Tommy Dorsey in the Elmore Band. In the early 1930s, Robel formed his own ban and played regularly scheduled 'hours' on local radio. Performing a mix of American and ethnic tunes, especially polkas, his band quickly gained popularity. In 1936, he first introduced the "Beer Barrel Polka" and recorded it. In six months, the record edged into the big time. While on tour he came across a European record, revised it, added a few modern licks and recorded it for Decca. It racked up $780,000 in sales. Later he came back with "Let's Roll Out the Barrel Once Again" and recorded about 60 more records. He sang, conducted, played clarinet, bass, violin and harmonica and had his own 12-piece orchestra. He had a radio program on WAZL in Hazletown, and another on WPAM. In 1950, Universal Motion Pictures in Hollywood selected Jolly Jack Robel as winner of their "Harvey Happiness Award."

Charles J. Roberts (orig. Karoly Kraushaar) (1868–1957), b. Košice, Slovakia, was a composer, arranger, flutist and editor. In 1890, he emigrated with his wife from Košice to the US, settling in New York City, where he used the name Carl Kraushaar privately and Charles Kraushaar professionally. He was a flutist in the New York Philharmonic. In 1892-93, he toured as flutist with the Mozart Symphony Club. In 1895-1910, he was conductor at Hoffman House in New York. In April 1899, he became naturalized American and changed his name to Charles J. Roberts. In 1899, he was employed by Otto Langey, residing at 13 West 113th Street. In 1899-1901, he was editor/arranger for Edward Schuberth in New York. In 1910, he was owner of a music publishing company, residing at 260 West 135th Street in Manhattan and, in 1920, at 547 West 149th Street in Manhattan. In 1920-45, he worked as editor/arranger for Carl Fischer, New York. In 1925-30, he was residing at 99 Murray Avenue, Larchmont Mamaroneck. In 1940, as a music publisher, was residing at 400 Perkins Street in Oakland, CA, and, in 1947, at 360 Forest Avenue, in Palo Alto California.

Charles Vaclav Rychlik (1875–1962), b. Cleveland, OH, was a composer and violinist. He studied at the Prague Conservatory (1891–95). He was a member of the Prague Opera Orchestra and performed with the Bohemian String Quarter in Europe. In 1897, he joined the Chicago Symphony Orchestra (1897-98) and in 1901, came back to Cleveland and played violin in the forerunner of the Cleveland Orchestra. In 1908, he replaced Carl Dueringer as 2nd violinist in the Philharmonic String Quartet, playing with the group until its demise in 1928. Rychlik also played with the Cleveland Orchestra from its inception in 1918 for 2 years. During this time, Rychlik began teaching and composing. He was a violin teacher in Cleveland in 1920s. He wrote numerous works for violin. Rychlik was internationally known through his 25-volume *Encyclopedia of Violin Technique*, which took 20 years to complete. It is said that 40 of his students became Cleveland Orchestra musicians.

Vincent Frank Šafránek (1867–1955), b. Dobrovitov, Bohemia, was a musician educated at Prague Music Conservatory. He was a chief musician and bandmaster of the 25th Infantry, Ft. Missoula, MT. He soon began to experiment with instruments and added such instruments as alto and bass clarinets, oboes, French horns and flugelhorns to US band. He perceived the need for arrangements that were suitable for the modern band. Most of the published American arrangements were designed for brass brand with reed parts indiscriminately added without regard for balance or blend. He was subsequently hired by the Carl Fischer publishing house to rearrange and modernize many of their publications. He also made many new arrangements of the more demanding overtures and operatic transcriptions. He was the composer of the very popular *Atlantis*.

Vladimir G. Sasko (1875–1975), b. Slovakia, was a concert pianist, composer, professor of music, director of the Sasko Music School, Chicago. He studied at the State Conservatory in Budapest (1894–97) and in Vienna (1899–1901), with Leschetitsky, teacher of Padereski. After immigrating to the US in 1906, he was on staff of the Chicago Piano College (1907–09); the South Lake Conservatory in Utah (1911–14); the Chicago Piano College (1915–20) and, since 1921, he had been Director of the Sasko Music School. He was also director of several Slovak singing societies, such as Nitransky Sokol, Sokol Slavia and Spevokol Lipa, and teacher of Polish, Bohemian and Croatian singing societies. He had contributed to national concerts in Europe and America free of charge. In the US, he had appeared on many stages and accompanied noted performers, among them Otakar Mařák, first tenor of the Prague Opera, when on his visit to America. He also had a number of piano compositions.

Hanuš A. Schimmerling (1900–1999), b. Brno, Moravia, was a pianist, composer, teacher, and musicologist. He received music education at the Academy of Music in Prague and Univ. of Vienna. He immigrated to US in 1939, where he became Dir., Harmony Hill Music Center, Woodstock, NY (s. 1951); musical dir., Opera Workshop, Hunter College, NYC (1953–54); opera dept., and professor of music theory, Chatham Square Music School, NYC (1954–57). He was the author and composer of *The Ballad of the Golden Threshold* (1941), *Te Deum* (1942), *Humphrey Potter* (1943), *Memories of Czechoslovakia* (1944), *A Millennium of Earliest Christian Hymn Writing* (1948), *Folk Dance Music of Slavic Nations* (1952), *Cantus Contra Bella* (1957), *Joseph Luitpold and His Composers* (1862) and many others.

Artur Schnabel (1882–1951), b. Lipník, Moravia, was a classical pianist and composer. In 1922, he made his debut in US and returned to this country in 1933, as pianist and teacher. He was accepted as one of the greatest interpreters of the music of Beethoven, as well as of Mozart and Schubert. Schnabel edited all the Beethoven piano sonatas, and wrote two volumes on music, and composed a piano concerto, three string quartets, several sonatas, and many pieces for piano.

Arnold Schoenberg (1874-1951), b. Vienna, of Slovak father and Bohemian mother (Náchod), was a composer, music theorist, teacher, writer, and painter. He was associated with the expressionist movement in poetry and art and the leader of the Second Viennese School. He immigrated to the US in 1934. He gained fame as a musical innovator and pioneer of modernism in 20th-century Western music. He created new methods of musical composition involving atonality, namely serialism and the 12-tone row. He was also one of the most-influential teachers of the 20th century; among his most significant pupils were Alban Berg and Anton Webern.

Edmund P. Sedivy (1911-1995), b. Verdigre, NE, of Czech ancestry, was a teacher and musician trained at Nebraska State Teachers College, Northwestern School of Music and Juilliard School of Music. He was member and director of the 46th Army Montana National Guard Band, director of the Algeria Shrine Band and was director of bands, Montana State Univ. (1946-69); and also, music professor of music education at Montana State University (1970-77). He was former City Commissioner elected for five consecutive terms and former Mayor of the City of Bozeman, Montana for three terms.

Tibor Serly (1901-1978), b. Lošonec, Bratislava, was a violist, violinist, and composer. He immigrated to America with his family in 1905. Spending much of his childhood in New York City, Serly played in various pit orchestras led by his father. In 1922, he returned to Hungary to attend the Franz Liszt Academy of Music in Budapest, where he studied composition with Zoltán Kodály, violin with Jenö Hubay, and orchestration with Leó Weiner. After his return to America (1927), he played and played the violin for ten years in Cincinnati in addition to composing, and then in the Philadelphia and NBC Symphony Orchestras. He lived in New York from 1937, and from then on was primarily engaged in teaching and composing. Serly taught composition at the Manhattan School of Music in New York City (among other institutions) and was also a featured composer/conductor with the Danish radio orchestra.

William R. Sima (1892-1965), b. Baltimore, of Bohemian ancestry, at the age of 15, began his professional career as a musician as the musical director at the Wilson Theatre. Prior to his military band service, he conducted pit bands in New York and Washington, performed as violinist at the old Caswell Hotel, and at the age of 18 played for Lillian Russell in a musical comedy, and for Margaret Anglin in *Lady Windermere's Fan*. In the summer of 1918, he played with Victor Herbert in the *Red Mill* and *Naughty Marietta* at the premiere performance at Ford's Theatre. For 19 years after coming to Annapolis, he played in various theatres and picture show houses, up until movietones replaced the silent films. He joined the Naval Academy Band in 1910 at the age of 18 and served as Assistant Leader for many years. He became H. J. Peterman's successor in 1933 and served as USNA Band Leader until 1946. Lt. Sima has a creditable number of musical compositions to his credit, including the *Victory March* and many football songs, as well as innumerable scores for academy shows such as *Gangway* and *Cease Firing*.

Mathias 'Math' J. Sladky (1931-2009), b. Wahoo, NE, of Bohemian ancestry, was a Polka Band leader. His band began playing 'live' every Sunday on KLMS Radio in Lincoln, Nebraska for over 7 years. During the week his music was taped. With playing on the radio, his band popularity flourished that there were some weeks he played every night and several years he played over 300 jobs. At the height of their popularity, *Bill Board* magazine rated Math Sladky and his KLMS Polka Band as #1 in Nebraska. After his military service call-up, he started another band. Sladky has released 21 recordings of polkas and waltzes with his band. His band has played from Canada to Texas and Ohio to Wyoming. Sladky has even taken polkas to the pulpit. In 1987, Sladky was inducted into the Sokol Omaha Polka Hall of Fame and in 2002, he was inducted in the Musicians Hall of Fame in Milligan, Nebraska.

Walter Smetak (1913-1984), b. Zurich, Switzerland, of Czech ancestry, was a cellist, composer, and inventor. He migrated to Brazil in 1937. He was a composer and inventor of instruments with which he would then play and conduct. Relatively unknown, he is considered a forerunner and early influence on the musicians and artists who would form the core of Tropicalia, such as Caetano Veloso, Gilberto Gil, Tom Zé and Torquato Neto. One of his best-known works is the experimental album titled *Smetak*, released in Brazil in 1974. Deeply involved in the Brazilian music scene of the 1960s and 1970s, Walter Smetak would collaborate with the likes of Gilberto Gil, Tom Zé, Uakti and others.

Gitta Hana Steiner (1932-1990), b. Prague, Czech., is a pianist, composer and teacher educated at Juilliard School of Music. She was a private instructor of piano (s. 1960); with Brooklyn Cons. of Music (s. 1963), as prof. of composition (s. 1983). She performed orchestral and chamber music throughout the US and abroad.

Josef Stránský (1872-1936), of Humpolec, Bohemia, was a conductor of the New York Philharmonic. He succeeded Gustav Mahler as the principal conductor of the New York Philharmonic Soc., holding the post from 1911 until 1923. Subsequently, he directed the New York State Symphony Orchestra which had been founded for him.

Fritz Stiedry (1883-1936), born in Vienna, of Bohemian ancestry, was a conductor and composer, whose talent was originally noticed by Gustav Mahler who appointed him his assistant at the Vienna Court in 1907. In 1937, Stiedry left for the US, where he conducted long-neglected works of Bach, Haydn and Mozart and premiering Schoenberg's Second

Chamber symphony. From 1945 onwards, he returned to opera, conducting the Lyric Opera of Chicago and the Metropolitan Opera of New York.

Jan Walter Susskind (1913-1980), from Prague, Bohemia, became music director of the Toronto Symphony Orchestra, of the Aspen Music Festival, CO, and the St. Louis Symphony Orchestra.

Edward E. Svoboda (1913-2012), was one of ten children. He was a leader of the Red Raven Orchestra for over 70 years, member of South Omaha Eagles #38 for 50 years, member of Bellevue Rod and Gun Club, inducted into Sokol Polka Hall of Fame in 1974.

Tomáš Svoboda (1939-2022), b. Paris, France, of Czech ancestry, is a Czech American contemporary classical composer, performer, and conductor. After escaping from Czechoslovakia at the beginning of World War II, the family lived in Boston, where three-year-old Tomas started piano lessons with his father. After the war, the family moved to Prague, where Svoboda studied at the Prague Conservatory. He graduated in 1962 with degrees in percussion, composition, and conducting and was recognized as a piano virtuoso. In 1964, the family fled the Communist regime in Czechoslovakia and returned to the United States. Svoboda's catalog contains over 200 compositions, including six symphonies and five concerti. His music is performed worldwide and recordings of more than 50 works have now been released. Svoboda's Piano Trios CD recording received a 2001 "Critics Choice Award" from the American Record Guide. A versatile chamber pianist, Svoboda composed for and performed in the Composers' Ensemble and Cascadia Composers. For fifteen years, he led Trio Spektrum, the flute, clarinet, and piano trio for which he wrote six works.

Henry Swoboda (1897-1990), b. Prague, Bohemia, was a Czech conductor and musicologist, educated under Zemlinsky and Talich. From 1931 to 1938, he was conductor with Prague Radio. After coming to US in 1938, he conducted mainly for record companies and also taught music. In 1964, he was appointed conductor of the University Orchestra at the Univ. of Texas in Austin.

George Szell (1897-1970), b. Budapest, of Czechoslovak ancestry, was a conductor and composer. He is widely considered one of the twentieth century's greatest conductors. He is remembered today for his long and successful tenure as music director of the Cleveland Orchestra of Cleveland, Ohio, and for the recordings of the standard classical repertoire, he made in Cleveland and with other orchestras. Szell came to Cleveland in 1946 to take over a respected if undersized orchestra, which was struggling to recover from the disruptions of World War II. By the time of his death, he was credited with having built it into what many critics regarded as the world's keenest symphonic instrument.

VIII. CULTURE: ARTS & LETTERS

Peter Elyakim Taussig (1944-), b. Prague, Czech., grew up in Israel, where his parents emigrated following the Communist take-over in 1949. At age 11, Taussig began studying composition at the Israeli Academy of Music, during which time he began giving concert and radio performances. After leaving Israel, Taussig moved to Canada, where he enrolled at the University of Toronto. His debut with the Toronto Symphony launched his solo and chamber music career. In 1973, Taussig began a long relationship with the Canadian Broadcasting Corporation. Over the next decade, Taussig recorded over 200 chamber music broadcasts for the CBC - including the complete works of Beethoven, Schubert, Mendelssohn, Schumann, and Brahms. In 1979, Taussig founded the Stratford Summer Music Festival in Ontario and became its first artistic director.

Walter Taussig (1908-2003), b. Vienna, of Bohemian ancestry, was a graduate of the Music Academy in Vienna, where he studied composition with Franz Schmidt and conducting with Robert Heger. He worked as a conductor at the Chicago Opera, the Montreal Opera, and San Francisco Opera before being hired by the Metropolitan Opera as its assistant chorus master. He established himself as an invaluable coach, especially in German repertoire, serving as a mentor to several generations of Met singers, from Birgit Nilsson. Who called him 'the father' of her Elektra, to Placido Domingo, who coached the role of Parsifal with him, and Deborah Voigt.

Wilson Touchet (1961-), b. Abbeville, St. Martin Parish, LA, of Bohemian ancestry, was a band leader and accordion player. He was raised in the cajun parish of St. Martin, LA, on a farm, producing mostly cotton and cayenne pepper. His Dad was a sharecropper, and they moved several times between Cypress Island and Breau Bridge, LA. Wilson Touchet spoke only Cajun French until he started school and was taught English. He was raised listening to traditional Cajun music and brings this heritage to the music of La Touché, a famed 5-piece band. Some of the venues La Touché has appeared at are, the John Anson Ford Theater in Hollywood, CA., on river boats in New Orleans, The University of Miami, Blossom Music Center in Akron, Ohio for MCA Records, Walker and Grand Portage, Minn., Michaul's Restaurant and Mulate's Restaurant in New Orleans, New Year's Eve Public Street Party in Mobile, Alabama, and the International Celtic Festival in Glasgow, Scotland. In 1999, La Touché had four albums available in the U.S. and one available in Europe.

Adolph Torovský (1867-1945), b. Prague, Bohemia, studied with prominent musicians in Vienna, including the famed waltz king, Johann Strauss, Jr. In 1892, he joined the Naval Academy Band, becoming director (s. 1916). In 1913, he was also conductor of the St. John's College Band.

Jiří (George) Traxler (1912–2011), b. Tábor, Bohemia. was a Czech Canadian jazz and swing pianist, composer, lyricist and arranger, and was considered a founder and co-creator of the swing music era in Czechoslovakia. He was the last surviving collaborator of the renowned Czech pre-war composer Jaroslav Ježek. In 1951, he emigrated to Canada, and lived with his wife, Jarmila, in Edmonton until his death in the summer of 2011. He gradually ended up finding fulfillment as a composer and arranger. He settled in Montreal and worked as a drafter in the company Canadair Ltd. Traxler published his memoires *Já nic, já muzikant* (Don't Blame Me, I'm Just a Musician) in 1982.

Jaroslav Vajda (1919–2008), b. East Chicago, IN, of Slovak descent; son of Lutheran pastor Rev. John Vajda, ordained as Lutheran minister, was noted as an American hymnist. Vajda did not write his first hymn until age 49. From that time until his death in 2008 at age 89, he wrote over 200 original and translated hymns that appear worldwide in more than 65 hymnals. He also published two collections of hymn texts, numerous books, translations, and articles. Vajda served on hymnal commissions for Hymnal Supplement (1969) and Lutheran Book of Worship (1978). He was named a Fellow of The Hymn Society in the United States and Canada.

Miroslav Ladislav Vitouš (1947–), b. Prague, Czech., is a Czech jazz bassist, composer and bandleader, who is known for his extensive career in the US. He studied under F. Posta at the Prague Conservatory. After winning a scholarship to the Berklee College of Music in Boston, he came to the U.S. a year later in 1966, he moved to New York and collaborated with musicians such as Bob Brookmeyer, Chick Corea, Miles Davis, Art Farmer, Stan Getz, Charlie Mariano, and Herbie Mann. In 1970, the group Weather Report was formed along with Wayne Shorter and Joe Zawinul. Three years later, he formed the Miroslav Vitous Group along with John Surman, Kenny Kirkland and Jon Christensen. In 1979, Vitous became the director of the Jazz Department at the New England Conservatory in Boston. In 1988, he removed himself from academia in order to focus all his energy on composing and performing.

Ernst von Dohnanyi (1877–1960), b. Bratislava, Slovakia, was one of the most distinguished pianists of his time, besides being a composer, conductor, and teacher. In 1919, after being forced out of the Academy for political reasons, Dohnányi became the chief conductor of the Budapest Philharmonic Society (1919–44) and later with the New York State Symphony Orchestra (1925 on). In 1949, he accepted the position at Florida State College in Tallahassee. His output includes three operas, two symphonies and wealth of chamber music.

Jaromír Weinberger (1896–1967), b. Prague, Bohemia, a pupil of Hofmeister, Křička and Reger, was a prolific Czech composer of operas, operettas, and orchestral works. He was a prodigy of near-Mozartian proportions, starting piano at the age of five and composing by his tenth year. In 1926, Weinberger completed Švanda Dudák (Schwanda the Bagpiper) which became one of the most popular operatic works between the wars, with thousands of performances in hundreds of theaters including the Metropolitan Opera in New York. While unable to duplicate that level of success in his subsequent works, Weinberger was a prolific, productive, and highly effective composer for several decades. He permanently settled in US in 1939.

Hugo David Weisgall (1912–1997), b. Ivančice, Moravia, was an was an American composer and conductor, who studied at the Peabody Institute and at the Curtis Institute of Music and later earned a Ph.D. in German literature at Johns Hopkins University. After the war he became a professor, and taught at Queens College, the Juilliard School, and the Jewish Theological Seminary, all in New York City. One of America's most important opera composers, Hugo Weisgall's output also included orchestral, chamber and choral works, eight major song cycles, and music for ballet. His opera *Six Characters in Search of an Author* brought Weisgall national acclaim when it was first performed by the New York City Opera in 1959. His other operas include *Athaliah*, *The Gardens of Adonis*, *Jenny/or The Hundred Nights*, *Will You Marry Me?*, *The Tenor*, and his most frequently performed opera, *The Stronger*.

Philip Yosowitz (ca. 1950–), b. Cleveland, OH, son of Czech immigrant father., is a Houston surgeon by day and composer by night. He completed his medical training at UCLA and at Walter Reed Army Hospital in Washington, D.C., and began his private practice in Houston, TX where he now resides. While Dr. Yosowitz's love for composing began in childhood, 'The Gold' is his first completed musical theatre work. The story of 'The Gold' was inspired by his love of athletics and his childhood memories of living with family members who were Holocaust survivors that had recently immigrated to the United States. Dr. Yosowitz is a lover of history, who later wrote a musical based on Joan of Arc.

Jeronym Zajíček (1926–2007), b. Krásné Březno, Czech., was a composer of orchestral works. He studied musicology with Josef Hutter at the Charles University in Prague from 1946 to 1949, he also took private lessons in conducting and orchestration with Otakar Jeremiáš. In 1949, he left the country and worked from 1950 to 1952 for the Czech section of Radio Free Europe in Munich. From 1952 to 1955 he studied privately, then until 1960 at Roosevelt University in Chicago with Karel Boleslav Jirák, Paul Amadeus Pisk, Oswald Jonas and Rudolph Ganz. From 1958 to 1964, he conducted the children's choir at Phil Sheridan Middle School in Chicago, lectured on music theory for the next two years, and conducted the choir at Chicago's Fenger College. Finally, in 1966, he became professor of conducting and composition at Loop College (later Washington College). He worked here until his retirement in 1996. As a composer, he emerged with choral works, chamber music and orchestral works.

John Stepan Zamecnik (1872–1953), b. Cleveland, OH, of Czech immigrant parents, was a composer, a pioneer in the scoring of Hollywood film music. Zamecnik studied at the Prague Conservatory of Music under Antonín Dvořák in the mid-1890s, completing his classes there in 1897. In 1899, Zamecnik returned to the United States. While living in Cleveland, where he worked as a violinist and composer, he also played in the Pittsburgh Symphony Orchestra as a violinist under Victor Herbert. In 1907, Zamecnik became music director of the newly constructed Hippodrome Theater in Cleveland, Ohio. When the Hippodrome commenced with the screening of silent films, Zamecnik began to compose music scores for them. They were published by Samuel Fox, whose company was the first to publish original film scores in the United States. Among his compositions, he provided musical numbers for the early shows of the Hermit Club and won a contest against 900 competitors to compose the California state song in 1915. In 1925 he went to Hollywood, where he contributed the scores to such films as *Abie's Irish Rose*, *Old Ironsides*, *Wings*, and *Betrayal*. By the time of his death in Los Angeles, he was credited with nearly 2,000 compositions.

John Zdechlik (1937–2020), b. Minneapolis, MN, of Czech heritage, was an American composer, music teacher, and conductor. Zdechlik was elected to the American Bandmasters Association and many of his compositions became standard concert band repertoire, including *Chorale and Shaker Dance*.

Eric Zeisl (1905–1959), b. Vienna, of Bohemian mother, was a composer. He studied at Vienna Academy of Music. After coming to US, he became a composer of music for MGM, Hollywood (1941–43). He also taught at So. California School of Music (1943–49) and Los Angeles City Coll. (1949–59). His compositions include operas *Leonce and Lena* (1937) and *Job*, ballets *Uranium 235*, *Jacob and Rachael* and a number of orchestral and chamber music pieces, as well as songs.

Fritz Zweig (1893–1984), b. Olomouc, Moravia, was a conductor. He studied composition and theory with Arnold Schoenberg in Vienna and Berlin. After conducting in Germany, he became first conductor with German Theater in Prague (1934–38). In 1940, he emigrated to US and during 1944–46 he conducted throughout the US. In 1946, his conducting activities halted due to ill health. He then turned to teaching conducting in Hollywood, CA.

2. Musicians

Austin Mark Adamec (1988–), b. Jacksonville, FL, of Czech and Slovak descent, is a guitarist, who primarily plays Christian pop music. Adamec earned a baccalaureate in Marketing from the University of Florida, in 2010. He has released one studio album, *All the Brighter*, in 2015. The song, "My Only Answer", charted on the *Billboard* magazine Christian Airplay chart.

George Antheil (1900–1959), b. Trenton, NJ, of Bohemian ancestry, studied with Constantin von Sternberg, Ernest Bloch, and with Clark Smith at the Philadelphia Conservatory. In 1922, he traveled to Europe to pursue a career as a concert pianist, performing in recital many of his own works such as *Mechanisms*, *Airplane Sonata*, and *Sonata Sauvage*. In Berlin, he met Stravinsky who became an important influence on his compositional style. Antheil wrote over 300 musical works in all major genres, including symphonies, chamber works, film music, and operas. He was extremely outspoken and articulate, and wrote numerous articles, as well as an autobiography, *Bad Boy of Music*. As a young composer, he considered himself to be quite the revolutionary, and his music, especially in his early career, employed many unusual sound sources and combinations of instruments. In many ways, both musical and technical, he was far ahead of his time. His concerts routinely caused riots all over Europe, which at the time was considered a sign of genius.

Kajetán Antonín Attl (1889–1976), b. Czech., studied harp with Czech teacher Hanuš Trneček. He emigrated to US in 1909, first to Chicago (1909–10), Denver (1910–1913), San Francisco from 1914. He was principal harp with San Francisco Symphony Orch. (1914–41) and principal harp with San Francisco Opera (until 1952). He was injured in an automobile accident in 1952 which compelled him to retire from the San Francisco Opera. He also played with the orchestra of the San Francisco Panama-Pacific International Exhibition (summer of 1915). As a conductor, 1934 he gained a Federal CWA grant to hire 50 union musicians to form the Chamber Orchestra of San Francisco, which Attl conducted without remuneration.

Vojmír Attl (1894–1967), b. Czech., studied harp with Czech teacher Hanus Trnecek. He was a harpist with San Francisco Symphony Orch. (1928–30). He was also Cincinnati Symphony harpist in 1930s and 1940s.

Christian Ferdinand Balatka (1861–1899), b. Chicago, of Bohemian ancestry, was a pianist and teacher. He studied under his father Hans Balatka and at the age of 13, was playing difficult compositions. He completed his studies at the Royal Academy of Music in Berlin, and in Leipzig. He then returned to Chicago. He was asst. dir. of the Balatka Musical Coll. for twenty-two years, and then became president. He was also director of the piano dept. of Dyrenforth College and devoted his attention to concert work, teaching and composing.

George Bareither (1842-d.), b. Bohemia, was double bassist with Boston Symphony Orchestra (1882-85, 1887-1907). He also toured the Chautauqua Circuit in 1899 with the International Symphony Club with Nikolai Sokolof violin, W. W. Swornsbourne violin, A. S. Martin viola, and Eric Loeffler cello.

Jacob Bareither (1847-1915), b. Bohemia, was third oboist with Chicago Symphony Orchestra (1891-98). He joined the Chicago Orchestra during its initial season 1891-1892 as third oboist. In 1910s, he became a hotel orchestra musician in Chicago.

Libushka Bartusek-Brown (1897-1999), b. Chicago, of Czech ancestry, was a pianist and dancer, and translator of opera librettos. She was trained at Charles Univ. and Conservatory of Music in Prague. She began her performance career at the age of three—at her father's Christmas party—then went on to spend years as a solo dancer with the Chicago Grand Opera and the Chicago Civic Opera, as well as appear on stage, screen and radio. She became very popular due to her masterful translation of the libretti of Smetana's *Bartered Bride* and Jaromir Weinberger's *Schwanda the Bagpiper*, which were produced in Chicago in the Garrick Theater and at the Univ. of Chicago, respectively, and scored tremendous success. She also authored two children's books and at the age of 97, she published her memoir *Everything but Circus and Burlesque: Libuska's Memoirs* (1994).

Prof. Paul Eugene Beck (1871-1934), b. Lititz, PA, the son of Abraham R. Beck (1833-1928) of Moravian ancestry, and Joanna Salome Huebener, was a musician and a teacher. He was educated at the Beck Family School in Lititz, Dr. Lock's Prepar Joanna Salome Huebener Atory School in Norristown, Moravian College in Bethlehem, and New York University. He taught for a time in the Beck Family School, and later was an art and music teacher in the Lancaster County schools. He was state supervisor of music and art during the superintendency of Dr. C. N. Schaeffer. During his late years, he has been a professor of literature in Moravian College, Bethlehem. For many years, Prof. Beck was organist and choirmaster of the Lititz Moravian Church and served in the same capacity at the Moravian Church in Nazareth. He was well-known in Lancaster and nearby counties as the leader of the Beck Concert Band, of Lititz. He was married to Elizabeth Loeffler, and they had 2 children.

Joseph C. Bejcek (1919-1998), b. Illinois, was asst principal trombonist with the Chicago Symphony Orch. (1947-54). He also played trombone at J. Sterling Morton High School in Cicero, Illinois and taught at Roosevelt University (1956-1958).

Henry Bielo (1895-1956), b. Bohemia, brother of Julius Bielo, emigrated with his brother, to the US in 1920. He played bassoon for two seasons in the Philadelphia Orchestra (1920-22). Later he became a teacher in Pittsburgh. He spent most of his career in Pittsburgh, PA.

Julius Bielo (1885–1955), b. Bohemia, brother of Henry Bielo, emigrated with his brother to the US in 1920. He played double bass with the Philadelphia Orchestra (1920–22). He also taught at Carnegie Institute, Pittsburgh, and played double bass at Pittsburgh Symphony in 1940s under Fritz Reiner. He spent most of his career in Pittsburgh, PA.

Harry J. Brabec (1927–2005), b. Oak Park, IL, of Czech parents, was a percussionist and virtuoso snare drummer, greatly admired by his peers not only for his exceptional music talents, but for his keen sense of humor and gutsy approach to life. His name became legend when, at the peak of his career as principal percussionist of the Chicago Symphony Orchestra in 1956, Fritz Reiner dismissed him for purely personal reasons, effectively destroying his career and leading to the failure of his first marriage. His comeback story is told by his second wife Barbara in her book *The Drummer Drives! Everybody Else Rides* (2010).

Frederick Brandeis (1832–1899), b. Vienna, of Bohemian ancestry, was a pianist and accompanist and composer. After the 1848 Revolution, came to New York, where he made appearance as a solo pianist and accompanist. After traveling through the country with various concert companies, he settled in NYC and devoted himself to composition and teaching. He was also the organist of Sts. Peter and Paul's R.C. Church, Brooklyn and of the Forty-fourth Street Synagogue, NYC. He wrote a number of compositions.

Frank Brouk (1913–2004), b. Chicago, IL, of Bohemian immigrant parents, was a horn player. Brouk studied with fellow Bohemian Frank Kryl in Chicago, and with Louis Dufrasne who also taught CSO horns Philip Farkas, Helen Kotas, and Clyde Miller. He was Principal horn player with the Indianapolis Symphony (about 1939–42); Rochester Philharmonic (1941–42); Cleveland Orchestra Principal horn (1947–50), horn (1946–47). He was Principal horn with the Chicago Symphony Orchestra (1961–63, 1965–66), horn (1961–62, 1963–65, 1966–78). Brouk was joint owner of the Carl Geyer horn store in Chicago.

Milan Bohumil Bučil (1936–), b. Prague, Czech., graduated from the Prague Conservatory of Music and studied musicology at Charles Univ. For seven years, he then toured Europe, playing all kinds of music, from classical to jazz to pop. In 1967, he played in Bern where he joined the Gunter Moritz Quartet and then went to Interlachen and Geneva. In 1968, he came to Canada. He taught at Scarborough HS and also at the Royal Conservatory of Music. He also played in various bands, including his own Umpa-Pas Band. Bučil also composed songs, scenic and stage music and wrote two books.

Pavel Burda (1942–), b. České Budějovice, Czech., is a timpanist, and percussionist educated at Prague Conservatory of Music and State Univ. of New York. He toured with orchestra in Europe and North Africa. He was a solo timpanist, Brazilian Symphony Orchestra (1968–69); principal timpanist and percussionist, Orchestra de Camera, NY. Developed the Music with

Percussion Ensemble at Univ. of Wisconsin at Milwaukee. Founder of the Milwaukee Twentieth Century Ensemble (1979). He was assoc. professor of music, Conservatory of Music, PR (1975-76), Univ. of Wisconsin. He was also TV and radio broadcaster.

Joseph Ottokar Čadek (1868-1927), b. Prague, Bohemia, was a prominent Czech violinist who settled in Chattanooga in 1892. There he founded the Cadek Conservatory of Music at the Univ. of Tennessee in 1904.

Ottokar Theodore Cadek (1897-1927), b. Chattanooga, TN, of Czech ancestry, violinist, teacher and conductor, was educated in Zurich and Birmingham Cons. of Music. Appeared in concerts in Chattanooga, Knoxville, Ashville, Baltimore, Washington, DC (for President McKinley). He was first violinist of New York String Quartet and New York Chamber of Music Soc. He was president and owner of Cadek Conservatory of Music, Chattanooga, TN (s. 1904). Cadek was also concertmaster, Chattanooga Symphony Orch., Cadek String Quartet.

Albert Vojtěch 'Vojta' Černý (1872-1964), b. Jilove, Bohemia, was a violoncellist of note and piano teacher and virtuoso. He immigrated to the US in 1888, settling in Chicago. He was a successful music teacher (piano, cello, violin, voice) and the founder of the first Bohemian Conservatory of Music in Chicago, where he was also a professor.

Milada Cerny (1892-1973), b. Chicago; of Czech ancestry, was a pianist. She was a daughter of Albert Vojtěch Černý, who immigrated to the US in 1888. He was a successful music teacher (piano, cello, violin, voice) and the founder of the first Bohemian Conservatory of Music in Chicago. Milada was a child prodigy, who began piano at the age of 3, becoming a virtuoso pianist and touring the United States at about age 9 and Europe at about age 10. In 1905-06, the artist Alfonse Mucha, who stayed several months with the Černy family in Chicago, painted several pictures of Milada.

William Cerny (1928-), b. New York, NY, of Czech ancestry, a pianist, after completing his studies at Yale, worked for 5 years (1954-59) as a professional accompanist out of New York City, touring the US, with such artists as cellist Aldo Parisot, Anna Russell, Angna Enters. His professional work in NYC also included accompanying artists in town hall recitals. Subsequently, he served for 13 years on the faculty of the Eastman School of Music (1959-72). After that, he became chairman of the music department at the University of Notre Dame (1972-81). Solo and chamber performances, along with master classes, have taken Prof. Cerny to scores of university campuses throughout the US. He has also made five separate guest appearances with the Chicago Symphony String Quartet. Prof. Cerny has made over 65 cassette recordings of solo piano literature, including over 150 separate titles.

VIII. CULTURE: ARTS & LETTERS

Joseph Edward Chapek (1895-1977), b. Chicago, IL, of Bohemian ancestry (son of the violinist Joseph Horomyr Chapek), was a violinist and teacher. He studied at Prague Cons. under Otakar Ševčík and Jindřich Feld. He was prof. of violin, Chicago Cons. of Music and Chapek Music School. After his father's death, he became director of the Chapek Music School (s. 1932).

Joseph Horymír Chapek (orig. Čapek) (1858-1932), b. Jestřebice, Bohemia, was a violinist, conductor, and composer. He introduced the Ševčík Violin Method in America (1883). He became first violinist with Mendelssohn Quintet Club, Milwaukee, WI (1883-85) and concert master of the Bach Symphony Orchestra, Milwaukee, WI (1885-88). In 1888, he came to Chicago to take charge of the violin dept. of the Chicago Conservatory and later at the Apollo School of Music. He was professor of violin, Kemper Hall, Kenosha, WI (1904-10); and director of his own Chapek Music School (s. 1910).

Stephanie Ann Chase (1957-), b. Evanston, IL, is the daughter of two musicians, the noted arranger and composer Bruce Chase and violinist Fannie Paschell, the latter being of Czech ancestry, her father having been born in Rokytnice, Bohemia. She is an American classical violinist. A remarkably versatile artist, Stephanie Chase excels in the virtuoso's repertoire and contemporary music, as well as historically informed performance practice. She gave her first public performance when only two years old and was recognized as a child prodigy. She made her debut with the Chicago Symphony at age eight. Her Carnegie Hall debut at eighteen was followed by appearances as soloist and in recital at major venues throughout the world. Her recordings include the first ever of Beethoven's 'Violin Concerto' on period instruments, which features her own cadenzas and is acclaimed as "one of the twenty most outstanding performances in the work's recording history." Additional performances by Ms. Chase in 2013/2014 include a recital of Russian music at New York's prestigious Kaufmann Hall and appearances with the Boulder Chamber Orchestra, Seattle Collaborative Symphony and the Stanford Philharmonia Orchestra at the newly opened, acoustically superlative Bing Concert Hall. She is married to Stewart S. Pollens (1949-).

Jaroslav Čimera (1885-1972), b. Přikosice, nr. Plzeň, Bohemia, was a noted trombone and euphonium player. He became soloist and assistant director in Kryl's Band, first trombonist in Sousa Band in 1914, member of Innes Band, and in 1915, he organized a Czechoslovak Band of his own and toured the country for Ellison White, and Redpath Lyceum and Chatauqua Bureau. He was a member of the Chicago Symphony Orchestra and since 1923, had been broadcasting regularly over station KYW.

Fred J. Divisek (1908-1998), b. Douglas, WI, of Czech ancestry, was educated at the Oshkosh State Teachers College and Hrusa Conservatory of Music. He was one of the youngest men given the post of snare drummer and middle man in the percussion section of Chicago Civic Opera Co. He performed with more than 20 different orchestras and bands. He also taught at the Joliet Musical College-Illinois and then prior to the San Francisco Symphony, worked in a music store and taught music in Oregon. He was with San Francisco Opera Orchestra (1954-59). After the San Francisco Symphony, he played in the Long Beach Municipal Band in the 1960s and the Long Beach Symphony.

Charles Dobias (1923-2001), b. Klàtova Novà Ves, Czech., was a prominent Canadian violinist. He arrived in Toronto at age seven. He won a Canada Council Grant to study in Prague with the great violinist Josef Suk during the summers of 1972 to 1974. As a member of the Toronto Symphony, he toured Japan, England, Scotland, and France with Seiji Ozawa conducting, and as concert master and soloist with the National Ballet Company of Canada, he toured all of Canada and the U.S. and performed as soloist in Mexico. In 1970, he accepted the position of Concert Master of the Edmonton Symphony and in 1972, came to Winnipeg as Concert Master for the Royal Winnipeg Ballet and as Associate Concert Master of the Winnipeg Symphony.

Robert Dolejsi (1892-1976), b. Chicago, IL. studied violin for more than four years with Otakar Ševčík. Dolejsi was a celebrated violinist, not only because he was a great violinist and viola expert but also because he was one of five exponents of the Viole d'Armour, that rare instrument which had received attention of ever-increasing number of serious students. Dolejsi was a member of the musical staff of the National Broadcasting Co. and was associated with the music department of the University of Chicago as director of chamber music and string ensemble. He authored *Modern Viola Technique* (1939).

Darry Dolezal (1961-), b. Lawrence, KS, of Czech ancestry, attended the University of Kansas, where he earned his Bachelor's degree in cello performance in 1982 with highest distinction and received the coveted Presser Award. An accomplished cellist, Dolezal has performed thousands of concerts in venues ranging from Carnegie Hall in New York City to the Copacabana Palace in Rio de Janeiro. His performances have been broadcast on major radio and television stations, including TV Cultura in Brazil, CBC Radio and Television in Canada, Netherlands Public Radio, WNYC in New York, WFMT in Chicago and WGBH in Boston. He has recorded for the Albany, Capstone, Centaur and CRI record labels.

Paul Desmond (orig. Paul Emil Breitenfeld) (1924-1977), b. San Francisco, CA, of Bohemian ancestry, was an American jazz alto saxophonist and composer, best known for the work he did in the Dave Brubeck Quartet and for penning that group's greatest hit, "Take Five". He was one of the most popular musicians to come out of the West Coast's cool jazz scene, and the possessor of a legendary and idiosyncratic wit. In addition to his work with

Brubeck, he led several of his own groups and did significant collaboration with artists such as Gerry Mulligan, Jim Hall and Chet Baker. After years of chain smoking and general poor health, Desmond succumbed to lung cancer in 1977 following one last tour with Brubeck.

Les Dudek (1952-), b. Naval Air Station, Quonset Point, RI, of Bohemian ancestry, is an American guitarist. He had built quite a reputation around the Florida area as a proficient guitar player, having started playing in local bands as a teenager. He is in constant demand as a sideman, and his playing has graced such all-time classic albums as the Allman Brothers' *Brothers and Sisters*, Boz Scaggs' *Silk Degrees* and the Steve Miller Band's *Fly Like an Eagle* and *Book of Dreams*, not to mention recordings by Stevie Nicks, Cher, Maria Muldaur, Dave Mason and others.

Steve Eckels (Steven Zdenek Eckels) (1955-2023), b. Las Vegas, New Mexico, of Czech grandfather (Zdeněk Ginsburg), is classical guitarist. He began playing guitar in 1965 at the age of 10 in Danville, Virginia where he was influenced by Afro-American soul music and country music, including the music of Chet Atkins. He received his formal training at Berklee College of Music and New England Conservatory where he studied jazz and classical music. His current repertoire of original music reflects his formal training and cultural influences. He was the instructor of guitar for School District #5 and Flathead Valley Community College and is the published author of numerous guitar books.

Frank Elias (1889-1958) b. of Bohemian ancestry, was a drummer who played drums in the pit orchestra at the Orpheum Theater during the days of vaudeville and the days of musical road shows. He organized the Shrine Band in 1918 and was the leader of the band for several years. He was a past president of the Omaha Musicians Association.

Fred Elias (1891-1970), b. Czech., is a trumpeter. He was a member of the Omaha Symphony Orchestra in Nebraska. He wrote three books, entitled *Secrets of the Trumpet*, *The Elias Buzz System*, and *The Emboucher Developer*, in which he described his system of playing every scale on a trumpet without touching the valves. He won a gold trumpet from a musical instrument company in 1931 in recognition of the unusual playing method.

Stephen A. Erst (1888-1956), b. Chicago, IL, of Czech ancestry, was an organist and pianist educated at the Chicago Musical Coll. and the Prague Conservatory. He made his debut as concert pianist at Chicago's Music Hall in 1910. For many years he held the position of organist and choirmaster of St. Ignatius Church. He was also on the faculty of the Auditorium Cons. of Music (1913-20) and director of the Smetana Singing Society (1914-27), in addition to maintaining his private studio in piano, organ and voice (s. 1910).

Eva Fabian-Reihs (1947–), b. Bratislava, Czech., is a pianist, and music teacher. She studied at Manhattan School of Music (B.M., 1972; M.M., 1974), and Julliard School of Music (Dipl., 1973). She resided in Jackson Heights, NY.

Marion Leona Fabry, b. Chicago, of Slovak parents, was an organist and choir director, Chicago. She entered De Paul University, Chicago and obtained Bachelor of Musical Education in 1931. She was a music teacher in the junior and Senior high schools of Chicago (1931-32) and then became organist and choir director at the Assumption Slovak Catholic Parish.

Chris Falteisek (1966–), b. Prescott, WI, of Czech ancestry, started playing organ and piano for church as a 6th grader. After attending the St. John Vianney Seminary at the College of St. Thomas in St. Paul, MN, Falteisek graduated from the University of Wisconsin, River Falls in 1988. He currently works as Minister of Worship at Christ Episcopal Church in Woodbury and is an accompanist at St. Elizabeth Ann Seton Catholic Church in Hastings and St. Thomas Aquinas Catholic Church in St. Paul Park. He has composed and recorded 15 albums. His musical performances have taken him to Sweden, Norway and around the United States. Falteisek's musical style is eclectic and mirrors his love of various historical periods.

Vincenc František Faltis (1856-1951), b. Jihlava, Moravia, was a self-taught violinist and horn player. He played in military bands throughout Europe and later organized bands in Bulgaria, Russia and Egypt. For a time, he was a professor at the Imperial Cons. at St. Petersburg. In the early 1900's, he came to US and became American citizen. For several years, he was a conductor at Barnum and Bailey's and finally became choir dir. at the Presbyterian Church in Brooklyn, NY. He composed several successful melodic pieces with Oriental themes for Barnum's pagans, such as *Cleopatra* and *The Queen of Sheba*, etc.

Philip Farkas (1914-1992), b. Chicago, IL, of Czechoslovak parents, was a horn player. He was the principal horn player in the Chicago Symphony Orchestra for many years (1947-60). In 1960, he left to join the music faculty at Indiana University, Bloomington. Before that, he was principal horn with Kansas City Philharmonic (1933-36), starting at age 18, Chicago Symphony (1936-41), Cleveland Orchestra (1941-45); a co-principal horn at Boston Symphony (1945-46).

Rudolf Firkušný (1912-1994), b. Napajedla, Moravia, was an eminent Czech American pianist. He emigrated to US in 1940 and devoted considerable part of his career to the promotion of Czech music abroad, including the works of B. Smetana, L. Janáček and B. Martinů. He also performed piano concertos of Dvořák, Martinů, Mendelssohn, Schumann, Brahms, Beethoven, and Mozart and with the Juilliard String Quartet and several etudes. He gave master classes at the Juilliard School of Music, NY.

Elias Beck Fischbach (1921–), b. Prague, Bohemia, is a cellist. He was first cellist, with Worcester, MA Orchestra (4 yrs.); with Denver Symphony (15 years).

Pamela Frank (1967–), b. New York, NY, of Czech mother (Lilian Kalier), is an American violinist, with an outstanding international reputation across an unusually varied range of performing activity. Her musicianship was recognized in 1999 with the Avery Fisher Prize, one of the highest honors given to American instrumentalists. In addition to her career as a performer, Pamela Frank joined the faculty of the Curtis Institute of Music in 1996. She is also on the faculties of the Peabody Institute of Johns Hopkins University, and the State University of New York at Stony Brook. Since 2012, Pamela Frank is chair of the jury of the Yehudi Menuhin International Competition for Young Violinists.

Josef Franzl (1882–1955), b. Bohemia, was a French horn player. He studied horn with Anton Janousek at the Prague Conservatory of Music. Before emigrating to the United States, he appeared as a soloist in Czechoslovakia and Paris. He made his debut with Pittsburgh Symphony Orchestra. In 1905, he toured as solo horn with Frederick Neil Innes' famous Concert Band. He was for many years a soloist with the New York Symphony under Walter Damrosch, the New York Chamber Music Society, the Kneisel Quartet, the Mannes Trio, the Georges Barrère Ensemble of Wind Instruments and the Columbia Broadcasting System Concert Orchestra. He also played during summers with the Chicago Symphony Orchestra and also performed in the orchestra for operas produced at the New York City Center. Mr. Franzl taught at the Julliard Graduate School, Institute of Musical Arts, the National Orchestra Association, and for eleven years, was head of the horn department of the Dalcroze School of Music in Manhattan.

Edward J. Freund (1886–1947), b. Bohemia, was a concert violinist. He studied violin with Prof. Otakar Ševčík (1904-09) and theory with Prof. Hornik (1904-06) at Prague Conservatory. He was Prof. Ševčík's assistant (1906-09) before coming to the US. He was a member of Bruno Steindel Trio, Chicago (1912-13). He also taught violin. He was the head of Violin Dept., Madison Musical Coll., IL (1913-14), head of the Violin Dept., Rockford Coll., IL (s. 1914), as well as the dept. head at Lake Forest School of Music (1916-17).

Alfred Friese (1876–1971), b. Czech, is one of the world's foremost timpanists and teachers. He was originally trained as a violinist, and his musical proficiency on this instrument won him the prized Artist Diploma and subsequently, a position in the Leipzig Gewandhaus Orchestra. It was during this time at Leipzig that he became interested in the timpani and began to study with the orchestra's timpanist, Hermann Schmidt. His first major timpani engagement was with Hans Winderstein's Orchestra. In 1902, he was invited by Franz Scheel to come to the United States to become one of the founding members of what would later become the Philadelphia Orchestra. Mr. Friese then moved on to become timpanist with the Pittsburgh Symphony under Emil Paur. When Gustav Mahler established the New York Philharmonic on a regular salaried basis in 1909, he chose Alfred Friese from among nine competitors for the solo timpani chair. In 1926, Mr. Friese opened his School for Timpani, the first of its kind. He also served as chairman of the percussion department of the Manhattan School of Music. His method of timpani instruction, the Friese-Lepak Timpani Method, has become a standard text for the instrument. In 1978, Friese was inducted into Percussive Arts Society Hall of Fame.

Ernest Goldman (1913–2014), b. Vienna, of Czech ancestry, was a pianist and accompanist. He grew up in a village in Moravia, near the border with Bohemia. As a youth, he spoke both German and Czech; English was his fifth language, after Latin and French. When he was 15, his family moved to Vienna, where he lived for 10 years until emigrating to the U.S. in December 1938. He was co-founder of 'Sounds of Stow' and served as pianist and accompanist for several decades. He received his musical training from teachers in a direct line leading back to Beethoven. Audiences in the Stow/Concord area knew him for his solo and chamber music work spanning more than 30 years. Over this period, he was soloist in more than twenty-five different piano concertos. He was an engineer and physicist by profession until his retirement in 1983, after which he devoted himself full-time to furthering music in the Stow area. He passed away in January 2014.

Frank J. Hain (1866–1944), b. Teplice, Bohemia, was a horn player. He began to study music at the age of seven, and at fourteen became a student in the Conservatory of Prague. The following year, he was engaged as the first hornist in the Genebehaus and Phihlarmonic Orchestras, under Nicode, afterwards as first hornist in the Philharmonic at Hamburg and at Karlovy Vary. While holding this position, he was engaged for the position of third horn in the Boston Symphony Orchestra and arrived in the United States in September 1891. He was a member of Boston Symphony Orch. (1891–1925), where he played third horn. He also played horn with Molé Chamber Music Concert Club, which included Charles Molé flute, Friedrich Mueller oboe, G. Goldschmidt clarinet, Adolf Guetter bassoon and Frank Hain horn. Hain was also a member of the Longy New York Modern Chamber Music Society.

Gaby (Gabriel) Haas (1920–1987), b. Františkovy Lázně, Czech., was Canadian accordionist and a composer. He moved to Saskatoon at 18 and began playing accordion at local dances and on CFQC radio. His broadcasts from Edmonton 1940–58 on CFRN and after 1944 on CKUA were carried 1946–55 on the CBC's national networks, establishing him as a popular old-time and country music performer. On CKUA, Haas was host for more than 40 years of *Continental Musicale* and was also heard on other ethnic-music programs including *The German Show* and *European Music Shop*. Concurrently on CFRN-TV, he starred 1955–69 on

Chuckwagon, 1956–71 on *The Noon Show* and 1969–74 on *Country Music*. Haas was later the host for such QCTV programs as *QC on Country Music* and *World Showcase of Music*.

Mark Halata (1967–), b. nr. Houston, TX, of Moravian ancestry, is a popular Texas accordion player, who was the Texas State Accordion Champion at the age of 13. He is proficient in country, Cajun, zydeco, tex-mex and even rock 'n' roll. He is the founder and leader of Texavia, a Houston-based Czech polka band with country music flair.

Louis Hanzlik (1975–), b. Wayne, NE, of Czech ancestry, is a graduate of the University of Iowa (B.M., 1998), the Juilliard School (M.M., 2000) and Teachers College, Columbia University (Ed.D., 2010). A trumpeter, he has established himself as an accomplished chamber musician, orchestral player, and educator. He is a member of the American Brass Quintet, Grammy Award-winning Orpheus Chamber Orchestra, the Orchestra of St. Luke's, and the Riverside Symphony. With Orpheus, Hanzlik has performed as a soloist and ensemble musician at Carnegie Hall on dozens of occasions and has toured nationally and internationally with the orchestra since 2000, including recent performances in Singapore, Scotland, Germany, Japan, Russia, Austria, and Colombia. In May of 2014, Hanzlik completed a three-week tour of Australia with the American Brass Quintet. Dr. Louis Hanzlik is associate professor of trumpet at the University of Connecticut. He also serves on the faculties of the Juilliard School and the Aspen Music Festival and School. As an educator, Dr. Hanzlik promotes the inclusion of chamber music within a student's learning. Prior to joining the American Brass Quintet, Hanzlik served as a member of the Atlantic Brass Quintet (2002–14). Hanzlik has recorded frequently for commercial radio and television and for numerous public radio and television features, such as *Live from Lincoln Center*, *National Public Radio's Performance Today*, and for the NFL on NBC.

Tony Harmon (fl. 2008), b. Riverside, CA, Slovak American, is a classical guitarist. He was introduced to the guitar at an early age by his father and began studying the instrument at the age of eleven at the local YMCA. By the time Tony was 13 years old, he was becoming an accomplished guitarist and he would devote 6 to 8 hours every day to his practice. He was known to take his guitar everywhere he went even on family holiday. At 14, Tony was asked to perform at Loma Linda University by the music faculty and gave his first public performance there to an audience of over 2500. Tony studied guitar with Patrick Read, Miguel Rubio, Philip Rosheger, George Sakellariou, Ray Reussner, Frederick Noad and Christopher Parkening. He performed on numerous television shows and special events. He composed and performed the musical soundtrack for ABC television's *The William Randolf Hearst Story*, and was asked to play at the Western White House for Ronald Reagan.

Charles (Karel) Havlicek, b. Omaha, NE, was a noted violinist in Nebraska who studied music in Berlin, Dresden, Paris and Prague. He made many concert tours throughout the United States, and then became a member of the Boston Symphony Orchestra. Later, he taught violin at Washington State College.

Maria Heritesová-Kohn (1881-1970), Vodňany, Bohemia, was a violinist and violin teacher. She studied at Prague Conservatory under Prof. Otakar Sevčík. She had concert appearances in Prague and also in Paris, London and Russia. She concerted with the Czech Philharmonic in Vienna, Budapest and Terst. She also performed in St. Louis at the World Exposition and in other American cities, also with Ema Destinnová. In 1916, she returned to the US and taught at Northwestern Cons. in Minneapolis, then in Oklahoma and Denton, TX, where she accepted the position of director of the Violin Dept. at the State Coll. Afterwards, she had her studio in NYC and later lived in Duluth, MN, Chicago, Johnson City, TN and finally St. Petersburg, FL. Her specialty were compositions of Paganini and of Czech composers, esp. Smetana and Dvořák. She was honored by SVU Honorary membership.

Otto Herz (1894-1976), b. Prešov, Slovakia, was a pianist and soloist. He studied the piano in Prague and Frankfurt and was a professor at the Fodor Music Conservatory in Budapest until he come to this country on a concert tour with Zino Francescatti, the violinist, and was offered a post at the music college here. He was a professor at the Manhattan School of Music and veteran of nearly 5,000 concerts. Dr. Herz joined the Manhattan School in 1972, after having, taught at New York University and the now defunct New York College of Music, with which he was associated from 1940 to 1998. Throughout his career, Dr. Herz appeared in public as a soloist, a member of chamber orchestras and accompanist, a role in which he was best known here from hundreds of recitals at Town Hall and Carnegie Recital Hall. The artists whom he accompanied on those occasions usually were making their debuts, but he also appeared with many of the world's great established artists.

Helen Kotas Hirsch (née Kotas) (1916-2000), b. Chicago, IL, of Czech parents, was an American horn player. She was a prominent female horn player with the Chicago Symphony Orchestra, in which she was principal horn from 1941 to 1947. She was one of the first principal horn players of a major US orchestra. Kotas subsequently left the Chicago Symphony to play principal horn with the Chicago Lyric Opera. She also taught horn at the American Conservatory and the Sherwood Conservatory. She grew up on the Southwest Side and played cornet at her parents' insistence at Harrison High School. She switched to horn before her graduation in 1932 and studied with prominent French horn players Frank Kryl and Louis Dufrasne while she played in the Civic Orchestra of Chicago. She made principal horn in the Woman's Symphony Orchestra in 1932 and played with the group while getting a psychology degree from the University of Chicago, which she received in 1936. She gained notice in Leopold Stokowski's All-American Youth Orchestra in triumphant summer tours in 1940 and 1941, the year Frederick Stock brought her to the CSO. She was married to the pathologist Edwin F. Hirsch (1886-1972) and they had 3 children.

James Robert Hladky (1926-2022), b. NE, of Czech ancestry, a cellist, was educated at the Eastman School of Music. He taught in higher education for forty-two years, the last thirty-three at the University of Oregon (1961-93). Before coming to the University of Oregon, Hladky was a member of the faculties of Eastman School of Music and Ohio Wesleyan University. As a professional cellist, he appeared as soloist with the Rochester Philharmonic Symphony, Columbus Symphony, Chamber Orchestra, Oklahoma City Symphony, Eugene Symphony, and the Oregon Bach Festival Orchestra.

Emil 'Bash' Hofner (1919-2002), b. Mouton, TX, of Czech mother, was the well-known steel guitarist from San Antonio. He will always be remembered for playing steel in his older brother Adolph's bands from 1939 to the early '90s. He was also one of the earliest electric guitarists to record, playing steel on Jimmie Revard's first Bluebird session in October 1936. He was a pioneer of Western swing music.

Alfred Holý (1866-1948), b. Oporto, Portugal, of Czech parents, was a harpist. He was trained as a harpist at the Prague Cons. (1882-85). He was first harpist with Boston Symphony Orchestra from 1913-1928. Before, he was principal harpist at German Opera, Prague (1885-96), Royal Court Opera, Berlin Opera (1896-1903), Vienna State Opera (1903-1913). He published studies for harp, arranged from the symphonic works of Richard Strauss.

Anton Horner (1877-1971), b. Bohemia, was a horn player. He studied his horn playing with father, Frank Horner and with Friedrich Gumpert at the Leipzig Conservatory. He was with Philadelphia Orchestra (1902-46), as principal horn player (1902-29), as co-principal (1929-31) and as third horn (1931-46). Before that, he was principal horn in the Pittsburgh Symphony (1898-1902) and was with Panama-Pacific International Exposition orchestra, San Francisco (1915). Horner also taught at the Curtis Institute until 1942. Anton Horner was an early advocate of the double horn working with his teacher, Friedrich Gumpert, and passed this on to his many Curtis Institute students.

Joseph P. Horner (1882-1944), b. Bohemia, brother of Anton Horner, was a hornetist. He studied with his horn playing father, Frank Horner and at the Vienna Conservatory. He was a second hornetist with the Philadelphia Orchestra (1900-01, 1902-38). Before, he was a member of the Henry Gordon Thunder Orchestra (1899-1900). After the 1900-1901 season at the Philadelphia Orchestra, he joined the Pittsburgh Symphony under Victor Herbert

(1901-02), where his brother Anton Horner had previously been principal horn. In 1902, he returned to Philadelphia Orchestra.

Joseph Houdek (1881-1944), b. Nový Etink, Bohemia, was a contra bassist. He studied five years at Vienna Conservatory of Music with the highest degree and also spent two semesters at the University of Munich. He became member of the Vienna Concertverein Orchestra (1905-06) and then professor at the Conservatory of Music, Athens Greece (1909-13). He was a member of Cincinnati Symphony Orchestra (1913-14), before becoming a member of the Chicago Symphony Orchestra (1914-44). He composed *Babinský*, an operetta in one act, choruses and songs for violin, piano and contra bass. His office was in Chicago o in Orchestra Hall.

Miloslav Hrdlík (1941-), b. Prague, Czech., is a double-bassist, who studied at the Prague Conservatory with the prominent pedagogue Prof. František Pošta. He was the double bass virtuoso and the principal double bassist of the Czech Philharmonic for 32 years. In 1969 he became a member of the New Orleans Symphony. Since 1991 he was a member of the Louisiana Philharmonic Orchestra until 2003.

John Hronek (1865-d.), was a musician, baritone horn player and a bandleader, residing in Cleveland. Hronek's Marine Band played at the Chicago World' Fair in 1893. His sons played with orchestras in Cleveland theatres.

Oldřich Hrousek (1897-d.), b. Královské Vinohrady, Bohemia, was a cellist educated at Prague Conservatory and the Burian Master School. He came to US in 1922 as a member of Czech Trio. He taught also at Chicago Music Conservatory.

Edward J. Hruby (1896-1982), b. Minnesota, of Czech ancestry, was a cornet player. He enlisted in US Navy in 1917 and remained until his retirement in 1947. He graduated in 1919 from New England Conservatory of Music and in 1920s, the Navy 'lent' him for a season to be cornet soloist with the John Philip Sousa band. From 1932-36, he was the cornet soloist with the US Navy Band. He is credited with writing the song 'Hail to the Redskins' for the Washington Redskins football team and he started the marching band for that organization. Moving to St. Paul, MN in 1962, he was a member of the City Police Marching Band from 1965-1978.

William Hruby (1899-1965), b. Cleveland, OH, of Czech ancestry, was a trumpeter, percussionist, xylophonist. He toured Europe with Hruby Family Orch. (1912). He was also a member of Cleveland Symphony Orch. (1925-26, 1927-56), where he played trumpet (1925-26) and percussion (1953-56). He was also a prize-winning bandleader for various northern Ohio American Legion posts.

Otto Hyna (1886-1951), b. Czech., was a double bass, having been a member of the Chicago Symphony Orchestra (1930-50). Before he was a member of Minneapolis Symphony (1921-1923) and during World War II, at age 55, Otto Hyna played in a US Army band. He played clarinet. Otto Hyna was to have been a concerto soloist with the Chicago Symphony in the 1950-1951 season, however, he unfortunately became ill and later died in January 1951.

Pierre Jasmin (1949-), b. Montreal, Canada, of Slovak descent, is a pianist, and teacher. He taught 1979-84 at Queen's University and 1979-88 at Vanier Cegep. He began to teach at the Université du Québec à Montréal (UQAM) in 1981, where he was director 1984-6 of the Music Department. In addition to Canada, Jasmin has performed in Austria, England, France, Italy, Taiwan, the USA, the USSR, and Yugoslavia. He has been a soloist with the McGill Chamber Orchestra and the Montreal Symphony Orchestra, and he inaugurated the first regular season of the Orchestre Métropolitain at the Place des Arts in 1985. His repertoire covers music from Bach to Stockhausen and Couperin to Messiaen; he has a particular affinity for Slavic music and the works of Beethoven, whose 32 piano sonatas he has performed in lecture-recitals 1989-90 and 2004. He has also given recital series of the solo piano works of Mozart (2001, 2004-5), and the preludes and fugues of Bach. From 1991 to 2003, he taught and performed annually in the Czech and Slovak Republics.

Ken Javor (1948-2019), b. Cleveland, OH, of Czech and Slovak descent, is a string bass player. Since the 1960s, he has been playing initially in Cleveland in the famous Buckeye Road Hungarian neighborhood. A mainstay of Slovak music in Cleveland with a wide repertoire of Slovak folk music reflecting his over 40 years of experience, Ken has performed at concerts and community events in Europe and across the United States. He was the longtime bass player of the bands, Harmonia and The Johnny Pastirik Band.

Jerome M. 'Jerry' Jelinek (1931-2015), b. Detroit, MI, probably of Czech ancestry, was a cellist. He was trained as a cellist at the Royal Academy of Music in London. He joined the faculty of Univ. of Michigan in 1961 as Professor and Cellist of the Stanley Quartet. A former member of the Detroit Symphony Orchestra and the University of Oregon Trio, Mr. Jelinek had performed to critical acclaim both as recitalist and orchestral soloist in Europe, Canada, and the United States. He then performed with the Jelinek/Gurt Duo and the American Trio.

Stephen (Štěpán) Jelinek (1865-1954), b. Manitowoc, WI, of Czech ancestry, was a cornetist of ability and bandleader. He came to Saline County, NE with his parents, Frank and Marie Jelinek in 1865, settling on a homestead near Crete. He grew to manhood there and later went to Chicago where he studied music at Northwestern University and played in the orchestra of the Chicago Opera. He was appointed bandmaster of the 11th Arizona

Regiment in Puerto Rico (Nov. 1894), during the Spanish-American War. His band numbered thirty-five men. In 1896, they returned to Washington, where they played in the parade during President McKinley's inauguration. They remained there until the close of April, when they sailed for the Philippine Islands, arriving at Samar Island in June 1897.

Olda Jirousek (1897-1984), b. Prague, Bohemia, was a violoncellist. For seven years, he studied at the Master School of Music at the State Conservatory of Music in Prague, specializing in violoncello. He came to Chicago in 1923 with the Czech Trio. He taught violoncello at the Northwestern Music School, the Lawndale Conservatory, and the United Artists Conservatory. From 1928 to 1933, he broadcasted over station WGN. He was also employed by A Century of Progress. He was a member of the Bohemian Arts Club. He had his office in Chicago on Diversey Parkway.

Peter Jirousek (1964-), b. Chicago, IL, of Czech ancestry, is a hornist. He began teaching at Vander Cook College of Music, Chicago, IL, in 2009. He previously taught at Elmhurst College and Notre Dame University. Peter served as principal horn in the South Bend Symphony for 14 seasons and as the Chicago Chamber Orchestra's principal horn for 8 seasons. He has been second horn for the Northwest Indiana Symphony since 1990. He served as third horn in the Shreveport Symphony Orchestra and has performed with the Ravinia Festival Orchestra, Grant Park Orchestra, and Lyric Opera of Chicago and for the Members of the Chicago Symphony Orchestra programs. Recently, Mr. Jirousek was an orchestra member for Broadway in Chicago's productions of *Wicked*, *Billy Elliot*, *Mary Poppins*, *Les Miserable* and *Phantom of the Opera*.

Joseph Frank Jirovec (1884-1955), b. Morse Bluff, NE, studied music and trumpet. At age 19 he organized and directed own band. He was known throughout the state as a director of popular bands and orchestras. He was a director of Leigh Band, Clarkson Band, and Jirovec Band.

Václav Jiskra (1881-1962), b. Zinkovy, Bohemia, a contrabassist, was trained at Prague and in Vienna. After an appearance as a soloist in Chicago, he was acclaimed as the world's greatest contrabass soloist and, in 1908, became a member of the Chicago Symphony Orchestra, as the principal double bass (1908-49).

Kateřina Jurásková, b. Czech Republic, is a cellist. She holds a Doctorate in cello performance from McGill University; diplomas from the Conservatoire de musique, the International Menuhin Music Academy and the Conservatoire European de musique de Paris; and a Bachelor's degree from The Prague State Conservatory. She has had extensive orchestral experience as principal cellist of the McGill Chamber Orchestra, La Pieta Chamber Orchestra, the National Academy Orchestra, the Music Academy of the West Festival

Orchestra and the Prager Symphonikers. She has performed as a chamber musician to great acclaim at festivals in Canada, Belgium, Sweden and Japan. She just completed her first year of a two-year cello fellowship with the Montgomery Symphony Orchestra in Montgomery, Alabama. Jurásková's many prizes, including Second Place in the Beethoven International Competition and First Place in both the McGill/Canadian Broadcasting Company Concerto Competition and the Music Academy of the West Concerto Competition, have set her apart as a player of distinction. She was the recipient of the Fonorola Montreal Young Artist Award and the Esperia Foundation Award.

John A. Jurena (1906-1935), b. Chicago, IL, of Czech ancestry, was a pianist educated at Northwestern Univ. Following in the footsteps of his father, who for years was the conductor of the Orchestra of the Ludvik National Theatre in Chicago. Mr. Jurena became a piano teacher of note in Chicago. He was a member of the Chicago Federation of Musicians and of the Bohemian Arts Club.

Frank John Kaderabek (1929-2023), b. Chicago, IL, of Czech ancestry is a trumpet player. At West Point, he played solo cornet in the band, studying in New York with Harry Glantz and Nathan Prager. He was with Dallas Symphony (1952-57) and Grant Park Symphony (during summers), as Chicago Symphony third trumpet (1958-66), as Detroit Symphony principal trumpet (1966-75). He was principal trumpet player with the Philadelphia Orchestra (1975-95). In 1982, he was the first American invited to judge at the International Trumpet Competition in Czechoslovakia, a role he has continued to fill. While in Prague in 1992, he recorded his first solo CD *An American Trumpet in Prague* on the VARS label. For the past 32 years, he has been a faculty member at the Curtis Institute of Music and also teaches at West Chester University. He is a frequent performer with the Kennet Square Symphony and the Allentown Band. Mr. Kaderabek speaks fluent Czech, collects rare books about World War I, and lives on a farm in Berks County, Pennsylvania.

Jan Kalas (1868-1941), b. Czech., was a cellist. He emigrated to the USA in 1893. He played cello with Chicago Symphony Orchestra (1893-1911). After Chicago, he became a music teacher in San Jose, California and taught at San Jose State College. He was a member of the State College Trio, playing cello, with Miles Creskell violin and Carl Towner piano. He was also said to be substitute in Boston Symphony. Kalas composed music including 'Forest Idyl.' His daughters Bojena and Helen Kalas taught piano and music at the College of the Pacific in the 1920s.

Vladimír Kalina (1903-), b. Vienna, of Bohemian ancestry, was a double bass. He studies under Václav Machek and Václav Jiskra. He became member of Chicago Civic Orchestra, performing in the stage orchestra at Chicago Opera House. During depression he played at Chicago Theater for vaudeville. Later he joined the Cincinnati Symphony Orchestra, where he stayed a few years, before he became a member of the prestigious Chicago Symphony Orchestra for 40 years (1936–76).

Lilian Kallir (1931–2004), b. Prague, Czech., was a concert pianist, who studied at Mannes School of Music, NYC and at Tanglewood. After her debut with the Philharmonic, she began a performing career that took her to Europe, South America and across the United States. Kallir kept major musical company, performing with the orchestras of Boston, Chicago and San Francisco, as well as the Berlin Philharmonic, Royal Concertgebouw Orchestra of Amsterdam, London Symphony, Leipzig Gewandhaus Orchestra and others.

Joža Karas (1926–2008), b. Warsaw, Poland, of Czech ancestry, was a violinist and teacher. Karas emigrated to the United States in 1948 via Colombia and Canada. A violinist and music historian by vocation, he taught at the Hartt School of Music for more than 50 years. He also performed with the Hartford Symphony Orchestra until his retirement in 2006. He located and made public music composed by Jewish inmates who worked at the Nazi concentration camp Terezín during World War II. He was the author of *Music in Terezín*.

Martin Karlíček (1977–), b. Cheb, Czech., studied at the Music Conservatory in Plzeň (B.Mus., 1998), Academy of Music in Prague (dipl., 2001; M.Mus., 2004), Utrecht Academy of the Arts in Holland (M.A., 2002) and at McGill University in Montreal, Canada (D.Mus., 2010). He has taught piano at Schulich School of Music of McGill University (s. 2010) and gives concerts as a soloist and a chamber musician. He has been hailed as 'one of the most talented musicians of his generation, outstanding performer, mature experienced artist, first rate virtuoso musician.' His performances, master classes and lectures have been enthusiastically received by audiences in the Czech Republic, Germany, Austria, Canada, Greece, U.S.A., Thailand and Japan. Mr. Karlicek is a holder of the Bedřich Smetana Prize in the Bedřich Smetana International Piano Competition 1994 (2nd Prize: 1st not awarded) and the First Prize and Ferenc Liszt Prize in the South Bohemian International Piano Competition 1995. In addition, he received the Béla Bartók Prize, Leoš Janáček Prize, Bedřich Smetana Prize and Bohuslav Martinů Prize in the Prague-Vienna-Budapest International Summer Academy Competition in 2001 and in IBLA Grand Prize Competition in 2011.

Jaroslav Karlovský (1925–1997), b. Klatovy, Czech., was a violinist. He was a long-time viola teacher and string coach at the School of Music of McMaster Univ. He was a renowned musician, who played in the Czech Philharmonic Orchestra and the Prague String Quartet, and on numerous recordings. In his years at McMaster Univ., he was mentor to countless students. He was also a member of the Czech String Quartet, founded in 1968 by musicians trained in Czechoslovakia who moved to Canada in 1969. In addition to their concert tours, the musicians were members of the Hamilton Philharmonic Orchestra. The ensemble was also in residence at McMaster University.

John Wenceslaus Kaspar (1892–1967), b. Baltimore, MD, of Czech ancestry, was a pianist and organist, trained at the Peabody Conservatory of Music, Baltimore. He was an organist at St. Wenceslaus Church, Baltimore and at Catholic Chapel in MD State Penitentiary for 46 years. He was the founder and director of Kaspar School of Music. He also organized his own orchestra.

Catherine C. Kautsky (1950–), b. US, of Bohemian ancestry (she is a daughter of John H. Kautsky), is a pianist, who received her music education at the New England Conservatory and at the Juilliard School, and has a doctoral degree in performance from the State University of New York at Stony Brook. She is Professor of Music at the University of WI-Madison and chair of its piano department. She has concertized throughout the United States and abroad as a recitalist, soloist with orchestra, and chamber musician.

Václav Ignác Kec (1878–d.), b. Czech., was a horn player. He came to US in 1905. He was with San Francisco Symphony (1911–12, 1914–15) and also with Orpheum Theater Orchestra, San Francisco in 1920s prior to the Cleveland Orchestra (fifth horn during 1926–27 season).

Felix Khuner (1906–1991), b. Vienna, of Moravian ancestry, was a violinist. He was trained in Vienna in math and music, having thought of becoming a mathematician. However, when he was offered a place in the Kolisch Quartet at age nineteen and saw Arnold Schoenberg at one of the Quartet's rehearsals, he decided to join them instead. He was a second violinist of the Kolisch Quartet. He played and toured with the Quartet for fifteen years, performing premieres and signal works of Schoenberg, Berg, and Bartok. With the advent of Nazism, he decided to settle in the United States, where he played with the San Francisco Symphony and Opera Orchestras for more than forty years. In the 1970s, Khuner was an instructor in the music department of the University of California, teaching chamber music. He was also concertmaster of the Monterey Symphony in the late 1960s and early 1970s. Khuner also had private violin students, giving lessons in his home in Berkeley Hills. He also performed regularly with the San Francisco Chamber Orchestra conducted by Edgar Braun.

Helen Sadilek Khyl (1883–1971), b. Chicago, IL, of Czech ancestry, was a Nebraska pianist. She studied music in Berlin then returned to Omaha to open her own school teaching piano, coaching voice, and also giving many concerts throughout the United States.

Rudolf Kirs (1883-1943), b. Czech., was a cellist who emigrated to the US in 1905. He was with the San Francisco Symphony (1911-12, 1913-34, 1935-44). Before that, he played in the orchestra of the Alcazar Theatre, San Francisco in the late 1910s.

Alex Klein (1964–), b. Porte Alegre, Brazil, of Czech ancestry, is an oboist who began his musical studies in Brazil at the age of nine and made his solo orchestral debut the following year. During his teenage years, he toured and performed as a soloist, recitalist and as a member of several professional orchestras in Brazil. After a year at Oberlin, he won first prize in the first Lucarelli International Competition for solo Oboe Players held in Carnegie Hall. He has received many awards worldwide including at the 1988 International Competition for Musical Performers in Geneva, Switzerland. He has performed as soloist with the Chicago Symphony, Philadelphia Orchestra, the Suisse Romande and Chicago Sinfonietta. Klein won the 2002 Grammy Award for Best Instrumental soloist with Orchestra for his recording of Strauss Oboe Concerto with Danile Barenboim and the Chicago Symphony.

Robert Klier (1880–d.), b. Karlovy Vary, Bohemia, was a brilliant player of the zither and a talented leader of band and orchestra. He played at Buckingham Palace, in appreciation of which Queen Alexandra presented him with an exceptionally valuable zither. After departing from England, he came to the US and for forty-eight weeks appeared on the B. F. Keith vaudeville circuit, then made a personal tour of the whole US which covered a period of two and a half years. In 1907, he came to California on Easter Sunday, having been the only soloist and artist on that religious program. He next became the leader of his own orchestra and for twenty-five years so continued. Bob Klier and his Hoffbrau Syncopators, as the organization was termed, were known as one of the finest bands in the country, being a group of skilled and splendidly trained musicians and led by one of the few real masters of the baton. Klier has likewise achieved fame over the radio, the tones of his zither first going over the air from station KFRC for three years.

John Klima (1911-1972), b. Iowa, of Czech parents, as a student, played in the Chicago Civic Orchestra. He became member of the Chicago Symphony Orch. (1937-71), playing a double bass and since 1941, he was also its librarian. In 1940, he was also engaged as concertmaster by the Little Symphony Orchestra of Chicago, under Hans Lange, associate conductor of the Chicago Symphony.

Paul Kling (1929-2005), b. Opava, Czech., was a Canadian violinist, educated at Brno State Conservatory of Music and Prague State Academy. As a teenager, he was deported to Terezín concentration camp. He was soloist, recitalist, radio, and TV, in Europe, Asia, and USA. He was prof. of violin, Tokyo Univ. of Arts (1952-55); Kunitachi College (1952-55); Univ. of Louisville (s. 1959); and concertmaster, Louisville Philharmonic. In 1977, Kling moved to British Columbia, where he taught at the Univ. of Victoria for some 20 years and was Director of the Music School (1980-87). He later taught violin at the Univ. of British Columbia.

Franz Kneisel (1865-1926), b. Bucharest, of Moravian father, was a noted violinist. In 1885, though barely 20 years old, he was engaged as concertmaster of the Boston Symphony Orchestra. For the next 20 years, he was concertmaster and assistant conductor, appearing as soloist in many violin concertos and giving the first American performances of the concertos by Brahms. Shortly after his arrival in Boston, he formed and led the famed Kneisel Quartet with other BSO string players.

Agnes Knoflicek (1898-1931), b. Nebraska, was a noted violinist. At the age of fourteen, went to Prague, Bohemia, to study violin with Professor Suchý and Professor Ševčík. She gave many concerts throughout the United States as a solo violinist.

Jaromir 'Mirek' Kocandrle (1951-2012), b. Czech., was a trumpet player. As a bass player for many years, he performed with the Phil Wilson Big Band, Wayne Naus Big Band, Boston Jazz Conspiracy Big Band, George Smith Big Band, Roy Orbison, Drifters, Coasters, Platters, Bee Gees, Marvelettes, Mary Wells, the Seekers, and the Canberra Symphony Orchestra. As music was his passion, he left Australia, where he moved in 1968, to attend Berklee College of Music, Boston. Upon graduation, he spent more than 30 years teaching at Berklee., where he was promoted to full professorship in 2012. He earned his USGTF certification and taught at the Golf Teaching Center Inc. in Northborough for a number of years. Kocandrle was a bass player in the band Jordan Valentine and the Sunday Saints. He organized student spring concerts for over 20 years at the Berklee Performance Center.

Jaroslav Kocián (1883-1950), b. Ústí nad Orlicí, was a noted Czech violinist. He studied in Prague at Prague Conservatory, under Otakar Ševčík and is considered together with Jan Kubelík as the most important representative of Ševčík´s school. He was an interpreter of violin compositions of Johann Sebastian Bach. He is especially noted for his compositions for the violin, which have been recorded most often by his student Josef Suk. He taught at the Prague Conservatory. He traveled widely through US and other countries.

Victor Kolar (1888-1957), b. Budapest, of Czech parents, was a violinist. He studied at the Prague Conservatory, where he was a pupil of Otakar Ševčík (violin) and Antonín Dvořák (composition). From 1905 until 1920, he was a violinist with the Pittsburgh Symphony and New York Symphony, joining the Detroit Symphony in 1920 as an assistant conductor. He remained with the orchestra until 1941, eventually assuming the post of principal conductor. Active as a composer as well, he wrote a symphony, some tone poems, and a few orchestral suites. Of these last, his *Americana* won first prize in a 1914 contest sponsored by the Illinois State Teachers Association.

Rudolf Kolisch (1896-1978), b. Klamm am Semmering, Austria, of Moravian ancestry, was a violinist and leader of string quartets. The Kolisch String Quartet, which he founded in 1922, was renowned for its performances of modern music as well as its ability to play the classical repertoire from memory.

Zdeněk Koníček (1923-), b. Bosnia, of Czech ancestry, an eminent Czech cellist, began music training at the age of six. His first professional activity was playing in the opera pit. He soon joined the Prague Symphony as principal cellist and also played with the Czech Philharmonic. After he defected from the communist Czechoslovakia, he immigrated to Canada, settling in Hamilton, where he became one of the driving forces in the city's classical music scene.

Joe Kopecky (1967-), b. Racine, WI, of Czech ancestry, is a gifted guitarist who is equally adept on either 6 or 7 string guitars. He has garnered considerable praise worldwide for his complex, fluid, and intuitive style as the highly original guitarist, whose 2006 release *Blood* was also released on Unicorn Digital. He also performs in Secret Society of Starfish and Kopecky/Blake.

William Kopecky (1969-), b. Racine, WI, is an American musician, known internationally for his expressive bass playing. He is known for playing bass, keyboards, and sitar in the band Kopecky with his two brothers, Joe and Paul. His extensive discography includes CDs by Par Lindh Project, KOPECKY, Far Corner, Michael Angelo Batio, Parallel Mind, Yeti Rain, and many others. On "Bluewolf Bloodwalk", William plays both fretted and fretless electric basses.

Václav Jan Kopta (1845-1916), b. Bohemia, was a violinist educated at Prague Cons. After coming to the US in 1866, he made a successful concert tour of the country with M. Strakosch. He was prof. at Philadelphia Cons. (1869-72); and later became a member of the NY Philharmonic Soc. under Theodore Thomas. Dvorak consulted him about his planned trip to the US before making the decision to come here. He later taught at Stein Academy, Los Angeles.

Helen Kotas (1916-2000), b. Chicago, IL, of Czech parents, was a prominent female horn player with the Chicago Symphony Orchestra, in which she was principal horn from 1941 to 1947. She was one of the first principal horn players of a major US orchestra. Kotas subsequently left the Chicago Symphony to play principal horn with the Chicago Lyric Opera.

Arthur G. Koterba (1921-2013), b. Omaha, NE, was the youngest of nine children of Czech immigrants who spelled their name Kotrba. He grew up in the Brown Park area of South Omaha. At 14, Arthur Koterba would sneak into bars and play drums for money for the family. After graduating from South High, Art took his drums and his sticks and hit the road. He also played a lot locally. Art Koterba played with Johnny Carson's band for Johnny's magic show. He played gigs with the Mills Brothers and with the duo of Les Paul and Mary Ford. Koterba especially enjoyed playing jazz, big-band and swing music. For a time, many years ago, he promoted his own band using his stage name and the motto: "Dance and be gay with Artie Kay."

Petr Kotík (1942-), b. Prague, Czech., is a Czech American flutist and composer, educated in Prague and Vienna. In 1960 he settled in US where in 1970 he toured with SEM Ensemble. From 1971-72, he taught flute at SUNY Buffalo; taught composition at York Univ., Toronto (1975-76); and at Univ. of Buffalo (1976-77). He has had solo concerts and tours and performances with SEM Ensemble s. 1975.

George John Koudelka (1945-), b. Hallettsville, TX, of Czech ancestry, was educated at Southwest Texas State Univ. He was a professional percussionist with radio dance orchestras; instructor in percussion, Southwest Texas State Univ. (1967-69); and dir. bands, Flatonia public schools, Texas (s. 1969). He was a percussionist at Presidential Inaugural, Washington, DC (1965). He also has written compositions and made recordings.

Jan Josef Kovařík (1850-1939), b. Všeteč, Bohemia, was an organist, at R.C. Church of St. Wenceslaus, Spillville, IA. Antonín Dvořák resided in his house during his stay in Spillville in summer of 1893. From 1898, he was organist at New Prague, MN where he died at the age of eighty-nine.

Leopold Kramer (1870-d.), b. Prague, Bohemia, a violinist, studied at the Prague Conservatory. In 1897, Leopold Kramer came to Chicago to join Theodore Thomas's Chicago Symphony, as a concertmaster (1897-1909). After some disagreements with the music director, he quit and moved to the Chicago Grand Opera, later becoming Concertmaster of the New York Philharmonic for one season (1913-14). Leopold Kramer was later Concertmaster of the Metropolitan Opera Orchestra for one season (1922-23). Established in New York City, Kramer taught at the Institute for Musical Arts (later renamed Juilliard) (1920-24). In the summer of 1924, Kramer returned to Prague to teach, where he lived at least until 1936.

Lily Kraus (1903-1986), a native of Budapest, of Bohemian father, was a noted pianist, known as a specialist in Mozart and Beethoven. From 1967 to 1983, she taught as artist-in-residence at Texas Christian University in Fort Worth.

Jan Krejcar (1980–), b. Czech., is a pianist, organist, conductor, researcher, and composer based in Montreal, Quebec. Raised in rural Alberta, he returned to the Czech Republic where he graduated from the České Budějovice Music Conservatory in 2002 with an Artist diploma. After touring Germany and Austria with the Tschechische Filharmoniker orchestra, he came to Montreal with his wife, opera singer Marina Krejcarová-Černichovská and earned his Doctorate degree in music at McGill University (D.Mus.). As part of his performing career, he has received numerous prizes and performed in venues in North America, Europe, the Caribbean, and the Middle East. Currently, aside from actively performing as a pianist, he is music and choir director at St. John's United Church in Pointe-Claire, Quebec; as well as being involved in the world music scene in which he founded several groups using Eastern European and Jazz elements in a unique blend. He is also actively involved in research – particularly in Czech music of the first half of the 20th century and in Ukrainian piano music.

Matthew Krejci (1951–), b. Cleveland, OH, of Czech ancestry, is a flutist, who studied at Indiana University, and at Cleveland Institute of Music. He is now Professor of Flute in the Conservatory of Music at the University of the Pacific in Stockton, California and Principal Flute of the Sacramento Philharmonic Orchestra. Active in chamber music, he has performed with the contemporary music ensemble, Music Now in a concert at the Los Angeles Museum of Art and is a member of and President of the Board of the Chamber Music Society of Sacramento. He also performs with San Francisco's Earplay, an ensemble which specializes in new music.

William George Krieglstein (1884–1952), b. Czech., was a member of the Chicago Symphony Orch., playing bassoon, contrabassoon and bass. He was a principal contrabassoon in 1912–16 and 1923–29.

Otto Kristufek (1887–1958), b. Chicago, IL, of Czech ancestry, was a timpanist with St. Louis Symphony, as well as with the orchestra of Chicago's Lyric Opera and the American Opera Company.

Frank Kryl (1872–1938), b. Bohemia, who studied at Prague Conservatory, played horn with Chicago Symphony Orch. (1914–17). He also played in the 1893 Chicago World's Columbian Exposition Fair Orchestra, Cincinnati Symphony horn; was director of the Frank Kryl Band, also a theater orchestra musician at the Covent Garden Theater, Chicago in 1920s.

Antonín Kubálek (1935–2001), b. Libkovice, Czech., was Canadian classical pianist and teacher. He studied in Prague with Czech pianist František Maxián. He emigrated to Canada in 1968 and settled in Toronto. During his time in Canada, Kubálek performed in solo, chamber and orchestral concerts. He had frequent solo recitals with Toronto Symphony and CBS broadcasts, as well as other Ontario orchestras.

Jan Kubelík (1880-1940), b. Michle, n. Prague, Bohemia, was a famous Czech violinist educated at Prague Cons. He played with leading orchestras throughout Europe and America. His first tour in US was in 1901-02.

Keith Kubena (1969-), b. San Antonio, TX, of Czech ancestry, is a San Antonio classical guitarist who also performs in Austin, Houston and Central/South Texas. His style includes: Classical, Spanish and Pop (Beatles, etc.) Keith first picked up the guitar at age 10 and has not put it down since. Playing in different genres for some time, his passion was found when he was introduced to the classical guitar. "Nothing is more pure and beautiful than the innocent strings of the nylon guitar". Keith is a Masterclass student of world-renowned guitarist Christopher Parkening, where he received his certificate of study from Montana State University. Keith has also studied with Ana Vidovic from Croatia. In addition, Keith has taught guitar for many years both privately and publicly, including Saint Mary's Hall in San Antonio. He has performed all over the Central and South Texas area, playing at many weddings, corporate events, parties, and socials. From the Hill Country to Brownsville, he will accommodate his clients. He has also released 4 CDs as a soloist.

Henry Hank Kubik, Jr. (1917-2013), b. Coffeyville, KS, graduated from Monmouth College in IL and attended Harvard Law School. He taught and performed cello as a member of the Kubik Ensemble and the Florida Symphony Orchestra, now the Orlando Philharmonic. During World War II, he served as a naval aviator and flight instructor and worked for Piper Aircraft in PA before and after the war. He had a 50-plus year career in financial planning and was a CFP. As an Orlando resident from 1947-1970, Mr. Kubik played a crucial role in the formation of Loch Haven Park as a major cultural center. He was a founder of the Central Florida Museum and Planetarium, now the Orlando Science Center.

Ernest L. Kubitschek (1889-1968), b. Czech., was trained as a bassoonist in Vienna in his teenage years. He was principal bassoon with the San Francisco Symphony (1914-17, 1919-34, 1934-56) and San Francisco Opera Orchestra (1950-1960). He was also principal bassoon with Cleveland Orchestra (1935-36) under Artur Rodzinski. He also played with Henry Cowell's New Music Society, giving the premiers of several works by Henry Cowell and Charles Ruggles in 1926-1927.

Frank Kuchyňka (1879-1971), b. Prague, Bohemia, was a bass player, educated at Prague Conservatory of Music (1903), who played in the Conservatory orchestra when it was conducted by Dvořák. He came to US in 1906 and became member of Pittsburgh

Symphony Orchestra. Then he became a bass violinist with NY Symphony Orchestra; with Minneapolis Symphony Orchestra (1913–37) as principal bass. While in Minnesota, he was also a faculty member of MacPhail School of Music and of the Music Dept. of University of Minnesota. Kuchynka was a Hollywood studio musician in the 1940s and early 1950s, primarily at MGM studios. He held the position of principal bass player for Los Angeles Philharmonic Orchestra.

Anton Emil Kuerti (1938–), b. Vienna, Austria, son of Rosa Jahoda (1905–2004), of Czech ancestry, and the physicist Gustav Kuerti, was a classical pianist. As a child, he immigrated to the US and studied piano under Edward Goldman in Boston. Kuerti performed the Grieg Piano Concerto with the Boston Pops Orchestra at age eleven. Kuerti studied music at the Longy School of Music, at the Cleveland Institute of Music where he earned a Bachelor of Music degree, and at the Curtis Institute. His teachers included Arthur Loesser, Rudolf Serkin and Mieczysław Horszowski. He also studied at the age of 16 at The Peabody Conservatory, Baltimore, with Henry Cowell. Kuerti moved to Canada in 1965. He later joined the music faculty at the University of Toronto. Kuerti has toured extensively as a solo performer, performing in 150 communities throughout Canada and with every professional Canadian orchestra and many in the USA and elsewhere. He has also recorded many albums. His recordings include all the Beethoven concertos and sonatas, the Schubert sonatas, the Brahms concertos, and works by many other composers. He won the 1976 Juno Award for best classical recording for his album *The Beethoven Sonatas, Volumes 1, 2 and 3*, and has been nominated 7 times. Kuerti has received nine honorary degrees. In 1980, he founded the Festival of the Sound, a classical music festival in Parry Sound, Ontario. In 1998, he was appointed an Officer of the Order of Canada. He was married to cellist Kristina Bogyo (1947–2007), who bore him a son.

Julian Andreas Kuerti (1976–), b. Toronto, Ont., Canada, son of the pianist Anton Emil Kuerti (1938–) of Czech ancestry, and the cellist Kristina Bogyo (1947–2007), was a Canadian conductor. He read engineering and physics at the University of Toronto and graduated with an honors degree. He later began conducting studies at the University of Toronto, starting in 2000. He has also been a conducting student of Lutz Koehler, at the Berlin University of the Arts. Kuerti served as the founding artistic director and principal conductor of the Berlin-based group Solistenensemble Kaleidoskop from 2005 to 2008. He was Assistant Conductor of the Budapest Festival Orchestra in the 2006–2007 season. He held the same post with the Boston Symphony Orchestra from 2007 to 2010. In 2012, Kuerti became principal guest conductor of the Orquesta Sinfónica Universidad de Concepción in Chile, for an initial period of 2 years. In April 2013, the Orchestre Métropolitain announced the appointment of Kuerti as its first-ever principal guest conductor, with an initial contract of 3 years.

Anton Lada (1890-1944), b. Prague, Bohemia, was a ragtime, jazz and dance musician. He was a drummer. He played with and was the manager of the Louisiana Five. He recorded on Columbia Records and toured. He performed dancing and vaudeville shows and made a series of recordings for Emerson Records, Edison Records, and Columbia Records. He is credited as co-composer of a number of tunes with Spencer Williams, most successfully the "Arkansas Blues". After the breakup of his first Louisiana Five, he formed a series of his own bands before launching a new "Original Louisiana Five" band and moving to Hollywood to do film scores.

Václav Laksar (1914-1994), was bassoonist with Cleveland Orchestra (1955-81).

Max Robert Lanner (orig. Lamm) (1907-1991), b. Aust., of Bohemian father, a pianist, immigrated to US in 1939. He became accompanist to Enrica Morini, Nathan Milstein, Zino Ferancescati, Grace Moore and others (1939-46). He was associated with Colorado Coll., Colorado Spring (1946-75), serving as professor of music (s. 1954), as dept. chair (1951-67), and chair of humanities div. (1956-58). He also appeared as soloist with Colorado Spring Symphony.

Roger L. Latzgo (1949-), b. Pennsylvania, of Slovak descent, is a guitarist, pianist, and composer. Latzgo, who first learned music at his accordion-playing grandfather's knee, continued his formal studies at Rutgers College and the Mason Gross School of the Arts. Accompanied by piano and guitar, Roger travels his musical road with a style called ethnofunkology - a unique blend of folk music and jazz. Stops along the way include Rutgers College and Lehigh University, Prague, and New York, all the while performing in palaces and embassies, castles, wine cellars and beer gardens. In his repertoire are songs of celebration, adventure and triumph: music that explores the resonance of life. Roger brings his unique sound to festivals, concerts, special events, workshops and residencies. When he's not touring, he lives in Germansville, PA, USA. In addition to performing and recording, he teaches music privately and at the Lehigh Carbon Community College.

Stanley Barta Letovsky (1864-1934), b. Racine, WI. of Czech ancestry, was a cellist of note, who began studying on the violin at the age of seven. For 22 years, Stanislav Letovsky participated actively in the musical life of Omaha, composing, teaching and playing in various orchestras. He was cellist in the orchestra which opened the new Boyd Theatre in 1891. He was a charter member of the Omaha Musicians Association and served as its first secretary. He was also a member of the Omaha Symphony Orchestra. Stanislav Barta Letovsky composed several operas and was well-known for his ability to arrange music for road shows coming to Omaha.

Anne Preucil Lewellen, b. Iowa City, IA, of Czech ancestry, is currently the principal harpist with the Fort Wayne Philharmonic. She played viola in the orchestra at the All-State Music Festival from 1977 to 1979. For Lewellen, music has always been a family affair. All four siblings, as well as Lewellen's parents are professional musicians. Anne Lewellen is in her nineteenth season as the Philharmonic's principal harpist. Born into a musical family in Iowa City, she began her training on the violin at age four, switching to the harp at age eight. Ms. Lewellen completed her undergraduate studies at the Oberlin College Conservatory where her harp teacher was Alice Chalifoux. She then received an Artist's Diploma from the Curtis Institute of Music, where she studied with Marilyn Costello.

Doris Lederer, b. Istanbul, of Czech parents, is a viola player. She has been with Shenandoah Univ. (s. 2004), where she holds the position of director of instrumental music and professor of viola and chamber music. A graduate of the Curtis Institute of Music, Doris Lederer has performed with the Marlboro Music Festival and toured with Music from Marlboro. She has appeared as soloist with the Seattle Symphony, the Czech Philharmonic Chamber Orchestra, the Chicago Sinfonietta, and the Albuquerque Chamber Orchestra, among others. Ms. Lederer was on the faculty at the Shenandoah Conservatory in Winchester, VA, Kneisel Hall in Blue Hill, Maine, the Idyllwild Arts Summer Program in Idyllwild, California, and the Chautauqua Institution in New York. She has also served on the faculties of the International Festival at Round Top, Texas and the Apple Hill Center for Chamber Music, as well as the annual Audubon Quartet's Intensive String Quartet Seminars. As a member of the Audubon Quartet since 1976, she has performed extensively throughout the world and given master classes at the Cleveland Institute of Music, the Eastman School of Music, the Oberlin Conservatory, the Shanghai and Beijing Conservatories, the Yale School of Music, The Chautauqua Institute, as well as the Audubon Quartet's annual String Quartet Seminar.

Lev Zelenka Lerando (1877–d.), b. Prague, Bohemia, was State Univ. of Ohio trained musician. He was concert harpist with Duke of Devonshire; prof. at Swarthmore, Univ. of Pennsylvania and Lafayette Univ. (s. 1920).

Elena Letňanová (1942–), b. Bratislava; Czech., is a pianist, publicist, and pedagogue. She studied at the Academy of Performing Arts in Bratislava and at the Fryderyk Chopin University of Music in Warsaw. The promising career of a concert pianist was interrupted by normalization, and the artist was forbidden to perform. In 1984, she emigrated and resumed her concert career. In the USA, she was the head of the keyboard department at the University of Ohio (1987–92). In 1991, she published the *Piano Interpretation of the Seventeenth, Eighteenth and Nineteenth Centuries: A Study of Theory and Practice Using Original*

Documents in the USA. She then returned to Slovakia. Apart from Slovak festivals, she has appeared at festivals in Vienna, Rome, Ghent, Bacau, San Francisco, Dayton, Prague, Kroměříž, Ostrava, Zlín, Katowice, Turin etc. and recitals in Carnegie Hall in New York, Washington and other states of the USA, Canada, Europe (Germany, France, Italy, Spain, Holland, Belgium, England, Austria, Croatia, Slovenia, Romania, Poland, Czech Republic etc.), Asia (Israel) and Japan. She has appeared with the Dayton Philharmonic Orchestra, M. Jora Philharmonic Orchestra in Bacau, Bohuslav Martin Chamber Orchestra in Brno, Brno Philharmonia, Brno Chamber Soloists conducted by Georg Sebastien, Philip Magnusson, Henri van de Velde, Ovidio Balan etc.

Oscar Ludwig (1877-1937), b. Czech., was a double bassist with Boston Symphony Orchestra (1908-37). Before that he was a double bassist with Berlin Philharmonic.

Milan Lusk (1893-1932), b. Chicago, IL, of Bohemian parentage, was a distinguished violinist. He had been accorded one of the most phenomenal careers of any violinist of the day. At the early age of four, he displayed an inclination to music. First studying the piano, he soon evidenced an interest in the violin. In 1913, he began his studies with the great Otakar Ševčík, at the Vienna Akademie, where he won the coveted Royal Akademie Scholarship in 1914. He made his debut as soloist with the Tonkuenstler Orchestra in Vienna under the baton of Oskar Nedbal and was immediately engaged for numerous appearances as soloist with the Prague Philharmonic Orchestra and others. Literally hundreds of American concerts soon followed. In 1924, he again returned to Europe for an extensive tour, and, after hearing him play, the then Queen Marie, of Rumania, made him her protégé, and practically sponsored his third European tour in 1926. In 1927, shortly before his death, King Ferdinand, of Rumania, knighted him with the order of Chevalier of the Crown. President Masaryk of Czechoslovakia also honored him with one of that nation's rarest medals for the sixty benefit concerts he gave in Europe and America during the war. His hundreds of American concerts, radio appearances, and phonograph recordings have thoroughly established him as one of America's favorite violinists. He frequently donated the proceeds from his concerts to the Czech Army Fund.

Frank Linhart (1900-d.), b. Zbraslavice, near Louny, Bohemia, was a flutist. He arrived in America in 1923 and eventually settled in Chicago. He was a flute virtuoso of broad and varied experience. In Chicago, he was engaged in concert and opera, while studying with Mr. Qunsel and Theodore Yeshke. For three years, Linhart played with the Chicago Symphony Civic Orch. He was also a music instructor at the J. Sterling Morton HS in Cicero, IL. He was a member of the Bohemian Arts Club.

Frank J. Mach, Jr. (1887–d.), b. Omaha, NE, was a noted violinist who studied violin in Prague, Bohemia, under Professor Jan Mařák. He returned to Omaha to teach music and has taught leaders of many famous orchestras.

Ottokar Málek (1876–1923), b. Czech., when he was 20 years of age, graduated from the Prague Conservatory of Music. He was engaged as instructor to the Duke of Fuerstenberg. Later he went to Vienna, where he studied for 3 years with the famous Alfred Gruenfeld, the Court pianist to the Emperor. After this, he studied the celebrated Leschetinzky system of piano technique. In 1896, he began to tour Europe as concert pianist. Shortly before coming to the US, he held the position of professor at Eichelberg Conservatory in Berlin, besides being 'capellmeister' of the Berliner Tonkünstler-Orchester, of which Richard Straus was then first conductor. In 1902, Malek came to the US. Since 1908, he spent most of the time in teaching and coaching pupils for the concert stage, besides playing publicly and occupying the position of director of piano depts. of different large music schools in and around Chicago. He was the founder and director of Malek School of Music, Grand Rapids, MI. Later on, he joined the faculty of the Columbia School of music in Chicago.

Joseph F. Mann (1868–1953), b. Czech, was a trumpet player with Boston Symphony Orchestra (1891–1937). After retiring as player, continued as asst. librarian until 1952 (61 years of service).

Joseph E. Mares, Sr. (1875–d.) played cornet with the military band at the New Orleans lakefront and ran a fur and hide business. Like many New Orleans cornetists of his generation, Joe Mares Sr.'s main influence was 'King' Joe Oliver.

Joseph E. Mares, Jr. (1908–1991), b. New Orleans, LA, brother of Paul Mares, was an American clarinetist. In his youth, he played informally with the New Orleans Rhythm Kings. Around 1953, he formed his own record company, Southland, and during the 1950s recorded many New Orleans musicians. The social security death index gives his last known place of residence as New Orleans.

Ferdinand Maresh (1918–1986), b. Ohio, was a bass player, who studied at the Curtis Institute Class of 1940. He was with the Philadelphia Orchestra (1946–86), as assistant principal bass (1967–70) and double bass (1970–86). Before that he was with the All-American Youth Orchestra (1940), and Cleveland Orchestra (1941–42, 1945–48). He wrote the interesting book *Transatlantic Passenger steamships to Philadelphia* in 1985.

David Martinka (fl. 2018), b. Slovakia, is a self-taught flute musician and an award-winning recording artist. David Martinka is a 5th generation musician who successfully blends the beautiful sounds of handmade flutes from his native Slovakian roots and his love for the

Native American flute into songs that are healing, meditative, loving and spiritual. The result is a step back into a time when the flute was used, to heal the soul and to bring peace to people's hearts.

Edward William Masacek (1895-1983), b. Illinois, was a trumpet player with Chicago symphony Orchestra (1921-46), as a second trumpet (1921-33), as fourth trumpet (1933-46). He also played in the US Band 'Pershing's Own' and in the Hollywood Bowl Orchestra (in the summer of 1923). Left the CSO when World War 2 service musicians returned to the Chicago Symphony. After leaving the CSO, Masacek worked at the Chicago NBC radio station. Later he became a music teacher in Berwyn, Illinois, a Chicago suburb.

Douglas Masek (1947-), b. Cleveland, OH, of Czech ancestry, is a saxophonist. He was trained at University of Cincinnati Coll.-Conservatory of Music and Ohio State Univ. He completed his academic education with a Doctorate in Musical Arts at the University of Southern California, where he taught from 1975-1995. He is internationally renowned performer and lecturer of the saxophone. Currently, Dr. Masek is a Leblanc/Yanagisawa saxophone clinician, and Vandoren Artist, and is Professor of Saxophone at UCLA and Cal State Northridge.

Marianne Matousek Mastics (1919-2011), b. Cleveland, OH, of Czech ancestry, was a pianist. She has appeared with the Cleveland 'Pops' Symphony, with the Cleveland Women's Symphony, and has recalled throughout Northeastern Ohio. Mrs. Mastics was also heard annually in her recitals at the Cleveland Institute of Music.

Mark 'Sparky' Matejka (1967-), b. Houston, TX, of Czech ancestry, is an American Southern rock guitarist. He is a former student of the North Texas State University (now UNT) jazz program and studied under renowned guitar educator Jack Peterson. He is probably best known as a guitarist in Lynyrd Skynyrd. He joined the band in 2006, replacing Hughie Thomasson who had left to reform Outlaws. He first played with Skynyrd on their *Christmas Time Again* album in 2000 and was credited with guitar and vocals. Prior to joining Lynyrd Skynyrd, Matejka was a member of Hot Apple Pie, a country music band. He also played for Charlie Daniels Band and Sons of the Desert. He played guitar on tour with The Kinleys in 1998.

Bohumil Med (1939-), b. Czech., is a horn player. He graduated from the Prague Conservatory of Music, under Josef Schwarz, and Post-Graduate from the Janácek Academy of Arts, Brno. In 1968, he moved to Rio de Janeiro, where he joined Orquestra Sinfônica, as a horn player. He also played with various music ensembles and taught horn at the Instituto Villa-Lobos (FIFIEG). In 1974, he became professor of horn and music theory at Universidad de Brasilia. He founded the University Brass Quintet, with which he made several recordings and performed concerts in Brazil and abroad. He also founded the National Theatre Orchestra in Brasilia and became its leading horn player. He wrote several textbooks of which his *Teoria da música* is considered the best work of its kind in Portuguese. He also owns a small publishing house and is the owner of the largest store of musical instruments – Brazil MusiMed. In November 2011, Professor Bohumil Med, was elected Dean of the music market in Brazil. The selection criteria took into account the dedication, commitment and contribution to the development of the Brazilian music market. This recognition confirmed the national and international success of a company located in the capital of the Republic, which, in its 30 years of existence, has become the largest music bookstore in Latin America. He has been president of the Sociedade Cultural Brasil-Tchecoslováquia. Over the years, he has contributed to the promotion of the Czech Republic in Brazil.

James A. Melichar (1897-1994), b. near Prague, Bohemia, came to the US in 1914. Although he never earned a formal degree, he had considerable musical training. He was a clarinet player. He was a member of the 115th Field Artillery Band (1917); and later a member of Kryl Band, He was a director of Monahan Post Band in Sioux City, Iowa and then became the conductor of the Cedar Falls Band from 1929 to 1976. Melichar also taught at Cedar Falls High School for 22 years, after which he taught at Dike High School for 14 years. Melichar also made some rather important innovations in the Cedar Falls Band. It was under his leadership that women were first allowed to join the band in 1930 when they needed a few extra instruments and vocalists for the Chicagoland Music Festival and Melichar used women to fill these spots. During Melichar's tenure as director, a beginners' band was established to help train younger children to play instruments. This was to go along with the Auxiliary Band (Junior Band) which had already been established to train older kids and young adults. Talented musicians could graduate from the beginners' band to the Auxiliary Band to the Cedar Falls Band.

Bohumil Michalek (1885-d.), b. Chicago, IL, of Bohemian ancestry, was violinist who studied at Brussels, Belgium and Prague, Bohemia; he was pupil and assistant of Prof. Otakar Ševčík. He was appointed concert master of New Bohemian Opera in Prague (1907) but declined appointment in Prague Cons. of Music and other similar offers in Russia, Germany, France and Switzerland. He returned to US in 1908 and founded in Chicago, in the Fine Arts Building, the Michalek Master School for Violinists, of which he became director. He resided in Chicago.

Chris 'Buddha' Michalek (1971-2010), b. Minneapolis, MN, possibly of Czech ancestry, was an American harmonica player. He was an accomplished modern diatonic harmonica player in many styles including Jazz, Funk, Blues and World Music. Michalek was also the organizer of the Global Harmonica Summit in 2000. Michalek was known for using the overblow technique, which is used to play chromatically on the diatonic harmonica. When he was a teenager, Michalek's harmonicostic talents were discovered by members of the Twin Cities Harmonica Society, including the prominent harmonica player and one-time Harmonicat Dick Gardner. Chris quickly began to play jazz and to experiment with other styles of music. He was still playing until recently with well-known bassist Mahlon Hawk in the Buddha's Groove.

Joseph James Michalek, b. of Czech ancestry, was a violinist. He studied violin at Bush Conservatory, Chicago with John Weicher, CSO principal second violin. He was a member of the Chicago Symphony Orch. (1942–72), playing violin. In 1930s, he played first violin with Kansas City Philharmonic. He also played second violin with the Sebald String Quartet and the Robert Quick String Quartet in Kansas City.

Marienka Michna (1922–1993), b. Torrington, CT, of Slovak descent, was a concert pianist and opera coach.

Marie Mikova (1892–1962), b. Omaha, NE, of Czech ancestry, became a well-known concert pianist in the country. She studied piano in Omaha under August Mothe Borglum. In 1910, she studied piano with Wager Swayne in Paris and played concerts with the Touche Orchestra. She made many concert tours throughout the United States. She was a soloist with Los Angeles Philharmonic, Hollywood Bowl Orchestras and Oakland Symphony. She also taught music in California State University in Berkeley.

Joseph Mischka (1846–1911), b. Heřmanův Městec, Bohemia, was an organist, conductor and teacher. He came to Buffalo in 1852 and began his musical career as organist of Westminster Church, and musical director of the Anon Singing Society. He held a position of organist in some of the Christian churches of this city, and for thirty years has held the position of organist at the Temple Beth Zion. In 1870, he became musical director of the Liedertafel, in which position he remained until 1894. He was prominently identified with the great musical festivals given here in 1883, 1884, 1885 and 1886.

August Molzer (1880–1967), b. Slaný, Bohemia, was a violinist. He studied violin under the renowned Prof. Otakar Ševčík, Prof. Štefan Suchý in Prague, as well as piano under Antonín Dvořák, was a concert violinist and teacher of violin in Nebraska. Upon his return to Nebraska, he taught two years as head of the violin department at Wesleyan University, Lincoln, and two years in the University School of Music. In 1911, he established the Molzer School of the Violin, of which he became director. Since 1925, he was on the University of Nebraska faculty as professor of violin. He also composed a number of violin pieces.

Joseph E. Mourek (1910-2003), b. Illinois, of Czech parents, at the age of 8, studied in Chicago with Czech-born horn musician Václav Basta and composer Thorwold Otterstrom. He played with the Chicago Civic Orchestra (1927-29) when he was hired as assistant third horn. At the age of 19, he was the youngest member of CSO. He was promoted to third horn the next year and moved to fourth horn a decade later. He retired from the symphony in 1976. Mourek wrote his interesting Memoirs in his Publish America book *Evolution of a Symphony Musician* (2001).

J. Gerald Mraz (1874-1952), b. Iowa, of Czech parents, was a violinist. Born in Iowa shortly after the American Civil War to Czech parents, Mraz attended Chicago Musical College before traveling to Europe to study at the Conservatory of Music in Prague, where he performed in an orchestra led by Czech conductor and composer, Antonín Dvořák. While in Europe, Mraz also performed in an orchestra under the direction of Richard Strauss. By the year 1920, Mraz made a home for himself in Oklahoma City and founded the Mraz Violin School. He taught at Oklahoma City University from 1924 to 1927, and before the founding of OKCU, Mraz was involved in teaching violin at the University's predecessor, Epworth University. Mraz contributed two works to the field of violin pedagogy, *Systematized Intervals* (1909) and *The Art of Violin Bowing* (1927). These works were both serialized in the publication, *The Violinist* and were standard repertoire for many students of violin around the world.

Karel Netolička (1920-), b. Vilimovec, Czech., is a bass player, educated at State Conservatory, Brno and Janáček Academy of Music. He was asst. principal bass, Milwaukee Symphony Orchestra (1972-82); and teacher of bass at Univ. of Wisconsin.

Eugenia Fichtenová Newman (1913-2011), b. Czech., was a violinist. She studied first in Prague, coming to the US in 1929. She was a violinist with the Indianapolis Symphony (1942-46), Buffalo Philharmonic under William Steinberg (1946-47), Cleveland Orchestra under George Szell (1947-48) and also with Eastbay String Quartet, as the first violinist. She has been with the San Francisco Symphony Oakland Symphony from 1964-79.

John Novacek (1964-), b. Los Angeles, CA, of Czech ancestry, is international concert pianist. He was the winner of the Leschetizky and Joanna Hodges International piano competitions, in addition to numerous national competitions. He divides his solo work between recitals and concertos with orchestra.

Frank Joseph Novak, Jr. (1901-), b. Chicago, IL of Czech parents, was a drummer and composer, educated at Univ. of Chicago and Czech Conservatory of Music in Prague. He had his debut with Bohumir Kryl's Band as a drummer. He appeared in concert tours of western states and others. He was also composer of concert and light operatic numbers. He resided in NYC.

Donald Andrew Novy (1930-), b. Oak Park, IL, was a trumpeter, composer, and conductor. Educated at Northwestern Univ. (M.A., 1955) and Univ. of Colorado. He was soloist with Northwestern Univ. Band, Denver Municipal Band and had performances with Nat Cole, Jerry Lewis, Red Buttons, Billy May, etc. He was a teacher of instrumental music in Denver Public Schools; private teacher; trumpet music director, Denver Winter Sports Show (1965-66), Alpine Musicamp, Inc., Aspen, CO (1968-71). He was also inventor of acoustic coil – an insert to the bore designed for Woodwinds, saxophones, and bass instruments to improve their response acoustically.

Joseph F. Novy (1901-1964), b. Illinois, of Czech parents, played cello with the Chicago Symphony Orch. (1923-40). In the 1940s, he was a musician with the orchestra of Chicago Radio Station WCFL.

Vincent C. Nowotný (1828-1887), b. Bohemia, had played the flute and piccolo in the West Point Band, and in later life in several Springfield (OH) bands and orchestras.

Emanuel Ondříček (1880 -1958), b. Plzeň, Bohemia, was a violinist, composer and teacher, educated at Prague Cons. of Music. After immigrating to US in 1912, he taught in Boston and NYC. Shortly before his death, he was appointed prof. of violin at Boston Univ. He was the author of *Mastery of Tone Production and Expression on the Violin* (1931).

Karel Ondříček (1865-1943), Prague, Bohemia, was a Czech violin virtuoso. He was one of the four famous Ondříček violinist brothers. He received his basic musical education from his father, Jan Ondříček, who was a violinist and conductor, and had studied music theory with Antonín Dvořák. He became a military band conductor, performed as a solo violinist in chamber ensembles, and taught music. Among his pupils was Jan Kubelík. He was involved in premiere performances of several pieces by Antonin Dvořák, including the String Quartet No. 1, the Terzetto in C, the 'Cypresses' for string quartet, and the Romantic Pieces. From 1887-93, he was Concertmaster of the National Theatre in Prague. In 1893, he received an offer from America, which he accepted. He performed at the World's Fair in Chicago and became Concertmaster of the Symphony Orchestra of the Music Hall in Boston. He played the second violin in the Kneisel Quartet from 1899-1902, and about 1910, led his own musical trio.

James (Václav) Paleček (1914-aft. 2002), b. Czech., emigrated to the US as a child with his family in 1922. He was with Chicago Symphony Orchestra (1956-76), as a double bass, librarian, and stage manager.

Ernst Panenka (1905-1990), b. Vienna, of Czech ancestry, was a bassoonist. An alumnus of the Vienna Music Academy, was a 25-year-old bassoonist with the Vienna Opera, when he auditioned in his native Vienna before Serge Koussevitzky, then the Boston Symphony's conductor, who hired him. He was bassoonist with Boston Symphony Orchestra (1930-75) – a total of 45 sessions. He was also a long-term teacher at the New England Conservatory of Music (1945-55). He also played bassoon with the Boston Pops and Esplanade orchestras. He was also an avid amateur astronomer, constructing several telescopes, grinding all of his own lenses.

Robert Pangborn (1934-), b. Painesville, OH, of Czech ancestry, is principal percussionist and assistant principal timpanist of the Detroit Symphony Orchestra. He began studying piano at the age of seven and percussion at nine with his uncle, William Hruby at the Hruby Conservatory of Music in Cleveland and later studied at the Cleveland Institute of Music, Eastman School of Music and at Juilliard. Before joining the Detroit Symphony Orchestra in 1964, Pangborn held the positions of Principal Timpanist with the Indianapolis Symphony, Mallet Percussionist with the Cleveland Orchestra, and Timpanist/Percussionist with the Metropolitan Opera Orchestra in New York City. Pangborn spent many years as a private percussion instructor and served on the faculties of the Cleveland Institute of Music and Oakland University.

Peter 'Pete' Parada (1973-), b. Arkport, NY, of Slovak paternal grandfather, is an American drummer and songwriter. Parada's drumming career began in 1995 when he joined L.A. band World In Pain on a recommendation from future Korn drummer Ray Luzier and then Steel Prophet in 1996 with whom he recorded one album a year later. Subsequently, he joined Face to Face and Saves the Day, and in 2007 became the new drummer for The Offspring. Parada was also associated with the metal band Engine and Rob Halford's solo project Halford, and briefly played drums in the punk band Alkaline Trio. He was also a member of Hot Mess.

Walter Parazaider (1945-), b. Maywood, IL, possibly of Czech ancestry, is an American woodwind musician best known for being a founding member of the rock band Chicago. He plays a wide variety of wind instruments, including saxophone, flute, and clarinet. He also occasionally plays guitar.

Theodore Pashkus (1905-1970), b. Bratislava, Slovakia; was a violinist and teacher. He and his wife Alice Pushkus, used original, modern and unique method of teaching the high art of violin playing, which had won worldwide recognition. Among their artist-pupils were violin virtuosi of international reputation such as Ossy Renardy, Ivry Gitlis, Michèle Auclair, Blanche Tarjus and many others. Theodore and Alice Pashkus divided their teaching activities between New York and Paris. Through "Young Violinist's Recordings" and the "Young Violinist's Editions" together with the "Young Violinist's Practice Guide",

Theodore and Alice Pashkus made available for the first time their unique method to average violin students all over the world.

Joe Pat Paterek (1919–1981), b. Chicago, of Slovak descent, was an accordionist. Joe became interested in music at an early age and began taking music lessons while attending local schools. After developing a serious pursuit of music, Joe formed his first band in 1932. For several years he continued to lead his band and on Thanksgiving Day of 1942, Joe was married to Irene Desecki. Three months after marriage, Joe was inducted into the Army Air Corps and was assigned to a unit entertaining the troops at USO shows and other military social functions. After being discharged from the service in 1946, he enrolled in the Midwestern Conservatory of Music where he later graduated with honors. In 1946, 'Joe Pat' also organized his new ten-piece band and played his first return engagement at the popular Pulaski ballroom. Through the years, he developed a vast acumen for music as it related to recordings, orchestrations, radio, television, and entertaining live audiences. Joe was active as a professional musician, bandleader, and entertainer for over 45 years at the time of his induction to International Polka Association (IPA) Hall of Fame in 1978. His versatile band, which exceled in playing various styles of ethnic and polka music performed repeatedly on radio and television; and at the popular dance halls, ballrooms, country clubs, hotels and major social functions throughout the country. In January of 1973, 'Joe Pat' Paterek and his band had the honor of having performed at the Presidential Inaugural salute to American Heritage in Washington, D.C. Joe and his musicians toured seven countries in Europe and performed in Hawaii. He and his band recorded a Polka Mass album of special music, which received considerable national attention and acclaim.

Pamela Pecha (1951–2018), b. New York, NY, of Czech ancestry, was an oboist of note.

Neyla Pekarek (1986–), b. Denver, CO, of Slovak paternal grandfather, is a cellist, vocalist, and pianist for the American folk-rock band, The Lumineers. She began playing the cello at age nine, performing in her school's orchestra. She attended college at the University of Northern Colorado, where she initially majored in vocal performance and musical theatre. She changed majors, however, graduating with a degree in music education; she initially planned on becoming a choir teacher. Although she did not play the cello much while attending college, she earned some income post-graduation as a cellist at weddings. After finishing her degree in music education, Pekarek responded to a Craigslist ad posted by Wesley Schultz and Jeremiah Fraites. Schultz and Fraites were looking for a cellist to join their band, The Lumineers. While her contribution to the band was most noticeable as a cellist, she had a larger role as a vocalist in live performances, including performing a duet with Schultz. She took a passive approach to songwriting, with no credits on their first album and two credits on their second album. On October 18, 2018, it was announced that

Pekarek would be leaving the band to pursue a solo career. Pekarek wrote a "folk opera" called Rattlesnake about Katherine McHale Slaughterback, popularly called "Rattlesnake Kate," who was a renowned snake hunter of Colorado. Pekarek enjoys singing barbershop music competitively as a member of Sweet Adelines International, seeing plays, and conducting musical training workshops with schoolchildren of her native Colorado.

John Frederick Peter (1746-1813), b. Heerendijk, Holland, of Moravian ancestry, was a pioneer organist, serving with the Moravian Brethren Church in Bethlehem, PA. Peter was educated in Holland and Germany before coming to America with his brother Simon in 1770. He began to compose music for the church shortly after his arrival in America and for a time served as an organist and violinist in the Moravian congregations of Nazareth, Bethlehem and Lititz in Pennsylvania before eventually going to Salem, North Carolina in 1780 in the same capacity. In his time, he was considered one of the greatest American composers.

Gordon B. Peters (1931-2023), b. Cicero, IL, of Czech ancestry, a noted percussionist, studied with a who's-who of percussion: Roy Knapp, Otto Kristufek, Clair Omar Musser, Morris Goldenberg, Saul Goodman, and William Street. He was with Chicago Symphony Orchestra (1959-2001), as principal timpani and assistant principal timpani. Before that he was with Rochester Philharmonic (1954-59), and US Military Academy Band (1950-53). He also served as a conductor of Elmhurst Symphony Orchestra (1968-73) and percussion professor and founder/director of Percussion/Marimba Ensemble programs at Northwestern Univ. (1963-68). In 2004, Peters was inducted into Percussive Arts Society Hall of Fame.

Miloš Petrák, b. Prague, Czech Republic, is a double bass player. He began his musical training at age six, taking violin lessons from his father, a member of Czech Philharmonic. At age fifteen he switched to the double bass and continued his training at the Prague Conservatory of Music, where he studied under Frantisek Posta, principal double bass player of Czech Philharmonic, where, for seven years, he played under the direction of Vaclav Neumann. In 1981, he emigrated via Japan to Canada, settling in Toronto. In 1988, he joined the Kitchener-Waterloo Symphony. For the last eleven summers, he has participated in the Colorado Music Festival in Boulder.

Krystof Pipal, b. Czech., grew up in Prague. Starting on piano, Pipal switched to horn when twelve years old and at eighteen appeared on Czech national television with the Bohemia Brass Quintet as a winner of the Prague Concertino Competition. Graduating from Prague Conservatory in 1994, Mr. Pipal accepted a scholarship to study at Harid Conservatory, Florida, graduating with honors in 1998. He also attended Sewanee, Bowdoin and Nove Straseci festivals. In his career, Mr. Pipal was a member of Nova Philharmonia Portuguese,

Prague Radio Symphony, Palm Beach Opera, Milwaukee Chamber Orchestra, among others. His teachers include Gregory journalists, Alois Cocek, Robert Rouch, and Bedrich Tylsar. He has been an associate principal horn with the Milwaukee Symphony Orchestra since 1999.

Edward Pique (1815–fl. 1892), b. Prague, was one of the oldest professional musicians on the coast. He had a successful career in Europe before immigrating to America in 1848. He taught guitar in Philadelphia, where he also developed a business relationship with C.F. Martin. He and his wife, an English-born dancer, moved to California in 1852, where Pique resumed his teaching career in California and became a frequent performer in San Francisco and Sacramento concerts. Pique also was a composer and arranger for the guitar. Pique had been engaged in teaching for over forty years.

Kazi Pitelka (1953–), b. of Czech ancestry, is a violist and musician of Pop, Folk and Rock. She is principal violist of L.A. Opera, of the Long Beach Symphony, and of the Los Angeles Master Chorale, and is active in Los Angeles, recording and motion picture industry. Kazi Pitelka has participated in the Monday Evening Concerts since 1980, first as a regular with the MEC Ensemble and later as a member of XTET in its annual appearances.

Edward Pitlik (1930–2010), b. Chicago, IL, of Czech ancestry, was a percussion player educated at Northern Illinois Univ. and Univ. of Illinois. He was a member of the Illinois Air National Guard Band (1948–57), director (s. 1958); and 566th Air Force Band, Chicago.

Gene Pokorny, b. California, of Czech ancestry, is a tuba player. He has been a principal tuba player with the Chicago Symphony Orchestra (s. 1989). Before that, he was with Israel Philharmonic (1975–78), the Utah Symphony (1978–83), the St. Louis Symphony (1983–89), and Los Angeles Philharmonic (1992–93). While in California, Pokorny played in Hollywood for films such as *Jurassic Park* and *The Fugitive*.

Vladimír Polivka (1896–1948), b. Prague, Bohemia, was a pianist and composer, trained at Prague Conservatory of Music. He came to US in 1922 as a member of Czech Trio. He taught piano in Chicago (1923–30) and traveled in Europe and America.

Walter Preucil (ca. 1965–), b. Iowa City, IA, of Czech ancestry, is a cellist. He is a graduate of the Eastman School of Music. He has been an orchestra member of the Lyric Opera of Chicago since 1988. His solo performances with orchestras have included works by Bloch, Brahms, Dvořák, Haydn, Miakovsky, Milhaud, Tchaikovsky, and a critically acclaimed appearance at the Casals Festival in Prades, France. He has performed in the Classic Arts Trio since 1993.

William Preucil (1931–), b. Joliet, IL, of Czech ancestry, is a graduate of the Eastman School of Music, former principal violist of the Detroit Symphony Orchestra, a founding member of the Stradivari Quartet, and is Emeritus Professor at The University of Iowa, where he received its annual M.L. Huit Award for Teaching Excellence in 1992. He is the recording artist for the method books of the Suzuki Viola School, and has served as Chair of the Board of Directors of the Suzuki Association of the Americas, vice-president of the International Suzuki Association, and vice-president of the American Viola Society, which gave him its Creative Achievement Award in 2008. He is also the recipient of the American String Teachers Association 2009 Artist Teacher Award. An SAA registered Teacher-Trainer, Preucil has performed concerts and taught classes in more than thirty-five countries on six continents.

Zachary Preucil (1991–) b. of Czech ancestry (son of Walter Preucil), is a cellist. He was trained in cello performance at New England Conservatory of Music (B.M., 2012), Eastman School of Music (M.M., 2014) and at University of Wisconsin-Madison (D.M.A., 2020). He has been engaged as principal cello by La Crosse Symphony Orchestra (since 2018), and as cello instructor by Farley's House of Pianos (since 2019) and Virtu.Academy (since 2021).

Tom Ptak (1895–1997), b. South Dakota, of Czech parents, taught himself to play the button accordion, the tuba, and the bells, but it was the drums with which Tom was to fall in love. When Tom's brother, Steve, a banjo and fiddle player, moved to Dante to begin teaching in the mid-1920s, Tom saw his chance to begin a musical career. He pulled together a diverse collection of musicians from the Wagner area, and put together his first band, a dance band called 'The Royal Serenaders.' The powerful AM radio station, WNAX, located in Yankton, which began broadcasting in the 1920s, included their performances as a part of its regular programming. In March 1927, The Royal Serenaders entered a competition at WNAX and won first prize.

Fred (Ferdinand) Anton Ressel (1899–1999), b. Liberec, Bohemia, was a violist. He privately studied violin and viola with Suchý and Prada in Prague. He was principal violist (s. 1936) for 41 years with the Buffalo Philharmonic Orchestra, which he helped found. Together with his wife, Ruby Sherrad Ressel, he was the founder, organizer, and conductor of Buffalo Symphonette (s. 1948), while she was a business manager. He also taught privately and at local colleges and high schools.

Jeanne Preucil Rose, b. US, the daughter of William Preucil, of Czech ancestry, is a violinist. She joined the Cleveland Orchestra's first violin section in January 1999. Born into a musical family, Ms. Preucil Rose began violin lessons at the age of four and soon joined the rest of her family in performances across the United States and Japan. She earned a

Bachelor of music degree from the Cleveland Institute of Music and a Master of music degree and performer's certificate from the Eastman School of Music in Rochester, New York. Before becoming a member of the Cleveland Orchestra, Ms. Preucil Rose was concertmaster of the Midland-Odessa Symphony and a member of the award-winning Everest Quartet. She has also participated in many summer music festivals. She is married to the violinist Stephen Rose.

Feri Roth (1899–1969), b. Zvolen, Slovakia, was a violinist. In 1922, he founded the String Quartet which bore his name for forty-seven years. Two years later, the quartet made a successful debut in Paris, then embarked on a tour of Europe and Africa. In 1928, the quartet, made its first appearance in the United States at the Pittsfield (Massachusetts) Music Festival. Subsequently, the quartet concertized throughout the United States, Canada, and Mexico, participating in concerts at the Library of Congress, giving many concerts of modern works in New York City and Washington, and performing all of Beethoven's string quartets including his *Grosse Fuge*. In 1947, Roth began his long association with UCLA, joining the Department of Music as Lecturer. In 1960, he was named full professor.

Christopher 'Chris' Lee Rybak (1977–), b. Hallettsville, TX, of Czech ancestry, is a famous musician and singer, performing at various festivals, concerts and cultural events throughout the USA and Europe. Chris Rybak, nicknamed the 'Accordion Cowboy', is best known as an accordionist, a music teacher and arranger, and a recording artist with over 10 albums to date. Professionally performing since the age of 12 with his father's band Leroy Rybak Swinging Orchestra, then performing solo and later adding more musicians and founding the Chris Rybak Band, he's been playing various styles of music including Czech & German polkas & waltzes, country & western, Cajun, Tex-Mex and gospel. Passionately promoting Czech heritage, language, music and culture through his performances, co-founding an educational website www.texasczechs.com (with his wife Edita Rybak) and organizing European tours, he is widely recognized as a prominent accordion player and Czech personality in the Texas music scene. Past performances have included many special occasions, such as performing for the dignitaries from the Czech Republic (Prime Minister and other ministers and the Czech Ambassador in Washington). His daughter Kristina Nicole Rybak has been following in his footsteps and is a part of his performances.

Dagmar Rydlo (1932–2024), b. Prague, Czech., is a pianist. She studied at the State Conservatory of Music in Prague (dipl., 1968) and at McGill Univ. (B.Mus., 1970). She taught in the music dept. of McGill Univ. for 12 years (1971-83). She also taught music majors at Marianopolis College, Montreal (1976-83). In 1987, she was appointed chief administrator for the Mississauga Branch of the Royal Conservatory of Music and worked in that position for five years. In 1990-93, she was a member of the Faculty of Music at

Univ. of Toronto. She has performed in numerous concerts throughout her musical career as a soloist and with chamber groups.

Anne Dolores Zvara Sarosy (1923-2015), b. Campbell, OH, of Slovak descent, was an accomplished accordionist. She had her own orchestra on WKBN Radio in the late 30s and 40s. She earned a Bachelor of Science Degree in Education, Cum Laude, from Youngstown State University and a Master in Education/Counseling degree at Westminster College, New Wilmington, PA. In addition, she did Slovak language studies at the University of Akron, University of Pittsburgh and the Slovak Jesuit Institute in Toronto, Canada.

Robert Haven Schauffler (1879-1964), b. Brno, Moravia, where his parents were missionaries. By the time he was two, he was back in the United States where his family founded the Schauffler College in Cleveland in 1886 for Bohemian immigrants who were interested in social or religious work. Schauffler's first successful career was as a cellist, and he studied with several notable musicians. His academic studies started at the Northwestern University, but he completed his degree at Princeton before going on to study at the University in Berlin in 1902-03. By this time, he had already been editor of the *Nassau Literary Magazine* for a year. On his return from Berlin, he combined his skills as a music editor for another magazine. He was also an American writer of poetry and a number of biographies of famous musicians such as Brams and Beethoven. He is also remembered as the author of a series of travel books on American and European destinations aimed at Americans contemplating a holiday, either at home or abroad.

Clara Tesar Schneider (1902-1993), b. South Omaha, NE, was a noted violinist. At the age of 8, she studied under the supervision of Professor F. Mach. She has done a great deal of concert work in Omaha. She toured Colorado, Nevada, Utah, California, and Oregon with the Southern Festival Circuit of Ellison White Co., from September 1924 to December 1924. Mrs. Tesar was for two seasons concert master and soloist of the Omaha Little Symphony. She resided in Omaha.

Peter Serkin (1947-2020), b. New York, NY, son of Rudolf Serkin, is an outstanding pianist. In 1958, at age 11, Serkin began studying at the Curtis Institute of Music, where his teachers included the Polish pianist Mieczysław Horszowski, the American virtuoso Lee Luvisi, as well as his own father. He graduated in 1965. He also studied with Ernst Oster, flutist Marcel Moyse, and Karl Ulrich Schnabel. He taught at the Curtis Institute of Music, the Juilliard School, Yale University, and Bard College. He is known for his performances of Mozart, Beethoven, Brahms, Schubert, Schoenberg, Stravinsky, etc.

Rudolf Serkin (1903–1991), from Cheb, Bohemia, was an eminent pianist, known for his interpretations of the Viennese classics. He helped to establish the Marlboro Festival in Vermont and served as its artistic director.

Steve Seventy (1927–1988), b. Pittsburgh, Pa, of Slovak father; accomplished accordion player, owner of Seventy's Music, Pittsburgh, teacher; elected to PA House of Representatives in 1978, served 4 more consecutive terms.

Jaroslav Šiškovský (1888–1979), b. Cleveland, OH, of Czech ancestry, was a violinist. He studied with Anton Machar at Cleveland and Otakar Ševčík in Vienna. He toured as 2nd violinist with NY String Quartet. He was a member of NY Chamber Music Soc. He was the author of *Fiddler on the Hoof: The Odyssey of a Concert Violinist.* (1975).

Mary Elizabeth Skalicky (1931–2014), Dallas, TX, of Czech ancestry, was a pianist and organist. She earned many accolades, including the Viola Cassidy Memorial Award for most outstanding organ student, first place recipient in the National Federation of Music Club's auditions, one of the few women members of the Guild of Carillonneurs of North America, a chosen performer in recital at historic St. Jacob's Church in Prague, invited performer at the Fifth International Organ Festival at St. Maurice's Church in Czechoslovakia, the Rockefeller Memorial Carillon at Riverside Church in New York, being the first woman to play the mammoth 74 bell carillon, and the Niagara Falls recital in Rainbow Bridge. Mary accepted the position of professor of music, Howard College and relocated to Big Spring, TX in 1968.

Ernie Skuta (1935–), b. Detroit, MI, of Moravian parents, is a trumpet player. He attended John Marshall Elementary School, where he began playing trumpet at nine years of age, when the band director, needing trumpeter, selected him. He began playing popular music and performing at dances with various bands. He also played with various Czech, Polish and German bands. He graduated from Cass Tech in 1953 and then enrolled at Lawrence Inst. of Technology (B.A., 1957), and then went on to Univ. Michigan to study nuclear engineering (M.S., 1958). He was a very talented musician who played variety instruments and various types of music. He was a popular trumpeter and band leader.

Luis Slabý (1951–), b. Buenos Aires, Argentina, of Czech ancestry, is Argentine clarinetist. In 1988, he created a series of chamber music concerts featuring music of Czech composers. He is a member of the National Symphony Orchestra and the Philharmonic Orchestra of the Theatre Colón and Symphonic Orchestra of Buenos Aires. He is professor at the Music Conservatories 'San Martin' and Julian Aguirre.'

Meyer Benjamin Slivka (1923-2012), b. Indiana, was a percussionist with San Francisco Symphony (1953-55), as a principal percussion (1955-56). Before, he was a cruise ship musician between San Francisco and Japan (1952) and also with Little Orchestra of San Francisco (1956-58) and Seattle Symphony timpanist, Washington beginning 1958-1959 season. Also with CBC Chamber Orchestra, Canada in 1960s. When Meyer Slivka played in the Seattle Symphony, he also constructed and experimented with a Theremin (electronic instrument). Slivka was also an active composer and experimented with electronic music.

František Smetana (1914-2004), b. Ohnišťany, Bohemia, was a cellist educated at State Conservatory of Music, Prague. He taught cello Iowa State Univ. (1966-73) and Virginia Commonwealth Univ., Richmond (s. 1973). He was a principal cellist, Richmond Symphony and Simfonia (1973-75), and a member of Smetana Trio. Has made extensive recordings.

Jennifer Sokol (ca. 1950-), b. Seattle, WA, of Czech ancestry, being a daughter of Vilem Sokol, is a violinist. In 1977, Jennifer was Concertmaster of the American Youth in Concert Orchestra and performed in venues such as Carnegie Hall, Royal Albert Hall in London, Victoria Hall in Geneva, and Notre Dame Cathedral in Paris. In 1976, she attended the Blossom Chamber Music Festival and studied with members of the Cleveland Symphony Orchestra. In 1979, she attended the Julliard String Quartet Seminar in 1979 and worked under the direction of Earl Carlyss and Samuel Rhodes. She is a member of the Cameo String Quartet. A freelancer for many years in the Puget Sound area, she has performed with groups such as the Seattle Symphony, the Seattle Opera and the Pacific Northwest Ballet Orchestra, and is a member of the St. James Cathedral Chamber Orchestra. She does recording studio work for Seattle Music and other companies and is the first violinist and manager of the Cameo String Quartet, performing many weddings and events each year.

Kyle Sokol (1974-), b. St. Petersburg, FL, of Bohemian ancestry, is an American bassist and also a skateboarder. He is known for his style of bass playing that mostly consists of fast technical bass lines. Kyle Sokol has played in bands such as Rude Squad, Noble Jones, Philistines, Basmistist, Stretch, Leadfoot, Cadaveric Mass, The Lazarus Machine, Strict-9, Must Not Kill and even the controversial Tampa industrial metal band Hell on Earth. His playing is very jazz-oriented, and he has provided a lot of new ideas for metal bass lines in the metal scene of Tampa, FL.

Mark Sokol (1946-2014), b. Oberlin, OH, of Czech ancestry, was a violinist. He studied violin with his father, Vilem Sokol, and with Dorothy DeLay and Robert Mann at the Julliard School of Music in New York. He initially performed with the United States Military Academy Quartet and at the Center for the Creative and Performing Arts. From 1971 to 1987, Sokol was first violinist of the Naumburg Award-winning Concord String

Quartet, which performed extensively in the US and abroad, appeared frequently on radio and television, and recorded over 40 works on the CRI, Nonesuch, RCA, and Vox Turnabout labels. After the quartet disbanded Sokol moved to Sebastopol California and began teaching at the San Francisco Conservatory of Music as chair of the chamber music department. Concurrently he spent many summers teaching at the Tanglewood Music Center (Lenox MA) and Kneisel Hall Chamber Music School (Blue Hill ME).

Vilém Sokol (1915-2011), b. Ambridge, PA, of Czech ancestry, was a violinist. He taught at Shorter College in Georgia, the University of Kentucky, and the Kansas City Conservatory of Music. In 1948, he joined the University of Washington faculty (s. 1948), where he became a music professor, teaching violin, viola, conducting, and his popular music appreciation classes. He was also violist with String Quartet. Among his many contributions to Seattle's music life, he founded and directed the Seattle String Society, and appeared frequently on local television and radio programs. He was principal violist of the Seattle Symphony Orchestra from 1959-62. The years of 1960 marked the year Vilem began his legendary career as conductor of the Seattle Youth Symphony. Under his direction, the orchestra attained national and international recognition, and became the standard bearer for youth symphonies the world over. During his 28-year tenure, the SYSO performed many world premieres, USA premiers, and first performances in Seattle and the Northwest. Sokol was one of the first American teachers to meet Shinichi Suzuki and apply aspects of his teaching method.

Paula Sokol-Elliott (1950–), b. Seattle, WA, is a violinist. She began violin studies at the age of 5 with her father, the renowned teacher and conductor, Vilem Sokol, and later graduated from Indiana Univ. with the legendary Josef Gingold. Stanislaw Skrowaczewski invited her to join the Minnesota Orchestra (1974-78), where she recorded the complete works of Ravel and Bartok for Vox Records. She performed as violinist with the Vancouver Symphony, and as associate concertmaster of the Kalamazoo Symphony. She performed with various orchestras, most recently with the Michigan Chamber Players (1994-present), and the Chelsea Chamber Players (1994-present). She also had numerous solo appearances. Paula has been on faculties of a number of schools, most recently with the Meadowmount School of Music in New York (2005).

Eva Solar-Kinderman, b. Sweden, of Czech ancestry, studied piano in Prague where she won the Czech Youth Music Competition in 1965. She holds advanced degrees from the Zürich Conservatory and the Vienna State Academy of Music (with distinction). She has been privileged to work with such renowned artists as Wilhelm Kemff, Sir Alfred Brendel, and Andras Schiff. An active performer of both solo and chamber music repertoire, she has been heard on the CBC and US Public Radio. Her recording of the last two Schubert Sonatas was released on the Bayer label in Germany in 1999. Since 1980, Ms. Solar-Kinderman has taught on the faculty of the University of Victoria and the Victoria Conservatory of Music. She is also a faculty member at Vancouver Community College and the International Piano Masterclass held yearly in the summer in the Czech Republic. Her concert career has taken her on tours of Canada, the USA, Europe and Japan. She has adjudicated music festivals in BC and given numerous master classes and workshops in Canada, the USA, and Central Europe.

Ella Spravka-Oumiroff (1873–d.), b. Bohemia, was a pianist. In 1920, she came to the US with her husband, Boža Oumiroff, the famous Bohemian singer. She was trained at Vienna Conservatory of Music, where she won first prize in a contest. Later she studied a year with Leschetizky, and two years with Edward Dannreuter of London. She made her debut at the Crystal Palace in London, appeared with the London Symphony, the Prague Philharmonic, the Bohemian String Quartet, the Ševčík Quartet and was associated in concerts with Kubelík, Kocián, Marie Hall Huberman, Ondříček, Mme Albany, Melba, and others. For more than twelve years she had been a member of the Bush Conservatory in Chicago. Her office was in Chicago, in Kimball Hall.

Otakar C. Šroubek (1923–2008), b. Prague, Czech, was a violinist, who started playing violin at age six. From a musical family, he studied first with his father, a composer, and a trumpet player, and then at the Prague Conservatory. He was with Prague Broadcast Orchestra and in 1945, he landed a position as Concert Master at the prestigious Czech Philharmonic, under conductor Rafael Kubelik. During those turbulent years, Nazi officials forced the orchestra to entertain them privately. Also, Otakar played for numerous radio shows, toured various countries and won awards including the revered Bela Bartok Competition in Hungary. After succeeding to escape, Šroubek quickly netted a position, as 1st violinist, with the New Orleans Symphony. After two seasons, he got on board with the Cleveland Orchestra under the direction of Rafael Kubelik. Otto's musical masterpiece of life escalated when he came to Chicago and caught a coveted spot as first violinist with the Chicago Symphony Orchestra (CSO) (1956–2004). There he "reeled in" night after night of concerts, applause, fanfare, and touring for a whopping 48 years with the CSO. During his time with the CSO, Otto was instrumental in forming the distinguished Contemporary Arts Quartet.

Lydia Smutny Sterba (1922–2014), b. Chicago, IL, of Czech ancestry, was a musician trained at American Conservatory of Music and Roosevelt Univ. She was a concert pianist, piano teacher, and chairman of the piano dept. at Morton Coll. for many years, retiring in 2010. She has been a soloist with many symphony orchestras in IL, MI and IN area.

Emil Straka (1866–1928), b. Suez, Egypt, of Czech ancestry, was a violinist and teacher educated at Prague Cons. under Ševčík. He came to US in 1885 and became Concert Master of Frank Danz Symphony Orch., Twin Cities, MN (1898) and asst. conductor of the Metropolitan Opera House. He was orch. leader of the Shubert Theater Orch. (8 years) and also played with St. Paul Symphony Orch. He was the founder of the Straka's Music School in Saint Paul and member of the Minneapolis Symphony Orchestra. He was an instructor in Northwestern Cons. of Music.

Jessica Suchy-Pilalis (1954–), b. Milwaukee, WI, the daughter of Raymond W. Suchy, who was a physicist of Czech ancestry, and the lawyer Labros E. Pilalis, studied harp at the University of Wisconsin, Milwaukee (B.F.A., 1976); harp performance (M.M., 1979) and music theory (M.A., 1982) at the Eastman School of Music; and received Doctorate at Indiana University (D.Mus., 1991). She had additional education in Byzantine music at the School of Byzantine Music of the Holy Metropolis of Thessalonica, Greece (dipl., 1984) and Macedonian Conservatory, Thessalonica, Greece (dipl., 1985). She also pursued graduate studies in Byzantine music at Holy Cross Greek Orthodox School of Theology, Brookline, MA. She was an adjunct instructor in music theory and harp at Butler University (1989-93), and a sabbatical replacement in music theory at the University of Wisconsin, Milwaukee (1993-94), before joining Crane School of Music, the State University of New York at Potsdam, as professor of music theory, harp and Byzantine music (s. 1996). She is also director of Crane Harp Ensemble and principal harpist in the Orchestra of Northern New York. In Byzantine music she specializes in theory, history and the practice of Byzantine chant. In 1984, she became what is thought to be the first officially titled and salaried female 'psalti' (precentor, cantor) of the Greek Orthodox Church of North and South America. In harp performance, she covers music of all periods (solo, chamber, concerto, orchestral) and in historical harp, her focus is on music for single-action harp, specifically the music of Madame Delaval. She serves as vice-president of the Historical Harp Society and is on the editorial board of the *American Harp Journal*.

Adalbert B. Suhany (1888–1950), b. Nitranska, Slovakia, was a teacher, choir master, and organist. He immigrated to the US in 1905, settling in Chicago. He is a music teacher, choir master and organist, was connected with several churches: the Holy Rosary Catholic Church (1908-09), the St. Joseph Catholic Slovak Church (1914-22), the Holy Rosary Catholic Slovak Church (1914-1922) and since 1922, he was with the St. Michael's Archangel Slovak church. He was also the organizer and director of the United Slovak Catholic Choirs.

Zdeněk Šváb (1938–), b. Czech., studied at Prague Conservatory, specializing in horn. He played in various orchestras and later became first horn in Prague FOK Symphony Orchestra. In 1968, he left for Brazil, where he became first horn player and soloist in the

Orquestra sinfonica Brasileira in Rio de Janeiro. Subsequently, he became first horn player in the national orchestra, as well as in municipal orchestra of Rio de Janeiro. He founded several chamber music groups and made a number of recordings of both classical and popular music. Since 1984, he also served as professor of French horn and chamber music at University of Rio de Janeiro.

Erin Svoboda (1983–), b. US, a daughter of Richard Svoboda, is in her first season with the Utah Symphony. Originally from the East Coast, Erin began her musical studies with the piano at the age of five and added the clarinet at ten. She spent her summers at the Tanglewood Music Center, Marlboro Music Festival, Pacific Music Festival, and Aspen Music Festival. Erin freelanced in New York City after she graduated, playing with such ensembles as the New York Philharmonic, Metropolitan Opera, and American Symphony Orchestra. She spent a year as the Assistant/2nd/E-flat clarinetist in the Colorado Symphony before moving to Utah. Also an active chamber musician and soloist, she recorded the trio Tibetan Dances on Spring Dreams with Cho-Liang Lin on violin and the composer, Bright Sheng, on piano. Erin also premiered Michael Gandolfi's Concerto for Clarinet and Bassoon.

George Svoboda, b. Cheb, Czech., a guitarist, has gained recognition not only as an immaculate and entertaining performer, but also as a composer and arranger of music for solo guitar, small ensembles and full orchestra. As a co-founder of the Benedetti/Svoboda Guitar Duo and member of the well-known Second Avenue Klezmer Ensemble, he has performed throughout the US, Canada, Taiwan, Hawaiian Islands, Mexico and Europe. Mr. Svoboda has performed for President and Mrs. Clinton at the world-renowned Hotel Del Coronado. He co-wrote and performed music for the Old Globe's production of *Much Ado about Nothin'* under the direction of Tony award winning director, Jack O'Brien. He has also performed with the San Diego Symphony, San Diego Ballet, Young Artists Symphony and San Diego Opera. In September 2006, Mr. Svoboda performed in a star-studded world premiere of *Primal Twang: The Legacy of the Guitar*, the first definitive theatrical journey through the guitar's colorful 3500-year history. In his native Czechoslovakia, he taught guitar and music theory in Public Schools of Art and since arriving in the U.S., he has taught in the San Diego City Schools as an Artist in Residence, as professor at Mesa College and as a guitar instructor at San Diego State University. He also published successful instructional books on guitar technique including a book of Rhythmic Exercises.

John Svoboda (ca. 1974–), b. Cheb, Czech., now residing in San Diego, CA, studied guitar and history of music at the State Conservatory of Music in Pilsen, Czech. Svoboda has gained recognition not only as an immaculate and entertaining performer, but also as a composer and arranger of music for solo guitar, small ensembles and full orchestra. His music is rooted in the folk traditions of Central Europe and his transcriptions have won him consistent praise from musicians and critics alike. As a co-founder of the Benedetti/Svoboda Guitar Duo and member of the well-known Second Avenue Klezmer Ensemble, he has performed throughout the US, Canada, Taiwan, Hawaiian Islands, Mexico and Europe. Mr. Svoboda has performed for President and Mrs. Clinton at the world-renowned Hotel Del Coronado. Svoboda has been performing and recording for nearly thirty-five years. Mr. Svoboda has also been actively involved in teaching for over twenty-five years. In his native Czechoslovakia, he taught guitar and music theory in Public Schools of Art and since arriving in the U.S., he has taught in the San Diego City Schools as an Artist in Residence, as Professor at Mesa College and as a guitar instructor at San Diego State University. He also published successful instructional books on guitar technique including a book of Rhythmic Exercises.

Richard Svoboda (1956–), b Pocatello, Idaho, USA, of Czech ancestry, is a bassoonist. He was bassoonist with Lincoln Symphony (1977–78) and Omaha Symphony (1977–78); principal bassoonist with St. Louis Philharmonic (1978–79), with Jacksonville Symphony Orchestra (1979–89), with Boston Symphony Chamber Players (s. 1989) and with Boston Symphony Orchestra (s. 1989). His academic positions have included being a faculty member of Symphony School of America (1981–84), adjunct instructor of bassoon, Boston Univ. (1995–2002); faculty member at Tanglewood Music Center (s. 1989), faculty member (s. 1990) and Woodward Chair (s. 2011) of New England Conservatory; faculty member at Sarasota Music Festival (s. 2009). He has given master classes throughout the world. Mr. Svoboda is an active chamber music collaborator, orchestral soloist, and recitalist. Among his solo appearances with the Boston Symphony Orchestra have been performances of John Williams' bassoon concerto *Five Sacred Trees* with the composer conducting and the Weber Concerto for Bassoon under the baton of Seiji Ozawa. In October of 2007, he premiered Michael Gandolfi's Concerto for Bassoon, and in March of 2011, along with his eldest daughter, clarinetist Erin Svoboda, premiered Mr. Gandolfi's Concerto for Clarinet and Bassoon, both times collaborating with Yoichi Udagawa and the Melrose Symphony Orchestra. In November of 2013 Richard Svoboda premiered Marc Neikrug's Concerto for Bassoon and Orchestra with conductor Rafael Frühbeck de Burgos and the Boston Symphony Orchestra.

Bohumil Sýkora (1893–1953), b. Glinsk, Russia, of Czech ancestry, was a violoncellist and composer. He was educated at Imperial Conservatory of Music in Kiev and Royal Conservatory of Music, Leipzig. He was a member of faculty of the Academy of Allied Arts, NY (s. 1937). He was the first European to perform before the Japanese Mikado.

Frank Sýkora (1898–d.), b. Prague, Bohemia, was a violoncellist. He was a graduate of the Prague Conservatory and two Imperial Conservatories, those of Kiev and St. Petersburg He was a well-traveled musician, having given performances in Europe, Russia, the Malay

States, Indo-China, China, Japan, the Philippines, Hawaii, and the Western Hemisphere, including Hong Kong, Singapore, Tokyo, Moscow, and Vienna. Sykora's band experience in Russia was substantial. He served Lieutenant Bandmaster in a sharpshooter regiment; for his service, he earned decorations in the orders of St. Anne and St. Vladimir. He immigrated to US in 1920. In the US, he had been a cellist with the Cincinnati Symphony Orchestra (1920–21), member and solo cellist of the Kansas City Philharmonic Orchestra (s. 1937). In early 1943, he joined Florida State University. At FSCW, Sykora taught cello and presented his own frequent recitals; he also proved to be a tireless interim band director. He was also and a member of faculty, Conservatory of Music, Kansas City, MI and Sherwood Music College, Chicago.

Clara Schneider Tesar (1902–1993), b. South Omaha, NE, was a noted violinist who, at the age of 8, studied under the supervision of Professor F. Mach. She toured many eastern states giving concerts and was also concertmaster and soloist for the Omaha Symphony Orchestra. She was or two seasons concert master and soloist of the Omaha Little Symphony.

Dennis Thompson (orig. Dennis A. Tomich) (1948–2024), b. Michigan, of Slovak descent, is an American drummer. He is most famous or being a member of the 1960s–70s Detroit proto-punk/hard rock group MC5, which had a No. 82 US single with "Kick Out the Jams" and a No. 30 US album with the same name. Thompson was given the nickname "Machine Gun" because of his "assault" style of fast, hard-hitting drumming that sonically resembles the sound of a Thompson machine gun (commonly referred to as a "Tommy Gun"). His drumming pre-figured and influenced punk, metal, and hardcore punk drumming styles. After MC5 broke up, Thompson was a member of the 1975–1976 Los Angeles-based supergroup 'The New Order,' the 1981 Australia-based supergroup 'New Race', 'The Motor City Bad Boys,' and' The Secrets.' In 2001, he guested for Asmodeus X on the song, "The Tiger" (St. Thomas Records). Thompson was in the band DKT/MC5 with the surviving members of MC5, from 2003–2012.

Jacob C. Till (1799–1882), b. Hope, NJ, of Moravian ancestry, was a pioneer Moravian Church musician. Besides filling for a time the position of organist of the Moravian Church in Bethlehem, and for fifty years or more a member of its Trombone Choir, he was an active member of the Philharmonic Society and the once celebrated 'Bethlehem Band.' While a member of the latter organization, he performed principally on the clarinet. He was instructor of the first military band formed in Mauch Chunk. Many years before that, Till became a resident of Easton, PA, and was appointed organist of St. John's Church.

Johann Christian Till (1762–1844), b. Gnadenthal, PA, of Moravian ancestry, was an early Moravian Church organist. His great music talent was recognized and developed by Rev.

Simon Peter and in 1785, he began to teach in the Bethlehem school. He served as teacher and organist of their church in Hope, NJ until its abandonment in 1808. Afterwards, he made musical instruments and since 1811, for 33 years, he was the faithful and efficient organist of the Bethlehem Church.

Godfrey Bohumir Antonin Tomanek (1925–2015), b. Chicago, IL, of Czech ancestry, was an organist. His family returned to Moravia (part of the Czech Republic) when he was seven years old. He remained in Czechoslovakia for 17 years. It was during his years at the gymnasium that Godfrey began serious music lessons with acclaimed composer Vaclav Nelhybel. He went on to the State Conservatory of Music in Prague where he received a bachelor's degree (summa cum laude) in organ and church music. He returned to Chicago in 1949, narrowly escaping the stormy political situation in Czechoslovakia. In Chicago, he received a master's degree in music in organ and pedagogy (harmony and counterpoint) from the American Conservatory of Music. He eventually settled in Connecticut in 1959, where he remained for the rest of his life. Godfrey was a noted conductor, composer, organist, teacher, and piano technician. Godfrey also taught piano, organ, improvisation, and theory. He was an expert in Gregorian chant and had extensive experience with Latin liturgical music.

Jerry (Jaroslav) Toth (1928–1999), b. Windsor, Ont., Canada, of Slovak father, was a saxophonist, clarinetist, flutist, arranger, composer, and producer. He also studied orchestration with Nimmons. Toth played alto saxophone 1945–53 in the dance bands of Stan Patton, Bobby Gimby, Trump Davidson, and others and was co-leader in 1952–7 with the trombonist Ross Culley and the saxophonist Roy Smith of a 17-piece jazz band. He was a member of Phil Nimmons' jazz bands from 1956–74. Toth began playing in CBC orchestras in 1954 under Jack Kane and in later years was a leading Toronto studio musician. He was chief arranger or music director for the CBC's *Parade* ca. 1957–60 and in the mid-1960s, began writing and producing jingles with his brother Rudy and others.

Tony Toth (ca. 1928–2003), b. Windsor, Ontario, Canada, of Slovak father, as an oboist, English hornist, saxophonist, clarinetist, and copyist. He worked in radio, TV, theater and recording orchestras. In the 1970s, he was the baritone saxophonist and copyist for Nimmons 'N' Nine Plus Six and during the 1980s played in Peter Appleyard's All-Star Swing Band.

Alois Trnka (1883–1923), b. New York, NY, of Czech ancestry, was a graduate of Prague Conservatory (1903), having studied under Ševčík. He appeared in concerts throughout Austria winning high praise. He opened studio in New York (1907) and gained reputation as a great teacher. He taught the Ševčík method. He appeared frequently in concert in the US.

Alois C. Trnka (1904-1990), b. Chicago, IL, of Czech ancestry, became a professional musician in his teens. He studied music at Wiliam Peace College, Raleigh, NC (1922-24). He played first cello with the Chicago Theater Orchestra, where he was featured with fan dancer Sally Rand. In 1928, Trnka became first cellist with the Minneapolis Symphony and, in 1930, he returned here to join the Chicago Symphony Orchestra, where he became first cellist. He remained with the orchestra until his retirement in 1978. He was featured as a soloist in 1950 under conductor Fritz Reiner. He had a host of other activities. In the 1920s, he founded the Fine Arts Quartet, which played around the nation and at the White House. He later founded the Chicago Arts Quartet, which played for public school children. Trnka played on WMAQ radio in 1922 and with the NBC-TV studio orchestra in Chicago in the 1950s. He taught music at Morton East High School in Cicero for 52 years. For 43 years, he directed a large boys' choir at Ascension Catholic Church in Oak Park, where he was assisted by other members of the Chicago Symphony Orchestra. He also taught at the Sherwood Music Conservatory, 18th Street and Michigan Avenue, for 25 years. After Trnka retired from the Chicago Symphony, he played 5 years with the Elmhurst Symphony.

Richard J. Urbis (1953-), b. Waco, TX, of Czech ancestry, is a pianist. He was graduated from Corpus Christian Univ. (B.S., 1975; Artist Dipl.) and then pursued studies in music at Juilliard School of Music (M.A., 1978) and at Univ. of Arizona (1995-96). He started as professional touring artist and also taught at Texas A&M, Kingsville and at Texas A&M, Corpus Christi. He is an internationally renowned pianist, who has successfully competed and performed in numerous national and international competitions, including the Tchaikovsky Competition (Moscow), the Chopin Competition (Warsaw), the Beethoven Competition (Vienna), and was a finalist in the International New York Chopin Association Competition. His playing has been featured on numerous national and international radio shows, and he has performed concerts throughout the United States, the Czech Republic, Austria, Germany, Slovakia, Italy, Mexico, Poland and Russia. As a composer, Professor Urbis has received world premieres by many notable ensembles. The Dallas Symphony premiered his 'Suite for Chamber Orchestra' and the Catalina Chamber Orchestra of Tucson, Arizona, premiered his symphony, 'St. Joan of Arc.' Professor Urbis teaches advanced music theory, orchestration, counterpoint and analysis, and applied piano. His recently released CD titled *Music from Prague: 200 Years of Czech Piano Music* is a critically acclaimed success.

Al Vanek, b. TX, of Czech ancestry, sometimes referred to as 'Starý Chlap' (old guy), has been a Polka DJ for KNON (North Texas Polka Radio) since 1997. Following the footsteps of his paternal and maternal grandfathers, Al has performed in several polka bands for over 40 years. He currently manages the Vanek Czech Band and performs with his two sons and other relatives.

VIII. CULTURE: ARTS & LETTERS

Bedřich Váška (1879-1979), b. Mladá Vožice, Bohemia, was a cello player who studied at Prague Cons. and was a pupil of Antonín Dvořák. He was a member of the famous Ševčík Quartet. After coming to US in 1911, he founded the Bohemian Trio; later became a member of the Eastman Quartet and from 1919 to 1930 he played with the New York String Quartet.

Julie Vaverka (1978-2007), b. Marshall, of Czech ancestry, was a clarinetist educated at Eastman School of Music. She was principal clarinet and soloist with the Pro Arte Chamber Orchestra of Boston. As a freelance clarinetist, she performed with the Boston Symphony, Boston Symphony Pops and Esplanade Pops, Boston Ballet Orchestra, Rhode Island Philharmonic, Boston Conservatory Chamber Players, and Monadnock Music Festival. She also taught at the Boston Conservatory of Music, Boston University and Philips Academy.

Bohumir C. Vesely (1881-1964), b. Illinois, of Czech ancestry, was a theater musician in the 1910s, and a musician at the La Salle Hotel. He then joined Chicago Symphony Orch. (1918-1946), as percussionist (1918-32), and as principal percussionist (1932-46).

Stanley 'Stan' J. Vesely, Jr. (1914-2008), b. Cedar Rapids, IA, of Czech ancestry, studied violin and tuba at Coe College (graduated in 1937). He was a member of Kryl Symphony orchestra (1940-43); bandmaster, Anamosa High School, Iowa (1943-45), of Wilson High School Cedar Rapids (1945-51); director of Coe College Band (1953-90). Under his direction the band never achieved the level of success accomplished by his father. For the next twenty years, the Coe Band had its up and down years. Highlights of this period included trips to Europe and the Far East and performances at the College Band Directors National Association under the direction of Tom Slattery.

Joseph Alois Vilim (1861-1938), b. Chicago, IL, of Czech parentage, was a violinist and teacher, trained at the famous Prague Conservatory. He returned to Chicago in 1883 and, after giving concerts for a year, he became a violin teacher at the Chicago Musical College, where he remained for three years. He then accepted the post of director of the violin department in the American Conservatory of Music, Chicago, where he remained for twelve years, having spent the year 1887 abroad in study. He founded the Beethoven String Quartet of Chicago, the Vilim Trio and the Vilim Family Trio. From 1904 to 1906, he played first violin in the Thomas Orchestra, and had participated in all branches of orchestral playing. His time at present is largely taken up with his work as a teacher.

Mark Washington Vilim (1889-d.), b. Chicago, of Czech ancestry, was a pianist, organist, and musical director. He was educated at Illinois and Northwestern Universities and was a graduate Columbia School of Music. He was director and organist at Riverside Presbyterian Church; manager and accompanist at Vilim American Violin School; pianist in Vilim Trio. He resided in Berwyn, IL.

Richard Vilim (1886-1973), b. Chicago, IL of Czech ancestry, was violinist and teacher, who studied violin with his father. He was a member of Chicago Philharmonic Orchestra; instructor of violin at American Vilim School, Chicago (for 7 years); manager of Vilim Music Bureau. He invented the 'echo mute' and the 'palm bracer.' He resided in San Diego., CA.

Ludmila Vinecká (1949–), b. Czech., is a violinist. She studied at Prague Conservatory. She moved to Brazil and in 1971, she performed as a soloist with the Orquestra Filharmonica de Sao Paulo. Since 1975, she taught violin at the music conservatory, Escola de musica de Brazilia, and later at the state university, Universidade de Brazilia. She founded the popular string quartet, Quarteto de Brazilia, in which she played first violin. She toured with them at home and abroad and made a number of recordings. She is considered one of the best violin virtuosos in the country.

Marguerite Volavý (1886-1951), b. Brno, Moravia, was a concert pianist, extensive recording artist, music editor, and pedagogue. She studied at Vienna Conservatory and graduated at age 15, with first prize in piano. Volavý debuted with Prague Philharmonic in 1902 and toured extensively in Europe, until settling in New York in 1912, where she debuted at Carnegie Hall as soloist with the Russian Symphony Orchestra in 1915. She had an extensive concert career in America, including raising funds for WWI with Paderewski, until an injury on a subway about 1924. As a recording artist and music editor, she worked for the American Piano Company (AMPICO), QRS Music Company, Welte-Mignon, and the Aeolian Corporation, with all major pianists of the era. After 1932, she devoted her life to teaching in her studio in White Plains, NY. The prolific recordings of Madame Volavý, as she was known, are still available today, including many of Czech composers and her own transcription of Czech folk music.

Ralph Votapek (1939–), b. Milwaukee, WI, of Czech ancestry, is a pianist and teacher, notable for winning the First Van Cliburn International Piano Competition in 1962. From the age of nine, he studied music at the Wisconsin Conservatory in Milwaukee, as well as Northwestern University, Manhattan, and Juilliard. Votapek was awarded the Naumburg Award in 1959 and performed his debut recital at New York's Town Hall. After winning the First Van Cliburn International Piano Competition in 1962, Votapek signed contracts with RCA and Sol Hurok, and made his debut at Carnegie Hall. Votapek was a professor of piano and Artist in Residence at the Michigan State University College of Music, East Lansing and served there for 36 years before retiring.

Sydney Vrana (ca. 1957–), b. of Czech ancestry, is a graduate of Marianopolis College, where he majored in music (dipl., 1979). He studied elementary and secondary education at Univ. de Quebec à Montréal (B.A., 1994) and music performance and education at McGill Univ.

(B.A., 1998). Since 2002, he has worked full-time as public school music teacher for the Sir Wilfrid Laurier School Board and as a solo classical guitarist and ensemble musician for concerts and music festivals as well (s. 1983). He has over 30 years' experience in concert performance, recordings, arranging, composition and as a music educator in the public and private sectors. He is first prize winner at the Canadian music competitions, finalist in Radio Canada's 'Jeune Virtuoses.' He travelled on concert tours in the 1990s in Europe, North and South America.

Čeněk Vrba (1947–), b. Brno, Czech., is a violinist and concertmaster of the Calgary Philharmonic Orchestra. He is one of Canada's foremost violinists, being described as a 'True inheritor of the Czech string tradition...violinist of a rare distinction.' His early music training started at the State Conservatory of Music in the Czech Republic. While there, he won many prizes including first place in the highly acclaimed Beethoven National Violin Competition. After immigrating to Canada in 1968 following the Warsaw Pact invasion of Czechoslovakia, he pursued further studies in the United States and Europe. Vrba was appointed concert master of the Calgary Philharmonic Orchestra in August 1975 and remained there for 36 years until his retirement in 2011. Winning the CBC National Radio Competition has launched his many solo recordings for CBC Radio and Television. Since then, Mr. Vrba has recorded and toured in recitals and with various orchestras in the United States, Japan, China and many European countries.

James Vrhel (1920–1987), b. Chicago, IL, of Czech ancestry, was an American double-bass musician. He studied at Northwestern University, Indiana University, and the University of Chicago. He was with the Chicago Symphony Orchestra, performing in the orchestra for 40 years, as double bass (1944–52; 1961–83), as principal double bass (1952–61). He was also with the Grant Park Symphony, the Indianapolis Symphony, the National Symphony of Washington, DC, and the Hans Lange Symphonietta. Vrhel was a Fellow at the Berkshire Music Center. He also was a noted businessman in the city, with interests that ranged from investment counseling to citrus groves in Texas.

Mark Vyhlidal (1961–), b. Morse Bluff, NE, of Czech ancestry, attended High School in North Bend, Nebraska, graduating in 1980. His music career began at age 8 playing polka music on the drums and has continued playing this music for over 42 years. He has played with several Nebraska polka bands. He started his own band as a Combo in 1973 at the age of 12. By 1976, the band grew to 6 members and is still performing and promoting polka music today. This talented musician plays several instruments: accordion, trumpet, valve trombone, tuba, keyboards, drums and bass guitar. He also arranges most of the music for the band which totals over 400 polkas and waltzes. The Maryann Polka was selected as the number one song in the country in May, 2000 on Chuck Stastny's Polka Countdown Radio

Show. Mark has also arranged music charts for several bands in Nebraska. Since 1982, the Mark Vyhlidal Orchestra produced ten recordings that include all of his compositions. Mark's band has performed extensively throughout the Midwest and has traveled to: Texas, Colorado, Ohio, Michigan, Canada and the Grand Polka Festival in Las Vegas, Nevada. Awards include the Ennis, Texas National Polka Festival Recognition of Czech Heritage Award in May, 2003, and he was honored and inducted into the Sokol Omaha Polka Hall of Fame in September, 2004.

Albert Weatherly (1895-1960), b. Harper, KS, of Czech mother, was a cello player, educated at Juilliard School in NYC. He became a specialist on the trumpet, cello, in voice and conducting. He had taught at Mississippi State, Tulsa University and Central State College in Edmond, OK. Mr. Weatherly served two years as a band director in the A.E.F. in World War I and with the Air Force and the Navy in WWII. He then moved to California, where he was active as chairman of the Music Department of Inglewood High School where he had taught since 1943.

Albert Weatherly, Jr. (1924-2009), b. Coffeyville, KS, of Czech ancestry, was a noted flutist. He resided in NYC where he became known as one of the top-class flute repairman and flute dealers in the world. At 19, performed with Sigmund Romberg. Also performed with the Boston Symphony. With highest artistry ran Albert Weatherly Flutes for over 50 years. His clientele included James Galway, Jean-Pierre Rampal and James Moody.

Robert Weatherly (1922-2005), Coffeyville, KS, of Czech ancestry, was widely known as the greatest trumpet player in the world in the 1940s. For three years, he was principal trumpet of the U.S. Air Force Band in Washington, D.C., under George S. Howard, touring Europe and the U.S. He then became principal trumpet of the St. Louis Symphony for 15 years, performing with virtually every great conductor and world-class soloist of the era. Having always wished to teach, in 1961, he became director of bands at Southeastern Louisiana University. His group became the first small-college band ever chosen to appear at a biennial National Conference of College Band Directors. At Southeastern, he was head of the department of music for seven years where he also taught conducting. His works included dozens of full productions of grand opera, major choral works with orchestra, musical shows and countless performances of smaller orchestral and wind ensembles. In 1989, he was awarded the Southeastern Louisiana University's Presidents Medal for Artistic Excellence. In 1990, he was inducted into The Louisiana Music Educators Association Hall of Fame. He considered his highest honor to be the large number of former students and friends now enjoying successful musical careers.

John Weicher (1904-1969), b. Chicago, IL, of Czech parents, was a violinist. He was a member of the Cleveland Symphony Orch., of the Gordon String Quartet and concertmaster of the Seattle Symphony Orch. After moving to Chicago, he was the founder and the first violinist of the Philharmonic String Quartet, later he became asst. concertmaster of the Chicago Symphony Orch. He was a member of the Bohemian Arts Club. His office was located in Chicago in the Orchestra Hall.

Charles Wels (1825-1906), b. Prague, Bohemia, was an organist but also a pianist, composer and teacher of church music. He received his music education in Prague under Václav Tomášek. He came to the US and settled in NYC. He became well known organist and was connected with St. Mark's All Saints, St. Cecilia's, St. Stephen's and other leading churches. In the US, he wrote piano compositions and a funeral march for Abraham Lincoln.

John Anthony Wilfahrt (1893-1961), b. New Ulm, MN, of Bohemian ancestry, was a professional polka musician, who got his start playing the accordion at local gatherings and concerts in and around his community. In the 1920s, 'Whoopee' John and his band relocated to Saint Paul, MN where they became regulars at live shows and on the radio. Wilfahrt first began recording commercially in the 1920s and would sign with the newly formed U.S. division of Decca Records in 1934 as the label's second act (The first act signed to the label being Bing Crosby). Whoopee John Wilfahrt and his band enjoyed popularity through the 1940s and 50s on the polka circuit. Over the course of his professional career, Wilfahrt would record nearly 1,000 songs, some of the most popular being 'Mariechen Waltz' and 'Clarinet Polka.'

Rosemary 'Rosie' Williams (née Zika) (1950-2007), b. Chicago, IL, of Czech ancestry, was a resident artist in piano and harpsichord, and a lecturer in music at Ohio Northern Univ. (ONU) since 1973. Since her high school days, Williams has been an active performer as a solo recitalist, accompanist, and chamber musician. She has performed in all capacities throughout the Midwest and in Austria. Since 1973, Williams has been an avid composer and arranger. Her works have been performed both in the United States and Europe including performances at the National Gallery of Art in Washington, D.C., and the Toledo Symphony.

Felix Winternitz (1872-1948), b. Austria, of Czech ancestry, was a violinist and composer. He immigrated to the US in 1889. He was a member of the Boston Symphony Orch. (1889-1890), where he played violin. He was also with Emil Mollenhauer Boston Festival Orchestra, long-time New England Conservatory professor, Worcester Festival - Massachusetts (1893). Minot Beale and Sheldon Rotenberg were Winternitz New England Conservatory violin students. The actor Roland Winters, who played Charlie Chan in 1940s B movies and later Elvis Presley's father in Blue Hawaii was Felix Winternitz's son.

Anton Witek (1872–1933), b. Žatec, Bohemia, studied violin at the Prague Cons. He became Concertmaster of the Berlin Philharmonic (1894–1909) and in 1903, Witek founded the Berlin Philharmonic Trio. In 1910 he came to Boston to take up the Concertmaster position with Max Fiedler 1910–18). Witek also formed a trio with Avita Witek and Joseph Malkin in Boston, and after the Boston Symphony, Anton Witek taught in Boston for the next decade), of Czech ancestry, was an accomplished violinist, who began playing at age 11. He was a member of the Chicago Symphony (1932–80) for 48 years and continued to play the violin after his retirement.

Paul Wittgenstein (1887–1961), b. Vienna, of Bohemian ancestry on maternal side, was a concert pianist. He lost his right arm in World War I but continued to give concerts playing with only his left arm and commissioned several works from prominent composers. He devised novel techniques, including pedal and hand-movement combinations that allowed him to play chords previously regarded as impossible for a five-fingered pianist. He became an American citizen in 1946 and spent the rest of his life in the United States, where he did much teaching as well as playing piano.

Ede Zathureczky (1903–1959), b. Spišská Nová Ves, Slovakia, was a violin virtuoso and pedagogue. His teacher was the exceptional Jenő Hubay. In 1920, he started playing concerts in Austria, Holland, Switzerland, Italy, Bohemia, Poland, Scandinavian countries and many cities around the world. In 1929, he became Hubay's assistant and later the Music Director at the Liszt Academy in Budapest. It is here that he performed frequently with his colleague, pianist Bela Nagy. The final few years of his life, he taught at Indiana University, where both Nagy and Menahem Pressler were also on the faculty. Ede Zathurecky played a concert with Béla Bartók at the hall of the Korona Hotel in Nyíregyháza on January 10, 1934. From 1943 to 1957, he was the director of the Budapest Music Academy.

Fannie Bloomfield-Zeisler (1863–1927), Bílsko, on Silesian/Moravian border, was one of the most eminent women pianists of her generation. At the age of ten, she played at a public concert in Chicago, and two years later went to Vienna to study with Leschetizky. At the expiration of five years, she returned to the United States, where, from 1883 to 1893, she repeatedly gave recitals, playing with all the leading orchestras throughout the country. In 1893, Bloomfield-Zeisler made a tour through Europe; and such was her success at Berlin, Leipzig, Frankfurt, Vienna, and elsewhere, that she prolonged her stay abroad until 1895. During the season 1895–96, she gave upward of fifty concerts in America, and in 1897, made a tour of the Pacific states. In 1898, she again went abroad and gave a series of concerts in Great Britain and France. She resided in Chicago. Considered at one time to be 'America's greatest virtuoso,' Zeisler played the piano until her death.

Charlie Zeleny (aka Charlie Z.) (1981–), b. Northern New Jersey, of Czech ancestry, is an American drummer, music director and producer. He became popular for his work playing duo with Jordan Rudess from Dream Theater and his drum duet work with Terry Bozzio for The Drum Channel. He also gained notoriety playing a nonstop 8-minute drum solo called 'Drumageddon' while walking up and taking an elevator in a Brooklyn building, using drums placed in the building and parts of the building, in one continuous take. Charlie has toured 39 US states, 19 countries and is on 70+ album releases and was an original member of progressive metal bands Blotted Science and Behold the Arctopus.

Jan Zellen (orig. Jan Žižka), b. Prague, Czech, is guitarist, who was one of the pioneers of bluegrass in Czechoslovakia. He immigrated to US after 1984. Less than two years after his arrival in the US, his band 'West Coast 77 String Quartet' outperformed many auditioning bands to win a performing contract at Disneyland in Anaheim. Jan Zellen was awarded Best Musical Program prize at Disneyland, USA, was finalist at the USA national Gibson Guitar Contest in Nashville, won many other US and international contests and performed on European TV and Radio. Jan played with Tommy Emmanuel, David Grisman, Dan Crary, Victor Wooten, Russ Barenberg, Mark O'Connor, Beppe Gambetta and others. One of America's newspapers wrote about Jan's music: "an unusual style of picking involving a flat pick and two finger picks that sound more like a guitar duet than a solo performer. The resulting unique sound was one so rich that Zellen soon drew notice from music lovers and the music industry."

Radim Zenkl (1966–), b. Opava, Czech., is a mandolin player, composer and instructor. Zenkl escaped from Czechoslovakia four months before the fall of communism for political freedom and to be closer to his musical influences. Once in America, he settled in the San Francisco Bay Area, California. After only a short period of time, Zenkl was performing at major music festivals and sharing the stage with artists such as Jerry Garcia/David Grisman, Tuck & Patti, Bela Fleck & The Flecktones, David Grisman Quintet, Preservation Hall Jazz Band, Tim O'Brien, Peter Rowan, John McCutcheon, Dan Hicks and many others. Radim's style features progressive original and eastern European traditional music flavored with string jazz, new age, bluegrass, flamenco, rock, classical and other. The US Mandolin Champion is redefining the mandolin and its role in music by designing new mandolin-family instruments and creating new playing styles. He has invented a masterful technique, the 'Zenkl style,' in which a single mandolin sounds like two. Besides collaborating with the top musicians of the acoustic music scene, he has built up an extensive repertoire for solo mandolin. In the recent years, he added a variety of ethnic flutes to his concerts and recordings.

3. Classical & Opera Singers

Maurice Anger (1885-1963), b. Prague, Bohemia, a tenor, studied piano and violin with Conrad Wallerstein in Prague and later with W. Batchelder, D. Crandall and Alfred Cogswell in San Francisco. He was soloist in various churches and appeared in concerts, musicales, and light opera. He specialized in Bohemian folk songs. He resided in Berkeley, CA.

Kurt Baum (1908-1989), b. Prague, Bohemia, was an American operatic Tenor. He is best remembered for his 25 seasons spent with the Metropolitan Opera, between 1941 and 1966. He was noted throughout his career for stentorian top notes.

Julia Nessy Backer (1889-1981), b. Prague, Bohemia, a Soprano, was a concert and opera singer. She originally studied violin and harp at Prague Cons. Later switched to singing.

Rudolf Berger (1874-1915), b. Brno, Moravia, was an operatic baritone and later tenor. He made his American debut at the Metropolitan Opera in N.Y. in 1914 and remained there until his death. His repertoire included 76 baritone and 18 tenor roles.

William Franklin 'Frank' Birnbaum (1922-2005), b. Czech, was a well-known 20th century chazzan within Conservative Judaism in the United States. Serving congregations and performing concerts across America, his music was well known for its eclectic and melodious nature. As a tenor, his voice was widely acclaimed as one of the finest cantorial tenor voices in the latter half of the 20th century. In 1949 he came to the US where he settled in NYC and studied at Columbia University.

Lída Brodenová (née Dokulíková) (1902-1990), b. Brno, Moravia, was a singer, producer, and teacher of Czechoslovak opera. At an early age, she began playing the piano and taking singing lessons, with the Czech soprano Emma Destinnová as her inspiration. She studied under Leoš Janáček, with her principal voice teacher Sigmund Auspitzer at the Music Conservatory in Brno, Czechoslovakia. She began her career in the French theatre in Brno and spent most of the 1930s performing operettas in various German and Czech troupes. Her knowledge of five languages enabled her to play in German theater in Brno and Alliance François, while the Prague listeners knew her for her performances in Reduta. Brodenová came to the United States in 1940 and settled in New York with her husband, Boris Brodenov. She began performing on the radio in New York City. She played at the Italian Mascagni Opera and thanks to her knowledge of Russian, she was engaged by the New York Russian Opera company. She demonstrated her piano ability in solo recitals in New York Town Hall and Carnegie Hall and her performances received acclaim in *New York Times* reviews. She also made guest appearances with the Chicago Lyra Singing Society and also in Cleveland, Washington, DC, and elsewhere. Using the libretto of Otto Simetti, she composed operetta *White Gardenia*, excerpts of which have been recorded. It was the beginning of a long career in the theatre in which she performed, wrote, and taught Czech repertory. She also organized benefit performances for war refugees. Since moving from New York to the Washington area in 1954, she staged performances of 17 operas, 12 of them Czechoslovak. Most were produced on low budgets and presented in high school and college auditoriums. Among her productions were Smetana's *Bartered Bride*, *The Kiss* and *Two Widows*, and the folk opera *Rusalka* by Dvořák.

Karel Burian (1870–1924), b. Rousínov, Bohemia, a famous Czech tenor, made his debut in Metropolitan Opera, NY during 1906–13. He is particularly remembered for his performance in the operas of Wagner, Smetana, and R. Strauss.

Soňa Červená (1925–2023), b. Prague, is a Czech operatic mezzo-soprano who has had an active international career since the 1950s. She has enjoyed particularly lengthy and fruitful associations with the Frankfurt Opera and the San Francisco Opera. In 1962, Červená made her United States debut at the San Francisco Opera in the title role of Georges Bizet's *Carmen*. She returned almost annually to this house through 1971 in such roles as Anna in *Les Troyens*, Azucena in *Il trovatore*, Berta in *The Barber of Seville*, Clarion in Strauss's *Capriccio*, Countess de Coigny in *Andrea Chénier*, Countess Geschwitz in *Lulu*, the First Norn in *Götterdämmerung*, Fricka in *Das Rheingold*, Herodias in *Salome*, The innkeeper in *Boris Godunov* etc. In 1971, she made her debut at the Lyric Opera of Chicago as Herodias.

Josepha Chekova (ca. 1905–d.), b. New York, NY, of Czech parents, performed in both Europe and in the United States until at least the late 1940s. In the late 1920s and early 1930s, she often performed with the (touring) San Carlo Opera Company, and also as a recitalist. Her voice was variously described by reviewers as "fresh and dewy" and of outstanding range. In 1942, Chekova performed with the 21-year-old Lanza at one of the latter's first concerts. Chekova was married to Czechoslovakian tenor Vladimir Domansky. She can be heard in duet with baritone Dennis King on a 1929 recording of 'Love Me Tonight' from Friml's *The Vagabond King*. Thirty years later, Lanza would also record the song.

Janet Marie Chvatal (1964–), b. Boynton Beach, FL, of Czech ancestry, is an American classical soprano and musical theatre singer. She created the leading role of the legendary historical Empress Elizabeth of Austria in the musical *Ludwig*.

Emmy Destinn (née Kitlová) (1878–1930), from Prague, Bohemia, was a famous Czech dramatic Soprano of notable power and intensity. She made her American debut in 1908 in *Aida* with the Metropolitan Opera in NY, Toscanini conducting, and remained with the company until 1916. She returned again in 1919 and stayed until 1921.

Joseph Diskay (1886–d.), b. Topoľčany, Slovakia; opera singer, tenor, voice coach.

Anna Drasdil (orig. Drazdil) (1841–1929), b. Pustý Mlýn, nr. Blatná, Bohemia, was a Contralto. She lived abroad for 22 years (1864–86). 'A pioneer songbird to appear in US.' She performed with world celebrities, such as Adelina Patti. She sang in London Crystal Palace and Buckingham Palace for the British Royal Family and for Russian czarina and Danish Queens. During her stay in New York, she sang at Grace Church for $2000 annually.

Ludmila Dvořáková (1923–2015), b. Kolín, Czech., was a Czech operatic soprano. She began her career in 1954 with the Prague National Theatre, later with the Vienna State Opera, and in 1960 with the Berlin State Opera, the Bayreuth Festival and in 1966 with the New York Metropolitan Opera and performed until 1985. She was famous for her Wagner arias. She bowed at the Metropolitan Opera on January 12, 1966 as Leonora and was to be heard 16 more times at both the Old and New Mets up thru 1968, her assignments including Isolde, Ortrud, Senta, and Chrysothemis.

Jacqueline Marie Evancho (2000–), b. Pittsburgh, PA, of Slovak descent; an American classical crossover singer. She gained wide recognition at an early age and, since 2009, has issued an EP and five albums, including a platinum and gold album, and three Billboard 200 top 10 debuts.

Hedda Graab Evans (née Grab) (1899–1990), b. Prague, Bohemia, was an opera singer. She was interned in concentration camp during World War I. She came to US in 1950 and resided in Denver, CO.

Renée Fleming (1959–), b. Indiana, PA, of Czech ancestry, is an American Soprano opera and jazz singer. She is one of the most sought-after sopranos of today, appearing at such renowned opera houses as the La Scala, Metropolitan Opera House, Vienna State Opera, Royal Opera House at Covent Gardens and Carnegie Hall.

Mark Freiman, b. New York City, of Czech ancestry, lyric bass, has sung the roles of both Bartolo and Figaro numerous times. He has performed with the opera companies of Sarasota, Ft. Worth, Kansas City, Virginia, Nashville, and Central City, as well as with Summer Opera Theatre, the Metropolitan Opera Guild, and two national tours with NY City Opera. He began his career singing the boy's solo in *La Bohème* for the very first live Metropolitan Opera telecast with Luciano Pavarotti. He is featured as William Jennings Bryan on the Sony Newport Classics CD of *The Ballad of Baby Doe* and spent a year in

Hamburg in the German-language production of *The Phantom of the Opera*. He has appeared as a soloist at both Carnegie Hall and Avery Fisher Hall.

Anni Frind (1900-1987), b. Mikulasovice, Bohemia, was one of the most highly recorded lyric sopranos in Germany during the 1920s and 30s. To avoid collaborating with the Nazis, Anni Frind curtailed her activities in Germany upon the rise of Hitler. During the war, she sang for Allied soldiers at the front and worked as a volunteer nurse. Anni Frind-Sperling moved to New Orleans in 1951 and became a singing teacher at Newcomb College Tulane University.

Maria Mattei Georgevich (1918-2009), b. Bratislava, Czech., was an opera singer, Montclair, NJ.

Etelka Gerster (1855-1920), b. Košice, Slovakia, was an opera singer, Soprano. Her first American tour in 1873 was with the cast of Her Majesty's Opera Company under the direction of James Henry Mapleson. She also appeared in San Francisco, where it was reported she became ill. In 1884, she again appeared in New York working with Mapleson at the Academy of Music. Adelina Patti and Christine Nilsson, and Gerster were considered the leading singers of their time. Gerster opened a voice school in Berlin where she trained many famous singers from 1896 until 1917. Among her students were Ilona Durigo, Matja von Niessen-Stone, and Lotte Lehma. She died in Italy.

Elsie Gilfond (née Elsa Lee Dobesh) (1924-2011), b. Richmond, Texas, of Moravian parents, graduated from Aldine High School at the age of fifteen and attended the University of Houston where she received her undergraduate degree in voice and music and a Master's degree in psychology. While attending the University of Houston, she was very active in the Dramatic Club, performing in many operettas. She enjoyed studying under scholarships at the Julliard School of Music and the Chicago Musical College. After returning to Houston, she gained a bi-weekly TV program where the cast performed excerpts from Broadway musicals. She moved to New York City in 1954 to pursue a career on stage. She was chosen for the role of one of the brides in the Broadway musical *Seven Brides for Seven Brothers*. After getting married, together with her husband, Albert Kenneth Gilfond, an engineer, she spent three years in Peru, nine in Venezuela and another in Panama. While living in Caracas, Elsie started the Venezuelan National Opera Company and sang in its first season. She also made three concert tours of South America. One took her through Venezuela, Colombia and Bolivia, another took her through Colombia, Venezuela and Panama, and a third took her down to Argentina. Everywhere she was hailed as a lyric soprano with an uncommonly rich voice. Elsie returned to Texas in the 1970's. In 1976, 1977, and 1978, she studied Czech along with other Texans at Charles University's summer school in Prague.

Marinka Gurewich (nee Revész) (1902–1990), b. Bratislava, was an American voice teacher and Mezzo-soprano of Jewish Czech descent. She is best remembered for teaching several successful opera singers, including Martina Arroyo, Marcia Baldwin, Grace Bumbry, Joy Clements, Ruth Falcon, Melvyn Poll, Florence Quivar, Diana Soviero, Sharon Sweet, Carol Toscano, Beverly Vaughn, and Mel Weingart among others. Gurewich trained as a singer and pianist at the Berlin University of the Arts where she was a pupil of Lula Mysz-Gmeiner. She also studied privately with Elena Gerhardt and Anna von Mildenburg in Munich. Her career as a singer in Germany was hindered by World War II and she fled Europe for the United States in 1940. Prior to the war, she had appeared in concerts and recitals in Europe. After coming to the United States, she appeared in a few recitals and concerts in New York City; but ultimately began devoting her time to teaching. During the 1960s and 1970s, she taught on the voice faculties of the Manhattan School of Music and the Mannes College of Music. She continued to teach privately until her death in 1990.

Maria Halama, b. Turčiansky Sv. Martin, Slovakia, was a concert singer. At the age of eight months, she was brought to America by her parents. She studied at the Bratislava Academy of Music (1921–1924). She appeared as a Mezzo-soprano soloist in concerts in most of the large cities of Europe and America. She played the role of Maddalena in opera *Rigoletto*, Annina in *La Traviata* and Hata in *Bartered Bride*. Her work was highly acclaimed by critics on both continents.

Maria Ludmila Havelka (1904–1971), b. Prague, Bohemia, was a singer. She studied at the M. Wallerstein Opera School for two years. She was with České divadlo in Moravská Ostrava (1906–08), with the Opera divadlo in Prague (1908–10), with the Smíchovské divadlo in Prague (1910–11), with Ceske divadlo at Moravská Ostrava (1911–14), with Narodní divadlo in Bratislava (1920–21). In 1921, she came to America. She appeared in various operas, such as *Bartered Bride*, *Carmen*, *Faust*, *William Tell*, and *Rusalka*, both in Europe and in America. In Chicago she sang in the Studebacker Theater, the Blackstone Theater, at the Auditorium, and other localities.

Margaret Maria Hecht, b. Prague, Bohemia, was a Soprano. She was a pupil of Adolph Robinson and others. She appeared in opera houses in Bohemia, Austria and Germany. She resided in Atlanta, GA, where she was one of the leading vocal teachers.

Hans Joachim Heinz (1904–1982), b. Vienna, of Moravian mother, was singer, tenor, and teacher. He studied music in Berlin. After getting married, he and his wife moved in 1929 to Berlin. They experienced the early Nazi years in Germany. In 1937, the couple toured with a group of musicians in the United States and decided not to return. Hans Heinz got positions in Baltimore and New York. In 1956, he became a teacher at the Juilliard School of Music.

Mildred Grey Heller (1910–d.), b. New York City, a Soprano, had her European debut in title role of Countess Maritza in Prague in 1937. She had her American debut in Moniuszko's *Haunted Castle* in Chicago Civic Opera (1940). She sang role of Silvana in *La Fiamma* and title role of *Lucrezia* by Respighi for the first time in Czechoslovakia. She had leading roles for dramatic soprano as prima donna of National Theater in Olomouc (4 years). In 1939, she returned to US and lived in Chicago.

Růžena G. Herlinger (nee Schwartz) (1890–1978), b. Tábor, Bohemia, was Can. soprano and teacher. She arrived in Montreal in August 1949, and taught there, at first privately and then 1957-62 at the Conservatoire de Musique du Québec à Montréal and 1963-1970 at McGill Univ.

Mme. Hesse-Sprotte (orig. Anna Růžena Sprotte) (1871–d.) b. Prague, Bohemia, was contralto opera singer and a teacher. She studied piano with Prof. Hahlfeldt in Prague and singing with Mme. Marchesl. She had her debut as Azucena in *Il Travatore* in Germany (1893). She sang in Berlin, Wiesbaden, Darmstadt, Prague, Mayence. In America, she sang with Thomas Orchestra, St. Paul, and Minnesota Symphony Orchestra; in Omaha and Seattle music festivals; with Seattle Philharmonic Orchestra; in California, etc. In Seattle, she organized an opera company and presented 14 operas. She had repertoire of seventy operas and a wide stage of experience. She had her studio in Los Angeles.

Růžena Horáková-Firkušná (née Bendáková) (1909–2001), b. Jičín, Bohemia, was an opera singer, mezzo-soprano, trained in Prague and at German Music Academy. She debuted in Liberec in 1937. The same year she began singing in the Brno Opera. She took part especially in Dvořák's operas, as well as Smetana's and Leoš Janáček's. Her repertoire included some 400 songs. She also sang in Prague Hlahol. She was with Národní divadlo (National Theater) in Prague from 1945-48. She had concerts in Vienna and in England. She was also a soloist of the opera Teatro Colón in Buenos Aires, Argentina. She remained in Buenos Aires, where she promoted the Czech music. Besides Buenos Aires, she also sang in provincial cities, e.g. Tucumán, Cordoba, Junin and elsewhere. Together with her second husband, musicologist Leoš Firkušný, she also edited a collection of Czech songs.

Helen Hájnik Janeček (1925-1993), b. Vranov nad Topľou, Czech., was a Canadian singer, Soprano, residing in Saskatchewan. She came to live in Assiniboia, Saskatchewan, Canada in 1935. She began her vocal training at the Regina Conservatory and continued her studies since 1948 in Peterborough, Ont. She received her A.R.C.T. dipl. and then attended the Royal Cons. of Music. She appeared in CBC recitals, as well as TV opera productions.

In 1960, she made extensive tour of Saskatchewan as a guest artist with Regina Male Voice Choir. She also toured Ontario for the Dept. of Education and sang for Czechoslovak communities in Toronto, Hamilton and Battawa.

Maria Jeritza (orig. Marie Jedličková) (1887–1982), a native of Brno, Moravia, was a celebrated Soprano singer. Her rapid rise to fame, beauty and personality earned her the nickname 'The Moravian Thunderbolt.' She made her debut as Elsa, in Wagner's *Lohengrin*, at Olomouc. The Emperor Franz Josef heard her and immediately ordered that she be offered a contract at the Imperial Hofoper, Vienna. She created the roles of Blanchefleur in Kienzl's opera *Der Kuhreigen* (1911), Ariadne in Strauss's *Ariadne auf Naxos* (1912), the Empress in his *Die Frau ohne Schatten* (1919), and Hariette/Juliette in Korngold's *Die tote Stadt* (Hamburg, 1920), though later became famous for her leading role of Marietta/Marie in the same opera in its January 1921 Vienna premiere, which was also the role in which she debuted at the Metropolitan Opera on 19 November 1921. In November 1926, she starred in the title role of Puccini's *Turandot* in its North American premiere at the Metropolitan, where she also created the title or leading soprano roles in Janáček's *Jenůfa* (1924), Wolf-Ferrari's *I gioielli della Madonna* (1925), Korngold's *Violanta* (1927), Richard Strauss's *Die Ägyptische Helena* (1928), and Suppé's *Boccaccio* (1931) and *Donna Juanita* (1932). She was as popular at the Metropolitan as in Vienna, especially as Tosca, Carmen and Massenet's *Thaïs*. She appeared in an early sound film *Grossfürstin Alexandra* for which Franz Lehár wrote the song "Du und ich sind für einander bestimmt."

Clementine Kalas (aka Klementina Kalašová) (1851–1889), b. Horní Borkovice, Bohemia, was a famous Czech mezzo-soprano. She was educated at Roudnice nad Labem, and studied music in Prague, Milan, and St. Petersburg. She sang in Covent Garden, Germany, Italy, Spain, Russia, as well as in the US, and in South America. She was particularly known for her role as Carmen, Azucena and Amneris. She died in Brazil while on concert there.

Anne Marie Kenny (1951–), b. US, the daughter of Veronica Margaret Janda (1920–2006), of Moravian ancestry, the attorney Daniel Leroy Kenny, is a noted singer, soprano, married to John Howard Bull. She is a singer and voice instructor with her own Vocal Performance Studio in Omaha, Nebraska. She loves to work with singers at all stages of development, from accomplished professionals to beginners. Her students have won first or second place in their category at NATS competitions. Her vocal method is based on the traditional bel canto technique mixed with an individualized contemporary approach to meet the interests and goals of each student. Besides the American musical theater and classical repertoire, her specialties are in French and Italian music, pronunciation and diction. Anne-Marie continues to perform in the United States. Anne-Marie continues to perform in the United States and abroad. For 20 years she lived in Europe, where she performed regularly at venues such as the Paris Ritz Hotel, the Monte Carlo Beach Regency, and Théatre de Cannes. In Prague, she was invited at the request of President Vaclav Havel to perform at the famous Reduta Club. Anne-Marie continues her vocal study with Janine Reiss of Paris, France, one of the greatest vocal coaches of our time. She has also studied in courses and/or master classes at the École Normale de Musique de Paris, the Juilliard School of Music in New York, and the Peabody Conservatory in Baltimore.

Štefan Kocán (1972-), b. Trnava, Czech.; opera singer, Bass. His American debut was at the Metropolitan Opera as Il Re in *Aida*, under the baton of Daniele Gatti in the 2009-10 season. The following season, he made his debut at the Lyric Opera of Chicago as Banco in a new production of *Macbeth* and returned to sing the role of Ramfis there the following season in *Aida*. Engagements with the Los Angeles Philharmonic followed in 2013, with Stefan Kocan singing the role of Il Commendatore in a new staged production of *Don Giovanni* and then as Ramfis in a concert version of *Aida* at the Hollywood Bowl, both under the baton of Gustavo Dudamel.

Ardis Krainik (1929-1997), b. Manitowoc, WI, of Czech ancestry, was an American Mezzo-Soprano opera singer who was the general director of the Lyric Opera of Chicago for 15 years.

Marta Krásová (1901-1970), b. České Budějovice, Bohemia, was a Czech operatic mezzo-soprano who had an active international career with major opera houses in Europe from 1922-1966. She also toured the US in the thirties.

Elise Kutscherra (1872-1921), b. Prague, Bohemia, was an operatic soprano. Her Paris Opéra debut was on June 15, 1896 as Sieglinde in *Die Walküre*. She had her American concert debut under the direction of Walter Damrosch in 1894. In 1914, she performed at the Metropolitan Opera in New York City and announced that she would move her school to the United States. Her school in the Rue Miromesnil was a music center in Paris for some ten years previously.

Hulda Lashanska (Rosenbaum) (1894-1974), b. New York City, of Czech ancestry, was a lyric Soprano, known professionally as Hulda Lashanska. Initially, she studied for a career as concert pianist, but later studied voice. She made her singing debut in 1910. Throughout her career, she appeared with some of the world's leading musicians, including Micha Elman, Lawrence Tibbett, Emanuel Feurermann, Rudolf Serkin, as well as with singers of pop music, such as Morton Downey, Frank Crumit, Jack Smith, and Gene Austin. She also appeared in concert in 1928 with George Gershwin.

Karla Lebedová (née Bernardiová), b. Vienna, of Czech ancestry; opera singer. After emigrating to Uruguay, she was engaged as voice teacher at the Kulischer Conservatory in Montevideo.

Eva Líková (1919-2004), b. Prague, Czech., was an American operatic Soprano. She was notably one of the major sopranos at the New York City Opera during the company's early years. She also made guest appearances with a number of opera houses in North America and Europe, enjoying a particularly fruitful partnership with the Philadelphia Grand Opera Company. After retiring from the opera stage in 1966, she embarked on a second career as a voice teacher. She made her professional opera debut in 1943 as Mařenka in Bedřich Smetana's *The Bartered Bride* at the Brno National Theatre where she was committed for two years. In 1947, Líková came to the United States on a two-year contract with the Detroit Symphony. Following reports of a communist coup in 1948, she decided to stay here for the rest of your life. She first performed in the USA as a concert singer, making her American debut on February 6, 1947 with the Detroit Symphony Orchestra under conductor Karl Krueger. In 1948, she received critical acclaim after appearing with the New York Philharmonic under the direction of Alfredo Antonini before an audience of over 14,000 at the landmark Lewisohn Stadium performing selections from Giacomo Puccini's *Madama Butterfly* and Ruggero Leoncavallo's *Pagliacci*. In 1949, made her American opera debut as Violetta in Giuseppe Verdi's *La traviata* at the New York City Opera (NYCO). She was a guest performer for opera companies and orchestras in Chicago, Detroit, Philadelphia, and around Europe. Ms. Líková participated in operatic productions for television in the early 1950s with NBC and CBC, including leading roles in *Pagliacci, La traviata, Carmen, La Boheme,* and others. In 1966, Ms. Líková joined the University of Michigan School of Music and taught young singers until her retirement in 1983. She later taught privately in New York and Philadelphia.

Karel Martin Ludvik, b. Montreal, of Czech ancestry, is a bass baritone. He studied with Winston Purdy at McGill University where he received a Bachelor of Music. A full scholarship from the German Government brought him to Augsburg where he studied at the Hochschule für Musik. He received his Master's in Opera from the Dutch National Opera Academy, under the tutelage of Margreet Honig, with whom he continues to coach today. Further significant impulse was received from Tom Krause. He continued his training as a member of the Operastudio Nederland and at the Académie du Festival d'Aix en Provence. Further training includes masterclasses with Thomas Hampson, Brigitte Fassbaender, and Helmut Deutch, among others. At home on the opera stage, as well as in concert, his repertoire encompasses a wide range from the baroque (Monteverdi) to 20th century works (the title role in Britten's *Owen Wingrave* with Opera Trionfo under the baton of Ed Spanjaard). As a soloist, Karel Martin Ludvik has performed with De Nederlanse Opera,

Opernfestspiele Heidenheim (Papageno), the Augsburg Mozartfest, the Festival d'Aix-en-Provence, at the Concertgebouw Amsterdam, and has sung with the Bochumer Symphonikern, the Nürnberger Symphonikern, among others. Thanks to his linguistic abilities (English, Czech, German, Italian, and French) he can be cast in almost all genres of the operatic and concert repertoire.

Milo Luka (1890–d.), b. Prague, Bohemia, was a Baritone, who received voice instructions in Prague. He came to US in 1920 and his debut performance was in the Carnegie Hall in NYC. Having scored a great success, he was immediately engaged as first baritone for the Chicago Civic Opera. His principal roles were in *Rigoletto, Aida, Barber of Seville, Pagliacci, Othello, Tannhauser, Il trovatore*. In 1926 he received first prize and gold medal in Philadelphia.

Otakar Mařák (1872–1939), b. Prague, Bohemia, was a famous Czech tenor. He was a member of the National Theater in Prague and the Vienna Opera. From 1934–37, he resided in US and taught voice in Chicago. He was particularly noted for his roles as Vítek, Dalibor, Jeník, Cavaradossi, Lohengrin and Don Jose.

Fritzi Massary (orig. Frederike Massaryk) (1882–1969), b. Vienna, of Moravian ancestry, was an American actress and soprano singer. She was one of the leading operetta singers in Berlin and Vienna, closely associated with Oscar Straus, creating roles in six of his operettas, including *Der letzte Walzer* in 1920. Despite her 1903 conversion to Protestantism, Massary fled Germany in late 1932 because of her Jewish heritage. She traveled through Austria and Switzerland to London, where she was befriended by Sir Noël Coward and starred in his *Operette* in 1938. Shortly thereafter, in February 1939, she moved to Beverly Hills, California, where she lived until her death in 1969. Beginning in 1952, she regularly spent summers in Germany.

Otto Morando (orig. Brandeis) (1869–1953), b. Prague, Bohemia, was a tenor. After study in Austria and Italy, he sang in opera in various European centers before turning to teaching. During his years in Toronto, teaching privately and at the Canadian Academy of Music 1913–24 (and also teaching during the summers 1920–2 in Victoria, BC), he developed the voices of many young singers, among them Eva Baird, Mary Bothwell, Douglas Stanbury, Margaret George, Gideon Hicks, John Mocrieff, Nellye Gill, and Victor Edmonds (orig. Edmond Petch). Morando moved to California in 1924 and was active there as a voice coach for film celebrities, notably Franchot Tone, Bebe Daniels, Joan Crawford, Marion Davies, and Charlotte Greenwood.

Stephanie Novacek (1970–), b. Iowa City, IA, of Czech ancestry, is an American operatic Mezzo-Soprano who has appeared at many of the world's opera houses. A regular performer at the Houston Grand Opera and Opera Atelier, Novacek is especially known for her performances in contemporary operas and in obscure operas, particularly baroque works, outside of the standard repertory. She made her professional opera debut that year as The Page of Herodias in Richard Strauss's *Salome* with HGO and her career has largely been based with that company ever since.

Jarmila Novotná (1903–1994), b. Prague, Bohemia, was a celebrated Czech soprano and actress and, from 1940 to 1956, a star of the Metropolitan Opera. student of Emmy Destinn, Novotná made her operatic debut at the Prague Opera House, on June 28, 1925, as Mařenka in Smetana's *The Bartered Bride*.' Six days later, she sang there as Violetta in Verdi's *La traviata*. In 1928, she starred in Verona as Gilda opposite Giacomo Lauri-Volpi in Verdi's *Rigoletto* and at the Teatro San Carlo in Naples as Adina opposite Tito Schipa in Donizetti's *L'elisir d'amore*. In 1929, she joined the Kroll Opera in Berlin, where she sang Violetta as well as the title roles of Puccini's *Manon Lescaut* and *Madama Butterfly*. She made her debut at San Francisco as Madame Butterfly (1939) and first sang at Metropolitan Opera, NY as Mimi in *La bohème* (1940). She remained until 1951 and returned again in 1952 and 1956. In January 1933, she created the female lead in Jaromir Weinberger's new operetta *Frühlingsstürme*, opposite Richard Tauber at the Theater im Admiralspalast, Berlin. In 1934, she left Berlin for Vienna, where she created the title role in Lehár's *Giuditta* opposite Richard Tauber. Her immense success in that role led to a contract with the Vienna State Opera, where she was named Kammersängerin. She appeared as Pamina in the 1937 Salzburg Festival production of Mozart's *The Magic Flute*, conducted by Arturo Toscanini. She also appeared in twelve other roles at the Met: Euridice, Violetta, Cherubino, Massenet's Manon, Marenka, Donna Elvira, Pamina, Octavian, Antonia, Freia, Mélisande and Prince Orlofsky, the role in which she made her farewell performance on January 15, 1956. Of her 208 appearances at the Met, 103 were in the breeches roles of Prince Orlofsky, Cherubino and Octavian. She appeared in several films, including Max Ophüls's 1932 version of *The Bartered Bride*. In 1948, she won acclaim for her leading role as an Auschwitz survivor who searches for her young son, played by Ivan Jandl, in *The Search* which co-starred Montgomery Clift. In 1951, she appeared in *The Great Caruso*, starring Mario Lanza.

Rose Paidar (1909–d.), b. Iowa, of Czech parents, was a concert singer and an actress. She appeared as Mezzo-Soprano with John Charles Thomas in *Blossomtime*, both in Los Angeles and San Francisco and in the Max Reinhardt production of Goethe's *Faust* in Los Angeles and San Francisco. She also toured with another Max Reinhardt production *Sister Beatrice*. She is known for her role in the movies *Ziegfield Girl* (1941) and *Meet Me in St. Louis* (1944).

Phyllis Pancella (1963–), b. St. Louis, MO, of Czech ancestry, is a Mezzo-Soprano. Her career has taken her to opera houses in the United States and abroad. At Glimmerglass Opera in 1996, she sang the title role in Jack Beeson's *Lizzie Borden*, which she repeated at

New York City Opera in 1999, telecast live on PBS. In the concert hall, she has appeared with the National Symphony, the Minnesota, Baltimore, Cleveland, Cincinnati, and New World Symphony orchestras, as well as the Orchestra della Toscana and the Opéra de Lyon. An active recitalist, she has toured with the Chamber Music Society of Lincoln Center and appeared with it at Lincoln Center for the New York premiere of Dominick Argento's *Miss Manners on Music*, a song cycle composed for her.

Rose Pauly (orig. Pollak) (1894–1975), b. Prešov, Slovakia, was a dramatic Soprano. Pauly studied in Vienna with Rosa Papier-Paumgartner, and during the 1917–18 season, made her debut in Hamburg in a minor role in *Martha*. She next went to Gera and Karlsruhe before singing the title role in the German premiere of *Káťa Kabanová* in Cologne in 1922. 1923 saw her appear at the Vienna Staatsoper, where she would go on to sing Sieglinde, the Empress, and Rachel, and where in 1931 she created the role of Agave in *Die Bakchantinnen* by Egon Wellesz. From 1927–31, she was on the roster of the Kroll Oper, and she won acclaim for her performances at the Berlin Staatsoper as well. In 1933, she appeared in Salzburg as the Dyer's Wife; the following year she returned in *Elektra* in the title role, which she would debut at the Royal Opera House, in 1938, and at the Metropolitan Opera.

Rudolf Petrak (1918–1972), b. Sučany, Czech., was a leading tenor with the City Opera Company (1948–1956). He began his career with the Bratislava Opera and the Prague Opera and made his American debut in 1948 at the New York City Center as Rodolfo in the City Opera's production of *La Boheme*. He was a leading tenor with the City Opera Company from 1948 to 1956. His later roles with the company included Cavaradossi in *Tosca*, Pinkerton in *Madame Butterfly*, Walther in *Die Meistersinger* and the title role in Charles Gounod's *Faust*.

Gertrude Pitzinger (1904–1997), b. Šumperk, Moravia, was an opera singer, Contralto. Pitzinger studied in Vienna at the Musikakademie. She graduated in 1926 as music teacher. She studied singing Lieder with Julia Culp, and then moved to Liberec, Czech Republic, where she performed in oratorios and in concerts. She toured in several European countries, and in the United States in 1938 and 1939. Hubert Giesen accompanied her in recitals, including at Carnegie Hall and the New York Town Hall. In England, the United States, and Canada, she became known as 'the German Lieder singer.'

Lucia Popp (1939–1993), b. Záhorská Ves, Czech., was an opera singer, Soprano. She began her career as a soubrette soprano, and later moved into the light-lyric and lyric coloratura soprano repertoire and then the lighter Richard Strauss and Wagner operas. Her career included performances at Vienna State Opera, the Metropolitan Opera, Covent Garden, and La Scala. Popp was also a highly regarded recitalist and Lieder singer.

Sondra Radvanovsky (1969–), b. Berwyn, IL, of Czech ancestry, is an American Soprano. She studied theater and voice at University of Southern California and University of California, Los Angeles. She sang her first full length opera in Richmond at the age of 21. Specializing in 19th-century Italian opera, Radvanovsky has been called one of the leading Verdi sopranos of her generation. Her signature roles include Elvira in *Ernani*, Leonora in *Il Trovatore*, Elena in *I vespri siciliani* and Élisabeth in *Don Carlos*.

Jan Rubeš (1920-2009), b. Volyně, Czech., was Can. bass, actor and director. He was a soloist 1949-58 with the CBC Opera and an original member (1950) of the Opera Festival Company of Toronto (later the Canadian Opera Co.). He appeared more than 1,000 times during 1949-89 in more than 50 COC productions of over 30 operas and participated in some 20 national tours.

Leonie Rysanek (1926–1998), b. Vienna, of Czech ancestry, is a dramatic Soprano who has appeared in world's foremost opera houses. She made her operatic debut in 1949 in Innsbruck. Her Metropolitan Opera debut came in 1959 as Lady Macbeth in Verdi's *Macbeth*, replacing Maria Callas who had been fired from the production. Over her lengthy career, she sang 299 performances of 24 roles there. She starred in productions of Verdi's *Nabucco*, in the title role of *Ariadne auf Naxos* by Richard Strauss, the Empress in *Die Frau ohne Schatten*, also by Strauss, and Janáček's *Káťa Kabanová*. She made her farewell there as the Countess in Tchaikovsky's *The Queen of Spades* in January 1996.

Ernestine Schumann-Heink (née Rössler) (1861–1936), b. Libeň, Bohemia, was a celebrated American operatic Contralto, noted for the size, beauty, tonal richness, flexibility, and wide range of her voice. Schumann-Heink made her debut in Dresden, Germany, in 1878 as Azucena in Giuseppe Verdi's *Il trovatore*. She sang in Wagnerian operas in Bayreuth, Germany, between 1896 and 1906 and created the role of Klytemnestra in Strauss's *Elektra* in 1909. From 1899 to 1904, she sang at the Metropolitan Opera in New York City. She often gave recitals and once toured the United States with the operetta *Love's Lottery*. Although known primarily as a Wagnerian singer—her most noted role was Erda in Wagner's *Siegfried*—her repertory included about 150 roles, among them Georges Bizet's' *Carmen*, Fidès in Giacomo Meyerbeer's *Le Prophète*, and Orlovsky in *Die Fledermaus* by Johann Strauss. In the latter part of her life, she was known for her radio broadcasts in the United States, and she appeared in the film *Here's to Romance* (1935). Schumann-Heink, who took the names of two of her husbands, Ernst Heink and Paul Schumann, enjoyed a remarkably long career. In her prime, she was considered the greatest contralto in the world, and in addition to her operatic work, she was a notable interpreter of lieder. Her powerful, rich voice of remarkable range, her command of the grand manner, and her personal warmth and manifest kindliness made her a favorite with audiences for nearly a half century.

Leo Slezák (1873–1946), from Šumperk, Moravia, was a world-famous tenor. Slezák secured a three-year contract with the New York Metropolitan Opera in 1909. Met audiences acclaimed him in performances of works by Wagner and Verdi.

Anna Růžena Sprotte (1910–1987), b. Prague, Bohemia, was a contralto opera singer and a teacher. She made her debut at Meinz and had sung on the operatic stages of Germany. She sang with Berlin Philharmonic, Chicago, Minneapolis, St. Paul and Los Angeles Symphony Orchestras. In Seattle, she organized an opera company and presented 14 operas. She had repertoire of seventy operas and a wide stage of experience. She had her studio in Los Angeles.

Suzanne Sten (1908–1995), b. Eberswalde, was a Mezzo soprano, educated in Berlin. She was a member of the German Theater in Prague. She appeared in leading opera houses of Central Europe and had recital tours in Europe and US. In 1938, she immigrated to the US and found work immediately on the radio and in concert. She made her operatic debut with the San Francisco Opera in 1940 as Amneris and sang elsewhere in the US in opera and concert. She was a soloist with the Chicago Symphony Orch., Boston Symphony, as well as San Francisco Opera. Following the War, she appeared at the Vienna Staatsoper and later taught at Juilliard. Her favorite role was Carmen. In 1940, she made a beautiful recording singing Mahler's 'Ich atmet 'einen linden duft.' She was married to pianist Leo Taubman.

Rudolph Rezso Szekely (1889–1981), b. Vrútky, Slovakia, was a singer, voice teacher, with Detroit Philharmonic Orchestra, MI.

Josef Turnau (1888–1954), b. Kolin, Bohemia, was an opera singer, tenor, intendant, and stage director. Because of his Jewish descent, he had to emigrate to the USA during the Nazi era. Turnau attended school in Prague and Vienna and then studied law and singing in Vienna. In 1918, he got his first engagement as a hero tenor and director in the Stadttheater am Brausenwerth in Elberfeld. After stints in Neustrelitz, Rostock and Karlsruhe, he was appointed senior director and assistant to Richard Strauss at the Vienna State Opera in the early 1920s. From 1925 to 1929, he was director of the Wroclaw City Theater. In August 1929, the city of Frankfurt am Main appointed him to succeed Clemens Krauss as artistic director of the Frankfurt Opera House. At times he also taught as a lecturer at the Institute for Social Research. Soon after taking office, he was in the ethnically-national press as Ostjude denounced and publicly attacked. In March 1933, the National Socialists came to power in Frankfurt. Turnau was given leave of absence on March 28, 1933, and dismissed on May 22, 1933, due to his Jewish descent together with general music director Hans Wilhelm Steinberg and acting director Alwin Kronacher. As a Czechoslovak citizen, he left Germany and became a director at the Prague National Theater. In 1939, he emigrated to New York where he worked on opera productions at Carnegie Hall and head of the opera department at the New School for Social Research. From 1946 until his death, he taught at Hunter College.

Georgia Tuzar (1912–2000), b. Prague, Czech., was a concert singer and former English teacher. In the 1920s and 1930s, She attended the Opera Studio of Mrs. Rosenkrancová in Prague, which then was a training ground for professional singers. She also studied and taught English at the English Institute of the British Embassy in Prague and was a member of a Prague choral society. She had a very beautiful, clear soprano voice and was a very expressive singer. After moving with her second husband, Jaroslav Tuzar to the US in 1948, they settled in Hyde Park. While her husband was completing his postgraduate studies in mathematics at the University of Chicago, Mrs. Tuzar gave charity concerts at the university and in the Czechoslovakian community. She and her husband moved to Berwyn in the 1950s, when she became active in several Czechoslovakian-American organizations, which had all sorts of musical activities in which she took part. In 1959, the family moved to Niles, IL.

Boža Umirov (aka Bogea Oumiroff, orig. Bohumír Nepomucký) (1864–1929), b. Mělník, Bohemia, was a Czech baritone opera singer. He commenced his singing studies under Wallerstein in Prague and continued under Vyskocil for Bohemian opera repertoire; later went to Milan and worked under Sabatini, thence to Paris, taking further lessons with Madame Rosine Laborde, who introduced him to the celebrated baritone Faure, with whom he completed his studies. He made a great reputation in Paris and was decorated 'Officer' of the Academie Franncaise. Then followed triumphs all over the continent and in London, where he was commanded to sing before many members of the Royal Family. He made three visits to the US, singing at the White House and several embassies.

Milena Vavřinová (1926–), b. Prague, Czech.; concert, radio and opera singer. She studied voice with Professor Zdeňka Schwarzová-Krejčová. For 9 years she was a soloist with Kuehn's Children's Choir in Prague radio. She was used to being a member of the City Theater in Olomouc. In 1951, she was engaged by RFE Czechoslovak broadcasting in Munich, Germany. After her emigration, she became a member of the State Theatre Sobre in Montevideo, Uruguay.

Thelma Votipka (1898–1972), b. Cleveland, OH, the daughter of Emil and Jessie Votipka, of Czech ancestry, was an opera singer, a mezzo-soprano who sang 1,422 performances with the Metropolitan Opera, more than any other woman in the company's history. She studied at Oberlin Conservatory and with Lila Robeson in Cleveland and Anna Schoen

Rene in New York City. Her operatic debut was as the singing countess in the 'Marriage of Figaro' for the American Opera Co. in 1927. She sang with the Chicago Opera from 1929-31, the Stadium Opera in 1930, and the Philadelphia Opera in 1932. In 1935, Votipka joined the Metropolitan Opera Co., remaining with the Metropolitan for 28 years. She specialized in small roles, never wanting to become a prima donna. Her most notable roles were Marianne in *Der Rosenkavalier*, Mamma Lucia in *Cavalleria Rusticana*, Flora in *La Traviata*, and Marthe in *Faust*. Her favorite role was that of the witch in *Hansel and Gretel*. After retiring in 1961, she made a brief return to the stage of the Metropolitan for the 1962-63 season. During her years with the Metropolitan, she also sang in San Francisco, Hartford, Conn., Cincinnati, and Puerto Rico. She married a church organist John C. Growth.

Dagmar White (née Hasalová) (1926–), b. Prague, Czech., began her studies at the Prague Conservatory and Charles University. She left Czechoslovakia with her family in 1948 for the US, settling in Washington, D.C. She holds undergraduate degrees from the University of Kansas (B.A., 1950) the Juilliard School of Music (B.S., 1952), a Master's degree in music education from Columbia University (M.A. 1956) and a Doctorate from Charles University (PhDr., 1992). She taught at the National Conservatories in Bogota, Colombia; Santo Domingo, Dominican Republic; and Managua, Nicaragua. As a soprano, she has had an extensive career in opera, concert, radio, and television, and has appeared as a soloist with symphony orchestras. She sang the title roles in four American premieres of Czech operas, among them *The Devil and Kate* at the Kennedy Center. She is a member of the music faculty of Northern Virginia Community College and also teaches voice in her private studio. She is also a dedicated promoter of Czech opera and Czech vocal music in America. As a founder and director of the Vienna Light Opera Company, she has produced and directed many light operas and operettas, among them Smetana's *The Bartered Bride*. She is also actively involved with the Czech community in the Washington, DC area.

Dolora Zajick (1952–), b. Salem, OR, of Czech ancestry, is an American Mezzo-Soprano who specializes in the Verdian repertoire. Zajick has been described as having one of the greatest voices in the history of opera. In 1982, she won the Bronze Medal at the 7th International Tchaikovsky Competition in Moscow, the only non-Soviet medalist that year and the first American musician to place in the contest in over twelve years. After this and graduating from the Manhattan School of Music, she was offered a place in the San Francisco Opera's Merola Program, she debuted with the San Francisco Opera as Azucena in *Il trovatore* in 1986, which launched her to international acclaim. Zajick is well known for her interpretations of Amneris and Eboli (in Verdi's *Aida* and *Don Carlos*, respectively). Zajick has also performed in other Verdi roles, including Ulrica in *Un ballo in maschera* and Lady Macbeth in *Macbeth*. She has also appeared as the Princess in Cilèa's *Adriana Lecouvreur*, Marfa in Moussorgsky's *Khovanshchina*, Ježibaba in Dvořák's *Rusalka*,

Joan of Arc in Tchaikovsky's *The Maid of Orleans*, Santuzza in Mascagni's *Cavalleria rusticana*, Adalgisa in Bellini's *Norma*, Dalila in Saint-Saëns' *Samson et Dalila*, the title role in Massenet's *Hérodiade* and Léonor in Donizetti's *La favorite*. In 2005, she created the role of Elvira Griffiths in Tobias Picker's *An American Tragedy* at the Metropolitan Opera. In recent years, while continuing to sing her established repertoire, she has added the roles of the Countess in Tchaikovsky's *The Queen of Spades*, La Zia Principessa in Puccini's *Suor Angelica*, made her Wagner debut as Ortrud in *Lohengrin*, her Poulenc debut as Madame de Croissy in *Dialogues des Carmélites*, and her Britten debut as Mrs. Grose in *The Turn of the Screw*.

4. Cantors

Solomon Baum (1868–1956), b. Šebeš, Slovakia, son of was a Rabbi and Cantor. He was educated in Budapest. Cantor's diploma was conferred by Professor Moritz Friedman, of the Budapest Conservatory. He was officiated as Cantor in Europe, and as Rabbi and Cantor in Congregation Beth Jacob, Brooklyn, N. Y. He was Cantor of Congregation Beth Israel Bikur Cholim, New York City (since 1894). He resided at 214 East 79th, New York City.

Alois Kaiser (1840–1908), b. Sobotište, was an American chazzan and composer, considered to be the founder of American cantorate. He received his early education in the religious school of the Vienna congregation under Dr. Henry Zirndorf, and then studied at the Realschule and the Teachers' Seminary and Conservatory of Music in Vienna. From the age of 10, he sang in the choir of Salomon Sulzer, and in 1859, became an assistant cantor in Fünfhaus, one of the suburbs of Vienna (now a part of Rudolfsheim-Fünfhaus). From 1863 to 1866, he was cantor at the Maisel Synagogue at Prague. Kaiser arrived in New York City in June, 1866, and in the following month was appointed cantor of the Oheb Shalom congregation in Baltimore, Maryland. He was for several years president of the Society of American Cantors. From 1895, he was honorary member of the Central Conference of American Rabbis, which in 1892 entrusted him and William Sparger with the compilation of the musical portion of a Union Hymnal, published in 1897. With Samuel Welsh, Moritz (Morris) Goldstein, and J. L. Rice, Kaiser published the *Zimrat Yah* (1871–86, 4 vols.), containing music for Shabbats and festivals. Kaiser died in Baltimore.

Lenka Lichtenberg (1955–), b. Prague, Czech., an award-winning composer, vocalist, arranger, producer, ethnomusicologist, and bandleader, is of Jewish origin, most of whose mother's family died during the Holocaust. After visiting Israel in 1987, Lichtenberg started learning Yiddish. Since this time, she's a Yiddish and cantorial singer who contributed to the rebuilding of Jewish life in Czech Republic. She's a chazanit in the Darchei Noam Congregation in Toronto. In 2008 and 2012, Lichtenberg was the recipient of the *Canadian Folk Music Award*.

Sister Charlotte Vesely, O.S.B. (1918–2008), b. Cicero, IL, of Czech ancestry, a daughter of Charles and Mary Vesely, was a Catholic nun and a teacher. Sister Charlotte was a faithful cantor and choir member at the monastery.

Samuel Weltsch (1835–1901), b. Prague, Bohemia, was cantor. Belonging to a family of 'hazzanim.' He early entered the profession and became cantor of the Meisel Synagogue at Prague while quite a young man. He received his musical education at the Conservatory of Music at Prague. In 1865, he received a call from the Ahawath Chesed Congregation in New York, and remained its cantor until 1880, when he resigned the position in order to return to his native city. During his stay in New York, he was active in improving the musical service of the American synagogue and was one of the collaborators on the first three volumes of the *Zimrat Yah*, a fourth volume of which was later added by Alois Kaiser of Baltimore. This work contains the music for all the seasons of the year and is still extensively used. In addition, Weltsch published Psalm 93 with German words for solo and chorus, and *Todtenfeier*, two hymns for the memorial service. He was a very prominent member of the order B'nai B'rith and took great interest in communal affairs in Prague, being the leading spirit in various charitable and educational organizations.

5. Popular Singers & Songwriters

Carmel Buckingham (1998–), b. Anchorage, AK, of Slovak descent, is a Slovak-American singer and the lead singer of pop-punk group 'The House United' based in Nashville.

Celeste Buckingham (1995–), b. Zurich, Switzerland, of Slovak descent was Carmel Buckingham's older sister, is a Slovak-American singer and songwriter. She grew up in Slovakia.

Jerry (Fulton) Cantrell, Jr. (1966–), b. Tacoma, WA, son of Gloria Jean Krumpos (1943–1987) of Bohemian descent, and Jerry Fulton Cantrell, is an American musician, singer, songwriter, and guitarist. He is the founder, lead guitarist, co-lead vocalist, and main songwriter of the band Alice in Chains. Layne Staley was also a member of the band.

John Čapek (1946–), b. Prague, Czech, even though trained as chemical engineer, is a noted Can. composer, arranger, keyboardist, producer and songwriter. In 1973, he emigrated to Canada. He became a director of the Songwriters Association of Canada and the Canadian Songwriters Hall of Fame and was a founding faculty member of the songwriting program at the Royal Conservatory of Music in 2005. He is an exceptionally prolific pop songwriter. Capek is noted for his use of complex harmonies, mostly associated with Tin Pan Alley. His biggest success to date has been "Rhythm of My Heart," with Rod Stewart.

Exene Cervenka (born Christene Lee Cervenka) (1956–), b. Chicago, IL, of Czech ancestry, is an American singer, artist, and poet. She is best known for her work as a singer in the California punk rock band X. One of the pioneers of punk rock in the United States during the years when she first sang lead vocals for the band X, Exene Cervenka has been an extremely influential figure, even if something less than a household name.

Greyson Michael Chance (1997–), b. Wichita Falls, TX, of Czech ancestry, is an American singer-songwriter and pianist. His April 2010 performance of Lady Gaga's "Paparazzi" at a sixth-grade music festival went viral on YouTube, gaining widespread attention and over 54 million views as of June 2015, as well as an appearance on *The Ellen DeGeneres Show* shortly afterward. Two of his original compositions, "Stars" and "Broken Hearts", gained over six and eight million views respectively on his YouTube channel. His debut single, "Waiting Outside the Lines", was released in October 2010. Chance's debut album, *Hold On 'Til the Night*, was released on August 2, 2011. Two years after releasing his last single, Chance was set to release his second studio album, *Planet X*, in 2015. The debut single from the album, "Thrilla in Manila" was released on August 11, 2014. The second single "Meridians" was released on March 24, 2015.

Annabelle Chvostek (1973–), b. Toronto, Ont., Canada, of Slovak descent, is a popular songwriter and multi-instrumentalist, raised in Toronto. She made her professional debut with the Canadian Opera Company at just seven years old, earned a degree in interdisciplinary fine arts at Concordia University and stayed on in Montreal after graduation. There, she began composing for dance and film, playing in bands and performing solo shows on the Montreal-Ontario-New York circuit. Between 1997 and 2004, she released three independent albums and an EP, toured Europe with a new-media performance piece called the Automatic Prayer Machine, a collaboration with Anna Friz, and performed across North America with artists like Po'Girl, Rae Spoon and Barlywick. In 2004, she was selected to replace Cara Luft in the Juno-winning 'Wailin' Jennys', a gig that took her from obscurity to international acclaim. Chvostek's songs were repeatedly singled out by critics as highlights of the Jennys' Juno-nominated CD, *Firecracker*. "Devil's Paintbrush Road" was the most downloaded song from the album on iTunes for months. It was also the #1 Canadian song at U.S. folk radio in 2006, and it remained at #3 in 2007. During her two and a half years with the Jennys, Chvostek toured Europe, performed on A Prairie Home Companion, sang on the Juno Awards telecast and earned a Juno nomination for Best Roots and Traditional Album Group. Then, in 2007, she left the Jennys and reprised her solo career, signing to Borealis Records and releasing what many see as her solo debut: *Resilience*. It was nominated for a Canadian Folk Music Award for Contemporary Album of the Year and became the second most-played Canadian album at U.S. folk radio at the start of 2009. Since the album's release, Chvostek has done yearly tours of the U.K., crisscrossed Canada and the U.S. and completed a 2009 tour through Poland and Slovakia. She also released a *Live from Folk Alley* live album in 2010. And last year, her two co-written duets with Bruce Cockburn were released on his Juno-winning album *Small Source of Comfort*.

Paul Dresser (orig. Dreiser) (1857–1906), b. Terre Haute, IN, of Bohemian ancestry, was an American singer, songwriter, and comedic actor of the late nineteenth and early twentieth centuries. He composed more than 100 songs on Tin Pan Alley, in New York City. At the peak of his fame, in the 1890s, he was the most popular songwriter in America. He created his own publishing house in 1901 to produce his works. Paul Dresser is best-known for composing what would become the state song of Indiana, "On the Banks of the Wabash, Far Away", a million-seller that made him a lot of money. He also wrote patriotic tunes with names like "We Are Coming, Cuba, Coming", "Your God Comes First, Your Country Next, Then Mother Dear", "Come Home, Dewey", "We Won't Do a Thing to You", "The Blue and the Gray", "Give Us Just Another Lincoln", and "Wrap Me in the Stars and Stripes." Despite his popularity, he died without a penny, apparently having been too generous with his money. His brother, Theodore, who spelled his name Dreiser, would eventually eclipse his sibling's fame, writing classic novels such as *Sister Carrie* and *An American Tragedy*. He depicted his brother's life in *Twelve Men*.

Anabel Englund (1992–), b. New York, NY, of Czech ancestry, being the granddaughter of the Academy Award-winning actress Cloris Leachman, is an American singer, songwriter, record producer and DJ from Southern California. She is best known for her collaborative work with electronic and house music artists such as Hot Natured and MK. Her debut album, *Messing with Magic*, was released in December 2020, with a deluxe edition dropping a few months later. It consisted of a compilation of all the singles released by Englund throughout that year under Ultra Music and AREA10, and featured "So Hot", "Picture Us", "Underwater" and "Waiting for You" which reached number one on U.S. dance radio.

Jacqueline Marie Evancho (2000–), b. Pittsburgh, PA, of Slovak descent, is an American crossover singer. She gained wide recognition at an early age and, since 2009, has issued an EP and five albums, including a platinum and gold album, and three Billboard 200 top 10 debuts.

Martina Fišerová (fl. 2019–), b. Prague, Czech., singer / songwriter and musician, now lives in the NYC, where she works on a new album with her original music. She graduated from J. Ježek Jazz College in 2011. She has performed with the following legendary bands: Impuls, Laco Deczi & Celula New York, Phishbacher Trio, Jan Kořínek and Groove, and others.

Schuyler Elizabeth Fisk (1982–), b. Los Angeles, CA, of Moravian ancestry (the daughter of actress Sissy Spacek), is an American actress and singer-songwriter. Fisk began acting in school plays as a child and eventually progressed to film. Her first role was as a bumblebee in a community theatre production of Charlotte's Web. She played her first lead role, as the title character in Annie, in sixth grade. Fisk got her film breakthrough in 1995 as Kristy Thomas in *The Baby-Sitters Club*. Her next appearance came in the 2000 film *Snow Day* as Lane Leonard. She is perhaps most well known for her supporting role as Ashley in the 2002 teen comedy *Orange County*, starring opposite Colin Hanks and Jack Black. Fisk plays the guitar, which she learned from her mother, and sang in various musicals as a child. She began writing and playing her own songs at age 15 and, in 2004, signed with Universal Records. In 2006, she put her acting career on hold in favor of honing her skills as a musician and recorded a demo with Joshua Radin, with whom she toured for two years. In 2008, Fisk amicably left Universal. Plans to release an EP were scrapped in favor of releasing a full-length album, which was released digitally on January 27, 2009, as a download at several online retailers. in March 2011, Fisk released her second album, *Blue Ribbon Winner* (through her label Cassidy Barks), then toured alongside the band Harper Blynn.

Jack Gilinsky (1996–), b. Omaha, NE, of Slovak ancestry; singer, part of the pop-rap duo Jack & Jack, along with Jack Johnson. They have released several songs and EP's but are mostly known for their new single "Beg" and the most recent collaboration with Jonas Blue "Rise". Starting off on Vine helped build their platform but now they are known for their extremely amazing music. They have several successful tours around the US and all over the world. The duo has also released their debut *A Good Friend Is Nice* and toured around North America and Europe promoting it.

Adam Green (1981–), b. Mount Kisco, NY, singer-songwriter, artist, and filmmaker. Green is well known for his involvement in the Anti-folk music movement and as one half of the band 'The Moldy Peaches.' Green has found success as a solo artist, enjoying increasing popularity in the United States as well as a number of European countries, particularly Germany.

Hanka Gregušová (aka Hanka G) (1980–), b. Mongolia, of Slovak parents, is in Us s. 2016; a jazz, gospel & world-music, singer and lyricist.

George Grossman (1953–), b. Prague, Czech., is a guitarist and prolific songwriter in Canada, educated at the Guildhall School of Music in London. Has lived and played music on three continents, specifically in the U.S., Canada, Iceland, the UK, Israel and the Czech Republic. He has recently relocated to Orlando and is now active on the Central Florida music scene. George performs widely as a jazz guitarist and vocalist, focusing on the

Classic American songbook, as well as gypsy jazz tunes and other 'ethnically flavored' jazz. He is also a composer.

David Lawrence Hlubek (1951–2017), b. Jacksonville, FL, of Czech ancestry, was the lead guitarist and founding member of the Southern rock band Molly Hatchet. In addition to writing the early hits Molly Hatchet was known for, such as "Flirtin' with Disaster", "Gator Country", Whiskey Man" and "Fall of the Peacemakers" among others, Hlubek is credited with motion picture soundtracks, including the feature films such as *Monster* starring Charlize Theron, *The Dukes of Hazzard*, *Suspect Zero* and *Delta Farce*. His music also appeared on television commercials, on *Hulk Hogan's Celebrity Championship Wrestling* TV show, and on the soundtracks of the video games *Rock Band*, *NASCAR 98* and others. Dave Hlubek had seven gold and platinum selling album awards with sales totaling approximately 24 million in album sales.

Marketa Irglová (1988–), b. Valašské Meziříčí, Czech., is a Czech songwriter, musician, actress, and singer, who, as of 2010, resided in New York City. Irglová began playing music at age 7 and began playing piano at the age of 8 when her parents bought her a piano and sent her for lessons. Irglová collaborated with Glen Hansard of the Irish rock band The Frames, whom she met when he was visiting Valašské Meziříčí, and performed with him in The Swell Season. In 2007, she co-starred with Hansard in the indie movie *Once*, written and directed by John Carney. Hansard and Irglová wrote all but one of the songs featured in the film. The movie won the World Cinema Audience Award for a dramatic film at the 2007 Sundance Film Festival. Among the songs Irglová wrote with Hansard for *Once* was "Falling Slowly" which received an Academy Award for Best Original Song. Irglová became the first Czech woman to win an Oscar, and at age 19, she was the youngest person to win an Oscar in a musical category. Hansard and Irglová performed the song live on the Oscar broadcast at Los Angeles' Kodak Theater on February 24, 2008. She now resides in Reykjavik, Iceland.

Ben Jelen (1949–), b. Scotland, UK, of Czech father, is a New York City-based multi-instrumentalist. He writes lush, orchestral pop songs that celebrate the breadth and complexity of human emotion. The nomadic tunesmith - he's lived in England, Scotland, Texas, and New Jersey - spent his formative years honing his skills on the guitar, violin, and piano, occasionally sitting in with friends' bands. He made a self-produced demo while working as an engineer at a local studio, and was discovered by a Calvin Klein marketing executive at a Jane's Addiction concert who wanted to offer Jelen a shot at a modeling career. Jelen declined but piqued the interest of the now-revealed CEO of Fearless Management, Joseph Janus, with his enthusiasm for a career in music. Janus signed on as the young artist's manager and figured prominently in his signing with

Madonna's Maverick Recording Company. Jelen released his debut, *Give It All Away*, in March 2004. The ecologically themed *Ex-Sensitive* arrived in 2007.

Jon Bon Jovi (orig. John Francis Bongiovi, Jr.) (1962–), b. Perth Amboy, NJ, of Italian and Slovak ancestry on his father's side is an American singer, songwriter, record producer and actor and philanthropist.

Tomas Kalnoky (1980–), b. Prague, Czech., is a Czechoslovak-born American musician. He is the lead singer/guitarist and songwriter of the bands Streetlight Manifesto and Bandits of the Acoustic Revolution, and goes by the pseudonym Toh Kay as a solo performer.

Anne Marie Kenny (1951–), b. Omaha, NE, of Czech ancestry on her mother's side (Janda), is a singer and voice instructor, who studied at the École Normale de Musique de Paris (1985), the Juilliard School of Music in New York (1982), and the Peabody Conservatory (1981). She also had private vocal training with three renowned teachers: Janine Reiss in Paris, France; Diana Morrison in Washington D.C.; Mary Fitzsimmons Massie in Omaha (1976–92). In 2005, Anne Marie went back to graduate school and earned a Master's in organizational leadership degree at the College of Saint Mary in Omaha. She has her own vocal performance studio in Omaha, Nebraska. Her vocal method is based on the traditional bel canto technique mixed with an individualized contemporary approach to meet the interests and goals of each student. Besides the American musical theater and classical repertoire, her specialties are in French and Italian music, pronunciation, and diction. In 1989, when the Iron Curtain fell in Germany and the Soviet bloc countries gained their freedom, Anne-Marie was a professional singer living in France and was inspired by the Czech Velvet Revolution and the writings of Vàclav Havel, the Czech dissident and newly elected President. She wrote a song and sent the poem to President Havel with a heartfelt congratulatory letter. Soon after, she was contacted by Pragokoncert on behalf of the President, inviting her to perform at the Reduta Club in the heart of Prague. Visiting Prague in 1990, for the first time, prompted Anne Marie and her husband, John H. Bull, to move from France to Czechoslovakia. In early 1992, Anne Marie made a career change from music to business owner and founded and directed one of the very first employment and training agencies in the country. Her company, AYS Placements and Workshops, eventually became the second largest employment agency in Prague. She built a client list of over 250 companies in the Czech Republic including Microsoft, Proctor and Gamble, Coca Cola, Citibank, and top law and accounting firms. In 1999, only seven years from its inception, AYS was purchased by Vedior, the world's fourth largest staffing firm. Anne Marie remained part owner and consultant for the following two years. Since the sale, Vedior merged with Randstad which has been highly successful in continuing to offer quality employment services in the region.

Jerome David Kern (1885-1945), b. New York City, of Bohemian ancestry on his mother' side (Fanny Kakeles), a notable composer, was also a songwriter. He had his first professional success on London's West End, and by the age of 20, his songs had been sung on stage on New York's Broadway. He wrote more than a thousand songs for more than a hundred stage productions and movies, including such American standards as "Ol' Man River," "A Fine Romance" (the delightfully flirtatious number sung and danced by Fred Astaire and Ginger Rogers in *Swing Time*), "Smoke Gets in Your Eyes," and "The Way You Look Tonight." Songs from his shows are still frequently performed and adapted. Although Kern detested jazz arrangements of his songs, many have been adopted by jazz musicians to become standard tunes.

Kaiulani Kimbrell (1980-), b. New York City, the daughter of the activist Andrew C. Kimbrell (1954-) of Czech ancestry, and the actress Kaiulani Lee, is a singer/songwriter, actress, documentary filmmaker and Ambassador for the Love Global Movement. Kaiulani writes on the piano, sings and produces her own original songs. She has toured the United States as a singer, and songwriter. She holds a degree in visual journalism/documentary filmmaking and launched her own documentary media production company, "A New Awareness Media" where she has shot extensive videos for the food and environmental movement, including the video series *Food Voices* that she developed and produced. In 2016, she began working abroad, serving as a Global Love Ambassador for the Love Button movement, joining forces with Chris Martin from Coldplay and the Global Citizen's Music Festival. She lives in Los Angeles and Mumbai, India where she is writing music and working with American and Hollywood artists.

Natálie Kocábová (1984-), b. Prague, Czech., the daughter of the Czech rock musician Michael Kocáb and an American born lyricist Marsha (née Crew) from North Carolina, is a noted Czech vocalist, musician, poet, and writer. Her discography consists of three solo studio albums, one extended play, four music videos and a number of other appearances. She is also well established in the Czech literary scene since she proves to be a prolific writer whose rebellious style does not leave the criticism unmoved (so far, she has published three works of prose *Monarcha Absint*, *Schola Alternativa* and *Růže*) and a poetess whose surrealistic poetry is peculiar to the Czech spirit (two collections of poetry published to date, when she was 18 years old).

Rob Kolar (1980-), b. US, of Czech father (film producer Evzen Kolar) is an American singer-songwriter, producer, composer and actor. Kolar has been a founding member of such bands as Lemon Sun, He's My Brother She's My Sister (formed with his sister, Rachel, and future wife, Lauren Brown) and KOLARS (with wife Lauren). As a member of He's My Brother She's My Sister, he toured extensively throughout the US, including such festivals as

Bonnaroo, Summerfest, Firefly, Secret Garden Party and Austin City Limits. He performed with the group on an April 2013 episode of *The Late Late Show with Craig Ferguson*. A composer for television, Kolar scores *The Detour.* on TBS. As an actor, Kolar co-starred in Monte Hellman's 2010 romantic thriller, *Road to Nowhere*.

Katarina Korcek (fl. 2017) b. Bloomfield Fields, MI, of Slovak descent, is an American singer. She went to Slovakia in the early 90s, teaching English, and did not return.

Josh Krajcik (1981–), b. Wooster, OH; singer and songwriter, bandleader.

Irene Kral (1932–1978), b. Cicero, IL, of Czech parents, was an American jazz singer who settled in Los Angeles in the early 1960s. Her older brother, Roy Kral, was a successful musician when she started singing professionally as a teenager. She sang with bands on tours led by Woody Herman and Chubby Jackson, former Herman bass player. She joined Maynard Ferguson's band in the late 1950s and sang with groups led by Stan Kenton and Shelly Manne. She then started a solo career until her death at 46 years of age. She was a ballad singer who stated that Carmen McRae was one of her inspirations. She became more famous posthumously when Clint Eastwood used her recordings in his 1995 movie *The Bridges of Madison County*.

Diana Krall (1964–), b. Nanaimo, British Columbia, Canada, the daughter of Stephen James Krall and Adella A. Wende, the former being of Czech descent, is a Canadian jazz pianist and singer, known for her contralto vocals. She has sold more than 6 million albums in the US and over 15 million worldwide. On December 11, 2009, Billboard magazine named her the second Jazz artist of the 2000–09 decade, establishing her as one of the best-selling artists of her time. Krall is the only jazz singer to have eight albums debuting at the top of the Billboard Jazz Albums. To date, she has won five Grammy Awards and eight Juno Awards. She has also earned nine gold, three platinum, and seven multi-platinum albums. In 2000, she was awarded the Order of British Columbia. In 2003, she was given an honorary Ph.D. (Fine Arts) from the University of Victoria. In 2004, she was inducted into Canada's Walk of Fame. In 2005, she was made an Officer of the Order of Canada. She is married to pop/rock musician Elvis Costello.

Georg Kreisler (1922–2011), b. Vienna, of Slovak ancestry, was a songwriter, playwright, composer, satirist, and cabaret performer. Kreisler went to high school in Vienna, where he studied music theory, and learned to play violin and piano. In 1938, he was forced to flee with his parents to the US, due to increasing Nazi restrictions on Jews. He enlisted in the Army and was stationed in Europe. He wrote songs for soldiers in Britain and France with the help of Marcel Prawy. After the war, he went to Hollywood and worked on movies with Charlie Chaplin, as a pianist. He performed at nightclubs and bars to make ends meet.

His songs were characterized by black humor and uncompromising criticism of society and politics. In 1947, he was rejected by the record companies because his songs were 'un-American,' especially songs with titles such as "Please Shoot Your Husband". In 1955, he returned to Europe, first to Vienna, then Munich in 1958, Berlin in 1976, Salzburg in 1988, Basel in 1992, and back to Salzburg in 2007. He was known for "Lola Blau" (1988), "|New Wine" (1941) and "Das Orchester" (1979).

Katrina Elizabeth Leskanich (1960–), b. Topeka, KS, of Czech ancestry, is an American musician and the former lead singer of British-American pop-rock band Katrina and the Waves. Their song "Walking on Sunshine" was an international hit in 1985. In 1997, the band won the Eurovision.

Lenka Lichtenberg (1955–), b. Prague, Czech., is a singer, an award-winning composer, arranger, chazanit, producer, ethnomusicologist, bandleader, and animal rights activist. She is of Jewish origin, most of whose mother's family died during the Holocaust. At the age of 9, Lichtenberg became an actress at the Music Theatre in Prague, but a few years later, she moved to Denmark, where she studied music at Arhus Universitet and worked as a club singer. In 1981, Lichtenberg moved to Canada and settled in Vancouver, where she continued her studies at the University of British Columbia and sang in a rock band. After visiting Israel in 1987, Lichtenberg started learning Yiddish. Since this time, she's a Yiddish and cantorial singer who contributes to the rebuilding of Jewish life in Czech Republic. She's a chazanit in the Darchei Noam Congregation in Toronto. She performs at many Jewish culture festivals, folk and world music festivals in the United States, Canada, Poland, France or Argentina. In 2008 and 2012, Lichtenberg was the recipient of the Canadian Folk Music Award.

Terezka Lihani (1929–2015), b. Vrbice, Czech. is a singer, composer, writer, producer, and director, residing in Cleveland, OH.

George (Gary) Lucas (1952–), b. Syracuse, NY, of Czech ancestry, is an American guitarist, a Grammy-nominated-songwriter, an international recording artist with over a dozen solo albums to date, and a soundtrack composer for film and television. He obtained a degree in English from Yale University (1974), before establishing his career in music first as a college DJ and then as music director at the college radio station, WYBC FM. Lucas is Jewish. He was a member of Captain Beefheart's band. He formed the band Gods and Monsters in 1989. Lucas has collaborated with Leonard Bernstein, Jeff Buckley, John Cale, Nick Cave, David Johansen, and Lou Reed. His album total to date is 30 plus, and he has included many genres and styles into his work, such as, Jazz, Blues, Avant-Rock, Classical,

World, Folk and Electronica. He has been hailed, 'without question, the most innovative and challenging guitarist playing today.'

Austin Mahone (1996–), b. San Antonio, TX, of Slovak descent in his mother's side, is an American singer and songwriter.

Waldemar Matuška (1932–2009), b. Košice, Czech. was a Czechoslovak singer who became popular in his homeland in the 1960s and 1970s. In 1986, he immigrated to the US.

Samuel Timothy 'Tim' McGraw (1967–), b. Start, LA, of Czech ancestry on his father's side, is an American country singer, actor, guitarist, and record producer. McGraw has released 16 studio albums (11 for Curb Records, four for Big Machine Records and one for Arista Nashville). 10 of those albums have reached number one on the Top Country Albums charts, with his 1994 breakthrough album *Not a Moment Too Soon* being the top country album of 1994.

Bret Michaels (orig. Bret Michael Sychak) (1963–), b. Buttler, PA, of Slovak descent, is an American singer-songwriter and musician. He gained fame as the lead singer of the glam metal band Poison who has sold over 40 million records worldwide and 15 million records in the United States alone. The band has also charted 10 singles in the Top 40 of the Billboard Hot 100, including six Top 10 singles and a number-one single, "Every Rose Has Its Thorn".

Jason Thomas Mraz (1977–). b. Mechanicsville, VA, of Czech ancestry, is an American singer-songwriter and guitarist. He rose to prominence with the release of his debut studio album, *Waiting for My Rocket to Come* (2002), which spawned the single "The Remedy (I Won't Worry)", that peaked at number 15 on the Billboard Hot 100 chart. His second studio album *Mr. A-Z* (2005) peaked at number five on the Billboard 200.

Vladimir John Ondrasik, 3rd (1965–), b. Los Angeles, CA, of Slovak paternal grandfather, is an American singer, songwriter, record producer, and philanthropist. He is best known for his piano-based rock, such as the top 40 hits, "Superman (It's Not Easy)" (2001), "100 Years" (2003) and 'The Riddle" (2006). Ondrasik has recorded six full-length studio albums, one EP, and several live albums as Five for Fighting. Ondrasik's song "Superman" was nominated for a Grammy in 2002. In his early years, he learned the piano; in his teens, he learned to play the guitar and started to write music. While he also learned to sing opera briefly, he soon decided that he would like to be a singer and songwriter. While in college, Ondrasik continued to pursue music in his spare time. He graduated from UCLA with a degree in applied science and mathematics.

Christopher Otcasek (1964–), of Czech ancestry (the son of Ric Ocasek), was the lead vocalist and a founder of a very obscure pop band from the late 1980s called Glamour Camp. He was also an actor, known for 'Pretty Woman' (1990) and 'Elvis is Alive' (2001).

Richard Theodore Otcasek (1944–2019), b. Baltimore, MD, of Czech ancestry, known as Ric Ocasek, was an American musician, singer, songwriter, and record producer. He was the primary vocalist, rhythm guitarist, songwriter, and frontman for the American new wave band the Cars. In addition to his work with the Cars, Ocasek recorded seven solo albums, and his song "Emotion in Motion" was a top 20 hit in the United States in 1986 Ric Ocasek, singer-songwriter, musician, and record producer.

Nicholas Perloff-Giles (1994–), b. US, the son of Carey Perloff of Czech ancestry, and the lawyer Anthony Giles, known globally as Wingtip, is a songwriter and producer. After signing to Republic Records in late 2016, he spent the entirety of 2017 on the road touring behind the success of his breakout single "Rewind" which quickly amassed over 36 million streams and counting on Spotify. Throughout 2017, he released multiple follow-up singles to "Rewind" including "Walls" featuring Delacey, "Space for Us" featuring UK singer Youngr, and "Cross Your Mind" featuring Morgxn, which Perloff-Giles co-wrote with multiplatinum artist Lauv.

James 'Jim' Michael Peterik (1950–), b. Berwyn, IL, of Slovak descent, is a musician and songwriter, rock singer, and guitarist. He is the founder of the band Survivor.

Jana Pochop (ca. 1983–), b. South Dakota, of Czech ancestry, raised in Albuquerque, NM, is a singer-songwriter and guitarist. She earned a degree in history from the University of New Mexico (B.A., 2005). She says it was at the University where she learned how to learn—a skill that she uses constantly while maneuvering the ever-changing music business. She honed her performance chops at open mics and opening slots, and in 2006, moved to Austin to close the gap in her pursuit of a career in music. Since then, she has been a singer-songwriter. She plays originals about love, loss, and some other stuff. Lots of the 'other,' actually. It has been described as acoustic-folk-pop for people who like shiny things. She has been changing her strings a lot lately with shows at the GoGirls South by Southwest Showcase, the Austin Woman's Film, Music, and Literary Festival, residencies at various Austin venues, GoGirlsMusicFest 2007 in Houston and Dallas, sharing the stage with Terri Hendrix and Lloyd Maines, touring New Mexico with CMA Songwriter of the Year Susan Gibson, and recording an EP with Daniel Barrett from Austin band porterdavis. She is also the owner of Social Thinkery, Austin, TX, a social media consulting for musicians and businesses.

Rainer Ptacek (1951–1997), b. East Berlin, Germany, of Czech parents, was a guitarist and singer-songwriter. His family fled East Germany for the United States when he was five years old. They eventually settled in Chicago, where young Ptacek was first exposed to blues music. He moved to Tucson in the early 1970s, where he began his own musical career. His guitar technique, which incorporated slide, finger-picking, tape loops and electronic manipulation, earned him admiration of some notable musicians such as Robert Plant and Billy Gibbons. He was diagnosed with a brain tumor in early 1996 and died nearly two years later after the illness recurred.

Vlasta Průchová (1926–2006), b. Ružomberok, Czech., is a jazz singer. She is the mother of the renowned American pianist and composer Jan Hammer. In 1968, she and her family moved to the US.

Peter Sabla, b. Czech., is a singer and song-writer based in New York. Speed Dial produced his debut album *Kecam*. According to Album Notes, *Kecam* (pronounced 'ketzum') in Czech (correctly should be spelled 'Kecám) "basically means chatting, kibitzing, shooting the sh*t.? It's a singularly appropriate title for the debut album from Speed Dial, since the album's 15 songs offer differing sounds, ideas, and opinions, kinda like an animated conversation." *Kecam* moves from plaintive pop to driving psychedelic rock and gentle ballads. According to James Kiffel, "Czech-born singer Peter Sabla has a fascinating, almost Native American-sounding accent with hard r's and unexpected twists on the vowels that make thoughtful lines sound downright prophetic. Sabla flexes his mastery of falsetto, making it sound like a natural expansion rather than a gimmicky Axl Rose stretch."

Isaac Slade (1981–), b. Boulder, CO, of Slovak descent, is an American musician and the lead vocalist, main songwriter, pianist, and co-founder of Colorado-based rock band The Fray. He attended Faith Christian Academy in Arvada, Colorado and later attended the University of Colorado, Denver, as a music and entertainment industry studies major. He received a Bachelor of Music. Slade started singing when he was 8 years old, and began playing the piano at 11, after temporarily losing his voice. He wrote his first song when he was 16 and learned to play guitar when he was in high school.

Sasha Sökol (1970–), b. Mexico City, Mexico, of Czech descent, is a Mexican singer, composer, actress and TV host. She attended the Peterson College of Mexico City, a prestigious and expensive private school that is dually accredited in Mexico and the US. When she released her debut album in November of 1987, she became the biggest female Pop artist of the 80s in Mexico and many other Latin American nations, and she maintained that position well into the early 90s. She has starred in the popular Mexican soap operas, *Alcanzar Una Estrella II* (1991), *El Premio Mayor* (1995), *La Vida En El Espejo* (1999), and she even starred in the popular Mexican series, *Tres Generaciones* (1989). Earlier in her career, she attended Televisa's talent school (CEA), and she was chosen to be a member of Pop group, Timbiriche. In 2005, Sasha took part in one of Mexico's versions of the reality series, *Big Brother*, titled "Big Brother VIP", which only features celebrities. Sasha actually became the big winner of Big Brother VIP and won a cash prize of 3.5 million Mexican pesos.

Robert E. Stolz (1880–1975), b. Graz, of Bohemian ancestry, was a songwriter and conductor, as well as a composer of operettas and film music. He was the great-nephew of the Bohemian soprano Teresa Stolz. He gave his first public piano recital at the age of seven to an audience which included Brahms, a family friend and shortly after his eleventh birthday he composed his (unpublished) opus 1, a piano piece, "Dedicated to my kind, beloved Papa". His formal music studies under Robert Fuchs and Engelbert Humperdinck led to his first professional engagement as répartiteur at the Graz Stadttheater at the age of 17, followed by conducting appointments at Marburg-an-der-Drau, Salzburg and Brno. In 1907, he became conductor at Vienna's Theater an der Wien, presiding over early runs of operettas such as Leo Fall's *Dollar Princess* (1907), Oscar Straus's *Chocolate Soldier* (1908) and Franz Lehár's *Merry Widow* (1905) and *Count of Luxembourg* (1909). In a life spanning almost ninety-five years, Stolz wrote in excess of 2,000 songs, dances and marches, as well as the music for more than 50 stage works, 60 films and 19 ice revues. With Hitler's forcible annexation of Austria in 1938, Stolz distinguished himself by aiding the escape of innumerable Jews and political refugees across the Austro-German border, before he himself sought refuge in the USA in 1940. This internationally-fêted 'Grand Old Man of Viennese Light Music' returned to Vienna in 1946, devoting himself to an unflagging schedule of composing, conducting, and recording until his death in Berlin on 27 June 1975.

Chip Taylor (orig. James Wesley Voight) (1940–), b. Yonkers, NY, of Slovak descent, brother of actor Jon Voight; American songwriter, noted for writing "Angel of the Morning" and "Wild Thing."

Timbuktu (orig. Jason Michael Bosak Diakité) (1975–), b. Lund, Sweden, of US-born Swedish human rights lawyer and Slovak mother; a rapper and reggae artist.

Marta Topferová (1975–), b. Ostrava, Czech., is a singer and songwriter who found her passion in Latin American music. She weaves Caribbean and South American music into her flowing and folksy vocals, which extend over the rhythmic textures of her back-up grooves. Topferová also masters the four-string South American guitar, the cuatro. She has performed in many venues in New York City and across the United States in cities such as Boston, San Francisco and Portland.

Ken Totushek (ca. 1954–), b. of Czech ancestry, graduated from Bethel Univ., majoring in Biblical and theological studies/psychology (B.A., 1981) and went on to study business administration at Univ. of Rhode Island (M.B.A., 1996). He worked for RexCut Products, Inc., Fall River, MA, as CEO and chairman (1982-2012). He has been an owner of Graceworks Music, Barrington, RI (s. 1996). He is an independent musician. As an acoustic guitar instrumentalist, singer and songwriter, he has been described as a 'musician with a mission.' He is primarily self-taught, though he has had the opportunity to study on occasion under some of his favorite guitarist/musicians—Ed Gerhard, Howard Emerson, Paul Asbell, and the late Artie Traum. He is continually studying the impact of various guitar construction effects on tone—variations such as shape and size, woods used, age, vintage guitars, boutique guitar builders (luthiers) of our day, strings, technique, etc. He writes and performs his own compositions, as well as those of others that he has arranged. He does all his own recording, as well as that of others at Graceworks Music and Recording, his 24-track digital, project recording studio.

Kate Elizabeth Voegele (1986–), b. Bay Village, OH, of Czech ancestry, is an American singer-songwriter, and actress. She made her musical debut in 2003, with the release of her *The Other Side* extended play. She performed numerous local live shows to promote the album and toured with artists such as John Mayer. In 2005, she released her second extended play, *Louder Than Words*. Both had local success and helped raise awareness of Voegele as an artist. During this time period, Voegele performed at events such as 'Farm Aid' to promote her music and began posting her music on popular social media network MySpace. She also won numerous awards and honors for her songwriting abilities. Voegele officially signed with Interscope Records in 2006, and immediately began working on her official debut album. Her first studio album, *Don't Look Away*, was released in 2007 to generally positive reviews. Voegele released her second studio album, *A Fine Mess* in 2009. In 2011, Voegele released her third studio album, *Gravity Happens*. This was her first album to be released through ATO Records.

John Keith Wozniak (1971–), b. Minneapolis, MN, of Czech mother, is an American musician, best known as the lead singer, guitarist, and songwriter of the band Marcy Playground. Wozniak learned how to play the guitar at the age of 14.

6. Musicologists & Historians

Fanny Brandeis (1892-1971) b. Louisville, KY, of Bohemian ancestry (a niece of Supreme Court Justice Louis D. Brandeis), was a musicologist and philanthropist. She was active for over 50 years in Louisville philanthropic and artistic endeavors. One of the founders and active members of the Louisville Orchestra Board; she wrote the program notes for its concerts for many years. She was also one of the founders of the Louisville Chamber Music

Society and served as its secretary-treasurer for many years. She supervised the Federal Music Project in Kentucky during the 1930s, and as a correspondent for *The Courier-Journal* covered the 1950 Bach Festival held in the Pyrenes by famed cellist Pablo Casals. In more recent years, she had served as a volunteer at Central State Hospital, where she had done much to bring music to the lives of its patients and also at Senior House.

Richard Cohn (1955–), b. US, of Bohemian ancestry on his mother's side (Zucker), received his Ph.D. from the Eastman School of Music in 1987, with a dissertation on transpositional combination in atonal music, under the supervision of Robert D. Morris. Early articles focused on music of Bartók and Schenkerian theory. He taught in the Music Department at the University of Chicago from 1985, where he served as Department Chair from 1998 to 2001. In 2004, he founded Oxford Studies in Music Theory, which he edited for Oxford University Press for ten years. In 2005, he was appointed Battell Professor of the Theory of Music at Yale University. He is currently executive editor of the *Journal of Music Theory*.

Edmund Cykler (1903–1988), b. San Jose, CA, of Czech ancestry, was a musicologist. He was with the Univ. of Oregon, Eugene for 37 years (s. 1947), professor of music (s. 1952), and Assoc. Dean, School of Music (1969–72). He was known for establishing the Chamber Music Series, serving as the UO symphony conductor, and being deeply involved with the Eugene music community. He helped found the International Society for Music Education (ISME). Cykler was awarded the Eugene Arts and Letters Award in 1985, which honors individuals who have made an exceptional contribution to the arts and culture of Eugene. His legacy will live on thanks to his $1 million gift establishing a faculty chair in his name.

Anthony Donato (1909–1990), b. Prague, NE, of Czech ancestry, was a composer and a musicologist trained at Eastman School of Music. From 1931 to 1937, Donato was head of the violin department and conducted the orchestra at Drake University. He also headed the violin departments at Iowa State Teachers College (1937–39), and at the University of Texas (1939–46), where he also taught composition. In 1947, he came to Northwestern Univ., where he advanced from associate professor of music to professor of theory and composition (s. 1950). From 1947 to 1958 and in 1961, Donato also directed the University Chamber Orchestra.

Frederick Dorian (orig. Friedrich Deutsch) (1902–1991), b. Vienna, of Bohemian ancestry, was an American musicologist and critic. In 1925 he took the Doctorate at the University of Vienna, where he worked with Adler. He was trained in composition and conducting at the Vienna Music Academy and was a member of the Schoenberg seminar in Vienna; he also studied theory and conducting with Webern and the piano with Edward Steuermann. He was music critic of the *Berliner Morgenpost* from 1930 to 1933. In 1934, he became

Parisian music correspondent for the *Frankfurter Zeitung* and from 1935 to 1936, he wrote for the *Neues Wiener Journal*. In America, he held the position of professor of music at Carnegie-Mellon University from 1936 until 1971, when he was appointed Andrew Mellon Lecturer in Music there; he became professor emeritus in 1975. In 1977, he was visiting professor of musicology at the Hebrew University, Jerusalem, and later visiting professor of music history at the Curtis Institute of Music, Philadelphia and served as a faculty member and program coordinator at the Marlboro Festival in Vermont.

Henry Sandwith Drinker, Jr. (1880–1965), b. Philadelphia, PA, of Moravian ancestry, apart from his successful legal career, had a passion for music. During his lifetime he was recognized as a leading musicologist and published numerous music-related books. These included translated and annotated scores of most of Bach's choral works and all of Mozart's choral music, Robert Schumann's songs, Franz Schubert's and Hugo Wolf's solo songs, and Johannes Brahms's vocal works. Drinker also published a major study of Brahms' chamber music. A talented baritone, Drinker was especially interested in choral music, and during the 1920s he organized 'singing parties' that gathered regularly at the spacious Drinker home in Merion, a Philadelphia suburb, to sing choral masterworks. Formally named the Accademia dei Dilettanti di Musica (the Academy of Musical Dilettantes) in 1930, the group included as many as 150 singers, gifted amateurs as well as the occasional professional. The Academia was accompanied by an orchestral ensemble that often included his pianist wife, his sister Catherine (on violin), and other family members. It continued for three decades before disbanding in 1960.

Leoš Firkušný (1905–1950), b. Napajedla, Moravia, an older brother of the pianist Rudolf Firkušný, was a Czech musicologist. He studied at Masaryk Univ. (PhDr., 1934). As a 25-year-old he was a music critic for *Národní listy* and later for *Lidové noviny* in Brno. He became secretary for Zemské divadlo in Brno (1935–39) and after the War, he occupied important position in the music department at the Ministry of Education. In 1948, he organized a lecture tour about Czechoslovak music to Great Britain but did not return. He then emigrated to Buenos Aires, Argentina, where he later died. He was an expert on Leoš Janáček and did much to bring his music to the listeners abroad. He was also one of the founders of the music festival Prague Spring.

Zdenka E. Fischmann (1923–1998), b. Prague, Czech., was a musicologist. She received a PhDr. in Musicology from Charles University in Prague in 1948. After the Communist takeover of Czechoslovakia California, she worked for many years as a music therapist for Patton State Hospital and published many works.

Petra Gelbart (1978–), b. Ústí nad Labem, Czech., considers Prague her home. She is the granddaughter of Holocaust survivors, was introduced to Romani language, music, and culture at a young age. At the age of 10, her parents moved the family to the USA. Her personal background drove her passion to study Romani culture further and to become an educator in Romani music, history, and other socio-political issues. She first studied musicology at UC Berkeley. Shortly after finishing her degree, she went on to pursue her postgraduate studies and earned a Ph.D. in ethnomusicology from Harvard University. Dr. Gelbart co-founded the Initiative for Romani music at New York University and is currently the music curator for the Romani Archive. She has also taught ethnomusicology, music psychology, as well as Romani music and language at the university level. Her research has focused on interethnic communication, the Holocaust, music psychology, and institutional ethnography. She is married to musicologist Matthew Benjamin Gelbart (1973–).

Anthony Ginter (1932–), b. Windsor, Ont., Canada, of Czech ancestry, is a music historian, musicologist and conductor. He studied Russian at University of Toronto (B.A., 1963), music education at Indiana University (M.M.E.) and music history at Ohio State University (Ph.D., 1976). He was assoc. prof. of music at Univ. of California, Riverside. He also conducted UCR Orchestra. He authored Six Sonatas for two violins, Op 5. (1999). The UCR's Anthony Ginter Award was named in his honor.

Hermann Grab (1903–1949), b. Prague, Bohemia, trained as a lawyer, was a music teacher and music critic. After short juridical practice, Grab became a music teacher and music-critic of *Prager Montagsblatt*. In 1934, he published the first of his short stories in Prague magazines and in 1935, his first book *Der Stadtpark*, a Prague novel, for it he was said to be 'Prague Proust'. After the occupation of his country by Hitler between 1938 and 1939, Grab escaped to Paris. When Hitler's armies defeated France, he escaped (and lost all his manuscripts) through France, Spain, Portugal, and finally to the USA. Grab settled in New York City and established a small music school, married a Belgian exile, and wrote his second book *Hochzeit* in Brooklyn. Serious illness prevented him from returning to Prague after World War II.

John Hajda, Jr. (1963–), b. Manhattan, KS, of Czech immigrant parents, studied mechanical engineering at Stanford Univ., but later switched to music and received Ph.D. at UCLA. He has been associated with Univ. of California, Santa Barbara, as a director of graduate student services (2001–04), as asst. professor in the dept. of music (2006–01), as assoc. director at the SAGE Center for the Study of the Mind, Department of Psychological & Brain Sciences (s. 2011). He specializes in music perception and cognition, which is a combination of musicology and psychology.

Leo Horacek (1919–), b. Topeka, KS, of Czech ancestry, was a music education specialist and musicologist. He was a graduate of the University of Kansas (B.M.E., 1941). After a stint in the US Navy during World War II, he went back to UK to complete his education (M.M., 1949; M.M.E., 1951; Ph.D., 1955). He taught at a variety of levels and locations, including being asst. professor at Cent. MO State Coll. (1958-60). He then joined West Virginia Univ., Morgantown, where he had risen from assoc. to professor of music education (s. 1960), as dept. chair. (s. 1965). He retired in 1981. Since his retirement, he has kept busy as a flight instructor, playing the organ and directing the choir at St. Thomas á Becket Episcopal Church in Morgantown.

Frank M. Hruby (1918-2012), b. Emporia, KS, of Czech ancestry, was Univ. of Rochester educated musicologist (M.Mus., 1941). He was head of composition and theory dept., Mississippi Southern College (1946-48); chairman of music and humanities dept., Univ. School Shaker Heights (1948-70), on humanities faculty (1970-75). He was also a music critic and columnist for Cleveland Press (1956-82); president, Exec. Rewrites (s. 1983). He was also a composer.

Heinrich Jalowetz (1882-1946), b. Brno, Moravia, was a musicologist and conductor. He was one of the core members of what became known as the Second Viennese School in the orbit of Arnold Schoenberg. A musicology pupil of Guido Adler, Jalowetz was among Schoenberg's first students in Vienna, 1904-1908. From 1909 to 1933, he worked as a conductor in Regensburg, Danzig, Stettin, Prague, Vienna and Cologne (as successor to Otto Klemperer). After emigrating to the USA in 1938, he taught at Black Mountain College, North Carolina.

Nelson Moreau Jansky (1903-1978), b. Au Sable, MI, of Czech ancestry, was a pianist and music critic educated at Univ. of Wisconsin School of Music. He was music and drama editor, *The Wisconsin Journal* (1925-26), as Sunday editor (1926); assistant music critic *The Boston Evening Transcript* (1927-32); advertising dir. for C. C. Birchard & Co. (s. 1932) and pres. Music Publishers Assn. (s. 1947).

Karel Boleslav Jirák (1891-1972), b. Prague, Bohemia, was a Czech composer, conductor and musicologist. Jirák became a pupil of Josef Bohuslav Foerster and Vítězslav Novák at Charles University and at Music Academy in Prague. From 1915-18, he was the Kapellmeister at the Hamburg Opera and worked from 1918 to 1919 as a conductor at the National Theatre in Brno and Ostrava. From 1920-30, he was a composition teacher at the Prague Conservatory, and principal conductor of the Czechoslovak Radio Orchestra until 1945. In 1947, he emigrated to the United States, where from 1948 to 1967, a professor at Roosevelt University, Chicago, and, in 1967, a composition teacher at the Conservatory College in Chicago. He remained in this position until 1971. In addition to the opera, *Apollonius of*

Thyane, Mr. Jirák was the author of a great many symphonies, serenades, sonatas, sonatinas and other composition and songs. He was a chevalier of the Légion d'Honneur (France), officer of the Order of the Roumanian Star, officer of the Yugoslav Order of St. Sava. He won many prizes, including the Czechoslovak State Prize for Composition (three times), Smetana Prize, prizes of the Czech Academy of Sciences and Arts, and the International Prize in Edinburgh (1951) for his 5th Symphony.

Leon Charles Karel (1919–2001), b. Iowa, of Czech parents, attended the State University of Iowa where he received a Bachelor of Music in 1940, an M.A. in 1941 and, after serving in the Army Air Corps during World War II, a Ph.D. in 1947. He then joined the faculty of Northeast Missouri State (now Truman State University) as professor of music in 1948 and left 35 years later as Professor Emeritus of aesthetic education and humanities. Dr. Karel retired to Florida in 1983 but remained active in professional organizations and as a composer, music critic and book editor until his death. He was the author of *Avenues to the Arts: A General Arts Textbook* (1966) and other monographs. He was also a well-known piano teacher in the Kirksville area.

Julius Leopold Korngold (1860–1945), b. Brno, Moravia, a musicologist, and a noted music critic, who is credited with discovery of pianist Arthur Schnabel, Erica Morini, Nathan Milstein and others. He is most notable for championing the works of Gustav Mahler at a time when many did not think much of him. He was the father of composer Erich Wolfgang Korngold. He co-wrote the libretto of the opera *Die tote Stadt* with his son (under the collective pseudonym Paul Schott).

Gertrude Prokosch Kurath (1903–1992), b. Chicago, IL, the daughter of historical linguist Eduard Prokosch (1876–1938) from Cheb, Bohemia, was an American dancer, researcher, author, and ethnomusicologist. She graduated from Bryn Mawr College, receiving a B.A. in 1922, and an M.A. in art history in 1928, concurrently studying music and dance in Berlin, Philadelphia, New York, and Providence, Rhode Island from 1922 to 1928. She then studied music and dance at the Yale School of Drama at Yale University, from 1929 to 1930. She danced under the stage name of Tula, starting in 1922. From 1923 to 1946, she was a teacher, performer, producer, and choreographer of modern dance. In the mid-1940s, she turned her focus to the study of American Indian dance, doing extensive fieldwork on the musical traditions of Michigan's Anishinaabe and others. She researched and wrote extensively on the study of dance, co-authoring several books and writing hundreds of articles. Her main areas of interest were ethnomusicology and dance ethnology. She made substantial contributions to the study of Amerindian dance, and to dance theory. Her other scholarly interests included the fields of folk liturgy and rock music. From 1958 to January 1972, she was dance editor for the journal *Ethnomusicology*.

Jaroslav Mracek (1928-1999), b. Montreal, Can., of Czech parents, received his B.A. in music in 1951 from the University of Toronto and Ph.D. in musicology from the Indiana University School of Music. In 1965, he joined the San Diego State Univ. (SDSU) faculty. In the mid-1980s, he organized a musical festival and conference that celebrated the career of famed Czech composer Bedřich Smetana. The Smetana Music Centennial of 1984 attracted musicians, composers and scholars from throughout Europe and the US and spawned a group called the Friends of Czechoslovak Music. Through this organization, Mracek helped organize several concerts at SDSU and established the Jan Löwenbach Scholarship for music students. The Czech Ministry of Culture awarded him the Smetana Medal for his efforts.

Martin Nedbal (1979-), b. Valašské Meziříčí, Czech., came to the United States in 1998 to pursue an undergraduate degree at Hamilton College in upstate New York, where he received his B.A. in German and Russian Studies in 2002. In 2004, he received his M.M. in Clarinet Performance from Syracuse University, followed by a Ph.D. in historical musicology from the Eastman School of Music (University of Rochester), completed in 2009. Since 2009, Nedbal is assistant professor of musicology in the Fulbright College of Arts and Sciences at the University of Arkansas. His musicological research focuses on German opera in late eighteenth-century Vienna and nineteenth-century Czech opera. Nedbal's articles on the operas of Mozart, Beethoven, and Dvorak appeared in the journals *The Musical Quarterly*, *Opera Quarterly*, *Current Musicology*, and *Acta Musicologica*. His edition of early nineteenth-century German adaptations of Mozart's *Don Giovanni* and *Così fan tutte* is forthcoming with the Hollitzer Wissenschaftsverlag in Vienna, Austria. His research has been supported by grants from the American Musicological Society and the Scholarship Foundation of the Republic of Austria.

Anna Nekola (1974-), b. Minneapolis, MN, of Czech ancestry, is a musicologist and professional oboist. She received a Bachelor of Arts cum laude from St. Olaf College (1996) where she majored in music, and in 1998 she received a Master of Music in oboe performance from Wichita State University where she studied with Emily Pailthorpe. At the University of Wisconsin-Madison, she earned a Master of Arts in musicology in 2000, followed by the Ph.D. in musicology in 2009. She has been on the faculty of Denison University since 2009 as a visiting assistant professor where her teaching duties are shared across three departments: Music, Communication, and Queer Studies. She is currently writing a monograph that analyzes the disputes over worship music within contemporary American evangelical Christianity, exploring how ideological and theological disputes are reconfigured as spiritual battles over the most appropriate musical style for organized worship services. In addition, Anna is a professional oboist and has held positions with orchestras in Kansas and Wisconsin and has also performed with ensembles in Norway, Canada, and Singapore.

Bruno Nettl (1930–2020), b. Prague, Czech., is an ethnomusicologist. He emigrated to the USA with his parents at the age of nine, settling first in Princeton, N.J., and then in Bloomington, Indiana. He studied principally at Indiana University (Ph.D., 1953) and, after several years on the faculty of Wayne State University (1954–64) and the University of Kiel, Germany, has spent most of his career, since 1964, teaching at the University of Illinois at Urbana-Champaign, as professor of musicology and anthropology (s. 1967), as chairman of div. of musicology (1967–72, 1975–77, 1982–85), and where he is now Professor Emeritus of Music and Anthropology. Bruno Nettl's main research interests are ethnomusicological theory and method, music of Native American cultures, and music of the Middle East, especially Iran. Professor Nettl has done field work with the Blackfoot people of Montana, and in Iran, Israel, and India, and he has an interest in the music history and folk music of his native Czech Republic. Professor Nettl has been focusing in recent years on the study of improvisatory music, the understanding of musical change throughout the world, and especially the intellectual history of ethnomusicology. He has published many articles and more than a dozen books, the best known being *The Study of Ethnomusicology* (1983, rev. ed. 2005), *The Western Impact on World Music* (1985), *Blackfoot Musical Thought: Comparative Perspectives* (1989), *Heartland Excursions: Ethnomusicological Perspectives on Schools of Music* (1995), *Nettl's Elephant: On the History of Ethnomusicology* (2013), as well as *Encounters in Ethnomusicology* (2002), a professional memoir, and *Becoming an Ethnomusicologist: A Miscellany of Influences* (2013), Certain of his books have been translated into French, Spanish, Portuguese, Japanese, Korean, Chinese, and Persian.

Paul Nettl (1889–1971), b. Vrchlabí, Bohemia, was trained as a musicologist at Univ. of Prague and Vienna. He was professor of musicology, Indiana Univ. (1946–60). He was an authority on Mozart in Bohemia, dance music. His works include: *Alte juedische Spielleute und Musiker* (1923); *The Story of Dance Music* (1947); *The Book of Musical Documents* (1948); *The Other Casanova* (1950) concerning Lorenzo da Ponte; *Forgotten Musicians* (1951); *Beethoven Encyclopedia* (1956); and *Mozart and Masonry* (1957).

Frederick Neumann (1907–1994), b. Bílsko, Silesia, was a musicologist, educated at Univ. of Berlin and Columbia Univ. He was professor of music history, strings and orchestra at Univ. of Richmond (1955–78). He was a specialist in music history, violin technique, and historical performance.

John K. Novak (1961–), b. New York City, is associate professor of music theory at Northern Illinois University. He holds a Bachelor's of Music Theory, a Master of Music in Piano Pedagogy and Literature, and a Ph.D. in Music Theory from the University of Texas at Austin, where he was awarded the Kent Kennan Scholarship in Music Theory and the John Maresh Scholarship in Czech Culture. He has taught at Austin Community College, the

University of Texas at Austin, and Oberlin Conservatory. He joined the faculty of the School of Music at Northern Illinois University in 1996, where he teaches undergraduate and graduate courses in music theory and aural skills, with a specialization in music of the twentieth century. Novak has published articles for *College Music Symposium, Indiana Theory Review, the International Journal of Musicology, Bulgarian Musicology, Kosmas*, and *Hudební Věda*, as well as for Oxford and Clerendon Presses. The subjects of his articles include the music of Dvořák, Bartók, Janáček, Suk, and various styles of popular music. He has presented at symposia and conferences throughout the U.S. as well as in London, Prague, Brno and Sofia. Novak is currently co-authoring a book of 90 songs which continue to be sung in Texas in the Czech language.

Diane M. Paige (1968–), b. Cedar Rapids, IA, of Czech ancestry, is a musicologist. She holds the position of Professor and Department Chair at Hartwick College, Oneonta, NY. Diane M. Paige received her B.M. in Music Education from Colorado State University where she minored in Slavic Studies. Her Master's degree in Musicology was awarded by Iowa State University where she wrote a Master's thesis entitled *Dvorak in Spillville*. She received her Ph.D. in Musicology from the University of California, Santa Barbara. Her dissertation, entitled *The Women of Leoš Janáček's Operas*, explored the archetypes and female roles of the Czech composer's mature operas. She has published in *The Musical Quarterly*, with Princeton and Cambridge (forthcoming) Presses, and is currently at work on a book about music and war from the American Revolution to present. She has presented her research at a wide variety of venues including BBC Radio 3, Lincoln Center for the Arts, and the Bard Music Festival. At Hartwick, she teaches the three-semester music history sequence, an introductory world music course, and courses on specialized topics such as Music of the African Diaspora, Music and World Wars I and II, and Music of the Roma (Gypsies). She has led off-campus courses to Anguilla, B.W.I. (student practica), Brazil (carnival and its music), and Ghana (dance, drumming, and oral history).

Paul Amadeus Pisk (1893–1990), b. Vienna, of Moravian ancestry, was a composer and musicologist. Pisk earned his Doctorate in musicology from Vienna University in 1916, studying under Guido Adler. Afterwards, he studied conducting at the Imperial Academy of Music and the Performing Arts, graduating in 1919. Pisk also studied privately with Arnold Schoenberg from 1917 to 1919. He then taught at the Vienna Academy and gave adult education lectures, especially at the Volkshochschule Volksheim Ottakring, where from 1922 to 1934, he was director of the music department. He also taught at the New Vienna Conservatory from 1925 to 1926 and the Austro-American Conservatory near Salzburg from 1931 to 1933. In 1936, he immigrated to the United States and taught at the University of Redlands (1937–1951), the University of Texas at Austin (1951–1963), and Washington University in St. Louis (1963–1972). He composed orchestral works, ballets, chamber music and songs, as well as writings in music theory. His notable students include Leopold Spinner, Samuel Adler, Gary Lee Nelson, and Thomas F. Hulbert.

Felix Salzer (1904–1986), b. Vienna, of Bohemian ancestry, on his mother's side, was an American music theorist, musicologist, and pedagogue. He was one of the principal followers of Heinrich Schenker and did much to refine and explain Schenkerian analysis after Schenker's death. He studied musicology with Guido Adler at the University of Vienna, finishing his Ph.D. in 1926 with a dissertation on sonata form in the works of Franz Schubert. At the same time, he studied music theory and analysis with Heinrich Schenker and Hans Weisse. In 1939, Salzer emigrated to the United States and became a citizen in 1945. While in the US he taught at several schools, including the Mannes College of Music, and Queens College of the City University of New York. His contributions to Schenkerian theory were twofold: first, he brought Schenker's ideas to the attention of American music theorists and musicologists, and second, he applied the analytical technique to music outside of the common-practice era music in which Schenker had exclusively worked, particularly to the music of the Renaissance, the Middle Ages, and to some music of the 20th century. Salzer's works include *Structural Hearing* (1952 and 1962), *Counterpoint in Composition: The Study of Voice Leading* (with Carl Schachter, 1969), and the periodical *The Music Forum* (initiated 1967).

Thomas Paul Sovik (1953–), b. Youngstown, OH, of Czech ancestry, is currently a Professor of Music Theory in the College of Music at University of North Texas, with a dual appointment as Director of Central European Studies & Exchanges. Following seminary studies, Dr. Sovík earned degrees at Ashland University (B.A., 1974) and the Ohio State University (M.A., 1975; Ph.D., 1985). After holding positions at the University of Northern Iowa and with Yamaha Music International, he joined the Univ. of North Texas (UNT) College of Music faculty in 1987 and served as the first chair of the Division of Music History, Theory, & Ethnomusicology (1990–97). He held the position of Dean of Fine & Performing Arts at Mississippi University for Women (1998-99), returning to Dallas for surgery and therapy after being run down by a drunk driver, and thereafter served two additional terms as Division chair at UNT. Since his return to the University of North Texas, Dr. Sovík has been promoted to the rank of full professor, has received UNT's coveted Professor Graham award for his 'Outstanding Teaching & Dedication to Students,' and has been recognized as an 'Outstanding Teacher of the Honors College.' Dr. Sovík's primary research field is the history of music theory in Central Europe during the Medieval and Renaissance Eras. Dr. Sovík's secondary research field is 'Popular Music in American Culture,' with enrollment in his popular music classes typically exceeding 1,700 students during the course of any academic year. As tour director and organist, Dr. Sovík led 34 visits to the Czech Republic; these visits provided the opportunity for 1,428 faculty and students to offer 162 academic presentations and 117 concerts.

Paul Stefan (orig. Paul Stefan Grünfeld) (1879-1943), b. Brno, Moravia, was a music historian and critic. Paul Stefan came to live in Vienna in 1898. He attended courses in law, philosophy and art history at the University of Vienna, before studying music theory with Hermann Graedener and composition under Arnold Schoenberg. From 1922 to 1937, he edited the Austrian music journal *Musikblätter des Anbruch* (entitled simply *Anbruch* from 1929). He was also, for many years, a music and dance critic for the Viennese newspaper *The hour and the stage*, as well as other European and American newspapers, including the *Neue Zürcher Zeitung* and *Musical America*. After the 'Anschluss' of Austria in 1938, he was forced to emigrate as a Jew and because of his anti-Nazi articles. He first went for half a year to Switzerland and then to Paris, until the occupation of France in 1940, where he worked primarily for broadcasting. The next stop on his escape was Lisbon, where Stefan, on behalf of the government, wrote a book about Portuguese music and translated some of his works into Portuguese. In April 1941, he arrived in the United States, where he continued to be successful as a music journalist and lecturer. He wrote also books about Gustav Mahler (1910, 1912), *Neue Musik und Wien* (1921), *Die Wiener Oper* (1922), *Arnold Schoenberg* (1924), *Arturo Toscanini* (1935), *Richard Wagner, Franz Schubert* und *Bruno Walter* (1936).

Frederick William Sternfeld (1914-1994), b. Vienna, of Bohemian ancestry, was a musicologist who emigrated to US in 1938. He studied at NY College of Music and then at Yale Univ. He was with Wesleyan Univ. (1940-46); Hanover College (1946-56), as professor of music (1955-56); member, Institute of Advanced Study, Princeton. NJ (1955). In 1956, he moved to UK and became lecturer and then reader in music at Oxford Univ. and Exeter College. In 1963-64, he was a Mellon Professor at Univ. Pittsburgh and in 1964, research fellow at Folger Shakespeare Library, Washington, DC. He was the author of a number of music history books and co-editor of *New Oxford History of Music* and editor of *Proceedings of the Royal Musical Assoc.* (1957-62). He was a specialist on music for films and renaissance music.

Richard Stöhr (1874-1967), b. Vienna, of Bohemian mother (Porges), was a composer, music author and teacher. He studied composition with Robert Fuchs at the Vienna Conservatory. After working there as a repetiteur and choral instructor from 1900, he taught music (theory of harmony, counterpoint, form) from 1903 to 1938, being professor from 1915. Among his students were Herbert von Karajan, Rudolf Serkin, Erich Leinsdorf, Samuel Barber, Erich Zeisl, Louis Horst, Marlene Dietrich, Alois Hába and Hellmut Federhofer. He was fired from the Vienna Academy due to his Jewish heritage in 1938, emigrated to the US in 1939 and taught at the Curtis Institute of Music in Philadelphia. His students there included Leonard Bernstein and Eugene Bossart. From 1941 to 1950, he taught at St. Michael's College in Vermont, where he maintained emeritus status until 1960. His published works include *Praktische Leitfaden der Harmonielehre*_(1906), *Musikalische Formenlehre* (1911), *Praktische Leitfaden des Kontrapunkts* (1911), and *Praktische Modulationslehre* (1915), and other works.

Frank Strnad (1960-), b. Arcadia, CA, of Czech ancestry, was on the Fullerton College Voice faculty from 2004-10, and is now pursuing a Ph.D. in musicology at Claremont Graduate University (s. 2010). He has performed a wide-ranging list of opera and oratorio roles. A member of the Los Angeles Opera Company from 1992-2003, he has sung leading and character roles in much of the standard opera repertory, including Verdi's *La Traviata* and Rossini's *Barber of Seville*. Additionally, he sang the lead in Puccini's *Gianni Schicchi*, Mozart's *Don Giovanni*, and Creon in Stravinski's *Oedipus Rex*. His oratorio experience includes the bass/baritone solos in Bach's *Magnificat*, Britten's *Rejoice in the Lamb*, Brahms *German Requiem*, Faure's *Requiem*, Handel's *Messiah*, and Mozart's *Coronation Mass*. A regional winner in the Metropolitan Opera National Auditions, and a Phyllis Curtin Vocal Fellow at the Tanglewood Festival, Strnad was also a Rotary Foundation Scholar to the Hochschule fur Musik in Vienna Austria (1981-83) and holds a Master's Degree in Vocal Arts from the University of Southern California (1990).

Lee Teply (?-2014), b. US, of Czech ancestry, held degrees in organ performance, music theory and literature from Oberlin College Conservatory (B.M.) and Eastman School of Music (M.M., 1977; D.M.A.). He studied conducting with William Weinert, Robert Fountain, Harriet Simons and Robert DeCormier. He became a full-time church musician in Lewiston, N.Y. Teply came to Norfolk in 1986 to teach music theory and music history at Old Dominion University (ODU). He is credited with starting the school's Collegium Musicum, an early instruments ensemble. He took over direction of the Madrigal Singers in 1988. He also was involved with ODU's Opera Workshop, conducting the productions of *Dido and Aeneas*, *The Telephone* and Douglas Moore's *Gallantry*. He was also the music director at First Lutheran Church of Norfolk. In addition to being the music director at First Lutheran, Teply also had been associated with the music at St. Andrew's Episcopal, Royster Memorial Presbyterian Church and Epworth United Methodist Church. A harpsichordist, Teply also played with the Virginia Pro Musica/McCullough Chorale and the Virginia Symphony Orchestra. For several years, he provided program notes for the chorale and the symphony and recently continued to do so for the Feldman Chamber Music Society. He was also a freelance music reviewer for *The Virginian-Pilot*.

Edith Vogl-Garrett (1904-1995), b. Nýrsko, Bohemia, was a musicologist and a pianist. She studied musicology and classical archeology at Charles Univ. (Ph.D., 1928). She also studied piano at the Academy of Music, Prague. Subsequently, she became a music critic and wrote a column on music for Prague newspapers. She entered the US in 1938 and taught musicology and piano at Keuka College (1939-42), German and Italian at the Northeast Conservatory of Music, Boston (1942-45), musicology at Boston Univ. (1950-62) and Wheaton College (1962-63). Subsequently, she became lecturer in musicology at Harvard Univ. She was a specialist on Baroque opera, Czech music of the 18th century.

Arnold M. Walter (1902-1973), b. Hanušovice, Moravia, was a Canadian musicologist and a farsighted and intellectual music educator. He studied law at the University of Prague, then musicology at the University of Berlin. In addition, he had private music lessons in piano and composition with Rudolf Breithaupt, Frederic Lamond, and Franz Schreker. In the early 1930s, Walter wrote the music column for *Die Weltbühne*, and was music critic for the *Vorwärts* magazine. In 1937, he immigrated to Canada and taught at Upper Canada College. From 1952 to 1968, Walter was music director of the music faculty of the University of Toronto. Walter established the Senior School as the Toronto Cons. of Music's advanced studies department and initiated the opera school. He received an Honorary Doctor of Music from Mount Allison University in 1966. In 1972, Walter was appointed Officer of the Order of Canada.

Emanuel Winternitz (1898-1983), b. Vienna, of Bohemian ancestry, was curator emeritus of the Department of Musical Instruments of the Metropolitan Museum of Art and a musicologist of international standing. He came to the US in 1939 and joined the Metropolitan Museum as a lecturer in 1941. A year later, he was appointed keeper of musical instruments. He presided over systematic reorganization and rehabilitation of the Crosby Brown Collection of Musical Instruments of All Nations, and in 1949, was given the title of curator when the Metropolitan made the Musical Instrument Collection an official department of the museum. Winternitz established new fields of research, especially in musical iconography, and for many years, he taught the history of musical instruments and related subjects at Yale, the City University of New York and elsewhere.

7. Music Critics

Leoš Firkušný (1905-1950), b. Napajedla, Czech., an older brother of the pianist Rudolf Firkušný, was a Czech musicologist and music critic. He studied at Masaryk Univ. (PhDr., 1934). As a 25-year-old, he was a music critic for *Národní listy* and later for *Národní* and *Lidové noviny* in Brno. He became secretary for Zemské divadlo in Brno (1935-39) and after the War, he occupied important position in the music department at the Ministry of Education. In 1948, he organized a lecture tour about Czechoslovak music to Great Britain but did not return. He then immigrated to Buenos Aires, Argentina, where he later died.

He was an expert on Leoš Janáček and did much to bring his music to the listeners abroad. He was also one of the founders of the music festival Prague Spring.

Max Graf (1873-1958), b. Vienna, of Bohemian ancestry, was Univ. of Vienna trained as a music critic and musicologist. He was a lecturer at New School of Social Research (1939-47) and also vis. professor. at Carnegie Inst. of Technology and Temple Univ. In 1947, he returned to Austria. He often championed new works of Gustav Mahler.

Frank M. Hruby (1918-2012), b. Emporia, KS, of Czech ancestry, was Univ. of Rochester educated musicologist (M.Mus., 1941). He was head of composition and theory dept., Mississippi Southern College (1946-48); chairman of music and humanities dept., Univ. School Shaker Heights (1948-70), on humanities faculty (1970-75). He was also a music critic and columnist for *Cleveland Press* (1956-82); president, Exec. Rewrites (s. 1983). He was also a composer.

Nelson Moreau Jansky (1903-1978), b. Au Sable, MI of Czech ancestry, was a pianist and music critic educated at Univ. of Wisconsin School of Music. He was a music and drama editor, *The Wisconsin Journal* (1925-26), as Sunday editor (1926); assistant music critic *The Boston Evening Transcript* (1927-32); advertising dir. For C. C. Birchard & Co. (s. 1932) and pres. Music Publishers Assn. (s. 1947).

Leon Charles Karel (1919-2001), b. Iowa, of Czech parents, attended the State University of Iowa where he received a Bachelor of Music in 1940, an M.A. in 1941 and, after serving in the Army Air Corps during World War II, a Ph.D. in 1947. He then joined the faculty of Northeast Missouri State (now Truman State University) as professor of music in 1948 and left 35 years later as Professor Emeritus of aesthetic education and humanities. Dr Karel retired to Florida in 1983 but remained active in professional organizations and as a composer, music critic and book editor until his death. He was the author of *Avenues to the Arts: A General Arts Textbook* (1966) and other monographs. He was also a well-known piano teacher in the Kirksville area.

Jan Loewenbach (1880-1972), b. Rychnov n/Knežnou, Bohemia, although trained as a lawyer, he devoted his entire career to music as a music critic, writer, librettist, and translator. He wrote studies, critical articles and commentaries on music and musicians for the American and Czech press and magazines and also lectured widely. He also wrote librettos for Jaroslav Křička's opera *The Gentleman in White* and for Bohuslav Martinů's *The Soldier and the Dancer*.

Jan (Vladimír) Matějček (1926-2017), b. Hamburg, of Czech parents, is Can. music editor, critic and administrator. He emigrated to Canada in 1969 and in 1970 served as executive secretary of the Ontario Federation of Symphony Orchestras and subsequently became first executive director of the Ontario Choral Federation, which he had helped to establish and edited newsletters for both organizations.

8. Music Publishers

Anita M. Smisek (1941–), b. Faribault, MN, of Czech ancestry, is an American Dominican nun, music publisher, pianist. and organist. In 1960, she became a member of the Sinsinawa Dominican Sisters in Sinsinawa, Wisconsin. She holds academic degrees from Rosary College (B.A., 1964) and University of Minnesota (M.A., 1976). She is committed to the dissemination of contemporary Czech music in the USA and published the hymnbook *Give Glory* during her time as organist at St. Wenceslaus Church in New Prague, which contains 77 well-known Czech chorales in English translation. She took traditional Czech songs on the albums *Koledy - Czech Christmas Carols*, *Ryba - Czech Christmas Mass* and *Give Glory, Earth, and Heaven*. In 1989, she founded with Joel Blahnik the publisher Alliance Publications, the particularly the publication of music education and church music works, and promotion devoted to contemporary and particularly Czech compositions.

Anthony J. Stastny (1885–1923), b. Cleveland, OH, of Czech ancestry, was an American composer and founder of A. J. Stastny Music Co., one of the largest music publishing firms in North America during the 1920s, with branch offices in 18 large cities, including Philadelphia, Chicago, San Francisco, and London – with over 200 employees and grossing over one million dollars a year. Stastny and his publishing company were originally located in Cleveland. In 1910, he relocated to New York City. He composed numerous popular songs and piano solo works.

Julius Victor Tupa (1931-2002), b. TX, of Czech parents, was a well-known Houston area musician, music promoter and radio disk jockey, and publisher of *The Texas Polka News*. He formed his first country western band in 1956 and recorded an LP on the Guide Record Label in the 60s. He organized a second country and western swing band in 1973. His involvement with the Houston music scene then continued as he owned and operated a recording and video studio.

9. Music Instrument Makers

Joseph Bohmann (1848–1928), b. Neumarkt, Bohemia, a stringed instrument maker, immigrated to America in 1873 and founded Bohmann's American Musical Industry in Chicago in 1878. He produced several kinds of instruments, including flattop acoustic guitars, mandolins, banjos and violins. Bohmann's Perfect Artists violins won international honors. His American mandolin model was the top of the line. His guitars are available in many different configurations and sizes. Never lacking in hubris, he repeatedly described himself as 'The World's Greatest Musical Instrument Manufacturer' and offered a $125,000 reward to anyone who could prove him wrong. While perhaps not the single greatest instrument maker, he did win an impressive number of international awards.

John Dopyera (orig. Ján Dopjera) (1893–1988), b. Šaštín-Stráže, Slovakia, was an inventor and entrepreneur, and maker of stringed instruments. His inventions include the resonator guitar and important contributions in the early development of the electric guitar. His father, Jozef, played and constructed his own violins; the makers of which were popular around Slovakia for their craftsmanship. Under his father's guidance, John built his first fiddle still in his boyhood days in Dolná Krupá. In 1908, the Dopyeras emigrated from Slovakia to California, sensing a war would erupt in Europe. In the 1920s, Dopyera founded his own store in Los Angeles where he worked making and repairing fiddles, banjos, and other wooden string instruments. Around this time, Dopyera patented several improvements on the banjo. A local vaudeville promoter, George Beauchamp asked John to come up with a loud guitar to cut through the sound of the small orchestras at his shows. John's solution was a metal guitar body with three aluminum cones under the bridge which picked up and amplified the vibration of the strings, causing the body of the guitar to act like a speaker cabinet. John and his brothers helped to set up the National Stringed Instrument Corp. in 1927. A single-cone resonator, or 'biscuit' design was developed and this and the original tri-cone design went on to sell in tens of thousands. The following year, John and his brothers set up their own 'Dobro' company (a contraction of Dopyera Bros. which also translates in Slovak as 'good') to continue developing their resonator guitars with wooden bodies.

Alois Fogl (1925–2021), b. Mistrovice, Czech., Bohemia, a violin builder, son-in-law of Anton Wilfer, took over the management of Wilfer's violin shop and concentrated mainly on restoration of violins. He also studied in Luby, specialized in the making of bows (about 24 by 1978) and the building and repair of violins. He settled in Montreal in 1949. The shop flourished, servicing the community of Montreal string players, including those from the Montreal Symphony, the freelance pool, teachers, and students, who enjoyed conversation with the two luthiers (the other, Ewald Fuchs) as much as their professional expertise. The shop closed in 1996.

Ewald Fuchs (1932–1991), b. Luby, Czech., a violin builder, son in law of Anton Wilfer, took over the management of Wilfer's violin shop and concentrated mainly on restoration of violins. He studied for three-and-a-half years in Mittenwald and worked 1950–55 in Switzerland before settling in Montreal in 1956. He made violins, violas, cellos, and guitars. The shop flourished, servicing the community of Montreal string players, including those from the Montreal Symphony, the freelance pool, teachers, and students, who enjoyed conversation with the two luthiers (the other, Alois Fogl) as much as their professional expertise. The shop closed in 1996.

John Rudolph Janac (1913-1981), b. Slovakia; music instrument manufacturer; partner of White Eagle Rawhide Mfg. Co. (WERCO), Chicago (1944-67), president and owner (s. 1967).

Joseph Jiran (1869-1957), b. Bohemia, was owner of two musical instrument stores in Chicago and Berwyn, IL. He arrived in the US in 1897. While still in Bohemia, he learned the trade of a musical instrument maker. He opened his first store in 1900 in the heart of the Pilsen district of Chicago and gradually enlarged his business and opened another store in the city of Berwyn. The latter was managed by his son Charles J. Jiran.

Ladislav Kaplan (1874-1962), b. Czech., was an American violin maker. He was a string maker and inventor of string-making tools and machines. He owned Kaplan Musical String Company, Rowayton, South Norwalk, CT. His violins were hand-made. They were not ordinary violins, but the kind bought by concert violinists, orchestra members and music teachers from all over the United States. Some said his violins were better than the famous Stradivarius. "My violins have been tested against his many times," Mr. Kaplan said simply "and they generally always sound better." The Rowayton inventor's instruments were hand-made after his own design, measured with scientific equipment for wood and string thickness and varnished with a mixture he formulated after years of painstaking experimentation. He was seven years old, when he first took violin lessons from teachers in Czechoslovakia. At 12, he presumably played first violin with a symphony orchestra and has played in many concerts. He moved to America when he was 19 and started his lifework with the violin by designing machines for the manufacture of strings. He made 14 machines, he said, and his strings became so well known that they were even exported to Germany, from which they all came. "Our strings are known all around the world," he said. Contrary to popular conception, Kaplan said, violin strings are made from the intestines of sheep, not cats. His company was located in a private home at the rear of the 12-room Victorian residence in which he lived alone. The Kaplan company turned out approximately 4,000 strings a week ranging in price from 25 cents for a violin E string to $7.50 for a base-fiddle string.

Martin Klema (1976-), b. Ilava, Slovakia, is an acoustic guitar maker. He studied guitar production in Luby near Cheb with Master Pavel Jung, a member of the Czech Violin and Guitar Master Association. He started making his own line of acoustic guitars at the beginning of the new Millennium.

Joseph Kun (1930-1996), b. Košice, Czech., was a bow maker and violin maker. He was a renowned violin pedagogue in his native Czechoslovakia before emigrating to Canada in

1968. He began crafting fine bows around 1972 and is credited with training Reid Hudson in the late 70's. Joseph won many awards throughout his lifetime and has co-authored *The Art of Bowmaking* along with Joseph Rech. Kun products have been known and appreciated worldwide for over 35 years. The first Kun rest was designed and patented by Violin and Bow Maker Joseph Kun. Prior to the introduction of Kun rests in the marketplace, there were very few such devices available, with players often having to struggle with limited and makeshift solutions to correct or avoid discomfort while playing their violin or viola. The early Kun rest possessed two breakthrough characteristics: a new ergonomic shape for ease and comfort in playing and simple mechanisms allowing the rest to be adjusted in three directions. As well, the Kun rest had been designed with sound quality in mind. The objective was minimal contact with the instrument, so that vibrations would not be absorbed. Thus, Kun basically established the world market for shoulder rests. Kun's original prototype pioneered the market, and its original shape remains popular today. Together with all of the important features of Kun rests, it provides the ideal in shoulder rest functionality.

Peter Mach (1945–), b. Brezce, Czech., studied the art of violin-making under Joseph Kun, a fellow Czech and a luthier and bow maker. In 1976, Mach enrolled in the International School of Violin-Making in Cremona, Italy. After graduating in 1980, Mach opened his own luthier's shop in Aylmer, Quebec, where he makes violins, violas, cellos, and double basses, and bows, and repairs string instruments and bows. In 1997, Mach developed a shoulder rest, which he called the Mach One Shoulder Rest. This rest is available for violin and viola. This is the first wooden rest on the market to be hand-crafted out of maple. The rest has an ergonomic "S" shape that hugs the shoulder and a simple design that allows width and height adjustments. The attaching feet of the rest are molded out of a single piece of rubber. This means that the rest has minimal direct contact with the instrument, which prevents scratches on the instrument. Musicians such as André Rieu (a Holland-based musician who conducts and owns the Strauss orchestra) have praised the natural look of the rest's wood, which matches the back of the instrument. Some players, especially violists, have noticed that the rest actually improves the sound of their instruments.

Sigurd Sabathil (1939–), b. Prameny, Bohemia, became co-partner, with his father Simon, of the firm Sabathil & Son Ltd. Vancouver harpsichord makers, in Vancouver, Canada, where they immigrated. By the 1970s, the company was producing three clavichord models and nine harpsichord models, including three with double keyboards and one with pedal. Other instruments have been custom-made, including a double-ended one. By 1980, the company had turned to the manufacture of historical reproductions, e.g. 17th-century Flemish single keyboard (after Andreas Ruckers) and 18th century French single and double keyboard models. Sabathil & Son have employed aluminum frames in their instruments to achieve stable tuning and audibility in modern halls and by 1991 were using 300-year-old cedar in the soundboards. The keyboards and some basic materials were formerly imported, but in 1980, the firm began to make its own keyboards. The quality of sound and craftsmanship and decoration are particularly impressive. Sabathil instruments have been purchased by colleges, conservatories, and individuals in North America and Europe. About 30 per cent of the instruments (produced in the 1970s at a rate of about 100 annually but by the early 1990s at a rate of between 10 and 30 annually) have been sold in Canada. The company has issued three demonstration records.

Simon Sabathil (1896–1980), b. Prameny, Bohemia, was a harpsichord and organ manufacturer. In 1960, he and his son Sigurd emigrated to Canada from Mariánské Lázněe where they moved from Prameny in 1945. Simon Sr. was a prominent leader of the Prameny Choir, which he accompanied as a piano master in performances, often on the organ. Under his leadership, the spring choir won the greatest honors in the area and gained the greatest fame during the years of its operation. In Vancouver, Sabathil & Son founded a harpsichord and organ company in 1970. During the 1970s, they managed to create a new original way of creating tones in these instruments, mimicking the sound that these instruments had in the 17th and 18th centuries. Their method is generally applied today. This made it possible to use these instruments in large modern halls while maintaining the fidelity of the tones. Today, Sabathil & Son is one of Canada's best-known musical instrument companies.

Fredolin Schimmel (1862–1929), b. Stará Oleška, Bohemia, was a piano manufacturer. He learned cabinet making in Riesa (1879) and piano making trade in Leipzig (1882). He worked at his trade in Germany and came to the US in 1890. He was employed in Mehlin Piano Factory Minneapolis (1890–92) and then was with Bush & Gerts Co., Chicago in 1892. He moved to Faribault, MN in 1893 and established a piano factory under firm name of Schimmel & Nelson Inc., manufacturing the Schimmel pianos using his exclusive patents.

David Tanneberger (1728–1804), b. Suchdol, Moravia, a joiner, who came to America in 1749, was an all-round musician, who is especially known for his organ building. In 1765, he and his family moved to the Moravian town Lititz, PA, where he set up his workshop and participated in the musical life of the community as a vocalist and violinist. He began building organs at the rapid rate of about one a year for Moravian, Lutheran and Reformed churches, as well as instruments for the Catholic church in Lancaster and for various individuals. His organs were installed in Pennsylvania, New Jersey, New York, Maryland, Virginia, and North Carolina. In all, Tanneberger produced nearly fifty organs during his lifetime. Tanneberger's reputation for building excellent, well-drafted and beautiful organs spread throughout the mid-Atlantic region and received rave reviews in the newspapers.

Carl Toth (1905-1958), b. Krásno pod Kysucou, Slovakia; in Canada s. 1925, settling in Toronto; gypsy fiddler and master cabinet maker; made 10 cimbaloms (dulcimers), modifying traditional design and also a few violins; founder of Carl Toth Gypsy orchestra, Toronto.

Joseph Urban (1821-1893), b. Černuc, Bohemia, was trained as a violin maker in Homlka. He worked in Prague before immigrating to New York in 1847. In 1852, he moved to California. After returning briefly to Prague in 1863, he settled in San Francisco, where he worked as a violin and guitar maker until his death in 1893. According to experts, Urban was the best violin maker in America, if not the best of the day.

Anton Wilfer (1901-1976), b. Luby, Czech., was a violin maker. He studied and practiced violin making in his home town before travelling in 1946 to Mittenwald, Bavaria, to perfect his work with master craftsmen. In 1951, he moved to Montreal and opened a workshop, Anton Wilfer Co Ltd., first located on Saint Catherine Street above the International Music Store. He made about 75 violins, 15 violas, 10 cellos, and 3 string basses. Wilfer worked together with his sons-in-law, Alois Fogl and Ewald Fuchs. In 1956, the shop relocated to a building they purchased at 2002 Mackay Street where it would remain a fixture for 40 years.

C. Dramatic Art

1. Stage Actors

Angélica Aragón (orig. Angélica Espinoza Stransky) (1953–), b. Mexico City, Mexico, of Czech ancestry, is a Mexican stage, film and telenovelas actress. She is known for her performances in several Mexican and American film productions, as well starred the classic Mexican telenovelas *Vivir un poco* (1985) and *Mirada de Mujer* (1997). She studied at London Academy of Music and Dramatic Arts" (LAMDA). There, for almost seven years, Angélica studied acting, pantomime, interpretative art, as well as canto and dance. In order to complete her histrionic education, she followed courses offered by The London School of Contemporary Dance, The National Dance Academy of India and by the Indian Kerala Kelandam Dance School. Back to Mexico in the early 80s, she started working in the telenovelas industry, for a local television company Televisa. After giving life to a wide range of characters, either weak or strong, subdued, or independent, sociable or secluded, kind or evil, she decided to change her production company and signed for a young, but far from intimidating production house Argos Televisión, which also brought her international acclaim for the extraordinary interpretation in *Mirada de Mujer* (A Woman's Glance). Apart from that, she had starred in no less than 24 movies, both Mexican and North American, among which the best known are *The Evil That Men Do* or *A Walk in the Clouds*. As a theater actress, Angélica, who performed plays like *Maquillaje* or *Aquila Real*. In 1999, she first directed a play, focusing on social themes *Tengamos el Sexo en Paz*. At the beginning of 2000, Angélica was back on the world's stage, with another telenovela inspired by Mexico's social, political, and educational realities, called *Todo Por Amor*, produced by Argos Televisión and broadcast by TvAzteca.

Peter Aterman (1961–), b. Halifax, NS, Canada, of Czech ancestry, is an award-winning writer, actor and stand-up comedian from Canada. He began his performing career in improv comedy and from there moved into writing and performing his own sketches. He performed his first full-length solo show, *City of Heroes*, at the Toronto Fringe Festival in 1999, and followed this a year later with his second and third solo shows, *Slaves of Starbucks* and *Donut Shop Vampires* in 2000. *Slaves of Starbucks* was remounted in 2001 in Toronto and New York, and then performed at the Edinburgh Festival Fringe in 2002, where it garnered critical acclaim and won two awards. It has since been toured in the United Kingdom. In 2004, Aterman won the Hackney Empire New Act of the Year, which *Time Out* magazine called one of the most important comedy awards in Britain. He premiered his fourth solo show, *Love and Despair: A Comedy*, at the Edinburgh Fringe in August 2004, where he won a Spirit of the Fringe award. He performs stand-up comedy in and around London, where he is now based.

Karen Blanche Black (née Ziegler) (1939–2013), b. Park Ridge, IL, of Bohemian ancestry, was an American actress, screenwriter, singer and songwriter. She graduated from Northwestern University, where she majored in theatre arts. She studied acting in New York City and performed on Broadway before making her major film debut in Francis Ford Coppola's *You're a Big Boy Now* (1966). She followed this with roles in *Easy Rider* (1969), *Five Easy Pieces* (1970), and *The Great Gatsby* (1974), the latter two of which she won Golden Globe awards for Best Supporting Actress; her performance in *Five Easy Pieces* also garnered her an Academy Award nomination for Best Supporting Actress. In 1975, she appeared in Dan Curtis's cult horror films *Trilogy of Terror* and *Burnt Offerings*; Robert Altman's *Nashville*, and *The Day of the Locust*, which earned her a third Golden Globe nomination. Other roles include *Airport 1975* (1974), Alfred Hitchcock's *Family Plot* (1976), *Come Back to the Five and Dime, Jimmy Dean* (1982), and Tobe Hooper's *Invaders from Mars* (1986). In the 1990s, Black starred in a variety of arthouse and horror films, as well as writing her own screenplays before appearing in Rob Zombie's *House of 1000 Corpses* (2003), which cemented her status as a cult horror icon. Black continued to star in low-profile films throughout the early 2000s, as well as working as a playwright before being diagnosed with ampullary cancer in 2010. Black's career spanned over fifty years and includes nearly two hundred film credits.

VIII. CULTURE: ARTS & LETTERS

Egon Brecher (1880–1946), b. Olomouc, Moravia, was a Czech-American stage actor and director. He was a 1900 graduate of the University of Heidelberg in Germany and then toured Austria and Germany acting on the stage. He also served as the chief director of the Stadts Theatre in Vienna before going to the U.S. in 1921. In the mid-1930s, he appeared in classic horror films and in the 30s and 40s in the espionage films. In 1906 and 1911, he visited to New York to act in plays in that city's robust Yiddish Theatre. In 1921, he moved to New York to act on Broadway. In the latter half of the 1920s, he was stage director and leading man for the theatrical troupe headed by Eva Le Gallienne. He moved to Hollywood in the late 1920s to appear in foreign-language versions of American films. In the mid-1930s he appeared in classic horror films *The Black Cat, Werewolf of London, The Black Room, Mark of the Vampire* and *The Devil-Doll*, and worked steadily in the espionage films of the 1930s and 1940s, his Slavic accent landing him roles both noble and villainous. One of his largest screen roles was in 1946's *So Dark the Night*.

Barbara Brecht-Schall (1930–2015), b. Berlin, of Moravian ancestry on her mother's side, was a stage actress. Brecht-Schall frequently appeared on stage with the Berliner Ensemble, founded in 1949 by her father, Bertolt Brecht and her mother, Helene Weigel. Brecht-Schall made sporadic appearances in East German films. She is especially known for her work on *Der Held der westlichen Welt* (1959), *Lotte in Weimar* (1975) and *Castles and Cottages* (1957). She was married to Ekkehard Schall. Most notably, she took over administration of her family's estate and notoriously fiercely protected her father's legacy. In theatrical and academic circles, Barbara Brecht-Schall enjoyed a fearsome reputation. As the administrator of the estate of her father, the German playwright Bertolt Brecht, she was stubborn, controlling and confrontational, frustrating and provoking of directors, editors and translators alike. Her unchanging view that "Anyone can perform papa's pieces on one condition: not a word could be added" frequently led to court battles. In February, she halted a Munich production of *Baal* reset in postwar Vietnam, saying it had too little of "papa's spirit."

Claiborne Cary (née Leachman) (1932–2010), b. Lone Tree, IA, of Czech ancestry, was a stage actress and cabaret performer. She was the younger sister of actress Cloris Leachman. Cary made her Broadway theater debut in *Silk Stockings* in 1956, later touring with the production's national tour with actor, Don Ameche. In 1957, she starred in *The New Girl in Town* at the Rialto Theater on Broadway. Her many other Broadway credits included *Hellzapoppin 67, The Supporting Cast* and the production of *Beg, Borrow or Steal*, opposite Betty Garrett and Eddie Bracken. She also appeared in television, including *Law and Order, The Dick Van Dyke Show* and *Young Dr. Kildare*. She also appeared in numerous television commercials. However, she began to focus more on cabaret productions and regional theater following the birth of her son, Berkeley Northrop. Within cabaret, she starred in and produced *Grand Slam* with Murray Grand.

Joe Chvala (1956–), b. Wisconsin, of Czech ancestry, growing up in Madison, WI set the stage for his career in theater and dance. At age 12 Chvala was cast in the title role of *Oliver!* at a community theater. He had rigorously practiced the show's tune *Where is Love?* and obviously made a strong impression at auditions. From that point on, he played Hansel, Pinocchio, and Peter Pan at the Madison Children's Theater. Chvala went on to enroll at the University of Wisconsin, Madison where he earned a B.S. in English education. During college, he auditioned at Wilson Street East Dinner Playhouse to be a singing waiter but found himself cast in the role of Lucky in *Dames at Sea*. Chvala went on to enhance various Madison stages during his college years. Acting credits from those years include *Stop the World - I Want to Get Off*, *Child's Play*, a Nixon spoof, *Trust Me*, and *Ah, Wilderness*. He has scaled the heights of the Twin Cities performing arts scene. He navigates the experimental and the mainstream with joyous assurance as both a choreographer and as a director. Chvala's innovative Flying Foot Forum percussive dance company has played in the U.S., France, and Russia. He has directed the Guthrie Theater's *A Christmas Carol* three times, is putting the finishing choreographic touches on their production of *The Music Man*; and has choreographed the Children's Theatre's staging of *Peter Pan*. It was Minnesota Opera's production of *My Fair Lady* that that put him in touch with actors and other theater artists soon after his move to Minneapolis in 1990. It was the Guthrie's 2014 production of *My Fair Lady* that he choreographed which became the biggest box office hit in the fabled regional theater's history.

Carrie Coon (1981–), b. Copley, OH, of Slovak descent, is a Chicago-based theatre, television, and film actress. Coon began her career in regional theater. After graduating from the University of Wisconsin-Madison, Coon was immediately recruited by the Madison Repertory Theatre and made her professional stage debut in a production of *Our Town*. After her debut with the Madison Repertory Theatre, Coon joined the American Players Theatre and stayed with them for four seasons. Coon moved to Chicago in 2008 and made her Chicago debut with a production of *Brontë* at Remy Bumppo Theatre Company. Coon is best known for starring as Nora Durst in the HBO drama series *The Leftovers* (2014–2017), for which she received widespread critical acclaim, winning a Critics' Choice Television Award for Best Actress in a Drama Series.

Paul Franklin Dano (1984–), b. Manhattan, NY, of Slovak and Bohemian ancestry, is an American actor and producer. Dano started his career on Broadway before making his film debut in *The Newcomers* (2000). He won the Independent Spirit Award for Best Debut Performance for his role in *L.I.E.* (2002) and received accolades for his role as Dwayne Hoover in *Little Miss Sunshine* (2006). For his roles as Paul & Eli Sunday in *There Will Be Blood* (2007), Dano was nominated for the BAFTA Award for Best Supporting Actor. He has also received awards and accolades for roles such as John Tibeats in *12 Years a Slave* (2013) and

Alex Jones in *Prisoners* (2013). His recent acting credits include the portrayal of musician Brian Wilson in *Love & Mercy* (2014).

Ernst Deutsch (aka Ernest Dorian) (1890–1969), b. Prague, Bohemia, was worldly acclaimed 'expressionist style' actor, on stage from 1914 at the Wiener Volksbuehne. He had a distinguished theatrical career under Max Reinhardt at the Deutsches Theater in Berlin. He appeared in German silent films, often playing intense, dramatic roles. In 1916, his performance as the protagonist in the world première of Walter Hasenclever's Expressionist play *The Son in Dresden* was praised. Deutsch also played the antihero Famulus in Paul Wegener's *The Golem: How He Came into the World* in 1920. As a Jew, he left Germany in 1933, moving to the U.S. in 1938. He had theater performances and recitals in NY (1938–46) and also film work in Hollywood, primarily in anti-Nazi movies. He is known by English-speaking audiences for his role as Baron Kurtz in Carol Reed's 1949 film noir, *The Third Man*. He acted under the nom de plume Ernest Dorian in English-speaking films. He returned to Vienna after the war, from 1951 he lived in Berlin, Germany. He then played in character roles, latterly white-haired, during the 1950's and 60's.

Gertrude Elliott (1874–1950), b. Rockland, ME, of Moravian ancestry, actress, was Maxine Elliot's younger sister. After making her New York debut in 1894, she acted with Marie Wainwright (1895) and Net Goodwin (1897–99), playing Emily in *In Mizzoura*, Lucy in *The Rivals*, and Angelica Knowlton in *Nathany Hale*. She made her London debut in 1899 as Midge in *The Cowboy and the Lady* and remained in England to play Ophelia in Forbes-Robertson's *Hamlet*. After the two were married in 1900, she returned to America several times, playing Maissie in the *Light that Failed* (1903), a character in the mold of Hedda Gabbler, and creating the role of Cleopatra in G. B. Shaw's *Caesar and Cleopatra* (1906). Critics praised her girlish spirit, playful humor, eloquent speech and dusky beauty. After her husband retired, she managed London's St. James Theatre (1918).

Maxine Elliott (1868–1940), b. Rockland, Maine, of Moravian ancestry, an actress, is said to have been one of the most photographed and beautiful actors at the beginning of the twentieth century. She was the star of the stage and motion pictures. In 1908, she built the Maxine Elliott Theatre on 39th Street, in the Times Square area off Broadway in New York – the first woman to finance and build a theatre there. Her first professional stage appearance was in the role of Felicia Umfraville in *The Middleman* at Palmers Theatre in New York on 10th November 1890. That was with the company of the great English actor/producer Edward S. Willard, in his first US production. She remained with Willard for the next three years, touring the USA and Canada in various productions, most notably *The Professor's Love Story*, one of Willard's greatest successes. She began to use the stage name Maxine Elliott at the suggestion of the great actor and dramatist Dion Boucicault.

Her sister Gertrude would adopt the same surname for her own stage career. As a young actress, her many boyfriends included baseball's Hall of Famer John Montgomery Ward and heavyweight champion and actor 'Gentleman' Jim Corbett. She quit her acting career during World War I to finance and staff a floating hospital to nurse wounded soldiers in France. She met her husband Nat C. Goodwin, the leading comic actor of his era, en route to Australia in 1896. Goodwin was a dedicated baseball fan/gambler, and the stage idol of George M. Cohan.

Elena Eustache (1974–), b. Czech., is a Czech-French actress. She began acting at the age of six, and at ten, began her professional studies at The Dramatic School of Arts in the Czech Republic. During this time, Elena performed on-stage in various foreign language productions at several professional theaters. Today, she speaks 12 languages. She attended high school in America at the School for Film and Television in New York City, where she studied acting. Elena attended Columbia University where she majored in Directing. She went on to study acting for three years at the William Esper Studios, in New York City-with Bill Esper as her main teacher. She took a course in stand-up comedy at "Carolines on Broadway" in New York, with Linda Smith and became a stand-up comedienne. She has since done various shows at "Carolines on Broadway," "The Comedy Store", "The Laugh Factory" (in N.Y./L.A.) and "The Improv" (in N.Y./L.A.). Elena was a contestant on *The Search for the Funniest Mom in America,* which aired on Nickelodeon TV. She was featured in the film, *The Informant* with Matt Damon. She was the star of her own televised, radio show, *Elena E, In the Heart of the Stars,* sponsored by Fred Siegel. Elena has appeared on the Comedy Central TV show, *The Burn* with Jeffrey Ross. She is currently working on her first TV comedy series, *The Ring Masters,* which she created, wrote, starring in-alongside some noted comedians. She also stars in her own TV show called, *Dr. Elena Eustache Show.* You can see her on a regular basis at, "The Comedy Store", "Laugh Factory", and the "The IMPROV". In addition to acting, directing, creating, writing and performing stand-up comedy, Elena is also a voice-over actress who specializes in foreign accents and languages.

Jack Garfein (1930–2019), b. Mukačevo, Czech., survived imprisonment in the Auschwitz concentration camp during WW2 and came to the US at age 15. After a few years of college, he became a stage actor, then a director. Garfein made his Broadway debut as a director with *End as a Man* starring Ben Gazzara. Notably Garfein produced two plays by Arthur Miller, *The Price* and *The American Clock,* and went on to direct other Broadway productions such as *The Shadow of a Gunman, The Sin of Pat Muldoon,* and *Girls of Summer.* He also directed 3 films. Garfein became director of the Studio's Los Angeles branch in 1966, and created The Harold Clurman Theatre on Theatre Row in New York City. Instructing for more than 40 years, he is one of the most experienced teachers of Method Acting.

VIII. CULTURE: ARTS & LETTERS

Sean Grandillo (1992-), b. Cleveland, OH, of Slovak descent; an American actor, singer, and musician, composer, and writer. Sean started training in theater at 17 and landed the title role on the National Tour of *The Adventures of Tom Sawyer* when he was just 19 years old. After joining SAG-AFTRA, Sean relocated to Los Angeles to take part in the Deaf West Theater's 2014 production of *Spring Awakening*, ultimately transferring to Broadway with the show in 2015. Along with voicing the role of Otto in the Broadway company, he served as the conductor for the orchestra and played multiple instruments. He was a regular on the 2nd season of MTV's *Scream* series, led the YouTube Premium series *Youth and Consequences* alongside Anna Akana, and has recurred in shows on networks including ABC, NBC, Netflix, and HBO Max. Sean also appeared in James Franco's *King Cobra* alongside Franco, Christian Slater, and Keegan Allen.

Teo Lucas Halm (1999-), b. Los Angeles, CA, of Czech ancestry, is an American teenage actor. In 2009, he was cast as a Neanderthal boy in a popular TV series *Nova*. In 2010, he was hired to play "Will Campbell" a fictitious UCLA spokesperson in a fund-raising e-solicitation to UCLA alumni. In 2012, Halm played the lead in a short coming of age film, *Waltham Vanguar*, written and directed by Bill Barke, Halm played opposite Jaime P. Gomez of *Nash Bridges* fame. In 2013, he was cast in the Disney Channel *Boy Meets World* follow-up series *Girl Meets World* as Elliot, the son of Cory (Ben Savage) and Topanga (Danielle Fishel). In 2014, he starred as vulnerable foster child Alex in the sci-fi fantasy film *Earth to Echo* receiving the Best Actor award at the 9th Annual PICK Awards for his performance. He was cast to play Frank Sullivan, Charles Bukowski's childhood best friend, in James Franco-directed movie '*Bukowski*.' He was also cast in a supporting lead role as Alex, a rebellious skater kid, in the movie *Memoria* which premiered at the Austin Film Festival October 29, 2015.

Arthur Hanket (1954-), b. Ft. Belvoir, VA, of Bohemian ancestry (son of Gen. Arthur P. Hanket), is a stage actor. He had his New York debut in 1979. He is known for *God is an Astronaut*, *American Playhouse* (1980) and *The Unit* (2006).

Václav Havelka (1885-d.), b. Borovany, Bohemia, was an actor. Since 1913, he was engaged by various operatic organizations and appeared in a number of plays. From 1905 to 1907, he was with the National Theater in Brno and from 1908-10, with Operatic Theater in Prague; with Smíchov Theater in Prague (1910-11), Moravská Ostrava National Theater (1919-20); Bratislava National Theater (1920-21). In 1921, he immigrated to America where he was active in various Bohemian theatrical enterprises in Chicago.

Božena Helclová-Snížková (1906-1997), b. Vrchotovy Janovice, studied at the Drama School of Marie Hűbnerová in Prague. She was a member of the National Theater in

Prague, a screen actress, and a member of Jan Snižek's cast in his Prague theatre. After she escaped to Germany in 1954, she began working for the Radio Free Europe in Munich, as an announcer. After immigrating to the US, together with her husband, Jan Snižek, they founded Krajanské divado (Compatriot Theatre) with which they toured across the US, visiting various Czechoslovak communities. When her husband died, she supported herself as a teacher of Czech.

Matt Iseman (1971–), b. Denver, CO, of Bohemian ancestry, is a comedian, actor, TV host and physician. He followed his father into a medical career, earning a B.A. with honors from Princeton University and an M.D. from Columbia University College of Physicians and Surgeons. He did his internship and residency in internal medicine at the University of Colorado Hospital in his home town of Denver, and later relocated to the Los Angeles area. Iseman began doing stand-up comedy, with a routine based partly on his experiences as a doctor. He worked with the improvisational comedy troupe The Groundlings, and in 2002 became a full-time professional comedian. In addition to comedy club work, Iseman's medical background has led to performing for medical and health-related organizations. He has performed at USO shows in Afghanistan, South Korea, Bosnia, and Hungary. He is best known for his role as play-by-play announcer of *American Ninja Warrior*. He became the first (and only) winner of *The New Celebrity Apprentice* in early 2017.

Fanny Janauschek (1829–1904), b. Prague, Bohemia, residing in the US since 1867, was an American stage character actress, who established an international reputation as a performer of the great tragic roles. She spent most of her career in US playing opposite Edwin Booth and other leading actors. One of her performances, especially Medea, were compared to the revered Italian tragedienne Adelaide Ristori. She became famous acting in great Shakespearean parts and other famous parts. She was particularly noted for playing Meg Merrilies, a role Charlotte Cushman made famous. In 1873, Janauschek starred in an adaptation of Charles Dickens's *Bleak House*, in which she played both the heroine Lady Dedlock and her murderous French maid Hortense, demonstrating Janauschek's range as an actress. While a famous tragic actress, Janauschek, like Sarah Bernhardt, could also perform comedy.

Peter Jurasik (1950–), born in Queens, NY, of Czech ancestry, is an American actor. He attended the University of New Hampshire, where he appeared in several plays. Peter Jurasik began his professional career as a stage actor working in off Broadway productions in New York and later in tours and regional theaters up and down the east coast. In 1975, he moved to Los Angeles beginning a twenty-five-year run as a character actor continuing to act on stage, but additionally working in feature films, in nightclubs doing comedy and especially on television with hundreds of TV appearances in both comedies and dramas.

He is known for his television roles as Londo Mollari in the 1990s science fiction series *Babylon 5* and Sid the Snitch on the 1980s series *Hill Street Blues* and its short-lived spinoff *Beverly Hills Buntz*. Peter Jurasik also portrayed Oberon Geiger, Diana's boss, in the T.V. series *Sliders*.

Markéta Kimbrell (née Markéta Nitschová) (1928–2011), b. Prague, Czech., was an American actress and professor of acting and film directing. She wed an American Army major named George Kimbrell, whom she met at a refugee camp in Germany following World War II. She moved to the United States with Kimbrell and was cast in stage, television shows and film. George Kimbrell died in 1952. She taught as a full-time professor of acting and film directing at the Tisch School of the Arts of New York University from 1970 until her retirement in 2006. In 1970, she and actor Richard Levy founded the New York Street Theater Caravan, a theater company which brought stage productions to audiences who otherwise might not have access to theater. Her target audiences included prisoners, coal mining towns, rural communities, Native American reservations, and low-income inner-city neighborhoods.

Werner Klemperer (1920–2000), b. Cologne, of Czech ancestry (son of the renowned conductor Otto Klemperer), was a comedic and dramatic actor, and singer, best known for his role as Colonel Klink on the CBS television sitcom, *Hogan's Heroes*. He twice won the award for Outstanding Supporting Actor in a Comedy Series at the Primetime Emmy Awards in 1968 and 1969. After serving in the United States Army during World War II, he began performing on the Broadway stage in 1947. Klemperer then appeared in several films during his early acting career such as *The Wrong Man* (1956), *Judgment at Nuremberg* (1961), and *Houseboat* (1958), and numerous roles in television shows such as *Alfred Hitchcock Presents* (1956), *Perry Mason* (1956), *Maverick* (1957), *Gunsmoke* (1958), *The Untouchables* (1960), and *Have Gun Will Travel* (1961), prior to his *Hogan's Heroes* role.

Jára Kohout (1904–1994), b. Prague, Bohemia, was a Czech stage and movie actor, singer and writer who emigrated in 1948 to US. During his life, he starred in about 54 Czech films, of which only four after World War II until 1948, when he emigrated. He first went to Germany and France, and later moved to the United States. He was associated with Radio Free Europe, NY, for whom he wrote numerous plays and movie scripts. He was one of the most popular film actors of the First Czechoslovak Republic, even in difficult conditions in exile eventually managed to establish itself and became very popular in the USA. After the Velvet Revolution on April 3, 1990, after 42 years of emigration, he returned to his homeland, played episodic roles in several new Czech films, appeared on radio and television, and managed to remarry a woman 60 years younger, with whom he then he also performed in public. He was known for *Ve dvou se to lépe táhne* (1928), *Vdavky Nanynky Kuličhovy* (1938) and *Nevinátka* (1929).

Leopoldine Konstantin (1886–1965), b. Brno, Moravia, was an actress who achieved the attention in 1910, for the first time, when she played Maria in the play *Gawan in Berlin*. Since 1912, she acted on the Berliner Reinhardt stage but after a lawsuit with Reinhardt, she changed to Vienna in 1916. Starting in 1912, she also played in silent movies, initially in title roles. She turned away from this medium when, after the First World War, she was offered increasingly minor parts. From 1933, she returned to film work, and in 1935, she went back to Austria. During Second World War, she was forced to exile, first to London, where she lost her son during a bombardment and later exiled to Hollywood. She is fondly remembered as Claude Rains dominant mother in Hitchcock's film *Notorious* (1946). Her works also include *Sumurûn* (1910), *Die Insel der Seligen* (1913), *Lola Montez* (1918), *Saison in Kairo* (1933), *Prinzessin Turandot* (1934), *Andere Welt* (1937) and The Swan for television in 1950. Sometimes, she was credited as Madame Konstantin.

Fritz Kortner (orig. Fritz Nathan Kohn) (1892–1970), b. Vienna, possibly of Bohemian or Moravian ancestry, was a stage and film actor and theatre director. He studied at the Vienna Academy of Music and Dramatic Art. After graduating, he joined Max Reinhardt in Berlin in 1911 and then Leopold Jessner in 1916. After his breakthrough performance in Ernst Toller's *Transfiguration* in 1919, he became one of Germany's best-known character actors and the nation's foremost performer of expressionist works. He also appeared in over ninety films beginning in 1916. His specialty was in playing sinister and threatening roles, although he also appeared in the title role of *Dreyfus* (1930). He originally gained attention for his explosive energy on stage and his powerful voice, but as the 1920s progressed, his work began to incorporate greater realism as he opted for a more controlled delivery and greater use of gestures. With the coming to power of the Nazis, the Jewish Kortner fled Germany in 1933, emigrating first to Vienna, then to Great Britain, and finally to the United States, where he found work as a character actor and theater director. He returned to Germany in 1949, where he became noted for his innovative staging and direction of classics by William Shakespeare and Molière, such as *Richard III* (1964) in which the king crawls over piles of corpses at the finale.

Ernie Kovacs (1919–1962), b. Trenton, NJ, of Slovak descent, was an American comedian, actor, and writer. He was educated at the New York School of Theatre and received the Sylvania Television Award. Joining the American Society of Composers, Authors, and Publishers (ASCAP) in 1957, he composed a number of songs and themes, a number of which were used in his famed television comedy sketches including Mr. Question Man. His other popular-songs included "Ugly Duckling", "So Good to Me", "The Patty Cake", "The Irving Wong Song", and many more. Kovacs's visually experimental and often spontaneous comedic style influenced numerous television comedy programs for years after his death. Kovacs has been credited as an influence by many individuals and shows, including Johnny

Carson, David Letterman, Chevy Chase and others. Some of Kovacs's unusual behaviors included having pet marmosets and wrestling a jaguar on his live Philadelphia television show.

Tomáš Kubínek (1965–), b. Prague, Czech., is a Canadian comedian, magician, acrobat, clown, 'certified lunatic, master of the impossible,' whose internationally acclaimed solo performances play to packed theaters around the world. At the age of three, he was smuggled out of the country by his parents to escape the 1968 Soviet invasion of Czechoslovakia, eventually settling in Canada. He became passionately interested in clowns, circus, theater, and magic and his perplexed, yet well-adjusted, parents took him to see every show that passed through town. At age 9, he presented his first performance before a circle of elderly magicians. By age 13, he had an agent. He performed in coffeehouses between folk-music acts and while still in his teens, he made his circus debut with a Brazilian clown duo as the rear half of a two-person horse. There was no turning back. Working any and all jobs related to showbiz, the enterprising Mr. Kubínek was able to save money and travel to Europe to study with some of the world's greatest teachers of theatre including; Monika Pagneaux, Pierre Byland, Jaques Lecoq and Boleslav Polívka. These studies, combined with his own tireless experiments in the art of live performance, led to the creation of his award-winning solo stage shows which play to capacity crowds at theaters, international arts festivals, and in television broadcasts throughout the world. Besides his solo work, Mr. Kubínek has had the great fortune of working with brilliantly talented theatre artists around the globe. Kubínek is the recipient of numerous international awards including; The Moers Comedy Prize from The International Comedy Arts Festival in Germany, The Schneestern Award from the International Festival of Humor in Arosa, Switzerland, and The Samuel Beckett Theatre Award from The Dublin Theater Festival in Ireland.

Cloris Leachman (1926–2021), b. Des Moines, IA, of Czech ancestry, was an American actress of stage, film, and television. She won many accolades, including eight Primetime Emmy Awards from 22 nominations, making her the most nominated and, along with Julia Louis-Dreyfus, most awarded actress in Emmy history. She won an Academy Award, a British Academy Film Award, a Golden Globe Award, and a Daytime Emmy Award. Leachman attended Northwestern University and began appearing in local plays as a teenager. After competing in the 1946 Miss America pageant, she secured a scholarship to study under Elia Kazan at the Actors Studio in New York City, making her professional debut in 1948. In film, she appeared in Peter Bogdanovich's *The Last Picture Show* (1971) as the jaded wife of a closeted schoolteacher in the 1950s; she won the Academy Award for Best Supporting Actress and the BAFTA Award for Best Actress in a Supporting Role for her performance, and the film is widely considered to be one of the greatest of all time.

Additionally, she was part of Mel Brooks's ensemble cast, appearing in roles such as Frau Blücher in *Young Frankenstein* (1974) and Madame Defarge in *History of the World, Part I* (1981). Leachman won additional Emmys for her role on *The Mary Tyler Moore Show*; television film *A Brand New Life* (1973); the variety sketch show *Cher* (1975); the ABC Afterschool Special production *The Woman Who Willed a Miracle* (1983); and the television shows *Promised Land* (1998) and *Malcolm in the Middle* (2000-06). Her other notable film and television credits include *Gunsmoke* (1961), *The Twilight Zone* (1961; 2003), *Butch Cassidy and the Sundance Kid* (1969), *WUSA* (1970), *Yesterday* (1981), the English-language dub of the Studio Ghibli's *Castle in the Sky* (1998), *Spanglish* (2004), *Mrs. Harris* (2005), and *Raising Hope* (2010-2014). Leachman released her autobiography in 2009 and continued to act in occasional roles.

Marjorie Lord (née Wollenberg) (1918-2015), b. San Francisco, of Bohemian ancestry, on her mother's side, was an American television, stage, and film actress. She was fifteen when she enrolled in both acting and ballet classes at the American Academy of Dramatic Arts and the Chaliff School of Dance in New York. Her first job was in 1936 as an 18-year-old on Broadway in *The Old Maid*. After signing with RKO Studios, she was cast in the feature films *Border Cafe* (1937) and *Forty Naughty Girls* (1937). She moved to Hollywood by the late 1930s and appeared in a string of B-movies and Westerns, and in the early 1950s, she appeared in such TV series as *The Adventures of Kit Carson*, *Ramar of the Jungle*, *Four Star Playhouse* and *Fireside Theatre*. She met actor John Archer after they appeared together in the stage production of *The Male Animal* and the couple married at the end of 1941. She earned a Universal Pictures contract and throughout the 1940s and 1950s, alternated between theater and movies, appearing in such films as *Johnny Come Lately* (1943) with James Cagney and *Sherlock Holmes in Washington* (1943) with Basil Rathbone and Nigel Bruce. In 1953, she became a household name when she was cast as the second wife of widower Danny Thomas in TV's *Make Room for Daddy* for seven seasons first on ABC and then on CBS. In February 1960, she was honored with a star on the Hollywood Walk of Fame. After the series ended, she continued to appear in theatre productions and would return to TV occasionally, appearing in the television series *Make Room for Granddaddy* (1971) and *Sweet Surrender* (1987). In 1988, she helped found the USC Libraries Scripter Award, an honor bestowed annually by the Friends of the USC Libraries. In 2005, she published her memoir *A Dance and a Hug*, which was followed up by an audio CD in which she read her book, with the prologue and epilogue read by her daughter, actress Anne Archer.

Peter Lorre (orig. László Löwenstein) (1904-1964), b. Ružomberok, Slovakia, was an actor. Lorre began his stage career in Vienna before moving to Germany where he worked first on the stage, then in film in Berlin in the late 1920s and early 1930s. Lorre caused an international sensation in the Weimar Republic-era film *M* (1931), directed by Fritz Lang, in which he portrayed a serial killer who preys on little girls. Of Jewish descent, Lorre left Germany when Adolf Hitler came to power. His second English-language film, following the multiple-language version of *M* (1931), was Alfred Hitchcock's The *Man Who Knew Too Much* (1934) made in Great Britain. Eventually settling in Hollywood, he later became a featured player in many Hollywood crime and mystery films. In his initial American films, *Mad Love* and *Crime and Punishment* (both 1935), he continued to play murderers, but he was then cast playing Mr. Moto, the Japanese detective, in a B-picture series. From 1941 to 1946, he mainly worked for Warner Bros. His first film at Warner was *The Maltese Falcon* (1941), the first of many films in which he appeared alongside actors Humphrey Bogart and Sydney Greenstreet. This was followed by *Casablanca* (1942), the second of the nine films in which Lorre and Greenstreet appeared together. Lorre's other films include Frank Capra's *Arsenic and Old Lace* (1944) and Disney's *20,000 Leagues Under the Sea* (1954). Frequently typecast as a sinister foreigner, his later career was erratic. Lorre was the first actor to play a James Bond villain as Le Chiffre in a TV version of *Casino Royale* (1954). Some of his last roles were in horror films directed by Roger Corman.

Bohumila Ludvíková (1856–d.), b. Dobrovice, Bohemia, was a stage actress. She came, together with her husband František Ludvík, to America in 1893. She was a member of the Ludvík Theater in Chicago and also its director.

Luba Mason (fl. 2018), b. Astoria, Queens, NY., of Slovak parents, was an American actress, jazz vocalist, songwriter, and dancer. She starred on Broadway, Off-Broadway, regional theaters in plays and musicals and television and film. As a singer, she has performed in International Jazz and Music Festivals as well as major jazz and music clubs around the country. Mason has trademarked her own musical format called Mixtura, "a blend of different musical currents."

Allison McAtee (1980–), b. Erie, PA, of Slovak maternal grandmother, is an American actress, best known for her role as Maggie Day in the Oprah Winfrey Network primetime soap opera, *The Haves and the Have Nots* and was promoted to the main cast in the fourth season.

Ryan McCartan (1993–), b. Excelsior, MN, of Slovak descent, is an American actor and producer, and singer. As an actor, he is known for or playing Jason "J.D." Dean in the original off-Broadway production of *Heathers: The Musical* (2014) and for playing Brad Majors in the 2016 Fox musical television film *The Rocky Horror Picture Show: Let's Do the Time Warp Again*. McCartan is also known as half of the former pop duo 'The Girl and the Dreamcatcher.' McCartan played the recurring role of Diggie Smalls on the Disney

Channel sitcom *Liv and Maddie*. Further Broadway credits include Fiyero in *Wicked* and Hans in *Frozen*.

Joshua Dylan 'Josh' Meyers (1976–), b. Bedford, NH, of Czech ancestry, is an American actor, writer and standup comedian. He went on to graduate from Northwestern University in Evanston, Illinois. After graduating, Josh moved to Amsterdam to be an actor at the famed 'Boom Chicago Theatre' which for twenty years has been a thriving European outpost for American improv comedy. While there, Josh wrote and performed with noted 'Boom Chicago' alums, including Jason Sudeikis, Jordan Peele and his brother, Seth Meyers. From Boom Chicago, Josh was hired into the cast of *MADtv* (1995), where he became known for his celebrity impressions, such as Owen Wilson and Matthew McConaughey. The sketch, 'Football Thing,' which he wrote and performed with frequent partner Ike Barinholtz, is historically one of *MADtv*'s biggest viral hits, with over 5 million views on YouTube. Meyers left *MADtv* for another Fox show, when he starred in the final season of *That '70s Show* (1998), replacing Topher Grace. Josh made his Broadway debut in *The Pee-Wee Herman Show on Broadway*, where he joined friend Paul Reubens and recreated various iconic roles - most proudly the voice of Conky Josh has been a regular contributor to *Late Night with Jimmy Fallon* (2009), starring in their parody series, 'Jersey Floor,' and is a frequent guest when he and his brother Seth play the 'SiblingWed Game,' where they compete to see who better remembers their childhood days. Recent television roles include *The Mindy Project* (2012) (as a singing male prostitute) and a regular role on *The Awesomes* (2013), an animated superhero series, where he plays the insufferable Perfect Man. Film works include Sacha Baron Cohen's *Brüno* (2009), where he played "Kookus" and the role of Liberace's attorney in the Emmy-winning *Behind The Candelabra* (2013). Josh is developing the sitcom, *Untitled Meyers Brothers Project*, for Lorne Michaels' Broadway Video along with fellow 'Boom Chicago' alum, Peter Grosz *The Colbert Report* (2005). Josh performs improv comedy regularly at the Hollywood Improv as well as stand-up comedy throughout Los Angeles and in Pasadena's famous Ice House.

Donna Murphy (1958–), b. Corona, Queens, NY, of Bohemian ancestry, is an accomplished stage and film actress, known for her most recent role as "Mother Gothel" in Disney's animated film, *Tangled*. A five-time Tony Award nominee, she has twice won the Tony for Best Actress in a Musical for her role as Fosca in *Passion* (1994–95) and as Anna Leonowens in *The King and I* (1996–97). She was also nominated for her roles as Ruth Sherwood in *Wonderful Town* (2003), Lotte Lenya in *LoveMusik* (2007) and Bubble/Raisel in *The People in the Picture* (2011). Murphy made her Broadway debut as a replacement in the 1979 musical *They're Playing Our Song*. Her other stage credits include the original Off-Broadway productions of *Song of Singapore* (1991) and *Hello Again* (1993). In 1997, she won a Daytime Emmy Award for Outstanding Performer in a Children's Special for her role in *Someone Had to be Benny*, an episode of the HBO series *Lifestories: Families in Crisis*. Her film roles include Anij in *Star Trek: Insurrection* (1998); Rosalie Octavius in *Spider-Man 2* (2004); Mother Gothel in the animated film *Tangled* (2010), and as one of the government secretaries in *The Bourne Legacy* (2012). Murphy's career also included work as a singer. She was in a band called Blessed Soul with fellow actor Eric Balfour in the early 1990s. On June 6, 2006, Murphy and Paul Oakenfold released the single "Faster Kill Pussycat," from the album *A Lively Mind*. The song became a club hit and hit number one on Billboard's Hot Dance Club Play chart. It also hit number seven in Oakenfold's native United Kingdom in June 2006. She dabbled in music again with the release of the film *Happy Feet*, in which she covered Queen's "Somebody to Love" and Earth, Wind & Fire's "Boogie Wonderland."

Pola Negri (1897–1987), b. Lipno, Poland, of Slovak immigrant father (Juraj Chalupec), was a Polish and American stage and film actress during the silent and golden eras of Hollywood and European film. Negri signed with Paramount in 1922, making her the first European actor in history to be contracted in Hollywood. She spent much of the 1920s working in the United States appearing in numerous films for Paramount, establishing herself as one of the most popular actresses in American silent film. In the 1930s during the emergence of the sound film, Negri returned to Europe where she appeared in multiple films for Pathé Films and UFA, and also began a career as a recording artist. She would make only two films after 1940, with her last screen credit in Walt Disney's *The Moon-Spinners* (1964).

Karel Neumann (1901–d.), b. Prague, Bohemia, became an actor at the age of 17. In 1923, he arrived in the US and for 5 years was employed by the Chicago Fuse Co. Later on, he became an advertising agent. He was co-editor and publisher of Gazette of Czechoslovak Theatrical Amateurs. Occasionally, he appeared on the stage where he felt at home. He was also active as an announcer for the radio hour of the Czechoslovak Radio Club, of which he was one of the founders.

Angelica Page (orig. Torn) (1964–), b. NYC, of Czech ancestry (a daughter of Rip Torn and the late Geraldine Page), is a notable actress, director, producer, and screenwriter. She began her career as an understudy in the 1993 Broadway revival of *Anna Christie*, and made her feature film debut in *Nobody's Fool* (1994). In 1998, she starred in a Broadway production of *Side Man*, which earned her a Helen Hayes Award for Best Actress. She subsequently appeared in the films *The Sixth Sense* (1999), and the political drama *The Contender* (2000). She continued to appear Off-Broadway throughout the 2000s, returning to Broadway with a supporting part in a 2012 revival of *The Best Man*. In 2015, she starred as her mother, Geraldine Page, in the touring stage production *Turning Page*, a biographical play which she also wrote. Additional film credits include Michael Imperioli's *The Hungry Ghosts* (2009), and the thriller *Never Here* (2017). On stage, Page received the Helen Hayes Award (Best Actress

2000) for her work in the Tony Award-winning *Side Man* at the Kennedy Center. This followed closely after being honored with the New York People's Choice Award in the Best Supporting Actress category (1999) for her portrayal of Patsy, a role she originated for the same production. Nominated for her second Helen Hayes Award (Best Actress 2010) for her portrayal of Ivy Weston in the Pulitzer Prize- and Tony Award-winning *August: Osage County* (Broadway and National Tour), her performance was heralded as "revelatory" by the *Chicago Tribune*. On television, she appeared as Julia Brinn in *Law & Order: Special Victims Unit* (2005); other television credits include *Law & Order: Criminal Intent*, *The Sopranos*, *100 Centre Street*, and *As the World Turns*. In 2009, she had a supporting role in the Michael Imperioli-directed drama *The Hungry Ghosts*.

Lisa Pelikan (1954–), b. Berkeley, CA, of Czech ancestry, is an American stage, film and TV actor. She attended the Juilliard School with a full scholarship to its drama division. Pelikan is primarily a stage actor and director but is also known to film audiences for her film debut as the younger version of Vanessa Redgrave's title character in *Julia* (1977). She also had the role as the widowed mother Sarah Hargrave in the film sequel *Return to the Blue Lagoon* (1991). Her first regular TV work was as maid Kate Mahaffey on the CBS soap opera *Beacon Hill*. Other high points in her career include her performances as the lusty Lucy Scanlon in the Television miniseries *Studs Lonigan* (1979), and the title character of the horror film *Jennifer* (1978). She won a Drama-Logue Award for her role in *Only a Broken String of Pearls*, a one-woman play about Zelda Fitzgerald by Willard Simms. Her stage credits are numerous.

Robert Petkoff (1963–), b. Sacramento, CA, of Slovak descent, is an award-winning American stage actor. He attended Illinois State University, studying theater. After finishing college, he began acting with the Illinois Shakespeare Festival, then continued his career in Chicago, working with the Oak Park Festival Theatre and Chicago Shakespeare Theater. While in Chicago, Robert was cast in the TV pilot *Mona*, a spin-off from *Who's The Boss*. He moved to Los Angeles and lived there for five years, where along with television work, he also worked in local theaters. He is known for his work in Shakespearean productions and more recently on the New York City musical theater stage. Petkoff has performed on Broadway, the West End, regional theatre, and done work in film and television. Petkoff was featured as "Perchik" in the Tony award-nominated 1994 revival cast of *Fiddler on the Roof* but is perhaps best known for his role as "Tateh" in the 2009 revival of *Ragtime* on Broadway. Petkoff has also provided the voices for over two dozen audiobooks, winning awards for his reading of Michael Koryta's *So Cold the River*. Married to actress Susan Wands, Petkoff has lived in New York City for the last twenty years, and often performs in benefit concerts for theater-district-related charities.

Lenka Pichlíková-Burke (1954–), b. Prague, is a Czech-American actress, director, author, and teacher. She is the seventh generation of her family to appear on stage since the eighteenth century. In 1977, Lenka Pichlíková finished her studies at the Faculty of Theatre of the Academy of Performing Arts in Prague (M.F.A.) She also studied acting with Uta Hagen and Herbert Berghof and mime with Marcel Marceau. She was a member of the Jiří Wolker Theatre company in Prague, where she had originally performed at the age of nine. While in Czechoslovakia, she performed on stage in many theatres, played in twelve films, and created over 40 television roles, rising to the rank of Advanced Master Artist. In addition to performing as a speaking actress, she was also involved professionally in classic pantomime. Since the 1980s, she has resided in the United States. In the United States, she has performed onstage in speaking roles as well as in pantomime productions for more than 25 years. Since 1988, she has been a member of the Actors' Equity Association, the union which represents professional actors. Lenka's writing credits include the full-length mimodramas, *Medea* and *Seven Sins and a Virtue*; one-person shows, including Katherine Luther; plays for children (*The Emperor and the Rabbi's Golden Secret*); and school performances (*Mother Goose, Time for Mime*) and others. In 2006, she was named the "Best Mime" of Fairfield County, Connecticut. She teaches performing arts, dramatic literature, and cultural history at SUNY Purchase and Fairfield University, and translates plays.

Nicholas Anton Podany (1996–), b. Santa Monica, CA, of Czech ancestry, has attended the Juilliard School, New York, graduating with a degree in Drama in 2018. He began his professional career onstage at age fourteen and has since then acted both in theater and in film. He is also a musician and a songwriter/composer. He is a member of Group 47 at the Juilliard School in New York.

George (Jiří) Prokop (1890–1961), b. Liberec, Bohemia, was a stage actor. As a child, he was early initiated to the theatre and played several Prague companies. He came to US in 1912 and was soon engaged by the Ludvik Stock Co., which had arrived in Chicago some two decades earlier. He was playing regularly in Thalia Theater and was very popular. He played leads in various musicals, comedies, farces, dramas, etc. and had a large following. At the height of his popularity, World War I broke out and George enlisted in the Czech unit of the French Legionnaires in the War. In 1927, he and his wife Libuše Zdenek were asked to form a theatrical group in the new building of the Sokol Slavský. The Prokops formed a group of twenty actors and opened in 1928 with the operetta *The Black Eagle*. The Prokops played to a full house with an auditorium seating two thousand people.

Vanessa Ray (née Liptak) (1981–), b. Livermore, Alameda, CA, of Slovak descent, is an American actress and singer. She is known for her role on *Pretty Little Liars* as Charlotte Drake; and also for her roles as Jenny on the legal drama series *Suits*, Teri Ciccone on the soap opera *As the World Turns*, Officer Eddie Janko-Reagan on long-running family-police drama *Blue Bloods*, and Maggie "Rocker" Sheldon on *White Collar*.

Frederick 'Fritz' Ritter (1896–1987), b. Vienna, of Moravian father, was an actor, academic and writer. He studied in Vienna and served as a soldier in World War I. After the War, Ritter worked as an actor, radio announcer and contributor to periodicals in Berlin and Munich. Most significantly, Ritter was a cast member of the first production of Bertolt Brecht's *Die Dreigroschenoper* (Threepenny Opera) in Berlin. As a 'non-Aryan,' his career as an actor in municipal theaters was cut short. He became a well-known figure of the Kulturbund deutscher Juden and performed in its production of Shakespeare's *Othello* in the Berliner Theater on Charlottenstrasse, as well as at its offshoots in other German cities. In November 1938, his contract was terminated, when the regime ordered the closure of all Jewish institutions. He gave up acting and immigrated to the Bahamas via London with his wife, the painter Ida (Ady) Lauinger (1900–1975), where, expecting to enter the United States, he gave Latin and Greek lessons. In 1944, he immigrated to the United States. Initially employed in a factory, he subsequently worked as a school teacher and studied German philology at the University of Chicago, where he received his M.A. in 1951 and his Ph.D., with honors, in 1955. He was then a professor of German language and literature at the Illinois Institute of Technology and at Indiana University from 1952–1968. During this time, he also frequently gave recitations of German works in the original and, starting in 1947, published several novels. In 1968, he retired from teaching. From 1969, he was a freelance writer and lecturer in Minusio, Switzerland (and later Chiemgau).

Susan Douglas Rubeš (1928–2013), b. Vienna, raised in Czech., is a stage actress. She had enjoyed a Broadway career where she won the Donaldson Award for best supporting actress in 1946. Breaking into American TV she played the character "Kathy" for 10 years on the daytime drama, *The Guiding Light* (1952). Moving to Canada with her actor husband, Jan Rubeš, she continued her acting career and also found time to return time to her profession by founding the Young Peoples Theatre in 1965. In 1979, she became head of Radio Drama for C.B.C. (Canadian Broadcasting Corp) Drama Canada. She was awarded the Order of Canada in 1977 and was Woman of the Year of the Toronto B'nai Brith in 1979.

Joseph Schildkraut (1896–1964), b. Vienna, of Slovak ancestry on mother's side (Ernestine Weinstein), was a stage and film actor. He began stage training with Max Reinhardt in Berlin and began his career on the stages of Germany and Austria, then made the transition to film in a few silent pictures. Schildkraut moved to the U.S. in 1920 and appeared in many Broadway productions. Among the plays in which he starred was a notable production of *Peer Gynt*. He made his U.S. screen debut in *King of Kings* (1927). A popular box office attraction, his many credits include *Marie Antoinette* (1938), *The Man in the Iron Mask* (1939), *The Three Musketeers* (1939), *Flame of the Barbary Coast* (1945) and *The Diary of Anne Frank* (1959). For television, he appeared on *Hallmark Hall of Fame, Dr. Kildare, Twilight Zone, The Untouchables* and *77 Sunset Strip*. He won an Oscar for his performance as Captain Alfred Dreyfus in the film *The Life of Emile Zola* (1937); later, he was nominated for a Golden Globe for his performance as Otto Frank in the film *The Diary of Anne Frank* (1959) and a Primetime Emmy for his performance as Rabbi Gottlieb in a 1962 episode of the television series *Sam Benedict*. He died of a heart attack at age 67 in New York City and has a star on the Hollywood Walk of Fame.

Stefan Schnabel (1912–1999), b. Berlin, Germany, of Moravian father, was an actor who worked in theatre, radio, films, and TV. He was the younger son of the classical pianist Artur Schnabel. He and his family left Berlin when the Nazi regime came to power in 1933. He eventually studied acting in London and the Old Vic Theatre. He was featured in Laurence Olivier's first production of *Hamlet* and became a friend of George Bernard Shaw after appearing in a production of *Major Barbara*. After moving to the United States in 1937, he became one of the original members of Orson Welles's Mercury Theatre repertory company. He portrayed Dr. Stephen Jackson on the CBS daytime TV series, *The Guiding Light*, for 17 years. Schnabel appeared frequently on the stage and was also in over sixty films.

Lizabeth Scott (1922–2015), b. Scranton, PA, of Slovak descent; an American actress, known for her 'smoky voice 'and being "the most beautiful face of film noir during the 1940s and 1950s." After understudying the role of Sabina in the original Broadway and Boston stage productions of *The Skin of Our Teeth*, she emerged in such films as *The Strange Love of Martha Ivers* (1946), *Dead Reckoning* (1947), *Desert Fury* (1947), and *Too Late for Tears* (1949). Of her 22 films, she was the leading lady in all but one. In addition to stage and radio, she appeared on television from the late 1940s to early 1970s.

Libby Skala (1967–2019), b. Englewood, NJ, of Czech ancestry, is a Canadian–American actress and writer best known for plays about her Austrian-American relatives. She has written three one-woman shows, *Lilia!, A Time to Dance* and *Felicitas*, and has performed them in North America and Europe. Skala is the eldest daughter of Mary and Martin Skala, a Canadian textile designer and Austrian-born financial writer for The Christian Science Monitor. After graduating from Oberlin College with a degree in English Literature/Theatre Emphasis and attending cattle calls in New York, Skala moved to Seattle where she earned her union cards and studied with Gary Austin, founder of the improvisational theatre company, The Groundlings. In 1995, Gary Austin encouraged Skala to write a one-woman show about her Academy Award-nominated actress grandmother Lilia Skala, months after her grandmother's passing. The show *Lilia!* was developed in Austin's workshop and went on to receive rave reviews internationally.

Lilia Skala (née Sofer) (1896–1994), b. Vienna, of Bohemian ancestry on her mother's side, was an actress. Before Skala decided to be an actress, she practiced architecture as a profession. She is one of the first women architects in Austria. She appeared on countless television shows and serials from 1952 to 1985 (for example, *The Alfred Hitchcock Hour* in 1965), and as Grand Duchess Sophie, kept company on Broadway with Ethel Merman in *Call Me Madam* not too many years after toiling in a Queens zipper factory as a non-English-speaking refugee from Austria. She was nominated for a Best Supporting Actress for her most famous role as the Mother Superior in 1963's *Lilies of the Field*, opposite Oscar-winning Sidney Poitier. Skala also appeared in *Ship of Fools* (1965), *Charly* (1968), *Deadly Hero* (1976), *Eleanor and Franklin* (1976), *Roseland* (1977), *Heartland* (1979), *Flashdance* (1983) and *House of Games* (1987).

Erika Alena Slezak (1946–), b. Hollywood, CA, of Moravian ancestry (a granddaughter of Leo Slezák), is a stage actress. At age 17, she became one of the youngest individuals ever accepted into London's prestigious Royal Academy of Dramatic Art, later graduating in 1966. Establishing a noteworthy reputation in theater, she performed in Milwaukee, Chicago. and Houston. She is best known for her role as Victoria Lord on the American daytime soap opera *One Life to Live* from 1971 through the television finale in 2012 and again in the online revival since April 2013. She is one of the longest-serving serial actors in American media. For her portrayal of Viki, she has won six Daytime Emmy Awards, the most of any daytime drama actress.

Walter Slezak (1902–1983), b. Vienna, of Moravian ancestry, was a character actor whose range stretched from the villainous Nazi in Hitchcock's *Lifeboat* to singing in the Metropolitan Opera's *Gypsy Baron*. He made his Broadway debut in operetta *Meet My Sister*. Other stage roles followed, including *My Three Angels* and *Fanny*. His film roles included *This Land is Mine*, *The Fallen Sparrow*, *Till We Meet Again*, *The Spanish Main*, *The Pirate*, *Call me Madam*, etc.

Otilie Splavcová-Stropnická (1866–d.), b. Prague, Bohemia, was a member of the Ludvik Theater in Chicago. She studied drama in Prague and in Paris. She had her first performance in the National Theater in Prague at the age of 18. She was then engaged for 7 years in the theater in Plzeň. Two years later, she left with her husband for America and joined the Ludvik Theater in Chicago. They toured with the company all over the US. In 1891, they came with the Ludvik Theater to Bohemia for a 3-months tour and performed in Prague – in the Píštěk and the Švanda Theatres, in Plzeň and Roudnice. She remained in America for 35 years. Afterwards she returned to Bohemia where she continued in her acting career.

Maruška Staňková (1934–2000), b. Prague, Czech., was a Czech Canadian actress and drama teacher. She had roles in Czech theatre, most notably with Laterna Magika, before moving to Canada with her husband Záviš Zeman in 1967. Before she came to Canada she acted in about 12 countries, and in about 8 different languages. Her first prominent acting role in Canada was as Mata Hari in an episode of the docudrama series *Witness to Yesterday*. She had a number of guest and supporting roles in film and television in the 1970s, 1980s and 1990s. She was known for *Quintet* (1979), *Almost Golden: The Jessica Savitch Story* (1995) and *Dreams Beyond Memory* (1988). For many years she taught the Directing, Acting and Writing for Camera workshop, teaching many of Canada's prominent filmmakers, screenwriters and actors of the era.

Brian Stepanek (1971–), b. Cleveland, OH, of Czech ancestry, is an American actor, voice actor, comedian, director, and writer. From 1985 to 1989, he attended Gilmour Academy, and went on to attend Syracuse University. He was awarded the 1998 Joseph Jefferson Award for Actor in a Principal Role in a Musical for *Me and My Girl*, at the Drury Lane Theatre in Oakbrook, Illinois. He is known for his role as Arwin Hawkhauser in the Disney Channel Original Series *The Suite Life of Zack & Cody* (2005). He was a Sector Seven Agent in the 2007 Michael Bay film *Transformers* (2007) and had a supporting role in another Michael Bay movie *The Island* (2005). He is also known for *Nicky, Ricky, Dicky & Dawn* (2014), and *Young Sheldon* (2017).

Charles Stransky (1946–), b. Boston, MA, probably of Czech ancestry, is an actor of stage, television, and film. He studied theatre arts at So. Illinois Univ., Carbondale (B.S., 1973). He performed on TV, film and stage. From Regional to Off-Broadway to Broadway theatres, the range of roles for Stransky are from Mamet to the Elizabethans. On Broadway, he was seen in the original production of *Glengarry Glen Ross* playing the hapless James Lingk. TV shows include *Newhart*, *Murphy Brown*, *Law & Order* and a recurring role on *All My Children*, plus many others. Film roles include three written & directed by David Mamet; independent films and industrials. He also narrates audio books ranging from fiction to non-fiction. Currently, he serves as producing artistic director with the Chicago Actors Theatre, Chicago. He was nominated for a 1980 Joseph Jefferson Award for Actor in a Supporting Role in a Play for *The Primary English Class* at the St. Nicholas Theater Company in Chicago, Illinois.

Nicolas Surovy (1944–), b. New York, NY, of Bohemian ancestry, was son of Walter Surovy, is a stage and screen actor. Nicolas attended Juilliard, paid for with the G.I. Bill after he completed a tour of duty in Vietnam. In 1984, he performed in *You Can't Take It With You* on Broadway, with Jason Robards and Colleen Dewhurst, while playing Mike Roy on ABC's daytime serial *All My Children*, (1970), a role to which he returned in March of 1998 for six months. As a film actor, he is known for *Anastasia: The Mystery of Anna*, (1986) *Forever Young* (1992), *12:01* 1993).

Walter Surovy (aka Szurovy) (1910–2001), b. Vienna, of Czech ancestry, was a stage and film actor. He appeared in leading roles at the Theater in der Josefstadt, the Salzburg Festival, and the Neues Deutsches Theater. He starred in several European films before moving to Hollywood, where a brief acting career led to a role in Howard Hawks' *To Have and Have Not* (under the name Walter Molnar). He was the manager and husband of mezzo-soprano singer, Metropolitan Opera star, Risë Stevens. The couple wed in 1939 and remained together until Surovy's death in 2001. They had one child, a son, actor Nicolas Surovy. In 1941, he founded the Polk-Szurovy Agency. After his wife retired, he managed the career of Erich Leinsdorf.

Elmore Rual 'Rip' Torn (1931–2019), b. Temple, TX, of Czech ancestry, is an American stage, TV and film actor whose career spanned more than sixty rears. Torn was a member of the Texas A&M University Corps of Cadets, although he graduated from the University of Texas where he studied acting under the Shakespeare professor B. Iden Payne. After moving to Hollywood, Torn made his film debut in the 1956 film *Baby Doll*. Torn then studied at the Actors Studio in New York under Lee Strasberg, becoming a prolific stage actor, appearing in the original cast of Tennessee Williams' play *Sweet Bird of Youth*. The play was a hit, closing on January 30, 1960, after 375 performances. He won a 1960 Tony Award nomination as Best Featured Actor in a Play and a Theater World award for his role as "Tom, Jr.," a role he recreated in the 1962 film. Torn earned a reputation as an actor's actor on stage, both Broadway and off-Broadway, as well as on screen. He won two Obie awards for his work off-Broadway, for Distinguished Performance in Norman Mailer's *The Deer Park* and for Distinguished Direction for *The Beard*. He had his own stage company, Torn, made his feature film directorial debut with *The Telephone* (1988). He was constantly in demand as a character actor. His best performance on film came in 'Payday' (1973), and he was nominated for a best supporting actor Oscar for *Cross Creek* (1983). Most of Torn's roles were in drama, though he was adept at comedy. His role in Albert Brooks' comedy *Defending Your Life* (1991) led to his being cast in *The Larry Sanders Show* (1992), on which he played talk show producer "Artie." Torn won six consecutive Emmy nominations for the role, winning once for Best Supporting Actor in a comedy series in 1996.

Jan Tříska (1936–2017), b. Prague, Czech., is a Czech-American actor. At the age of 19, he joined the Prague DAMU, where he studied from 1955–1959. Already during his studies, he performed on the stage of the National Theater. After graduating from DAMU, he became the youngest member of the National Theater. In 1966, he changed his engagement and went to the Krejčov Theater behind the gate. After the end of the theater, he was a guest in Kladno. In the years 1974-77, he performed on the boards of the Municipal Theaters of Prague. After signing the Charter 77 manifesto aimed at the Communist regime, he succeeded to immigrate to Canada via Cyprus and from there to the US. Thanks to Jiří Voskovec and Miloš Forman, he acquired his first theatrical role in New York a few months after arrival. In 1982, he moved to Los Angeles. His most notable film role in the U.S. was probably that of Milos, the loyal butler and personal assistant to Mr. Terry Silver, in *The Karate Kid Part III*. He also played the assassin in Miloš Forman's *The People vs. Larry Flynt*, and appeared in *Highlander: The Series* (season 5, episode 10), *Highlander: The Raven, Blizzard*, The *Osterman Weekend Ronin, Apt Pupil* (as Isaac Weiskopf), and the sequel to Stanley Kubrick's 1968 science fiction epic *2001: A Space Odyssey*, Peter Hyams' *2010: The Year We Make Contact*, among many others. After the Velvet Revolution of 1989, Tříska visited the Czech Republic to perform in movies such as *The Elementary School* (1991), *Horem pádem* (2004), the Academy Award nominated *Želary* (2003) and *Máj* (2008; based on the poem Máj by Karel Hynek Mácha). In 2002, Tříska received an Alfréd Radok Award for his performance as Lear in *King Lear* at the Summer Shakespeare Festival at Prague Castle. Although he occasionally visited the Czech Republic, Tříska remained a resident of the United States.

Robert Urich (1946-2002), b. Toronto, OH, of Rusyn and Slovak ancestry, was a stage, TV and film actor, and TV producer. He earned his Bachelor's degree in Radio and Television Communications from Florida State University in 1968 and his Master's degree in Broadcast Research and Management from Michigan State University in 1971. He joined WGN radio in Chicago as a sales account representative. He then briefly appeared as a TV weatherman, and soon realized that he wanted to become an actor. Urich's big break came in 1972 when he played Burt Reynolds's younger brother in a stage production of *The Rainmaker*. Reynolds and Urich were both alumni of FSU. Reynolds brought him to California and let him stay in his home until he got his acting break. He also recommended Urich to producer Aaron Spelling for the TV series *S.W.A.T.* (1975). Although that series lasted only one season, Spelling remembered Urich and later cast him in *Vegas* (1978), which had a longer run. He was starring in the TV series *The Lazarus Man* (1996) when he was diagnosed with cancer, which caused the cancellation of the series. The cancer went into remission after treatment, and he resumed acting again with his role as Captain Jim Kennedy III on *Love Boat: The Next Wave* (1998). The cancer would eventually claim Urich's life on April 16, 2002, at the age of 55.

George (Jiří) Voskovec (orig. Jiří Wachsmann) (1905-1981), b. Sázava, Bohemia, was a Czech-American actor, playwright, dramatist, director, translator, and poet. Throughout much of his career, he was associated with actor and playwright Jan Werich. In 1927, together with Werich, he joined the Osvobozené divadlo (Liberated Theater), where the two students had created a sensation with their 'Vest Pocket Revue' that year. In 1929, Voskovec and Werich took control of the theatre. The Liberated became a center for Czech clownery, a reaction to contemporary political and societal problems. Their performances began with the primary goal of evoking laughter through fantasy, but with the changing political situation in Germany, their work became increasingly anti-fascist, which led to the closure of the Liberated Theater after the Munich agreement in 1938. Both Voskovec and Werich fled to the United States in early 1939. For the rest of his life, Voskovec lived primarily in the United States, interrupted only by brief stays in Czechoslovakia in 1948 and in France from 1948 to 1950. Until the mid-1940s, Voskovec worked and wrote mostly with Jan Werich, but after Werich's return to Communist Czechoslovakia, they met only a few more times. Voskovec acted in 72 movies. Only the first five of these were Czech; the rest were American or British. His most famous American movie was as the 11th juror in *12 Angry Men* with Henry Fonda – where being a very recognizable European immigrant to the US was central to his role. His most famous British film was *The Spy Who Came in from the Cold*. His last movie was *Barbarosa*, with Willie Nelson and Gary Busey. In 1975, he published the Czech spoken LP record *Relativně vzato*, where he reflects on his life and world in general. Voskovec also appeared in the 1978 television film *The Nativity* and the 1980 film *Somewhere in Time*, starring Christopher Reeve and Jane Seymour.

Ruby Wax (orig. Wachs) (1953–), b. Evanston, IL, of Moravian ancestry, is an American actress, comedian, mental health campaigner, and author. After arriving in Britain from the United States in 1977 and training as an actress, Ruby Wax began her career with the Royal Shakespeare Company. She went on to a hugely successful career with BBC television as an interviewer and comedian, and has written, and edited numerous scripts for TV and film including *Absolutely Fabulous*. Ruby then turned her attention to the study of psychotherapy and neuroscience, graduating from Oxford University in 2013 with a Master's degree in Mindfulness Based Cognitive Therapy. She is also an Alumna and Honorary Senior Fellow of Regent's University London's with an MA in Psychotherapy and Counselling, and is a Visiting Professor in the School of Mental Health Nursing at the University of Surrey as well as holding an Honorary Doctorate from the School of Psychology from The University of East London. She is known for her work on *Shock Treatment* (1981), *Girls on Top* (1985) and *Chariots of Fire* (1981). She is the author of 2 best-selling books *Sane New World* and *A Mindfulness Guide for the Frazzled* which combine neuroscience, mindfulness and comedy. The hardback copy of *A Mindfulness Guide for the Frazzled* sold over 100,000 copies and is distributed in over 20 countries.

Matt Wayne (orig. Matthew Wayne Tomasko) (1986–), b. York, PA, of Slovak ancestry, is an American illusionist, producer, and television personality. He is best known for his work and skill as a performer of close-up magic. In 2005, Wayne moved to Fukuoka, Japan and lived solely by performing magic tricks. In 2006, Wayne moved back to the United States and moved to Manhattan, New York. Since September 2008, Wayne has been the sole producer behind Emmy-award winner Ted Greenberg from *Late Night with David Letterman*, and the off-Broadway comedy, *The Complete Performer*.

Helene Weigel (1900–1971), b. Vienna, of Moravian ancestry, was a distinguished actress and artistic director. She was the second wife of Bertolt Brecht and was married to him from 1930 until his death in 1956. Between 1933 and 1947, as a refugee from Adolf Hitler's Germany, she was seldom able to pursue her acting craft – even during the family's six-year stay in Los Angeles. Weigel became the artistic director of the Berliner Ensemble after Brecht's death in 1956. She is most noted for creating several Brecht roles, including: Pelagea Vlassova, *The Mother* of 1932; *Antigone* in Brecht's version of the Greek tragedy; the title role in his civil war play, *Señora Carrar's Rifles*; and the iconic *Mother Courage*. She died in 1971, still at the helm of the company, and many of the roles that she created with Brecht are still in the theatre's repertoire today.

Elmarie Louise Wendel (1928–2018), b. Howard Co., IA, of Czech ancestry, was an American actress. She spent her childhood traveling with her musical parents and dancing with her sisters in and around the Midwestern U.S. in club and concert hall venues, including the Grand Ole Opry. She eventually made her way to New York City, where she enjoyed success in both Broadway and off-Broadway theatrical productions. Elmarie's musical theater credits include *Wonderful Town, Cole Porter Revisited, Little Mary Sunshine* and *Gigi*. A national touring company of Annie took her to Los Angeles, where she made a successful transition into film and television. She garnered the role of the eccentric Mrs. Dubcek on *3rd Rock from the Sun*. She made appearances on such shows as *Seinfeld, Love & War, Murphy Brown, Murder, She Wrote*, and *Empty Nest*. She appeared in *And the Band Played On* and the 1989 film *Far from Home*.

Gisela Werbezirk (aka Giselle Werbesik) (1875–1956), b. Bratislava, Slovakia, was an actress and cabaret performer. She was a Viennese superstar of stage and screen of several decades before 1938, when she came to the US. She was known for *Jobra én, balra te* (1918), *Frau Braier aus Gaya* (1926), *Das Kabinett des Dr. Larifari* (1930), *A Scandal in Paris* (1946). She was an unattractive woman with an extraordinary stage presence and inborn sense of dramatic timing. Werbezirk quickly became a star, with her mastery of the nuances of language.

Jan Werich (1905-1980), b. Prague, Bohemia, was a notable Czech actor, playwright, writer – a legendary figure of the Czech stage and screen. He studied law at the Charles University Law School from 1924 to 1927, from which he made an early departure to begin his artistic career and forge one of the most important trio partnerships of his life with Jiří Voskovec and Jaroslav Ježek, representative of the interwar theater avant-garde and later also post-war Czech theater culture. His collaboration with Jiří Voskovec and Jaroslav Ježek lasted for more than 10 years. They formed a unique comedy act and quickly became stars of Prague's new Liberated Theatre, the First Republic's most dazzling political cabaret. Dressed as clowns and engaging in Dadaesque jokes and wordplay, the roly-poly Werich and skinny Voscovec pointedly, and often profoundly, satirized all aspects of post-World War I life. Fascism was a frequent target, but so was Communism, Nationalism, Depression-era woes, and basic human foibles. Along with the third member of their team, the brilliant composer Jaroslav Ježek, they wrote and produced 20 hit plays and revues between 1928 and 1938, among them *Fata Morgana* (1929), *Don Juan & Co.* (1930), *Golem* (1931), *Caesar* (1932), and *Robin Hood* (1933). Songs from these shows are still Czech standards. Unluckily, the Nazis didn't find them amusing and with the 1938 Munich Agreement, the Liberated Theatre was shut down. Werich, Voskovec and Ježek fled into American exile, where Ježek died in 1942. After World War II, the comedians returned to Prague and reopened their theatre in 1947, but with the Communist takeover the following year, Voscovec left his homeland for good. Werich carried on with a new partner, Miroslav Horníček, and then as a solo act, albeit with the teeth taken out of his humor by government censorship. His film work of this period is more noteworthy. He co-wrote and starred in the fairy tale feature *Once Upon a Time There Was a King* (1955), which acquired the status of a Yuletide classic and is still shown annually on Czech TV; and he lent his voice to a 1954 series of puppet films based on Hašek's *Good Soldier Švejk* by the great animator Jiri Trnka. The gradual de-Stalinization of Czechoslovakia in the 1960s led to a resurgence in Werich's topical humor and he allied himself with Dubček's 'Prague Spring' liberal reforms. Once these were crushed by the 1968 Soviet invasion, the comedian was virtually banned from performing for the rest of his life. He was restored to official honor, posthumously, after the fall of the Communist regime in 1989. A bit of trivia for fans of the James Bond films: Werich was originally cast as archvillain Blofeld in *You Only Live Twice* (1967) but had to bow out at the last minute due to illness. He was replaced by Donald Pleasence.

Cornel Wilde (orig. Weisz) (1912-1989), b. Prievidza, Slovakia, was an actor and film director. After studying at Theodora Irvine's Studio of the Theatre, Wilde began appearing in plays in stock and in New York. He made his Broadway debut in 1935 in *Moon Over Mulberry Street*. He also appeared in *Love Is Not So Simple*, *Daughters of Etreus*, and *Having Wonderful Time*. It was not until he was hired in the dual capacities of fencing choreographer and actor (Tybalt) in

Laurence Olivier's 1940 Broadway production of *Romeo and Juliet* that Hollywood spotted him. He played a few minor roles before leaping to fame and an Oscar nomination as Frederic Chopin in *A Song to Remember* (1945). He spent the balance of the 1940s in romantic, and often swashbuckling, leading roles. In the 1950s, his star dimmed a little, and aside from an occasional blockbuster like *The Greatest Show on Earth* (1952), he settled mainly into adventure films. A growing interest in directing led him to form his own production company with the goal of directing his own films. Several of his ventures into film noir in this period, both his own and other directors', are quite interesting – *The Big Combo* (1955) and *Storm Fear* (1955) - for example. He produced, directed, and starred in *The Naked Prey* (1965), a tour-de-force adventure drama that brought him real acclaim as a director. His later films were of varying quality, and he ended his career in near-cameos in minor adventure films.

Rebecca Wisocky (1971–), b. York, PA, of Slovak descent, is an American film, television, and stage actress. She is best known for her role as Evelyn Powell in the Lifetime comedy-drama series Devious Maids. She began her acting career in York at York Little Theatre, a community theater, where she said she spent most of her childhood. She also attended the Pennsylvania Governor's School for the Arts. Wisocky later moved to New York City, and graduated from the New York University Experimental Theatre Wing. Wisocky began work in the theatre, appearing on Broadway in 1995 in *The Play's the Thing*. Wisocky later performed in many stage productions, primarily playing strong women, like Lady Macbeth and Medea. In 2008, she won the Obie Award for Distinguished Performance by an Actress for her role as Nazi-era German filmmaker Leni Riefenstahl in Jordan Harrison's *Amazons and Their Men*. She also acted in several other Off-Broadway plays, including *Don Juan Comes Back from the War*, *The Tooth of Crime*, and *Hot 'N Throbbing*. Wisocky had supporting roles in number of films, including *Pollock* (2000), *Funny Money* (2006), and *Atlas Shrugged: Part I* (2011). She made her television debut in 2000, on an episode of HBO comedy *Sex and the City*. In later years, she also guest starred on *Law & Order*, *Law & Order: Criminal Intent*, *Law & Order: Special Victims Unit*, *The Sopranos*, *NCIS*, *Bones*, Emma Smith in *Big Love*, and as Queen Mab on *True Blood*.

Ed Wynn (orig. Isaiah Edwin Leopold) (1886–1966), b. Philadelphia, PA, of Bohemian father, was a popular comedian and actor. He was noted for his Perfect Fool comedy character, his pioneering show of the 1930s and his later career as a dramatic actor. He ran away from home in his teens, worked as a hat salesman, and as a utility boy, and eventually adapted his middle name 'Edwin' into his new stage name, 'Ed Wynn,' to save his family the embarrassment of having a lowly comedian as a relative. Wynn began his career in vaudeville in 1903 and was a star of the Ziegfeld Follies starting in 1914. Wynn wrote, directed, and produced many Broadway shows in the subsequent decades, and was known for his silly costumes and props as well as for the giggly, wavering voice he developed for the 1921 musical revue, *The Perfect Fool*. He became popular for roles throughout the 1950s and 1960s, best remembered for *The Ed Wynn Show* (1949), and for *Mary Poppins* (1964) as Uncle Albert, who reflects his old-style charm. He continued to perform, until he died in 1966.

Keenan Wynn (1916–1986), b. New York, NY, of Czech ancestry, was an American character actor. He was the son of vaudeville comedian Ed Wynn. Wynn began his career as a stage actor. He appeared in several plays on Broadway, including *Remember the Day* (1935), *Black Widow* (1936), *Hitch Your Wagon* (1937), *The Star Wagon* (1938), *One for the Money* (1939), *Two for the Show* (1940), and *The More the Merrier* (1941). He also appeared on radio. Wynn appeared in hundreds of films and television series between 1934 and 1986. He was a Metro-Goldwyn-Mayer contract player during the 1940s and 1950s. Wynn's film career flourished into the 1960s and 1970s, during which time he frequently appeared in such Disney films as *The Absent-Minded Professor* (1960) and *The Love Bug* (1968) as apoplectic villain Alonso Hawk. Wynn also starred in such TV series as *Troubleshooters and Dallas*.

Blanche Yurka (orig. Jurka) (1887–1974), b. St. Paul, MN, of Czech immigrant father, was an American theatre and film actress until the late 1960s. She made her Broadway debut in 1910 and established herself as a character actor, also appearing in several films.

2. Screen Actors

Anne Archer (1974–), b. Los Angeles, CA, of Bohemian ancestry, is an American actress. She was nominated for the Academy Award for Best Supporting Actress for the 1987 film *Fatal Attraction*. Her other film appearances include 'Paradise Alley' (1978), 'Patriot Game' (1992), 'Short Cuts' (1993), 'Clear and Present Danger' (1994) and 'Lullaby' (2014). On stage, she starred as Mrs. Robinson in the West End production of 'The Graduate' in 2001, and in the title role of The *Trial of Jane Fonda* at the 2014 Edinburgh Festival Fringe.

Buddy Baer (1915–1986), b. Omaha, NE, of Bohemian ancestry (younger brother of world heavyweight champion Max Baer), was an American boxer and later an actor. He moved with his family to California in 1928, living first in Livermore in 1926 and then Hayward, before settling in Sacramento in the early 1930s where he would later retire. Both Buddy and his brother Max had a large Jewish following, for they claimed Jewish ancestry on their father's side and frequently wore a Star of David on their boxing trunks. As an actor, he had important parts in seventeen films, as well as roles on various television series in the 1950s and 1960s. In films, he played giants in 'Quo Vadis' (1951) and 'Jack and the Beanstalk '(1952). When television westerns were in vogue in the 50s and 60s, he often played the heavy to super-sized heroes James Arness, Clint Walker and Chuck Connors.

VIII. CULTURE: ARTS & LETTERS

Max Baer, Jr. (1937–), b. Oakland, CA, of Bohemian ancestry, is an American actor, screenwriter, producer, and director. Baer earned a bachelor's degree in business administration from Santa Clara University, with a minor in philosophy. Baer's first acting role was in *Goldilocks and the Three Bears* at the Blackpool Pavilion in England in 1949. He began acting professionally in 1960 at Warner Bros., where he made appearances on television programs such as *Maverick, Surfside 6, Hawaiian Eye, Cheyenne, The Roaring 20s,* and *77 Sunset Strip*. His career took off two years later, when he joined the cast of *The Beverly Hillbillies* and he is best known for playing Jethro Bodine and in January 2015, after the death of Sonna Douglas, Baer became the last surviving member of the show's cast. Following the cancellation of *The Beverly Hillbillies* in 1971, Baer made numerous guest appearances on television, but he found his TV acting career hampered by typecasting. He concentrated on feature motion pictures, especially behind the camera, writing, producing, and directing. Baer wrote and produced the drama *Macon County Line* (1974), in which he played Deputy Reed Morgan, the highest-grossing movie per dollar invested at the time. Made for US$110,000, it earned almost US$25 million at the box office, a record that lasted until *The Blair Witch Project* superseded it in 1999. Baer also wrote, produced, and directed the drama *The Wild McCullochs*. Baer is credited with being one of the first to use the title of a popular song as the title and plot anchor of a film, acquiring the rights to Bobbie Gentry's hit song and producing the 1976 film *Ode to Billy Joe*, which he also directed. Made for US$1.1 million, the film grossed $27 million at the box office, and earned over US$2.65 million outside the US, US$4.75 million from television, and US$2.5 million from video. He directed the 1979 comedy *Hometown U.S.A.* before retiring to his home at Lake Tahoe, Nevada. He the continued to make occasional guest appearances on television.

Blanche Baker (orig. Garfein) (1956–), b. NYC, of Czech father, is an American stage, screen and TV actress and filmmaker. After attending Wellesley College, she took her mother's surname and made her television debut by playing the character Anna Weiss in the miniseries *Holocaust*. She won the Emmy Award for Outstanding Single Performance by a Supporting Actress in a Comedy or Drama Series in 1978 for her performance. Her feature films include *Sixteen Candles, The Handmaid's Tale* with Robert Duvall, *Raw Deal* with Arnold Schwarzenegger and the Kevin Bacon HBO film *Taking Chance*. She was part of the Yale Repertory Theatre and Anna Sokolow's dance troupe. Her theatre roles include *Steel Magnolias* and Edward Albee's *Lolita* with Donald Sutherland. Blanche is Senior Faculty at the New York Film Academy where she teaches in both the Acting and Musical Theatre Departments.

Scott Stewart Bakula (1954–), b. St. Louis, MO, of Bohemian ancestry, is an American actor and director. He attended Jefferson College, followed by the University of Kansas for a time, when he left to pursue acting, having been cast in the leading role of *Godspell*. In 1976, he was first hired professionally in the role of Sam in 'Shenandoah' and went to New York. After several small roles on television, he starred opposite Dean Stockwell in the science fiction series *Quantum Leap* (1989). Bakula played Dr. Sam Beckett, a physicist who was trapped by a malfunction of his time machine to correct things gone wrong in the past. He won a Golden Globe in 1992 for Best Performance by an Actor in a TV series – Drama for *Quantum Leap* (1989) and was nominated for a Tony Award in 1988. He also starred in the prequel series *Star Trek: Enterprise* (2001) as Jonathan Archer, the captain of Earth's first long-range starship. Today, he lives in Los Angeles, California and has a farm in upstate New York.

Michael John Berryman (1948–), b. Los Angeles, CA, of Czech ancestry on his mother's side, is an American character actor. Berryman was born with hypohidrotic ectodermal dysplasia, a rare condition characterized by the absence of sweat glands, hair, and fingernails. His unusual physical appearance has allowed Berryman to make a career out of portraying characters in horror movies and B movies, portraying mutant bikers, evil undertakers, monsters and other frightening characters. Berryman as a young man worked as a florist in Venice Beach, California, before embarking on his acting career. It was while he was working at the plant and flower shop that he was offered a role in legendary Director and producer George Pal's production of *Doc Savage: Man of Bronze*. Shortly after his acting debut, Iconic Film Director Milos Forman offered Michael the role of Ellis in the Oscar-winning film *One Flew over the Cuckoo's Nest*. Michael's major breakthrough came with his role as Pluto in Wes Craven's *The Hills Have Eyes*. Additionally, Berryman has appeared in such films as *Weird Science, Star Trek IV, Armed Response, Cut and Run, Solar Crisis, The Devil's Rejects*, and many more. He also has appeared in more mainstream roles, such as the comedy *Spy Hard* and family favorite *Scooby Doo*. Michael's many television credits include *Tales from the Crypt, X Files, The Star Trek* series as well as a recurring role in *Z Nation*.

Turhan Bey (orig. Turhan Gilbert Selahattin Sahultavy) (1922–2012), b. Vienna, of Bohemian mother and Turkish father, was an American actor. He attended the Ben Bard's School of Dramatic Art in California in order to improve his English. He later enrolled at the Pasadena Playhouse where he was discovered by Warner Bros, was given the new name of Turhan Bey, and placed into films. Popular leading man in 1940's Hollywood who, with his suave demeanor, exotically handsome looks, and well-modulated voice, was first called upon to portray mysterious or villainous characters. Soon he would be teamed with other 'exotics' (e.g. Maria Montez and Sabu) in a series of escapist adventures, filmed in glorious Technicolor and set in lands of fable, which proved most popular with movie audiences of the World War II years. But with the end of the war, his career (like that of Montez) would decline. He ultimately returned to his city of birth to pursue opportunities in commercial photographer and stage director. Returning to Hollywood after a 40-year hiatus, he made several guest appearances in 1990s television series including *SeaQuest DSV*, *Murder, She Wrote* and *Babylon 5* as well as a number of films. After retiring he appeared in a number of documentaries, including a German-language documentary on his life.

Mayim Hoya Bialik (1975–), b. San Diego, CA, of Czech ancestry, is an American actress and neuroscientist. From early January 1991 to May 1995, she played the title character of NBC's *Blossom*. Since May 2010, she has played Dr. Amy Farrah Fowler on CBS's *The Big Bang Theory*. She was nominated twice for the Primetime Emmy Award for Outstanding Supporting Actress in a Comedy Series for her work on *The Big Bang Theory*.

Camren Bicondova (1999–), b. San Diego, CA, of Slovak descent, is an American actress and dancer. Bicondova first got her start as a performer when she was enrolled in dance class at the age of 6. After her family relocated to Hawaii, Bicondova began to study at a local studio where she took heavily to jazz-funk and hip-hop styles of dance. By age 11, she had become an 'Elite Protégé' for The Pulse on Tour dance convention, traveling the country as an assistant to some of the nation's top teachers and choreographers. Bicondova first came to mainstream prominence when she was featured in the 2012 dance-drama film *Battlefield America*. That same year, her all-girl dance group 8 Flavahz was runner-up on the seventh season of *America's Best Dance Crew*. In 2014, Bicondova landed the role of a young Selina Kyle on FOX's television series *Gotham*. She earned a Saturn Award nomination for "Best Performance by a Younger Actor in a Television Series" for Season 1. In September 2015, she was listed in Variety's annual Youth Impact Report, as an artist who "represents the next wave of Hollywood savvy and talent".

Jessica Biel (1982–), b. Ely, MN, of Slovak ancestry, is an American actress, model, producer, and singer. Biel's family moved frequently during her childhood, living in Texas, Connecticut, and Woodstock, Illinois, before finally settling in Boulder, Colorado. From 2000 to 2002, she attended Tufts University in Medford, Massachusetts. As a child, Jessica initially pursued a career as a vocalist, performing in musical theater. At age nine, she appeared in several musical productions in her hometown, playing lead roles in productions such as *Annie*, *The Sound of Music* and *Beauty and the Beast*. A natural beauty, Jessica soon turned to modeling and commercial work by competing in The International Modeling and Talent Association's Annual Conference in 1994. Her television series acting debut, playing Mary Camden on the WB's #1–rated show, *7th Heaven* (1996), helped her emerge as a breakout star. She then excited and terrified moviegoers with her portrayal of Erin, "Leatherface's" greatest nemesis to date, in New Line Cinema's *The Texas Chainsaw Massacres* (2003), a remake of the famous original. Having finished filming, *Blade: Trinity* (2004) in Vancouver with Wesley Snipes, Ryan Reynolds, and Kris Kristofferson, she transported her toned and trained body of a vampire hunter/killer to Australia to fill the uniform and project the integrity of one of filmdom's first female jet-fighter pilots in Columbia/Sony Pictures new film, *Stealth* (2005), starring Josh Lucas, Jamie Foxx, and Sam Shepherd, for director Rob Cohen. Jessica's film career began at age 14 when she played alongside Peter Fonda in his Golden Globe-winning performance in *Ulee's Gold* (1997). Her other film credits include *I'll Be Home for Christmas* (1998), *Summer Catch* (2001), Roger Avary's *The Rules of Attraction* (2002), and *Cellular* (2004), which stars Chris Evans, Kim Basinger, and William H. Macy.

Karen Blanche Black (née Ziegler) (1939–2013), b. Parke Ridge, IL, of Bohemian ancestry, was an actress, screenwriter, singer, and songwriter. Black studied theater at Northwestern University at 19, before dropping out, two years later, and relocating to New York City. She studied under Lee Strasberg in New York and worked in a number of off-Broadway roles. She made a critically acclaimed debut on Broadway in 1965 in *The Playroom*. Her first big film role was in *You're a Big Boy Now* (1966), directed by Francis Ford Coppola. Shortly afterwards, she appeared as Marcia in the TV series *The Second Hundred Years* (1967). The film that made her a star was *Easy Rider* (1969), where she worked with Dennis Hopper, Peter Fonda, and a supporting actor named Jack Nicholson. She appeared with Nicholson again the next year when they starred in *Five Easy Pieces* (1970), which garnered an Academy Award nomination and a Golden Globe for Karen. Her roles mainly consisted of waitresses, hookers and women on the edge. Some of her later films were disappointments at the box office, but she did receive another Golden Globe for *The Great Gatsby* (1974). One role for which she is well remembered is that of the jewel thief in Alfred Hitchcock's last film, *Family Plot* (1976). Another is as the woman terrorized in her apartment by a murderous Zuni doll come to life in the well-received TV movie *Trilogy of Terror* (1975). After a number of forgettable movies, she again won rave reviews for her role in *Come Back to the 5 & Dime Jimmy Dean, Jimmy Dean* (1982). Since then, her film career has been busy, but the quality of the films has been uneven. She received numerous accolades throughout her career, including three Golden Globe Award nominations, two of which she won, as well as an Academy Award nomination for Best Supporting Actress.

Tyler Jordon Blackburn (1986–), b. Burbank, CA, of Czech ancestry, is an American actor and singer and a model. Blackburn started his acting career at the age of 17. He began performing in 2004 and appeared on the series *Unfabulous* on Nickelodeon. In the following year, he was a teacher in the short film *The Doers of Coming Deeds*. In 2008, he made a cameo in the film *Next of Kin*. In 2007, Blackburn appeared in *Cold Case* and *Rockville CA*, a web series launched by Josh Schwartz. In 2010, he appeared on *Days of Our Lives*, *Gigantic*, and was also in the independent film *Peach Plum Pear*. In 2010, he was cast in a recurring role as Caleb Rivers in the TV series *Pretty Little Liars*. Blackburn also starred as Pete in the six-episode web series *Wendy*, a project developed by Alloy Entertainment and

Macy's that was based on Peter Pan which premiered in September 2011. In 2012, he starred in drama *Hiding*, alongside Ana Villafañe, Jeremy Sumpter, Dean Armstrong and Dan Payne. In 2013, Blackburn starred in the *Pretty Little Liars*' spin-off *Ravenswood*. In March 2018, Blackburn joined the cast of The CW series *Roswell, New Mexico*.

Nicole 'Nikki' Margaret Blonsky (1988–), b. Great Neck, NY, of Bohemian ancestry on her mother's side, is an American actress, singer, and dancer, and Internet personality. She daily attended the after-school theatre program at William A. Shine Great Neck South High School, where she participated in productions of *Les Misérables*, *Sweeney Todd*, *Kiss Me, Kate*, and the title role of the opera *Carmen*. Blonsky began acting in 2007, first portraying Tracy Turnblad in the musical film *Hairspray*, an adaptation of the musical of the same name. The film went on to become a commercial and critical success and became Blonsky's breakthrough role. She received for it a Critics' Choice Award and a nomination for a Golden Globe Award and a Screen Actors Guild Award. She is also known for her starring role as Willamena Rader in the ABC Family series *Huge* (2010), for which she received a Teen Choice Award nomination. Her other television credits include *Valmont* and *Smash*.

Marcus Paul 'Marc' Blucas (1972–), b. Butler, PA, of Czech and Slovak ancestry, is an American actor. After Blucas failed to make it into the NBA, he moved to England, where he played professional basketball for a year with British Basketball League's Manchester Giants. He later decided to become a lawyer but changed his mind and went into acting instead. Blucas's first television role was in the television movie *Inflammable*, made in 1995. From there, he found roles in both television and film. He starred as the Basketball Hero in Gary Ross's *Pleasantville* (1998). However, Blucas finally landed his first major role in 1999 as Agent Riley Finn in *Buffy the Vampire Slayer*. After his departure from the series, he went on to act in such films as *Summer Catch* (2001), *We Were Soldiers* (2002), alongside Mel Gibson and Chris Klein, and *First Daughter* (2004), with Katie Holmes. In 2007, Blucas began to land leading roles in films such as *Thr3e* and *The Killing Floor*. In 2010, Blucas joined the cast of the ABC television drama pilot *True Blue*. Blucas was part of the regular cast of the USA Network show *Necessary Roughness* for the first two seasons, playing Matthew Donnelly. The series premiered in June 2011.

Karlheinz Böhm (aka Carl Boehm or Karl Boehm) (1928–2014), b. Darmstadt, Germany, of Bohemian ancestry, was an actor and philanthropist. Faked papers (claiming he had a lung disease) enabled him to emigrate to Switzerland in 1939, just around the beginning of World War II, where he attended the Lyceum Alpinum Zuoz, a boarding school. In 1946, he moved to Graz with his parents, where he graduated from high school the same year. He originally intended to become a pianist but received poor feedback when he auditioned. His father urged him to study English and German language and literary studies, followed by studies of history of arts for one semester in Rome after which he quit and returned to Vienna to take acting lessons with Prof. Helmuth Krauss. From 1948 to 1976, Böhm acted, first in the theater and later in some 45 films and numerous TV productions. Böhm's international breakthrough came playing opposite Romy Schneider as Austrian Kaiser Franz Joseph in the historic melodrama *Sissi* (1955). The film was a global hit and spawned two sequels. Their success led to international offers, including the leading role in Michael Powell's serial killer classic *Peeping Tom* (1960), where he plays the creepy, cinematic voyeur Mark Lewis. In the U.S., Bohm appeared as Jakob Grimm in *The Wonderful World of the Brothers Grimm* (1962) for MGM and as Ludwig van Beethoven in *The Magnificent Rebel*, part of a Walt Disney television anthology, which was released theatrically in Europe. He appeared as the Nazi-sympathizing son Paul Lukas in the MGM film *Four Horsemen of the Apocalypse* (all 1962), a remake of the 1921 silent Rudolph Valentino film. In the 1970s, Bohm worked extensively with groundbreaking New German cinema director Rainer Werner Fassbinder, appearing in four of his films between 1974 and 1975, including *Effi Briest*. He later said it was Fassbinder who opened his eyes to politics and turned him into an activist on global issues. Activism overtook acting in Bohm's life after he lost a bet on German TV show *Wanna Bet?* and agreed to found the charity Humans for Humans (Menschen fur Menschen), which raises money to help people in Ethiopia. He received numerous honors for his charitable work, including the Balzan Prize in 2007 and the Essel Social Prize in 2011 as well as, in 2003, honorary Ethiopian citizenship.

Melissa Bolona (1989–), b. Greenwich, CT, of Czech mother, is an actress and model. She grew up in New Jersey and Lima, Peru. Boloña went into acting at the age of twelve. She took acting more seriously while studying international marketing in Paris, enrolling in acting classes which she continued while studying for her degree. Upon graduation, she began pursuing acting as a profession. Boloña's acting debut was in the movies of the week *Grace of God* and *The Saint*. In the summer of 2015, she had her feature film debut as the supporting female lead in the theatrical release of *In Stereo*. She has continued her acting career regularly appearing in films since, most recently as Lisa in *The Final Wish*. Boloña has modeled for numerous magazines. She became a model for Beach Bunny Swimwear in 2013 after beating out 20,000 others in a model search. She appeared in campaigns for the brand which were shot alongside Irina Shayk. She has appeared on numerous magazine covers, most recently for *Vanidades*.

David Boreanaz (1969–), b. Buffalo, NY, of Slovak descent, is an American actor, producer and director. He graduated from Ithaca College in Ithaca, New York, in 1991 with a degree in cinema and photography. After graduating from college, David moved to Los Angeles in order to pursue a career in the movies. He is known for playing the roles of vampire-turned-private investigator Angel on *Buffy the Vampire Slayer* (1997–2003) and its spinoff *Angel* (1999–2004); FBI Special Agent Seeley Booth, a homicide investigator, on the television crime procedural comedy-drama series *Bones* (2005–17); and United States Navy SEALs Master Chief Special Warfare Operator Jason Hayes in the military drama series *SEAL Team*.

Barbara Bouchet (née Gutsler) (1943–), b. Liberec, Czech., is an American actress and entrepreneur, living in Italy. She has acted in more than 80 films and television episodes and founded a production company that has produced fitness videos and books. She also owns and operates a fitness studio. She appeared in *Casino Royale* (1967) as Miss Moneypenny, as Patrizia in *Don't Torture a Duckling* (1972), *The Scarlet and The Black* (1983) and as Mrs. Schermerhorn in Martin Scorsese's *Gangs of New York* (2002).

Adrien Brody (1973–), b. Woodhaven, Queens, New York, of Bohemian ancestry on his mother's side (son of Sylvia Plachy), is an American actor and film producer. He made debut as a 13-year-old orphan from New York City who finds a new life in Nebraska in *Home at Last*. He received widespread recognition and acclaim after starring in Roman Polanski's *The Pianist* (2002), for which he became the youngest actor to win the Academy Award for Best Actor at age 29.

Gail Brown (née Ziegler) (1937–), b. Parke Ridge, IL, of Bohemian ancestry, is an American actress, best known for her role as Clarice Hobson on the soap opera *Another World*. She played the role from 1975 to 1986 with sporadic on-off appearances following her departure. In his book, *Eight Years in Another World*, head writer Harding Lemay stated that he intended the character of Clarice to last only two days, but he was so taken by Brown's performance that he decided to add the character to the storyline. Her sister was actress Karen Black. Brown took her professional name from her first husband, Michael Quinlan Brown.

Alice Calhoun (1901–1966), b. Cleveland, OH, of Czech ancestry, was a silent screen western star. She made her film debut in a role not credited in 1918 and went on to appear in another forty-seven films between then and 1929. As a star with Vitagraph in New York City, she moved with the company when it relocated to Hollywood. For her contributions to the film industry, Calhoun was inducted into the Hollywood Walk of Fame with a motion picture star located at 6815 Hollywood Boulevard.

Sarah Anne Wayne Callies (1977–), b. La Grange, IL, of Czech ancestry, after graduating from high school, entered Dartmouth College in Hanover, New Hampshire. In conjunction with her studies, Callies remained involved in theatre. She continued her education at Denver's National Theater Conservatory, where she obtained her Master of Fine Arts degree in 2002. Callies moved to New York in 2003 and then quickly landed her first television role as Kate O'Malley, a recurring part on the short-lived CBS show *Queens Supreme*. Her first starring role was as Detective Jane Porter on The WB's *Tarzan*. After making various guest appearances on *Law & Order: Special Victims Unit*, *Dragnet* (2003), and *NUMB3RS*, Callies gained a starring role on Fox's *Prison Break* as Sara Tancredi. Her role lasted from 2005 through 2009. In 2010, Callies was cast in her biggest role to date, main character Lori Grimes on the AMC horror/drama series *The Walking Dead*, based on the comic book series of the same name, from the show's start until season three. Callies has also starred in two feature films – Universal Pictures' *Whisper* and an independent film, *The Celestine Prophecy*. In April 2010, she appeared on the Fox Television drama *House M.D.* as a patient of the week, whose open marriage fascinates House and the team. In August 2010, Callies' first screenplay, an adaptation of Campbell Geeslin's children's book *Elena's Serenade*, was optioned by producer Cameron Lamb and Canadian production company The Film Farm. Callies starred in the Nigerian movie *Black Gold* (2011) and one of the female lead roles in the Canadian thriller *Faces in the Crowd* (2011). In 2015 she co-starred Nicolas Cage, in Uli Edel's thriller film *Pay the Ghost*.

Sue Carol (née Evelyn L Jeanette Lederer) (1906–1982), b. Chicago, IL, of Czech father, was an American actress and talent agent. While at a social function in Los Angeles in 1927, a director offered her a part in a film. She took it and began playing minor parts. Carol's film career lasted from the late 1920s into the 1930s; when it ended, she became a talent agent. The last of her three marriages was to one of her clients, Alan Ladd, from 1942 until his death in 1964. One of the WAMPAS Baby Stars, she performed in motion pictures from 1927 until 1937. Among the movies in which she appeared are *Fox Movietone Follies* (1929) and *Girls Gone Wild* (1929). Her films were made in association with producer Cecil B. DeMille and Metro-Goldwyn-Mayer. After retiring from acting in the late 1930s, Carol established her own talent agency, the Sue Carol Agency. For her contribution to the motion picture industry, Sue Carol has a star on the Hollywood Walk of Fame at 1639 N. Vine Street.

Hunter Carson (1975–), b. Los Angeles, CA, of Bohemian ancestry, is the son of actress Karen Black and actor, producer, screenwriter, and director L. M. Kit Carson. He is an American actor, screenwriter, producer, and director. He is a graduate of Wesleyan University. Carson's first acting role was in the film *Paris, Texas*, portraying the character of Hunter Henderson. The film *Paris, Texas* was adapted for the screen by his father, L. M. Kit Carson. Hunter Carson received strong reviews for his performance in the film. He then starred in the 1986 remake of *Invaders from Mars*, where he co-starred with his mother Karen Black, and appeared in the 1988 comedy drama *Mr. North*, which also featured his *Paris, Texas* co-star Harry Dean Stanton. He played Bud Bundy in an unaired early pilot of *Married... with Children*. He played a 'crazy killer boyfriend' in the 2010 horror film *She's Crushed*. He co-directed with Alejandro Itkin the 2013 feature film *Single in South Beach*, a romantic drama starring Kevin Sorbo. He also directed the short *With It* (2004).

Jim Caviezel (1968–), b. Mount Vernon, WA, whose paternal grandmother was of Slovak descent, is a film and TV actor. He earned his Screen Actors Guild card with a minor role in the 1991 film *My Own Private Idaho*. He then moved to Los Angeles to pursue a career in acting. He was offered a scholarship to study acting at New York's Juilliard School in 1993, but he turned it down to portray Warren Earp in the 1994 film *Wyatt Earp*. He later appeared in episodes of *Murder, She Wrote* and *The Wonder Years*. He is known for his portrayal of Jesus Christ in *The Passion of the Christ* (2004) and for starring as John Reese on the CBS series *Person of Interest* (2011–16). His other notable roles include Slov in *G.I. Jane* (1997), Private Witt in *The Thin Red Line* (1998), Detective John Sullivan in *Frequency* (2000), Edmond Dantès in *The Count of Monte Cristo* (2002), Willard Hobbes in *Escape Plan* (2013), and Bob Ladouceur in *When the Game Stands Tall* (2014).

JoBe (or Jo Be) Cerny (1948–), b. Cicero, IL, of Bohemian descent, is a voice-over personality, character actor, producer, and director. He is best known as the voice of Pillsbury Doughboy and as Procter & Gamble's silent spokesman, *The Cheer Man*. In addition to appearing in advertising spots and commercials, Cerny has appeared in numerous films, including *Legally Blonde 2* (2003), *Road to Perdition* (2002), and *My Best Friend's Wedding* (1997). Cerny has also been featured in televised series and talk shows including *Chicago Hope* and *Oprah*, as well as appearing in numerous theatrical performances.

Alexandra Chando (1986–), b. Bethlehem, PA, of Slovak descent, is an American actress and director. Chando attended Manhattan College before becoming an actress. She is known for her role as Maddie Coleman in the CBS soap opera, *As the World Turns* and for her dual role as identical twins, Emma Becker and Sutton Mercer in the ABC Family drama series, *The Lying Game* (2011). She is also known for *Dead People* (2015) and *Construction* (2021) and was featured on MTV's *True Life: I'm Getting My Big Break* (2006). She also worked in film, including a part on *The Bleeding House* (2011) with Patrick Breen. Most recently, Chando acted on *Outcast* 2016.

Anna Chlumsky (1980–), b. Chicago, IL, of Czech ancestry on both sides of her parents, is an American film, stage and television actress. She graduated from Walther Lutheran High School and in 2002 from the University of Chicago. She rose to prominence for her role as Vada Sultenfuss in *My Girl* (1991), as well as in its 1994 sequel. Chlumsky abandoned her acting career in 1999 to study at the University of Chicago and pursued other work before returning to acting in her late twenties, starring in independent films such as *Blood Car* (2007) and *In the Loop* (2009). As of 2012, Chlumsky has a starring role in the HBO series *Veep*, for which she was nominated in 2013 for the Primetime Emmy Award for Outstanding Supporting Actress in a Comedy Series.

Kelsey Asbille Chow (1991–), b. Columbia, SC, of Czech ancestry, is an American actress. She is best known for her role as Mikayla in the Disney XD sitcom *Pair of Kings*. From 2005 to 2009, she had a recurring role as Gigi Silveri in the drama *One Tree Hill*.

George Cisar (1912–1979), b. Cicero, IL, of Czech parents, was an American actor. He performed in more than one hundred roles in two decades as a character actor in film and television, often in prominent Hollywood productions. He frequently played background parts such as policemen or bartenders. He made his motion picture debut in *Call Northside 777* (1948), followed by *Batman and Robin* (1949). In 1949, Cisar co-starred with a young Mike Wallace in the short-lived police drama *Stand by for Crime*. Among Cisar's more frequent roles was from 1960 to 1963 as Sgt. Theodore Mooney in thirty-one episodes of CBS's *Dennis the Menace*. Oddly, series co-star Gale Gordon took the name 'Theodore Mooney' and added the middle initial 'J.' for his character, Theodore J. Mooney, a tough-minded banker on Lucille Ball's second sitcom, *The Lucy Show*. Cisar portrayed character Donald Hollinger's father in *That Girl*, the Marlo Thomas sitcom which aired on ABC, and Cyrus Tankersley on CBS's *The Andy Griffith Show* and its sequel *Mayberry, R.F.D.*

Gaelan Alexander Connell (1989–), b. Washington, DC, of Czech ancestry, is an American actor, singer and film director. He graduated from Bethesda-Chevy Chase High School and attended the Tisch School of the Arts. He is the lead singer of the band, Sweet 16. Connell appeared in 2000 in *Chocolat* as Didi Drou and in *A Dirty Shame* as Horny Kid. He also guest starred in an episode of *Law & Order*. He played the lead role in *Bandslam* – a high school outcast who becomes popular after he manages a band and discovers he doesn't have to change himself to fit in. In 2011, he appeared as Wyatt Black in Cartoon Network's TV Movie *Level Up*. In 2012, he was one of the founders of California Burrito, a quick-service restaurant chain in southern India.

Tony Curtis (orig. Bernard Schwartz) (1925–2010), b. Bronx, NYC, of Slovak ancestry, is film actor. His career spanned six decades but who achieved the height of his popularity in the 1950s and early 1960s. He acted in more than 100 films in roles covering a wide range of genres, from light comedy to serious drama. In his later years, Curtis also made numerous television appearances.

Jamie Lee Curtis (1958–), b. Santa Monica, CA, of Slovak descent, a daughter of Tony Curtis, is an American actress and author. She got her big break at acting in 1978 when she won the role of Laurie Strode in *Halloween* (1978). After that, she became famous for roles in movies like *Trading Places* (1983), *Perfect* (1985) and *A Fish Called Wanda* (1988). She starred in one of the biggest action films ever, *True Lies* (1994), for which she won a Golden Globe Award for her performance. Curtis also appeared on *Buck Rogers in the 25th Century* (1979) and starred in *Death of a Centerfold: The Dorothy Stratten Story* (1981) as the title role. Her first starring role was opposite Richard Lewis on the ABC situation comedy *Anything But Love* (1989). In 1998, she starred in *Halloween H20: 20 Years Later* (1998) in which she reprised her role that made her famous back in 1978.

Henry Czerny (1959–), b. Toronto, Ont., Canada, possibly of Czech ancestry, is a Canadian American film, stage, and television actor. He is known for his roles in the films *The Boys of St. Vincent*, *Mission: Impossible*, *Clear and Present Danger*, *The Ice Storm*, *The Exorcism of Emily Rose*, *Fido*, *Remember*, and *Ready or Not* and has appeared in numerous television programs in both guest and starring roles, including a regular role as Conrad Grayson on the ABC primetime soap opera *Revenge*. Czerny has received the Theatre World Award and two Gemini Awards, and was nominated for the Canadian Screen Award for Best Supporting Actor for his performance in *The Other Half*.

Alexandra Anna Daddario (1986–), born in New York City, of Czech and Slovak ancestry, is an American actress, known to film audiences as Annabeth Chase in the 2010 film *Percy Jackson & the Olympians: The Lightning Thief*. She also appeared in films like *Texas Chainsaw 3D*, *Bereavement* and *Hall Pass* and guest-starred in TV shows including *White Collar*, *Its Always Sunny in Philadelphia* and *True Detective*.

Matthew Daddario (1987–), b. New York, NY, of Slovak ancestry, is an actor, producer, and director. He is the younger brother of actress Alexandra Daddario. He is best known for his role as Alec Lightwood on the Freeform television series *Shadowhunters* (2016–19).

Brant Daugherty (1985–), b. Mason, OH, of Slovak descent, is an American actor, known for his recurring role as Noel Kahn on the teen drama television series, *Pretty Little Liars*.

Lucy DeCoutere (1970–), b. Canada, of Czech mother, is a Canadian actress best known for her role as the character Lucy in the hit television series *Trailer Park Boys*.

Donald John 'Don' DeFore (1913–1993), b. Cedar Rapids, IA, of Czech ancestry on his mother's side, was an American film, radio, and television actor. DeFore is best known as Erskin 'Thorny' Thornberry, the Nelson family's neighbor on the long running sitcom *The Adventures of Ozzie and Harriet* and as George 'Mr. B.' Baxter on the 1960s sitcom *Hazel*. A longtime Republican, DeFore was a delegate at the 1980 Republican National Convention. His friend, former actor and 40th President Ronald Reagan, appointed him to the Presidential Advisory Council to the Peace Corps.

Lya De Putti (1897–1931), b. Vojčice, Slovakia; film actress of the silent era, noted for her portrayal of vamp characters; in US s. 1926.

Debra Dusay (1956–), b. Venice, CA, of Czech ancestry (a daughter of Marj Dusay), is an actress. She is known for *Police Academy 2: Their First Assignment* (1985), *Remington Steele* (1982) and *Equinox* (1992). She is married to David Blocker.

Marj Dusay (orig. Marjorie Ellen Pivonka Mahoney) (1936–2020), b. Russell, Kansas, of Czech ancestry on her mother's side, is an actress known for her roles on American soap operas. She is especially known for her role as Alexandra Spaulding on *Guiding Light*, a role she played on and off, from 1993 through the show's 2009 cancellation.

Ann Dvorak (orig. Anna McKim) (1911–1979), b. New York City, of Bohemian ancestry, on her mother's side, was an American film actress. She came to international prominence in *Scarface* (1932) with Paul Muni.

Geraldine Dvorak (orig. Jeraldine Matilda Dvorak) (1904–1985), b. TX, of Czech ancestry, was an actress. She is known for her work on *No Limit* (1931), *The Story of Mr. Hobbs* (1947) and *Nothing Ever Happens*, (1933). She was used by Irving Thalberg as a stand-in for Greta Garbo (at a time when the star may have been pregnant) for long-shots and at costume fittings. Apparently, Dvorak not only possessed Garbo's exact physical dimensions (height, weight, shape), but was also able to walk and talk (affecting a fake Swedish accent) exactly like Garbo.

Charles 'Chip' Esten (1965–), b. Pittsburgh, Pa, of Slovak descent, known professionally as Chip Esten and Charles Esten, is an American actor, singer, and comedian. He graduated from The College of William and Mary. Esten is best known for his role as country singer Deacon Claybourne on the ABC/CMT drama *Nashville* from 2012 to 2018 which subsequently kickstarted his own musical career and for his role as Ward Cameron on the Netflix teen drama series *Outer Banks*. He is also best known for his comedic role in the improvisation show *Whose Line Is It Anyway?* as a series regular between 1999–2005 and returned in 2019 as a regular.

Patrick Joseph Fabian (1964–), b. Pittsburgh, PA, of Slovak paternal grandfather, is an American film, stage, and TV actor and produce. He attended Penn State University and received his Bachelor of Fine Arts in Performance. He moved to California, where he earned a Master's degree from California State University, Long Beach. He is best known for his role on *Better Call Saul* as Howard Hamlin. His film roles include *End Game* (2006), *The Last Exorcism* (2010), *Pig* (2011) and *Jimmy* (2013).

Peter Falk (1927–2011), b. New York City, of mix of Russian, Polish and Czech ancestry, was an American actor, best known for his role as Lt. Frank Columbo in the television series *Columbo*.

Oakes Fegley (2004–), b. Pennsylvania, of Slovak descent; American child actor. He is known for his supporting role as Paul Swann in the film *Fort Bliss*, for playing Samaritan's human avatar Gabriel in the series *Person of Interest*, and for starring as Pete in the 2016 Disney film *Pete's Dragon*.

Hans Feher (1922–1958), b. Vienna, of Bohemian mother (son of Magda Sonja), and also of Slovak ancestry, was born as Johannes Weiss. He was an actor, known for *Haunted People* (1932), *Když struny lkají* (1930) and *Ihr Junge* (1931). He died on April 1, 1958, in Los Angeles, California.

Tibor Feldman (1947–), b. Slovakia, of Czech-Jewish descent, is an American actor, having played roles in movies, television shows, television commercials, and stage plays. He has appeared in television dramas including: *Law & Order*, *Conviction*, *The Sopranos*, *Third Watch*, and *New York Undercover*. He has played roles in films including *Kissing Jessica Stein*, *Nothin' Goes Right*, in which he co-starred with Rodney Dangerfield and *Fat Guy Goes Nutzoid*. In 2006, he played Elias-Clark president Irv Ravitz in the film *The Devil Wears Prada*. He has starred in television commercials for companies including Microsoft, AT&T and FedEx. In 2001, he graced the cover of the *Maxwell House Haggadah*. This edition remains annually distributed during the Passover period in supermarkets across the United States. Feldman has also appeared in numerous Off-Broadway plays. He resides in New York City.

Regina Marie Fischer (aka Jenna Fischer) (1974–), b. Fort Wayne, IN, of Bohemian ancestry on her mother's side, is an American actress and director. She is known for her Emmy-nominated portrayal of Pam Beesly-Halpert on the NBC situation comedy *The Office*. She has also appeared in films such as *Blades of Glory* (2007), *Walk Hard: The Dewey Cox Story* (2007), *The Promotion* (2008), and *Hall Pass* (2011).

Dennis Franz (orig. Dennis Franz Schlachta) (1944–), b. Maywood, IL, of Bohemian ancestry, is a retired American actor. He is a graduate of Wilbur Wright College and Southern Illinois University, Carbondale, graduating from the latter with a Bachelor's degree in speech and theater in 1968. He is best known for his role as Detective Andy Sipowicz in the ABC television series *NYPD Blue*. He has also guest starred in shows such as *The A-Team*. Other major roles were on the television series *Hill Street Blues* in which he played two characters over the run of that show. Franz first played the role of Detective Sal Benedetto, a corrupt cop in the 1983 season, who later kills himself. Due to his popularity with fans, he returned in 1985 as Lt. Norm Buntz, remaining until the show's end in 1987. He also starred in the short-lived *Beverly Hills Buntz* as the same character. Franz went on to win four Emmy Awards for his portrayal of Andy Sipowicz on *NYPD Blue*. The character of Sipowicz was ranked #23 on Bravo's 100 Greatest TV Characters list.

Brendan James Fraser (1968–), b. Indianapolis, of Czech ancestry, is a Canadian-American film and stage actor. He portrayed Rick O'Connell in the three-part *The Mummy* film series (1999, 2001, and 2008), and is known for his comedic and fantasy film leading roles in major Hollywood films.

Rudolf Friml, Jr. (1910–1972), b. Los Angeles, CA, of Czech father, was an actor, known for *Sweetheart Serenade* (1943), *Up in Arms* (1944) and *Wild Weed* (1949). He was a son of the composer Rudolf Friml. He had been seen also in movies such as *Night and Day* (1946), *Hollywood Canteen* (1944), *Nobody Lives Forever* (1946), *Painting the Clouds with Sunshine* (1951), and *John Loves Mary*.

Willie Garson (orig. William Garson Paszaman) (1964–2021), b. Highland Park, NJ, of Slovak descent; an American actor. He has appeared in over 75 films, and more than 300 TV episodes. He is known for playing Stanford Blatch on the HBO series *Sex and the City* and in the related films *Sex and the City* and *Sex and the City 2*, and for his role as Mozzie, in the USA Network series *White Collar* from 2009 to 2014. He appears on *Hawaii Five-O* as Gerard Hirsch.

Sara Gilbert (née Sara Rebecca Abeles) (1975–), b. Santa Monica, CA, of Czech ancestry, is an American actress, best known for her role as Darlene Conner on the ABC sitcom *Roseanne* from 1988 to 1997, as co-host and creator of the daytime talk show *The Talk* that premiered October 18, 2010. The show features Julie Chen, Sharon Osbourne, Sheryl Underwood, and Aisha Tyler. She is also known for her guest role as Leslie Winkle on CBS's *The Big Bang Theory*. Gilbert appeared in two films alongside Drew Barrymore, in *Poison Ivy* in 1992 and *Riding in Cars with Boys* in 2001. Gilbert also had a feature role in *Light It Up* in 1999. She has had several minor roles following *Roseanne*, including short film *$30* (aka *30 Bucks*) as part of the *Boys Life 3* feature, and *High Fidelity*. She directed her short film *Persona Non Grata* in 1998.

Jack Gilinsky (1996–), b. Omaha, NE, of Czech ancestry, is an American singer. He is part of the pop-rap duo Jack & Jack, along with Jack Johnson.

Michael Gladis (1977–), b. Houston, TX, of Slovak descent, an American actor. He played Paul Kinsey in the television series *Mad Men*; he appeared in the series' first three seasons, and as a guest star in the show's fifth season.

Bruce Herbert Glover (1932–), b. Chicago, IL, of Czech ancestry, is an American character actor. In the 1950s, Glover began to teach acting. In the 1970s, he conducted acting classes with 'The Indian Actors Workshops' and had various acting studios around Los Angeles, California. He began acting with numerous appearances on various television shows including *My Favorite Martian* (1963), *Perry Mason: The Case of the Golden Girls* (1965), *The Rat Patrol* (1966), *Hawk* (1966), *The Mod Squad* (1968), *Mission: Impossible* (1970), and *Bearcats!* (1971). In 1971, Glover and jazz musician Putter Smith portrayed the assassins Mr. Wint and Mr. Kidd, respectively, in the James Bond film *Diamonds Are Forever*. Glover played a motorcycle gang leader known as Bach in the *Adam-12* episode "Log 103: A Sound like Thunder" (1969). He also played a redneck thug harassing well-meaning teenagers in the drama *Bless the Beasts & Children* (1971), appeared in *Black Gunn* (1972) and *One Little Indian* (1973), was leaning on hustler James Coburn to repay his debts in *Hard Times* (1975), and contributed another icy performance as Duffy in *Chinatown* (1974). Glover also appeared as deputy Grady Coker in the film *Walking Tall* (1973) and the sequels: *Walking Tall Part II* (1975) and *Walking Tall: Final Chapter* (1977). He remained busy through the 1980s and 1990s with more guest spots on TV shows including *T.J. Hooker* (1982), *The Dukes of Hazzard* (1979), *CHiPs* (1978), and *The A-Team* (1983). He also appeared in the films *Killcrazy* (1989), *Popcorn* (1991), and *Warlock: The Armageddon* (1993). More recently, Glover was interviewed by Chris Aable on the cable television show *Hollywood Today* (1995) and appeared in the films *Night of the Scarecrow* (1995), *Die Hard Dracula* (1998), and *Ghost World* (2001). He is the father of actor Crispin Glover.

Crispin Hellion Glover (1964–), b. NYC, of Czech ancestry, is an American film actor, director, screenwriter, recording artist, publisher, and author. Glover is known for portraying eccentric people on screen such as George McFly in *Back to the Future*, Layne in *River's Edge*, unfriendly recluse Rubin Farr in *Rubin and Ed*, Andy Warhol in *The Doors*, the Thin Man in the big screen adaptation of *Charlie's Angels*, etc.

Anna Gunn (1968–), b. Santa Fe, NM, of Slovak descent; an American actress. She is best known for her role as Skyler White on the AMC drama series *Breaking Bad*, for which she won the Primetime Emmy Award for Outstanding Supporting Actress in a Drama Series in 2013 and 2014.

Ivan G'Vera (orig. Ivan Šplíchal) (1959–), b. Prague, Czech, is a film and TV actor. He is know for Terminator Salvation (2009), Casino Royale (2006) and The Hunt for Red October (1990).

Hugo Haas (1901–1968), b. Brno, Moravia, was a Czech-American film actor, director, and writer. He appeared in over 60 films between 1926 and 1962, as well as directing 20 films between 1933 and 1962.

Wolf Harnisch (1918–1992), b. Brno, Moravia, was an actor, known for *The School Girls* (1970), *Battle of Britain* (1969) and *Roselyne and the Lions* (1989).

Juliet Hartford (1968–), b. New York, NY, of Bohemian ancestry, is the daughter of A&P heir Huntington Hartford. Her father was the original owner and developer of Paradise Island in the Bahamas. Juliet is an artist (painter) and part-time fashion model, spending time in London, Paris and New York. She has worked with Elite Model and has done shoots for both the German and American *Vogue*. Juliet appeared in the film *Plain Clothes* (1988), and she also played herself in *Born Rich*, a documentary on HBO.

Teri Lynn Hatcher (1964–), b. Palo Alto, CA, of Czech ancestry on her mother's side, is an American actress, writer, presenter, and former NFL cheerleader. She is known for her television roles as Susan Mayer on the ABC comedy-drama series *Desperate Housewives*, and portraying Lois Lane on the ABC comedy-drama series *Lois & Clark: The New Adventures of Superman*. For her work on *Desperate Housewives*, she won the Golden Globe Award for Best Actress and three Screen Actors Guild Awards, as well as a Primetime Emmy nomination.

James Haven (aka James Haven Voight) (1973–), b. Los Angeles, CA, of Slovak ancestry, is an American actor and producer. He is the son of Jon Voight and the brother of actress Angelina Jolie. Following graduation from high school, he enrolled at the USC School of Cinema-Television. While at the University of Southern California, he received a George Lucas Award for a student film he directed starring his sister. Haven began his professional acting career in 1998. He had minor roles in several films starring his sister, Angelina Jolie, namely *Gia* (1998), *Hell's Kitchen* (1998), and *Original Sin* (2001). He also appeared in *Monster's Ball* (2001). He appeared in a 2004 episode of *CSI: Crime Scene Investigation* and a 2007 episode of *The Game*. In 2005, Haven was the executive producer of the documentary *Trudell*, which chronicles the life and work of Santee Sioux musician and activist John Trudell; it won the Special Jury Prize for Best Documentary at the Seattle International Film Festival. In 2011, he served as executive producer to the short comedy film *That's Our Mary*, which follows two actresses awaiting the final casting decision for the role of the Virgin Mary at a faith-based film studio. Since 2006, James has been the executive board director of Artivist, a Los Angeles festival that highlights movies, addressing human rights, animal rights, and environmental issues.

Julie Lynne Hayek (1960–), b. La Canada Flintridge, CA, of Czech ancestry, was an American beauty queen and actress who was Miss USA 1983. She is a trained actress and has starred in successful shows such as *Dallas*, *Twin Peaks* and *As the World Turns*.

Glenne Headly (1955–2017), b. New London, CT, of Slovak descent; an American actress. She was widely known for her roles in *Dirty Rotten Scoundrels*, *Dick Tracy*, and *Mr. Holland's Opus*. Headly received a Theatre World Award and four Joseph Jefferson Awards and was nominated for two Primetime Emmy Awards.

VIII. CULTURE: ARTS & LETTERS

Logan Phillip Henderson (1989-), b. North Richland Hills, TX, of Czech ancestry, is an American actor and singer. He is best known for his role as Logan Mitchell on the Nickelodeon series, *Big Time Rush*, as well as being a member of the Big Time Rush band itself. He, along with the band, have won and been nominated for multiple awards over the past few years.

Paul Henreid (1908-1992), b. Trieste, Italy, of Bohemian ancestry, was an American actor and film director. He grew up in Vienna and studied at the prestigious Maria Theresa Academy (graduating in 1927) and the Institute of Graphic Arts. He debuted on the stage under the direction of Max Reinhardt and began his film career acting in German films in the 1930s. In 1935, he emigrated from Austria to Great Britain one year after the 1934 Austrian Civil War which ended with installation of Austrofascism. With the start of World War II, Henreid risked deportation or internment as an enemy alien, but Conrad Veidt spoke for him, and he was allowed to remain free in England. A small role in *Goodbye, Mr. Chips* (1939), and third billing as a Nazi Major in *Night Train to Munich* (1940), led to his shifting to a Hollywood career. His first film for RKO was *Joan of Paris* (1942). In 1942, Henreid also appeared in his two most important films. In *Now, Voyager*, he and Bette Davis created one of the screen's most imitated scenes, in which he lights two cigarettes and hands one to her. Henreid's next role was as Victor Laszlo, heroic anti-Nazi leader, in *Casablanca* with Humphrey Bogart and Ingrid Bergman. He made regular film appearances throughout the 1940s, and in the early 1950s began directing for both film and television. His film credits include *Between Two Worlds* (1944), *The Spanish Main* (1945), *Of Human Bondage* (1946), *Song of Love* (1947), *Thief of Damascus* (1952), *Siren of Bagdad* (1953), and *Four Horsemen of the Apocalypse* (1961). His television directorial credits include *Alfred Hitchcock Presents*, *Maverick*, *Bonanza* and *The Big Valley*. In 1964, Henreid directed *Dead Ringer*, which starred Bette Davis and featured, in a minor role, the director's daughter, Monika.

Audrey Hepburn (orig. Audrey Kathleen Ruston) (1929-1993), b. Ixelles, Belgium, of Bohemian father, was a prominent actress, model, and dancer, and humanitarian. Recognized as both a film and fashion icon, Hepburn was active during Hollywood's Golden Age. She shot to stardom after playing the lead role in *Roman Holiday* (1953), for which she was the first actress to win an Academy Award, a Golden Globe Award, and a BAFTA Award for a single performance. That same year, Hepburn won a Tony Award for Best Lead Actress in a Play for her performance in *Ondine*. She went on to star in a number of successful films, such as *Sabrina* (1954), *The Nun's Story* (1959), *Breakfast at Tiffany's* (1961), *Charade* (1963), *My Fair Lady* (1964), and *Wait Until Dark* (1967), for which she received an Academy Award, Golden Globe, and BAFTA nominations. Hepburn won three BAFTA Awards for Best British Actress in a Leading Role. She was ranked by the American Film Institute as the third greatest female screen legend in the history of American cinema and placed in the International Best Dressed List Hall of Fame.

Ashley Holliday (orig. Popelka) (1985–), b. Burbank, CA, of Czech ancestry on her mother's side, is an American actress best known for playing Chloe Delgado on the 2010 ABC Family series *Huge* and Melissa Sanders on the 2012 Nick at Nite serial drama *Hollywood Heights*. She grew up in Los Angeles and was trained at The Theatre School at DePaul University in Chicago, until she moved back to Los Angeles where she studied at the acclaimed Playhouse West, Lesly Kahn Institute and John Rosenfeld Studios. Holliday began her career at an early age, as the daughter of Stanley Tucci's character on the *Miami Vice* episode 'Baby Blues' in 1986. Her breakout role came in 2010, when Holliday booked a leading role in the ABC Family series *Huge*. In 2012, she played quirky Melissa Sanders on TeenNick's *Hollywood Heights*, followed by Rita in the film *The Man Who Shook the Hand of Vicente Fernández* and a cameo in Team Unicorn's latest music video "For the Win". In 2013, she appeared in two episodes of the *Pretty Little Liars* spin-off, *Ravenswood*.

Oskar Homolka (1898–1978), b. Vienna, of Czech ancestry, was a character film and theatre actor. Although he often played villainous roles, he was nominated for an Oscar for his portrayal of the crusty uncle in *I Remember Mama* (1948). Homolka also acted with Marilyn Monroe in *The Seven Year Itch*, with Ronald Reagan in *Prisoner of War* and with Katharine Hepburn in *The Madwoman of Chaillot*.

Steve Ihnat (1934–1972), b. Jastrabie pri Michalovciach, Czech., was an American actor, director, producer and writer. He immigrated to Canada when he was five years old, and later became a United States citizen. Ihnat moved to the United States in 1956 to pursue a career in acting and attended the Pasadena Playhouse. He was popular character performer best remembered for his role as Fleet Captain Garth of Izar on the original *Star Trek* science fiction television series. His other television credits include *Bonanza*, *Gunsmoke*, *Mission: Impossible*, *Mannix*, *Rawhide*, *The Fugitive* and many more. For feature films, he appeared in *Strike Me Deadly* (1963), *The Chase* (1966), *In Like Flint* (1967), *Madigan* (1968), *Zig Zag* (1970) and *Fuzz* (1972).

Milan Jablonský (1935–), b. Oravské Veselé, Czech., was trained as a physical educator and a coach, but decided to be an actor. He defected with his wife in 1969 to Canada, after the Soviet troops invaded Czechoslovakia, and resides in Ottawa. He is known for *Chingachgook, die grosse Schlange* (1967), *Janosik* (1963) and *The Young Lady from the Riverside* (1959).

Lisa Jakub (1978–), b. Toronto, Ont., Canada, of Slovak descent, is Canadian actress and writer, speaker, and yoga teacher. She had more than forty movies and TV shows to her name. She is best known for her role as Lydia Hillard in the comedy-drama film *Mrs.*

Doubtfire (1993) and as Alicia Casse in the 1996 film *Independence Day*. After retiring from acting, Jakub moved to Virginia and married her longtime partner, former Hollywood theater manager Jeremy Jones, in 2005. Jakub later became a writer, authoring two books called *You Look Like That Girl* (2015) and *Not Just Me* (2017) and regularly contributes to online blogs. Jakub is also a qualified Kripalu yoga teacher.

Walter Janowitz (1913–1997), b. Teplice-Šanov, Bohemia, was a character actor. He worked in Hollywood films and shows during the 1960s, 1970s and early 1980s. This includes his role of Oscar Schnitzer on the sitcom, *Hogan's Heroes* (1965–1970), *The Incredible Hulk* (1979) and *It Takes a Thief* (1968–1969).

Jessica Jaymes (1979–2019), b. Anchorage, AK, of Czech ancestry, on her mother's side, is an American actress. She is known for being *Hustler*'s first contract model and the 'Hustler Honey of the Year' in 2004 and the August 2008 'Penthouse Pet of the Month.' Jaymes played a small role in two episodes of the television series *Weeds* in 2006 and 2007 and made appearances on various reality shows such as VH1's *Celebrity Rehab Sober House* and HBO's *Vivid Valley*, as well as *The Howard Stern Show*.

Cameron Jebo (1990–), b. Santa Clara, CA, is of Slovak descent, his mom's grandfather (Robert Andrew Dopyera) was born in Krupá, Slovakia. He is an American actor, known for *NCIS* (2003), *Austin & Ally* (2011) and *Power Rangers Megaforce* (2000).

Jenteal (orig. Reanna Lynn Rossi) (1976–2020), b. Oklahoma, of Czech and Slovak descent, is the stage name of a former American pornographic actress. She had a brief appearance in the Jon Favreau/Vince Vaughn movie *Made* where she played the role of an erotic dancer and was credited under the name Reanna Rossi. Jenteal also appeared in an episode of the TV comedy program *The Man Show*, and two episodes of Playboy TV's *The Helmetcam Show*. She has at some time been a contract performer with Vivid Entertainment.

Angelina Jolie (orig. Angelina Jolie Voight) (1975–), b. Los Angeles, of Slovak ancestry, is a film actress, a former fashion model and a Goodwill Ambassador for the UN Refugee Agency. She is often cited by popular media as one of the world's most beautiful women and her off-screen life is widely reported. She has received three Golden Globe Awards, two Screen Actors Guild Awards and Academy Award. Jolies acting career began with the low budget production *Cyborg 2* (1993), and she played her first leading role in a major film in *Hackers* (1995). She appeared in the critically acclaimed biographical films *George Wallace* (1997) and *Gia* (1998) and won an Academy Award for Best Supporting Actress for her performance in the drama *Girl, Interrupted* (1999). She achieved international fame as a result of her portrayal of video game heroine Lara Croft in *Lara Croft: Tomb Raider* (2001). She was ranked among the highest-paid actresses in Hollywood with the sequel *The Cradle* of Life (2003). She continued her action-star career with *Mr. & Mrs. Smith* (2005), *Wanted* (2008), *Salt* (2010) and *The Tourist* (2010). Her biggest commercial success was the fantasy film *Maleficent* (2014). She received critical acclaim for her performances in the dramas *A Mighty Heart* (2007) and *Changeling* (2008), which earned her a nomination for an Academy Award for Best Actress. Jolie made her directorial debut with the 2007 documentary, *A Place in Time*, followed by the wartime drama, *In the Land of Blood and Honey* (2011).

January Kristen Jones (1978–), b. South Dakota, of Czech ancestry, is an American actress and model. She is best known for playing Betty Draper in the television series *Mad Men* (2007–2015), as well as for roles as Cadence in *American Wedding* (2003), Elizabeth Harris in *Unknown* (2011), and Emma Frost in *X-Men: First Class* (2011). Jones was ranked No. 82 on the Maxim Hot 100 Women of 2002. She appeared on the cover of "The Hot Issue" of British *GQ* magazine in May 2009. She appeared on the cover of the November 2009 issue of American *GQ* magazine, and has been a 'topic' in the magazine several times. On November 14, 2009, Jones hosted an episode of *Saturday Night Live* which featured the musical guest 'The Black Eyed Peas,' giving a performance that was met with negative reviews. Currently, she appears in the Fox television show *The Last Man on Earth*, playing the character of Melissa Shart. For her work on *Mad Men* she has received two Golden Globe nominations and one Emmy nomination.

Bianca Kajlich (1977–), b. Seattle, WA, of Slovak father and Italian mother, is a TV and film actress. She attended Washington State University in Pullman, Washington. Kajlich has had starring and supporting roles in television and film including the role of Jennifer on the CBS comedy *Rules of Engagement* (2007–13). Kajlich was an actress on *Bosch* as Christina Henry during Season 5 of the Amazon Prime series. She is also for *Halloween: Resurrection* (2002), *Bring It On* (2000) and *10 Things I Hate About You* (1999).

Andrew Keegan (orig. Andrew Keegan Heying) (1979–), b. Los Angeles, CA, of Czech ancestry, is an American actor best known for his roles in television shows including *Party of Five* and *7th Heaven* and in films such as *10 Things I Hate about You*, *The Broken Hearts Club* (2000) and *O* (2001).

Casey Keegan (orig. Casey Keegan Heying) (1980–), Los Angeles, of Czech ancestry, is an American actor. He is brother of actor Andrew Keegan. He is best known for *Rhythm & Jam* (1993), *Americans* (2015) and *Crossroads* (2002).

Kate Kelton (1978–), b. Bamberg, Ger., of Czech parents, is a Canadian artist, model and actress, notable for appearing as the 'Tic Tac Girl' in television advertisements for Tic Tac mints for almost a decade throughout Canada, Australia, South Africa and Israel. She is probably best known for her recurring role on Syfy's *Haven* as Jordan McKee from 2012 to

2013, appearing in 14 episodes. She first discovered acting during her final year of film school. She had her big-screen debut during the Toronto International Film Festival in *The Republic of Love* (2000), which was directed by Deepa Mehta. Her film credits include *Harold & Kumar Go to White Castle* and *American Psycho II: All American Girl*. She has also appeared in numerous music videos including Shaggy's "It Wasn't Me", Jet Set Satellite's "Baby Cool Your Jets" and "Abused" by Jason Englishman. Kate has appeared in several indie films and TV guest spots including *Detention* which starred Josh Hutchinson, and Devin Zimmerman's *Growth*. On July 16, 2012, she appeared in the music video "Love All Humans" alongside musician/composer Gingger Shankar, guitarist Anthony Gallo, model Tara Bre and others. Her artwork is exhibited internationally.

Markéta Kimbrell (née Markéta Nitschová) (1928–2011), b. nr. Prague, Czech., was an American actress and professor of acting and film directing. As an actress, she was known for *The Pawnbroker* (1964), *Playhouse 90* (1956) and *Reaching Out* (1983). In 1970, she and actor Richard Levy founded the New York Street Theater Caravan, a theater company which brought stage productions to audiences who otherwise might not have access to theater. Her target audiences included prisoners, coal mining towns, rural communities, Native American reservations, and low-income inner-city neighborhoods. She taught as a full-time professor of acting and film directing at the Tisch School of the Arts of New York University from 1970 until her retirement in 2006.

Susan Kohner (1936–), b. Los Angeles, of Czech ancestry, was a leading lady in Hollywood films of the late 50s and early 60s, as well as on stage and TV. She is best known for her role as Sarah Jane in *Imitation of Life* (1959), for which she was nominated for an Oscar and won a Golden Globe award. She played a mixed-race African-American woman who 'passed' for white as a young adult. After Kohner married menswear designer and writer John Weitz in 1964, she retired from acting to devote time to her family. Her two sons, Paul Weitz and Chris Weitz, have both become film directors and producers, screenwriters, and occasional actors.

Harley Jane Kozak (1957–), b. Wilkes-Barre, PA, of Slovak descent, is an American actress and aa writer. She made her film debut in the horror film *The House on Sorority Row* (1982) and had a recurring role as Mary Duvall on the soap opera *Santa Barbara* between 1985 and 1989. She later had supporting parts in *Clean and Sober* (1988) and *When Harry Met Sally...* (1989), before starring in the major studio films *Parenthood* (1989) and *Arachnophobia* (1990). Kozak continued to act in film throughout the remainder of the 1990s and into the 2000s but turned her focus to writing. She has published five mystery novels since 2004. Her debut novel, *Dating Dead Men*, earned her an Agatha, Anthony, and Macavity Award.

Nita Krebs (1905–1991), b. Czech., was an actress, a folk figure. She played the part of a Lullabye League Munchkin in the beloved 1939 classic *The Wizard of Oz*. She was a member of the famous Leo Singer Midgets. Nita's favorite love was ballet. She was featured in many of the Munchkin reunions.

Pavel Kříž (1961–), b. Brno, Czech., a Czech stage actor, in 1988 immigrated to Canada, settling in Vancouver. After some time, he began acting in theatre. His film credits include: *Sleeping Dogs* (1998), *The Scarlet Pimpernel* (1999), *The Summer of my Deflowering* (2000), *Dune* (2000), *Anne Frank* (2001), *Resurrection* (2001), *Dr. Zhivago* (2002), *Children of Dune* (2003), *Colditz* (2005), *Cold War* (2005).

Candace Kroslak (1978–), b. Chicago, IL, of Slovak descent, is an American actress. She known for *Take Me Home Tonight* (2011), *Planet of the Apes* (2001) and *Ocean Ave.* (2002). She has been married to Thomas E. van Dell since 2013.

Vladimír Kulich (1956–), b. Prague, a Czech stage actor, upon coming to America, was immediately cast in guest-starring television and feature roles. He is best known for his roles as Buliwyf in the film *The 13th Warrior*, Tiberius in the film *Ironclad*, Erik in the television series *Vikings*, as well as the voice of Ulfric Stormcloak in *The Elder Scrolls V: Skyrim* and as The Beast in the television series *Angel*. In 1995, he appeared as Olafsson in the *X-Files* episode 'Død Kalm.' While living in Montreal, Quebec, Canada as a young adult, he was a professional ice hockey player.

Alana Ladd (1943–2014), b. Hollywood, CA, of Czech ancestry, was an actress, known for *77 Sunset Strip* (1958), *Hawaiian Eye* (1959), *Guns of the Timberland* (1960), *Duel of Champions* (1961), and *Young Guns of Texas* (1962). She was married to radio commentator Michael Jackson. She was Sue Carol's daughter. Alana was stricken with a stroke around 2001 which limited her mobility for the rest of her life.

Carol Lee Ladd (orig. Stuart) (1932–2010), b. Los Angeles, CA, of Czech ancestry, on her mothers side, was Sue Carols daughter. She was an actress, known for *The Deep Six* (1958) and *Matinee Theatre* (1955). She was previously married to John Veitch and Richard Anderson.

Jordan Elizabeth Ladd (1975–), b. Los Angeles, CA, of Czech ancestry, is an American actress. She is known as a scream queen, having appeared in several horror films. She began taking small film roles before landing her first high-profile role in *Never Been Kissed* (1999). Since then, Ladd has portrayed supporting as well as lead roles in films, including *Cabin Fever* (2002), *Club Dread* (2004), and *Death Proof* (2007). She has also earned acclaim for her lead role in the horror film *Grace* (2009).

VIII. CULTURE: ARTS & LETTERS

Shane Ladd (1985–), b. Los Angeles, CA, of Czech ancestry, is an actress, known for her work on *The Dark Knight Rises* (2012), *The Smurfs* (2011) and *Journey 2: The Mysterious Island* (2012). She is the daughter of David Ladd.

Christine Lakin (1979–), of Czech ancestry, actress and director. Her most well-known performance was in the 1990s ABC/CBS sitcom *Step by Step*, where she played Alicia "Al" Lambert. In addition, she voiced Joyce Kinney in *Family Guy*, appeared as Joan of Arc on Showtime's *Reefer Madness*, and served as Craig Kilborn's sidekick on his 2010 Fox talk show *The Kilborn File*.

Hedy Lamarr (orig. Hedwig Eva Maria Kiesler) (1914–2000), b. Vienna, of Moravian ancestry, was an Austrian and American inventor and film actress. After an early and brief film career in Prague, which included a controversial love-making scene in the film *Ecstasy* (1933), she fled with her husband and secretly moved to Paris. While there, she met MGM head Louis B. Mayer, who offered her a movie contract in Hollywood where she became a film star from the late 1930s to the 1950s. Mayer and the studio cast her in glamorous parts alongside popular leading men and promoted her as the 'world's most beautiful woman.' During her film career, Lamarr co-invented the technology for spread spectrum and frequency hopping communications with composer George Antheil. This new technology became important to America's military during World War II because it was used in controlling torpedoes. Those inventions have more recently been incorporated into Wi-Fi, CDMA and Bluetooth technology, and led to her being inducted into the National Inventors Hall of Fame in 2014. Lamarr appeared in numerous popular feature films, including *Algiers* (1938) with Charles Boyer, *I Take This Woman* (1940) with Spencer Tracy, *Comrade X* (1940) with Clark Gable, *Come Live With Me* (1941) with James Stewart, *H.M. Pulham, Esq.* (1941) with Robert Young, and *Samson and Delilah* (1949) with Victor Mature.

June Lang (orig. Winifred June Vlasek) (1917–2005), b. Minneapolis, MN, of Czech ancestry, a blue-eyed blonde with a striking, open-faced beauty, was an American film actress. She made her film debut in 1931 and caught the eye of Darryl F. Zanuck at 20th Century-Fox, gradually securing second lead roles in mostly B movies. Noted for her fragile and demure appearance, she was usually cast as the little sister or the heroine's best friend in light comedies and adventure films. She soon graduated to leading roles, most notably in *Bonnie Scotland* (with Laurel and Hardy, 1935), in *The Road to Glory* (with Fredric March, Warner Baxter and Lionel Barrymore—written in part by William Faulkner—1936), and in *Wee Willie Winkie* (directed by John Ford, with Shirley Temple, Cesar Romero, and Victor McLaglen, 1937). This approachable actress had a very encouraging career going for her in 30s Hollywood, but extenuating circumstances hurt her chances in the long run. In less than a decade and a half, June Lang was out of pictures altogether (after appearing in over 30) and therein was glimpsed here and there on TV and commercials until her full retirement. Although June never lost her stunning looks and vivacity, she never managed to return, although she indeed contemplated it from time to time.

Dagmar Lassander (orig. Dagmar Regine Hager) (1943–), b. Prague, Czech., of a French father and Chilean mother, and began her career as a costume designer in the Berlin Opera. Her first role was in 1966 in *Sperrbezirk* by Will Tremper. Starting from 1969, she began to work regularly, especially in Italian crime, horror and erotic movies. In the 1980s, she was featured in several Italian TV series and the French-German feature film *S.A.S. à San Salvador*. The character of Lassander Dagmar in the Italian-influenced 2015 horror film *We Are Still Here* is named after her. She is known for *The House by the Cemetery* (1981), *Blood Brides* (1970) and *Forbidden Photos of a Lady Above Suspicion* (1970).

Lauren Bush Lauren (née Lauren Pierce Bush) (1984–), Texas, of Czech ancestry, is an actress, and also fashion model and designer, and activist. She is a daughter of Neil Bush and Sharon Bush (née Smith), a granddaughter of former President George H. W. Bush and niece of former President George W. Bush and former Florida Governor Jeb Bush. She studied fashion design at BEBE and Central Saint Martin's College of Art and Design and graduated from Princeton University in 2006 with a B.A. in anthropology and a certificate in photography. She is known for *Scatter My Ashes at Bergdorf's* (2013), *Celebrity Page* (2013) and *Rachael Ray* (2006). Bush was signed with Elite Model Management before launching FEED. She has been featured on the covers of *Vogue* and *Vanity Fair* and has frequently modelled for Tommy Hilfiger, as well as for Abercrombie & Fitch and designers Gai Mattiolo and Isaac Mizrahi. Bush was an intern on the television sitcom *Friends*, making a cameo in one episode, and interned alongside Ashley Olsen with designer Zac Posen. In 2005, Bush traveled to Chad as a Student Ambassador for the World Food Program. In 2007, Lauren launched FEED Projects, a social business to fight world hunger on behalf of the UN World Food Programme. She has been married to David Lauren since September 4, 2011.

Francis Lederer (1899–2000), b. Prague, Bohemia, was a leading man in Hollywood from 1933. He was getting top billing and Irving Thalberg had planned to make Lederer 'the biggest star in Hollywood' but Thalberg's untimely death put a stop to that. But Lederer continued successfully in film and TV for many years.

Otto Lederer (1867–1965), b. Prague, Bohemia, was an American actor. He appeared in 120 films between 1912 and 1933, most notably *The Jazz Singer* (1927), the first full-length film to have sound sequences, and the Laurel and Hardy short *You're Darn Tootin'* (1928). His other credits include: *Behind Two Guns* (1924), *Wizard of Oz* (1925), *Sailor Izzy Murphy* (1927),

The King of Kings (1927), *Celebrity* (1928), *Little Bit of Heaven* (1928), *One Stolen Night* (1929) *The Sign of the Cross* (1932), *Rasputin and the Empress* (1932), and *Forgotten* (1933).

Pepi Lederer (orig. Josephine Rose Lederer) (1910-1935), b. Chicago, IL, of Bohemian ancestry, was an American actress and writer. She was the niece of actress Marion Davies. After her aunt Marion began a long-term affair with William Randolph Hearst, Hearst took responsibility for the accommodation of Pepi and her several siblings, who included Charlie Lederer, later a well-known screenwriter. She spent a good deal of her youth at Hearst Castle. The Hearsts took the ambitions of her brother seriously and relegated Pepi to a few small parts in movies such as *The Cardboard Lover* (1928). She did some writing for the *Los Angeles Examiner* newspaper. She later moved to London. A known lesbian, she ran around with Tallulah Bankhead and Louise Brooks who became one of her best friends.

Ryan Scott Lee (1996-), b. Austin, TX, of Czech ancestry, is an American actor. He is best known for his role as Warren in the show *Trophy Wife* and as Cary in the 2011 film *Super 8*.

Anna Lehr (1890-1974), b. of Bohemian parents, was an American silent film and stage actress. She was a respected actress in her day and worked regularly throughout the 1910s and into the 1920s. Lehr began making films for the Majestic Motion Picture Company in the early 1910s. In 1914, she toured the Orpheum vaudeville circuit with her daughter in tow, performing a skit called *Little California*. Lehr eventually relocated to Los Angeles where she made films for companies such as Triangle and Universal.

Liana Daine Liberato (1995-), b. Galveston, TX, of Czech ancestry on her mother's side, is an American television and film actress. She is known for her role as young Amanda Collier in the 2014 film *The Best of Me*. She is also known for her starring role in the 2010 film, *Trust* She starred in the Fox Faith film *The Last Sin Eater* and appeared in the fourth season of *House* in the episode "It's a Wonderful Lie". She was featured in the cover story of the June 4, 2006, issue of *The New York Times Magazine* titled "Hollywood Elementary" with her friend Hannah Marks.

Herbert Lom (orig. Herbert Charles Angelo Kuchačevič ze Schluderpacheru) (1917-2012), b. Prague, Bohemia, was a versatile actor whose personality adapted itself equally well to kindness or villainy.

Celia Lovsky (1897-1979), b. Vienna, a daughter of Břetislav Lvovsky (1857-1910), a Czech opera composer, was an American actress. She studied theater, dance, and languages at the Austrian Royal Academy of Arts and Music. She made a name for herself playing slightly exotic roles such as the deaf-mute mother of Lon Chaney in *Man of a Thousand Faces* with James Cagney and Apache Princess Saba in the Jane Russell film *Foxfire*. As she grew older, she was given dignified dowager roles, such as Romany matriarchs, elderly Indian women, expatriate Russian princesses, and a brief but memorable role as the widowed mother of Reinhard Schwimmer, one of the victims of the St. Valentine's Day Massacre in the 1967 film of the same name. Her final movie appearance was of the Exchange Leader in 1973's *Soylent Green*.

Heidi Lucas (1977–) is a former teen Czech-American actress. She was an actress during the 90s. She is best known for her role as Dina Alexander on the Nickelodeon show *Salute Your Shorts* which ran from 1991–1992. She is also known as Noriko 'Max' Matsuda in the 1996 sci-fi series *Hypernauts*. She has been in many movies, TV shows and commercials which include: *Saved by the Bell: The New Class*, *Boy Meets World*, *The Wayans Bros.* and the 1992 action/adventure film *Ghost Ship*. She has also been in TV Commercials for Coca Cola (1998), Clearasil (1997), Sunny Delight (1996), Noxyma (1995 & 1996) and Secret Ultra Dry Deodorant, Johnson & Johnson Persa Gel, and Skittles. She won Young Artist Award for best young actress in 1993 for Salute Your Shorts. In 1998, Lucas quit acting, pursuing higher education instead.

Paul Lukas (1894–1971), b. Budapest; resided in Košice; actor, specializing in comedy; winner of the Academy award for best actor (1943).

Jes Macallan (née Jessica Lee Liszewski) (1982–), b. Sarasota, FL, of Slovak descent; an American actress. She is best known for her role as Josslyn Carver in ABC drama series *Mistresses* and Ava Sharpe in The CW superhero comedy-drama *Legends of Tomorrow*.

Karl Malden (1912–2009), b. Chicago, IL, of Czech mother, was an Emmy Award-winning, Oscar-winning and Golden Globe-nominated American actor, known for his expansive manner. In a career that spanned over seven decades, he starred in films such as *A Streetcar Named Desire*, *On the Waterfront* and *One-Eyed Jacks*, with the late Marlon Brando, and also starred in the blockbuster movie, *Patton*. Among other notable film roles are Archie Lee Meighan in *Baby Doll* and Zebulon Prescott in *How the West Was Won*, both starring Caroll Baker. His best-known role was on television as Lt. Mike Stone on the popular 1970s crime drama, *The Streets of San Francisco*. Towards the end of his acting career, he guest-starred on an episode of *The West Way*. In 2006, he was the oldest living male Hollywood star.

Thomas Randall Mann, Jr. (1991–), b. Portland, OR, of Czech ancestry, who grew up in Dallas, TX, is an American actor. He attended Plano East Senior High School briefly before moving to California at the age of 17 to give acting a serious go. He is best known for his roles as Thomas Kub in the 2012 black comedy film *Project X* and as Greg Gaines in *Me and Earl* and the *Dying Girl*.

VIII. CULTURE: ARTS & LETTERS

Gina 'Gia' Cristine Mantegna (1990–), b. NYC, of Czech ancestry on her mother's side, is an American actress. She made her acting debut at age 13 in the 2003 film *Uncle Nino*, alongside Anne Archer, Trevor Morgan and her father, Joe Mantegna. She later appeared in *13 Going on 30*. In 2006, Mantegna portrayed the character of Grace Conrad in Warner Brothers' winter feature, *Unaccompanied Minor*. She was cast in one of the main roles in an American television pilot show *Murder Book* for Fox. She starred in *The Neighbor* alongside Matthew Modine, Michele Laroque and Ed Quinn. In 2008, Mantegna made a guest appearance in the Season 3 episode, for television show *Criminal Minds*, in which her father stars, where she portrayed an abducted teen who witnesses her best friend's death in Chula Vista, California. She appeared on *The Secret Life of the American Teenager* in a recurring role as Patty Mary. In 2010, Mantegna starred in the independent feature *And Soon the Darkness*. She also appeared in the TeenNick television series *Gigantic*. On December 9, 2010, Mantegna was announced as the 2011 Miss Golden Globe for the 68th Annual Golden Globe Award Ceremony. In 2011, Mantegna starred in the found footage feature *Apartment 143* and in the independent romantic comedy, *Getting That Girl*. In addition to film roles, she currently plays recurring characters on *The Middle* and *Under the Dome*.

Florence Marley (née Hana Smékalová) (1919–1978), b. Obrnice, Moravia, was an alluring actress, discovered by renown French director Pierre Chanal, whom she later married. She had leading roles in a number of movies and won the Best Motion Picture Actress award for her performance in *Les Maudits* (The Damned) at the Cannes Film Festival.

Luba Mason (1961–), b. Astoria, Queens, NY., of Slovak parents; American actress, jazz vocalist, songwriter and dancer. She has starred on Broadway, Off-Broadway, regional theaters in plays and musicals and television and film. As a singer, she has performed in International Jazz and Music Festivals as well as major jazz and music clubs around the country. Mason has trademarked her own musical format called Mixtura, "a blend of different musical currents.

Mark McGraw (1972–), b. New York City, of Czech ancestry on his father's side, is an actor, known for 'No Boundaries' (2009), 'Dead & Deader' (2006) and 'Watching the Detectives' (2010). He grew up in New York and Philadelphia, PA., and later moved to Oregon to go to college and for his love for the outdoors. After graduating, Mark had a 10-year career as a firefighter/paramedic with the city of Springfield, Ore. On his days off, he enjoyed woodworking, construction projects as well as working/studying as an actor. After losing his father to brain cancer, Mark made the decision to move to Los Angeles to pursue his love of acting. He has appeared in several national commercials, independent films and TV shows.

Seth Adam Meyers (1973–), b. Evanston, IL, of Czech ancestry, is an American actor, voice actor, writer, producer, television host and comedian. He currently serves as head writer for NBC's *Saturday Night Live* and hosts its news parody segment 'Weekend Update.' In 2013, it was announced that Meyers had been chosen to replace Jimmy Fallon the following year when his edition of *Late Night* ceases production in 2014.

Dashiell 'Dash' Mihok (1974–), b. New York, NY, of Slovak and Czech ancestry, is an American actor, most well known for playing 'Bunchy' Donovan in the Showtime drama, *Ray Donovan*. He attended Fordham University for some pre-college courses but started working around the age of 18 so never pursued a degree. Mihok has been featured in roles in films such as *The Day After Tomorrow*, *The Perfect Storm*, *The Thin Red Line*, *Lifted*, *Romeo + Juliet*, and *Silver Linings Playbook*. He has had starring roles in independent features such as *Telling You* and *Loveless in Los Angeles*. Mihok studied Shakespeare to prepare for *Romeo + Juliet* and had five extensive audition sessions with director Baz Luhrmann before landing the role. He played Detective Martin Soap in the film *Punisher: War Zone*, which was released in December 2008. Mihok also studied dance and is a photographer.

Martin Miller (orig. Rudolph Muller) (1899–1969), b. Kroměříž, Moravia, was a prominent legit film and TV actor in Great Britain and also in US. His biggest legit hits were a three-year run in *Arsenic and Old Lace* and playing 1,000 performances in *The Mousetrap*.

Isabela Merced (orig. Isabela Moner) (2001–), b. Cleveland, OH, of Slovak descent; an American actress and singer. She is known for her lead role as CJ Martin on the Nickelodeon television series *100 Things to Do Before High School*, her film roles as Izabella in *Transformers: The Last Knight* and Lizzie in *Instant Family*.

Noah Munck (1996–), b. Mission Viejo, CA, of Bohemian ancestry, is an American actor and music producer. He is best known for his role as Gibby in the Nickelodeon series *iCarly*, and for his appearances as Bobby Sinclair, the junior lawn-mowing entrepreneur in the 'TruGreen' commercials. Munck produces trap and electronica music under the name NoxiK. He also makes independent comedy videos on YouTube and releases music under the aliases Noah Praise God and Sadworldbeats.

Brittany Anne Murphy (née Bertolotti) (1977–2009), b. Atlanta, GA, of Italian, Irish and Slovak ancestry, was an American actress and singer. Murphy moved to Los Angeles as a teenager and pursued a career in acting. Her breakthrough role was as Tai Frasier in *Clueless* (1995), followed by supporting roles in independent films such as *Freeway* (1996) and *Bongwater* (1998). She made her stage debut in a Broadway production of Arthur Miller's *A View from the Bridge* in 1997 before appearing as Daisy Randone in *Girl, Interrupted* (1999) and as Lisa Swenson in *Drop Dead Gorgeous* (1999).

Rudolf Myzet (1888-1964), b. Horoměřice, Bohemia, was an actor, director. In Hollywood, he is best known for his portrayals of character roles and as technical adviser to the Studios for pictures dealing with the Central European and Slavic countries.

Anastacia Carmel Nemec (1970-), b. Burbank, CA, an older sister of Corin Nemec, is an actress. She is known for her work on *3:10 to Yuma* (2007), Lee Daniels' *The Butler* (2013), and *Knight and Day* (2010).

Corin Nemec (orig. Joseph, 4th) (1971-), b. Little Rock, AR, of Czech ancestry, is an actor. Corin Nemec's name comes from his nickname, Corky, given to him as a child by his grandmother. He was born in Little Rock, Arkansas but later moved to Atlanta. He now lives in California. His first acting parts were in the series *Webster* (1983) and *Sidekicks* (1986). He then got a part in *Tucker: The Man and His Dream* (1988), directed by Francis Ford Coppola, followed by lead roles in *I Know My First Name is Steven* (1989) and *My Son Johnny* (1991), and the lead role in the TV series *Parker Lewis Can't Lose* (1990). Nemec is also known for playing Jonas Quinn in *Stargate SG-1*, and Harold Lauder in the ABC miniseries *The Stand*. He is also a Master Mason of the Freemasonic Order, having joined the Lodge in the year 2000. He is accredited with a documentary video detailing the hidden geometric meaning of the Master Mason's Apron for the Grand Lodge of Texas in early 2002.

Elinor 'Nell' Teresa Newman (1959-), b. New York, NY, of Slovak ancestry, is child actress, environmentalist, and biologist. She is the eldest child of actress Joanne Woodward and the late actor, businessman, and philanthropist, Paul Newman. As a is child actress, she performed under the name of Nell Potts. She is an actress, known for *The Effect of Gamma Rays on Man-in-the-Moon Marigolds* (1972) and *Rachel, Rachel* (1968). She worked professionally as an actress during the 1960s and 1970s. Under the direction of her father, she played the title character as a child in *Rachel, Rachel* (1968), in which her mother, Joanne Woodward, portrayed the adult Rachel. She has been married to Gary Irving since February 17, 2005. She is also an environmentalist, biologist, and a prominent supporter of sustainable agriculture, who became an entrepreneur when she founded an organic food and pet food production company, Newman's Own Organics.

Melissa 'Lissy' Newman (1961-), b. Hollywood, CA, of Slovak ancestry, is a screen actress, artist, and pop singer. She is known for *Hawkins* (1973), *Mr. & Mrs. Bridge* (1990) and *The New Perry Mason* (1973). She appeared at the 30th Annual Primetime Emmy Awards. Newman is married to Raphael 'Raphe' Elkind, a middle-school teacher and they reside in Westport, Connecticut.

Paul Newman (1925-2008), b. Shaker Heights, OH, of Slovak ancestry, was an actor, film director, producer, activist, race car driver.

Scott Newman (1950-1978), b. Cleveland, OH, of Slovak ancestry, is film and TV actor, stuntman. He was the only son of Academy Award-winning actor Paul Newman. After Scott Newman's death from a drug overdose in 1978, his father established the Scott Newman Center, which is dedicated to preventing drug abuse through education.

Becki Newton (1978-), born in New Haven, CT, of Czech descent, is an American actress best known for her role as Amanda Tanen on the television series *Ugly Betty* and Quinn Garvey on *How I Met Your Mother.*

Matt Newton (1977-), b. CT, of Czech descent (Becki Newton's brother), is an American actor, who began acting at the age of 15. He landed his first starring role opposite Karen Allen and Oscar nominee Michael Lerner in the controversial indie film *Poster Boy* (2004), which was released nationwide in 2006, and for which he received rave reviews.

Eva Novak (1898-1988), b. St. Louis, MO, of Bohemian ancestry, was a silent screen lady. In 1920 she starred opposite Tom Mix in *The Daredevil*, one of six film roles she would have that year, and one of ten films in which she starred opposite Tom Mix. From 1921 to 1928, she appeared in and starred in 48 films, including an early version of *Boston Blackie*. She also co-starred with Betty Bronson and Jack Benny in *The Medicine Man* (1930) and appeared in the 1922 film *Chasing the Moon*, which was an early forerunner of the 1950s film *D.O.A.* In the late 1920s, she and her husband moved to Australia, where she made numerous films, including *The Romance of Runnibede*.

Jane Novak (1896-1980), b. St. Louis, MO, of Bohemian ancestry, was an actress, a silent screen leading lady in the early 1900s. She was the sister of actress Eva Novak.

Kim Novak (1933-2012), b. Chicago, IL, of Czech ancestry, was a motion picture and TV actress. She began her film career in 1954 after signing with Columbia Pictures. There she starred in a string of movies, among them the well-received *Picnic* (1955). She later starred in such films as *The Man with the Golden Arm* (1955) and *Pal Joey* (1957). However, she is perhaps best known today for her performance as Madeline Elster/Judy Barton in Alfred Hitchcock's thriller *Vertigo* (1958) with James Stewart. She was named one of 10 most popular movie stars by *Boxoffice* magazine (1956) and All-American favorite (1961). Her contributions to world cinema have been honored with two Golden Globe Awards, an Honorary Golden Bear Award, and a star on the Hollywood Walk of Fame among others.

David Nykl (1967-), b. Prague, Czech., is a Canadian actor of film, TV, commercials and theater. He is known to science fiction fans as the recurring *Stargate Atlantis* character of Dr. Radek Zelenka, a Czech scientist on Earth's expedition to the 'lost city' of Atlantis.

Jodi Lyn O'Keefe (1978–), b. Cliffwood Beach, NJ, of Czech ancestry, is an American award-winning actress and model, who rose to fame at age 17 as Don Johnson's daughter, Cassidy Bridges on *Nash Bridges*. She is also known for playing Gretchen Morgan on *Prison Break* (2007–09), and for her roles as Jo Laughlin on *The Vampire Diaries* (2014–17) and Lionel Davenport on *Hit the Floor* (2014–18). Her film credits include *Halloween H20* (1998) and *She's All That* (1999).

Timothy Omundson (1969–), b. St. Joseph, Missouri, of Slovak descent, is an American actor. He is notable for his supporting roles as Sean Potter on the CBS television series *Judging Amy*, Eli on the syndicated series *Xena: Warrior Princess*, Carlton Lassiter in *Psych*, as King Richard on the musical series *Galavant* and as Cain in *Supernatural*.

Eron Otcasek (1977–), b. Boston, MA, of Czech ancestry (son of Ric Ocasek), began an acting career that has led him to lead roles in both the Hollywood movie *Inscrutable Americans* (1999), and the lead role in the film *Roomates* (2001). Since then, his film roles have varied from a 'street punk' in the 2003 Tribeca film festival hit *Wholey Moses* (2003) to a runaway with an anger management problem in the upcoming short *Who Is Don Berdi?*

Annette O'Toole (1952–), b. Houston, TX, of Czech ancestry, is an American actress, dancer, and singer-songwriter. She is probably best known for portraying Lisa Bridges in the TV series *Nash Bridges*, Beverly Marsh in the *It* miniseries, Lana Lang in *Superman III*, Elaine, the girlfriend of Nick Nolte's character in *48 Hrs.* the leading role, Kathy, in the romantic-comedy *Cross My Heart*; and more recently for portraying Martha Kent, the mother of Clark Kent, on the television series *Smallville*.

Cameron Palatas (1994–), b. Los Angeles, CA, of Slovak paternal grandfather, is an American actor. He is best known for playing a younger Gideon Malick in *Agents of S.H.I.E.L.D.* and Kane in *F the Prom*.

Nick Palatas (1988–), b. Bethesda, MD, of Slovak descent, is an American actor. He is known to play 'Shaggy' in the film *Scooby-Doo! The Mystery Begins* (2009) and reprise the role in *Scooby-Doo! Curse of the Lake Monster* which aired in 2010.

Betsy Palmer (nee Patricia Betsy Hrunek) (1926–2015), b. East Chicago, IN, of Czech immigrant father, is an American actress. She is best known as a regular panelist on the game show *I've Got a Secret*, and later for playing Pamela Voorhees in the slasher film *Friday the 13th*.

Annie Parisse (née Cancelmi) (1975–), b. Anchorage, AK, of Italian, Slovak and Syrian ancestry, is an American television, film, and theater actress. She portrayed Alexandra Borgia on the drama series *Law & Order*. Parisse has also starred as Julia Snyder on the soap opera *As the World Turns*, for which she was nominated for a Daytime Emmy Award, and as FBI special agent Debra Parker on the thriller series *The Following*.

Jacob 'Jake' Lynn Pavelka (1978–), b. Dallas, TX, probably of Czech ancestry, is a pilot and Reality Show contestant. He took first flying lesson at age 12 and became an airline captain flight instructor at 23. He appeared on several commercials and television programs under the alias Jake Landrum. First TV appearance was on *Walker, Texas Ranger*.

Joaquin Phoenix (orig. Joaquin Rafael Bottom) (1974–), b. San Juan, Puerto Rico, of Slovak descent, is an American actor, producer and activist. For his work as an actor, Phoenix has received a Grammy Award, a Golden Globe Award and three Academy Award nominations.

Liberty Phoenix (1976–), b. Caracas, Venezuela, of Slovak ancestry, is an American former child actress. She is younger sister of Rain Phoenix. In the 80s, Phoenix appeared in several TV productions. Among those were *Kate's Secret* and *Seven Brides for Seven Brothers*, after which she stopped acting. She founded a punk band with her sisters Rain and Summer Phoenix, called The Causey Way, which no longer exists. However, she occasionally supported Rain's band the 'Papercranes' with her backup vocals.

Rain Phoenix (aka Joan of Arc Phoenix) (1972–), b. Crockett, TX, of Slovak descent, is an American actress, musician and singer. Over the years, Rain has starred along celebrities like Julia Stiles, Josh Hartnett and Uma Thurman. Her love of music has led her to appear in such bands as Aleka's Attic, whom her brother River also was in, 'The Causey Way' with her sister Summer and her current band, 'The Paper Cranes' with her husband, Michael Tubbs. She also toured with the Red Hot Chilli Peppers as a backup singer during their 'One Hot Minute' tour in 1996.

River Phoenix (orig. River Jude Bottom) (1970–1993), b. Madras, OR, of Slovak descent, is an American actor, musician, activist. Phoenix's work encompassed 24 films and television appearances, and his rise to fame led to his status as a "teen idol".

Summer Phoenix (1978–), b. Winter Park, FL, of Slovak ancestry, is an American actress, model and designer. She is the youngest sister of Rain Phoenix and Liberty Phoenix. Phoenix was a child actor, working with agent Iris Burton along with her brothers and sister at the age of two, and went on to have guest roles in *Murder, She Wrote*, *Growing Pains*, *Swamp Thing* and *Airwolf*. She appeared in the TV movie *Kate's Secret* and in *Russkies*, playing the younger sister of real-life brother Joaquin. Phoenix later appeared in *Wasted*, *The Laramie Project*, *SLC Punk*, *Dinner Rush*, *The Believer*, and *The Faculty*. She played leads in *Esther Kahn* (2000) and *Suzie Gold* (2004). In 2002, Phoenix starred in a three-month run of *This is Our Youth* at the Garrick Theatre alongside Matt Damon and Casey Affleck.

Danny Pintauro (1976–), b. Milltown, NJ, of Slovak decent, is an American actor. He is best known for his role as Jonathan Bower on the popular American sitcom *Who's the Boss?*, as well as his role in the 1983 film *Cujo*.

Pete Ploszek (1987–), b. Hinsdale, IL, of Slovak descent, is an American actor. In 2009, he graduated from Princeton University, where he was a four-year member of the Princeton Tigers football team. He graduated with an MFA in Acting from the USC School of Dramatic Arts in 2012. He is best known for his roles a Leonardo in the *Teenage Mutant Ninja Turtle's* films. He is also known for his role as Garrett Douglas on the MTV supernatural drama series *Teen Wolf*.

Matthew 'Matt' Prokop (1990–), Victoria, TX, of Czech ancestry, is a retired American actor and producer. Moved to Los Angeles to pursue his dreams of acting at the age of 16, Matt Prokop is quickly becoming one of Hollywood's hottest, most-coveted young stars. After making appearances on the hit comedies *The Office* (2005) and *Hannah Montana* (2006), Prokop competed globally and was cast in a highly sought-after role Disney's *High School Musical 3: Senior Year* as Jimmie 'The Rocket Man' Zara (2008). He guest starred on *Medium* (2009) as Kyle "K.C." Covington for one episode. Prokop landed a role in the Brendan Fraser film *Furry Vengeance* (2010), playing Fraser's son and he played the role of Josh Rosen in the Disney Channel original movie *Geek Charming* (2011) based on author Robin Palmer's novel. In 2012, he appeared in an episode of *Modern Family*.

Fatima Ptacek (2000–), b. US, is a Czech-American child actress and model. Ptacek has appeared in more than 60 television commercials and on the covers of numerous national magazines. She is best known as the current voice of Dora in Nickelodeon animated television series *Dora the Explorer*, and a lead in the Academy Award-winning 2012 short film *Curfew*.

Vladimír Pucholt (1942–), b. Prague, Czech., is a Czech-Canadian actor. He made his first film at the age of 12, *Návstěva zoblak*, which established him as a child star in his home country. He successfully made the transition from child actor to adult actor, and in his early twenties, he established a working relationship with Miloš Forman. The famed director first hired Pucholt for the film *Competition* and later brought him aboard for two more films, *Černý Petr* and *Lásky jedné plavovlásky*. Pucholt would continue to act until 1967, when he abruptly left the profession and moved to Canada, where he became a doctor. In 1999, after an absence of over 30 years, Pucholt made a return to acting with the film *Návrat ztraceného ráje*.

Michael Rady (1981–), b. Philadelphia, PA, of Slovak descent, is an American actor. Rady made his acting debut in the feature film *The Sisterhood of the Traveling Pants*, playing Kostas

Dounas, a role he reprised in the sequel, *The Sisterhood of the Traveling Pants 2*. He has appeared in other feature films with small parts including *The Guardian*. Rady also starred in the independent film *InSearchOf*. Rady had a recurring role in the CBS summer series, *Swingtown*, playing philosophy teacher Doug Stephens. He appeared in the second season of Showtime's TV drama *Sleeper Cell*. Rady appeared as a guest star in two seasons of the ABC Family series *Greek*, playing the Honors Polymer Science major and Honors Engineering Floor Resident Advisor Max Tyler. In 2009, he was cast in The CW series *Melrose Place* as Jonah Miller, an aspiring filmmaker. Since 2014, he has appeared in a number of made-for-television movies airing on the Hallmark Channel.

Charles H. Radilak (orig. Karel Hradilák) (1909–1972), b. Dolní Žukov, Czech., was a Czech actor. He left Czechoslovakia in 1946 and then worked in Hollywood under a new name and acted in a number of American films. His credits include *Dr. Kildare* (1961), *Perry Mason* (1963), *77 Sunset Strip* (1963), *Genghis Khan* (1965), *Hogan Heroes* (1966), *The Virginian* (1968), *The Sunshine Patriot* (1968), *Ironside* (1969), *It Takes a Thief* (1966), etc.

Mary Lynn Rajskub (1971–), b. Detroit, MI, of Czech ancestry on her father's side, is an American comedic actress, best known for her leading role as Chloe O'Brian in the Fox action-thriller *24*. While she has been mainly a television star, Rajskub also played bit parts on the big screen in *Magnolia* (1999), *Man on the Moon* (1999), *Road Trip* (2000), among her other works. She offered mesmerizing performances in *Mysterious Skin* (2004), *Sweet Home Alabama* (2002), and in *Punch-Drunk Love* (2002), then played a few more visible roles such as Janet Stone in *Firewall* (2006), opposite Harrison Ford, and as Pam in *Little Miss Sunshine* (2006). In 2006, Harrison Ford presented Rajskub with the Female Breakthrough Award for her "high concept comedic stage productions, as well as her TV and film acting skills."

Věra Hrubá Ralston (1919–2003), b. Prague, Czech., was a Czech figure skater and actress. She moved to Hollywood with her mother and signed a contract in 1943 with Republic Pictures. During her career, she was known as Vera Hrubá Ralston and later Vera Ralston. She normally played an immigrant girl, because of her limited English skills. Among the 26 films Ralston starred in were *Storm Over Lisbon* with Erich von Stroheim (1944), *Dakota* (1945) with John Wayne, *I, Jane Doe* (1948) with Ruth Hussey and John Carrol, *The Fighting Kentuckian*, also with John Wayne (1949), *A Perilous Journey* with David Brian (1953), and *Fair Wind to Java* with Fred MacMurray (1953). She retired from films in 1958. In 1952, Ralston married Republic studio head Herbert Yates, who was nearly 40 years her senior.

Dylan Ramsey, b. Prague, Czech., is a young Canadian actor, film producer and writer. He is known for his portrayals of dark dramatic and comedically eccentric characters of diverse ethnicity. Recent major roles include the leading role of Ginger in HBO's *Donny &*

Ginger, guest-starring as the ethereal suicide bomber Saaed Hotary on FX's *Nip/Tuck* and the title role of Jack Belmont in *Visual Purple*. He also starred in *Air Crash Investigation's* "The Killing Machine" episode as Bobby "The Killer", and *Air Crash Investigation's* "Death of the President" episode on the Polish Air Force Crash in 2014.

Vanessa Ray (née Liptak) (1981–), b. Livermore, Alameda, CA, of Slovak descent, is an American actress and singer. She is best known for her role on *Pretty Little Liars* as CeCe Drake (Charlotte DiLaurentis), Jenny on the legal drama series *Suits*, Teri Ciccone on *As the World Turns*, and Officer Eddie Janko on *Blue Bloods*, and Maggie "Rocker" Sheldon on *White Colar*.

Catherine Reitman (1981–), b. Los Angeles, CA, of Slovak ancestry (daughter of the film director Ivan Reitman), is an actress, producer, and film critic. Reitman starred in the television series *The Real Wedding Crashers*, based on the hit movie *Wedding Crashers*. She appeared in the films *Knocked Up* (2007) and *I Love You, Man* (2009). She has also had roles on the series *Hollywood Residential*, *It's Always Sunny in Philadelphia*, *How I Met Your Mother*, *Weeds*, and *Blackish*.

Alan Michael Ritchson (1984–), b. Grand Forks, ND, of Czech ancestry on his mother's side, is an American actor, model, and director and also a writer. He is known for his modeling career as well as his portrayals of the superhero Aquaman on The CW's *Smallville* and Thad Castle on Spike TV's *Blue Mountain State*. Ritchson also starred as Gloss in 2013's *The Hunger Games: Catching Fire* and Raphael in 2014's *Teenage Mutant Ninja Turtles* reboot.

Maria (Sieber) Riva (1924–), b. Berlin, Germany, of Bohemian father, is an American actress, memoirist and activist. Her father, Rudolf Sieber (1897–1976), producer and cinematographer, was a native of Ústí nad Labem. Her mother, the screen icon Marlene Dietrich (1901–1992), about whom she published a memoir in 1992, was born in Berlin. Maria was married to esteemed Italian art director William Riva (1920–1999). She is known for *Scrooged* (1988), *The Scarlet Empress* (1934) and *Studio One in Hollywood* (1948). She primarily worked on television in the 1950s.

Karel Roden (1962–), b. České Budějovice, Czech., is an actor. He is a graduate of the Prague Dramatic Academy of Fine Arts, hailing from a long tradition of Czech actors. Roden's feature film career began almost simultaneous with his theatre work in 1984 as Honza, a medical student in the 2nd part of a trilogy entitled 'How the poets are losing their illusions' (Jak básníci přicházejí o iluze), a lighthearted, comic look at life through the lives of young university students. Roden's Honza also appeared in the final installation of the trilogy, 'How poets are enjoying their lives' (Jak básníkům chutná život). Other comic turns include Roden's Captain Tuma in *What Kind of Soldier* (Copak je to za vojáka), a humoristic look at life as a soldier in the socialist Czech army, the character Dragan in the action-thriller *Dead Fish* with Gary Oldman and Terence Stamp. In the comedy crime-thriller *Shut Up and Shoot Me*, Roden plays the hen-pecked husband hired to assassinate a grieving widow. He is an internationally known actor who was most recently seen in the United States in director Jaume Collet-Serra's *Orphan*, starring Vera Farmiga and Peter Sarsgaard, and in Guy Ritchie's *RocknRolla*, opposite Gerard Butler, Tom Wilkinson and Thandie Newton. His work can also be seen in such films as the hit comedy *Mr. Bean's Vacation*, starring Rowan Atkinson; Wayne Kramer's *Running Scared*, opposite Paul Walker and Vera Farmiga; Paul Greengrass' wildly successful *The Bourne Supremacy*, the second film in the franchise starring Matt Damon; Guillermo del Toro's comics-based action thrillers *Hellboy* and *Blade II*; *Bulletproof Monk*, starring Chow Yun-Fat and Seann William Scott; and *15 Minutes*, starring Robert De Niro and Edward Burns. Roden has been nominated several times and recently won a prestigious Czech Lion Award for Best Actor for his work in the film *Guard No. 47*, produced in his native country. He has acted in numerous Czech films, as well as in a variety of films produced throughout Europe.

Nicholas 'Nick' Edward Roux (1990–), b. Los Angeles, CA, of Slovak descent, is an American actor and singer. His breakthrough was the role of Scott Pickett in the Disney Channel original movie *Lemonade Mouth* (2011). He is known for *Tomato Red: Blood Money* (2017), *Jackals* (2017) and *Jane by Design* (2012).

Anne Schaefer (1870–1957), b. St. Louis, MO, of Bohemian ancestry, was a silent movie actress. She appeared in 147 films between 1911 and 1938. She was known for *Saturday's Children* (1929), *The Little Princess* (1917) and *The Price of a Good Time* (1917). She was married to F. Medek. She was the aunt of fellow actresses Eva and Jane Novak.

Lola Montes Schnabel (1980–), b. New York, NY, of Moravian ancestry, daughter of the artist Julian Schnabel, is a painter, printmaker, photographer, and filmmaker. She studied at Cooper Union School of Advancement of Science and Art (B.F.A., 2008). She has exhibited internationally, including Tripoli Gallery, Southampton, NY; Ace Gallery, Los Angeles, CA; The Hole, New York, NY, among others. Recent exhibitions include Heaven, which was on view at the Shelbourne Hotel during Art Basel Miami 2014, and Forms Wrestling with Existence, at Eden Rock Gallery, Saint Barthélemy. She has collaborated with Max Mara Carte Blanche (2012) and Alice + Olivia (2015) on textile designs created from her watercolors, and her film work includes *Training Day*, a Nike commercial featuring Steve Nash, and projections for Lou Reed's concert and feature film, *Berlin*, both in 2007.

Stella Madrid Schnabel (1983–), b. New York, NY, of Moravian ancestry, daughter of the artist Julian Schnabel, is an actress, producer, poet, and fashion designer. She is known for known for *At Eternity's Gate* (2018), *Rampart* (2011) and *Spring Breakers* (2012).

Olga Schoberová (later known as Olinka Bérová) (1943–), b. Prague, Czech., is a Czech-American actress, who is often compared with Brigitte Bardot and Ursula Andress. She acted in 22 Czech, German, Italian and American movies. She was married to Brad Harris (1967-1969), now divorced, have one daughter, Babrinka. She is now married to John Calley and lives in the US. She became the Czech sex-symbol, years before Paulina Pořízková and many current fashion models, because she was the first beauty from Czech Republic to appear in Playboy, and made it on the front cover, too.

Arnold Alois Schwarzenegger (1947–), b. Vienna, was of Czech ancestry on his mother's side (Aurelia Jadrny), while his paternal great-grandfather, Wenzel Mach, was also Czech and came from the village of Chocov, nr. Mladá Vozice, Bohemia. As a young man, Schwarzenegger gained widespread attention as a highly successful bodybuilder. He later gained worldwide fame as a Hollywood action film icon. Perhaps his most famous role is in the *The Terminator* series. In October of 2003 Schwarzenegger, running as a Republican, was elected Governor of California in a special recall election of then governor Gray Davis. The "Governator," as Schwarzenegger came to be called, held the office until 2011.

Stefanie Noelle Scott (1996–), b. Chicago, IL, of Czech ancestry, is an American actress and singer. Her maternal grandfather John Paul Kipta was born in Indiana, to Czech parents. Scott is known for her roles as Quinn Brenner in the film *Insidious: Chapter 3*, Dana Tressler in the film *Flipped*, for which she won a 2011 Young Artist Award, and Lexi Reed on Disney Channel's *A.N.T. Farm*. Scott's discography has consisted of her EP *New Girl in Town* (2009), some Disney Channel promotional singles, released between 2008 and 2012, and the 2015 film soundtrack album from her role in *Jem and the Holograms*.

Adolph Seidel (1887-1962), b. Bohemia, was an actor. He was known for *The Big House* (1930). He died on March 12, 1962, in Los Angeles, CA.

Thomas 'Tom' William Selleck (1945–), b. Detroit, MI, of Slovak descent, is an American actor and film producer. His breakout role was playing private investigator Thomas Magnum in the television series *Magnum, P.I.* (1980–88). Since 2010, Selleck has co-starred as New York City Police Commissioner Frank Reagan in the series *Blue Bloods*, and the show has been renewed for its twelfth season in 2021–22. Beginning in 2005, he has portrayed troubled small-town police chief Jesse Stone in nine made-for-TV movies based on the Robert B. Parker's novels. In films, Selleck has played bachelor architect Peter Mitchell in *Three Men and a Baby* (1987) and its sequel *Three Men and a Little Lady* (1990). He has also appeared in more than 50 other film and television roles since *Magnum, P.I.*, including the films *Quigley Down Under*, *Mr. Baseball*, and *Lassiter*. He appeared in recurring television roles as Monica Geller's love interest Dr. Richard Burke on *Friends*, as Lance White, the likeable and naive partner on *The Rockford Files*, and as casino owner A.J. Cooper on *Las Vegas*. He also had a lead role in the television western movie *The Sacketts*, based on two of Louis L'Amour's books.

Emil Sitka (1914-1998), b. Johnstown, PA, of Slovak descent, was a veteran American actor, who appeared in hundreds of movies, short films, and television shows, is best known for his numerous appearances with *The Three Stooges*. He is one of only two actors to have worked with all six Stooges (Shemp Howard, Moe Howard, Larry Fine, Curly Howard, Joe Besser, Joe DeRita) on film in the various incarnations of the group (Harold Brauer, a recurring villain who appeared in three 1940s shorts, was the other).

Karl Slover (orig. Karl Kosiczky) (1918-2011), b. Prakovce, Slovakia, was an American actor best known as one of the Munchkins in *The Wizard of Oz* (1939). Diagnosed at an early age with pituitary dwarfism, Slover was barely two feet tall by his eighth birthday. When Slover was just nine years old, his father sent him to work for a traveling show based out of Berlin, Germany. After working with the show for several years, Slover moved to the United States where he joined another traveling show. It wasn't long before Slover began appearing in films like *The Terror of Tiny Town*, *Block-Heads*, *Bringing Up Baby*, and *They Gave Him a Gun*. Slover was working in Hawaii when his circus manager sent him to Hollywood, where little people were needed for an upcoming film called *The Wizard of Oz*. At the age of 21 and standing just 4 feet 4 inches, Slover played the parts of four Munchkins in the movie; the first trumpeter, a soldier, one of the sleepy heads, and was among those who sang "Follow the Yellow Brick Road." After filming Oz, Slover began working for the 'Original World Famous Singers Midget Show' where he sang and danced throughout the United States. When the show ended in 1942, Slover joined the Royal American Carnival in Tampa, Florida. At this time, he took the last name Slover, the last name of his stage manager. Slover remained very active in his later years and participated in several celebrations related to *The Wizard of Oz*. Every June, Slover attended festivities celebrating Judy Garland's birthday at the Judy Garland Museum & Birthplace in Grand Rapids, Minnesota.

Magda Sonja (1886-1974), b. Hradistko, Bohemia, was a silent movie actress, known for *The Robber Symphony* (1937), *Ssanin* (1924) and *Verbotene Liebe* (1927). She was married to Friedrich Feher. She was a dark-haired cabaret performer and chansonnière, on stage in Vienna since at least 1907. She became a noted silent screen diva with Sascha Films in the 1920's, invariably in productions directed by her husband Friedrich Feher. She did not make the transition to sound. Evaded the Nazi persecution of Jews by fleeing to Britain, she emigrated to the U.S. in 1937. She died in Los Angeles.

Maelcum Soul (orig. Patricia Ann Soul) (1940-1968), b. Baltimore, MD, of Bohemian ancestry, was an American bartender, artist's model, and actress. In the 1960s, she portrayed leading characters in two of filmmaker John Waters' earliest works, *Roman Candles* and *Eat Your Makeup*. She was known for her wild looks, with burnt red hair, white chalk makeup, and very long eyelashes. Soul was reportedly considered the "Alice Prin" of Baltimore. She was known for dyeing her hair an "iron-ore red" and wearing heavy eyeliner and "hip haberdashery" drawing from the style of the Berlin cabaret.

Mary Elizabeth 'Sissy' Spacek (1949–), b. Quitman, TX, of Moravian ancestry, is an Academy-Award-winning American actress and singer. Spacek came to international prominence in the 1970s for her BAFTA Award nominated role as Holly Sargis in Terrence Malick's film *Badlands* (1973) and as Carrie White in Brian De Palma's horror film *Carrie* (1976), based on the first novel by Stephen King, for which she earned her first Academy Award nomination. She won the Academy Award for Best Actress for her role as country star Loretta Lynn in the film *Coal Miner's Daughter* (1980). and also earned a Grammy Award nomination for the song "Coal Miner's Daughter" from the film's soundtrack. She went on to receive further Oscar nominations for her roles in *Missing* (1982), *The River* (1984) and *Crimes of the Heart* (1986). *Coal Miner's Daughter* and *Crimes of the Heart* also won her the Golden Globe Award for Best Actress in a Musical or Comedy. A six-time Oscar nominee, she received her sixth nomination for *In the Bedroom* (2001), which also won her a third Golden Globe, this time for Best Actress in a Drama. Her other films include *3 Women* (1977), *Raggedy Man* (1981), *JFK* (1991), *Affliction* (1997), *The Straight Story* (1999), *Nine Lives* (2005) and *The Help* (2011).

John Spencer (orig. Speshock) (1946–2005), b. Paterson, NJ, of Ukrainian-Irish ancestry, but based on his own testimony, he also had Czech roots. He attended the Professional Children's High School in New York City, and while a student, adopted the stage name John Spencer. Spencer began acting in his teens and landed his first big break when he was cast as Henry Anderson on the TV series *The Patty Duke Show*. After the end of the show's run, Spencer resumed his education, enrolling at Fairleigh Dickinson University in Teaneck, NJ; he later transferred to New York University. In the early 70s, Spencer began pursuing a career as a stage actor in New York City, and in 1981, he won an Obie award for his performance in the play *Still Life*. In 1983, Spencer began working in film, appearing in supporting roles in two movies that year, *War Games* and *Echoes*. By the mid-80s, Spencer was working steadily in movies and making frequent television guest shots; he was also earning increasing acclaim for his stage roles, receiving a Drama Desk Award nomination for his role in *The Day Room* in 1988. However, Spencer's first real brush with fame came in 1990, when he won the role of Tommy Mullany, a tough but good-hearted lawyer, on the hit TV series *L.A. Law*. While Spencer's regular guy looks seemed to rule him out of leading man roles, his success on *L.A. Law* established him as a first-call character actor, and he began scoring higher-profile roles in a variety of higher-profile films, while earning higher billing in made-for-TV movies and appearing in stage roles as his schedule permitted. In 1999, Spencer's career received yet another boost when he was cast as Chief of Staff Leo McGarry on the acclaimed television series *The West Wing*. Spencer's work as part of the ensemble cast earned him a Screen Actors Guild award in 2001 and 2002, and he was nominated for an Emmy five times for Best Supporting Actor, winning in 2002. In the same year that his character Leo suffered a heart attack on *The West Wing*, Spencer sadly suffered the same fate. After a severe attack, he died among friends and family in a Los Angeles hospital in December 2005. He was 58 years old.

Frederick Stafford (orig. Friedrich Strobel von Stein) (1928–1979), b. Piestany, Czech., was an American actor. He was a leading man in spy movies. In 1949, he emigrated to Australia, where he qualified as a doctor of chemistry, after studying at University of Sydney and Perth. Fluent in five languages, in the 1950s he held a series of positions in the pharmaceutical industry, last being a regional manager in Hong Kong. In 1964, French director André Hunebelle discovered Stafford on holiday at a hotel in Bangkok and asked him "How would you like to make movies with me?" Stafford replied, "Why not?" That's how it all began. He was rushed off to Brazil to make his first film in Rio de Janeiro and had been busy ever since. He played a starring role in his first film, as an agent code-named OSS 117 in *OSS 117 Mission for a Killer* (1965) with Mylène Demongeot. The film was the eleventh biggest movie of the year in France. He followed this with the similar *Agent 505: Death Trap in Beirut* (1965) and a second OSS117 film, *Atout cœur à Tokyo pour OSS 117* (1966). He made several other films of this type. These movies brought the attention of Alfred Hitchcock, who signed him in 1968 to play the leading role as agent André Devereaux in *Topaz* (1969), which was not successful. He made a comeback in 1972 as Commissario Luca Micelli in the Italian Giallo *Shadows Unseen*. Five years after *Topaz*, he starred in the Italian thriller *Special Killers* (1973). His last successes were the Spanish Movies *Metti che ti rompo il muso* (1975) and *White Horses of Summer* (1975), the Italian thriller *Werewolf Woman* (1976) and the Spanish-Italian-French coproduction *Hold-Up* (1977). He also made *La trastienda* and *Sfida sul fondo*.

Martin Starr (orig. Martin James Pflieger Schienle) (1982–), b. Santa Monica, CA., of Czech ancestry, is an American actor and comedian. He is known for his television roles as Bill Haverchuck on the short-lived NBC comedy-drama *Freaks and Geeks*, Roman DeBeers on the Starz comedy series *Party Down* (2009–2010) and Bertram Gilfoyle in the HBO series *Silicon Valley*, as well as for his film roles in *Knocked Up* (2007), *Cheats* (2002), *Adventureland* (2009), and *Dead Snow: Red vs. Dead* (2014), and *Spider-Man: Homecoming* (2017).

Sarah Jane Steele (1988–), b. Philadelphia, PA, of Czech ancestry, is an American actress. Steele graduated from Columbia University in 2011 with a B.A. in comparative literature. After her breakout role as Bernice in the 2004 film *Spanglish*, Steele continued acting, appearing on an episode of *Law & Order* and in the films: *Mr. Gibb*, which co-stars Hayden

Panettiere, Tim Daly and Dan Hedaya; and *Margaret*, which co-stars Matt Damon, Matthew Broderick, Anna Paquin, Mark Ruffalo, and Allison Janney. Steele was seen on the New York stage in an off-Broadway production of *The Prime of Miss Jean Brodie*, which ran for a few months at the Acorn Theater. From 2007 to 2008, she appeared in the off-Broadway play *Speech & Debate*. From January to March 2012, she appeared in the off-Broadway play *Russian Transport* at the Acorn Theatre, playing the role of Mira. She has also appeared in other off-Broadway and regional productions. In late 2014, Steele made her Broadway debut in *The Country House* by Donald Margulies, playing the granddaughter, Susie, opposite Blythe Danner. In 2009, Steele appeared on *Gossip Girl* as Kira Abernathy, Jenny Humphreys rival at Cotillion and Eric van der Woodsens friend. Steele appeared in three episodes of *The Good Wife* in 2011 as Marissa Gold, the daughter of Eli Gold (Alan Cumming). She reprised the role during season six in 2014.

Miroslava Stern (orig. Miroslava Šternová) (1926–1955), b. Prague, Czech., was a Mexican actress who appeared in thirty-two films. Miroslava moved to Mexico as a child with her mother and adoptive Jewish father in 1941, seeking to escape war in their native country. After winning a national beauty contest, Miroslava began to study acting. She appeared in a number of Hollywood and Mexican films.

Silvia Šuvadová (1973–), b. Ružomberok, Czech., is an actress and producer. She studied acting at Academy of Performing Arts in Bratislava (Dipl., 1994). She worked as a presenter and played in TV ads and TV movies. In 2002, she moved to Los Angeles. She is known for *The Fast and the Furious: Tokyo Drift* (2006), *Behaving Badly* (2009), *Violent Blue* (2011) and *Starwatch* (2017).

Emerson Tenney (1997–), b. Los Angeles, CA, of Czech ancestry on her mother's side (daughter of Teri Hatcher), is an actress. She is known for *Caroline* (2009) and *Planes* (2013).

Angela Trimbur (1981–), b. Bucks County, PA, of Slovak descent, is an American actress, comedian, writer and dancer. She is best known for her role as Isabel in *Trash Fire*, starring opposite Adrian Grenier, Tina the wild '80s party camp counselor in the horror comedy film *The Final Girls* (2015), and Penny Whitewall on FXX's animated series *Major Lazer*. In 2014 she created the L.A. City Municipal Dance Squad, a team of dancers to perform a halftime show for the Los Angeles Women's Community Basketball pickup league, which quickly grew a large following. Angela began offering workshops and the squad began creating events called "Slightly Guided Dance Party" hosted by the Museum of Contemporary Art with 300+ in attendance. The squad was featured in *Time* magazine in 2018, for building a unique community for women. In July 2018, Trimbur was diagnosed with breast cancer. After undergoing treatment, Trimbur began hosting breast cancer support groups on Marco Polo to help others.

Arianne Ulmer (1937–), b. New York City, NY, of Moravian father, is an actress, known for her work on 'Beyond the Time Barrier' (1960), 'The Naked Venus' (1959) and 'Edgar G. Ulmer: The Man Off-Screen' (2004). She was previously married to Jay Cipes and Giorgio Andrea Puglisi. In 1994, she established the Edgar G. Ulmer Preservation Corporation, a nonprofit dedicated to the preservation and promotion of the artistic works of her father. In addition to her work preserving her father's legacy, she has built a career of her own in the family business. In 1982, she founded AUC Films Inc., a consulting business for international and domestic film sales. She has also served as Executive Vice President for the American Film Marketing Association, Vice President of International Film Distribution for Best International and was co-founder and Senior Vice President of Sales and Services for the Producers Sales Organization.

Justin Urich (1978–), b. USA, of Slovak ancestry, is an actor and screenwriter. He is the son of Tom Urich. He is known known for *How High* (2001), *Serial Killing 4 Dummys* (2004) and *Monster Man* (2003).

Ryan Urich (1978–), Henderson, NV, is an actor. He is the son of Robert Urich. He is alumnus of Ross University Medical School and California Polytechnic State University, San Luis Obispo, CA. He is known for his work on *The Killer Within Me* (2003), *Survive the Savage Sea* (1992) and *Night Walk* (1989).

Tom Urich (1935–2022), b. Hollidays Cove, WV, of Slovak ancestry, was an actor. He was older brother of Robert Urich and father of Justin Urich. He was known for *Murder at 1600* (1997), *JAG* (1995), and *Midnight Witness* (1993).

Apollonia Váňová (fl. 2018), b. Slovakia, raised nr Vancouver, BC, Canada, is an actress and opera singer, known for her roles as Silhouette in the film version of 'Watchmen' and as the leading Wraith Queen and leader of a Wraith Alliance in the *Stargate: Atlantis* episode 'The Queen.' She played a role in ABC Family's *Samurai Girl*. She also played as Nadira, one of General Zod's Kryptonian soldiers in *Man of Steel*.

Marek Vašut (1960–), b. Prague, Czech., is a Canadian film, stage, and television actor. Vašut had first travelled to New York City to attend the Lee Strasberg Theatre and Film Institute. Vašut also attended and the Academy of Performing Arts in Prague. He is best known for his appearances in *Mission Impossible* (1996), *Solomon Kane* and *Blade II* (2002). He voiced the character Tommy Angelo for the Czech version of the video game *Mafia: The City of Lost Heaven*. Vašut later reprised his role as Tommy in the 2020 remake *Mafia:*

Definitive Edition. He is also known or his appearances in *Help! I'm a Teenage Outlaw* and *Thief Takers*.

Anton Vaverka (1872–1937), b. Prague, Bohemia, was a veteran of the Austrian theatre. He appeared in supporting character roles in U.S. films during the late silent era. In 1923, he made his film debut, playing Emperor Franz Joseph of Austria in Erich von Stroheim's film, *Merry-Go-Round* (1923). He also played in another Stroheim film, *The Wedding March* (1928). He also played prompter in the *The Phantom of the Opera*, released in 1925 and was known for *The Love Parade* (1929). In 1930, he appeared in *Melody Man*. In 1932, he played his final film role in *Broken Lullaby*.

Ingrid Veninger (1968–), b. Bratislava. Czech., is a Canadian actress, writer, director, multitalented filmmaker, producer, and film professor at York University. She began her career in show business as a child actor in commercials and on television; as a teen, she was featured in the CBC series *Airwaves* (1986–87) and the CBS series *Friday the 13th: The Series* (1987–90). In the 1990s, she branched out into producing, and, in 2003, she founded her own production company, pUNK Films, through which she began to work on her own projects as a writer and director. Veninger's directorial debut came in 2008, with the release of her low-budget feature film, titled *Only*, which cost $20,000 to produce. She has written and directed six feature films—*Only* (2008), *Modra* (2010), *I am a good person / I am a bad person* (2011), *The Animal Project* (2013), *He Hated Pigeons* (2015), and *Porcupine Lake* (2017), all of which have screened at film festivals around the world. In 2011, she won the Toronto Film Critics Association's Jay Scott Prize for an emerging artist. In 2013, she won an EDA Award from the Alliance of Women Film Journalists at the Whistler Film Festival. *The Globe and Mail* has dubbed Veninger "The DIY Queen of Canadian Filmmaking."

Lavínia Gutmann Vlasak (1976–), b. Rio de Janeiro, of Czech descent, is a Brazilian actress, and former model. She has always been compared to Audrey Hepburn. In 1980, she moved to the United States when her father, an official of a multi-national org., was transferred there. After only seven years, on her return to Brazil, she learned Portuguese. When Vlasak returned, she studied at the British School in Rio de Janeiro. The school's curriculum focused on art education, and she became interested in the acting profession. She began her professional life working as a model at the age of 15. As an actress, she is known for *The King of the Cattle* (1996), *Celebrity* (2003) and *Opposite Lives* (2006).

Jon Voight (1938–), b. Yonkers, NY, of Slovak father, is an American actor. In 1956, he enrolled at The Catholic University of America in Washington, D.C., where he majored in art and graduated with a B.A. in 1960. After graduation, Voight moved to New York City, where he pursued an acting career. He graduated from the Neighborhood Playhouse School of the

Theatre, where he studied under Sanford Meisner. He came to prominence in the late 1960s with his Academy Award-nominated performance as Joe Buck, a would-be gigolo in *Midnight Cowboy* (1969). During the 1970s, he became a Hollywood star with his portrayals of a businessman mixed up with murder in *Deliverance* (1972); a paraplegic Vietnam veteran in *Coming Home* (1978), for which he won an Academy Award for Best Actor; and a penniless ex-boxing champion in the remake of *The Champ* (1979). His output became sparse during the 1980s and early 1990s, although he won a Golden Globe Award and was nominated for an Academy Award for his performance as the ruthless bank robber Oscar "Manny" Manheim in *Runaway Train* (1985). He made a comeback in Hollywood during the mid-1990s, starring in Michael Mann's crime epic *Heat* (1995) opposite Robert De Niro and Al Pacino. He portrayed Jim Phelps in *Mission: Impossible* (1996), a corrupt NSA agent in *Enemy of the State* (1998), and the unscrupulous attorney in Francis Ford Coppola's *The Rainmaker* (1997), which earned him a Golden Globe nomination for Best Supporting Actor. Voight gave critically acclaimed biographical performances during the 2000s, appearing as sportscaster Howard Cosell in *Ali* (2001) for which his supporting performance was nominated for the Academy Award, the Golden Globe Award and a Critics Choice Award, and also as Nazi officer Jürgen Stroop in *Uprising* (2001), as Franklin D. Roosevelt in Michael Bay's *Pearl Harbor* (2001) and as Pope John Paul II in the eponymous miniseries (2005). Voight also appears in' Showtime's' television series *Ray Donovan* as Mickey Donovan, a role that brought him newfound critical and audience acclaim and his fourth Golden Globe win in 2014. He is the winner of one Academy Award, having been nominated for four. He has also won four Golden Globe Awards and has been nominated for eleven. In November 2019, he was awarded the National Medal of Arts.

Vlasta Vrana (1950–), b. Norway, of Czech parents, is a Canadian actor. He moved to Canada at the age of four. He has appeared on many television shows and films such as *The New Avengers*, *The Littlest Hobo*, *Choices*, *Spearfield's Daughter*, *The Kiss*, *War of the Worlds*, *After Amy*, *All Souls*, *Friday the 13th: the Series*, *Windsor Protocol*, *Lobby*, *Highlander III: The Sorcerer*, *Sirens*, *All Souls*, *Mom P.I.*, *The Hitchhiker*, *Press Run*, *Waking the Dead* and *The Blue Man*. He also played Fire Chief Wickersham in *Secret Window* and Booker (MPC) in *The Day After Tomorrow*. His work as a voice actor includes *Assassin's Creed*, *Splinter Cell*, *Heavy Metal*, *Heavy Metal 2000*, and *The Mysterious Cities of Gold*, as well as documentaries and thousands of radio and television commercials. He also narrated *Canada Vignettes* films and several other films for The National Film Board of Canada. He was awarded the 2005 Award of Excellence by ACTRA Montreal and the Richard Kind Award for best actor at the 2005 Trenton Film Festival.

Jennifer J. C. Wendel (1964–), b. US, of Czech ancestry, the daughter of Elmarie Wendel, is an actress. She is best known for *Quantum Leap* (1989), *Dave's World* (1993), *The X-Files* (1993), *Yesterday's Target* (1996) and *Shrinking Violet* (2001).

Devon Werkheiser (1991–), b. Atlanta, GA, of Slovak descent, is an American actor, voice actor, singer, songwriter and musician. He is known for his starring role as Ned Bigby in Nickelodeon's hit TV series *Ned's Declassified School Survival Guide* (2004). The show has upheld a fan base of people ages 20–30 all over the world and garnered him two Kid's Choice Awards orange blimps. Moving to Los Angeles from Atlanta as a kid, he has over 20 years of acting experience. More recent credits include *Where's The Money* (2017), *Santa Girl* (2019), and *Sundown* (2016). He is also seen in *Crown Vic* (2019), opposite Thomas Jane, produced by Alec Baldwin. More than just an actor, Devon is an independent musician with years of released music. He continues to engage his fans and grow his platform on all forms of social media.

Tanya Wexler (1970–), b. Chicago, IL, of Bohemian ancestry, on her mother's side, has been a professional actress from age five. She has numerous commercial and local theater credits as an all too precocious child actor. Five years ago, she realized that she would much rather be behind the camera and enrolled in Columbia University's Film School where she earned an M.F.A. She has written and directed several video and short film projects including behind the scenes of *Fallen Angel* at Circle in the Square. *The Dance*, her first short film, was shown at The Telluride International Film Festival, The Seattle International Film Festival and the *First Look Series* at the Tribeca Film Center. Her thesis film *Cool Shoes* was awarded the bronze medal at the Houston Worldfest. *Finding North* is her first feature. She is best known for her 2011 comedy *Hysteria*.

Keala Wayne Winterhalt (2007–), b. US, of Czech ancestry (daughter of Sarah Wayne Callies), is a child actress. She was successful to grab the public attention in her early age of just seven years after a short role in *Into the Storms* which was released in 2014. In 2019, she appeared in *Unspeakable*.

Roland Winters (1904–1989), b. Boston, MA, of Czech ancestry (son of Felix Winternitz), was an American actor who played many character parts in films and television but today is best remembered for portraying Charlie Chan in six films in the late 1940s. After the series finished, Winters continued to work in film and television until 1982. He was in the movies *So Big* and *Abbott and Costello Meet the Killer, Boris Karloff*, played Elvis' father in *Blue Hawaii* and a judge in the Elvis film *Follow That Dream*. He made appearances in the early TV series *Meet Millie* as the boss. In one episode of the *Bewitched* TV series, he played the normally unseen McMann of *McMann and Tate*. He also portrayed Mr. Gimbel in *Miracle on 34th Street* in 1973.

Tom Wopat (1951–), born in Lodi, WI, of Czech ancestry, is an American actor, singer and guitarist. Wopat attended the University of Wisconsin–Madison and made his television debut on *One Life to Live*. He achieved television fame on the television series *The Dukes of Hazzard* (1979–85), then embarked on a music career. He has recorded eight albums. Musically, he switches between rock and roll and country music styles, though his two most recent albums have been of classic pop standards. Wopat first appeared on the Broadway stage as a replacement in the 1977 musical *I Love My Wife*, as Wally. He later appeared as a replacement in the stage musicals *City of Angels* and *Guys and Dolls*. In 1981, he played the main character, Billy Bigelow in the musical *Carousel*, at the Augusta Barn Theatre in Augusta, Michigan. He appeared in the opening cast of the 1999 revival of *Annie Get Your Gun* as Frank Butler, opposite Bernadette Peters, Susan Lucci and Crystal Bernard, who played Annie Oakley (in consecutive order); he was nominated for a Tony Award in 1999 for his performance as Butler. He later appeared in revivals of *Chicago* and *42nd Street*. In 2005, Wopat appeared in the Broadway revival of David Mamet's Pulitzer Prize-winning play *Glengarry Glen Ross* as James Lingk. He starred in the North Carolina Theatre's production of *The Music Man* as Harold Hill in November 2006. In 2008, Wopat starred on Broadway as the father in *A Catered Affair*, written by Harvey Fierstein (book) and John Bucchino (score), which opened in April 2008 at the Walter Kerr Theatre. He received his second Tony nomination for that performance. In July 2009, he originated the role of Frank Abagnale Sr. in the musical *Catch Me If You Can* (based on the film of the same name) in July and August 2009 at Seattle's 5th Avenue Theatre. He was featured in the new musical revue *Sondheim on Sondheim*, conceived and directed by James Lapine, presenting the life and works of Stephen Sondheim. The revue premiered on Broadway at the Roundabout Theatre's Studio 54 in March 2010 in previews and closed in June. He portrayed Ryan Hutton in the musical *Lovestruck*.

Trevor Wright (1980–), b. San Diego, CA, of Czech ancestry, is an actor. His breakthrough acting lead role was in the 2007 film *Shelter* as Zach. His very first break came through his involvement in music videos when, in 1989, Wright, along with fellow actor Elijah Wood, appeared in the video for Paula Abdul's single *Forever Your Girl*, directed by David Fincher. He subsequently starred opposite singer Stacie Orrico in the videos for her singles *Stuck* (2003), and *I Could Be the One* (2004). His first feature-film role was in 1993's *Memories* by Joe Frank, but his first major role was as "Zach" in the 2007 independent film *Shelter*, directed by Jonah Markowitz and co-starring Brad Rowe, Tina Holmes and Ross Thomas. His role brought him three awards for Best Male Lead at the Dallas Out Takes, and Best Actor and Audience Awards at Tampa International Gay and Lesbian Film Festival. Wright's film roles include *Vicious Circle*, in which he appeared in the role of the character "Fin." He was the lead actor in *Vacancy 2: The First Cut*, that had a straight to DVD release in January 2009. His 2010 films include *The Social Network* and *2001 Maniacs: Field of Screams*.

VIII. CULTURE: ARTS & LETTERS

Ned Wynn (1941–2020), b. NYC, of Bohemian ancestry, was an American actor and screenwriter. He was the son of actor Keenan Wynn and the grandson of Ed Wynn. He attended Lycée Jaccard School in Switzerland, the University of Pennsylvania and California Berkeley and worked at Fox as a script analyst. He was a background actor in several *Beach Blanket Bingo* films of the sixties and a number of other films and TV shows. His featured role in the movie, *California Dreaming* (1979), which he also wrote, was a proof, according to Ned, that he should stick to writing. He has become an accomplished screenwriter and he penned screenplays for the surfing movie *California Dreaming* (1979), starring Glynnis O'Connor and Seymour Cassel; for telefilms starring Dennis Weaver, Shari Belafonte and John Ritter; and for a 1983 episode of ABC's *Matt Houston*. He even co-wrote a song, "Available," that none other than Frank Sinatra recorded in the '60s. In 1990, he wrote his extraordinary autobiography *We Will Always Live in Beverly Hills* which describes his jaunty, sad, hilarious, and heartwarming path to his eventual career as an author.

William 'Billy' Zabka (1965–), b. New York, NY, of Czech ancestry, is an American actor, producer and screenwriter. Billy launched his film career starring as the main antagonist in 1984's classic movie *The Karate Kid*. He spent the next fifteen years acting in more than thirty feature films, including *Back To School*, *European Vacation*, *Just One Of The Guys* and had a four-year recurring role on the *Equalizer*. In 2001, Billy wrote and produced his first film, *Most* (a 33-minute Czech language live-action short film). *Most* had its world premiere at the Sundance Film Festival 2003 and went on to win numerous awards from prestigious film festivals, including the Crystal Heart Award at the Heartland Film Festival and Best of Festival in the Palm Springs International Film Festival. The film ultimately earned Zabka an Academy Award Nomination in 2004. In 2007, Billy wrote, directed and starred in a short film/music video called "Sweep The Leg" for Astonish Records and the band, No More Kings. The video spoofs his character from *The Karate Kid* and reunites many of the original cast. This video has had more than 2.5 million unique Internet views since its release.

Jacob Zachar (1986–), b. Chicago, IL, of Czech ancestry, is an American actor and singer. His roles include Russell "Rusty" Cartwright on the ABC Family TV Series *Greek*. Zachar booked his first starring role in *Greek* after living in Los Angeles for only two months. He played the part of Ernest in the film *Little Big Top* and then appeared as a cashier in the movie *Bodega*, also in 2006. He has also done commercials for Carl's Jr. and Dunkin' Donuts. He has performed in various theater roles such as *On Golden Pond*, *Prairie Lights*, *Big: The Musical*, *Les Misérables* and *Guys and Dolls*. Zachar provided voices for the movie *Surf's Up* and an episode of the animated television series *King of the Hill* where he was a cashier. In 2005, Zachar completed the film *Drunkboat* in which he stars along with Dana Delany, John Malkovich and John Goodman. While living in Chicago, he was in a metal band called

Megaband. Zachar also sang in a punk/ska group Not Too Good. He now plays in a blues and funk band part-time.

Winter Ave Zoli (1980–), b. New Hope, PA, of Czech father, is an American actress and model. At the age of 11, she moved with her family to Prague, Czech Republic, where she was able to fully plant her Czech roots. At 17, she attended the Carnegie-Mellon summer school theater program and, at 19, enrolled in the Atlantic Theater Company acting school in New York City. She appeared in the 2007 film *Sex and Death 101* as Alexis the fast food beauty. She held the main role of legendary Libuše in the 2009 Czech film *The Pagan Queen*. In 2016, Winter starred in the feature film *Deserted* (2016) opposite Mischa Barton, Jackson Davis, Trent Ford, Dana Rosendorff, Lance Henriksen, Jake Busey and Gerry Bednob. Winter gained further international recognition with her main role as Lyla Winston on the hit American TV series *Sons of Anarchy*.

Chris Zylka (orig. Chris Settlemire) (1985–), b. Warren, OH, of Czech and Slovak ancestry, is an American actor and model. He attended the University of Toledo. Zylka began his career with a guest appearance on *90210* in 2008. He was soon cast in a recurring role in *Everybody Hates Chris* before also having guest appearances on the shows *Hannah Montana*, *Cougar Town* and *Zeke and Luther*. Zylka then landed a sixteen-episode recurring role as Joey Donner in *10 Things I Hate about You*. Zylka began to move into films around this time, appearing in *The People I've Slept With* before starring in the horror television film *My Super Psycho Sweet 16*. Zylka would later reprise this role in the sequel, *My Super Psycho Sweet 16: Part 2*. Zylka also appeared in *Kaboom* in 2010. He starred in two animal attack-themed films, *Shark Night* (2011) and *Piranha 3DD* (2012). Zylka portrayed Flash Thompson in *The Amazing Spider-Man*. He played the role of Jake in the television drama *The Secret Circle*. Buddy TV ranked him number ninety on its list of "TV's Sexiest Men of 2011."

3. Dancers & Choreographers

Olga Maria Bibza Adkins (1912–1998), b. Duquesne, PA, was a dancer. She was very musically gifted and in early years studied piano. She graduated from State Conservatory of Music in Prague, Czech., with a Bachelor of Arts degree in 1934. She continued her education with a Master's degree in Fina Arts at Women's College of the University of North Carolina, Greensboro, NC, in 1954. She then taught at the following colleges: Mississippi State College for Women, MS (1941–43), Alabama Polytechnic Institute, Auburn, AL (1943–52), Women's College of the University of North Carolina, Greensboro, NC (1952–53), University of Georgia, Athens, GA (1952–55). In 1955, she came to Miami University, Oxford, OH as a professor of dance. She specialized in contemporary dance and folk dance (1955–77).

Adele Astaire (née Adele Marie Austerlitz) (1898-1981), b. Omaha, NE, of Bohemian ancestry (a sister of Fred Astaire), was acclaimed vaudeville and musical theater dancer and actress. She built a successful performance career with her younger brother, Fred Astaire. The brother and sister act initially worked their way through vaudeville circuits, finally achieving a breakthrough with their first Broadway roles in 1917. She became known for her talents as a skilled dancer and comedienne, starring in hit Broadway musicals such as *Lady, Be Good!* (1924), *Funny Face* (1927) and *The Band Wagon* (1931).

Fred Astaire (orig. Frederick Austerlitz) (1899-1987), b. Omaha NE, of Bohemian ancestry, was an American dancer of stage and motion pictures who is best known for a number of highly successful musical comedy films in which he starred with Ginger Rogers. He is regarded by many as the greatest popular-music dancer of all time. He was also choreographer, actor, and singer.

Otokar Bartík (1868-1936), b. Prague, Bohemia, was a ballet dancer and choreographer. He was a solo dancer and dancing master choreographer of the Metropolitan Opera House in NYC for 24 years of service (1908-32). Before his arrival in New York, he had worked in several European theatres. In America, he first got an engagement with Barnum and Bailey's, and later organized great ballets at Madison Square Garden until the success of the first performance of the *Bartered Bride* was staged, according to the original plan of Conried, by Andreas Dippel, who engaged the best possible conductor of the time, Gustav Mahler, and the best singer for the role of Mařenka, Emmy Destinn. At the suggestion of J. E. Vojan, Dippel, recognizing the true nature of the work, he had the dances performed by a group of Czech boys and girls under the direction of Bartík and thus brought out the national and popular character of the opera.

Augustin Berger (1861-1945), b. Boskovice, Bohemia, was a dancer, ballet master and choreographer. During 1923-32, he was in charge of ballet in Metropolitan Opera, NY.

Helena Bolehovská (née Schmausová) (1928-ca. 2003), b. Prague, Czech., in Brazil s. 1950); dancer, choreographer, and teacher. She studied law at Charles University but did not finish. She also attended the 8-year Dance school of R. Remislavsky, a ballet master of the National Theater in Prague. After her marriage at the end of 1949, she escaped with her husband, from Czechoslovakia and in 1950, they immigrated to Brazil. She became an active member of the cultural organization, União Cultural Tcheco Brasileira, of which she became president for number of years. Almost immediately, she began forming a dance group, which was not easy at that time. Nevertheless, she organized a group with several couples, and they soon began performing the Czech Beseda, as well as the Moravian Beseda. Eventually she established a 35-member dance ensemble which performed publicly and took part in contests with other dance groups. She also included folklore dancing, with dancers wearing the authentic Czech folk and national costumes. Her group apparently won the first folk dancing prize in Brazil. She also established a large library for her club and regularly organized discothéque and videotheque showings of Czech films. Bolehovská was the only teacher of Czech language in Brazil, and she also prepared her own language texts. She was also an active translator from Portuguese, English, German, and Spanish to Czech.

Nina Brzorad (1954–), b. New York City, of Czech parents, began her formal ballet training at age 11 at the Balanchine School of American Ballet, where she received a full scholarship at the age of 12. Also studied at the American Ballet Theatre School as well as modern dance and jazz at the Alvin Ailey American Dance Center. While still a student at the School of American Ballet, she was chosen by Stanley Williams to perform the leading roles in his restaging of the Bournonville classics, Napoli, Konservatoriet and La Sylphide, for the annual workshop performances. At age 16, she received her first professional engagements with Eglevsky Ballet Company in NY and Ballet Spectacular, performing classical pas de deux such as Flower Festival and Don Quixote, with fellow student partner, Fernando Bujones. She then joined American Ballet Theatre where she danced for four years, touring the USA and participating in the movie *The Turning Point*, featuring M. Baryshnikov. She became a principal dancer with the Iranian National Ballet in Teheran, Iran. She danced a variety of leading roles in full length classics as well as John Butler's *Carmina Burana* and *After Eden*, plus other repertory. Due to the political upheaval in Iran, returned to the US where she went on to join the New Jersey Ballet Company as principal dancer. She danced leading roles in the company's classical and contemporary repertory, as well as numerous Balanchine ballets. She became principal dancer with Essener Ballett in Germany. For three years, she danced all the leading roles in the repertory, including working with Dutch choreographer, Hans Van Manen and appearing as a guest in various dance festivals with the Essener Ballett in Köln, Frankfurt, Hanover and on television. Upon her return to N.Y., Nina Brzorad became principal dancer, co-founder and associate artistic director of the Dance Theatre of Long Island in N.Y., under the artistic direction of Ali Pourfarrokh, as well as co-founder and faculty member of the North Shore School of Dance. She was also an associate professor and artist in residence at the Hofstra University Dance Department in NY. During the last ten years, she has been working in the Czech Republic, mainly in Prague as a freelance company teacher for the National Theatre Ballet, Prague Chamber Ballet, Laterna magika and conducted several master classes for the dance department at the Charles University in Prague. She also continues to guest-teach for the Gärtnerplatz Theatre in Munich, Germany, as well as in N.Y. Since 2002, Nina Brzorad is the main company teacher for the National Theatre Ballet in Prague, under the Artistic Direction of Peter Zuska as well as rehearsal assistant and coach.

Gertrude Bunzel (née Goldschmied) (1910-1986), b. Vienna, of Moravian ancestry, was a contemporary dancer and choreographer, trained at Vienna State Academy of Music. Since 1939, she was in US where she was engaged as teacher of creative dance and eurhythmics and recreational leader in Baltimore and Pittsburgh (1940-44), then taught at Carnegie Inst. of Technology, etc.

Eva Cernik, b. Brazil, of Czech ancestry, is a dancer, who has danced since her childhood in Brazil. She is known for her sizzling Turkish Oriental dance style. Eva was first introduced to the dance by Anahid Sofian of New York whose Turkish style left a strong impression. She has worked in many countries and performed on a regular basis with the Erdogan Turkish Oriental Dance Troupe, Inosis Berber Ballet, and the Colorado Bedouin Ballet. She researched Oriental dance, its music and content with 19 trips to Egypt and 5 to Turkey, as well as lengthy study and work in Iran, Syria, Spain, Morocco and 13 other countries. In her present home in Denver, she produces grand shows, with live music from bands such as Sherefé, utilizing dance to express themes concerning spirit and life.

Joe Chvala (1956-), b. Wisconsin, of Czech ancestry, is a dancer and choreographer, and the founder and artistic director of 'Flying Foot Forum,' a percussive dance/theater company. Joe Chvala has spent most of his adult life based in New York City, Gothenburg, Sweden, and since 1990 Minneapolis. During this time, he has worked as a director, choreographer, writer, composer, performer, and teacher for opera companies, experimental and nonexperimental theatres, concert dance venues, performing arts academies, and universities. After moving to the Twin Cities in 1990, Joe worked with a variety of theater companies while developing his own choreographic dance/theater work for his company of percussive dancers, the Flying Foot Forum. Since the premiere of their first full concert (May '93), the Flying Foot Forum has been presented in a variety of venues around the world from Paris to New York City, Jacob's Pillow to England.

Jean Tachau Haas (1926-2016), b. Louisville, KY, of Bohemian ancestry, was a dancer. She studied dance with Mary Long Burke in Louisville and Ted Shawn at Jacob's Pillow. After high school, she moved to New York City to pursue a dance career and performed on Broadway in *Allegro* and *Kiss Me Kate*. Jean returned to Louisville in 1953 to raise a family and opened the Jean Tachau Haas School of Ballet, which she operated until 1969. She also taught dance at Sacred Heart Model School and the Brown School. Jean's second career was in early childhood education. She taught at Edgecliff Daycare, Crescent Hill Presbyterian and Highland Presbyterian pre-schools.

Audrey Ichida (ca. 1968-), of Czech-Japanese ancestry, studied ballet for 12 years and began studying Middle Eastern dance in 1999. She is a Level I certified dancer with The

Suhaila Salimpour School of Dance, Albany, CA. She joined Silk Road Dance Company in 2001, performing with the ensemble that year in their first appearance at the Kennedy Center.

Thomas Ivanec (1949–), b. Cleveland, of Slovak ancestry, is the founder and director of Lučenec Folk Ensemble, and the children's Lučínka Golk Ensemble. With a sparkling renewed interest in his Slovak ancestry, he acquired knowledge of Slovak folk dance and ultimately formed the Lúčina Slovak Folklore Ensemble.

Francesca Jandasek (1974–), b. Namibia, Africa, of Czech ancestry, is a dancer and a dance teacher. She lives in Washington, DC and currently dances with local dance companies Sharna Fabiano Tango Company, Dakshina, Daniel Phoenix Singh Dance Company and Deviated Theatre.

Jozef Jantoška (fl. 1990), b. Slovakia, is an actor, director, and choreographer. He was a folklore choreographer of the Toronto Slovak Dancers (1985–87). Jantoska returned in 1990 and enriched the repertoire with four new dances which include 'Horehronska Veselica, Cerkany, Perinarky Janosik and Veselica na Detve.' Through its dances, the ensemble has laid a great deal of importance upon the intimate knowledge of the folk character of the given region, and the development of individual abilities of all the members. By choosing music from different regions of Slovakia, the ensemble's repertoire demonstrates the beauty and variety of Slovak folklore.

Albia Kavan (ca. 1917), b. Chicago, IL, of Czech ancestry, was a ballet dancer who performed for Pres. Roosevelt in White House in 1935. She danced with the American Ballet, the Metropolitan Opera Corp. and with the Ballet Caravan.

Gabriel de Korponay (aka Gábor Korponay) (1809–1866), b. near Košice, Slovakia, was a celebrated teacher of dancing. He came out to the United States in the early 1840s or even earlier to become a famous polka dancer here, so the fashionable polka dance was a success in New York and other cities in the states after Europe. Between 1846–48, during the Mexican-American War, he was captain of the Third Volunteer Cavalry Regiment in Missouri. During Civil War, he was colonel of a PA Regiment.

Harold Kreutzberg (1902–1968), b. Liberec, Bohemia, was a dancer and choreographer. He was trained at the Dresden Ballet School, he also studied dance with Mary Wigman and Rudolf Laban. Beginning in 1927, he appeared in plays directed by Max Reinhardt and in 1929, went with Reinhardt to New York City. Kreutzberg then toured the US, Canada, and Europe with the dancer Yvonne Georgi. He founded a school in Bern in 1955. Its ballets combined the drama and humor, with an emphasis on inventive scenes. He danced in US in early 30s and again in 1937, 1947, 1948, and 1953. His last appearance in US was with Chicago Opera in 1965 when he danced four roles in a version of Orff's *Carmina Burana*. In 1932-1936, Kreutzberg, along with his partner Ruth Page, created a new and unlikely partnership. Kreutzberg was a German modern dancer, while Page was an American ballerina. They first performed together on 25 February 1933 in Chicago. This partnership helped Kreutzberg perform his solo acts in other venues, which is what people really enjoyed watching him do. Kreutzberg's performances were described as including everything from strong actions to flowing movements and even some pantomime.

John Kriza (1919-1975), born in Berwyn, IL, of Czech ancestry, was a ballet dancer who was one of American Ballet Theatre's best-known male principals. He went to Chicago where he studied with Bentley Stone and Walter Camryn. He danced with Page-Stone Ballet Company. In New York City, he studied with Anton Dolin and Pierre Vladimirov before joining Ballet Theatre in 1940. Kriza created roles in Jerome Robbins' *Fancy Free* in 1944, and *Interplay* in 1945. Also Michael Kidd's *On Stage* in 1945, Agnes de Mille's *Fall River Legend* and Herbert Ross's *Caprichos*. He will be remembered for his interpretation of Billy in Eugene Loring's *Billy the Kid*. He retired from dancing with Ballet Theatre in 1966 and became assistant to the director. John Kriza died in a freak accident while swimming in Florida.

James Kudelka (1955-), b. Newmarket, Ontario, Can., of Czech ancestry, is Can. choreographer, dancer, and director. James Kudelka is acknowledged internationally as the leading Canadian ballet choreographer of his generation. He has evolved a unique style that draws from both classical ballet and modern dance to produce works of unusual technical inventiveness and emotional power. Kudelka's musical tastes are exceptionally wide-ranging, from pop to classical – The Beatles to Bartok. He has also commissioned several original scores. He was the artistic director for the National Ballet of Canada from 1996 to 2005, now serving as the National Ballet's artist in residence.

Gertrude Prokosch Kurath (1903-1992), b. Chicago, IL, of Czech ancestry, was an American dancer, researcher, author, and ethnomusicologist. She graduated from Bryn Mawr College, receiving a B.A. in 1922, and an M.A. in art history in 1928, concurrently studying music and dance in Berlin, Philadelphia, New York, and Providence, Rhode Island (1922-28). She then studied music and dance at the Yale School of Drama at Yale University, from 1929-1930. She researched and wrote extensively on the study of dance, co-authoring several books and writing hundreds of articles. Her main areas of interest were ethnomusicology and dance ethnology, with some of her best-known work being the book *Music and Dance of the Tewa Pueblos*, co-written with Antonio Garcia (1970). She made substantial contributions to the study of Amerindian dance, and to dance theory. From 1958 to January 1972, she was dance editor for the journal *Ethnomusicology*. Her other scholarly interests included the fields of folk liturgy and rock music. In 1962, she founded the Dance Research Center in Ann Arbor, Michigan.

Linda Lehovec (1961-), b. Pittsfield, MA, of Czech ancestry, is a choreographer and performer, working from a home base in the rural Midwest. She is currently an associate professor with tenure and co-director of the BFA Program. Lehovec began her training in Pittsfield, Massachusetts, with Madeline Cantarella Culpo. She holds a BFA degree from the Juilliard School (1982?) and an MFA degree from the University of Illinois at Urbana-Champaign (1994). Linda teaches ballet, contemporary modern technique, and yoga (certified in 2011 from the Temple of Kriya Yoga, Chicago). Her research focuses on the creation of contemporary modern dance works. Linda danced in the works of many contemporary choreographers, including Joe Goode, Ralph Lemon, Stephen Koester, Bill Young, Tere O'Connor, Sara Hook, and David Parker. Her work has been performed internationally in Canada, Korea, and Chile and nationally in San Francisco, Seattle, Chicago, Detroit, Atlanta, Oklahoma, Florida, Minnesota, and Wisconsin. Linda has been awarded two fellowships in choreography from the Illinois Arts Council and was recently awarded a College of Fine and Applied Arts Creative Research Award and a University Research Grant to collaborate with Chilean choreographer Francisca Silva-Zautzik. Their new work, Gone, featuring a cast of American and Chilean performers, was premiered in Santiago, Chile, in August 2013 and was presented at Krannert Center as part of February Dance: *Hybridity* in 2014.

Maria Ley-Piscator (née Friederike Czada) (1898-1999), b. Vienna, of Bohemian ancestry, was a dancer and choreographer. Maria Ley sought to create a theatrical career for herself as a dancer in Paris and Berlin. Later, she turned to choreography and helped in several stage productions with Max Reinhardt, including *A Midsummer Night's Dream*. Maria Ley also studied literature at the Sorbonne, where she met Erwin Piscator (her third husband) during his exile in 1936. After marrying in Paris, the couple moved to Manhattan in 1939, where they founded the Dramatic Workshop at the New School for Social Research. Their students included Harry Belafonte, Marlon Brando and Tony Randall. Ley-Piscator directed several theatrical productions off Broadway. During the 1970s, she worked as a teacher at the Southern Illinois University Carbondale and at Stony Brook University. Ley-Piscator died in New York in 1999 at the age of 101.

Angela M. Jumba-Lipchick (aka Angie Lipchick) (1954-), b. Pittsburgh, PA, of Slovak ancestry, is a director and choreographer of Pittsburgh Area Slovak Folk Ensemble, and a librarian at St. Maurice Catholic School. She has a degree from Carlow College and graduate work at Duquesne University in Ethnomusicology. She is the Director of The Pittsburgh Area Slovak Folk Ensemble (PAS) - a world-class-performing ensemble. PAS has performed at Deťva, Slovakia representing the United States for their International Festival. PAS also performed at the Bicentennial Celebration and at the Statue of Liberty rededication in New York. Other venues include Disneyworld in Florida, the National Slovak Festival in New Jersey, and The Slovak Embassy in Washington DC among other places. Angela has authored papers about Slovak traditions and customs and was also privileged to experience the many cultures of the world by being the Executive Director of the Pittsburgh Folk Festival from 1995-1997. Besides PAS, her greatest loves are being on the staff of East Catholic School. She serves on the Advisory Board of the Czech and Slovak School of Pittsburgh.

Florentina Lojeková (1939-), b. Bratislava, is a prima ballerina and choreographer. She was one of the first graduates at department of dance at the State Conservatory in Bratislava. It was during her studies when Jozef Zajko, ballet director and Slovak choreographer, offered her to perform a role in the ballet the *Sleeping Beauty*. At the age of 16, she presented this role. On the top of her career, she was forced to leave the country. In 1968, she came to Canada, joining the Canadian National Ballet. For 25 years, she served as professor at Ryerson University in Toronto.

Vladimír Marek (1928-2020), b. Užhorod, Czech., was a ballet dancer. He was trained in his native Czechoslovakia and Russia. He was a soloist, National Theater Ballet, Prague (1947-50); principal dancer Bratislava (1950-69), ballet master (1958-68). He came to San Antonio in 1968. In 1970, he and Nancy Smith founded the San Antonio Ballet, this city's first professional company. Dancers were hired from auditions across the U.S. as well as from Europe and Asia. An inspired teacher, Marek identified talented young San Antonio dancers and began a scholarship program to nurture their gifts and give them a start on dance careers. Students trained at the Vladimir Marek Ballet Academy, went on to dance in numerous companies across the U.S. and in Europe. He was also a ballet teacher, Our Lady of Lake Univ., San Antonio (1970-78); and owner, teacher V. Marek Ballet Acad., San Antonio. He danced dancing leading roles in the classics like *Swan Lake*, *Giselle*, and *Sleeping Beauty*.

Milada Mladova (née Annabelle Milada Mraz) (1921-2015), b. Oklahoma City, is a ballet dancer and film performer. She studied dance at Fronie Asher's School of Dance in Oklahoma City until 1936, when Leonide Massine held auditions in Oklahoma City. Following the audition, she studied in Paris with Olga Preobrojenska for six months before joining the Ballet Russe de Monte Carlo, where she took the stage name Milada Mladova. She danced with the Ballet Russe de Monte Carlo from 1937-42, beginning as a corps member and moving up to soloist. She danced solos in *Rodeo*, *Gaite Parisienne*, *Devil's Holiday*, *Poker Game*, and *Les Sylphides*. She left the company in 1942 after Massine left as director and went on to be a featured dancer in films such as *The Merry Widow, Night and Day, Atlantis, Escape Me Never* and *Ali Baba.*

Milica (Hasalová) Moravčík (1933–2022), b. Prague, is a ballet instructor and choreographer. She studied education at George Washington Univ. (B.S., 1954; M.S., 1978). She is a member of the original Washington Ballet; former member of the National Ballet, Washington, DC; choreographer for the Washington Civic Opera, Washington, DC, choreographer for the Vienna Light Opera Company, VA; member of the teaching staff of The Holton Arms School and Junior College (1954–1960); lecturer at George Washington University (1975–78); owner and director of the Kemp Mill School of Ballet s. 1958).

Rebecca Nettl-Fiol (1953–), b. Indiana, of Czech father, is a dancer, and choreographer. She holds the position of professor of modern dance, University of Illinois. She specializes in the Alexander technique and dance training. Her choreography has been presented in New York City, Chicago, and Quito, Ecuador, annually at Krannert Center for the Performing Arts, at many College Dance Festivals and throughout the Midwest. She is the co-author of *Dance and the Alexander Technique: Exploring the Missing Link.*

Andre Oliveroff (orig. Oliver Smith Grymes) (1896–1952), desc. f. Augustine Heřman, was a ballet dancer. He was a member of Anna Pavlova's ballet troupe. He toured with Mme. Pavlova from 1916 till 1923. He collaborated with John Gillon on the ballerina's biography *Flight of the Swan: A Memory of Pavlova* (1932).

Nadia Oros (fl. 1992), b. Prešov, Slovakia, is an instructor/choreographer. She was with Lučenec Folk Ensemble and the children's Lučínka Folk Ensemble; formerly with Slovak Folk Ensemble, 'ŠARIŠAN.' In 1992, Nadia made her debut in the United States and Windsor, Canada. She performed in cities across the United States, including Chicago, Pittsburgh, and Detroit. It was in Cleveland that the tour ended and where she decided to stay to explore American culture.

Dean Poloka (1971–), b. Pittsburgh, of Slovak descent, is a choreographer and ethnic researcher of traditional Carpatho-Rusyn music, song and dance. Dean holds a Bachelor's Degree in History with an Eastern European concentration and an undergraduate certificate from the Center for Russian and East European Studies, both from the University of Pittsburgh. Dean has researched and studied Carpatho-Rusyn history, language, music, song and dance for over 20 years. He is currently the Program Director and choreographer of the Slavjane Folk Ensemble, a children's Slavic dance ensemble. Dean served as Vice-President of the Carpatho-Rusyn Society as well as President of its Pittsburgh Chapter. Since 2004, Dean has hosted the Carpatho-Rusyn Society Heritage Program, a weekly radio broadcast that propagates Carpatho-Rusyn music and information to a worldwide audience.

Jack Poloka (1938–2010), b. Pittsburgh, PA, of Slovak descent, was an activist. Apart from his management position at Equitable Gas, he was a driving force behind the preservation of Carpatho-Rusyn heritage in Pittsburgh. With his son, Dean, he hosted a weekly ethnic radio program on WPIT 730 and led heritage tours back to Eastern Europe. A longtime board member of the Pittsburgh Folk Festival, Mr. Poloka also served was served recently as director of its annual festival. Starting in 1956, he taught Carpatho-Rusyn dancing to thousands of children, including his own children and all of his grandchildren old enough to participate. As director of the Slavjane Folk Ensemble, which he founded, Mr. Poloka was involved with every facet of the group, from making the posters to selling the tickets to cooking the food for the group's Christmas banquet.

Miroslava 'Mira' Pospisil (1956–), b. New Haven, CT, of Czech parents, is a dancer. She studied philosophy at Yale Univ. (B.A., 1979) and elementary school education at Bank St. Coll. of Education (M.S., 1984). She also holds a painting certificate from Pennsylvania Academy of Fine Arts. She studied modern dance (Humphrey technique) with Ernestine Stodelle for 30 years. She taught creative dance at Brooklyn Coll. and was engaged as a dance teacher at the Princeton Ballet, Philadelphia College of Art, Bryn Mawr College, National Ballet Academy and the Dutch National Ballet.

Irena Prochotsky (1941–2003), b. Klagenfurt, Austria, of Slovak descent, was a ballet dancer. She was the owner of Ballet School Bethesda, MD.

Ivo Váňa Psota (1908–1952), b. Kiev, Ukraine, of Czech parents, ranked amongst the most renowned Czech dancers and choreographers. He was the ballet master and ballet art director for the National Theatre in Brno starting in 1928 and taught dance at the Brno conservatories. He worked in the ballet group Ballet Russe de Monte Carlo (1932–36). He also established his own ballet school in Brno. Psota left Brno for the USA in 1941 and became the ballet art director of the Metropolitan Opera in New York where he, amongst other things, presented excellent choreography of Dvořák's Slavonic Dances under the name Slavonica. He consequently met with success once again with Original Ballet Russe, primarily in Latin America (1941). He rejected an offer to become director of the Teatro Colón in Buenos Aires as well as the post of ballet director of the National Theatre in Prague and returned to Brno in 1947. His ballet consequently became the leading professional dance troupe in Czechoslovakia.

Thomas (Tomáš) Schramek (1945–), b. Bratislava, Czech., is a Canadian ballet artist. He has been a professional dancer since the age of 15. Tomáš started studying with The National Theatre Ballet School and continued at Slovak Folk-Dance Ensemble SLUK, where he became a professional dancer. While performing, he studied for and obtained a Bachelor of

Fine Arts from the Academy of Musical and Theatrical Arts (VSMU) in Bratislava. He joined The National Ballet of Canada in 1969 and was promoted to Principal Dancer in 1973. Tomas became a Principal Character Artist in 1990 and a Guest Principal Artist in 2020. He was appointed Company Teacher in 1992 and was the Assistant Ballet Master from 2005 to 2010. As a Principal Dancer, Tomas performed most of the leading male classical roles, including Prince Florimund in *The Sleeping Beauty*, Prince in *Swan Lake*, Albrecht in *Giselle*, James in *La Sylphide*, Romeo and Mercutio in *Romeo and Juliet*, Colas in *La Fille mal gardée*, Franz in *Coppélia* and Catalinon in John Neumeier's *Don Juan*.

Pavel Šmok (1927-2016), b. Levoča, Slovakia, of Czech father, is a ballet dancer and choreographer. He was trained at Prague State Conservatory, graduating age 26. He danced with the Army Ensemble (1952-55) and in Pilsen (1955-58) but injury forced him to retire from the stage. He was ballet master in Usti and Labem (1958-60) and in Ostrava (1960-64) then in 1964 he co-founded Prague Ballet with Lubos Ogoun. He remained there as ballet master until 1970, after which he was director of Basle Ballet (1970-73). Between 1973 and 1975 he worked as a freelance choreographer until forming the Chamber Ballet Prague in 1975. His ballets for that company such as 'Intimate Letters' (mus. Janáček, 1969), 'Sinfonietta' (mus. Janáček, 1971), and 'Stabat Mater' (mus. Dvořák, 1995), frequently used Czech and Slovak scores, the tense angular style of his early ballets softening into a more rounded lyricism in the later works. In 1990, he was appointed professor in the music faculty of the Prague Academy of Arts. He is known in US for the dances he staged in *Jenufa* for the Am. Opera Center and the *Bartered Bride* for the Metropolitan Opera (1978).

Ruth A. Sobotka (1925-1967), b. Vienna, of Bohemian ancestry, was a dancer, costume designer, art director, painter, and actress. Ruth Sobotka immigrated to the United States from Vienna with her parents in 1938. She studied set design at The University of Pennsylvania and graduated from the Carnegie Institute of Technology. After studying at the School of American Ballet, Sobotka became a member of George Balanchine's Ballet Society (1946-1948) and its successor The New York City Ballet from 1949-1961. She also designed the costumes for and danced in the Jerome Robbins' controversial ballet *The Cage* (1951) and played Robbins' wife in *Tyl Eulenspiegel* (1951). Sobotka appeared in many successful Balanchine ballets including *The Four Temperaments* (1946); *Serenade, Apollo, Symphony in C* (1946); *Swan Lake* (pas de quatre) (1951); *Concerto Barocco, The Nutcracker* (1954); *Ivesiana* (1954) *Agon* (1957) and *The Figure in the Carpet* (1961). Sobotka also danced in James Waring's company and for major American choreographers and designed costumes for works by Paul Taylor, Erick Hawkins, and John Taras. She danced on Broadway in the musicals *Sadie Thompson* (1944) and the Balanchine revival of *On Your Toes* (1954). A young Sobotka appeared as "The Girl" in Man Ray's segment "Ruth, Roses and Revolvers" in the groundbreaking avant-garde film by Hans Richter, *Dreams That Money*

Can Buy (1946). Ruth Sobotka was the second wife of film director Stanley Kubrick (1928–1999). She and Kubrick met in 1952; they married in January 1955; separated in 1958 and divorced in 1961. Sobotka appeared in a cameo role of the ballerina "Iris" in Kubrick's *Killer's Kiss* (1954) and served as art director on the sets of *Killer's Kiss* and Kubrick's subsequent feature, *The Killing* (1956). After her resignation from the NYC Ballet in 1961, Sobotka choreographed for the Shakespeare Festival in Stamford, Connecticut and studied acting under Herbert Bergoff, Uta Hagen and later Lee Strasberg at The Actor's Studio. She appeared in a number of off-Broadway productions and was a member of the Seattle Repertory Theatre during their first season in 1963, playing Cordelia in *King Lear*.

Dagmar Spain (ca. 1964–), b. Czech Republic, is a choreographer, actor, dancer and dance teacher. She received her dance training in Frankfurt, Germany and in New York (MFA) where she resided for 20 years. At age ten, a ballet teacher planted the seed of her joy in improvisation, which eventually led to her discovery of choreography. In 1999, she founded her company Dance Imprints. Her work has been commissioned for a student-production at Brown University, at the Kyurian Theater in Tokyo, and at the Taipei Theater in New York, as well as presented at many other theaters in New York.

Matt Steffanina (1986–), b. Charlottesville, VA, of Slovak descent, is an American hip hop dancer, choreographer, and YouTuber. He is the most followed dancer in the world with over 10 million followers and a billion views on YouTube. Matt was originally a competitive snowboarder and didn't become interested in dance until the age of 18 after watching dance videos online. After winning a dance competition, he was offered the position as the head choreographer of the University of Virginia hip hop dance crew. After doing choreography near his home state, he decided to move to Los Angeles, California to pursue a dance career full time in 2010. He started dancing and doing choreography for artists such as Chris Brown, Lil Wayne, Jermaine Jackson, Snoop Dogg, DJ Tiesto, Busta Rhymes and Tyga. He also appeared on nationally televised shows such as *So You Think You Can Dance*, *Jay Leno*, and *Ellen*. In 2012 he started posting videos of his dance classes on YouTube with his students where he ended up gaining a large following and becoming a YouTube star. His videos usually consist of him and his students performing new dances he has choreographed for current hit songs. The students in Matt's videos range from kids to adults. He's amassed millions of subscribers and his videos have been viewed over a billion times. In 2016, he appeared on the *Amazing Race* in Season 28 with his fiancé and dance partner at the time Dana Alexa. They would go on to win the competition and the million-dollar grand prize.

Dušan Týnek (ca. 1975–), b. Czech, is an internationally known dancer. He came to the US in 1992 and received his B.A. from Bard College, with a concentration in dance performance and composition as well as studies in the natural sciences. The Czech-born choreographer has studied and performed with several modern dance pioneers, owing much of his training and inspiration to Lucinda Childs as well as Merce Cunningham who personally tutored him while Týnek served as an understudy for the Merce Cunningham Dance Company. Týnek also performed and toured with Dance Works Rotterdam in the Netherlands. Since founding his own 8-member company – Dušan Týnek Dance Theatre – in 2003, Týnek has created over 20 major dances, choreographed an opera, and held seven critically-acclaimed seasons in major dance venues in NYC. Týnek has received commissioning grants from the NEA and from the Harkness, Greenwall, and O'Donnell-Green Music and Dance foundations. He has taught and/or set work on students at schools across the U.S. and abroad. He is recently the recipient of a prestigious Bogliasco Fellowship. Týnek has been awarded also the Hermitage Artist Residency and most recently the Djerassi Residency. In addition to choreographing dance for stage and opera, he has created site specific works at flooded quarries. Most recently, Tynek completed a commission for a site-specific dance in The Skyspace at the Ringling Museum of Art alongside the light installation of James Turrell. The company has received ongoing support from the Ford Foundation, NYCDCA, Czech Center NY, Trust for Mutual Understanding, and Mid Atlantic Arts Foundation, among others.

Jana 'Jaja' Vaňková (1992–), b. Česká Kamanice, Děčín, Czech., is a Czech-American dancer, choreographer, and artist. She found her passion for dance, performance, and movement when she was a little child. At that time joining the small dance crew Tizzians, leading her to then join a professional dance crew Out Of Bounds in her teenage years. She was studying choreography, theater, and performance with her group while actively researching and working on herself in numerous other styles and the history of street dance. After many successes in the Czech Republic, Jaja received the opportunity to start her dance career in Los Angeles with IaMmE Crew. This led her to become America's Best Dance Crew champion and the opportunity to stay in the US. Since then, Jaja has traveled to 40+ countries to share her knowledge, give performances, and work on numerous projects around the whole world. She has worked with numerous artists, such as choreographing for Justin Bieber and dancing for Selena Gomez, Taylor Swift, Kevin Hart, Ludacris, and more. She's notably known as a finalist of *So You Think You Can Dance* season 12, as Robot Girl from *Step Up All In*, or for her own project *The Puppet & The Puppet Master*. Jaja is the founder and director of RUR Alliance where she's leading the next generation of artists to become powerful individuals in all aspects of dance and arts.

Petr Zahradníček, b. Brno, Czech., is a choreographer. In 2001, he decided to move to the United States where he danced with Colorado Ballet. Since joining Milwaukee Ballet in 2003, Zahradnícek has created many pieces for the Company, the Nancy Einhorn Milwaukee

Ballet II Program and Milwaukee Ballet School & Academy. He has also choreographed three pieces for Ballet Memphis in Tennessee.

4. Models

Markéta Bělonoha (1982-), b. Tábor, Czech., currently lives in Hradec, Kralove. She has done nude modeling for numerous websites and adult magazines including MET Art, *Hegre Art*, *Perfect 10* and *Playboy* and was rated one of the sexiest women alive by the French editions of both *Playboy* and Lui. In May 2006, she earned a special Red Diploma Degree certificate for exceptional excellence in informatics management, for which she is entitled to carry the professional title, Ing. Marketa is and has been one of the most photographed nude models in the world, and presently ranks as the highest paid nude model in all of Eastern Europe. She has also done fashion modeling in both the US and Europe since 2005 and is working on a website devoted to her fashion work, in sharp contrast to the nude website she presently maintains. In 2007, she made her mainstream acting debut in *Deep Gold 3D* (2011), a suspense film shot in the Philippines.

Scarlett Chorvat (1972-), b. Bratislava, Czech., is an American model and actress. She moved to the US at the age of five. She started playing tennis semi-professionally at the age of 15, but moved on to become a model, and finally an actress. Scarlett attended and graduated from Barbizon Modeling and Acting School in Michigan. She is best known as a model, counting numerous covers of magazines, advertising and TV commercials. As an actress, she is known for *Dodgeball: A True Underdog Story* (2004), *Buying the Cow* (2002) and *Frank McKlusky, C.I.* (2002).

Skin Diamond (orig. Raylin Christensen) (1987-), b. Ventura, CA, of Czech ancestry, is the stage name of an American actress and nude model. Diamond started her career as a mainstream model and posed, among others, for Louis Vuitton, American Apparel and Atsuko Kudo. She entered the adult film industry in 2009 and did her first scenes with Joanna Angel and James Deen for *Burning Angel*. In 2012, Diamond posed for comic book artist David Mack, who portrayed her as Echo in the Marvel Comics miniseries *Daredevil: End of Days*. In 2014, Diamond was on CNBC's list of "The Dirty Dozen: Porn's Most Popular Stars." Diamond also starred (with Allie Haze) in the music video for American hip hop recording artist B.o.B, for his song "John Doe", which features Priscilla Renea. Diamond was the Penthouse Pet of the Month for July 2014.

Amy Fadhli (1965-), b. Galveston, TX, of Czech mother and Iraqi father, is an American fitness model, and an actress. She is a qualified dental hygienist and after graduating from college, she moved to Northern California, where she first encountered serious fitness training. However, she eventually moved to Dallas and started swimsuit modeling and competing in bikini contests in which she won several swimsuit titles and many prizes including money and trips. She then decided to continue in pursuing her career in modelling, so she submitted her photo and resume to the promoter of the Fitness America Pageant, and she was then invited to compete in the National Championships that year. She managed to win the physique round, but only came in ninth overall in the pageant. After enjoying competing in the first year, she competed again in the following year, and finished as first runner up, and soon she became the Fitness America National Champion in 1996. Besides being a fitness model, she is also an actress and has made appearances in many television shows such as *The Young and the Restless*, *Heaven & the Suicide King* (1998), *The Lobo Paramilitary Christmas Special* (2002) and *Con Games* (2001). Her career has enabled her to travel the world, she has been to places such as Hong Kong, Italy, Germany, Mexico, Guam, Spain, Hungary, Slovakia, Malaysia, Jamaica and Lebanon.

Nargis Fakhri (1979–), b. Queens, NY, is an American fashion model and actress. Her father is Pakistani, and her mother is Czech. Fakhri appeared on *America's Next Top Model* Cycles 2 and 3 in 2004. She posed for the 2009 Kingfisher Swimsuit Calendar. In 2011, she made her feature film debut in the Hollywood film, *Rockstar*, alongside Ranbir Kapoor which was released on November 11, 2011.

Roxanne Galla (1975–), b. Houston, TX, of Czech ancestry, in 1998, was selected to be part of the Texas Bikini Team, which served as a platform for her to display her many talents. In 2000, she did her first photo shoot – a test shoot with *Playboy* in Chicago and 2001, she became a *Playboy* staple and was named 'Cyber Girl of the Week.' After she was featured as the model of the month on Lisa Boyle's website, Roxanne started her own site and her popularity skyrocketed. She also appeared in Playboy productions such as *Playboy: Wet & Wild Live!* (2002) and *Playboy: No Boys Allowed, 100% Girls 2* (2004).

Eva Herzigová (1973–), born in Litvinov, Czechoslovakia, is a Czech model and actress. Her first important appearance was as the model for the first Wonderbra campaign in 1994. She has appeared in the Victoria's Secret catalog and *Sports Illustrated*. She was a member of Thomas Zeumer's Metropolitan Models. In 2006, she was 'Venus' at the 2006 Winter Olympics Opening Ceremony.

Markéta Jánská (1981–), b. Most, Czech., is a model. She began modeling as a teenager and appeared in European magazines, swimsuit calendars and TV commercials. In 2001, she left her home in the Czech Republic to travel to Western Europe. While there she got a modeling offer in Los Angeles. She accepted and moved to LA. After testing for *Playboy*, she was chosen to be Playmate of the month for July 2003. She currently lives in Los Angeles and is continuing to pursue her modeling career as well as a singing career. She appeared in the

2005 Playmates at Play at the Playboy Mansion swimsuit calendar as calendar girl of October. The calendar was the inaugural Playmates at Play calendar, and it was shot on the grounds of Playboy Mansion in 2004.

Justin Jedlica (1980–), b. Poughkeepsie, New York, to Slovak parents; model, known as the 'Human Ken Doll'; noted for multiple cosmetic surgeries.

Adriana Karembeu (née Sklenaříková) (1971–), b. Brezno, Czech.; Slovak; fashion model and actress; a former Guinness record holder for the longest legs among female models (at almost 1.24 m).

Karolina Kurková (1984–), b. Děčín, Czech., is a Czech model, best known as a former Victoria's Secret Angel and *Vogue* cover star. *Vogue* editor Anna Wintour called her the 'next supermodel.' She began her career at a young age. Photos of her were sent to a modeling agency in Prague, and right away she began getting work in print ads and on catwalks. As she began to get more and more serious about her line of work, at 15 she traveled to Milan to gain experience at the center of the fashion world. While there, she was signed almost immediately to a contract with Prada. The editors of *Vogue* magazine also took notice, and the result was a move to New York, where Kurková constantly found plenty of work. After her cover appearance on the February 2001 issue of *Vogue*, she gained recognition that resulted in deals with Yves Saint Laurent, Tommy Hilfiger, and Victoria's Secret. She also quickly racked up the magazine covers and became one of the most demanded models. The constant and hard-working Kurková was even named 'Model of the Year' by *Vogue* at the 2002 VH1/Vogue Fashion Awards, after putting over 23 straight weeks of work. Kurková is among the world's top-earning models, having earned an estimated $5 million in the year 2007. She was placed 6th in the Forbes annual list of the highest earning models. Most in the fashion industry see her as bright and energetic, and her great attitude has made her a favorite of designers and photographers. She currently lives in New York City.

Michaela Kocianová (1988–), b. Trenčín, Czech.; a Slovak model. She won second place in the 2004 Elite Model Look Slovak fashion contest. She has since been featured in advertisements for Monique Lhuillier and Vivienne Westwood. She has appeared in magazines such as *Italian Vogue, Velvet, Spanish Vogue, Elle, British Elle, Amica*, and *L'Officiel*. In 2009, she became the face for Piazza Sempione, an Italian designer. She resides in New York, NY.

Janet Paula Lupo (1950–2017), born in Hoboken, NJ, of Czech and Italian ancestry, is an American model. She was *Playboy* magazine's Playmate of the Month for its November 1975 issue. Her centerfold was photographed by Pompeo Posar. Lupo posed for an April 1984 Playboy pictorial, 'Playmates Forever! Part Two.'

Jay Manuel (1972–), b. Springfield, IL, of Czech ancestry on his mother's side, is a Canadian American make-up artist. He is most recognizable as the director of photo shoots on the popular reality television show *America's Next Top Model*. Manuel is also the host and lead judge of the second and third cycle of *Canada's Next Top Model*, a spin-off to the original. He attended Dr. Norman Bethune Collegiate Institute and York University. Before entering the fashion industry, Manuel was a pre-med student and also studied opera, which included working for the Metropolitan Opera at one point.

Annalaina Marks (1983–), b. Erie, PA, of Slovak descent; American model, actress, and television personality. She is known for being a contestant on the third season of *America's Next Top Model*. She is also known for her work on *Made of Honor* (2008), *The Good Wife* (2009) and *Person of Interest* (2011).

Claire Muzik (1986–), b. Prague, Czech., is a glamour model, residing in Las Vegas, NV. She became internationally known for her appearances in many international and national men's magazines across the globe such as *Maxim* and *FHM*. She moved to the Sun City in 2011 and within one year she became the first Czech model to become a finalist of Las Vegas Top Model beauty contest. She has worked as a promotional model full-time since 2010 and has appeared in numerous commercials and several music videos in the United States and Europe. She has been featured in several international and national magazines (across Europe, USA, Asia) and can be seen in *FHM*, *MAXIM*, *Easyriders* (The World's Best-Selling Motorcycle Magazine for Men), *Radikal Magazine*, *Players Magazine* and many more.

Petra Němcová (1974–), born in Karviná, Czech., is a Czech model, television host, author, and philanthropist. She is the founder and chair of the Happy Hearts Fund. In December 2004, she was injured in Thailand by a tsunami resulting from the 2004 Indian Ocean earthquake. Němcová gained attention outside the fashion industry after featuring on the cover of the 2003 *Sports Illustrated Swimsuit Issue*, from a shoot in Barbados by Walter Iooss. She also appeared in the 2002, 2003, 2004, 2005 and 2006 editions. She was the object/subject of Joanne Gair's body painting work. In January 2015, Němcová replaced Abbey Clancy as the face of Ultimo underwear. She also serves as the global face of Chopard.

Lucia Oskerova (1990–), b. Bratislava; Slovak-Canadian model and actress. She became a Fashion Week star, walking for Dolce & Gabbana, Prada, Dior, Chanel, Fashion Rocks, Leone, Boboli and Vetrina. She was cast in several outstanding network TV series including *Smallville*, *Battlestar Galactica*, *The Guard*, *Painkiller Jane*, *Very Bad Men* as well as in the feature film *National Lampoon*. She now lives between Istanbul and Los Angeles where she continues her work as a model and actress.

Daniela Peštová (1970–), b. Teplice, Czech., is a Czech model. She was discovered by the Madison Modeling Agency's Dominique Caffin. She had plans to attend college but after winning a modeling contest, she moved to Paris to sign with Madison Modeling Agency. She moved to New York and from there, her career took off. She has appeared on the covers of *GQ*, *Marie Claire*, *Cosmopolitan*, *Glamour* and *ELLE*. She appeared in the *Sports Illustrated Swimsuit Issue* (second of Czechoslovak descent, after Paulina Pořízková) and has been modeling for the magazine for years, appearing on the cover three times, in 1995, 2000 and 2006. In addition to working with photographers on her *Sports Illustrated* shoots, she was the subject of Joanne Gair's inaugural body painting works as part of the *Sports Illustrated Swimsuit Issue*.

Paulina Pořízková (1965–), born in Prostějov, Czechoslovakia, is a Czech-American supermodel and actress. At the age of eighteen, she became the first woman from Central Europe to be on the cover of the *Sports Illustrated Swimsuit Issue*. She was the second woman (after Christie Brinkley) to be featured on the swimsuit issue's front cover in consecutive times (1984 and 1985).

Tori Praver (1987–), b. San Diego, CA, of Czech ancestry; American model and swimwear fashion designer.

Stephanie Romanov (1969–), b. Las Vegas, NV, of Slovak descent, was an American model and an actress. She first began modeling in Europe and was discovered at 15 by Elite Model Management founder, John Casablancas. Her first professional modeling job was in Europe, shooting fashion layouts for Italian and French Bazaar. She then moved to New York to pursue a professional model career, leaving her family in Las Vegas. She appeared in *ELLE*, *Vanity Fair* and *French Vogue*. In 1993, Romanov decided to leave modeling in favor of acting. She landed her first role as Teri Spencer on Aaron Spelling's *Models, Inc.* She went on to land guest starring roles in *Homicide: Life on the Street*, *The Sentinel*, *Just Shoot Me!* and *Burke's Law*. She starred on *Angel* for four seasons, playing Lilah Morgan from 2000–2003. Romanov has also appeared in several films, including '*Spy Hard*' and *Menno's Mind*. She played Jacqueline Kennedy in the critically acclaimed *Thirteen Days* and appeared in *The Final Cut*, alongside Robin Williams.

Antonio Sabato, Jr. (1972–), b. Rome, Italy, of Bohemian mother, is an American model and actor. His father is Antonio Sabàto Sr., a film star of Italian heritage born in Sicily. His mother, Yvonne Kabouchy, is a realtor from Prague and is of Czech Jewish heritage; her own mother was a Holocaust survivor. His family moved to the United States from Italy in 1985 and he received his high school diploma from Palisades Charter High School in Los Angeles, California. He first became known as a Calvin Klein model and for his role on the soap opera *General Hospital*. He continued appearing in films and television series throughout the 1990s and 2000s.

Viera Schottertova (1982–), b. Topoľčany, Slovakia; a Slovak mode. Schottertova moved to Vienna after participating in the Elite Model Look Contest. From there her international career quickly took off and she featured on covers and editorials for magazines such as *Elle*, *Marie Claire*, *DS*, *Vogue* and major advertising drummer campaigns for Armani, Bernd Berger, Bolero, Chanel cosmetics, Custo Barcelona, Gant, Horizons, Lou lingerie, Mango, Marc Cain, Olivier Strelli, Red Point, Rimmel, Tag woman, TaiFun, Trixi Schober, Walter Leder, Women's Secret, Yera. She has also appeared in Victoria's Secret catalogs.

Christi Shake (1980–), born in Baltimore, MD, of Czech ancestry, is an American model and actress. Shake was chosen as *Playboy* magazine's Playmate of the Month for May 2002. She has been featured in *Playboy* videos and appeared as herself on episodes of the TV shows *The Girls Next Door*, *My Antonio*, and *Howard Stern*. Moreover, Christi was in the music video for 'God Knows Why' by Kid Rock.

Hana Soukupová (1985–), born in Karlovy Vary, Czech., is a Czech model. She has participated in the Victoria's Secret fashion shows and modeled for the Victoria Secret Catalog.

Jenna Talackova (1988–), b. Vancouver, B.C., Canada, of Czech parents, is a Canadian model and television personality, who gained media attention in 2012 when she successfully waged a legal battle to be allowed to compete in the Miss Universe Canada after being initially disqualified for being a trans woman.

Ivana Trump (née Ivana Marie Zelníčková) (1949–), b. Zlín, Czech., is a former Olympic athlete, socialite, and fashion model noted for her marriage to mogul Donald Trump. They married in 1977 and divorced in 1992.

Katarina Van Derham (née Ambrusova) (1975–), b. Ľubochňa, Slovakia, is an American model, actress and publisher. She is best known for being the longest-serving St. Pauli Girl, playing Bob Saget's girlfriend on *Entourage* and being the founder of *Viva Glam Magazine*.

Lucky Joseph Vanous (1961–), b. Lincoln, NE, of Czech ancestry, is an American model and actor. He became nationally known in 1994 after appearing in a series of commercials for Diet Coke. He studied at University of Nebraska at Lincoln. He was discovered while visiting New York City, and he moved there to model and continue his studies at New York University and Fordham University. His notable acting roles include playing Matt Dunning for a season on *Pacific Palisades* and playing Chance Bowman on *18 Wheels of Justice*.

Veronika Vařeková (1977–), born in Olomouc, Czech., is a Czech model. Veronica moved to New York City at the age of 19 to attend the Parsons School of Design. Upon arriving in Manhattan, Veronica met with Next Models at the urging of a close friend and was signed immediately. With Next Models, Veronica's career took off, landing her the covers of *Vogue, Marie Claire, Cosmopolitan*, and, the most coveted of all, the *Sports Illustrated Swimsuit Issue*.

5. Internet Personalities – You Tube Stars

David Dobrík (1996–), b. Košice, Czech., is a YouTuber and podcaster. His family moved to Vernon Hills, Illinois, when Dobrik was six years old. He attended Vernon Hills High School, where he played tennis, which led him to qualify for the 2014 Boys Tennis State Tournament where he won third place in the doubles tournaments. After graduating high school, he moved to Los Angeles to pursue his Vine career. He is known for his work on *An Interrogation* (2015), *FML* (2016) and *Airplane Mode* (2016). He has a successful channel on YouTube with over 6 million subscribers, where he posts vlogs about skits and his daily life.

Breanne Ezarik (1987–), b. Pittsburgh, PA, of Slovak descent, was trained as a pharmacist, working at Target. However, she is also an American internet personality. Before fame, she was an honor student at Bentworth high school and one of the school's best volleyball players as well as class president. Following the footsteps of her younger sister, iJustine, she has started her own YouTube Channel and she debuted in July 2012. With years of struggle, her YouTube channel has managed thousands of subscribers and over half-million views as of March 2018.

Jenna Ezarik (1989–), b. Pittsburgh, PA, of Slovak descent; an American internet personality and a video blogger. Jenna Ezarik is a YouTuber who has over 646k subscribers. Jenna is famous for her bubbly nature and humor she shows in her videos. Though Jenna does not have a million subscribers like other YouTubers, she surely is the one who made her videos as she likes. Jenna has over 334k Instagram followers and 175k Twitter followers. She manages her Instagram and Twitter accounts herself and is active in both. Jenna is definitely a hit and not miss in the internet world. Her videos have collaborations with her sister iJustine as well.

Gabrielle Jeannette Hanna (1991–), b. New Castle, PA, of Slovak descent, is an American YouTuber, Viner, author, comedian, actress, singer, and songwriter. Hanna graduated from the University of Pittsburgh with a degree in psychology and communications. After college, she worked for a marketing company that sold products out of a Sam's Club; she became the top salesperson in the U.S. for the company and moved to Cleveland, Ohio, to help start a new branch of the company. However, she departed after realizing that they relied on a pyramid scheme. She has risen to fame through YouTube, gaining over 6,000,000 subscribers. She is known for her YouTube channel *The Gabbie Show*. Hanna released a poetry book titled *Adultolescence* in September 2017, and her follow-up book, titled *Dandelion* was released in October 2020. She ventured into the music industry with her debut single "Out Loud" (2017), and her debut extended play, *2WayMirror*, was released on May 31, 2019. Her second EP, *Bad Karma* was released on May 15, 2020.

iJustine (née Justine Ezarik) (1984–), b. Pittsburgh, PA, of Slovak descent, is a YouTube personality, TV host, comedian, actress and model. She is best known as iJustine, with over a billion views across her YouTube channels since 2006. She gained attention as a life caster who communicated directly with her millions of viewers on her Justin.tv channel, ijustine.tv. She acquired notability in roles variously described as a 'lifecasting star,' a 'new media star,' or one of the Web's most popular lifecasters. She currently posts videos on her main channel iJustine.

6. Film & TV Directors & Producers

Norbert Auerbach (1922–2009), b. Vienna, of Czech father, grew up in Prague. His family left Prague just before the Germans invaded, landing first in Paris and then Brazil before settling in Maryland. After starting at UCLA, Auerbach enlisted in the US Army, then returned to college to study business. Originally intending to manage his father's orange orchards in Israel, he studied soil science but instead turned to working on his father's film productions. Striking out on his own, he began working in international distribution, principally for United Artists. The multilingual executive traveled in Europe with the Beatles to help promote "A Hard Day's Night," helped bring Ian Fleming's James Bond novels to United Artists and was brought in to help stabilize UA during the "Heaven's Gate" debacle. As an international distribution exec, he oversaw international releases for films such as *And God Created Woman* with Brigitte Bardot, as well as several installments of the *James Bond* and *Pink Panther* franchises. After serving as UA's head of international distribution, Auerbach was named president of United Artists; he made the announcement at the 1981 Cannes fest that UA had been purchased by MGM. He soon ankled MGM/UA to become president of United Intl. Pictures, which distributed films overseas for Universal, Paramount, United Artists and MGM. Filmgoing was at a low point in the U.K. and European territories at the time, and Auerbach and co-prexy Pana Alafouzo played a part in helping to increase the importance of international box office for U.S. studios.

Martin Beck (1867–1940), b. Liptovský Mikuláš, Slovaki, was a vaudeville theater manager, owner, and impresario. He founded the Orpheum Circuit, and built the Palace and Martin Beck Theatres in New York City's Broadway Theatre District. He was a booking agent for and became a close personal friend of the prominent magician, Harry Houdini.

Michael Bergmann (1953–), of Czech ancestry, is an American writer, director, and producer. He is the son of two Freudian psychoanalysts and the grandson of Hugo Bergmann, a philosopher who was one of the founders of Hebrew University in Jerusalem. Michael Bergmann graduated with a B.A. in Latin from Columbia University in 1975 and studied film concurrently at N.Y.U. Undergraduate Film School. He went on to study at the N.Y.U. Graduate School of Film and Television. In 1995, he made his first commercially released feature, *Milk and Money*, on 35 mm film produced by RKO Pictures, but as early as 1976, he began making narrative films on video from his own scripts. His prize-winning short in *Bed with My Books*, which explores the interior lives of older women, was an audience favorite at the Montréal festival. In 1999, Bergmann wrote one of the first how-to books on digital filmmaking, *Trifling With Fate: How to Make a Digital Video Feature Film*. He has also appeared as a lecturer and panelist at independent film conferences, speaking on the latest trends in state-of-the-art technology. He has also directed many plays and worked with musicians, dancers and artists in other genres, including his wife, the sculptor and writer Meredith Bergmann, who has been the production designer on many of his film and theater projects. In 2008, he co-wrote *What Silent Love Hath Writ: A Psychoanalytic Exploration of Shakespeare's Sonnets* with his father, Martin Bergmann.

Jana Boková (1948–), b. Prague, Czech., is a film director, photographer, journalist, and script writer. She left Czechoslovakia in August 1968 to attend a conference of art students in Austria, then emigrated to Paris, France to study at the Sorbonne. She has a Doctorate in Fine Arts, specializing in photography and surrealism. She then lived in the United States where she worked as a photographer for *Rolling Stone* and other magazines. She then lived in the United Kingdom for many years, studying at the National Film and Television School, and producing documentary films for British television. She wrote and directed the 1986 drama film *Hôtel du Paradis*, which was shown out of competition at the Cannes Film Festival in 1987. In 2001, Boková was approached by musician Eric Clapton to direct a music video but ended up filming a feature length documentary film called *Eric Clapton and Friends* which covered Clapton's band's rehearsals and preparations for a world tour. In 2003, the Cinémathèque Française hosted a complete retrospective of Boková's work. Her most recent film, *Bye Bye Shanghai* (2008), examines the concept of 'exile' as it relates to Czech émigrés including herself. Boková currently lives in Buenos Aires, Argentina.

Ester Brymová (1978–), b. Prague, Czech., is a film director, producer, and editor. In 1997, she moved to New York City to pursue studies in film-making. She worked as an editor in independent cinema until 2008 when she decided to move to Los Angeles to direct her first feature film *Butterflies*. *Butterflies* has premiered at Action on Film International Film Festival in Pasadena, California on 27 July 2009 and won the Alan J. Bailey Excellence Award in

Documentary Filmmaking. It was also nominated for Best Social Commentary. It showed at ArcLight's first ever Documentary Festival written up by *L.A. Times*.

Hanuš Burger (1909–1990), b. Prague, Bohemia, was a theater, film, and television director, playwright and author of books and screenplays, including the documentary film *Crisis* (1939), and the German language version of *Death Mills* (1945), supervised by Billy Wilder. He studied set design in Munich and dramatic art at Univ. of Munich. He was with Deutsches Theater in Prague (1932–36). In 1938, emigrated to US. He worked as set designer in New York. Member, Screen Dirs' Guild (1940–50). He was a co-founder of Assn. of Documentary Film Producers. He was also Director of C.B.S. film dept., New York (1946–47). He produced the first color film to inaugurate C.B.S. TV color broadcasts. He became film prog. Officer at U.N. (1947–50) and prod. dir. of films on political and humane topics for UN. member. nations. In 1950, he moved back to Prague following harassment during McCarthy investigations. In 1968, he emigrated to Munich after the Soviets invaded Czechoslovakia.

Katerina Cizek (1969–) b. Waterloo, Ont., Canada, the daughter of Czech immigrants, is a Canadian documentary filmmaker and web creator. Cizek studied anthropology at McGill University in Montreal and worked as an independent filmmaker before joining the National Film Board of Canada, where she works as a filmmaker-in-residence. Her father Jiří Čížek taught quantum physics at the University of Waterloo. He is known for introducing Coupled cluster theory. As of 2011, Cizek has been directing the National Film Board of Canada's *Highrise* series on life in residential skyscrapers, including the 2010 web documentary *Out My Window*, winner of the inaugural IDFA DocLab Award for Digital Storytelling at the International Documentary Film Festival Amsterdam and an International Digital Emmy for best digital program: non-fiction, and the 2011 webdoc *One Millionth Tower*, which lets users explore a high-rise complex in 3D virtual space, as Toronto residents re-imagine their neighborhood. Until mid-2014, Cizek collaborated with the Massachusetts Institute of Technology's OpenDocLab unit to develop the next production in the Highrise project. As part of MIT's Visiting Artists Program, she worked with scholars and apartment residents to ask how new technological forms are reshaping personal lives in suburban high-rise communities. Prior to working on Highrise, Cizek directed an NFB crossmedia documentary project about life inside Toronto's St. Michael's Hospital. Called Filmmaker-in-Residence, it garnered a Webby Award for Best Documentary Series. Prior to joining the NFB, her films included *Seeing is Believing: Handicams, Human Rights and the News*, co-directed with Peter Wintonick. Cizek and NFB producer Gerry Flahive have also collaborated on academic research with urbanist Roger Kiel on how cities are changing, with the Global Suburbanisms program at York University. Cizek has also taught new media approaches to documentary creation.

Chris Columbus (1958–), b. Spangler, PA, of Czech descent, is an American film director, Oscar nominated producer and screenwriter. After graduating from John F. Kennedy High School in Warren, Ohio, he went on to study at New York University's film school at the Tisch School of the Arts. Columbus had his largest success with the first two films in the Harry Potter series, *Harry Potter and the Sorcerer's Stone*, and *Harry Potter and the Chamber of Secrets*, along with *Home Alone*, the last receiving a British Comedy Award for Best Comedy Film.

Breck Eisner (1970–), b. California, of Bohemian ancestry (the son of Michael Eisner) is an American TV and film director. He attended Harvard High School (now Harvard-Westlake School) and majored in English and Theatre at Georgetown University. He attended USC School in Cinematic-Television where he received his Master's degree. He is director and producer, known for *The Crazies* (2010), *Sahara* (2005) and *The Last Witch Hunter* (2015).

Miloš Forman (1932–2018), b. Čáslav, Czech., was an actor, screenwriter, professor and film director. Forman was one of the most important directors of the Czechoslovak New Wave. His 1967 film *The Fireman's Ball*, on the surface a naturalistic representation of an ill-fated social event in a provincial town, was seen by both movie scholars and authorities in Czechoslovakia as a biting satire on Eastern European Communism, resulting in it being banned for many years in Forman's home country. Since Forman left Czechoslovakia, two of his films, *One Flew Over the Cuckoo's Nest* and *Amadeus*, have acquired particular renown, both gaining him an Academy Award for Best Director. *One Flew Over the Cuckoo's Nest* was the second to win all five major Academy Awards (Best Picture, Actor in Lead Role, Actress in Lead Role, director, and Screenplay) following *It Happened One Night* in 1934. Forman was also nominated for a Best Director Oscar for *The People vs. Larry Flynt*. He had also won Golden Globe, Cannes, Berlinale, BAFTA, Cesar, David di Donatello, European Film Academy, and Czech Lion awards.

Peter R. Gimbel (1927–1987), b. NYC, was an American filmmaker and underwater photojournalist. He was the son of Bernard Gimbel and heir to the Gimbels department store chain. After serving in the United States Army occupation force in Japan in 1946-1947, he graduated from Yale University in 1951, earning degrees in both English and economics. He spent ten years as an investment banker but after the death of his twin brother at age 29, he left banking to pursue a career in exploration. He parachuted into the Peruvian Andes with G. Brooks Baekeland (grandson of Leo Baekeland, the inventor of Bakelite) and Peter Lake in search of the lost Inca city of Vilcabamba. He was the first to dive the wreck of the SS *Andrea Doria* and his photos of the ship were published in *Life* magazine in August 1956. He produced two documentaries about the ship *The Mystery of the Andrea Doria* and *Andrea Doria: The Final Chapter*. He opened the safe of the Andrea Doria on live television in 1984. Gimbel also directed and produced the 1971 film *Blue Water, White Death* which was the first cinematic filming of the 'Great White Shark,' featuring Ron and Valerie Taylor, Rodney Fox, Stan Waterman and Peter Lake. The shark's attack on Lake's cage at the end of the film inspired Peter Benchley's book, *Jaws*.

Kate Guinzburg (1957-2017), b. NYC, of Bohemian ancestry, is a film producer. Kate Guinzburg worked as Michele Pfeiffer's producing partner. Together they formed their own production company, Via Rosa Productions from 1990 until the year 2000.

Philip Hoffman (1955-), b. Kitchener, Ont., Canada, of Czech mother, is a film maker of memory and association. He creates 'personal' yet highly universal works which weave and question fact and fiction in an experimental 'diarist' cinema. A film maker with an extensive list of productions, his short films have won many awards, including three in 2002, A Golden Gate Award, New Visions, from the San Francisco International Film Festival, as well as the Gus Van Sant Award from the Ann Arbor Film Festival, both for *What These Ashes Wanted* (2001). He now teaches at York Univ. In 2001, Hoffman's films were featured at the Images Festival for Independent Film and Video in Toronto, where a new book about his films was launched; *Landscape with Shipwreck: First Person Cinema* and the *Films of Philip Hoffman* contains over 25 essays/writings by academics and artists.

Allen J. Holubar (1888-1923), b. San Francisco, CA, of Bohemian ancestry, was an American actor, film director, and screenwriter of the silent film era. He was a well-known as a leading man of the legitimate stage. Later he became one of the screen's foremost producers. His stage experience consisted of leading roles in the New York productions of David Belasco and Henry W. Savage. From the legitimate, he went to the silent drama, where he appeared in Jules Verne's *Twenty Thousand Leagues under the Sea*. Since that time, he has spent every minute of his life in training for the production of super-films. Picture fans will remember him as the author-director of such masterworks as *The Heart of Humanity*, *The Right Happiness*, *Once to Everywoman* and *Man, Woman, & Marriage*, a teeming, vital drama showing a struggle between the sexes from the earliest caveman era to the present day. Holubar's knowledge of drama, history and human nature, and his ability as an executive and an artist were the foundation stones upon which he had built his directorship.

Jim Jarmusch (1953-), b. Cuyahoga Falls, OH, of Czech ancestry, is an independent film director, screenwriter, actor, producer, editor, and composer. He is known for directing such works as *Down by Law*, *Dead Man*, *Ghost Dog: The Way of the Samurai* and *Only Lovers Left Alive*. Jarmusch studied film at NYU's Graduate Film program in the late 1970's. Jarmusch developed his first feature film, *Permanent Vacation*, while a student at NYU. The film premiered at the International Filmfestival Mannheim-Heidelberg and won the Josef von

Sternberg Award. Jarmusch went on to make *Stranger Than Paradise*, which was released in 1984 to widespread critical acclaim. From there, Jarmusch has gone on to direct 12 more feature films, winning several awards including the Cannes' Grand Prize of the Jury for *Broken Flowers*, the 2005 Gotham Tribute Award, and the 2013 International Cinephile Society's Best Director Award for *Only Lovers Left Alive*.

Vojtěch Jasný (1925-2019), b. Kelč, Czech., was a prominent Czech film director, screenwriter and professor in the sixties, who has written and directed over 50 films. After coming to the US, he has taught film directing classes at Columbia University. Jasný made feature and documentary films in Czechoslovakia, Germany, Austria, USA & Canada, and was a notable figure in the Czechoslovak New Wave movement of the 1960s. He is best remembered for his movies *The Cassandra Cat* and *All My Compatriots*, both of which won prizes at Cannes Film Festival. In addition to his film career, he taught directing at film schools in Salzburg, Vienna, Münich and New York.

Zuzana Justman (née Pick) (1931-), b. Prague, Czech., left Czechoslovakia in 1948 with her mother, after surviving two years at Terezín concentration camp during World War II. They emigrated to Argentina, but detesting the Peron regime, Zuzana Pick left Buenos Aires in 1950 to study at Vassar College (B.A., 1954) and then studied Slavic linguistics at Columbia Univ. (Ph.D., 1981). She settled in NYC, and after working as a writer and translator in the late 1980s, she started filmmaking. She has filmed most of her documentaries in the Czech Republic and other European countries, and her topics have been the Holocaust of World War II and postwar history. Her films include *Terezin Diary* (1989), *Czech Women: Now we are Free* (1993), *Voices of the Children* (1996) and *Trial in Prague* (2000). She was recipient of the 1999 National Emmy Award for Outstanding Historical Program and other film festival and TV competition awards.

Ján Kadár (1918-1979), b. Budapest, of Slovak descent, was a film director and writer, who was important in the "New Wave" of Czechoslovak cinema of the early 1960s. Kadár attended Charles University, Prague, and the Film School at Bratislava (1938). During World War II, he was interned in a Nazi labor camp, after which he worked as a scriptwriter and assistant director, first at the Koliba Studios in Bratislava and from 1947 at the Barrandov Studios, Prague. Most of his films were directed in tandem with Elmar Klos. The two became best known for their Oscar-winning *The Shop on Main Street* (Obchod na korze, 1965). As a professor at the FAMU (Film and TV School of the Academy of Performing Arts) in Prague, Kadár trained most of the directors who spawned the Czechoslovak New Wave in the 1960s. After moving to the United States, he became professor of film direction at the American Film Institute in Beverly Hills.

Alexandra Forbes Kerry (1973–), b. Concord, MA, of Moravian ancestry, is the elder daughter of politician John Forbes Kerry. She is an American filmmaker. She is a partner at Locomotive Films and co-founder of Fictional Pictures, a film production company based in New York and Los Angeles. Kerry graduated from the Milton Academy and then attended Brown University where she studied anthropology and modern culture and media. In 2004, she graduated with an MFA in directing from the AFI Conservatory's two-year masters filmmaker program. Kerry's short film *The Last Full Measure* premiered at the 2004 Cannes Film Festival and earned her top honors at the Austin Film Festival. The film also earned her the 'Director of the Year' award from American Film Institute. She is a co-producer of the 2008 documentary film *Be Like Others*. Kerry has also had several roles in television and in film. She has appeared in two David Mamet films, *State and Main* in 2000 and *Spartans* in 2004. As a television director, she has directed the commercial, including the pilot and first season of MTV's *The Hills* – and the pilot for the 2002 film *The Forest*. She has also co-produced several documentaries including the award winning *Be Like Others* for HBO and has won two Silver Tellies for producing and directing on an online ad campaign for Allstate Insurance. In 2011, Kerry joined Locomotive, a New York-based independent film production and financing company.

Milo Kubík (1929–2013), b. Čadca, Czech., was a producer. He attended the famous Prague school FAMU. In 1968, he came to Toronto, Canada. In 1971, he formed an independent firm Animete Canada and produced the whole series of animated films for children. He later became in charge of the Czech and Slovak TV program in Toronto.

Pancho (orig. Paul Julius) Kohner (1939–), b. Los Angeles, CA, of Czech ancestry, is a producer, director and writer. He has been president of Capricorn Productions, Inc. (since 1978). He is known for *The New Adventures of Madeline* (1995), *The Bridge in the Jungle* (1970) and *Mr. Sycamore* (1975).

David Alan Ladd (1947–), b. Los Angeles, CA, of Czech ancestry on his mother's side, is an American producer and former actor. His professional career in Hollywood began in 1957 with a supporting role in a film starring his father titled *The Big Land*. As a result of that film's success, Samuel Goldwyn Jr. offered him a role as a mute in the 1958 movie *The Proud Rebel*, once again playing opposite his father and co-starring Olivia de Havilland. For this role, Ladd won a Golden Globe award as the "Best Newcomer of 1958" as well as a special award for "Best Juvenile Actor" and received a Best Supporting Actor nomination. He was also included in Film Daily's Filmdom's Famous Five critic's award. Ladd followed this success with a series of films including *The Sad Horse* (1959), *A Dog of Flanders* (1960), *Raymie* (also 1960) and *Misty* (1961), as well as appearing in numerous television shows including *Bonanza*, *Zane Grey Theatre*, and *Shirley Temple's Story Book Theatre* (as Tom Sawyer). Ladd was again included in Film Daily's Filmdom's Famous Five in 1961 for *A Dog of Flanders*. Ladd's other feature film credits include *RPM* (1970), *The Day of the Locust* (1975), *The Treasure of Jamaica Reef* (1975), *Jonathan Livingston Seagull* (1977) and *The Wild Geese* (1978). In 1982, Ladd began working at Columbia Pictures as a creative executive. Shortly thereafter, his brother-in-law, John Veitch, stepped down as president of Columbia and asked Ladd to join him in establishing a new production company based at Columbia. Ladd became a senior production executive at MGM and was part of the key team responsible for the resurgence of the studio (1989–1997). He was responsible for a variety of films, including the smash hit *Get Shorty* (1995).

Fritz Lang (1890–1976), born in Vienna, of Moravian ancestry, was a filmmaker, screenwriter, and occasional film producer and actor. Lang's most celebrated films include the groundbreaking futuristic *Metropolis* (1927) and the influential *M* (1931), a film noir precursor that he made before he moved to the United States. His other major films include Dr. *Mabuse the Gambler* (1922), *Die Nibelungen* (1924), *Fury* (1936), *You Only Live Once* (1937), *Hangmen Also Die!* (1943), *The Woman in the Window* (1944), *Scarlet Street* (1945) and *The Big Heat* (1953). Although he was not honored by the American film establishment until a retrospective of his work at the Los Angeles County Museum of Art in 1969, France, Germany, Austria, and Yugoslavia gave him many awards for his contribution to film from the 1950s through the 1970s. He also received an award for his film *M* from the German Motion Picture Arts Association in 1931.

Terry Hamlisch Liebling (1942–2001), NYC, of Moravian ancestry, on her father's side, was a prominent casting director on both coasts. Her extensive list of credits included *Apocalypse Now*, *The Two Jakes*, *Nine to Five*, *Brubaker*, *The Postman Always Rings Twice* and *The Adventures of Buckaroo Bonzai*. TV credits included numerous Movies of the Week, *Rhoda*, starring Valerie Harper (1974–79) and *Doc* from MTM Prods., through the feature film *Trial and Error*, starring Michael Edwards and Jeff Daniels (1997). Among the other major films she helped cast were *The Empire Strikes Back*, *Paternity*, and *Sharky's Machine*. Liebling was a past board member of the Casting Society of America, a member of the Academy of Motion Picture Arts & Sciences, the Academy of Television Arts & Sciences and Women in Film.

Gustav Machatý (1901–1963), b. Prague, Bohemia, was a Czech film director, screenwriter and actor. He directed 17 films between 1919 and 1955, including *Ecstasy* (1933). He also was the screenplay writer for 10 films between 1920 and 1955. In the early 1920s, he emigrated to the United States taking up residence in Hollywood where he learned filmmaking as an apprentice to two masters, D.W. Griffith and Erich von Stroheim. After serving a four-year apprenticeship in Hollywood, he returned to Prague to make his own films. Two movies, *Erotikon* (1929) and *Ekstase* (1933) made him internationally famous. Released as *Ecstasy* in the U.S. with the advertising tag-line "The Most Talked About Picture in the World," *Ekstase* featured young Hedy Kiesler in the nude. Kiesler, who would become internationally famous herself as Hedy Lamarr, played a sexually frustrated hausfrau who achieves orgasm (ecstasy) in the arms of a young swain who has espied her in the buff making like one of Busby Berkeley's water nymphs, sans bathing suit. When exhibitor Samuel Cummins imported the film in 1935, the U.S. Customs Service seized the print, acting under the aegis of the 1930 Customs Act that forbade importing obscene material.

Peter Nýdrle (1954–2014), b. Czech., was an award-winning commercial and music video director, producer, and director of photography. He continued to direct various commercial spots and run his company, Nydrle, Inc. located in West Hollywood, California.

Mark Randolph Osborne (1970–), b. Trenton, NJ, of Czech ancestry, is an American film director, writer, producer and animator. He began his career by studying Foundation Art at Pratt Institute in New York before receiving his Bachelor of Fine Arts Degree in Experimental Animation from the California Institute of the Arts in June 1992. His thesis film, *Greener*, won numerous awards and was screened at more than 40 film festivals worldwide. He has received two Academy Award nominations, including one for Best Animated Feature of the year for the 2008 critically acclaimed *Kung Fu Panda* which he directed alongside John Stevenson. *Kung Fu Panda* has netted more than $630 million worldwide to-date. The action-comedy was Osborne's first major studio project. It also won him and Stevenson the Annie Award for Directing in an Animated Feature.

Georg Wilhelm Pabst (1885–1967), born in Roudnice nad Labem, Bohemia, was a film director and screenwriter. While growing up in Vienna, he studied drama at the Academy of Decorative Arts and initially began his career as a stage actor in Switzerland, Austria and Germany. In 1910, Pabst traveled to the United States, where he worked as an actor and director at the German Theater in New York City. When World War I began, Pabst returned to Europe, where he was interned in a prisoner-of-war camp in Brest. While imprisoned, Pabst organized a theatre group at the camp. Upon his release in 1919, he returned to Vienna, where he became director of the Neue Wiener Bühne, an avant-garde theatre.

Ivan Passer (1933–2020), b. Prague, Czechoslovakia, was a film director and screenwriter. A significant figure in the Czech New Wave of the mid-1960s, Passer worked closely with Miloš Forman on many of his films and directed his first feature in 1965. Following the Soviet invasion in 1968, Passer defected to the West, aided by Carlo Ponti and has been living and working in the United States since then. He made some worthy movies, such as his American debut *Born to Win* (1971), a complex portrait of a heroin-addict hairdresser; his satire on civil surveillance, *Law and Disorder* (1974); the comedy about money-laundering bankers *Silver Bears* (1977), and the cult film *Cutter's Way* (1981), in which a war veteran investigates a crime, despite he only has one eye, one arm and one leg. For television he directed the biopic *Stalin* in 1992. Passer taught film at the University of Southern California, and lectured students in foreign film academies.

Irving Pichel (1891-1954), b. Pittsburgh, PA, possibly of Bohemian ancestry, was a movie director and actor. He had wanted to be in the theater from childhood. Pichel attended Harvard University and tried other lines of work, before acting finally won out. His pronounced Semitic features prevented Pichel from becoming a movie leading man in the white-bread 1930s, but he proved a valuable character player and villain in such Paramount films as *Murder by the Clock* (1931), *An American Tragedy* (1931), and *The Cheat* (1932). Pichel began his directing career in collaboration with Ernst B. Schoedsack on *The Most Dangerous Game* (1932). His directorial efforts of the 1930s were largely potboilers, but the quality improved when he joined the Fox directing staff in the 1940s. His better efforts include *Hudson's Bay* (1940), *The Pied Piper* (1942), *The Moon Is Down* (1942), and, for Paramount, *A Medal for Benny* (1945). He also partnered with George Pal on the fanciful features *The Great Rupert* (1950) and *Destination Moon* (1950) and was producer of the 1941 Fox melodrama *Swamp Water*. Irving Pichels last films as a director were those sectarian church-basement favorites *Martin Luther* (1953) and *Day of Triumph* (1954).

Noam Pitlik (1932-1999), b. Philadelphia, PA, of Slovak ancestry, was an American television director, screenwriter, and actor. He was a graduate of Gratz College and Temple University. In 1957, he starred in an Off-Broadway production of Kurt Weill's *The Threepenny Opera*. During the 1960s and 1970s, Pitlik became a familiar character actor on television, making guest appearances in around 80 different TV series. Though he largely retired from acting in the mid-1970s to concentrate on directing, Pitlik still made a handful of widely spaced acting appearances over the next two decades. Pitlik directed episodes of 29 different TV series including Barney Miller (102 episodes, more than anyone else). In 1979, Pitlik won an Emmy for Outstanding Directing for a Comedy Series for his work on the ABC sitcom *Barney Miller*. In addition to the Emmy, he also received the Peabody Award and Directors Guild of America Award.

Bill Pohlad (1955-), b. Hennepin, MN, of Slovak ancestry, is an American film producer and director. Pohlad was the executive producer of the movies *Brokeback Mountain*, *A Prairie Home Companion*, and *Food, Inc.*, and a producer of *Into the Wild* and *12 Years a Slave*. On January 24, 2012, he was nominated for an Academy Award (as producer) for the film *The Tree of Life*. Almost 25 years after his directorial debut with *Old Explorers* (1990), Pohlad's biopic of Brian Wilson, *Love & Mercy*, was screened at the 2014 Toronto Film

Festival. Pohlad is the President of the River Road Entertainment company, which he founded in 1987.

Marek Pošíval (1963–), b. Prague, Czech., is a Czech Canadian producer, actor, screenwriter and film director. He emigrated to Toronto and attended the York University in the 1980s (B.F.A., 1992). He is best known as a producer of feature films, primarily of the thriller, horror or drama genre. A script penned by Posival, *The Tortured*, which was directed by Robert Lieberman, was released in 2010. Posival also worked on the project as one of the film's producers, together with Mark Burg, Oren Koules and Carl Mazzocone of Twisted Pictures. Posival also wrote and directed a highly regarded short film called *Hold Up* and worked with Deepa Mehta as Associate Producer on the feature film *Water* which was among the five nominees for Best Foreign Language Film at the 2006 Academy Awards. Posival's latest film is *Phantom Punch*, a period drama about the life of the controversial heavyweight boxing champion Sonny Liston, which he produced together with Hassain Zaidi and Ving Rhames.

Emil Radok (1918–1994), b. Czech., was a Czech film director. He was co-inventor of the multi-media show Laterna Magika, which was a star attraction at the Czechoslovakia pavilion at Expo 67. In 1968, he left to exile to Canada. Radok's most monumental project was the 'kinetic mosaic' which he designed for the Universe of Energy Pavilion at Walt Disney World's EPCOT theme park, opening in 1982. Working with WED (Walt Disney Imagineering), Radok created a pre-show film projected on a 90-foot-wide screen. The projection surface was composed of some 100 triangular revolving modules arrayed in four horizontal rows, 25 modules in each row. Each module had two white projection surfaces and one black surface, each 3 ½ feet square. Each module was revolved by its own interior servo-motor. Computerized, the modules could create one large flat screen, but were also programmed to revolve in a variety of displays, combining into patterns of triangular wedges, flat panels, and black panels, precisely coordinated with the changing film images. The rippling movement of the units gave a unique "third dimension" to the projection surface. The theater accommodated 580 spectators. In 1987, Radok received the Canadian Special Achievement Genie Award for the film *Taming of the Demons*, which played primarily at Vancouver's Expo '86.

Rudy Ralston (1918–1984), b. Prague, Czech., was a Czech-American film producer. He was the brother of figure skater turned actress Vera Ralston, who was married to the head of Republic Pictures Herbert Yates. Rudy was employed by Republic Pictures, making B westerns during the 1950s. His memorable films include: *Marshall of Cedar Rock* (1953), *El Passo Stampade* (1953), *Double Jeopardy* (1955), *Hell's Crossroads* (1957) and *The Man Who Died Twice* (1958).

Andrew Reichsman (1953–), b. US, of Moravian ancestry, is a producer and cinematographer and production manager. He is known for *Lilac Ridge: Life on a Family Farm* (2011), *Signs of Life* (1989) and *Music for the Movies: Bernard Herrmann* (1992).

Gottfried Reinhardt (1913–1994), b. Berlin, Germany, of Bohemian and Slovak ancestry (son of Max Reinhardt), was an American film director and producer. In Hollywood, he became assistant director of Ernst Lubitsch, later a production assistant at the Metro-Goldwyn-Mayer studios, contributing to the making of the 1938 film *The Great Waltz*. In 1941, he produced *Two-Faced Woman* starring Greta Garbo in her final film role.

Karel Reisz (1926–2002), b. Ostrava, Czech., was a British filmmaker who was active in post–World War II Britain, and one of the pioneers of the new realist strain in 1950s and 1960s British cinema. In 1974, Reisz resurfaced in America with *The Gambler*, a dark odyssey in which a compulsive gambler, by day a New York professor of literature given to lucid analysis of his own malady in his lectures on Dostoevsky, desperately tries to stave off brutal retribution by raising the money he owes.

Ivan Reitman (1946–2022), b. Komárno, Slovakia, is a Canadian film and T.V. producer and director, and screenwriter. His parents were Jewish; his mother survived the Auschwitz concentration camp, and his father was an underground resistance fighter. His family came to Canada as refugees in 1950. Reitman attended Oakwood Collegiate in Toronto and was a member of the Twintone Four singing group. Reitman attended McMaster University, receiving a Bachelor of Music in 1969. At McMaster, he produced and directed many short films. He is best known for his comedy work, especially in the 1980s and 1990s. He is the owner of The Montecito Picture Company, founded in 1998.

Jason Reitman (1977–), b. Montreal, Canada, of Slovak ancestry, is a Canadian-American film director, screenwriter, producer and actor. He is the son of director Ivan Reitman. He is best known for directing the films *Thank You For Smoking* (2005), *Juno* (2007), *Up in the Air* (2009), and *Young Adult* (2011). He has received one Grammy Award, one Golden Globe, and four Academy Award nominations, two of which are for Best Director.

David Riva (ca. 1961–), b. US, of Bohemian ancestry on his mother's side (a son of Maria Sieber Riva and grandson of Marlene Dietrich), is a producer, director, and production designer. He is known known for *Marlene Dietrich: Her Own Song* (2001), *Back in Business* (1997) and *Precious Find* (1996).

Rick Sebak (1953–), b. Bethel Park, PA, of Slovak descent, is American film director and producer. He attended the University of North Carolina at Chapel Hill. He lives and works in Pittsburgh. Sebak is the creator of the 'scrapbook documentary' genre, many of which he has created for WQED and PBS. He calls his quirky cultural travelogues 'scrapbook documentaries.' For 11 years, he worked at the South Carolina Educational Television Network. There, he made an award-winning documentary about the official state dance, entitled 'Shag.'

Jaroslav Siakel (1896–1997), b. Blatnica, Czech., was a Slovak film director and cinematographer. Baptized as Ludvik Jaroslav, he emigrated to the USA in 1912, where he used the name Ludwig Jerry Siakel. During the First World War, he completed an aerial photography course, later making short documentaries and feature films for Rothacker Film Mfg. Co, several thematically focused on Czechoslovakia. He also dealt with issues of simplification of the production of propagating film materials. In November 1920, they founded the American Slovaks in Chicago company Tatra Film Corporation for the purpose of filming in the old country. In 1921, he made the first feature-length silent film *Jánošík* in a Slovak-American co-production, which is one of the first feature films in the world. Together with his brother Daniel, he held several patents in the field of film and camera technology.

Michael Sucsy (1973–), b. New York, NY, of Slovak descent, is Golden Globe and Emmy Award-winning film director, screenwriter, and producer. He is a graduate of Deerfield Academy, Georgetown University's Edmund A. Walsh School of Foreign Service, where he earned a degree in International Relations, Law & Organization, and the Art Center College of Design in Pasadena, CA, where he received a Master's in Fine Arts. He pursued work as a production assistant, an art department coordinator, a production secretary, and an assistant director on feature films, commercials, and music videos in Washington DC, New York City, and Los Angeles. He later went on to earn a Master's of Fine Arts in film from Art Center College of Design in Los Angeles. Sucsy then began directing commercials and was soon dubbed by *Shoot! Magazine* "as one of the industry's crop of new directors to watch." He was subsequently nominated for the Young Director of the Year Award given in conjunction with the 2002 Cannes Lions International Advertising Festival. He is best known for creating the HBO film *Grey Gardens*. He was a Director for the fourth season of Netflix's *13 Reasons Why*.

Václav Táborský (1928–), b. Prague, Czech., is a documentary film producer and a screenwriter. From 1947 to 1952, he studied directing at FAMU. After two years of military service, he returned to the Short Film of the Documentary Film Studio, where until his emigration in 1968, he managed to make over 80 films, including the feature films for young people *Escape in the Wind* and *The Wonderful Border*. After leaving for Canada in the fall of 1968, he served on the National Film Board of Canada in Montreal. He later founded the first production-oriented film school in Canada in Kitchener. From 1975 to 1979, he worked in the film department of Algonquin College in Ottawa, then in the film department of York University in Toronto. In addition to films, he is also involved in literature, especially writing humorous books. He also published his biography under the title *Paměti točomana*. In memory of his wife, Dagmar, he founded the Dagmar and Václav Táborský Foundation, which annually awards financial rewards to FAMU students.

Edgar G. Ulmer (1904–1972), born in Olomouc, Moravia, was an American film director, with low-budget productions. Ulmer studied architecture while designing sets in Vienna. Max Reinhardt hired the teenage Ulmer to design his stage productions, and in the early 1920s, he traveled with Reinhardt to New York City. He is best remembered for the movies *The Black Cat* (1934) and *Detour* (1945). These stylish and eccentric works have achieved cult status.

John Vasicek (1974–), b. San Francisco, CA, of Czech ancestry, is an American filmmaker. He received his Master's degree in Motion Picture and Television from the Academy of Art University (2005), San Francisco, CA. His undergraduate work was in business. Vasicek became a certified public accountant, while working for the international accounting firm KPMG before entering filmmaking. His debut film *Voyeur*, was selected for the 2007 Sonoma film festival. Two years later he produced *My Movie Girl*, which was screened at more than 25 film festivals. His latest script, *Rhodes to Love*, which won both an Odysseus Award (Best Script) and the Greek Film Lovers Award (Audience Favorite) at the 2013 London Greek Film Festival, was directed by the acclaimed Australian Filmmaker Nadia Tass. His 2015 script, *Adam & Eve*, won the 2015 Stage 32 Happy Screenwriters Competition.

Erich von Stroheim (orig. Erich Oswald Stroheim) (1885–1957), b. Vienna, of Bohemian mother (Johanna Sara Bondy, was American director, actor, and producer, most noted as a film star and avant-garde, visionary director of the silent era. He was one of the most critically respected motion-picture directors of the 20th century, best known for the uncompromising realism and accuracy of detail in his films. His 1924 film *Greed* (an adaptation of Frank Norris's 1899 novel *McTeague*) is considered one of the finest and most important films ever made. After clashes with Hollywood studio bosses over budget and workers' rights issues, Stroheim was banned for life as a director and subsequently became a well-respected character actor, particularly in French cinema. He also wrote screenplays and won recognition as an actor, notably for roles as sadistic, monocled Prussian officers.

Jon Watts (1981–), b. Fountain, CO, of Czech ancestry, is an American film director, producer, and screenwriter. He studied film at New York University. Before directing movies, Watts directed commercials for production company Park Pictures. He directed the films *Clown* and *Cop Car* and episodes of the Onion News Network. Watts directed

Spider-Man: Homecoming, *Spider-Man: Far From Home*, and *Spider-Man: No Way Home*. When trying to get the job directing *Spider-Man*, Watts got a tattoo of Spider-Man on his chest to make himself "stand out in the field."

Jiří Weiss (1913–2004), b. Prague, Bohemia, was a film director and screenwriter; playwright. Against the will of his father, he began to shoot documentary and advertisement films in Czechoslovakia and later in England where he fled from the Germans and joined Czechoslovak units in RAF. After the war, he returned to Prague and as director-screenwriter made many successful films such as *Wolf Trap* (1957) and *Romeo, Juliet and Darkness* (1959). In 1968, he left Prague again after the Russian occupation and settled in the US. There he taught film at Hunter College, New York and in Santa Barbara. After the Velvet Revolution, he shot his last film again in his homeland, *Martha and I* (1991).

Chris Weitz (1969–), b. New York City, a son of actress Susan Kohner, is an American producer, writer, director, and actor. He is best known for his work with his brother, Paul Weitz, in the comedy films *American Pie* and *About a Boy*, as well as directing the film adaptation of the novel The Golden Compass and the film adaptation of New Moon from the series of Twilight books.

Paul John Weitz (1965–), b. New York City, a son of actress Susan Kohner, is an American film director, film producer, screenwriter, playwright and actor. He is the brother of filmmaker Chris Weitz. Weitz attended Collegiate and, in 1988, he graduated from Wesleyan University. While at Wesleyan, Weitz studied under film instructor Jeanine Basinger. He is known for *Grandma* (2015), *About a Boy* (2002), and *Mozart in the Jungle* (2014), for which he won a Golden Globe.

Stanley 'Stan' William Zabka (1924–2023), b. Des Moines, IA, of Czech ancestry, was assistant director of *The Tonight Show*, starring Johnny Carson during the first two years of Carson's tenure. He has worked as production manager on a number of motion pictures, including the Chuck Norris vehicle *Forced Vengeance*. Stan Zabka is known for his work on *Romancing the Stone* (1984), *Midnight Run* (1988) and *The Doctors* (1963).

Peter Zinner (1919–2007), b. Vienna, of Moravian ancestry, was an American filmmaker who worked as a film editor, sound editor, and producer. Following nearly fifteen years of uncredited work as an assistant sound editor, Zinner received credits on more than fifty films from 1959–2006. He studied music in the Theresianum and at the Max Reinhardt Seminar. Following the occupation of Austria by Germany in 1938, Zinner and his parents, who were Jewish, emigrated. They went first to the Philippines, and in 1940 to the United States. As a young man, Zinner worked in Los Angeles as a taxi driver and occasionally as a pianist at screenings of silent films. He was Oscar winning film editor who did sound effects editing at Universal from 1947 to 1949 and music editing at MGM from 1949 to 1960. Zinner was nominated for the Academy Award for Best Film Editing three times for his work on *The Godfather* (1972), *The Deer Hunter* (directed by Michael Cimino-1978), and *An Officer and a Gentleman* (directed by Taylor Hackford-1982). He won the Oscar, a BAFTA, and an Eddie for *The Deer Hunter*. His work (with Barry Malkin and Richard Marks) on *The Godfather Part II* (1974) earned a second BAFTA nomination. Zinner was nominated four times for Emmy Awards, and won for the miniseries *War and Remembrance* (1988) and for *Citizen Cohn* (1992). His peers in the American Cinema Editors honored him with six Eddie nominations of which he won four.

7. Stage Directors & Producers

Martin Beck (1867-1940), b. Liptovský Mikuláš, Slovakia, was a vaudeville theater manager, owner, and impresario. He went with a group of actors on the *SS Elbe* from Bremen, Germany, to the United States in May 1884, where he worked as a waiter in a beer garden in Chicago, Illinois. He went to San Francisco with the Schiller Vaudeville Company, then gained citizenship in the United States in October 1889. When the Orpheum Theatre in San Francisco was bought by Morris Meyerfeld Jr. in 1899, he worked with Morris to acquire more theaters. By 1905, Beck was running the organization. In 1910, he formed the United Booking Offices with Alfred Butt. He built the Palace and Martin Beck Theatres in New York City's Broadway Theatre District. He was a booking agent for and became a close personal friend of the prominent magician, Harry Houdini. In 1932, he managed the booking office at RKO. In 1934, he brought the D'Oyly Carte Opera Company from London to America.

František Deák (1940-), b. Bratislava, Czech., was a dramaturg. He studied at the Academy of Music and Dramatic Arts in Bratislava (M.F.A.) and at Carnegie-Melon (Ph.D.). He served as dramaturg at the Centre Universitaire International de Recherches et de Formations Dramatiques in France and as contributing editor to The Drama Review for several years. He has published widely in theatre journals in the US and Europe and has published a major book on Symbolist Theatre. He was professor of department of theatre and dance (1974-94), dept. chair (1991-94), Dean, Division of Arts and Humanities (1994-2004), University of California, San Diego.

Jiří Fisher (1947-), b. Brno, Czech., is a multimedia executive producer in the Washington DC Metropolitan area. He studied at Janáček's Academy of Performing Arts, where he received his Master's degree in 1970. He spent 12 years in Czech theatres and played numerous roles for television, radio and films. After arriving in the United States in 1980, he starred in the NBC soap opera, *Another World*, in the long running principal role as Anton Čapek. On stage, he played Václav Benda in the off-Broadway production of John Foster's play *Ceremony in Bohemia*. He created NO CURTAIN THEATRE in Washington, D.C.

Sold-out performances of Havel's play, *Audience*, directed by Jiří Fisher and performed by Dick Stilwell at GW's Marvin Center Theatre, The Resident Associates Program of the Smithsonian Institution in the Baird Auditorium led to the theatre's founding. The same year, Fisher toured his native Czechoslovakia with the production, followed by performances in New York, Minnesota, Pennsylvania and at the Joseph Papp Public Theatre in New York City. As the featured guest artist at George Washington University in the Department of Theatre and Dance, he directed *Stars in the Morning Sky* by Russian playwright Alexander Galin. Fisher has translated numerous theater plays from English to Czech language and is always looking for new dramatists and quality plays.

Charles Gilfert (1787-1829), b. Prague, Bohemia, was a theatrical manager. He began his career in the US as a composer and teacher of music and became a manager of concerts and oratorios. Eventually he led the orchestra of the Park Theatre in New York City, and was the conductor of the Musical-fund society. In 1815, he relinquished his musical career, and became lessee of the theatre in Charleston, South Carolina. At the close of an unsuccessful season, he went to Albany, New York, with his wife, and for several years managed the theatre in that City. In 1826, when the noted New York or Bowery theatre was built, he was offered the management, and became its lessee. Here he produced in rapid succession spectacular novelties, ballets, and operatic ensembles superior to any that had been seen in this country. But he was of an over-sanguine temperament, regardless of obligation, and reckless in money matters. As a consequence, his affairs became disordered, he was continually harassed, and not seldom imprisoned for debt within the 'jail liberties' of his theatre.

Vít Hořejš (1950–), b. Prague, Czech., received a BA (equivalent) in philosophy in 1974, and MA (equivalent) in French language and literature from Charles University and a diploma in acting from Lidová škola umění in 1975. The same year, he joined a professional repertory theatre company in Šumperk, as an actor. He directed several independent theatre productions between 1972–1977 and translated from French and Italian. He left Czechoslovakia in 1978 to consult with Primo Levi on his translation of *Il Sistema Periodico* into Czech and never looked back. After spending a year in Paris, he came to New York in 1979. He worked as a taxi driver and a theatre technician, before he joined Ta Fantastika Black Light Theatre with which he toured the world during the '80s as a performer and associate director (1982–89). In 1984, Vít found a treasure trove of 69 marionettes, aged 80 to 180, at Jan Hus Church in Manhattan. He ultimately founded the Czechoslovak-American Marionette Theatre (CAMT) in 1990 with other émigrés from Prague and has been its artistic director ever since. Vít has translated, written, adapted and directed over twenty plays for CAMT. Vít has also performed on stage, in films and on TV. On screen, he was most notably Krojack in Woody Allen's *Don't Drink the Water*. His published works include *Twelve Iron Sandals* (1985), a collection of Czech and Slovak fairy tales retold in English. He co-produced an award-winning documentary film about Czech puppetry, *Faust on a String*. A collection of his small-scale plays appear in *Vít Hořejš's Rare & New Plays* (2007).

Erich Juhn (1895–1973), b. Přerov, Moravia, was a journalist and a theater impresario. Educated at Univ. of Vienna, he immigrated to New York in 1941. He was contributor to Red Book and, after 1942, to Aufbau, New York. He became a co-manager of political German-language cabaret, *Die Arche*, at Master Theatre, New York (1942–45). Thereafter he became a professor at Georgian Court Coll., Lakewood, NJ. After 1948, he was with Berlitz Language School, first as dir. of schools in Baltimore and Washington, DC. He was a co-founder of theatre enterprise, Contemporary Plays, Inc., New York (s. 1949–); dir. of research in New York (s. 1952), prod. and script writer for Aufbau – New World Club Cabaret, New York (s. 1963).

Adolph Klauber (1879–1933), b. Louisville, KY, of Bohemian ancestry, was a drama critic, was also theatrical producer. He scored a modest hit with his first solo offering *Nighty-Night* (1919). In 1920, Klauber was the un-credited co-producer of two Eugene O'Neill's plays, *The Emperor Jones* and *Diff'rent*. His 1922 production of *The Charlatan* was well received but had only a mediocre run. With the Selwyns and his wife, Jane Cowl, he produced many of her starring vehicles, such as *Lilac Time* (1917), *Smilin' Through* (1919), *Pelleas and Melisande* (1923), and *Antony and Cleopatra* (1924), although he remained a silent partner in these enterprises.

Milo Kubik (1929–2013), b. Čadca, Czech., was a producer, founder of independent firm Animette Canada, later in charge of the Czech and Slovak program in Toronto.

George Lederer (ca. 1862–1938), b. Wilkes-Barre, PA, of Bohemian parents, was an American producer and director on Broadway from 1894 to 1931. Lederer began his career when he joined a touring opera company at age 13, as a soprano singer. When he reached the age of 17, he collaborated with the producer Thomas Canary and leased the Casino Theatre, in New York City. In 1897, at age 25, he produced the musical *The Belle of New York*, which became one of the first American musicals to enjoy enduring success in England, where it ran for over two years. Lederer was one of the first producers of musical *Revues* in the U.S., when together with Sydney Rosenfeld, he presented *The Passing Show* in 1894. In 1903, while he was manager of the New York Theatre he presented the all-black musical *In Dahomey*, with music by Will Marion Cook and lyrics by poet Paul Dunbar. It starred the prominent black vaudeville team of Bert Williams and George Walker. Then crossing the

Atlantic, it played for seven months, and received a Royal Command Performance at Buckingham Palace in England.

František Ludvík (1843-1910), b. Bohemia, a hatter by trade, developed interest in theater at early age. Since 1867, he was a member of City Theater in Plzeň. In 1893, he left for America where he founded his own theater in Chicago, the Ludvik Theater – the first permanent Czech theater in America.

Joseph Ondrejkovic (1890-1964), b. Turčiansky Sv. Martin, Slovakia, was the founder and director of the Slovak National Theater, Chicago, residing in Berwyn, IL.

Peter Peřina (1944-), b. Czech., graduated from the School of Fine Arts in Prague in 1964 and worked professionally in Czechoslovakia for 3 years before moving to Ottawa in 1967. He was an assistant professor at the University of Saskatchewan from 1970-1972 and joined the faculty of the Dalhousie's Department of Theatre in 1972. He has designed 343 productions and guest lectured in Canada, USA, and the Czech Republic. He is the Chair of the Baroque Theatre Foundation at the Castle of Český Krumlov and a member of the Board of Perspectiv, Association of Historic Theatres in Europe.

Max Reinhardt (1873-1947), b. Baden, nr. Vienna, of Moravian ancestry on his mother's side, was an American stage and film actor and director, and theatrical producer. In 1935, Reinhardt directed his first film in the US, *A Midsummer Night's Dream* that included James Cagney, Mickey Rooney, Joe E. Brown and Olivia De Havilland, amongst others.

Kurt Robitschek (later Ken Robey) (1890-1950), b. Prague, Bohemia, was a popular cabaret and theatre director. He was raised in Vienna. He was active there as an actor and lyricist. He co-founded 'Kabarett der Komiker' in Berlin. Until 1933, he was proprietor and landlord of this most important pre-1933 political and lit cabaret. He engaged famous actors and cabaret artists. In 1933, he returned to Prague and then resided in Vienna. His attempt to stage similar cabaret in Vienna met with little success. In 1936, he went to France and then to U.K. In 1937, he emigrated to the US. He reopened his Kabarett der Komiker there. Until 1945 he successfully toured cities with renowned émigré actors. In 1942, his attempt to establish a permanent German theatre in New York failed.

Štěpán Šimek (1963-), b. Prague, Czech., initially moved to Switzerland in 1982 and then emigrated to the US in 1987. He received a B.A. in Theatre from San Francisco State University in 1991, M.F.A. in Theatre Directing from the University of Washington in 1995, and he was the 1996 Drama League of New York Directing Fellow. He is now a director, translator, adaptor and a Professor of Theatre, and the Chair of the Theatre Department at Lewis & Clark College in Portland, OR. Previously, he was a faculty member at The Evergreen

State College in Olympia Washington, and Reed College in Portland. Over the past twenty-five years, Professor Šimek has directed over thirty theatre productions in New York, Seattle, San Francisco, and Portland, both professionally and in College and University settings; translated plays from Czech, German, and French, and adapted several novels, including Michael Bulghakov's *Heart of the Dog*, Franz Kafka's *Amerika* for the stage. He is one of the authorized translators of the former President of the Czech Republic, Václav Havel's work, and his various translations and adaptations have been staged in New York, Philadelphia, Baltimore, Seattle, Portland, Los Angeles, San Diego, and San Francisco, and published in a number of anthologies. His translations of Petr Zelenka's *Theremin* and Iva Volankova's *Three Sisters* (2002). He received the 2006 PEN America Translation Award, and his version of Havel's *The Increased Difficulty of Concentration* is widely produced in the English-speaking theatre.

Robert Vrtis (1980–), b. Fort Belvoir, VA, of Czech ancestry, studied theatre arts at Longwood Univ. (B.F.A., 2003) and at the University of Oregon, Eugene (M.A., 2008; Ph.D., 2011), having completed his doctoral dissertation, *Plague and Mirror: Metaphors of Emotional Transfer and their Effect on the Actor-Audience Relationship in Theatre*. There, he directed *Arabian Night*, *The Highest Tide*, *Atomic Farmgirl*, and an original adaptation inspired by the works of Anton Chekhov Masha. While in Eugene, OR, he was regularly involved with the Lord Leebrick Theatre / Oregon Contemporary Theatre, directing *Fahrenheit 451*, *Boom*, and *The Santaland Diaries*. Other directing credits include Lee Blessing's *Eleemosynary*, *Twelfth Night*, *Macbeth*, *Tartuffe*, and *WASP*. Currently he is an assistant professor at Luther College, Decorah, IA, where he teaches acting and directing in the Visual and Performing Arts program. There, he has directed *Cabaret*, *In the Next Room* (or the vibrator play), *Metamorphoses* and original adaptation of *La Dispute*. His research interests are in the area of contemporary acting theory and pedagogy, Clown, Shakespeare in performance and adaptation, theories of affect in relation to theatre arts, and dramatic literature.

Dennis Zacek (1940–), b. Pilsen suburb of Chicago, of Czech ancestry, graduated from DePaul Univ. (B.A., 1963), and studied theater at Northwestern Univ. (Ph.D., 1969). He was an artistic director of Victory Gardens, Chicago, retiring in 2011, after 34 years at its helm. He is also professor emeritus of Loyola University. He began working with the company in 1977 and has directed more than 250 productions in his career. As the artistic leader of the company, he established a playwright ensemble of 14 members. Across the ensemble, virtually every major accolade has been bestowed on its members, including the Tony Award, Emmy Award and the Pulitzer Prize. The accomplishments of the theater and its ensemble led to receiving the Tony Award for Outstanding Regional Theatre in 2001, and local and national media have recognized Victory Gardens as one of the most important playwriting theaters in the country. These accolades propelled the company, under Zacek's leadership, to renovate the historic Biograph Theater, a new state of the art facility which includes the Zacek McVay Theater, the Richard Christiansen Theater, a rehearsal room, and administrative offices. Dennis Zacek recently accepted the Actors' Equity Association's (AEA) Spirit of Diversity Award, which is given to institutions that 'have made non-traditional casting a way of life.' He also received the 2005 Jeff Award for Outstanding Achievement in Chicago Equity Theatre and the 2004 Artistic Leadership Award from the League of Chicago Theatres. Zacek and Marcelle McVay, his wife and former VG Managing Director, received the 1999 Rosetta Lenoire Award from Actors' Equity and the 1998 Sidney R. Yates Arts Advocacy Award from the Illinois Arts Alliance Foundation.

8. Cinematographers

Fred 'Béďa' (Bedřich Baťka) Batka (1922–1994), b. Czech., was a Czech-American cinematographer of note. He held the position of professor of film and TV, New York Univ. Tisch School of the Arts., New York.

Robert Buchar (1951–), b. Hradec Králové, Czech., is an American cinematographer, filmmaker, film director and producer. He studied cinematography at FAMU, the Film Academy of Fine Arts. He worked as a cinematographer mainly for the documentary section of Krátký film, before defecting to the United States in 1980. There he worked as a cameraman for CBS until 1989, photographed over twenty films and documentaries in the U.S. and Europe. He also works as director of photography on independent films and commercials. Since 1989, he teaches cinematography at the Columbia College in Chicago, where he became head of the Cinematography Concentration, the faculty's cinematography program, an advanced production course he developed.

Karl Freund (1890–1969), b. Dvůr Králové, Bohemia, was a cinematographer and film director. He worked as a cinematographer on over 100 films, including the German Expressionist films *The Golem* (1920), *The Last Laugh* (1924) and *Metropolis* (1927). Freund emigrated to the United States in 1929 where he continued to shoot well remembered films such as *Dracula* (1931) and *Key Largo* (1948). He won an Academy Award for Best Cinematography for *The Good Earth* (1937). In 1937, he went to Germany to bring his only daughter, Gerda Maria Freund, back to the United States, saving her from almost certain death in the concentration camps. Between 1921 and 1935, Freund also directed ten films, of which the best known are probably *The Mummy* (1932) starring Boris Karloff, and his last film as director, *Mad Love* (1935) starring Peter Lorre. At the beginning of the 1950s, he was persuaded by Desi Arnaz at Desilu to be the cinematographer in 1951 for the television series *I Love Lucy*. Critics have credited Freund for the show's lustrous black and white cinematography, but more importantly, Freund designed the "flat lighting" system for shooting sitcoms that is still in use today. This system covers the set in light, thus eliminating shadows and allowing the use of three moving cameras without having to modify the lighting in-between shots. And where Freund did not invent the three-camera shooting system, he did perfect it for use with film cameras in front of a live audience. Freund and his production team also worked on other sitcoms produced at/through Desilu such as *Our Miss Brooks*.

John C. Hora (1940-2021), b. Pasadena, CA, of Czech ancestry, was a cinematographer. He earned a Bachelor of Arts degree from the University of Southern California Cinema School (now the School of Cinematic Arts) in 1962 and was Phi Beta Kappa. He is an American cinematographer active from the 1970s to the 2000s. He has also worked as an actor in the 1980s and 1990s. Hora worked with director Joe Dante in numerous films, including *The Howling* (1981), *Twilight Zone: The Movie* (1983), *Gremlins* (1984) and its sequel, *Gremlins 2: The New Batch* (1990), *Explorers* (1985), and *Matinee* (1993). He also served as a cinematographer for Michael Jackson's 1988 film *Moonwalker*; and for the pilot for the television series *Eerie, Indiana*. As an actor, Hora performed in Dante's film *Innerspace* (1987). He later appeared in '*Honey, I Blew up the Kid*' (1992), the sequel to *Honey, I Shrunk the Kids*. Hora also worked as the director of photography for *Honey, I Blew up the Kid*. Later, Hora worked for The Los Angeles Film School and as secretary for the American Society of Cinematographers. In May 2005, he was honored by the magazine *American Cinematographer*. John has served for a number of years on the Scientific and Technical Awards Committee at the Academy of Motion Picture Arts.

Eduard Ingriš (1905-1991), b. Zlotnice, Czech., apart from his other talents, was also an excellent photographer and cameraman. As a cameraman, Ingriš worked for film studios in Czechoslovakia, Germany, and Peru. He filmed a series of thirteen travel and adventure films for the American Production Company, Hollywood. For Movius Productions, Hollywood, he filmed *Jungle Sabotage*, a movie starring Pilar Pallete, wife of actor John Wayne. He assisted the late author Ernest Hemingway in filming *The Old Man and the Sea*, based upon Hemingway's, Pulitzer Prize-winning novel. He also wrote music for another film, produced by Stell Productions in Hollywood, called *The Gallant One*. His own high adventure films *From High C's to High Seas*, depicting his two balsa raft expeditions across the Pacific, *Untamed Amazon* and *Sailing the South Seas* of his return voyage on a ketch from Tahiti to Lima, Peru, are scored with his own compositions, and were personally presented on lecture tours for several years throughout USA, Canada and Hawaii and later transferred to videos.

Robert Jay Kositchek, Jr. (1952-), b. Santa Monica, CA, of Bohemian ancestry, was raised in Los Angeles. His education was at the Art Center College of Design, Pasadena, CA, where he studied photography (B.F.A.). His real education began in the studios of Hollywood as an assistant cameraman, working up to director of photography. At this time, he teaches cinematography at the University of Southern California. He has extensive experience in television, feature, documentary, and commercial production. Over the years, he has worked on cutting edge projects such as *24*, *The X-Files* and *Roswell* and *The Pretender*. He lives in Santa Monica, CA.

Antonín Lhotský, b. Czech., a cinematographer, editor, and producer. He is a graduate of F.A.M.U., the Czechoslovakia Film Academy in Prague. He has taught film at a number of Canadian film schools and has been a professor of film and video production at York University in Toronto for the last 10 years. As a Canadian filmmaker, he has accumulated more than 100 film credits, mostly in cinematography but also as producer, director and editor in documentary and theatrical films. He has also worked on several multi-screen projects including *Taming of the Demons* (1986) which received a special Genie Award (Canada's top film honor) for outstanding film achievement.

Miroslav Ondříček (1934-2015), b. Prague, Czech., was a Czech-American cinematographer. He studied filmmaking at the Barrandov Studio Training School and began making movies during the Czech New Wave. His first feature film work was on Miloš Forman's *Talent Competition*. He continued his long working relationship with Forman in the US on such films as *Hair* (1979), *Ragtime* (1981) and *Amadeus* (1984). He also collaborated with the British film director Lindsay Anderson on two films: *If....* (1968) and *O Lucky Man!* (1973). Ondříček earned Oscar nominations for *Ragtime* in 1982 and *Amadeus* in 1985.

Franz Planer (1894-1963), b. Karlovy Vary, Bohemia, was a cinematographer. Planer had trained as a portrait painter, but realizing that photography was becoming very popular, and would replace the requirement for talented artists changed his career path. He changed direction into films, and thus began his career as a director of photography for films in Germany and later throughout Europe in the early 1900s until 1933. In 1937, he left the failing Austrian film industry, to begin work in Hollywood. He shot over 130 movies, including *Letter from an Unknown Woman* (1948), *The Big Country* (1958) and *Breakfast at Tiffany's* (1961).

František Valert (1932-1993), b. Czech., was a Czech cameraman and pedagogue. He graduated from FAMU (1952-59), majoring in camera. He became a close collaborator of Zdeněk Podskalský. As a cinematographer, he participated in the production of films in the period 1953-69, the most famous of which are, *The White Lady*, *The Madly Sad Princess*, and *Saints*. In 1969, he left for England and a year later for Canada where he first worked at the Conestog University Institute of Technology and Advanced Learning in Kitchener, Canada.

In 1975, he became a professor of film and television production and cinematography at Univ. of California, Los Angeles (UCLA).

9. Film Editors

Matthew Hamachek (1980–), b. Washington, DC, of Czech ancestry, received his schooling and training at Denison Univ. He began his career working on the Oscar-nominated documentary *Street Fight* with Marshall Curry and went on to collaborate with Curry again on *Racing Dreams* (best documentary, Tribeca Film Festival) and *If a Tree Falls*, which won the Documentary Editing Award at the 2011 Sundance Film Festival and was nominated for an Academy Award for Best Documentary. Hamachek went on to win the editing award at the 2013 Sundance film festival for *Gideon's Army*. Since then, he has edited *Mistaken for Strangers* about the band The National and *Console Wars* (executive producers Scott Rudin and Seth Rogen) about the battle between Sega and Nintendo in the 90s. He then edited Matthew Heineman's (Escape Fire) film *Cartel Land*.

Lee Unkrich (1967–), b. Cleveland, OH, of Slovak descent on his mother's side, is an American director, film editor, screenwriter, and animator. He is a longtime member of the creative team at Pixar, where he started in 1994 as a film editor. He later began directing, first as co-director of *Toy Story 2*. After co-directing *Toy Story 2*, *Monsters, Inc.* and *Finding Nemo*, Unkrich made his solo directorial debut with *Toy Story 3* in 2010, and most recently directed *Coco* in 2017, both of which won the Academy Award for Best Animated Feature and the Academy Award for Best Original Song. After working at the studio for 25 years, Unkrich left Pixar and the film industry in January 2019 to be able to spend more time with his wife and three children.

10. Scenic Designers & Art Directors

Lisa Aronson (née Jalowetz) (1920–2013), b. Prague, Czech., was a set designer. For over 35 years, Lisa Jalowetz Aronson was part of the Broadway theater design team, with her husband Boris Aronson, garnering six Tony awards. After graduating from Black Mountain, Lisa Jalowetz moved to New York. There, she won work sketching theatre scenes for newspapers. She later became an assistant to such set designers such as Jo Mielziner (working on *Carousel*). She and Boris Aronson married in 1945. Thereafter, she worked only in conjunction with him. She assisted her husband on such iconic shows as *Detective Story*, *The Country Girl*, *I Am A Camera*, *The Crucible*, *Bus Stop*, *J.B.*, *Fiddler on the Roof*, *Follies* and *A Little Night Music*.

Frank J. Drdlík (1901–1985), b. Zenica, Bosnia, of Czech parents, reached Hollywood by chance and in 1922 started designing in the MGM studio. He designed sets for such pictures as *The Thief of Baghdad, Iron Mask, Black Pirate, Gaucho, Romeo and Juliet, Mission to Moscow, Dual in the Sun, Spellbound* and many other.

Christopher Horner (1955–), b. Los Angeles, CA, of Czech ancestry, was an American anthropologist and scenic designer. Before graduating high school, he had already studied anthropology and been involved in exchange programs on Hopi Reservations. Graduating from UC Berkeley in 1976 with a degree in architecture and environmental design, he accepted a job with MGM as a set designer. He worked on films such as *Winter Kills, Comes a Horseman, Altered States, The Jazz Singer* and the Emmy-award-winning *Friendly Fire* for CBS, among many others.

Harry Horner (1910–1994), a native of Holice, Bohemia, was wo-time Academy Award-winning production designer, director and producer. After graduating from the University of Vienna with a degree in architecture, he worked as an architect for a year, then turned to acting under the guidance of Max Reinhardt. For two years (1933–35), he appeared in a number of Reinhardt productions in Vienna and Salzburg, and then in 1935, he traveled to New York with 'The Eternal Road' as Reinhardt's assistant, and in 1937, took over as designer of the show (succeeding Norman Bel Geddes). From this success, he went on to design a number of Broadway productions. He won an Oscar in 1949 for his work on William Wyler's *The Heiress* and another in 1961 for Robert Rossen's drama *The Hustler*.

Emil Kosa, Sr. (1876–1955), b. Solovice, Bohemia, was a painter and draftsman. Kosa worked with his father making marionettes for his theater. He moved to Paris to work as an assistant to his longtime friend, the renowned Czech painter, Alphonse Mucha. In Paris, he met his first wife, Jeanne Mares Kosa, a French pianist at the Paris opera. She gave birth to their first son, artist Emil Kosa Jr., in 1903. Three years, later she died of tuberculosis. Kosa remarried and in 1908, the family moved to Cape Cod, Massachusetts, so that Kosa could continue designing theatrical posters and painting murals with Mucha. In 1912, the family moved back to Brno, Czechoslovakia, but soon became caught in the middle of World War I. After the War, the family went back to America. By 1924, Kosa settled in Los Angeles with his son, who was following his father's footsteps and becoming a great painter. Kosa Sr. worked at T. C. Fox matte painting department under Fred Sersen. Emil Kosa Sr. made puppets which he used as models for his paintings. He continued to exhibit locally in Los Angeles until his death on May 11, 1955.

Emil Kosa, Jr. (1903–1968), b. Paris, France of Czech ancestry, was a painter, muralist and lithographer. In 1912, Emil Kosa Jr. moved from France to the U.S. with his family at age four. The family subsequently returned to Czechoslovakia, where he attended the primary and secondary school during and after World War I. After the War ended, Kosa Jr. trained in art at the Academy of Fine Arts, Prague. After a mere three semesters, he moved to the United States in January 1921. He took art courses at the California Institute of the Arts in Valencia. In 1928, he spent the year in Paris, studying at the École des Beaux Arts and with Pierre Laurens and Frank Kupka, and returned to California the same year. In 1933, he joined the newly formed special effects department at 20th Century-Fox (later 20th Century Studios). He was quickly promoted to art director, a position he held for the next 35 years. In 1964, he became the first person to win the Best Visual Effects after the Academy Awards changed the name from Special Effects. He won at the 36th Academy Awards for his work on the film *Cleopatra*. He also helped to create the first logo for 20th Century Pictures (later 20th Century Fox, later 20th Century Studios).

Adolf Lešovský (1885-1972), b. Humpolec, Bohemia, was a painter and designer. Lesovsky settled in Los Angeles in 1906. He worked there both as a portraitist and as an artist for the Garret Corporation (air research) until his death on Dec. 30, 1972. He studied art at YMCA and worked in commercial art (1908-11). He first engaged in jewelry designing for Waltan Co. (1911-16) and also worked for Tiffany, NY (1920-23). He received medal for jewelry designing. Subsequently, he became art director for Hollywood productions and interior decorator (1923-41).

Joseph C. Nemec, 3rd (1948-), b. Little Rock, AR, of Czech ancestry, is production designer and art director. He is known for his work on *'Fatal Beauty'* (1987), *'The Abyss'* (1989) and the TV show *'Midnight Caller'* (1988). He has also worked in the Art Department for such movies as *American Flyer* (1985), *The Color Purple* (1985) and the mini-series *V* (1983). He was also production designer for *Terminator 2 - Judgement Day* (1991), *Patriot Games* (1992), *Twister* (1996) and *Speed 2: Cruise Control* (1991) and *The Hills Have Eyes* (2006), to name but a few of the many. The list of movies is phenomenal.

J. Michael Riva (1948-2012), b. Manhattan, NY, of Bohemian ancestry on his mother's side (a son of Maria Sieber Riva), was an American production designer. Riva had a long and prestigious career as an art director and production designer on numerous films, including the 1985 film The Color Purple, for which he was nominated for the Academy Award for Best Art Direction. Other credits include *The Goonies* (1985), *Lethal Weapon* (1987), *A Few Good Men* (1992), *Spider-Man 3* (2007), *Iron Man* (2008) and *Iron Man 2*. His final films, *The Amazing Spider-Man* and *Django Unchained*, were released posthumously. He was the production designer for the opening ceremony of the 1996 Summer Olympics in Atlanta, as well as for the 74th and 79th Academy Awards in 2002 and 2007, respectively. He won a Primetime Emmy Award for his work on the latter.

J. Paul Riva (1957–), b. US, of Bohemian ancestry on his mother's side (a son of Maria Sieber Riva), is art department administrator, Los Angeles. He is known for *Six Days, Seven Nights* (1998).

Richard Rychtařík (1895–1982), b. Prague, Bohemia, was American set and costume designer. In 1923, came to the US and soon began to design sets and costumes for the Cleveland Playhouse. While in Cleveland, he also became associated with the Cleveland Orchestra. In the late 1930s, he went to work for the New York City Center as scenic advisor and then designed sets for the fledgling City Center Opera. After having provided the sets for some Metropolitan Opera productions, he was engaged by the Metropolitan in 1947 as its technical director. He joined CBS two years later as their scenic designer for its TV shows.

Fred Sersen (orig. Sršeň) (1890–1962), b. Veselí nad Moravou, Czech., was a painter and cinema special effects artist. At the age of 17, he moved to the United States (1907) and made his home in Los Angeles around the year 1920. Having completed an extensive education at the Los Angeles School of Art and Design, the Portland Art Academy and the San Francisco Institute of Art, he went on to become a prodigious painter of watercolour landscapes, many of which have been exhibited in galleries along the West Coast. Sersen also began forging a career in the film industry. By 1930, he worked in the art department of Fox as a set designer and scenic artist. He was among the first to successfully combine live action scenes with both matte shots and miniatures. Becoming the leading visual effects photographer at the re-formed 20th Century-Fox, Sersen set up one of the best special effects departments in Hollywood by 1937 supervising a large team of matte painters, optical effects experts, miniature builders, editors and cameramen. His first credited film was *A Connecticut Yankee* (1931). In 1937 he recreated the 1871 Great Chicago Fire on the screen for the film *In Old Chicago*. Other notable effects for which he is credited include the fire in *Hangover Square*, the flying saucer in *The Day the Earth Stood Still*, and the sinking of the ship in Titanic. Sersen was nominated for no less than eight Academy Awards, winning two: for Best Effects, Special Effects (photographic), in 1940 for *The Rains Came*, and in 1944 for *Crash Dive*.

Klára Zieglerová (1969–), b. Prague, Czech., is a set and graphic designer, working primarily as an award-winning theatre designer. Her degrees include M.F.A. in book culture and typography from the Academy of Arts, Architecture and Design in Prague; M.F.A. from the Theatre School, Miami University; and M.F.A. from School of Drama, Yale University. She lives now in New York City. She has been designing extensively for theatre in the United States, Europe and Asia. Her work has been seen on Broadway, where Ms. Zieglerová designed Sister Act directed by Jerry Zaks. Klara has designed numerous productions all over the United States at theaters such as the New York Public Theater, Manhattan Theatre

Club, New York Theatre Workshop, Irish Repertory Theatre, La Jolla Playhouse, Cincinnati Playhouse, Dallas Theater Center, Portland Center Stage, Seattle Rep, Williamstown, and others. In Europe, Ms. Zieglerová has worked for Stage Entertainment on productions such as *Saturday Night Fever* in Holland and *Sister Act* in Hamburg, Vienna, Milan, and UK & Ireland Tour. In Ireland, she designed productions of *Eden* (by Eugene O'Brien) and *Wrecks* (by Neil LaBute). Klara designed the interior of the New World Stages in New York – the home of five Off Broadway Theaters. She also designed the US National Exhibition at the Prague Quadrennial 2015 and is a member of the International Board of Prague Quadrennial 2019 as well as a curator of its Fragments exhibition. Ms. Zieglerová won The Green Room Award 2010 (Australia) for Best Design of a Musical, The Best Set Design of the 2009 Theatregoers' Choice Award London (both for *Jersey Boys*), 2005 Lumen Award (New World Stages), 2003 Grammy Award for Best Set Design; 2000 Carbonell Award for Best Set Design; sets for the Best Touring Production, 2003 L.A. Ovation Award.

11. Drama & Film Critics

Adolph Klauber (1879–1933), b. Louisville, KY, of Bohemian ancestry, was an American drama critic and theatrical producer. He left Louisville after high school to attend the University of Virginia, after which he moved to New York and took a position with the Empire Theatre Company. In 1900, he began working as a reporter for *The New-York Commercial Advertiser*. From there he moved to the *New-York Tribune*, and thence to the New York Times, where he became drama critic in 1906, a post he held for twelve years. It was during this time that he married the actress and playwright Jane Cowl. He then began working with Archibald and Edgar Selwyn, two of the founders of Goldwyn Pictures, later to become part of MGM, and worked for a while there as a casting director.

Effie Wise Ochs (1860–1937), b. Cincinnati, OH, of Bohemian parents, was a communal worker, drama and book critic for *Chattanooga Times*. She was the daughter of Rabbi Isaac Mayer Wise, founder of Reform Judaism.

12. Performing Arts Educators & Historians

Thomas F. Bradac (1947–), b. South Gate, CA, of Czech ancestry, studied at Long Beach State Univ. (B.A., 1969; M.A., 1971). He has been a theatre professional for over forty years. He is associated with the dept. of theater at the Chapman Univ., Orange, CA, as asst. professor (1990–97), as assoc. professor (1997–2014), as professor (s. 2014). He is the founder of Shakespeare Orange County (1992–2013), where he has directed and produced over 50 productions. He also founded the Grove Shakespeare Festival (1979–1991), guiding it through a thirteen-season tenure where he produced and/or directed 110 productions including *Cyrano De Bergerac, A Midsummer Night's Dream, The Dresser, The Merry Wives of*

Windsor, Quilters, Mrs. California, and *The Merchant of Venice.* Tom was awarded the prestigious Hollywood Drama Logue Publisher's Award for Exceptional Achievement in Theatre for his work with Grove Shakespeare Festival, The Helena Modjeska Award for Service to Orange County, CA by OC Weekly and Kennedy Center/ American College Excellence in Education Award for his teaching. As an actor, he has performed as Bottom in *A Midsummer Night's Dream*, Dogberry in *Much Ado About Nothing* and Falstaff in *The Merry Wives of Windsor*, among others. He is a founding director of the Shakespeare Theatre Association, an international service organization for theatres dedicated to producing Shakespeare and has served as the organization's President.

Joseph Brandesky (1954–), b. Karnes City, TX, of Moravian ancestry, graduated from Texas State Univ. (B.A., 1978) and studied theatre in the same institution (M.A., 1982). Subsequently, he studied Russian and East European theatre and drama at Univ. of Kansas (Ph.D., 1991). He has been associated with Ohio State Univ. (OSU), Lima, as asst. professor (1998–95), as assoc. professor (1994–2003), as full professor (s. 2003), as Martha W. Farmer Endowed Professor in Theatre (s. 2012); joint appointment at OSU, Lima and OSU, Columbus (s. 2012); as assoc. director of the Center for Slavic and East European Studies at OSU, Columbus (s. 2013). Most of his professional career has been devoted to bringing visually expressive examples of Russian and East European theatre to the attention of American audiences. In 2000, he co-created and edited the catalog for the U.S. exhibit *Metaphor and Irony: Czech Scenic and Costume Design 1920-1999*, and in 2004, he produced the exhibit *Metaphor and Irony 2: František Tröster and Contemporary Czech Theatre Design* and co-created and edited its catalog. In 2007 he edited a volume of essays *Czech Theatre Design in the Twentieth Century: Metaphor and Irony Revisited* (2007). He was recipient of Faculty Scholar Award, OSU, Lima (2008).

Jarka Marsano Burian (1927–2005), b. Passaic, NJ, of Czech ancestry, was educated at Cornell Univ. He was Professor emeritus, Dept. of Theater, SUNY Albany. He taught English at Cornell University from 1951 to 1955. Beginning in 1945 and continuing through the 1960s, Burian acted in regional, summer, and off-Broadway productions. Burian joined the New York State College for Teachers (the predecessor of the State University of New York, Albany) in 1955, working as an assistant professor (1955–59), associate professor (1959–63), professor (1963–1993), and professor emeritus (s. 1993). From 1971 to 1974, and again from 1977 to 1978, Burian served as the chairman of the Department of Theatre at the State University of New York at Albany. He directed many theatrical productions at the State University theatre during the academic year. During the late 1950s and 1960s summer sessions, Burian also served as producer/director at the Arena Summer Theatre which was open to all members of the Capital District community. Burian published articles on the theatre, particularly on the subjects of arena theatre and contemporary theatre in Czechoslovakia. Burian wrote a book on *The Scenography of Josef Svoboda* (1971) and used Svoboda as the guest designer for the sets for two productions he directed at the State University. He also authored *Modern Czech Theatre: Reflector and Conscience of a Nation* (2000) and *Leading Creators of Twentieth-Century Czech Theatre* (2013).

Joan Copjec (1946–), Hartford, CT, of Czech ancestry, has an M.A. in English from the University of Wisconsin; a diploma in film from the Slade School of Fine Art, University College, London; and a Ph.D. in cinema studies from New York University. She is the author of *Read My Desire: Lacan against the Historicists* (1994) and *Imagine There's No Woman: Ethics and Sublimation* (2002). A former editor of the influential journal, *October*, she has also edited numerous books, including: *October: The First Decade* (1987; with A. Michelson, R. Krauss, and D. Crimp); *Jacques Lacan: Television* (1990), *Shades of Noir* (1993); *Supposing the Subject* (1994); *Radical Evil* (1995) and *Giving Ground: The Politics of Propinquity* (1999, with Michael Sorkin). Her primary fields of research are psychoanalysis, film and film theory, feminism, and art and architecture. She has taught intermittently at various schools of architecture: the Institute for Architecture and Urban Studies, NYC; Sci-Arc, LA; and the School of Architecture, Urban Design and Landscape Architecture at the City College, NYC.

Ján Marian Dafčík (1923–1981), b. Žabokreky nad Nitrou, Slovakia, was a professor of drama and film, playwright, theater director, editor, literary critic, and publicist. After graduating from high school in Bratislava (1942), he studied in 1942–47 Theater Studies at the Universities of Berlin and Vienna. In 1947–48, he was prof. at the acting and opera school Št. Bruckner Conservatory in Linz, prof. history of film and dramaturgy at the Alpfilm Film School in Linz and Salzburg, dramaturg of the Municipal Theater in Braunau. He lived in Argentina from 1948, where he was director and director of the Immigrant Theater from 1950 to 1954, director of the German stage *Die Insel*, collaborator of the German daily *Freie Presse* in Buenos Aires, foreign correspondent for the German film magazine *Film-Echo*, director of amateur performances in Slov. Cultural Association of Buenos Aires. Since his student years, he has regularly published theater critiques, reviews, reflections and commentaries in several domestic periodicals (*Naše divadlo*, *Javisko*, *Nový svet*, Slov. rozhlas, Slov. magazín, Slov. pravda, etc.). He also continued his writings in emigration and his numerous contributions were published in Austrian (*Die Furche*, *Welt am Montag*, *Maske und Kothurn*, *Linzer Volksblatt*, etc.), German (*Freie Presse*, *Film-Echo*, etc.) and Slovak newspapers and magazines (*Jednota*, *Slovak in America*, *South American Slovak*, *Mladost*, etc.). Author of radio games *Laugh, bajazzo!* (1942), *Cherries for Rome* (1943), the drama *At the End of the Road* (1951), *And the Stars Go Out* (1953).

Everard d'Harnoncourt (1921-1996), b. Velké Losiny, Moravia, received his Doctorate in theater arts from the University of Vienna in 1951. He was professor emeritus of dramatic art and a founding member of the program, Univ. of California, Davis. During his nearly 30 years at Univ. of California (UC), Davis, he helped build the dramatic arts program, contributing significantly to the creation and development of its graduate programs. Professor d'Harnoncourt was also instrumental in assembling a collection of films at UC Davis that will constitute the base for a new program in film studies. As part of his contributions to the stage, he directed more than 25 plays. His career in the department also included the original production of a musical comedy on the history of American film that used music and scenery from films dating back to the 1930s and 1940s. Professor d'Harnoncourt also translated several plays into English from French and German. One of them, *The Architect and the Emperor of Assyria* by Fernando Arrabal, was first produced at UC Davis and later professionally by the American Conservatory Theatre in San Francisco.

Evžen Drmola (1927-1981), b. Prostějov, Czech., was professor of theater arts, Univ. of Massachusetts, Boston. He was also a playwright and translator. As an actor, he was known for *Letišět nepřijímá* (1960), *The Black Dynasty* (1962) and *Kissing-Time Ninety* (1965).

Mojmír Drvota (1923-2006), b. Prague, Czech., was a writer, film historian, theorist, screenwriter, and director. After the end of the Second World War, during which he was totally deployed in the Semtín factory, he studied at the Faculty of Arts of Charles University. After expulsion in 1948, he completed his studies in Olomouc. The beginning of his literary activity can be dated to the mid-1940s when he wrote the humorous novel *Holiday in Pajamas*. After the war, he began contributing short stories to several magazines, for which he also wrote a humorous novel to continue the Pension for Artists. These texts already contained very distinctive dialogues, which formed the basis of his later philosophical texts. In addition to the first book, other books were prepared for printing, such as *Burning Pýr*, but were not published until the 1990s. In 1957, Drvota went into exile, first living in Germany, then landing in New York. After various short-term jobs, he collaborated with Columbia and later New York University, and after relocating to Ohio, he lectured at Ohio State University. He was professor of photography and cinema, Ohio State Univ., Columbus, OH (until 1979). Drvota wrote a number of plays, novels, and poems. He wrote and directed the film *A Distant Journey*. Drvota taught film making at both Columbia and Ohio State University.

Nataša Durovičová (1954-), b. Bratislava, Czech; editor, International Writing Program, editor of *91st Meridian* – an electronic publication, cinema historian, University of Iowa, Iowa City.

Ivan Dušek, of Willmar, MN, studied at Univ. of Minnesota (Ph.D., 1972). He was a member of faculty, Speech and Theatre at Ridgewater Coll. (1967-99). Subsequently, he became Trustee, MN State Colleges and Universities (2000-06) and then a member of Board of Directors, Clear Way Minnesota (2006-12).

Marinka Gurewich (nee Revész) (1902-1990), b. Bratislava, Slovakia, was an American voice teacher and mezzo-soprano of Jewish Czech descent. Gurewich trained as a singer and pianist at the Berlin University of the Arts where she was a pupil of Lula Mysz-Gmeiner. She also studied privately with Elena Gerhardt and Anna von Mildenburg in Munich. Her career as a singer in Germany was hindered by World War II and she fled Europe for the United States in 1940. Prior to the war, she had appeared in concerts and recitals in Europe. After coming to the United States, she appeared in a few recitals and concerts in New York City; but ultimately began devoting her time to teaching. During the 1960s and 1970s, she taught voice at the Manhattan School of Music and the Mannes College of Music. She continued to teach privately until her death in 1990.

John Franklin Hruby (1914-1992), b. Cleveland, OH, was educated at Western Reserve Univ. and at Univ. of Denver, with B.A., M.A., M.F.A. degrees. He was asst. prof. of speech, Wayne State Univ. (1955-61), assoc. prof. and head of dept. of speech and theatre (1961-68); assoc. prof. of theater, Rider Coll. (1968-72), assoc. prof. of drama, Macon, GA (s. 1974).

Diane L. Kvapil (ca. 1955-), b. US, possibly of Czech ancestry, is assoc. professor of drama at College-Conservatory of Music (CCM), Univ. of Cincinnati. She studied at Catholic University, Washington, D.C. and the Neighborhood Playhouse, New York City, with Sanford Meisner. She studied with Eric Morris, summer 1987. At CCM, Diane has directed productions of *Trojan Women*, with original music by Richard Oberacker, *Our Town*, *Three Sisters* (Acclaim Award winner for Outstanding Ensemble) and Tom Stoppard's *Arcadi*. In 2011, she was named Outstanding Theatre Educator by the ACCLAIM Awards in Cincinnati. She has been featured in numerous regional and national touring productions as well as WNET and NBC telecasts. She has performed with National Players in Japan, Korea, Hawaii, Canada, North Africa and Bermuda. She is in demand for on camera commercial work as well as voice over for radio and television. She authored one teleplay recently produced for NBC's Young People's Specials.

Josef 'Pepi' Lustig, b. Czech., holds M.A. degree in film studies from American University and NYU, and a Ph.D. from the world-famous Prague film and media school, FAMU. He has taught screenwriting and various aspects of film making for Yale and NYU, among numerous other U.S. and European institutions. Lustig has written, directed and produced numerous shows for Czech television, and has worked on such American movies as *The*

World According to Garp, *Ragtime*, and *Cutter's Way*. His documentary work for the US Holocaust Memorial Council, the American Jewish Congress, and *LIFE Magazine* has been extensive. Lustig's publications and translations reflect his incredibly diverse interests and trans-Atlantic perspective. His numerous awards include a grant from the Czech Minister of Culture Fund for Cinematography and a grant from the National Endowment for the Humanities.

Jane Manner (orig. Jennie Mannheimer) (1878–1943), b. New York, of Bohemian ancestry, was a teacher, elocutionist, teacher of speech and drama and acting coach. She began her teaching career, when she accepted a position as a teacher and director of the Drama Dept. of the Cincinnati College of Music (now the College-Conservatory of Music at the Univ. of Cincinnati), where she remained until 1907. Believing that Americans did not take the time to pay attention to correct and proper language and that success was very much tied to careful speech, she founded her own school, the Cincinnati School of Expression where she served director until 1912. Mannheimer's focus was on the interpretation of literature and the teaching of speech. In 1913, she began a series of modern drama readings that were presented at the Cincinnati Women's Club. With the success of these performances, Mannheimer presented a similar series at the Plaza Hotel in New York. Later she moved to New York to continue her career as reader and teacher and as a director of the Manner Drama Studio. As she had done in Cincinnati, Mannheimer gave numerous recitals and readings, and she directed many plays. She performed at Carnegie Hall, the Brookings Institute of Arts and Sciences, and the Waldorf Astoria, where she gave recitals for seven consecutive years. Over the course of her career, Mannheimer taught many students who went to distinguished careers on stage, screen and radio. She also published books on drama and speech, including *The Silver Treasury of Prose and Verse for Every Mood* (1934), which dealt with the teaching and interpretation of literature.

Peter Peřina (1944–), b. Czech., graduated from the School of Fine Arts in Prague in 1964 and worked professionally in Czechoslovakia for 3 years, before moving to Ottawa in 1967. He was an assistant professor at the University of Saskatchewan from 1970–72 and joined the faculty of the Dalhousie's Department of Theatre in 1972. Currently, he is professor emeritus of technical scenography in Dalhousie Univ. Fountain School of Performing Arts. He has designed 343 productions and served as guest lecturer in Canada, USA, and Czech Republic. He is the chair of the Baroque Theatre Foundation at the Castle of Český Krumlov and a member of the Board of Perspectiv, Association of Historic Theatres in Europe.

Lisa A. Peschel (1965–), b. Madison, WI, of Bohemian ancestry, studied playwriting at Univ. of Texas and theatre historiography at Univ. of Minnesota. At the University of Texas, she researched theatrical performance in the World War II Jewish ghetto at Terezín, completing and staging a play about the cultural life of the ghetto for an MFA degree in playwriting. During her Doctoral studies at the University of Minnesota she spent several semesters in the Czech Republic, interviewing Terezín survivors and searching for previous unpublished scripts. In 2008, her annotated volume of plays and cabarets from the ghetto was published in Czech and German. Afterwards, she received postdoctoral fellowships at the US Holocaust Memorial Museum in Washington, DC, and the Center for Jewish Studies at Harvard University. In 2011, she was appointed a lecturer in theatre at the Department of Theatre, Film and Television at the University of York, Heslington (East), York, UK. She is the author of *The Prosthetic Life: Performing Captivity* and *Performing Escape: Cabarets and Plays from the Terezin/Theresienstadt Ghetto* (2013).

Josef Škvorecký (1924-2012), b. Náchod, Bohemia, studied philology at Charles Univ. Škvorecký taught fiction, creative writing and film at the Faculty of Arts and Science at the Erindale College campus of Univ. of Toronto from 1971 until his retirement in 1990. He wrote several books on the Czech cinema, i.e., *All the Bright Young Men and Women: A Personal History of the Czech Cinema* (1971), *Jiri Menzel and the History of The Closely Watched Trains* (1982) and *Talkin' Moscow Blues: Essays about Literature, Politics, Movies & Jazz* (1988). He also wrote for film and television and translated American classics into Czech, having been drawn to American literature from an early age, particularly to Hemingway, Fitzgerald and Twain. He is best known however for his novels.

Wendy Sterba (1956-), b. Kansas City, KS, of Czech ancestry, received her B.A. from Reed College and MA and Ph.D. from Rice University in German Studies in 1988. She received a DAAD scholarship to study at the Ludwig Maximillians Institut, University of Munich in 1974 and also attended Passau University in 1985. She joined the Department of Languages and Cultures, College of St. Benedict/ St. John's University in 1989, where she teaches courses on film history and theory as well as German culture and language. She received tenure and the rank of associate professor in 1996 and was promoted to full professor in 1999. She is a teacher devoted to pressing students to think critically and credits her Czech ancestry for giving her a strong belief in a broad, international humanism and for this reason, has directed numerous study abroad programs in places such as Australia, Austria, England and Japan. She specializes in film and medieval German literature with a focus on critical theory and feminist studies, served as dept. chair (2010-2012), and has been invited to present at international conferences worldwide from Transylvania to Paris to Kalamazoo and Los Angeles, among others. She has published on a variety of topics ranging from Hartmann von Aue's Erec, to dystopian film, the new media, the use of the photograph in film, and topics of women's presentation, capitalism and prostitution in the film and televisual works of Joss Whedon.

Pavel I. Trenský (1929-2013), b. Ostrava, Czech., was educated at Comenius Univ., Harvard Univ. and at Fordham Univ. He came to Fordham in 1964 and joined what was then Fordham's Russian Institute, which he eventually led. For 44 years, he taught Russian literature and comparative drama in the Modern Languages Department, earning him the Bene Merenti medal in 2004 for 40 years of service to the University. During this time, he published widely, including two books, *Czech Drama Since World War II* (1978) and *The Fiction of Josef Škvorecký* (1991). He also contributed frequently to Czech theater journals on New York, Berlin, and Czech theater and cultural topics. After retiring in 2008, he continued submitting annual essays on the Salzburg Festspiele and the Berliner Theattertreffen, to the Prague journal *Svět a divadlo* (World and Theater), which he had done since 1993.

Jan Uhde (1942-), b. Brno, Czech, is a film historian. He studied at Masaryk Univ., Brno (Dipl., 1965) and at the University of Waterloo, Ontario, Canada (Ph.D., 1974). Since 1970, he has been teaching at the University of Waterloo where he founded a General and Honours BA program in Film Studies in the Department of Fine Arts. He holds the position of professor (film studies) at the University of Waterloo. His professional and research interests focus on the area of identification and distancing of the film viewer, the non-authored modifications and manipulation of film works on their journey from the filmmaker to the viewer, and specific questions of film history, including the Central European cinema. He is the editor of *Kinema*, a Journal for Film and Audiovisual Media, which he founded in 1993.

Thomas Valasek (1946-), b. Pittsburgh, PA, of Czech ancestry, received education in English and cinema studies at New York Univ. He holds the position of professor of film and communication studies at Raritan Valley Community College at Branchburg, NJ. He is the author of film textbook, *Frameworks: An Introduction to Film Studies* and co-authored a public speaking textbook, *The Confident Speaker's Handbook: A Practical, Hands-on Approach to Public Speaking*. He has a special interest in and passion for Czech cinema, and has received two International Research Exchange (IREX) fellowships to pursue research projects in the Czech Republic and a Fulbright fellowship to teach at Charles Univ.

George E. Wellwarth (1932-2001), b. Vienna, of Czech ancestry on his mother's side, emigrated to US in 1946. He attended New York Univ. and Columbia Univ. and received Ph.D. from Univ. of Chicago. He was asst professor at Staten Island Coll. (1960-63), and assoc. professor (1963-64). He then became associated with Pennsylvania State Univ. (s. 1964), as assoc. prof. of English and comparative literature (1966-70). Since 1970, he served as prof. of theater and comparative literature, SUNY Binghamton. He did research on modern, especially avant-garde, theater in Europe and America; also on the history of drama.

13. Talent Agents

Paul Kohner (1902-1988), born in Teplice, Bohemia, was talent agent and producer. He came to Hollywood in 1920 after having been a news reporter in Prague. In 1938, he opened the Paul Kohner Talent Agency and managed the careers of Marlene Dietrich, Greta Garbo, Dolores del Río, Maurice Chevalier, Billy Wilder, Liv Ullmann, Henry Fonda, David Niven, Erich von Stroheim, Ingmar Bergman and Lana Turner. In the same year, he founded the European Film Fund (EFF).

Walter Kohner (1914-1996), b. Teplice-Šanov, Bohemia, was a Hollywood agent. He worked along with his brother Paul in his legendary Paul Kohner Agency on Sunset Blvd. in Hollywood, CA. They represented numerous actors and writers with great success.

D. Visual Art

1. Painters

Monika Abbott (1948-), b. Prague, Czech; was originally trained as a lawyer at Charles University. In 1975, she emigrated to Holland, where she began to study drawing and painting. Three years later, she exhibited her first paintings. In 1985, Abbott came to the United States to study at Parsons Institute, and she has been showing her works ever since. She has exhibited at the Kuks Castle in the Czech Republic; International Images in Pittsburgh; and the Artsforum Gallery and the Metropolitan Museum Staff Show in New York.

Egon Adler (1892-1963), b. Karlovy Vary, Bohemia, was a painter and graphic artist. In 1940, he immigrated to US where he helped to promote abstract expressionism.

Irena Altmanová (1923-2019), b. Plzeň, Czech., is an artist and painter, educated at Prague: Graphic School and UMPRUM. Paris: Academie Andre Lhote, Ecole des Beaux-Arts. Florence: Santa Reparata Graphic Art Center. Albany: SUNY, Albany (M.A., in 1970). She exhibited her paintings in individual shows at Albany, Glens Falls, NY, Saratoga Springs, NY and Florence, Italy, as well as in many group shows. She is the author of *A Lifetime of Pastels* (2011), which is her specialty. She was a recipient of several awards and other honors. Her works are included in a number of public and private collections.

Dina Babbitt (née Dina Gottliebová) (1923-2009), born in Brno, Czechoslovakia, was an artist and Holocaust survivor. She resided in Santa Cruz, California.

Adolf Benca (1959-), b. Bratislava, Czech., is a painter. His family emigrated to the United States when he was ten years old, in 1969. He studied at Cooper Union (B.F.A., 1981);

Columbia university (M.F.A., 1987) and University of Bologna. His works are exhibited in many galleries around the world, many of his paintings ending up in private collections.

Jolán Gross-Bettelheim (1900-1972), b. Nitra, Slovakia; artist, painter, active in New York, NY, resided in US from 1925-1956, working in the graphics art division of the works Progress Administration.

Gorge Biddle (1885-1973), b. Philadelphia, PA, desc. f. Augustine Heřman, was an American painter, muralist, and lithographer. He is best known for his social realism, combat art, and his strong advocacy of government-sponsored art projects. Biddle was a lawyer by training whose passion for art led him to abandon his original profession.

Franz A. Bischoff (1864-1929), b. Kamenický Šenov, Bohemia, was an American artist known primarily for his beautiful floral paintings and California landscapes. Spending less time with ceramic painting, Bischoff painted local farms, fishing wharfs, and coastal landscapes. Recognized during his career for use of color and vivid composition, his paintings always displayed reverence for nature.

Albert Bloch (1882-1961), b. St. Louis. MO, of Bohemian father, was an American Modernist artist and the only American artist associated with Der Blaue Reiter (The Blue Rider), a group of early 20th-century European modernists. At an early age he produced caricatures for the St. Louis satirical weekly *The Mirror*. He was in Munich from 1909-1921, where he met and worked with Kandinsky and Mare, the founders of the revolutionary art movement the Blue Rider Group. On his return to America, he became a professor of art at the University of Kansas at Lawrence. In 1997, the Albert Bloch retrospective exhibition took place at three locations.

Joseph Bodner (1925-1982), b. Florence Township, NJ, of Slovak descent; an American painter, illustrator. He often chose the vanishing West and white stallions as favorite subjects but his painting "The Resurrection of Jonathan," which was exhibited at the motion picture premiere of *Jonathan Livingston Seagull*, is probably his best-known work.

Rudolf Bohůnek (1875-1939), b. Bohemia, was both a painter and printmaker. He studied art in Prague at the School of Art and in 1907 traveled to America. In 1909, he made his way down south and worked in New Orleans for four years. While in New Orleans, he received a large commission to paint the Louisiana Sugar Planters Association's members' portraits. Bohůnek also produced a series of portraits of historic Louisiana figures. Later, he moved to Chicago where he became art instructor at the Chicago Academy of Fine Arts. He established a studio in Chicago's Loop. After arriving in Chicago, he also started an art school (about 1913).

Darina Boldizar (fl. 2015), Slovak Canadian, b. Košice, Slovakia; immigrated to Canada in 1980; after retiring from a successful real estate business, she became an oil painter.

John Beale Bordley (1800–1892), b. Wye Island, MD, desc. f. Augustine Heřman of Prague, a prominent planter and lawyer, distinguished himself as an artist. He was a portraitist in Baltimore. Thirty-two of his portraits were exhibited at the Maryland Historical Soc. in 1954. He painted the large (60" x 90") portraits of the Signers: Samuel Chase, Wm. Paca, and Thomas Stone in the Md. State House.

Maurice Braun (1877–1941), b. Bytča, Slovakia, was an artist, and landscape impressionist. He was one of the most popular California impressionist painters and one of the most popular artists in San Diego.

Marta Brestovansky (1937–1999), b. Košice, Czech., was a painter, residing in Orillia, Ont., Canada. At 14, she entered the College of Fine Arts in Bratislava. Because of her young age, she was granted admittance by special permission due to the merit of her portfolio. She escaped from Czechoslovakia in 1968 and eventually settled in Canada. She was proficient in a myriad of techniques - Portraits, landscapes, fantasy, graphic all compose her oeuvre. Marta has exhibited throughout Canada, the United States of America, Europe, and Japan.

Zdenka Buresch (1913–1994), b. Kunvald, Czech., was a painter and art restorer.

Vojen W. Čech-Colini (1924–2010), b. Kolín, Czech., first studied art with professor Kutil, then an exponent of German expressionism. In 1943, Colini moved to Prague, where he was exposed to the work of the leading Czech surrealist, Karel Maly, a disciple of de Chirico. Leaving Prague in 1947, Colini began a 12-year journey of self-discovery, living in Switzerland, France, West Indies, South America, and Canada. In 1959, this sojourn came to an end in New York, where he took up his greatest challenge, i.e., of distilling his rich and haunting life experiences into graphic images. Since then, however, he is returning frequently to Germany and Italy where he felt equally at home. In 1972, Colini was invited to join the Gallery Schreiner in Basel - which in those times was affiliated with the famous Gallery Peithner-Lichtenfels from Wien - and thus was the focus of Ars Fantastica movement in Switzerland. Since his acceptance into this group, Colini's work has travelled to the major cities of Switzerland, West Germany and France. Finally in the year 1975, Colini was accepted as a member in the prestigious 'Kunstlergilde e.V' in West Germany. This important success opened the doors to the German art scene and Colini began to exhibit in the Gallery Koelner Kunst Kabinett, Gallery Scholler, and Gallery Blankenborgh. His work was accepted in the prominent 'Inter Art Galerie – Cologne' and he joined 'Phainesthai' a group of Koeln artists. He took active part in the evolution of the organization into the 'Gruppe 82 Koeln. He became fascinated with Italian art of the

Renaissance Era and decided to paint only in Egg Tempera. He began to find ways to improve the Surrealists weaknesses by overlaying a Renaissance flavor.

Barbara Cervenka, O.P. (1939-), b. Cleveland, OH, probably of Czech ancestry, is a Dominican Sister of Adrian, Michigan. She is a painter who works primarily in watercolor. Her work has been exhibited at the Detroit Institute of Art, the University of Michigan Museum of Art, the Dennos Museum in Traverse City, Central Michigan University and the Art Gallery of Winsor, and many other places here and abroad. For the past thirty years, she has taught at the University of Michigan in Ann Arbor and at Siena Heights University in Adrian. She holds the position of associate professor of art at the latter.

Howard Gardiner Cushing (1869-1916), b. Boston, MA, desc. f. Augustine Heřman was a portrait painter. He established a studio in New York City in 1898 and worked there until his death. In his early work he confined himself to a portraiture, later he specialized in mural and decorative paintings. Recipient of numerous awards.

Lily Dulany Cushing (1909-1969), b. New York, NY, desc. f. Augustine Heřman of Prague, was an artist whose paintings are exhibited at the Metropolitan Museum, the Whitney, and the Museum of Modern Art in New York and in many private collections. Lily Cushing was known for still life and landscape paintings.

Lydia Darvaš (née Hacaj) (1935-2024), b. Lošonec, Czech., is an artist, abstract and surrealistic painter, residing in North Miami Beach, FL. She was trained at Fine Arts Academy in Bratislava (M.F.A., 1953). Recipient Bicentennial award, American Heritage Organization, 1976, First prize paintings, Arvida Corporation, 1980, First prize collages, Hollywood Fashion Center, 1980. She was a member of Smithsonian Institution, National Museum Women in Arts.

Charles Demuth (1883-1935), b. Lancaster, PA, of Moravian ancestry, was a notable painter who had major influence on American art by introduction of modern European movements, such as cubism. He graduated from Franklin & Marshall Academy before studying at Drexel University and at Philadelphia's Pennsylvania Academy of Fine Arts. He later studied at Académie Colarossi and Académie Julian in Paris, where he became a part of the *avant garde* art scene.

Jan De Ruth (1922-1991), b. Karlovy Vary, Czech., a Holocaust survivor, enjoyed special popularity as a portraitist and has been one of the best known painters of the nude female in the world. He exhibited at 34 national juried exhibitions, 14 museum solo shows and 51 gallery solo exhibitions. He was the author of *Portrait Painting* (1964) and *Painting the Nude* (1968).

Frank Dolejska (1921–1989), b. Houston, TX, of Moravian mother, was the first generation child of immigrant. Dolejska, along with Robert Preusser, were two of the first non-objective painters in Texas, with early works dating from 1938. Basically self-taught, Dolejska was a student with McNeill Davidson for a brief period. After serving in World War II, Dolejska returned to Houston where he became the curator for the new organization, the Contemporary Arts Association. Leaving the CAA in 1956, Dolejska took up metal work, creating sculptures with copper and lead. His early paintings are rare because he burnt many of them. A founding member of the Contemporary Arts Association in Houston, his work was shown in many exhibitions including the 1940 Texas General Exhibition and shows in Houston. His work was the focus of a one-man show at the Corpus Christi Art Museum, the Dallas Museum of Fine Arts and the Museum of Fine Arts, in Houston.

Jan Doubrava (1912–1972), b. Brno, Moravia, was a painter, who resided in New York. He was asst. head of art dept. at the New School of Social Research.

Joseph Drapell (1940–), b. Humpolec, Czech., is one of Canada's most important abstract painters. He immigrated to Canada in 1966. From 1968-1970, he studied at the Cranbrook Academy of Art in Bloomfield Hills, Michigan. He moved permanently to Toronto in 1970. Drapell began his formal career as an artist when he was 28 and has participated in numerous exhibitions. He developed a technique of applying paint with a broad spreading device attached to a movable support. Drapell is a member of the Royal Canadian Academy of Arts.

Oskar Ember-Spitz (1892–1952), b. Spišská Nová Ves, Slovakia; painter, portraitist.

Alois Fabry, Jr. (1912–1986), b. New York, NY, of Czech father, was an artist, teacher, and author. He was a 1936 graduate of the Yale University School of Fine Arts. Early in his career, during the Depression, Mr. Fabry painted two of the largest murals commissioned for the Works Progress Administration. Painted on the rotunda of Brooklyn Borough Hall, the murals covered 1,900 square feet and became the subject of controversy. Primarily a water colorist of seascapes and landscapes, exhibited widely on the East Coast. He was also contributing artist to the *New Yorker,* where his drawings appeared regularly over the 40 years. He became the director of the mural-painting dept. of the Beaux-Arts Inst. of Design and taught at Columbia Univ. and the Pratt Inst. From 1956 to 1971, he was the director of art for the New Canaan school system.

Paul (Pavol) C. Fallat (1908–1973), b. Bardejov, Slovakia, was a portrait painter. He was also administrator at Slovak Catholic Sokol, Passaic, NJ.

Velen Fanderlík (1907-1985), b. Prague, Czech., displayed artistic ability from an early age, but followed family tradition and became a lawyer. He and his father were instrumental in organizing the Czechoslovakian Boy Scouts, of which Velen Fanderlík became president. World War II forced him to flee his homeland. He practiced law in England, and also in France, where he worked as an evacuation officer for Czechoslovak refugees. He served as a military judge and became a member of the prosecuting team at the Nuremberg war crime trials. After the communist takeover in 1948, he and his wife fled Czechoslovakia illegally to the American zone of West Germany, where they involved themselves in the work of the International Relief Organization. About a year later, they returned to England, but before long, made the decision to relocate in Canada. The couple settled in Vancouver, where Fanderlík worked at the YMCA and studied at the University of British Columbia (U.B.C.) to become a teacher. In 1955, he accepted a teaching position at J.L. Crowe Secondary School in Trail. Here, he taught Latin, history, social studies, law and art until his retirement. He also taught the history of art at night school classes in Trail and Castlegar and at summer schools at U.B.C. and Notre Dame University in Nelson. Fanderlik never abandoned his art. He studied at the University of Brno, St. Martin School of Art in London, Cambridge University, the Academy of Art in San Francisco, University of British Columbia and the Banff School of Fine Arts. His favorite medium was watercolors, but he also liked oil paints, pastels and other mediums. He became known as a miniaturist and for his lino cuts.

Velenka Fanderlik (aka Stanislava Eliška Fanderlíková) (1914-1980), b. Skalica, Czech.; painter. Her formal training started only after she came to Canada. At the University of Vancouver, she studied under Jean-Paul Lemieux and Jacques de Tonnacour. Several years, she studied in Banff School of Fine Arts. She also studied at the Academy of Arts in San Francisco. The dominant note of Velenka's personal approach to art was her universal compassion, flowers and children being her favorite subjects.

Aldrich Otto Farsky (1895-1968), b. Chicago, IL, of Bohemian father, was a landscape and figure painter who was formerly from Chicago and was a resident of Los Angeles in 1925-1928. His paintings include scenes of Antelope Valley near Palmdale. He died in Berwyn, Illinois.

Edward Aldrich Farsky (1900-1973), b. Chicago, IL, of Bohemian father, a brother of Aldrich Otto Farsky, was also a painter. Edward Farsky is known for genre, historical themes and portrait paintings. He was a resident of Los Angeles in 1928. He died in Crystal Lake, IL in December 1973.

Oldřich Farský (1860-1939), was an American landscape, still life, portrait, marine and figure pointer. He was a Czech immigrant to the US, who studied at the Art School in Prague. He had a studio in Karlovy Vary, Bohemia and traveled and painted in Italy, France and Holland before moving to Chicago in 1893. Throughout the early 20th century, Farský was a prominent member of the Czech immigrant community in Chicago and became a member of the Czech Artists Club. He exhibited his works in a number of exhibitions, including an exhibition held in Cleveland by the Slavic Alliance of Cleveland. Farský lived in Los Angeles in 1925–1928, and during his travels, painted the mountains of Colorado and Canada.

Fred (Bedřich) Feigl (1884-1965), b. Prague, Bohemia, was a Czech-Jewish painter, graphic designer, and illustrator. Feigl studied at the Prague Academy of Fine Arts with Vlaho Bukovac and František Thiele. Feigl lived for a long time in Berlin and New York. Feigl created the best work of his expressionistic period with his landscapes of Copenhagen, Berlin, and the fishing villages on the French Riviera. He is, however, best known for his sketches of Prague ghetto life. Feigl also did book illustrations. His works are placed in galleries around the world.

Brian Fencl (1968-), b. Englewood, CO; of Czech ancestry, studied illustration at the Art Center College of Design (B.F.A., 1990) and drawing at New York Academy of Art (M.F.A., 2000). He was a member of the adjunct faculty at the University of Colorado at Denver (2000-2002); and a lecturer and was a demonstrator at the Carnegie Museum of Arts, Pittsburgh (2007). He joined the faculty at West Liberty Univ., West Liberty, WV, as asst. professor of art (2002-07), as assoc. professor (2007-2010), as full professor (s. 2010) and chair of the dept. of journalism, communication studies and visual art (s. 2009). During the period of 2008-10, he was master instructor for the visual arts at the West Virginia Governor's School for the Arts. In 2005, he was in Umbria, Italy, as an artist in residence at the International School of Painting, Drawing and Sculpture. During 2006-07, he was voted by the students Professor of the Year. In 2008 and 2009, he was awarded 'Best of Show', by West Virginia Arts and Crafts Guild 7th Annual Juried Competition, Parkersburg Arts Center, Parkersburg, WV, and by Persad Center Celebrate Life, Celebrate Art Auction, Pittsburgh, PA, respectively.

John Fery (1859-1934), b. Austria, of Bohemian father, studied painting in Vienna, Munich and Düsseldorf. In 1886, he traveled to America and began making extended trips to the West to paint the magnificent scenery and abundant wildlife of the Rocky Mountains region. In 1910, Louis Hill, president of Great Northern Railway, hired Fery to paint vast panoramic landscapes depicting Glacier National Park. Hill used these paintings as part of the 'See America First' campaign which extolled the natural wonders of the pristine mountain wilderness and encouraged people to travel on his railway and stay in his hotels and lodges. From 1910 to 1913, Fery completed an astounding 347 paintings for Great Northern, ranging in size from 40 x 40 inches to 48 x 192 inches. Company records in 1913 itemizing Fery's salary, supplies and rent indicate an average cost to Great Northern of $31.70 per painting.

Irena Fiala-Zedníček (1943–2011), b. Czech., was a graduate of the New York Inst. Technology with a major in architecture and rounded up her unique painting style at the Art students League in NYC. Upon her arrival in the US in 1970, she co-founded Fiala Gallery in NYC with her late husband Karel Zedníček, a known Czech architect and painter. She later went on to exhibit her work in the New York area and participated in several painting competitions. Her accomplishments include an exhibit at New York City's Frish Gallery, at the Roslyn Museum of Fine Art and annual exhibits of her work at the International Art Expo at the Javits Convention Center in New York City. Throughout her career of over twenty years as an oil painter, Irena's style had undergone several evolutionary developments while maintaining an underlying architectural presence. Her early 1980's work depicts representational images and reflects a gentle sensitivity in its expression of the human form and nature. In the early 1990's, her work evolved into an abstract expression of geometry, this time representing the human form as sculpture.

Hugo Anton Fisher (1854–1916), b. Kladno, Bohemia, was an artist known for his skill in watercolor painting of landscapes. Fisher came to the United States in 1874. He lived in New York City for a period, and then moved with his wife to Alameda, CA in 1886, setting up a studio in nearby San Francisco. He sketched scenes during his commute by ferry to and from his studio and became well-known on both coasts. He lost many earlier works by San Francisco Earthquake in 1906. His work has received favorable mention, finding places in this city and also in galleries of Eastern cities, and in Europe, and received the silver medal at Sacramento. He exhibited in New York and California and his works can be found in the collections of: St. Mary's College, Fine Arts Museums of San Francisco, Society of California Pioneers, Crocker Art Museum, Washington University and Oakland Museum.

Hugo Melville Fisher (1876–1946), a native of Brooklyn, NY, of Bohemian father (son of Hugo Anton Fisher) was a California-based impressionist painter. At age eight, Hugo Melville moved with his family to Alameda, CA where he grew up. By that time, his father had taught him to paint. After graduating from high school, he was in Hawaii for two years. Shortly after the turn of the century, he went to Europe and spent the next 16 years there. While in Paris, he studied with Whistler, Bouguereau, Laurens, and Benjamin-Constant. His exhibitions in London and Paris received favorable reviews from the local press. While there, he was a member of the American Art Assn. and Friars Club. Upon his return to New York in 1920, his paintings of the French Modernist school caused quite a stir. After 1925, he traveled constantly and made trips around the world. Returning to

Alameda in 1938. Fisher remained there until a brain tumor ended his life on Sept. 30, 1946. He was known for landscapes, winterscapes and seascapes.

Frank Daniel Fousek (1913-1979), b. Cleveland, OH, was a painter, etcher, lithographer and a photographer.

Maru Prokop Fried (1906-1997), b. Pardubice, Czech.; artist, painter; also a singer, residing in Brookfield, IL.

David Friedmann (1892-1980), b. Moravská Ostrava, Moravia, was an accomplished Czech artist before World War II, who survived the Holocaust. In 1949, he fled Communist Czechoslovakia to Israel and later immigrated to the US. During his lifetime, Friedmann produced a large body of work including various still life and genre themes, portraits, landscapes, and abstract art. He also created a unique exhibition entitled, 'Enjoyment in Libraries with the Candid Pencil of David Friedman.' This series, about 100 drawings, consists of life studies of people in various St. Louis libraries between 1962-1972.

Joseph Gabanek (1923-2011), b. Budapest, Hungary, and grew up in Czechoslovakia. His art education began in Vienna, later in Bratislava and from 1945-50, he studied figure painting and printmaking at the Academy of Fine Arts in Prague, where he received honorary award for figure composition. Though portraiture and figure painting has always been a major part of Gabanek's work – he finds outdoor sketching and painting a rewarding experience. In Czechoslovakia, he exhibited his work in solo and group shows and was a member of Czechoslovak Federation of Artists. After the 1968 Soviet invasion of Czechoslovakia, he came to Canada and settled in Vancouver B.C. He began to show his work in newly created Gastown in the Exposition Gallery, where he had solo shows and participated in group exhibitions until 1973. He exhibited throughout B.C. extensively. He was represented by Alex Fraser Galleries. His paintings are in many private and corporate collections. Among prominent Canadians who commissioned portraits by Joseph Gabanek are Dr. Hugh Keenleyside, former chairman of B.C. Hydro, Hon. John Nicholson, former Lieut. Governor of B.C., in Government House, Victoria, Prof. Dr. Vladimir Krajina, University of B.C. Soon after he settled in Canada, he was commissioned to execute a life size copy of Rembrandt's *Night Watch*, which was much admired in former Rembrandt Hotel, Vancouver.

Maria Gabánková (1951-), b, Prague, Czech, immigrated to 1968, eventually settling in Toronto. She studied at the Ostrava Art School (1966-68), the University of British Columbia (1970-71) and the Vancouver School of Art, graduating in printmaking in 1977. Gabankova has illustrated books, magazines and album covers, painted commissioned portraits, and also teaches. Currently, she holds the position of associate professor at Ocad Univ., Toronto.

Her areas of expertise are figurative painting and oil painting. Maria Gabanková has been commissioned to paint many portraits in Canada and US. Among her sitters are several renowned personalities such as the Czech-Canadian novelist Josef Švorecký, Czech poet Karel Kryl, Canadian pianist Antonín Kubálek, composer Oskar Morawetz, Dr. J. D. Corbett, principal of Knox College, professor W. Klempa, principal of Presbyterian College, McGill University, NHL hockey player Miroslav Frycer, and world ice-skating champion Aja Vrzáňová. Her works can be found in private collections in Vancouver, New York, Toronto, Montreal, Ottawa, Kingston as well as in Germany, Czechoslovakia, France, Switzerland, and Italy. She had solo exhibitions at Wilfrid Laurier University, Waterloo (1993) and at Regis College, Univ. of Toronto (1995) and participated in group exhibitions at Isaacs Gallery, Toronto (1995) and at Newman Centre, Toronto (1996).

Anton Gág (1859-1908), b. Stráž, nr. Tachov, Bohemia, was a well-known painter and studio photographer, known for his portraits, still lives, landscapes, and murals. He immigrated to the US at the age of 14 with his family in 1873, eventually settling in New Ulm, MN. Together with other local painters, Gag decorated altars and walls of several churches in the area. He and a partner also produced a large panorama with eleven panels on the Dakota War of 1862.

Frank John Gavencky (1888-1966), b. Chicago, of Czech immigrant parents, was a painter. He studied at the Chicago Academy of Fine Arts and the Chicago Art institute. He was pictorial painter for Thomas Cusack Co., and then owner of the Arrow Display Co. He held 'one-man' exhibits at the O'Brien Galleries, Chicago (1930); and at the Pasadena an Art Institute, CA (1931). In 1925, he was awarded the Palette and Chisel Club Gold Medal and in 1930, won the Clyde M. Carr Prize at the Art Institute of Chicago. His office was located in Chicago on South Crawford Avenue.

Ladislav Guderna (1921-1999), b. Nitra, Czech.; surrealist, painter, art teacher.

Herman Carl Hanatschek (1873-1963), b. HerZnojmo, Moravia, was a painter educated in Vienna and Munich. He permanently settled in New York City where he opened a portrait studio. He painted portraits of notables, such as Queen Elizabeth of Belgium, Arch Duke Ferninand of Austria, Prince Leopold, and others. In US, he painted Pres. Calvin Coolidge, Chief Justice Harlan F. Stone, Gov. of New Jersey George S. Silzer, Sen. Thomas F. Bayard and many other personalities.

Olaf Haněl (1943-2022), b. Prague, Czech., is a painter, graphic artist, sculptor, curator, and art critic, one of the leading representatives of Czech action art of the 1970s and 1980s. From 1960 to 1965, he studied at a teaching college in Pardubice. Between 1967 and 1970, he was director of the Gallery of Visual Art in Havlíčkův Brod, where he prepared shows for the likes of Ladislav Novák, Bohdan Lacina, Naděžda Plíšková and Bohuslav Reynek. It was in this period that he began creating his own conceptual projects. Following a move to Prague in 1971, he became part of the circle around the Crusaders' School of Pure Humour Without Jokes, whose members also took part in his events. After signing Charter 77, he was employed as a water pumper and stoker. In February 1979, he emigrated to Vienna, from where he moved to Canada's Montreal six months later. There, between 1982 and 1983, he worked occasionally as a printer for Sixty Eight Publishers. He created land art sculptures and began painting. In 1990, he moved back to Prague, where for almost 20 years he worked as curator of the Czech Museum of Fine Arts. Olaf Hanel's early work is linked to humorous drawings and caricatures. Drawing also influenced his later work, specifically conceptual events in which he worked with linear constructions and graphic ideas. In the mid-1970s, he ceased doing action art for political reasons and began looking for new means of expression. A visit to the southern French town of Vence was a formative moment; there, inspired by the creative genius loci and local vegetation, he began producing abstract paintings employing a kinetic method.

Juliet Hartford (1968–), b. New York, NY, of Bohemian ancestry, is the daughter of A&P heir Huntington Hartford. Her father was the original owner and developer of Paradise Island in the Bahamas. Juliet is an artist (painter) spending time in London, Paris and New York. She has worked with Elite Model and has done shoots for both the German and American Vogue. Juliet appeared in the film *Plain Clothes* (1988), and she also played herself in *Born Rich*, a documentary on HBO.

Fritz Hirschberger (1912–2004), b. Dresden, Germany, of Czech mother, was a Holocaust survivor and painter. After the war, having married, Hirschberger and his wife moved to New York where he continued his art, teaching at the New School in New York. In 1984, he moved with his wife to San Francisco. His exhibitions have been shown in museums, memorials, and galleries throughout the world.

Iva Hladis (1965–), b. Czech., was exposed to fine art early in life, as both her father and mother were fine art painters. Two principal artistic influences on this budding young talent were Josef Šíma and Jan Zrzavý. As with Šíma's vaguely identifiable objects and Zrzavý's dark world of the fantastic, her paintings emerged as resolutely in the school of Czech modernism, her art in its almost violent emotionalism, carrying on the story of loss told in Czech art throughout the twentieth century. In the summer of 1985, Iva escaped Czechoslovakia and made her home in Rome, Italy. A year later, she was granted political asylum in the United States. Her painting changed: abstracted figures dominated, and an intense symbolism was employed. By 1988, she began working as a painter for Robert Walker. He introduced her to the Los Angeles art scene and helped establish her place within the art community. During the '88–'89 school year, she also worked as an assistant in a drawing class at West Los Angeles College, where she studied at the time. In the fall of 1989, the sudden exhilaration unleashed in Czechoslovakia, by the Velvet Revolution and the end of communist rule, created a reverse effect on her paintings and a return to the old dissident themes she thought were left behind. The reunion with her mother, shortly after, inspired a series of works filled with injustice and despair. It was this body of work that earned Iva a first exhibit at the Los Angeles County Museum of Modern Art's (LACMA) rental division. In her more recent paintings, the abstraction has faded, and the figures are recognizably human. Currently, Iva continues to work and live in Los Angeles.

Emery Donaldson Horsky (1885-1964), b. Helena, MT, of Bohemian ancestry, was a painter known for his landscape and western genre. Horsky moved to California in 1924. While a resident of Canoga Park in the 1930s, he was active on the Federal Art Project.

Charles Houska (1965-), b. Springfield, Illinois, possibly of Czech descent, earned a Bachelor's degree in art/visual communication from Illinois State University in 1987. He is a pop-artist who has been a working artist for more than 20 years and opened his St. Louis, MO Houska Studio in 1998. Colorful, bold, intense art that commands attention and triggers a smile that is the essence of artist Charles E. Houska's work. Inspired by such famous artists as Roy Lichtenstein, Andy Warhol and Keith Haring, Houska creates his own pop-art style, using a whimsical cast of characters and bright colors, bordered obsessively by black lines.

Olinka Hrdy (1902-1987), b. Prague, OK, of Czech ancestry, as an abstract painter and muralist.

Vince Hron (1961-), b. Omaha, NE, of Czech ancestry, studied painting and drawing at Drake University in Des Moines (B.F.A., 1984) and painting at the University of Michigan in Ann Arbor (M.F.A., 1987). Subsequently, he was awarded a graduate scholarship to participate in an exchange program through the University of Michigan with Germany's State Art Academy in Karlsruhe. In 1988, he returned to his hometown, Omaha, NE, where he continued developing and exhibiting his paintings. In 1996, he accepted a teaching position at Bloomsburg University where he has continued to refine his paintings. He holds the position of professor of painting and chair of the department of art and art history. He has received numerous awards including a Pollock-Krasner Foundation Grant and has exhibited his work nationally. In his work, he has endeavored to imbue our daily experiences with heightened significance through a rigorous analysis of each subject's formal potential. His objective is to remedy our detachment from the routines of life by revealing their beauty and symbolic potential. To that end, he has brought historical iconographic traditions into a contemporary context to engage and question cultural assumptions about aesthetics, spirituality, and social responsibility.

William Hubacek (1871-1958), b. Chicago, IL, was a painter of realistic still life and landscapes. Hubacek came to San Francisco by covered wagon as a child of five and began painting at age twelve. He studied at Mark Hopkins Institute and later in Europe. He had his studio at San Bruno, CA. Hubacek was a realist, mainly of landscapes and is known as one of the greatest American still life painters of the early 20th century.

Antonín Hudeček (1872-1941), b. Loučka, Bohemia, was a landscape artist in oils. He studied in Prague under prof. M. Pirner and prof. Václav Brožík. He received a Bronze Medal at St. Louis Expn. (1904).

Rudolph Frank Ingerle (1879-1950), b. Vienna, of Czech ancestry, was a painter. He came to America in 1890. He studied at Art Institute of Chicago. His paintings are found in the Friends of American Art Collection, at the Chicago Art institute, the Municipal Art Leagues Collection, etc. He was recipient of numerous honors, including Gold Medal from Bohemian Arts Club (1916), Assn. of Painters and Sculptors (1926) and William Randolph Hearst Prize (1928). He was first president of the North Shore Art League, president of the Chicago Society of Artists, vice-president of the Chicago Association of Painters and Sculptors, director of the Municipal Art League. His office was located in Chicago on E. Wacker Drive.

Pavel Janáček (1950-), b. Czech., is an artist who immigrated to Canada in 1969. He was educated at the Ontario College of Art and Design (OCAD) and has been an artist for over 30 years. He works in oil on canvas, depicting mainly landscapes. His work is held in private and institutional collections and has been exhibited in Minnesota and throughout Toronto.

Catherine Drinker Janvier (1841-1922), a native of Philadelphia, PA, of Moravian ancestry, was a prominent painter and art teacher, who at the age of 27, was the first womn to teach at the Pennsylvania Academy. Aside from teaching, Janvier also created marketable paintings of people, still-life, and genre scenes that sold for about $300 (equivalent to $6,443 in 2015) each painting in New York City. The paintings of *Geoffrey Rudel and the Countess of Tripoli* (1870), *James Madison* (1875), *Daniel at Prayer* (1876) and the lithograph *Blessed Are the Meek* (1871), all helped to develop her reputation as an artist. *Geoffrey Rudel and the Countess of Tripoli* were exhibited at the Union League of Philadelphia and *James Madison* was purchased by the city of Philadelphia and is now in the collection of the Independence National Historical Park. Drinker won the Mary Smith Prize in 1880 for *The Guitar Player*, which in 1922 was among the collection of the Neighborhood Guild at Peace Dale, Rhode Island.

Hans Jelinek (1910–1992), b. Vienna, of Czech ancestry, was graphic artist and professor emeritus of art at City College. He was famous for his woodcuts, which won many awards, including first prize in the 1943 Artists for Victory National Graphic Art Exhibition for his series on the Czechoslovak town Lidice, and the Pennell Prize of the Library of Congress. After coming to the US in 1938, he became a medical illustrator at the University of Virginia. In 1945, he moved to New York, where he was a professor of art at City College for 31 years.

Jana Jeníček (1941–), b. Prague, Czech., is Canadian painter who obtained her training at Akademie výtvarných umění, Prague (dipl. 1968) and at Centro Internazionale di Studi del Mosaico, Ravenna, Italy (Cert., 1969). She has been engaged as an art teacher at Centre Cultural de Longueuil Quebec, Canada. Her specialty is symbolic and surrealistic painting.

Joseph W. Jícha (1901–1960), Czech., was a figure, genre, and landscape painter, commercial artist and watercolorist, who came to Cleveland with his family as an infant. Jicha worked for Fawn Art and Creative Artists on advertisements for the Hotel Statler, Sherwin Williams Co., and Libbey-Owens-Ford Glass Co. His work appeared in the *Saturday Evening Post* and *Life* magazine. He won the Art Director's Show in New York City in 1936. His paintings were described by critics as having great line strength and composition, with blazing colors.

Dušan Kadlec (1942–2018), b. Prague, Czech., studied at the Academy of Fine Arts in Prague where he received a Master's Degree in 1967. His undergraduate and graduate training focused on traditional painting techniques but also explored aspects of sculpture, jewelry design, art restoration, and architecture. After completing his Master's, he was fortunate to be able to make a living as an artist in his homeland. Most of his early works were commercial art projects but he also contributed to a number of exhibitions and was invited to participate in the design of 'Man and His World,' the Czech pavilion at the 1967 World Expo in Montreal. When the Soviet Union invaded Czechoslovakia during the Prague Spring revolution of 1968, Kadlec fled his homeland and immigrated to Canada, settling in Halifax, Nova Scotia. He immediately began to look for work as an artist, and within two weeks, secured his first commission – a portrait. Since then, he has continued painting in his old-world style, gradually expanding his subject matter to include historic images from around the globe. His work is included in the Burrichter/Kierlin Marine Art Collection which is considered one of America's largest and finest privately owned marine art collections. In 2008, Dušan Kadlec received the Rudolph J. Schaefer Maritime Heritage Award from Mystic Seaport Museum.

Ferdinand Kallik (1912–1984), b. Prague, Bohemia, was an artist, painter and architect of note who was trained at the Academy of Arts, Architecture and Design in Prague (1932–

36) and at the Academy of Fine Arts in Prague (1939–46). He was only 24 years old when he received a prize for his ceramics. He received some 75 different prizes in his life. He died in Beverly Hills, CA.

Frederick Kann (1894-1965), b. Jablonec, Bohemia, was a painter, sculptor, designer, educated at Technical College of Prague and the Academy of Fine Arts in both Prague and Munich. By 1910, he moved to New York, supporting himself as a freelance and commercial artist. By 1928, he moved to Paris, where he taught studio art. It was during that period that Kann began painting abstractions. In 1936, Kann was offered a position teaching painting at the Kansas City Art Institute. In 1943, Kann left his teaching position in Kansas to accept a teaching position at the Chouinard Art Institute in Los Angeles. In California, he opened the Frederick Kann-Frank Martin Gallery, also called the Circle Gallery, exhibiting his own work and other abstract artists. The gallery was one of the few to exhibit abstract art at the time. In 1953, Kann retired from the Chouinard Art Institute and established the Kann Institute of Art in West Hollywood.

Alfred Kantor (1923–2002), b. Prague, Czech, a Holocaust artist and survivor, had finished one year of a two-year commercial art course at the Rotter School of Advertising when he and all the other Jews were expelled. His watercolors and sketches recreating daily life in Auschwitz, Terezín and Schwarzheide constitute one of the few visual records of existence in a Nazi concentration camp. His 127 paintings and sketches of concentration camp life were published in 1971 by McGraw-Hill as *The Book of Alfred Kantor*, which included his account of his experiences. The paintings, done in a rapid, Impressionist style, first show daily scenes in the 'model ghetto' that the Nazis created for Czechoslovak and other Jews in Terezín. Reaching the US at the end of the war, Mr. Kantor served in the Army, playing a glockenspiel in a military band. He spent the rest of his working life as a commercial artist in New York.

George Karger (1924–2010), b. Opava, Czech., received his art training at the Academy of Art in Zlín, State Graphic School in Prague and at Vysoká škola umělecko-průmyskvá (UMPRUM) in Prague (dipl., 1949) and, after coming to the US, also at UCLA (M.F.A., 1966). He was a painter of note. He began exhibiting his paintings already in Munich's Kunstwerein in 1949, while still a political refugee from communist Czechoslovakia. He spent some time in Norway and in Sweden, still as a refugee, where he also had several art exhibits. After coming to the Pacific Coast, he lectured at Pierce College, in Hollywood Art Center and also at UCLA. In 1967, he was named arts director with CBS TV in Los Angeles, where he worked until his retirement. He gained international prominence with his large projects in New York (relief in front of Thomson Building), and elsewhere.

NEW WORLD VISIONARIES, SEEKERS, AND CREATORS WITH CZECHOSLOVAK ROOTS

Stephen Kasala (1864-1943), b. Czechoslovakia, came to the US in 1890. In 1903, he settled in Los Angeles where he remained until his demise on Feb. 26, 1943. He was a painter, who resided in California.

Leo Katz (1887-1982), b. Rožnov, Czech., was a modernist painter and muralist. During the 1930s, he was a resident of Los Angeles. While there, he taught art at the Chouinard School and painted a mural for the Federal Art Project in the Wiggins Trade School which was removed in 1935 due to its nudity and violent content.

Enit Kaufman (1897-1961), b. Rosice, Moravia, was a landscape and portrait artist. She held teaching positions at City College New York City and Southern Vermont Art Club. She exhibited in Paris at Gallery Tedesco in 1937 and then emigrated to the United States where she exhibited widely including Arizona, California, Kansas, and Ohio. She was a co-author of *American Portraits* (1946).

William Jurian Kaula (1871-1953), b. Boston, MA, of Czech ancestry, was a landscape painter in Boston. He worked in both watercolors and oils, was renowned for capturing the New England landscape in its true form by allowing the mood of the scene to dictate the tone of the painting, while adding or subtracting details to heighten natural effects. In 1915, Kaula won a bronze medal at the Panama-Pacific Exposition in San Francisco.

Jiří (George) Kayser (1918-2016), b. Písek, Czech., was educated at the Prague Academy of Fine Arts and Charles University. Later, he became a professor of fine arts, as well as member of various artistic advisory committees to architects and city planners. He participated in numerous national and international exhibits in Czechoslovakia, Austria, Italy, Denmark, Belgium, Australia and New Zealand. His work is very much influenced by Picasso, Salvador Dali and his contemporaries. After fleeing with his family to Canada in order to escape the political turmoil in 1968, he taught art at Ecole de Beaux Arts in Quebec City and elsewhere and exhibited throughout eastern Canada and USA. In 1977, he became a graphic artist and artist-in-residence for IATA (International Air Transport Association) in Montreal. In 1989, he retired to a quiet life of an artist in Cambridge, Ontario. His extensive work during his years in Canada has ranged from electrifying landscapes and urban scenes, nudes and still lives to detailed etchings that clearly reflect his classical heritage. He was awarded the Czech Republic's 50th Anniversary Prize for Modern Painting in 1995. His work can be found in numerous permanent exhibitions including Albertina Museum (Vienna, Austria), Czech National Gallery (Prague), IATA Administrative Offices in Montreal and Geneva, and private collections on five continents.

Charles H. Kellner (1890–1979), b. Košice, Slovakia; became a well-known painter in Chicago in the early 20th century. His most well-known subjects were still lifes, landscapes, portraits, and figures.

Joe Klamar (1965–), b. Jasná, Slovakia; immigrated in 1987 to Canada; photographer. He is the chief photographer of the French agency Agence France-Presse for the Central Europe. His specialties include political events, memorial celebrations, and celebrities. In 2009, he won the first prize in the Czech Press Photo competition for Barack Obama picture in Prague.

Jerome Jaroslav Klapka (1887–1965), b. Bohemia, was a painter and illustrator. The early part of his career in Chicago was devoted to commercial and advertising. Later, Klapka painted figural works and landscapes in oils and in watercolors. *Over the Top* in 1933 probably was Klapka's best-known image. The American Legion reproduced it on brochures for its conventions in 1934 and again in 1946 and 1952.

Alice Ellen Klauber (1871–1951), b. San Diego, CA, of Bohemian ancestry, was a portrait, landscape, and still life painter who studied art locally at the School of Design and the Art Students League. She further studied with William M. Chase, Robert Henri in Spain and Hans Hofmann at UC Berkeley.

Amy Salz Klauber (1872–1928), b. Stockton, CA, of Bohemian ancestry, was a still-life painter. Amy began her art studies in San Francisco at the Mark Hopkins Institute and ASL under Emil Carlsen in the late 1880s followed by study at the AIC. She was the mother of artist Amy J. Wormser.

Leda Josephine Klauber (1881–1981), b. San Diego, CA, of Bohemian ancestry, was a landscape and still-life painter and a craftsperson. After 1951, she was on the Asian Arts Committee at the San Diego Fine Arts Gallery. Her work includes landscapes and still lives in watercolor and gouache. She exhibited at San Diego FA Gallery (1927) and at Calif.-Pacific Int'l Expo, San Diego (1935).

Leo Kober (1876–1931), b. Brno, Moravia, was a portrait painter, cartoonist, and draftsman. He resided in NYC and was staff artist for *The Sunday World*. He was also a writer.

John Michael Anthony Koerner (1913–2014), b. Novy Jičín, Moravia, was a painter, printmaker, etcher, muralist, educator, and author. He moved to Vancouver, British Columbia, Canada in 1939. His media were oil, acrylic, watercolor, casein, crayon, ink, collage, lithograph and etching. His subjects were the Canadian west coast landscape, shoreline and seascape; still life; flowers. John Koerner is the oldest still-active member of the Vancouver School of painters, a group that developed modernism in Canadian art. He also taught at the Vancouver School of Art and the University of British Columbia. His work also appears in the collections of the Tate in London, of Clare Hall at Cambridge University and of the Hirshhorn Museum in Washington, DC. His work was influenced by German philosopher Bo Yin Ra. Following his 100th birthday, Koerner had a show at the Burnaby Art Gallery and the exhibition John Koerner: The Hidden Side of Nature at the Penticton Art Gallery. He died at home in Vancouver at the age of 100.

Maxim Kopf (1892-1958), b. Vienna, a noted painter, was raised in Prague. He first came to the United States in 1923 to do scenic work for Ziegfeld and assisted in painting murals in the Ziegfeld Theatre. Kopf was in Prague when Hitler took over. He escaped to Paris and was interned as an enemy alien. After a few months, he was released and went to Morocco and was interned again. Altogether, he spent two and a half years in camps. Kopf again reached the United States in 1941. He met Dorothy Thompson in 1942. He was a painter and sculptor, known chiefly for his liturgical works. His paintings were strongly influenced by expressionism and later created works with biblical themes and landscapes. His works are held in the Everson Museum of Art, the Hood Museum of Art, the Memorial Art Gallery, the Brooklyn Museum of Art, the Museum of Modern Art - New York, the Saint Louis Art Museum, and the National Gallery in Prague.

Lenka Konopasek (1967–), b. Czech Republic, where she attended School of Applied Arts in Prague. She lived for several years in Germany before emigrating to the United States in 1989. After immigrating to the United States, she received BFA degree from University of Utah and MFA degree from Maine College of Art in Portland, Maine. She attended artist residencies in Vermont Studio Center, Chicago Art Institute and Little Falls, Minnesota. Her paintings have been exhibited widely throughout United States, Taiwan, Germany, India and Czech Republic. She also completed several large public art projects in Utah. Her work has been featured on the back cover of the *New American Painting* and in other publications. Lenka has been involved in co-owning an art gallery in Salt Lake City and in Denver and working for the Salt Lake Art Center, Visual Art Institute and Utah Arts Festival. She has been teaching at University of Utah and Westminster College in Salt Lake City and other art institutions and schools throughout the city.

Matthew Kousal (1902-1990), b. Czech., immigrated to Chatham, Ontario, Canada in 1927, where he established his reputation as a landscape artist. In 1948, he moved to Waterloo, Ontario. He became a prolific painter of landscapes and seascapes, completing over 12,000 works. Working in oil, he painted seascapes in Nova Scotia and landscapes in northern Ontario especially near Lake Huron and Algonquin. He was also a teacher, giving lessons from his studio.

Peter Kovalik (1956-), Czech., son of Tibor Kovalik; Canadian artist, painter, residing in Toronto.

Tibor Kovalik (1935-), b. Poprad, Czech; Canadian surrealistic painter, designer and illustrator of children's books, recipient of awards, residing in Lac-Beaport, Quebec.

Stephen Kratochvil (1876-d.), Czech., was an American architectural, genre and landscape painter, educated in Czech; he lived in NYC.

Mikuláš Kravjanský (1928-2020), b. Czech.; painter, designer, poet, residing in Ontario, Canada.

Helmut Krommer (1891-1973), b. Opava, Moravia, was a painter and graphic artist and also a journalist. He lived in Boston, MA.

Kamil Kubík (1930-2011), b. Olomouc, Czech., was a contemporary painter, specializing in urban landscape, who began his formal art training in Prague. When the Communists seized power in 1949, he escaped, starting a long journey of study and work around the world. Kubik did set design in Australia, and painted portraits in London and San Francisco. His works are owned by collectors on five continents including the collections of Mrs. Lyndon B. Johnson, Mr. and Mrs. John V. Lindsay, Paul Mellon, Count de La Lanne-Mirrlees and Robert Sarnoff.

Anne Kutka (1902-1994), b. CT., of Czech parents, was a notable painter. She lived and worked, with her husband David McCosh, also a painter, in Eugene, OR. In 1991, the University of Oregon sponsored a lifetime retrospective of her work. She created more than 650 oils, drawings, watercolors, and prints in her lifetime.

Jiří Ladocha (1942-2021), b. Czech., emigrated to Toronto in 1968. Over the span of his 35-year career as a professional fine artist, he has achieved an international reputation as a critically acclaimed, highly skilled, and original painter and sculptor. A master in the application of mixed media including plaster, gold and silver leaf, graphite and pigment, Ladocha is renowned for his ever-evolving exploration and evocation of the textures, hues and sensibilities of the Old and the New Worlds. His symbolic portrayals of a visual universe have been celebrated in such notable series as Urbs Perdita, Lost Souls, The New Alchemy and Dreaming of a Story, The Story of a Dream. Ladocha's work has been exhibited widely, in both commercial galleries and public museums, across Canada, the United States and Europe. He is represented in numerous public, private and corporate collections on both sides of the Atlantic, including the Guggenheim Museum in New York.

His work, life and philosophy have been the subject of more than thirty publications and documentaries.

Antonia Laník-Gabanek (ca. 1925–), b. Brušperk, Czech., graduated at the Academy of Fine Arts in Prague, where she studied figure painting and printmaking. After she completed her studies in 1950, she exhibited regularly in state galleries and in addition, executed numerous designs for stained glass windows, graffito and mosaics for public buildings. After the Soviet invasion of Czechoslovakia in 1968, she left her homeland and settled in Vancouver, British Columbia. Her mediums are water colors, acrylics and oils. For her sketches, she uses pen and ink with water color washes. She enjoys painting landscapes, flowers and still life arrangements. Her landscapes and city scenes come alive with men, women and children. When she paints portraits, she depicts not only the likeness of the subject but also tries to capture their inner qualities and emphasizes the essential humanity of the person. She has been exhibiting in Vancouver since 1970 as well as in other cities of British Columbia and the US. She was featured in the CBC documentary *Painting Canada*, 1986, received an honorable mention in the Coho Art Festival in Vancouver, and her water color *Grandma Knitting* was accepted in the Provincial Festival of Arts in Kimberley, B.C.

Lawrence Lebduska (1894–1966), b. Baltimore, MD, of Bohemian ancestry, is one of the most interesting self-taught American artists of the 20th century. Lebduska achieved a great deal of fame in the 1930s, especially when his work was widely exhibited including at a notable one-man show at the Contemporary Gallery in 1936. This exhibition was said to have influenced Abby Aldrich Rockefeller to begin her famous folk art collection.

Alois Lecoque (orig. Kohout) (1891–1981), b. Prague, Czech., was a painter known for his beautifully colored post-impressionist paintings. His work ranged from still life to harbor life to the city views of Prague. He painted magnificent buildings and waterfronts in Paris. He came to California, first to Laguna Beach and then settled in Los Angeles.

Tosca Lerch (fl. 1960–), b. Teplice-Šanov, a painter, came to Canada in 1939 and subsequently studied with Margaretta Stevens, Dorothy Stevens, Aba Bayefsky, Jas. Williamson, Hayward Veal (from Pitman College of Art, London, Eng.) and Mashel Teitelbaum of the New School, Toronto. The Forest Hill Journal described her work as follows, "The paintings of Tosca Lerch are abstract landscape studies. Mood of seasons and an impassioned use of personal color are trade-marks of this gifted painter. Over a period of years, she has developed from the representational studies of flowers and nature to the joyous tone poems on the Canadian Seasons." She has exhibited her work at the East York Public Library, the Canadian

National Exhibition, the Pollock Gallery, and Eaton's Fine Art Gallery. She resided in Toronto.

Anna Lesznai (pseud.) (real name: Amália J. Moskowitz) (1885–1966), b. Budapest, who grew up in Nižný Hrušov, Slovakia, on the country estate belonging to her father Geyza Moskowitz, a physician, was an American painter, designer, writer and key figure in the Jewish Hungarian / Slovak avant-garde. Multi-talented, she was recognized equally for her artwork and her writing. She studied art in Budapest with Károly Ferenczy and Simon Hollósy, later in Paris with Lucien Simon. In 1909, she joined the Constructivist-Expressionist group of Hungarian artists known as Nyolcak ("The Eight"), and in 1911, her work was shown as part of their second exhibition. Her painting and embroideries drew much of their inspiration from Hungarian folklore and folk art. Lesznai's early published writing includes essays, poetry, and original fairy tales. Beginning in 1908, she was a regular contributor to the literary journal *Nyugat*. In 1919, Lesznai emigrated to Vienna along with sons George and Andrew and her companion Tibor Gergely (1900–1978), an artist and illustrator fifteen years her junior whom she knew from the Sunday Circle. The couple eventually married and, faced with the rising tide of anti-Semitism in Europe, immigrated to the United States in 1939. Settling in New York City, Lesznai continued her work in art education, lecturing and teaching classes in Hungarian art and design. In 1946, she opened her own school of painting. Her autobiographical novel *Kezdetben volt a kert* ("In the Beginning was the Garden"), on which she worked for thirty years, was published in German translation in 1965 and in the original Hungarian the following year.

Adolf Lešovský (1885–1972), b. Humpolec, Bohemia, was a painter who settled in Los Angeles in 1906. He worked there, both as a portraitist and as an artist, for the Garret Corporation (air research) until his death on Dec. 30, 1972.

Henry L. Levy (1868–1940), b. Hartford, CT, of Bohemian ancestry, grandson of Samuel Kakeles of Prague, was a figure, interiors and still life painter. Still in his teens, he was the first American student to win the prestigious French Beaux-Arts Prize which enabled him to study at the École des Beaux Arts School in Paris.

Barbara Pejsar Linder (1929–2013), b. Plattsmouth, NE, Czech ancestry; artist. She was first taught by her artist mother and later studied in workshops taught by nationally known artists. Her work encompasses a variety of subjects, mediums, and techniques. Her style is noted for its softness and purity of color. She has been very active in the local art world and has won numerous awards and honors. She is the mother of four, a graduate of the University of Nebraska-Lincoln, and is a former high school teacher. She has traveled extensively to Europe and is proud of her Czech roots. She hopes that her artwork may bring joy to the viewer by capturing a feeling, a memory, or something beautiful that may be lost in time.

George Lowy (1926-2016), b. Ostrava, Czech., was a corporation executive, later becoming a watercolor painter, Silver Spring, MD.

Andrew Leonard Lukachko (1927-), b. Czech.; watercolor painter, residing in Toronto, Canada (s. 1936).

George Lusk (1902-1977), b. Chicago, of Czech ancestry, was a mural and portrait painter who was educated at Art Institute of Chicago, New York Univ., National Academy, etc. His works are held in Village Hall, Wilmette, Chicago Academy of Fine Arts. He was a Federal Art Project artist.

Marie Koupal Lusk (1862-1929), b. Czech., came to Chicago with her parents in 1867. While attending the public schools of Chicago she showed talent in drawing and drew the attention of a Mr. Carpenter, of the Chicago Art Institute, then known as the Chicago Art School. In 1880, Mrs. Lusk was sent to New York, where she studied at the Art Students' League under William M. Chase. She also studied at the Academy of Design in New York and won the Suydam medal there in 1880 for the best drawing from life. Following her studies in New York, Mrs. Lusk was sent to Paris, where she studied in 1882 and 1883 under one of the leading masters, Brožík. Her paintings were exhibited at the Paris Salon. Returning to this country in 1884, she married Charles Lusk, who was one of the oldest practicing Bohemian lawyers in Chicago. Mrs. Lusk continued her painting work after her marriage and from 1884 to 1924, exhibited at the Chicago Art institute. She has also exhibited on the north shore many times. Mrs. Lusk is better known to the older generation of artists. She was the founder of the Ladies' Bohemian Arts Club in Chicago.

Leokadia Makarska-Čermák (or Lily Čermák, in Czech: Leokadia Čermáková), b. Poland, is known in the US for painting US Senator Charles Schumer, New York City Mayors Rudy Giuliani and Michael Bloomberg. She received a merit-based full scholarship from the Ministry of Culture that allowed her to study the five-year program in interior design and wood technologies at the Technical University in Zvolen, Czechoslovakia. After graduation, Leokadia married Jiří Čermák and moved to Ostrov, a town not far from Karlovy Vary. She worked in Karlovy Vary first as an interior and furniture designer and later, as a teacher at a technical high school. She now resides in the US.

Hana Mrázová Malik (1941-), b. Ostrava, Czech., is Czech Canadian painter. She settled in Canada with her family in Saskatchewan in 1969 and resides in Toronto since 1985. She studied at Fine Art College, Brno (1955-59); printmaking at University of Regina (1982-

85); and at School of Classical Studies, Toronto (1998-2001). Recent Inspiration of her creative work is in the Canadian prairie landscape. She was especially known for her drawings and painting of landscapes in Saskatchewan and Cuba. Her techniques range from drawing and watercolor, to printmaking, and recently, acrylic on canvas. She had exhibitions in Saskatchewan, Toronto, Aregua, Paraguay, Rio De Janeiro, Brazil and in Prague, Czech Republic.

John A. Mallin (1883-1973), b. Hlohovec, Moravia, was a Czech-American mural and fresco painter. He came to the United States in 1907 and settled in Chicago and eventually opened a studio in the Fine Arts Building at 410 S. Michigan Avenue in the Chicago Landmark Historic Michigan Boulevard district. He specialized in church decoration and ecclesiastical painting as well as art glass and mosaics. His business flourished. In one of his brochures, he lists over 50 churches as references, most in Chicago, but some in Indiana, Michigan, Iowa and Tennessee. Eventually, he moved his studio to 2252 W. Devon Avenue. His son joined the studio and specialized in gold leaf applications. He decorated more than 100 churches in his lifetime.

Gabriele Ella Margules (1927-2016), b. Tachov, Czech., attended Cambridge School of Art (1944-47), and has diploma in fine arts from the Royal Academy School, London (1950) and did postgraduate work at New School, NYC (1952). She held various publishing companies' executive positions but is known as an artist and painter. Her media are watercolors, and ink. She was recipient of the 1st prize, Royal Academy (1949), Best Oil award, Putnam Arts Council, Merit award, first place award (1990). She is a member of Garrison Art Center, Putnam History Association, Ulster Arts Alliance, Kingston Artist Association, Woodstock Artist Association, Artists Equity, Barrett House. Her works are at Forbes College, Kerlan College, University of Minnesota. Media: watercolors, ink. Awards: Silver medal first prize for life drawing, Royal Academy, London (1949); best one hundred illustration children's books, American Institute of Graphic Arts (1968-70).

Jan Matulka (1890-1972), b. Vlachovo Březí, Bohemia, was a Czech-American modern artist. His style ranged from abstract expressionism to landscapes, sometimes in the same day.

Karl May (1901-1976), b. Bohemia, studied at the academies in Vienna and Prague. His extensive travels throughout the Middle East and Europe led to his association with the celebrated Bruke and Blaue Reiter groups in Germany. By 1926, he had been appointed professor at the Prague Academy and he won the coveted Rome Prize. World War II interrupted his professional and personal life and many of his paintings were confiscated as 'degenerate art' and later burned in Berlin together with works by Klee, Nolde, Kirchner, Beckman and others. After the war, he spent several years teaching in Teheran and served as artistic advisor for the foundation of the Iranian Academy. He emigrated to Canada in 1952 settling in the Laurentians, north of Montreal. He continued to teach, paint and travel until his death.

Anka Mayer (fl. 1956), b. Prague, Czech., travelled to South America where she studied with Oskar Kokoschka at the Academies of Fine Arts in Santiago, Chile and Buenos Aires. She has held one-woman shows in Buenos Aires (1956, 1960), Montevideo (1958), Santiago, Chile (1959, 1962), Milano, Italy (1963), Toronto (1966), Madrid, Spain (1966). She has been living in Toronto, Canada.

Anne Kutka McCosh (1902–1994), b. Danbury, CT, of Czech parents, studied and worked at the Art Students League in New York, with Kenneth Hayes Miller and Kimon Nicolaides. The Van Courtland Express, painted in 1933, portrayed the subway she rode to art classes. The humorous Dressing Room, Klein's Department Store shows yet another aspect of the life she experienced in New York. When she married David McCosh in 1934 and moved to Eugene, she brought an East Coast urban perspective. Soon she was painting her new environment 'shoulder to shoulder with the cornerstones of the regionalist movement.' She stressed the characteristic features of the people and events of this college town. In 1991, the University of Oregon sponsored a lifetime retrospective of her work. Her Leaving the Lecture, Faculty Wives shows how she drew on real life experiences for inspiration. Its formal composition with underpainting, modeling and glazing is striking, but her emphasis is on what is going on inside the subjects, rather than outward appearance. She created more than 650 oils, drawings, watercolors and prints. She taught in her home studio and at the Maude Kerns Art Center for more than twenty years.

Ervine Metzl (1899–1963), born in Chicago, of Bohemian immigrant parents, was an American graphic artist and illustrator best known for his posters and postage stamp designs.

Frank Mikuska (1930–2021), b. Canada, of Slovak father; painter, residing in Manitoba, Canada.

Vincent Mikuska (1956–), b. Manitoba, Canada; painter, abstract painter, residing in Manitoba, Canada.

Josef Moravec (1951–), b. Czech., is a Czech paleoartist and painter currently living in the USA. He specializes in paintings of dinosaurs and has studied fossils for over 35 years to gain the necessary knowledge about them.

Paul Moschcowitz (1873–1942), b. Giraltovce, Slovakia, was an artist.

Irene Moss (née Greenfield) (1910-d.), b. Czech., studied art at the Brooklyn Museum School of Art and at the School of Visual Arts, and, privately, with the painter Moses Soyer, all in NYC. She held many solo exhibitions of her painting at galleries and universities, e.g. Contemporary Art Gallery (1961-63), East Hampton Gallery (1966, 1968, 1970), Columbia Univ. (1970, 1971), Bacardi Gallery, Miami (1974), New York Univ. (1970), etc. Her works are represented in private and public permanent collections, including Akron Art Inst., Brooklyn College, Lehigh Univ., Brandeis Univ. She was one of the founders of Women in the Arts (W.I.A.) and of *The Feminist Art Journal* (1972).

Magdalena 'Magda' Mráz (1948-), b. Liberec, Czech., graduated from CUNY (B.A., 1972) and holds an M.F.A. (1976) from Queens College of the City University of New York, and D. Min. degree from the Wisdom University in San Francisco, California. She uses oils, silk, design, mixed media, ceramics and ceramic sculpture. She has painted, exhibited and taught art both in the USA and Europe, and now lives in Connecticut. Her work has been a spiritual quest into the purpose of our existence and the nature of our consciousness. Her works develop a contrast between the disintegrating environment of public places and the focused figures of young people facing the viewer. The transient reality of existence is brought to focus in painted and sculpted figures who attempt to escape the limitations of their physical boundaries.

Alphonse Mucha (1860-1929), b. Ivančice, Moravia, was a Czech Art Nouveau painter and decorative artist, known best for his distinct style. He came to America in 1905 and taught at Art Inst. of Chicago and New School of Applied Design for Women.

Jan Müller (1922-1958), b. Hamburg, of Czech parents, was a New York figurative Expressionist of the 1950s. In 1933, his family fled the Nazis to Prague, and later to Bex-les-Bains, Switzerland. He visited Paris in 1938 and two years later, was apprehended and interned in a camp near Lyon. Shortly after the fall of Paris Müller was released, at which time he moved to Ornaisons, near Narbonne. Following an unsuccessful attempt to escape to the United States from Marseille, he was able to cross the border into Spain in 1941 and proceed via Portugal to New York. Jan Müller began to study art in 1945: the Art Students League of New York, New York City, NY for six months; and Hans Hofmann School of Fine Arts for five years. According to the poet John Ashbery, Müller "brings a medieval sensibility to neo-Expressionist paintings."

Francis R. E. Noga (1892-1988), b. Bohemia; was an American painter and an etcher.

Z. Vlasta Nosek (1925-), b. Czech., was a Canadian painter. Her works are in oil, acrylic, aquarelle, abstract, surrealism, and realism. (Versatile, Pluraliste, L'esprit Libre).

Olivia Darvaš Novak (1960–), b. Bratislava, Czech., is a professional artist; working as a painter, designer, book illustrator, and photographer. Graduated the Art Institute of Fort Lauderdale, Florida USA (1981). As a fine art painter, she trained under world renowned painter Lydia Darvas. Aside from being a Fine Art professional, Olivia has also had a very successful art career as a Corporate Artist and Designer, working for world media giants Knight-Ridder and Time Warner. While with Time Warner, she was employed by the book publisher Warner Bros. Publications where she designed over 1,600 projects, most of which were Books and Book Covers for the Music and Motion Picture industries. Designs were produced for Professionals and Superstars of music, the movies, theatrical stage, and included pop music, classical music, and country music. Books are still circulated worldwide with a name credit of design by Olivia D. Novak. As a fine artist, Olivia's artwork has been displayed locally and internationally at Galleries and Exhibits receiving numerous awards and honors in various categories, selling over 900 prints/originals. Her artwork has also been published in *Encyclopedia of Living Artists in America and New Art International.*

Elmer Ladislaw Novotny (1909–1997), b. Cleveland, OH, of Czech ancestry, was a long-time resident of Ohio, teacher at Kent State University and painter of portraits, figures, still-lives and landscapes. He studied at the Cleveland Institute of Art and London's Slade School of Art.

Vincent A. Novotny (1828–1883), b. New York, NY, of Bohemian ancestry, was a carriage painter, artist and musician. He was active in Springfield, OH from the mid-1870s or earlier until his death there. He possessed, according to his obituary, 'artistic abilities of no mean character and quite a number of his paintings show talent of high order.'

William Anton Oktávec (1885–1956), b. Vimperk, Bohemia, came to New York, in 1903 at 15 years old. He moved to Baltimore, MD in 1913, where he opened a grocery store, and began developing the folk art of painting pictures on window screens. He was the first person to introduce colorful scenes on woven wire. He had painted his first window screen while on the job at Eclipse Air Brush Company in New Jersey for a secretary whose work was often disturbed by people on the sidewalk outside her office. With the newly-painted screen, the secretary could see out, but no one could see in. In Baltimore, Oktávec painted a screen to shade the fruit at his corner grocery store at North Collington and Ashland Avenue. Before long, he began to get requests for painted screens, and others in neighboring ethnic communities started to join in the tradition. By the 1930s, East Baltimore row houses sported almost 100,000 painted door and window screens. Today, this folk art tradition is declining. It is estimated there are less than 3,000 painted screens in Baltimore. William had four sons, Albert, Bill, Bernie, and Richard. Al had done screens as well, but Richard kept the art form alive to pass it on down to John, Richard's son.

Klement Olšanský (1909-1963), b. Líšeň, Brno, Moravia, was a notable Czech Canadian painter. He was a graduate of Academy of Fine Arts in Prague and of the Art Inst. in Chicago. He resided in Montreal, QC.

William Pachner (1915-2017), b. Brtnice, Moravia, was an abstract painter and illustrator. Known as a colorist, Pachner's work includes satiric drawings, erotic figurative, biblical Judaic and Christian themes, photomontages, and paintings of great color intensity. Late in his career, he turned to black and white after losing sight in his one good eye.

Shawn Palek (1970-), b. IA, of Czech ancestry, studied commercial and advertising art at Des Moines Area Community College (A.A., 1994). He is an airbrush artist in Des Moines Iowa and has been painting since 1989 for a living, along with several odd jobs along the way. He was initially employed by Mid Air & Ink, Des Moines, IA, as airbrush artist and manager (1995-2000) and also opened his own firm Artwork by Shawn Palek, Des Moines, IA (s. 1988). He co-owned and served as a design director of Custom Paint Specialists, Des Moines, IA (2002-09). He paints any subject on canvas, and murals, he does a lot of motorcycles, cars and helmets. He paints clothing and also does body painting. His shop in Des Moines is a full service body and paint shop, they have a mechanic on staff that works on gas, diesel and marine. He has a gallery of artwork featuring his work along with several other artists in the area. His studio is set up as a classroom, he teaches airbrushing for Des Moines Area Community College. He did tattoos for several years but enjoys painting so much more and has recently been experimenting with engraving.

Lillian Gaertner Palmedo (1906-), b. NYC, of Bohemian father, was a muralist, set designer and costume designer who worked in New York City during the 1920s and 1930s. When she was 14 years old, her skill as an artist was recognized by architect and theatrical designer Joseph Urban, who made her his protégé. He packed her off to art school in Vienna where she studied under the architect and designer Josef Hoffmann. Back in Manhattan, Palmedo was commissioned to paint murals at various hotels, theaters, restaurants, clubs and office buildings throughout the city, including the original Ziegfeld Theater (1927), the Persian Room at the Plaza Hotel (1934), the Hotel Pennsylvania, and the Essex House. As a costume and set designer she contributed to productions at Carnegie Hall and the Metropolitan Opera.

Hana E. Pánek (1958-), b. Prague, Czech., studied architecture at Penn State University (B.S., 1984) and University of Pennsylvania. She was licensed as an architect in 1987. Today, she is a successful practicing architect at MOSAIC Associates. In addition to her design education, she started painting regularly in the 1990's. Primarily a self-taught painter, she has participated in many painting workshops and learned much from many artists. She now primarily paints in acrylic, often mixes media and adds collage, and has also painted in pure watercolor and oil. She started in 'en plein air' – at first architectural pencil/ink sketches, and later watercolor landscapes. Her abstract paintings, on the other hand, have been created in her cramped studio. She mixes colors and moves shapes, textures, and paint around; playing, remembering and learning. Themes, structures or concepts develop, which she then expands to give a painting its final direction. Her paintings are in private collections in several states and overseas. She has participated in solo, and group shows, shows in several galleries, and has won numerous awards.

John Ignatius Perl (1806-1972), b. Galanta, Slovakia; physician, surgeon, in US s. 1924, practicing in Chicago. At the age of 46, Dr. Perl took up painting as a serious avocation and on his first attempt at a major exhibition, his work was accepted into an Art Institute of Chicago watercolor show in 1942. He exhibited at the Art Institute in 1942, 1943, 1946 and 1948 and was best known for his scenes of Chicago. He had local gallery representation at a prominent Chicago gallery at that time called The Little Gallery on Delaware Pl. Dr. Perl was an important patron to many Chicago artists, including Boris Anisfeld. In 1972, Dr. Perl died in Chicago at the age of 76.

Adele Pierce (née Stalmach) (ca. 1973-), b. Ottawa, of Czech ancestry, is self-taught as an artist and has been passionate about painting since early childhood. While a student at Lester B. Pearson High School in the 1980s, she worked primarily in watercolors and was fortunate to receive many portrait and some landscape commissions and thus grew in her ability to achieve a likeness working both from photographs and from life. In 1995, she graduated from Carleton University with undergraduate degrees in art history and English and a Master's Degree in art history. Travels through Europe and the West Coast of the United States and Canada between 1989 and 1995 inspired in her an immense love of architecture and architectural detail and she hurried to depict this new love on canvas. Between 1995 and 1998, she successfully exhibited and sold her work in restaurants in Ottawa, including at Sante, Clair de Lune, Memories Café, The Manx Pub, The Mud Oven, The Upstairs Bistro and in exhibitions through Art East and The Nepean Fine Arts League. She then took a sabbatical from painting in order to raise her children and, having now returned to full-time painting, she has been inspired to depict life in New York City and California after thrilling visits to those places. Although she has enjoyed brief forays into landscape painting and some whimsical work, her true love remains architecture. Her paintings can be found in private collections in Canada, the United States, Australia, Denmark and the Vatican.

Joseph Plavcan (1908-1981), b. Braddock, PA, of Slovak parents; an American painter and teacher.

Max Pollak (1886–1970), b. Prague, Bohemia, studied at the Vienna Academy of Art before settling in San Francisco in 1927. He exhibited landscapes and portraits locally and was active in the local art scene until his death in May 1970 in Sausalito, CA.

Ida Hrubesky Pumberton (1890–1955), b. Schuyler, NE, of Bohemian ancestry, was a painter and illustrator. She created 64 botanical watercolors during the 1930s and 1940s, taking inspiration from plants she grew and nurtured at her Denver home. She is revered among botanical artists who applaud her work for its beauty and painstaking detail. Her art has been exhibited at several prestigious institutions.

Emil Purgina (1937–), b. Bratislava, Czech.; painter, graphic artist.

Frank Reichenthal (1895–1971), b. Lehnice, Slovakia; artist, abstract expressionist.

Ruth Rogers-Altmann (née Karplus) (1917–2015), b. Vienna, of Moravian ancestry; painter, fashion designer, NYC.

Helen A. Salz (née Arnstein) (1883–1957), b. San Francisco, CA, of Bohemian ancestry, was a painter and poet who helped to found the Northern California branch of the American Civil Liberties Union. Early in her career, she worked in oil and watercolor, but later switched to pastels. Inspired by the Fauves, her subjects include landscapes, floral still lives, portraits, and genre subjects.

Gordon Samstag (1906–1990), b. New York, NY, of Bohemian ancestry, was a painter, sculptor, illustrator and educator, who studied at the National Academy of Design and the Art Students League in NYC. He also studied with Charles Hawthorne at Provincetown and was in Paris where he enrolled in the Academie Colarossi. He was Director of the American Art School in New York City from 1951 to 1961 and then moved to Australia, where he was Director of the South Australian School of Art from 1961 to 1971. During the 1930s, Samstag was a WPA artist for the Federal Art Project.

Lola Montes Schnabel (1980–), b. New York, NY, of Moravian ancestry, daughter of the artist Julian Schnabel, is a painter, printmaker, photographer, and filmmaker. She studied at Cooper Union School of Advancement of Science and Art (B.F.A., 2008). She has exhibited internationally, including Tripoli Gallery, Southampton, NY; Ace Gallery, Los Angeles, CA; The Hole, New York, NY, among others. Recent exhibitions include Heaven, which was on view at the Shelbourne Hotel during Art Basel Miami 2014, and Forms Wrestling with Existence, at Eden Rock Gallery, Saint Barthélemy. She has collaborated with Max Mara Carte Blanche (2012) and Alice + Olivia (2015) on textile designs created from her watercolors, and her film work includes *Training Day*, a Nike commercial featuring Steve Nash, and projections for Lou Reed's concert and feature film, *Berlin*, both in 2007.

Orlando V. Schubert (1844–1927), b. Erie, OH, of Bohemian ancestry, was an early Cleveland artist especially noted for his marine paintings.

Alvena Vajda Seckar (1915–2012), b. McMechen, WV, of Slovak immigrant parents, was a painter and activist. She was recognized primarily for paintings expressing social and political commentary, also wrote children's books featuring Slovak-immigrants' families. Her parents were poor, often living under unhealthy conditions. One of Alvena's teachers in Allentown, Pennsylvania recognized her artistic talent, and made it possible for her to find a patron and study at the Pennsylvania Museum School of Industrial Art. She continued her education at the University of Pennsylvania, transferred to New York University and received her Bachelor's in 1939 and her Master's in 1949. In 1952, her book *Zuska of the Burning Hills* was a *New York Herald-Tribune* Spring Festival Honoree and was placed on *The New York Times* list of the Hundred Best Books published for children. *Zuska* is only one of her fabulous works, the rest of which are equally compelling.

Richard Sedlon (1900–1973), b. Philadelphia, PA, of Bohemian ancestry, was an American painter living in Bedford, OH. He started already at the age of 18. He was a journeyman lithographer with Morgan Lithography in Cleveland – the largest printing outfit of its time nationwide. Richard was also a professional artist who dabbled in carvings, oil paintings and sketches.

Jaroslav Šejnoha (1889–1982), b. Sebranice u Litomyšle, Bohemia, graduated from the Academy of Fine Arts in Prague and then studied art at the Graphic School of Max Švabinský and later also in Paris. He joined the Czechoslovak Legion in France and since 1919, he worked for the Czechoslovak Embassy in Paris. In 1925, he was named Czechoslovak commissioner for the Exhibition of Decorative Arts in Paris. As a member of Czechoslovak Foreign Service, he held a number of diplomatic posts. In 1944, he was appointed Czechoslovak Ambassador to Egypt and in 1948, the first Czechoslovak Ambassador to India. After the communist putsch in 1948, he left New Delhi and emigrated to Canada, where he returned to his artistic career.

Zoltan Leslie Sepeshy (1898–1974), b. Košice, Slovakia painter, Bloomfield Hills, MI.

Frederick B. Serger (orig. Sinaiberger) (1889–1965), b. Ivančice, Moravia, was a painter. He studied at art schools in Brno, Vienna, Munich, and later Paris. Prior to the outbreak of World War II, the Sergers moved to London, then Panama, Mexico, and Guatemala before reaching New York in 1941. Serger settled on West 57th Street in New York and bought a summer home in artistic Woodstock, NY in 1947. His paintings were shown in the Van Diemen-Lilienfeld Gallery, the Schonemann Gallery and the Le Boite Gallery owned by his wife, Helen Serger.

Marketa Sivek (1969–), b. Vsetín, Czech., a self-taught artist living and working in Chicago for past 25 years. Established as one of the leading artists in the community, her work has been featured in numerous publications such as *Elle Decor* and is included in many private collections in the United States, London, Australia, and Finland, as well as in the private collection of Oprah Winfrey among others. She is the owner of Marketa Sivek Gallery in Chicago.

Pavel Skalník (1941–), b. Prague, Czech., studied in Prague and Paris, France. He was professor of visual arts of Universite de Moncton in New Brunswick and Ontario College of Art in Toronto. His work was presented in more than a hundred one man shows and more than forty group exhibitions in Canada, USA, Europe, Africa, South America and Asia. His work is in collections of Canada Council Art Bank, National Library of Canada, N.B. Government, Universite de Moncton, University of New Brunswick, University of Oregon, Mount Saint Vincent University, College de Bathurst, Academy of Fine arts in Prague, Open Studio, New Brunswick Hall of Fame and private collections.

Yvonne Slipka (1948–), Canadian Czech artist. A graduate from York Memorial Collegiate, Yvonne won the first prize for her drawings and paintings in all Canadian Eagle Art Scholarship contest and received honorable mention in the Hallmark art scholarship contest. She studied fine art at the University of Toronto.

Joseph S. Smutný (1855–1903), b. Bohemia, was a portrait painter. He received his art education in Vienna. He came to New York around 1888.

Božena Sochor (1901–1963), b. Šonov, Bohemia, was a painter who resided in Uniontown, PA. She came to America in 1920 and studied art at Carnegie Inst. Technology. She also attended Waynesburg College and Pennsylvania State Univ. She was director of McCrum Training School (1957–63). She exhibited in Butler, AL (1944); Parkersburg (1943–46); Ohio Univ. (1945); Uniontown, PA (1941–58).

Trude (Gertrud) Sojka (1909–2007), b. Berlin, Germany, of Czech parents, was a Czech-Ecuadorian painter and sculptor, creator of an original technique using recycled materials and concrete. She began to show her artwork, both sculptures and paintings, in Berlin until the outbreak of World War II, when the Nazis first sent her to Theresiendstadt. Here she tried raising the morale of the children by encouraging them to draw and forget their horrific conditions. It did not take long before she, her newborn baby daughter, husband,

and mother were transferred to Auschwitz, where only she survived, while the rest of her family was murdered. The Soviet Army liberated Auschwitz in the year 1945, and after getting news that her brother had moved to Ecuador, Trude Sojka followed in 1946. She again began to paint and produce sculptures that were displayed not only in Ecuadorian galleries but in the United States, France, and ironically, in Germany. The Ecuadorian House of Culture honored her by naming her Artist Emeritus in the year 2000. Trude Sojka passed away at the age of 97 in the year 2007 and in 2009, her daughters made the decision to create a museum in memory of their mother. Anita Steinitz and Miriam Steinitz Kannan opened the Trude Sojka Cultural House in her old home, which brings the lives of Jewish refugees in Ecuador to life. Hundreds of students have visited the Trude Sojka Cultural House and have come away from the experience fulfilled and emotionally drained, yet with great respect for Trude Sojka, as she was able take her pain and grief and turn it into masterpieces. The centre also educates the public on the Holocaust and the atrocities that were suffered during this time. The Trude Sojka Cultural Centre is located in Quito, and features a Holocaust Memorial Room, interactive projects and of course, numerous art pieces created by Trude Sojka.

Koloman Sokol (1902–2003), b. Liptovský Sv. Mikuláš, Slovakia; painter, graphic artist, illustrator, Bryn Mawr, PA, later resided in Tucson, AZ.

Jiří Stavovčík (1971–), b. Banská Bystrica, spent his childhood in Cuba and Czechoslovakia. He was educated in the Czech Republic and subsequently in the US, where he earned M.B.A. and another degree in accounting at the Moravian Coll. He also studied figurative drawing at Fleisher Art Memorial in Philadelphia and Spring Studio in New York City. When his promising business career hit a temporary snag, he decided to paint. He divides his time working in Washington D.C. and New York City. His art was featured at various group shows and solo exhibitions in New York City, Washington D.C., and Nagano (Japan). He is currently represented by Artspace 109 in Alexandria, Virginia.

Hugo Steiner-Prag (1880–1945), b. Prague, Bohemia, was a painter, etcher, and book illustrator. He made his reputation as an illustrator and book designer in Germany where he held professorship in Leipzig. He also became art director of the Propylaeen publishing house in Berlin and organized several book exhibits, including the first international book exhibit in Leipzig in 1927. When the Nazis abolished his position, he returned to Prague and established a private school for book arts and graphic design, called the 'Officina Pragensis'. In 1937, the publishing house of the Officina Pragensis released fifty stone drawings done by Steiner-Prag of the Jewish Ghetto and cemetery. He arrived in the US in June 1941, where he was offered a position as professor at the Division of Graphic Arts at New York University.

VIII. CULTURE: ARTS & LETTERS

Daniel Stein-Kubin (1958–), b. Czech., was trained at Charles Univ. in Jewish mysticism, is a Czech-American artist, poet, philosopher, and pataphysicist. His paintings are loaded with esoterical, metaphysical, and mythological ideas and generally have strong impact on his artistic work where images, colors, and symbols communicate and are of utmost importance. The influence of Dada / surrealism is also evident.

Antonín Štěrba (1875–1963), b. Heřmanice, Bohemia, was a portrait painter and etcher. He immigrated to America in 1880. He was educated at Chicago Art Inst., Smith Art Academy in Chicago, as well as in Paris at Julian Acad. From 1902 to 1910, he was instructor at the Smith Art Academy and in 1929, visiting instructor at the Los Angeles Art Institute and later, instructor at the Chicago Art Institute and at the American Academy of Art. His portraits were exhibited in national exhibitions in universities and clubs, including Pennsylvania Academy of Fine Arts, Corcoran and Chicago galleries. He was recipient of Gold Medal from Bohemian Arts Club (1923) and prizes from Chicago Gallery Assn (1930), Art Institute of Chicago (1938). His office was in Chicago on East Ohio Street.

Richard Štípl (1968–), b. Šternberk, Czech., an artist, now lives and works both in Canada and the Czech Republic. He graduated from the Ontario College of Art in Toronto with an Honors Diploma in 1992 and was awarded Canada's prestigious Governor General's Award in the same year. Working initially as a painter, Štípl has recently turned to making sculpture. Using himself as a model, Richard focuses exhaustively on the indefinite nature and moment-to-moment paradoxes inherent in the act of continuously recreating oneself throughout the course of a lifetime. Characteristically, Štípl's paintings and sculptural works alike force us to reconsider the role of boundaries and consequent categories of choice that comprise contemporary attitudes and approaches to art-making and art-consumption. Štípl has exhibited in Toronto, Montreal, New York, Miami, Berlin, Los Angeles, Madrid, Stuttgart, and the Czech Republic, and is included in many important public and private collections worldwide.

Helena M. Stockar (née Kubásek) (1933–2013), b. Bratislava, Czech., who resided in the US since 1968, was a designer, abstract painter, and illustrator. As a child, she lived through the horrors of the Second World War in Prague. The war was replaced by an uneasy life behind the Iron Curtain. She earned a Bachelor's Degree in industrial design at Grafická škola Prague (1948–52), and a Master's Degree in classical piano at the Prague Conservatory of Music. The two were always intertwined in her inspiration. She brings to her work a deep knowledge of the history of art, as well and obsession with people and color. While in Prague, she was influenced by the Czech painter, Jan Zrzavy, and his impressionist style and Cubism. She also counts Marc Chagall as an influence, as well as old Masters like Greco, Tintoretto, and others. Her paintings are in Johnson & Wales University and Hasbro

Children's Hospital, both in Providence, Rhode Island, in addition to being in galleries and private collections around the world. Helena Stockar lived the majority of her married life in Rhode Island, moving to Pennsylvania to be close to her grandchildren in 2012.

Antonín Švehla (1875-1963), b. Heřmance, Czech., is best known for his luminous portraits. He was also accomplished as a landscape and still life painter, and a printmaker. He joined the Art Institute of Chicago and later was a faculty member of Chicago's American Academy of Arts.

Antonín (Tony) Švehla (1935-), b. Prague, Czech, graduated with an MFA degree from George Washington University and taught art at Doug Hammarskjöld College and in Washington, DC public high schools. Tony Svehla is an abstract expressionist painter. His works are in many private collections in the United States, England, France and the Czech Republic. Instead of exhibiting in galleries, he supports humanitarian causes by donating his works for auctions. His paintings were auctioned at the newly opened Hoskins Cancer Research Center in Savannah, Georgia; at the Second Presbyterian Church in Richmond, Virginia for its mission to Malawi, Africa and for scholarships for women from underdeveloped countries sponsored by the World Bank, etc.

Josef Čestmír Svoboda (1889-1953), b. Prague, Bohemia, was a painter. He came to America with his parents in 1902. He studied painting in Prague with František Bizy and at the Art Institute of Chicago with Ralph Clarkson, Walter Ufer and Charles Hawthorne. He exhibited in Chicago at various Czech artist shows, at the Art Institute in the 1920s and 1930s, and at the Palette and Chisel Club. He exhibited in Arizona at the State Exhibition of 1926. He was a member of the Bohemian Arts Club in Chicago. He distinguished himself not only as a painter but also as a lithographer, an illustrator and a lecturer on fine art. He was based in Dallas, where he was the artistic director for the Herbert Rogers Co. He belonged to the Dallas Art Association and the Dallas Museum of Fine Art as well as to the American Federation of Artists and the Bohemian Art Club.

Joseph Tománek (1889-1974), b. Strážnice, Moravia, was a Chicago area artist, who came there in 1910. He received professional training at the Decorative and Design School and the Academy of Fine Arts in Prague and at the Art Institute in Chicago. Formerly an interior decorator, later became a commercial artist. Joseph Tomanek was best known for his paintings of nude figures against lush foliage or marine backgrounds. He traveled to Santa Fe, New Mexico, where he established himself as a recognized artist. His works are found at the Art Museum of Arizona and the Phoenix Art Museum.

Rita Svoboda Tomanek (1941-), b. Cedar Rapids, IA, of Czech ancestry, is an artist. She graduated from Regis High School and earned her B.F.A. in Studio Art from the University of Iowa where she also did graduate work in Religion and Health. Her paintings, mixed media, sculptures, and photographs have been exhibited throughout Iowa. She developed the Art Cart Program within Project Art at the University of Iowa and Clinics. The artworks of Rita Svoboda Tomanek express her experiences that act like threads woven into her works, intended to create a spiritual or emotional response. Painting and photographing nature's delicacy and grace is another way that she expresses her odyssey of art. Her more recent abstract art invites curiosity. Her sculpture has a sensual dimension, whereas her clay portraitures seek out the subject's personality.

Mym Tuma (1940-), b. Berwyn, Il, of Czech ancestry, studied at Northwestern University, where she earned her Bachelor's degree in education, majoring in art (1962). She was the Harley J. Earl scholar in the art and architecture department at Stanford University (1963-64), which awarded her an M.A. in painting and philosophy. Her post-graduate study was at New York University under Esteban Vicente and Irving Sandler (1964-65). Continuing her education at schools in Guadalajara in anatomy and mineralogy she earned the friendship of Georgia O'Keeffe for her pastel drawings and synthesis of sculptured paintings when visiting her (1968, 1969 and 1971), respectively. After leaving her studio in Mexico, Tuma joined the faculty at Tuley High School in Chicago for a year in 1972. From 1973-76, she was introduced to David Alfaro Siqueiros and traveled to the Outback of Australia. During this time, she focused on writing a book of essays on creative development and meditations on growth and form, later published: *The Sea, The Simplicity of the Sea and Other Poems*. In 1978, she moved to the Chicago area, working as a typesetter for RK printers to support her studio (1979-1986). It was there that she began to divide her attention to designing Come to Life Graphics TM. until the studio drawing based on garden flowers and the basic shapes of nature: spirals, helix, spherical and radial forms were created. In these drawings, her interpretation of science is based upon inspired energy statements. One woman shows of her principal works, Pastel Drawings and Abstract Sculptured Painting were at the Art League, La Grange, IL, 1987 also at the Eden's Gallery. In 1987, Tuma was a guest lecturer at the Columbia College, SC O'Keeffe Centennial Celebration. She continued to contrast her minimalist synthesis called Sculptured Painting as distinct from modeling on O'Keeffe's flowers. Quogue Gallery, Quogue Library, NY 2009, and Galerie Belage, in Westhampton, NY 2010. Starting in October 1990 she worked on the East End of Long Island as a tutor.

Yaroslav (Jaroslav) Henry Valenta (1889-d.), was a painter and graphic artist residing in Brooklyn, NY. He studied in Portland. He exhibited his work at the Federal Art Gallery in NYC and at the American Artists Congress. His works can be found in Indianapolis Museum of Art.

Andrew Valko (1957–), b. Prague, Czech., is a Canadian artist trained at Red River College in Winnipeg and he also studied woodblock printing in Japan. Valko is known for his photo-realist paintings, many of them dimly lit or night scenes, which make seemingly mundane scenes seem disquieting. He often explores themes from contemporary culture, including motels and drive-in movies. Andrew is a recipient of numerous awards and commissions including the Royal Canada Academy of the Arts, Manitoba Arts Council, and Canada Post Corporation. His work appears in a wide range of public, corporate, and private collections.

Frank Vavruska (1917–1974), b. Antigo, WI, of Czech parents, was an abstract painter. In the late 40s, his work began to shift from its expressionist figurative basis it initially had towards a purer form of abstraction and his work from the early 50s bears some resemblance to the work of COBRA (an avant-garde movement active from 1949 to 1952) artists of Northern Europe, some of which he may have seen at the time. Vavruska's beautiful, rough abstract paintings were included in exhibitions at the Metropolitan (American Painting Today, 1950), Pennsylvania Academy of Fine Arts (1957), Madison Square Garden.

Godfrey Francis Veselý (1886–1966), b. Czech., was a self-taught landscape painter. He specialized in desert landscapes of Utah, California and Arizona. His works are held at National Hotel, Nevada City, New Deal Corp., Grass Valley, CA, Ebell Club, Long Beach.

Edouard Antonín Vysekal (1890–1939), b. Kutná Hora, Bohemia, was a painter, trained at Chicago Art Institute. He was an instructor and lecturer at Art Students League and Otis Art Institute, Los Angeles. Vysekal is best known for his bold modern figure studies. He was a recipient of numerous awards, e.g. Harrison Prize (1921), Ackerman Prize (1922–24), gold medal, California Art Club (1926), etc.

Václav Vytlacil (1892–1984), b. New York City, of Czech ancestry, was a painter educated at Chicago Art Institute and Art Students League of New York. He was an instructor at Minneapolis School of Arts (1917–21), California Coll. of Art (1935–36); chairman, arts dept., Queens Coll., NYC (1942–45); instructor, Art Students League (s. 1967). He was a recipient of many awards, such as: honorable mention, Art Institute of Chicago (1913), gold medal, Art Institute of Chicago (1930), gold medal, France (1936), etc.

Sonja Waldstein (1926–), b. Prague, Czech., is a portrait painter. She came to Montreal in 1951. She attended commercial art school in Prague, Academie d'art de Bruxelles and School of Art in Montreal. She resided in Montreal and worked as an art monitor for Montreal recreational program.

Charles A. Wilimovsky (1885-1974) b. Chicago, IL, of Czech ancestry, was an impressionist painter. He taught at the Art Institute of Chicago and in 1920 at the Kansas City Art Institute.

Amy Josephine Klauber Wormser (1903-1988), b. San Diego, CA, of Bohemian ancestry, an easel painter and fabric and wallpaper designer, was educated at Mills College, Oakland and in Vienna at the Kunstgewerbeschule. She later returned to the CSFA for further study with emphasis on applied design. Her paintings were done between 1920-1940s. She then specialized in fabric and wallpaper design. She was a member of San Diego Museum of Art.

Ella Klauber Wormser (1863-1932), b. Carson City, NV, of Bohemian ancestry, had many talents, including painting portraits and still lives, photography, literature, and music. She was best known in the art world for her painting and photography skills.

Jaroslav Zetek (1929-1982), b. Prague, Czech., was an outstanding modern painter and watercolorist. He studied and practiced art in his native Prague before immigrating to Canada in 1968. He first administered the Skylon Gallery in Niagara Falls (1970) before opening his own studio and gallery in Toronto in 1974. His work with acrylics, such as the fine example entitled *Journey* date mostly from this period. He was a master of figure studies and landscapes, deriving both from his acute observation of life forms and from the depths of his fertile imagination.

John Zwara (1880-1951), b. Horní Štěpánov, Moravia, was a painter educated at Academy of Fine Art in Prague. He is best known for his landscape, frontier scene, and still life paintings, as well as his schizophrenic personality. He painted many landscapes in and around Brown County, Indiana.

2. Illustrators

René Robert Bouché (orig. Robert August Buchstein) (1905-1963), b. Prague, Bohemia, in 1926, at the age of 21, studied art history at Munich University, while earning a living as an illustrator of children's books. In 1927, he moved to Berlin and adopted the name René Robert Bouché. Having left Berlin for Paris, after Hitler came to power, Bouché started making drawings for the magazine *Plaisir de France* and advertising for Nestlé. In 1938, he began his work for *Vogue*. While in France, Bouché was separated from his first wife Margo Schoenlank and their son Michael and forced to escape from advancing German forces. From Lisbon, he crossed the Atlantic for the United States where he gained US citizenship and continued his work for *Vogue*. He illustrated advertisements for Saks Fifth Avenue and Elizabeth Arden. In 1948, he became interested in abstract expressionism and became a member of The Eighth Street Avant-Garde Painters Club before deciding to concentrate on portraiture. *Time* magazine regularly featured his work on their covers. Throughout the fifties, Bouché was sent on a number of travel assignments for Condé Nast that took him to Japan to study the rituals of the geishas, to Dublin for the horse races and the French Riviera to witness the European Aristocracy at play. The works produced on these trips are some of the most evocative of the period and reveal Bouché to be an artist with an exceptional eye, flair and extraordinary confidence. He also travelled regularly to Paris to cover the couture collections.

Gene Deitch (1924-2020), b. Chicago, based in Prague, is an American illustrator, cartoonist, animator, film director. He has been based in Prague, Czech., since 1959. After 1968, Deitch has been the leading animation director for the Connecticut organization Weston Woods/Scholastic, adapting children's picture books.

Will Eisner (1917-2005), b. Brooklyn, NY, of Czech mother, was an innovative and influential illustrator and writer, often referred to as the 'grandfather of the graphic novel.'

Jaro Fabry (1912-1953), b. New York, NY, of Czech ancestry, was a painter and a leading illustrator and cartoonist for national magazines. He employed a modernist approach related to Held's and Patterson's beauties in creating his drawing of Katharine Hepburn for the cover of Cinema Arts. Applying watercolor with loose, free brushwork, Fabry achieved a fresh, spontaneous portrait of Hepburn.

Harrison Fisher (1875-1934), b. Brooklyn, NY, of Bohemian ancestry, was a popular commercial artist and illustrator of the cover of *Cosmopolitan* magazine from the early 1900's through 1934. He was known as 'The Father of a Thousand Girls.' He became famous in America with his unusual ability of painting the most beautiful women. Fisher illustrated most *Cosmopolitan* covers - nearly 300 between 1913 and his death in 1934. He also did 80 covers for *the Saturday Evening Post* between 1900 and 1915.

Wanda Hazel Gág (1893-1946) of New Ulm, MN, of Bohemian ancestry, was an American artist, author, translator, and illustrator. In 1917, Gág won a scholarship to the Art Students League of New York where she took classes in composition, etching and advertising illustration. By 1919, Gág was earning her living as a commercial illustrator. In 1928, she published *Millions of Cats,* the first of a number of children's books written and illustrated by her which won several awards, the oldest American picture book still in print. Throughout the 1930s and 1940s, Gag worked as a printmaker, winning praise for her landscapes, still lives, and interior subjects, which display her distinctive personal style. The American Institute of Graphic Arts honored Gag by including her work in its annual selections of fifty outstanding prints.

VIII. CULTURE: ARTS & LETTERS

Vladyana Langer Krykorka, b. Prague, Czech., enrolled at the Ontario College of Art, graduating with a degree in graphic design and began working as an art director for a business magazine, which in turn led to illustrating math and spelling textbooks. Her career in illustrating children's picture books started with *A Promise is a Promise*, written by Robert Munsch and Michael Kusugak. Illustrating Munsch' and Kusugak's book (1988) sparked Vladyana's love for the Inuit culture. Since then, she has flown to the Arctic many times to meet, paint and photograph the people and their land. She has illustrated all the titles by acclaimed Inuit storyteller Michael Kusugak. Since then, she has illustrated more than 25 books from her Toronto studio including *Northern Lights: The Soccer Trails*, which won the Ruth Schwartz Award and was listed on the Aesop Accolade list. She was also awarded the silver medal of the Mr. Christie Book Award for both *The Twelve Months* and *The Polar Bear's Gift*.

Jiřina Marton (1946-), b. Prague, Czech., is a graduate of School of Applied Art in Prague, who later moved to Paris where she continued her studying. In Paris, she had her first exhibitions and received her first commissions to illustrate children's books. Her illustrations have been exhibited in Italy, Japan and Canada. Currently, she lives in Toronto. She is a published author and an illustrator of children's books. Some of the published credits of Jiřina Marton include *Marja's Skis, Arctic Adventures: Tales from the Lives of Inuit Artists, Little Book of Northern Tales: The Bear Says North*, and *The Bear Says North: Tales from Northern Lands*. She won the prestigious Governor General's Award for illustration for her work on the children's book, *Bella's Tree*.

Emanuel Václav Nádherný (1866-1945), b. Tusovice, Bohemia, was an illustrator. He came to Chicago in 1882. He studied at the Art Institute, Chicago and the Julian Academy, Paris. His illustrations appeared in *Harper's, Collier's, The New York Herald, Le Monde Illustre, Zlatá Praha* and other publications. His paintings were exhibited at the Academy of Design in NYC, Buffalo, and Chicago.

August Petrtýl (1867-1937), b. Bohemia, was a historical figure painter, portraitist and above all, an illustrator. He studied at Chicago Art Inst. and at Academy of Prague. He had his studio in Chicago and exhibited at Chicago Art Inst.

Miroslav Šašek (1916-1980), b. Prague, Czech., was a book illustrator. From 1951-57, he worked for Radio Free Europe before launching his popular book *This Is...* series, starting with *This is Paris* (1959). Then came in succession: *This is London* (1959), *This is Rome* (1960), *This is New York* (1960), *This is Edinburgh* (1961) *This is Washington, DC* (1969), etc. He received a number of awards, such as *New York Times* Choice of Best Illustrated Books of the Year 1959 (for his *This is London*) and 1960 (for his *This is New York*).

Thomas A. Sindelar (1867-1923), b. Cleveland, OH, of Bohemian ancestry, was an illustrator, and designer. He studied in Paris, presumably with Alphonse Mucha. His name first appears in the New York City directory in 1894, and he was listed as designer. He later lived in Elmhurst, NY and in Flushing, Queens where he died. He was an instructor at New York School of Design for Women. He was a life member of the Lotos Club, a New York men's group of distinguished professional, literary, and academic pursuits. For years, Sindelar designed the menus of the Lotos Club, and these were elaborate, symbolic and allegorical works.

Peter Sís (1949-) b. Brno, Czech., is an internationally acclaimed illustrator, author, and filmmaker. He attended the Academy of Applied Arts in Prague and the Royal College of Art in London. Peter is a seven-time winner of *The New York Times Book Review* Best Illustrated Book of the Year, a two-time Boston Globe-Horn Book Award Honoree, and has won the Society of Illustrators Gold Medal twice. Peter's books, *Starry Messenger: Galileo Galilei, Tibet through the Red Box,* and *The Wall: Growing Up Behind the Iron Curtain* were all named Caldecott Honor books by the American Library Association. *The Wall* was also awarded the Robert F. Sibert Medal. In addition, Peter Sís is the first children's book illustrator to win the prestigious MacArthur Fellowship.

Frederick J. Sklenar (1938-), b. Staten Island, NY, of Czech ancestry, has been a professional illustrator for international publications and ad agencies. He specialized in editorial concepts and portraits of business leaders, and national sports celebrities. Fred became art director for such publishing entities as Sport Magazine, McGraw-Hill, Penton Publishing, *Look* and *Venture* magazines, and for over a decade, was the creative director of his own marketing and advertising agency.

Jan Sovák (1953-), b. Tábor, Czech., is a paleoartist, an illustrator, designer and fine artist recognized as one of Canada's foremost natural history illustrators. His work has been published in over 170 books in more than 15 languages. More than 40 museums around the world house examples of his art on prehistoric animals, and his illustrations also have appeared on educational television in 12 films on Discovery Channel Worldwide.

Josef Čestmír Svoboda (1889-1953), b. Prague, Bohemia, was a Texas illustrator known for his landscapes and portraits. He was Art Director of the Herbert Rogers Company in Dallas, Texas. He studied painting in Prague with Frantisek Bizy and at the Art Institute of Chicago with Ralph Clarkson, Walter Ufer and Charles Hawthorne. He exhibited in Chicago at various Czech artist shows, at the Art Institute in the 1920s and 1930s, and at the Palette and Chisel Club. He exhibited in Arizona at the State Exhibition of 1926. He also painted in Taos and Santa Fe, New Mexico and exhibited his work in Taos at the Harwood Foundation.

Received several prizes for his work and honorable mentions, including first and second prizes at Arizona State exhibition (1926).

Walter Trier (1890–1951), b. Prague, Bohemia, was an illustrator, best known for his work for the children's books of Erich Kästner and the covers of the magazine *Lilliput*. In 1936 he emigrated to London and during the Second World War, Trier helped the Ministry of Information produce anti-Nazi leaflets and political propaganda. In 1947, he moved to Toronto, Canada. On his arrival in Canada, Trier started work on illustrations for the company Canada Packers. Trier held an exhibition of oils and water-colors in the University of Toronto in 1951 but died of a heart attack on 8 July of that year.

Edward 'Ed' Ignatius Valigursky (1926–2009), b. Arnold, PA, of Slovak descent; American illustrator; freelance artist; an art director for Ziff-Davis Publications, NYC. He illustrated books for such publishers as Bantam Books, Ballantine Books, Lippincott, MacFadden Publications, and Time-Life Books. In 1970s, he was invited to NASA to illustrate the spectacular space program for *Popular Mechanics*, where he continued to work until the 1980s. After retiring from commercial illustration in the 1990s, he began to produce fine art paintings that celebrated the history of aviation.

Anna Vojtěch (1946–), b. Prague, Czech., studied art and toy design at the School of Applied Arts and animation film and graphics at the Academy of Applied Arts in Prague. After the Soviet invasion of her country in 1968, she attended the Royal Academy in Antwerp, Belgium and the Academy of Fine Arts in Hamburg, Germany. Here she met her husband, Roland Baumgaertel. In 1971, they moved to Canada. Since 1982, she has lived with her husband Roland and their sons, Mathis, and Lukas, in Massachusetts. She has exhibited her work in the Boston Athenaeum, the Peabody Museum and various galleries and museums. She has cooperated with several educational and children's books publishers. Since 1992, her illustration work has been represented by Studio Goodwin Sturges. Anna Vojtěch has illustrated various books for children, mostly folktales and stories about nature. Her pictures are full of flowers and animals, of giraffes and elephants or of little birds and chipmunks. Folktales are also about people, their nature, and their spirit. Through her illustrations, Anna has brought readers closer to our Native American heritage as well as the traditions of other nations. Nature has been always a strong source of inspiration for Anna. She spent years combing through the northern forests and meadows searching out rare wildflowers. Parts of her extensive collection of botanical paintings were published in different magazines and as a book *Wild Flowers for All Seasons*. They have been exhibited in the USA, Canada, and England.

James Warhola (1955–), b. Smock, PA, of Slovak-Rusyn ancestry (Andy Warhol's nephew), is an illustrator of more than two-dozen children's picture books, since 1987. Warhola has worked for several major publishing houses, among them Warner Books and Prentice Hall. He serves as a consultant to the Andy Warhol Museum of Modern Art in Medzilaborce, Slovakia, near the Warhola ancestral village of Miková.

Emil Weiss (1896–1965), b. Moravia, was an illustrator, one of the last 'press artists' that old journalistic specialty superseded by photography. In 1948, he emigrated to the US and became the *Monitor*'s artist-reporter covering national events and politicians both on assignment as well as freelance until his death in 1965. Illustrator of some 40 children's books (originals now in the Kerlan Collection of the University of Minnesota Library), he illustrated Harper & Row's young readers' edition of JFK's *Profiles in Courage*; Emily Neville's 1964 Newbery medal winner *It's like this, cat* (1963.) He was author of *My Studio Sketchboook, Marsland* (1948); with Karla Weiss the children's cookbook *Let's have a party* (1946); as well as *Slavische Märchen* (1952).

3. Caricaturists & Cartoonists

Brad Benischek, b. probably of Czech ancestry, received his Bachelor of Fine Arts from the Parsons School of Design and his Master of Fine Arts from the Savannah College of Art and Design in Savannah, Georgia. He is a contemporary visual artist, educator, writer and actor, living and working in New Orleans, Louisiana. While Benischek is primarily a cartoon and graphic artist, he also works in multiple media such as video. He is one of the founding members of the Press Street literary and visual arts collective, a New Orleans-based non-profit which promotes art and literature in the community through events, publications and arts education. Benischek's work has appeared in numerous publications, and in galleries and art spaces across the South.

Christian Beranek (1974–), b. Council Bluffs, IA, is a writer, producer, musician and consultant. She has worked in comics with such companies as Zenescope, Markosia, Image, and IDW. From 2000–2008, she co-ran Silent Devil Productions with his family. In 2008, she signed a producer deal with Disney to launch Kingdom Comics. In 2010, she helped launch the successful website The Webcomic Factory.

Oscar Berger (1901–1977), a native of Prešov, Slovakia, attained considerable fame, as a caricaturist, who focused on world celebrities, from kings and presidents to movie stars. During the 1950s, Berger attended many sessions at the United Nations and illustrated virtually every important world leader to be seen there.

Joe E. Buresch (1916–2004), b. Pittsburgh, PA, took a correspondence course on cartooning and had two years of art instruction. Since the mid-1930s, he had been active as a syndicated artist, starting with features like 'Detective Nehi and Skihi', 'Cowboy Joe', 'Fireman Sam', 'Jimmy Rivers', 'Cousins' and 'Ride 'em Cowboy' in the 1930s. Then came 'Crosby's Country Cousins' (1939-42) and the long running daily 'Dinah Mite' panel (1953 throughout the 1980s), as well as 'The Fletcher 4–H'R' in the 1970s. Since 1978, he did the monthly 'Cy's Super Service' strip for *Electrical Apparatus* magazine, which he continued until shortly before his death. Way back in the 1930s, Buresch had also done comic book art for *Centaur Comics*. He was a writer/artist for 'Detective Picture Stories' and 'Western Picture Stories,' 'Keen Detective Funnies' and the author of features like 'Buck Rush', 'The Caveman Cowboy', 'Double Trouble', 'Hezzy of the Hills', 'Jimmy and Jean', 'Mountain Murder', 'Pat O'Day', 'Pete Kid Calahan' and 'Roadhouse Racket'.

Will Eisner (1917–2005), b. Brooklyn, NY, of Czech mother, was an innovative and influential illustrator and writer, often referred to as the 'grandfather of the graphic novel.'

Peter George Estin (1927–1963), b. Prague, Czech., was a cartoonist, illustrator and commercial artist. He was born to a banker's family that narrowly escaped Hitler's genocide of eastern Europe in 1938. He eventually immigrated to the US, settling in Boston. Peter graduated from Phillips Academy Andover, then Dartmouth as ski team captain and an MS in international relations (Slavic Languages and Literature) from Harvard. He then served in the US Air Force Reserves as 2nd Lieutenant (Intelligence) in the early 1950s. Afterwards, he spent a few years as a Boston-based financial analyst for HC Wainright & Co., but the lure of the mountains always beckoned. He left the business world to became an ambassador - or promoter - of sorts as Director of Ski Schools at Sugarbush, VT, Portillo, Chile and La Parva, Chile attracting east coast high society and media attention to those resorts in the 1950s and early 1960s. With his brother and best friend, Hans, an Andover-Tabor Academy-Harvard educated Boston investment banker, the two founded Ski Club 10 at the base of Sugarbush Mountain, the first American on-mountain ski social club of true 'jet set' notoriety. He wrote the book *Skiing the American Way* considered by many a ski teaching classic. He was a speechwriter for Ted Kennedy in his first successful Senate race in 1962 and a cartoonist with works published in *The Saturday Evening Post* and Colliers, amongst others. A book of Peter's cartoons, *Jestin with Estin*, was published posthumously in the 70's. He died at age 35 of ski related injuries.

Joseph Keppler (1838–1894), b. Vienna, of Bohemian ancestry, was an American caricaturist and founder of *Puck*, the first successful humorous weekly in the United States. The English version lasted until 1918, 22 years longer than the German. Initially, Keppler drew all the cartoons for *Puck*, and, although later many other artists contributed, his influence remained strong. His cartoon 'Forbidding the Banns,' published on behalf of anti-Garfield forces in the Garfield-Hancock presidential campaign of 1880, attracted widespread attention. According to Thomas Čapek, Kepler knew Czech. Around the year 1882, he published in *Puck* in Czech language a joke about Dr. F. L. Rieger, which was brought about by a bet.

Harold Hering Knerr (1882-1949), b. Bryn Mawr, PA, of Moravian ancestry on his mother's side, was an American comic strip creator who signed his work H. H. Knerr. He was best known as the writer-artist of *The Katzenjammer Kids* for 35 years. Knerr was extremely prolific, producing more than 1,500 Sunday comic pages between 1901 and 1914 for a half-dozen continuing features in three different Philadelphia newspapers.

John Francis Knott (1878-1963), b. Plzeň, Bohemia, was a political cartoonist and artist. He immigrated to Sioux City, IA, with his widowed mother at the age of five Knott started working at *The Dallas Morning News* in 1905 and drew daily cartoons in the paper during Woodrow Wilson's first presidential campaign and World War I. It is believed his cartoons supporting American entry into World War I helped increase the sales of Liberty Bonds and donations towards the war effort. During his fifty-year career as a cartoonist, he created more than 15,000 cartoons.

Jeffrey Koterba (1961-), b. Omaha, NE, of Czech ancestry, is an American editorial cartoonist based in Omaha, Nebraska. He has been *Omaha World Herald*'s cartoonist since 1989 and his work is syndicated nationwide to over 400 newspapers by King Features Syndicate. His work regularly appears in many major U.S. newspapers including *The New York Times*, *Chicago Tribune*, *USA Today*, *The Atlanta Journal Constitution*, *Washington Post* and CNN.

Grady (Gray) Lyda (1954-2015), b. Dayton, OH of Czech ancestry (grandson of painter Charles A. Wilimovsky), is an American comic book artist and writer best known for his time travel series, 'Tempus Fugit', in *Star Reach* magazine.

Frank V. Martinek (1895-1975), b. Chicago, IL, of Bohemian ancestry, was a cartoonist. He was a cartoonist, a creator of 'Don Winslow of the Navy' and 'Bos'n Hal - Sea Scout,' newspaper adventure strips (s. 1934). He attended business college and Academy of Fine Arts, Chicago. He was a copy boy and cub reporter *Chicago Record Herald* (1910-13); Identification inspector Chicago Civil Service Commission (1913-17); Enlisted in US Navy as seaman (1917), served as intelligence officer, Special agent US Department of Justice (1921-25); with Standard Oil Corporation of Indiana (since 1925), assistant vice president, from 1928.

Jiřina Marton (1946–), b. Liberec, Czech., is a Canadian artist and illustrator. She studied at the School of Applied Arts in Prague and continued her studies in Paris. Marton had her first exhibitions there and also began illustrating children's books. She came to Canada in 1985 and now lives in Toronto. She authored some 26 children's books, such as *The Little Plane Goes on a Journey, Lady Kaguya Secret, Flowers for Mom*. She was the winner of the Grand Prize, Itabishi Picture Book Contest (1995), and now lives and works in Toronto, Ontario. Her books have been published in France, Canada, Switzerland, Spain, Japan, China and Korea. Her illustrations have appeared in exhibitions in Italy, Japan and Canada.

Paul Peter Porges (1927–2016), b. Vienna, of Bohemian ancestry, is an American cartoonist. He established himself at *Mad* magazine, where he continued his slapstick drawings for kids, and also at prestigious magazines such as the *Saturday Review of Literature* and *The New Yorker*, where he developed a very clever style. He also contributed to *Harper's* and the *Saturday Evening Post*.

John Sikela (1907–1996), b. Veľké Kozmálovce, Slovakia, was a cartoonist. Along with Wayne Boring, he was one of the most important and long-lasting ghost artists on Joe Shuster's *Superman* comic. He joined the studios in 1940, where he worked close with Joe Shuster, doing penciling and inking work. His solo work featured dynamic panels with big aerial views. Later on, he was one of the main artists on the spin-off 'Superboy' series. After the introduction of *Superboy* #1 in 1949, Sikela enjoyed a long run on the title through the latter half of the 1950s and also illustrated several stories for *Adventure Comics*.

George Sixta (1909–1986), b. Chicago, IL, of Czech ancestry, was an American cartoonist, best known for his syndicated comic strip, *Rivets*, about a wire-haired terrier. During his Navy PR job, Sixta got the idea for *Rivets* when he saw many photos of Navy mascots. *Rivets* first appeared in *The Saturday Evening Post* in 1944 and was syndicated from 1953 to 1985. Sixta also drew two newspaper features, *One for the Book* and the sports humor cartoon series *Hit or Miss*, which ran from November 1, 1948 to January 9, 1954. *Hit or Miss* featured the character Louella, as noted by comics historian Allan Holtz.

Frederick A. Sklenar (1918–1992), b. Bayonne, NJ, of Czech ancestry, had his last home and studio in Brooksville, Florida. He was an editorial cartoonist for *The Hernando Times* and other publications. He taught painting and won numerous awards and recognition over the years.

Vincent A. Svoboda (1877–1961), b. Prague, Bohemia, was painter and cartoonist. He came to this country as a boy. He received three prizes when he graduated from the National Academy of Design. Later he studied in Prague, Czechoslovakia, and in Paris, where he worked with Mucha, the Czechoslovak poster artist. He belonged also to the Allied Artists of America and the Cartoonists Club. Initially he did illustrations for the old *New York American*, *Harper's Magazine* and *The Saturday Evening Post*. In the 1920's, he did posters for motion picture theaters. He was a former cartoonist with the *Brooklyn Eagle* from 1940 to 1952. In 1925 and 1937, Svoboda won Salmagundi Club awards.

Otakar Valášek (1884-1954), b. Moravany, Bohemia, was political cartoonist for the old *Chicago Herald Examiner* before World War I, and later a commercial artist. Emigrated to the United States at the age of 17 and studied at the Art Institute of Chicago. Was in commercial art advisory business, Chicago (1914-1917). With *Chicago Herald* (August 1917–April 1918). Staff Committee on Public Information until end of the war. Author: *American War Cartoons* (1917), *100 Cartoons—200 Years of Slavery* (Slavic), 1918, serial cartoons *Creepers on the Earth*, published in Russia (1919).

4. Comic Book Artists

Stephen J. Ditko (1927-2018), b. Johnstown, PA, of American Rusyn and Slovak ancestry, was a comic book artist and writer, co-creator of the Marvel Comics heroes 'Spider-Man' and 'Doctor Strange.' Ditko was inducted into the comics industry's Jack Kirby Hall of Fame in 1990, and into the Will Eisner Award Hall of Fame in 1994.

James Kochalka (1968-), b. Springfield, VT, of Czech ancestry, is an American comic book artist and writer, and rock musician. His comics are noted for their blending of the real and the surreal. Largely autobiographical, Kochalka's cartoon expression of the world around him includes such real-life characters as his wife, children, cat, friends and colleagues, but always filtered through his own observations and flights of whimsy. In March 2011, he was declared the cartoonist laureate of Vermont, serving a term of three years.

Grady (Gray) Lyda (1954-), b. Dayton, OH of Czech ancestry (grandson of painter Charles A Wilimovsky), is an American comic book artist and writer best known for his time travel series, 'Tempus Fugit', in *Star Reach* magazine.

Joel F. Naprstek (1947-), likely of Czech ancestry, is an American painter and comic book cover artist who provided painted cover art for the series *Predator: Homeworld* and contributed to the jam comic *Aliens: Havoc* for Dark Horse Comics. A graduate of New York's School of Visual Arts, Joel taught painting and illustration there for nine years, and currently teaches at the Joe Kubert School of Cartoon and Graphic Art in Dover, New Jersey. Narpstek has been a freelance illustrator for over 25 years. His clients have included NBC, CBS, Time Inc., McGraw-Hill, Business Week, Financial World, Fortune, and numerous ad agencies.

Jan Steven Strnad (1950–), b. Wichita, KS, of Czech descent, is an American writer of comic books and science fiction. He is most known for his work in the *Star Wars* expanded universe, the majority of which has been published by Dark Horse Comics. His career in comics began at Warren Publishing; he has since written material for DC Comics, Marvel Comics, Eclipse Comics, and Fantagraphics Books. Jan Strnad has collaborated frequently with artist Richard Corben.

5. Graphic Artists & Designers

Fritzi Brod (née Schermer) (1900–1952), b. Prague, Bohemia; textile designer, graphic designer. Brod came to Chicago in 1924 after studying art in Prague and Vienna. Already an accomplished designer of textiles in the modern manner, she continued her work with Raymond Katz in his 'Little' Gallery. Brod's work was critically acclaimed at Chicago's first outdoor art fair in 1932, and she was featured in C. J. Bulliet's column, "Artists of Chicago" in 1936. She wrote two books, *200 Motifs and Designs* and *Flowers in Nature and Design*. She did a painting for Millikin University, Decatur, IL entitled 'Landscape.' Her work is in the New York Public Library and in Vanderpool College.

Charles (Karel) Bruml (1912–1998), b. Prague, Bohemia, was a graphic artist, whose talent helped him survive Nazi concentration camps of World War II. In Terezín and Auschwitz camps he was put to work painting numbers on uniforms and in the printing and engineering department. He survived the 40-mile death march in January 1945 from Auschwitz to Gleiwitz, where prisoners were being moved away from invading Russians. Charles Bruml was liberated by British troops later that year. He met his wife, Dr. Hana Bruml, a clinical psychologist, who had been in the same camps, for the first time at an office in Prague after the war. The couple married and then moved to the Washington area in 1947, Charles Bruml studied at the Corcoran School of Art. He displayed his paintings at galleries in the Washington area and at the Jewish Community Center of Northern Virginia. His artifacts from the war, including the suitcase he carried on deportation transport, are part of the collection of the US Holocaust Memorial Museum. A videotaped interview with the Brumls, who had traveled back often over the years to the concentration camp sites, is also at the Museum.

Jan Burka (1924–2009), b. Postoloprty, Czech., in 1940, he studied at a private art school, and then attended a course in graphics at the Vinohrady Synagogue, led by Petr Kien. After some time in Prague, he was deported as Geltungsjude, and was sent to Terezín on 10 August 1942. In Terezín, he was once again reunited with Petr Kien, and even in the difficult conditions in the ghetto, continued to study drawing. In Terezín, he lived to see liberation. He also met his future wife, renowned figure skater Ellen Burka (née Danby), in Terezín, who was raised in the Netherlands. After World War II, Burka (with Danby) settled in Amsterdam, where he studied at the Royal Academy of Fine Arts (Rijksakademie beeldende van Kunsten), under Lütke and Westerman. From 1945-1951, he worked as a graphic artist in Amsterdam. In 1951, he moved to Toronto, Canada, where he studied at the Ontario College of Art & Design. There he was linked to Henri Chopin. He also founded his own graphic arts studio, and together with Alain Fleming, was a co-founder of a Canadian group of designers. From 1961-1968, he lived in France, where he made his first reliefs and sculptures. In 1968, he went back to Toronto, where he lived and worked until 1978. Most of these works are now located in Canadian museums. Burka attended more than a hundred exhibitions in Europe, Canada, and the United States. His works are exhibited in a number of Canadian, American, and European museums and are part of important private collections. In 1968, he received the Ontario prize Centenaire du Canada. Burka also won numerous awards for his graphic work and his "Concrete poetry", part of an anthology of experimental poetry, published in 1967.

Vlasta Cihlář (1929-2004), b. Brno, Czech., was a graphic artist, painter and also made patent drawings. She was trained at Státní grafická škola (1948). She resided in Jackson Heights, NY.

Michael Engelmann (1928-1966), b. Prague, Czech., an American designer, possessed a strong signature style—simple and bold, utilizing sans serif type with minimal imagery, often photography. Through the 1950s and 60s, Engelmann's work took him around the globe including Amsterdam, Munich, Milan, Dusseldorf and New York. His client list included Pirelli, Volkswagen and Geigy.

Želmíra "Myra" Hatala (1942-2013), b. Michalovce, Czech.; graphic artist, fashion designer, in art advertising and printing, art director, *The Washington Post*.

Hans Jelinek (1910-1992), b. Vienna, of Bohemian ancestry; graphic artist, professor of art at City College, NYC. He studied at the Academy of Applied Art and the University of Vienna. After coming to the United States in 1938, he became a medical illustrator at the University of Virginia. In 1945, he moved to New York, where he was a professor of art at City College for 31 years. He also taught at the New School and the National Academy of Design, and was a member of the National Academy, the Society of American Graphic Artists and a Benjamin Franklin Fellow of the Royal Society of Art in England. Jelinek was famous for his woodcuts, which won many awards, including first prize in the 1943 Artists for Victory National Graphic Art Exhibition for his series on the Czechoslovak town Lidice, and the Pennell Prize of the Library of Congress.

Jon Jicha (1950-), b. Cleveland, OH, of Czech ancestry, received training in graphic design at Kent State Univ. (B.F.A., 1972; M.F.A.). He was associated with Coker Coll., Hartsville, SC as asst. professor (1976-81), as assoc. professor and coordinator of graphic design (1981-

84). He then joined Western Carolina Univ., Cullowhee, NC as assoc. professor (1984-93), as professor and coordinator of graphic design and media arts (1993-2004), as director of Master of Fine Arts Program (2004-07), as professor of graphic design and media arts (s. 2007). His area of specialization is graphic design, interactive design, information design, painting, drawing, and photography.

Anna Lesznai (pseud.) (real name: Amália J. Moskowitz) (1885-1966), b. Budapest; she grew up in Nižný Hrušov, Slovakia, on the country estate belonging to her father Geyza Moskowitz, a physician. She immigrated to the US in 1939, settling in New York City. She was an American writer, painter, designer, and key figure in the avant-garde. In 1946, she opened her own school of painting. Her autobiographical novel *Kezdetben volt a kert* ("In the Beginning was the Garden"), on which she worked for thirty years, was published in German translation in 1965 and in the original Hungarian the following year.

Pavel Liháni (1922-2008), b. Hňúšťa, Czech., was a commercial and fine artist, graphic artist, poet, journalist. He studied at Cleveland Institute of Art (1947), Famous Artist Institute of Arts (1947) and Famous Artists School (1960). He was a co-owner of Creative Arts Studio and Terry Art Productions, Parma, OH.

Ervine Metzl (1899-1963), b. Chicago, IL, of Jewish Bohemian ancestry, was a graphic artist and illustrator, best known for his posters and postage stamp designs. As a young man, he attended the School of the Art Institute of Chicago and showed an interest in poster design. In July 1917, in the midst of the First World War his Red Cross poster earned an honorable mention at the Art Institute's Exhibition of Posters for National Service. He created several posters for a series commissioned by the Chicago Transit Authority in the early 1920s. Metzl's posters, *The Evanston Lighthouse by the Elevated Lines* and *The Field Museum by the Elevated Lines* (featuring a toucan) are still reproduced today. From 1957-1960, Metzl designed ten postage stamps for the United States Postal Service. In addition to his stamp design work, Metzl served on the U.S. Postal Service Citizens' Advisory Committee. In recognition of his contributions, he was one of the inaugural recipients of the Benjamin Franklin Award in 1960. He wrote *The Poster: Its History and Its Art,* published by Watson-Guptill Publications shortly before his death.

Vojtěch Preissig (1873-1944), b. Světec, Bohemia, was a graphic artist, designer, illustrator, and painter. In 1897, he moved to Paris and worked for two years with the Czech Art Nouveau artist, Alphonse Mucha. He returned to Prague in 1903 where he founded the periodical *Česká grafika* (Czech Graphics) and opened his own graphic studio 1905. He moved to the United States in 1910 and worked as an art instructor. Preissig remained in the United States until 1930. He taught at Columbia University and the Art Students League of New

York starting in 1912, then moved to Boston by 1916 and taught a course in graphic arts for the Wentworth Institute, becoming the director of the School of Printing and Graphic Arts, until 1926. In the US, he was noted for his 'legionnaires' recruitment posters.

Liba Puchmajer (orig. Libuše Puchmajerová-Girsová) (1936–), b. Prague, Czech, is a graphic artist. She graduated from Academy of Applied Art (dipl., 1961). She worked in Prague advertising agency as an art director and manager (until 1964). In 1965, she and her husband emigrated to the US. Liba then worked in New York and Connecticut as an art dir. Later, she taught as a visiting professor at the Graduate School of New Rochelle and at SUNY, Farmingdale.

Miloš Reindl (1923–2002), b. Czech., was a Czech painter and graphic designer and one of the most interesting poster designers of 60s in former Czechoslovakia. After his schooling at the School of Applied Art in Prague, Reindl worked in the team of artists preparing the famous World exhibition Expo 58. He also worked as a textile and vinyl covers designer and created some of the most iconic movie posters of 1960s. After the Russian occupation in 1968, Miloš Reindl, among several other artists, immigrated to Canada where he continued his career as an artist and teacher of drawing at the University of Laval, Quebec. In the early 1970s, he began a career as an art professor, teaching for nearly thirty years at Laval University. During his years as a teacher, Reindl continued to paint, creating hundreds of oil paintings, gouaches, and drawings over the course of his career, however his work was only shared with only a few close friends until after his death in 2002.

George Sadek (1928–2007), b. Ústí nad Labem, Czech., was trained as a graphic designer. He was with Indiana Univ. (1960–66); as professor of graphic design, Cooper Union, NYC (s. 1966), chairman of art dept. (1966–68), Dean, School of Art (s. 1968). He was the founder of Cooper Union's Center for Design and Typography, who transformed graphic design education by having students work on actual projects for nonprofit institutions.

Koloman Sokol (1902–2003), b. Liptovský Sv. Mikuláš, Slovakia, was one of the most prominent Slovak painters, graphic artists, and illustrators. He was a founder of modern Slovak graphic art. He lived in New York City during the World War II and left for the US again in 1948, when Communists took power in Czechoslovakia. He settled in Bryn Mawr, PA and in the 1990s in Tucson, AC, where he died at the age of 100.

Hugo Steiner-Prag (1880–1945), b. Prague, Bohemia, was a painter, etcher, and book illustrator. He made his reputation as an illustrator and book designer in Germany where he held professorship in Leipzig. When the Nazis abolished his position, he returned to Prague and established a private school for book arts and graphic design, called the

Officina Pragensis. He arrived in the US in June 1941, where he was offered a position as professor at the Division of Graphic Arts at New York University.

Ladislav Sutnar (1897–1976), b. Plzeň, Bohemia, was a graphic artist who is considered one of the great pioneers of the modern period. Sutnar was brought to the United States to design the exhibition for Czechoslovakia at the New York World Fair in 1939. In 1941, he became art director of F.W. Dodge's Sweet's Catalog Service from 1941 until 1960 where he led the development of information design along with Knud Lonberg-Holm. He continued his typographic design for advertising and corporations as he was art director for *Theatre Arts* magazine for ten years. He also created trends in glassware and flatware products. Sutnar was one of the first designers to actively practice in the field of information design.

Ivana Vaváková (1965–), b. Prague, Czech., is a graphic designer. She was trained at Cleveland St State University (B.A.), specializing in fine and studio arts. She served as senior art director with Scott Key, Inc., Teaneck, NJ (2010–11); graphic designer with Zindigo Inc, NYC (7 months); creative director with Beauty Solutions, Ltd., NYC (2012–14); senior graphic designer with McIntire Direct, Portland, OR; and senior graphic designer with Lund International / Bushwacker, Inc., Buford, GA (s. 2014).

Jan V. White (1928-2014), b. Prague, Czech., was a designer, communication design consultant, and graphic design educator and writer. He was educated in England at Leighton Park School and held degrees in architecture from Cornell University and Columbia University School of Architecture, Planning and Preservation. From 1951 to 1964, he worked on two of TIME's architectural magazines: *Architectural Forum* (1951–56) as associate art director, and *House & Home* (1956–1964) as art director. Since 1964, he has worked as a consultant, writer and teacher. He redesigned more than 200 periodical publications on four continents and influenced many more with his books and articles about design for print. Initially focused on periodical design in the mid-1980s, White brought his analysis of the visual rhetoric of structure, white space and typographic hierarchy to bear on corporate publishing in a way that shared common ground with information design.

Alex W. White (ca. 1956–), b. US, of Czech father, studied graphic design in a number of universities, including Kent State Univ. (B.F.A., 1978), Univ. of Illinois, Urbana (M.F.A., 1981) and Syracuse Univ. (M.F.A., 1983). He is an associate professor and chairman of the Master of Professional Studies program in Design Management at the Shintaro Akatsu School of Design at the University of Bridgeport (s. 2012). He is past chairman of the Type Directors Club (tdc.org), an international arts organization based in New York City. He has worked with dozens of companies and hundreds of art directors and writers around the world and wrote seven industry-leading books on design and typography and many articles that have appeared in industry publications. He taught design and typography at six prominent colleges for thirty years. He designed award-winning identity programs and magazines.

Henry Wolf (1925–2005), b. Vienna, of Bohemian Jewish ancestry, was a graphic designer, photographer, and art director. Wolf studied art in Paris, but after hiding from the Germans and living in two detention camps in Morocco, the family relocated to the United States in 1941. He continued his art studies at New York City's School of Industrial Art. He worked with photographers Richard Avedon, Melvin Sokolsky and Art Kane before he launched his own photography studio on the Upper East Side of Manhattan. He became the art director of *Esquire* in 1952, his designs becoming the sophisticated image for which the magazine is now known. In 1958, he became the art director of *Harper's Bazaar*, succeeding Alexey Brodovitch and worked with Richard Avedon and Man Ray. After a tenure of three years at *Harper's Bazaar,* he left to start a new a new progressive arts magazine *Show* for A&P heir Huntington Hartford. In 1965, Wolf began working for McCann Erickson where he directed high-profile advertisement campaigns like Alka Seltzer, Buick, Gillette, and Coca-Cola. He later joined advertising executive Jane Trahey, forming Trahey/Wolf, serving as vice president and creative director. In 1971, Wolf launched Henry Wolf Productions, a studio devoted to photography, film, and design. For the next three decades, he worked as both photographer and designer, creating over 500 television commercials and nine films, shooting for Van Cleef & Arpels, RCA, Revlon, Borghese, Olivetti and Karastan among others. His work was published in many magazines, including *Esquire, Town and Country, Domus,* and *New York.* Wolf taught graphic design at Parsons School of Design in New York City, as well as the School of Visual Arts and The Cooper Union.

6. Engravers & Etchers

Jaroslav Brožík (1904–1986), b. Plzeň, Bohemia, was an etcher, lithographer, and painter. He grew up in Illinois and studied at the Art Institute of Chicago. Brozik taught at the Davenport Municipal Art Gallery in the early 1930s, and later, in 1935, became an art instructor at Flint Institute of Arts, Flint, Michigan, where he remained until 1945. Brozik was among the 5000 artists commissioned in the WPA sponsored Federal Project No.1, which created jobs for artists by employing them with commissions to enhance public buildings with their art. His mural "Rural Delivery" (1941) is extant today at the Howell, Michigan post office. He was a recipient of Chicago Society of Artists prize (1932) and Gold Medal from Detroit Institute of Art. He was a recipient of Chicago Society of Artists prize (1932) and Gold Medal from Detroit Institute of Art.

Rudolph Růžička (1883-1978), b. Bohemia, was a celebrated Czech-American wood engraver, etcher, illustrator, book designer, and topographer. Růžička designed typefaces and wood engraving illustrations for Daniel Berkeley Updike's Merrymount Press, and was a designer for, and consultant to, the Mergenthaler Linotype Company for fifty years. He designed a number of seals and medals, including the American Institute of Graphic Arts (AIGA) and the Dartmouth Medal of the American Library Association.

7. Bookbinders & Book Artists

Tatana 'Tana' Kellner (1950-), b. Prague, Czech., is a visual artist. She is a daughter of two Holocaust survivors. She came to Toledo, OH with her family in 1969. She received a BA from the University of Toledo in 1972 and an M.F.A. from the Rochester Institute of Technology in 1982. Her practice encompasses artist's books, printmaking, papermaking, drawing, photography, and installation. She uses these media to comment on contemporary culture. She has created many artist books, and her work is in many public collections. Tatana Kellner is the founding member and artistic director of Women's Studio Workshop, an artist's workspace in Rosendale, NY. WSW is the only women's studio facility and residency program in the US. She had over 20 solo exhibitions in USA and Canada. She has received the Ruth & Harold Chenven Foundation Award and has been awarded residences at Visual Studies Workshops in Rochester, New York, Artpark in Lewiston, New York and also MacDowell Colony in Peterborough, New Hampshire.

Jan Bohuslav Sobota (1939-2012), b. Hromnice, Czech., in 1954, was enrolled at the School of Applied Arts in Prague. He studied bookbinding in Masters' Studios of Karel Silinger in Plzeň, Czech., and Emil Perták in Prague, completing his studies in 1957. In 1969, he was awarded the title 'Master of Applied Arts' and ten years later in Germany the title 'Meister der Einbandkunst' (MDE). He came in 1984 as a Czech émigré via Switzerland to Cleveland, sponsored by the Rowfant Club, a private group of book collectors. He found immediate employment at the book conservation labs of Case Western Reserve University. Later on, he settled in Texas. Together with his wife Jarmila Helena, who is a bookbinder restorer, they owned the firm J. Sobota Book Arts. He was also director of Conservatorium Laboratory at Bridwell Library, Southern Methodist Univ. in Dallas, TX. In 1997, he returned to Czech Republic, where, together with his wife, they opened J&J Sobotas' Book Art Studio, in Loket. Jan Sobota's contribution to modern bookbinding spans a broad spectrum, from creative art form to the painstaking craft and science of conservation and restoration work, which depends upon his substantial theoretical knowledge, and fifty years of experience. He is best known in the international bookbinding scene for his original and unusual book sculptures and objects. His work has been exhibited in countries on four continents, including the Metropolitan Museum of Art. Since 1969, he has participated in 137 group and thirty-two individual exhibits and has received some twenty-one prizes. He has lectured and taught in USA and in Europe, and his work has been published widely in numerous international journals and books.

8. Industrial Designers

Arthur Nicholas BecVar (1911–2003), b. Cleveland, OH, of Czech ancestry, was an industrial designer. He was trained at Notre Dame (B.F.A., 1933), received an engineering certificate from Purdue University and M.F.A. at Institute of International Education, Charles University, Prague (1934). He was art director, Stearn Advertising Co. (1935–36); Jeffrey Manufacturing Co. (1936–37); assoc., J.G. Rideout & Assoc. (1937–40); research industrial designer, Revere Copper & Brass Co. (1940–41); advisor to director of design, General Electric Co., Bridgeport (1945–51); manager, industrial design, Louisville (s. 1951). He served as president of American Soc. of Industrial Designers (1955–56), as director (s. 1956). In 1957, he and Robert W. Blee designed a new Kitchen Center for GE. The nine-foot-long grouping included a combination washer/dryer, a disposal-equipped sink, a dishwasher and a range with oven—all under a single, seamless stainless-steel countertop. By 1965, he had a staff of 45 in Louisville. General Electric opened a new Applied Research and Design Center in 1971 in Louisville for major appliances, which included the Industrial Design Operation and a staff of 50 under Arthur's direction. He remained there until his retirement in 1976.

Antonin Heythum (1901–1954), b. Most, Bohemia, was a noted Czech architect, scenographer, and furniture designer. In 1924, he studied architecture, civil engineering and ship construction at the Czech Technical University in Prague. He joined the Devětsil art association and took part in the beginnings of the Liberated Theater, where he worked as a set designer from 1924 to 1925. He became famous for his projects at the national glass exhibition in Prague in 1933 and in the exhibition pavilions at the World's Fair in Brussels from 1934 to 1935. For the World's Fair in Paris in 1937, Heythum created a glass department for exhibits of 120 Czechoslovak glass companies. In 1938, Heythum left for the USA to prepare a Czechoslovak pavilion with Kamil Roškot for the world exhibition in New York planned for the years (1939–40) and for the exhibition in San Francisco. After the outbreak of World War II, he remained in the United States. In 1940, the Heythums held a showcase of his work at Columbia University in New York. The exhibition was incomplete due to the circumstances, yet on the basis of it, the President of California Tech in Pasadena offered Heythum a place at the school, which he accepted. He founded the Department of Industrial Design at the school and obtained the title of professor. In 1945 he still worked at Columbia University as a professor of architecture. Since 1946, he was a professor of industrial design at Syracuse Univ. and other places. He was co-author of book *Design for Use* (1944).

VIII. CULTURE: ARTS & LETTERS

Leo A. Jiranek (1901–1990), b. Grand Rapids, MI, of Czech ancestry, graduated from Princeton Univ. He was a furniture and interior designer. He had been in the furniture business for 62 years and had contributed designs to many furniture companies. He was a consultant to Ethan Allen, Inc., Danbury, CT until his death. He founded and served as first president of the American Designers Inst., now the Industrial Designers Soc. of America. In the 1960s, he founded and was president of the Jiranek School of Furniture Design and Technology in Manhattan, NYC.

Jeffrey Kapec (1950–), b. Jersey City, NJ, of Czech ancestry, graduated with honors from Pratt Institute, receiving a Bachelor of Industrial Design (1972). He started his career with Montalbano Development, as a senior designer, promoted to project manager (1972–76), human factors industrial design project director and designer (1976–80). In 1980, he co-founded Tanaka Kapec Design Group, Inc. (TKDG), a full-service engineering design and industrial design consulting firm, of which he is a Principal and Executive Vice President. He has more than 44 years industrial design and consulting and strategic product development experience in medical instrument design, including orthopedic instrument design and other surgical instruments, medical diagnostic equipment, pharmaceutical packaging, drug delivery systems, technical instruments, office equipment, office furniture design, and consumer products. He is also a professor in the Industrial Design Department at Pratt Institute, Brooklyn, NY, and is actively involved in numerous professional design organizations, including the IDSA, Human Factor and Ergonomics Society, Rowena Reed Kostellow Fund and Core77. He is a primary inventor and co-inventor of 40 US utility patents, 6 patents currently pending, 10 international utility patents and recipient of numerous international design awards. Jeffrey has published articles on industrial design, ergonomics, advanced manufacturing technology, medical packaging, bio-materials and design applications. In addition, he has been engaged as an expert witness in civil cases that involved patent litigation and design patent infringement.

Joseph Koncelik (1940–), b. Islip, NY, of Czech descent, studied industrial design at Pratt Inst. (B.I.D., 1961), received M.A. degree in arts at Stanford in 1963 and did postgraduate research at Royal College of Art in Great Britain (1965–66). He is a professor emeritus in the Department of Industrial, Interior and Visual Communication Design at College of the Arts, the Ohio State University; and retired professor of industrial design, College of Architecture, Georgia Institute of Technology. Formerly he was director, Center for Assistive Technology and Environmental Access and professor of industrial design, College of Architecture, and interim director, Advanced Wood Products Laboratory, 1995–2001, Georgia Institute of Technology. He was professor of industrial design, the Ohio State University (1973–95) and vice president for research and development, Zoetech Corporation (1990–95); assistant professor, Department of Design and Environmental

Analysis, Cornell University (1966-73); president, Design and Research Services, Inc. (1978-83). He is the author of two books: *Designing the Open Nursing Home* (1976) and *Aging and the Product Environment* (1983), covering research and design development related to issues in gerontology. Koncelik is the recipient of the IBD Silver Medal in 1980, Designer's Choice Award in 1981, NEA Grants Recognition in 1980, and the NEA Outstanding Research in Design Award in 1983.

Francis (Frank) A. Ruzicka (1924-2003), b. Chicago, of Czech ancestry, was raised in Racine, WI. He studied engineering at the University of Michigan. He served in the United States Marine Corps during World War II and completed his Bachelor's degree in 1946. After working as an engineer, he returned to school and earned a BFA in drawing and painting from the Art Institute of Chicago. Following a teaching assignment at the University of Wisconsin, he joined the faculty of Parsons School of Design in 1957, and taught drawing in the Design in Industry and Editorial and Fashion Illustration departments. While teaching at Parsons, he earned an MFA in painting (1963) and an MS in art education (1965) from the Pratt Institute in Brooklyn. Ruzicka served as an assistant dean and an administrative dean before becoming president of Parsons School of Design in 1963 and served until 1969. After leaving Parsons, Ruzicka became dean at Ohio State University's College of the Arts and, in 1976, was elected chair of the Lamar Dodd School of Art at the University of Georgia, Athens. He retired in 1993.

Eva Striker Zeisel (1906-2011), b. Budapest, Hungary, of Slovak ancestry was an industrial designer. She immigrated to the US in 1938. She was known for her work with ceramics, especially from the period after she immigrated to the US. She was 'maker of useful things,' as she called herself. Her forms are often abstractions of the natural world and human relationships. Work from throughout her prodigious career is included in important museum collections across the world. To support her painting, she decided to pursue a more practical profession and apprenticed herself to Jakob Karapancsik, the last pottery master in the medieval guild system. From him she learned ceramics. Though best known for her ceramics, she also worked in glass, wood, metal and plastics. Eva was imprisoned under Stalin, had the first one-woman show at MoMA and was honored at the White House, with many adventures in-between. She continued designing until she died at 105 years old in 2011. Her work is in permanent collections of major museums around the world, including the British Museum, MoMA and The Metropolitan Museum of Art.

9. Photographers

Adam Bouska (1983-), b. Decatur, IL, of Czech ancestry, is an award-winning American fashion photographer who runs a photography studio based out of West Hollywood, California. Known for pictures of male models in particular, he is considered a rising 'superstar photographer' in the gay community. Bouska is most recognized for co-creation of the internationally recognized NOH8 Campaign. In addition to his published work, Bouska has made appearances on TV shows including: *Running Russell Simmons, Giuliana & Bill, Keeping Up with the Kardashians, The Real Housewives of Orange County, The Millionaire Matchmaker, Million Dollar Listing, The World According to Paris, Hollywood Exes, Mel B: It's a Scary World*, and *Dog the Bounty Hunter*.

Talisman Brolin (ca. 1982–), b. New York, NY, of Bohemian and Slovak descent, trained as a cultural anthropologist, is a commercial and documentary photographer with background in photojournalism. She has been owner, photographer, Talisman PHOTO LLC, NYC (s. 2004); co-founder / owner, Top Floor White Door, NYC (s. 2016).

Sonja Bullaty (1924–2000), b. Prague, a Holocaust survivor, was a photographer noted for lyrical composition and startling use of color and light in a vast body of work created during a five-decade collaboration with her husband, Angelo Lomeo.

Vladimír Chaloupka, b. Prague, Czech., a still photographer, is an experienced photojournalist with a number of associated press awards. He lived in Seattle, WA, but now he is based in Santa Fe, NM.

Yuri Dojc (1946–), b. Humenné, Czech., is a Slovak Canadian fine arts photographer known for his portraits of Slovak World War II veterans from his Last Folio project. Yuri Dojc left Czechoslovakia in 1968 when Soviet tanks rolled into Prague. He settled in Toronto, where he embarked on a four-decade journey from refugee to internationally acclaimed photographer. His work is included in the collections of the National Gallery of Canada and the Slovak National Museum. The Library of Congress in Washington recently acquired a number of selections for its photography collection. In 2001, he received the Medal of Honor from the Slovak Ambassador to the United States for *We Endured*, a series of portraits of Slovak Holocaust survivors. Dojc has been profiled in dozens of magazines around the world, including Communication Arts, Applied Arts and Creativity, and he has been the subject of feature stories on both Apple and Microsoft's websites. In 2010, Dojc published his sixth solo book, *Honour,* which pays homage to Canadian World War II veterans, and a retrospective of his work was exhibited at Bratislava's Mirbach Palace. Dojc's *Last Folio* exhibition opened at the Museum of Jewish Heritage in New York City in March 2011. It had since been seen in numerous other venues on both sides of the Atlantic.

Helena Kolda Ducháček (1928–1997), b. Brno, Czech., was a photographer and video artist, residing in NYC.

Jan Faul (1945–), b. Port Chester, NY, of Czech father, is a photographer who has developed and explored many styles professionally but is now specializing in panoramic landscape photography, with a focus on American Civil War National Battlefields, World War II Military Airfields of East Anglia, and the environment in Scotland's Highlands and Western Isles. Jan's first job was as Chief Photographer for the Office of Economic Opportunity. While at OEO, he traveled across America portraying the poor. Following his year at OEO, he moved to the Appalachian Regional Commission for two years. Concurrently with the ARC assignments, he was on contract to *Time* magazine. In 1979, he moved to Denmark and there, his work took him all over Scandinavia and Europe. During this period, he traveled extensively while doing photography for advertising. He returned to the US after a decade. In March 1993, he began a two-month residency at Yaddo and developed new styles. In 1994–95, Jan was awarded a grant from the Graham Foundation to photograph disappearing family farms in Waukesha County Wisconsin. Thereafter, he worked mostly on 'scapes' of New England, as well as California and the West. By 1996, his landscapes more specifically had become panoramic. In 1996, he began working on American Civil War battlefields stretching from Pennsylvania to New Mexico and continues to shoot these places today.

Fred Fehl (1906–1995), b. Vienna, of Moravian ancestry, was an American photographer of Viennese upbringing. He was the first person in America to make a career of performance photography, for over forty years he covered Broadway as well as dance, opera, and music. His pictures have appeared in *The New York Times*, major national magazines, and in hundreds of books on theater, dance, and music. Fehl took photographs of over 1,000 Broadway plays.

Frank Freedle (ca. 1854–1911), b. Bohemia, was a professional photographer in Cleveland. He was the founder and proprietor of the firm Freedle & Brother.

Eva Fuka (née Podešvová) (1927–2015) was a Czech-American photographer whose artwork is characterized by surreal and melancholic effects, which she achieved by using her environment to create unreal settings with a dreamlike atmosphere. She ranks among the founding figures of Czech photography who introduced different approaches to the practice.

Tibor Gasparik (1922–1993), b. of Slovak descent, was a photographer, Cleveland, OH.

Anita H. Grosz (1955–), b. Warren, PA, of Czech father, trained as a lawyer, was a photographer and an artist. She was awarded a Bachelor of Arts in psychology in 1978 from Indiana University (IU), Bloomington and a Juris Doctor in 1987, Honors from Benjamin Cardozo School of Law, New York, where she was on the Moot Court Board and participated in the Alternative Dispute Resolution Clinic and was editor-in-chief of the

Cardozo Law Forum. She also is a recipient of the Master's degree in photography and multimedia (MPhil, 2016). Before moving to the UK in 1987, she lived in New York City and practiced intellectual property law. During this period, as a volunteer lawyer, she assisted artists with a variety of needs. At night, she was sculpting at the Arts Student League. While in NYC, she also practiced criminal law with the Brooklyn District Attorney's Office. Part of her law preparation involved working with a publishing attorney, a District Court Judge, the US Attorney's Office (fraud, art theft), and the Strike Force Against Organized Crime. Before 1985, she lived in Chicago, working as a research assistant in a law and economics firm and studied photography at night at the SAIC. She was involved in a number of exhibitions, participated in theatre productions, and assisted in filmmaking. She also trained individuals in testing techniques in the field of neuropsychology. Prior to returning to photography as an art form, Anita has worked with ceramics and sculpture. Occasionally these art forms merge together to express Anita's message.

Bedřich Grünzweig (1910–2009), b. Prague, Bohemia, following university studies and service in the Czech army, he took an administrative post in a sugar mill. In 1939, he escaped from Nazi-occupied Czechoslovakia. Arriving in the U.S., he settled permanently in New York City, whose architectural forms, visual excitement and relentless pace would inform and inspire his photography throughout his life. Following a job at the Czech Pavilion of the 1939 World's Fair and service with the wartime Czech government-in-exile, he joined the newly formed United Nations where he worked until his retirement in 1974. In each case, he worked in the field of communications, media and public information. Since the 1940s, Bedřich Grunzweig had been photographing life in a wide range of locations, with a particular interest in his adopted hometown, New York City. His best-known images include *Between Heaven and Earth*, a spectacular shot of a window cleaner at the United Nations building which won *U.S. Camera* magazine's first prize in 1951, as well as being published in *Popular Photography*'s 1952 Annual and in the 1952 Annual of American Photography. In 1964, he won the Saturday Review first prize for his photograph of architect Eero Saarinen's ground breaking TWA Terminal at Kennedy Airport. In 1973, his work was exhibited at the solo show "Return to Prague: A Personal Sojourn" at the Jewish Museum in New York City and at the Koffler Centre for the Arts in Toronto. Grunzweig returned to Prague, the city of his birth, three times between 1969 and 1983 and again in 1991 and in 1998. This last visit marked the opening of the one-man retrospective show "Between Heaven and Earth," Grunzweig's first exhibit in the city of his birth. In addition to documenting life in New York City, Grunzweig traveled and photographed in diverse locations, including the American Rockies, Congo, Czech Republic, Israel, Vermont, Toronto, Mexico, and more.

Alexandr Hackenschmied (1907–2004), b. Linz, but grew up and lived in Prague, Czech. He was a leading photographer, film director, cinematographer, and editor in Czechoslovakia between the two world wars. He immigrated to the U.S. in 1938 and became involved in American avant-garde cinema.

James Hajicek (1947–), b. St. Paul, MN, of Czech ancestry, received his B.F.A. from the Kansas City Art Institute (1970) and his M.F.A. from the University of New Mexico (1978). He is a professor emeritus at Arizona State University where he taught fine art photography for 34 years. His area of specialization is late 19th century photographic printing processes. His work has been exhibited internationally over the last thirty years and can be found in many significant public collections including the International Museum of Photography at the George Eastman House, Rochester, New York, the San Francisco Museum of Modern Art, and the Bibliotheque Nationale, Paris, France. He is presently co-director of Alchemy-Studio.net and directs art and photography workshops in Tuscany, Italy.

Leo Millard Holub (1916–2010), b. Decatur, AR, of Bohemian ancestry, was an artist trained at the Art Inst of Chicago. He was famous for his landscapes and architectural images of San Francisco, and photographs of Yosemite. His contemporaries and close friends included Ansel Adams and Imogen Cunningham. Throughout his career, Holub worked in various design firms, advertising agencies, and print shops throughout the Bay Area. He also taught drawing at the California School of Fine Arts, and in 1960, he took a job in the University Planning Office at Stanford University. In 1969, Holub founded the photography program in the Department of Art and built the University's first darkroom. For the next decade, Holub taught classes in photography until he retired as a senior lecturer emeritus in 1980.

Following his decade-long career as a professor, Holub left Stanford University to pursue work as a freelance photographer and typographic designer. In 1986, Bay Area collectors Harry W. and Mary Margaret Anderson commissioned Holub to photograph numerous American artists represented in their private collection. He traveled to San Francisco, New Mexico, and New York, capturing portraits of artists such as Frank Stella, Roy Lichtenstein, and Robert Rauschenberg at their homes and studios. Over the course of a decade, Holub photographed more than 100 individuals, making this project one of his most exhaustive efforts.

Robert Hupka (1919–2001), b. Vienna, of Moravian ancestry, was a recording engineer for RCA and later for Columbia Records and, until his retirement, a cameraman for CBS Television in New York. He emigrated to the U.S. at the onset of World War II to escape the Nazi persecution which took his parents' lives. His grandfather was the composer Ignaz Brüll, a native of Moravia, who was a friend of Brahms. Hupka took thousands of photographs, secretly or not, of conductor Arturo Toscanini while Toscanini was leading the NBC Symphony Orchestra. The greatest of these were published in the book *This Was*

Toscanini (1963) accompanying an uncompleted essay by Samuel Antek, a violinist in the NBC Symphony. Photos of Toscanini, taken by Hupka, were used as set pieces in the television show, *The Odd Couple*; the photos can be seen in Felix Unger's bedroom. In the late 1980s, he worked with engineers at NBC International on the audio/video synchronization of the Toscanini telecasts, which were finally issued by BMG/RCA in the early 1990s. Hupka was also the author of *Michelangelo: Pieta*, a collection of a hundred photographs, from various angles and with different lighting, of Michelangelo's Pieta, taken in 1964 when this sculpture was exhibited at the New York World's Fair.

Paul Ickovic (1944–2023), b. England, of Czech parents, is a photographer. He makes his home on the East Coast but has traveled the world carrying a concealed camera to capture emotionally laden pictures of people, places, and their interactions. He concentrates on ordinary people in ordinary neighborhoods and his photographs 'capture a quiet, bleak poetry of place, and find hope and humor in images of children in gritty city spaces.'

Fred Iltis (1923–2008), b. Brno, Czech., an American entomologist, was also an exceptional photographer. Many photos of his vast archive are about the Civil rights movement in the 60s, the student protest against the Vietnam War, the struggle of the Chicano agricultural workers led by César Chávez and Dolores Huerta, the strikes and boycott of the American fruit companies. In his journeys south of the border, he portrayed the life of the Mexican Indians, particularly in Michoacán. Fred developed and printed his photos using the slow and complicated archival process system, by which the prints can last for many decades.

Patrik Jandak (1977–), b. Malacky, Czech., is a Slovak photographer, residing in Canada s. 2005. After first year at University, he went to England where he purchased his first camera. During his stay in the United Kingdom, he became a member of Windsor Photographic Society. In 1998, he started to study photography in London. In 2000, he returned to Slovakia and few months later, he got a job as a photo lab assistant in Bratislava which eventually led him to the position of the official photographer of the president of Slovakia, Rudolf Schuster. Since December 2001 till June 2004, he worked as official photographer to President of Slovakia Rudolf Schuster and since June 2004 till April 2005, as photographer of Slovak President Ivan Gasparovic. In Canada, he transformed from documentary photographer to studio portrait and Fine Art nude photographer. In October 2010, he started publishing monthly photography magazine *PH Magazine*.

Charles B. Kaufmann (1881–d.), b. Humpolec, Moravia, was a commercial photographer. He was president of Kaufmann and Fabry Co. Photographers, Chicago (s. 1908). Charles Kaufmann and Herman Fabry opened their first studio together in 1903, becoming one of the staples of Chicago's documentary and news related photo services. Many of their images included large panoramas of the city as well as many photos of the Chicago Cubs and Chicago White Sox teams. Charles Kaufmann served as president of the National Commercial Photographers Assn.

Edward Klauber (1835–1918), b. Bohemia, was a professional photographer and Daguerreian artist. He settled in Louisville, KY and established a photo studio there. His studio had been compared to that of Matthew Beatty at New York City, lavishly furnished, which was popular with stage performers, who said to have preferred Klauber portraits to all others. The Fils Club has many examples of his documentary photographs of bridges, locks and dams. Klauber also did the documentary work for the Kentucky Geological Survey and made the portraits of prominent Louisvillians that appeared in *Louisiville Past and Present* (1875).

Russell Lee Klika (1960–), b. Appleton, WI, of Czech ancestry, US Army Staff Sergeant, is a self-taught photojournalist. At age 17, he joined the Marines to become a machine gunner. Soon after, he purchased a 35mm film camera on a whim. The strength of his photos earned him a spot in the Eddie Adams Experience in Photojournalism workshop where he was the first military photographer to attend. In 1990, Klika transitioned from the Marines to the civilian world and was assigned to several large newspapers on both US coasts. As a civilian photojournalist, he has covered a myriad of events including daring military aerial maneuvers and the emotionally charged LA riots. In 2003, Klika returned to the military and volunteered for two tours in Iraq, both with the Tennessee Army National Guard where he served as NCOIC of Public Affairs, 278th Armored Cavalry Regiment and later as a Team Leader, for the 133rd Mobile Public Affairs Detachment. He credits his close personal relationships with his comrades as what allowed him to return with a wealth of powerful and compelling images from the frontlines. Klika is the recipient of over 50 First Place honors and Best of Show Designations; his work has been featured in over 35 magazines, newspapers and web-based galleries worldwide, to include *TIME*, *Newsweek*, *NY* and *LA Times*, *World Literature Today*, *American Photo*, *French Photo* and *Soldier of Fortune*. He is also a frequent contributor to the *Guard Experience* magazine. Upon his return from Iraq, Klika was assigned as a photography trainer to First Army Operation Warrior Trainer program for Public Affairs where he mentored other military photographers.

Joe (Jozef) Klamár (1965–), b. Jasná, Slovakia. Emigrated in 1987 to Canada. Photographer for the Canadian Press Agency, the Slovak Press Agency TASR and Reuters. He returned to Slovakia in 1998 and since 2012, lives in Los Angeles and works for the French company Agence France Presse. His specialties include political events, memorial celebrations, and celebrities.

Robert Jay Kositchek, Jr. (1952–), b. Santa Monica, CA, of Bohemian ancestry; Director of photography, teacher of cinematography.

Antonín Kratochvíl (1947–), b. Lovosice, Czech., is one of the finest world's photojournalists. He gained a BFA in Photography from Gerrit Rietveld Academie, Amsterdam. He is a founding member of VII, the esteemed cooperative picture agency. As a photojournalist, he has tackled a good deal of upheaval and human catastrophe, whilst going about his documentation of the times in which we live. His own refugee life has in many ways reflected what he has rendered on film. Over the years, Kratochvil's unconventional work has ranged from photographing Mongolian street children to a portrait session with David Bowie; from covering the war in Iraq for *Fortune* magazine to shooting pictures of Deborah Harry for an American Civil Liberties Union campaign. His work has appeared in a range of top-ranking international magazines and newspapers, and he has brought out five books of his own. Among his array of awards are a Lucie Award for Outstanding Achievement in Photojournalism, a Leica Medal of Excellence, and three World Press Photo first prizes.

Vilém Francis Kříž (1921–1994) b. Prague, Bohemia, was a photographer. When Kriz was fourteen, his father gave him a large format Linhoff camera, which he continued to use throughout his career. He later attended the State Graphic School in Prague (1940–46), where he was exposed to the methods and philosophy of surrealism and studied under leading Czech photographers Jaromír Funke, Josef Ehm, and František Drtikol. He continued to explore the possibilities of surrealism, even after it ceased to be fashionable. In 1946, after World War II, Kriz moved to Paris, a vibrant site of creative activity for photographers throughout the 1930s and 1940s, where he befriended Jean Cocteau. There he focused his lens on the ruined forms of the city and worn, discarded objects, portraying dreamlike aspects of the world around him. In 1952, Kriz immigrated to the United States with his wife and son to Berkeley, California, and then to New York. For the next decade he made very few photographs. It was only in 1964, after moving back to Berkeley and starting to teach at California College of Art and Crafts in Oakland, that he returned to photography in earnest. Unlike in Paris, where he sought out the fantastical in an urban environment, in the later period of his career, Kriz devoted himself to photographing small surrealist constructions he made at home or in his backyard.

In images representative of this later period, such as the two untitled works in the MoCP's collection, Kriz combined various objects and found materials to create tightly framed, enigmatic compositions. He printed these photographs on eleven by fourteen-inch paper and individually toned his prints with custom solutions. Several monographs of Vilem Kriz's work have been published, including *Surrealism and Symbolism* (1971), *Sirague City: Photographs* (1975), *Séance* (1979), Vilem Kriz, Photographs (1979), and *Vilem Kriz Photographs* (1999).

David Kruta (1986–), b. Nuremberg, Germany, of Czech political refugee parents, is an award-winning self- taught photographer, specializing in high-speed photography. David Kruta's lifetime has taken him through a variety of cultures, experiences and locations spanning the globe, naturally bringing him to New York City to fulfill his passion for cinematography and storytelling. David's career in the arts included not only still and moving pictures, but also the culinary arts, graphic design and fine art — all of which have inspired him to create cutting-edge visuals in his pursuit for the perfect image. David has shot short films, commercials, documentaries, fashion and music videos and feature films. David has an extensive list of clients, including Porsche, Mizuno, Canon, Gilette, Starbucks, Sony, Amtrak, Bose and Penske, and is always on the lookout for new and interesting projects.

Jan Lukas (1915–2006), b. České Budějovice, Bohemia, was a legendary Czech photographer who moved to the US in 1966. From 1946 to 1948, he was editor of the magazines *Sobota* and *Pramen*, and after that he worked as a freelance photographer. His works include photojournalism conceived in a humanistic tone, travel snapshot, landscape photography, portraits and photos of Braun's sculpture work. In his snapshots, he frequently and successfully used striking details, and less traditional pictorial composition. From 1967, he lived in New York City. Lukas's work gained notable attention again in the 1990s when his exhibitions were held in the Prague Mánes gallery (1995), in the Czech Center in New York (1998), and also when the Prague publishing house Torst issued his book *Pražský deník 1938-1965* (A Prague Journal 1938–1965) in 1995. His American portfolio consisted of twenty-five albums, not including translated versions, new editions, or his participation in group projects.

Vivian Maier (1926–2009), b. Bronx, NY, of Slovak descent; an American street photographer. She took more than 150,000 photographs during her lifetime, primarily of the people and architecture of Chicago, New York City, and Los Angeles, although she also traveled and photographed worldwide. Her life and work have been the subject of books and documentary films, including the film *Finding Vivian Maier* (2013), which premiered at the Toronto International Film Festival, and was nominated for the Academy Award for Best Documentary Feature at the 87th Academy Awards.

Duane Michals (1932–), b. Mc. Keesport, PA, of Slovak ancestry; American photographer. Michals's work makes innovative use of photo-sequences, often incorporating text to examine emotion and philosophy.

Joseph W. Molitor (1907–1996), b. US, of Czech ancestry, is recognized as one of the leading 20th-century American architectural photographers. Molitor turned exclusively to architectural photography in the late 1940s, maintaining his studio in suburban Westchester County, New York. Working primarily in black and white, Molitor's images appeared in *Architectural Record, The New York Times, House & Home,* and other national and international publications. His iconic photograph of a walkway at architect Paul Rudolph's high school in Sarasota, Florida, won first place in the black and white section of the American Institute of Architects' architectural photography awards in 1960. He served several terms as president of the Architectural Photographers Association and published *Architectural Photography in* 1976, a guide to photographing the built environment that included many examples of his own work. Molitor retired from practice in the mid-1980s.

Sylvia Plachy (1943–), from Budapest, of Bohemian Jewish mother, is a notable American photographer. Plachy's work has been featured in many New York city magazines and newspapers and she was an influential staff photographer for the *Village Voice.* Plachy's first book, *Sylvia Plachy's Unguided Tour,* won the Infinity Award from the International Center of Photography for best publication in 1991.

Anita Lily Pollitzer (1894–1975), b. Charleston, SC, of Czech ancestry, was an American photographer. Pollitzer may be best known for her friendship with Georgia O'Keeffe whom she met at Columbia University. Pollitzer introduced O'Keeffe to Alfred Stieglitz helping to forge one of the most significant artist relationships in the 20th century.

Frank Powolny (1902–1986), b. Vienna, of Czech ancestry, was the photographer who snapped the famous World War II swimsuit picture of Betty Grable. As head portrait and still photographer at 20th Century-Fox, and a predecessor company, from 1923 to 1966, Mr. Powolny captured thousands of stars in photos that ended up in newspapers, magazines and theater lobbies around the world. His subjects included Janet Gaynor, Tom Mix, Shirley Temple, Lana Turner, Gene Tierney, Humphrey Bogart, Bing Crosby, Jennifer Jones, Joan Collins and Ann-Margret. In 1962, Mr. Powolny took the last known still photographs of Marilyn Monroe on the set of *Something's Got to Give,* a week before her death. But he was best known for the pin-up of Miss Grable that many G.I.'s carried during World War II. The photo showed the actress in swimsuit and pumps, peeking coyly over her shoulder. He lived in Newbury Park, CA. During this long period, he photographed thousands of Hollywood actors, and is often referred to as "the greatest Hollywood photographer of all time."

Ernst Raba (1874–1951), b. Frýdlant, Bohemia, where he received training as an apprentice photographer, came to San Antonio in 1891. Before the turn of the century, he opened his own studio and established himself as a portrait photographer of some merit. He not only collected photographs of his subjects, but also of the city that he loved, focusing on its unique buildings, plazas, and streetscapes.

Emiline Royco Ott, b. St. Louis, MO, of Slovak parents; photographer, residing in Chevy Chase, MD.

Johnny Rozsa (1949–), b. Nairobi, of Jewish Czech parents, is a New York-based photographer, specializing in fashion, portrait, and celebrity photography. Rozsa studied architecture, painting, and communications at Manchester College of Art and Design, and communications at Polytechnic of Central London. Afterwards, he interned at *Vogue* under Barney Wan. He later ran a vintage shop called Nostalgia in Covent Garden, where he met fashion editors, models, actors, and photographers on a daily basis. In the late 1970s Rozsa began his photography career, working in Nairobi, Kenya, London, England and the U.S. By 1978, he had a series of four full-page celebrity portraits in *Ritz*, with accompanying interviews. Johnny Rozsa collaborated with top Japanese hairstylist Fumio Kawashima, who is the owner of Peek A-Boo salons in Tokyo, on six published books shot in different locations including Los Angeles, New York, Rio de Janeiro and London. Rozsa has been photographing celebrities such as Hugh Grant, Halle Berry, Nicolas Cage, John Malkovich, and Natasha Richardson since the late 1970s. His photographs have appeared in numerous publications, including *Vogue*, the *Sunday Times*, *The Observer i-D*, *Maxim*, *The Face*, *The New York Times*, and *People*. In 2010, Rozsa published a book, *Untouched*, featuring unretouched photos of 115 now world-famous celebrities, from their days before airbrushing, Photoshop, digital cameras and enhancements, cosmetic surgery, and perfect images.

Drahomír Růžička (1870–1960), b. Trhová Kamenice, Bohemia, trained as a physician, became a photographer. He came from a Czech family that immigrated to the United States in 1876. He studied medicine at the University of Vienna and finished his studies in New York. In 1894, he opened his own private medical practice in New York. He started to photograph intensively in 1909, took a course in photography with Clarence Hudson White, and in 1916, became a founding member of the Pictorial Photographers of America. From 1921 to 1923, he lived in Czechoslovakia where he helped his family. Later, he returned to Czechoslovakia regularly until 1936. His exhibition in Prague in 1921, where he exclusively exhibited straight photographs without the use of pigment processes, influenced a number of Czech photographers. His earlier work, emphasizing a luminous atmosphere and soft drawing, belongs among the most marked examples of purist Pictorialism. His photographs, which were inspired by the beautiful nature of Central Park, became very popular. He got acquainted with photographic technique when he was getting acquainted with roentgen apparatus which he used in his medical practice.

VIII. CULTURE: ARTS & LETTERS

Alice Schalek (1874–1956), a native of Vienna of Bohemian parents, made a name for herself as Austria's first female war photographer during World War I and went onto a stunning career as a photojournalist and travel writer. She continued to travel after the War but, in 1939, after being arrested by Gestapo, succeeded in escaping to New York.

William Schleisner (1912–1962), b. Baltimore, of Bohemian ancestry, was a noted photographer of architecture and a partner of the Gottscho-Schleisner photography firm. Mr. Schleisner's photographs survived in a number of collections around the country.

Věra Prášilová Scott (1899–1996), b. Kutná Hora, Bohemia, worked as a stills photographer for Lasky Famous Players in New York. After relocating to Houston in 1926, she opened and operated her photography studio on San Jacinto St. which soon became well known for her portraits, whose highlights and shadows, finished in oil or gum print have the effect of rich charcoal. Her subjects were not posed in a 'look pleasant' stereotype, but their moods are caught and held and veiled just enough to capture their allurement.

Peter Sramek (1951–), b. Toronto, Ont., of Czech ancestry, has been a photographic artist for over 38 years. He studied photography at the Massachusetts Institute of Technology under Minor White and has taught at the Ontario College of Art & Design University since 1976. Over this time, his administrative roles at OCAD U, in addition to the Chair of Photography and of Cross-Disciplinary Art Practices, have included Associate and Assistant Dean positions and Acting Dean in the Faculty of Art. As a founding member in 1979 of Gallery 44 Centre for Contemporary Photography in Toronto and as its Financial Coordinator for 15 years, Sramek has contributed considerably to the Canadian photography community. His photographic practice spans many interests, from history, to urban spaces, to social and gender issues and the aesthetics of everyday life. Handmade artist books form a portion of his output. Walking as a meditative and observational practice has resulted in a series of small books from different world cities, as well as a series of panoramas taken over a 300 km walk through the countryside of Japan. His work incorporates photography, digital imaging, hand-binding, and video installation.

Julian H. Stein (1885–1937), b. Milwaukee, WI, of Bohemian father, was a professional photographer in Milwaukee, WI. He was associated with father in conducting Stein Studios, taking over management upon the death of his father. He won 34 medals and cups in national and state conventions.

Simon Leonard Stein (1854–1922), b. Mariánské Lázně, Bohemia, first located in Chicago but in 1873, established residency in Milwaukee, WI. He took up profession of portrait photography and became a well-known Milwaukee portrait photographer. He was winner of twenty-nine cups at national and international expositions. He was presiding judge of liberal arts at Pan Am Exposition in San Francisco and elected twice president of Photographers Assn. of America. In conjunction with the Wisconsin Historical Society, he established a collection of leading Wisconsin citizens with detailed biographical information for the use by genealogists, and historians, which has been preserved. Prior to his death, he donated a total 382 portraits. His son, Julian, who took over the establishment, continued his father's work, contributing another 47 to the collection.

Ralph Steiner (1899-1986), b. Cleveland, OH, of Bohemian ancestry, was an American photographer, pioneer documentarian and a key figure among avant-garde filmmakers in the 1930s.

Ian Stendal (1913-1992), b. Prague, Bohemia, was a famous American photographer, who initially immigrated to Canada, but eventually settled in Los Angeles. Stendal became fascinated by Los Angeles street life and turned his lens toward capturing the vast diversity of life he found in the city. Much of his street photography is marked by a brightness and vitality unusual in that art form and he was one of the few street photographers to embrace Kodachrome film, eschewing the black and white standard to celebrate the vigor and energy of California life.

Lynn Stern (1942-), b. New York, NY, of Bohemian ancestry, is a photographer. She began to pursue photography as a career in the late 1970s. She creates black and white photographs highlighting natural light. The central concern in Stern's work is luminosity. Five books of Stern's work have been published: *Unveilings* (1988), *Dispossession* (1995), *Animus* (2000), *Veiled Still Lifes* (2006) and *Frozen Mystery* (2010), which accompanied her retrospective exhibition at the Museo Fundación Cristóbal Gabarrón in Spain.

George Stoklas (1902-1979), b. Vamberk, Bohemia, was a professional photographer, who studied at New York Institute of Photography. From 1934 to 1944, he managed his own photo studio. From 1948, he was the owner of Embassy Camera Center, Washington, DC. Upon his retirement, his son, George Stoklas, Jr. took over.

Paul Strand (orig. Stransky) (1890-1976), a New Yorker, of Bohemian-Jewish parents, was one of the most important figures in American twentieth-century photography. In the 1930s, he became seriously involved with documentary film and, from the 1940s until the end of his life, he was committed to making photographic books of the highest quality.

Antonín Štupl (1834-1917), b. Mnichovo Hradiště, Bohemia, was a pioneer portrait photographer in Texas. He trained as a tinsmith before coming to the United States with his family in 1852. After arriving in Galveston on December 1 of that year, they traveled to Cat Spring in Austin County, where they joined a friend who had settled there six months previously. Stupl helped on the family farm until the Civil War, when he and his three brothers were forced to join the Twentieth Regiment of Texas Infantry. They helped to defend Galveston from Union forces for two years. The Stupl brothers and several other Czechs subsequently deserted the Confederate Army while on leave. Although they were captured, they later succeeded in eluding Confederate forces and found refuge in Austin County until the end of the war. After the war, Stupl farmed with his family until 1870, when he traveled to Bohemia to study photography for a year. Upon his return to the United States, he helped on the family farm until one of his brothers died, at which time he established a photography studio in Brenham. Between 1872 and 1883, he lived in Industry, where he was a very successful portrait photographer. He worked primarily in the inexpensive tintype medium and supplemented his income by raising and selling tobacco and making cigars.

Albert F. Svasek (1900-1960), b. Baltimore, of Bohemian ancestry, was a veteran *Sunday American* and *News-Post* photographer.

Arthur Taussig (aka Harry A. Taussig) (1941-), b. Los Angeles, of Bohemian ancestry, is a physicist, biophysicist, collage artist, photographer, film analyst, author, and fingerstyle guitarist. Prior to his career in visual arts, Taussig worked as a physicist and musician. He began studying art and photography in 1964. In 1967, he made his first limited edition solo recording, *Fate Is Only Once* (which has since been reissued on Tompkins Square records). While doing advanced studies at the UCLA Brain Research Institute, he continued his studies in photography with Robert Heinecken and Robert Fichter. He received his Master's in Biochemistry and a Doctorate in Biophysics in 1971 while beginning to exhibit his photography internationally. He accepted a teaching position in Photography at Orange Coast College where he later also taught film. The Robert Freidus Gallery in New York City represented his photographs and placed them with many collectors and museums. Taussig's work has been included in over 300 exhibitions worldwide and in 1982, he received the National Endowment of the Arts Visual Artist's Grant. Currently, in addition to continuing his photographic works, he has produced a series of illuminated books of classic works: Dante's *The Divine Comedy*, James Joyce's *Ulysses*, Shakespeare's *Hamlet,* and so on. Taussig has also embarked on a series of collage works based on Jungian Psychology: Alex's *Adventures in the Five Rivers of the Underworld* and Alice's *Alchemical Adventures*. In this vein, he has done what he calls "a 21st century" set of Tarot Cards.

Marie Tomanová (1984-), b. Czech., is New York-based photographer. She received BFA in Studio Art from Masaryk University in 2007 and MFA in Painting from Faculty of Fine Arts at University of Technology, Czech Republic in 2010. After finishing her studies, she left to United States and currently lives and works in NYC. Since then, her work has changed dramatically in approach, mediums, and themes. She has been dealing with issues of displacement, identity, inclusivity, gender, and sexuality through photography and video in her current two main projects: photo-based *Self-portraits*, in which she addresses the issue of displacement and finding place in the American landscape and *Young American*, which was released as a solo show at Czech Center New York (2018) and addresses issues of displacement, belonging and fitting into the American landscape in a social aspect.

Rudolph Adams Torovsky (1897–1990), b. Annapolis, MD, of Bohemian father, was a medical photographer of note for the St. Elizabeth Hospital, Washington, DC.

John Paul Trlica (1882–1977), b. Vsetin, TX, of Moravian ancestry, is a photographer. He opened his photography studio in Granger, TX in 1909 which remained in business into the mid-1950s. During his career, he made portraits of nearly everyone in the area and documented family, business, and community activities such as anniversary celebrations, parades, and fairs. Taken as a whole, his photographs thoroughly document the society of this Central Texas community for the first half of the twentieth century.

Jiří Turek (1965–), b. Prague, Czech., is a celebrated Prague-based photographer. As a reporter, he accompanied President Havel all over the world. Since 1998, he has been a freelance photographer and he is becoming one of the most acclaimed portrait photographers of the Czech Republic. From 2002 to 2006, he lived and worked in New York, where he continued with his work for magazines and publicity.

Robert Vano (1948–), b. Nové Zámky, Czech., is a Slovak photographer living in Prague. After his exams in 1967, instead of joining the armed forces for duty, he emigrated via Yugoslavia and Italy to the United States where he made a living as a hairdresser and makeup artist. Later on, he worked as an assistant for photographers (Horst P. Horst, Marco Glaviano or Leo Castelli). Since 1984, he has worked as an independent photographer. He worked in New York City, Paris, Milan and Prague, where he photographed for fashion magazines such as *Cosmopolitan*, *Harper's Bazaar*, and *Vogue*. Since 1995, he lives in Prague where in 1996 to 2003, he worked as artistic director of the Czech edition of the *Elle* magazine, and then in 2009 to 2014, as creative director at Czechoslovak Models. Since then, he has worked as a freelance photographer. Vano is primarily a fashion and commercial photographer. He makes black and white portraits and male nudes on film and also a now little-used technique of platinotype. He prefers photographing in daylight. In 2010, he was awarded the European Trebbia award for creative activities.

10. Printmakers & Lithographers

Wulf Barsch (orig. Wulf Erich Barsch von Benedikt) (1943–), b. Roudnice, Czech., is a painter and printmaker. Barsch's metaphorical painting interprets mystical and spiritual themes. He lives in Boulder, Utah. Barsch graduated from Werkkenschule in 1968. He began his art training in Germany with the master students of Paul Klee and Wassily Kadinsky. He received his MA in printmaking from Brigham Young University in 1971 and his M.F.A. in painting from BYU in 1972. He joined the BYU faculty in 1972. Barsch won the American Academy in Rome fellowship in painting in 1975. He won the Western States Foundation Printmaking Award in 1980. His work was included in the 38th Corcoran Biennial. Other awards include the Printmaking Award from the Western States Art Foundation, an award for Excellence in Art from the Snowbird Institute, and the Directors Award from the Springville Museum of Art. *Book of Abraham* (1984), *Toward Thebes* (1985), and *Anduat* (1982) which won the purchase award, are featured in the Springville Museum of Art permanent collection.

Michael John Biddle (1934–), b. New York City, desc. f. Augustine Heřman, is a contemporary American painter, lithographer, and printmaker. He is the son of the famous social realist artist, George Biddle (1885–1973). Michael Biddle began his artistic education at Harvard College (1952–56) and furthered his studies at the Fine Arts Academy, Vienna (1959), the Central School of Art and Crafts, London (1959–60) and at the Skowhegan School of Painting and Sculpture, Skowhegan, ME (1961). He had over 50 one-man exhibitions in Paris, Vienna, Rome, Mexico City and most American cities. His works are in permanent collections, such as Metropolitan Museum, Whitney Museum, Museum of Modern Art, NY Public Library, Berlin, and Mexico City. He has done fresco and paintings in many public buildings.

Jaroslav Brožík (1904–1986), b. Plzeň, Bohemia, was an etcher, lithographer, and painter. He grew up in Illinois and studied at the Art Institute of Chicago. He was a recipient of Chicago Society of Artists prize (1932) and Gold Medal from Detroit Institute of Art.

Bernice Ficek-Swenson (1951–), b. Jamestown, ND, of Czech ancestry, is a printmaker. She studied fine arts at the Univ. of North Dakota, Grand Forks (B.A., 1974; M.F.A., 1994) and at the State University of New York, Oswego (M.A., 1977). She was co-director of fine-art printmaking atelier, Land Mark Editions, Minneapolis, MN (1980–91), before becoming professor, with specialty in fine-art print making (1992–2014), and professor of art at University of Wisconsin, River Falls, WI (2001–14). She has been a visiting professor at the Hong Kong Institute of Education, as well as an Artist-in-Resident at Anchor Graphics, Chicago, Memorial University of Newfoundland, Canada and the Athens School of Fine Arts, Greece. As an artist, she specializes in copper plate photogravure, a 19th century photographic process. Her artwork explores the elemental forces of nature using stone, ashes, fire and water to create constructed photographs. She has exhibited her work extensively in the US and internationally in Sweden, Canada, France and Greece. In 2012, she was awarded the UWRF College of Arts & Sciences Excellence in Research, Scholarship & Creative Activities Award.

Ladislav R. Hanka (1952-), b. Cedar Rapids, IA, of Czech ancestry, is a printmaker, craftsman and book maker. He studied engraving in Prague and received training in printmaking in the US, in addition to his biology background. He received a BA in Biology from Kalamazoo College (1975), an MS in Zoology from Colorado State University (1979), and an MFA in Printmaking from Western Michigan University (1981). In addition, Mr. Hanka was a guest student at the Rheinische Friedrich Wilhelms Universität in Bonn, Germany (1973) and at the Hochschule für Angewandte Kunst in Vienna, Austria (1979-1980). He also served a private apprenticeship in Prague with Jindra Schmidt, master engraver of stamps and currency (1979). Hanka has had a number of traveling exhibitions including: Visions of a Wandering Naturalist (1997-2001), 50 x 25 Book Arts Exhibit (1993-1999), Boreal Meditations (1995), and County Survey (1989-2001) to name a few. His art may be found at the Fogg Museum of Art in Cambridge, MA., the Princeton University Print Collection in Princeton, NJ, the Kalamazoo Institute of Art, the New York Public Library, and the Library of Congress. His work may also been seen abroad at the National Museum (Prague, Czech Republic), the British Library (London, Great Britain), the Rembrandt House (Amsterdam, Netherlands), The Bookplate Society (Eubonne, France), Huang Zhe Temple (Sichuan Province, China), Jatson Chumig Special School (Lhasa, Tibet), and at the Graphic Arts Institute and Francisco Toledo Museum (Oaxaca, Mexico).

Thomas Lax (1948-), b. Ostrava, Czech., studied art at York Univ. (B.A., 1974; M.F.A., 1976). He has been associated with the Dept. of Art, Alberta College of Art, Calgary, where he has held the position of professor. He also taught at York University, Toronto, Ont., and at Fanshaw College in London, Ont. He is primarily known as a printmaker. He was awarded the Jury Prize at the Alberta Artists Association Exhibition in 1979, the Jury Selection Award for the Edition I Ontario Arts Council Printmaking Competition and Exhibition in Toronto, Ontario in 1974, and the Jury Selection Award for Printed Matter, the Printmaking Competition and Exhibition at Mount Allison University in Sackville, New Brunswick, that same year.

Louis Novak (1903-1983), b. Žilina, Slovakia, was a printmaker, printer, and teacher. He came to the US, with his parents, at the age of 4. They lived first in New York, before moving to Cambridge, MA. He studied at the Massachusetts School of Art in Boston, where he earned a degree in education, and the Museum of Fine Art School. Novak later became an instructor of architectural drawing at the Wentworth Institute in Boston. Novak's works were exhibited at the Art Institute of Chicago in 1927, the Library of Congress in 1943 and 1946, the National Academy of Design in 1943, Jordan Marsh of Boston in 1946, and the Cambridge Art Association in 1952. He was a member of the Cambridge Art Association, Prairie Printmakers, and the Watertown (MA) Arts Association. Works by Novak are in the collection of a number of institutions, including the Peabody Essex Museum in Salem, MA; the Delgado Museum of Art; and the Reading Public Museum. He died in Cambridge, MA in 1983.

Frank Novotný (1873-1926), b. Bohemia, was an engraver. He was active in Cleveland at the turn of the 20th century and died in Cleveland.

Rudolph Růžička (1883-1978), b. Kouřím, Bohemia, was a wood engraver, etcher, illustrator, typeface designer, and book designer. Ruzicka designed typefaces and wood engraving illustrations for Daniel Berkeley Updike's Merrymount Press, and was a designer for, and consultant to, the Mergenthaler Linotype Company for fifty years. He designed a number of seals and medals, including the American Institute of Graphic Arts (AIGA) and the Dartmouth Medal of the American Library Association. He emigrated to the United States of America at age ten, living first in Chicago where he took drawing lessons at the Hull House School before becoming an apprentice wood engraver. In 1910, Ruzicka set up his own shop at 954 Lexington Avenue in New York City. He received his first major art commission from *System* magazine. Many exhibitions followed, including such venues as the Societe de la Gravure, Paris, the Grolier Club, and the Century Association, New York. In 1916, Ruzicka built a house and a workshop in Dobbs Ferry, New York. In 1935, Ruzicka was awarded the Gold Medal from the American Institute of Graphic Arts, and in that same year began work with the Typographic Development staff at Mergenthaler Linotype Company, for which he was to produce typeface families. In 1948, he moved to Massachusetts, and eventually he settled in Vermont.

Axel Jakob Salmson (1807-1876), b. Stockholm, Sweden, of Bohemian father, a pioneer lithographer, pioneered color printing in Sweden. Salmson and C. F. Ström opened a lithographic printing business in 1847. In 1851, the companionship ended and Salmson continued by himself. In 1862, he had to leave the country because of financial problems. He settled in Amsterdam, NY.

T. F. Simon (1877-1942), b. Železnice, Bohemia, Czech., was a major Czech painter, etcher, and woodcut artist much of whose career took place in Prague, New York City, and Paris. His style was strongly influenced by the French impressionists and, presumably through them, by Japanese printmaking techniques, in particular color aquatints with soft ground etching. Simon was also a master of the mezzotint but completed very few prints in this difficult medium, with most being female nudes in subtle tones of black.

John C. Vondrous (1884-1935), b. Bohemia, a painter, illustrator, etcher, won a bronze medal for printmaking at the 1915 Panama Pacific Exposition in San Francisco. He studied at the National Academy of Design. He exhibited extensively in Europe, America and with the Chicago Society of Etchers, Brooklyn Society of Etchers and the California Society of Printmakers.

11. Sculptors

Pearl Amsel (1931-), b. Czech., is a sculptor who creates monuments in bronze, embodying both ancient myth and recent experience. Her work is sometimes dedicated to commemorating the memory of the victims of Auschwitz, where Pearl Amsel was sent during the war. Although her sculpture is mostly abstract in form, it effectively conveys the heaviness of the material and the extraordinary strength of beings that employ resistance in order to remain free.

Barton Lidice Benes (1943-2012), b. Hackensack, NJ, of Czech ancestry, was rather an unconventional and provocative sculptor who lived and worked in New York City. He worked in materials that he called artifacts of everyday life, expanded his definition of 'everyday' as he went. He transformed fragments of our throwaway culture into art that sometimes addressed taboo subjects and often used unconventional materials including cremation ashes, shells, bodily fluids, currency and shredded money, relics, celebrity artifacts and found objects. Benes' reliquaries, displays of thematically composed collectibles and relics, were celebrated in the book *Curiosa* (Abrams, 2002).

Charles Biederman (1906-2004), b. Cleveland, OH, of Bohemian ancestry, was an American Modernist painter, sculptor and theorist who made his mark in New York in the 1930s. Biederman created reliefs consisting of richly colored vertical and horizontal elements.

Emilie Beneš Brzezinski (1932-2022), b. Geneva, Switzerland, of Czech parents, is an American sculptor, who earned a fine arts degree at Wellesley College in Massachusetts. Since the 1980s, most of her works have been in wood. Her monumental 1993 work *Lintel*, constructed from cut cherry trees and then cast in bronze, is in the collection of Grounds for Sculpture, a 35-acre (140,000 m²) sculpture park and museum in New Jersey.

Casper Buberl (1834-1899), a native of Kynšperk and Ohří, was one of the first sculptors of Czech origin in America. He is best known for his Civil War monuments for the *terra cotta* relief panels on the Garfield Memorial in Cleveland. OH, and for the 1,200-foot-long frieze on the Pension Building in Washington, DC.

VIII. CULTURE: ARTS & LETTERS

Tony Chytka (1954-), b. Yankton, SD, of Czech ancestry, a sculptor, combines his love for rodeo with art to create unique bronze sculptures that replicate the rodeo lifestyle. Chytka was a founding member of the Professional Rodeo Cowboy Artists Group, and his work has been displayed at the Pro Rodeo Hall of Fame in Colorado Springs.

Hana Geber (née Kraus) (1910-1990) b. Prague, Bohemia, was a Canadian sculptor, educated in Prague and at Art Students League and Sculpture Center, New York. She is known for her modern sculpture of Biblical subjects in bronze, silver, and terra cotta. She was a designer of ceremonial objects for use in home and synagogues. She was a recipient of gold medal from National Assn. for Women Artists and first prize from American Society of Contemporary Artists.

Nicola Ginzel (ca. 1970-), b. Hollywood, CA, of Bohemian father, is a mixed media artist, who transforms everyday items normally slated for tossing – a plastic shopping bag, a retail receipt, a fast-food wrapper – into thoughtful works of art. Nicola Ginzel has exhibited both internationally and nationally, with most recent shows at Jenny Jaskey Gallery in Philadelphia, the Corridor Gallery in Reykjavik, Iceland, and the Udi Alioni Project Room in NYC. Her work has been included in exhibitions curated by Lydia Yee, Bill Arning, and Lisa Phillips. She lives and works in Brooklyn, NY.

Frederick Victor Guinzburg (1897-1978), b. New York, NY, of Bohemian ancestry, was a sculptor, draftsman, medalist, and landscape artist. He was educated at Art Students League and School of American Sculpture. He founded the Westchester County Arts and Crafts Guild, White Plains, N.Y. Works by Mr. Guinzburg, a Fellow of the National Sculpture Society, are on exhibit at the San Francisco Museum, The Fine Arts Museum in Chicago, galleries in London and Paris and in outdoor— displays in Westchester County. One of his last works was a bronze head of his friend, the late William G. Wilson, who founded Alcoholics Anonymous. Mr. Guinzberg was an active supporter of legislation designating alcoholism as a disease. He was a recipient of Bronze Medal at Sesquicentennial Exposition, Philadelphia (1926) for his work *Bobby*, and hon. mention for *The Bride of the Man Horse*, shown at National Acad. Arts.

Dan Havel (1959-), b. Minnesota, of Czech ancestry, has been a Houston local artist for 22 years. An active member of the 90's era underground art scene in Houston, he is best known for his large-scale installations in alternative public settings. In his time in the city's art scene, he has collaborated with Dean Ruck as part of Havel Ruck Projects. Their partnership brought several public art works to Houston and has also been the recipient of several awards and print reviews, with inclusion in exhibitions and special collections, including at the Museum of Fine Arts Houston. He serves as an art educator at St. John's School in Houston, since 1995. In 2010, Havel was named the Texas Artist of the Year.

Joseph Havel (1954–), b. Minneapolis, MN, of Czech ancestry, is a postmodernist American sculptor. Havel earned a B.F.A. in Studio Arts from the University of Minnesota and an MFA from Pennsylvania State University. He received a National Endowment for the Arts Artist Fellowship in 1987 and a Louis Comfort Tiffany Artist's Fellowship in 1995. He is Glassell School of Art School Director and director of the Core Program, Museum of Fine Arts (MFAH), Houston. He is a man of international artistic fame. Featured in galleries all over the world, he calls Houston home and has work in several major locations in the city, including The Menil Collection, the MFAH, the Hiram Butler Gallery and others. He is the recipient of a number of prestigious awards and fellowships, including a National Endowment for the Arts Fellowship and a Louis Comfort Tiffany Fellowship.

Jaroslav F. Huta (1940–), b. Charvatská Nová Ves, Czech., received his training at Academy of Fine Arts in Prague (1961–64) and at Academy of Fine Arts in Munich (dipl., 1974). He is a sculptor of note, residing in Toronto, Canada. He designed medals for the Opera of Vienna and the Schiller Series. In Canada, he created the Meta Olympic Stamp Sculpture Series IV and V, an official issue of the government of Canada and relief portrait of Her Majesty Queen Elizabeth II for the Canada Post 12-cent stamp.

Michael Jankovsky, b. Colorado, of Czech ancestry, while hunting and fishing on the plains and in the Rocky Mountains, spends much of his time studying and observing animals in their natural habitat. He studied photography at the Colorado Institute of Art and has been a professional taxidermist since 1974. He is a student of wildlife anatomy, sculpts animal manikins, and is highly proficient in all phases of the taxidermy profession. His experience in these disciplines inspired his interest in original wildlife sculpture and in 1984, he began sculpting limited edition bronzes. Applying artistic standards to his taxidermy, Michael's work has won numerous competitions including 1st place Juror's Choice Award, Safari Club International, the Wasco Award and the Onno Van Veen Award for most artistic mount. His work has also been featured in *Breakthrough Magazine*. Jankovsky's sculptures have been exhibited in numerous juried shows including Allied Artists of America Exhibition, National Arts Club, New York, NY; 'Birds in Art,' Leigh Yawkey Woodson Art Museum, Wausau, WI (including the "Birds in Art" national tour and the 'Birds in Art' tour of Japan), The North American Sculpture Exhibition, Foothills Art Center, Golden, CO; 'Sculpture in the Park' Loveland High Plains Arts Council, Loveland, CO; 'State of the Arts '93,' New England Fine Arts Institute, Boston, Massachusetts; and 'Sedona Sculpture Walk,' Red Rocks Arts Council, Sedona, Arizona. Sculpture awards include the Runyan Fisher Foundries Award at the North

American Sculpture Exhibition, the third place award in the *Artist's Magazine*, and the Juror's Award at the 'Sedona Sculpture Walk.'

Frank L. Jirouch (1878–1970), b. Cleveland, OH, of Bohemian father, was a sculptor known mainly for his work in Cleveland's Cultural Gardens. Jirouch did as many as 25 of the busts, statues, and commemorative plaques of groups sponsoring the Gardens, the greatest contribution of any single sculptor.

Cyril Jurečka (1884–1959), b. Příkazy, Moravia, was a sculptor, educated at the Academy of Fine Arts, Prague. By 1919, he had moved to southern California and was active in the Los Angeles art scene. He started the sculpture department for Famous Players-Lasky Corporation in 1918. This company became Paramount Pictures. He initiated instruction in sculpture at Pomona College when he joined the Pomona Faculty in 1952. He retired in 1949.

Christina Kenton (fl. 2017), b. Vancouver, BC, Canada; of Slovak descent; a self-taught lighter/ mixed media artist, inspired heavily from her late surrealist grandfather Ladislav Guderna; surrealistic sculptor.

Vladimíra Klumpar (1954–), b. Rychnov nad Kněžnou, Czech., a glass sculptor of note, studied at specialized School of glassmaking, Železný Brod (B.A., 1973) and at the Academy of Arts, Architecture and Design, Prague (M.F.A., 1981). For much of her adult life, she lived between homes in the United States, Mexico, Portugal, and the Czech Republic. She is the recipient of a Pollock-Krasner Foundation Grant. Her work has been widely exhibited in Europe and the Americas and is represented in public and private collections on both continents. Her works can be found at Corning Museum of Glass, American Arts and Crafts Museum, NYC, Lannan Foundation, Palm Beach, FL, etc. She has been recipient of many awards.

Mario Korbel (1882–1954), b. Osík, Bohemia, was an American sculptor. He worked in bronze, often experimenting with this media, trying new patinas and textures. He often depicted idealized female nudes and worked in the neoclassical style. He was elected to the National Academy of Design in 1937 as an Associate member and became a full Academician in 1944.

Gyula Košice (orig. Ferdiand Fallik) (1924–2016), b. Košice, Czech., was an Argentine sculptor, plastic artist, and a poet. Along with Carmelo Arden-Quin, he founded the Madí movement and wrote the *Madí Manifest* in 1946. Later on, he also participated in the abstract-only 'Arte Concreto-Invención' movement. He is considered one of the vanguards of kinetic and luminance art, being one of the first to experiment with new materials and abstraction. He studied drawing and modeling at three different academies. In 1946, he created luminance structures with neon gas, used for the first time in the worldwide plane. In 1949, he also became the innovator behind the hydraulic sculpture, and he uses the water as an essential element in his works. He also held the Retrospective Exhibition *A Hundred Works of Kosice, a Forerunner* at the Di Tella Institute (1968) and the Retrospective Exhibition in the National Museum of Fine Arts (1991) in Buenos Aires. Also worthy of note is Kosice's participation in the *Multiple Modernities* exhibition at the Centre Pompidou in Paris in 2014. He was given a whole room to exhibit his work, which included his notable 1944 *Röyi* wooden sculpture, considered today one of the pieces that paved the way to Argentinean abstraction. He has also published 14 books of essays and poetry and has made 30 personal exhibitions and participated in more than 600 group exhibitions. He was distinguished as 'Caballero de las Artes y las Letras' (Lord of the Arts and Literature) by the government of France and named Honorary Citizen of the City of Buenos Aires. He made monumental sculptures, hidro-spatial routes, and hydro-murals. His works appear in museums and private collections in Argentina, Latin America, the United States, Europe, and Asia.

Tom Kotík (1969–), b. Prague, Czech, studied studio art New York University (B.S.) and continued at Hunter College, where he was the recipient of the Graf Travel Grant and received his MFA in 2004. He has also attended the School of Applied Arts in Prague and Glasgow School of Art in Scotland. He is a sculptor. His work has been widely exhibited in New York and abroad, including shows at Smack Mellon, Socrates Sculpture Park, and Sculpture Center in New York and Prague National Gallery in the Czech Republic. He is also a rock musician and as such, he explores the interaction of music and sculpture and is interested in how to make the invisible waves of sound visual.

Joseph M. Kratina (1872–1953), b. Prague, Bohemia, a sculptor, studied at Ecole des Beaux Arts and Julien Academy in Paris. He was a noted sculptor who lived in New York. Unfortunately, little is known about him.

Milan Kříž (1945–), b. Náměst n. Osl., Czech., is a Czech-Venezuelan sculptor and painter. He emigrated to Venezuela where he obtained citizenship in 1983. His art pieces are made from a wide spectrum of classical and modern raw materials, including sculptures of wood, marble, coral, bronze, and even epoxy resin and bronze-ready positive originals in clay. Milan Kriz's paintings are usually made with oil on canvas, but he uses oil on formic too; his engravings were made mostly on hard paper with linoleum plates or ancient wood.

Michael Krondl (1960–), b. Prague, Czech., is a Czech/Canadian artist, trained at Cooper Union and living in New York. He uses both sculpture and photography to create site specific installation pieces. Over the years, he has designed outdoor installations using very large-scale prints of clouds in spaces usually reserved for billboards. Particularly intriguing is the way these pictures erase part of the cityscape while, at the same time pointing to the actual sky the buildings have usurp.

Dalya Luttwak (fl. 2018), b. Northern Galilee, Israel, of Slovak immigrant parents, is an Israeli-American sculptor, living in Chevy Chase, MD. She was educated at the Hebrew University of Jerusalem. Her path, like that of her parents, was inspired by intrusion: a tornado overturned a large silver maple tree in her front yard. The exposed roots evoked her family's uprooting and inspired her. Since 2007, she has been working on a series of large-scale metal sculptures that symbolically represent the root systems of various plants. Her sculptures are site-specific or site-responsive. At times, she works from the roots themselves, which she digs out of the earth, other times, she photographs, copies or draws roots as the basis of her work. She tries to uncover the hidden beauty of roots, exploring the relationship between what grows above the ground, and the invisible parts below. Her sculptures reveal what nature prefers to conceal. She aspires to uncover and discover roots even when they are hidden. Roots – to each other and to the earth – anchor, structure and nourish us.

Pina Macků (1947-), b. Brno, Czech., is a sculptor. She emigrated in 1968 to Switzerland and in 1978 to Canada. She studied clinical psychology at Masaryk Univ. in Brno; has graduate diploma and was a dance and movement instructor with Team 70 Basel Tanz & Gymnastik. After coming to Canada, she studied graphic art at Dawson College. She has been an artist/member of Tour des Arts studio tour, Quebec (s. 1994) and is also an owner of B&B Pinorama (s. 1994). She creates sculptors from recycled materials, i.e., recycled clothes, hats & accessories, barn wood sculptures. Inspired from a background in the world of theatre and dance, she creates unique garments, whimsical wooden sculptures, hats, painted stones, jewelry and much more, all at affordable prices! Her art work reinvents the ordinary and makes it special. Humor is inseparable in all her creations. Pina lives in Sutton, Quebec and still teaches exercise classes.

Anna Justine 'Gucki' Mahler (1904–1988), b. Vienna, of Bohemian father (she was a second child of the composer Gustav Mahler and his wife Alma Schindler), was a sculptor. They nicknamed her 'Gucki' on account of her big blue eyes (gucken is German for 'peek' or 'peep'). Anna Mahler's exposure to the visual arts began early when she would visit Oskar Kokoschka's studio. She was also a model for her mother-in-law, the painter Broncia Koller-Pinell. After her divorce (she was married five times), Anna studied art and painting on and off in Berlin, Rome, and Paris throughout the 1920s. At the age of twenty-six, she discovered that sculpture was the medium in which she could best express her creativity. Having taken lessons in sculpting in Vienna in 1930 from Fritz Wotruba, she became an established sculptor there, and was awarded the Grand Prix in Paris in 1937. As well as sculpting successfully in stone, Anna Mahler produced bronze heads of many of the musical giants of the 20th century including Arnold Schönberg, Alban Berg, Artur Schnabel, Otto Klemperer, Bruno Walter, Rudolf Serkin and Eileen Joyce.

Zdeno Mayercak (1953-), b. Žilina, Czech.; came to US as a political refugee in 1985; sculptor; professor of art, Montgomery College, Rockville, MD.

Peterpaul Ott (1895-1992), b. Plzeň, Bohemia, was a sculptor and draftsman. He studied in Dresden, Germany at the Royal College of Fine and Applied Arts. He served in World War I and followed his service by studying at the Austrian State Academy of Fine Arts. In 1924, he moved to New York where he studied with Alexander Archipenko at Cooper Union. He also worked in a factory, carving furniture and received architectural sculpture commissions for the interiors and exteriors of buildings. In 1931, he moved to Chicago where he taught at Northwestern University and the Evanston Academy of Fine Arts. From 1936 to 1939, he was the Chicago WPA supervisor of sculpture. He did the interior and exterior decoration for the Oak Park, Illinois Post Office. In 1940, he moved to Laguna Beach, California where he taught at several high schools including Laguna Beach, South Pasadena, Whittier and San Juan Capistrano. He may have been the artist for the wood sculptures at the Green Bay Road School, now the District 112 Administrative Building. He worked in wood, bronze, terra cotta, tiles, and aluminum, Ott made sculptures in all sizes. He is the recipient of the Logan Medal of the Arts (1934).

Albin Polášek (1879-1965), from Frenštát, Moravia, was one of the American foremost sculptors of the 20th century. He worked in classical style, using a variety of mediums including stone, bronze, plaster, and wood. At age 37, after periods of residence in Rome and New York City, he was invited to head the sculpture department at the Art Institute of Chicago, where he remained for nearly thirty years. While there, he created the original *Forest Idyll*; *Victorious Christ* for St. Cecelia's Cathedral in Omaha, Nebraska; Kenilworth Memorial relief, Kenilworth, Illinois; *The Spirit of Music* in Grant Park in Chicago; the *Woodrow Wilson Memorial* in Prague, Czech Republic; Governor Richard Yates sculpture, capital grounds, Springfield, Illinois; and many other works. He created more than 400 works during his career, 200 of which are displayed in the Albin Polasek Museum & Sculpture Gardens in Winter Park, Florida. Polášek was elected an Associate Member of the National Academy of Design in 1927, and full member in 1933.

Maria Porges (1954-), Oakland, CA, of Bohemian ancestry, is an artist, sculptor, draftsman and writer. She received her education at Yale Univ. (B.A., 1975) and at Univ. of Chicago (M.F.A., 1979). She holds the position of an associate professor at California College of the Arts (CCA), Oakland, CA, serving primarily in the Graduate Program in Fine Arts. Her work has been exhibited nationally in solo shows and group exhibitions since the late eighties. Porges' critical writing has appeared in many publications, including *Artforum, Art in America, Sculpture, American Ceramics, Glass,* the *New York Times Book Review,* and a host of other now-defunct art magazines. She has also authored essays for more than 70 exhibition catalogues and dozens of scripts for museum engineer tours. Porges' studio practice focuses on sculpture and drawing. She received a SECA award from the San Francisco Museum of Modern Art and has twice been in residence at the Headlands Center for the Arts.

Denisa Procházka, b. Czech., daughter of Ludmila Procházka, is a sculptor. She lives in Canada since mid-eighties. She is an award-winning Canadian artist living in Ottawa, Ontario, Canada. She grew up playing in her mother's ceramic studio. She is a classically trained figurative sculptor with a passion for portrait sculpture and figurative clay reliefs. Many of her sculptures depict female subjects and feminine forms created to empower and inspire the feminine balance in this world. Denisa has attracted many special commissions and has participated in over thirty exhibitions in Canada and USA. She has been commissioned to create Awards of Excellence for the Nelson Mandela Legacy and Ottawa University BHM, Women Excellence Awards, Guinean Excellence Awards and Women Who Work Excellence Awards. Manhattan Arts International has awarded her with the Featured Artist Art Award, Second Place Special Recognition Arts Award, and an Award of Excellence.

Lyuba Durdakova Prusak (1922-2010), b. Košice, Czech., was a freelance artist, sculptor, and teacher, Pacific Design Center, Melrose, CA. Her father died in Mauthausen concentration camp. Lyuba had a lifelong passion for art, especially sculpture. After the war, she was accepted into The Academy of Fine Arts in Prague and graduated in 1950. Though persecuted for her religious beliefs and for refusing to join the Communist Party, Lyuba successfully exhibited her art in several venues and countries. When the Soviet Bloc invaded Czechoslovakia in 1968, Lyuba, with her daughter and her first husband Josef Janousek, escaped to the United States and settled in Southern California, where she continued to study sculpture and produce and exhibit her art locally. She received a second Master's degree from The California State University at Northridge and exhibited her work in international exhibitions in Greece, Spain, France, and the Czech Republic. After her first husband died, she married Mirek Prusak. Together they settled in Pasadena, California from which they traveled extensively and until Mirek died in 2006. The next year, Lyuba resettled in Provo, Utah, to be near her family.

Josef Randa (1933-2005), b. Prague, Czech, was a sculptor. He studied at the Ceramic School of Prague from 1952 and apprenticed thereafter. After coming to Canada, he began to work as a sculptor in Winnipeg in mid 70s. His experience and knowledge of various media allowed him to create works in bronze, plaster, glass and fiberglass. He created several magnificent works, including the *Meeting of Rivers* which graces one of Winnipeg's parks and *Crucified Again*, a statue dedicated to victims of Communism that has been erected in Masaryktown in Scarborough, Ont.

Dennis Rechcygl (1950-), b. WI, of Bohemian ancestry, is a figurative sculptor. He also paints (in water color and acrylic) and works with ceramics. He now lives in Goffstein, NH.

Richard Rezac (1952-), b. Lincoln, NE, of Czech ancestry, studied fine arts at Pacific Northwest College of Arts, Portland, OR (B.F.A., 1974) and at Maryland Inst., College of Art, Baltimore (M.F.A., 1982). Early in his career, he was active in Oregon, serving as Gallery Director of Pacific Northwest College of Art in Portland from 1977 to 1980 and then teaching at Mount Hood Community College and Portland State University. From 1985, he has been an instructor at the School of the Art Institute of Chicago where he was made an associate professor in 1991. Presently, he holds there the position of adjunct professor of sculpture, painting and drawing and graduate advisor. Richard Rezac is known for refined forms in a variety of media, primarily object sculpture but also large-scale public works. In a diverse range of materials, Rezac examines multiple relationships of elements at once architectural and organic. In free standing objects, wall pieces and ceiling suspended works, Rezac has investigated polychrome strategies and serial orders. He has had solo exhibitions at the Portland Art Museum, Oregon, Museum of Contemporary Art, Chicago, Feature Inc., New York, James Harris Gallery, Seattle, Rhona Hoffman Gallery, Chicago, Marc Foxx, Los Angeles and many others. He was awarded the Rome Prize by the American Academy in Rome.

Klára Katherina Sever (née Klein) (1935-), b. Trebišov, Czech., is a sculptor, residing in Falls Church, VA. Being of Jewish faith, Klara and her family were forced to the concentration camp in Žilina. There they stayed until her uncle was able to convince a local official to vouch for the family and were released under supervision. Klara Sever studied at the School of Art and Design and at the Comenius University in Bratislava, Czechoslovakia. She worked as a sculptor and restorer on some of Czechoslovakia's most beautiful baroque castles, and also designed new architectural sculpture for the interior of the National Theater. In 1969, she and her husband moved to New York City. There she was employed to reproduce sculptures. Since immigrating to the United States, Mrs. Sever has dedicated all her time to sculpting, exhibiting in Washington at the Marlboro Gallery, the Art Barn, the Gallery House, and the George Meany Center. She has received awards at the National Small Sculpture Competition.

Antonín C. Skodik (1870-1908), b. Modrá, Moravia, was a craftsperson and a sculptor, educated at Art Students' League in NYC. He resided in NYC and exhibited in New York and in Philadelphia. He was a recipient of Henry O. Avery Prize for sculpture.

Jana Štěrbák (1955–), b. Prague, Czech., is a Canadian sculptor, who immigrated in 1968 to Canada with her parents. She is best known for her conceptual sculptures that are made about and in relation to the body. She has used a surprising variety of materials in her sculpture, including electrical wire, dressmakers' measuring tapes, and beefsteak, as well as more common materials such as lead, glass, and bronze.

Jan Peter Stern (1926–), b. Berlin, of Czech ancestry, is a sculptor, specializing in monumental sculptures, using stainless steel and metals. He came to the US in 1938. He graduated from the College of Fine Arts, Syracuse University and has lived in Los Angeles since 1958. His work can be seen at Storm King in New York, the Hirshhorn Museum in Washington, D.C. as well as other major museums. In addition, he has completed public art installations in New York, Chicago, and San Francisco.

Richard Štipl (1968–), b. Šternberk, Czech., is a sculptor, who lives and works both in Canada and the Czech Republic. He graduated from the Ontario College of Art in Toronto with an Honors Diploma in 1992 and was awarded Canada's prestigious Governor General's Award in the same year. Working initially as a painter, Stipl has recently turned to making sculpture. Using himself as a model, Richard focuses exhaustively on the indefinite nature and moment-to-moment paradoxes inherent in the act of continuously recreating oneself throughout the course of a lifetime. Characteristically, Stipl's paintings and sculptural works alike force us to reconsider the role of boundaries and consequent categories of choice that comprise contemporary attitudes and approaches to art-making and art-consumption. Over the past several years, Richard's work has captured extensive media and critical attention wherever he has exhibited. Stipl has exhibited in Toronto, Montreal, New York, Miami, Berlin, Los Angeles, Madrid, Stuttgart, and the Czech Republic, and is included in many important public and private collections worldwide.

Victoria Thorson (1943–), b. NYC (?), of Moravian ancestry; daughter of painter Ruth Rogers-Altmann and the granddaughter of architect Arbnold Karplus; New York-based sculptor, editor, art historian. She is most known for being one of the world's leading authenticators of French Sculptor Auguste Rodin's drawings, and, along with Kirk Varnedoe, was one of the first to discover fake Rodin drawings in numerous major private and public collections.

Lea Vivot (orig. Drahomíra Lea Hekelová) (1954–), b. Šumperk-Horní Temenice, Czech., is an internationally-renown sculptor, residing in Ont., Canada. Vivot's over life-sized bronze sculptures are figurative and often depict families, couples, mothers, children, and other subjects of humanity. Most of her sculptures include benches, which have become her trademark. She is also active in drawing and printmaking.

Ruth Vodicka (1921–1999), b. New York, NY, was a sculptor. An alumna of the Sculpture Center and of the City College of New York, Vodicka began working in welded metal in the 1950s. Early in her career, she would repair items with her welder's torch in order to afford more art supplies. She was also a member of the Sculptors Guild. Vodicka donated a collection of her papers to the Archives of American Art at the Smithsonian Institution in 1977.

Anthony Vožech (1892–1965), b. Bohemia, was a sculptor. He studied at Industrial Art School, Prague. His works are maintained at Thayer Museum of Art, University of Kansas., University of California, Bohemian National Cemetery, Chicago, Toledo Public Library, Toledo Museum of Art (1936–39). He was a recipient of several art prizes.

Albert S. Vrana (1921–1994), b. Cliffside, NY, probably of Czech ancestry, was an American sculptor who is best known for his mid-twentieth century monumental architectural sculptures done in the Modernist style, using novel materials, such as ferrocement, and new techniques, such as sand casting using plastic Styrofoam molds to shape sculptural concrete panels and metal sculptures.

Jan Zach (1914–1986), b. Slaný, Bohemia, was a much-respected sculptor of large-scale wood and metal works. In 1938, he came to the United States to work on the Czech Pavilion at the New York World's Fair, and never returned to his native country because of World War II. In 1940, he settled in Rio de Janeiro, Brazil, where he remained until 1951. He had large exhibitions of his paintings and drawings at the National Museum of Fine Arts in 1943 and the Institute of Brazilian Architects in 1948. He also worked as a commercial artist in Rio. He then moved to Victoria, British Columbia, to open a school of painting and sculpture. In 1958, he joined the University of Oregon faculty, as professor of fine arts, where he remained until his retirement in 1979. His work has been exhibited in five countries, and he was active in national and international sculpture organizations. He worked in a variety of media to create sculptures that celebrate courage and freedom in the face of oppression.

Helen Zelezny (or Helene Scholzová-Železná) (1882–1974), b. Chropyně, Moravia, was a sculptor and architectural sculptor. She is widely considered one of the most influential figures in the sculpture of north Moravia and Silesia, at the end of the nineteenth and beginning of the twentieth centuries. Her sculptures largely featured sculpted portraits, including members of the Habsburg family, Count Franz Conrad von Hötzendorf, Lady Sybil Grahamová,'Il Duce' Benito Mussolini, and 1st President of Czechoslovakia Tomáš Garrigue Masaryk (1932) with whom she gained a close relationship. She also lived in the United States for a short time, from 1946 to 1949, where she taught mixed media at the Philadelphia

Museum of Art and Swarthmore College, among other institutions in and around Philadelphia. From 1949 until her death, she had regular classes in her old studio in Rome.

12. Craft, Decorative & Folk Artists

Neda Al-Hilali (1938–), b. Cheb, Czech., who lived in Bagdad, is an American fiber artist. She moved to southern California in 1961. She trained as an artist in Europe, and at the University of California Los Angeles. Her early works in the 1960s consisted of flat weavings and knotted hangings. These were followed by large, room-filling installations and a series of giant brown-paper *Tongues* installed on Venice beach. Her work is in the collections of various museums, including the Renwick Gallery, Museum of Art and Design, and Utah Museum of Fine Arts. Her papers are at the Archives of American Art.

Peter Bauer (1932–), b. Liberec, Czech, is Master Artisan Inspired Designer. In today's world, when even the most expensive jewelry is mass produced, Peter Bauer's hand-wrought jewelry is prized for its refreshing individuality and superb handcrafting. Peter grew up in a central European town steeped in jewelry-making tradition. His mother was a talented designer, and his uncle owned a jewelry manufacturing business, where Peter made his first piece of jewelry at age 5. He went on to learn jewelry fabrication skills from his uncle. He completed extensive metalworking and art courses at the University of Vienna, where he earned two engineering degrees. He studied industrial design at London University and earned a Master's degree in physics from Cambridge University, England. Peter's limitless imagination and innate curiosity drive his compelling designs and sensuous textures. Wildly exciting and always wearable, Peter's jewelry is sold in fine shops and has been exhibited in galleries in Canada and the US. His work is included in prestigious private collections around the world.

Betty Rose Kepka Belton (née Vanek) (1934–2019), b. Wilson, KS, of Czech ancestry; the name Kepka comes from her grandmother who had major influence on her. She is known for her beautifully decorated Czech eggs ('kraslice'), the art she learned from her grandmother. After high school, Kepka attended Emporia State University where she earned a degree in art. While in college, she continued to make kraslice, but she never made more than a dozen or so a year. The eggs she made during this period were usually given to relatives as gifts. After graduation she worked as an apprentice to a jeweler in Omaha, Nebraska, for $30 a week. After a year in Omaha, she moved to Kansas City, Missouri, and went to work for Hallmark Cards. While at Hallmark, she began to call up her Czech heritage while designing greeting cards. She recalls that one day she was drawing a peacock and in the eyes of the feathers she placed Czech eggs. She received encouragement from other artists to explore her Czech heritage in her work. After spending two years in Kansas City, Missouri, Kepka moved back to Kansas to become a teacher. It was during this period that she began displaying her work at festivals and fairs. A teaching job soon drew her back to her hometown of Wilson, where she became actively involved in promoting the Czech heritage of the community of which her egg decoration became an essential part. In 1980, a journalist for the Associated Press wrote an article on the "Egg Lady" of Kansas. People of Czech heritage from throughout the United States wrote to Kepka asking for recipes, wanting to buy her eggs, and sharing their own experiences as Czech-Americans.

Frank Bily (1884–1965), b. nr. Spillville, IA, of Czech parents, a farmer and carpenter by trade, was a noted carver of clocks. He worked with his older brother Joseph. While Joseph developed designs, drew up plans and joined the woods, Frank did nearly all of the actual carving. The brothers used very simple tools, many of them homemade. Nearly all of the main clocks had moveable mechanical figures and musical chimes. They generally constructed the mechanisms themselves, except for the clock works and chimes, which were factory made. However, for one clock they carved wooden works. Although the Bily Brothers received many offers for their clocks, they accepted none. In 1947, arrangements were made whereby the entire clock collection would become the property of Spillville after their deaths. It would never be broken up and would always remain at its present location. The clocks are housed in the building occupied by composer Antonin Dvorak during his visit to Spillville in 1893.

Joseph Bily (1880–1964), b. Calmar, IA, of Czech parents, a farmer and carpenter by trade, was a noted wood carver of clocks. He was the older brother of Frank Bily, with whom he worked as a team.

Dale Chihuly (1941–), b. Tacoma, WA, of Slovak descent, is an American glass sculptor and entrepreneur. Dale Chihuly was introduced to glass while studying interior design at the University of Washington. After graduating in 1965, Chihuly enrolled in the first glass program in the country, at the University of Wisconsin. He continued his studies at the Rhode Island School of Design (RISD), where he later established the glass program and taught for more than a decade. In 1968, after receiving a Fulbright Fellowship, he went to work at the Venini glass factory in Venice. There he observed the team approach to blowing glass, which is critical to the way he works today. In 1971, Chihuly cofounded Pilchuck Glass School in Washington State. With this international glass center, Chihuly has led the avant-garde in the development of glass as a fine art. His work is included in more than 200 museum collections worldwide. He has been the recipient of many awards, including twelve honorary doctorates and two fellowships from the National Endowment for the Arts.

Moritz Fuerst (1782–1840), b. Pezinok, Slovakia; US Mint engraver, medalist. Prior to immigrating, he was enlisted by the American consul at Livorno, Italy in 1807 and came to the United States to work as an engraver. In 1808, he settled in Philadelphia where he set up business as a seal and steel engraver and die-sinker. He was subsequently employed by the United States Mint in Philadelphia and soon received recognition as an early American medalist. Thirty-three of his patriotic commemoratives and portraits, including his best-known work which honored heroes of the War of 1812, are still issued by the U.S. Mint. He struck the official portraits of Presidents James Monroe, John Quincy Adams, Andrew Jackson and Martin Van Buren.

Helen Frances Gregor (1921–1989), b. Prague, Czech., was a Czech-Canadian artist who specialized in textile art. She was considering a career in theatrical design but moved with her family to England in 1940 to escape the Second World War. She studied art at Newark Technical College, Birmingham College of Art, and at the Royal College of Art's School of Design in London. She exhibited at the Czechoslovak Club, and at Liberty in London. She also studied at the American School of Craftsmen in Rochester, New York. She moved to Canada with her husband Tibor Gregor and became a teacher at Ontario College of Art and Design in Toronto in 1952, where she founded and became head of the textile department. She worked in textile art, creating tapestries, and challenged the distinction between fine art and applied art. She exhibited at the Triennial of Tapestry in Łódź twice. Examples of her works are held by the Canadian Museum of Civilization, the National Gallery of Canada, and the Art Gallery of Ontario. She won Ontario Crafts Council's Mather Award in 1982 and was appointed as a Member of the Order of Canada in 1987. The Ontario Crafts Council established the Helen Frances Gregor scholarship in her honor. Her book *The Fabric of My Life: Reflections of Helen Frances Gregor* was published in 1987.

Trude Guermonprez (née Gertrud Jalowetz) (1910–1976), b. Danzig, Germany, of Moravian father; weaver, textile artist and designer, teacher at California College of Arts and Crafts.

Rudolph Heinrich (1875–d.), b. Bohemia, a glass artist, learned the glass making in Bohemia. Coming first to Canada, he remained there until 1917, then came to Pittsburgh, and established the business which had made him famous in the glass trade. He was proprietor of the Dresden Art Works, Pittsburgh, PA, where he decorated the choicest glass for the most exclusive markets of the US, and also for export. He did only the most exclusive decorating of glass and bric-a-brac, and his work went into every State in the Union, some being exported. Among artists, especially in his own line, Mr. Heinrich achieved wide distinction, and his work was classed with the very finest to be obtained. He employed sixteen artists, and the opportunity to see his studio was a rare treat. His plant was 26 x 112 feet, two stories in height, making a total floor space of 5,824 square feet. He was assisted by his eldest son.

Carl V. Helmschmied (1863-1934), b. Kamenický Šenov, Bohemia, was a glass artist and designer, educated at the Imperial Technical School. He was employed at Smith Brothers, Jesse Dean and Mount Washington Glass Companies. Starting in 1886, he was employed by C.F. Monroe Company of Meriden, CT. When the company was incorporated, he became a stockholder and was made superintendent of the plant. In 1903, he opened his own corporation called the Helschmied Mfg. Company, Reservoir Avenue, Meriden, CT. He was a member of the Woodmen of America and the Colonial Club in Meriden.

John Kebrle (orig. Kebrdle) (1895-1959), b. Plzeň, Bohemia, immigrated to Galveston, TX in 1913. He was gifted in art and music and played the violin, viola, guitar, trumpet and saxophone. However, he is best known for Kebrle Stained Glass Studio, which he established in 1920, which is now managed by his son John Kebrle, Jr. Kebrle Stained Glass Studio has designed and fabricated thousands of stained glass windows worldwide and is the preeminent studio in the southwest. Works include hundreds of churches, such as St. Michaels and All Angels Episcopal Church in Dallas, First United Methodist Churches in Houston, Duncanville, Hurst, and Denton, St. Elizabeth Catholic Church and St. Jude Catholic Chapel in Dallas, Heights Baptist Church in Richardson, and St. Paul's United Methodist, in Muskogee, OK, etc. In addition to classical painted stained glass, the studio successfully implemented Dalle de Verre, also known as faceted glass, in Zion Lutheran, Spring Valley United Methodist, and Ursuline Academy Chapel, all in Dallas, and also many more. The Studio is also credited for the restoration of a turn of the century church in Honeygrove. The studio designed and fabricated windows for 43 Hard Rock Cafes around the world including Dallas, Philadelphia, Boston, Cancun, Paris, Berlin, Edinborough, Barcelona, Stockholm, and 7 in Japan. The Studio works also includes windows for estate residence and homes, universities, hospitals, and libraries.

John Kebrle, Jr. (1927-), b. Dallas, TX, of Czech parents, is son and grandson of stained-glass artists. He received his B.A. from SMU. He learned his art and his craft through studies at Dallas Art Institute; Famous Artists School of Westport, Connecticut; and Southern Methodist University and through apprenticeships to George Brozius and John Kebrle, Sr. He has headed the Kebrle Stained Glass Studio since 1958 and has served the Stained Glass Association of America as a board member (1965-1984) and president (1980-1981). He has juried numerous stained-glass competitions throughout the country and presently serves as committee chairman for SGAA at the Corning Museum of Glass at Corning, New York. His dedication to his work is reflected in his tour of Greece to study the remnant evidence there, of the Classical mythology which provides the theme for the Library windows.

VIII. CULTURE: ARTS & LETTERS

Jay Kvapil (1951–), b. Phoenix, AZ, of Czech ancestry, is a ceramic artist who served as School of Art Director and College Dean. He received his B.A., cum laude, in literature from the University of the Pacific in 1973, spending an equal amount of time in the ceramics lab as he did studying English literature and film. Although his original intent was to go into law practice, he decided to follow his passion for ceramics first. To that end, he studied tea ceremony ceramics in 1974 and 1975 at the Takatori Seizan Pottery on the island of Kyushu in Southern Japan. There, he achieved the rank of Journeyman Potter. Returning to the United States, he received both his M.A. (1979) and M.F.A. (1981) from San Jose State University. His teaching career began at University of Hawaii in 1984, moving to California State University Long Beach (CSULB) in 1986. Kvapil joined the faculty at Cal State Long Beach as an assistant professor of art. He rose through the ranks. He chaired the art department and eventually became Director of the School of Art in 2011. Between those posts, he has been associate dean and interim dean of the College of Arts. In May 2014, he was named the new Dean of California State University, Northridge's Mike Curb College of Arts, Media and Communication. While pursuing his academic career, Kvapil has continued to create art. His work in ceramics shows deep meditation on the relations of Asian and American art — on the delicate shapes and intimate scale of the tea ceremony, as well as the richly textured and organic shapes of mid-century American expressionism. His work has been included in numerous exhibitions, including 'American Porcelain, New Dimension in an Ancient Art' at the Smithsonian Institution's Renwick Gallery in Washington, D.C.; the Taipei Fine Arts Museum in Taiwan; at the Oakland Museum; and a one-person exhibition at the Downey Museum of Art. His work also can be found in the public collections of the Long Beach Museum of Art and the San Jose Museum of Art.

Eva Lapka (1944–), b. Czech., received diploma in ceramics, sculpture and design from the College of Arts and Crafts, Brno (1959–1963). She emigrated to Montréal, Québec in 1968. Eva Lapka was professor of ceramic perfecting at the Institut des metiers d'art and the Commission de formation professionnelle in Montréal from 1988 to 1995 and is professor of ceramics at the Montréal Visual Arts Centre since 1991. She has also received several grants and won the first prize at the "Passions paralleles" exhibition in Blainville, Québec in 1991. Together with her husband Milan, they work closely together on ceramic projects. Eva is responsible for the form of the figures, Milan for the glazes and firing.

Milan Lapka (1942–), b. Czech., studied at the School of Arts in Prague. He emigrated to Montréal, Québec in 1968. Milan Lapka taught ceramics technology at the Institut des metiers d'art and the Commission de formation professionnelle in Montréal from 1988 to 1993, and from 1996 to 1998, was a teacher of art in the program for children with learning disabilities and the program for mentally challenged children, also at the Visual Arts

Centre in Montréal. Together with his wife Eva, they work closely together on ceramic projects. Eva is responsible for the form of the figures, Milan for the glazes and firing.

Tatiana Krizová Lizoň (1942–), b. Ústi nad Oravou, Czech., is a freelance artist, artist craftsman, fiber and quilt artist, Knoxville, TN. According to her, she has been influenced by the folk art of her native Czechoslovakia – weaving, costume, embroidery, woodcarving and some of the architecture. That is where her love of bright colors originated. In this country, she became aware of the beautiful quilts, especially the quilts of the Amish, with their simple but powerful designs. She wants to draw from these traditions in her work and would like her work to bring warmth and aesthetic feeling into people's environments, which are often so cold and colorless.

Greta Loebl Schreyer (b. Greta Loebl) (1917–2005), b. Vienna, of Slovak descent, was a Jewish jewelry designer and painter. She followed in her father's footsteps at 18 to become a master goldsmith. She survived the Holocaust and died in New York City. Greta Schreyer's jewelry design included lapel pins she created to make a living as a newly-arrived immigrant – they became an immediate fashion hit, and were advertised in *Vogue*, *Harper's Bazaar*, and *Mademoiselle* magazines. From a goldsmith, she evolved into an artist and from 1956, the year of Schreyer's first solo exhibition, until her death, her work was displayed in many solo and group exhibitions in the United States, Austria, and Czechoslovakia. Her paintings and watercolors included symbols of her flight from peril, her dream-world, and her optimism. One series was of burning synagogues in Poland, reflecting the destruction of Polish Jewry by the Nazis. As of her death, her work was in the permanent collections of Brandeis University Library, The Jewish Museum in New York, Museum Haaretz in Tel Aviv, Israel, and The Albertina and The Oesterreichische Galerie-Belvedere Palace in Vienna, Austria.

Joseph Mrázek (1889–1959), b. Poděbrady, Bohemia, was an apprentice artist, before leaving to live in America. Joseph continued his artistic education at the St. Louis Academy of Arts. He became a gifted painter and muralist. Joseph Mrazek's most enduring legacy can be found, however, in the brilliantly-colored, hand-painted pottery that he created from 1918–1933. Between the two World Wars, Joseph Mrazek was the largest producer of hand-painted pottery in Czechoslovakia, most of which was exported to the United States. With the advent of the Second World War, he invented and manufactured a critically important military aircraft component that was integrated into more than 70,000 U.S. warplanes.

Daniela Mahoney (née Šípková) (1956–), b. Prague, Czech., in US s. 1983, is an egg artist and cultural educator. She first experienced traditional egg decorating as a child during Easter. Under the guidance of her grandmother, she learned the basic wax resistant technique and practiced the craft as a seasonal hobby during her childhood and adolescence. Since arriving in the United States Daniela, returned to traditional egg decorating at Easter time as a hobby and soon developed the craft into a full-time business. Since 1982, Daniela participated in hundreds of art shows, craft shows and ethnic festivals nationwide. She also developed educational programs to teach cultural crafts as part of the Czech and Slovak heritage preservation in community-based settings. She became a resident artist for Young Audiences of Oregon and Washington and the Regional Arts & Culture Council in Portland, Oregon. Daniela is known for organizing large scale egg decorating events for children, such as "1000 eggs with 1000 children in four hours." She also published children's coloring and activity books.

Marjorie 'Marj' A. Kopecek Nejdl (1936–), b. Cedar Rapids, IA, of Czech ancestry, is a folk artist. Her specialty is egg decorating. Nejdl learned the techniques as a child from her uncle, Martin Polehna. He and her father, Charles Kopecek, owned Polehna's Meat Market in what is now Czech Village. At the first Festival of Czech Arts held in Cedar Rapids in 1971, Polehna was slated to demonstrate egg decorating, while Nejdl planned to present Czech-style Sokol gymnastics, which she coached for 27 years. But her uncle got sick and wasn't able to present, so he asked Nejdl to take his place. "I am so thankful it happened, because it's been my life ever since. It was an accident," Nejdl said. Ever since that first demonstration, Nejdl has both produced her own art and taught regular classes, working to pass the techniques down to the next generation. Her hobby took her to the Iowa State fair in 1982 where she was acclaimed officially as an Iowa Folk Artist. In 1996, Marj went to Washington D.C. to attend and demonstrate at the Festival of Arts at the National Sesquicentennial Festival of the Arts. She has illustrated many posters. She designed the shirt for the International Czechoslovakian Sokol Festival which was held in Omaha, Nebraska. Marj's love of Czech music and song puts her into the ranks of charter member of the Czech Heritage Singers of Cedar Rapids, Iowa.

Michael Pavlík (1941–), b. Prague, Czech., received a B.A. at the School of Glass Art in Železný Brod, and in Prague (1973), and his M.F.A. at the Academy of Arts and Architecture in Prague (1981). After coming to the United States in the early 80s, he worked at the Penland School of Crafts. He produced abstract glass sculptures unusually composed of linked elements of simple geometric forms with highly polished surfaces. He received immediate recognition, including a grant from the National Endowment for the arts in 1984. From 1982 to 1998, Pavlik created two seemingly different bodies of work, one made from encasing layers of molten glass, and the other by techniques of casting and gluing elements together. As different as the processes were, the common denominator was the exploration of complex spatial relationships. In 1999, Pavlik and his wife Vladimíra Klumpar began casting sculpture together and in 2001, moved back to the Czech Republic to oversee the casting of their work. In 2003, Pavlik retired leaving an impressive body of work in the hands of collectors and over 30 museums.

Dušan Petran (1955-) b. Brno, Czech., a master carver, and puppeteer, carries on the art and craft of puppetry, as well as the tradition of the marionette theater of his native Czech Republic. As a child, he learned about puppetry in Moravia, the region where he grew up, which has a long tradition of wood carvers, many of whom chose the art form of puppet making to make a living. His marionettes are hand carved in wood and represent traditional Czech puppet characters. He demonstrated his technical skill by carving puppets and displaying finished marionettes, showing how he develops their expressive qualities, and strings and balances all the parts to achieve the movement wanted. In addition to carving, he created Yorick's Marionette Theatre, which draws on traditional Czech puppet characters. He has performed extensively in the US and Europe, and has received numerous awards for his work, including a traditional arts fellowship from the Rhode Island State Council on the Arts. He lived and worked in United States in 1989-2009 and in France since 2010.

Vince Pitelka (ca. 1949-), b. California, of Czech ancestry, studied art at Humboldt State Univ. (B.A., 1971). After a ten-year career as a studio potter in Blue Lake, California, he returned to school in 1985 for his M.F.A. in ceramics at University of Massachusetts, Amherst. He was with Univ. of Massachusetts (1989-91); with North Dakota State Univ., Fargo (1991-94). Currently, he is assoc. professor of clay, and head of the Clay Center, Tennessee Technological Univ.'s Appalachian Center for Crafts, Smithvillle, TN.

Ludmila Procházka, b. Czech. is a ceramic sculptor. She is a Canadian artist, living and working in Ottawa. She completed her art education in the Czech Republic and established herself as a professional artist. She has been exhibiting and selling her artwork in Canada and abroad for over 30 years. She is a member of the National Capital Network of Sculptors in Ottawa, Ontario, Canada. Her work can be found in many countries around the world including Canada, United States, Czech Republic, Germany, Austria, Switzerland, and Australia. Her charming and authentic ceramic sculpture reliefs are sculpted in clay, then glazed and fired in the kiln. She assembles them into wall size reliefs, transforming her environment into a breathtaking scenery. She defines her artwork through two- and three-dimensional forms that meet between the ancient and modern world of art.

Axel Jakob Salmson (1807-1876), b. Stockholm, Sweden, of Bohemian father, was a visual artist and graphic artist, lithographer and pioneer of color printing. He was a student at the Academy of Fine Arts, painted miniatures, and performed lithographs for the collection. He published several, at that time popular works such as, *Swedish kings and their epochs*, with text by A. L. Arvidsson 1830-1843, *the most remarkable people of the Thirty Years' War*, 1844–1856, also *Gripsholmsgalleriet*, all according to his own drawings. He founded in Stockholm, around 1854, a fairly large lithographic printing house, but lacking equity to run it properly. He ran into serious financial troubles, committed criminal proceedings and escaped in 1862 from his native country to North America, where he died in 1876.

William 'Bill' Schiffer (fl. 1970), b. New York, NY, of Slovak descent, artist, jewelry designer, NYC. Schiffer was a student at 'The Castle on the Hill,' also known as The High School of Music & Art in Harlem. This magnet school eventually combined to become the Fiorello H. LaGuardia High School of Music & the Arts. Schiffer was surrounded by creativity from a young age and experimented with paint, paper collage cutouts, and sculpture, not being constrained by his materials or environment. He conveyed his ideas through colorful murals and large-scale abstract street art. In 1973, he started creating jewelry that could be worn as art. Bloomingdales was the first store to carry his designs, and Saks Fifth Avenue followed shortly after. His jewelry counters remained in place for ten and twelve years, respectively, as permanent fixtures in the departments. Each handcrafted item is unique or limited to one. In 1980, Bill Schiffer and his wife Sally Hawkins launched an art gallery on West Broadway in the Soho area of New York City. There, on the side of the building that came to represent Soho, he painted a well-known mural that became a symbol of the times. Even though Schiffer is best known for his handcrafted jewelry, he stopped making new pieces that could be worn in 2006 after his wife passed away. Schiffer is still producing high-quality, multi-dimensional artwork. In 2017, he finished a new wall mural on the side of Bistro Les Amis in New York, leaving his mark on Soho once more.

Sidonka Wadina (ca. 1985–), b. Milwaukee, WI, of Slovak descent, is a Slovak Master folk artist, graphic designer, egg decorator, straw weaver, and folk painter. Sidonka Wadina grew up in a Slovak neighborhood in Milwaukee, Wisconsin. Her grandmother, Johanna Biksadski, told folk tales and stories of Slovakia, while teaching Wadina to decorate eggs and weave straw talismans for the annual Holiday Folk Fair, an ethnic festival in which the family has participated since 1943. Her grandmother told her: "You are the future; it is up to you to pass this along so it will never be lost." When Biksadski lectured and gave presentations on Slovak culture at schools and colleges, her granddaughter demonstrated. When relatives returned from Slovakia with examples of straw work, Wadina took them apart to understand how they were made. Later, she studied harvest mythology, visited museums in Slovakia and learned to recreate the traditional straw talismans. She became proficient in dozens of straw plaits and egg-decorating techniques from villages throughout the Czech Republic and Slovakia. She has also conducted master classes in straw weaving in Poland, Hungary, Ukraine and Belarus.

13. Pop Visual Artists

Bozidor Brazda (1972–), b. Cambridge, Canada, of Slovak descent; the grandson of the award-winning journalist Andrej Brázda-Jankovský. He is an artist living in New York City. Brazda's work consists of silk screens, wall texts, and audio recordings. In recent years, the artist has moved away from his earlier "narrative-driven" installations to a minimalist Pop Art that reflects his continued interest in the 'edges of popular culture.' His work has appeared in purple.com, Artforum, Flash Art, artnet.com, *The New York Times*, *Architectural Digest (France)*, *Art in America*, *Interview Magazine* and *Maximum Rocknroll*. Brazda plays in the post-punk band TXTR with model and singer Ruby Aldridge.

Miloš Reindl (1923–2002), b. Czech. is one of the most remarkable, yet unknown artists of his generation. Trained in the ateliers of Emil Filla and Antonin Kybal, Reindl arrived in Canada in 1968 as a political refugee. Following in the tradition of Czech Cubism, Reindl's style was greatly influenced by European modern art, in particular Pablo Picasso, Henri Matisse, Marc Chagall and Jean Dubuffet. He studied at the Academy of Arts, Architecture and Design in Prague, and graduated in 1951. Following the Soviet invasion of Czechoslovakia in 1968, Reindl emigrated to Montreal, Canada. In the early 1970s, he began a career as an art professor, teaching for nearly thirty years at Laval University. During his years as a teacher, Reindl continued to paint, creating hundreds of oil paintings, gouaches, and drawings over the course of his career, however his work was only shared with only a few close friends until after his death in 2002. His art has its own unique style, recognizable by the masterful lines of his drawings and the unfettered colors of his paintings.

Edward Joseph Ruscha, 4th (1937–), b. Omaha, of Czech ancestry, is an American artist associated with the pop art movement. He has worked in the media of painting, printmaking, drawing, photography, and film, and the creation of artist books. Though born in Nebraska, Ruscha lived some 15 years in Oklahoma City before moving to Los Angeles in 1956 where he studied at the Chouinard Art Institute (now known as the California Institute of the Arts) under Robert Irwin and Emerson Woelffer from 1956 through 1960. While at Chouinard, Ruscha edited and produced the journal *Orb* (1959–60) together with Joe Goode, Emerson Woelffer, Stephan von Huene, Jerry McMillan, and others. Ruscha spent much of the summer of 1961 traveling through Europe. After graduation, Ruscha took a job as a layout artist for the Carson-Roberts Advertising Agency in Los Angeles. By the early 1960s, he was well known for his paintings, collages, and photographs, and for his association with the Ferus Gallery group, which also included artists Robert Irwin, John Altoon, John McCracken, Larry Bell, Ken Price, and Edward Kienholz. He worked as layout designer for *Artforum* magazine under the pseudonym 'Eddie Russia' from 1965 to 1969 and taught at UCLA as a visiting professor for printing and drawing in 1969. He is also a lifelong friend of guitarist Mason Williams. Ruscha achieved recognition for paintings incorporating words and phrases and for his many photographic books, all influenced by the deadpan irreverence of the Pop Art movement. His textual, flat paintings have been linked with both the Pop Art movement and the beat generation. Ruscha lives and works in Culver City, California.

Andy Warhol (orig. Andrew Warhola) (1928–1987), b. Pittsburgh, PA, of Slovak-Ruthenian descent, was an artist, a leading figure in the visual art movement known as pop art whose works explore the relationship between artistic expression, advertising, and celebrity culture that flourished by the 1960s, and span a variety of media, including painting, silkscreening, photography, film, and sculpture. Some of his best-known works include the silkscreen paintings *Campbell's Soup Cans* (1962) and *Marilyn Diptych* (1962), the experimental films *Empire* (1964) and *Chelsea Girls* (1966), and the multimedia events known as the *Exploding Plastic Inevitable* (1966–67). Warhol initially pursued a successful career as a commercial illustrator. After exhibiting his work in several galleries in the late 1950s, he began to receive recognition as an influential and controversial artist. His New York studio, 'The Factory,' became a well-known gathering place that brought together distinguished intellectuals, drag queens, playwrights, Bohemian street people, Hollywood celebrities, and wealthy patrons. He promoted a collection of personalities known as Warhol Superstars and is credited with inspiring the widely used expression '15 minutes of fame.' In the late 1960s, he managed and produced the experimental rock band The Velvet Underground and founded *Interview* magazine. He authored numerous books, including *The Philosophy of Andy Warhol* and *Popism: The Warhol Sixties*. Warhol has been the subject of numerous retrospective exhibitions, books, and feature and documentary films. The Andy Warhol Museum in his native city of Pittsburgh, which holds an extensive permanent collection of art and archives, is the largest museum in the United States dedicated to a single artist.

14. Costume & Fashion Designers

Sarah Ann Courtney Dano (aft. 1984–), b. New York, of Bohemian descent on her mother's side, is a costume designer. Since 2015, she has been a set costumer at New Line Productions, Inc. She studied arts management at College of Charleston.

Rudi Gernreich (1922–1985), b. Vienna, of Bohemian ancestry, was an avant-garde fashion designer of the 1960s. Gernreich immigrated to the United States in 1938 and, from 1942 to 1948, was a dancer and costume designer for the Lester Horton Modern Dance Troupe. From 1951 to 1959, he worked as a designer for a Los Angeles boutique. In 1960, Rudi Gernreich Inc. was formed, but he continued to design knitwear and swimsuits for other manufacturers. He became interested in developing nonrestrictive and contemporary clothing for women. His innovative designs were intended as an alternative to the conservative styles of the then-dominant Parisian fashion houses. In 1964, he designed a topless swimsuit ('monokini') that gained him worldwide notoriety. The unisex look, invisible undergarments, transparent tops, miniskirts, knit tank suits, and brightly colored stockings were his trademarks.

Anne Jaros (1954–), b. Berwyn, IL, of Czech ancestry, was trained in technical theatre, technical design at Univ. of Illinois, Urbana (B.F.A., 1976) and in design at Northwestern Univ. (M.F.A., 1981). She was asst. professor and costume designer at SUNY Geneseo, NY (1982–87), before becoming professor of theatre and costume designer at Missouri Southern State Univ. (s. 1989). She has both designed professionally and/or taught at the college level for over 35 years. Anne is a member of United Scenic Artists Association, the professional designers' union. Her current goal is to teach students to do high quality theatre work while maintaining their physical and emotional health.

Lauren Bush Lauren (née Lauren Pierce Bush) (1984–), b. Denver, CO, of Bohemian ancestry, is the CEO, Creative Director, and Co-Founder of FEED Projects. She is also a fashion model and designer. She is the daughter of Neil Bush and Sharon Bush (née Smith), granddaughter of former President George H. W. Bush and niece of former President George W. Bush. She was raised in Houston, Texas. She studied fashion design at BEBE and Central Saint Martin's College of Art and Design and graduated from Princeton University in 2006 with a B.A. in Anthropology and a certificate in Photography. Bush is signed with Elite Model Management. She has been featured on the covers of *Vogue and Vanity Fair* magazine and has frequently modeled for Tommy Hilfiger, as well as for Abercrombie & Fitch and designers Gai Mattiolo and Isaac Mizrahi. Bush was an intern on the television sitcom *Friends*, making a cameo in one episode, and interned alongside Ashley Olsen with designer Zac Posen. In 2005, Bush traveled to Chad as a Student Ambassador for the World Food Program. In 2007, Lauren Bush launched FEED Projects, an initiative to fight world hunger on behalf of the UN World Food Programme. Bush relaunched her fashion label on September 11, 2008, under the name 'Lauren Pierce.' In 2012, Lauren Bush was announced as the first National Lady Godiva Honoree of the Lady Godiva Program. She became the 2013 Advocacy Award recipient from World of Children Award in celebration of the significant work she and her organization, FEED Projects, has done for hungry children worldwide.

Mallory Prucha (1981–), Omaha, NE, of Czech ancestry, as an undergraduate majored in studio arts (B.A.) and studied theatre arts (M.A.), both at Univ. of Nebraska, Omaha. Subsequently, she studied costume design and technology (M.F.A.) at Johnny Carson School of Theatre and Film, Univ. of Nebraska, Lincoln. She also taught courses at the latter institution, and designed costumes for the first non-professional Regional Premiere of Mary Zimmerman's adaptation of Leonard Bernstein's *Candide*. Her artwork for the poster is currently housed in the Leonard Bernstein Permanent Archive. Currently, she is a resident faculty member in Costume Design and Costume Shop Supervisor at Mesa Community College, AZ. She has also taught at the University of WI-Eau Claire and Iowa Western Community College. In the summer of 2008, Prucha completed her 8th season of work with the Nebraska Shakespeare Festival; her duties ranging in capacity from costume designer to special projects assistant in which she created a rendering presented to former NEA Chairman Dana Gioia. She has also spent several seasons designing costumes at the NE Repertory Theatre. Furthermore, she has been the recipient of a two-week fellowship with the Kennedy Center American College Theatre Festival, which granted her the opportunity to study Theatrical Design with world-renown designers Ming Cho Lee and Constance Hoffman at the Kennedy Center in Washington, D.C. She has also published illustrations for A Primer in Theatre History by Dr. William Grange and has illustrated two volumes of poetry for author Toni Poll-Sorensen. Her artwork has received numerous awards, including the distinction of winner of the Westminster Mint's International 'Green Coin' design competition, which yielded the minting of her design in a limited edition the 1-oz silver coin.

Jan Skalicky (1929–2006), b. Joliet, IL, of Czech ancestry, studied in Paris and London, and then at the Academy of Applied Arts in Prague. In the 60s, he designed costumes for Czech theatre and opera stars. After 1968, he returned to the US where he became quite known. He worked with Metropolitan Opera in New York, with Montserrat Cabellé in Paris, etc. Among other, he also designed, on four different occasions, costumes for Smetana's *The Bartered Bride*. In 1977, he was recipient of primetime Emmy Award for outstanding achievement in costume design for music-variety.

Betty Yoková (1901–1995), b. Prague, Bohemia, is a fashion designer. She was employed by With Neustadter Furs, Inc., New York, NY. She was a recipient of Coty Award (1964).

15. Architects

David Adler (1882–1949), b. Milwaukee, WI, of Bohemian ancestry, was a prolific architect, designing over 200 buildings, who largely practiced around Chicago, Illinois. He was also a long-time Board member of the Art Institute of Chicago.

Felix Augenfeld (1893–1984), b. Vienna, of Moravian ancestry, was a Vienna trained architect and interior designer. He was in US s. 1939 as freelancer. From 1941, he had his own architectural studio in NYC. Augenfeld's designs included the Buttinger residence and research library on East 87th Street. He also created a special chair to accommodate the position Sigmund Freud liked to sit in. Photos and diagrams of his work are at Columbia Univ. Library.

David Peter Baycura (1953–), b. Pittsburgh, Pa, of Slovak descent, is a landscape architect and real estate developer. He was trained in landscape architecture at Penn State University (B.S.) and in business administration at University of Pittsburgh (M.B.A.).

Tibor (Eliahu) Beerman (1925–2015), b. Berehovo, Czech., was an architect in the United States. His work, much of it modernist, includes synagogues, residences, and the 1966 Galveston County Courthouse. His brother died at Buchenwald, and Beerman wrote about his own experiences during the Holocaust.

Miroslava M. Beneš (1953–), b. San Francisco, CA, of Czech ancestry, studied history of art at Princeton Univ. (B.A., 1974) and at Yale Univ. (M.A., 1977, M.Phil., 1977; Ph.D., 1989). She was associated with Harvard Univ., as asst. professor of landscape architecture (1988–94), as assoc. professor (1994–2000) and as sr. lecturer (1994–2000). Subsequently, she joined Univ. of Texas, Austin, as assoc. professor of landscape architecture (s. 2006). Her scholarly research focuses on the city of Rome, its urban, architectural, and landscape histories, including vernacular landscapes. She publishes on Roman Baroque architecture and gardens and on relationships between the design of landscape and landscape painting. She is preparing a book on Landscape, Architecture, and Experience in Baroque Rome: Gardens and Parks in the Age of Claude Lorrain. Beneš co-edited, with Michael G. Lee, *Clio in the Italian Garden: Twenty-First-Century Studies in Historical Methods and Theoretical Perspectives* (2011), and with Dianne Harris she co-edited *Villas and Gardens in Early Modern Italy and France* (2001). She is particularly concerned with methodological and historiographical issues in the history of landscape architecture and has published on this topic. She has held numerous fellowships and lectures nationally and internationally. Beneš has twice been a Fellow of the American Academy in Rome and twice a Fellow of Dumbarton Oaks Center for Garden and Landscape Studies, a Harvard Research Institute in Washington, D.C.

W. Dominick Beneš (1857–1935), b. Prague, Bohemia, was a prominent architect, responsible for some of Cleveland's most splendid classical revival buildings, including the Cleveland Museum of Art, as well as major early modern commercial structures, including the Ohio Bell Telephone Co. He immigrated to the US with his family in 1866. In 1876, Benes began with the Cleveland architectural firm of Coburn & Barnum, later Coburn, Barnum, Benes & Hubbell (1896). Benes and Hubbell subsequently established their own partnership, Hubell & Benes (1897–1939), whose major projects included the Citizens' Bldg. (1903); the Cleveland School of Art (1905), demolished; the Mather College Gymnasium (1908); the West Side Market (1912); the YMCA (1912); the Illuminating Bldg. (1915); the Masonic Auditorium

(1921); the current business wing (1922) of the Cleveland Public Library; the Phillis Wheatley Assoc. (1927); and St. Luke's Hospital (1927). Benes was president of the American Institute of Architects Cleveland Chapter and the Cleveland Architectural Club.

John Virginius Bennes (1867–1943), b. Peru, IL, of Bohemian ancestry, was an American architect in Baker City and Portland, OR. In Baker City he designed the Geiser Grand Hotel, several homes, and the Elks Building.

Benjamin C. Bloch (1890–1977), b. Chicago, IL, of Bohemian ancestry, was Cornell Univ. trained architect. He was a partner, arch. firm, The Bloch & Hesse, New York City (s. 1913). He was the architect of Free Synagogue Bldg, New York City, White Plains Community Center, Beth El, Great Neck, L.I., Coney Island Jewish Center, Brooklyn, NY, Hunts Point Hospital, Park E. Hospital, etc.

Titus de Bobula (1878–1961), b. Budapest, of Slovak descent; American architect; in US s. 1897, living and working at times in New York City and Marietta, Ohio. In 1903, he arrived in Pittsburgh, Pennsylvania, where he designed buildings for the next eight years. One of his major commissions was St. John the Baptist Greek Catholic Church in Munhall, Pennsylvania, patterned after the Rusyn Greek Catholic Cathedral of the Exaltation of the Holy Cross in Uzhhorod. The church's twin towers, which rise 125 feet, are composed of white brick in a Greek cruciform pattern set into sandstone. His last building in Pittsburgh was St. Peter and Paul Ukrainian Orthodox Greek Catholic Church in Carnegie, Pennsylvania.

Richard Bondy-Charvát (1893–1978), b. Trnava, Slovakia, was a landscape architect and politician. He studied agriculture and economics at Leipzig University and graduated from the Institute of Agricultural Engineering in Prague. During the Nazi occupation of Czechoslovakia, he escaped to Yugoslavia and joined in organizing Czechoslovak foreign legion units. He then left with Czechoslovak volunteers to France but when France capitulated, he left for England. After the war, he returned to his homeland but later left for England again., where he managed his estate in South Wales. Since 1962, he was engaged in landscaping in Fontana, WI.

Jiří W. Boudník (1970–), b. Plzeň, Czech., is an architect, residing in New York City. He is also known as a photographer. At the age of seventeen, he emigrated with his mother and sister to the United States. He graduated from the Civil Engineering School. He later studied art at the Munson Williams Proctor Institute School of Art (1989–91) and architecture at Cooper Union (1991–97). In September 2001, he worked as a design engineer on the construction of the Federal Court Building on the Brooklyn Bridge. After 9/11, he was heavily involved in rescue work and the removal of the wreckage of the towers of the World Trade Center in New York, which became one of the targets of the attacks of September 11, 2001. He assembled for the rescuers the first model of the site of the tragedy and the models of the wreckage, which helped rescuers rescue people from the destroyed twins. It was six months of volunteering. Later, in February 2002, he worked in a team of experts tasked with investigating the collapse of buildings. His return to normal life was accompanied by severe depression after this event. He later founded his own company Brain Storm, which deals, among other things, with 3D modeling of buildings. The book, *Towers Book -The Story of September 11* tells the story of Jiří Boudník, as a direct participant in the fall of the New York towers. It points to the author's dedication and use of his expertise to save many lives and speed up the removal of WTC debris. It offers an insight into the greatest tragedy of modern history. A number of technical details and human destinies appear in the book, giving the whole story another dimension. The book was also loaded into the form of an audiobook by the actor of the National Theater, Pavel Baťek.

Paul Buřík (1954–), b. České Budějovice, Czech, escaped from Czechoslovakia in 1968 after the Soviet invasion and settled in Cleveland. He attended Kent State University where he received a degree in architecture (dipl. 1977). He spent much of his professional career working for the City of Cleveland as chief architect, now retired. While there, he had an opportunity to work on numerous city buildings including the famed West Side Market. He became involved with the Cultural Gardens as a representative of the Czech Garden. He is the immediate past president of the Cleveland Cultural Gardens Federation, an umbrella organization of all the 30+ gardens, representing the various nationalities. During his presidency, the Gardens experienced a renaissance with a new Garden being added each of the past four years. Currently there are several nationalities waiting to build a new Garden.

Robert George Cerny (1908–1985), b. La Crosse, WI, of Czech ancestry, was Univ. of Minnesota and Harvard Univ. trained architect. He practiced architecture in Minneapolis in partnership with Thorshov, later pres. of the Cerny Assoc., Inc., architects, Minneapolis and St. Paul. He also held position of prof. of architecture at Univ. of Minnesota.

Eugene Cizek (1942–), b. Louisiana, of Czech ancestry, studied architecture at Louisiana State Univ. (B.A., 1964), city planning (M.C.P., 1966) and urban design (M.U.D., 1966) at MIT; city building at Delt Inst. of Technology (D.Sc., 1967) and environmental social psychology at Tulane Univ. (Ph.D., 1978). Cizek taught architecture and landscape architecture at Louisiana State Univ. (LSU) from 1967 to 1970; served as acting director of architecture and planning in New Orleans for the City Improvement Agency from 1970 to 1978; and was the founder and first president of the Faubourg Marigny Improvement Association. A founding Board member of the Preservation Resource Center of New Orleans, he is also a founding member of the Historic Bourbon Street Foundation, the

Riverfront Coalition, and the Priestley School of Architecture and Construction. Cizek's passion for preserving the built environment led him to create the nationally acclaimed Education through Historic Preservation Program, for which he served as co-director from 1977 to 2011. In 1978, he became a professor of architecture and Latin American Studies at Tulane School of Architecture, where he founded the Preservation Studies Program. He has restored numerous historic houses in New Orleans and has served as a consultant to historic structures throughout the region. Among the many organizations to grant him honors are the National Trust for Historic Preservation, the Louisiana Landmarks Society, the Foundation for Historical Louisiana, Save Our Cemeteries, and the National Council of Preservation Education.

Dorothy Wormser Coblentz (1894–1988), b. Deming, Luna Co., NM, of Bohemian ancestry, was the first Jewish female architect in the American West. In fact, the first 'girl' architect licensed by the state of California. In 1918, she began working for renowned San Francisco architect Julia Morgan. Eventually Wormser worked at San Simeon for Morgan on her massive commission there for publisher William Randolph Hearst, helping to catalog the art and antiquities that arrived by railroad carloads. Wormser also began work in 1921 on Morgan's commission for a Jewish women's group to design a residential facility for Jewish working girls in San Francisco, the Emanuel-El Sisterhood Residence. The three-story, brick residence club, completed in 1922, lists Dorothy Wormser as an Associate Architect. The building survives today as the San Francisco Zen Center.

Dana Čupková (fl. 2012), b. Slovakia; architect. She holds assistant professorship at the Carnegie Mellon School of Architecture and is a co-founder and design director of EPIPHYTE Lab, an architectural design and research collaborative. Cupkova was a founder and design director of DCm-STUDIO, an architectural design practice in New York City, and has extensive international professional experience in Europe, the United States, and Southeast Asia. She was previously in practice with Smith-Miller+Hawkinson Architects, RUR Architecture in New York City, and TR Hamzah & Yeang in Malaysia.

John Jacob Desmond (1922–2008), b. Denver, CO, of Bohemian ancestry on his mother's side, was an American architect in Baton Rouge, Louisiana, who designed such public buildings as the Baton Rouge River Center, the Louisiana State University Student Union, Bluebonnet Swamp Interpretive Center, Louisiana Arts and Sciences Center, Louisiana State Archives, etc.

John Michael Desmond (1953–), b. New Orleans, LA, of Czech ancestry, studied architecture at Louisiana State Univ. and graduated from Grad School of Design at Harvard and MIT. He holds an architectural license and has practiced in Louisiana and Massachusetts, most recently with an AIA design award for the Bluebonnet Swamp Interpretive Center in Baton Rouge. He is prof. of architecture at the Louisiana State Univ. His teaching responsibilities include architectural history and urban design. He is coordinator of the Master of Architecture Program in the School of Architecture. His areas of interest include: history, theory and criticism of architecture, architecture and the city, American architecture, and cultural mythology.

James B. Dibelka (1869-1925), b. Bohemia, was an architect of note who designed many large public buildings in the Chicago area, including the Univ. of Illinois. During 1913-17, he held the position of the State architect for the State of Illinois. He was recipient of International Medal at San Francisco international exposition.

Francis J. Dittrich (1892-1973), b. Zlonice, Bohemia, was an architect. He obtained his architectural education in a Technical Coll. in Prague. He came to America in 1912, settling in Chicago. He became a designer and chief draftsman with C. W. Corbusier, architect, Chicago (1916-19); designer and chief draftsman with B. K. Gibson, architect, Chicago (1919-23) and as designer with Graham Anderson Probst & White Architects, Chicago (1923-30). Since then, he was in partnership with C. W. Nicol and B. K. Gibson, architects. His office was in Chicago on Van Bren Street.

Cyrus Lazelle Warner Eidlitz (1853-1921), b. New York City, of Bohemian father, was a New York architect best known for designing One Times Square, the former New York Times Building on Times Square.

Leopold Eidlitz (1823-1908), b. Prague, Bohemia, exponent of Gothic revival in architecture who built in that style some of the most beautiful buildings in New York. H is best known for his work on the New York State Capitol in Albany, as well as 'Iranistan,' P. T. Barnum's house in Bridgeport, Connecticut, St. Peter's Church in Bronx, the former Temple Emanu-El, the Broadway Tabernacle, etc. He was America's first Jewish architect.

Robert James Eidlitz (1864-1935), b. New York City, of Bohemian ancestry, was educated at both Cornell University, from which he graduated in 1885, and later at the Berlin Polytechnic, where he studied architecture. After completing his schooling, Eidlitz went to work for his father in the latter's building firm, Marc Eidlitz & Son, Inc. In 1928, Eidlitz was named president of the company, following the death of his older brother. Many of New York City's most prominent buildings—including the ANS's expanded Audubon Terrace facility—were built by Eidlitz's company. These buildings include the Federal Reserve Bank, Cloisters museum, New York Academy of Medicine, Yale Club, Astor Library, AT&T building, and New York Stock Exchange.

Martin Eisler (1913–1977), b. Vienna, of Moravian ancestry, studied architecture in his home country. In 1938, he moved to Buenos Aires, Argentina, where he started his work as a designer and architect and exhibiting his furniture designs. From the early 1950's to the late 1970's, he worked mostly in Brazil, on his own designs, mostly self-produced and he collaborated with the Brazilian company Forma. Eisler worked in the height of the Mid-Century Modern period. He used many local exotic woods, like jacaranda and civiona, but he also experimented with black lacquered wood, reverse painted glass, glass, bronze, and cane materials. He frequently collaborated on designs and, with E. J. Wolf, who became the company's director, founded Forma to sell their own designs as well as pieces licensed from Knoll International. Eisler also opened Forma in Buenos Aires, along with partners Arnold Hakel and Susi Aczel, as an architectural, industrial and interior design firm also known as Interieur Forma. His sleek and curvaceous pieces were masterly crafted and mixed exotic local woods with precious materials like bronze, painted glass or lacquered panels. His warm color palette and bright prints clearly evoke his Brazilian environment.

Francis Augustus Flaks (1886–1945), b. Měčín, Bohemia, was an architect. He came to America in 1903. He attended evening classes at the Armour Institute and the Chicago Art Institute and passed the state examination for architects in 1914. From 1904 to 1920, he was an architectural draftsman for James B. Dibelka and Michin, and since 1920, he had been chief draftsman for Schmidt, Garden & Erickson. He was a member of the Illinois Society of Architects and the Bohemian Arts Club. His office was located in Chicago on Michigan Ave.

Petr Franta (1948–), b. Prague, Czech., studied at the Faculty of Architecture, Prague (Ing. Arch., 1972). Starting in 1977, he lived in Montréal, Canada, where he began working at De Nova Associates in Montreal as designer of exhibition and interior projects, later collaborating with various architects on individual projects. He joined the firm Fiset, Miller, Vinois Architects in 1982, where he worked as design architect until 1985. The same year, he was associated with a New York architect and formed Roberto Brambilla & Petr Franta, Architects and Planners, becoming registered in the state of New York in 1989. With the Montréal architect James Ogden, he founded the firm Ogden Franta Architects in 1986, a partnership which lasted until 1993. In the second half of the nineteen-eighties, he collaborated with the sculptor Magdalena Jetelová on monumental sculptures for public locations and museums. He became a member of the Architekten Kammer Nord Rhein Westfalen in Düsseldorf in 1990, at which time he returned to Prague and joined with Michal Brix to form the architectural atelier Brix & Franta Architects & Assoc., Ltd. in 1991. This partnership was dissolved in 1997, when he formed the studio Petr Franta Architects & Assoc., Ltd.

Joseph Fuller (1926-2003), b. Pacov, Czech., was an architect trained at Charles Univ. He was a designer and architect with Crow, Lewis & Wick, NYC (1952-59) and then established his own firm, NYC (1960-65); architect, with Max O. Urbahn, NYC (s. 1965); and then founded the firm Fuller and D'Angelo, Architects in Elmsford, NY (1972).

Victor Fürth (1893-1984), b. Horažďovice, Bohemia, was a Czech architect working in Prague until 1939. Between 1928 and 1930, he and Ernst Mühlstein designed the Villa Schück in Prague. He also joined with Ernst Mühlstein in the design of the large apartment complex in Prague called Molochov on Milady Horákové Street in the years 1936-1938. When the Adolf Hitler regime came to power in Czechoslovakia, he had to leave and fled to the United States through Great Britain. In Oxford, Ohio, Victor Furth joined the faculty at Miami University as a professor of architecture. Among his designs were the Bern Street Apartments having large bedrooms and hardwood floors and numerous houses for Miami faculty often employing a cathedral ceiling.

John Gustav Gabriny (1923-2000), b. Rajec, Czech., was an architect, Washington, DC.

Ray Weld Gray (1880-1944), b. Boston, MA of Moravian ancestry, was an architect trained at Harvard Univ. and Ecole des Beaux Arts in Paris. He engaged in independent practice in Boston. His outstanding work includes the River St. Bridge between Boston and Cambridge. He was also known for his domestic architectural designs. He was awarded the Parker Medal of Boston Soc. Arch. In additional to architectural work, he was known for his paintings and water colors.

Victor Gruen (orig. Grünbaum) (1903-1980), b. Vienna, of Moravian ancestry, was an American architect best known as a pioneer in the design of shopping malls in the United States.

Kamil Stephen Gschwind (1931-2005), b. Plzeň, Czech., studied architecture at School of Architecture and Urban Design of the Technical Univ. of Prague (Dr. Arch. Eng., 1955) and at Academy of Fine Arts (M. Arch., 1958). He first worked as director of design with William Dorothy and Assoc. and then as a project architect with Hisaka and Assoc. Subsequently, he opened his own architectural firm Kamil S. Gschwind in Richmond Heights, Ohio. He also lectured at Kent State Univ. He specialized in rendering and design work and was consultant for seven architectural firms until his death.

Tomáš Gulíšek (ca. 1970-), b. Slovakia; architect, registered in New York (s. 2000). He is a Design Principal with AE7. He is an internationally recognized designer who has worked in the US, Europe and MENA for over 17 years. Previous to AE7, Tomas was one of the founding Principals of the Burt Hill Dubai office and has been living in the MENA region for over 5 years.

John Quentin Hejduk (1929-2000), b. New York, NY, of Czech ancestry, an architect trained at Harvard, became Dean of Cooper Union School of Art and Architecture, post he held for 25 years. He was one of the most original architects in the United States, noted for his use of attractive and often difficult-to-construct objects and shapes. He had also a profound interest in the fundamental issues of shape, organization, representation, and reciprocity. He was known more for his visionary works of architecture on paper and his influence on graduates of Cooper Union.

Oswald Constantin Hering (1874-1941), b. Philadelphia, PA, of Moravian ancestry, was the son of civil engineer Rudolph Hering. He attended MIT (1893-97) and studied art and architecture further at the atelier Ginain and Ecole des Beaux Arts in Paris (1897-99). In 1901, he opened his own architectural practice in NYC, which he ran for a period in partnership with Douglas Fitch. He specialized in country and suburban homes and pioneered residential use of reinforced concrete. He designed a number of residences for both Garden City and Jamaica Estates, Long Island, NY. His nonresidential projects included the old Brentano bookstore in NYC and the Lakewood Theater, Skowhegan, Maine. He was the author of several books on architecture, including *Concrete and Stucco Houses* (1912), *Economy in Home Building* (1924) and *Designing and Building the Chapter House* (1931).

Martin Holub (1938-), b, Prague, Czech., trained at the Czech Technical Univ. in Prague, is the principal of Martin Holub Architects and Planners, a New York architectural firm, established in 1971. Between 1975 and 1979, the firm maintained a branch office in Teheran, Iran and in 1990, after the fall of communism, the firm established a subsidiary ARA-Praha/New York.

Franziska Hosken (née Porges) (1919-2006), b. Vienna, of Bohemian father, was an architect trained at Harvard Univ. From 1948, she was a freelance display designer and architectural worker. She became an owner, manager and designer-in-chief, Hosken Inc., contemporary furniture (1948-54); interior design consultant and instructor, Garland Coll. (1958-61); prof. of urban design, Experimental Coll., Tufts Univ. (s. 1970); assoc. prof., Univ. Without Walls, Boston (1971-74). She was also a social activist.

Frank M. Hrachovský (1907-2002), b. Strážnice, Moravia, was an architect trained at Brno Polytechnic and Armour Inst. of Technology. He also did graduate work in the history of art at Univ. of Chicago. He was practicing architect (until 1946), in the capacity of chief designer for Friedman Altschuler and Sincere Architects in Chicago. He was with Illinois

Inst. of Technology, where he had risen from asst. professor to assoc. prof. of engineering graphics. He was very active in various Czech-American organizations.

J. W. Hrádek (1855-1936), b. Bohemia, came to Cleveland in 1882 where he studied architecture. He was employed by Andrew Mitermiler for five years and Lehman and Schmitt for three years. In 1890, he went into business for himself. Hruby Conservatory of Music in Cleveland, which he designed, is on the National Register of Historic Places.

Henry Hradílek (1886-1938), b. Moravia, was a Cleveland architect. He designed numerous single family homes in Cleveland Heights. His Weizer Building built in 1928 is a Cleveland landmark.

Ladislav Hudec (1893-1958), b. Banská Bystrica, Slovakia; architect active in Shanghai from 1918 to 1945 and responsible for some of that city's most notable structures. After leaving Shanghai in 1947, Hudec moved to Lugano and later to Rome. In 1950, he moved to Berkeley where he taught at the University of California.

Miloš B. Jakl (1923-), b. Pátek, Czech., studied architecture at Royal Melbourne Inst. of Technology, Australia (dipl., 1960). He has his own firm, Creamer-Jakl & Assoc. Architects at Sherman Oaks, CA. His interests are in town planning in residential field and development.

Albert F. Janowitz (1867-1936), b. London, of Bohemian parents, worked for the Peoria, Illinois-based architectural office of Wechselberger, Janowitz s. 1894). He was active in Cleveland in the first three decades of the 20th century. He designed the B'Nai Jeshurun Temple and, most notably, Anshe Emeth Synagogue (now Cory Methodist Church). He was also the architect of several apartment buildings along Clifton Boulevard, Lake Avenue, and East Boulevard.

Hugo Kafka (1843-1915), a Czech-American architect, was a founding associate of the predecessor firm of Alfred B. Mullett & Sons, as well as William Scheckel & Company. He ran his own firm, Hugo Kafka in the early twentieth century, later renamed Hugo Kafka & Sons.

Arnold Karplus (1877-1943), b. Vitkov, Moravia, was an architect in New York.

Gerhard Emanuel Karplus (1909-1995), b. Vienna, of Moravian ancestry, was an architect in Florida.

Robert Michael Kliment (1933-2017), b. Prague, Czech., graduated from Yale Univ. (B.A., 1954) and studied architecture also there (M.A., 1959). In 1961, he removed to Philadelphia to work with Ehrman Mitchell and Romaldo Giurgola. He also taught in the Dept. of Architecture, Univ. of Pennsylvania and later at Columbia Univ. In 1972, he opened his own practice, jointly with his wife Frances Husband in NYC. He also taught at Yale Univ. (1978-84), Univ. of Virginia (1979-80) and at Harvard (1980-81). His works include Computer Science Building Princeton University (National Honor award American Institute of Architects 1994), University Virginia Life Sciences Building, Columbia University Computer Sciences Building (National Honor award American Institute of Architects 1987, award NYSAA 1985, Tucker award Building Stone Institute 1985, other awards), Mercantile Exchange Building, New York (Bard award for excellence in architecture City Club New York 1989), Burke Chemistry Building, Dartmouth College, Adelbert Administration Building, Case Western Reserve University (American Institute of Architects National honor award 1994), Sudikoff Computer Science Building, Dartmouth College, MTA/Long Island R.R. Entrance Building, Penn Station, New York (Bard award for excellence in architecture City Club New York 1995, American Institute of Architects national honor award 1996, NYSAA & New York City American Institute of Architects awards 1995), etc. He was recipient of American Institute of Architects Architectural Firm Award (1997), and Medal of Honor New York City American Institute of Architects (1998).

Stephen Alexander Kliment (1930-2008), b. Prague, Czech., was MIT and Princeton Univ. educated architect. He was editor of *Architectural and Engineering News* (1961-69); vice-pres., Candill Rowlett Scott, NYC (1969-72); editor-in-chief, *Advertising and Publishing News* (1978-80); exec. editor, Whitney Library of Design (1981-85); vice pres., Practice Management and Assoc. Ltd. (1985-87); editor, science and technology div., John Wiley and Sons (1987-90), editor, *Architectural Record* 1990-96).

Dennis Kobza (1933-2022), b. Ulysses, NE, an architect, is the founder (s. 1965) of the firm Dennis Kobza & Associates, located in Mountain View, CA. It is an architectural firm with experience with commercial projects such as corporate campuses, biotech facilities and many others. It does master planning, site planning, selection and analysis. It also provides interior design services, consulting services, and building design. Architect Dennis Kobza was Palo Alto's first resident to install solar power in his home, and after 28 years, he became the 500th when his system reached the end of its life, and he installed a whole new solar system; recipient of solar Pal Award for home using photovoltaic solar system generating electricity.

Estanislao Kocourek (1930-), b. Argentina, of Czech ancestry, studied architecture at Buenos Aires (dipl., 1955). In 1958, he took over his father's firm Kocourek SA Construcciones. He designed one of the first skyscrapers in Buenos Aires. He is also an excellent athlete.

Carl Koechlin (1858-d.), b. Vienna, of Bohemian ancestry, was a well-known architect of Peoria, IL, with an office at Observatory Building, where he had been located since 1907.

Jan Jaroslav Kofránek (1939-), b. Prague, studied at Czech Technical Univ. (dipl., 1962). He came to the US in 1969, settling in Seattle, WA. He worked as project architect for Quinton-Budlong (1969-71) and then for J. Graham & Associates (1971-73), WWA, Honolulu (1973-74). Subsequently, he was engaged as vice president by Campisell Associates, Seattle (1974-79), before he opened his own private practice in Seattle, under the title Kofranek Architects on Mercer Island, WA. (s. 1979).

Karl Kohn (1894-1979), b. Prague, Bohemia; architect, Quito, Ecuador. He is considered a pioneer of modern Ecuadorian architecture.

Roger H. Kolar (1944-2023), b. San Diego, CA, of Czech ancestry, studied art and interior design at Southern Methodist University (B.A., 1966) and architecture (B.Arch., with highest honors, 1972) and architectural history (M.Arch., 1979), both at Univ. of Texas, Austin. He is Registered Architect and Registered Interior Designer in the State of Texas. He is partner in the firm Cotera, Kolar and Negrete Architects, Austin, TX. With degrees in both architecture and interior design, Kolar counts among his specialties programming, interior architecture, and space planning. He works extensively on the design of educational facilities for public school districts and for higher education, and in the course of his career, has designed and managed facilities for educational clients throughout central and south Texas. Kolar has maintained historic architecture as an area of primary interest. Thus, he has sought involvement in the firm's projects with a historic component. His advocacy for preservation has led several public bodies to adaptive reuse projects when demolition was being considered.

Otto Kollisch (1881-1951), b. Vienna, of Moravian ancestry, was an architect and master builder in Vienna. After the Austrian Anschluss, he and his family emigrated to the US.

Vlastimil Koubek (1927-2003), b. Brno, Czech., was a Czech American architect who designed more than 100 buildings, most of them in the Washington, D.C. Metropolitan area. Most of his work is modernist in style, although he developed a few structures in other vernaculars.

George Kuska (1921-2003), b. Lincoln, NE, of Czech ancestry, was trained as an architect at Univ. of Nebraska. He designed numerous schools, churches, libraries, and other buildings in and around Central California. At Univ. of Nebraska in Lincoln he designed the Ralph Mueller Bell Tower.

VIII. CULTURE: ARTS & LETTERS

James J. Kuska (1973-2002), b., Nebraska, of Czech ancestry, was a landscape architect, trained at Michigan State Univ. and Univ. of Illinois. He was professor of landscape architecture, University of Idaho (s. 1973) and department chair (1983-92). He has worked as an independent Architecture and planning professional in Spokane, WA since then.

Robert Kuzelka (ca. 1940-), b. Nebraska, of Czech ancestry, holds degrees in architecture from University of Nebraska, Lincoln (UNL) (B.A., 1962) and community and regional planning from the University of Texas at Austin (M.A., 1967). He also conducted post-graduate research in town and country planning at Sydney University in Australia (1968), under a Fulbright Post Graduate Fellowship. His professional experience includes work as an architect, a planner for a neighborhood in Tulsa, Oklahoma, and a policy coordinator on the staff of the Nebraska State Office of Planning and Programming (now the Governor's Policy Research Office). He was a full-time faculty member at UNL from 1979 to 2004. During those years, he was affiliated with the Conservation and Survey Division; Department of Community and Regional Planning; Department of Forestry, Fisheries and Wildlife; University of Nebraska Water Center; and the School of Natural Resources. From 2001 to 2008, he served as the director of UNL's interdisciplinary environmental studies program. His academic research interests are in the areas of public policy and planning. He still advises undergraduate and master's level students in thesis and professional projects for topics that interest him.

Christopher La Farge, Jr. (1897-1956), b. New York City, desc. f. Augustine Heřman, was an architect trained at the Yale Architectural School. He specialized in designing homes, first in the Beaux Arts style and later in modified contemporary and English country manor styles. He designed residences in Charlestown, SC., the Hamptons on Long Island, the Hudson Valley in New York and in the New Haven area. He also shaped the Caneel Bay Resort in the Virgin Islands.

Max Levy (1857-1926), b. Detroit, MI, of Bohemian ancestry, studied architecture, Detroit, 1875. After serving an apprenticeship of three years with an architect, he became chief draftsman in his brother's (Louis E. Levy's) photoengraving establishment in Baltimore during the early struggle to establish and perfect that branch of the graphic arts. He accompanied his brother to Philadelphia, and for a time, was in charge of the entire business. Introduced modern screen for half-tone process; prominent in advances in half-tone illustration in the dev. of the theory of the subject. Received from Franklin Inst., Philadelphia John Scott medal; Royal Cornwall Polytechnic silver medal; gold medals, Chicago, 1903; Paris, 1900, Buffalo, 1901, St. Louis, 1904, medal of honor, San Francisco Expn., 1915. In 1917, he patented counting chamber for hemocytometer, new construction adopted in army and med. institutions and awarded the Edward Longstreth Medal from Franklin Inst. in 1918.

Goodhue Livingston (1867-1951), b. New York City, desc. f. Frederick Philipse, was Columbia Univ. trained architect. He practiced architecture in NYC (s. 1896). Among his most notable designs were buildings for J. P. Morgan & Co., Bankers Trust Co., Chemical National Bank, Bank of America, NY Stock Exchange, Hayden Planetarium, all in NYC. In 1936, he won an architectural contract for new state capitol in Oregon. He won Medal of Honor from AIA and Architectural League of NY for his outstanding work.

Peter Lizoň (1938-), b. Lučenec, Czech.; architect, professor of architecture, University of Tennessee, Knoxville.

Adolph Lonek (1864-1938), b. Čižice, Bohemia, was an architect educated at Charles Univ. He designed and supervised construction of many private residences in Chicago and the western suburbs. Among the business structures he designed was the Adams S. Bank and the Pilsen Brewery.

Miroslav J. Macalík (1935-), b. Zlín, Czech., studied architecture at Technical Univ. of Brno (Ing. Arch., 1958) and Dalhousie Univ., and building economics at Univ. of Karlsruhe (1978). He has been associated with Dalhousie Univ., Halifax, as professor of architecture for some 30 years (1968-97). In addition, he was engaged as a consultant (s. 1980) and president of Caneur Limited, Halifax (1980-2014).

Frank J. Machlica, 3rd (1945-2015), b. Endicott, NY, of Slovak ancestry; architect, with Veterans Administration, Cincinnati, OH; US Air force in Dayton, OH and Camp Spring, MD; and US Navy, Washington, DC.

Ricardo de Jaxa Malachowski (1887-1972), b. Prochorowa, nr Odessa, Ukraine, of Polish father and Slovak mother; a Peruvian architect; known as the main architect of Government Palace of Peru in Lima (1938).

Rudolf Mikuta (1907-1989), b. Nýdek, Moravia, was trained as an architect at Czech Technical Univ. of Prague. He practiced architecture in Connecticut and New York City (1950-55), Miami, FL (1956-63), Los Angeles (1963-67). He was principal architect and chief designer, for Ralph M. Parsons Co., Pasadena, CA (1967-77); subsequently, he had his own business under the name, Rudolf Mikuta, AIA, Cons. & Dev., Alhambra, CA (s. 1977).

Andrew Robert Mitermiler (1840-1896), b. Choceň, Bohemia, was an architect who practiced in Cleveland from 1871-96 designing business blocks, social halls, breweries, and churches for Czechs and Germans. He was educated at the University of Vienna as a civil engineer and worked on the Innsbruck Tunnel in Austria. When about to be conscripted into the Austrian army, he escaped to Baltimore, MD in 1861 where he practiced engineering before coming to Cleveland ca. 1871, working as foreman in the office of architect J. M. Blackburn before setting up his own office in 1873.

Joseph Molitor (1874–1917), b. Bohemia, was an architect with a noteworthy legacy in church architecture. As an independent architect, Molitor drew up the architectural plans for a number of churches, mostly in Chicago, that are noted for their refined architectural stylings.

Josef M. Mrázek (1888–d.), b. Prague, Bohemia, resided in US since 1900. He settled in Chicago and studied at Art Inst. of Chicago and Chicago Tech. Coll. Since 1926, he was acting as architect of the City of New York.

Joseph Jerome Nadherny (1891–1986), b. Chicago, IL, of Czech parents, was an architect. For four years, he studied at the university of Pennsylvania and in 1916, he obtained a certificate of proficiency from that institution. He was a draughtsman for the Marshall & Fox Architects from 1909 to 1914, and then became partner in the firm. Some of the buildings he designed include: Triner Scale and Mfg. Co., Oakridge Cemetery entrance gateway, office and conservatory, Oakridge Abbey mausoleum and Golfmore Hotel in Grand Beach, MI. He was a member of the American Institute of Architects, the Illinois Society of Architects and of Česká Beseda. He had the office in Chicago on South Dearborn Street.

Antonín Nechodoma (1877–1928), b. Prague, Bohemia, was a Czech architect who practiced in Puerto Rico and Dominican Republic from 1905 to 1928. He is known for the introduction of the Prairie Style to the Caribbean and the integration of Arts and Crafts elements to his architecture.

Rudolph James Nedvěd (1895–1971), b. Teplice, Bohemia, was an architect. He came to the US with his mother in 1906. He graduated from Armour Institute of Technology (B.S., 1921). He won the Chicago architectural foreign fellowship for the year of 1923–24 and the Sketch Club scholarship for travel in summer of 1925. He was Assistant professor of design in architecture at Armour Institute (1924–28) and was a member of the firm of Rudolph & Elizabeth Kimball Nedved Architects (1925–28) and designer for Hamilton Fellows & Nedved Architects (s. 1928). He designed many small and large residences and elementary and high schools. He was president of the Chicago Architectural Exhibition League and a member of the Exec. Board of the Am. Inst. of Architects. He had office in Chicago on Tower Court.

Dion Neutra (1926-2019), b. Los Angeles, CA, is a modernist, International style American architect and consultant who worked originally with his father, Richard Neutra. He became president of the Neutra company upon his father's death.

Richard Neutra (1892-1970), b. Vienna, of Moravian ancestry, is considered to have been one of modernism's most significant architects, living and building for the majority of his career in Southern California. He studied under Moravia-born Adolf Loos at the Vienna University of Technology (1910-1918). Neutra moved to the United States by 1923 and became a naturalized citizen in 1929. He worked briefly for Frank Lloyd Wright before accepting an invitation from his close friend and university companion Rudolf Schindler to work and live communally in Schindler's Kings Road House in California.

Hana E. Panek (1958-), b. Prague, Czech, is an architect. She studied architecture at Penn State University (B.S., 1984) and University of Pennsylvania. She has been a licensed architect since 1987. Today, she is a successful practicing architect at MOSAIC Associates. In addition to her design education, she started painting regularly in the 1990s.

Victor Papanek (1923-1998), b. Vienna, of Moravian ancestry, attended public school in England and emigrated to the U.S. where he studied design and architecture. Papanek worked with Frank Lloyd Wright in 1949. He earned his Bachelor's degree at Cooper Union in New York (1950) and did graduate studies in design at the Massachusetts Institute of Technology (M.A., 1955). He was a designer and educator who became a strong advocate of the socially and ecologically responsible design of products, tools, and community infrastructures. He disapproved of manufactured products that were unsafe, showy, maladapted, or essentially useless. His products, writings, and lectures were collectively considered an example and spur by many designers. Papanek was a philosopher of design and as such he was an untiring, eloquent promoter of design aims and approaches that would be sensitive to social and ecological considerations. He wrote that "design has become the most powerful tool with which man shapes his tools and environments.

Ernst Denis Payer (1904-1981), b. Vienna, probably of Czech ancestry, was an architect trained in Vienna and Harvard Univ. He was architect, NYC (1939-46), prior to opening his own studio, Architect Ernst Payer and Assoc., Cleveland (1946-81). He was a recipient of the First Medal Housing, Ohio Soc. Of Architects (1947), First Medal Craftsmanship, Cleveland Museum of Art (1951), First Award Ohio Soc. of Illuminating Engineers (1966).

Joseph Roman Pelich (1894-1968), b. Prague, Bohemia, was trained as an architect at Cornell Univ. and at Sorbonne. He was initially active in Cleveland but after completing his military duty at Fort Worth, TX, he remained there and started his architectural practice. He became the first architect to receive the Texas Restoration Award for the restoration of the birthplace of former president Dwight D Eisenhower in Denison.

Ina Podivinský (ca. 1940–), b. Brno, is an architect. She was trained at Vysoké učení technické Brno (Ing. Arch., 1963). She been practicing architecture in Edmonton, Alta., Canada, where she immigrated.

Jan Hird Pokorný (1914–2008), b. Brno, Moravia, was Columbia Univ. trained architect. He was the owner, of the firm Jan Hird Pokorny, Architect, NYC (1945–71); partner, Pokorny and Pertz (1971–77). He was with Columbia Univ. School of Architecture (s. 1958), as professor of architecture (1974–82).

Ernst Preisler (1855–1934), b. Prague, Bohemia, was trained in both architecture and engineering at the Imperial Technicum in Vienna. He worked as an engineer for the Austrian Government Railroad Service, before coming to the United States in 1877. His position as engineer and supervisor of buildings and bridges for the Frisco Railroad brought him to St. Louis in 1887. Preisler established an independent practice as an architect in 1892. Many homes designed by him are still standing in South St. Louis. He received a number of important commissions, including the 1907 Carondelet Branch Library and the Regent Hotel at 14th and Chestnut (demolished). He designed 12 houses in the Compton Heights neighborhood, as well as numerous medium-priced houses and flats for real estate investors.

Jiří Procházka (1923–1998), b. Prague, Czech., received his architectural training at ČVUT in Prague. He was professor, School of Architecture, Universite Laval, P.Q., Canada.

Walther Prokosch (1911–1991), b. Madison, WI, of Bohemian ancestry, was Yale Univ. trained architect. He practiced architecture in NYC (s. 1949). He designed Pan Am Terminal, NY International Airport, Puerto Rico Intl. Airport, San Juan, PR, Little Dix Bay resort in British Virgin Islands, etc. In 1970, with his son Andrew, he co-founded Shelter Kit, Inc., Tilton, NH, manufacturers of house and barn kits.

George J. Puchmajer (1931–2006), b. Klatovy, Czech, after graduation from Prague Technical University, practiced in Prague as an architect. He was a winner of several architectural competitions. After emigrating to the US in 1965 and after passing American license exams, George became a member of AIA (American Institute of Architecture) and was a principal designer in several architectural firms in NY. George was also a landscape painter with interest in architectural subjects. He had several exhibits in US, Canada and Czechoslovakia. His paintings are in several private and public collections.

Ladislav Rado (1909-1993), Čadca, Slovakia; architect, partner of the firm Raymond Rado, New York City and Tokyo, Japan (1946-82).

Zdenko Rakušan (1923-2005), b. Hradec Králové, Czech., held a degree of 'Academic Architect' from the Academy of Fine Arts in Prague (dipl., 1958). After coming to the US, he practiced architecture in Washington, DC, being part of the firm Weihe Partnerships. He specialized in the design of offices, apartment buildings and residences. He was also a writer and the author of two monographs *Být či nebýt* (To be or not to be) (1963) and *Kniha o erbech* (Book about coats-of-arms) (1970).

Frank Randák (1861-1926), b. Bohemia, studied architecture before emigrating to the US in 1888. He located in Chicago, where he advanced steadily until he was recognized as one of the best and most successful of the younger architects of the city. He had designed many of the buildings there and prepared the plans for the Douglas Park Natatorium and gymnasium, the Bohemian Plzensky Sokol Hall gymnasium, Ashland Avenue Bohemian-American Hall; Pilsen Station post office, and many other important buildings, including private residences, business houses and flat dwellings.

Antonín Raymond (1888-1976), b. Kladno, Bohemia, was a famed architect who explored traditional Japanese building techniques with the latest American building innovations. He pioneered modern architecture in Orient, resulting in several hundred internationally known buildings, including US Embassy and consular establishments, French Embassy, USSR Embassy, St. Luke's International Hospital Center, Rising Sun Building, etc.

James B. Rezny (1871-1945), b. IL, of Czech ancestry, was one of the first Chicago architects to receive a certificate to practice under the new Illinois architectural law that was adopted in 1902. He began work as a draftsman in the office of Adler & Sullivan. Later, he was employed by Jarvis Hunt as head of the architectural staff in the office. Most of the buildings Rezny designed were two-story single-family homes. He commonly used unstuccoed Chicago bricks, a plain front porch, stuccoed lintels, bay windows, and a generally undecorated look. Rezny also built Saint Agnes Church at 2659 Central Park Avenue, a Bohemian church in South Lawndale.

John R. Rockart (orig. Rochac) (1872-1951), b. US, of Czech ancestry, an architect, was a member of the renowned firm of Cass Gilbert, Cass Gilbert Jr. and John R. Rockart. Among their many accomplishments, they designed and constructed the US Supreme Court Building, the Minnesota State Capitol Building, the West Virginia Capitol Building, the Fine Arts Building and Festival; Hall in St. Louis and the Woolworth Building in New York City. But of all these accomplishments, the U.S. Supreme Court is the most acclaimed artistic masterpiece of its time (or anytime). While the Supreme Court Building was in the early stages of construction, Cass Gilbert died, and Rockart was left to complete this magnificent structure. In fact, Rockart had the additional responsibility of designing the interior of the building. In the building's majestic vestibule are massive Bohemian glass crystal chandeliers, and Rockart's hand is further evident in the intricate work of the rosette designs that form the geometric décor of the courtroom's ceiling.

Emery Roth (1871–1948), b. Sečovce, Slovakia; architect; the founder of the New York architectural firm Emery Roth & Sons. Without formal training, he became one of New York's best-known architects. His buildings, characterized by rich Renaissance details, included the Belleclaire, San Remo, Normandy, Ritz Tower, St. Moritz, Drake, Dorset and Oliver Cromwell.

Julian Roth (1902–1992), b. Manhattan, NY, of Slovak descent; American architect. Following the death of his father, founder Emery Roth, he and his brother Richard took over at Emery Roth & Sons, one of the oldest and most prolific firms in New York City. National Real Estate Investor dubbed the brothers "New York's name-brand architects, designing much of Sixth Avenue in the 1960s and 1970s." They were also a key contractor in building the World Trade Center.

Richard Roth (1904-1987), b. Manhattan, NY, of Slovak descent, architect; chairman of the board of the firm Emery Roth & Sons. He guided the firm to a position of leadership in the design of more than 150 high-rise buildings and luxury hotels around the country. Most of them are in Manhattan, including the General Motors headquarters building on Fifth Avenue at 59th Street, the Park Lane Hotel on Central Park South and the Palace Hotel, a multi-use structure that incorporates a luxury hotel, apartments, stores, office space and the landmark Villard Houses on Madison Avenue, behind St. Patrick's Cathedral.

Emil Royco (1908–1996), b. St. Louis, MO, of Slovak descent; architect, Washington, DC.

Bernard Rudofský (1905–1988), b. Suchdol nad Odrou, Moravia, was an American writer, architect, collector, teacher, designer, and social historian. Rudofsky earned a doctorate in architecture in Austria before working in Germany, Italy, and a dozen other countries. He temporarily settled in Brazil in the 1930s and opened an architectural practice there, building several notable residences in São Paulo. An entry in a 1941 design competition brought an invitation from MOMA to tour the US; in the wake of Pearl Harbor, as an Austrian native, he was given the option of staying in the US. He remained based in New York City, although he continued to travel until his death. Rudofsky variously taught at Yale, MIT, Cooper-Hewitt, Waseda University in Tokyo, and the Royal Academy of Fine Arts in Copenhagen. He was a Ford, Fulbright and Guggenheim Fellow. Rudofsky was most influential for organizing a series of controversial MOMA exhibits in the 1940s, 1950s and

1960s. He is best remembered today for a number of urbane books that still provide relevant design insight that is concealed in entertaining, subversive sarcasm. His interests ranged from vernacular architecture to Japanese toilets and sandal design. Taken together, his written work constitutes a sustained argument for humane and sensible design.

Rudolph Michael Schindler (orig. Schlesinger) (1887–1953), b. Vienna, of Bohemian father, was an American architect whose most important works were built in or near Los Angeles during the early to mid-twentieth century. Although he worked and trained with some of its foremost practitioners, he often is associated with the fringes of the modern movement in architecture. His inventive use of complex three-dimensional forms, warm materials, and striking colors, as well as his ability to work successfully within tight budgets, however, have placed him as one of the true mavericks of early twentieth century architecture.

Marie Schneiderová-Zubaníková (1900–1966), b. České Budějovice, Bohemia, is an architect who resided in the US since 1924. She studied in Prague civil and architectural engineering, having been the first woman to attain the civil and architectural degree in Czechoslovakia. Worked as designer of Ready Cut Houses for Sears and Roebuck, Co., Chicago (1925–28). She was vice president of American Association of Czechoslovak Engineers. She was also excellent pianist and violinist.

Lilia Skala (née Sofer) (1896–1994), b. Vienna, of Czech ancestry, was an architect and actress. Before becoming one of the leading actresses in Austria and then in America, she was one of the first women to have received a degree in Architecture and Engineering from the University of Dresden, band then practiced architecture professionally in Vienna.

Joseph Škvařil (1934–), b. Czech., studied architecture at Univ. of Brno (Eng. Arch, 1958). He then pursued studies in city planning (1963–67), which he could not complete for political reasons. He escaped to Sweden and in 1973, he immigrated to Canada. He practices architecture and city planning in Edmonton.

Walter S. Sobotka (1888–1972), b. Vienna, of Bohemian father, enrolled at the Technischen Hochschule Wien, studying under Karl König. He completed his degree in 1912 with the title of Engineer-Architect. Sobotka served as an officer in the Austrian army during World War I. After the war, from 1919 to 1923, he worked for the Viennese firm of Karl Korn while also producing grave monuments and furniture for his family in Vienna and Czechoslovakia. In 1919, he married Gisela Schoenau. After leaving Korn's firm, Sobotka began to make a name for himself with some larger residential projects, eventually designing the interiors for Peter Behrens's house at the Weisenhoff Siedlung built for the Deutscher Werkbund Seidlung in Stuttgart (1927). He also designed two large housing projects for the city of Vienna and two houses for the 1932 Österreichischer Wekbund Seidlung. Sobotka was very involved with the Austrian Werkbund and served as vice-chairman on the Board of Directors for two years. Exhibitions, mostly of furniture, constituted another important part of Sobotka's practice, and in 1937, he designed the Austrian Pavilion for the World Exposition in Paris. When the political situation in Austria became too tenuous for those of Jewish descent, Sobotka emigrated to the United States. He made the trans-Atlantic crossing aboard the *Saturnia* arriving in New York on July 7th, 1938. In 1941, he began to teach at the University of Pittsburgh in the Research Bureau for Retail Training, becoming an assistant professor of textiles and applied arts five years later. He also taught architecture at the Carnegie Institute of Technology from 1941 to 1948. He was appointed assistant professor for interior decoration in 1946. Sobotka's practice in the United States focused mostly upon residential interiors and furniture design, for Thonet Brothers (1938–1939) and Russel Wright, among others. He also designed numerous theater interiors for RKO. His architecture can be classified as modernist, but he never fully embraced functionalism. His interiors reveal the decorative and ornamental influences of his training in early twentieth century Vienna. Sobotka maintained lifelong friendships with other Viennese architects, most notably Josef Frank.

Frank (František) Štalmach (1903–1985), b. Moravská Ostrava, studied architecture at Státní vyšší průmyslová škola in Brno and the Academy of Fine Arts in Prague. After communist putsch in 1948, he emigrated to Canada, settling first at Port Credit, Ont. and then in Toronto. During 1951–55, he was with the building firm in Toronto, afterwards he co-owned a private architectural firm. He specialized in modern architecture and was member of Royal Architectural Inst. of Canada and Ontario Association of architects. Among other, he designed the head office of Ontario Credit Union League, Ontario Bell Telephone Employees Credit Union, Autoworker Oshawa Credit Union, St. Antonius Church in Chatham, Ont. and many other churches and residential buildings. He also converted a shed and garage into a Czech Catholic church. He helped Czech refugees by employing many in his company.

Josef Staša (1923–2009), b. Zlín, Czech., studied architecture at Vysoká škola architektury a pozem stavitelství in Prague (Ing., 1950). The following year, he immigrated to Canada to escape communist-ruled Czechoslovakia in search of a 'free cultural life.' Eight years later, he received a Master's degree in city planning from the Massachusetts Institute of Technology (M.C.P., 1959). He worked as an urbanist for the Harvard University Planning Office for more than 25 years. Staša was a longtime member of Adams House Senior Common Room.

Clarence Stein (1882–1975), born in Rochester, NY, of Bohemian ancestry, was an American urban planner, architect, and writer, a major proponent of the 'Garden City' movement in the United States. He received many honors and awards for his work, including the Gold Medal Apartment House Award from AIA in 1940 and in 1941 AIA Medal of Honor for his work in field of low-cost housing. In 1955, he received an award for his development of new towns and in 1960, the Ebenezer Howard Memorial Medal for his work on garden cities.

Andrew Steiner (1908–2009), b. Dunajská Streda, was a Czechoslovak and American architect. In 1925, he moved to Brno and studied at German Technical University. After graduation, he worked for Ernst Wiesner and from 1934, he worked in his own atelier. During the Second World War, he was a member of an illegal group whose aim was to protect Jewish people. After the Communist takeover of Czechoslovakia in 1948, he left and moved to Cuba where he was offered the position of chief architect in an American design studio. In 1950, he settled in Atlanta in the USA. In the 1960s, he became the manager of the area and town planning division at Robert and Company Associates, an architecture company based in Atlanta. He also taught at the University in Atlanta. He was also Vice-president of the American Institute of Planners Urban Design Department. In 2004, he received an honorary degree from Masaryk University in Brno.

Eugene Sternberg (1915–2005), b. Bratislava, Slovakia, earned an architectural engineering degree in Prague, and was pursuing his graduate degree in architecture at Cambridge University in England when World War II broke out. He remained in London through the war teaching part-time at Cambridge, and then joined the firm of Sir Patrick Abercrombie, where he was involved in the rebuilding of housing destroyed by the German bombing of London. In 1945, like many European architects displaced by the war, Sternberg immigrated to the US. He is known for his passionate commitment and contribution to contemporary/modernist architecture and town planning in Colorado and other Rocky Mountain states between 1950 and 1990. He designed over 400 building projects and subdivisions, many of them iconic examples of Modernist architecture. Since his focus was on improving the quality of life of the general population, the structures he built were beautiful, useful, and cost-effective. Most of his projects were in the category of social architecture: affordable homes, senior housing projects, public housing, hospitals, medical clinics, public schools, community colleges, community centers, churches, buildings for credit unions, labor unions, and headquarters offices for Rural Electric Associations. As a planner, Sternberg designed a number of innovative housing subdivisions and master plans for college campuses, governmental complexes, county fairgrounds, and a number of small western cities.

Miroslav Šulc, b. Czech., is a licensed structural engineer with a Master's degree in architectural and structural engineering. He has over 30 years of experience in project management, structural design and analysis, and review of working and shop drawings. Šulc has a broad range of experience of building types and construction, with a specialization in wind analysis, shear walls, and foundation design. He is associated with the firm Teng and Associates, based in Chicago.

Radoslav Ladislav Sutnar (1929-2023), b. Prague, Czech., is an architect and city planner trained at Pratt Inst. and Harvard Univ. Practiced planning and architecture, Los Angeles (s. 1964), and as assoc. res., Univ. California, Los Angeles (s. 1966).

William Gabriel Tachau (1875-1969), b. Louisville, KY, of Bohemian ancestry, was an architect trained at Ecole des Beaux Arts, Paris. With Lewis Pitcher, he was a partner in the architectural firm of Pitcher & Tachau from 1904 to 1919 when he established the firm of Tachau & Vought. Both firms from 1918 onward specialized in mental hygiene hospitals. The firm moved from 109 Lexington Avenue to 102 East 30th Street around 1923 and remained at that address and that name even after Vought left.

Paul Tesar (1941-), b. Vienna, of Czech ancestry, was trained as an architect at Technical University of Vienna and at the Univ. of Washington in Seattle. He has been associated with North Carolina State Univ., Raleigh (s. 1975), advancing to assoc. professor (1980-93) and to full professor of architecture (s. 1993). His major teaching and scholarship areas include: architectural design, design fundamentals, design pedagogy, architectural theory, aesthetics, and vernacular architecture.

Norbert Troller (1900-1984), born in Brno, Moravia, was a Czech and American architect of Jewish descent. He was also an artist notable for his portrayal on life in the Theresienstadt concentration camp. He emigrated to the US soon after 1945. For the next 10 years, Norbert Troller designed Jewish Community Centers for the US, Canada and Columbia, the Building Bureau of the National Jewish Welfare Board in New York. He produced about 80 designs of those projects. The local architects had realized many of them. Simultaneously, he had developed and implemented planning and construction design standards for the Jewish Community Centers' buildings. In 1958, he opened his own practice, and was involved in the design of residential houses, interiors of offices, showrooms, retail shops and restaurants in New York City and the metropolitan area.

Joseph Urban (1872-1933), b. Vienna, of Bohemian ancestry, was an architect, illustrator, and scenic designer. He immigrated to the US in 1911 to become the art director of the Boston Opera. In 1914, he moved to New York and for the next two decades, his studio was a major theatrical presence, designing productions for New York theaters, the Ziegfeld Follies and the Metropolitan Opera.

Elo John Urbanovsky (1907-1988), b. West, TX, of Czech ancestry, received training in architectural design from Texas A&M Univ. He joined the faculty at Texas Tech University in 1949 and served as professor of park administration and landscape architecture until his retirement in 1975. He was a landscape architect for the US Department of Agricultural regional office in Dallas and for Veterans Administration hospitals in Texas, Louisiana, and Mississippi. Urbanovsky worked closely with Lady Bird Johnson on a number of beautification projects, including those at the Lyndon B. Johnson Ranch.

Miroslav Vanek (1927-1980), b. Chicago, IL, of Czech ancestry, was a graduate of Michigan College (B.A., 1945) and studied architecture at Univ. of Illinois (B.S., 1952). He was with the firm Nicol & Nicol, Chicago (1955-59), partner and vice president (1959-61); member, architectural firm Pratt & Vanek (1961-64); pres., Nicol & Nicol, Inc. (1969-73); president, Nicol, Chaney &Vanek, Inc., Chicago (s. 1973).

Stefan Andrew Yarabek (1952-), b. Dobbs Ferry, NY, of Czech and Slovak descent; landscape architect, president / owner, Hudson & Pacific Designs, Saugerties, NY.

Liane Zimbler (née Juliana Fischer) (1892-1987), b. Přerov, Moravia, was one of the first European women to obtain an architecture degree. After running a highly successful business in Vienna, she emigrated to the United States in 1938 where she specialized in interior design.

16. Interior Designers

Lidye Bauer Alexander (fl. 2019-), b. Czech., is a professional residential St Petersburg interior designer and allied member of American Society of Interior Designers. After graduating from the International Academy of Design and Technology in Tampa, FL, she formed AL Interiors, later AL Interiors International, Inc., St. Petersburg, FL.

Helena T. Dunn, b. Prague, Czech., left Czechoslovakia in 1968 and lived in Holland and in Canada. In 1984, she moved to the United States. She is a licensed interior designer with 25 years of international interior design experience. She has a B.A.A. in interior design from Ryerson Polytechnical University in Toronto, Canada, and an architectural technology diploma from the Technical Collegiate Institute in Prague. In 1984, Helena T. Dunn joined the Interior Design Department of Marriott International and for 17 years, she has been involved in all areas of senior living and hospitality design. In 2002, she established in Chevy Chase, MD her own company under the name Helena T. Interior Design LLC. This company provides Interior Design solutions for both new construction and refurbishment projects in domestic and international markets. Helena T. Dunn offers creative and fully coordinated design, production and project management for the client.

Frances Adler Elkins (1888–1953), b. Milwaukee, WI, of Bohemian ancestry, was interior designer. She was the sister of architect David Adler. Their travels together in Europe inspired her passion for design. She became one of the twentieth century's most prominent female designers. She found inspiration in the work of Jean-Michel Frank and Alberto Giacometti. She developed an eclectic and bold style through the use of color and furnishings. Elkins had the tendency to mix time periods and styles in nearly every room she completed. During the 1930s, Elkins' reputation spread, giving her the title 'decorator of choice' in San Francisco. By the end of her career, she had collaborated with Adler to complete fifteen large scale houses.

Elsie Wise Gross Herzog (1911–1992), b. Cincinnati, OH, of Czech ancestry; an interior designer for more than 50 years. Working under the business name of Elsie May Gross Interiors, she specialized in designing for residences throughout the New York metropolitan region. She also worked on civic buildings in New Rochelle, including two schools and City Hall. For three years in the 1960's, she was the host of "Ask Elsie," a call-in radio show on design that was broadcast in Westerly, R.I. She was a graduate of the Parsons School of Design and an officer and member of the American Society of Interior Designers, which cited the quality of her work in awards. She was also a member of the Decorators Club and served on the board of the Thomas Paine Historical Association.

Irene Olga Stříbrná (1925–), b. Prague, Czech., is an architect and interior designer. She was trained at ČVUT (Ing. Arch., 1950). She practiced in Edmonton, Alta., Canada, specializing in the design of hospitals and industrial and residential buildings. She worked as an interior designer for the Nordick Woodwork, Edmonton.

17. Kinetic Artists

Frank Malina (1912–1981), b. Brenham, TX, of Czech parents, was an aeronautical engineer who later in his career left his position with UNESCO to pursue an interest in kinetic art. In 1968 in Paris he founded *Leonardo,* an international peer-reviewed research journal that featured articles, written by artists on their own work, and focused on the interactions between the contemporary arts with the sciences and new technologies. The *Leonardo* journal is still published as of 2024 as a project of Leonardo/ISAST, the International Society for the Arts, Sciences and Technology.

18. Animators

Art Babbitt (orig. Arthur Harold Babitsky) (1907–1992), b. Omaha, NE, of Czech ancestry, was an American animator, best known for his work at the Walt Disney Company. He was a developer of the character 'Goofy.' He received over 80 awards as an animation director and animator. Babbitt worked as an animator or animation director on films such as *Snow*

White and the *Seven Dwarfs*, *Pinocchio*, *Fantasia* and *Dumbo*, among others. Outside of Disney, he also animated *The Wise Quacking Duck* for Leon Schlesinger Productions.

Paul Fierlinger (1936–), b. Ashiya, Japan, son of Czech diplomat, is an American creator of animated films and shorts, especially animated documentaries. He is also a part-time lecturer at University of Pennsylvania School of Design. In 1955, he graduated from the Bechyne School of Applied Arts. After two years of military service, he freelanced in Prague as a book illustrator and gag cartoonist for cultural periodicals under the pen name Fala. Fierlinger established himself in 1958 as Czechoslovakia's first independent producer of animated films, providing 16 mm films from his home studio for Prague TV and the 16 mm division of Krátky Film. Thus, he created approximately 200 films, ranging from 10-second station breaks to 10-minute theatrical releases and TV children's shorts. In 1967, Fierlinger escaped from Czechoslovakia to the Netherlands, where he pitched for a number of station breaks for Dutch television in Hilversum. He then went to Paris to work for a short stint as a spot animator for Radio Television France and ended up in Munich for half a year, having been offered the job of key animator on a feature film at Linda Films, *The Conference of the Animals*. In Munich, prior to his departure to the United States, he married a Czechoslovak compatriot and photographer, Helena Strakova. In 1971, he formed AR&T|AR&T Associates Inc., his own animation house. Since 1971, AR&T produced over 700 films, of which several hundred were television commercials. Many of these films received considerable recognition, including an Academy Award nomination for *It's So Nice to Have a Wolf Around the House*.

Jan Jaroslav Pinkava (1963–), b. Prague, Czech., studied computer science (B.Sc.) and then robotics (Ph.D.), both at Univ. of Wales, Aberystwyth. After university, he turned to a career in computer animation initially in London, with Digital Pictures, specializing in TV commercials. In 1993, he joined Pixar and moved to the USA. His *Arrows* TV commercial for Listerine won the Gold Clio Award in 1994. He is the director and writer of the Pixar Oscar-winning 1997 short film *Geri's Game* and the originator and co-director of Pixar's Oscar-winning 2007 film *Ratatouille*. His last work at Pixar Animation Studio was as storyboard artist on the feature film *Toy Story 3*. He left the studio shortly after. He subsequently joined Laika and then Motorola. Since 2013, he directs his own Pinkava Production, LLC.

Břetislav Pojar (1923–2012), b. Sušice, Czech., is a puppeteer, animator and director of short and feature films. In the mid-1960s, Pojar emigrated to Canada, where he began a long collaboration with the National Film Board. His Canadian work is some of his best known, and it has won awards at prestigious international film festivals. His film *To See or Not to See* (Psychocratie) won the Canadian Film Award for Film of the Year in 1970. Pojar's work is characterized by strong social commentary, such as in *Balablok*, where armies of small circle- and square-shaped beings war with each other until they are all wounded into indistinguishable shapes. Often, Pojar's shorts contain little or no spoken dialogue. In the mid-2000s, Pojar moved back to the Czech film business in order to co-direct the collaborative animated feature film *Fimfárum 2* (based on the stories of Jan Werich), which was released in 2006.

Ludmila Zeman (1947–), b. Zlín, Czech., is a Czech-Canadian artist, animator, and children's book author/illustrator. Her talent for painting, puppetry, and film-making was nurtured by her father, a famous film-maker, who had his own studio. By the age of ten, she was already painting and taking pictures for his prize-winning films. By her early 20s, as she continued to work with her father, she also began to study art and design at university. Later, she published a best-selling picture book and, with her husband, developed a successful yet personal and unique style of film-making by creating award-winning shorts. An offer to teach at the Emily Carr College of Art in Vancouver led to the family's eventual emigration to Canada in 1985. Ludmila Zeman became a Canadian citizen in 1988. Since coming to this country, she and her husband have made a film about West Coast Native peoples for the television program *Sesame Street*. Another film, based on legends of the Pacific North West, was prepared for the National Film Board. The husband-and-wife team are presently working on a full-length feature-film presentation, based on her extensively researched, highly acclaimed picture-book trilogy about Gilgamesh, the mighty king of Uruk, in Mesopotamia at the dawn of civilization. The concept was eventually developed into a trilogy of children's books written and illustrated by Zeman: *Gilgamesh the King* (1991), *The Revenge of Ishtar* (1993), and *The Last Quest of Gilgamesh* (1995). For Ludmila Zeman, film is the ultimate. In 1995, she was the recipient of the Governor General's Literary Award / Children's Literature (for best illustrations) for The Last Quest of Gilgamesh.

19. Multi-Genre Visual Artists

Jozef Bajus (1958–), b. Kežmark, Czech.; award winning fiber and mixed media artist; associate professor of design and director of fiber program, Buffalo State College, NY. Bajus received his MFA from the Academy of Fine Arts and Design (AFAD), Bratislava. He began his teaching career in 1990 during the Velvet Revolution. Since that time, he has held positions of visiting scholar, instructor, and coordinator at various colleges and programs in the United States and abroad including, the Rhode Island School of Design, Slippery Rock University, Haystack Mountain School of Crafts, Penland School of Crafts, Arrowmont School of Arts & Crafts, Split Rock, Kanazawa College of Art (Japan), and Jianxing University (China). Currently, Bajus is an Associate Professor at SUNY Buffalo State College, Buffalo, NY. His career has earned him numerous prestigious awards and recognition. Bajus' work has exhibited in numerous one-person, and groups exhibitions, nationally and internationally, and is in the collection of many museums, art galleries worldwide.

Jozef G. Cincík (1909–1992), b. Clopodia, Rumania, of Slovak descent, was a painter, sculptor, graphic artist, scenographer, art historian. He studied at the Faculty of Law of Charles University in Prague (1928–32), later also in archeology and art history at the Faculty of Arts of Comenius University in Bratislava (1932–36). From the mid-1930s, he wrote in numerous periodicals on the history of older and modern Slovak art, on history and archeology. He was the author of several art monographs and was actively involved in art (especially painting and graphics). He designed several stamps during the existence of the war-torn Slovak Republic (an eight-part series of "Slovak princes") as well as designs for banknotes (in 1944). In March 1945, Cincík emigrated, first to Austria, then to Bavaria and in October 1945, to Italy. From 1946, he lived and worked in the United States, taught at St. Beda's College and also worked as an artist and graphic artist (he painted several churches in the USA). In his spare time, he researched the fate of the French soldier and participant in the American war for US independence, Ján Ladislav Polerecký. At the end of his life, he worked as a cataloger for the Public Library in Cleveland.

Eva (Tlustá) Eisler (1952–), b. Prague, Czech., has lived and resided in New York since 1983. Her work ranges from drawing to sculptures, furniture, product, interior design, as well as jewelry design. After her interrupted studies in Prague, she studied at Parsons School of Design, New York, where she also taught for number of years. Presently, she teaches at the New York University at the Art and Art Professions Dept.

Ruth Francken (1924–2006), b. Prague, Czech., was a Czech-American sculptor, painter, and furniture designer, living mostly in Paris. After studying painting from 1939–1940 at the Ruskin School in Oxford, England, she moved to New York, where she studied at the Art Students League of New York. After becoming an American citizen in 1942, she worked as a textile designer until 1949, when she left the United States for Europe. After a two-year period in Venice (1950–1952), she moved to Paris, where she lived until her death in 2006. She was considered an Abstract Expressionist in her early career, until around 1964. After this point she began working with object sculptures, collage, and different textiles and techniques, and her art took on a more surrealist and pop-art aesthetic. She focused heavily on problems and disconnects in communication. Her work was featured in an international exhibit, initially created by Tate Modern in London, titled "The World Goes Pop."

Vera Frenkel (1938–), b. Bratislava; Czech., is a multidisciplinary artist, independent video artist, writer, first recognized as a printmaker, and sculptor.

Dagmar Frinta (ca. 1956–), b., a native of NYC, of Czech parents, was born on the tip of Manhattan during the year the Broadway Bridge was being built over the northern bend of the Harlem River, a few blocks away. She studied at the Scuola Niccolò Machiavelli in Florence, Italy from 1968 to 1969, and obtained a BFA from Syracuse University in 1978. Since then, she has published in major magazines, and newspapers, including a six-page article in *Graphis* in 1985. In 1983, she won a Silver Medal from the NYC Art Director's Club. Her work has been shown in galleries in Italy, the Czech Republic, and New York. Dagmar has been commissioned to create book jackets, posters, and worked as a bookbinder, architect, fabricator, painter and illustrator. Her notable clients include: Robert Musil, Sherwood Anderson, Charles Portis, Lou Reed, and Peter Lynch. Throughout the 1980s and 1990s, she taught at Syracuse University, the Rhode Island School of Design, and the School of Visual Arts in New York City. In 2006, she was a founding member of the Bau Institute workshops, collaborating with architect Paola Iacucci. She is currently a faculty member of Parsons New School for Design.

Nicola Ginzel (ca. 1970–), b. Hollywood, CA, of Czech father, is a mixed-media artist. She never had an art class—the only exposure she had to art was through the drawings and sculpture that her mother did in art school and on trips to Europe. She has exhibited, both internationally and nationally, with most recent shows at Jenny Jaskey Gallery in Philadelphia, the Corridor Gallery in Reykjavik, Iceland, and the Udi Alioni Project Room in NYC. She is the recipient of grants from the Robert Rauschenberg Foundation, Artists' Fellowship Inc., SIM (The Icelandic Visual Arts Association), Reykjavik Art Museum Residency, and The Skaftfell Cultural Center Residency in Seydisfjördur, Iceland. Her work has been included in exhibitions, curated by Lydia Yee, Bill Arning, and Lisa Phillips. She lives and works in Brooklyn, NY.

Ian Hornak (1944–2002), b. Philadelphia, PA, of Slovak descent, was American draughtsman, painter and printmaker and one of the founding artists of the Hyperrealist and Photorealism art movements. Hornak attended University of Michigan–Dearborn before transferring to Wayne State University in Detroit where he earned Bachelor of fine arts and Master of fine arts degrees. Between 1966 and 1968, he taught studio art courses at Henry Ford Community College, and Wayne State University. He became known for elaborate, extremely detailed paintings of flowers, food and tableware that recall the 17th-century Dutch vanitas tradition. At the same time, his pictures have a sharply focused hyper-real look that verges on Surrealism and Photorealism. Mr. Hornak began exhibiting in 1972 at the Tibor de Nagy Gallery and moved to the Fischbach Gallery in 1977. Since 1988, he had had seven solo shows at the Katharina Rich Perlow Gallery. Among the institutions that own his work are the Corcoran Gallery of Art in Washington, the

Indianapolis Museum of Art and the Smithsonian Institution's National Museum of American Art.

Ali Hossaini (1962–), b. West Virginia, of Slovak descent on his mother's side, is a video artist philosopher and businessperson, described as a 'biochemist turned philosopher turned television producer turned visual poet.' He has served as an executive in a number of media and technology-oriented businesses. In 2017, Hossaini published the *Manual of Digital Museum Planning* and subsequently became co-director of National Gallery X, a King's College London partnership that explores the future of art and cultural institutions. Prior to National Gallery X, Hossaini worked with King's College to develop Connected Culture, an action research program that tested cultural applications for 5G supported by Ericsson. As a working artist and producer, Hossaini's genre-spanning career includes installations, performances and hundreds of media projects. Since 2018, Hossaini has worked with security think tank Royal United Services Institute and, in a 2019 special edition of its journal, he assessed the threat from AI from the perspective of biology.

Jaroslav Hovadik (1935–2011), b. Zlín, was a Czech graphic artist, illustrator, and sculptor. He studied at the Academy of Fine Arts in Prague (1956–57). He entered the art scene as a painter and since 1962, also as a graphic artist and author of objects and assemblages. In 1968, he immigrated to Canada, where he worked for 11 years. From Canada, he moved to France and in 1986, settled in Mühlheim Germany, where he became a member of the Association of German Artists. After the Velvet Revolution, he returned to the Czech Republic, settling in Litoměřice, where he continued working until his death. He exhibited in the US, Australia, India and Africa, among other.

Olinka Hrdy (1902–1987), b. Prague, OK, was a painter, muralist, sculptor, and lithographer. She studied at Univ. of Oklahoma and Roerich Academy of Art in NYC. As an employee of Federal Art Project, she painted murals and executed sculptures. Her works are held at Casadena Jr. College, Univ. of Oklahoma, etc. She was Oklahoma's first modernist painter, Hrdý was an artist ahead of her time, among the first to exhibit European Bauhaus influences—something that most American artists wouldn't pick up on for another few years.

Susan E. Jahoda (1952–), b. Bolton, England, of Czech ancestry, studied art education at Rhode Island College, Providence (B.S., 1974) and photography at Rhode Island School of Design (M.F.A., 1979). She works in a range of genres, including video, sound, photography, text, performance, and installation. Her works have been exhibited widely, including venues in London, Paris, Venice, Basel, Seoul, Russia, Rome, and New York. Additionally, she has received grants from the National Endowment of the Arts, the New York Foundation for the Arts and The Trust for Mutual Understanding. Jahoda has co-curated a number of exhibitions and screenings including Martha Rosler Library, an E-flux project in collaboration with Martha Rosler and *Beyond the Instance of an Ending* (2009), *Setting in Motion* (2006), and *Global Priority* (2002), with the intent of bringing together a varied group of international individuals engaged in critical artistic practice. She has also published short stories and essays including "Spring Flowers" in Class and its Others (2000) and "Theatres of Madness" in Deviant Bodies (1995). In 1993, Jahoda began serving as the arts editor for the journal *Rethinking Marxism*, a position that has enabled her to collaborate with other artists and writers on numerous projects. In addition to her work as a visual artist, curator and editor, Jahoda taught at Princeton University (1981-86), The Museum School of Fine Arts (1986-87), and Sarah Lawrence College (1987-88). In 1989, she began teaching at the University of Massachusetts, Amherst, where she is currently a professor in the Department of Art, Architecture, and Art History. Other teaching affiliations include serving as a visiting artist for the Graduate Program in Photography at The Rhode Island School of Design, (2003-08), and as visiting faculty at the International Center of Photography (1981-present). Jahoda resides in New York City.

Martin Kastner (1974-), b. Czech., was originally trained as a blacksmith and worked fashioning doors, gates, and weaponry for a 16th century castle. Later, he enrolled in the Fine Arts Institute in Ústí nad Labem, Bohemia, pursuing studies in natural materials design. Kastner then received his M.F.A. in metal sculpture from Academy of Arts, Architecture and Design in Prague. He has been working in the United States since 1998. He founded Crucial Detail, a multidisciplinary design practice that houses myriad projects, from product development and graphic design to photography and corporate image management. Expanding his medium well beyond the blacksmiths' range. Kastner saw Crucial Detail as a way to blur the lines between design and art—much the same way a chef fuses the technical perfection of cuisine with interpretive license. Kastner is best known for his Alinea service ware concepts, which landed him on The Future Laboratory's list of the 100 most influential individuals in contemporary design. *Alinea* book, which Kastner designed in collaboration with Naissance Inc., was one of the winners in 2009 Communication Arts Design Annual for Best Book Design and is included in Altitude's "The Best of Cover Design." Beyond appearances at events like Alimentaria (2004), Madrid Fusion (2009), and Gravity Free (2012), his work has been featured in numerous publications, including *Gourmet, Wired Magazine, The Huffington Post, Fast Company*, and the *Bon Appetit* blog.

Tatana Kellner (1945-), b. Prague, Czech., is a photographer and book artist, who now resides in Kingston, NY. She has an M.F.A. from Rochester Institute of Technology and a B.A. from the University of Toledo. She had over 20 solo exhibitions in USA and Canada. Her practice encompasses artist's books, printmaking, papermaking, drawing, photography, and installation. She uses these media to comment on contemporary culture. Her work is in many public collections. Kellner is the founding member and Artistic Director of Women's Studio Workshop (WSW), an artists' workspace in Rosendale, NY. WSW is the only women's studio facility and residency program in the United States. For the past 28 years, Kellner has been instrumental in designing and implementing programs which provide opportunities for women artists in all stages of their careers. As a working artist, Kellner is active in creating and exhibiting her work. Kellner's most recent exhibition was a mid-career retrospective at CEPA Gallery in Buffalo, NY. She has completed a large-scale memorial piece entitled Requiem for September 21, which is installed at the Atrium of the Market Arcade on Main Street in Buffalo. Kellner is a recipient of several grants, awards, and residencies.

Christina Kenton (1979–), b. Vancouver, BC, Canada; of Slovak descent, is a self-taught lighter/ mixed media artist, inspired heavily from her late surrealist grandfather Ladislav Guderna. Along with her grandfather, dreams, animals, forensics, and surrealism pay a big part of influence in her work She is especially known for her miniature sculptures.

John Michael Anthony Koerner (1913–2014), b. Nový Jičín, Moravia, was a painter, printmaker, etcher, muralist, educator, and author. His mediums were oil, acrylic, watercolor, casein, crayon, ink, collage, lithograph, and etching. Koerner was exposed to art at an early age in Paris and Italy. Although his ultimate goal was to become an artist, on his father's advice, he studied law at Charles University in Prague and at the Sorbonne. With the rise of the Third Reich in Germany, he left Prague with his father and uncles, settling in Paris. However, it became necessary for the family to leave again and, the following year, they arrived in Vancouver, British Columbia. He worked in the family lumber business for twelve years before returning to his first love, art. He also taught at the Vancouver School of Art and the University of British Columbia. A number of his works were acquired by the National Gallery of Canada. He also became friends with painter Lawren Harris, who invited him to join the exhibition committee of the Vancouver Art Gallery. His work also appears in the collections of the Tate in London, of Clare Hall at Cambridge University and of the Hirshhorn Museum in Washington, DC. Following his 100th birthday, Koerner had a show at the Burnaby Art Gallery and the exhibition John Koerner: The Hidden Side of Nature at the Penticton Art Gallery.

George Alois Frederick Laisner (1914–1984), b. Czechoslovakia, studied at the University of Chicago and AIC. Most of his career was spent in Pullman, WA as a professor at the State College. George Laisner is known for abstraction, sculpture, and graphics. He was active and lived in Washington, California. He exhibited in SFAA, 1930s, 1940s; Seattle Museum,

1937, 1939; GGIE, 1939; SFMA, 1939, 1943, 1948; Oakland Art Gallery, 1940, 1947. His works can be found at Seattle Museum; SFAA.

Renata Loree (ca. 1963–), b. Czech., a self-taught mixed media artist. She studied by copying old master paintings, and then moving onto painting portraits for her friends. She eventually acquired enough skill to earn commissions for her art. As a single mom, she did not have much of a chance to devote full time to her passion, and so she earned her living as a designer. The work in a corporate world was not very satisfying to her free spirit, and by a strike of disaster and luck at the same time, she has moved onto teaching yoga and eventually owning a yoga studio. Through love for the practice and teaching of yoga, she recognized that her expression in art has to come from a deeper experience that comes from within, rather than from the outside. She also recognized that the outer circumstances help us recognize who we are and how we respond to them and that her creative journey was leading her into an exploration on a canvas – the story behind the face. She now teaches classes online and in person and lives in Natick, MA.

Magda Mraz (1948–), b. Liberec, Czech, is a multi-genre designer. Her early interest in art found focus on her studies of painting and sculpture at the Industrial School for Ceramics in Karlovy Vary, Czechoslovakia. In 1967, her family emigrated to the US and after a short interruption, Magda was able to continue her education at Queens College in New York City, where she earned her B.A. (1972) and M.F.A. (1976) degrees. After her graduation, Magda used her skills and qualification in the fields of textile, stage design and illustration, as well as in her teaching jobs. Her original textile designs created with silk and dye were featured in *The New York Times, Vogue, Mademoiselle, Harper's Bazaar* and purchased by Ralph Lauren, Liz Claiborne, Dan River and Spring Mills. Her children's books' illustrations appeared in Macmillan and Doubleday publications, and she participated in set designs for the Columbia University School of Film. In her teaching, Magda combined the interesting presentation style with her ability to motivate and inspire students on all levels. In her classes they learned how to use the charcoal, pastels, watercolors, oil and acrylic paints, as well as clay, fabric and papier mache. She also introduced them to the artists and styles of various historical periods and encouraged them to express their individual creativity. Magda's spiritual interests led her to further studies at Wisdom University in San Francisco, CA, where she received her Doctorate in Ministry in 2008. While pursuing her various practical careers, Magda also continued to develop her personal painting style and philosophy. She has displayed her work in numerous art shows in the US and abroad. The theme of gradual evolution of the human spirit toward greater liberty is further explored in the group of seven large paintings based on the sacred geometry, which permeates all creation in our universe, including the structures of our consciousness.

Ann Pachner (1944–), b. New York, NY, of Bohemian father, is an American artist. Her body of work consists of range of genres, including drawings, archival digital prints, and wood carvings. The digital prints explore both the nature of print as variations on a theme and the more personal exploratory process of sifting into a generative place of silence. Through mark-making with pencil or chisel or grinder Pachner's lines suggest hair, water, and fire. The work points to that which lies beyond form, No Thing —the multi-dimensional, layered, vibrational experiencing of being. Pachner has had ten one-person shows at A.I.R. gallery in New York City. She is a recipient of a National Endowment for the Arts grant and a New York Foundation for the Arts grant. Working Artist Ink, her fine arts printing service is established to partner with artists to achieve their individual vision.

Beata Pies (1956–), b. Bratislava, Czech., is a freelance artist, painter drawing artist, graphic artist, tapestry artist, science artist. She studied at Vysoké vytvorné umenie in Bratsislava (dipl. 1983).

Zuzana Rudavská (1962–), b. Bratislava, Czech., is a textile designer, jewelry designer, graphic artist, and painter. She was a student at the College of Fine Arts and Crafts in Bratislava (1982) and at the University of Fine Arts and Crafts in Prague (1986). Zuzana Rudavská has mostly exhibited in Slovakia, but also had exhibitions in United States, Croatia. Rudavská had 3 solo shows and 14 group shows over the last 22 years. She has also been to art fairs, but in three biennials. The most important show was Statues Objects Drawings at Stredoslovenská galéria / Central Slovakian Gallery in Banská Bystrica in 2007. Other important shows were at Dom umenia/Kunsthalle Bratislava in Bratislava and Slovak Union of Visual Arts in Bratislava. Zuzana Rudavská has been exhibiting with Ondrej Rudavský and Andrej Rudavský. Her art is in one museum collection, at Museum Kampa - The Jan and Meda Mládek Foundation in Prague.

Ondrej Rudavský (1966–), b. Bratislava, Czech.; painter, graphic artist, sculptor, art photographer, animated film maker. In 1986, he emigrated to New York and in 2000, he moved to Los Angeles. He returns to Slovakia on a regular basis. Rudavsky works in a multitude of media: film, animation, painting, photography, video installation, digital art, jewelry, costume design, sculpture, music and illustration. Within each medium, he creates a universe of captivating and compelling subconscious worlds that are hypnotic, surreal, and dream-like. Rudavský's works have been shown world-wide at hundreds of film festivals, museums, and galleries including: Museum of Modern Art, New York, 1991; Bronx Museum of Arts, New York, 1991; XLVII Venice Biennial, Italy, 1997; EXPO in Hannover, Germany, 1999; University of Arizona Museum of Art, Tucson, 2000; Los Angeles International Biennial, 2005. He has received numerous awards.

Gordon Samstag (1906–1990), b. New York, NY, of Bohemian ancestry, was a painter, sculptor illustrator, educator. He was an impressionist and modern artist. He studied at the National Academy of Design and the Art Students League. He also studied with Charles Hawthorne at Provincetown and was in Paris where he enrolled in the Academie Colarossi. During the 1930s, Samstag was a WPA artist for the Federal Art Project, and from this period, his painting of a black cleaning woman, Proletarian, is in the collection of the Toledo Art Museum. A 1981 exhibition at the Wichita Art Museum, Kansas, The Neglected Generation of American Realist Painters 1930–1948, confirmed his status as a significant social-realist painter of the *American Scene*. His work was featured in several exhibitions at key galleries and museums, including the Art Gallery of South Australia and the Samstag Museum of Art.

Tibor Spitz (1929–), b. Dolný Kubín, Czech., is a Jewish artist of Slovak origin and a Holocaust survivor. After escaping from communist Czechoslovakia to the West, he lived and worked in Canada and the United States. Currently he lives in Kingston, New York. Besides painting, he has been also sculpting, making ceramics, woodcarvings, and wood burnings. When he discovered that impressionists have not fully exhausted all their artistic possibilities, his painting techniques gradually gravitated toward pointillism and neo-impressionism. Besides initial hounding faces and figurative scenes associated with Holocaust, Judaism and Jewish mystical teachings Kabbalah, he also added fishing scenes, musicians, horses, still-life and landscapes.

Melanie Kent Steinhardt (1899–1952), b. Lemberg, Poland, of Bohemian parents, was a Bohemian American painter, expressionist, printmaker, and ceramicist. She was raised in her father's hometown, Žatec, Bohemia. Together with her first husband, she initially resided in Berlin where, for a privileged decade, she honed her painting techniques with distinguished professors, such as Willi Jaekel, at the Verein der Berliner Künstlerinnen (Union of Berlin Women Artists' School). She eventually emigrated to the US, by then divorced from her first husband and remarried to Alfred Kent, settling in New York City and in 1943, she moved to Inglewood, CA. By the end of World War II, the artist returned to painting and etching. She manufactured handmade ceramic tableware under the brand Kent Handmade, which she initially glazed and fired in the Kent's garage in Inglewood. From 1948 until her death, Kent Steinhardt owned and operated the Home Decorators Hobby Shop on Robertson Boulevard in Los Angeles. She produced and taught ceramics, painting, sewing, and crafts. Her compositions, portraits and landscapes blend European expressionism with an émigré's troubled impressions of her new American life. Much of the work Kent Steinhardt created in her final years depict complex existential themes, reminiscent of the work of post-World War I Expressionists Käthe Kollwitz, James Ensor,

Max Beckmann, and George Grosz. Melanie Kent Steinhardt died due to carbon monoxide poisoning in her Robertson Boulevard shop in January 1952. She was 52 years old.

John Regis Tuska (1931–1998), b. Yukon, PA, the only son of a Slovak immigrant coal miner, was a ceramist, painter, sculptor, papier-macheist, and art historian. Tuska cast himself as a teacher who created art along the way. Tuska graduated from an alternative high school for the arts and worked proofreading Collier's Encyclopedia for 25 cents a day. Tuska was educated at the New York State College of Ceramics at Alfred University. After graduating, he moved to Kentucky for a teaching job at the Murray State University. After three years, Tuska moved to University of Kentucky, where he lectured for over 30 years. Tuska continued to create and teach until his death in 1998. Tuska's body of work can be found in collections and public spaces, both regionally and internationally. He created thousands of pieces of art including drawing, collage, ceramics and papier-mache. His last major work was *Illumine*, a "series of 56 bronze figures celebrating individual human expression that are mounted on the façade of UK's Fine Arts Building". He was working on it for 10 years – from 1985 to 1995. Other works include Study of 4 Squares mixed media on paper.

Marja Vallila (1950–2018), b. Prague, Czech., was as an American artist, painter, printmaker, ceramicist, and sculptor, and experimental filmmaker. She exhibited internationally and taught for 25 years in the Art and Art History department at the University at Albany. Her early research often led to large outdoors architectonic sculptures made of steel, sometimes with the addition of granite, cement or wood. She then went through a period of small-scale metal sculptures, already incorporating objects of daily life in her carving and casting processes, paradoxically resulting in a precious like object.

Thomas R. Yanosky (1918–2014), b. Colver, PA, of Slovak parents, was a cartographer by trade, a noted artist whose media included etchings, oils, acrylics, constructions, watercolors and collages, Herndon, VA. He has works in the Library of Congress, George Washington University's Dimock Gallery, and many private collections. He was befriended as a young man by Duncan Phillips who purchased one of his oils (*Blue Mosaic*) for the Phillips Collection in the early 1950's. He studied at the Corcoran School of Art and was a past president of the Washington Society of Artists. He also was a master of scratch-built model airplanes, some of which are in the Museum of Model Aeronautics, Muncie, IN.

20. Visual Activists

Federico Díaz (1971–), b. Prague, Czech, of Czech-Argentinean descent, attended the Prague High School of the Creative Arts from 1987 to 1990 and then spent seven years at the Academy of the Plastic Arts and Painting, also in Prague. He has won numerous grants and awards for his work and has exhibited worldwide. He also leads the creative team of the company E-Area, which was founded in 1998. He is based in Prague and in Buenos Aires but also spends much time in Milan and Paris. Since the 1990s, he has used new media to reveal immaterial aspects of everyday reality of our natural environment which are elusive through primary human senses. Díaz's work is typified by the language of algorithmically-generated art and systems art, increasingly more intense channels of direct communication with the viewer and the ability to follow his basic creative premise, which says that art is created without the touch of the human hand. He uses media and technologies as a socio-political catalyst of social changes. He has exhibited at the Mori Art Museum Tokyo, Institute of Contemporary Arts London, Center for Art and Media Karlsruhe, Ars Electronica Linz, Massachusetts Museum of Contemporary Art, MoMA PS1, Miami Art Basel, the Florence Biennale and at the 53rd Venice Biennale. In 2010, he represented Czech art at the World Expo 2010 in Shanghai. In 2007, he received the Premio Internazionale Lorenzo il Magnifico for digital media at the Florence Biennale.

Stefan Eins (1940–), b. Prague, Czech., grew up in Vienna and Gresten, Austria. He settled in New York City in 1967. Eins graduated from the University of Vienna with a degree in theology (1965) and attended the Academy of Fine Arts in Vienna from 1964–1967. He does not distinguish between creating art and doing science research. He is the founder of Fashion Moda as a cultural concept. An important manifestation of Fashion Moda was the Museum of Science, Art, Invention, Technology and Fantasy (1978–1993) in the Bronx. It quickly became a strong voice in the New York art world during the late 1970s to mid-1980s. Fashion Moda also pioneered in the featuring of Graffiti art and showed artists such as Jenny Holzer and Keith Haring among others early on. It was a Multicultural project of the Hip-Hop culture of artists, writers, rappers, and break dancers. While continuing activities with Fashion Moda, Eins also pursued his own talents, having shows in the National Gallery in Vienna (1991), MoMA PS1 in New York (2007), the notable Now Gallery and other museums and galleries in US, Europe and Asia.

21. New Media Artists

John Klima (1965–), b. Redondo Beach, is an American new media artist, who uses hand-built electronics, computer hardware and software to create online and in gallery artworks. He has had solo exhibitions at Postmasters Gallery and the Whitney Museum's Artport in New York City, and the Bank Gallery in Los Angeles. He lives and works in Brooklyn and is currently adjunct professor at the Rhode Island School of Design and Brooklyn Polytechnic University. Klima was a resident at Eyebeam.

Jan Jakub Kotík (1972–2007), b. Buffalo, NY, of Czech parents, the son of composer Petr Kotík, was an artist and rock drummer. He attended Fiorello H. LaGuardia High School of Music & Art and Performing Arts in New York City and received a Bachelor of Arts degree from the Cooper Union. He played drums with the Mommyheads, Beekeeper, and Church of Betty, among many other bands in New York City. In 2000, he moved to Prague, where he became a highly acclaimed visual artist. In 2007, he received the prestigious Jindřich Chalupecký Award. On 13 December 2007, he died after a three-year battle with cancer.

22. Art Historians

Kamila Alleyn (1930–2015), b. Žamberk, Czech., is an art historian trained at Charles Univ. and California State Univ. at Northridge. She has been professor of art history, Santa Clara, CA.

Miroslava M. Beneš (1953–), b. San Francisco, CA, of Czech ancestry, studied history of art at Princeton Univ. (B.A., 1974) and at Yale Univ. (M.A., 1977, M.Phil., 1977; Ph.D., 1989). She was associated with Harvard Univ., as asst. professor of landscape architecture (1988–94), as assoc. professor (1994–2000) and as sr. lecturer (1994–2000). Subsequently, she joined Univ. of Texas, Austin, as assoc. professor of landscape architecture (s. 2006). Her scholarly research focuses on the city of Rome, its urban, architectural, and landscape histories, including vernacular landscapes. She publishes on Roman Baroque architecture and gardens and on relationships between the design of landscape and landscape painting. She is preparing a book on Landscape, Architecture, and Experience in Baroque Rome: Gardens and Parks in the Age of Claude Lorrain. Beneš co-edited, with Michael G. Lee, *Clio in the Italian Garden: Twenty-First-Century Studies in Historical Methods and Theoretical Perspectives* (2011), and with Dianne Harris she co-edited *Villas and Gardens in Early Modern Italy and France* (2001). She is particularly concerned with methodological and historiographical issues in the history of landscape architecture and has published on this topic. She has held numerous fellowships and lectures nationally and internationally. Beneš has twice been a Fellow of the American Academy in Rome and twice a Fellow of Dumbarton Oaks Center for Garden and Landscape Studies, a Harvard Research Institute in Washington, D.C.

Eve Blau (1951–), b. London, England, of Czech ancestry; historian of architecture. Eve Blau is Adjunct Professor of the History of Urban Form in the Department of Urban Planning and Design at Harvard university's Graduate School of Design. She teaches courses in the history and theory of urban formation and design. Before coming to Harvard, Blau was Curator of Exhibitions and Publications at the Canadian Centre for Architecture in Montreal, and editor of the *Journal of the Society of Architectural Historians*. Her research engages a range of issues in urban and architectural history and theory and the productive intersection of urbanism and media.

Adele Brandeis (1885–1975), b. Louisville, KY, of Bohemian ancestry, was a niece of United States Supreme Court Justice Louis D. Brandeis. She was an art historian and art administrator. During the Great Depression of the 1930s, Brandeis worked for the WPA Federal Art Project and the Section of Painting and Sculpture. Brandeis did art research for the Index of American Design, a comprehensive collection of American material culture, and managed the creation of visual artwork by local artists. Brandeis was the Director of Louisville Art Association in 1937. She wrote for the *Louisville Courier-Journal* starting in 1945. Among other jobs, she did research for the editorial page. She was on the Board of Trustees of the University of Louisville and various Kentucky art organizations.

Andrea Bubenik (1975-), b., St. John's, Newfoundland, Canada, of Czech ancestry, studied history and philosophy at Memorial Univ. (B.A., 1997) and art history at Queen's Univ. (M.A., 2001; Ph.D., 2007). She was a lecturer at Univ. of Guelph, Canada (2007-08), before moving to Australia in 2009 to take up her position at Univ. of Queensland (UQ), Brisbane St. Lucia. Andrea Bubenik's research and teaching is focused on the Renaissance and Baroque periods, and especially the art and science of Albrecht Dürer. She is author of *Reframing Albrecht Dürer: The Appropriation of Art, 1528-1700* (2013), which focuses on aspects of Dürer's reception. In her role as an Associate Investigator with the ARC Centre of Excellence for The History of the Emotions, Andrea is researching the role of the passions in early modern art theory. At UQ, Andrea lectures on Italian and Northern Renaissance Art, Baroque Art, and the historiography of art. She is also interested in cross disciplinary enquiry, and teaches a course entitled 'Art, Science and New Technologies'. Most recently, she has developed a study abroad option for UQ Art History students, 'Art and Architecture in Venice', which takes place on site in Venice, Italy.

Margaret Deutsch Carroll (ca. 1943-), b. US, of Bohemian ancestry, is an art historian, educated at Harvard Univ. She holds the position of professor of art at Wellesley Coll. Her primary research is in the field of 16th- and 17th-century Dutch and Flemish painting, with specialized work on Hieronymus Bosch, Pieter Bruegel the Elder, Rubens, and Rembrandt.

Charlene Ann Cerny (1941-), b. Jamaica, NY, of Bohemian ancestry, is an art historian, formerly curator and now museum director. She was educated at SUNY-Binghamton. She served as director or the Museum of International Art, Santa Fe, NM (1984-99). Prior to that she was a curator of Latin American folk art (1974-1984). She was also founder and executive director of the Santa Fe International Folk Art Market, the largest event of its kind in the world.

Anne d'Harnoncourt (1943-2008), b. Washington, DC, of Czech ancestry, was an American museum director and historian of modern art. She was the director and CEO of the Philadelphia Museum of Art, a post she held from 1982 until her sudden and unexpected death in 2008. Before that, she was a curator of the 20th century art at Art Inst. of Chicago

(1969–71) and then a curator of the 20th century art at Philadelphia Museum of Art (1971–82). She was an expert on the works of Marcel Duchamp, who had been an acquaintance of her father René d'Harnoncourt, the director of the Museum of Modern Art in New York.

Lorenz E. A. Eitner (1919–2009), b. Brno, Czech., was an art historian and museum director. He spent his childhood in Frankfurt and Berlin. The family first emigrated to Brussels and then to the US, settling in South Carolina in 1935. He received his first university degree in 1940 *summa cum laude* from Duke University. He worked for the American Office of Strategic Services during World War II, with assignments in Washington DC, London, Paris and Salzburg. During the Nuremberg Trials, he worked in the research department under chief prosecutor Robert H. Jackson. After the War, he studied at Princeton University, receiving his M.F.A. in 1948 and Doctorate in 1952. In 1949, he began teaching art at the University of Minnesota. He left Minnesota to chair of the Department of Art and Architecture at Stanford University in 1963, which included, on a volunteer basis, the administration of the Stanford Art Museum. Under his tenure, he refocused university art museum to be a center for art; it previously had held a variety of realia including a railroad car and biological specimens. Eitner received both the Mitchell Prize for the History of Art and a Charles Rufus Morey Book Award of the College Art Association in 1983 for his book *Géricault: His Life and Work*. He retired from the University in 1989.

Philipp Fehl (1920–2000), b. Vienna, of Czech ancestry, was an artist and art historian. He was the cousin of the renowned ballet photographer Fred Fehl. He became a refugee in 1938, eventually emigrating to the United States in 1941. Fehl attended the School of the Art Institute of Chicago, where he studied painting. In 1943, he transferred to Stanford University, where he got his B.A. in Romance Languages. In 1948, Fehl received his M.A. in History of Art from Stanford University. Fehl was at the University of Chicago from 1948 to 1952, eventually gaining a Ph.D. in the History of Art in the Committee on Social Thought in 1963. He became an artist, author and lecturer at several universities. He was Lecturer in humanities at the University College, Chicago (1950–52), Instructor at the University of Kansas City (1952–54), Assistant Professor of Art at the University of Nebraska (1954–52), Associate Professor (1962–63) and from 1963, he had been associated with the University of North Carolina, where he held the position of Professor of History of Art. He retired as Professor Emeritus from the University of Illinois at Champaign-Urbana in 1990. His special fields of interest were history of art criticism, and Renaissance painting and sculpture.

Raina Fehl (née Schweinburg) (1920–2009), b. Vienna, of Moravian father, was an American classicist, art historian, writer, and editor. She resided in US s. 1939. She studied history, English, German philosophy, and classics in various US universities. She then taught at University of Chicago, University of Nebraska, and University of North Carolina. She was best known as a multitalented scholar for her writings and editing. Among other, she edited a two-volume *The Literature of Classical Art* (1992). Being married to Philipp Fehl, a prominent art historian, she also collaborated with him. Among other, she collaborated with him on The Leopoldo Ciognara Project, of which she was a director, at the University of Library, Vatican Library, Vatican City, dedicated to the study of and promulgation of literary sources in the history of art.

Hugo Feigl (1889–1960), b. Prague, Bohemia, was an art historian, art collector and art dealer. He received a Doctor of Laws degree from Prague University in 1919, but never practiced law. Instead, he owned and operated the prestigious Feigl Gallery in Prague from 1924 to March 15, 1939. The gallery specialized in French and German Expressionist paintings. He fled Prague from the Nazis on March 15, 1939, to Paris and from there to New York. He was the founder of his Feigl Gallery in New York City in 1942, specializing in French and German Expressionist paintings.

Jaroslav Thayer Folda, 3rd (1940–), b. Baltimore, MD, of Czech ancestry, studied history of art at the Johns Hopkins Univ. (Ph.D., 1968). He has been with the University of North Carolina at Chapel Hill (s. 1968), where he advanced from instructor to professor of history of art (1978–96) and then to N. Ferebee Taylor Professor (1996–2008), retiring as Professor emeritus in 2008. He is an art historian, a medievalist, in which field he is a Haskins Medal winner and a scholar in the history of the art of the crusades. From 1973 to the late 1990s, he spent most summers in the Near East pursuing this research. He is the author of a number of books, including *Crusader Manuscript Illumination at Saint-Jean d'Acre: 1275–1291* (1976), *The Nazareth Capitals and the Crusader Shrine of the Annunciation* (1986), *The Art of the Crusaders in the Holy Land, 1098–1187* (1995), *Crusader Art in the Holy Land, from the Third Crusade to the Fall of Acre: 1187–1291* (2005) and *Crusader Art: The Art of the Crusaders in the Holy Land, 1099–1291* (2008).

Paul Frankl (1878–1962), b. Prague, Bohemia, was an American art historian, historian of architecture. Paul Frankl first took up a degree in architecture, from 1907 he studied art history in Munich. In 1910, he received his doctorate under Heinrich Wölfflin. From 1914 to 1921, he was employed at the University of Munich. In 1921, he was appointed professor in Halle (Saale). His academic students include Ludwig Grote and Hans Werner Schmidt. In 1933, he was dismissed and banned from publishing due to his Jewish descent. Charles Crodel, who was also dismissed, continued his lessons in Frankl's private apartment. In 1938, Frankl emigrated to the USA, where he worked at the Institute for Advanced Study in Princeton from 1940. He is the brother of the Austrian women's rights activist Olly

Schwarz. Frankl is most known for his writings on the history and principles of architecture, which he famously presented within a Gestalt-oriented framework.

Jiří Frel (1923–2006), b. Czech., was an art historian trained at the Sorbonne École normale supérieure. He taught classical art at Charles Univ. from 1948 to 1968. During the 1968 Czech revolt, he defected from Czechoslovakia, then under communist rule, to the US. He joined the staff of Metropolitan Museum of Art, New York, in 1970 as associate curator of Greek and Roman Art. In 1973, he became curator of ancient art at the J. Paul Getty Museum. After Getty's death in 1976, the museum became the wealthiest in the world and Frel was assigned to acquire the best classical works of art available.

Mojmír Svatopluk Frinta (1922–2015), b. Prague, Czech., was an art historian, art restorer and a practicing artist. He studied painting at the Prague School of Graphic Arts and the School of Decorative Arts, and history at Charles University, Prague. He also attended the Académie André Lhote and École des Beaux-Arts and École du Louvre in Paris. His paintings and lithographs were exhibited in Paris, where he specialized as restorer of old paintings. He entered the US in 1951, graduated from the University of Michigan, Ann Arbor (M.A., 1953; Ph.D., in history of art, 1960). Since 1955, he had been on the staff of the Metropolitan Museum of Art as Senior Restorer at the Cloisters. In 1963, he became Assistant Professor, and the Associate Professor, Fine Arts Dept., State University of New York at Albany. His major interest was in Medieval and Early Renaissance painting and sculpture, conservation and restoration of works of art, medieval art technology, and was also a practicing artist (painting and print making). He is the author of *The Genius of Robert Campin* (1966).

Albert Eugene Gallatin (1881–1952), b. Villanova, PA, desc. from Frederick Philipse, was a collector, art historian, and founder of the first museum gallery devoted exclusively to modern art in the US. Called 'one of the great figures in early 20th-century American culture,' he was a leading proponent of nonobjective and later abstract and particularly Cubist art whose 'visionary approach' in both collecting and painting left "an enduring impact on the world of modern art."

Anna Gonosová (ca. 1945–), b. Slovakia is an art historian, specialist on Byzantine and Medieval art and architecture, University of California, Irvine, CA.

Beverly F. Heisner (1937–), b. Detroit, MI, is an art historian. She studied history of art at Univ. of Michigan (Ph.D., 1970). She held the position of professor of history of art and architecture at Tulane University and Univ. of South Carolina, Columbia. She authored *Hollywood Art: Art Direction in the Day of the Great Studios* (1991) and *Production Design in Contemporary American Film* (2004).

Renata Hejduk (1964–), b. New York, NY, of Czech ancestry, is an Associate Professor who teaches architectural history and theory. She is a faculty affiliate of The Barrett Honors College at Arizona State University (ASU) and the Center for Nanotechnology in Society at ASU. Previous to her academic career, she was the assistant curator of European and contemporary art at the Yale University Art Gallery, and the curatorial associate in the Department of Photographs at Harvard's Fogg Art Museum. She is trained and does research as both an architectural and art historian with a Ph.D. in architectural history and theory from Harvard University, an M.A. in art history from Tufts University, and an A.B. in fine arts from Columbia University, Barnard College. Her research is focused on European and American avant-garde architecture and urbanism from around 1960 to the present and its development relative to the art, culture, and philosophy of that period. Her work was most recently published in the Journal Culture and Religion; a special issue of the *Journal of Architecture* called 'Architecture and Dirt'; the edited volume *Transportable Environments 3*, Taylor and Francis, 2006; and *The Nature of Dwellings: The Architecture of David Hovey* (2005). She co-edited (with Jim Williamson) *The Religious Imagination in Modern and Contemporary Architecture: A Reader* (2011).

Jan-Christopher Horak (1951–), b. Germany, of Czech immigrant parents, received a B.A. in history from the University of Delaware, a M.Sc. (1975) in film from Boston University and a Ph.D. (1984) from the Dept. of Communications at the Westfälische Wilhelms-Universität in Münster, Germany. For three decades, film scholar and historian Jan-Christopher Horak has been a leader at prestigious archives around the world and has an international reputation as a scholar in the field of moving image studies. In 1998, he became founding director of Archives & Collections at Universal Studios (1998–2000), then moved to the Hollywood Entertainment Museum, where he was curator (2000–2006). Horak was a visiting professor at UCLA in both the Cinema and Media Studies and Moving Image Archive Studies (MIAS) programs for more than 10 years and has served as director of the UCLA Film & Television Archive since December of 2007. Horak has also taught as an adjunct professor at the University of Rochester, the Munich Film Academy, the University of Salzburg and Wayne State University's Program Abroad. He has published numerous books in German and English, including *Saul Bass: Anatomy of Film Design* (2014), *Making Images Move: Photographers and Avant-Garde Cinema* (1997), *Lovers of Cinema: The First American Avant-Garde* (1995), *The Dream Merchants: Making and Selling Films in Hollywood's Golden Age* (1989).

Gregor Kalas (1963–), b. Lake Forest, Illinois, of Bohemian ancestry, studied art history at Williams Coll. (B.A., 1985), The Johns Hopkins Univ. (M.A., 1989) and at Bryn Mawr Coll. (Ph.D., 1999). He taught at Texas A & M Univ., as an asst. professor of the history of art and architecture (2002–06). Subsequently, he joined the Univ. of Tennessee, Knoxville, as asst. professor in the School of Architecture (2006–13), as assoc. professor of history and theory of architecture (s. 2013). His research focuses on the architecture and urbanism of the later Roman Empire and the early medieval Mediterranean. He investigates the architecture of late antiquity and the early Middle Ages with a particular focus on the post-classical adaptations of ancient buildings and monuments. In his publications, Kalas explores the reuse of ancient structures by highlighting that architectural reconstruction engages with historical memories and the reconstitution of lapsed time. Kalas has pursued investigations of late antique urban landscapes by digitally reconstructing the center of Rome in order to reveal the ritual function of buildings and the topographical linkages between significant city spaces. Currently, Kalas' research concerns the late antique revitalization of public architecture in the Roman Forum, Rome's chief monumental precinct. He is the author of *The Restoration of the Roman Forum in Late Antiquity: Transforming Public Space* (2015). He also serves as a co-editor of *Arris: The Journal of the Southeast Society of Architectural Historians* (s. 2011).

David Gordon Karel (1944–2007), b. North Carolina, of Czech ancestry, received both BS and MS in Music, with an emphasis in clarinet, finishing in 1966 from Northeast Missouri State Teachers College. He was awarded a Ph.D. in Art History at the University of Chicago in 1974 and since then has been a professor of art history at Laval University. David Karel explored the field of art in Quebec. In 1986, he compiled the catalogue of paintings by Horatio Walker that was exhibited at the Museum of Quebec. He wrote the monumental *Dictionary of the Artists of French Language in North America: Painters, Sculptors, Draughtsmen, Engravers, Photographers and Goldsmiths* (1992). In addition, he wrote "André Biéler or the shock of the cultures" and "Edmond-J. Massicotte, illustrator." In 1991, he wrote *The Collection of Maurice Duplessis*, the catalogue of the collection of the former Prime Minister of Quebec. In 2006, David Karel was elected to the Royal Society of Canada.

Adeline Lee Karpiscak (ca. 1948–), b. of Slovak descent is an art historian. Karpiscak received her Bachelor of Arts in art history from New York University in 1970 and began her distinguished foray into the museum world at the American Museum of Natural History. She came to the University of Arizona Museum of Art in 1977 as an assistant curator of collections. In 1979, she received her Master of arts in art history from the University of Arizona. Her thesis on Ernest Lawson evolved into a retrospective exhibition and the publication of an accompanying catalog. In her 26 years at the Museum of Art, Karpiscak has worn many hats (and beautiful shoes) as curator, assistant director, associate director and interim director. As a curator, Karpiscak has produced more than 20 exquisite exhibitions and catalogs showcasing the art of Maynard Dixon, James McNeil Whistler, and Arizona artists Jim Waid, Nancy Tokar Miller, David Andres and Ann Simmons-Myers. She broke new ground by establishing an international bridge of art and ideas from Slovakia to the United States. She has been the conduit for Slovakian visiting artists and curators as well as the curator of a remarkable series of exhibitions of Slovak art beginning in 1990 and continuing this spring with "East of the Danube". In April 2002, she was honored by the Minister of Culture of the Slovak Republic for her promotion of Slovak culture in the United States. She is an author of numerous books.

Ruth Kolarik (1947–), b. Caldwell, KS, graduated from Univ. of Kansas, majoring in art history and German (B.A., 1969), and continued her studies in art history, also at Univ. of Kansas (M.A., 1970), and fine arts (art history) at Harvard Univ. (Ph.D., 1982). She is a professor of art history at Colorado College in Colorado Springs. She teaches survey courses in the history of architecture and garden design that combine historical perspectives with discussions of crucial issues in contemporary architecture, landscape architecture and urbanism. She also advises students interested in pursuing careers in architecture. Her scholarly research focuses on the art and architecture of Late Antiquity, the period from 200 to 600 CE that saw the end of classical culture and the establishment of Christianity as the official religion of the Roman Empire. As an archaeologist at the ancient city of Stobi in Macedonia, she studied the mosaic floors that decorated residences, a synagogue and churches. Her publications center on the late antique and early Byzantine floor mosaics as well as early Christian architecture from the Balkan Peninsula and Greece. In more recent years, she has researched the monuments of Turkey as well as the revival of late antique mosaics in nineteenth-century France.

František Kovárna (1905–1952), b. Krpy, Bohemia, was an art historian, critic and prosaist. He specialized in modern Czech painting of the first half of the 20th century. After escaping from the communist Czechoslovakia, he lived in Germany, France and then in the US.

Joseph J. Krakora (1939–), b. Cleveland, OH, studied theatre arts at Denison University and Union Theological Seminary. After graduation, he took on important posts primarily in the field of performing arts, including Associate Director of Development at the Lincoln Center for the Performing Arts in New York, Executive Vice President at the City Center Joffrey Ballet in New York, Director for the Dance Program at the National Endowment for the Arts, and General Director at the Chicago City Ballet. Since 1985, for a total of 27 years to date, he has served as Executive Officer in charge of external and international affairs at the National Gallery of Art in Washington, D.C. The National Gallery of Art has held three major exhibits devoted to Japan over the past few decades: 'Japan: The Shaping of Daimyo Culture' in 1988, 'Edo: Art in Japan' in 1998, and 'Colorful Realm: Japanese Bird-and-Flower Paintings by Ito Jakuchu' in 2012. These exhibitions were of an unprecedented scale and quality for Japan-related exhibits held outside of Japan and Mr. Krakora continually played a pivotal role in arranging and promoting them. In particular, 'Colorful Realm', the exhibit of works by Ito

Jakuchu, which was held to commemorate the 100th anniversary of the gift of cherry blossom trees from Japan to the United States, received the seventh-highest daily average attendance in the history of the National Gallery of Art. Mr. Krakora has also played an active role in promoting exchange between the museums of Japan and the United States by coordinating requests for loans of works of art from the National Gallery's collection for exhibitions in Japan. In 2011, the exhibition 'Impressionist and Post-Impressionist Masterpieces from the National Gallery of Art' was held in both Tokyo and Kyoto directly after the Great East Japan Earthquake. Despite various uncertainties, the exhibit was eventually held as planned. To realize this exhibition, Mr. Krakora worked tirelessly to convey the importance of lending works in support of Japan during the time of crisis. He also developed the concept of establishing a Global Initiative for Cross-Cultural Understanding and Exchange to create a partnership including the cultural institutions of Japan and the National Gallery of Art.

Stella Kramrisch (1896–1993), b. Mikulov, Moravia, was an American art historian and curator. She was well known as a specialist in Indian art and Hinduism. She enrolled at the University of Vienna, studying Indian art, Sanskrit, anthropology, and Indian philosophy, and earned her Doctorate in 1919. In 1922, she was invited to India to teach at the Visva-Bharati Univ. in Santiniketan. She was appointed professor of Indian art at the University of Calcutta in 1924, where she taught until 1950. She then moved permanently to the United States. Stella Kramrisch was the professor of South Asian Art at the University of Pennsylvania for a long period of time. She was also the curator of Indian art at the Philadelphia Museum of Art from 1954 until 1972 and was a Curator Emeritus until her death. In 1981, she curated Manifestations of Shiva, a large-scale exhibition of Indian art and sculpture at the Museum, which was met with both critical and popular success. She is famous for her books on the *Hindu Temple*, *Principles of Indian Art*, and the encyclopedic *The Presence of Siva*. In 1982 the Indian government awarded Kramrisch with its Padma Bhushan award. In 1985 she was awarded the prestigious Charles Lang Freer Medal by the Smithsonian Institution. She died in Philadelphia.

Ernst Walter Kris (1900–1957), b. Vienna, of Bohemian ancestry on his mother's side (Schick), a psychoanalyst and art historian. Kris received his doctorate in art history from the University of Vienna in 1922 and was appointed an assistant curator at the Vienna Kunsthistoriches Museum, soon gaining a reputation as a leading authority on gems, intaglios, and goldwork. In 1924, he was asked by Sigmund Freud to assist with Freud's collection of cameos and intaglios. He continued his work at the Museum, while undergoing training in psychoanalysis until 1933. He was asked by Freud in 1933 to co-edit, with Robert Waelder, the journal *Imago*. Kris left Vienna in 1938, going first to England, then to Canada;

and finally, in 1940, to the United States, where he joined the New School for Social Research.

Karil Kucera (1963-), b. West Bend, WI, of Czech ancestry, is an art historian. She received training in Asian Studies and French at Univ. of Wisconsin (B.A., 1987); and art history at Univ. Oregon (M.A., 1995) and at Univ. of Kansas (Ph.D., 2001). For her Ph.D. she has chosen as a major area – Buddhist sculpture of Tang and Song China and as minor areas – Japanese Kamakura Buddhist art and Chinese painting of the Song and Yuan. She was visiting asst. professor of art at Lewis and Clark Coll., Portland (2000-01) and at Univ. of Washington, Seattle (2001-02). She then joined St. Olaf Coll. as a tenured assoc. professor (s. 2002) in the dept. of art and art history and Asian Studies. Her areas of expertise include sacred sites of Asia, with special expertise in Buddhist sites in China; contemporary Chinese art and its connections with the past; digital humanities projects related to Asia.

Viktor Lowenfeld (1903–1960), b. Linz, Aust., of Bohemian ancestry, was an art educator and curator. Dr. Lowenfeld graduated from the College of Applied Arts in Vienna, as well as the Academy of Fine Arts in the same city. He later received his Doctorate in education from the University of Vienna, and during this time, served as an elementary and secondary school teacher. While in Vienna, he also served as the director of art in the Blind Institute. In 1938, Lowenfeld fled to England before arriving in the United States. He became a citizen in 1946 after serving in the Navy as a wartime visual aids consultant. Lowenfeld joined the Hampton Institute in Virginia in 1939 as assistant professor of Industrial Arts, studio art teacher, and later chairman of the Art Department. In 1945, he was named curator of the distinguished collection of Black African Art at the Hampton Institute. Lowenfeld came to the Pennsylvania State University as professor of art education in 1946. Ten years later, he became head of the newly founded Department of Art Education. He stayed in this position until his death in 1960. Dr. Lowenfeld is well known for his Visual-Haptic theory in Art Education which was assimilated from Viennese sources.

Edward A. Maser (1923–1988), b. Detroit, MI, of Bohemian mother, attended the University of Michigan for two years before entering the Army Air Corps in 1943 during World War II. He resumed his studies after the war, earning a Master's degree from the University of Chicago in 1948 and a Doctorate in 1957. He did post-graduate work at the University of Frankfurt on the Main, in West Germany, from 1949 to 1950 and at the University of Florence, in Italy, from 1950 to 1952. He spent a year as an instructor at Northwestern University before joining the University of Kansas faculty in 1953. He joined its faculty after spending eight years at the University of Kansas as associate professor of art and director of that university's museum of art. He had been on the University of Chicago faculty since 1961 and served as chairman of its art department from 1961 to 1964. He also was a founding director of the University's David and Alfred Smart Gallery of Art, 5550 S. Greenwood Ave. Maser was an expert on the art of central Europe in the 17th and 18th centuries. Fluent in German, his position at the university was professor in art and Germanic languages and literatures. Although the art of the baroque was his specialty, as director of the Smart Gallery from 1972 to 1983, he sought to support all aspects of art history, encouraging exhibits from other artists and periods.

Joseph Daniel Masheck (1942–), b. New York, NY, of Czech ancestry, was trained as an art historian at Columbia University (B.A., 1963; M.A., 1965; Ph.D., 1973) and at Dublin. He has been associate professor of art history, Hofstra Univ., Hempstead, NY (1987-94), as full professor (since 1994). Prior to that he taught, as assistant professor, at Barnard College (1973-82) and lecturer at Harvard University (1983-86). He is the author of *Van Gogh 100* (1995).

Nancy Mowll Mathews (1956–), b. Baltimore, MD, of Czech ancestry, graduated from Goucher College and went on to complete an MA in art history at Case Western Reserve University and a Ph.D. at the New York University Institute of Fine Arts. Before joining the Williams College faculty in 1988, she was a professor at Randolph-Macon Woman's College from 1977 to 1987. She was Eugénie Prendergast Senior Curator of 19th and 20th Century Art at the Williams College Museum of Art, from 1988 to 2010. She is currently an independent scholar, curator, professor, and host of the television show *Art World with Nancy Mathews*. She graduated from Goucher College and went on to complete an MA in art history at Case Western Reserve University and a Ph.D. at the New York University Institute of Fine Arts. Mathews is the author of *Mary Cassatt: A Life* and of several other books on Mary Cassatt, and of *Paul Gauguin: An Erotic Life* (2001). She curated the exhibition 'Moving Pictures: American Art and Early Film, 1880–1910' and edited the related book of the same title. She co-authored the catalogue raisonné of the works of Maurice and Charles Prendergast, as well as several other books and exhibitions on the American artist-brothers, under the auspices of the Prendergast Archive and Study Center at the Williams College Museum of Art.

Thomas M. Messer (1920-2013), b. Bratislava, Czech., raised in Prague, was an art historian. He was the director of the Solomon R. Guggenheim Foundation, including the Solomon R. Guggenheim Museum in New York City and the Peggy Guggenheim Collection in Venice, Italy, for 27 years, a longer tenure than any of the city's major arts institutions' directors. He was a graduate of Boston University (B.A.) and earned a Master's degree in art history and museology from Harvard University (M.A., 1951). From 1947 to 1961, he worked in a series of art and museum administration positions, the last of which was director of the Institute of Contemporary Art, Boston. In 1961, he became director of the Guggenheim Museum in New York. There, he was able to establish the usefulness of the spiral-shaped Frank Lloyd Wright-designed Guggenheim as a venue for the display of art, despite the doubts of critics and artists. Messer was instrumental in expanding the museum's collection during his tenure, especially by persuading Peggy Guggenheim to donate her collection to the Guggenheim Foundation. Messer served as director of the Guggenheim Foundation from 1981 to 1988.

Zdenka Műnzer (née Roubíčková) (1902–1986), b. Čelakovice, was a historian of art and architecture, and a librarian. She studied history of art and architecture at Charles Univ. (PhDr., 1929). She specialized in the Medieval and Byzantine art. While still in Czechoslovakia, she was editor of cultural section of the *Prague Radio-Journal*. She published monographs on early medieval architecture. After the Nazi invasion in 1939, she and her husband, Jan Műnzer, emigrated to the US. She received a scholarship at Simmons College in Boston, where she studied library science. Since 1942, she was a librarian in the public library in Providence, RI. Later on, she became librarian at Columbia Univ. in NYC and, when the UN was established, she worked in the UN Library, where she remained until her retirement. Subsequently, she was offered a librarian position at the Rockefeller Institute in New York, from where she later moved to the Metropolitan Museum Library.

Max Page (1966–), b. Northampton, MA, of Czech. ancestry, is professor of architecture and history at the University of Massachusetts in Amherst. He received his education at Yale University (BA, magna cum laude in History, 1988) and from the University of Pennsylvania (Ph.D., 1995). He is the author and editor of eight books: *The Creative Destruction of Manhattan, 1900-1940* (1999), which won the Spiro Kostof Award of the Society of Architectural Historians, for the best book on architecture and urbanism; *The City's End: Two Centuries of Fantasies, Fears, and Premonitions of New York's Destruction* (2008); *Building the Nation: Americans Write About Their Architecture, Their Cities, and Their Environment* (2003, co-edited with Steven Conn); *Giving Preservation a History: Histories of Historic Preservation in the United States* (2003, co-edited with Randall Mason); *The Future of Higher Education* (2011, with Dan Clawson); *Reconsidering Jane Jacobs* (2011, co-edited with Tim Mennell); *Campus Guide to the University of Massachusetts* (2013, with Marla Miller); and *Memories of Buenos Aires: Signs of State Terrorism in Argentina* (2013). He writes for a variety of publications about New York City, urban development, and the politics of the past. For the hundredth anniversary of Times Square in 2004, he was curator for an exhibition on the history of the Square at the AXA Gallery in New York City. He is a recipient of fellowships from the Howard Foundation, Fulbright Commission, and Guggenheim Foundation. He was a Rome Prize Fellow at the American Academy in Rome, working on a book on the future of historic preservation.

Zuzana Trepková Paternostrová (1944-), b. Budapest, of Slovak descent; art historian, living in Brazil. She studied at the School of Art Industry in Bratislava (1958-62) and then at the Department of History and Theory of Fine Arts at Comenius University (1962-67). She did postgraduate work on restoration and conservation of paintings at the Academy of Fine Arts at the University of Rio de Janeiro, Brazil (1977-79). She held the position of Head Curator at the Department of Foreign Paintings at the Museu Nacional de Belas Aries in Rio de Janeiro (1982-2006); and then Senior Curator of the Directorate of the Museu Nacional de Belas Aries, Rio de Janeiro (2006-11).

Jerry Charles Podany (1951-), b. Omaha, NE, of Czech ancestry, studied fine arts at Univ. of Nebraska (B.F.A., 1975) and at Claremont Graduate School (M.F.A., 1982) and holds the Certificate in Archaeological Conservation (with distinction) from the Univ. of London (1982). Jerry Podany joined the Department of Antiquities Conservation at the J. Paul Getty Museum in Malibu, California in 1978. He has been senior conservator/ head of Department since 1985. From 1999 to 2003, he served as president of the American Institute for Conservation and from 2006 to 2012, served as president of the International Institute for Conservation (IIC). Mr. Podany is now IIC president emeritus. He is a fellow of the Society of Antiquaries of London. He received the Rutherford John Gettens Award from the American Institute for Conservation and the Engineering Research Institute's Heritage Innovation Prize. He served as an adjunct professor at University of Southern California and has regularly lectured at Columbia University, NYU and UCLA.

Zdenka Pospíšil (1923-), b. Brno, Czech., is an art historian who studied at Univ. of Oregon (B.A., 1951; M.S., 1952) and Yale Univ. (Ph.D.) She has been associated with Southern Connecticut State College, New Haven, as professor of history of art. Her interests are in Central European popular art and primitive art.

Kristina Potuckova (ca. 1984-), b. Slovakia, is an art historian. She received her Magister degree in the History of Art and Culture from the University of Trnava (Slovakia). She also holds an M.A. in Art History from Tufts University (2014) and an M.A. in Medieval Studies from Central European University (2007). Currently she is a Doctoral candidate in Western medieval art history at Yale University.

Robin Louis Ptacek (ca. 1958-2012), b. Chicago, IL, of Czech ancestry, was an art historian and curator of modern art. He graduated from Beloit Coll. and studied art history at Univ. of California, Santa Barbara (M.A., 1982; Ph.D., 1989). In addition to teaching at various universities (California, Maryland and Texas), he also served as a curator of modern art at the National Gallery of Art in Washington, DC. After retiring from his professional career, he became involved in community activism, primarily around senior and LGBT issues.

While he had maintained an interest in modernist and pop art throughout much of his life, his interest in researching and collecting Melmac was sparked during a vacation in Palm Springs, CA.

Heinrich Schwarz (1894–1974), b. Prague, Bohemia, was an art historian, curator, and historian of photography. He immigrated to the US, where by 1941 he had settled as a research scholar at the Albright Art Gallery, Buffalo, New York. In 1943, he moved to the Museum of the Rhode Island School of Design (RISD), Providence, R.I., as curator of paintings, drawings, and prints. In 1954, Dr. Schwarz finally settled at Wesleyan University in Middletown, CT, in the position of professor of history of art and curator of the Davison Art Collection, where he remained until his retirement in 1972. Throughout this period, Dr. Schwarz wrote and lectured primarily on the machine's interjection into art through the centuries, early photography, and iconography, including most specifically the symbolism of the owl and the mirror in art.

Suzanna Simor (1940–), b. Prague, Czech., studied fine arts (M.A., 1974) and history of art (Ph.D. 1994) New York Univ., and library science at Pratt Inst. (M.L.S., 1977). She is assoc. prof. and head of the art library and coordinator of Art and Music Libraries, Queens College, NY. She is also director of the Art Center there.

Jerry Stefl (ca. 1948–), b. US, of Czech ancestry, studied fine arts at (B.F.A., 1970), at (M.F.A., 1980). He taught art at Carl Sandburg High School for 33 years. Currently he has been associated with the School of the Art Institute of Chicago, where he holds the position of adjunct assoc. professor of art education (s. 1997). Concurrently, he is also senior content editor for Studio Art/The College Board Website and C.A.P.E. consultant. He is past president of the Illinois Art Education Association. He was selected as the Illinois Art Educator of the Year; the Illinois Alliance of Arts Education Arts Educator of the Year; and the National Secondary Art Educator of the Year; and was recipient of the International Kohl Award for Exemplary Education.

Hans Tietze (orig. Taussig) (1880–1954), b. Prague, Bohemia, was Univ. of Vienna educated art historian. He emigrated to US in 1938 and became vis. prof. of art history, Toledo Art Museum (1938–39); and then res. assoc., Metropolitan Museum of Art (1939–54). He was primarily known as an authority on Venetian painting, author of beautiful books on Titian and Tintoretto, and, jointly with his wife Erica Tietze-Conrat, of the standard work on Venetian drawings.

Erica Tietze-Conrat (1883–1958), b. Vienna, of Moravian ancestry, was an American art historian. She studied art history at the University of Vienna from 1902 until 1905 under Franz Wickhoff and Alois Riegl and in 1905, received her Doctorate with dissertation about the contributions to the history of Georg Raphael Donner. She was the first woman who completed the study of art history at the University of Vienna with a doctorate. She was a strong supporter of contemporary art in Vienna and an art historian specializing in Renaissance art and the Venetian school drawings. She and her husband Hans Tietze were friends with many contemporary artists including Oskar Kokoschka who was commissioned to paint them in 1909, the portrait is now at the Museum of Modern Art in New York. The sculptor Georg Ehrlich created two bronze busts of Hans and Erica Tietze which are now in the Österreichische Galerie Belvedere in Vienna, as well as numerous portrait drawings of Erica Tietze. In 1938, the couple emigrated to the US for political reasons during World War II. Erica Tietze worked as a researcher, academic lecturer at Columbia University and published art historical publications on Renaissance artists as well as contemporary Vienna artists until her death.

Hans Karl Tietze (orig. Taussig) (1880–1954), b. Prague, Bohemia, was art historian. In 1893, his family moved to Vienna. He studied archaeology, history, and art history at the University of Vienna (Ph.D., 1903). In 1909, he was appointed lecturer in art history at the University of Vienna. After World War I, he became assistant professor and began editing the art journal, *Die bildenden Künste*. After the annexation of Austria by the Nazis in 1938, he and his wife went to London and then to the United States, where he was appointed visiting professor at the Toledo Museum of Art in 1938–39. In 1940, he settled as a private scholar in New York City, where he wrote introductions to some museum catalogs and "great art" surveys for the general public.

Jan Tumlir (1962–), b. probably of Czech ancestry, is an art writer, teacher, and curator who lives in Los Angeles. He holds the position of Wallace Herndon Smith Distinguished Professor of Art at Sam Fox School of Design & Visual Arts at Washington University in St. Louis. He is a founding editor of the local art journal *X-TRA*, and his articles appear regularly in *Artforum*, *Aperture*, and *Flash Art*. He has written catalog essays for such artists as Bas Jan Ader, Uta Barth, John Divola, Jorge Pardo, Cyprien Gaillard, and, most recently, James Welling. Tumlir is a member of the Humanities & Sciences faculty at Art Center College of Design; previously, he taught at Otis College of Art and Design, CalArts, University of Southern California, UCLA, and University of California, Riverside. He has authored several books, including *LA Artland* (2005), a survey of contemporary art in Los Angeles, co-written with Chris Kraus and Jane McFadden, *Desertshore* (2008), and *Hyenas Are...* (2011), a book about artist Matthew Brannon. Tumlir's recent curatorial project, *In the Good Name of the Company*, which focused on artists who had worked with the Colby Poster Printing Company, was mounted at ForYourArt Gallery in Los Angeles and at New York Book Fair in 2013. It has yielded a book of the same name, published by Picturebox.

George (Jiří) Velinger (1938–), studied at VŠU Prague (1960–65) and continued his studies in sculpture, with focus on metals at Rhode Island School of Design (dipl., 1969). After coming to Canada, he taught and was chairman of the Dept. of Arts at Johns Abbott College (1977–78), as director of Gallery 89 (1989–92) and as professor of sculpture (1973–95). As an artist, he has worked for over forty years with metal – it has been the dominant material of his career – 'welded steel but also soldered sheets, cut, bent, torn, shaped into endless abstract forms, expressing a personal vision that at times has been bleak, at other times playful, often rebellious or provocative, sometimes even a little difficult to pin down.'

Zdenka Volavka (1929–1990), b. Czech., received her PhDr. from Charles University, Prague. She immigrated to Canada in 1968, and was professor in the Department of Visual Arts, York University, Downsview, Canada. One day, Zdenka Volavka found a lost treasure: the investiture regalia of the African Kingdom of Ngoyo, dating from the Iron Age of the second millennium. These objects became the focus of Volavka's research in her remaining years, and formed the subject of her book, *Crown and Ritual: The Royal Insignia of Ngoyo* (1998).

Harry Brandeis Wehle (1887–1969), b. Louisville, KY, of Bohemian ancestry, was a curator of the Metropolitan Museum of Art, NYC. Wehle was the nephew of Supreme Court Justice Louis Brandeis. As an undergraduate at Harvard, Wehle took the famous 'Museum Course" lead by Paul J. Sachs. He graduated from Harvard in 1911. He was appointed curator in 1918. Under his tenure, the collections of Bache, Griggs, Havemeyer and Lewisohn came to the Met. He retired as curator of European Painting in 1948, succeeded by Theodore Rousseau, but retained the title curator of collections until 1953.

23. Art Collectors & Art Dealers

Maria Altmann (née Maria Victoria Bloch) (1916–2011), b. Vienna, was a Jewish refugee from Nazi Austria, noted for her ultimately successful legal campaign to reclaim five family-owned paintings by the artist Gustav Klimt, stolen by the Nazis during World War II, from the Government of Austria. The family name was changed to Bloch-Bauer the following year. She was a niece of Adele Bloch-Bauer, a wealthy Jewish patron of the arts who served as the model for some of Klimt's best-known paintings. In 1937, Maria married Fredrick 'Fritz' Altmann. Not long after their Paris honeymoon, the 1938 Anschluss incorporated Austria into Nazi Germany. Under the Nazis, Fredrick was arrested in Austria and held hostage at the Dachau concentration camp to force his brother Bernhard, by then safely in France, to transfer the Bernhard Altmann textile factory into German hands. Fredrick was subsequently released, and the couple fled for their lives. Traveling by way of Liverpool, England, they reached the United States and settled first in Fall River, Massachusetts, and eventually in Los Angeles, California. Briefly after moving to Los Angeles, Bernhard Altmann mailed Maria Altmann a cashmere sweater – something

America hadn't seen yet – accompanied with the note: "See what you can do with this." Maria took the sweater right to Kerr's Department Store in Beverly Hills, and shortly thereafter attracted a multitude of buyers in both California and across the United States for Bernhard Altmann's cashmere sweaters. Maria became the face of cashmere in California and eventually started her own clothing business with her own clients, among them Caroline Brown Tracy, the mother of actor Spencer Tracy.

Hugo Feigl (1889–1961); art dealer, owner of Feigl Gallery, NYC.

Hans Peter Kraus (1907–1988), b. Vienna, of Bohemian father (Dr. Emil Kraus of Karlovy Vary), was a book dealer described as "without doubt the most successful and dominant rare book dealer in the world in the second half of the 20th century" and in a league with other rare book dealers such as Bernard Quaritch, Guillaume de Bure and A.S.W. Rosenbach. Kraus specialized in medieval illuminated manuscripts, incunables (books printed before 1501), and rare books of the 16th and 17th centuries, but would purchase and sell almost any book that came his way that was rare, valuable and important. He prided himself in being "the only bookseller in history…to have owned a Gutenberg Bible and the Psalters of 1457 and 1459 simultaneously," stressing that "'own' here is the correct word, as they were bought not for a client's account but for stock." He started his own rare book business in 1932, which prospered despite the Depression. In 1938, after the German annexation of Austria, Kraus was arrested for being Jewish and sent to the Dachau concentration camp. After several months, he was transferred to Buchenwald. After eight months in Buchenwald, he was released, returned to Vienna and ordered to leave Austria within two months. Kraus restarted his rare book business in New York, which soon began to prosper. Over the years, Kraus bought and sold major medieval illuminated manuscripts, incunables and assorted rare books and manuscripts.

Hans P. Kraus, Jr. (ca. 1958), b. of Bohemian ancestry, has been established in New York since 1984 as a private dealer in nineteenth and early twentieth century photographs, specializing in the paper negative era which flourished before 1860. The gallery is a member of the Art Dealers Association of America, the Private Art Dealers Association, and The Association of International Photography Art Dealers. Publications include monographs on early photographers, and catalogues under the series title Sun Pictures. The gallery has two annual exhibitions with public hours and participates regularly in international art fairs: Art Basel, The Art Show (ADAA), The Photography Show (AIPAD), Winter Antiques Show, Maastricht (TEFAF), and Paris Photo.

Meda Sokolová Mládek (1919–2022), b. Zákupy, Bohemia was trained as an art historian at L'Ecole de Louvre, Univ. of Paris and the Johns Hopkins Univ. Together with her husband

Jan, she has been dedicated to promoting and collecting art from Central European painters and sculptors who were persecuted, exiled or forced to go underground by the Communist regime. When the Sova Mill in Prague became available, Mrs. Mladek saw it as a one-time opportunity to realize her dream of sharing with the Czech people the hundreds of paintings, sculptures, drawings, and graphic works she had accumulated over the years – in the newly established Kampa Museum for Central European Modern Art.

Vito Maria Schnabel (1985–), b. New York, NY, of Czech ancestry, is an art dealer and the owner of Vito Schnabel Gallery, founded in Switzerland in 2015, and Vito Schnabel Projects, founded in New York in 2003. He is the son of artist and filmmaker Julian Schnabel. Schnabel attended Saint Ann's School in Brooklyn and Columbia University for one year. Schnabel organized his first exhibition at the age of 16, a group show in New York in 2003. Two years later, he presented a solo show of Ron Gorchov's paintings. Other early exhibitions presented by Schnabel include a show of Terence Koh's paintings at Richard Avedon's former studio in New York in 2008, several exhibitions of Rene Ricard's paintings in New York, Los Angeles, and London, and an exhibition of Laurie Anderson's paintings and drawings in New York in 2012. Schnabel has organized several major group exhibitions in temporary exhibition settings, such as DSM-V, curated by David Rimanelli, at the Farley Post Office in New York in 2013, and First Show / Last Show, presented in 2015 at the Germania Bank Building on the Bowery, which had not been open to the public since the mid-1960s. In 2013, Schnabel opened an office and showroom in New York where he presents public exhibitions. Vito Schnabel Gallery opened in St. Moritz in 2015.

Heinrich (Jindřich) Waldes (1876–1941), b. Nemyšl, Bohemia, a manufacturer, was also a passionate art collector of contemporary Czech art. In 1918 in Prague, he founded Waldes Museum for his collection of buttons which had over 70 thousand items. The collection was transferred after the Second World War to Museum of Decorative Arts (Uměleckoprůmyslové muzeum) in Prague. Apart from buttons, he collected works of Czech painters, especially František Kupka's paintings. They became friends in 1919 and remained so until 1938. Waldes supported Kupka throughout his career by buying his canvases. Part of Jindřich Waldes' collection held by the National Gallery in Prague had been returned to his descendants living in the United States. In 2007, the Prague City Court rendered the decision to return fifty percent of the Czech Koh-i-Noor holdings to the Waldes family heirs. However, in 2010, the Constitutional Court in Brno reversed the decision, stating that the Beneš decrees of 1945 handed the property to the Czech State, not the Communist seizures in 1948.

IX. Humanities

A. History

June Granatir Alexander (1948–), b. Steubenville, OH, of Slovak ancestry, is a historian. She was educated at the University of Cincinnati (M.A., 1971) and the University of Minnesota (Ph.D., 1980). She specializes in USD history and Slovak emigration and immigration. She is on the faculty of the Russian and East European Studies Program at the University of Cincinnati. She is the author of *Ethnic Pride, American Patriotism: Slovaks and Other Immigrants in the Interwar Era* (2004) and *The Immigrant Church and Community: Pittsburgh's Slovak Catholics and Lutherans 1880–1915* (1987).

Josef Anderle (1924–2014), b. Prague, Czech., was a historian. He studied history at Charles University (dipl. 1948; PhDr., 1991), the University of Munich (1952–53) and the University of Chicago (Ph.D.). He was research assistant in the Center for American Foreign and Military Policy at the University of Chicago (1956–59) and a Bibliographer for Social Sciences and Slavic Studies at the University of Chicago Library (1960–62). He also taught at Univ. of Chicago, before joining the University of North Carolina at Chapel Hill in 1962, becoming a full professor of history there in 1970. He was a specialist on Czechoslovak history. He was a co-author of *Latvia: An Area Study* (1966) and a co-editor of *Progressive Czech* (1965). He was instrumental in establishing the Czechoslovak History Conference.

Elinor G. Barber (1924–1999), b. Prague, Czech., received her B.A. in History from Vassar College in 1945 and was elected Phi Beta Kappa. She earned the M.A. and Ph.D. degrees in History from Radcliffe College in 1946 and 1951, respectively. She held the position of editor for biographies, Int. Encycl. Soc. Sci. (s. 1961); project dir., international div., Ford Foundation (s. 1967); manager of research dept., Inst. of International Education; research associate in the Provost's Office at Columbia University. She was the author of *The Bourgeoisie in 18th Century France* (1955), *Bridges to Knowledge: Foreign Students in Comparative Perspective* (1984) and co-author of *Increasing Faculty Diversity: The Occupational Choices of High-Achieving Minority Students* (2003).

Susan Groag Bell (1926–2015), b. Opava, Czech., in 1939, found refuge in England; studied history at Stanford University and Santa Clara University; historian and affiliated scholar at the Stanford Institute for Research on Women and Gender. She was a Czech-American pioneer in Women's Studies. At a time when there were no academic courses nor textbooks, offered in women's history, Bell compiled images of women's participation in society from artworks and began presenting lectures to present roles women had held in society. In 1971, a year after the first women's studies course was offered in the United States, Bell taught her own class on the subject and prepared a reading guide for the course which would become one of the first textbooks to treat women's history from an academic perspective. She taught and researched for more than four decades as an independent scholar at the Clayman Institute for Gender Research.

Harry Jindřich Benda (1919–1971), b. Liberec, Czech. was a social and political historian. He studied at Victoria University College, Wellington, NZ (B.A., 1950), University of New Zealand (M.A., 1952) and Cornell University (Ph.D., 1955). He was with University of Rochester (1955–59), Yale University (1959–71), as prof. of history (1966–71). He specialized in South East Asian history, Indonesian history and politics and comparative elite structures. He was the Founding Director of Institute S.E. Asian Studies, Singapore (1968–69). He was the author of *The Crescent and the Rising Sun: Indonesian Islam during the Japanese Occupation, 1942-45* (1958). He was editor of Yale's *Southeast Asia Monograph* series from 1960 through the turbulent years of the Vietnam War, until his untimely death on October 26, 1971.

Karel D. Bicha (1937–), b. La Crosse, WI, of Czech ancestry, is Univ. of Minnesota educated historian (Ph.D., 1963). He has been associated with Marquette Univ. (s. 1969), as prof. of history (s. 1977). He specializes in agricultural history, immigration history and U.S. history. He is the author of *Western Populism* (1976) and *Czechs in Oklahoma* (1980).

Livia Bitton-Jackson (orig. Elli L. Friedmann) (1931–2023), Šamorín, Czech., is a historian, an author and a Holocaust survivor. She was 13 years old when she, her mother, father, aunt and brother Bubi, were taken to Ghetto Nagymagyar. Eventually, they were transported to Auschwitz, the largest German concentration camp. She, her mother and brother were liberated in 1945. Bitton-Jackson came to the U.S. on a refugee boat in 1951 to join Bubi, who was studying in New York. She then studied at New York University, from which she received a Ph.D. in Hebrew Culture and Jewish History. She has been a professor of history at City University of New York for 37 years, and has won numerous awards, including the 1998 Christopher Award for her book, *I Have Lived a Thousand Years*.

Eve Blau (1951–), of Vianna, of Czech descent on her mother's side, is an American historian and educator, who teaches at the Graduate School of Design at Harvard University as Adjunct Professor of the History and Theory of Urban Form and Design, as well as Director of Research. Blau has contributed to a scholarship on the history of architecture and urban design. In 2018, she was named Fellow of the Society of Architectural Historians. Blau attended the University of York and received a Bachelor of Arts degree in English and Sociology. Her postgraduate studies in the History of Architecture took her to Yale University. There, Blau was awarded a Master of Arts in 1974 and a Doctor of Philosophy in

1978. Blau began her teaching career in the Art and Art History Department at Wesleyan University. She was the Head of the Department of Exhibitions and Publications (1984-1991) then Curator of Exhibitions and Publications (1991-2001) at the Canadian Centre for Architecture. She was a Professor of the History of Architecture (2004-2011) in the Department of Architecture at the Harvard University Graduate School of Design, while Toshiko Mori was chair. Blau served as Director of the Master in Architecture Degree Programs (2008-2011). She has been part of the school's Department of Urban Planning and Design as Professor of the History and Theory of Urban Form and Design. In 2019, Blau was appointed as Director of Research by Mohsen Mostafavi.

George Erwin Blau (1911-1999), b. Vienna, the son of Edith Beatrix Khuner (1890-1970) of Moravian ancestry, and the physician Gustav Blau, was a historian. He was chief historian for the U.S. Government in Europe. He was married, in 1947, to Gertrude Marle (1918-2012) who bore him 2 children.

John Bodnar (1944-), b. Victoria, Texas, of eastern Slovak descent, grew up in Forest City, PA. He is a Distinguished Professor of History at Indiana University, described as 'the doyen of American immigration history.' He is a co-director of the Center for the Study of History and Memory. He was nominated for a Pulitzer Prize. He was trained at Joh Carroll University (B.A., 1966; M.A., 1968) and University of Connecticut (Ph.D., 1975).

Stephen Borsody (1911-2000), b. Prešov, Czech., was a historian. He was educated at Charles Univ. in Prague, receiving a Doctor's degree in law and political science in 1934. He then studied history at Univ. of Budapest, becoming docent of East European history in 1946. He also studied in Dresden, Rome, Paris and London. In 1957, he started his career as a journalist. He worked in Prague and in 1938, he moved to Budapest. In 1945, he was foreign editor of *Szabad Szó*, the Peasant Party daily and also assoc. editor of *Új Magyarország*, a weekly specializing in international news. He then joined the Hungarian Foreign Service and was appointed counselor and press attaché of the Hungarian Legation in Washington (1946-47). Following his resignation from diplomatic post in 1947, he entered academic profession, becoming professor of history at Chatham College (s. 1947). He is the author of *The Tragedy of Central Europe* (1960).

Edita Bosak (1950-2022), b. Stockholm, Sweden, of Slovak descent; is a historian, trained at Brock University (B.A., 1973), University of Waterloo (M.A., 1974), and University of London (Ph.D., 1982). She held the position of Associate Professor in the Department of History, at the Memorial University of Newfoundland, St. John's, Newfoundland, Canada. Her interests were in Central and East European history, nationalism, Slovak national movement and Slovak women.

Leila Leah Bronner (née Amsel) (1930–2019), b. Czech., was an American historian and biblical scholar. She immigrated to the United States in 1937, growing up in Williamsburg, Brooklyn. In 1949, she married Rabbi Joseph Bronner, who had escaped Berlin with his family in 1941. They moved with their newborn daughter to Johannesburg, South Africa in 1951, where she began her career. She taught at the University of the Witwatersrand, and she co-founded the Yeshiva College of South Africa. In 1984, the family moved to Los Angeles, California where Leila Bronner taught at American Jewish University and the University of Southern California. She became president of Emunah Women, and was involved in Amit Women, Builders of Jewish Education, and the Jewish Federation. She authored four books, including two books about biblical women, in which she showed that they are represented in many different ways, and another book about the afterlife, in which she tackled both Hassidic and Kabbalistic approaches.

Laura Burian (1970–), b. Boston, MA, of Czech ancestry, studied comparative area studies (East Asian Studies) at Duke Univ. (B.A., 1991), and Chinese/English translation and interpretation at the Monterey Institute of International Studies (M.A., 1995). She also studied abroad at National Taiwan Normal University, Chinese University of Hong Kong, and Nanjing University. Her expertise is in the area of simultaneous and consecutive interpretation between Chinese and English, and pedagogy for the teaching of simultaneous and consecutive interpretation. In the late 90s, she worked as an in-house translator, interpreter, and legal assistant in the Beijing office of Skadden, Arps, Slate, Meagher & Flom, and freelanced as both a translator and interpreter in the US, mainland China, and Taiwan (s. 1995). In Jan 2000, she joined the faculty of the Middlebury Institute of International Studies at Monterey (MIIS, formerly the Monterey Institute of International Studies). There she has served as president (2007–09) and vice president (2013–15) of the faculty senate and was awarded the Outstanding Teacher of the Year award in 2004, the Allen Griffiths Excellence in Teaching Award in 2005, and the Dr. Leslie Eliason Teacher of Excellence Award in 2008. Beyond teaching, Professor Burian is an active freelance translator and interpreter. Her private sector clients are primarily in the fields of law, medicine, IT, mobile internet, venture capital, new energies, biology, human rights, and education. Her US government clients include the Departments of State, Energy, and Commerce, the US Embassy in Beijing, among others. She is also a freelance violinist/violist/fiddler with groups such as the Monterey String Quartet and Heartstrings (s. 2001).

Peter Burian (1943–), b. Hanover, NH, of Czech ancestry, graduated from Univ. of Michigan, Ann Arbor, majoring in classical studies (B.A., 1964). He then continued his studies at Princeton Univ. (M.A., 1968; Ph.D., 1971). He has been associated with Duke Univ. as instructor (1968–71) and asst. professor in the dept. of classical studies (1971–77), as assoc. professor (1977–96), as full professor (s. 1996), as professor of theater studies (s.

2001), as chair of classical studies (2003-07), as professor emeritus (s. 2015). He was also visiting professor at Dartmouth College (1989) and professor in charge at the Intercollegiate Center for Classical Studies in Rome (2009-10, 2013-14), as well as a fellow of the Center of Hellenic Studies, Washington, DC (1980-81) and senior associate of King's College, Univ. of Cambridge, UK (2003). He specializes in dramatic literature, theater history, and literary and cultural criticism. His research interests are in the area of Greek literature, particularly drama; theory and practice of literary translation; reception of Greco-Roman antiquity in later thought and arts. He is the author of *Euripides, Helen* (2007), *Aeschylus, The Oresteia* (2003), *Aeschylus, The Suppliants* (1991), *Aristophanes, Birds* (1991), *Euripides, The Phoenician Women* (1981). He also edited a number of monographs and edited the complete Oxford Greek Tragedy in New Translations.

Thomas Čapek (1861-1950), b. Chrášťovice, Bohemia, besides being a lawyer, banker and NE State legislator, was also a journalist and a noted historian. He emigrated to the US in summer 1879, being approximately eighteen years old and was naturalized in the mid-1880s. In 1883, he became editor of the *Pokrok Západu* in Omaha and in the fall of 1886 entered Ann Arbor, to study law at University of Michigan (LL.B., 1888) and initially practiced law in Omaha, Nebraska (1890-91). About the same time, he was elected a member of the Nebraska Legislative House of Representatives (1890-91). In 1894, he married Anna Vostrovský and subsequently practiced law in New York, NY (1895-1910). After serving first as vice president of the Bank of Europe, New York, NY. (1910-2), he became president of the Bank (1912-32). He started publishing his historical writings with the monograph, *Bohemia under Hapsburg Misrule (1915).* Then followed many others, including *Bohemian (Czech) Bibliography* (1918), *The Čechs (Bohemians) in America* (1920), *The Czechs and Slovaks in American Banking* (1920), *The Czech Community of New York* (1921), *Augustine Herrman of Bohemia Manor* (1930), *Moje Amerika* (1930), *Ancestry of Frederick Philipse, First Lord and Founder of Philipse Manor at Yonkers* (1939), *Czechs and Slovaks in the United States Census* (1939), *American Czechs in Public Office* (1940), *Návštěvnici z Cech a Moravy v Americe v Letech 1848-1939* (1940), *Slavs in the United States Census, 1850-1940, with Special References to Czechoslovaks* (1943).

Bořivoj (Boris) Čelovský (1923-2008), b. Ostrava, Czech., was a Czech Canadian historian, member of the post-1948 Czechoslovak political exile and former political adviser. He studied modern history at the University of Heidelberg and then at the Université de Montréal. He was mostly dealing with historical and contemporary reflections of the Czech-German relationships. His books often escalated strong reactions, both positive and negative and initiated broad debates.

Christian William Ceplecha (1927–2002), b. Berwyn, IL of Czech ancestry, was Catholic Univ. educated historian. He was associated with Illinois Benedictine Coll., for more than three decades, as a prof. of history and dept. chair from 1960 to 1980. He specialized in the 19th century Europe, reformation and historiography.

Joseph Chada (aka Čada) (1896–1992), b. Chicago, IL of Czech ancestry, was a historian, who specialized in Czech American history. Mr. Chada received a Bachelor of Arts degree in history from the University of Chicago in 1919. From 1919 to 1927, he taught in Indiana and Illinois high schools. He taught history at Chicago Junior College until 1943. From 1945 to 1961, Mr. Chada was professor of history and chairman of the social studies department at Chicago Teachers College, now Chicago State University. From 1961 to 1972, he was a professor of European history and chairman of the Slavic Center at St. Procopius College, now Illinois Benedictine. During his teaching career, Mr. Chada made 12 films on world history for use in elementary schools. Mr. Chada was knighted in 1954 by Pope Pius XII for his work on behalf of displaced persons. He was a past director of the Catholic Charities of Chicago and was active in the Czechoslovak Society of Arts and Sciences (SVU).

Robert Cherny (1943–), b. Marysville, KS, graduated from Beatrice High School, Beatrice, Nebraska, and received his B.A. from the University of Nebraska, Lincoln in 1965, and his M.A. and Ph.D. from Columbia University in the City of New York in 1967 and 1972. He was a member of the history faculty of San Francisco State University from 1971 to 2012, when he became professor emeritus. Cherny's research interests are in U.S. political history, especially for 1865–1940, and the history of California and the West. He is the author of three books on U.S. politics, 1865–1925, and more than two dozen published essays in journals and anthologies; co-author of two books on the history of San Francisco, a US survey textbook now in 7th edition, and a California history textbook now in 2nd edition; and co-editor of anthologies on the Cold War and labor and on California women and politics. His most recent book, now in press, is a biography of Victor Arnautoff, an artist who was born in Russia and lived in San Francisco for much of his life; Cherny is now completing a biography of Harry Bridges, a long-time San Francisco labor leader. While a faculty member at San Francisco State, Cherny served as chair of the academic senate, chair of the system-wide academic senate, chair of the history department, acting dean for social and behavioral sciences, and interim dean of undergraduate studies.

Bohdan Chudoba (1909–1982), b. Brno, Czech., was a historian, archivist, journalist and Czechoslovak politician, who lived abroad s. 1948. He was a specialist on political and cultural history of the 16th and 17th centuries and esp. on the Spanish influences on the European countries, history of various circumstances relating to the Battle of White Mountain and the struggles between Protestants and Catholics. He was professor of history at Iona College (1949-1978). He studied history at Universities in Brno, Oxford, Rome, Vienna and Madrid. In 1933, he graduated as Doctor of Historical Sciences at the Royal Spanish Universidad de Alcalá.

Joseph Chytry (1945-), b. Tehran, Iran, of Czech ancestry, received his D.Phil. in politics and the history of ideas from the University of Oxford (1973), a Master of International Affairs degree from Columbia University (1973), and a B.A. with special honors in international affairs from the George Washington University. He was a Humboldt Postdoctoral Fellow in Philosophy at the University of Tuebingen, Germany, as well as a graduate student in philosophy at the University of Heidelberg. He has been associated with the dept. of history of Univ. of California, Berkley as res. associate (1977-84), (1992-94). Currently he holds the position of instructor in humanities at Univ. of California, Berkeley Extension Program (s. 1989) and a senior adj. professor of critical studies at California Coll. of the Arts, Oakland (s. 1996). He serves also as founding managing editor of *Industrial and Corporate Changes* (s. 1993). He is the author of a number of books, including *Mountain of Paradise: Reflections on the Emergence of the Civilization of Greater California as a World Civilization* (2013), *Unis vers Cythère: Aesthetic-Political Investigations in Polis Thought and the Artful Firm* (2009), *Cytherica: Aesthetic-Political Essays in an Aphrodisian Key* (2005), *The Aesthetic State: A Quest in Modern German Thought* (1983).

Marshall Clagett (1916-2005), b. Washington, DC, desc. f. Augustine Heřman, was an American historian of science who specialized in medieval science. Clagett began his undergraduate education in 1933 at the California Institute of Technology. In 1935, he transferred to George Washington University, there completing his Bachelor's degree and in 1937, his Master's degree. He then studied history at Columbia University with Lynn Thorndike, receiving his Ph.D. in 1941. He was with Univ. of Wisconsin, Madison (s. 1947), as prof. history (s. 1954), eventually becoming Vilas Research Professor there. From 1959 to 1964, he was also director of the University's Institute for Research in the Humanities. In 1964, Clagett moved to Princeton as a professor in the Department of Historical Studies of the Institute of Advanced Study. It was here that he began to publish his major work on Archimedes and his followers, and later began his work on ancient Egypt. At the time of his death, he was working on the fourth and final volume in the series. Clagett twice won the John Lewis Prize of the American Philosophical Society. In 1995, he was awarded one of two newly-created European Prizes in the History of Science, Technology and Industry, and in 1996, he won the Italian International Galileo Galilei Prize, given to foreign scholars who have made an outstanding contribution to the study and diffusion of Italian culture. He specialized in medieval history of science. He wrote more than a dozen volumes on the history of science, many of them focusing on the role of mathematics in natural philosophy and on pure mathematics. He was the author of *Giovanni Marliani and Late Medieval Physics*

(1941), *Greek Science in Antiquity* (1956), *Mechanics in the Middle Ages* (1959), *Archimedes in the Middle Ages* (1963).

Jesse D. Clarkson (1897–1973), b. Brooklyn, NY, desc. f. Frederick Philipse, studied history at Columbia Univ. He was with Brooklyn Coll. (s. 1930), prof. of history (s. 1945), as dept. chair (1937–50). He was an authority on Russian history, recent European history and Irish history.

Konštantin Čulen (1904–1964), b. Brodské, Slovakia; was a journalist and politician, turned historian, author, second director of the Slovak Institute in Cleveland (1956–1959).

Zdeněk David (1931–), b. Blatná, Czech., did graduate work at Harvard (M.A. in Russian area studies, 1954; Ph.D. in history, 1960). He taught historiography, and Russian and East European history at the University of Michigan in Ann Arbor from 1960 to 1965. During this time, he spent a year in Helsinki, Finland, on a fellowship from the American Council of Learned Societies (1964–1965). From 1966 to 1974, he served as a Slavic bibliographer and history lecturer in Russian and East European history at Princeton University, and from 1974 to 2002, as librarian at the Woodrow Wilson International Center for Scholars. Since then, he has been senior scholar at the Woodrow Wilson Center. With the late Robert Kann, he is co-author of the *Peoples of the Eastern Habsburg Lands, 1526-1918* (1984). He compiled the "Bibliography of Works in the Philosophy of History for 1978-82" and "for 1983-87" (1984-89). His book, *Finding the Middle Way: The Utraquists' Liberal Challenge to Rome and Luther* was published in 2003. David's next book appeared in 2010 as *Realism, Tolerance, and Liberalism in the Czech National Awakening: Legacies of the Bohemian Reformation*.

Gotthard Deutsch (1859–1921), born in Dolní Kounice, Moravia, was an American scholar of Jewish history. He was Prof. of Jewish history and philosophy of religion at Hebrew Union Coll. s. 1891. Matriculating in 1879 at the University of Vienna, two years later he received his Ph.D. in history. While attending the university, he enrolled in a Talmudic course taught by Isaac Hirsch Weiss at Beth Hammidrash. During his studies in Vienna, Deutsch drew inspiration and guidance from both Weiss and Adolf Jellinek, an authority in Midrashic research. Shortly after his graduation, Deutsch received Semichah (ordination) from Weiss. In 1891, at the invitation of Isaac Mayer Wise, Deutsch moved to the United States to accept the chair of Jewish history and philosophy at Hebrew Union College in Cincinnati. After eleven years of teaching there, he was appointed Dean. In February 1903, after the death of Moses Mielziner, he was designated acting president of the college, a position he held until October of the same year.

Francis Dvorník (1893–1975), b. Chomýž, Moravia was a Catholic priest and academic scholar. He was considered one of the leading twentieth-century experts on Slavic and Byzantine history, and on relations between the churches of Rome and Constantinople. He graduated from the Archdiocesan School in Kremeříž, after which he continued his education at the Faculty of Theology of the University in Olomouc. He graduated in 1916 and was ordained a priest. After serving briefly as vicar in the towns of Bílovec and Vítkov, Fr. Francis continued his studies at the Charles University in Prague. In 1920, he received his Doctorate in Theology from the Theological Faculty in Olomouc. Fr. Francis then attended the University of Paris simultaneously studying in several specialties. He graduated in 1926 after defending his postdoctoral studies and received a Doctor of Letters degree from the Sorbonne. In 1927, he returned to Czechoslovakia. Receiving his appointment in 1928, he became professor of ecclesiastical history at the Faculty of Catholic Theology at Charles University in Prague. There, he became one of the founders of the Institute of Slavic Studies in Prague and co-founder of the journal *Byzantinoslavica*. After the German occupation of Czechoslovakia in 1939, Fr. Dvornik immigrated to Great Britain in 1939, and to France in 1940. In France, he taught at the Collège de France and the Paris Ecole des Hautes Etudes. In 1948, Fr. Dvornik was appointed Professor of Byzantine Studies at the Dumbarton Oaks Center at Harvard University. Between 1962 and 1965, he was an Advisor for History and Ecumenism of the Second Vatican Council. In 1965, he became professor emeritus. He was an authority on Byzantine history, Slavic history and civilization and on relations between the churches of Rome and Constantinople. His scholarly work culminated with the synthetic survey and interpretation of the history and civilization of the Slavs in the European context. He was the author of *Les Slaves, Byzance et Rome au IXe siècle* (1926), *La vie de St. Grégoire la Décapolite et les Slaves Macédoniens au IXe siècle* (1926), *Les Lègendes de Constantin et de Mèthode vues de Byzance* (1933), *National Churches* (1944), *The Photian Schism. History and Legend* (1948), *The Making of Central and Eastern Europe* (1949), *The Slavs, Their Early History an Civilization* (1956), *The Idea of Apostolocity in Bazantium and the Legend of the Apostle Andrew* (1958), *The Ecumenical Councils* (1961), *The Slavs in European History and Civilization* (1962), *Early Christian and Byzantine Political Philosophy, Origins and Background* (1967) and *Byzantine Missions among the Slavs* (1970); *Origins of Intelligence Services: The Ancient Near East, Persia, Greece, Rome, Byzantium, the Arab Muslim Empires, the Mongol Empire, China, Muscovy* (1974).

Robert Dennis Fiala (1938-2018), b. St. Louis, MO, of Czech ancestry, graduated from Concordia Teachers Coll., Seward, NE (B.S.Ed., 1960) and studied history at Municipal Univ. of Omaha (M.A., 1963) and at Wayne State Univ. (Ph.D., 1967). He taught history and political science at Concordia from 1965 until he retired in 2004, although he continued to teach some East Asian and Chinese history. He served as adjunct professor of history at the University of Nebraska, Lincoln for ten years and as visiting professor of history at Wayne State University, Detroit; Tunghai University in Taichung, Taiwan (1975-6); the Normal College of Foreign Languages, Beijing, China (1987-1988) and Oak Hill College,

London (1997). Fiala served as founding Director of International Education at Concordia from 1993-1997 and was a member of the Seward City Council (1984-2010). He has published scholarly articles on topics ranging from colonial American Quakers to British radicalism and Asian nationalism and has written and illustrated numerous travel articles on European and Asian politics and culture.

Eleanor Flexner (1908-1995), b. Georgetown, KY, of Bohemian ancestry, after graduating from Swarthmore College, with high honors in English and history in 1930, she attended Somerville College at Oxford University. She was an American distinguished independent scholar and pioneer in what was to become the field of women's studies. Her much-praised *Century of Struggle: The Woman's Rights Movement in the United States*, originally published in 1959, relates women's physically courageous and politically ingenious work for the vote to other 19th- and early 20th-century social, labor, and reform movements, most importantly the push for equal education, the abolition of slavery, and temperance laws.

James Thomas Flexner (1908-2003), b. Manhattan, of Bohemian ancestry; was an American historian and biographer best known for the four-volume biography of *George Washington* that earned him a National Book Award in Biography and a special Pulitzer Prize. In 1929, His one-volume abridgment, *Washington: the Indispensable Man* (1974) was the basis of two television miniseries, *George Washington* (1984) and *George Washington II: The Forging of a Nation* (1986), starring Barry Bostwick as Washington. Flexner graduated cum laude from Harvard University, and found work as a reporter for the *New York Herald Tribune*. In 1931, he took a position at the New York City Department of Health as an executive secretary. The following year, he left his job to devote his full energies to writing. Although untrained in art history, he gravitated to art subjects as part of his interest in writing about American history. He wrote other historical biographies, including *The Young Hamilton* (on Alexander Hamilton), *Mohawk Baronet* (on Sir William Johnson, 1st Baronet), and *The Traitor and the Spy: Benedict Arnold* and *John André*. He wrote many books on the history of American art, including a highly regarded life of the American painter John Singleton Copley.

John Fousek (1959–), b. New York, NY, of Czech ancestry, studied history and sociology at Columbia Univ. (B.A., 1981) and history at Cornell Univ. (Ph.D., 1994). He became adjunct asst. professor at St. Francis College (1993–94) and then visiting asst. professor of history at Franklin and Marshall College (1995–97). He then joined Rutgers Univ., as assoc. director of Center for Global Change and Governance (1997–2001), as assoc. member of the Graduate Faculty in History and Global Affairs (2002–06) and as a senior fellow of the Center for Global Change and Governance (2002–06). From 1997 to 2004, he was executive director of the World Order Models Project, a non-profit research organization. Subsequently, he moved to Yeshiva Univ., as program director of the Center for Ethics (2006-10) and as academic adviser and special assistant to the dean of Stern College for Women (2010-2012). In 2013, John Fousek joined the faculty of New York University's MA Program in International Relations in 2013. Professor Fousek's research and teaching focus on U.S. foreign relations and global history from the 18th century to the present. His long-standing interests include: the dynamics of international power and global cultural change; public opinion, American nationalism and U.S. foreign policy; the Cold War and its legacy; and problems of world order in the post-Soviet era (before and after Sept. 11, 2001). His book, *To Lead the Free World: American Nationalism and the Cultural Roots of the Cold War* has been in press continuously since its publication in 2000. He is co-editor of a collection of essays on *Ethics and the U.S. Presidency* (2010). He has written on terrorism, political ethics and the prevention of genocide as well as culture and US foreign policy.

Marianka S. Fousek (1930-), b. Prague, Czech., studied history at Wellesley Coll. (B. A., 1952) and theology at Union Theol. Sem. (B.D., 1955) and church history at Harvard Univ. (Th.D., 1960). She was Associate Professor of History, Rosary Coll., River Forest, IL and Miami Univ., Oxford. Her specialty was Bohemian reformation. She was the author of *The Eclipse of Lutheranism in the 17th Century Czechoslovakia* (1966), *The Church in a Changing World - Events and Trends from 250 to 600* (1971) and *The Church from Age to Age: From Galilee to Global Christianity* (2011).

Alexander Fried (1925-), b. Czech., a historian, after a boyhood in Nazi concentration camps, lived in postwar Prague from 1948 to 1950 as communism's grip on the country tightened, then lived in exile in Vienna, Belgium and Canada. Now a part-time resident of Prague again, he has been a witness to years of economic shock therapy, since 1989. He received his first Doctorate from Vienna University as a young exile in 1952 after having submitted a 386-page dissertation on the former president of the First Czechoslovak Republic. 1967, Fried's younger brother Ferdinand, a successful pharmaceutical industry entrepreneur in Montreal, called him up in Brussels, where Fried had been looking for work, and invited him for a visit to Canada. After a brief sojourn in Montreal, an offer came through in April 1968 from Toronto to head up the Farband, a Yiddish community organization in the city. After a year, Fried proved himself, far more, than a simple administrator and won an offer from Prince of Wales College in the Canadian seaside idyll of Charlottetown, Prince Edward Island, to head its nascent history department. Soon, Fried found himself on a flight bound for the then-backwater of the Maritimes to head up a department of 80 professors and more than 3,000 students.

Saul Friedländer (1932-), b. Prague, Czech., is an award-winning historian. He is a scholar of the Third Reich and the Holocaust who has transformed our understanding of this period by weaving into a coherent whole the perspectives of ordinary Germans, party activists, military and political figures, and, most importantly, victims and survivors. He was raised in France and lived through the German Occupation of 1940-1944. From 1942 until 1946, Friedländer was hidden in a Catholic boarding school in Montluçon, near Vichy. While in hiding, he converted to Roman Catholicism and later began preparing for the Catholic priesthood. His parents attempted to flee to Switzerland, were arrested instead by Vichy French gendarmes, turned over to the Germans and were gassed at the Auschwitz concentration camp. After 1946, Friedländer grew more conscious of his Jewish identity and became a Zionist. In 1948, Friedländer immigrated to Israel on the Irgun ship *Altalena*. After finishing high school, he served in the Israel Defense Forces. From 1953-1955, he studied political science in Paris. Friedländer served as secretary to Nachum Goldman, then President of the World Zionist Organization and the World Jewish Congress. In 1959, he became an assistant to Shimon Peres, then vice-minister of defense. In 1963, he received his Ph.D. from the Graduate Institute of International Studies in Geneva, where he taught until 1988. Friedländer taught at the Hebrew University of Jerusalem and at Tel Aviv University. In 1988, he became Professor of History at the University of California, Los Angeles. Saul Friedländer is one of the most significant historians of the Holocaust. He has written some of the major works on the Holocaust, including *Pius XII and the Third Reich* (1965), *When Memory Comes* (1979), *Reflections on Nazism* (1984), and *Nazi Germany and the Jews, Volume One: The Years of Persecution, 1933-1939* (1997). The second volume *Nazi Germany and the Jews, Volume Two: The Years of Extermination, 1939-1945* appeared in 2017.

Adelaide Lisetta Fries (1871-1949), b. Salem, NC, of Moravian ancestry, was the foremost scholar of the history and genealogy of the Moravians in the Southern United States. She made important contributions to the field as archivist, translator, author and editor. In 1911, the Provincial Elders' Conference of the Moravian Church in America, Southern Province, appointed Fries as archivist of the Southern Province, and granted her the use of a warehouse in Salem as repository and offices. She immediately began collecting, organizing, translating and publishing records, a work that continued until her death. Fries was never satisfied that the warehouse was a safe repository, and over the years, her friends and supporters raised enough money to convert the former office of the Vorsteher (business manager) of the Salem community into a fireproof repository. The archives moved into the new building in 1942. One of Fries' best-known books is *The Road To Salem* (1944), an account of the life of Anna Catharina (Antes) Ernst (1726-1816). Another well-known book, *The Moravians in Georgia*, has entered the public domain and is available online. *Forsyth County* was revised and updated in 1949, and a further revision and update was issued in 1976 under the oversight of J. Edwin Hendricks of Wake Forest University. She was the editor of the *Records of the Moravians in North Carolina*, 8 vols. (1922–54).

Alexander Grab (1946–), b. Tel Aviv, Israel, of Bohemian ancestry, is a historian. He attended UCLA, receiving Ph.D. in 1980. He has been with Univ. of Maine (s. 1982), where he now holds the chair of Adelaide and Alan Bird Professor of History. He offers courses in early modern and modern European history. His area of research has focused on Italian history in the 18th and early 19th centuries. Initially, he studied eighteenth century Lombardy, when that region was a part of the Habsburg Empire. He is the author of *Napoleon and the Transformation of Europe* (London, McMillan-Palgrave, 2003) which won the 2004 Literary Book Award of the International Napoleonic Society.

Arthur Gustav Haas (1925–2016), b. Vienna, of Moravian ancestry, is Univ. of Chicago educated historian. He has been associated with Univ. of Tennessee, Knoxville (s. 1963) and as prof. of European history (s. 1969). He specialized in German and Central Europe and the 17th and 20th centuries.

Fred Hahn (1906–2003), b. Staňkov, Bohemia, was a historian. He studied at University of Prague (JUDr., 1929), Sorbonne (Cert., 1928) and Columbia University (M.A.T.C., 1951). He was with Trenton State Univ. (s. 1964) and as prof. of history (1969–77). He specialized in modern Central and East European history.

Walter Karl Hanak (1929–2016), b. Trenton, NJ., of Czech ancestry, was a historian. After serving on active duty in Korea, Walter attended the University of Texas, Austin earning a Bachelor of Arts degree in History. He earned his Master's Degree and a Doctorate of Philosophy from Indiana University, Bloomington. Upon completing his Doctorate, Walter became an assistant professor of history at The University of Virginia, Charlottesville. In 1970, he joined the faculty of Shepherd University, where he advanced from asst. professor to assoc. professor of history (1978), as professor (s. 1978). He specialized in history of Byzantine Europe, history of the Kievan Russia, history of the Great Moravian Empire and Bohemia/Moravia before 1200.

Milan L. Hauner (1940–2022), b. Gotha, of Czech father, lived in Prague where he went to school. In 1957, he entered Charles U. to study history and Czech lang. and lit. He completed his Ph.D. with a topic on Anglo-German naval rivalry 1908–12. Leaving Czechoslovakia at the time of the Soviet invasion in 1968, he settled in England, studying for his second Ph.D. at St. John's Coll. in Cambridge. In 1971, he joined St. Antony's Coll. in Oxford for three years. Thereafter he moved to London, working from 1974 in the research dept. of Amnesty International in charge of Eastern Europe. Two years later, he joined the German Historical Inst. in London where he published his major book based on his Ph.D., *India in Axis Strategy:*

Germany, Japan, and Indian Nationalists in the Second World War (1981). In 1980, he joined his family in the US. Since then, he has been affiliated with the University of Wisconsin-Madison, He taught and conducted research at various universities in England (Oxford, London, Warwick, L.S.E., Open U.), Germany (Freiburg, Leipzig) and America (Philadelphia, Berkeley, Hoover Inst. Stanford, Georgetown, Columbia, US Naval War College) - and after 1990, again in Eastern Europe, mostly in the Czech Republic. In 1990-91, he was director of East European Studies at the Woodrow Wilson International Center for Scholars, Washington. He is the author and co-editor of ten books and more than 100 scholarly articles on the modern history of India, Central Asia, Czechoslovakia, Germany, and Russia.

Martin Joseph Havran (1929-2000), b. Windsor, Ont., Canada, probably of Czech ancestry, was trained as a historian at Detroit University (B.A., 1951), Wayne State University (M.A., 1953) and Case Western Reserve University (Ph.D., 1957). He was with Kent State Univ. (s. 1957), as assoc. prof. (1964-68); as assoc. prof. history, Univ. of Virginia (1968-72), as prof. (1972-99), as chairman of dept. (1974-79); dir., Self-Study Program (1984-86). He was the author of *Catholics in Caroline England* (1962), *England: Prehistory and Present* (1968), *Life of Lord Cottington* (1973); and editor of *Readings in English History* (1967). His interests were in Tudor and Stuart England, English reformation, and history of Canada. He was President of American Catholic Historical Assn (1982).

Jana Srba Hearn (1939–), b. Prague, Czech., is a historian, trained at Indiana Univ. (Ph.D., 1971). She was an asst. professor of history, Carnegie-Mellon Univ., Pittsburgh, PA. She also taught the second grade at the Hillside School in Hastings-on-Hudson, N.Y. She was the author of *The Schoolmaster of Liberty, or The Political Views of Benjamin Constant de Rebecque* (1970).

Jean Frances Herskovits (1935-2019), b. Evanston, IL, of Slovak Jewish ancestry (the daughter of anthropologist Melville J. Herskovits), was a research professor of history at the State University of New York at Purchase specializing in African (particularly Nigerian) history and politics. Herskovits taught at Brown University, Swarthmore College, City College of the City University of New York and Columbia University. She held a D. Phil. in African history from Oxford University.

Dagmar Horna Perman (1925-1978), b. Bratislava, Czech.; historian, political scientist, social activist. She had fled her native Czechoslovakia in 1948 at the onset of the communist takeover there. After settling in the United States in late 1948, she won a grant from the Federation of Women's Clubs of Kansas that enabled her to pursue a Master's degree at the University of Kansas in Lawrence. She later went to the University of California at Berkeley for her Doctorate. She held the position of associate professor of history at Georgetown

University, Washington, DC. She was the author of *The Shaping of the Czechoslovakian State*, a book that is now the standard text on the subject. From 1953 to 1956, she played a crucial role in microfilming and classifying captured German war documents, an effort of lasting use to American and international scholars.

George Huppert (1934-), b. Těšín, Czech., studied history at Univ. of California, Berkeley (Ph.D., 1962). He has been with Univ. of Illinois at Chicago Circle (s. 1960), as prof. of history (s. 1976). He specializes in early modern and French Renaissance history, intellectual and social history, and history of historiography. George Huppert is the author of several books, including *The Idea of Perfect History*, as well as *The Style of Paris* and *After the Black Death* and *Les Bourgeois Gentilshommes*.

Stephanie Olga Husek (1909-1994), b. Cleveland, OH, of Slovak descent, was a historian. She graduated from Seton Hall College (A.B.) and studied history at Charles Univ. in Prague (Ph.D.). She was professor of history at Bridge Water State College (1956-74). Before that she taught at Georgia Court College, where she held the position of associate professor (s. 1949). She specialized in modern European and Russian history.

Oskar Jászi (orig. Jakubovits) (1875-1957), b. Nagykaroly, of Slovak descent; social scientist, historian, politician; in US s. 1925. He joined the faculty of Oberlin College, where he settled down to a career as a history professor and wrote a series of books, the best known of which is *The Dissolution of the Habsburg Monarchy*, first published by the University of Chicago Press in 1929.

Lawrence James Jelinek (1943-2017), b. Detroit, OH, of Czech ancestry, was trained as a historian at Univ. of California, Los Angeles (Ph.D., 1976). He was with Dept. of History, Loyola Marymount Univ., Los Angeles, CA (s. 1977), becoming full professor in 1989. He was a member of the Editorial Board for the California Historical Society's journal, *California History,* and the author of *Harvest Empire: A History of California Agriculture*. He taught courses in U.S. and Western history.

Yeshayahu A. Jelinek (1933-2016), b. Prievidza, Czech., was a pioneer historian of Central Europe. The family immigrated to Israel in 1949. In 1951 to 1953, he served in the army. He later studied history, sociology and contemporary Judaism at the Hebrew University of Jerusalem and graduated in 1963 with a Master's degree. In 1966, he received his Doctorate (Ph.D., 1966) from Indiana University, and according to fellow students, he was the only Indiana University graduate student who ever wrote his Doctoral Dissertation in Slovak. He has been teaching at various universities since 1966, initially until 1969 as Visiting Assistant Professor at the University of Colorado in Denver and the University of Minnesota. He later taught at Haifa University, the Hebrew University of Jerusalem, New

York's Columbia University, Denison University in Granville, Ohio, Ben Gurion University of the Negev, and Hanegev College in Sha'ar HaNegev. Since 1988, he has been a visiting professor and visiting scientist at the University of Hamburg, the University for Jewish Studies in Heidelberg, the Carl von Ossietzky University in Oldenburg, the Simon Dubnow Institute in Leipzig and the Herder Institute in Marburg. He published in English, Slovak and German on German-Israeli relations and the history of the Jews in Slovakia. He made use of oral history long before it became fashionable in Holocaust studies.

Marcel Jesenský (ca. 1969–), b. Slovakia, is a historian, with specialization in international relations and diplomacy. He attended Technical University in Košice (dipl., 1991), Comenius University (dipl., 1993), Carleton University (M.A., 2006) and University of Ottawa (Ph.D., 2012). He is a part-time professor, Department of History, University of Ottawa. He is a former diplomat who worked at the UN in New York. Marcel Jesenský's current research looks into the bilateral relations between Canada and the former Czechoslovakia (1918-1992) and the history of the United Nations (1945-2012).

John T. Juricek (1938–), b. Chicago, IL, of Czech ancestry, studied at Univ. of Chicago (B.A., 1959; M.A., 1962; Ph.D., 1970). He was a lecturer at University of Chicago (1964); Roosevelt University, Chicago (1964–65), before joining Emory University, Atlanta, GA, as instructor (1966–70), as assistant professor (1970–73), as associate professor (1973–2010), as professor (s. 2010), now emeritus. He has long been interested in early America, especially the English colonies, most especially the interactions of those colonies with the native Indians. He is the author of *Colonial Georgia and the Creeks: Anglo-Indian Diplomacy on the Southern Frontier, 1733-1763* (2010), and editor of *Georgia Treaties, 1733-1763* (1989) and *Georgia and Florida Treaties, 1763-1776* (2002).

Erich Kahler (1885-1970), b. Prague, Bohemia, of Jewish family, was a historian, and literary scholar and essayist. He studied philosophy, literature, history, art history, sociology, and psychology at the University of Munich, the University of Berlin, the University of Heidelberg, and the University of Freiburg before earning his Doctorate at the University of Vienna in 1911. He settled in Munich in 1913 and remained there until 1933, when he was deprived of his citizenship by the Nazi regime. Between 1934 and 1938 he lived in Czechoslovakia, then in Switzerland and in 1938, came to US. In the U.S., he taught at The New School for Social Research, Black Mountain College, Cornell University, and Princeton University. He was the author of *Über Recht und Moral* (1911), *Das Geschlecht Habsburg* (1920), *Israel unter den Völkern* (1936, poetry), *Der Deutsche Character in der Geschichte Europas* (1937).

Anthony S. Kalina (1903-1984), b. Blatná, Bohemia, was Georgetown Univ. educated historian. He was director of social sciences, Sci. Res. Inst., Cleveland, Ohio (s. 1959). He was an authority on diplomatic history, political science, international law and organization.

Josef Kalvoda (1923-2000), b. Maleč, Czech., was a historian political scientist and publicist. After the communist coup in February 1948, he was arrested and charged with anti-state activities. When he was released from custody, he escaped and, from 1949 to 1951, he lived in Norway. In 1951, he immigrated to the US. He studied political science and history at Hunter College (B.A., 1956) and public law and government at Columbia University (M.A., 1957). In 3 years, he earned his Doctorate also at Columbia (Ph.D., 1960). He was with St. Joseph College, (1957-61) and then at Univ. of San Diego Coll. for Women, where he attained full professorship of history in 1964. He then taught at Louisiana State Univ. (1966-68), until he accepted professorship of history and political science at St. Joseph College, West Hartford, CT (s. 1968). He specialized in diplomatic history, political science and international law and organization. In his work, he focused mainly on the foreign policy of the Soviet Union. He argued that only a drastic approach, as Ronald Reagan later practiced, toward the Soviet Union could be an effective US foreign policy toward the state. He rejected the cooperation of the Western world with the communist states, the financial support of Tito's Yugoslavia or communist Poland. In his works, he was also critical of Edvard Beneš. Dr. Kalvoda has published seven books, four of which were published in Czechoslovakia.

Robert Joseph Kerner (1887-1956), b. Chicago, IL, of Czech ancestry, was an American historian of note, specializing in modern European history. He attended University of Chicago (A.B., 1908; A.M., 1912) and Harvard University (Ph.D., 1914). He was professor of modern European history at University of Missouri (1921-28) and acting Dean of Graduate School (1925-26). Subsequently, he joined University of California, Berkeley, as professor of modern European history (1928-41), as Sather Professor of History (1941-54), and as Director of Slavic Studies (1948-56). He was appointed by President Woodrow Wilson to serve on a committee to study ways to peace in 1917. From 1917 to 1919, he served on the committee in Paris that led to the establishment of Czechoslovakia. Many of his publications were dedicated to interpreting the Slavic peoples to the English-speaking world. They included: *Slavic Europe* (1919); *Bohemia in the Eighteenth Century* (1932); and *The Balkan Conferences and the Balkan Entente* (1935). He was also editor of the *Journal of International Relations* (1919-22) and the *Journal of Modern History* (1929-31), and ten volumes on the United Nations. His many awards include the Czechoslovakia state prize in literature in 1941. He was designated by Czechoslovakia as Commander of the Order of the White Lion, the Order of Leopold II medal by Belgium and Officer of the Star by Romania. He traveled, advising world leaders and speak extensively on the politics of Eastern Europe and Russia.

Alice Kessler-Harris (née Kessler) (1941–), b. Leicester, England, of Czech ancestry, is a historian. She received her B.A. from Goucher College in 1961 and her Ph.D. from Rutgers University in 1968. She was with Hofstra University (s. 1968), as professor (1981–88); professor of history at Temple University (1988–90); professor of history and director of women's studies at Rutgers University (1990–95); Gordon Hoxie Professor of American History at Columbia University (s. 1995). She is a specialist in the American labor and comparative and interdisciplinary exploration of women and gender. Her newest book, *A Difficult Woman: The Challenging Life and Times of Lillian Hellman*, was published in 2012. Her other books include *Gendering Labor History* (2007), which collects some of her best-known essays on women and wage work; *In Pursuit of Equity: Women, Men, and the Quest for Economic Citizenship in Twentieth Century America* (2001) which won several prizes including the Joan Kelly Prize, the Philip Taft award, and the Bancroft Prize. Among her other fellowships and awards, Kessler Harris has been a Fellow at the National Humanities Center in Durham, North Carolina and at the Radcliffe Institute for Advanced Study. She is the past president of the Labor and Working-Class History Association and a former president of the Organization of American Historians. She was married to the psychiatrist Jay Evans Harris.

Rebekah Klein-Pejšová (1972–), a Slovak American historian, earned her Ph.D. from Columbia University in 2007, after completing her M.A. degree at the Central European University in Budapest, and her B.A. degree at Bard College. She is Jewish Studies Assistant Professor of History at Purdue University. She specializes in Modern Jewish and East Central European social history, with research interests focusing on the problem of loyalty in state/society relations in the region of today's Hungary, Slovakia, and the Czech Republic since the early 20th century. She has also taught at Columbia, Rutgers, and the City University of New York.

Kimberley 'Kim' Klimek (1970–), b. Denver, CO, of Czech ancestry, studied history at Univ. of Colorado, Colorado Springs (B.A., 1994), at Colorado State Univ. (M.A., 1997) and at Univ. of New Mexico (Ph.D., 2008). She has been with Metropolitan State Coll. of Denver (s. 2004), as asst. professor of history (s. 2004). Her fields of specializations and areas of interest include Medieval Europe – 300–1450 (social and cultural), women and gender, intellectual life and philosophy, Anglo-Saxon and Anglo-Norman worlds, and authority and social minorities.

Franz Kobler (1882–1965), b. Mladá Boleslav, Bohemia was an attorney and historian of Jewish origin. He studied law and philosophy in Prague, Vienna and Berlin. He received his Doctorate in law in Prague in 1906 and became a lawyer in Vienna in 1914. He became a pacifist. Kobler immigrated to San Francisco via Switzerland and Great Britain in 1938.

Among other, he authored *Violence and Non-violence* (1928); *The Age of Emancipation* (1938); *Letters of Jews through the Ages* (1952); *Napoleon and the Jews* (1976); *From Sonnenfels to Kelsen*.

Hans Kohn (1891-1971), b. Prague, Bohemia, was an American philosopher and historian of Jewish origin. He studied philosophy, political science and law at the German part of the Charles-Ferdinand University in Prague (JUDr., 1923). He moved to Palestine in 1925, but visited the United States frequently, eventually immigrating in 1934. Kohn taught modern history at Smith College in Northampton, Massachusetts. From 1948 to 1961, he taught at City College of New York. He also taught at the New School for Social Research, Harvard Summer School. He wrote numerous books on nationalism, Pan-Slavism, German thought, and Judaism. He was an early contributor to the Foreign Policy Research Institute in Philadelphia, where he died. In 1944, he published his major work *The Idea of Nationalism* about the dichotomy between Western and Eastern Nationalism. Kohn sought to understand the emergence of nationalism through the development of Western civilization and the rise of liberalism. He also authored: *Nationalism and Liberty* (1956), *American Nationalism* (1957), *Basic History of Modern Russia* (1957), *West Germany. New Era for German People* (1958), *Mind of Germany* (U1960), *The Age of Nationalism* (1962), *Reflections on Modern History* (1963), *Living in a World of Revolution* (1964), *Absolutism and Democracy* (1965), *Prelude to Nation-States* (1967), *Nationalism and Realism* (1967), *Europe in Crisis, 1850-1914, State, Class, Faith* (1969). Kohn was a prominent leader of Brit Shalom, which promoted a binational state in Palestine.

Thomas Kolský (1942-), b. Buzuluk, Russia, of Czech parents, was raised in Czechoslovakia. He studied US diplomatic history at Univ. of Hawaii (M.A., 1967), international relations at Univ. of Pennsylvania (M.A., 1970) and history with emphasis on Middle Eastern and Jewish history at George Washington Univ. (Ph.D., 1986). Dr. Kolský has been associated with the Montgomery County Community College, Blue Bell, PA, as asst. professor of history (1971-75), as assoc. professor (1975-85), as full professor (1985-2015). A political humorist, caricaturist, and lover of classical music, he enjoys creating and sharing humor. Since 1985, he has lectured extensively on politics, Middle Eastern and Jewish history, as well as on humor. His career in humor began at a very tender age. He was deeply influenced by observing life's absurdities as he grew up in Czechoslovakia, Israel, and the United States. East European, Middle Eastern, and American cultures left an indelible impression on him and contributed to shaping his outlook. A political maverick, Kolský advocates peace, intellectual freedom, religious pluralism, liberal democracy, social justice, and market economy with a human face. Dr. Kolský is interested in American, European, Middle Eastern, and Jewish history, Czechoslovak history and culture, as well as most fields of political science. He is the creator, host, and moderator of the college lecture and interview/talk show *Issues and Insights*. Dr. Kolský is the author of *Jews against*

Zionism (1990) and contributor to *Philadelphia Jewish Life, 1940-2000* and the *Encyclopedia of the Jewish Diaspora*. He was a recipient of the Lindback Distinguished Teaching Award (2003) and the Council for the Advancement and Support of Education (CASE) and Carnegie Foundation for the Advancement of Teaching Pennsylvania's 2004 Professor of the Year. He is conversant in English, Hebrew, Czech, German, and Arabic.

Michael J. Kopanic, Jr. (1954-), b. Youngstown, OH, of Slovak parents, is a historian, trained at Youngstown State University (B.A., 1976), University of Notre Dame (M.A., 1977) and University of Pittsburgh (Ph.D., 1986). He was first with St. Francis University of Pennsylvania; and then with University of Maryland University College, Adelphi (s. 2007), as adjunct professor (s. 2012). He specializes in interwar trade unions, Slovak history and Slovak-American history and customs.

Valerie Joyce Korinek (1967-), b Toronto, Ontario, Canada, of Czech ancestry, is a graduate of Branksome Hall School in Toronto. She graduated with distinction from the University of Toronto, Mississauga (BA, 1984). Subsequently, Korinek did graduate work in Canadian cultural and gender history at Univ. of Toronto (M.A., 1990; Ph.D., 1996). In 1996, she was appointed assistant professor in modern Canadian history at the University of Saskatchewan (US), Saskatoon, Canada. She was awarded tenure and promoted to associate professor in 2000. In 2005, she was promoted to professor of history in the Department of History in the US. Her areas of research interest are: food history, Canadian cultural history (with a strong emphasis on popular culture, media, and print culture) and histories of sexuality. She is the author of *Roughing it in the Suburbs: Reading Chatelaine Magazine in the Fifties and Sixties* (2000), which was awarded the Laura Jamieson Prize by the Canadian Research Institute for the Advancement of Women, 2001, for 'Best feminist book by a Canadian author.' She also co-edited *Edible Histories, Cultural Politics: Towards a Canadian Food History* (2012) and *Finding a Way to the Heart: Feminist Writings on Aboriginal and Women's History in Canada* (2012).

Daniella Jane Kostroun (1970-), b. Ithaca, NY, of Czech father, after graduating from Ithaca High School (1987), pursued a B.A. in history at Cornell University (1992, magna cum laude). In the summer of 1991, she spent two months teaching English in Mariánské Lázně as a Masaryk Fellow through the Charter 77 Foundation (now the Foundation for a Civil Society). She received a M.A. (1995) and Ph.D. (2000) from Duke University in history with a special focus on early modern Europe, French history, and women's studies. She was an assistant professor at Stonehill College, Easton MA (2002-2004) and then at Indiana University-Purdue University, Indianapolis (2005-10), where she continues to work. She is associate professor (s. 2011) and is the author of *Feminism, Absolutism, Jansenism: Louis*

XIV and the Port-Royal Nuns (2011) and co-editor of Women, Religion, and the Atlantic World (1600–1800) (2009).

Nikolaus Kozauer (1930–2020), b. Mukačevo, Czech., was a historian. In 1947, following the war, he and his family settled in Bethlehem, PA. He went on to earn his Bachelor's degree from Lehigh University, his Master's degree from Muhlenberg College, and his Doctorate in Russian history from Rutgers University. In 1966, Nick became one of the founding faculty members of Ocean County College, in Toms River, NJ, where he held the position of professor of history (s. 1967). He was the first faculty member to be promoted to the rank of full professor in the community college system in the state and was recognized as the college's first Professor Emeritus upon his retirement in 1996. He authored the book The Carpatho-Ukraine between the Two World Wars: With Special Emphasis on the German Population (1964).

Paul Kubricht, b. Chicago, IL, of Czech ancestry, grew up in the Chicago area. He attended Greenville College in Illinois where he received his Bachelor of Arts degree in history and political science. For graduate work, he attended Ohio State University and received a Master of Arts and Doctorate, while serving as a teaching associate. His major field was Eastern European studies and his minor fields were Soviet Russia and American foreign policy. He also spent time studying in Prague, Czech Republic, and Vienna, Austria as a result of grants from the American Council of Learned Societies and the International Research and Exchanges Board. In 1974, he came to LeTourneau University, where he became Professor of History and Political Science. His desire and calling was to teach at a small Christian college. Kubricht has received grants from the National Endowment of the Humanities and has spent a number of grant-supported summers studying at major research libraries.

Věra Láska (née Oravec) (1928–2006), b. Košice, Czech., a Holocaust survivor, was a historian. She joined the resistance when she and her friend, both expert skiers, agreed to lead from Slovakia to Hungary two men who lacked proper identification papers. Over the next several years, Vera made about a dozen such trips leading political and Jewish refugees as part of an underground railroad from Slovakia to Hungary to Yugoslavia and beyond. In spring 1943, Vera was arrested after being caught with false papers she had used during her trips across the border. After being jailed in her hometown for about a month, Vera was deported to Auschwitz II-Birkenau as a political prisoner. Along with some of her friends, Vera was transferred to work at a textile factory at Gross-Rosen. To impede production, Vera and other workers would participate in slowdown strikes and acts of sabotage when the guards were not looking. In early 1945, as the Soviet Army approached Gross-Rosen, the Nazis evacuated their prisoners to the concentration camp Dora-Mittelbau in central

Germany. Vera then worked in a tunnel, measuring parts used in the German V-2 missile program. Her task was to divide the good rings from the bad, but she sabotaged the contents by arbitrarily dividing the parts. In March 1945, this camp too was evacuated, and the prisoners were forced on a death march to the Mauthausen concentration camp in Austria. Vera seized her chance to escape in a moment of confusion, when hundreds of starving prisoners descended on a cauldron of soup. She fled into a nearby barn where she hid for the next four days. On the fifth day, a Ukrainian forced laborer who apparently knew of her hiding place, came into the barn and told her to come down because the war was over. She subsequently went to Prague and worked for the Czech War Crime Commission while also studying at the city's Charles University. In 1946, Vera's professors at Charles University decided Vera should go to America to study American history, so Vera chose to attend the University of Chicago. Vera continued her education and earned her Doctorate in American history from the University of Chicago in 1959. She was associated with Regis Coll. Weston, MA (1972–80), as professor (s. 1980) and chair dept. of social sciences (s. 1968). She was a specialist on American diplomatic and immigration history, Latin America, the Holocaust. She was author of a number of books, including some about women and resistance during the Holocaust.

Herman Lebovics (1935–), b. Czech., a historian, trained at University Connecticut, Storrs (B.A., 1956); Yale University (M.A., 1957; Ph.D., 1965) and Freie Universität Berlin (1959–60); He was professor, SUNY at Stony Brook, NY (s. 1966). He is the author of *True France: The Wars over Cultural Identity, 1900-1945*, also from Cornell, *and Bringing the Empire Back Home: France in the Global Age*.

Igor Lukeš (1950–), b. Prague, Czech, studied philosophy at Charles Univ. (PhDr., 1976) and international relations at the Fletcher School of Law and Diplomacy, Tufts University (Ph.D., 1985). He was associated with the Fletcher School of Law and Diplomacy, as an asst. professor (1985-88), before joining Boston Univ. as an associate professor in 1988, advancing to university professor & professor of history and international relations. Lukes writes primarily about Central Europe. His publications deal with the interwar period, the Cold War, and contemporary developments in East Central Europe and Russia. He is the author of *On the Edge of the Cold War: American Diplomats and Spies in Postwar Prague* (2012), *Rudolf Slansky: His Trials and Trial* (2006), *Czechoslovakia between Stalin and Hitler: The Diplomacy of Edvard Benes in the 1930's* (1996). Lukeš is also a co-author and co-editor of *The Munich Conference, 1938: Prelude to World War II* (1999), *Inside the Apparat: Perspectives on the Soviet Union* (1990), and *Gorbachev's USSR: A System in Crisis* (1990).

Radomir Luža (1922-2009), b. Prague, Czech., was New York Univ. educated historian. He was associated with Tulane Univ. (s. 1967), as prof. of history (s. 1970). He specialized in

European history, Nazism and Communism and European resistance. He was a prominent member of the Czech resistance during the Second World War. In 2003, he published his autobiography, *The Hitler Kiss* (2004), by far the most mainstream and successful of his seven books.

Alexy N. Malyshev (1926-1989), b. Prague, Czech., was a historian trained at Columbia Univ. and Univ. of Colorado. He was associated with Colorado Coll. (s. 1960), where he held the position of prof. of history. He specialized in Russian history.

Victor S. Mamatey (1917-2007), b. North Braddock, PA, of Slovak descent, spent his childhood years in Bratislava. Subsequently, he earned a diploma from the Comenius University in Bratislava and then completed his undergraduate work at the University of Chicago before earning his Master of Arts from Harvard University. In 1942, Mamatey enlisted into the United States Army Air Corps and served in the China India-Burma theatre. After demobilization, Mamatey enrolled at the Sorbonne in Paris where he earned a Ph.D. In 1949, Mamatey moved to Tallahassee, Florida, to accept a faculty position with the history department at Florida State University. He was promoted to chairman of the department in 1964. In 1967, he moved to the University of Georgia. At the University of Georgia, he assumed the duties of research professor and served for a year in 1972, and 1973 as acting dean of the Franklin College of Arts and Sciences. In 1984 he retired. A recognized expert in East European history, Mamatey authored, co-authored and edited a number of books and other publications. He won the American Historical Association's George Louis Beer Prize in 1958 for The United States and East Central Europe, and a Guggenheim fellowship.

Thomas D. Marzik (1941-2007), b. Bridgeport, CT, was a historian. He was a graduate of Fairfield College Preparatory School, College of the Holy Cross and Columbia University. For 36 years, he taught as a professor of European History at St. Joseph's University, Philadelphia. He was an internationally respected scholar in East Central European history and was past officer of the Slovak Studies Association and the Czechoslovak History Conference. In 1998, the President of the Slovak Republic honored him for his contributions as a historian of Slovaks and Slovakia.

Vojtěch Mastný (1936-), b. Prague, Czechoslovakia, is an American historian and political scientist, trained at Columbia University (Ph.D.). He has specialized in the history of Cold War. He has been professor of history and international relations at Columbia, University of Illinois, Boston University and the Johns Hopkins School of Advanced International Studies, as well as professor of strategy at U.S. Naval War College, Fulbright professor at the University of Bonn, Senior Research Scholar at the Woodrow Wilson International Center for Scholars and Senior Fellow at the National Security Archive. He is the coordinator of the Parallel History Project. In 1996–1998, he was the first researcher awarded Manfred Wörner Fellowship by NATO. Mastny's books include *Continental Europe under Nazi Rule*, which won him the Clarke F. Ansley award in 1971, *Russia's Road to the Cold War* (1979), *The Helsinki Process and the Reintegration of Europe* (1992) and *The Cold War and Soviet Insecurity: The Stalin Years*, which won the American Historical Association's 1997 George L. Beer Prize.

Todd Michael Michney (1971–), b. Cleveland, OH, of Slovak descent, is a historian, specializing in US history. He was trained at Case Western Reserve University (B.A.) and University of Minnesota (M.A.; Ph.D.). He is an Assistant Professor in the School of History and Sociology at Georgia Institute of Technology. His work focuses on urban history, digital history, African American history, and the history of race and ethnicity. Dr. Michney is the author of *Surrogate Suburbs: Black Upward Mobility and Neighborhood Change in Cleveland, 1900-1980* (2017), as well as articles in the *Journal of Social History, Journal of Urban History, Journal of Planning History,* and *Reviews in American History*. His current research interests include black building tradesmen and the extent of African American access to New Deal mortgage supports. Michney has sat on the board of the Urban History Association and twice served as a National Endowment for the Humanities (NEH) grant evaluator.

Susan Mikula (1943–), Bratislava, Slovakia, who came to US as a child, is a historian. Mikula earned a Bachelor's degree in History from the former University of Detroit and a Ph.D. in Russian and Eastern European History from Syracuse University. She joined the faculty at Benedictine University, Lisle, IL in 1981, teaching Russian and Eastern European History. Along the way, she developed a women's history course, became division chair of Arts and Humanities, a departmental chair, scholars director and most recently, acting dean of the College of Liberal Arts. She has written on political and economic condition of Slovaks in Czechoslovakia and now in Slovakia. She is recipient of the Judith Ann Whinfrey Distinguished Faculty Award for Leadership (2015).

Maxim William Mikulak (1929–2009), b. New York, NY, of Slovak descent, was a historian. He had Ph.D. degree. He was professor of history at New York Institute of Technology, Old Westbury, NY (s. 1980), where he taught world history and the history of science and technology. He offered a one-year course in the history of science and developed a course on the history of science in Russia at the State University College, Fredonia, NY. He was the author of *Jesus: The Controversial Messiah*, CreateSpace Independent Publishing Platform, 2014.

Joseph A. Mikuš (1909-2005), b. Krivá, Slovakia, was professor of history and international relations at St. John's University, Jamaica, NY and Georgian Court College (1968-77), Lakewodd, NJ.

Leo Mucha Mladen (1913-1989), b. Řepy u Prahy, studied at Charles Univ. (Th.C., Ph.C., 1939, 1948), and at Columbia Univ. (M.S.L.S., 1954; Ph.D.). He was associated with Indiana State Univ., Terre Haute, where he held the position of asst. professor of history. He was also associated with the Institute for Medieval and Renaissance Studies, City College, City University of New York. His interests were in the area of history of ideas (religion, philosophy, law) and cultural forms (heraldry, onomastics, sphragistics).

Rudolf Mrázek (1942-), b. Prague, Czech, was trained as a historian at Charles Univ. and ČSAV, specializing in Southeast Asian history (dipl. 1964; CSc./Ph.D., 1980). He has been associated with Univ. of Michigan (s. 1990), as professor of history (1999-2013), as professor emeritus (s. 2014). He taught courses in modern Southeast Asia, comparative history, intellectual history, history of colonial expansion, technology and nationalism, and oral history. He specialized in Southeast Asian modern history. He wrote a number of books, including: *A Certain Age: Colonial Jakarta through the Memories of its Intellectuals* (2010), *Engineers of Happy Land: Technology and Nationalism in a Colony* (2002), *Sjahrir: Politics and Exile in Indonesia, 1906-1966* (1994), *United States and the Indonesian Military, 1945-1965* (1978).

Václav Mudroch (1924-1969), b. Prague, Czech., studied law at Charles Univ. (JUDr., 1949) and history at Univ. of British Columbia (B.A., 1954) and University of Toronto (M.A., 1956; Ph.D., 1960). He fled to West Germany in 1950 and subsequently became a history professor in Kansas and Ontario. He was assoc. prof. of history, Carleton Univ. (s. 1963). He was a specialist on medieval history. He was the author of *Essays on the Reconstruction of Medieval History* (1974) and *The Wyclyf Tradition* (1979).

Reinhold Christopher Mueller (1940-), b. St. Louis, MO, of Bohemian ancestry on his father's side, graduated from Coll. of St. Thomas (B.A., 1962) and studied history at the Johns Hopkins Univ. (M.A., 1965; Ph.D., 1969). He was assistant-associate professor of history at University Arizona, Tucson (1973-79); associate professor, University Venice, Italy (s. 1979). He was Fellow, Harvard Center for Italian Renaissance Studies, Florence, Italy (1975-76), American Council of Learned Societies (1978-79), Institute for Advanced Studies, Berlin (1989-90). He is the co-author of *Money and Banking in Medieval and Renaissance Venice, Vol. 1: Coins and Moneys of Account* (1985), *The Venetian Money Market: Banks, Panics, and the Public Debt, 1200-1500 (Money and Banking in Medieval and Renaissance Venice, Vol. 2)* (1997).

Ludvík Němec (1912–1988), b. Staré Město-Velehrad, Moravia, was a R.C. priest and a noted historian-theologian. He attended the Theological Faculty of Charles University, Prague (S.T.B., 1939), and was ordained a Catholic priest in Prague (1940). He studied at international Papal University of Angelicum, Rome (S.T.L., 1949), Catholic University of America, Washington, DC (S.T.S., 1953), was chaplain of New Castle Hospital and then Professor of Church History at Rosemont College (s. 1963), and chair dept. of theology (1967–80). He was an authority on church history, Slavic and Byzantine history. He published over ten books, including *Church and State in Czechoslovakia* (1955), *The Great and Little One of Prague* (1959), *The Infant of Prague* (1958) and *Our Lady of Hostyn* (1981), etc. He also contributed over thirty major studies in Byzantine and Slavic History to various learned journals.

Marie L. Neudorfl (1940–), b. Czech., studied history at Charles University and at University of Alberta (Ph.D., 1981). She has been a freelance historian, Ottawa, Ont., Canada. She is a specialist on modern East and West European history, Czech and Slovak history, women's movement before 1914.

Otakar Odložilík (1899–1973), b. Kostelec na Hané, Moravia, was a Czech historian and Moravia. He began his scholarly career as an archivist, after receiving a Ph.D. in history from Charles University in Prague (1923). At the university, he had studied under the famous Czech medievalist, Václav Novotný. From 1926 to 1939, he taught at Charles University, first as a *docent* and later as a professor. He immigrated to US in 1938 and then taught at University of Colorado at Boulder, then University of Pennsylvania and finally at Columbia. After the war, he returned to teaching as professor of history at Charles University in Prague. Following the communist takeover, he left for the US where he assumed teaching at University of Colorado, University of Kansas, Columbia and finally University Pennsylvania. He was an authority on the late Middle Ages, pre-Hussite, Hussite and Reformation thought and history. He authored *Wycliff and Bohemia* (1937), *The Czechoslovak Inheritance* (1945), *The Caroline University* (1948), *The Hussite King* (1965).

Stanley Zdeněk Pech (1924–1985), b. Hradec Králové, Czech., came to Canada in the wake of the Communist takeover in Prague in 1948. A graduate of Charles University (1947), he obtained M.A. at the University of Alberta in 1950. He then proceeded to University of Colorado, Boulder, where he studied under Professor S. Harrison Thomson, a well-known authority on Czech history, and wrote a Dissertation on Francis L. Rieger (1818–1903), a leading Czech politician and statesman from the revolution of 1848 to the end of the century. His first teaching post was at the Western Montana College of Education in 1955–56. In 1956, he joined the University of British Columbia (UBC) Department of Slavonic Studies, as an assistant professor and was promoted to associate professor in 1962. After the reorganization of the area studies program in the 1960s, he transferred to the history department in 1967 and was promoted to the rank of professor in 1971. Throughout his UBC career, Professor Pech taught East-Central European history. He authored *The Czech Revolution of 1848* (1969). He was president of the Canadian Association of Slavists (1966-67) and vice-president of the Czechoslovak History Conference (1980-18).

Dagmar Horna Perman (1925-1978), b. Bratislava, of Czech parents, was a historian and activist. Her father, professor of law, was sent to Bratislava to help organize the School of Law of the newly founded Comenius University. Her schooling in Bratislava was interrupted by the Munich conference in 1938, which led to the breakup of Czechoslovakia and her family's return to Prague, where she completed her secondary school education. After World War II, she matriculated in the graduate school of business administration at the Prague Institute of Technology. After the 1948 Communist coup in Prague, she fled to Switzerland, where she attended the Handelshochschule of the University of St. Gallen. She subsequently immigrated to the US and continued her studies at the University of Kansas and the University of California-Berkeley. She received her A.M. degree in Kansas in 1949 and her Ph.D. in political science and history at California in 1954. Her doctoral dissertation, which was prepared under the direction of the late Professor Robert J. Kerner, dealt with the Czechoslovak question at the Paris Peace conference. After receiving her doctorate, she worked as director of the American Historical Association's 'Alexandria project' in 1957-59, microfilming and cataloging captured German documents. In 1972, she joined the Department of history at Georgetown University. She authored *The Shaping of the Czechoslovak State: Diplomatic History of the Boundaries of Czechoslovakia, 1914-1920* (1962); and *Bibliography and the Historian* (1968). She was married to a psychiatrist Gerald P. Perman (1923-2015) and they had 2 children. Mrs. Perman earned national attention in the early 1970s when she helped organize a group of southeastern Pennsylvania citizens in a legal fight against Charnita Inc., a land development company then thriving in that area. Mrs. Perman, along with her husband, Dr. Gerald Perman, Washington psychiatrist, owned property near the Charnita operation.

Laura Matild Polanyi (1882-1959); b. Vienna, of Slovak father; married to Slovak-born businessman Sándor Striker. She was trained as a historian and economist and was the first woman to get a Ph.D. from the University of Budapest. She was active as feminist and prolific nonfiction writer; author of a biography about the American hero Captain John Smith (of Pocahontas fame), the founder of Virginia in the 17th century.

Nicholas S. Popper (1947-), b. Chicago, IL, of Bohemian ancestry, was raised in New Jersey, before attending Haverford College as an undergraduate. He received his Ph.D. in history of science from Princeton University in 2007, specializing in early modern European intellectual history and was a Mellon Postdoctoral Fellow at the California Institute of Technology (2008-09). Since then, he has been with the history dept. of the College of William and Mary in Williamsburg, VA, as asst. professor of history. In his research, he specializes in early modern British history with a particular focus on intersections between intellectual and political culture and on the transmission of scholarly practices from continental Europe to Britain. His research interests also extend to early modern history of science, history of the book, travel and geographical learning. These interests come together in his book, entitled *Walter Raleigh's History of the World and the Historical Culture of the Late Renaissance* (2012).

David Prochaska (1945-), b. Alhambra, CA, of Czech ancestry, was trained as a historian at Stanford Univ. (B.A., 1968) and Univ. of California, Berkeley (Ph.D., 1981). He has been associated with Univ. of Illinois, Urbana, where he advanced from asst. to associate professor of history. He specializes in history and comparative colonial studies and visual culture. He authored *Making Algeria French: Colonialism in Bône, 1870-1920* (1990, 2004) and co-authored *Renoir in Algeria* (2003), *Beyond East and West: Seven Transnational Artists* (2004), *Genealogies of Orientalism: History, Theory* (2008), *Postcards: Ephemeral Histories of Modernity* (2010).

Frank Prochaska (1941-), b. Cleveland, OH, is an historian of modern Britain and the author of a number of books on modern British and American history, with a particular interest in philanthropy, the monarchy and political thought. After serving in the United States Air Force (1959-1963), he graduated with a degree in history from the University of Maryland in 1965, before going on to complete a Ph.D. in British history at Northwestern University in 1972. He has taught British history on both sides of the Atlantic, including the University of Missouri, Columbia (1973-74), the University of Wisconsin, Madison (1976), University College, London, (1976-86), and Yale University (2001-10). He was a research fellow at the Welcome Institute for the History of Medicine, London University (1987-90), and a visiting fellow of All Souls College, Oxford (1997-98). He moved from Yale to Oxford University in 2010, where he is a member of the history faculty and Somerville and Wolfson Colleges. He is an honorary fellow, Institute of Historical Research, London University, and a fellow of the Royal Historical Society. He is the author of *Women and Philanthropy in Nineteenth Century England* (1980), *The Republic of Britain* (2000), *Eminent Victorians on American Democracy* (2012), *The Memoirs of Walter Bagehot* (2013), etc.

Francis Paul Prucha (1921-2015), b. River Falls, WI, of Czech ancestry, was educated at Wisconsin State Teachers College, at River Falls, which awarded him a Bachelor's of Science degree in 1941. After a year and a half of high school teaching and then three and a half of service in the United States Army Air Force, he enrolled in the University of

Minnesota and received an M.A. degree in 1947. Harvard University awarded him a Ph.D. degree in history in 1950 under the direction of Frederick Merk. Prucha joined the Society of Jesus in 1950 and was ordained in 1957, after studying at Saint Louis University and Saint Mary's College in St. Mary's, Kansas. Three years, later he began teaching at Marquette and is remembered by generations of alumni as a model of the teacher-scholar. Since 1960, he has been on the history faculty at Marquette University. He has served as visiting professor at the University of Oklahoma and at Harvard and was the Gasson Professor at Boston College. In the late 1960s, while studying under a Guggenheim Fellowship, Prucha began work on a comprehensive history of US Indian policy. His research culminated with the two-volume *The Great Father: The United States Government and the American Indians.* The book was a finalist for the Pulitzer Prize in history in 1985 and is regarded as a classic among professional historians. *The Great Father* was awarded the Billington Prize by the Organization of American Historians in 1985. The recipient of six honorary degrees, Prucha was awarded his emeritus appointment in 1988. Father Prucha is also the author or editor of 25 other books and numerous articles, and scores of book reviews. He is known internationally for his expertise on the American West and United States policy towards Native Americans. Prucha also helped to establish Marquette's rich research collections documenting Catholicism among Native Americans. As a tribute to Prucha, Marquette University's Archives and Special Collection's reading room in its newly constructed Raynor Library was named in his honor. Father Prucha was also inducted into the Milwaukee Central Library's Wisconsin Writers Wall of Fame.

Theodore K. Rabb (orig. Rabinowicz) (1937–), b. Teplice-Šanov, Czech., an American historian, was raised in London. He studied at Queen's College, Oxford (B.A., 1958; M.A., 1962) and at Princeton University (M.A., 1960; Ph.D., 1961). Rabb was a professor of history at Stanford University, Northwestern University, and Harvard University before becoming an Associate Professor at Princeton University in 1967. There, he taught, both in the History Department and in Humanistic Studies, an interdisciplinary program. He also directed Princeton's Community College programs. In 1970, he co-founded the *Journal of Interdisciplinary History* with Robert I. Rotberg. He was also an advisor for the 1993 television series *Renaissance*. He has chaired the National Council for History Education and the New Jersey Council for the Humanities. He specialized in English history, 16th and 17th centuries and interdisciplinary history.

Oskar K. Rabinowicz (1902–1969), b. Aspern, Austria, of Bohemian ancestry, was raised in Boskovice, Moravia. Rabinowicz attended the nearby University of Brno and then Charles University in Prague, where he received a Doctorate in Philosophy in 1924. In 1924, Rabinowicz moved to Brno, where he became a correspondent for the *Jüdische Volkstimme*, edited by Max Hickl. He wrote regular columns on Zionist and cultural issues until the newspaper's demise in 1932. He also wrote for *Selbstwehr, Židovské zprávy*, and *Tagesbote aus Böhmen*. Barred from holding a post at the University of Brno (which required that all faculty be baptized), Rabinowicz turned to teaching at the secondary level, becoming the cofounder of a new Jewish gymnasium in Brno, where he also taught history. His chief concern, however, was Zionism. Rabinowicz established the Czechoslovak branch of the Revisionist Party. In 1931, he went to Berlin to study for the rabbinate at the Hochschule für die Wissenschaft des Judentums. He was ordained in 1933 but never practiced as a rabbi. Throughout the 1930s, Rabinowicz lectured widely in central and Eastern Europe on behalf of Revisionist Zionism. He helped organize immigration to Palestine and continued to write, publishing three books in the 1930s. In 1934, he founded the weekly *Medina Iwrit-Judenstaat* (The Jewish State), which he edited until it ceased publication in 1939. Rabinowicz's career after 1939, when he and his family fled to London, was increasingly involved with banking and finance, which his father had taken up in the 1920s with his son's occasional help. Rabinowicz wrote many articles and five books in English, in addition to editing Volume 2 (1971) of *The Jews of Czechoslovakia*. In 1956, he moved to the United States, where he died in 1969. He was a co-founder and director of the Society for the History of Czechoslovak Jews.

Miloslav 'Mila' Rechcigl (1930–), b. Mladá Boleslav, Czech., apart from his scientific and administrative science career, has been a prolific immigration historian, bibliographer and archivist. He was trained as a biochemist, nutritionist and a food scientist at Cornell University (B.S., 1953, M.S., 1954; Ph.D., 1958). He was one of the founders and past President, for many years, of the Czechoslovak Society of Arts and Sciences (SVU). He is considered an authority on Czech and Slovak American immigration history. He authored numerous books on the subject, including: *Notable American Women with Czechoslovak Roots*; *Notable Americans with Slovak Roots*; *American Jews with Czechoslovak Roots*; *Czechs Won't Get Lost in the World, Let Alone in America*; *Beyond the Sea of Beer. History of Immigration of Bohemians and Czechs to the New World*; *Encyclopedia of Bohemian and Czech-American Biography 3 vols.*; *Czech It Out. Czech American Biography Sourcebook*; *Czech American Timetable. Chronology of Milestones in the History of Czechs in America*; *Czech American Bibliography. A Comprehensive Listing*.

Barbara Kimmel Reinfeld (1935-2020), b. Prague, Czech., was a historian. She fled to the West with her family in 1948. They settled in America, where she completed her undergraduate education at Carleton College (B.A., 1958) and her postgraduate education in history at Columbia University (M.A., 1959; Ph.D., 1979). Her dissertation led to the publication of her book, *Karel Havlíček (1821-1856): A National Liberation Leader of the Czech Renascence* (1982). She also published on Františka Plamínková, Charlotte Masaryk, and Milada Horáková. She taught for many years at New York Institute of Technology in Old Westbury, NY, where she served as chair of the Department of Social Sciences. After her retirement from NYIT, she taught as an adjunct at Hofstra University in Hempstead, NY.

Her last course at Hofstra was part of a summer program in Prague in 2007. Barbara was the first woman to be president of the Czechoslovak Studies Association (Czechoslovak History Conference), holding the office from 1990-1992. She is a specialist on modern East European history and Czech history.

Carl Peter Resek (1929-2016), b. Prague, Czech., fled Prague with his parents and sister within six-weeks of the Nazi invasion. He graduated with honors from Brooklyn Technical High School, where he was on the Chess team. He completed his undergraduate degree at the University of Wisconsin, Madison and received his Ph.D. from the University of Rochester. Dr. Resek was a scholar of American Social and Intellectual History, with a particular interest in the progressive movement of the early 20th Century. His publications included "Lewis H Morgan, American Scholar," "The Progressives; and War and the Intellectuals," and "The Collected Essays of Randolph Bourne." He received several academic awards and fellowships including a Guggenheim fellowship, Wilson Center Fellowship, and a Fulbright. He taught American History at Columbia, Sarah Lawrence, SUNY Binghamton, and Northwestern University, before becoming the Dean of Humanities at SUNY Purchase, where he built the first humanities department and served on the faculty until 1991. He also taught American History at the Ionian University in Corfu, Greece.

Thomas Říha (1929-d.), b. Prague, Czech., came to the U.S. in 1947. He received a Master's degree at the Univ. of Calif., Berkeley, and a Doctorate in Russian history from Harvard Univ. He also served in an intelligence capacity in the U.S. Army during the Korean War. From 1960 to 1967, he taught at the Univ. of Chicago, then moved to Univ. of Colorado, Boulder, where he held the position of assoc. prof. of Russian history (s. 1967). On March 15, 1969, he vanished without a trace. Tied to his disappearance was Galya Tannenbaum, a self-proclaimed confidante, who took her own life, in 1971, by swallowing cyanide pills in the State Mental Hospital in Pueblo.

Rev. Joseph Charles Roubik (1888-1962), b. Chicago, IL, of Czech ancestry, S.J., was Charles Univ. educated historian. He was prof. of history at St. Louis Univ. (1924-25), Univ. of Detroit (1929-31) and prof. of history and head, dept. of history and political science at Loyola Univ. (s. 1933). He was also a clergyman.

Benjamin Irving Rouse (1913-2006), b. Rochester, NY, of Czech maternal grandfather, was an American archaeologist on the faculty of Yale University best known for his work in the Greater and Lesser Antilles of the Caribbean, especially in Haiti. He also conducted fieldwork in Florida and Venezuela. He made major contributions to the development of archaeological theory, with a special emphasis on taxonomy and classification of archaeological materials and studies of human migration.

Stephen Quade Ruzicka (1946–), b. Greenwich, CT, of Bohemian ancestry, studied history at Univ. of Chicago (M.A., 1973; Ph.D., 1979). He has been associated with the Univ. of North Carolina, Greensboro (s. 1980), where he advanced from asst. professor of history to associate professor (1985–2011) and full professor (s. 2011). He specializes in ancient Greek and Persian history. He authored *Politics of a Persian Dynasty: The Hecatomnids of Caria* (1992) and *Trouble in the West: Egypt and the Persian Empire 525-332 BC* (2012) and numerous articles on 4th century BC Greek and Persian affairs.

Milton C. Sernett (1942–), b. IA, of Czech ancestry on his father's side, attended Iowa State University at Ames for a year and then enrolled at Concordia College, St. Paul, 1961-62 before transferring to the Senior College at Ft. Wayne, Indiana. He is a graduate of Concordia Seminary, St. Louis, Missouri, (M.Div., 1968), and received the M.A. and Ph.D. in American history from the University of Delaware (1969; 1972). He joined the faculty of Syracuse University in 1975 after teaching church history for three years at Concordia Theological Seminary, Springfield, Illinois. Sernett is currently professor emeritus of African American studies and history and adjunct professor of religion at Syracuse University. His principal areas of teaching and research have been African American religious history, the American South, the abolitionist movement, the 'Underground Railroad', and American social reform movements. Sernett has published seventeen books and numerous scholarly essays.

Anthony E. Sokol (1897–1982), b. Vienna, after his discharge from the Austrian Navy, his fluency in at least five languages brought him to the United States in 1924 to teach languages, especially German, at Mississippi State Teacher's College. After a brief return to Vienna, where he studied philosophy and history, he came to Stanford in 1929 as a teaching assistant in the Department of Germanic Languages. He obtained his Ph.D. in 1932 and was appointed assistant and then associate professor in that department. World War II brought a sharp shift of emphasis in Tony Sokol's career. His knowledge of the Dutch and Malay languages, as well as of Indonesia, led to his becoming co-director of Stanford's Far Eastern Area and Language Program, one of the Army's Specialized Programs in anticipation of post-war occupation of the Pacific and Southeast Asian islands. This in turn led to his helping organize and administer the post-war Pacific Asiatic and Russian Program, an interdisciplinary area studies program for undergraduates. When Stanford organized a new Department of Asiatic and Russian Studies in 1945, Tony became executive head and professor of Asiatic Studies. That department was reorganized in 1957 for Asian Languages only, at which time he transferred to the Hoover Institution and, in 1958, to the Department of Political Sciences as professor of International Security Affairs. He never lost interest in naval and military power in world affairs. He was a prolific writer on a variety of cultural and historical subjects, but the works for which he is best known were *Sea Power in the Nuclear Age* (1962) and an official history of the Austrian Navy entitled *The Imperial and Royal Austro-Hungarian Navy* (1968). The latter, translated and reprinted in an elaborate illustrated edition in Austria, was a huge sales success and led to his being awarded by the Austrian Government in 1976 the highly prestigious decoration, The Cross of Honor, First Class, in Science and Art. He was, indeed, a major contributor to the study of naval power and history.

Daniela Spenser (1948–), b. Prague, Czech.; historian. Following the Soviet-led military invasion in 1968, she left for England, studied Spanish and Latin American literature at King's College, London, and anthropology at the London School of Economics and Political Science. In 1972, she immigrated to Mexico and lived and worked in Chiapas for a number of years, with Paolo Freire's texts under her arm. Spenser earned her M.A. degree at the Universidad Nacional Autónoma de México in Latin American studies and a Ph.D. in Latin American history at the University of North Carolina at Chapel Hill, under the guidance of Gilbert Joseph. Daniela Spenser has been a researcher at the Centro de Investigaciones y Estudios Superiores en Antropología Social in Mexico City since 1980. She joined CIESAS to participate in a group project dealing with the history of the German entrepreneurial community in Mexico since the nineteenth century, during the Second World War and the postwar years. That research led her to a long-standing interest in political history. Spenser has worked on the history of Mexican and Latin American communism and the study of the Cold War. Her publications in Mexico and in the United States have become standard classroom assignments. Chief among them are *El triángulo imposible: México, Rusia Soviética y Estados Unidos en los años veinte*, foreword by Friedrich Katz (2008); published in English as *The Impossible Triangle* (1999), based on research in the Soviet archives; *Los primeros tropiezos de la Internacional Comunista en México* (1999), in English as *Stumbling Its Way through Mexico* (2011); editor of *Espejos de la guerra fría: México, América Central y el Caribe* (2004), and coeditor with Gilbert M. Joseph of *In from the Cold: Latin America's New Encounters with the Cold War* (2008). Spenser also published a biography of the Mexican politician and labor leader Vicente Lombardo Toledano (1894–1968), a controversial figure in Mexico's labor history, *In Combat: The Life of Lombardo Toledano (2018)*.

Matthew Spinka (1890–1972), b. Štítary, near Kolín, Bohemia, was a church historian. He entered the US and studied at Coe College, Cedar Rapids (B.A., 1918), the Chicago Theological Seminary (B.D., 1916), University of Chicago (M.A., 1919; Ph.D., *magna cum laude*, 1923). He was Professor of Church History, Central Theological Seminary (1919–26), Librarian and Associate Professor of History of Eastern Christianity, Chicago Theological Seminary (1926–38), and Associate Professor of Church History, Chicago Seminary and Divinity School of the University of Chicago (1936–43). He was Waldo Professor of Church History, Emeritus, the Hartford Seminary Foundation, Hartford, CT and Professor of

Historical Theology, University College, Claremont, CA. He held many distinguished appointments, such as President of the American Society of Church History (1946) and editor of its quarterly, *Church History* (1938-48). He received many honors, among them Th.D. from the John Ev. Theological Faculty in Prague (1946), D.D. from Coe College (1948), Th.D. from the University of St. Andrews, Scotland (1954), D.D. from Chicago Theological Seminary (1962), etc. He was an authority on Orthodox Eastern and Czech Church history and the author of some 20 books, among them *John Hus and the Czech Reformation* (1941), *Jan Amos Comenius* (1943), *Comenius' Labyrinth of the World* (1942) and *Comenius' Bequest of the Unity of Brethren* (1940), *Advocates of Reforms* (1953), *John Hus and the Council of Constance* (1965), *John Hus' Concept of the Church* (1966), etc.

Thomas Spira (1923-2005), b. Bratislava, Czech., moved to the United States just before the outbreak of World War II. He enrolled in the Bachelor of Arts program at the City College of New York in 1964, and later completed his M.A. and Ph.D. in History at McGill University in Montreal. Spira began teaching at the University of Prince Edward Island in 1980 and was named Professor Emeritus by its Board of Governors in 1998. Among other, he is the author of *German-Hungarian Relations and the Swabian Problem: from Károlyi to Gömbös, 1919-1936* (1977) and *Nationalism and Ethnicity Terminologies: An Encyclopedic Dictionary and Research Guide* (1999).

Joseph Sramek (1976-), b. Poughkeepsie, NY, of Czech ancestry, received his B.A. in history, *magna cum laude*, from State University of New York at Binghamton in 1998, and his M.Phil. and Ph.D., both also in history, from the City University of New York Graduate Center in 2002 and 2007, respectively. He has been associated with Southern Illinois Univ., Carbondale, as asst. professor of history (2007-13), as assoc. professor (s. 2013), specializing in the history of Britain and its empire, with a particular focus on colonial India during the eighteenth and nineteenth centuries. He is the author of "'Face Him Like a Briton': Tiger Hunting, Imperialism, and British Masculinity in Colonial India, ca. 1800-1875" published in *Victorian Studies* (2006), and *Gender, Morality, and Race in Company India, 1765-1858* (2011).

M. Mark Stolarik (1943-), b. St. Martin, Czech., is a specialist in the history of immigration and ethnic groups in North America, with emphasis on the Slovak experience. He studied at University of Ottawa (B.A., 1965; M.A., 1967) and University of Minnesota (Ph.D., 1974). He is Professor of History and holder of the Chair in Slovak History and Culture at the University of Ottawa. From 1979 to 1991, he was President and CEO of the Balch Institute for Ethnic Studies in Philadelphia, and Director of its press. He has published a number books, including *Slovaks in Bethlehem, Pennsylvania, 1880-1976* (1985), *The Slovak Americans* (1988), *Immigration and Urbanization: The Slovak Experience, 1870-1918* (1989) and *Where is my Home? Slovak Immigration to North America* (2012). He recently edited *The Slovak Republic: A Decade of*

Independence (2004) and *The Czech and Slovak Republics: Twenty Years of Independence, 1993-2013* (2016).

George J. Švejda (1927–2020), b. Horní Velimec, Czech., was a historian. Before reaching his 24th year of age, he fled from Czechoslovakia to Germany and eventually immigrated to the US. He graduated from Illinois Benedictine Coll. (B.A., 1952) and was trained as a historian at Georgetown Univ. (Ph.D., 1959). He served as a historian with Division of History, Office of Archeology and Historic Preservation, National Park Service, US Dept. of Interior (s. 1962). He was an authority on US diplomatic and immigration history. He authored *History of the Star-Spangled Banner from 1814 to the Present* (1969).

Katherine H. Tachau (ca. 1950–), b. Louisville, KY, of Bohemian ancestry, is a historian. She has been a member of the History Department at the University of Iowa, Iowa City, since 1985 and is currently Professor of History. Her training as a Medievalist began at Oberlin College (BA in Spanish and Medieval Studies in 1972) and continued at the University of Wisconsin-Madison. From 1979–81, she was a researcher at the Institute for Medieval Greek and Latin Philology at Copenhagen University in Denmark and subsequently held faculty positions at Montana State University and Pomona College before coming to the department. Katherine's research, like her teaching, is deeply interdisciplinary, bringing together the histories of medieval science, philosophy, and religious thought (with special emphasis on their development at the 13th and 14th-century medieval universities) with the history of medieval art. At Iowa, she has become active in both the University's Center for the Book and the Medieval Studies Program. She is married to an art historian John Beldon Scott (1945–).

Michael Taussig (1940–), b. Sidney, Australia, of Bohemian ancestry, is an American anthropologist. Although he has published on medical anthropology, he is best known for his engagement with Marx's idea of commodity fetishism, especially in terms of the work of Walter Benjamin.

Michael K. Taussig (1938–2010), b. Prague, Czech., came to the United States as an infant. The family moved to Colorado where he attended high school, graduating as one of the first Merit Scholars. He studied history at Univ. of Colorado (B.A., 1960) and earned a Ph.D. in economics from M.I.T. (1966). He was a faculty member at Rutgers University for 29 years, where he held the position of professor of economics. His interests were in the area of income distribution and the Social Security System. He particularly enjoyed teaching students. He was author of books, including *The Objectives of Social Security* (1968), *Social Security: Perspectives for Reform* (1968), *Alternative Measures of the Distribution of Economic Welfare* (1973), *Environmental Economics* (1974) and numerous other studies.

Kathryn Tomasek (1961–), b. Austin, TX, of Moravian ancestry, received training in US history at Univ. of Wisconsin, Madison (M.A., 1989; Ph.D., 1995). She has been associated with Wheaton Coll., Norton, MA, as asst. professor (1995–2002), as assoc. professor (s. 2002). She is also a co-director of the Wheaton College Digital History Project. Her research interests are in the area of digital humanities, XML, XQuery, and developing markup models for historical financial records that is compatible with the Guidelines of the Text Encoding Initiative, tei-c.org.

Rosemarie 'Rosie' Tong (née Behensky) (1949–), b. Chicago, IL, of Czech ancestry, is an American feminist philosopher. The author of 1998's *Feminist Thought: A More Comprehensive Introduction*, an overview of the major traditions of feminist theory, she is the emeritus distinguished professor of health care ethics in the Department of Philosophy at the University of North Carolina, Charlotte.

Elizabeth Closs Traugott (1939–), b. Bristol, England, of Bohemian ancestry (granddaughter of the novelist Robert Priebsch), is a linguist, educated at the Univ. of California at Berkeley. She is now professor emeritus of linguistics and English at Stanford University where she taught from 1970-2003. She has written about syntax, pragmatics, semantics, lexicalization, socio-historical linguistics, linguistics and literature.

Edward Andrew Tuleya (1919–2008), b. Bridgeport, CT, of Slovak descent, was a historian. He was professor of history, Millersville University (1968-81), curator and archivist, Slovak Museum & Archives, Middletown, PA (1983-95).

Walter P. Ullmann (1924-2011), b. České Budějovice, Czech., attended Charles University in Prague before coming to Canada, where he earned a B.A. and an M.A. at the University of British Columbia. He received his Ph.D. from the University of Rochester. Prior to coming to Syracuse University in 1964, where he rose to the rank of full professor, he taught several years at Wayne State University (1959-64). A specialist in Eastern European history, Professor Ullmann was the author of a number of articles and a book, *The United States in Prague, 1945-1948*.

Jiří Theodor Vojta (1931–2013), b. Czech., came to US in 1957. He was assoc. professor of history, California State Univ., Chico, CA. He was a recipient of the Chancellor's Award for Excellence in Teaching in 1983. He retired in 1992.

Felix John Vondracek (1901-1984), b. Cedar Rapids, IA, of Czech ancestry, was a historian. He attended State University of Iowa (B.A., 1923; M.A., 1924) and Columbia University (Ph.D., 1937). He was with Univ. of North Dakota (s. 1929), as prof. of history (s. 1944), dept.

chair (s. 1946). He specialized in Central European modern history. He authored *The Foreign Policy of Czechoslovakia, 1918-1935* (1937).

George Waskovich (1896–1971), b. Greenwich, CT, of Slovak descent, was historian. He attended Tufts University (B.S., 1923), University of London, Harvard University and Charles University (PhDr., 1927). He taught history at the college of St. Teresa, Winona, MN (1928–32), St. John's University, Brooklyn, NY (1931–37) and since 1934, he had been associated with Hunter College, NY, where he was Professor of History; historian, trained at Charles University (Ph.D., 1927). He taught history at the College of St. Teresa, Winona, MN, St. John's University, Brooklyn, NY and Hunter College, New York, NY. He specialized in Slavic Central Europe and Russian history.

Jan Wiener (1920–2010), b. Hamburg, of Bohemian ancestry, was a historian. He grew up in a Jewish family in Prague. After the occupation of Czechoslovakia, he escaped to Yugoslavia (1940), after it was attacked, he wanted to cross Italy to get to Marseille, where certain Czechs lived who helped their countrymen to emigrate to north Africa. In Italy, he was captured, though he escaped two times and his second escape was successful. He crossed the front in southern Italy and got to the Allies. He joined the air force and remained there for the rest of the war, in the RAF's 311, Czechoslovakian bombing squadron. After the war, he returned to Czechoslovakia, spent five years in a communistic prison, then he emigrated to USA. In the last period of his life, he lived both in the USA and the Czech Republic. In the mid-1960s, Wiener settled in the United States and became professor of history at the American University in Washington, D.C. After the collapse of communism, he returned to his homeland on a regular basis and became a guest lecturer at Prague's branch of New York University. In 2001, he was awarded the medal "Za zásluhy" 1. stupně (Distinguished Service Medal of the First Grade). He died on November 24th, 2010 in Prague.

Charles Wojatsek (1916–2008), b. Dvory and Žitavou, Slovakia, was a historian. He studied in Bratislava (B.A.), Debrecen, Hungary (M.A.) and at U. Montreal (Ph.D.; Hum. Sc.D.). He held the position of professor of history, Bishop's University, Sherbrooke, Quebec, Canada (s. 1976). He was the author of *From Trianon to The First Vienna Arbitral Award: The Hungarian Minority in the First Czechoslovak Republic, 1918-1938* (1981).

Joseph Frederick Zacek (1930–), b. Berwyn, IL, of Czech ancestry, is a historian. He studied history at University of Illinois, Champagne-Urbana (B.A., summa cum laude, 1952; M.A., 1953; and Ph.D., 1962) and holds a Certificate from the Institute on East Central Europe, Columbia University (1962). He was a Research Assistant in European History at the University of Illinois (1957–58), then Teaching Assistant in European and Russian History

(1959–60), an Assistant Professor of History at Occidental College (1964–66). Subsequently, he joined the State Univ. of New York (s. 1968), as prof. of history (s. 1971) and dept. chair (1974–77). He was National Board consultant to National Endowment for Humanities, Washington (since 1975), Visiting scholar International Research & Exchanges Board Comenius U., Bratislava, and Charles U., Prague, Czechoslovakia (1973), Columbia University (1977–78), University of Illinois, Champaign-Urbana (1987). He has specialized in modern European history, East Central Europe, Czechs and Slovaks, East European immigration to US. He authored *Palacký: The Historian as Scholar and Nationalist* (1970).

Ronald Edward Zupko (1938–2021), b. Youngstown, OH, is a historian. He is a professor of modern history, Marquette University, WI (1966–2002). He was an authority on historical metrology.

B. Philosophers

Alexander Altmann (1906–1987), b. Košice, Slovakia, was an Orthodox Jewish scholar and rabbi. Atmann received his Ph.D. in philosophy from the University of Berlin in 1931 and was ordained rabbi by the Hildesheimer Rabbinical Seminary of Berlin in the same year. From 1931 to 1938, he served as rabbi in Berlin and professor of Jewish philosophy at the Seminary. He immigrated to England in 1938. There, in addition to his responsibilities as a community leader, he continued to independently pursue his scholarly studies, publishing in 1946 a translation and commentary of Saadia's *Beliefs and Opinions*. His scholarly activities ultimately led him to found and direct the Institute of Jewish Studies from 1953 to 1958, which at the time was an independent institution. There he edited the *Journal of Jewish Studies* and *Scripta Judaica* and authored his work on Isaac Israeli. In 1959, Altmann left England to join the faculty of Brandeis University in Waltham, Massachusetts. Aged 53 at this time and the author of almost 100 publications, the Brandeis appointment was for Altmann his first university position. He served at Brandeis as the Philip W. Lown Professor of Jewish Philosophy and History of Ideas beginning in 1959 and until his promotion to Professor Emeritus and subsequent retirement in 1976. He was elected Fellow of the American Academy of Arts and Sciences in 1967. From 1976 to 1978, he was a visiting professor at Harvard and at Hebrew University, and from 1978 until his death, he was an Associate at the Harvard University Center for Jewish Studies. He is best known for his studies of the thought of Moses Mendelssohn and was indeed the leading Mendelssohn scholar since the time of Mendelssohn himself. He also made important contributions to the study of Jewish mysticism, and for a large part of his career, he was the only scholar in the United States working on this subject in a purely academic setting.

Martin F. Andic (1940-2005), b. New York, NY, of Slovak descent, was a philosopher. He grew up in New York City and spent most of high school at Bronx Science. He was younger than most of his classmates, after skipping two grades. He got his undergraduate degree at Dartmouth College, majoring in philosophy. He thought of going to medical school but after he won a Reynolds Fellowship and spent a year's study at St. John's College, Oxford, he enrolled in a philosophy graduate program at Princeton University where he received Ph.D. in 1967. He taught initially at Reed College in Portland, OR, but soon moved to University of Massachusetts in Boston. He taught a large variety of courses, from Greek and medieval philosophy to modern and contemporary philosophy, including the 19th century philosophy, the philosophy of mind, the philosophy of religion, metaphysics and the philosophy of science. His writings also ranged from works of Greek philosophy, medieval philosophy and religion to the writings of selected thinkers, such as Dostoevsky, Tolstoy and mystic Simone Weil.

Erich Beck (1883-d.), b. Prague, Bohemia, was trained as a philosopher at Univ. of Heidelberg. He held the position of prof. of philosophy at Univ. of Marburg (1928-35); at Univ. Heidelberg (1923-28); and after coming to the US, he became res. assoc. at Harvard Univ. (s. 1939).

Maximilian Beck (1887-1950), b. Pilsen, Bohemia, studied philosophy at universities of Vienna, Prague, Berlin and Munich. He was editor of *Philosnphische Hefte* in Berlin and Prague and a lecturer at Masaryk Peoples' Univ. (1935-37). After coming to US, he became a researcher in philosophy in NYC (1939-40); with Yale Univ. (s. 1940), as a researcher and hon. fellow.

Richard Marion Becka (1925-2007), b. Cleveland, OH, of Czech ancestry, studied philosophy at St. Louis Univ. and Univ. of Ottawa, He was with Univ. of Detroit (1954-62); St. Bernard College (1962-63); with Loyola College (1963-66); as assoc. professor of philosophy, Gonzaga Univ. (1966-68); Texas A & M Univ. (1968-1987). He lived in Bryan College Station for 38 years and retired from Texas A&M as professor emeritus. He was the author of *Notes on the Personal Being of Man* (1959), and *Jung, St Thomas and the Concrete Conditions of Human Knowing* (1960) and *The Subjectivity of the Individual Metaphysician* (1966). He was a member of the American Maritain Association and the Society of St. Thomas. He also served in WWII in the Army Air Force.

Gary Blahnik (1952-), b. Cleveland, OH, of Czech ancestry, earned a B.A. in linguistics and religion (California State University, Fullerton), an M.A. in English (Xavier University), an M.A. in counseling (Xavier University), an M.A. in philosophy (University of Cincinnati), and a Ph.D. in humanities (Union Institute & University). He has taught a wide variety of philosophy courses, focusing on ethics, at a variety of colleges and universities. Blahnik published four original works in philosophy developing a new philosophical perspective in which he seeks to integrate mind and body, spirit and matter, and traditional relativism with traditional objectivism, one work in psychology where he applies his philosophical perspective to psychotherapeutic theory and practice, seeking to challenge the assumptions of current theory and practice of psychotherapy, ten full-length plays where he seeks to push the boundaries of theater, and two novels. After working in social work and counseling for more than a decade, Dr. Blahnik developed a strong interest in human social hierarchies and the effects that these forms of human organization have upon mental and physical health.

Victor Benjamin Brezik (1913-2009), b. Hallettsville, TX, of Czech ancestry, entered St. Basil Novitiate in 1931. He then began undergraduate studies at St. Michael's College, earning a B.A. from the University of Toronto, and then began Theological studies at St. Basil's Seminary, being ordained in 1940. He was associated in various capacities with the Univ. of St. Thomas, Houston, TX over his 55-year tenure, from 1954-80 as a prof. of philosophy, and s. 1961 as dept. chair. He was a specialist on epistemology and metaphysics.

Charles Edwin Bures (1910-1974), b. Cedar Rapids, IA, of Czech ancestry, was a philosopher and educator. He studied at Grinnell College (B.A., 1933) and University of Iowa (M.A., 1936; Ph.D., 1938). He was professor philosophy and psychology College of Idaho, Caldwell (1938-42); with North America Aviation, Inc. (1943-45); and lecturer at University of Southern California (1947-48); and instructor at University of Oregon (1948-49). Subsequently, he joined California Institute of Technology, Pasadena, as assistant professor (1949-53), associate professor (1953-69), and professor (s. 1969). He was Fellow of the American Association for the Advancement of Science.

Richard Martin Burian (1941-), b. Hanover, NH, of Czech ancestry, is a historian-philosopher of biology. Burian retired from the Departments of Philosophy and of Science and Technology in Society at Virginia Tech in 2007. He maintains a wide range of research interests in history and philosophy of science and science studies. His undergraduate degree was in mathematics at Reed College (1963) and his Ph.D. was in philosophy from the University of Pittsburgh (1971). Before coming to Virginia Tech in 1983, Burian held faculty positions at Brandeis University (Waltham, MA) (1967-76) and Drexel University (1977-1983). He spent a year (1976-77) at the Museum of Comparative Zoology, Harvard University, where he learned enough biology to begin to work in history and philosophy of biology, focusing especially on epistemological issues raised in the biological sciences. He also profited greatly from residential fellowships at the National Humanities Center (1991-92) and the Center for the History of Recent Science (1999-2000) and from visiting faculty positions at Florida A&M University, the University of Pittsburgh, the University of California, Davis, and the University of Dijon, France. Among his administrative positions, he was the first head of the Virginia Tech's Department of Philosophy (1983-92), and the director of Virginia Tech's Science and Technology Studies Graduate Program (1992-97). He was one of the founding members of the International Society for History, Philosophy, and Social Studies of Biology, and served as its president (1999-2001). His publications have focused mainly on conceptual change in science and on the historical and philosophical problems involved in integrating knowledge about organismal development, evolution, and genetics. This line of work is prominent in his book, *The Epistemology of Development, Evolution, and Genetics* (2005).

Milič Čapek (1909-1997), born in Třebechovice, Bohemia, was a Czech–American philosopher. Čapek was strongly influenced by the process philosophy of Henri Bergson and to a lesser degree by Alfred North Whitehead. Much of his work was devoted to the relation of philosophy and modern physics, especially the philosophy of space and time and metaphysics. He studied philosophy at Charles University (Ph.D., 1935). Following the German occupation, he escaped from Czechoslovakia and studied at the Sorbonne in Paris, where he also directed Czech-language broadcasts back to his homeland. Ten days before the Nazi invasion, Čapek left Paris and went to America after an odyssey via Dakar, Casablanca and a Vichy concentration camp in Morocco. During the war, he taught physics in the Army Specialized Training Program at the University of Iowa, the V-12 Navy College Training Program at Doan College, and at the University of Nebraska. After the war, he returned to Czechoslovakia, where he taught briefly at the Palacký University of Olomouc. One month before the 1948 communist coup d'état, he was fleeing once again to take up permanent residence and citizenship in the United States. In 1948, he joined the Carleton College philosophy faculty. In 1962, he accepted a position as professor of philosophy at Boston University, where he served with distinction until his retirement in 1974. His visiting professorships included the Davis Campus of the University of California, Emory University, University of North Texas, Yale University, and, again, Carleton, as the Donald J. Cowling Distinguished Visiting Professor of Philosophy. In addition to many articles in Czech, American and French scholarly periodicals, he was the author of *Bergson a tendence současné fysiky* (1938), *Henry Bergson* (1939), *Key to Czechoslovakia: Territory of Kladsko* (1946) and *Philosophical Impact of Contemporary Physics* (1961).

Joan Copjec (1946-), b. Hartford, CT., of Czech ancestry, has an M.A. in English from the University of Wisconsin; a diploma in film from the Slade School of Fine Art, University College, London; and a Ph.D. in cinema studies from New York University. She has taught intermittently at various schools of architecture: the Institute for Architecture and Urban Studies (NYC); Sci-Arc (LA); and the School of Architecture, Urban Design and Landscape

Architecture at the City College (NYC). She is currently professor of modern culture and media at Brown University. Before moving to Brown, she was UB Distinguished Professor of English, Comparative Literature, and Media Study at the University of Buffalo, where she also directed the Center for the Study of Psychoanalysis and Culture. Her primary fields of research are psychoanalysis, film and film theory, feminism, and art and architecture. Copjec has been a prolific scholar. She has written or edited 11 books, published nearly 60 essays in books and journals, and has given lectures at more than 160 conferences in the United States and internationally. Her work has been translated into a dozen languages. She is the author of *Read My Desire: Lacan against the Historicists* (1994); *Imagine There's No Woman* (2002); and *Cloud: Between Paris and Tehran* (forthcoming), all from MIT Press. A long-time editor of the New York art journal, *October*, she also founded and edited a book series, S, from Verso Press and a journal of Lacanian psychoanalysis, *Umbr(a)*. Her edited books include the following titles: *Shades of Noir* (1993); *Supposing the Subject; Radical Evil* (1995); *Giving Ground: The Politics of Propinquity* (1999) (edited with Michael Sorkin); *Jacques Lacan's Television* (1990); and *Penumbra* (edited with Sigi Jottkandt).

Jaromir Daněk (1925–2011), b. Czech., studied philosophy in Prague (Ph.D.). He lived in Canada s. 1968, where he held the position of professor of philosophy at Laval Univ., Quebec, Canada. Mr. Daněk has distinguished himself throughout his career at Laval University, as much by his dedication to his students as by his commitment within the Faculty of Philosophy, of which he was an eminent representative. He is the author of a large number of publications. Mr. Daněk will have left his mark on the history of the Faculty of Philosophy of Laval University and greatly contributed to his fame. He translated Patočka's main works into French and wrote an important book about the life, *Etoiles Et Horizon Du Domicile: Cosmologie Et Monadologie De L'Homme* (1986). He also wrote *Les projets de Leibniz et de Bolzano: Deux sources de la logique contemporaine* (1975), *Ontologie et Critique Philosophique* (1986) and *Leibnitz - panlogisme monadologique* (1986).

Jozef Dieska (1913–1995), b. Dolná Lehota, Slovakia, was a philosopher. He graduated from the Faculty of Arts at Bratislava University (1936–40), where he was appointed, in 1943, associate professor. In 1945–47, he also worked as an editor of *Filozofický zborník MS* and was also politically active. In 1948, he left Czechoslovakia. He worked first at the University of Georgetown and then at the University of Dayton, Ohio (s. 1954). In America, he focused mainly on gnosis and philosophy of science and was also active in the Council of Free Czechoslovakia.

Robert J. Dostal (1947–), b. Fort Benton, MT, of Moravian immigrant parents, received a B.A. and M.A. in philosophy from the Catholic University of America in 1969 and 1971. He completed his Ph.D. at Pennsylvania State University in 1977 after two years at the

University of Cologne, Germany. His first teaching position was at Memphis State University (now Memphis University). He taught there from 1976–1980. In 1980, he took a position in the philosophy department at Bryn Mawr College, Bryn Mawr, PA, where he continues to work. He was promoted to full professor in 1992 and given the Rufus M. Jones Chair. He served as provost of Bryn Mawr College from 1994–2002. He is currently chair of the philosophy department and Chair of the Faculty. He teaches a variety of courses including the history of philosophy (ancient, modern, and contemporary), ethics, environmental ethics, literary theory, the philosophy of time, and seminars on phenomenology, hermeneutics, and the philosophies of Plato, Kant and Hegel. He has been a Humboldt Fellow at the Universities of Cologne and Freiburg. He has published numerous scholarly articles on the philosophies of Immanuel Kant, Edmund Husserl, Martin Heidegger, and Hans-Georg Gadamer. He edited *The Cambridge Companion to Gadamer* (2002).

Matthew L. Drabek (1983–), b. New Albany, IN, of Czech ancestry, was trained as a philosopher at Univ. of Iowa, Iowa City (M.A., 2010; Ph.D., 2012). He is a visiting asst. professor of philosophy at Univ. of Iowa (s. 2012) and content specialist II, Technical Team with ACT, Inc. (s. 2013). His research interests deal with the classification of people into groups in the social sciences and in everyday life. He has developed a model of how people think about their own classifications and how it affects them. His focus is particularly on some of the social ills that result from classification. He is the author of *Classify and Label: The Unintended Marginalization of Social Groups* (2014).

Richard L. Drtina (1935–), b. Náchod, Czech., graduated from Vysoká škola pedagogická, Prague (dipl., 1958) and studied aesthetics at Charles Univ. (dipl., 1966; CSc./Ph.D., 1968). He was associated with the Humanities Dept. of John Abbott College, Quebec, Canada. His research interests were in axiology, aesthetics and philosophy of art.

Rudolph Valentin Dusek (1941–), b. Toronto, Canada, studied philosophy at Univ. of Texas. Austin. He has been associated with Univ. of New Hampshire, as assistant professor of philosophy (1970–81), as assoc. prof. (s. 1981). Dusek has taught philosophy of science; science, technology and society; Eastern philosophy; logic; and the humanities. His primary research interests are in the philosophy of biology (sociobiology, biotechnology); philosophy of the history of science; social epistemology of science; alternative approaches to science (Romantic, Hermetic, Chinese); and Marxism. Dusek has written *Holistic Inspirations of Physics: An Underground History of Electromagnetic Theory* (1999) and co-edited, with Bob Scharff, *Philosophy of Technology: The Technological Condition, An Anthology* (2003). He is presently working on an introductory text in the philosophy of technology.

Herbert Feigl (1902-1988), b. Liberec, Bohemia, of Jewish family, was as a philosopher and an early member of the Vienna Circle. He coined the term 'nomological dangler.' He specialized in logic and methodology of physics, psychology, gen. theory of knowledge and moral philosophy. He matriculated at the University of Vienna in 1922 and studied physics and philosophy under Moritz Schlick, Hans Hahn, Hans Thirring, and Karl Bühler. Feigl received his Doctorate at Vienna in 1927 for his dissertation "Chance and Law: An Epistemological Analysis of the Roles of Probability and Induction in the Natural Sciences." He published his first book, *Theorie und Erfahrung in der Physik* (Theory and Experience in Physics), in 1929. In 1930, Feigl and his wife immigrated to the US, settling in Iowa to take up a position in the philosophy department at the University of Iowa. In 1940, Herbert Feigl accepted a position as professor of philosophy at the University of Minnesota, where he remained for 31 years. His close professional and personal relationship with Wilfrid Sellars produced many different collaborative projects, including the textbook *Readings in Philosophical Analysis* and the journal *Philosophical Studies*, which he and Sellars founded in 1949. In 1953, he established the Minnesota Center for Philosophy of Science (the first center of its kind in the United States) with a grant from the Hill Foundation. He was appointed Regents Professor of the University of Minnesota in 1967. He specialized in logic and methodology of physics, psychology, gen. theory of knowledge and moral philosophy.

Oscar Benjamin Frankl (1881-1955), b. Kroměříž, Moravia, was a literary scholar educated at Univ. Vienna. He was the founder and dir., Urania - Masaryk People's Univ. (1917-38). He came to US in 1940. He became freelance writer, researcher; member Rand School for Social Science, NYC (1940-42); broadcaster in German, Office of Research, Columbia Univ. (s. 1942). He was also the founder and exec. secy., Emerson-Goethe Soc. (s 1949). He was the author of *Einstein and Masaryk as Men, Philosophers and Pacifists* (1949-50), *Theodore Herzl. The Jew and the Man* (1950).

Viktor Emil Frankl (1905-1997), b. nr. Vienna, of Moravian father and Bohemian mother, was an Austrian neurologist and psychiatrist as well as a Holocaust survivor. Frankl was the founder of logotherapy, which is a form of existential analysis, the 'Third Viennese School of Psychotherapy.' He studied medicine at the University of Vienna and later specialized in neurology and psychiatry, concentrating on the topics of depression and suicide. His early development was influenced by his contacts with Sigmund Freud and Alfred Adler, although he would later diverge from their teachings. In 1942, Frankl, his wife, and his parents were deported to the Nazi Theresienstadt Ghetto. Liberated after three years in concentration camps, Frankl returned to Vienna, where he developed and lectured about his own approach to psychological healing. In 1948, Frankl earned a Ph.D. in philosophy. His dissertation – 'The Unconscious God' is an examination of the relation of psychology and religion. In 1955, he was awarded a professorship of neurology and psychiatry at the University of Vienna, and as visiting professor, he resided at Harvard University (1961), at Southern Methodist University, Dallas (1966), and at Duquesne University, Pittsburgh (1972). He lectured and taught seminars all over the world and received 29 honorary doctoral degrees.

Lubomír Gleiman (1923-2006), b. Trnava, Slovakia, was a political philosopher, professor at Newton College, Franklin, MA (1957-75).

Heinrich Gompers (1873-1942), b. Vienna, of Moravian ancestry, son of Theodore Gompers, was a philosopher educated at Univ. of Vienna. In 1935, he emigrated to US with invitation to Univ. of So. California, Los Angeles where he held the position of guest prof. of philosophy (until 1942). He was noted for development of pathempiricism and later developed theory on understanding purposeful and meaningful processes.

Robert Francis Harvanek (1916-1996), b. Chicago, IL, of Czech ancestry, SJ, was a philosopher. He received his Bachelor of Arts in 1939, his Master of Arts in 1941, both at Loyola University, Chicago, and in 1944 attained his Ph.D. at Fordham University in New York. He taught philosophy at Bellarmine School of Theology in North Aurora (1964-67) and in 1972, Father Harvanek began teaching philosophy at Loyola University, since 1974 as a professor and from 1979 to 1985 as the department's chairman. He was an authority on Greek and early Christian philosophy and on contemporary European and American philosophy.

Paul William Henle (1908-1962), b. New York, NY, son of Pearl A. Hahn (1880-?), of Bohemian ancestry, and Leo Henle, was a philosopher, holding the position of Professor of Philosophy at University of Michigan for some 25 years (1937-62). He joined the faculty in 1937, after having taught at his alma mater, Harvard University, and at Smith College. He earned the A.B., A.M. and Ph.D. degrees before beginning his teaching career. Professor Henle left the Michigan Campus in 1942, on leave of absence, to serve in the Army until 1945. Then he resigned in 1946 to become Chairman of the Philosophy Department at Northwestern University. However, he rejoined the Michigan staff in 1950. Professor Henle was co-author of a book, *Fundamentals of Logic*, which has been translated into the Chinese. He is currently Vice-President of the Western Division of the American Philosophical Association and has been consulting editor of the Journal of the Association for Symbolic Logic. He was married to Jeanne M. La Farge, with whom they had two sons.

Thomas Hurka (1952-), b. Toronto, Can., of Czech ancestry, earned a BA in philosophy from the University of Toronto in 1975, a B.Phil. (also called M.Phil.) in philosophy from Oxford University in 1977, and a D.Phil. in philosophy from Oxford University in 1980. He was assistant professor, then associate professor, then professor at the University of

Calgary from 1979 to 2002; from 2002 he's been professor of philosophy at the University of Toronto, being named Chancellor Henry N.R. Jackman Distinguished Professor of Philosophical Studies in 2003 and University Professor in 2013. He works primarily in moral and political philosophy plus the history of ethics. His major publications are the books *Perfectionism* (1993), *Virtue, Vice, and Value* (2001), *The Best Things in Life* (2011) and *British Ethical Theorists from Sidgwick to Ewing* (2014). He is a fellow of the Royal Society of Canada and past recipient of a Guggenheim Fellowship and a Killam Research Fellowship from the Canada Council, and several visiting fellowships at Oxford. He was elected to The Royal Society of Canada in 2001.

Douglas N. Husak (1948-), b. Cleveland, OH, of Czech ancestry, received both Ph.D. and J.D. degrees from Ohio State University (1976). He is a professor of philosophy and law at Rutgers University, where he began in 1977. He has been a visiting professor of philosophy or a visiting professor of law at 8 different colleges or universities. His specialty is philosophy of law. More narrowly, he is interested in the connections between moral philosophy and the substantive criminal law - especially decisions about criminalization and the moral limits of the criminal sanction. This latter interest has led him to critically examine the rationale for drug prohibitions. He has written six books. His most important are *Drugs and Rights* (1992); *Overcriminalization* (2008), and *The Philosophy of Criminal Law: Collected Essays* (2010).

John Peter Jelinek (1916-1998), b. Omaha, NE, of Czech ancestry, SJ, was Gregorian Univ. (Rome) educated philosopher. He served as a prof. of philosophy at Creighton Univ., Omaha (s. 1963) and dept. chair (1962-67). He specialized in ethics.

Leo Jung (1892-1987), b. Uherský Brod, Moravia., was a rabbi and educator. He was one of the major architects of American Orthodox Judaism. He studied at Univ. of Vienna and Berlin, Cambridge University (B.A., 1920; M.A., 1926) and Univ. of London. He received his Hebrew education in yeshivas in Hungary and in Berlin, where he was ordained in 1920. He came to US in 1920 to serve the Congregation of Knesseth Israel in Cleveland. In 1922, the Jewish Center in New York City called him to become its rabbi. Dr. Jung became a professor of ethics at Yeshiva Coll., in New York in 1931, at Yeshiva Univ. (s. 1945) and at Stern Coll, for Women (s. 1956). For many years, he served as president of the Jewish Academy of Arts and Sciences, which he helped to organize. He was an author and editor of 37 books, including *Judaism in a Changing World* (1939).

Ladimír Klácel (orig. František Matouš) (1808-1882), b. Česká Třebová, Bohemia, formerly a member of the Augustinian order and professor of philosophy at the Bishop's Inst. in Brno, because of his liberal views and acceptance of Hegel's thoughts, was removed from his professorship. In the revolutionary year of 1848, he left the order and became editor of *Moravské Noviny* in Brno but was deposed again. Disenchanted, in 1869 he decided to accept John Barta Letovsky's invitation to come to America and edit his paper *Slovan Amerikánský* published in Iowa City. As a respected literary figure and with ties with leading literary figures in the Czech Lands, he was received in US with great enthusiasm and expectations. He became the spiritual leader of the rationalistic movement among the American Czechs and as an advocate of new society, he urged his followers to establish congregations which in 1870 formed the Alliance of Free Thinkers. He established newspaper *Hlas Jednoty svobodomyslných* (Voice of the Alliance of Free Thinkers) and for the Bohemian Freethinkers in Chicago, he founded a bimonthly *Svojan*. 'Let us dare to grow intelligent' was his slogan. He strove to found a communal society where the individual (rid of tradition and human failings) would attain a sense of personal dignity and social responsibility and conduct his life in the path of harmony, beauty and universality. The spiritual and social doctrine founded by Klácel was embodied in the principle of his spiritual creed. His philosophy held that a universal law governed the world and that all creation was interdependent. Man was nature's most perfect and yet most dependent being. He was endowed with a will and mind which formed his ego but he was not free or self-sufficient since he too was subject to the universal law of interrelation with others. Human community existed only as a segment of a greater whole such as a nation, continent, or the world. Yet, even the world was interdependent on a greater unity, the universe. Universality necessarily encompassed all natural and human phenomena manifested to or conceived of by man. In spite of his advanced age, he developed enormous activity as a writer, translator, and teacher and in a period of eleven years he produced over eighty publications. Toward the end of his life, he turned to mysticism and in 1882 died destitute.

Roman Anthony Kocourek (1909-1964), b. Kilkenny, MN, of Czech ancestry, was Laval Univ. educated philosopher. He served as a prof. of philosophy at Coll. of St. Thomas (1939-61) and as a prof. and dept. chair at the Coll. of Women, Univ. San Diego (s. 1951). He was an authority on philosophy of nature.

Erazim Václav Kohák (1933-2020), b. Prague, Czech., is a philosopher. After communists took over Czechoslovakia in 1948, his family escaped to the United States. He studied at Colgate University, earning a B.A. in 1954, and then studied philosophy, theology and religious studies at Yale University (M.A., 1957; Ph.D., 1958). He also worked at Gustavus Adolphus College and Boston University (Professor in 1977). His special interest in philosophy was Plato and Platonism, and in history it was recent Central European history. After the Velvet Revolution in 1989, he returned to Czechoslovakia to become a professor at Charles University in Prague. Since 2006, he had been a senior research fellow in the

Centre of Global Studies in the Institute of Philosophy at the Czech Academy of Sciences in Prague.

Stephen Körner (1913–2000), b. Moravská Ostrava, Moravia, was Charles Univ. and Cambridge Univ. educated philosopher. He was with Bristol Univ. (s. 1946), as prof. of philosophy (1952–79), as dean (1965–66), as pro vice chancellor (1968–71). From 1970 to 1983, he lived in US as prof. of philosophy at Yale Univ. He was a specialist on philosophy of science.

Pavel Kovály (1928–2006), b. Prague, of Slovak father, was a Holocaust survivor. He held PhDr. and CSc. degrees. After marrying Hedvika Margolius, they immigrated to the US and settled in Boston, MA. He secured position as lecturer in philosophy at Northeastern Univ., Boston, while she found work as a librarian at the Harvard University Law School. He was the author of *Rehumanization or Dehumanization? Philosophical Essays on Current Issues of Marxist Humanism* (1973). In 1996, the couple returned to Prague, where Pavel Kovaly died in 2006.

Rudolph Krejčí (1929–2018), b. Hrušky, Czech., was a Czechoslovak-American philosopher and educator, who was the founder of the Philosophy and Humanities Programs at the University of Alaska, Fairbanks. Krejčí studied at high school in Kroměříž and Brno, where he was introduced to philosophy by Professor Antonin Kříž, who translated Aristotle's work into the Czech language. His studies were terminated on May 1, 1949 due to his membership of an anticommunist dissident student group. Krejčí had to go into hiding in a secret room of his father's apartment, where he stayed for five years. In May 1954, with the help of his father, he escaped Czechoslovakia hiding in a coffin under a coal wagon covered with vinegar and mustard, and made it to Vienna, Austria. From 1954–1959, Krejčí studied at the University of Innsbruck, Austria, majoring in philosophy, psychology, Russian history and literature. In 1959, he became a Doctor of Philosophy. Krejčí then went to the United States to work as an engineer for Bechtel Corporation and Bethlehem Steel, and in 1960, he was offered a contract to teach Russian and German at the University of Alaska in Fairbanks. Two years later, he established a Philosophy program, and 13 years after that, he added a Humanities program. After one year as a Dean of Arts and Letters, he formed a new College of Arts and Sciences. He has been associated with the Univ. of Alaska, Fairbanks (s. 1962), as prof. of philosophy (s. 1969), dept. head (1962–74), and dean, Coll. Arts and Letters (1974–75). Krejčí's career with the university almost ended during a political dispute with former University of Alaska president William Ransom Wood regarding Project Chariot, a scheme by the federal government to detonate up to six nuclear explosions along the northwest coast of Alaska to create a new deep water harbor for future mineral extraction. In response to Krejčí's opposition to the project, Krejčí said that "Wood came to me and told me: 'If you go on as you do now, there is only one way, one way from Alaska, direct, down to lower states.'" As a result of Krejčí's opposition, Project Chariot never happened. In 2009, Governor Sean Parnell presented Krejci with the Governor's Awards for the Humanities for 'Distinguished Service to the Humanities in the state of Alaska'. Krejčí lectured on philosophy in the USA, Canada, England, Europe and Asia and cooperated with the International Wittgenstein Symposium in Kirchberg, Austria, Siu's *Panetics* in Washington DC, Viktor Frankl's logotherapy in Vienna, and Takashima's humanistic anthropology in Tokyo. In 1997, Krejčí became Professor Emeritus of Philosophy and Humanities after 37 years of service at the University of Alaska, Fairbanks. He specializes in history of philosophy, epistemology, methodology of sciences and humanities.

Werner Josef Krieglstein (1941-), b. Blatnice, Czech., is an award winning and internationally recognized scholar, director and actor. Following the post-war expulsion of the Germans from Czechoslovakia, he relocated near Frankfurt, Germany. In the sixties, Krieglstein was a student at the Frankfurt School in Germany with Theodor W. Adorno. Before moving to the United States, Krieglstein also studied at the Free University of Berlin. Following his studies in Germany, Krieglstein pursued his Doctorate in philosophy at the University of Chicago as a Fulbright Scholar and University Fellow. Krieglstein has held teaching positions at the University of Helsinki, Finland, and Western Michigan University in Kalamazoo. He currently is professor emeritus of philosophy and religious studies at the College of DuPage, where he was awarded the Most Outstanding Teacher Award in 2003 and the Distinguished Regional Humanities Educator Award from the Community College Humanities Association in 2008. Krieglstein is the founder of a neo-Nietzschean philosophical school called Transcendental Perspectivism. After emigrating to the US and while teaching at Western Michigan University in 1976, he founded and directed a small rural theater company in Lawrence, Michigan known as the Whole Arts Theater, which later moved to Kalamazoo.

Will Kymlicka (1962-), b. London, Canada, of Czech ancestry, is a Canadian political philosopher mostly known for his work on multiculturalism. Kymlicka received his B.A. (Honours) in philosophy and political studies from Queen's University in 1984, and his D.Phil. in philosophy from Oxford University in 1987. He is currently professor of philosophy and Canada Research Chair in Political Philosophy at Queen's University at Kingston, and recurrent visiting professor in the nationalism studies program at the Central European University in Budapest, Hungary. He is the author of six books published by Oxford University Press. His main interests are liberalism, multicultural society, citizenship and minority rights.

Nicholas Lobkowicz (1931-), b. Prague, Czech., is a philosopher. He studied at University of Fribourg, Switzerland (Ph.D., 1958). He taught philosophy at the Univ. of Notre Dame (1960-67) and then became prof. of political theory and philosophy at Univ. of Munich (s. 1967) and president (1976-82). Subsequently, he became president of Catholic Univ. at Eichstaet. He is an authority on Marxism, philosophy of social science and metaethics.

Bernard Martin (1928-1982), b. Seklence, Czech., was a Rabbi, philosopher and educator. He was ordained as a rabbi at Hebrew Union College in 1951, receiving his M.H.L. degree with highest honors. He pursued a combined career as pulpit rabbi and scholar and received a doctorate in philosophy from the University of Illinois in 1960. He served as rabbi of Sinai Temple in Champaign, Ill., from 1951 to 1957, with a leave of absence to serve as a chaplain in the U.S. army in Japan from 1953 to 1955. He was associate rabbi of Sinai Temple in Chicago from 1957 to 1961 and then senior rabbi of Mount Zion Temple in St. Paul, Minn., until 1966. In 1966, Martin accepted a professorship at Case Western Reserve University in Cleveland, where he became prof. of Jewish philosophy and history of Judaism (s. 1968), and dept. chair (s. 1967); and Abba Hillel Silver Professor of Jewish Studies in 1968. He specialized in history of Jewish literature, contemporary Jewish philosophy and philosophy of religion. He was active in the American Academy for Jewish Research, Academy for Jewish Philosophy, and American Academy of Religion, among others, and served from 1975 to 1981 as editor of the *ccar Journal*, published by the Central Conference of American Rabbis. Martin's first book was *The Existentialist Theology of Paul Tillich* (1963). He then developed a specialty in the Russian Jewish existentialist Lev Shestov, editing *Great Twentieth Century Jewish Philosophers* (Shestov, Rosenzweig, Buber, 1969) and *A Shestov Anthology* (1970), and translating Shestov's *Athens and Jerusalem* (1966), *Potestas Clavium* (1968), and *Speculation and Revelation* (1982).

Martin Beck Matuštík (1957-), b. Bratislava, Czech., attended gymnasium in Prague (1972-76) and then continued his studies, majoring in psychology at Charles Univ. (1976-77). He was one of the student signatories of the Czechoslovak Manifesto for human rights issues by Jiří Hájek, Václav Havel and Jan Potočka. After coming to the US, he studied philosophy at St. Louis Univ. (M.A., 1985) and at Fordham Univ. (Ph.D., 1991). He joined Purdue Univ., as asst. professor of philosophy (1991-96), assoc. prof. (1996-2000) and full professor (2000-08). In the meantime, he also spent a year on the Fulbright Lectureship Grant at Charles Univ. (1995). In 2008, he was appointed Lincoln Professor of Ethics and Religious Studies at Arizona State Univ., Phoenix. His research and teaching specialization include: critical theory, social and political philosophy, continental philosophy of religion, nineteenth- and twentieth-century continental philosophy and post-Holocaust ethics and memory studies. Matustik has published six single author books, edited two collections, and co-edited *New Critical Theory*, a series at Rowman and Littlefield Publishers. Among his publications are

Postnational Identity: Critical Theory and Existential Philosophy in Habermas, Kierkegaard, and Havel (1993); *Specters of Liberation: Great Refusals in the New World Order* (1998); *Jurgen Habermas: A Philosophical-Political Profile* (2001); and *Kierkegaard in Post/Modernity* (1995), co-edited with Merold Westphal. His most recent book is *Radical Evil and the Scarcity of Hope: Postsecular Meditations* (2008).

Sister Mary Christine Morkovsky (1931-2024), b. San Antonio, TX, of Czech ancestry, professed vows as a Sister of Divine Providence of San Antonio, Texas in 1951. She held M.A. and Ph.D. degrees in philosophy and an M.A. in religious studies from St. Louis University. She has been a teacher, administrator, researcher, lecturer, writer, and spiritual director, associated with Our Lady of the Lake College, San Antonio. She had risen from asst. prof. to assoc. professor of philosophy (1966-77), and director of humanities (s. 1977). She is the author of *Living in God's Providence: History of the Congregation of Divine Providence of San Antonio, Texas, 1943-2000* (2009).

Charles (aka Karol) Murin (1913-1998), b. Žabokreky, Slovakia, was a philosopher and politician. After obtaining his Doctorate of Law from the University of Bratislava, he studied in Paris. From 1939 to 1945, he was personal secretary to Dr. Jozef Tiso, President of the wartime Slovak Republic. In 1948, he arrived in Canada with his wife Isabelle and daughter Janina. A few years, after his arrival in Canada, he started teaching philosophy at the University of Montreal, where he taught until his retirement. To his degrees from Europe, he added a M.A. and Ph.D. in philosophy from the University of Montreal. A specialist on Nietzsche and on Thomas Aquinas, Dr. Murín published *Nietzsche problème: Généalogie d'une pensée* (1979).

Ernest Nagel (1901-1985), b. Nové Mesto nad Váhom, Slovakia; was a philosopher of science. He was in US s. 1911, where he studied at CUNY (B.S., 1923) and Columbia University (A.M., 1925; Ph.D., 1931). He was with Columbia University, as an instructor of philosophy (1931-37), assistant professor (1937-39), as associate professor (1939-46), as professor (1946-55), as John Dewey Professor (1955-66), as University Professor (1966-70), and as emeritus (1977-85). He was the author of *On the Logic of Measurement. Sovereign Reason* (1954), *Logic without Metaphysics* (1957), *Gödel's Proof* (1958), *The Structure of Science* (1961), and *Technology Revisited* (1978). He was the editor of *Journal of Philosophy* (1940-56), *Philosophy of Science* (1956-59), and *Journal of Symbolic Logic* (1939-45).

David Neumark (1866-1924), b. Galicia, was an American Reform scholar. He was the rabbi in Rakovník, Bohemia and later became a professor of Jewish philosophy at the Veitel-Heine-Ephraimschen Lehranstalt in Berlin in 1907. Later that year, Neumark was appointed to the faculty of Hebrew Union College, Cincinnati, OH, by President Kaufman

Kohler. He became chair of philosophy in 1907 and served until 1924. In 1919, Neumark founded *The Journal of Jewish Lore and Philosophy*, which became *The Hebrew Union College Annual* in 1921. Neumark was a scholar and philosopher. He attempted, in his many works, to show that throughout the evolution of Judaism, the basic commitment of the Jew was to religion, and that the Jews remained true to Judaism through the ages only because their concepts of God and morality differed from and were superior to all other religions and philosophies of their time. Neumark was also an ardent Zionist. His magnum opus was *Geschichte der juedischen Philosophie des Mittelalters* (1907–1910) was translated into Hebrew under the title *Toledot ha-Filosofyah be-Yisrael*, (Vol 1, 1922, vol. 2, 1929). His essays in *Jewish Philosophy* (1929) contains a bibliography of his writings, which also included *The Philosophy of Judaism* (1925) and *The Philosophy of the Bible* (1918).

Michael Novak (1933–2017), b. Johnston, Pa, of Slovak ancestry, was a Catholic philosopher, author and publicist. Novak earned a Bachelor of Arts degree summa cum laude in philosophy and English from Stonehill College in 1956, a Bachelor of Sacred Theology degree from the Pontifical Gregorian University in Rome in 1958, and a Master of Arts degree in history and philosophy of religion from Harvard University in 1966. The author of more than forty books on the philosophy and theology of culture, Novak is most widely known for his book *The Spirit of Democratic Capitalism* (1982). In 1994, he was awarded the Templeton Prize for Progress in Religion, which included a million-dollar purse awarded at Buckingham Palace. He wrote books and articles focused on capitalism, religion, and the politics of democratization. Novak was George Frederick Jewett Scholar in Religion, Philosophy, and Public Policy at the American Enterprise Institute. Novak served as United States Ambassador to the United Nations Commission on Human Rights in 1981 and 1982 and led the US delegation to the Conference on Security and Cooperation in Europe in 1986.

Daniel D. Novotný (1975–), b. Chlumec nad Cidlinou, earned Ph.D. in philosophy at SUNY Buffalo in 2008 under Jorge J. E. Gracia, Barry Smith, and John T. Krearns. He is presently a post-doctoral researcher in 'analytical scholasticism' at the University of South Bohemia in České Budějovice. Since 2010, he has been editor-in-chief of *Studia Neoaristotelica: A Journal of Analytical Scholasticism*. He is a co-editor of a volume in analytical metaphysics and authored a book on Baroque scholastic metaphysics. At the moment, the primary focus of his research is scholastic logic/metaphysics/philosophy-of-nature/philosophy-of-mind of the Baroque era, especially in so far as the issues that were discussed at that time may be related to issues discussed in contemporary analytical metaphysics and philosophy of religion. In addition, he has also been involved in various other areas, such as epistemology, semantics, informatics, education, philosophical practice, interpretations of Laozi, etc.

Suzanne Obdrzalek (1975–), b. East York, Canada, of Czech ancestry, studied philosophy at Stanford Univ. (B.A., 1997) and at Univ. of California, Berkeley (Ph.D., 2004). She was a Mellon postdoctoral fellow at Yale from 2004–2006. She is associated with Claremont McKenna College, CA, as asst. professor (2006–2012), as assoc. professor (s. 2012). Her specialty is ancient philosophy.

Werner S. Pluhar (1940–), b. Berlin, Ger., of Bohemian ancestry, studied philosophy at Univ. of California, Berkeley (B.A., 1968) and philosophy and ethics at Univ. of Michigan, Ann Arbor (Ph.D., 1973). He taught philosophy at Grinnell College, Grinnell, IA (1973–78) and then at Penn State Univ., Eberly, as lecturer (1978–79), as asst. professor (1979–93); with Penn State Univ., Fayette, as affiliate professor of philosophy (s. 1994). He has devoted most of his efforts to translation of Immanuel Kant's main works from German to English *Critique of Judgment* (1987), *Critique of Pure Reason* (1996), *Critique of Practical Reason* 2002), and *Religion within the Bounds of Bare Reason* (2009).

Louis Paul Pojman (1935–2005), b. Chicago IL, grew up in Cicero, Illinois, where he attended Morton High School and Junior College. He went on to receive a B.S. degree from Nyack College and a B.D. degree from New Brunswick Theological Seminary, becoming an ordained minister in the Reformed Church of America. After serving an inter-racial church in Bedford Stuyvesant, Brooklyn, he returned to seminary, attending Union Theological Seminary at Columbia University in New York where he studied under Reinhold Niebuhr and earned a Ph.D. in Ethics. During this time, he received several fellowships to study abroad. In 1969–71, he was a Fulbright Fellow and a Kent Fellow at the University of Copenhagen, Denmark, and in 1970, a Rockefeller Fellow at Hamburg University, Germany. Upon receiving his Ph.D. from Union, he decided to study analytic philosophy and went to Oxford University where he earned his D. Phil. in 1977. He also lectured at Oxford. In 1977, he became a visiting assistant professor at the Univ. of Notre Dame. After this, he taught at the Univ. of Texas (Dallas), and became a Professor at the University of Mississippi, where he was chair of the Philosophy Department. He was also a visiting Scholar at Brigham Young Univ., Univ. of California, Berkeley and New York Univ. among others. He retired as professor of philosophy emeritus from the United States Military Academy at West Point, where he was a professor for nine years. In 2004–5, he was a visiting fellow at Clare Hall, Cambridge Univ., UK, where he became a Life-fellow. He had read papers at 60 universities in the USA, Europe and Asia. Dr. Pojman was the author or editor of many books and articles. He was best known perhaps for presenting extremely balanced perspectives in his writings on a variety of some of the most controversial and challenging contemporary issues, including abortion, affirmative action and the death penalty. He endeavored to explain why people disagree on such issues and presented the roots of the ideas, teachings and writings that help build an understanding of these differing viewpoints so that the reader can reflect on his or her own point of view on various issues.

Paul Theodore Pojman (1966–2012), b. New York City, of Czech ancestry (son of Louis Paul Pojman), spent seven of his early years in Copenhagen and Oxford, England. When he was 11, he moved with his family to Richardson, Texas. At 10, he was ranked eighth in his age group in the world in chess and played with such people as Nigel Short while in England. After high school, he attended Reed College in Oregon for two years, then traveled, farmed, and while a devotee in the International Society for Krishna Consciousness, studied Sanskrit at an ashram in India. He earned a Bachelor's degree in philosophy from the University of Mississippi in 1993, followed by a Master's degree in 1995, also in philosophy. Dr. Pojman earned a Ph.D. in the history and philosophy of science from Indiana University in 2000, his dissertation titled "Ernst Mach's Biological Theory of Knowledge." Dr. Pojman began his academic career as an assistant professor of philosophy in 2000 at the University of Central Arkansas in Conway, and the next year was named a visiting professor of philosophy at the University of Utah in Salt Lake City. He joined the faculty of Towson University in 2002 as an assistant professor of philosophy until being named an associate professor in 2008. Dr. Pojman's areas of specialization and interest included the philosophy of science, science and technology studies, environmental ethics, and anarchist theory. He was also a community activist. He died of cancer, when he was only 45 years of age.

Štefan Polakovič (1912–1999), b. Chtelnica, Slovakia, was a theologian and philosopher of Christian orientation. He studied theology and philosophy in Rome (Dr. Th., 1938; Ph.D., 1942). He was professor of philosophy of the Slovak University (now UK) (1944). He interpreted the ideology of Jozef Tiso and Slovak nationalism in the intentions of Blondelism. He contributed to the founding of the Philosophical Department of Matica slovenská in 1940 and to the publication of the first Slovak philosophical journal, the quarterly *Filozofický sborník*, which was published until 1950. Before the arrival of the Red Army, he emigrated to Austria, from there to Bavaria, and at the end of 1945, to Italy. In 1947, he emigrated to Argentina, where he first worked as a bank clerk and later built a prosperous electrical engineering company, which, however, did not survive due to the crisis. Here he focused mainly on the issue of the nation, especially the Slovak one. He developed into a leading figure in the South American cultural, especially the philosophical community. He developed a friendship with the important Argentine writer Ernest Sabat. He has also published extensively in Spanish and Italian in the field of philosophy, political science, political history and ethnography in numerous Slovak as well as in foreign language magazines and anthologies abroad and in 1933–1945 and 1990–1997 in Slovakia. After 1990, he maintained sensitive contact with Slovak culture in Slovakia and publicly distanced himself from some of his radical nationalist attitudes before 1945.

Sir Karl Raimund Popper (1902–1994), b. Vienna, of Bohemian ancestry, studied philosophy at Univ. of Vienna. He was with London School of Economics and Political Science (s. 1946); fellow, Stanford Univ. (1956–57); vis. prof. of philosophy, Univ. of California, Berkeley. He is counted among the most influential philosophers of science of the 20th century, and also wrote extensively on social and political philosophy. Popper is known for repudiating the classical observationalist / inductivist account of scientific method by advancing empirical falsification instead; for his opposition to the classical justificationist account of knowledge which he replaced with critical rationalism, 'the first non justificational philosophy of criticism in the history of philosophy' and for his vigorous defense of liberal democracy and the principles of social criticism which he took to make the flourishing of the 'open society' possible.

George Rebec (1868–1944), b. Tuscola, MI, of Czech ancestry, was a philosopher. He entered the University of Michigan at the age of nineteen and was graduated Bachelor of Philosophy in 1891. For the next two years he served as Instructor in English at the University but declined reappointment in order to take up graduate study abroad. The year 1893–1894 was spent at the University of Strasbourg, from which he was recalled in September 1894, to the University of Michigan to become Instructor in Philosophy. In 1897, he received the degree of Doctor of Philosophy on examination from the University, and in 1900, was advanced to the rank of Assistant Professor of Philosophy. Since 1904, he has been Junior Professor of Philosophy.

Augustin C. Riška (1935–), b. Brodské, Czech., is a philosopher. He studied philosophy (dipl., 1959) and logic (PhDr., 1967) at Comenius University. After coming to the US, he became associate professor of philosophy, St. John's University, New York, NY. His interests were in logic, philosophy of science, and history of philosophy.

Avital Ronell (1952–), b. Prague, Czech., trained as a comparative literature scholar at Princeton Univ., is an American philosopher who contributes to the fields of continental philosophy, literary studies, psychoanalysis, feminist philosophy, political philosophy, and ethics. She is University Professor in the Humanities and in the Departments of Germanic Languages and Literature and Comparative Literature at New York University where she co-directs the Trauma and Violence Transdisciplinary Studies Program. As Jacques Derrida Professor of Philosophy, she teaches, regularly at the European Graduate School in Saas-Fee. Her research ranges from Johann Wolfgang von Goethe dictating haunted writing and psychoanalysis, Alexander Graham Bell setting up electronic transmission systems in the early 20th century, the structure of the test in legal, pharmaceutical, artistic, scientific, Zen, and historical domains, to 20th-century literature and philosophy on stupidity, on the disappearance of authority, childhood and a diction of deficiency. Ronell is a founding editor of the journal *Qui Parle* and a member of Jewish Voice for Peace. Her books include: *The Test Drive* (2005); *Stupidity* (2001); *Finitude's Score: Essays for the End of the Millennium* (1994); *Crack Wars: Literature, Addiction, Mania* (1992); *The Telephone Book: Technology, Schizophrenia, Electric Speech* (2001); *Dictations: On Haunted Writing* (1986). He was with Univ. of Michigan (1891-1909) and then became prof. of philosophy and director of graduate div. at the Oregon State Univ. (1921-33) and Dean and dir. of graduate div., Oregon State System of Higher Education (1933-38).

Rev. Michael John Sablica (1920-1997), b. Czech., was a philosopher and theologian. He spent the first nine years of his life in Czechoslovakia, coming to Milwaukee, WI in 1929. Educated at Marquette University, he was ordained in 1956. He held a Master's degree from Marquette in religious studies and a Doctorate in philosophy from Duquesne University, Pittsburgh. In 1961, he was an associate pastor at St. John parish in Plymouth. He also served briefly as chaplain at Rocky Knoll Sanatorium, near Plymouth and at St. Joseph hospital in West Bend. As a teacher, he worked in grade and high schools in the Milwaukee archdiocese. Teaching college students, he spent the early 1970s at Mount Scenario College in Ladysmith and Christian Theological Seminary and the Catholic Seminary Foundation of Indianapolis. In 1977, he became assistant professor of philosophy and theology at Divine Word Seminary College, Epworth, IA, serving until 1986. Subsequently, he was engaged as a pastor at St. Cyril and Methodius Catholic Church, Sheboygan, WI.

Tamar Schapiro (1964-), b. Chicago, IL, daughter of Raya Czerner (1934-2007), a native of Prague, Czech, and the physician Joseph Solomon Schapiro, is a philosopher. She studied philosophy at Yale Univ. (B.A., 1986) and at Harvard Univ. (Ph.D., 1997). She then became Junior Fellow with the Harvard Society of Fellows (1997-2000). Subsequently, she was appointed assistant professor of philosophy at Stanford Univ. (2000-09) and assoc. professor (s. 2009), where she studies theories of morality, practical reasoning, and agency. She has received fellowships from the Andrew W. Mellon Foundation, the Harvard Center for Ethics and the Professions, the Mrs. Giles Whiting Foundation, and the Stanford Humanities Center, the Radcliffe Institute. Her areas of specialty are: ethics, history of ethics, Kant's practical philosophy, practical reasoning, moral psychology and philosophy of action. Her research interests are in the area of the nature of passion/inclination and its role in practical reasoning, the structure of agency, the role of ideal concepts in moral theory and Kantian nonideal theory.

Frederick Schick (1929-2022), b. Brno, Moravia, is Columbia Univ. educated philosopher. He was with Brandeis Univ. (1960-62) and then with Rutgers Univ., where he became prof. of philosophy (s. 1969) and dept. chair (1965-68). He is an authority on philosophy of science and inductive logic decision theory. He is the author of *Ambiguity and Logic* (2003).

Alfred Schütz (1899-1959), b. Vienna, of Bohemian mother, was a philosopher, social phenomenologist and sociologist, trained at Univ. Vienna. He moved to the US in 1939, where he became a member of the faculty of the New School for Social Research. He worked on phenomenology, social science methodology and the philosophy of Edmund Husserl, William James and others.

James P. Sterba (1943-), b. US, of Czech ancestry, was trained as a philosopher at Univ. of Pittsburgh (Ph.D.). He holds the position of professor of philosophy at Univ. of Notre Dame, which he joined in 1973. His areas of interests are ethics, political philosophy, environmental ethics, philosophy of peace and justice. He has written numerous books, including *The Pursuit of Justice: A Personal Philosophical History* (2014), *From Rationality to Equality* (2013), *Morality: The Why and the What of It* (2012), *Introducing Ethics for Here and Now* (2012), etc.; and also edited quite a few. A fellow of Notre Dame's Kroc Institute for International Peace Studies, Sterba also is past president of the International Society for Social and Legal Philosophy (the American Section), past president of Concerned Philosophers for Peace, and past president of the North American Society for Social Philosophy.

Joshua Stuchlik (1981-), b. Wichita KS, of Czech ancestry, is a professor of philosophy who currently works at the University of St. Thomas in St. Paul, MN. He received his B.A. in philosophy at the University of Notre Dame (2004) and completed his M.A. (2006) and Ph.D. (2011) in philosophy at the University of Pittsburgh, where he received an Andrew W. Mellon Fellowship in the Humanities (2004-2005). He has worked at the University of St. Thomas, MN, since 2011, and since 2012 has also served as assistant editor of the *American Catholic Philosophical Quarterly*. His interests include ethics, epistemology, and the philosophy of action, and he teaches a wide variety of courses including ethics, modern philosophy, and contemporary philosophy.

Ivan Sviták (1925-1994), b. Hranice, Czech., was a philosopher, critic and poet, who ranked among Europe's most prominent proponents of Marxist humanism. He studied at Charles University (JUDr., 1949), VŠPS (RSDr., 1952) and ČSAV (CSc., 1960). After the Warsaw Pact invasion of Czechoslovakia in August 1968, Sviták chose to emigrate, first to New York and in 1970 to Chico, California, where he was offered an academic position. Sviták worked at California State Univ., Chico until 1990, when he returned to Czechoslovakia after the end of Communist Party's rule.

Vincent Anthony Tomas (1916-1995), b. Cicero, IL, of Czech ancestry, received his Bachelor's degree from Knox College in 1936 and a Doctorate from Brown in 1941. He was a member of Phi Beta Kappa. During World War II, he served in the European Theater with the 11th

Armored Division and earned the Silver Star and service ribbons. Tomas joined the Brown faculty in 1946 where he remained until his retirement in 1980. He also served as a visiting professor at Dartmouth, Yale, Harvard, Northwestern, Minnesota and Calgary universities. He was a Guggenheim Fellow in Rome in 1959-60. In 1972, he was one of two Brown professors selected by the Board of Foreign Scholarships to teach American literature at the American University of Beirut in Lebanon. As a founding member of the American civilization program at Brown, Tomas also served as chairman of the philosophy department, in addition to serving on other University committees. He was a member and officer of the American Association of University Professors, the American Philosophical Association, the American Society for Aesthetics and the American Civil Liberties Union.

Peter Trnka (1964–), b. Prague, Czech., was educated in England, where the family moved in 1968, and the U.S., where he received his B.A. in philosophy and English from the University of Toronto in 1985, M.A. in Philosophy in 1987, and Ph.D., also in philosophy in 1993. He held research and teaching positions at Univ. of Prince Edward Island and York Univ. before receiving a tenured position at Memorial Univ. of Newfoundland (s. 1995). He was also a visiting researcher at Charles Univ. in Prague. Currently he is an associate professor of philosophy and coordinator of the Diploma in Applied Ethics. He published articles on radical politics, David Hume, and Gilles Deleuze. His book *The Best of Czech Cooking*, first published 1997, is now in an expanded second edition and still in print. Peter Trnka is currently writing a book on philosophy and food.

Ernst Tugendhat (1930-2023), b. Brno, Czech., of Jewish family, is a philosopher. In 1938, the family emigrated from Czechoslovakia to St. Gallen, Switzerland, and in 1941, travelled on to settle in Caracas, Venezuela. Tugendhat studied classics at Stanford from 1944 to 1949 and went on to do graduate work in philosophy and classics at the University of Freiburg, receiving his Doctorate with a work on Aristotle in 1956. During the years 1956-58, he did post-doctoral research at the University of Münster. From then until 1964, he was an assistant professor in the Department of Philosophy at the University of Tübingen, where, after spending 1965 lecturing at the University of Michigan in Ann Arbor, he gained his Habilitation in 1966 analyzing the concept of truth in Edmund Husserl and Martin Heidegger. Tugendhat became a professor at the University of Heidelberg (1966-1975), but as a protest against the situation at German universities in the 1970s, he gave up his position and moved to Chile, and later to Berlin, becoming an emeritus professor of philosophy at the Free University of Berlin. Tugendhat retired in 1992 but was a visiting professor in philosophy at the Pontificia Universidad Católica de Chile, Santiago (1992-96), a researcher at the Institute for Human Sciences, Vienna (1996), and visiting professor at Charles University in Prague (1997-98).

William 'Bill' Vitek (1957–), b. Schenectady, NY, of Bohemian ancestry, received a BA degree in philosophy from Union College in 1979 and MA and Ph.D. degrees in philosophy from the City University of New York in 1985 and 1989. He is currently professor of philosophy and chair of the Department of Humanities and Social Sciences at Clarkson University in Potsdam, New York, where he has taught for twenty-seven years. He is an environmental philosopher. His current research focus is on the substantial cultural and social changes that will be necessary - in our lifetimes - to live without easy access to cheap, carbon-based energy in the form of soils, forests, oil, natural gas and coal. He is the author of *Promising* and the co-editor of *Applying Philosophy*; and co-editor with Wes Jackson of *Rooted in the Land: Essays on Community and Place*; and *The Virtues of Ignorance: Complexity, Sustainability and the Limits of Knowledge*. He is currently writing a book titled *The Perennial Imagination*. Vitek was W. Ford Schumann Professor in Democratic Studies at Williams College in 2010–2011. He co-founded and directed Clarkson University's Environmental Science & Policy Program and served as Associate Director of Clarkson's Center for the Environment. He directed Clarkson's Campus Sustainability Initiative in 2001–2002.

Mark C. Vopat (1971–), b. Cleveland, OH, of Czech ancestry, studied philosophy at Cleveland State Univ. (B.S., 1994; M.A., 1996) and at Univ. of Western Ontario (Ph.D., 2003). He is associated with Youngstown State Univ. (YSU), as asst. professor of philosophy (2007–12), as assoc. professor (s. 2012). In addition, he is a senior lecturer at Univ. of Akron (s. 2002). He regularly teaches courses in logic, professional ethics and general ethics along with seminars in Children's Rights. His research interests include: Children's Rights, Social and Political Philosophy, Ethics, and Applied Ethics. He has presented papers at conferences across the United States as well as in the United Kingdom and Switzerland. He authored the book *Children's Rights and Moral Parenting* (2014).

Rev. Alois Vyoral (1920–1998), b. Komárov, near Napajedla, Moravia, joined Salesian Order and was ordained as R. C. priest. He studied theology at the Papal Univ. of the Salesians in Turin, Italy. He was sent to the missions in Mexico, where he was active from 1950 to 1965, as professor of philosophy. In 1965, on account of his bad health, he was then transferred to the State of New York, where he cared for Czech immigrants and refugees.

Vladimír Zeman (1937–2014), b. Brno, studied philosophy at Charles Univ. (dipl. 1960; CSc./Ph.D., 1967), with additional training in Austria and in Germany. Zeman began at Sir George Williams Univ., one of Concordia Univ.'s founding institutions, as a visiting professor in 1968. A year later, he was appointed asst. professor in the dept. of philosophy (1969–71), advancing to assoc. professor (1971–2002), and full professor (s. 2002). He also served as department chair (1971–1974), assistant dean (1979–1983) and acting department chair (1999–2000, 2008), and was co-director of the University Centre for

System Theory and Knowledge Engineering. He also served on a number of department and university committees throughout his career. He was instrumental in developing the department's graduate MA program and supervised numerous M.A. and Ph.D. theses. Zeman was well known among students and remembered for his courses on Kant, and also taught courses on philosophy of science, 19th century philosophy, Habermas and many other topics. At Concordia, he was a pioneer in thinking about technology and the environment, and teaching courses on this topic. He was expert in the history and philosophy of science, from the perspective of 20th century continental philosophy, particularly neo-Kantianism, and lectured abroad in the Czech Republic, Germany and Switzerland. He was a member of the Canadian Philosophy Association, Kant Society of North America, Leibniz Society, International Institute for System Theory and Cybernetics, and North American Fichte Society.

C. Languages and Literature

1. Classical Languages

Herbert Bloch (1911-2006), b. Berlin, Germany, of Bohemian ancestry, is a specialist on Greek and Latin. He attended Univ. of Rome. In 1939 emigrated to US. He was with the dept. of classics, Harvard Univ. (s. 1941), as assoc. professor (s. 1947), as professor of Greek and Latin (s. 1953), as Pope Professor of Latin Language and Literature (s. 1973). He was also a member of Institute for Advanced Study, Princeton (1953-54) and a member of the Board of Scholars, Dumbarton Oaks (1953-59). He contributed to classical and medieval scholarship, focusing on Latin epigraphy, especially on Roman brick stamps and their bearing in the chronology of buildings and the involvement of the Roman upper class in the brick industry.

Peter Burian (1943-), b. Hanover, NH, of Czech ancestry, graduated from Univ. of Michigan, Ann Arbor, majoring in classical studies (B.A., 1964). He then continued his studies at Princeton Univ. (M.A., 1968; Ph.D., 1971). He has been associated with Duke Univ. as instructor (1968-71) and asst. professor in the dept. of classical studies (1971-77), as assoc. professor (1977-96), as full Professor (s. 1996), as professor of theater studies (s. 2001), as chair of classical studies (2003-07), as professor emeritus (s. 2015). He was also visiting professor at Dartmouth College (1989) and professor in charge at the Intercollegiate Center for Classical Studies in Rome (2009-10, 2013-14), as well as a fellow of the Center of Hellenic Studies, Washington, DC (1980-81) and senior associate of King's College, Univ. of Cambridge, UK (2003). He specializes in dramatic literature, theater history, and literary and cultural criticism. His research interests are in the area of Greek literature, particularly drama; theory and practice of literary translation; reception of Greco-Roman antiquity in later thought and arts. He is the author of *Euripides, Helen* (2007), *Aeschylus, The Oresteia*

(2003), *Aeschylus, The Suppliants* (1991), *Aristophanes, Birds* (1991), *Euripides, The Phoenician Women* (1981). He also edited a number of monographs and edited the complete *Oxford Greek Tragedy in New Translations*.

Albert Miloslav Gessman (1916–1988), b. Vienna, of Czech ancestry, was educated at Charles Univ. (Abs., 1939) and at Rudolf Univ. in Vienna (Dr. phil., 1950). He was prof. of classics and ancient studies, Univ. of South Florida, Tampa (s. 1967), as dept. chair (s. 1961), as coordinator of ancient studies (s. 1975). He specialized in ancient studies, linguistics, religion and history of Near East. He was the author of *The Codes of Language* (1959, 1974), *The Tongue of the Romans* (1970); *The Tongues of the Bible* (1971); *The Gift from Thoth* (1975). He was also editor and publisher of *University of South Florida Language Quarterly* (1962).

Clement Lewis Hrdlicka (1896–1945), b. Wahoo, NE, of Czech ancestry, a R.C. priest, O.S.B., received his classical language training at Univ. Illinois and Catholic Univ. of America. He was prof. of Latin, Greek, and ancient history at St. Procopius College, Lisle, IL (1929–40). He was the author of *A Study of the Late Latin Vocabulary and the Prepositions and Demonstrative Pronouns in the Confession of St. Augustine*.

Jerry Lewis Kasparek (1939–), b. Sulphur, OK, is a classicist and an educator. He is a graduate of University of Oklahoma (B.A. in Letters), who then pursued studies in comparative languages and literature, classic and classical languages and linguistics at Vanderbilt University (Ph.D.). He has been with Ball State University, Muncie, IN, as associate professor of classical languages and comparative literature (s. 1971), as a chair of the department of foreign languages (s. 1973). He became director of the University's London Center. He authored *Molière's Tartuffe and the Traditions of Roman Satire* (1977). Since 1985, he has been the owner the Academic Consulting and Educational Services (ACES), in Charlotte, North Carolina area, helping students at the high-school level improve their scores on standardized test in ways that will maximize their potential to matriculate to colleges and universities at the competitive to most competitive levels.

Rev. Basil Charles Kolar (1899–1982), b. Chicago, IL of Czech ancestry, O.S.B., received his classical language training at St. Procopius College. He was with Illinois Benedictine College (s. 1925), as prof. of Greek, Latin and ancient history (s. 1956), as a head, dept. of Greek and Latin (1956–69).

Elemer Joseph Nagy (1916–2010), b. Oros, Slovakia; professor of classics, California State University, Fresno (s. 1969). He was president of Classical Association of the Pacific States.

Charles Frederick Pazdernik (1968–), Breckenridge, MN, of Czech ancestry, studied at Cornell University, earning the B.A. in Classics (1990); the University of Oxford, earning the

M.Phil. in Byzantine studies (1992); and Princeton University, earning the M.A. and Ph.D. in Classics (1995, 1997). He has held the Samuel I. Golieb Fellowship in Legal History at New York University School of Law (1997–98), a Mellon Fellowship in ancient Greek and Roman law at Emory University (1998–2000), and a junior research fellowship at Harvard University's Center for Hellenic Studies in Washington, DC (2005–06). He has taught at Brooklyn College, CUNY (1998), Emory University (1998–2000), and Trinity School in New York, NY (2000–2001). He joined the faculty of Grand Valley State University (GVSU), Allendale, MI in 2001, at the rank of assistant professor, subsequently associate professor (2005) and professor (2013) and chair of Dept. of Classics. He served as a Board member (1987–2014) and president (2000–2002) of Telluride Association, Inc., an educational nonprofit organization. His work focuses on the political and legal history of late antiquity, especially in the sixth century CE, and on classical and classicizing historiography, including contributions to *The Cambridge Companion to the Age of Justinian* (2005), the forthcoming *Code of Justinian: A New Annotated Translation*, and the forthcoming *Cambridge World History*.

Donald Miles Poduska (1934–), b. Chicago, IL, of Czech ancestry, received his classical language training at Ohio State Univ. (Ph.D., 1963). He was with John Carroll Univ. (s. 1960), as prof. of classical languages (s. 1973). He is a specialist of Roman comedy, Roman historians, and Virgil.

Robert John Sklenar (1963–), b. Detroit, MI, of Czech father, studied classics at Princeton University (M.A., 1988) and at University of Michigan (Ph.D., 1996). He also holds a law degree from University of Michigan (J.D., 1991). He first taught classics as a visiting professor at Swarthmore College (1997–2000, 2001–02), University of Michigan (2000–01) and Tulane University (2002–03), before joining University of Tennessee, Knoxville. There he advanced from assistant professor (2003–09) to associate professor (s. 2009) and finally Professor and Associate Head of the Department of Classics. His primary research interest is Latin poetry of the early imperial period (Augustus through Nero). He authored a book *The Taste of Nothingness: A Study of Virtus and Related Themes in Lucan's Bellum Civile* (2003).

Robert Jaroslav Smutny (1919–2008), b. New York City, of Czech ancestry, studied at College of the City of New York (A.B., 1940) and Columbia University (M.A., 1948) and received his classical language training at Univ. of California (Ph.D., 1953). He was with Univ. of New Mexico (1953–55); with Univ. of Pacific (s. 1955), as prof. of classics (s. 1959), as dept. chair (s. 1955). He was a specialist on classical literature, text history and criticism, Latin epigraphy. He authored *The Text History of the Epigrams of Theocritus* (2015). He was president of Classical Association of the Pacific States.

2. English Language

Rev. John F. Abbick (1911-1974), b. Kansas City, KS, of Slovak descent, R.C. priest, joined the Society of Jesus in 1931 and received a Master's Degree in English in 1939 from St. Louis University. In 1967, Father Abbick received a Ph.D. in English from the University of North Carolina at Chapel Hill. He was an English professor at Marquette University in Milwaukee for 20 years before joining the English department at Rockhurst College in 1969. Father Abbick was a member of the Modern Language Association and a member of the Conference on Christianity and Letters and the Gerard Manley Hopkins International Association.

Abraham Albert Avni (1921-1995), b. Brno, Czech., was professor of English and comparative literature, California State University at Long Beach (CSULB), whose teaching career spanned three decades in that University. His focus was romanticism. His classes included English Romanticism, Literary Criticism, Literature for Adolescents, Survey of Comparative English Literature, and Bible in English. Avni's educational endeavors took him to the Hebrew University in Jerusalem, where he earned three Master's degrees, one in literature, another in philosophy and the third in Hebrew. He was graduated in 1964 with a Doctorate in comparative literature from the University of Wisconsin. Besides his teaching career, Avni was a member of the Modern Language Association and acted as secretary to the Minister of Education in Jerusalem in the 1950s.

Herschel Clay Baker (1914-1990), b. Cleburne, TX, desc. f. Augustine Heřman, was an American professor of English literature, specializing in the intellectual history of Christian humanism and its erosion. He did his undergraduate work at Southern Methodist University and received a Ph.D. from Harvard in 1939. He taught at the University of Texas for seven years (1939-46), before joining the Harvard faculty in 1946, becoming full professor of English (s. 1956) and dept. chair (s. 1952). He was a specialist on intellectual history, Renaissance literature, and English stage history. Baker's 1947 book *The Dignity of Man* is a series of chronological studies tracing the development of Christian humanism until the Reformation.

Michael William Bartos (1930-1990), b. Chicago, IL, taught English at William Rainey Harper College in Palatine. He earned a Bachelor's degree from De Paul University, a Master's from Northwestern University and a Doctorate from Nova University in Florida. He had been a professor at Harper College for 22 years, as associate professor of English (1967-80) and as professor (s. 1980). He is specialist on English literature.

Barry Arnold Bauska (1945-), b. Shreveport, LA, was educated at Occidental College in Los Angeles and at Univ. of Washington. He served as asst. prof. of English, Univ. of

Puget Sound (1971–76), as assoc. prof. (s. 1976), as dept. chair (s. 1981). He is a specialist on American literature and creative writing. He co-founded the University's Creative Writing and Freshman Orientation programs. He was also a poet.

Donald Bedichek (1962–), b. Texas, of Bohemian ancestry, studied English and writing at Abilene Christian University (B.A., 1984). Initially, he was self-employed, teaching junior-level composition. Subsequently, he held the position of professor of English at the University of Texas, El Paso, TX (1996–2002), in addition to working as a Nonprofit Grant Writer for the Professional Writing Association of Abilene (1998–2002). Since then, he has been self-employed as a Tutor in Humanities, having his own company, Bedichek Writing Company and Educational Consultants (s. 2011).

Phillip Edward Bozek (1948–), b. Chicago, IL, studied English language and literature at St. Procopius Coll. (B.A., 1970) and Southern Illinois Univ., Carbondale (M.A., 1972). He got his Doctorate also at the latter University, majoring in English and Linguistics (Ph.D., 1979). He started his career at Illinois Benedictine College as Assistant Professor of English (1974–82), following which he taught literature and communications at California State College (1982–84). Subsequently, he became Senior Consultant with Shipley Associates at the Greater Salt Lake City Area (1984–90), and then Director of Curriculum Development at Franklin Institute (1989–90). Since then, he has been over 30 years, with communication Designs and Training Programs, which he founded and of which he has been President (s. 1990).

Robert Warren Burda (1932–2010), b. Chicago, IL, of Czech ancestry, studied history and English at Union Theol. Sem. and San Francisco State Coll. He was assoc. professor of English, Illinois Wesleyan Univ., Bloomington, IL. Before joining University of Maryland Division, where he has regularly taught a seminar about Ernest Hemingway, R. W. Burda, was chairman of the Department of English and coordinator of international studies at Illinois Wesleyan University. There he was named both Teacher and Fine Arts Person of the Year. In the late 1950s, he was associate pastor of the Congregational Church in Lansing, Mich.; in Eagle River, Wis.; and in the late 1950s in Paradox, CO.

John O. Cech (1944–), b. Chicago, IL, of Czech ancestry, grew up in the Chicago area, and went to the University of Illinois, graduating with honors and a degree in English and American Literature in 1966. He received a Ph.D. in English and American literature from the University of Connecticut in 1974. He has taught at Northeastern University in Boston (1972–76) and has been on the faculty of the University of Florida in Gainesville (s. 1976), where he is the Director of the Center for Children's Literature and Culture. John has written 14 books for young people, a novel for adults, three scholarly books and hundreds of critical essays, reviews, and feature articles for such publications as *The Christian Science Monitor*, *The*

New York Times Book Review, USA Today, The Hornbook Magazine, Child, Muse, and *Parabola*. From 2001 to 2009, John was the creator, producer, and host of the public radio program, *Recess*, which was distributed to public radio stations across the country. John is the recipient of numerous grants and awards for his scholarship and teaching - most recently, the Anne Devereaux Jordan Award for his lifetime contributions to the field of children's literature. John is married to Eve Belevtsov Cech and currently lives in Gainesville, FL.

Pavel Cenkl (1971–), b. Newton, Massachusetts, studied English at Brandeis Univ. (B.A., 1992), at the Univ. of New Hampshire (M.A., 1994), and at Northeastern Univ. (Ph.D., 2003). He has been associated with Sterling College, Craftsbury Common, VT, as professor of humanities and regional studies (2006–11), as Dean of the College (2007–2014), and as Professor of Environmental Humanities and Curriculum and Instructional Design Specialist (s. 2014). Since 2019, he has been the Head of Schumacher College, Totnes, Devon, UK. Cenkl is most interested in, on one hand, how literature has and continues to shape place, and, on the other hand, how ecosystems, topography, and bioregions can have profound and lasting effects on cultural identity. For more than twenty years, he has been able to share a passion for place, the humanities, ecological thinking, and appropriate technologies by teaching courses from literature of the Northeast and the politics of place and identity to adventure literature to field courses in Iceland and rock and ice climbing. In addition to a number of journal articles and book chapters on regional and environmental literature and place, he is also the author of *This Vast Book of Nature: Reading the Landscape of New Hampshire's White Mountains, 1785-1911* (2006) and editor of *Nature and Culture in the Northern Forest: Region, Heritage, and Environment in the Rural Northeast* (2010).

George Robert Cerveny (1902–1988), b. Idaho, was a University of Idaho graduate who taught in the English Department from 1930–1933 and again from 1935–1936. He also taught at New York University and Long Beach University in California., where he held the position of professor emeritus. He was an English philologist. He is the author of *Mark the Winds Power* (1983), a novel based on the lake country of Northern Idaho.

Lída Dutková Cope (1965–), b. Přerov, Czech., received training at Palacký Univ., and at Univ. of Arizona. She currently holds the position of assoc. professor at East Carolina Univ. Her research interests include child bilingualism, language contact and first language attrition, community language loss, language and ethnic identity, and cross-cultural communication. She has published on child first language attrition and on the issues of language, culture and identity in Czech Moravian communities in Texas.

Sandra Lee Maresh Doe (1940–), b. Oklahoma City, of Czech ancestry, graduated with a major in English from Doane College, Crete, NE in 1963 and completed her Master's degree at the University of Denver, in 1967 in English. She joined the faculty at Metropolitan State College in 1966, which was now renamed to Metropolitan State University of Denver (MSU). The MSU Denver awarded her an Outstanding Service Award in 1997-98. She commuted to the University of Northern Colorado to attain her Doctoral degree in rhetoric and composition in 1983. She has served as professor of English at MSU Denver for over thirty years, as full professor (s. 1992), teaching poetry writing workshops, nature writing, travel writing, and freshman composition. She writes poems about the Czech-American experience. She studied "Music and Travel in Europe and the Americas, 1500-1800" at the Newberry Library in Chicago, Illinois in 2013, having been awarded an NEH/Newberry grant to be a summer scholar.

Agnes McNeill Donohue (1917-2003), b. Sheboygan Co., WI, of Bohemian ancestry; daughter of Luella R. Weinberger McNeill. With a Doctorate from University of Chicago, she taught English and American Literature for more than 50 years, retiring in 1988. She taught at Barat College from 1942 to 1965 and was on the graduate faculty at the University of Illinois at Chicago from 1946 to 1954. She then taught at Loyola University Chicago from 1965 to 1988 and at Northeastern Illinois University from 1990 to 1994. An eminent Nathaniel Hawthorne scholar, Mrs. Donohue was the author of *Hawthorne: Calvin's Ironic Stepchild* and editor of casebooks on Hawthorne and John Steinbeck. In addition, she wrote many articles on a wide range of literary topics.

Nataša Durovičová (1954-), b. Bratislava, Czech.; editor, International Writing Program, University of Iowa, Iowa City. She divides her time between editing, teaching, scholarly work, and translating. She is the editor of IWP's imprint 91st Meridian Books at Autumn Hill Books, and the program's journal *91st Meridian*. She has also co-edited *World Cinemas, Transnational Perspectives* (2010; the winner of SCMS's 2011 Best Edited Collection award) and the essay collection *At Translation's Edge* (2019).

Doris Leonora Eder (1936-), b. Teplice, Czech., studied English at Hunter. She was with Ohio State Univ. (1966-70); with Univ. of Rochester, where she advanced from asst. prof. to assoc. prof. of English (1970-77); dean fac., Schenectady Co. Community Coll. (1977-78); dean, Keene State Coll. (1978-82); dean, School of Arts and Sciences, Univ. New Mexico (s. 1982). She is a specialist on modern and contemporary American, British and European literatures.

Sigmund Eisner (1920-2012), b. Red Bank, NJ, of Bohemian ancestry, studied English at Univ. of Arizona and Columbia Univ. (Ph.D., 1955). Eisner taught at Oregon State University (1954-58) and Dominican College (1960-66) before returning in 1966 to the University of Arizona, where he taught for over forty years, as prof. of English (s. 1967).

He was a noted expert on Geoffrey Chaucer. He enrolled at the University of Arizona in 1939 but joined the Army after World War II. He graduated from the University of California at Berkeley in 1947 and received his Ph.D. from Columbia University in 1955, then was a Fulbright Scholar in Ireland. Eisner taught at Oregon State University and Dominican College before returning to the University of Arizona, where he taught for over forty years. He died on December 18, 2012.

Anna Katherine Froula (1974–), b. Boulder, CO, of Czech ancestry, moved with her family to Knoxville, Tennessee, where she played varsity basketball, softball, and volleyball for Farragut High School. After graduating in 1993, she won the McWane Honors Scholarship and majored in English and minored in biology at Birmingham-Southern College in Alabama. After visiting Prague in 1997, she spent some time in the non-profit sector, working for Appalachia Service Project, Inc. in Johnson City, Tennessee, and running a welfare-to-work program in Maysville, Kentucky before returning to graduate school and earning an M.A. and Ph.D. in English at the University of Kentucky in 2007. She currently resides in Greenville, North Carolina, where she is an associate professor of film studies at East Carolina University and associate editor of *Cinema Journal*, with her husband Sean Morris, who teaches English at ECU. She has published several journal articles and book chapters on war, gender, trauma, and zombies and is co-editor of *Reframing 9/11: Film, Popular Culture*, and the *War on Terror* (2010) and *It's a Mad World: The Cinema of Terry Gilliam*.

Christine Froula (1950–), b. Louisville, MS, of Czech ancestry, attended Vanderbilt University (1967–68), University of Chicago (B.A. with Honors, 1971, M.A. with honors, 1972; Ph. D., English, with Honors, 1977). She was associated with University of Alabama (1977–78), before joining Yale Univ., as asst. professor of English (1977–78), as assoc. professor (1978–83). Subsequently, she moved to Northwestern Univ. as associate professor of English (1983–86), becoming associate professor of English and comparative literature and theory (1987–91), and professor of English, comparative literature, and gender studies (s. 1991). Her research interests are in the area the 20th- and 21st-century literature, art, culture, science, technology, and theory; interdisciplinary, international, and transnational modernism and modernity; women's literature and feminist theory; English poetry, poetics, and translation; textual scholarship and genetic criticism; law and literature; the Bloomsbury Group; the art of the short story; modern drama. Her publications include: *Virginia Woolf and the Bloomsbury Avant-Garde: War, Civilization, Modernity* (2005), *Modernism's Body: Sex, Culture, and Joyce* (1996), *To Write Paradise: Style and Error in Ezra Pound's Cantos* (1984); *A Guide to Ezra Pound's Selected Poems* (1983); libretto for composer John Austin's *Heloise and Abelard: Lyric Drama in Two Acts* (2012).

Alexander Gelley (1933–), b. Czech., studied English at Harvard (B.A.) and at Yale Univ. (Ph.D., 1965). He was with Cornell Univ. (s. 1967), as asst. prof. of comparative literature (1969–71); as assoc. prof. of comparative literature, Univ. of California, Irvine, CA (s. 1971), later full professor. His research interests are in the area of 18th century English and comparative literature, 19th century English and comparative literature, romanticism, contemporary theory, literature and philosophy; German-Jewish literature and culture

Peter Gibian (1952–), b. Northampton, MA, of Czech ancestry, studied English at Yale (B.A.), New York Univ. (M.A.) and Stanford (Ph.D.). He is director, Graduate Studies and associate professor of American literature, Dept. of English, McGill Univ. He is a specialist on American literature and culture before 1900, especially the 'American Renaissance,' American mass culture of the 19th and 20th centuries.

Richard L. Hanzelka (1939–), b. Belle Plaine, IA, of Czech ancestry, studied English-education with minors in administration and reading at the University of Iowa (Ph.D., 1974). He is professor of education (secondary education), in the School of Education, St. Ambrose Univ., Davenport, IA (s. 2001). Formerly secondary teacher (1961-1964) in Cedar Rapids, Iowa; assistant professor (1964-69) at State University of New York at New Paltz; consultant and director of general education (1969-99) in Bettendorf, Iowa; professor and Education Department chair at Marycrest International University (1999-2001), Davenport, Iowa. He is former president of ASCD (2006-2007) and member of the ASCD Board (2001-2009). ASCD is an education association of 175,000 members in 135 countries. Extensive ASCD travel to schools: China, India, Austria, Slovenia, Australia, New Zealand, Czech Republic, Puerto Rico, Russia, Finland. His areas of professional interest are secondary curriculum, school change, whole child education, international education and writing across the curriculum. He specializes in the uses of writing for learning by teaching in National Writing Project institutes since 1978. Focus is on building the confidence of K-12 teachers in their own abilities as writers so that they will use writing as a tool for learning for themselves and for their students.

Lloyd John Hubenka (1931-1982), b. Omaha, NE, of Czech ancestry, was a literary scholar, specializing in English. He attended Creighton University (B.A., 1952; M.A., 1952) and University of Nebraska (Ph.D., 1966). He was with Creighton Univ. (s. 1958), as prof. of English (s. 1968), as dept. chair (s. 1966); president of Harcum Jr. College. He was a co-author of *The Design of Drama* (1973), *The Narrative Sensibility* (1975); editor of John Ruskin's *Unto This Last* (1968).

Del Ivan Janik (1945-2013), b. Berwyn, IL, of Czech parents, studied English at Northwestern Univ. (B.A., 1966; Ph.D., 1971) and University of Michigan (M.A., 1967). He was an English professor at SUNY Cortland for 35 years (s. 1975), becoming full professor of English (s. 1979), earning the rank of professor emeritus before moving to Long Island and becoming an adjunct professor at Farmingdale State College in 2006. He was Fulbright exchange professor at Polytechnic of North London (1983–84). He is a specialist of English and American literature. He was the author and editor of several books, including *The Curve of Return: D.H. Lawrence's Travel Books* and *Modern British Women Writers: An A to Z Guide*, which he co-wrote with his wife.

Philip C. Kolin (1945–), b. Chicago, IL, of Czech ancestry, has taught in the Department of English at the University of Southern Mississippi since 1974 and in the fall of 2010 was made the Distinguished Professor in the College of Arts and Letters. In 2006, he won the Innovation Award in Applied Research, and was the first Charles W. Moorman Alumni Distinguished Professor in the Humanities from 1991–1993. Kolin has published 40 books and over 200 scholarly articles on Shakespeare, modern American and African American drama and business writing. Regarded as an international authority on Tennessee Williams, Kolin published *The Tennessee Williams Encyclopedia*, which debuted at the Kennedy Center, and books on *A Streetcar Named Desire*, Williams' late plays, and his influence on contemporary American playwrights. Kolin has also served as a guest editor for several journals. In 2012, Cengage/Wadsworth released the 10th Edition of his widely respected *Successful Writing at Work*. Further, Kolin is the general editor for the *Routledge Shakespeare Criticism Series*. His most recent books are *Suzan-Lori Parks: Essays on the Plays and Other Works* (2010), which was designated an 'Editors' Choice' by *Yale Theater*, and *Suzan-Lori Parks: In Person. Interview, Speeches, and Addresses* (with Harvey Young). A poet as well, Kolin has published four books of poems, including *Deep Wonder*, which won an award from the Catholic Press Association, and, most recently, *A Parable of Women: Poems*. He has also coedited the anthology *Hurricane Blues: Poems about Katrina and Rita*. Kolin is the founding editor of *Vineyards: A Journal of Christian Poetry*.

David L. Kubal (1936–1982), b. Cleveland, OH, of Bohemian ancestry, was raised in Chicago, and studied English at Univ. of Notre Dame (B.A., 1958; M.A., 1960; Ph.D., 1968). After teaching at Michigan State University, he came to California State Univ., Los Angeles, where he advanced from asst. professor to assoc. professor (1968–77) and full professor (1977–82). In 1972, Prof. Kubal published *Outside the Whale: George Orwell's Art and Politics*. He then devoted himself to graduate program in English, and from his efforts to strengthen and formalize the postgraduate teaching of literature, he was inspired to read and think with increasing depth and breadth in the entire Western literary tradition. This resulted in his teaching a series of seminars on the nineteenth-century novel and Victorian culture, and in his publishing articles in journals such as *The Yale Review* and *The Kenyon Review*. The thought and writing of these years culminated in *The Consoling*

Intelligence: Responses to Literary Modernism, a collection of essays published posthumously in 1982.

Julius Victor Kuchynka (1884–d.), b. Chicago, IL, of Czech ancestry, studied English at Univ. of Chicago. He first taught at the Astoria HS, Astoria, IL and then in the English department of the Iowa State Univ. Subsequently, he was appointed to the chair of prof. of English at Loyola Univ. where he served for over 20 years.

Benjamin Putnam Kuntz (1878–1950), b. Maui, Hawaii, desc. f. Augustine Heřman, studied English at Univ. of California, he was with Univ. of California (s. 1903), as prof. of English (1919–49). He was a specialist on criticism, poetry and Middle English literature. He was awarded gold medal by Commonwealth Club of San Francisco (1934).

Louis A. Landa (1901–1989), b. Hallettsville, TX, of Bohemian ancestry, graduated from the University of Texas (A.B., 1923) and earned a Master's degree from Columbia University (1926) and a Doctorate in English from the University of Chicago (1941), where he taught before going to Princeton in 1946. There he advanced from assoc. professor of English to full professor (1946–70), retiring in 1970. Professor Landa was an authority on Jonathan Swift and wrote and edited several books on the 18th-century English writer. He also edited *Essays in English Literature of the Eighteenth Century*, published in 1980 by the Princeton University Press. For 10 years, Professor Landa was a member of the Editorial Board of Publications of the Modern Language Association. He was a fellow of the Royal Historical Society.

Bridget Gellert Lyons (1932–), b. Prague, Czech., studied English at Oxford Univ. and Columbia Univ. She was with Rutgers Univ., New Brunswick (s. 1965), as prof. of English (s. 1978). She is a specialist on 16th and 17th century Renaissance English literature, and on Shakespeare.

Gloria Ptacek McMillan (1948–), b. Chicago, IL, of Czech ancestry, received her Ph.D. in English from the University of Arizona, and an M.A. in literature from Indiana University. She is a Research Associate at the University of Arizona and teaches at Pima Community College in Tucson. She published a mystery *The Blue Maroon Murder* in 2011 (Anaphora) and edited a collection of essays *Orbiting Ray Bradbury's Mars* (McFarland, 2013). She is a co-founder of the Arizona Theatre Company's Old Pueblo Playwrights, a group which works closely with ATC in developing new playwrights and play scripts. Her plays have been produced in Tucson and in the Chicago area. Her play *Universe Symphony*, about modern composer Charles Ives, was jointly produced by the Flandrau Planetarium and the Music and Theater Departments of the University of Arizona. She is a contributor to a number of academic journals, including *Rhetoric Society Quarterly, Across the Disciplines,*

Kairos, The Adjunct Advocate, Extrapolation: MLA Journal of Science Fiction and Fantasy, and *Text Technology.*

Rev. Edward E. Mehok (1932–), b. Akron, OH, of Slovak descent, Rev., is R.C. priest, ordained in 1960. He was an English literature specialist, professor of English, Borromeo College, OH (1961–73), vice president and Dean of men (s. 1967).

Donald Melichar, possibly of Czech ancestry, studied at Univ. of Montana (B.A.; M.A.) and at Arizona State Univ. (Ph.D.). He holds the position of dept. chair and assoc. professor of English at Univ. of Central Missouri, Warrensburg. His interests are in the area of English literature, literature for adolescents and Chicano's literature.

Maximillian E. Novak (1930–), b. Bronx, NE, of Czech ancestry, studied at UCLA (B.A., 1952; M.A., 1954; Ph.D., 1958) and at St. John's, Oxon. (D.Phil., 1961). Both of his Doctorates were in English literature. He was associated with Univ. of Michigan (1958–62); and then with the dept. of English, of UCLA, as asst. professor (1962–66), as assoc. professor (1967–72), as full professor (1973–2001), as professor emeritus (s. 2001), as distinguished professor emeritus (s. 2004); as assoc. director, UCLA Center for Seventeenth and Eighteenth Century Studies (1987–90). His specialty within English Literature was the period from 1660–1800. He has published over 200 books, editions, essays, and reviews, including studies of Daniel Defoe, William Congreve, and general work on the eighteenth century. His three studies of *Defoe: Economics and the Fiction of Daniel Defoe* (1962); *Defoe and the Nature of Man* (1963), and *Realism, Myth, and History in Defoe's Fiction* (1983), have established him as one of the foremost interpreters of Defoe's fiction among modern critics. A recent book, a 756-page biography, *Daniel Defoe Master of Fictions* (2001) was selected as one of the best books of the year by *The Economist*. He also wrote about a number of Jewish-American writers: I.B. Singer, I.J. Singer and Philip Roth. He was president of Western Society for Eighteenth Century Studies (1985) and honorary president of Defoe Society (2008).

Marianne Novy (1945–), b. Cleveland, OH, of Czech ancestry, studied English at Harvard Univ. (A.M., 1967) and Yale Univ. (Ph.D., 1973). She has been associated with Pittsburgh Univ., as asst. professor of English (1973–77), as associate professor (1978–82), as professor (s. 1992), as director, Women's Studies Program (1994–96). She was one of the leaders in the growth of feminist Shakespeare criticism in the 1970s and 1980s. Subsequently, she was one of the first critics to discuss the history of literary representations of adoption, adoptees, and adoptive families, and author of the first book-length treatment of the subject in fiction and drama. She has taught a variety of courses over the years; the major areas have been Shakespeare, Renaissance literature, literature by women (up to the present) and the representation of adoption in literature. These are also the main areas of her research. She is the author of several books, including *Love's Argument: Gender Relations in Shakespeare* (1984), *Cross-Cultural Performances: Differences in Women's Re-Visions of Shakespeare* (1993), *Transforming Shakespeare: Contemporary Women's Re-Visions in Literature and Performance* (2000).

Alex R. Page (1923–), b. Košice, Czech., resided with his parents in Berlin, Germany (s. 1926). When the Nazi regime began persecuting Jews after 1933, Alex and his family moved to London, England in 1937. In 1940, the family moved to Cleveland, OH, in the US. In 1944, he joined the U.S. army and served in the Counter Intelligence Corps in Shanghai, China. With support of the GI bill, Alex graduated with a BA from the University of Vermont and then attended Harvard University, graduating with a Ph.D. in English in 1953. Alex taught at Rutgers University's Newark campus and then came to the University of Massachusetts Amherst in 1955 where he taught in English department for 33 years, retiring in 1987. Alex's area of scholarship was 18th century English literature, especially Jane Austen, the modern novel and comparative literature. Among his publications, Alex translated works by Barlach, Goethe and the Czech dissident Pavel Kohout from German. He also wrote several radio plays which were produced in the United States and United Kingdom, including *The Cancelled Sky* about his relatives' last train ride to Auschwitz.

Jennifer Panek (1969–), b. Toronto, Ont., Canada, of Czech ancestry, studied English literature at Dalhousie Univ. (M.A., 1993; Ph.D., 1999). She has been associated with Univ. of Ottawa, as asst. professor (2003–05), as assoc. professor (s. 2005). Her specialty and research interests are in the area of early modern English drama, and her research focuses on issues of gender and sexuality. She has published a fair amount of work on the English playwright Thomas Middleton (1580–1627). She authored *Widows and Suitors in Early Modern English Comedy* (2004), and *The Roaring Girl: A Norton Critical Edition* (2011).

Marjorie Perloff (née Gabriele Mintz) (1932–), b. Vienna, of Moravian ancestry; in US since 1938; a poetry scholar and critic. After completing her degrees at Catholic University, Perloff taught at the school from 1966–71. She then moved on to become professor of English at the University of Maryland, College Park (1971–76) and professor of English and comparative literature at the University of Southern California (1976–86) and then at Stanford University (1986–90). She then became Sadie Dernham Patek Professor of Humanities at Stanford (1990–2000), prof. emeriti (s. 2001). She is currently scholar-in-residence and Florence Scott Professor of English Emerita at the University of Southern California. A prominent literary critic, she is best known for her work on contemporary American poetry, and, in particular, poetry associated with the avant garde.

George Michael Pisk (1932-2012), b. Vienna, of Moravian parents, was professor of English. After graduating from the Webb School in Claremont, California, in 1949 and Yale University in 1953, he came to Texas, where his father, Dr. Paul A. Pisk, was a professor of musicology at the University of Texas. While finishing his doctoral dissertation on Renaissance English literature at U.T., he taught English and German. Thereafter, he taught English at Stephen F. Austin in Nacogdoches. Upon returning to Austin, where he lived the remainder of his life, he taught at Southwest Texas (now Texas State) in San Marcos.

Joseph 'Joe' Benjamin Plicka (1977–), b. Provo, Utah, raised in California, of Moravian ancestry, completed a double major in English and Latin American Studies at Brigham Young University in Provo, Utah (B.A., 2002). He also received a post-graduate degree in English from BYU-Provo (M.A., 2006). He earned his Doctorate in English Language and Literature at Ohio University in Athens, Ohio (Ph.D., 2011). His dissertation was a collection of short fiction ("Stories for the Mongrel Heart"), with an essay analyzing the inner workings of storytelling and arguing for the unique and powerful place that fictional discourse holds in human culture. While at Ohio University, Joe also spent two years as the editor of *Quarter After Eight*, a national literary journal, and served as an organizer of Ohio University's long-running Spring Literary Festival. He has taught introductory literature and composition classes, beginning and advanced creative writing workshops and courses on the form and theory of fiction. Currently, he is an assistant professor of English at Brigham Young University—Hawaii in Laie, Hawaii (2012–present). He has published short stories, essays, reviews, poems, and is at work on a novel. He also worked as a reporter and staff writer (2001-03) for *The Daily Republic* and The Davis Enterprise, two northern California newspapers.

Tim Prchal (1958–), b. Hinsdale, IL, of Czech ancestry, received a B.A. (1983) in Communications from Northern Illinois University, M.A. (1990) in English from Boston's Northeastern University, and Ph.D. (1998) in English at the University of Wisconsin, Milwaukee. He was associated with SUNY, Cortland (1990-91), Cardinal Stritch Univ. (1992-94), Univ. of Wisconsin (1994-2001) and Marquette Univ. (1998-2001), before assuming the present position of visiting asst. professor of American literature at Oklahoma State Univ. (s. 2001). Prchal's specialties are in American literature of the 19th and early 20th centuries, especially, immigration fiction from that period, as well as the histories of Gothic, Mystery, and Science Fiction. Among his several journal publications, he authored "The Bohemian Paradox: My Antonia and Popular Images of Czech Immigrants," which appears in *Multi-Ethnic Literature of the United States*, 29, No. 2 (Summer 2004). More works pertaining to Czech immigration are part of an anthology Prchal co-edited with Tony Trigilio, titled *Visions and*

Divisions: American Immigration Literature, 1870-1930 (2008). Using the pseudonym Tim Prasil, he writes prose fiction as well as audio and stage plays.

Miroslav Renský (1927-1982), b. Prague, Czech., studied English at Charles Univ. (PhDr., 1951) and ČSAV. He was a professor of English and linguistics at Graduate Center of the City Univ. of New York and Brooklyn Coll. (s. 1970).

Treadwell Ruml, 2nd (1952-), b. New York, NY, US, of Bohemian ancestry, is associated with California State Univ., San Bernardino, where he holds the position of professor of English. He graduated from the St. Thomas Choir School in New York, Phillips Exeter Academy and magna cum laude from Harvard University A.B., 1974). He received a J.D. degree from Harvard (1977) and a Doctorate in English from Univ. of Virginia (Ph.D., 1989). He specializes in the 18th century studies, historical and fictional narrative, the English Bible and literature myth and epic. His grandfather, the late Beardsley Ruml, was an economist who was the chairman of R. H. Macy & Co. and the author of the 'pay as you go' withholding tax plan adopted by Congress in 1943.

Jaroslav Schejbal (1922-), b. Prague, Czech., is Charles Univ. trained literary scholar. He has been assoc. prof. of American literature at Univ. of Illinois, Chicago Circle (s. 1968), and now emeritus. He is a specialist on American and European picaresque novel, grotesque in American and European novel, literature of American renaissance. He is the author of *Days and Nights of America* (1964), *The Genius of Ezra Pound*. He also translated Kundera's *Někde za* (1984) and Vaculík's *Feuilletons* (1985), etc.

Barbara Sebek (1964-), b. Hammond, IN, of Czech ancestry, studied English at Univ. of Illinois (M.A., 1989; Ph.D. with distinction, 1994). She was associated with St. Ambrose Univ., Davenport, IA (1994-95), before joining Colorado State Univ., Fort Collins, CO. Starting there as an asst. professor of English (1995-2001), she advanced to assoc. professor (2001-10) and then to full professor (s. 2010). Her courses deal with colonial and postcolonial literatures. Her scholarly publications concern gift and commodity exchange, women as economic agents, global trade, early globalization, and how these topics reverberate in Renaissance drama and early modern literature. She has published several essays and reviews on Shakespeare and other writers, and is the co-editor of the book, *Global Traffic: Discourses and Practices of Trade in English Literature and Culture, 1550-1700* (2008). She was a recipient of Houston Distinguished Visiting Scholar Award (2010) from the University of Houston and was the winner of Shakespeare Association of America Open Submission Competition (2009).

Patrick 'Pat' Sebranek (1946-) b. Madison, WI, of Czech ancestry, received his Bachelor's degree in 1968 and his Master's degree in 1971 in English education from the University of

Wisconsin, La Crosse. Sebranek taught writing and speaking at the high school level for 16 years, where he developed several courses aimed at helping students use the writing process more effectively. He co-founded Write Source in 1976, along with Dr. Verne Meyer, after co-authoring their first writing book, *Basic English Revisited*. That handbook soon became such a phenomenon that it drew the attention of Boston-based publisher D. C. Heath, who contracted the authors to create an entire line of books and support materials for kindergarten through high school. When D. C. Heath was in turn acquired by the Houghton Mifflin company, the new publishers created a division named Great Source, largely to manage the multimillion-dollar annual sales of Write Source books. Having completed the K-12 line in 1999, Write Source went on to create *The College Writer, The College Writer's Handbook*, and *The Business Writer for Cengage Learning*. In addition, Sebranek and his co-authors developed COMP: Read and COMP: Write for Cengage's 4LTR Press division. With 25 years of experience running their own business, the founders recognized that business writing has its own unique demands. In 2001, they established UpWrite Press as a sister company to Write Source, each a division of Sebranek Inc. UpWrite Press's very first product, *Write for Business*, immediately garnered awards from such organizations as the Chicago Book Clinic. All in all, the educational materials Sebranek and his co-authors produced have been used by over 100 million students in classrooms across the United States.

John Dana Simecek (1948–2016), of Czech ancestry, is English/Writing Teacher with writing, editing, publishing experience. He holds two double-major B.A.s, one from Wayne State University, the second, from Madonna University, which was in academic/professional writing and journalism/public relations. His double-focus M.A., from Eastern Michigan University, is in academic/professional writing and writing pedagogy. Having served the local university and community college as a professor of English composition for 15 years, he is now a full-time freelance editor. The name of his company is WordWeave Editorial. The boilerplate that describes himself and his company is: "professional, personalized, scholarly assistance in academic research, editing, style formatting, writing, and publication preparation exclusively for graduate scholars and academic professionals in the humanities, the social sciences, the arts, and education." He is a member of the National Coalition of Independent Scholars (NCIS) and is affiliated with the ALA's Association of College and Research Libraries, the Modern Language Association, the National Council of Teachers of English, the Editorial Freelancers Association, the Professional Editors Network, and the Freelancers Union. John is also on NCIS's short list of Manuscript Critique Servicers/Editors. He mostly edits and formats such works as Journal Articles, Anthology Chapters, Reviews, Conference Papers, and Comps & Dissertations for those not quite finished with Ph.D. work or who are back for another. For M.A. students, he edits Final Course Projects and Theses.

Patricia Lyn Skarda (1946–2014), b. Clovis, NM, of Czech ancestry, earned a Ph.D. from the University of Texas at Austin, where she also taught before coming to Smith, where she holds the position of professor. Professor Skarda has spent two years away from Smith as an American Council on Education Fellow in Academic Administration (1978–79) and as a distinguished visiting professor at the United States Air Force Academy (1992–93). Besides publishing in the Romantic period and co-editing *The Evil Image: Two Centuries of Gothic Short Fiction and Poetry* (1981) with Nora Crow, Professor Skarda has also published two collections of literature written by Smith alumnae (*Smith Voices: Selected Works by Smith College Alumnae*).

Peter Spielberg (1929–), b. Vienna, of Bohemian ancestry, studied English at NYU and at SUNY, Buffalo. He was with Brooklyn College (s. 1961), where he advanced from assist. to prof. of English (1966–78). He was a specialist on 20th century fiction with emphasis on James Joyce. Spielberg has been awarded fellowships in fiction by the New York Foundation for the Arts and by the National Endowment for the Arts. He is the author of several books, including *Twiddledum Twaddledum* (1974), *Noctambulists and Other Fictions* (2001), *Hearsay* (1992), *Crash Landing* (1985) and *The Hermetic Whore* (1977).

Mark Spilka (1925–2001), was educated at Brown University and, following service in the U.S. Army Air Corps from 1944 to 1946, graduating with the class of 1949. He pursued graduate studies at the University of Indiana, completing his Ph.D. in 1956. Between 1968 and 1973, Spilka served as chairman of the Brown University English department. He was named the Israel J. Kapstein Professor of English in 1990. He was director of the National Endowment for the Humanities summer seminar in 1974. He served as president of the Conference Editors of Learned Journals and the Modern Language Association in 1974–1975. His published works included critical studies of D.H. Lawrence, Ernest Hemingway, and Charles Dickens. He was also an editor of various books, as well as the periodical *Novel: A Forum on Fiction*. He was previously an editorial assistant at *American Mercury* and an assistant professor at the University of Michigan. He served as a visiting professor at the Graduate Institute of Modern Letters at the University of Tulsa, Hebrew University in Jerusalem, and Indiana University. He was named a Harry T. Moore distinguished D.H. Lawrence scholar, an Indiana School Letters fellow, a Guggenheim fellow, and a National Endowment for the Humanities fellow. He had been president of the Dickens Society and the American Association of University Professors.

Frederic Joseph Svoboda (1949–), b. Hastings, Nebraska, of Czech ancestry, studied English at Michigan State Univ. (B.A., 1971; M.A., 1973; Ph.D., 1978) and the publishing industry at Harvard University's prestigious Radcliffe course in publishing procedures. He was initially associated with Michigan State Univ. as asst. professor of American thought and language (1978–80). He then joined the Univ. of Michigan at the Flint campus, as asst. professor of English (1984–85), as assoc. professor (1985–97) and as full professor (s. 1997), as chair of English dept. (1997–2002, 2008–11). He teaches courses at introductory, intermediate and advanced levels, including multi-semester courses on the American novel and American film open to both advanced, undergraduate, and graduate students. He also has served two terms as a director and treasurer of the Ernest Hemingway Foundation, which sponsors a literary prize in honor of the author, organizes international conferences and currently is involved in publishing a complete edition of Hemingway's collected letters. He also is a past president and current vice-president of the Michigan Hemingway Society. He is the author or editor of several books. He is the author of *Hemingway and The Sun Also Rises: The Crafting of a Style* and the coeditor of *Hemingway: Up in Michigan Perspectives.* The most recent (2011), co-edited with Suzanne del Gizzo, collects twenty-five years of criticism of Hemingway's posthumously published novel *The Garden of Eden*. Current projects in progress include a book on American novelist John Updike for the University of South Carolina Press and a collection of essays on how to teach Ernest Hemingway's short stories for Kent State, as well as a novel set during the American Civil War.

Thomas E. Tausky (1942–), b. possibly of Czech ancestry, studied English at Yale Univ. He was assoc. professor of English, Univ. of Western Ontario, London, Canada. He has edited several books about Canadian writer Sara Jeanette Duncan: *Sara Jeanette Duncan: Selected Journalism* (1978), *Sara Jeannette Duncan: Novelist of Empire* (1980), and also *Sara Jeannette Duncan* (1988) in the *Canadian Writers and Their Works* series. He has also edited several of Duncan's books *The Simple Adventures of a Memsahib* and *The Imperialist*.

Laura Skandera Trombley (1960–), b. Los Angeles, of Czech ancestry, the daughter of an elementary school principal and a second-grade teacher, enrolled at Pepperdine University at the age of 16, receiving her B.A. in English and humanities (1981) and graduating summa cum laude with a Master's in English (1983). She earned her Ph.D. in English from the University of Southern California (1989), where she received the Virginia Barbara Middleton Scholarship and was named the Lester and Irene Finkelstein Fellow for Outstanding Humanities Graduate Student. Prior to joining Pitzer Coll., as its 5th President, Laura Trombley was Dean of the faculty and vice president for academic affairs (1997–2001) and a professor of English (1997–2002) at Coe College in Iowa. She joined SUNY Potsdam in 1990 and earned tenure in three years, becoming an associate professor of English (1997–2002) and holding several administrative posts. While working on her

Doctorate, she discovered the largest known cache of Mark Twain letters to date. Trombley is the author of five books. Her most recent, *Mark Twain's Other Woman: The Hidden Story of His Final Years,* was published by Knopf in 2010.

Keith Tuma (1957–), b. Akron, OH, of Czech ancestry, was educated at the University of Akron, and the University of Chicago, where he received his M.A. (1980) and Ph.D. (1987) in English Language and Literature. While pursuing his degrees at the University of Chicago, he taught at several universities in Chicago and Indiana and served in the early 1980s first as poetry editor and later as general editor of *Chicago Review*. After receiving his Ph.D. he taught, as visiting assistant professor, at Reed College in Portland, Oregon from 1987 to 1988. He has taught at Miami University in Oxford, Ohio, where he is professor of English, since 1988. He was chair of the Department of English from 2002 to 2007 and associate dean of the College of Arts and Science from 2008 to 2013. Since 2004, he has directed and edited the Miami University Press, which publishes poetry, fiction, and books about Miami University. From 2005 to 2010, he directed Meshworks, a video archive of poetry in performance, and, in 2006, he curated 'Imageworks/Wordworks,' an exhibit about poetry and art, for the Miami University Art Museum.

Rev. Leo C. Vancura (1910–1987), b. Vienna, of Czech ancestry, was a noted teacher of English literature and of Shakespeare. He came to the United States at the age of 3. He graduated from Harrison Technical High School in Chicago. Before starting college, he worked for American Multigraph Co. as its representative in Chicago and San Francisco. He was professed a monk, OSB, of St. Procopius Abbey in 1934, earned his undergraduate degree in philosophy at Illinois Benedictine in 1936, and was ordained a priest in 1940.

Kathleen Vejvoda (1967–), b. Boston, MA, of Czech-American father, received her B.A. in English from the University of Massachusetts at Boston in 1989 and her Ph.D. in English with a specialty in Victorian literature from the University of Texas at Austin in 2000. She has been associated with Bridgewater State Univ., as asst. professor of English (2002–10), and as assoc. professor (s. 2010). Professor Vejvoda's research interests include childhood studies, including representations of children and childhood in various national cinemas and in memoir; Irish cinema and folklore; Victorian literature, particularly George Eliot, the Brontës, and Dickens; religion and literature; and the ghost story. She has published articles on Victorian fiction and poetry, Irish folklore, and Irish cinema in peer-reviewed journals including *Victorian Literature and Culture* and *Irish Studies Review*. She has essays on Irish cinema in *Screening Irish-America* (ed. Ruth Barton, 2009) and in a collection currently under contract with Palgrave Macmillan (ed. Barry Monahan). As Kathleen Chaplin, her poetry has appeared in *Irish Feminist Review* and *Southword*. Excerpts from her memoir-in-progress have been published in *New England Review* and NER Digital.

René Wellek (1903-1995), b. Vienna, of Czech father, was a Czech-American comparative literary critic. He studied English Literature at the Charles University in Prague (Dr. phil., 1926), and was active among the Prague School linguists there, before moving to teach at School of Slavonic and East European Studies (now part of University College London) in 1935. From 1939, the beginning of World War II in Europe, Wellek lived in America. He taught first at the University of Iowa for seven years, advancing from assoc. prof. to prof. of English (1941-46). Beginning in 1946, he was with Yale University, as prof. of Slavic and comparative literature (1952-72), as dept. chair (1959-72), and as Director of Graduate Studies in Comparative Literature, and also Chairman of Slavic Department (1948-59) and chairman of the Department of Comparative Literature (s. 1960). He was also Visiting Professor at the University Minnesota (1947), Columbia University (1948), University of Hawaii (1961), University of California, Berkeley (1967); Fellow, Huntington Library, San Marino, CA (1942), Guggenheim Fellow (1951-52, 1956-57), Fulbright research scholar, Italy (1959-60), etc. He was appointed a member of the Joint Committee on Slavic Studies of the American Council of Learned Societies and the Social Science Research Council (1948-57) and was recipient of Prize for Distinguished Service from the American Council of Learned Societies (1959). Prof. Wellek had been awarded many honors, 14 honorary degrees, including an Honorary Doctorate of Humane Letters from Lawrence College (1958), Litt.D. from Oxford and Harvard universities in 1960; from the University in Rome in 1961, from the University of Maryland in 1964, from Boston College, etc. In the United States, he was widely regarded as a founder of the study of comparative literature. Professor Wellek was the author of *Immanuel Kant in England, 1793-1838* (1931), *The Rise of English Literary History* (1941, *Literary Scholarship* (1941), *The English Romantic Poets* (1951), *Dostoevsky: A Collection of Critical Essays* (1962), *Essays on Czech Literature* (1963), *Confrontations: Studies in the Intellectual and Literary Relations between Germany, England, and the U.S. during the 19th Century* (1965). With Austin Warren, Wellek published a landmark volume entitled *Theory of Literature* (1956), one of the first works to systematize literary theory. The crowning work of Wellek's career was an eight-volume magnum opus entitled *A History of Modern Criticism: 1750-1950*, the last two volumes of which he dictated from his bed in a nursing home at age 90.

Joseph B. Zavadil (1929-1992), b. St. Louis, MO, of Czech ancestry, received his BA (1949) and MA (1954) degrees from Loyola University in Chicago and his Ph.D. from Stanford University (1961), in English, before joining the Univ. of New Mexico (UNM) faculty in 1962. Starting as asst. professor of English (1961-67), he advanced to assoc. professor (s. 1967), and chair of the dept. of English (1969-79). In training and teaching, Professor Zavadil's main focus lay in the interaction between religion and medieval English literature, having written on *Patience and Cleanness: A Study of Doctrinal Relationships and Literary Purpose*. Professor Zavadil was one of the four designers of the anthology *Western*

Literature in a World Context and the co-editor of the first volume of a major work. *Medieval Scholarship: History* (1995).

Zora Devrnja Zimmerman (1945–), b. Mariánské Lázně, Czech., studied English at SUNY Buffalo. She was with Iowa State Univ. (s. 1974), as prof. of English (s. 1985), as associate dean for Academic Programs (s. 1990). She is a specialist on Serbian traditional narrative and lyric, dynamics of change and persistence in folklore, English and European Romanticism.

3. Germanic Languages

Martin Anderle (1932–), b. Kroměříž, Czech., studied German at Univ. of Vienna. He was with Univ. of Massachusetts (1959–62); as prof. of German, Queens Coll. (s. 1969), as prof. of Scandinavian languages (s. 1970).

Herbert Anton Arnold (1935–), b. Bochov, Czech., was evacuated with other Germans from Czechoslovakia to Germany, after the World War II, in 1945. He studied German at Julius Maximilians Univ., University of Wurzburg (Ph.D.) and Wesleyan University (M.A.A.). He was with Wesleyan Univ., Middletown (s. 1962), as prof. of Germanic languages and literatures (s. 1980), as dept. chair (1982–85). He has been an authority on German literature of the 17th and 18th centuries, and modern German literature.

Robert Karl Arnold (1900–1992), b. Klosterneuburg, studied German at Univ. of Prague. He was prof. of German, Victoria Coll. Univ. or Toronto, Canada. He was a specialist on modern German literature.

Ingeborg H. Baumgartner (1936–), b. Horna Stubňa, Czech., was a foreign language educator. She studied at Univ. of Michigan (A.B., 1958) and at Univ. of Wisconsin (M.A., 1959; Ph.D., 1970). She has been with Albion Univ. (1966–2001), as professor of modern languages and cultures, presently professor emerita (s. 2001). She was a specialist on German drama, and 19th and 20th century German literature.

Angelika Cardew (née Kruliš-Randová) (1931–1978), b. Prague, Czech.; philologist. She left Czechoslovakia in 1950 and came to the US, where she attended the University of Michigan and obtained the degrees B.A. and M.A. Subsequently, she finished studies for a Ph.D. in Medieval German. She was a teaching fellow at the University of Michigan and instructor at Eastern Michigan University. She was a member of Phi Betta Kappa, German Honorary Society, Modern Language Association and American Association of Teachers of German.

Cynthia S. Chalupa (ca. 1969–), b. Chicago, IL, of Czech ancestry, completed a B.A. in German and English at the University of Michigan, Ann Arbor in 1991, an M.A. (1995) and Ph.D. (2001)

in Germanic languages and literatures at Ohio State University. Cynthia Chalupa is associate professor and director of the Basic German Language Program at Department of World Languages, Literatures, & Linguistics, West Virginia University (WVU), Morgantown, WV. Since arriving at WVU in 2001, Dr. Chalupa has developed courses on German literature and culture, business German, pronunciation and phonetics, and courses on nineteenth- and twentieth-century literature. She also teaches foreign language methods to teacher candidates at WVU and a Norse mythology FLIT course. Dr. Chalupa serves as an advisor to undergraduate German majors and leads the WVU-Fulda University Study and Internship abroad program. She specializes in contemporary German literature and culture, foreign language pedagogy, and assessment. In 2012, she co-authored an intermediate/AP textbook titled *Neue Blickwinkel: Wege zur Kommunikation und Kultur*. She has written on the mirror image in the works of Rilke, Trakl, and Aichinger, ETA Hoffmann, and on the link between the mirror and self-portraiture. Her work in pedagogy includes publications on international TA training, on assessment development, autonomous learning and motivation, and on the use of live television programming in the German classroom.

Charlotte H. Clark (1910-2001), b. Brno, Moravia, earned a Ph.D. in philology from the Charles University in Prague. Her first husband was Karel Hašler, the best-known Czech song writer prior to World War II, and an ardent nationalist, who died in the hands of the Nazis. After the communists took over Czechoslovakia, she emigrated to Australia, where she lived for nine years, and taught French and Latin, before coming to the US. She settled in Connecticut where she married her second husband, John Clark, who was involved in the import-export business. She became associated with the Univ. of Hartford (1960-76), where she rose from asst. prof. to prof. of German, and dept. head (1973-76).

Dorrit Cohn (née Zucker) (1924-2012), b. Vienna, of Bohemian ancestry, studied German and comparative literature at Radcliffe Coll. and Stanford Univ. She was with Indiana Univ. (1964-71); prof. of German, Harvard Univ. (s. 1971), as prof. of comparative literature (s. 1984), later becoming Ernest Bernbaum Professor of Literature. She was an authority on European romanticism, modern novel, 19th and 20th century German literature. She won the Modern Language Association of America's Aldo and Jeanne Scaglione Prize for Comparative Literature Studies.

Charlotte M. Craig (1929-), b. Ostrava, Czech. studied German at Univ. of Arizona and at Rutgers. She was prof. of German, Kutztown State Coll. (s. 1974). She previously taught at the University of Kansas, George Washington University, and Schiller International University in Heidelberg, Germany.

Peter Demetz (1922-), b. Prague, Czech., is a literary scholar and Germanist. He studied German and English at Charles Univ. (Dr. phil., 1948), German at Columbia Univ. (M.A., 1954) and comparative literature at Yale Univ. (Ph.D., 1956). He has been with Yale Univ. (s. 1956), as prof. of German and comparative literature (s. 1962), as dept. chair (1962-69), retiring in 1991. He is now Sterling Professor Emeritus of Germanic Language and Literatures. He is an authority on sociology of literature, literary theory, German 18th century thought and literature. Together with his wife, Hana Demetz, he translated from Czech into German the novel of Božena Němcová, *Babička*, under the title *Die Grossmutter* (1959) and short stories by Jan Čep, *Zeit und Widerkehr* (1962). He also edited *Twentieth Century Views: Bertolt Brecht* (1962) and a volume of Czech poetry in exile, *Neviditelný domov: Verše exulantů 1948-1953* (1953). His most recent book, *Prague in Black and Gold,* is a history and personal memoir of the city which was home and inspiration to many towering figures of European civilization such as Kepler, Mozart, Rabbi Judah Loew, Dvořák, Smetana, Rilke and Kafka. Other books by Demetz include *Marx, Engels and the Poets* and *After the Fires: Writing in the Germany, Austria and Switzerland*. Demetz was awarded a Medal of Merit in the fields of scholarship and culture from the Czech Republic in 2000. Previously Demetz has won two other major awards for his outstanding contributions to the study of German culture. In 1971, he received the Golden Goethe Award of the Federal Republic of Germany, and in 1984, he was given the Commander's Cross of the Order of Merit by the German government.

Ruth Deutsch (1912-2004), b. Prague, Czech., completed her undergraduate studies at the University of Prague before immigrating to the United States in 1938. Her parents and sister died in Auschwitz in 1944. She graduated from Radcliffe in 1941 with a degree in German literature. During World War II, she and her husband worked for the Office of Strategic Services in Washington. She later continued her graduate studies at Harvard, Stanford, and Yale. She taught at Wellesley Coll. from 1944 to 1977, taking time off when she and her husband, Karl, took on other assignments. Between 1958 and 1967, while her husband taught political science at Yale, Mrs. Deutsch held teaching positions at the University of Bridgeport and Southern Connecticut State College. At Wellesley, Mrs. Deutsch taught German language courses and both 18th-century and contemporary German literature, with a focus on the Enlightenment period and German Expressionism. When she retired in 1977, the Wellesley Board of Trustees gave her the title of lecturer emeritus. In 1994, the Wellesley German Department named its new departmental library for Mrs. Deutsch in appreciation for her years of service and the donation of a large portion of her personal book collection.

Lore Barbara Foltin (1913-1974), b. Vienna, of Bohemian ancestry, studied German at Univ. of Prague. She was with Univ. of Pittsburgh (s. 1949), as assoc. prof. of Germanic languages and literatures (s. 1961). She was a specialist on Franz Werfel, Rilke, Schnitzler.

Oscar Benjamin Frankl (1881-1955), b. Kroměříž, Moravia, was a Germanist, literary scholar, philosopher, freelance writer and researcher. He studied philology at Vienna Univ. In 1918, he founded in Prague the German Urania Inst. for Adult Education which he headed until 1938. He was appointed chief of German dept. of the Czechoslovak Govt. radio and became an international authority on broadcasting. In 1939, he managed to escape to the US through France. There he served as a researcher for Columbia Univ. (1942-55) and was appointed lecturer at the Rand School of Social Science. His *Der Jude in den deutschen Dichtungen des 15., 16. und 17. Jahrhunderts* on the image of the Jew in German literature of the 15th to 17th centuries, and *Friedrich Schiller in seinem Beziehungen zu den Juden und zum Judentum*, on Friedrich Schiller's relations to Jews and Judaism, are noteworthy. He also authored *Theodor Herzl, the Jews and the Man* (2008).

Markéta Goetz-Stankiewicz (1927-), b. Liberec, Czech. studied German and comparative literature at Univ. of Toronto. She was a professor of German studies, Univ. of British Columbia, Vancouver, B.C., Canada, as head of Germanic Studies (1980-85). She was a specialist on comparative literature, contemporary Czech and German literature.

Erich Heller (1911-1990), b. Chomutov, Bohemia, was a literary scholar. He studied at German University of Prague (Dr. Juris, 1925, at the age of 23) and later at Cambridge Univ. After initial stay in England, where he was associated with University College Swansea (1948-60), he moved to US, where he joined Northwestern Univ. (s. 1960), as prof. of German literature (s. 1967). He was an authority on modern German and European literature. Most of Heller's articles and books dealt with German philosophy and literature. He authored *The Ironic German, a Study of Thomas Mann* (1958); *Franz Kafka* (1974); and *The Importance of Nietzsche* (1988). Several other collections of Heller's essays were also published. He was a recipient of several awards.

Otto Heller (1863-1941), b. Karlovy Vary, Bohemia, attended the University of Prague, followed by the Universities of Munich, Vienna, and Berlin. He came to the United States in 1883 as a tutor and secured the post of instructor in Greek at LaSalle College in Philadelphia in 1887. Heller received his Doctor's degree from the University of Chicago in 1890. Heller taught briefly at the Massachusetts Institute of Technology before becoming a professor of German language and literature at Washington University in 1892. In 1914, Heller was made professor of modern European literature in addition to his original professorship, and in 1924, he became the first dean of the Graduate School of

Arts and Sciences, a post he held until he became dean emeritus in 1937. He was primarily known as a nonfiction author, with the focus on German literature.

Antonín Hrubý (1920-), b. Vienna, of Czech ancestry, studied at Charles Univ. (PhDr., 1946) and Univ. of Paris (License des Lettres). He was with Univ. of Washington, Seattle (s. 1961), as prof. of German languages and literatures (s. 1968). He is now professor Emeritus of Germanics and Comparative Literature. He is a specialist on mediaeval literature, textual criticism.

Wilma Abeles Iggers (1921-), b. Miřkov, Czech. studied German at Univ. of Chicago. She has been with Canisius Coll. (s. 1965), as prof. of German (s. 1975), as prof. emerita (s. 1991). She is a specialist on cultural history of the Jews in Bohemia and Moravia, recent Czech literature, Karl Kraus.

Erich Kahler (1885-1990), b. Prague, Bohemia, was a literary scholar and essayist. He studied philosophy, literature, history, art history, sociology, and psychology at the University of Munich, the University of Berlin, the University of Heidelberg, and the University of Freiburg before earning his Doctorate at the University of Vienna in 1911. In 1933, deprived of his German citizenship by the Nazi regime, he left Germany, emigrating to the United States in 1938 after a period of residence in England. In the U.S., he taught at The New School for Social Research, Black Mountain College, Cornell University, and Princeton University. Like Einstein, Kahler was a member of the Institute for Advanced Study. Kahler's many books often take up political themes, in addition to the relation of society to technology and science. He was an ardent Zionist.

Otto William Mandl (1916-1992), b. Ústí n/Labem, Bohemia, studied German at Univ. of Vienna. He was with Willamette Univ. (s. 1963), as prof. of German (s. 1969). He was a specialist on German literature, esp. in the 19th and 20th century English literature.

Walter Friedrich Neumann (1910-d.), b. Ústí n/Labem, Bohemia, studied German at Univ. of Bonn. He was with McPherson, KS (s. 1939); with Univ. of Wisconsin (1947-54); as professor of German, Ohio State Univ. (s. 1961). He was a specialist on German drama and lyrics, and contemporary European literature.

Heinz Politzer (1910-1978), b. Vienna, of Moravian ancestry, was educated in Vienna and in Prague. He was a writer, literary critic, Germanist, and historian of literature, particularly on Franz Kafka. Together with Max Brod, he edited the first four volumes of the first collected works of Kafka. He also lived in Israel, moving to Jerusalem in 1941, and then to the United States. He became a professor at Bryn Mawr College, then at Oberlin

Coll. (1952-60); and served as prof. of German at Univ. of California, Berkeley (1960-78). He was a specialist on Austrian literature, German literature, and psychology.

Rio Preisner (1925-2007), b. Mukačevo, Czech., was a literary scholar and Germanist, Czech poet and translator. At the end of the War, he studied in the German and English Departments of Charles University in Prague, obtaining his Doctorate in 1950 with a dissertation on Franz Werfel. For the next year, he taught in the German Department of Charles University, and worked as a literary translator for the Mladá Fronta and Státní nakladatelství krásné literatury publishing houses. In 1952, he was arrested and sentenced to hard labor in a Stalinist labor camp. After being released in 1954, he returned to Prague, where he taught German until 1965. That same year, after the Warsaw Pact's squelching of the Prague Spring, he, his wife Olga, and their daughter Ruth left Prague for exile, first in Vienna, and later, from 1969, in the USA. From 1969 to his retirement in 1992, Preisner was Professor of German at Penn State in University Park, Pennsylvania. There, he taught both graduate and undergraduate students, and directed many M.A. and Ph.D. theses in German, Czech, and Comparative Literature. After his retirement, he and his wife moved to the Pittsburgh area, where he continued to write. His works, banned for some two decades, were again being published in the Czech Republic, and received with critical acclaim. In 2000, President Václav Havel awarded him the "Za zásluhy" medal ("For Meritorious Service") in the field of culture and scholarship. He had an impact in the interest in Kafka in the United States and the publication of the first complete translated works of Kafka in the US, and he was a close associate to Kafka's protégé, Max Brod. He was awarded the Key to the City of Vienna and the Austrian Cross, among many other prizes and honors. Among the highlights of his career was giving the Eroeffnungrede to the 1976 Salzburg Music Festival.

Edward Prokosch (1876-1938), b. Cheb, Bohemia, was a historical linguist who specialized in Indo-European and, specifically, Proto-Germanic studies. He studied at University of Chicago (A.M., 1901) and University of Leipzig (Ph.D., 1906). Prokosch taught German and Germanic philology at many American educational institutions, including the University of Chicago, the University of Texas (1913), the University of Wisconsin-Madison (1905-09), Bryn Mawr College (1919-20) and New York University (1927-29). Prokosch finished his career as the Sterling Professor of Germanic Languages at Yale University, during which time he wrote his most influential work, *A Comparative Germanic Grammar*, which broke ground in the fields of Indo-European and Germanic studies. He was the father of the novelist Frederic Prokosch.

John Pustejovsky (1953-), b. Shiner, Texas, from a family of Moravian ancestry, has been both faculty member and administrator at Marquette University, which he joined in 1982 as assistant professor. Since 1990, he has held the position of associate professor of

German, in the Department of Foreign Languages & Literatures at Klingler College of Arts and Sciences, Marquette University. He earned his B.A. from Marquette University, a Ph.D. in German literature from The University of Texas at Austin and was a Fulbright-Hays Student Grantee to the Federal Republic of Germany. In his work, he has focused on the experiences that are crucial to successful undergraduate education: teaching, advising, and learning. His scholarly work has dealt with the German enlightenment, German pietism, and more recently contemporary poetry and spirituality, and the post-World War II German short story. Pustejovsky has been a vigorous advocate for the Socratic approach to teaching and textual discussion and has introduced the Great Books shared inquiry method at a number of colleges and universities, and for more than 25 years to school and community organizations. He was the recipient of the 2004 Faculty Award for Teaching Excellence, and the College's Faculty Award for Excellence in Academic Advising. In 2012, he was recognized as Wisconsin's Distinguished German Educator by the American Association for the Teaching of German and was recognized for lifetime service by the national Jesuit Honor Society.

Walter Albert Reichart (1903–1999), b. Bratislava, Slovakia, is a German scholar. He came to the United States while still a boy and attended grammar and high school at Toledo, Ohio. He studied at Univ. of Michigan. He was with Univ. of Michigan (s. 1925), as assistant professor of German (s. 1931), becoming full prof. of German (s. 1940). He was a specialist on Anglo-German literary relations, Gerhard Hauptmann.

Frederick (Fritz) Ritter (1896–1987), b. Vienna, of Bohemian ancestry, originally actor, later became a Germanist. He served as a soldier in World War I from 1916–1918. After the war, Ritter worked as an actor, radio announcer, and contributor to various periodicals, mainly in Berlin and Munich. Ritter was a cast member of the first production of Bertolt Brecht's Dreigroschenoper (Threepenny Opera) in Berlin. Due to the "Gesetz zur Wiederherstellung des Berufsbeamtentums" (Law for the Restoration of the Professional Civil Service), his career as an actor in municipal theaters was cut short. Furthermore, as a 'non-Aryan,' he was denied admission to the Reichstheaterkammer (Reich Theater Chamber)—the equivalent of an occupational ban. Subsequently, Ritter was among the first to join the Kulturbund deutscher Juden (Cultural League of German Jews), which was founded in July 1933. He became a well-known figure of the Kulturbund and performed in its production of Shakespeare's Othello in the Berliner Theater on Charlottenstrasse, as well as at its offshoots in other German cities. In November 1938, his contract with the Kulturbund was terminated because the National Socialist regime ordered the closure of all Jewish institutions—just one day before the November Pogroms. Like many of his colleagues, Ritter gave up acting. From December 1938 to May 1939, he took part in a training program at the Krankenhilfe der Jüdischen Gemeinde (Healthcare Center of the Jewish Community). He then immigrated to the Bahamas via London with his wife, the painter Ida (Ady) Lauinger (1900–1975), where, expecting to enter the United States, he gave Latin and Greek lessons. In 1944, he immigrated to the United States. Initially employed in a factory, he subsequently worked as a school teacher and studied German philology at the University of Chicago, where he received his M.A. in 1951 and his Ph.D., with honors, in 1955. He was then a professor of German language and literature at the Illinois Institute of Technology and at Indiana University from 1952–1968. During this time, he also frequently gave recitations of German works in the original and, starting in 1947, published several novels. In 1968, he retired from teaching and received a Swiss residence permit and from 1969, he was a freelance writer and lecturer in Minusio, Switzerland (and later Chiemgau).

Barbara Zeisl Schoenberg (1940–), b. New York, NY, of Bohemian ancestry, is the daughter of composer Eric Zeisl and Dr. Gertrud S. (Jellinek) Zeisl. She received her Ph.D. in German Language and Literature from University of California, Los Angeles and taught at Pomona College, as professor of German language and literature. She has published articles on the Viennese fin de siècle and exile studies and is a translator of German books and poetry. She is the mother of attorney E. Randol Schoenberg.

Hanna Spencer (née Fischl) (1913–2014), b. Kladno, Bohemia, was a Germanist. She achieved a rarity for a woman of that period, a Ph.D. (in Slavic and Germanic languages from the University of Prague). As a non-practicing Jew, she suffered the constraints placed on the lives of Jews by the invading Nazis in 1938. Hanna escaped the Holocaust by immigrating to Canada in 1939. Under Canada's anti-Semitic immigration laws, Hanna was admitted pretending to be a Christian and a glove-maker in an uncle's glove factory in Prescott, Ont. She soon put her education to use teaching in Elmwood, a private girls' school in Ottawa. Through a colleague, she met and married Elvins Spencer. She kept a diary of those pivotal years, published 60 years later under the title *Hanna's Diary 1938-1941* (still in print). Following Elvins in his career as an organic chemist to jobs in several Canadian cities, Hanna and Elvins ultimately settled in London, Ont. in 1951. Once her children Erica and Martin were in school, she resumed her own career, and joined the faculty of University of Western Ontario (s. 1959), as professor of German (s. 1977). She was not only recognized as an excellent teacher but became a world authority on the German poet and journalist Heinrich Heine, publishing two books and numerous academic papers. In addition to her distinguished academic career, Hanna was politically active and served as president of the National Council of Women. She also co-founded the Unitarian Fellowship in London. An intrepid traveler, accomplished pianist, and avid tennis player until the age of 90, she was one of the earliest participants in the Canadian Centre for Activity and Aging.

George Stefanský (1897–1957), b. Prague, Bohemia, was Germanist, literary and intellectual historian, and sociologist. He received his Dr. phil. degree at the Univ. of Prague in 1922. He was a member of the faculties at Univ. of Prague, Berlin, Műnster and Geneva (1927-39). In 1939, he emigrated to the US. He became vis. prof. of philosophy at Columbia Univ. (1943 and then dir. of research for the United Pal. Appeal (1943-53). He was also a lecturer in sociology at New York Univ. (s. 1943). Since 1953, he was dir. of research at Am. Fin. and Dev. Corp. for Israel. He was a specialist on German literary and intellectual history. He also conducted research on the economic, political and sociological problems of refugees.

Joseph Peter Strelka (1927–), b. Wiener Neustadt, of Czech ancestry, was a Germanist. From 1945 to 1950, he studied German philology with Oskar Benda and received his Doctorate with his dissertation, "Feudalromantic currents in Renaissance literature and its development," At the beginning of the 1950s, he headed the cultural office of the city of Wiener Neustadt. Until 1958, he headed the literary studies group at the Institute for Science and Art and habilitated at the University of Vienna. In 1964, he was appointed Associate Professor of German Literature at the University of Southern California in Los Angeles. From 1966 to 1971, he taught at Pennsylvania State University, then, at the State University of New York in Albany (1971-97). He is a specialist on literary theory, literature of the Renaissance, German literature of the 20th century.

Elisabeth Trahan (née Welt) (1924-2009), b. Berlin, Germany, of Moravian mother (née Silberstein) was raised by her grandparents in Ostrava, Moravia, after her mother's death in 1929. In January 1940, she rejoined her father, who had been living in Vienna since 1936, so that they could emigrate together. They did not succeed in leaving. In July 1947, she immigrated to the United States as a displaced person with the help of the American Jewish Joint Distribution Committee (AJDC). She graduated from Sarah Lawrence College (B.A., 1951), majoring in literature, and pursued her studies in German and Russian literature at Cornell University (M.A., 1953) and in comparative literature at Yale Univ. (Ph.D., 1957). She served as an instructor in the German Department from 1956-61. She later taught at the University of Pittsburgh and the Monterey Institute of International Studies in California. She retired in 1985. She returned as a visiting professor to Amherst College (1985-89), and also became actively involved in the International Writers Union. Since then, she was active as an independent scholar and writer. Occasionally she wrote under the pen name Lisa Mondo. Her interests were in Slavic, German and comparative literature of the 19th and 20th centuries. In addition to editing textbooks, she published a variety of professional articles on modern German and comparative literature. She was the author of *Walking With Ghosts: A Jewish Childhood in Wartime Vienna* (1998) and *Ten Dollars in My Pocket: The American Education of a Holocaust Survivor* (2006).

Hans Rudolph Vaget (1938–), b. Mariánské Lázně, Czech., received his academic training at the Universities of Munich and Tübingen, the University of Wales, Cardiff and Columbia Univ. Since 1967, he has been teaching at Smith College, where he now holds the position of Helen & Laura Shedd Professor Emeritus of German Studies. Aside from Smith Coll., Vaget has taught at the University of California-Irvine, Yale, Columbia, Princeton, the University of Hamburg and the Summer School at Middlebury College. He has published widely in the field of German studies from the 18th century to the present, focusing on Goethe, Wagner and Thomas Mann as well as music history and film.

4. Romance Languages

Paul Amann (1884–1958), b. Prague, Bohemia, a literary scholar specializing in Romance studies, was educated at Univ. of Prague, Vienna and Grenoble. He was also a writer. In 1939, he emigrated to France and in 1941, to US. From 1943 till 1953, he was engaged as professor at Univ. of New York. He was a prolific writer and poet, as well as a translator. His writings include *Verschonte Verse 1924 bis 1955* (1956), *Kristall meiner Zeit* (1956). For a good three decades, Amann carried on a notable correspondence with Thomas Mann (1915–52). Mann's letters to him were published in both German and English after Amann's death.

Věra Fischer Beck (1905–1975), b. Prague, Bohemia, studied at Charles Univ. (PhDr.) and at Rockford Coll. (B.A.). She was asst. professor of Romance languages and literatures, C. W. Post Center, Long Island Univ., Greenvale, NY. Her specialty was Spanish and Portuguese.

Olga Bernal (1929–2002), b. Czech., was a Holocaust survivor. After the War, she studied French literature at Columbia Univ. (Ph.D.). Subsequently, she taught at Vassar (1960–67) and at SUNY Buffalo (s. 1967), where she held the position of professor of French (s. 1970). She published several books with Gallinard in France. She was a specialist on 19th century French poetry and 20th century French novel. She was 1966 Guggenheim Fellow in humanities. In 1980, she moved to the south of France and dedicated herself to the creation of sculpture.

Dushan Břeský (1920–), b. Přerov, Czech., initially studied law at Charles Univ. (JUDr., 1948). After emigrating to Canada, he studied Romance languages and literatures at Univ. of Washington (M.A., 1958; Ph.D., 1962). He specialized in modern French literature, esp. Anatole France, and in comparative literature. His later research also focused on aesthetics. He held positions at the University of British Columbia and the University of Montana before coming to the Univ. of Calgary in 1963. He is the author of *The Art of Anatole France* (1969), *Cathedral of Symphony: Essays of Jean Christophe* (1973) and *Literary Practice* (2 vols., 1984, 1988). He also authored a Czech novel *Bez konce jsou lesy* (1943) and co-authored *Hory, lyže, sníh* (1947).

Frederico Abel Chalupa (1953–), b. Peru, of Moravian ancestry, earned his Ph.D. in Latin American Literatures & Cultures (1990) at Univ. of Arizona; his M.A. in Foreign Languages (1986) at Washington State University and his B.A. in Liberal Arts (1976) at Univ. de Piura (Peru). He has been associated with Bowling Green State Univ., OH, as asst. professor of International Studies and Spanish American Studies (1990–96), as assoc. professor (s. 1996), as director of International Studies Program (s. 2010). His research interests are in Andean narratives, and racial and gender studies.

Eugene H. Falk (1913–2000), b. Liptovský Sv. Mikuláš, Slovakia, studied at German University in Prague and the Sorbonne in Paris. He graduated from Charles University in Prague and earned his Doctorate in 1942 from the University of Manchester in England. He was associated with Univ. of North Carolina (s. 1967), and was awarded an endowed professorship in 1972, retiring in 1986. At Univ. of North Carolina, Falk was a director of graduate studies in French and comparative literature and chaired the comparative literature curriculum. Before coming to Carolina, Falk chaired the Romance Languages Department at the University of Minnesota and was a professor of French at Dartmouth College. He specialized in French literature and comparative literature. He authored *Renunciation as a Tragic Focus* (1954), *Types of Thematic Structure* (1967) and *The Poetics of Roman Ingarden* (1980). He won the French Order of Palmes Academiques in 1979.

Alexander Fischler (1931–), b. Liberec, Czech., is Univ. of Washington trained literary scholar. He has been with SUNY Binghamton (s. 1964), as assoc. prof. of French and comparative literature (s. 1966). He is a specialist of French literature of 19th and 20th centuries.

Miroslav John Hanák (1926–2012), b. Plzeň, Czech., studied political science at University of Illinois (B.A., 1951); comparative literature at University of Southern California (M.A., 1963) and Spanish at Universidad Central Madrid Espana (Ph.D., 1965). He was with East Texas State Univ., Commerce (s. 1968), as prof. of Spanish and philosophy (s. 1973). He is a specialist on comparative literature, esp. European Baroque, Nietzsche philosophy and Spanish thought of the 19th and 20th centuries.

Anna Heyberger (1874–1952), b. Bohemia, studied at the Universities of Vienna and Prague and was awarded a diploma in modern languages at the Carl-Ferdinand University in Prague and music teachers' diploma in Vienna. She was the director of the School of Modern Languages at Tabor, Bohemia. After coming to the US, she became professor of French and German at Beaver College, PA (1905–06) and then at Westminster College (s. 1906). Subsequently, she taught French and Czech at Coe Coll. (1912–41).

Vladimír Honsa (1921-2011), b. Netolice, Czech., studied at Charles Univ. and Univ. of Michigan. He was prof. of Spanish and linguistics, Univ. of Nevada, Las Vegas (s. 1970). He was a specialist of Spanish and linguistics

Eric H. Kadler (1922-2006), b. Plzeň, Czech., received his initial training at Vysoká škola obchodní (Univ. of Business) in Prague (Ing. Com., 1948). He continued his studies at Univ. of London (1949-52) and then at Univ. of Michigan, where he studied comparative literature (M.A., 1956) and Romance languages (Ph.D., 1959). He was with Lycoming Coll. (1960-70); prof. of French literature and foreign languages and dept. chair, Cent. Michigan Univ. Mt. Pleasant (s. 1970), now professor emeritus of French and contrastive linguistics. French language and French literature of the 18th century, applied linguistics, French theatre since the 17th century and applied and contrastive linguistics were his specialty. He was the author of *Literary Figures in French Drama* (1969), *Linguistics and Teaching of Foreign Languages* (1970) and numerous articles in professional journals.

Eliška Krausová (1946-), b. Prague, Czech.; in Colombia s. 1968. She studied French and Spanish at Charles University and initially moved to Bogota, Colombia in 1968 for postgraduate studies in linguistics and Latin-American literature. After the Soviet occupation of Czechoslovakia, she decided to remain there. She completed her studies there and began teaching at the university foreign languages, specializing in French. In 1970, she married Professor Ignacio Chavez, with whom she published a Spanish dictionary that was awarded the UNESCO prize. Since 1982, she has been engaged as professor of French at the university in Bogota, where she also heads the office of international relations. After the death of her husband, she founded in 2009 an association for Czech-Colombian friendship, Asocheca. After the Czech Embassy was closed in Bogota, the organization played a significant role towards maintaining Czech-Colombian relations. Among other, Krausová organized under its aegis an exhibition, which lasted for several years, about the Czech children jailed in Terezin. For her activities, she was awarded the Gratias agit.

John William Kronik (1931-2006), b. Vienna, of Bohemian ancestry, was Univ. of Wisconsin trained literary scholar and Romanticist. He was with Univ. of Illinois (1963-66); with Cornell Univ. (s. 1966), as dir. grad. studies (1970-73), as prof. of Romance studies (s. 1971). He was a specialist on Spanish literature of the 19th and 20th centuries, Franco-Spanish literary relationships.

Eva Dubská Kushner (1929-), b. Prague, Czech., studied French literature and philosophy at McGill Univ. She holds the position of professor emeritus of French and comparative literature, Univ. of Toronto, Canada. Eva Kushner works in comparative literature, Renaissance studies, contemporary French literature, and Québec poetry at Victoria

IX. HUMANITIES

College, University of Toronto. Kushner served as president of the International Comparative Literature Association (ICLA) (1979–82), as vice-president of International Federation for Modern Languages and Literatures (FILLM) (1987–93), and as its president (1996–99). She was representative for French Studies in the Renaissance Society of America (1997–2000) and served as Canadian representative to the International Union of Academies (2000–03).

Jaques J. C. Le Clercq (1898–1972), b. Karlovy Vary, Bohemia, was a Romanist. He was educated at Haileybury College, England; private schools in Paris; Haverford College (1914–17); University of California, Berkeley (A.B., 1920; M.A., 1921). He was Instructor in Romance Languages, University of California, Berkeley (1920–22); Field Service Fellow in Comparative Literature, Universities of Poitiers and Paris (1922–24); Instructor in Romance Languages, Columbia University (s. 1924). He was editor, Publishing Department, Brentano's, (1928–30); Chairman, Prix Brentano (s. 1929). By 1930, he was Professor at Columbia University in New York. During WWI, he had served in the US Army, and during WWII, he served with the Office of War Information in New York and France. He later (s. 1957), became professor of French Literature and Romance Languages at Queens College, CUNY, Flushing, NY, a post from which he eventually retired. He was a scholar, author, and translator of a number of literary works, he also wrote poetry under the pen name Paul Tanaquil.

John Lihani (1927–), b. Hnúšťa, Czech., is a specialist on Spanish literature and linguistics. He arrived in the US in 1937 and studied at Case-Western Reserve University (B.S., 1948), Ohio State University (M.A., 1950) and at the University of Texas (Ph.D., 1954). He was a Teaching fellow at Tulane University, New Orleans (1950–51); Teaching fellow and instructor at University Texas, Austin (1951–54); Instructor and then assistant professor at Yale University, New Haven (1954–62); Associate professor at the University Pittsburgh (1962–69); Fulbright professor at Institute Caro y Cuervo, Bogota, Colombia (1965–66); Professor of Spanish literature & linguistics at University Kentucky, Lexington (1969–92), professor emeritus (s. 1992). He was a founding editor of *La Coronica Journal* (1972) and co-editor of *Bulletin of Comediantes Journal* (1973–92).

Edward M. Malinak (ca. 1943–), b. US, possibly of Slovak ancestry, studied at Univ. of Michigan (B.A., 1965), Michigan State Univ. (M.A.) and at Univ. of Kentucky (Ph.D.). He holds the position of professor of Spanish and chair, Dept. of Foreign Languages, Nazareth Coll., Rochester, NY. He was also with the University of South, Sewanee, TN (1971–72).

Charles Carroll Marden (1867–1932), b. Baltimore, MD, of Bohemian ancestry, having descended from Augustine Heřman of Prague, studied at Johns Hopkins Univ. (B.A., 1989; Ph.D., 1894). He was the first professor of Spanish in United States, teaching at Johns

Hopkins from 1905 until 1917. His greatest scholarly contribution was as editor of ancient Spanish-language texts, such as *Cuatro Poemas de Berceo*, the works of the earliest known Castilian poet, Gonzalo de Berceo. Marden discovered parts of the text in a secondhand bookstore in Madrid then searched for the remaining portions of the manuscript and found the remaining thirty-two folios in a remote village in Spain. He then prepared the text for publication. In 1916, Marden became the newly created Emery L. Ford Chair of Spanish at Princeton University. After dividing his time between Johns Hopkins and Princeton, he moved to Princeton in 1917 and remained there until his death in 1932.

Thomas Mermall (1937–2011), b. Užhorod, Ruthenia, Czech., of Jewish family, was a Hispanist and professor of Spanish literature. During the War, he and his father survived by hiding, while his mother died in a concentration camp. In 1947, Thomas Mermall and his father managed to leave Europe and settle in Chile for three years before moving to the United States where his father's brother lived. Mermall completed his studies in the US, at University of Connecticut. He was with SUNY, Stony Brook (1968–72); with Brooklyn Coll. (s. 1973), where he advanced to the rank of professor of Spanish. He is a specialist on contemporary Spanish essay, history of ideas. His studies focused primarily on modern Spanish literature and thought, primarily the developments after the Spanish Civil War, including analyses and commentaries on the works of José Ortega y Gasset, Unamuno, Pedro Laín Entralgo, Juan Rof Carballo and Francisco Ayala, as well as comments on the importance of the essay in Spanish literature.

Erika Ostrovsky (née Spielberg) (1926–2010), b. Vienna, of Bohemian ancestry was an author and professor of French at New York University. Her interest in Louis-Ferdinand Céline stemmed from a 3-year stay in France, where she studied at the Alliance Française and the Sorbonne. She has been active in the discovery, identification, and acquisition of important unpublished Céline manuscripts for the New York University Libraries.

Anna Otten (1921–1997), b. Neštémice, Czech.; Romance scholar. She was trained as literary scholar at University of Western Ontario. She was with Antioch College, Yellow Springs, OH (s. 1956); as professor of French and German Languages and Literatures (s. 1970). Her specialty was in French and German radio drama, modern French and German prose.

Marija Petrovská (1926–), b. Zagreb, of Czech ancestry, studied at the Conservatory of Dramatic Arts in Prague (dipl., 1945), Institut des Hautes Etudes d'Interprétariat in Milan (dipl., 1855) and then at Univ. of Tennessee (M.A., 1965) and at the Univ. of Kentucky (Ph.D., 1972), in the latter two institutions majoring in French. She has had a varied career, starting as an actress in Czech theatres (1945–50) and then as a translator in Milan (1950–63), before entering the academic scene. She rose from asst. professor to professor of Italian, French and comparative literature at Univ. of Tennessee (s. 1963). She was also visiting professor of Italian at Indiana Univ., PA and at Masaryk Univ. in Brno. She is the author of *Prague Diptych* (1980) and two scholarly books on Victor Hugo (1977) and *Merope: The Dramatic Impact of a Myth* (1984). She also edited *A Brief Anthology of French Poetry* (1985).

Ernest Pick (1936–), b. Prague, Czech., is a Romanist. He emigrated to the United States as a boy, studied at the University of Pennsylvania (as well as a year at the University of London), went on to take a Doctorate in French, after studying at the University of Bordeaux, then Nancy. He taught at Lake Erie College (s. 1961), as assoc. prof. of modern languages (s. 1969).

George (Jiří) Pistorius (1922–2014), b. Prague, Czech., was a literary scholar. He was the grandson of Josef Jiránek, who was a noted concert pianist and pupil of Smetana. Pistorius attended Charles University (1945–48), where he studied French and comparative literature. He left Prague in 1948 for Paris, where he worked as a journalist, writing cultural and education programs for the French Broadcasting Company, and did postgraduate studies in Slavic philology at Université de Paris (1948–50). When he first came to the US in 1958, he taught French and German at Lafayette College in Easton, PA, while attending University of Pennsylvania, where he studied Romance languages, specializing in French (Ph.D.). In 1963, he moved to Williamstown to teach French at Williams College, where he taught for 29 years until his retirement in 1992. He was chair of the Romance Languages Department, 1971–1982. He was fluent in four languages and was interested in Franco-German literary relations. He was an active member of the Modern Language Association and wrote five books and numerous articles focused on 19th- and 20th-century French literature and 20th-century Franco-German literary relations. In Czech, he authored *Bibliografie díla F. X. Šaldy* (1948), *Padesát let Egona Hostovského* (1958) and *Doba a slovesnost* (2007). He became director of their mandatory study abroad program and was hired to direct the international programs of the 34 colleges and universities in the State of Georgia System, and subsequently taught also at Georgia Perimeter College. He was specialist on language methodology. He was married, lived in Atlanta, and has a daughter, Elisabeth, who lives in Ohio. He has been writing plays, poetry and an occasional novel throughout his lifetime. He often wonders whether he is living in a parallel universe.

John H. Polt (orig. Pollatschek) (1929–), b. Ústí n/Labem, Czech., is a Romanist and literary scholar. He studied public and international affairs at Princeton University (A.B., 1949); and Spanish (M.A., 1950) and Romance Languages and Literature (Ph.D., *magna cum laude*, 1956) at University of California, Berkeley. He has been with Univ. of California, Berkeley (s. 1956), as prof. of Spanish (s. 1970), as chairman of dept of Spanish and Portuguese (1974–78). He was visiting associate professor of Spanish at University of California, Santa Barbara (1956–57). He was a specialist on Spanish literature of the 18th and 19th century.

George Oswald Schanzer (1914-2011), b. Vienna, of Bohemian ancestry, was a specialist on Spanish. He was State Univ. of Iowa trained literary scholar. He was with St. John's Univ. NY (1952-64); with SUNY Buffalo (s. 1964), as prof. of Spanish American literature (s. 1964). He was a specialist on Spanish American literature, fiction, theater, Hispanic-Russian literary relations, La Plata literature.

Eva Maria Stadler (1931-), b. Prague, Czech., is Columbia Univ. trained literary scholar. She has been with Fordham Univ. (s. 1968), as assoc. prof. of French and comparative literature, chair, div. of humanities (s. 1973). She is a specialist on literature of the 18th century, the novel and theory of narration, prose, fiction and film.

Henry Anthony Stavan (1925-), b. Ostrava, Czech., was trained at Univ. of California, Berkeley as a literary scholar. He was with Univ. of Minnesota (1964-66); with Univ. of Colorado, Boulder (s. 1966), as prof. of French (s. 1975). He is a specialist on 18th century French literature.

Jiřina Anna Sztacho (1910-1984), b. Hradec Králové, Bohemia, was a literary scholar. She studied French Language and literature at Charles University (PhDr., 1936) and Russian language and literature at Columbia University (M.A., 1965). She was with Bronx Community Coll. (s. 1960), as prof. of French (s. 1965), as dept. head (1964-71). She was a specialist on modern French literature, European history, philosophy, ethics and morals, and bibliography.

Thomas J. Tománek (1931-), b. Hodonín, Czech., is Charles Univ. trained literary scholar (PhDr.) He has been with California State Univ., Hayward (s. 1971), where he is now professor emeritus of Spanish (s. 1985). Before he was assistant Professor of Romance Languages at University of Oregon, Eugene. He is a specialist on Spanish-American literature, Spanish language, modern novelists.

Ludmila Ondrujová Velinský (1905-1998), b. Bzenec, Czech., studied psychology and French at Masaryk Univ. She was professor of French, Southeast Missouri State Coll. (s. 1959), then with Northern Illinois Univ., DeKalb, IL. She was a specialist on French literature, teaching methods of modern languages.

Margaret Mary Vojtko (1930-2013), b. Homestead, PA, of Slovak ancestry; adjunct professor of French at Duquesne University,

Emil Volek (1944-), b. Rožnov pod Radhoštěm, Czech., studied Spanish, English, and aesthetics at Charles University, receiving Ph.D. in 1970. After graduation, he worked as a specialist in Ibero-American literatures at the Czechoslovak Academy of Sciences in

Prague (1968–74). Upon leaving the country, he was invited as visiting professor to the Romanisches Seminar at the University of Cologne, Germany (1974–75), and later joined the faculty at Arizona State University, Tempe. Starting there as an assistant professor (s. 1975), he advanced to assoc. prof. (1978–84) and then to full professor (s. 1984) at the School of International Letters and Cultures. He specialized in Latin American literature and culture, theory of literature, and in Slavic schools of literary and cultural criticism.

Helen Waldstein Wilkes (1936–), b. Czech., is an energized octogenarian who survived a lifetime of hardships ranging from fleeing Nazi Germany as a child (in 1939) to navigating personal and professional obstacles as an adult. Helen was educated in Canada but earned her Doctorate (Renaissance French literature) in the U.S. She spent 30 years teaching and developing research interests that include cross-cultural understanding, language acquisition, and neurolinguistics. She was professor of French in Canada and the US. She authored *Letters from the Lost: a Memoir of Discovery* (2009).

John F. Winter (1913–d.), b. Piešťany, Slovakia; professor of French literature, University of Cincinnati (s. 1967).

Irena Zátková, (?–2004), b. Czech., studied languages at Charles Univ. After coming to Canada, she taught Spanish at the Dalhousie Univ. and later at Sheridan Coll. in Oakville, Canada.

Joseph William Zdenek (1931–2009), b. Chicago, IL, is Univ. of Madrid trained literary scholar. He has been with Winthrop Coll., SC (s. 1966), as prof. of Spanish and chairman, dept. of modern and classical languages (s. 1970). He is a specialist on Spanish chronicles of the 16th and 17th centuries, Garcia Larca, 20th century Spanish drama.

Jindřich Zezula (fl. 2000), b. Czech., held the position of professor of French at New York Univ.

5. Slavic Languages

Veronika Ambros (1947–), b. Prague, Czech., studied Slavic languages and literatures at Free University of Berlin. She holds the position of assoc. professor of Slavic Languages and Literatures, Department of Slavic Languages and Literatures and the Centre for Comparative Literature, University of Toronto. She has published extensively on the semiotics of theatre and drama, literary theory, and modern Czech literature. Her research interests include Czech and Russian literature and literary theory.

Maria Němcová Banerjee (1937–), b. Prague, Czech., studied Slavic languages and literatures at Univ. of Montreal (M.A., 1957) and Harvard Univ. (Ph.D., 1962). She has been with Smith

Coll. (s. 1964), as assoc. prof. of Russian literature (s. 1972), and now she is prof. of Russian language and literature. She is a specialist on 19th and 20th century Russian, esp. Dostoevsky and symbolism, Pushkin, Russian and European realism in the novel. She wrote several books, including *Paradox: The Novels of Milan Kundera* (1990) and *Dostoevsky: The Scandal of Reason* (2006).

Luba Barna-Gulanich (1924–), b. Bratislava, Czech., is a Slavic linguist. She studied at Charles University, dipl., 1960), Case Western Reserve University (M.A., 1965) and Vanderbilt University. She was associate professor at Youngstown State University, Youngstown, OH.

Věra Žanda Bořkovec (1926–2014), b. Brno, Czech., but grew up in Teheran, Iran where her father Josef Žanda was sent in 1934 as director of the Škoda company. The family returned to Prague in 1945 and she began her studies at Charles Univ., majoring in English and Persian studies. After immigrating to the US, Věra got her M.A. in French from Hollins College in 1960, M.A. in Russian from American University in 1966 and her Ph.D. in Russian from Georgetown Univ. in 1973. After a teaching career of more than thirty years in the Department of Language and Foreign Studies at American University, where she taught Russian (sometimes also Czech) language, linguistics, literature and drama, she retired as professor emerita and devoted herself to her lifelong interests: theater, poetry, and literary translation.

Libor Brom (1923–2006), b. Ostrava, Czech., was a professor of Foreign Languages and Literatures and director of Russian Area Studies at the University of Denver. He received his education at the Czechoslovak Institute of Technology, School of Economics, the Charles University of Prague, School of law, the San Francisco State University, and the University of Colorado. In Europe, Dr. Brom served as an economist and lawyer in International Business and as the chief planner in the research. development, and normalization of Czechoslovak river shipbuilding. He studied Slavic languages and literatures at Univ. of Colorado. He was with Univ. of Denver (s. 1967), as assoc. prof. of foreign languages (s. 1971), later he became a prof. and director of Russian Area Studies. As a professor in the United States, he was selected by the Modern Language Association of America as the Teacher with Superlative Performance, named The American by Choice in Colorado, and received the National Americanism Medal. In the College Book by the Ballantine Books of New York (1984), he is named Denver University's best professor. He was a specialist on Russian émigré literature, Czechoslovak civilization and literature. He is the author of nine books and a great deal of studies in the field of Slavic culture and civilization. In addition, he has lectured at numerous institutions of learning and for many civic and religious groups on education, literature, and international relations. He has appeared on three continents and often on radio and television.

Verona Chorvathova-Conant (1942–), b. Bratislava, Czech. She studied at Comenius University (PhDr., 1978) and at University of Pittsburgh (1983). She resided in Rochester, NY. Her interests were in Slavic languages and literatures and in Czech and Slovak history and folklore and translations into Slovak.

Andrew Činčura (1917–2000), b. Divin, Slovakia, immigrated to the US in 1956. He was a literary scholar and a translator. He received his Doctorate in comparative literature at University of California in Riverside (Ph.D., 1973). He taught at University of California, Riverside, specializing in comparative literature and Slavic languages. He was the editor of *An Anthology of Slovak Literature* (1976).

Norma Comrada (1932–), b. Long Beach, CA, studied psychology and education at Whitman College, Walla Walla, WA (B.A., 1954) and education policy and management at Univ. of Oregon (UO) (M.S., 1982). Prior to 1979, she spent several years each as kindergarten teacher and administrator; adult literacy teacher and program supervisor; public affairs television scriptwriter and presenter; editor; Oregon State Legislature committee clerk and administrator; legislative lobbyist. During 1979–88, she served as assistant to the president and director of the University of Oregon Office of Affirmative Action; for two years during this period, she also was assistant director of the UO Russian and East European Studies Center. From 1989–1991 she was director of communications for the UO Foundation; later in the 1990s she worked as a consultant in human relations for Management/Marketing Associates, Inc. Currently she is a freelance writer, translator, lecturer, illustrator and editor. She has been appointed as courtesy professor of Slavic literature at the Univ. of Oregon, specializing in the life and work of Karel Čapek. For years she has conducted independent research at the Czech State Literary Archives and the ČSAV Inst. of Czech Literature.

Lubomír Doležel (1922–), b. Lesnice, Czech., was a literary theorist and one of the founders of the so-called fictional worlds theory. He was educated at Charles University in Prague and received his CSc. (roughly equivalent to a Ph.D.) in Slavic Philology from the Institute of the Czech Language of the Czechoslovak Academy of Sciences. In the 1960s, Doležel worked concurrently as research fellow in the Institute of Czech Language and as assistant, and later associate, professor of the Philosophical Faculty of Charles University. He was engaged primarily in the application of mathematics (especially statistics), information theory and cybernetics to the study of language and literature. He founded and co-edited a series entitled *Prague Studies in Mathematical Linguistics*. In 1965, Doležel was invited as visiting professor to the University of Michigan in Ann Arbor, where he stayed till 1968. He co-edited (with Richard W. Bailey) a collection of studies *Statistics and Style* (1969). On his return to Prague, he was appointed research fellow of the Institute of

Czech Literature of the Czechoslovak Academy of Sciences, but in the fall of 1968, he left the country after the Soviet invasion of Czechoslovakia. He was invited to the University of Toronto as visiting professor in the Department of Slavic Languages and Literatures, where he later became full professor. He established the study of Czech language and literature at the university. In 1982, he was cross-appointed to the Centre for Comparative Literature. His main research interest was the theory of literature, with a focus on narrative (narratology). Doležel's theoretical position was strongly influenced by analytic philosophy, especially by the conceptual framework of possible worlds. On his retirement in 1988, the Centre organized an international conference "Fictions and Worlds." He was visiting professor at the University of Amsterdam, University of Munich and Charles University. He published numerous papers on the history of poetics, narratology and fictional semantics, and a couple of books on the same subjects.

Andrew M. Drozd (1963–), b. Richmond, TX, of Czech father, received M.A. in history in 1986 and an M.A. in Russian literature in 1988 at Univ. of Texas, Austin. He went abroad for the first time in the summer 1988 when he participated in two summer schools in Czechoslovakia. The first was in Prague in July, the second in Olomouc in August. He followed this by going to the Soviet Union in September, where he studied at Leningrad State Univ. for the fall semester. He entered Indiana U. in the fall 1989 where he obtained a Ph.D. in Russian literature with a minor in Czech Studies (1995). He has been working at Univ. of Alabama since the fall of 1994. From a visiting instructor he advanced to assistant professor in the fall 1995 and received tenure and was promoted to associate professor in 2001. His research interests include: nineteenth-century Russian literature, Tolstoy and Dostoevsky, Russian intellectual history up to the revolution, Czech-Russian ties, Slavic folklore, Czech National Awakening.

George Gibian (1924–2000), b. Prague, Czech., was a literary scholar, specializing in Russian and comparative literature. With the Munich Agreement and its guarantee of a German takeover of Czechoslovakia, he was sent to England, for safety and for his studies. In 1940, after a harrowing journey across the Atlantic, the Gibian family settled in the United States. He returned to Europe as a member of the 94th Infantry Division, which landed in Normandy in 1944. He participated in the Battle of the Bulge, and at the end of the war, he was assigned to occupy the southern part of Czechoslovakia. George was decorated with the Bronze Star with the V device for Valor. After the war, received his Ph.D. degree in English from Harvard University. He taught at Smith Coll. (1951–61); Amherst, and the University of California at Berkeley, before joining the faculty at Cornell in 1961, as Goldwin Smith Professor of Russian and Comparative Literature, as dept. chair (1963–73). In the process, he shifted his specialization from English to comparative literature and Russian literature. He was an authority on Soviet literature, the novel. His honors include Fulbright, Guggenheim,

American Philosophical Society, and Rockefeller Foundation fellowships. He wrote and edited twenty-four books and published ninety-five articles on, among other things, Russian and Soviet literature, Czech literature, comparative literature, intersections of literature with history and politics, and Russian nationalism. He kept an active interest in Czech cultural life, returning regularly to Prague and maintaining contacts with Czech writers and artists there and here. Among his last publications was a 1998 volume of verse and prose by Jaroslav Seifert, with introduction and prose translations by George Gibian.

Šárka B. Hrbková (1878–1948), b. Cedar Rapids, IA, of Czech ancestry, received her training at the University of Nebraska. From 1908 to 1919, she was a member of the faculty of the University of Nebraska, where she was head of the Department of Slavonic Languages and Literature; in 1910 she received the title of adjunct professor; in 1914 assistant professor, with a position on the University Senate and in 1918 was made full professor.

Charles Kinzek (orig. Knížek) (1888–1923), b. Chvalovice, Bohemia, studied at the Univ. of Texas (A.B., 1915). Later became instructor and chair in Slavic and Germanic languages at the Univ. of Texas having the honor of pioneering the Czech language in Texas at university level. He taught Czech and Russian from 1915 to 1923, when Czech was discontinued due to lack of students. Knížek eventually changed his name to the more American spelling of Charles Kinzek and went on to teach in the Department of Foreign Languages at Compton Junior College in Compton, California.

Andrej Kodjak (1926–), b. Prague, Czech., was educated at Univ. of Montreal, St. Vladimir's Theological Sem. and Univ. of Pennsylvania. He has been assoc. professor of Slavic languages and literatures, New York Univ. (s. 1969). He is a specialist on formal literary criticism, stylistics and Pushkin and contemporaries.

Luděk Alois Kozlík (1927–1998), b. PA, of Czech ancestry, was professor of Russian, and Chairman in the Department of Germanic and Slavic Languages and Literatures, San Diego State Univ., San Diego, CA (1965–92).

Joseph R. Kupcek (1914–1986), b. Chicago, IL, of Slovak descent, was professor of Russian language and literature, Southern Illinois University, Carbondale, IL (s. 1970). Previously, he taught at Creighton University before (s. 1954).

Peter Kussi (1925–2012), b. Prague, Czech., was specialist on Czech literature, editor and translator. He was educated at Univ. of Wisconsin and Columbia Univ. He was adj. prof. of Slavic languages at Columbia Univ. He was a specialist on Slavistics, contemporary Czech literature, comparative literature and theory of translations. He was the translator into

English of works by Milan Kundera, Jaroslav Hašek, Josef Škvorecký, Karel Poláček and Jiří Gruša.

Alexander Levitský (1947–), b. Prague, Czech., became a political refugee in 1964 and since then has lived and worked in the West. He studied Slavic languages and literatures at Univ. of Michigan (Ph.D., 1977). He has been a professor of Slavic languages, and Director of Graduate Studies at Brown Univ. (s. 1975). Before coming to Brown in 1975, he held teaching positions at the University of Michigan and Middlebury College. He was a Visiting Professor at Charles University in Prague (2004) and at Harvard (2007). He is a specialist on Russian pre-modern and modern literature, Slavonic Baroque literature, Russian literary culture. He is author or editor of volumes, including *Creative Anthology of Czech Poetry* (1973), *Modern Czech Studies* (1999, 2000), etc.

Milan Loupal (1937–), b. Žilina, Czech., studied Slavic Languages and Literatures at University of Kansas (M.A., 1965). He taught at Dept. of Foreign Languages at University of California, Irvine, CA. He apparently also taught at Portland State Univ. He specialized in linguistics and Slavic literature and Russian.

Joe Malik, Jr. (1919–1997), b. Christopher, IL, of Czech ancestry, studied at Univ. of Pennsylvania. He was with Univ. of Texas (1949–60). In 1960, he was hired away from the University of Texas to start a Russian program at the University of Arizona. He was with Univ. of Arizona (s. 1960), as prof. of Russian (s. 1963), as dept. chair (1972–85), who retired in 1989. He was the first Russian professor in Arizona, his department became independent for the German Department in 1970. By the time he retired, he had built Bachelor's and Master's programs. He was a specialist on methods of teaching foreign languages.

Ladislav Matějka (1919–2012), b. Suché Vrbné, Czech., was a Czech scholar of semiotics and linguistic theory, who translated and published many contributions to Prague linguistic circle theory. He received his Doctorate in Charles University in Prague in 1948. In 1954. Matějka immigrated to the United States. After a year at the Radio Free Europe desk in New York, he enrolled at Harvard University where he earned a second Doctorate in linguistics in cooperation with the late Roman Jakobson. From 1956 until 1989, he taught at University of Michigan in the Slavic Department, as prof. of Slavic languages and literatures (s. 1969). In 1962, he founded *Michigan Slavic Publications*, a series that has published more than 100 volumes by authors such as Roman Jakobson and Nikolai Trubetzkoy. From 1982–1993, he edited the series *Cross Currents* that published material by Milan Kundera, Josef Škvorecký and Czesław Miłosz. His academic correspondence has been deposited at Howard Gotlieb Archival Research Center, Boston University.

IX. HUMANITIES

Eduard Míček (1891-1962), b. Frýdek, Moravia, was educated at Charles Univ. (1920), King's Coll. of University of London (Ph.D., 1924) and at Univ. of Chicago (1924-26). He came to Texas in 1926 having been offered by the University of Texas in Austin the position of instructor of Slavic languages. When the department of Slavic languages originated in 1929, he became its chairman; he served in that capacity until 1958. In 1936 Míček was vice president of the Czech Texas Centennial Association. During World War II, he spoke frequently to the Austin Forum of Public Opinion on the Nazi regime, the underground in Europe, and Russian-American relations. In 1942, he taught the first class in Russian offered at the university. He was elected vice president of the American Association of Teachers of Slavonic and East European Languages in 1949 and served as president the following year. For five years, beginning in 1954, he was president and organizer of the Czech Majales Festival. In the first thirty-two years of his thirty-six at the University of Texas, Míček never missed a class. He was the author of numerous books and articles, including *The Real Tolstoy* (1958), *Tolstoy the Artist and Humanist* (1961), and a series of four illustrated Czech readers. In addition to Czech and German, he was fluent in Russian and Polish.

Beatrice M. Nosco (1924-2001), b. Dublovice, Czech.; a graduate of Charles University, Prague (1947) and also studied at Uppsala University, Sweden (1947-49) and at Columbia University (M.A., 1951). She taught the Czech language and literature at the Royal University at Uppsala (1948-49) and then held the position of research associate at Columbia University, where she taught Czech since 1950. She was also instructor of German at Queens College. During her graduate studies, she was awarded the Swedish Government fellowship (1947-48) and a fellowship from the American Association of University Women (1956-57). Her fields of interest were activities and the fate of the Czech and Slovak religious emigrants during the 17th century and Czechoslovak-Scandinavian relations in general.

Hongor Oulanoff (1929-2010), b. Prague, Czech., spent his teenage and college years in Paris, France. He attended the University of Paris where he graduated with a Diplome de Licencie es Lettres in Arabic language and literature. He spent two post graduate years at the College of Europe in Bruges, Belgium. He was accepted into the University of Paris Sorbonne section Doctorial Program but chose Harvard University, Cambridge, MA. There he received his Ph.D. in Russian Literature in 1960. After a short teaching position at Harvard, he taught at Vanderbilt University from 1961-1963 and then from 1963-1991 in the Department of Slavic Languages and Literatures at The Ohio State University where he became one of the youngest Full Professors (s. 1970). He was a specialist on modern Russian prose, Soviet science fiction. Among his many distinctions, he received an Honorary Captain's Gold Shield from the New York City Police Department.

Peter Petro (1946–), b. Bratislava, Czech.; Russian language specialist; associate professor of Russian Studies, University of British Columbia, as professor (s. 1977); coordinator of Russian program a chair of program in modern European studies.

Hana Píchová (1961–), b. Prague, Czech., studied comparative literature (M.A., 1985) and Slavic languages and literatures (M.A., 1987; Ph.D., 1991), all at Univ. of Wisconsin, Madison. She was associated with Univ. of Texas, Austin, as asst. professor of Slavic languages and literatures (1991–98) and then as assoc. professor (1998–2009), before joining University of North Carolina, Chapel Hill as an assoc. professor of Slavic languages and literatures (s. 2009). Her specialization is in twentieth century Czech and Russian prose. Most of her published work focuses on literature in exile. Recently, she has been pursuing an interest in how Czech literature refracts various cultural and architectural events that occurred in Czechoslovakia after WWII.

Rostislav V. Pletnev (1903–1985), b. St. Petersburg, USSR, was trained as a philologist and linguist at Charles Univ. in Prague (PhDr.). He was professor of Slavic languages and literatures, Univ. of Ottawa.

Božena B. Pospishil (1910–2001), b. Čáslav, Bohemia. She was trained at Charles University (PhDr., 1938). She held the position of Lecturer in Czech, University of California, Berkeley, CA.

Jaromíra Rakušan (1940–), b. Prague, Czech., studied Slavic languages and literatures (dipl., 1964) at Charles University and Slavic studies (Ph.D., 1976) at University of Ottawa. She has taught several courses at Carleton University including: modern and historical Russian grammar, Old Church Slavonic, Czech language, introduction into general linguistics, phonology (introductory and advanced), morphology, semantics, sociolinguistics, historical grammar, language in cultural perspective, language as a toy and a weapon, as well as several courses on linguistic topics for the learning in retirement program. Her research has involved the following topics: Russian morphology, i.e., augmentatives and diminutives, language contacts, and Slavic and Germanic comparative phraseology. She co-authored a book, *Source Book for Linguistics* (3rd ed., 1999).

Josef Rostinský (1945–), b. Brno, Czech., studied at Univ. J. E. Purkyně (dipl., 1969), SUNY-Albany (M.A., 1970, Harvard Univ. (M.A., 1975) and at Brown Univ. (Ph.D., 1980). He has had varied careers, including being preceptor at Harvard University (1973–1975); instructor at United States Defense Language Institute, California (1977); lecturer University Texas, Austin (1975–77); and instructor at Brown University, Providence (1978–80). Since then, he has been professor of American civilization studies at Tokai University, Tokyo. He has also served as consultant, Information Communications Systems, Tokyo (1984); curriculum analyst at Brown University (1978-79); research analyst for National Academy of Sciences, Washington, DC (1974); and co-chairman for Koji Chikugo Fund. He specializes in Slavic languages and literatures and semiotics He is the author of *Credo* (1984).

Gerald J. Sabo (1945-), b. Bridgeport, CT, of Slovak descent; R.C. priest, S.J., associate professor of Slavic Languages and Literatures, John Carroll University. Cleveland, OH.

Míla Šašková-Pierce (1948-), b. Prague, Czech., studied at Univ. of Brussels, Univ. of Louvain and Univ. of Kansas (Ph.D., 1986). She has been associated with Univ. of Nebraska, Lincoln, as asst. professor of Czech and Russian (1989-96), as assoc. professor (s. 1996). Her areas of specializations and research are: methodology of second language learning and technology use in foreign language acquisition, émigré culture and language, language attrition, Czech émigré literature from the linguistic point of view, synchronic Slavic linguistics, language levels and language planning in Czech and Russian languages. She is the author of *Czech for Communication, Listening and Reading Comprehension, and Conversational Themes for Students of the Czech Language* (1995).

Walter Schamschula (1929-), b. Prague, Czech., was a literary scholar and translator. Since 1950, he studied Slavic, Romance, English and German languages at the University of Frankfurt am Main. This followed a year of study at the University of Sorbonne in Paris with Pierre Pascal and Victor Tapié. From 1954, he studied at the University of Marburg. In 1958, he followed his teacher Alfred Rammelmeyer as an assistant to Frankfurt, where, after his appointment, he helped to set up the Slavic seminar. There he received his Doctorate in 1960, with his dissertation 'The Russian Historical Novel from Classicism to Romanticism.' In 1970, he habilitated in Frankfurt with his work on 'The Beginnings of Czech Renewal and the German Spiritual Life (1740-1800),' In the academic year 1970-71, he was a visiting professor at the University of California at Berkeley, where he taught, among other things, Czech language and literature. He then taught at the University of Saarbrücken (1971-72). In 1972, he was a full professor at University of California in Berkeley. Later, he developed the Slavic seminar at the University of Bamberg (1981-84). In 1984, he returned to Berkeley, where he taught until his retirement in 1994. He is a specialist on Russian historic novel, Pushkin, and Czech literature.

Peter Zdeněk Schubert (1946-), b. Prague, Czech., graduated from Univ. of Waterloo, majoring in mathematics (B.Math., 1973). Subsequently, he switched fields and pursued studies in Russian literature at Univ. of Waterloo (M.A., 1975) and comparative literature at Univ. of Alberta (Ph.D., 1985). He taught at Univ. of Alberta and later served at US embassy in Vienna as an area specialist (1990-97). Currently, he is self-employed as translator and interpreter and resides in Edmonton, Alberta, Canada. His interests are in the area of the 20th century Czech literature, 19th and 20th century Russian literature and theory of literature. He is the author of *The Narratives of Capek and Chekhov: A Typological Comparison of the Authors' World Views* (1996).

Klement Šimončič (1912-2010), b. Krupá, Slovakia, was a Slavic philologist, trained at Comenius University (dipl., 1935). He was editor, Free Europe, Inc., New York, NY (1948-73); and also, lecturer with Columbia University. Because of his ability to speak several languages, he frequently served as translator. He served in the US Army during World War II in the European Theatre.

John Marion Skrivanek (1913-1972), b. Caldwell, TX, of Bohemian ancestry, was a Slavic philologist. He was a fourth generation Czech American whose great-grandfather settled in Texas in 1885. He attended the University of Texas (B.A., 1938; M.A., 1946) and Charles University in Prague (PhDr., 1948). He was an instructor in Slavic languages at the University of Texas (1941-46), Head, Dept. of Slavonic Languages, University of Houston (1948-51); Head, Dept. of Modern Languages, South Texas College (1951-52) and, since 1952, he had been Professor of Modern Languages (Russian, Czech, Spanish) at Texas A&M College, College Station, TX. He was a specialist on Slavonic philology, Russian, Czech. He authored several Czech textbooks which were used throughout the country. He also authored a textbook on Russian language, *Russian Conservation and Reading* (1962). He also wrote *Education of Czechs in Texas*. He was the founder of the Czech Educational Foundation of Texas. He was Fellow of Institute of International Education.

Elena Sokol (1943-), b. Chicago, IL, is a second-generation Czech-American, raised in Chicago by her immigrant grandparents and bilingual mother, while her father served in World War II. As a teenager, she began regularly traveling to Czechoslovakia to visit relatives. After completing her BA in Russian at the University of Colorado, Boulder, she earned her M.A. (1967) and Ph.D. (1974) in Slavic Literatures at the University of California, Berkeley. She was a visiting professor in the dept. of German and Russian at Oberlin Coll. (1984-87). Subsequently, she joined the dept. of Russian studies at the College of Wooster, OH, where she advanced from visiting assoc. professor (1987-88) to full professor (1998-2009), in addition to being chair. of the dept. of Russian studies, as well as chair of the Cultural Area Studies program. Her areas of expertise include Russian and Czech literature, language, and culture. Sokol is also an authority on life in Russia and the Czech Republic today. She has also taught courses in comparative literature and women's studies. She had previously served as resident director of study abroad programs in Leningrad, Moscow, and Krasnodar, as well as in Olomouc, Czech Republic. She is the author of *Russian Poetry for Children* (1984) as well as articles on Russian literature and theatre. Since the mid-1990s, her research has focused on contemporary Czech women prose writers. She is currently working on a book devoted to eight of these writers (born between 1945 and 1963), as well as translating novels by Daniela Hodrová.

Peter Steiner (1946–), b. Prague, Czech., is a specialist on Slavic languages and literatures. He studied at Yale Univ. (M.Phil., 1973; Ph.D., 1976). He has been with Univ. of Pennsylvania (s. 1978), becoming assoc. professor of Slavic languages and literatures (1985–99) and full professor (s. 1999); as chair of Slavic dept. (1990–93). Before coming to Penn, Peter Steiner taught at the University of Michigan (1976–77) and at Harvard University (1977–78). He is a specialist on modern Slavic literatures, theory of literature, semiotics. He is the author of *Deserts of Bohemia: Czech Fiction and its Social Context* (2000), *Making a Czech Hero: Julius Fučík through His Writings* (2000) and *Russian Formalism: A Metapoetics* (1984).

Jiří Stejskal (1961–), b. Prague, Czech., studied Slavic languages and literatures at Univ. of Pennsylvania (Ph.D., 1998) and business administration and management at Temple Univ. (M.B.A., 2000). He has taught undergraduate and graduate language courses as a part-time lecturer at the University of Pennsylvania since 1990. He is the founder and president of CETRA Language Solutions (s. 1997). He has more than 20 years of experience as a translator. He is an active member of the American Translators Association (ATA), where he served as president (2007–09). He also served as VP of Fédération Internationale des Traducteurs (2008–14) (AFTI), and chairman of the Status Committee of the International Federation of Translators (FIT). His specialties include: translation and interpretation services in the following industries: marketing research, legal, life sciences, government. He is holder of GSA Federal Supply Schedule for Translation and Interpretation.

Orin Stepanek (1888–1955), b. Crete, NE, of Czech ancestry, studied at Univ. of Nebraska (B.A., 1913) and at Harvard (M.A., 1914). He was with Univ. of Nebraska (s. 1920), as assoc. prof. (s. 1924). He then left for Czechoslovakia, to study Slavic philology at the Charles University in Prague. A year later, he again took up his post in Nebraska University, where he had first taught, second- and third-year courses in Czech continuously, offering also correspondence courses in that language, through the Extension Department. He had also given a beginning course in Russian. His courses in the Department of English were in composition, modern prose fiction and eighteenth-century literature.

Malynne Sternstein (1966–), b. Bangkok, Thailand, of Czech father, is an associate professor of Slavic Studies, specializing in Czech Studies, at the University of Chicago. Her research interests are in Czech literature of the 20th–21st centuries, Czech film, and Czech art, especially that of the Czech surrealists. She explored the latter movement in the book *The Will to Chance: Necessity and Arbitrariness in the Czech Avant-garde from Poetism to Surrealism*. She also has a strong interest in Czech political 'dissidence' internationally.

Her interest in Czech history inspired the book *Czechs of Chicagoland*. She has written articles on Czech film, art, literature, philosophy, and culture. Currently, she is working on a book length study comparing the Czech and French New Wave movements in cinema and the intellectual histories informing these movements.

Rudolf Sturm (1912–2000), b. Doubravice, Bohemia, was a philologist. He was drawn into world affairs as a young man. In 1936, he was sent to Brussels, Geneva, and Paris as a Czechoslovak delegate in a European movement attempting to preserve peace. Initially, he studied law and political science at Charles University in Prague (Abs., 1937). He fled his homeland in 1939, joining the Czechoslovak Government-in-exile in Paris, but in 1941 the Nazi invasion forced him to flee again, this time to the United States. He enlisted in the U.S. Army in 1942 and served in the North African and Italian campaigns. After the War, having returned to Czechoslovakia, he was appointed Head of the American Division, Ministry of Information, Prague, directing cultural relations between the US and Czechoslovakia (1946–48). The communist takeover again forced him to leave in 1948. He returned to the U.S. and worked for Radio Free Europe. He then went on to Harvard University to study Languages and Literatures (Ph.D., 1952). He taught at Boston College, Hershey Junior College, City College of NY, Union College, NY and served as a research associate at Yale University and the Mid-European Studies Center. Later, he was associated with Skidmore College (s. 1958), as professor of modern languages and literatures. He was a specialist on Czechoslovak and Italian literature. Along with extensive teaching and research at Skidmore, he founded its Employees Federal Credit Union. He also served the American Association of University Professors in several capacities and was active in the Modern Language Association and the Czechoslovakian Society of Arts and Sciences (SVU), where he held the position of Secretary General (1959–60, 1962–66). As a member of the National Executive Committee of American Professors for Peace in the Middle East during 1968–75, he traveled to Arab states and Israel to confer with government and intellectual leaders. He lectured frequently on Israel and the diaspora, and, as a Roman Catholic, he received Israel's Tower of David Award in 1984.

František Svejkovský (1923–2011), b. Suchdol n/Lužnicí, Czech., studied Slavic philology and literary history at Charles Univ. (PhDr., 1949). He was prof. of Czech and Slovak literature, Univ. of Chicago (s. 1971). He was a specialist on Czech and Slovak literature, comparative literature, and literary history.

George Jiří Svoboda (1933–), b. Bratislava, Czech., studied at Charles Univ. (Ph.D., 1967). He was associated with the dept. of Slavic languages and literatures, Univ. of California, Berkeley.

Jindřich Toman (1944-), b. Prague, Czech., studied Slavic and Germanic philology at Charles Univ., Univ. of Freiburg and Univ. of Köln. He has been with Univ. of Michigan, Ann Arbor, where he holds the position of professor of Slavic languages and literatures. He works in the area of Slavic and German linguistics. In addition, he has a broad range of research interests, including history of linguistics, Czech literature, and the East European avant-garde. He teaches courses in Slavic linguistics and Czech literature. He is a specialist on Czech literature and culture.

Robert Vlach (1917-1966), b. Prague, Czech., studied at Charles Univ. He emigrated to US in 1958 and until 1959 he taught at Bennet Coll., Greensboro, NC. Since 1959 he was associated with the Univ. of Oklahoma, Norman, where he held the position of assoc. prof. of Slavic languages and literatures. Since 1961 he was editor of the *Books Aboard* monthly. He also wrote poetry.

Bronislava Volková (1946-), b. Děčín, Czech., studied Slavic languages and literatures at Charles Univ. (dipl., 1969; PhDr., 1970). She also bears a certificate of fulfillment of all requirements for CSc./Ph.D. in Russian Language (1973), but the degree was not awarded for political reasons. She has been associated with Harvard Univ. (1978-79), prior to joining the Slavic Dept. of Indiana Univ., Bloomington. Starting as a visiting professor (1982-86), she progressively advanced to asst. professor of Slavic languages (1983-86), assoc. professor (1986-91) and full professor (s. 1991). Here, she also served as a director of the Czech Program for thirty years. For two years, she was active as a resident director of the Council on International Educational Exchange (CIEE) student exchange program in Prague (1999-2001). Since 2010, she is a professor emerita of Slavic Languages and literatures, comparative literature and Jewish studies. Her research interests include Semiotics, emotive language and Czech literature. Her scholarly publications include two books on linguistic and literary semiotics, *Emotive Signs in Language and Semantic Functioning of Derived Nouns in Russian* (1987) and *A Feminist's Semiotic Odyssey through Czech Literature* (1997). She also writes poetry.

Karen von Kuneš (1949-), b. Prague, Czech., received her first post-graduate training in business administration at Univ. of Texas (M.B.A., 1982), followed by a diploma in Slavic languages and literatures at McGill Univ. (Ph.D., 1980). Starting as a visiting professor in Czech language and literature at Univ. of Texas (1981-82), she then went on to Harvard as preceptor in Slavic languages and literatures (1984-97). She then joined Yale Univ. (s. 1995), where she is now a senior lecturer. She specializes in Czech language teaching, lexicography (historical and comparative), modern Czech literature, European literature, relation of literature to social psychology, Czech film identity of Czech expatriate writers and filmmakers, and creative fiction/screenwriting. She wrote a number of books, including

Czech Practical Dictionary Czech-English/English-Czech (2011), *Beyond the Imaginable: 240 Ways of Looking at Czech* (1999), *Barron's Travel Wise Czech* (1998), *72 Discussions of the Czech Language* (1995), *Fast & Easy Czech* (1992). She also wrote a novel *Among the Sinners* (2013) which addresses serious global immigration issues in a playful style.

Martin Votruba (1948-2018), b. Štrba, Czech., senior lecturer of Slavic languages and literatures, and head of Slovak studies program, University of Pittsburgh.

Thomas Gustav Winner (1917-2004), b. Prague, Bohemia, studied at Harvard and Columbia Univs. He was with Duke Univ. (1948-57); with Univ. of Michigan (1958-66); as prof. of Slavic languages and comparative literature, Brown Univ. (s. 1976), as dir. of Center Research Semiotics (s. 1977). He was a specialist on Russian literature of the 19th century, literary theory, semiotic theory.

Vladimír Zbořílek (1924-), b. Mořkovice, Czech., studied French and Spanish at Masaryk Univ., then in Paris and Madrid and at the end also at the Univ. of California, Berkeley. He then became asst. prof. of foreign languages at Univ. of Miami, FL, where he remained until his retirement in 1995. He specializes in Czech and Russian languages, and also Czechoslovak, Russian and Spanish history.

Gleb N. Žekulin (1922-2004), b. Prague, Czech., was educated at Univ. of Liverpool. After a year teaching in the US, he was appointed associate professor of Russian at McGill University and five years later, he moved to the Department of Slavic Languages and Literatures at the University of Toronto, where in 1978 he was appointed full professor. He was also director of the Centre for Russian and East European Studies at the University of Toronto, a post he held for five years (1979-84). He remained deeply concerned with Czech affairs; he offered courses in Czech language and literature and was closely involved with the '68' publishing house in Toronto, but his main interests were in Russian literature. He had made a name for himself with his work on the 'village prose' of the 1950s and later with a passionate involvement in the work of Solzhenitsyn. Most of his work, however, was devoted to the nineteenth century, and in particular to Pushkin, Gogol, and Dostoevsky.

6. Near Eastern Languages

Miloš Borecký (1903-1954), b. Prague, Czech., studied Classic and Oriental philology and history at Charles Univ. (PhDr., 1930). He worked at the University library in Prague and in 1947, he was sent on a grant to Iran to do research. At its termination, he emigrated to the US, settling in Washington, DC, where he was employed at the Library of Congress. His interests have been in Iranian philology and classic Persian poetry.

Bernhard Geiger (1881-1964), b. Bílsko, on Moravian/Silesian border, was a philologist trained at Univ. of Vienna, the University of Bonn, the University of Prague, the University of Göttingen and the University of Heidelberg. He came to US in 1938. He became prof. of Indo-Iranian philology, Asia Inst., NYC (1938-51); vis. prof. and then adj. prof., Columbia Univ. (1951-56). He was a specialist on Iranian and Sanskrit. He analyzed inscriptions from third century near Damascus.

Edeltraud Harzer (1943-), b. Karlovy Vary; Czech., in US since 1973. She graduated from Charles Univ., where she majored in Indian studies. After additional training in India, at Benares Hindu Univ. and at the University in Pun (1971-73), she immigrated to the US. She continued her studies at Univ. of Washington (Ph.D.), where she taught Hindu, Indian literature and Asian studies. Simultaneously, she also taught religion at State Univ. of Washington, Tacoma. In 1993, she taught Hindu studies at Stanford and from 1993-96, she taught Sanskrit and Hindu at Indiana Univ. Subsequently, she has been a senior lecturer at Univ. of Texas, Austin (s. 1998). Her research interests are Sanskrit, Indian philosophy and literature and material culture.

Ruth Goldsmith Kunzer (1915-2005), b. Prague, Bohemia, but raised in Germany. When Hitler came to power, she escaped with her family to England. In 1937, Ruth's Zionist affiliation began when she joined the staff of the Jewish Agency for Palestine in London where she worked with the leaders of the Palestine Jewish community, including David Ben Gurion and Moshe Sharett. In 1945, Ruth made her home in Israel as a Public Relations Officer of the Weizmann Institute of Science. In Israel's War of Liberation in 1948, she was a war correspondent attached to the Israeli Army, and later appointed press officer of the Government of Israel. In 1950, as the Director of Public Affairs of Israel's Consulate General in New York, Ruth was heard weekly over New York radio on "Life in Israel." In Los Angeles, Ruth completed her formal education which had been disrupted by Hitler, graduating summa cum laude from California State University, Northridge. She was professor of Jewish literature and history at Hebrew Union Coll., Los Angeles, CA.

Benno Landsberger (1890-1960), b. Frýdek, Moravia, was an Assyriologist, specializing in Semitic languages. Starting in 1908, he studied Oriental Studies at Leipzig. Amongst his teachers were August Fischer in Arabic and Heinrich Zimmern in Assyriology. After the War, in which he took an active part, he returned to Leipzig and was appointed to the position of extraordinary professor in 1926. In 1928, he was appointed successor to Peter Jensen at Marburg but returned to Leipzig in 1929 as Zimmern's successor. Landsberger was dismissed as a result of the Nazi-era Law for the Restoration of the Professional Civil Service which excluded Jews from government employment. Landsberger accepted a post at the new Turkish University of Ankara, working especially in the area of languages, history and geography. After 1945, he was appointed to the Oriental Institute of the University of Chicago, where he worked until 1955. Landsberger was an eminent and groundbreaking scholar, editing many important lexical texts and conducting fundamental linguistic studies.

Adolf Leo Oppenheim (1904-1974), b. Vienna, of Moravian father, was a specialist on Near East. He was one of the most distinguished Assyriologists of his generation. He was John A. Wilson Professor of Oriental Studies at the University of Chicago. He received his Ph.D. at the University of Vienna in 1933. His parents died in the Nazi Holocaust, and his wife Elizabeth barely escaped but he and she emigrated to the United States, where, after a couple of lean years, he became a research associate at the University of Chicago, 1947, and a faculty member in 1950. He became an associate editor of the University's Chicago *Assyrian Dictionary* in 1952. The Dictionary had been planned since 1921 and would eventually stretch to more than 20 published volumes. Assisted by Erica Reiner, Oppenheim remained editor-in-charge until his sudden death, still at the height of his intellectual powers. A. Leo Oppenheim's most famous work is *Ancient Mesopotamia: Portrait of a Dead Civilization*. His attempt to reform the field, embodied in *Assyriology— Why and How?*, was taken personally by some other Assyriologists. Its tone of pessimism at the impossible prospect of reviving a living understanding of Mesopotamian culture belied his personal optimism and sociability.

William Popper (1874-1963), b. St. Louis. MO, of Bohemian ancestry, was educated at Columbia Univ. (A.B., 1896; A.M., 1897; Ph.D., 1899). He then went abroad for postgraduate courses at the universities of Strasbourg, Berlin and Paris. He travelled in Germany, France, Austria, and Spain (1899-1901); Egypt, Syria, Palestine, the Hauran, North Syrian Desert, the Euphrates region, Bagdad, and Bombay (1901-1902). On his return to America, he served for three years (1902-05) as associate editor and chief of the Bureau of Translation of the *Jewish Encyclopedia*. For the last two years of this period (as well as later in 1919-1920), he was also Gustav Gottheil Lecturer in Semitic Languages at Columbia University. In 1905, he was invited to join the faculty of the University of California, Berkeley. From the rank of instructor (1905), he moved swiftly up to assistant professor (1906), to associate professor (1916) and was appointed professor of Semitic languages in 1922, and chairman of the Department of Semitic Languages - a post he held until his retirement as professor emeritus in 1945.

Samuel Rosenblatt (1902-1983), b. Bratislava, Slovakia; rabbi and scholar; professor of Jewish literature (1930-46) and thereafter Oriental languages, at Johns Hopkins University, Baltimore.

Stanislav Segert (1921–2005), b. Prague, Czech., was educated at Charles Univ. and the Czechoslovak Academy of Sciences. He was professor of Northwest Semitic Languages in the NELC department from 1969 until his retirement in 1991. Segert was perhaps best known for his textbook *Basic Grammar of the Ugaritic Language* (1984), but he also wrote a fundamental *Grammar of Phoenician and Punic* (1976) as well as the best Old Aramaic grammar, *Altaramäische Grammatik* (1975).

Andreas Tietze (1914–2003), b. Vienna, of Bohemian ancestry, was a language specialist on Turkish, trained at Univ. of Vienna. He emigrated to US in 1958. He was with UCLA (s. 1958), as prof. of Turkish (1960–74), as chairman dept. of Near-Eastern languages (1965–70). He then returned to Austria to head Inst. für Orientalistik at Univ. of Vienna. He was a specialist in Turkish language, including compilations, literature and translation, also folklore.

7. Far Eastern Languages

William M. Bodiford (1955–), b. Nashville, TN, of Czech ancestry on his mother's side, received his Ph.D. from Yale Univ. in the Department of Religious Studies, where he specialized in Buddhist Studies. He is a professor in the Department of Asian Languages and Cultures at the Univ. of California, Los Angeles.

Laura Burian (1970–), b. Boston, MA, of Czech ancestry, studied comparative area studies (East Asian Studies) at Duke Univ. (B.A., 1991), and Chinese/English translation and interpretation at the Monterey Institute of International Studies (M.A., 1995). She also studied abroad at National Taiwan Normal University, Chinese University of Hong Kong, and Nanjing University. Her expertise is in the area of simultaneous and consecutive interpretation between Chinese and English, and pedagogy for the teaching of simultaneous and consecutive interpretation. In the late 90s, she worked as an in-house translator, interpreter, and legal assistant in the Beijing office of Skadden, Arps, Slate, Meagher & Flom, and freelanced as both a translator and interpreter in the US, mainland China, and Taiwan (s. 1995). In Jan 2000, she joined the faculty of the Middlebury Institute of International Studies at Monterey (MIIS, formerly the Monterey Institute of International Studies). There she has served as president (2007–09) and vice president (2013–15) of the faculty senate and was awarded the Outstanding Teacher of the Year award in 2004, the Allen Griffiths Excellence in Teaching Award in 2005, and the Dr. Leslie Eliason Teacher of Excellence Award in 2008. Beyond teaching, Professor Burian is an active freelance translator and interpreter. Her private sector clients are primarily in the fields of law, medicine, mobile internet, venture capital, new energies, biology, human rights, and education. Her US government clients include the Departments of State, Energy, and Commerce, the US Embassy in Beijing, among others. She is also a freelance violinist/violist/fiddler with groups such as the Monterey String Quartet and Heartstrings (s. 2001).

Milena Doleželová-Velingerová (1932-2012), b. Czech., a sinologist, educated at Charles Univ. and at the Oriental Inst. of ČSAV, immigrated to Canada in 1969. She was with Univ. of Toronto (s. 1969), as assoc. prof. (1969-72), as prof. (1972-96); with Charles Univ. (1996-2000). She is the author of *Ballad of the Hidden Dragon. Translated with an Introduction* (1971), *The Chinese Novel at the Turn of the Century* (1980), *A Selective Guide to Chinese Literature 1900-1949. Vol. 1. The Novel* (1988); *The Appropriation of Cultural Capital. China's May Fourth Project* (2001).

Anthony (Antonín) V. Liman (1932-), b. Prague, Czech., studied first at Charles Univ. and then at Waseda Univ., Tokyo, Japan. He emigrated to Canada in 1968 and settled in Toronto, where he taught in the dept. of East Asian Studies at Univ. of Toronto (s. 1968), as assoc. professor (1972-89), as a full professor (s. 1989). He retired as professor emeritus in 1997 with 30 years of service. In 1997-99, he assumed post of senior visiting scholar at Otemae Coll., Kobe, Japan. In 2008, he was awarded Joseph Jungmann Prize for best translation of the novellas by Ibuse Masuji. In 2009, he was awarded main prize of the Japanese Soc. of Translators for complete translations of the four volumes of Manyoshu.

John William Nemec (1971-), b. Cleveland, OH, of Czech father, completed B.A. in religion, minor in philosophy at the University of Rochester in 1994; M.A. in Religious studies from the Univ. of California at Santa Barbara in 1997; and M.Phil. in Oriental studies (Classical Indian religions) from Oxford University, England in 2000, and Ph.D. in South Asia studies from the Univ. of Pennsylvania in 2005. From 2005-2012, he was assistant professor of Indian Religions and South Asian Studies in the Department of Religious Studies at University of Virginia. From 2012, he has been associate professor in the same department and under the same title. All his studies are in the area of classical and contemporary Indian and South Asian religion, philosophy, language, and culture. He works on classical Sanskrit literature and is the author of numerous scholarly articles in the subject and of a monograph titled *The Ubiquitous Siva: Somananda's Sivadrsti and His Tantric Interlocutors* (2011).

8. Other Languages

Magdalena Hauner (née Slavíková) (1944-), b. Brno, Czech., received her first degree from Charles University in 1965, with majors in African studies and English, and Ph.D. in Bantu languages from the School of Oriental and African Studies, University of London in 1975, and was lecturer there (1971-78). She joined the University of Wisconsin, Madison in 1979 in the Department of African Languages and Literature as assistant professor in Swahili and African linguistics, later promoted to associate professor (1986), and professor (1998). She directed Swahili language and culture instruction in the Department and taught it at all levels, as well as courses on African linguistics, translation, and other Africa-related courses. Bantu linguistics and Swahili language and culture are her special areas. Her research interests also include second language acquisition and the role of technology in teaching. She served as department chair (1999-2003), as associate dean for the arts and humanities in the College of Letters and Science (2003-2011). Currently she is professor emerita. Her publications include *Lexico-statistical Analysis as a Basis for Teaching Swahili* (1969) – three extensive online courses in Swahili language and culture – *Rosa Mistika* (Intermediate Level Swahili) (1999), *Magazeti Online* (2002), and *Utamaduni Online* (co-authored) (2008). She also co-authored a book for college instructors of Swahili, *Mwalimu wa Kiswahili* (1998).

František Lorenz (*aka* Francisco Valdomiro Lorenz) (1872-1957), b. Zbislav, Bohemia, was a polyglot and philosopher. He was one of the first Esperantists in the world and was able to communicate in over 100 different languages. In 1891, Lorenz moved to Brazil due to political reasons. Lorenz published over 36 books in 40 languages and was one of the most prominent promoters of Esperanto movement ever.

Alois Richard Nykl (1885-1958), b. Radlice, near Dolní Kruty, Bohemia, was a polyglot trained at Univ. of Chicago (Ph.D., 1921) During his lifetime, he learned dozens of languages, many of which he mastered as a native speaker, including Arabic and the languages of the Orient. He taught in a number of universities, including Northwestern Univ. (1921-25), Marquette Univ. (1926-29), Univ. of Chicago Oriental Inst. (1929-32), Harvard (1941-44), etc. He traveled widely around the world, including Mexico, Egypt, China, India, Japan, etc. During the First World War, he actively participated in the Czech national movement in America and led, together with Enrique Stanko Vráz, a campaign for the re-election of President Wilson for the US president.

9. Linguistics

Isaac Bacon (1914-2007), b. Svinov, Moravia, was a linguist trained at Masaryk Univ., Czech. Through incredible acts of bravery, the University awarded him Ph.D. on March 28, 1939, thirteen days after Adolph Hitler entered Prague. He was with Univ. of Colorado (s. 1946), as prof. of linguistics (1956-59); and with Yeshiva Coll. as prof. of linguistics (s. 1959) and dean (1960-75). He specialized in High German, early new High German and linguistics.

John Frederick Bailyn (1962-), is son of Bernard Bailyn and Lotte Lazarsfeld, the latter being of Czech ancestry. He is a linguist trained at Cornell University (Ph.D., 1995). He is professor of linguistics at Stony Brook University (s. 1994). He is the co-founder and co-director of NYI, as well as the Director of the State University of New York's Russia Programs Network. John Frederick Bailyn's research involves investigations of the workings of the linguistic component of the mind, with particular attention to the Slavic languages. Within theoretical linguistics, his primary interests lie in generative syntax, especially issues of case, word order and movement. Within cognitive science, he is interested in issues of modularity, creativity, and musical perception. Within Slavic Linguistics, he is interested in Russian Syntax, Morphology, and Phonology, comparative Slavic syntax, and historical linguistics. He authored *The Syntax of Russian* (2012), the winner of 2013 AATSEEL in Slavic linguistics.

Luba Barna-Gulanich (1924–), b. Bratislava, Czech., is a Slavic linguist, trained at Charles University (dipl., 1960) and Case Western Reserve University (M.A., 1965). She is associate professor Youngstown State University, Youngstown, OH, specializing in Russian phonetics.

Leonard Bloomfield (1887–1949), b. Chicago, IL, nephew of Maurice Bloomfield, was a linguist, pioneer in structural linguistics. Bloomfield was Instructor in German at the University of Cincinnati, 1909–1910; Instructor in German at the University of Illinois at Urbana-Champaign, 1910–1913; Assistant Professor of Comparative Philology and German, also University of Illinois, 1913–1921; Professor of German and Linguistics at the Ohio State University, 1921–1927; Professor of Germanic Philology at the University of Chicago, 1927–1940; Sterling Professor of Linguistics at Yale University, 1940–1949. During the summer of 1925, Bloomfield worked as Assistant Ethnologist with the Geological Survey of Canada in the Canadian Department of Mines, undertaking linguistic field work on Plains Cree; this position was arranged by Edward Sapir, who was then Chief of the Division of Anthropology, Victoria Museum, Geological Survey of Canada, Canadian Department of Mines. Bloomfield was one of the founding members of the Linguistic Society of America.

Vít Bubeník (1942–), b. Nové Město na Moravě, Czech, studied philology (dipl., 1967) and Greek language and literature (PhDr., 1969) at Masaryk Univ. He has been associated with the Memorial Univ. of Newfoundland, St. John's, Can. (s. 1971), where he advanced from asst. professor to assoc. professor of linguistics (1976–84), Univ. res. professor (1996–2001), professor of general and historical linguistics (2001–11), prof. emeritus (s. 2012). He specializes in Hellenic (Ancient and Modern Greek) and Indic (Sanskrit, Prakrits) branches of Indo-European. He is the author of *An Introduction to the Study of Morphology* (4th ed., 1997), *Historical Syntax of Late Middle Indo-Aryan* (1998), *Helenistic and Roman Greece as a Sociolinguistic Area* (1989), *The Phonological Interpretation of Ancient Greek: A Study in Pan-dialectal Analysis* (1983), *Etymology: How and Why* (1983), etc.

Lída Cope (1965–), b. Přerov, Czech., was initially trained as a teacher of Czech language and literature at Palacký Univ. After coming to the US, she continued her studies at Univ. of Arizona at Tucson, which awarded her M.A. in English (1994) and Ph.D. in second language acquisition and teaching (1998). She was associated with Univ. of Arizona, before becoming asst. professor in curriculum and instruction at University of Mississippi at University (1999–2000). Since then, she has been assoc. professor of applied linguistics at East Carolina

Univ. at Greenville. She is also an external research associate, Department of Slavic and Euroasian Studies, University of Texas at Austin (s. 2013). Her research interests relate to: Texas Czech; immigrant/heritage community language documentation, revitalization and maintenance; language, culture and ethnic identity; child bilingualism; language contact and first language attrition; and cross-cultural communication.

Antonin F. Dostál (1906–1997), b. Řimice, Czech., was educated at Charles Univ. (PhDr., 1931; DrSc, 1957). In 1930–45, he taught French at the Business Academy in Prostějov and continued his private study of Slavonic studies. From 1945, he worked in the Office of the Old Slavonic Dictionary in Prague. In 1948, he received his habilitation at the Faculty of Arts, Charles University. He lectured on the history of the Polish and Russian languages at the Faculty of Arts, Charles University, and Old Slavonic and comparative Slavic studies at the Faculty of Arts, Palacký University in Olomouc. From 1953 to 1960, he worked at the University of Russian Language and Literature in Prague, where he was appointed professor in 1954 and obtained the title of DrSc. He taught Old Slavonic and the history of the Czech language, held the positions of Vice-Rector and Head of the Department of Czech Language and General Linguistics, and was the editor-in-chief of the *School Bulletin* (1956–61). From the beginning of the 1950s, he also devoted himself intensively to Byzantology. In 1953, he became a co-editor of the magazine *Byzantinoslavica*, in which he participated in bibliography since 1949, and from 1959–69, he was its editor-in-chief. Until 1968, he chaired the Czechoslovak Byzantine Committee, from 1948, he was a member of the Association International des Études Byzantines. Until his departure for the USA, he also collaborated with the Slavonic Institute as executive director of the editorial board of the *Dictionary of the Old Slavonic Language* (1956–69). He also participated in the preparation of the exhibition Great Moravia (Brno 1963, Prague 1964). He obtained the Bulgarian Order of Cyril and Methodius I. From 1960 to 1968, he worked at the Faculty of Arts of Charles University as a member of the Department of Slavonic Studies, and also worked as the Vice-Dean for International Relations and the Director of the Summer School of Slavonic Studies. He emigrated in 1968 and was a professor of Slavonic studies at Brown University in Providence, RI, until 1976.

Eva Eckert (1957–), b. Prague, Czech., studied at Charles Univ., Univ. of Michigan and Univ. of California in Berkeley. She has been prof. of Russian at Connecticut Coll., New London. She is a specialist on Slavic linguistics, Czech and Russian. Eckert's primary research is in language contact, maintenance and death, and history of immigration.

Milan Fryščák (1932–2020), b. Dobrá u Frýdku, Czech., was a Slavic linguist. He attended preparatory high school in Místek and received his B.A. from Palacky University in Olomouc in 1956. In the Fall of 1957, Milan made a daring escape from Communist

Czechoslovakia when a ship he was on docked in Venice, Italy. He spent the next year and a half as a political refugee in camps in Cremona and Naples after which he immigrated to Racine, WI in January 1959. He moved to California in 1960. He studied at the University of California, Berkeley, where he obtained his M.A. in Slavic Languages and Linguistics in 1962. In 1964, he became an American citizen and started teaching in the Russian Language department of Wittenberg University. He received his Ph.D. in Slavic Linguistics from Ohio State in 1969. From 1971 until his retirement in 2008, Prof. Fryščák taught at New York University in the Department of Russian and Slavic Studies. He was also a graduate advisor to Master's and Ph.D. candidates in that department. From the 1970s through the 1990s, he spent the majority of his summers directing and teaching at the Russian School of Norwich University in Vermont. In 1988, he was selected by IREX for an academic exchange between the United States and Czechoslovakia. Following the Velvet Revolution in 1989, he was instrumental in establishing some of the first scholar exchanges between Charles University and NYU. He served as Director of NYU's Summer Program in Prague, lectured at Charles University, and taught in their Summer School of Slavonic Studies. In recognition of his efforts, on the occasion of the 650th anniversary of the founding of Charles University, he was honored with the Charles University Memorial Medal. He was a specialist on comparative Slavic linguistics and history of Russian language.

Paul Lucian Garvin (1919–1994), b. Karlovy Vary, Czech., was Indiana Univ. trained linguist. He was prof. of linguistics at SUNY Buffalo (s. 1969) and served two terms as Linguistics Department chairman. He retired in 1990. He was an internationally known expert in language problems, language policy and planning issues and language in education. He also did research in machine translation, problems of linguistic theory and method, semiotics and socio- and ethno-linguistics. Garvin taught under Fulbright grants in Argentina, Uruguay and Chile and traveled extensively in Latin America. He was consultant to the French Language Council of the Quebec government and was an honored guest of the Irish Language Board of the Republic of Ireland and the Second International Congress of the Catalan Language of the Catalan regional government in Spain. Since his retirement, he divided his time between Buffalo and Europe, where he held appointments in anthropological linguistics at Masaryk University in Brno, Czechoslovakia, and at the University of Prague. He taught occasionally at UB and continued to advise students there. He specialized in general linguistics and linguistic theory, semiotics and computation in linguistics.

Albert Miloslav Gessman (1916–1988), b. Vienna, of Czech ancestry, was a linguist. He studied comparative linguistics at Charles University (Abs., 1939) and at Rudolf University Vienna (Dr. phil, 1950). He was with Univ. of South Florida, Tampa (s. 1961), as prof. of classics and medieval studies (s. 1967) and dept. chair (s. 1961). He specialized in general and comparative linguistics and ancient studies. He authored *The Codes of Language* (1959, 1974), *The Tongue of the Romans* (1970), *The Tongues of the Bible* (1971), *The Gift from Thoth* (1975). He was also editor and publisher of *University of South Florida Language Quarterly* (1962).

Eugene Gottlieb (1894–1962), b. Spiš, Slovakia; linguist, assistant professor of Germanics and Slavonic languages, City College, New York, NY.

Věra M. Henzl (ca. 1931–), b. Ostrava, Czech., is a linguist trained at Stanford Univ. Since 1977 she has taught at Foothill College, Los Altos Hills, CA and Stanford Univ. She has returned to Europe several times to teach at the Universities in Rome, Hamburg, Prague and London. She has done research and published on diglossic language variation, language cultivation, maintenance of immigrant languages, and communicative patterns of various ethnic and professional groups in the USA.

Ruth Weir Hirsch (1926–1965), b. Czech., was Univ. of Michigan trained linguist. When the Charles University was reopened after the War, she enrolled in the field of linguistic studies for a year. In that time, she passed the State Board Examination in Principles of Education and was qualified as a teacher of English in secondary schools in Czechoslovakia. In 1947, she immigrated to the US. She obtained a Bachelor of Arts degree at West Virginia University in 1948. Her major subject was French, and her minor was German. As a graduate student she attended the University of Michigan in Ann Arbor. There she earned two Master's degrees in two successive years: in 1949 in Spanish literature with a minor in French literature, and, in 1950, in linguistics. Only one year later she received the degree of Doctor of Philosophy in Romance Linguistics. Ruth Hirsch's first full-time teaching position (1951–52) was in Washington, DC, at the School of Languages and Linguistics of the Foreign Service Institute of the US Department of State. She spent from 1952 to 1956 as an Instructor and Assistant Professor at Georgetown University's Institute of Languages and Linguistics. There she supervised the teaching of beginning and intermediate courses in French, German, Spanish, and Czech, and, on the graduate level, taught Phonetics and Phonemics, Romance structure and the methodology of Language teaching for elementary and secondary school teachers. In July 1954, she married Robert H. Weinstein, a Washington lawyer, by whom she had three children. When the family moved to California in 1956, their last name was changed to Weir. In September 1956, Ruth Hirsch Weir began teaching at Stanford University, where she had a joint appointment as Assistant Professor of Education and Spanish, which was later changed to Assistant Professor of Education and Linguistics. In 1963, she was promoted to Associate Professor of Linguistics. She also taught graduate courses in applied linguistics and, in the School of Education, courses in language teaching methodology. She was instrumental in the developing a new graduate Program in

Linguistics at Stanford University. In her last project, she returned to language acquisition in infants, the subject of the significant contribution which she had made in her book *Language in the Crib*. She died, suddenly and prematurely on November 13, 1963.

Vladimír Honsa (1921-2011), b. Netolice, Czech., was a linguist. He received his B.A. degree in Romance Philology from Charles University, Prague in 1947. His advanced graduate studies were at the University of Paris (1948-49) and at the University of Madrid (1948-51). He received his M.A. and Ph.D. in Romance Linguistics from the University of Michigan, Ann Arbor (1953-57). His teaching career in the Unites States and Latin America began as an assistant professor of Spanish at Marquette University, Milwaukee (1956-58). He became an assistant professor of Spanish and Linguistics and Acting Chairman of Linguistics at the University of Southern California, Los Angeles (1958-62). While serving as Associate Professor of Spanish Linguistics at Indiana University, Bloomington (1962-70), Vladimir received a Fulbright Professorship of Spanish Linguistics at the Instituto Caro y Cuervo in Bogota, Colombia (1964-65), and the University of Uruguay, Montevideo in 1965. He was also a Visiting Professor of Spanish and General Linguistics at Florida State University, Canal Zone Branch, Panama in 1970. From 1970-1988, he served as Professor and Chairman of Linguistics and Latin American Studies at the University of Nevada, Las Vegas. Vladimir retired in 1988. His extensive research was in the areas of Dialectology of Romance Languages, Modern Spanish Linguistics and Dialectology, Spanish Historical Linguistics, Medieval Spanish Literature, and General and Implied Linguistics. Vladimir collected samples of Spanish in every Spanish speaking country. He authored several books, including: *An Old Spanish Reader: Episodes from 'La Gran Conquista de Ultramar'* (1985); *Old Spanish Grammar of 'La Gran Conquista de Ultramar'* (1986); and *Six Books of Sonnets* (2000).

Roman Jakobson (1896-1982), b. Moscow, Russia, emigrated to Czechoslovakia and became Czechoslovak citizen. He was trained as linguist, first at Lazarev Inst. of Oriental Languages, Moscow (A.B., 1914) and at Moscow University (dipl., 1918). He left Moscow for Prague in 1920, where he worked as a member of the Soviet diplomatic mission while continuing with his Doctoral studies. In 1926, the Prague School of Linguistic Theory was established, of which Jakobson was a co-founder. He got his Doctorate at Charles University in Prague (PhDr., 1930). He became Professor of Russian philology at Masaryk University in Brno (1933-39). After coming to the US, he was named professor of general linguistics and Czechoslovak Studies, at Ecole Libre des Hautes Etudes, New York (1942-46) and then T. G. Masaryk professor of Czech Studies, at Columbia University (1946-49). He then joined Harvard University, as S. H. Cross Prof. Slavic Languages and Literatures, (1949-57), and gen. linguistics (1960-67); and Inst. prof., M.I.T. (1957-67). He was the author of numerous books, including *Preliminaries to Speech Analysis* (1952), *Fundamentals of Language* (1956), *Studies on Child Language and Aplasia* (1971), *Main Trends in the Science of Language* (1973), *The Sound Shape* of Language (1979), *The Framework of Language* (1980), *Brain and Language* (1980). He was recipient of numerous awards.

Laura A. Janda (1957–), b. New Brunswick, NJ, of Czech ancestry, earned degree in Slavic linguistics from UCLA. She is now professor of West Slavic linguistics and director, of Slavic & East European Language Resource Center at Univ. of North Carolina, Chapel Hill. She specializes in Slavic linguistics, historical linguistics and cognitive linguistics.

Richard Janda (1954–), b. Los Angeles, CA, of Czech ancestry, has been trained as a linguist at Stanford Univ. (M.A., 1977) and UCLA (Ph.D., 1987). He taught linguistics at Univ. of New Mexico (1985–88), Univ. of Pennsylvania (1988–91), Univ. of Chicago (1991–98), Ohio State Univ. (1998–2005), and Coll. of William and Mary (2005–06). Currently he holds the position of adjunct lecturer in the dept. at Indiana Univ. (s. 2006). His specialty is linguistics, especially morphology and phonology, both synchronically and diachronically, mainly in Germanic and Romance languages, with a strong uniformitarian focus on understanding change in the past via variation and change in the present, across a range of genres including even song texts and notetaking. His most representative work is "Introduction" to the *Handbook of Historical Linguistics*, Volume 1 (2003–2005) (primary author, with Brian D. Joseph).

Otilia Marie Kabeš (1920–2014), b. Prague, Czech.; concluded her studies with a Baccalaureate (History, Latin, German, Social Studies). After the Communist takeover, she left the country and resettled with her family in Washington, DC, where she obtained from George Washington University a degree in Clinical Chemistry. She studied and graduated from the University of Geneva (Switzerland), School of Translation and Interpretation. She worked as a freelance translator and interpreter for several UN organizations and at many important international conferences (Security and Cooperation in Europe, International Red Cross, etc.). Upon returning to the United States, she continued to work for both the US Government (Dept. of State, USIA, etc.) and private international organizations and businesses. She was also lecturing at the Institute for Learning in Retirement (LIR) of the American University in Washington, DC, where her subjects covered Russian, French and Central European history, advanced French history and literature, and Women's Studies. She volunteered hosting foreign visitors for the Meridian House and taught continuing education courses at American University. Using her fluency in Czech, English, German, Russian and French, she volunteered to translate wartime documents at the Holocaust Museum.

Vladimír Kajlik (1946–), b. Perecin, Czech.; theologian, librarian, Wayne State University, Detroit, MI; now residing in the Czech Republic, applied linguist and translator, with University of South Bohemia, České Budějovice.

Anne Stepan Keown (1972–), b. Little Rock, AR, of Czech ancestry, is a linguist. She studied Russian at Wake Forest University (B.A., 1994) and Slavic linguistics at University of North Carolina (M.A., 1999; Ph.D., 2004). Her specialization is Slavic linguistics, with emphasis on Russian, Czech, and Polish. Her dissertation is a cognitive linguistic analysis of pronominal address forms in Russian, Polish, and Czech.

Edward Stephen Klima (1931–2008), b. Cleveland, OH, of Czech ancestry, was an eminent linguist who specialized in the study of sign languages. Klima's work was heavily influenced by Noam Chomsky's then-revolutionary theory of the biological basis of linguistics and applied that analysis to sign languages. He was among the first to prove that sign languages are complete languages and have complex grammars that have all the features of grammars of oral languages. Klima studied linguistics at Dartmouth College, earning his Bachelor's degree in 1953. Two years later, he received a Master's in the same subject from Harvard University. Starting in 1957, Klima worked as an Instructor at the Massachusetts Institute of Technology under Noam Chomsky (1956-67). After earning his Ph.D. in linguistics from Harvard University in 1965, he joined the linguistics department at the University of California, San Diego. Later, he also became an adjunct professor at the Salk Institute for Biological Studies. He specialized in psycholinguistics and historical linguistics.

Rostislav Kocourek (1929–1978), b. Prague, Czech., studied Czech and English (dipl., 1952), English phonetics (PhDr., 1953) and English literature (CSc./Ph.D., 1962), all at Charles Univ. He has been associated with the Department of French at Dalhousie Univ., Halifax, Can., where he rose to the position of McCulloch Professor. Currently, he is professor emeritus. His interests are in linguistics and specialized terminology, lexicology and lexical semantics and Jacobean drama. He authored a dozen monographs, textbooks, readers, including *The Term and its Definition* (1965), *La langue francaise de la technique et de la science* (1982, 1991), *Reductivisme lexical* (1988), *Metaphors in Linguistic Terminology* (1994), *Essays in French and English linguistics* (2001).

Jozef J. Konuš (1904–95), b. USA, of Slovak descent, was an Anglicist. He was the author of *Slovak-English Phraseological Dictionary/Slovensko-Anglicky Frazeologicky Slovnik*. Passaic, NJ: Slovak Catholic Sokol (1969), and *Practical Slovak Grammar* (1939).

Henry Kučera (1925–2010), b. Třebařov, Czech., was a linguist. He studied at Charles University (1945–48), and at Harvard University (1949–52), where he was Graduate Research

Fellow and Research Associate of the Russian Research Center. He obtained the degree of Ph.D. from Harvard University in 1952, and then became Assistant Professor of Foreign Languages at the University of Florida (1952)54). He then went to Brown University (s. 1981), as prof. of Slavic languages and linguistics (s. 1963), as prof. of cognitive sciences (s. 1981), as chair., dept. of Slavic languages (1965-68). He was also a Guggenheim Foundation Fellow and Howard Foundation Fellow (1960-61). He was a specialist on general and Slavic linguistics, computers in linguistics research, language and cognition. He was a pioneer in corpus linguistics and linguistic software. He was the author of *The Phonology of Czech* (1961), *Computers in Linguistics and Literary Studies* (1975), etc.

Mark Richard Lauersdorf (ca. 1967-), is a linguist, trained at University of Kansas (Ph.D.), as well as at Komenský University in Bratislava. He is associate professor, Linguistic Institute, University of Kentucky, Lexington. He was visiting professor in the Department of English and American Studies at the University of Ljubljana, Slovenia, during the Summer Semester 2020. His research is in historical sociolinguistics, both macro- and micro-aspects. He authored *Protestant Language Use in 17th Century Slovakia in a Diglossia Framework* (2003).

Goldie Piroch Meyerstein (1928-2017), b. Liptovský Mikuláš, Czech.; in US s. 1939; linguist; professor at UCLA and later was engaged as a longtime teacher in the LA public school system.

Elizabeth Pribic (1916-1996), b. Šternberk, Bohemia, was Univ. of Munich trained linguist. She was with Univ. of Illinois, Chicago (1969-78) and then became prof. of modern languages at Florida State Univ. She specialized in Slavic linguistics, esp. Old Church Slavonic, history of Russian and Czech languages and comparative Slavic studies.

Eduard Prokosch (1876-1938), b. Cheb, Bohemia, was a historical linguist who specialized in Indo-European studies. He was the father of Frederic Prokosch. He studied law in Vienna, passing the Bar examination before immigrating to the United States in 1898. Prokosch taught German and Germanic philology at many American educational institutions, including the University of Chicago, the University of Texas, the University of Wisconsin-Madison, Bryn Mawr College and New York University. Prokosch finished his career as the Sterling Professor of Germanic Languages at Yale University, during which time he wrote his most influential work, *A Comparative Germanic Grammar* (1939), which broke ground in the fields of Indo-European and Germanic studies.

James D. Pustejovsky (1956-), b. Shiner, TX, of Moravian ancestry, studied linguistics and philosophy at MIT (B.S., 1978) and linguistics at Univ. of Massachusetts, Amherst (Ph.D., 1985). He has been associated with the dept. of computer science at Brandeis Univ., as asst.

professor (1986-92), as assoc. professor (1992-2000), as full professor and director of laboratory for linguistics and computation (s. 2002), as chair of language and linguistics program (s. 2006), and as director of computational linguistics MA program (s. 2007). In 2009, he was appointed to TJX/Feldberg Endowed Chair in Computer Science. He has made his name with his Generative Lexicon Theory. His expertise includes: theoretical and computational modeling of language, spec. computational linguistics; lexical semantics; knowledge representation; temporal reasoning and extraction, machine learning, language annotation models. He is co-author of *The Handbook of Linguistic Annotation* (2015), *Advances in Generative Lexicon Theory* (2013), *Interpreting Motion: Grounded Representations for Spatial Language* (2012), *and Natural Language Annotation and Machine Learning* (2012). He has also written or co-edited a number of other books, in addition to publishing numerous articles in professional journals.

Miroslav Renský (1927-1982), b. Prague, Czech., was Charles Univ. (Ph.D., 1951) and ČSAV educated linguist. Since 1970, he was associated with CUNY Grad. School and Brooklyn Coll., where he held the position of prof. of English and linguistics. He specialized in modern English syntax and phonology.

Anton J. Rozsypal (ca. 1946-), studied at Univ. of Alberta (Ph.D., 1972). He was associated with the Univ. of Alberta, where he has held the position of professor of emeritus in the Dept. of Linguistics.

Andrew Schiller (1919-), b. Czech., is State Univ. of Iowa educated linguist. He was with Univ. of Illinois, Chicago Circle (s. 1955), where he was prof. of English and linguistics (s. 1964), and chairman, dept. of linguistics (s. 1973). He specialized in morphology, applied linguistics, and metrics.

Julie Šedivý (1967-), b. Ústí nad Orlicí, Czech., emigrated with her family in 1969 and spent most of her childhood in Montreal, Canada. She earned a B.A. in linguistics from Carleton University in Ottawa (1988), an M.A. in linguistics from the University of Ottawa (1991) and a Ph.D. in linguistics from the University of Rochester (1997). In 1997, she joined the faculty at Brown University, first as an assistant professor of cognitive and linguistic sciences, and then as associate professor from 2003-2009. In 2009, she became an adjunct associate professor at the University of Calgary in Canada. As an academic, Julie Šedivý has published several dozen articles on psychological aspects of language, investigating the ways in which language is learned and processed in the human mind. She has lectured widely around the world, and in 2014, she published a textbook titled *Language in Mind: An Introduction to Psycholinguistics*. Dr. Sedivy has also been active in the Canadian literary community and served on the Board of Directors of the Writers' Guild of Alberta from

2009–2014, including a term as its president. She has often incorporated a scientific understanding of language in public lectures about the aesthetic or persuasive uses of language and has made numerous appearances in national and international media as a language commentator. She is the co-author of a popular science book title *Sold on Language: How Advertisers Talk to You and What This Says about You* (2011) and has regularly written for scientific magazines aimed at general audiences.

Stanislav Segert (1921–2006), b. Prague, Czech., began his studies at the Protestant Theological Faculty of Charles University in 1939. When, later that year, the Nazi occupation authorities closed down all universities, Stanislav Segert completed his studies in various illegal courses and in 1943, he was ordained a chaplain of the Evangelical church of Czech Brethren. In 1945–1947, Segert pursued his graduate studies at the Faculty of Arts and was awarded a degree of Doctor of Philosophy in Semitic and Classical philology and philosophy. Between 1945 and 1952, he was an assistant lecturer at the Protestant Theological Faculty, mostly teaching courses in Greek and Latin. In 1951, he started teaching at the Faculty of Arts and in 1952, he became a member of the Oriental Institute of the newly established Czechoslovak Academy of Sciences. In 1969, following the government repressions in the wake of the 1968 Soviet invasion of Czechoslovakia, he left for the United States where he became a Professor of North-West Semitic languages at the University of California, Los Angeles. He was an authority on Canaanite and Aramaic philology, bible and contacts between Semitic and Graeca-Roman civilizations. Segert was perhaps best known for his textbook *Basic Grammar of the Ugaritic Language* (1984), but he also wrote a fundamental *Grammar of Phoenician and Punic* (1976) as well as the best Old Aramaic grammar, *Altaramäische Grammatik* (1975). Besides these works, he wrote hundreds of articles on aspects of Hebrew, the Dead Sea Scrolls, and aspects of Ugaritic studies.

Stanley Starosta (1939–2002), b. Oconomowoc, WI, possibly of Czech ancestry, received a B.A. in physics (1961) and Ph.D. in linguistics (1967) from the University of Wisconsin-Madison. He was professor of linguistics at the University of Hawaii at Manoa. Professor Starosta spent extended periods doing research, teaching, and field work in the East, Southeast, and South Asia, and Western Europe. His primary area of research was Lexicase, a highly-constrained dependency grammar he developed. He also worked on natural language processing; morphological theory; and the synchronic analysis and historical reconstruction of languages of East, Southeast, and South Asia and the Pacific. An expert in Austronesian linguistics, he wrote countless papers and gave innumerable presentations on Formosan languages. Much of his work was based on his own field work in Taiwan. In addition to his work on Proto-Austronesian, he also did research on the prehistory of other languages of E/SE/S Asia and the Pacific. Additionally, he had considerable expertise in Chinese languages, German, Japanese, and Thai. He devoted much of his effort to issues in syntactic theory, such as case relations, ergativity and transitivity, and focus. His morphological theory, also highly constrained, holds that words have no internal structure, and, in essence, that the only morphological rule is analogy.

Nathan Süsskind (1906-1994), b. Stropkov, Slovakia; professor of German, City College of New York (1932-74), director of the Institute for Yiddish Lexicology.

Elizabeth Closs Traugott (1939-), b. Bristol, England, of Bohemian ancestry (granddaughter of the novelist Robert Priebsch), is a linguist, educated at the Univ. of California at Berkeley. She is now professor emeritus of linguistics and English at Stanford University where she taught from 1970-2003. She has written about syntax, pragmatics, semantics, lexicalization, socio-historical linguistics, linguistics and literature.

Karla Trnka, studied at Brown Univ. She became asst. professor at Univ. of Texas, Austin. She authored the book *A Generative Description of Temporal Adverbial Constructions in Contemporary Russian and Czech* (1973).

Robert S. Wachal (1929-), b. WI, of Czech ancestry, is a linguist trained at Univ. of Wisconsin (Ph.D., 1966). He has been associated with the Univ. of Iowa, where he is now Prof. Emeritus of linguistics. He specialized in lexicography, English grammar and usage and stylistics. He authored *Abbreviations Dictionary: A Practical Compilation of Today's Acronyms and Abbreviations* (1999).

Henry C. Werba (1934-2002), b. Prague, Czech., emigrated from the ruins of post-World War II Germany to the United States when he was 16, ultimately being granted citizenship through persistence and a special act of Congress. He earned a Ph.D. in German from the University of Connecticut and worked as professor of foreign languages at Southern Connecticut State University for many years until his retirement in 1992. He was fluent in six languages, including English, German, Spanish, Czech, Russian and French. He valued culture and the arts and was an accomplished concert violinist, composer, sculptor, painter, and award-winning photographer. He belonged to several professional associations. As a practical compliment to these artistic achievements, he also authored several college textbooks, built his own house, rode motorcycles, developed and managed residential rental properties, and reconditioned pianos for many years.

Thomas G. Winner (orig. Weiener) (1917-2004), b. Prague, Bohemia, was an eminent American linguist, Slavist and Semiotician. He studied at Charles University (1936-38), Harvard University (A.B., 1941; M.A., 1942) and at Columbia University (Ph.D., 1950). He rose from assoc. prof. to prof. Slavic languages, U. Michigan (1958-65); professor of Slavic languages and comparative literature, Brown University (1965-82), chairman of dept. Slavic languages (1968–72), prof. emeritus (1982–2004), director of Center for Research in Semiotics (1977–83), dir., Program in Semiotic Studies (1984–2004). He was the founder of first semiotic center in US, established at Brown University. He was a well-known Chekhov specialist, and a proponent of Tartu-Moscow semiotics school. He retired as Professor Emeritus of Slavic Languages and Comparative Literature at Boston University, Cambridge, MA.

Michael Zarechnak (1920–2016), b. Vydraň, Czech., was a linguist. He immigrated to US with his family in December 1948. First, he taught Russian at the Army Language School in Monterey, California. From the early 1950s until retirement several decades later, he taught linguistics and Russian at Georgetown University in Washington, DC. There he led the groundbreaking machine translation and computational linguistics programs. He received a Doctorate degree in linguistics from Harvard University.

Ladislav Zgusta (1924–2007), b. Libochovice, Czech., was a linguist and lexicographer, who wrote one of the first textbooks on lexicography. He graduated from Charles University, majoring in classical philology-Indology (PhDr., 1949) and habilitated at Masaryk University in the field of Indo-European comparative linguistics and, in the same year, he earned Doctor of Philological Sciences in Asia Minor linguistics. In 1948–52, he worked as an assistant at the Faculty of Arts, Charles University, from where he moved, as a researcher, to the Oriental Institute of the Czechoslovak Academy of Sciences, where he held the position of head of lexicography (1951–67) and linguistics department (1959–70) and deputy director (1954–58). For several years, he also worked as an external head of the lexicographic group at the Institut für Orientforschung AV GDR in Berlin. In the years 1955–70, he worked as an executive editor of the Oriental Archive and as a managing editor, he managed the non-periodical series of the Czechoslovak Academy of Sciences *Dissertationes orientales* (1964–70). In 1968–70, he lectured on comparative linguistics at the University of Brno. In 1970, he emigrated to the USA and became a professor of linguistics at Cornell University, Ithaca, NY. From 1971–95, he worked as a professor of linguistics at the Center for Advanced Studies of the University of Illinois at Urbana, IL, which he headed as its director in 1987–95. In 1995, he was appointed professor emeritus there. The main areas of his professional interest in Indo-Europeanism included the study of Scythian and Sarmatian idioms on the basis of names preserved in Greek inscriptions in southern Ukraine, deciphering ancient Ossetian and Pisidic inscriptions, critical classification of pre-Greek personal and local names from Greek sources. In addition, he prepared the first comprehensive treatise on the theory and methodology of lexicography. Dutch lexicographer Piet van Sterkenburg referred to Zgusta as "the twentieth-century godfather of lexicography." He was elected a Fellow of the American Academy of Arts and Sciences in 1992, and in the same year awarded the Gold Medal of the Czech Academy of Sciences for his work in Humanities.

X. Science

A. Biological Sciences

Helen M. Blau (1949-), b. London, England, of Czech ancestry, is a molecular biologist trained at Harvard. She is currently the Donald E. and Delia B. Baxter Professor and Director of the Baxter Laboratory for Stem Cell Biology in the Microbiology and Immunology Department and the Stanford Institute for Stem Cell Biology and Regenerative Medicine in the Stanford University School of Medicine. Her research area is regenerative medicine with a focus on stem cells. She is world renowned for her research on nuclear reprogramming and demonstrating the plasticity of cell fate using cell fusion. Her laboratory has also pioneered the design of biomaterials to mimic the in vivo microenvironment and direct stem cell fate. She is married to the psychiatrist David Spiegel (1945-) and they have 2 children.

William Victor Chalupa (1937-2016), b. New York, NY, likely of Czech ancestry, was trained as an animal nutritionist at Rutgers Univ. (M.S., 1959; Ph.D., 1962). He was employed in teaching and directing graduate students in the Dairy Science Department at Clemson University. He was then granted sabbatical leave to perform research at the U.S. Department of Agriculture in Beltsville, Md. He then was employed for 5 years, as manager of rumen metabolic research, by Smith Kline pharmaceutical at the research farm in West Chester, Pa., and for a short time at the University of Maryland. He did research on energy and protein utilization of feedstuffs by ruminant animals and the biochemistry of rumen metabolism. Lastly, he joined the School of Veterinary Medicine at the University of Pennsylvania, as assoc. professor of nutrition (1976-80), as a professor (s. 1980), conducting research at New Bolton Center and teaching in Philadelphia. During his career, Bill received several honors for his work. In May 2003, he was awarded the George Hammell Cook Distinguished Alumni Award. In July 2007, he was recognized by the Dairy Nutritionists of Mexico for his outstanding contribution to dairy nutrition.

John L. Cisar (1954-), b. Passaic, NJ, of Czech ancestry, earned his B.A. from Rutgers University, M.S. from Cornell University and Ph.D. from the University of Rhode Island. He has been associated with the Univ. of Florida (s. 1986), where he advanced to full professor in 1997. He currently holds the position of professor of turfgrass management and water there. He has conducted research and extension outreach on the environmental impacts of turfgrass management in Florida since 1986 and has cooperator projects with IFAS state-wide faculty. He has focused on the effect of turfgrass management systems on water quality and conservation, soil water repellency, pesticide fate, and nutrient leaching. Cisar was elected C-5 Turfgrass Division Board Representative of the American Society of Agronomy, 1999-2002. He is the current treasurer of the International Turfgrass Society and is the technical editor for the *Florida Turf Digest* and *Turf News*. Cisar served as International Turfgrass Society Director from 1993-2001. Dr. Cisar received the 2005 'Wreath of Grass Award,' the highest honor from the Florida Turfgrass Association.

Johanna Döbereiner (née Kubelka) (1924-2000), b. Ústí nad Labem, Czech., was a Brazilian agronomist. She received her degree from the Ludwig Maximilian University of Munich and settled, with her husband, becoming a Brazilian citizen in 1956. Her early work includes studies of Azospirillum and other bacteria that could be useful to Brazilian soil. She later played an important role in Brazil's soybean production by encouraging a reliance on varieties that solely depended on biological nitrogen fixation. The consequences of these research work, largely influenced by Johanna Döbereiner ideas, resulted that nowadays the soybean plantations in Brazil are completely supplied for nitrogen (N) by rhizobia and not using any N-fertilizers. It has large consequences, since Brazil is, together with USA, the main producers of soybean in the world (ca. 50% world production). This was one of the reasons that Johanna Döbereiner was indicated for the Nobel Prize in the 1990s. She was married to veterinarian Jurgen Döbereiner (1923-2018).

Michael F. Holick (1946-), Slovak American, was trained as biochemist and physician. He is Professor of Medicine, Physiology and Biophysics; Director of the General Clinical Research Unit; and Director of the Bone Health Care Clinic and the Director of the Heliotherapy, Light, and Skin Research Center at Boston University Medical Center. After earning a Ph.D. degree in biochemistry, a medical degree, and completing a research postdoctoral fellowship at the University of Wisconsin, Madison, Dr. Holick completed a residency in medicine at the Massachusetts General Hospital in Boston. As a graduate student, he was the first to identify the major circulating form of vitamin D in human blood as 25 hydroxyvitamin D3. He then isolated and identified the active form of vitamin D as 125-dihydroxyvitamin D3. He determined the mechanism for how vitamin D is synthesized in the skin, demonstrated the effects of aging, obesity, latitude, seasonal change, sunscreen use, skin pigmentation, and clothing on this vital cutaneous process.

Leslie Elizabeth Hornig (1957-2012), b. US, the daughter of eminent American chemist and later president of Brown University Donald F. Hornig and an equally notable American scientist Lilli Schwenk, the latter being a native of Ústí and Labem, Czechoslovakia. Leslie, who kept her maiden name, after getting married, moved from Washington, DC, in 1988, to pursue a Ph.D. in evolutionary biology at the University of Chicago and received her degree in 1995. Following three years of post-doctoral research in genetics, she decided to leave academia and share her love of science with younger learners at the Lab Schools, where she taught from 1998 to 2011. In 1980, she was a program officer at the Fund for the Improvement of Postsecondary Education (FIPSE) at the Department of Education and later, she was a public affairs specialist at the National Zoo in Washington. Before returning to school, Ms. Hornig spent two years working at the American Association for the Advancement of Science, producing the National Forum for School Science, a forward-looking effort to improve teaching quality. She was married to psychologist David Woolpy Kleeman (1957-) and they had 2 daughters.

Ales Hrdlicka (1869-1943), b. Humpolec, Bohemia, as a Czech anthropologist who lived in the United States after his family had moved there in 1881. He is considered the founder of American physical anthropology. Between 1898 and 1903, during his scientific travel across America, Hrdlička became the first scientist to spot and document the theory of human colonization of the American continent from east Asia. He argued that the Indians migrated across the Bering Strait from Asia, supporting this theory with detailed field research of skeletal remains as well as studies of the people in Mongolia, Tibet, Siberia, Alaska, and Aleutian Islands. Aleš Hrdlička founded and became the first curator of physical anthropology of the U.S. National Museum, now the Smithsonian Institution National Museum of Natural History in 1904 and held that position until 1941. He was elected to the American Academy of Arts and Sciences in 1915 and the American Philosophical Society in 1918. That same year, he founded the *American Journal of Physical Anthropology*.

Jiří Hulcr (1978-), b. Slaný, Czech., is a forest entomologist. He studied entomology at University of South Bohemia (B.Sc. and M.Sc., 2001) and received Doctorate at the same university in 2008. He then continued studies in entomology at Michigan State University (Ph.D., 2009). He had postdoc in bacteriology at University of Wisconsin, Madison (2009-10) and another postdoc in microbial symbiosis at North Carolina State University (2010-12). He has been with University of Florida since 2012, where he holds the position of Associate Professor of Forest Resources and Conservation. He has extensive experience with science and policy consultation to forestry and fruit industries, consulting on forest health for governments in the US, Europe, Asia and the United Nations. He has over 12 years of experience in systematics, ecology and symbioses of insects and fungi and years of experience with high-throughput surveys of microbial associates of insects.

Edward W. E. Janike (1910-2001), b. Rising City, NE, of Czech mother, an animal husbandman who became dean of extension at the University of Nebraska in 1963. Prior to that, he was director of the Nebraska Agricultural Extension Service. Trained at the Univ. of Nebraska and Colorado State Univ., he started his career at the University as an assistant extension animal husbandman in 1931. He was a district supervisor for the Agricultural Adjustment Administration from 1932 to 1939. In 1939, he returned to the University as an assistant extension animal husbandman, a post he held until 1945. He was State 4-H Club leader from 1949 to 1950. He was acting associate director of the Agricultural Extension Service in 1950 and associate director in 1951. He also has farmed and served as secretary of the Omaha Livestock Exchange. Janike has been a pioneer leader in Nebraska in the Rural Development Program. In the animal husbandry field, Janike pioneered the first sow testing work in Nebraska. He also demonstrated the use and importance of protein supplements for swine feeding.

Helen Beneš Kaiser (1952-), b. San Francisco, CA, the daughter of Bohuš Beneš, former Consul of Czechoslovakia in San Francisco (1943-48) and nephew of President Edvard Beneš, and Helen Dulik, both from Czechoslovakia, is a molecular geneticist. She studied at the Sorbonne (Université de Paris, France) and received her B.A. in French literature from Harvard University in 1973. She obtained her Ph.D. (1982) in anatomy and molecular biology at the University of Arkansas for Medical Sciences (UAMS) and did postdoctoral training in genetics and molecular biology at the Institut Jacques Monod (C.N.R.S.) in Paris, France (1983-85). She joined the department of biochemistry and molecular biology at UAMS in 1986 and then the department of anatomy and neurobiology (now neurobiology and developmental sciences), becoming asst. professor (1988-2002), assoc. professor (2002-07), rising to the rank of professor in 2007. She teaches gross anatomy in the College of Medicine and molecular biology in the Graduate School. Her research is in insect molecular biology, focusing on mechanisms of gene expression to develop novel techniques for control of mosquito populations and reduce the incidence of diseases spread by mosquitoes. Her laboratory also studies regulatory mechanisms for reduction of cellular damage from oxidative stress. She is married to the historian Thomas Ernest Kaiser (1947-).

Sonja Osaki Keller (1926-1992), a native of Trutnov, Czech. She was a biochemist. She and her family fled the country in 1938, when Germany occupied it. The family first went to England for a year and then immigrated to Bolivia. She came to the US in 1947. She earned a Bachelor's degree from MIT and her Doctorate from Harvard in 1954. She first concentrated her research in organic chemistry, but later became a biochemist. For the past ten years, her research had focused on the biosynthesis of lipids in the kidneys. Besides being a researcher, she also taught at Simmons College and Boston University. In 1967, she received a Radcliffe Institute for Independent Study research fellowship. From 1968 to 1971, she was a research associate in MIT's biology department. They had one son.

George 'Koz' Kozelnicky (1918-2005), b. Akron, OH, of Czech ancestry, graduated from the University of Georgia, where he was a member of Phi Beta Kappa. He became a member of its faculty in 1951 specializing in plant pathology and genetics. From 1961 until his retirement from the university in 1983, he researched and taught turfgrass management. He developed a corn that had more kernels on the cob and could therefore feed more people. As a turfgrass instructor, Kozelnicky instituted a turfgrass disease laboratory held on North Georgia's golf courses, the only one of its kind at the time. He served as the executive secretary of the Georgia Golf Course Superintendents Association of America from 1968 to 1989, while at the same time serving as the editor for the *Georgia Turfgrass News* (1971–92). From 1979 to 1984, he served the city of Atlanta, GA, and its golf courses on an ad hoc task force. While teaching at the University of Georgia, he also was a turfgrass instructor. He instituted a turfgrass disease laboratory held on North Georgia's golf courses, the only one of its kind at the time. He was inducted into the Georgia Golf Hall of Fame on January 4, 1992, for his work in identifying turfgrass diseases and turfgrass management.

Donald Thomas Krizek (1935–2020), b. Cleveland, OH, of Czech ancestry, was a plant physiologist. He studied botany at Western Reserve University, Cleveland (B.A., 1957) and at the University of Chicago (M.S., 1958; Ph.D., 1954). He held the position of res. plant physiologist at the Plant Stress Lab., Beltsville Agr. Res. Center, USDA (s. 1972). He was a specialist in plant growth and development, senescence of vascular plants, photoperiodism and photomorphogenesis, plant growth regulators, plant stress, and environmental physiology.

Arthur Francis Novak (1916–1979), b. Baltimore, MD, of Czech ancestry, was a food scientist. He was trained at the University of Alabama and at Purdue University. He was a prof. of bacteriology and chemistry at Univ. of Florida (1947–51); dir. of research Nutrilite Products Inc., Buena Park, CA (1951–54); prof. and head of the dept. of food science and technology, and prof. of marine sciences at Louisiana State Univ., Baton Rouge (s. 1954); president, Internat. Tech. Consultants, (1978–79); vice pres. for science & tech., Singleton Packing Corp. Tampa, FL (1979); cons., foods & drugs (s. 1947).

Rosa Kuerti (née Jahoda) (1905–2004), b. Vienna, was the daughter of Carl Jahoda and Betty Probst, the former being of Czech ancestry, his father having been born in Přerov, Moravia. She was a biologist and peace activist, Cleveland. She received her education in biology at Univ. of Vienna (RNDr., 1928). Her career includes being a teacher at Univ. of Istanbul, Turkey (1937–38), Buckingham School, Cambridge (1938–39); professor at Hathaway Brown School, Cleveland (1939–40), before joining Case Western Reserve Univ., Cleveland. She ended her career as professor emeritus of biology at CWRU. She was also a longtime activist in the Cleveland area, with years of involvement in Women Speak Out for Peace and Justice. She volunteered for a number of years, at the Free Medical Clinic and in tutoring inmates at the Cleveland Workhouse. Her love of music was passed on to her son, the famed pianist Anton Emil Kuerti, whom she had with the physicist Gustav Kuerti.

X. SCIENCE

Oksana Maslivec Lockridge (née Maslivec) (1941–), b. Czech., is a biochemist, biochemical pharmacologist, and biochemical geneticist. She is a graduate of Smith College (B.A., 1963), and received additional training in chemistry and biochemistry at Northwestern University (Ph.D., 1970). She was a research scientist at University of Michigan (1982–90), before her appointment as professor at University of Nebraska Medical Center. She is married to Kenneth Allan Lockridge (1940–).

Vera Marie Nikodem (1940–2018), b. Czech., was a Czechoslovak-American molecular biologist who served as a section chief at the National Institute of Diabetes and Digestive and Kidney Diseases. She graduated from Charles University in 1962 with degrees in chemistry and biology. She escaped communism and moved to the United States in 1967 to join her husband, Zdenek Nikodem who was pursuing graduate studies at Princeton University. Nikodem earned her Ph.D. in biochemistry at Rutgers University in 1975, followed by postdoctoral research at Princeton. Nikodem and her family moved to the Washington, D.C., area in 1978 and Nikodem began her 30-year career as a molecular biologist at the National Institutes of Health (NIH), culminating as a section chief at National Institute of Diabetes and Digestive and Kidney Diseases (NIDDK). Nikodem retired in 2008 and spent her time in both Georgetown and at her second home in Breckenridge, Colorado.

Frederick George Novy (1864–1951), b. Chicago, IL, of Czech ancestry, a bacteriologist, was an inventor of Novy jar and other laboratory equipment.

John Palka (orig. Pálka) (1939–), b. Paris, France, of Slovak refugee parents, was trained as zoologist, with specialty in neuroscience. He was educated at Swarthmore College (B.A., 1960) and UCLA (Ph.D., 1965). He has been with University of Washington, Seattle (s. 1969), where he rose from assistant professor to full professor of biology, retiring as professor emeritus. In 2002. He is the winner of numerous prestigious academic awards, including election as a Fellow of the American Association for the Advancement of Science, two Fulbright Fellowships for teaching in India, and a Guggenheim Fellowship for research in Cambridge, England. He also co-founded and co-directed the University of Washington's highly lauded Program on the Environment.

Sheila N. Patek (1972–), b. New York, NY, of Czech ancestry, is a biologist. She studied biology at Harvard Univ. (A.B., 1994) and at Duke Univ., Durham, NC (Ph.D., 2001). She also had Miller postdoctoral fellowship at Univ. of California, Berkeley (2001–04) and Radcliffe Fellowship at Harvard Univ. (2008–09). She held faculty positions at the University of California Berkeley (2004–09), University of Massachusetts Amherst (2009–13) and, currently, Duke University (s. 2013), where she is assoc. professor in the dept. of biology. She specializes in evolutionary biomechanics, ultrafast movements in biology, and marine bioacoustics. She received a number of awards, including Christopher Clavius, S.J. Award, Bartholomew Award and Brilliant 10 Award. She is married to a biological anthropologist Charles L. Nunn (1969–) home in Breckenridge, Colorado.

Paula (Marie) Pitha-Rowe (née Mahr) (1937–2015), b. Prague, Czech., was a pioneer in cancer research. She studied chemistry at Technical Univ. Prague (Ing., 1960) and biochemistry at ČSAV (CSc./Ph.D., 1964). She later trained at the Institute of Organic Chemistry and Biochemistry in Prague, the National Research Council in Ottawa, Canada, the Curie Institute in Paris, and the Salk Institute in California. She joined the faculty of the Johns Hopkins School of Medicine in 1971, becoming a full professor in oncology, molecular biology and genetics in Hopkins' biology department and at the medical school (s. 1985). She retired in 2013 but remained teaching. The focus of her research was on effects viral infection on the expression of cellular genes and in the novel approaches to modulation of the antiviral and anti-inflammatory responses, interferon-molecular mechanism of induction and action, regulation of gene expression, and RNA tumor viruses. She was an internationally renowned scientist whose research led the way for the development of interferon. She pioneered basic research towards the understanding of inflammatory cellular immune responses to viruses and other infectious agents, and how viruses may contribute to cancer. This work led to her international acclaim and honors in this field. She received the 1996 Milstein Award for excellence in interferon and cytokine research, and the 2005 G. J. Mendel Honorary Medal for Merit in Biological Sciences and was elected a Fellow of the American Association for the Advancement of Science (AAAS) in 2011.

Radmila B. Raikow (née Borůvka) (1939–), b. Prague, Czech, was a geneticist and immunologist. She was trained at University of California in Berkeley as a geneticist and immunologist. She has been a research scientist, doing cancer research at Allegheny Singer Res. Inst. in Pittsburgh (s. 1978). Her research interests are: autoimmunity in ophthalmopathy and immune functions in cancer etiology. She was married to Robert Jay Raikow (1940–2012).

John 'Jack' E. Rechcigl (1960–), b. Washington, DC, son of Czech immigrant parents, Míla Rechcigl (1930–) and Eva Edwards (1932–2024), graduated from the Univ. of Delaware, majoring in plant science (B.S., 1982) and studied soil science at Virginia Polytechnic Inst. and State Univ., Blacksburg (M.S., 1983; Ph.D., 1986). He joined the faculty of the Univ. of Florida in 1986, as asst. professor of soil science and water quality, in 1991 was promoted to associate professor and in 1996 attained full professorship. In 1999, he was named Univ. of Florida Research Foundation Professor. He also holds the Honorary Professorship at the Czech Univ. of Agriculture in Prague. He was initially based at the Range Cattle Research and Education Center at Ona, FL (1986–2000), prior to his appointment as Director of Gulf Coast Research and Education Center in Bradenton (2000–01) and then at a brand new, state-of- the-art Center in Balm (s. 2001). In 2020, he was given an additional responsibility by being also named Director of Fort Lauderdale Research and Education Center. Dr. Rechcigl is recognized nationally and internationally for his research on the beneficial uses of organic wastes and industrial by-products as fertilizers for agricultural crops. He has been a frequent speaker at national and international workshops and conferences and has consulted in various countries including Brazil, Nicaragua, Venezuela, Australia, Taiwan, Philippines, South Africa and the Czech Republic and Slovakia. He has authored over 300 publications, including contributions to books, monographs, and articles in periodicals in the fields of soil fertility, environmental quality, and water pollution. He served as associate editor of the *Soil and Crop Science Society Proceedings*, prior to assuming the responsibility as editor-in-chief of the *Agriculture and Environmental Book Series*. Among other, he edited monographs: *Soil Amendments and Environmental Quality* (1995), *Soil Amendments: Impacts on Biotic Systems* (1995), *Environmentally Safe Approaches to Crop Disease Control* (1997), *Agricultural Uses of By-Products and Wastes in Agriculture* (1997), *Biological and Biotechnological Control of Insect Pests* (1998) and *Insect Pest Management: Techniques for Environmental Protection* (2000).

John Allen Resko (1932–), b. Patton, PA, of Slovak/Croatian parents, was a physiologist and educator. He earned a bachelor degree from St. Charles Seminary and graduate degrees from the Marquette University and the University of Illinois. John Allen Resko was a professor of physiology at the Oregon Health and Science University in Portland Oregon (s. 1981). He has made many contributions for understanding the effects of steroid hormones before birth on the development of both heterosexual behaviors and male orientation in experimental animals. He spent most of his scientific career in Oregon, first at the Oregon Regional Primate Research Center and later as professor and chairman of the physiology department in the school of Medicine of the Oregon Health & Science University.

Blanka Říhová (1942–), b. Prague, Czech., is a Czech immunologist. Her research involves the development of targeted drug delivery methods for cancer. She is the former director at the Institute of Microbiology of the Czech Academy of Sciences. In 2018, Říhová was made President of the Learned Society of the Czech Republic. She studied science at the Charles University. She remained there for her graduate studies and joined the Czechoslovak Academy of Sciences in 1964. In December 1969, she defended her Doctorate at the Institute of Microbiology of the Czechoslovak Academy of Sciences. She spent much of her career in the United States, where she worked in Seattle, Salt Lake City and New York City. She visited the University of Utah where she worked alongside Jindřich Kopeček. Říhová was made Head of Research at the Czechoslovak Academy of Sciences in

1990. She served as Chair of the Czech Immunological Society from 1994 to 2000, sat on the Academic Council of the Academy of Sciences of the Czech Republic from 2004 to 2007, and was the vice-chairwoman of the Learned Society of the Czech Republic. Since 2007, she has acted as Head of the Department of Immunology. She was made European Ambassador for Creativity and Innovation in 2009. In 2018, she was elected President of the Learned Society of the Czech Republic. She is a member of the scientific council of the Czech Academy of Sciences.

Joseph G. Sebranek (1948–), b. Richland Center, WI, of Czech ancestry, is a meat, food, and animal scientist. He was a graduate of the University of Wisconsin-Platteville (B.S., 1970), where he majored in animal science. He continued his studies at the University of Wisconsin Madison, where he first specialized in meat and animal science (M.S., 1971) and then in meat and animal science and food science (Ph.D., 1974). He has been with Iowa State Univ. (s. 1975), as prof. of animal science and food technology (1984–97), as C. F. Curtiss Distinguished Professor of Agriculture and Life Sciences (s. 2008). Sebranek's research has defined the use of cryogenics for ground beef and investigated pressure and documented patterns of flow during meat grinder operation. He has written over 500 refereed journal articles and technical publications and is the author of *Meat Science and Processing* (1978) and holds two patents. He is a Fellow of the American Meat Science Association, the Institute of Food Technologists, and the American Society of Animal Science. He is the recipient of the R.C. Pollock Award. Dr. Sebranek was named a member of the Meat Industry Hall of Fame in 2017. Even with these prestigious credentials, his greatest contribution may be his service as a mentor to many leaders in the meat industry and the AMSA Press.

Joseph Stephen Semancik (1948–), b. Barton, OH, of Slovak descent, is a plant pathologist and virologist. He has been professor of plant pathology, University of California, Riverside (s. 1974).

Margaret Terzaghi-Howe (née Terzaghi) (1941–), b. Boston, MA, the daughter of Karl Terzaghi and Ruth Doggett, the former having been born in Prague, Bohemia, is a molecular biologist. She has been a molecular biologist and cancer researcher at Oak Ridge National Laboratory, TN (s. 1975). Her research focus has been on in vitro carcinogenesis induced by chemical carcinogens and radiation. She was married to Herbert Charles Howe, Jr. (1944–) but their marriage has not lasted.

Frank Zalom (1952–), b. Chicago, IL, of Slovak descent, is an entomologist. He was a graduate of Arizona State University, majoring in zoology (B.S., 1974) and ecology (M.S., 1975). He then pursued studies in entomology at the University of California in Davis, CA

(Ph.D., 1978). He is a Distinguished Professor of Entomology, Agricultural Experiment Station Entomologist and Extension Specialist at UC Davis where he teaches Arthropod Pest Management and conducts IPM research on the tree, vine, small fruit, and vegetable crops. He did a brief Post Doc at UC Berkeley in the late 1970s, before becoming an Assistant Professor at the University of Minnesota where he taught Economic Entomology and Insects in Relation to Plant Disease and conducted research on insect vectors of plant diseases. Frank returned to the University of California as Extension IPM Coordinator in 1980 at the inception of the Statewide IPM Program. He served as UCIPM's Associate Director and then as its director for 16 years before returning to the Entomology Department in 2002. He was the Department's Vice-Chair from 2005–08. Frank provides IPM leadership nationally and served as co-Chair of the APLU National IPM Committee from 1999–2015, IPM representative to the ESCOP Science and Technology Committee since 2003, and USDA Western Region IPM Competitive Grants Program Manager from 2004–14. He served on the USAID Board of Directors for the IPM CRSP from 2001–05. He is a Fellow of the California Academy of Sciences, the Entomological Society of America (ESA), the American Association for the Advancement of Science (AAAS), and the Royal Entomological Society (London). He served as ESA Pacific Branch President (2001) and as its Secretary-Treasurer (1983–89). He was elected to ESA national office as Vice President-Elect in 2012 and served as Vice President, then ESA President in 2014, presiding over the 62nd Annual Meeting in Portland, OR. He served as President of the Entomological Foundation in 2015 and continues to serve as a member of the Entomological Foundation Board of Directors and ESA's Science Policy Committee. He has authored over 335 peer reviewed journal articles, book chapters and books, including *Food, Crop Pests, and the Environment* (1992), published by APS.

Paul Charles Zamecnik (1912–2009), b. Cleveland, OH, of Bohemian ancestry, was an American scientist who played a central role in the early history of molecular biology. He was a professor of medicine at Harvard Medical School and a senior scientist at Massachusetts General Hospital. Zamecnik pioneered the in vitro synthesis of proteins and helped elucidate the way cells generate proteins. With Mahlon Hoagland, he co-discovered transfer RNA (tRNA). Through his later work, he is credited as the inventor of antisense therapeutics. Throughout his career, Zamecnik earned over a dozen US patents for his therapeutic techniques. Up until his death in 2009, he maintained a lab at MGH where he studied the application of synthetic oligonucleotides (antisense hybrids) for chemotherapeutic treatment of drug resistant and XDR tuberculosis in his later years. He attended Dartmouth College, majored in chemistry and zoology, and received his AB degree in 1933. He then attended Harvard Medical School and received his MD degree in 1936. Between 1936 and 1939, he worked at Collis P. Huntington Memorial Hospital in

Boston, Harvard Medical School, and Lakeside Hospital in Cleveland. During his Lakeside Hospital internship, Zamecnik became interested in how cells regulate growth, and hence, in protein chemistry. He was awarded a Finney-Howell Fellowship and a Moseley Traveling Fellowship to go to the Carlsberg Laboratory in Copenhagen where he worked with Dr. Kai Linderstrom-Lang. He returned to Boston where he became an assistant physician at the Huntington Memorial Hospital, studying the toxic factors involved in traumatic shock for a wartime Office of Scientific Research and Development project led by Huntington director Joseph Charles Aub. After a year in New York at the Rockefeller Institute for Medical Research studying protein synthesis with Max Bergmann, he joined the faculty of medicine at Harvard Medical School in 1942, becoming an instructor and then professor of medicine, where he served until retiring as the Collis P. Huntington Professor of Oncologic Medicine, Emeritus in 1979.

Vladimir Zbinovsky (1913–2013), b. Warsaw, of Slovak parents, was a pharmacologist and biochemist. He taught first at Clark University, MA; after settling at Nanuet, NY, he worked for American Cyanamid, also known as Lederle Labs. His years at American Cyanamid yielded several patents and the discovery of new antibiotics, among them minocycline.

B. Physical Sciences

Olga 'Ollie' Beaver (1942–2012), b. Prague, Czech., was a Czech American mathematician and Professor of Mathematics at Williams College. She was the recipient of the second Louise Hay Award from the Association for Women in Mathematics. She is noted for having founded the Summer Science Program at Williams. She served as the director of the SSP for many years and was the chair of the Mathematics Department at Williams for five and a half years.

Henry Victor Bohm (1929–2011), b. Vienna, son of Gertrude Rie (1897–1985) of Bohemian descent, and Victor Charles Bohm, was professor of physics at Wayne State University. He did his undergraduate work at Harvard, his graduate work at the University of Illinois, and his Ph.D. work at Brown University. Along with earning his full professorship, Dr. Bohm served at different times as chair of the department, V. P. for Graduate Studies & Research, V.P. for Special Projects, Provost, Dean of Faculties, and Dean of the College of Liberal Arts. He was instrumental in the construction of the new physics building at Wayne in the 1960s.

Otto Eisenschiml (1880–1963), b. Vienna, Aust., of Czech ancestry, a chemist, devised one of the earliest deodorants, transparent window envelopes, oiled baseball gloves, rustproof barbed wire (originally used in Flanders during World War I) and dozens of other useful contributions which have flowed unheralded into the stream of our necessities.

Rudi H. Ettrich (1970–), b. Bönnigheim, State of Baden-Württemberg, Germany, of Czech parents, is President and CEO of Larkin University, Miami, FL. After finishing undergraduate studies at Eberhard-Karls University in Tubingen, Germany, and Charles University, Prague, Czech Republic, he completed his Doctorate in physical chemistry focused on structural biology of protein complexes at Charles University in 2001. After a post-doc stay at the Institute of Physical Biology of the University of South Bohemia in 2002–2003, he was appointed in 2004 group leader in the department of structure and function of proteins of the Institute of Systems Biology and Ecology, Academy of Sciences of the Czech Republic, and in the same year head of the department. Since 2011, he had been the director of the Center for Nanobiology and Structural Biology of the Academy of Sciences, a research center and campus he has built up and shaped from ground in Nove Hrady, South Bohemia, for the last 14 years. In 2013, he was appointed full professor in biophysics at the University of South Bohemia. Since 2018, he has been with Larkin University, Miami, first as Professor and Dean (August-December) and then as President and CEO (since December 2018). Dr. Ettrich is a pioneer in providing structural insight on very fundamental processes in living organism, using a synthesis of theoretical and experimental methods to gain key insights into the relationship between the structure and function of proteins, dynamic changes related to functional processes on the level of proteins, and the mutual interaction of cofactors and subunits in protein complexes.

Martin Fleischmann (1927–2012), b. Karlovy Vary, Czech., an electrochemist, is best known for his controversial work with his former graduate student Stanley Pons on cold fusion, in the 1980s and '90s. On March 23, 1989, while Pons was a researcher at the University of Utah, he and Fleischmann announced the experimental production of cold fusion – a result previously thought to be unattainable. After a short period of public acclaim, the pair was attacked widely for sloppy, unreproducible research and inaccurate results, as Fleischmann predicted they would be. Fleischmann, Pons and the researchers who replicated the effect remain convinced the effect is real, but skeptics who oppose them are convinced it is not. In 1992, Fleischmann moved to France with Pons, to work at the IMRA laboratory (part of Technova Corporation, a subsidiary of Toyota). The pair parted ways in 1995, and Fleischmann returned to Southampton, where he remained as of 1999. In 2006, Fleischmann joined the San Francisco company D2Fusion.

Rudolf Gaertner (1873–1930), b. Prague, Bohemia, a ceramic chemist, trained at Liberec Polytechnicum, invented a jet-black glaze for hard feldspar china, an incandescent lamp refractor, and china insulators with inserted glaze lamelles for electric currents up to 50,000 volts. He established his own decalcomania plant at Mt. Vernon, NY which developed into one of the largest enterprises of its kind in the world.

Maryellen Lissak Giger (née Lissak) (1956–), b. Elmhurst, IL, of Czech ancestry, is a medical physicist and radiologist. She is a graduate of Illinois Benedictine College (B.S., 1978) and pursued physics at University of Exeter (M.Sc., 1979) and medical physics at University of Chicago (Ph.D., 1985). From a research assistant at University of Chicago (1983–85), she rose there to Professor in the Department of Radiology and Biological Sciences (s. 2003) and Director of Imaging Research Institute (s. 2008). She is the author of more than 400 publications. She was married to Dr. Charles C. Giger and they had four children.

David Jonathan Gross (1941–), b. Washington, DC, of Czechoslovak ancestry, is an American theoretical physicist and string theorist. Along with Frank Wilczek and David Politzer, he was awarded the 2004 Nobel Prize in Physics for their discovery of asymptotic freedom. Gross is the Chancellor's Chair Professor of Theoretical Physics at the Kavli Institute for Theoretical Physics (KITP) of the University of California, Santa Barbara (UCSB), and was formerly the KITP director and holder of their Frederick W. Gluck Chair in Theoretical Physics. He is also a faculty member in the UCSB Physics Department and is currently affiliated with the Institute for Quantum Studies at Chapman University in California. He is a foreign member of the Chinese Academy of Sciences. Gross received his bachelor's degree from the Hebrew University of Jerusalem, Israel, in 1962. He received his Ph.D. in physics from the University of California, Berkeley in 1966, under the supervision of Geoffrey Chew.

Arlene A. Halko (1933–2007), b. Chicago, IL, of Czech. immigrant father, was an American medical physicist and gay rights advocate, based in Chicago. She was on the staffs at Michael Reese Hospital and Cook County Hospital, both in Chicago. She was Clinical Assistant Professor of Radiology at the University of Illinois College of Medicine. She was the first lesbian president of Dignity/Chicago, an organization of gay Roman Catholics. In 1985, she co-founded Chicago House, a social service agency assisting people with HIV/AIDS who needed housing, hospice care, and other supports. From 1982 to 1989, she was a co-owner of Piggens Pub, a lesbian bar. In 2000, she and fellow activist Marie J. Kuda co-founded the Jeannette Howard Foster Memorial Sewing Circle and Book Club, dedicated to preserving Chicago lesbian history. She was inducted into the Chicago LGBT Hall of Fame in 1996.

Lili Hornig (née Schwenková) (1921–2017), b. Ústí nad Labem, Czech., was a Czech American scientist who worked on the Manhattan Project, as well as a feminist activist. In 1929, her family moved to Berlin. Four years later, she and her mother came to the United States, following her father who had moved there to escape the Nazis. As her parents were Jewish, her father was threatened with imprisonment in a concentration camp. She obtained her BA from Bryn Mawr in 1942 and her Ph.D. from Harvard University in 1950. In 1943, she married Donald Hornig and they had four children. Hornig went with her husband to Los Alamos where he had obtained a job; after being originally asked to take a typing test, her scientific skills were recognized and she was given a job as a staff scientist for the Manhattan Project, in a group working with plutonium chemistry. Hornig later became a chemistry professor at Brown University, and chairwoman of the chemistry department at Trinity College in Washington, D.C. She was appointed by President Johnson as a member of a mission to the Republic of Korea that began the founding of the Korea Institute for Science and Technology. A feminist, Hornig was the founding director of HERS (Higher Education Resource Services) under the auspices of the Committee for the Concerns of Women in New England Colleges and Universities first organized by Sheila Tobias. She served on equal opportunity committees for the National Science Foundation, the National Cancer Institute, and the American Association for the Advancement of Science. She was the research chair of the Committee for the Equality of Women at Harvard and consulted with and participated in many studies of women's science education and careers.

Karl Guthe Jansky (1905-1950), b. Norman, OK, of Bohemian ancestry, an American physicist and radio engineer. In 1931, he first discovered radio waves emanating from the Milky Way. He is considered one of the founding figures of radio astronomy.

Peter Edward Kaus (1924-2016), b. Vienna, the son of Gina Weiner (1893-1985) of Czech ancestry, and Otto F. Kaus, was a physicist, trained at UCLA (Ph.D., 1954). That's where he met his future wife, Eva Lewy, with whom he then moved to Princeton, NJ, where Peter worked for RCA Laboratories. His team at RCA designed the deflection yoke for the first commercially successful color TV tube, for which Peter shares the patent. Peter returned to Los Angeles in 1958 for a position at the University of Southern California. In 1963, the family moved to Riverside, where Peter became a physics professor at the then-new University of California, Riverside campus. He remained at UCR for the next 30 years, teaching and continuing his research in elementary particle physics. Peter's work spanned a broad range of topics from neutrinos to quarks. One of the key accomplishments of his life was his contribution to the establishment and success of the Aspen Center for Physics, a premier international institution for research in theoretical physics.

John Michael Kovac (1970-), b. Princeton, NJ, of Czech descent, is an American physicist and astronomer. His cosmology research, conducted at the Harvard Smithsonian Center for Astrophysics in Cambridge, Massachusetts, focuses on observations of the Cosmic Microwave Background (CMB) to reveal signatures of the physics that drove the birth of the universe, the creation of its structure, and its present-day expansion. Currently, Kovac is a Professor of Astronomy and Physics at Harvard University.

Paul Krutak (1934-2016), b. Pueblo, CO, of Slovak descent, was an eminent American micropaleontologist. He was a Professor of Geology at Eastern New Mexico University, Ball State University, and the University of Nebraska-Lincoln. After leaving the University of Nebraska in 1982, Krutak worked as a consulting geologist for ARCO Oil Company, primarily in Lafayette, Louisiana, with some time spent on the North Slope in Alaska.

Jarmila Kukalova-Peck (née Kukálová), (1930-), b. Prague, Czech., is a paleontologist well known for her controversial theories on insect evolution. She is currently an adjunct professor in the Department of Earth Sciences at Carleton University in Ottawa, Canada. She is married to a Canadian entomologist Stewart B. Peck.

Louis Edward Levy (1846-1919), b. Pilsen, Bohemia, was a U.S. chemist, inventor, communal leader and newspaper editor. He was brought to U.S. at the age of eight. In 1875, he invented the photochemical engraving process known as "Levytype," permitting newspapers to print halftone pictures from the stereotype plate and founded the Levytype Company in Baltimore. The company moved to Philadelphia in 1877. Levy, the first U.S. citizen to receive a patent in this field, also invented the Levy acid blast, an etch-powdering machine, and the Levy line screen. He published and edited the *Philadelphia Evening Herald*, an independent Democratic daily (1887-90), *The Mercury*, a Sunday paper (1887-91), and *The Jewish Year* (1895). Levy was a leader of the Philadelphia Jewish community and, reflecting his deep interest in the problems of Jewish immigration to the U.S., was a founder (1884) and president of the Association or Relief and Protection of Jewish Immigrants. He wrote *The Russian Jewish Refugees in America* (1895), a pamphlet; *Business, Money and Credit* (1896); and (with Hugo Bilgram) *The Cause of Business Depressions as Disclosed by an Analysis of the Basic Principles of Economics* (1914).

Max Levy (1857-1926), b. Detroit, MI, of Bohemian ancestry, invented, jointly with his brother Louis, the Levy half tone screen, an etched glass grating which they patented in 1893. For this invention, they received the John Scott Legacy Medal. Max then engaged in the manufacture of half tone screens and photographic plate holders and camera diaphragms of his own invention for photoengraver's use. He also patented the hemocytometer in 1917.

Joseph Mahler (1899-1981), b. Czech., a physicist, was an inventor of vectographs, polarizers, and stereoscopic viewers. A vectograph is a type of stereoscopic print or transparency viewed by using the polarized 3D glasses most commonly associated with projected 3D motion pictures. He was a cousin of composer Gustav Mahler. He immigrated to the US from Czechoslovakia in 1938 and was hired by the Polaroid Corporation, where he worked with its founder Edwin Land, to develop his idea into a practical process.

Jack Johnson Morava (1944–), b. TX, of Czech and Appalachian descent, is an American homotopy theorist at Johns Hopkins University. He was raised in Texas' lower Rio Grande valley. An early interest in topology was strongly encouraged by his parents. He enrolled at Rice University in 1962 as a physics major, but (with the help of Jim Douglas) entered the graduate mathematics program in 1964. His advisor Eldon Dyer arranged, with the support of Michael Atiyah, a one-year fellowship at the University of Oxford, followed by a year in Princeton at the Institute for Advanced Study. Morava brought ideas from arithmetic geometry into the realm of algebraic topology. He joined the Johns Hopkins University faculty in 1979 and was involved in organizing the Japan-US Mathematics Institute there. Much of his later work involves the application of cobordism categories to mathematical physics, as well as Tannakian descent theory in homotopy categories (posted mostly on the ArXiv).

Douglas (Dean) Osheroff (1945–), b. Aberdeen, WA, the son of Bessie Anne Ondov (1919–1996), the daughter of a Lutheran minister from Slovakia, and William Osheroff, is a physicist, known for his work in experimental condensed matter physics, in particular for his co-discovery of superfluidity in Helium-3. For his contributions, he shared the 1996 Nobel Prize in Physics along with David Lee and Robert C. Richardson. Osheroff received a Ph.D. in 1973 and began working at Bell Labs in Murray Hill, New Jersey, where he continued his research in low-temperature phenomena in ^{3}He. As a member of the Department of Solid State and Low Temperature Research under the direction of C. C. Grimes, he performed many interesting investigations with his team and measured many of the important characteristics of the superfluid phases which helped identify the microscopic states involved. In the late 1970s, he began to focus more on solid ^{3}He. Around this time, he partnered with Gerry Dolan to discover antiferromagnet resonance in nuclear spin ordered solid ^{3}He samples which they grew from the superfluid phase directly into the spin-ordered solid phase. From 1982 to 1987, he headed solid-state and low-temperature research at the labs. In 1987, he joined the Departments of Physics and Applied Physics at Stanford University as a professor and also served as department chair from 1993–96. His research also covers studies of transport properties in nuclear magnetically ordered solid ^{3}He and studies of the B phase nucleation in superfluid ^{3}He.

Wolfgang Ernst Pauli (orig. Pascheles) (1900–1958), b. Vienna, of Bohemian ancestry, was a physicist. He received his early education in Vienna before studying at the University of Munich under Arnold Sommerfeld. He obtained his doctor's degree in 1921 and spent a year at the University of Göttingen as assistant to Max Born and a further year with

Niels Bohr at Copenhagen. The years 1923–1928 were spent as a lecturer at the University of Hamburg before his appointment as Professor of Theoretical Physics at the Federal Institute of Technology in Zurich. During 1935–1936, he was visiting Professor at the Institute for Advanced Study, Princeton, New Jersey and he had similar appointments at the University of Michigan (1931 and 1941) and Purdue University (1942). He was elected to the Chair of Theoretical Physics at Princeton in 1940 but he returned to Zurich at the end of World War II. Pauli was outstanding among the brilliant mid-twentieth century school of physicists. He was recognized as one of the leaders when, barely out of his teens and still a student, he published a masterly exposition of the theory of relativity. His exclusion principle, which is often quoted bearing his name, crystallized the existing knowledge of atomic structure at the time it was postulated, and it led to the recognition of the two valued variable required to characterize the state of an electron. Pauli was the first to recognize the existence of the neutrino, an uncharged and massless particle which carries off energy in radioactive ß-disintegration; this came at the beginning of a great decade, prior to World War II, for his center of research in theoretical physics at Zurich. Pauli helped to lay the foundations of the quantum theory of fields, and he participated actively in the great advances made in this domain around 1945. Earlier, he had further consolidated field theory by giving proof of the relationship between spin and "statistics" of elementary particles. He has written many articles on problems of theoretical physics, mostly quantum mechanics, in scientific journals of many countries.

John C. Polanyi (orig. Pollacsek) (1929–), b. Berlin, Ger., of Slovak ancestry, is a Canadian chemist. He won the 1986 Nobel Prize in Chemistry, for his research in chemical kinetics. His family emigrated in 1933 to the United Kingdom where he was subsequently educated at the University of Manchester and did postdoctoral research at the National Research Council in Canada and Princeton University in New Jersey. Polanyi's first academic appointment was at the University of Toronto, and he remained there. In addition to the Nobel Prize, Polanyi has received numerous other awards, including 33 honorary degrees, the Wolf Prize in Chemistry and the Gerhard Herzberg Canada Gold Medal for Science and Engineering. Outside his scientific pursuits, Polanyi is active in public policy discussion, especially concerning science and nuclear weapons.

Hugh David Politzer (1949–), b. New York, NY, of Czechoslovak parents, was a theoretical physicist. He shared the 2004 Nobel Prize in Physics with David Gross and Frank Wilczek for their discovery of asymptotic freedom in quantum chromodynamics. He graduated from the Bronx High School of Science in 1966, received his Bachelor's degree from the University of Michigan in 1969, and his Ph.D. in 1974 from Harvard University, where his graduate advisor was Sidney Coleman. Politzer was a junior Fellow at the Harvard Society of Fellows from 1974 to 1977 before moving to the California Institute of Technology

(Caltech), where he is currently professor of theoretical physics. Politzer was also elected as a member of the American Academy of Arts and Sciences in 2011.

Aurora Pribram-Jones (née Pribram) (1987-), b. Stanford, CA, of Czech ancestry, is a chemist. She received training in chemistry at Harvey Mudd Coll. (B.S., 2009) and in theoretical chemistry at Univ. of California, Irvine (Ph.D., 2015). In her research, she is associated with the Burke Research Group at the University and also with Sandia National Laboratories. She is supported by the Department of Energy as a Computational Science Graduate Fellow. Her interests include chemistry education, density functional theory (DFT), and quantum theory. She likes to explore the interface of chemistry, physics, and mathematics. She is married to a mathematician David Gross (1986-).

Svante Procházka (1928-), b. Prague, Czech., was trained as a chemist at University of Technology in Prague and at MIT. He has been with General Electric Corp. He specialized in materials science and ceramics. He is an inventor and a holder of a number of patents. Among others, he invented a new materials-fabrication process which makes gas turbines for the generation of electric power more efficient, and aircraft engines less fuel-hungry.

Eva Saxl (1921-2002), b. Prague, Czech., as a self-taught manufacturer of insulin and an advocate for people with diabetes. In 1940, during World War II, she and her husband, Victor Saxl, fled to Shanghai, China. In Shanghai, a year later, Saxl was diagnosed with type 1 diabetes. When the Japanese attacked Pearl Harbor in 1941, the Japanese occupation of China was tightened, and soon all the pharmacies in Shanghai were closed. Saxl had no legal access to insulin. It was possible to buy insulin on the black market using one ounce gold bars for payment. But that was not the safest option; one of Eva's friends died from using the black-market insulin. Eventually, Victor and Eva decided to get insulin another—highly unconventional—way: make it themselves. The book "Beckman's Internal Medicine" described the methods that Dr. Frederick Banting and Charles Best first used to extract insulin from the pancreases of dogs, calves, and cows in 1921. A Chinese chemist lent them a small laboratory in the basement of a municipal building, where they attempted to extract insulin from pancreata of water buffaloes. After much work, they finally produced brown colored insulin. The insulin was tested on rabbits starved for twenty-four hours and then divided into two groups. One group was injected with the extracted mix, and the other with Eva's insulin. Without equipment to test the rabbits' urine or blood, the best way Victor could test the potency of the insulin was to see if the rabbits experienced the same hypoglycaemic shock as the other rabbits. After testing the insulin on rabbits for more than a year, Eva was running out of conventional insulin and cautiously tried it on herself—and it worked. In the Jewish ghetto where they were living, many other people with type 1 diabetes were also in dire need of insulin. Eva gave her insulin to two boys in a nearby hospital who was in diabetic comas. With a successful batch of homemade insulin, the Saxls began production of insulin for all people with diabetes in the Shanghai Ghetto. In all, over 200 people survived between 1941 and 1945 and there were no fatalities reported as a result of tainted insulin. The Saxls left Shanghai after World War II and emigrated to the United States. Eva and Elliott P. Joslin, MD, founder of today's Joslin Diabetes Center in Boston, Massachusetts, befriended each other, and soon Dr. Joslin began inviting Eva to give lectures to groups of children and diabetes organizations. She became the first vocal spokesperson for juvenile diabetes. Her husband worked for the United Nations. The Saxls' story was dramatized by the 1956–1958 CBS television show *Telephone Time* in an episode titled "Time Bomb".

Franz Charles Schmelkes (1899–1942), b. Prague, Bohemia, a chemist, was best known for his discovery of azochloramid, used to sterilize wounds and burns. This compound is also known by the name chlorazodin, but its formal name is 1-(amino-chloroimino-methyl) imino-2-chloro-guanidine.

Paul Schwarzkopf (1886–1970), b. Prague, Bohemia, developed physical purification method for molybdenum based on distillation of the volatile molybdenum oxide which he patented in 1927. He also developed multi carbide tool materials (1929) which revolutionized machining technique by permitting the high-speed machining of steel. He also developed copper filtrated iron and steel and initiated and directed research which led to the development of refractory borides for service at extremely high temperatures.

Trudy Enzer Smith (née Enzer) (1924–2002), b. Cheb, Bohemia, was trained as a physical chemist at Ohio State University, graduating in 1944. She did research on the kinetics and mechanisms of vapor phase pyrolysis, on gas chromatography and mass spectroscopy. She came to Connecticut College in 1962, after teaching chemistry for two years at the University of Connecticut. Previously, she had done chemical research for Aaerojet General Corporation of California and the Naval Ordnance Test Station at China Lake, California. She was professor of chemistry at Connecticut College, New London for over 30 years. She was married to chemist S. Raven Smith (1920–2003) and they had 6 children.

Carl Richard Sovinec (1963–), b. MN, of Czech descent, is an American physicist from the University of Wisconsin, Madison. Sovinec is the son of Dr. Richard and Cathleen Sovinec and a 1981 graduate of Winona Senior High School in Winona, Minnesota. He attended the United States Air Force Academy in Colorado Springs, Colorado. He was awarded the status of Fellow in the American Physical Society, after they were nominated by their Division of Plasma Physics in 2009, for using large scale magnetohydrodynamic simulation to elucidate the roles of reconnection, relaxation and transport in self-organization processes of low field magnetic confinement devices and for providing a primary scientific leadership role in the development of the NIMROD project.

Michael Sveda (1912–1990), b. West Ashford, CT, of Czech immigrant parents, a chemist, was a discoverer of cyclamates, an artificial noncaloric sweetener that was widely used in diet soft drinks and desserts before being banned by the Department of Health, Education, and Welfare as a possible carcinogen in 1969. He also invented method for production of pyrosulfyl chloride, thionyl chloride, vapor phase sulfonation hydrocarbons, with sulphur trioxide, method for separating two forms of DDT, first polymerization of silicon.

Olga Taussky-Todd (née Taussky) (1906–1995), b. Olomouc, Czech., was a mathematician. She was noted for her more than 300 research papers in algebraic number theory, integral matrices, and matrices in algebra and analysis. In 1945, the Todds emigrated to the United States and worked for the National Bureau of Standards. In 1957, she and her husband both joined the faculty of California Institute of Technology (Caltech) in Pasadena, California. She received an honorary Doctorate from the University of Vienna and an honorary D.Sc. by the University of Southern California in 1988. She was a Fellow of the AAAS, a Noether Lecturer and a recipient of the Austrian Cross of Honour for Science and Art, 1st class (1978). In 1993, the International Linear Algebra Society established a lecture series to honor the contributions to the field of linear algebra made by Taussky-Todd and her husband Jack Todd (1911–2007).

Edward Teller (1908–2003), b. Budapest, of Slovak ancestry, was a theoretical physicist, known as 'father of the hydrogen bomb.' He earned a degree in chemical engineering at the Institute of Technology in Karlsruhe, Ger. He then went to Munich and Leipzig to earn a Ph.D. in physical chemistry (1930).

Robin Thomas (1962–2020), b. Prague, Czech., was a mathematician working in graph theory at the Georgia Institute of Technology. Thomas received his doctorate in 1985 from Charles University in Prague, under the supervision of Jaroslav Nešetřil. He joined the faculty at Georgia Tech in 1989, and became a Regents' Professor there, briefly serving as the Department Chair. In 2011, he was awarded the Karel Janeček Foundation Neuron Prize for Lifetime Achievement in Mathematics. In 2012, he became a fellow of the American Mathematical Society. He was named a SIAM Fellow in 2018.

Hans Tropsch (1889–1935), b. Planá, Bohemia, chemist, along with Franz Fischer, was responsible for the development of the Fischer-Tropsch process. It is a collection of chemical reactions that converts a mixture of carbon monoxide and hydrogen into liquid hydrocarbons. The process, a key component of gas to liquids technology, produces a synthetic lubrication oil and synthetic fuel, typically from coal, natural gas, or biomass.

The Fischer-Tropsch process has received intermittent attention as a source of low-sulfur diesel fuel and to address the supply or cost of petroleum-derived hydrocarbons.

Arnold Weissberger (1898–1984), b. Chemnitz, Saxony, of Bohemian ancestry, a chemist, formulated and developed many of the organic compounds used in the color process photography, and was holder of more than 100 US and foreign patents.

Victor 'Viki' Frederick Weisskopf (1908–2002), b. Vienna, Austria, of Bohemian Jewish father, was an American theoretical physicist. He did postdoctoral work with Werner Heisenberg, Erwin Schrödinger, Wolfgang Pauli and Niels Bohr. During World War II, he was Group Leader of the Theoretical Division of the Manhattan Project at Los Alamos, and later campaigned against the proliferation of nuclear weapons. In the 1930s and 1940s, 'Viki', made major contributions to the development of quantum theory, especially in the area of Quantum Electrodynamics. One of his few regrets was that his insecurity about his mathematical abilities may have cost him a Nobel Prize when he did not publish results (which turned out to be correct) about what is now known as the Lamb shift. From 1937 to 1943, he was a Professor of Physics at the University of Rochester. After World War II, Weisskopf joined the physics faculty at MIT, ultimately becoming head of the department. Weisskopf was a co-founder and board member of the Union of Concerned Scientists. He served as director-general of CERN from 1961 to 1966. Weisskopf was awarded the Max Planck medal in 1956 and the Prix mondial Cino Del Duca in 1972, the National Medal of Science (1980), the Wolf Prize (1981) and the Public Welfare Medal from the National Academy of Sciences (1991). Weisskopf was a member of the National Academy of Sciences. He was president of the American Physical Society (1960–61) and the American Academy of Arts and Sciences (1976–1979).

Jon Zeleny (1872–1951), b. Racine, WI of Czech immigrant parents, was a physicist. In 1911, he invented the Zeleny electroscope. He also studied the effect of an electric field on a liquid meniscus. His work is seen by some as a beginning to emergent technologies like liquid metal ion sources and electrospraying and electrospinning. He attended the University of Minnesota (B.S., 1892), followed by Trinity College, Cambridge (B.A., 1899), and the University of Minnesota (Ph.D., 1906). Zeleny began his teaching career at the University of Minnesota after earning his BS. Zeleny was an elected member of the American Academy of Arts and Sciences. He was elected to the American Philosophical Society in 1915. That same year, he joined the faculty at Yale, where he was chairman of the physics department and director of graduate studies in physics until his retirement in 1940.

C. Earth Sciences

Richard J. Anderle (1926–1994), b. New York, NY, of Czech ancestry, was a geodesist. He was a graduate of Brooklyn College, where he majored in mathematics (B.A., 1948). He pursued graduate studies in mathematics and physics at American University, where he also taught as a lecturer in 1964 and 1965. He had a profound impact on the evolution of the field of a satellite geodesy during his career with the Department of the Navy, at what is now the Naval Warfare Center in Dahlgren, VA. As a geodesic mathematician for the Navy, he was responsible for developing Geodesic Satellites (i.e., global positioning). While working in the Naval Surface Weapons Center, he spent a large part of his career developing equipment to employ satellites for positioning purposes. First, the Doppler system provided positions to an accuracy of ± 1-meter in each component and second, GPS where in the relative mode, accuracies of 0.1 ppm are possible. He also developed the algorithm to track Sputnik I and II and sent several experiments up on the space shuttles. He received numerous awards, including being a winner of the Johannes Kepler Award. Anderle became a member of the American Geophysical Union (AGU), in 1965, was elected a fellow in 1981, and served as president of the Geodesy Section from 1980 to 1982. He also devoted much of his personal time to supporting the International Association of Geodesy, where he served on many scientific advisory committees and held several offices. He served as secretary of IAG's space techniques section from 1979 to 1983 and as president of the Section on Advanced Space Technology from 1983 to 1987. He was also active within the International Astronomical Union and the Committee on Space Research.

Luke Beranek (1980–), b. Eau Claire, WI, of Czech ancestry, holds a Ph.D. in geological sciences (2009) from the University of British Columbia, M.S. in geosciences (2005) from Idaho State University and a B.S. in geology (2003) from the University of Wisconsin-Eau Claire). Beranek is currently an assistant professor of earth sciences at Memorial University of Newfoundland, Canada. His research and teaching interests focus on the interactions between plate tectonics and earth surface processes.

Jiří Březina (1933–), b. Prague, Czech., was trained as a geologist at Charles Univ. He joined Univ. of Maryland in 1973 and taught geology and related subjects for 37 years. In 1976, he developed an equation for drag coefficient of a regimenting irregular body as a function of Reynolds' number and Shape Factor, from which all involved quantities can be calculated, such as particle (grain) size, shape, density, and sedimentation velocity. He constructed an advanced Sand Sedimentation Analyzer (MacroGranometer) and Sand Sedimentation Separator. Dr. Brezina has been president of the company that manufactures these instruments since 1973.

Vladimír Čermák (1937–), b. Prague, Czech., studied physics (dipl., 1960) and geophysics (CSc./Ph.D., 1967) at Charles Univ. In 1981 he also received Dr.Sc. degree. He has been associated with Geophysical Inst. of ČSAV (1960–68) and subsequently served as a postdoctoral Fellow at Dominion Observatory, Ottawa, Canada (1968–70). He then returned to the Geophysical Inst. in Prague, becoming head of the Dept. of Geothermics (1971–90) and then the director of the Institute (1990–98).

Petr Černý (1934–), b. Brno, Czech., attended Masaryk University for his B.Sc. (1956) in geology, and the Czechoslovak Academy of Sciences in Prague for CSc./Ph.D. (1966). As of 1968 he was associated with the University of Manitoba, Winnipeg, Canada as postdoctoral Fellow (1968–1971), professor of mineralogy at the Department of Geological Sciences (1971–2000), and professor emeritus (since 2004). His research interests were focused at a broad variety of aspects of granitic pegmatites: deposits of rare metals such as Li, Cs, Be, and Ta that are enormously important in present day technologies. He examined multitudes of regional populations of these deposits in North America and Europe, with particular attention to the pegmatites in Manitoba, notably the world-famous Tanco deposit and its regional setting. His exploration guidelines have been widely used in Africa and South America based on his studies in geologically analogous terranes. The significance of his studies has been appreciated by numerous Canadian and international awards.

Joseph V. Chernosky, Jr. (ca. 1945–), b. US, of Czech ancestry, graduated from Univ. of Notre Dame (A.B., 1966) and received training in geological sciences at Univ. of Wisconsin, Maine (M.A., 1969) and at MIT (Ph.D., 1973). He has been associated with Univ. of Maine where he held the position of geological sciences in the dept. of earth sciences, now professor emeritus. His specialties are metamorphic minerals and mineral assemblages which record information about the intensive conditions, temperature, fluid pressure, oxygen fugacity, etc. which they experienced during metamorphism. His research effort has two principal objectives: (1) to experimentally locate, in P(fluid)-T-X (CO2) space, the positions of key metamorphic equilibria in the model chemical system CaO-MgO-Al2O3-SiO2-H2O-CO2; and (2) to use the experimentally located equilibria to refine the thermochemical parameters for selected rock-forming minerals which occur in the model system.

Petr Chýlek (1937–), b. Ostrava, Czech., was trained as a theoretical physicist and physicist, resp., at Charles Univ. (dipl., 1966) and Univ. of California, Riverside (Ph.D., 1970). He was associated with SUNY, Albany (1973–75); with Purdue Univ., as an assoc. professor of geosciences (s. 1975); with dept. of physics at New Mexico State Univ., Los Cruces (s. 1988); with Dalhousie Univ., Halifax, Can., as professor of atmospheric physics (s. 2002). He also taught at Univ. of Oklahoma. He now serves as a researcher for Space and Remote Sensing Sciences at Los Alamos National Laboratory. His res. interests include: remote sensing, atmospheric radiation, climate change, cloud and aerosol physics, applied laser physics and ice core analysis. Chylek is best known for his work in remote sensing, aerosols and climate change.

Alan Milton Cvancara (1933–), b. Ross, ND, of Czech ancestry, was trained as a geologist at Univ. of North Dakota (M.S., 1957) and at Univ. of Michigan (Ph.D., 1965). He was with Univ. of North Dakota (s. 1963), where he advanced from asst. to assoc. professor of geology (1963–72), as professor (1972–91), as emeritus professor (s. 1992). He is a specialist on paleobiology and invertebrate paleontology, tertiary mollusks and stratography.

Heinz H. Damberger (1933–), b. Chomutov, Czech., was trained as geologist at Clausthal Tech. Univ. (dipl., 1960; Dr. rer. nat., 1966). He was with Illinois State Geological Survey (1968–76), as sr. geologist and head, coal sect., (s. 1978); and has served as adj. prof. of geology, at Univ. of Illinois, Urbana (s. 1992). His res. interests were in the area of coal geology, coalification, coal mining, geology and coal petrography, classification of coal, microstructure of coal.

Zdenko Frankenberger Daneš (1920–), b. Prague, Czech., was trained as a geophysicist at Charles Univ. He has served as prof. of physics at Univ. of Puget Sound (1962–84), as professor emeritus (s. 2006); president, Danes & Res. Assocs. (1978–89). He is a specialist on gravity, geomagnetism, constitution of earth, radiation, lunar physics, and electromagnetic theory.

Ernst Robert Deutsch (1924–2000), b. Frankfurt /M, of Moravian ancestry, was trained as a physicist at Univ. of London. He was associated with Memorial Univ. (s. 1963), as professor of geophysics (s. 1963) and professor of physics (s. 1968). He was a specialist on continental drift and polar wandering and research on the high-temperature characteristics of rocks.

Jaroslav Dostál (ca. 1947–), b. Prague, Czech., graduated from the Charles University in Prague, with a B.Sc. in geology and from McMaster University in 1974 with a Ph.D. in geology. He has been teaching in the Department of Geology at Saint Mary's University in Halifax since 1975, and where he is now prof. emeritus of geology. Dostal has over 35 years experience in geology, ore deposit studies, and geochemistry. He has been Director of Ucore Uranium Inc. since September 14, 2007. Dostal served as a director of Landmark Minerals Inc. since September 22, 2005. He has published more than 250 scientific papers, and is a widely acknowledged expert on tin and uranium mineralization in granitoids, mobility of uranium in metamorphic and volcanic rocks, and the use of trace elements in the search for volcanogenic massive sulfide deposits. Dr. Dostal has been director of Ucore

Rare Metals Inc. He is the recipient of the 2005 Career Achievement Award of the Volcanology and Igneous Petrology Division of the Geological Association of Canada and the 2007 Gesner Medal for Distinguished Scientist of the Atlantic Geoscience Society.

Vernon F. Dvorak (1928-), b. of Czech ancestry, is a retired American meteorologist from the National Oceanic and Atmospheric Administration. In 1974, he developed the Dvorak technique to analyze tropical cyclones from satellite imagery. He worked with the National Environmental Satellite, Data, and Information Service. Dvorak now lives in Ojai, CA.

William Clinton Elsik (1935-2011), b. Snook, TX, of Czech ancestry, was trained as a geologist at Texas A&M Univ. He attained a B.S., M.S., and Ph.D. in geology, finally specializing in palynology, the study of fossil pollen and spores. He joined Humble Oil & Refining Co. in 1962, retiring 28 years later from then Exxon Corp. He was a founding member and a president of the American Association of Stratigraphic Palynologists. He was a specialist in fossil fungal spores and classification.

Irene Fischer (1907-2009), born in Vienna, of Czech ancestry, was a geodesist. Fischer became one of two internationally known women scientists in the field of geodesy during the golden age of the Mercury and Apollo moon missions. Her Mercury Datum, or Fischer Ellipsoid 1960 and 1968, as well as her work on the lunar parallax, were instrumental in conducting these missions.

Otto Henry Haas (1887-1976), b. Brno, Moravia, was trained as a paleonthologist and geologist at Univ. of Vienna. He was with American Museum of Natural History, NY (1940-55); served as vis. prof. at Hofstra Coll., (1957-60); and was on faculty of Macay School of Mines, Univ. of Nevada (1960-71). He specialized in mesozoic invertebrates, paleontology and evolution of stratigraphy.

Susan D. Hovorka (1952-), b. New Orleans, LA, of Czech ancestry, was trained as a geologist at Univ. of Texas (M.A., 1981; Ph.D., 1990). She worked as a geologist at Bendix Field engineering Corp., Austin, TX (1979-81), before joining the Bureau of Economic Geography at the Univ. of Texas, Austin (s. 1981). She is interested in application of geological techniques to environmental problems, particularly focusing on the issue of permeability in both tight and very transmissive systems. This interest has led her to work on diverse problems, from characterization of salt as a containment material to analysis of carbonate fabrics to better understand flow in karst aquifers. Currently, she is leading teams in field CO2 injections to assess geologic sequestration as a mechanism for reducing atmospheric greenhouse gas emissions.

František Hron (1937-1999), b. Starý Klíčov, Czech., studied geophysics (dipl., 1961) and physics (CSc./Ph.D., 1967) at Charles Univ., spent eight years on the faculty in the Department of Mathematics and Physics at Charles University before coming to Canada in 1968. With the exception of the year 1973/1974 when he was working as a Senior Staff Geophysicist at Amoco Canada. Dr. Hron had been associated with the University of Alberta, where he held the position of professor of physics. He wrote over 70 scientific papers and 27 technical reports for the Amoco Research Center in Tulsa for which he was a consultant (s. 1972). He was elected Fellow of the Royal Astronomical Society in 1987 and was awarded a major research prize by the Russian Academy of Sciences in 1993 for the discovery of S* waves and subsequent development of its theory. Dr. Hron's interests included theoretical seismology, computational seismology; seismic numerical modeling and computer inversion of seismic data. He is a member of the SEC, CSEG, AGU, CGU, SIAM, EAEG and the Seismological Society of America.

Brian Michael Hynek (1976–), b. Cedar Rapids, Iowa, of Czech ancestry, was trained in earth science at Univ. of Northern Iowa, Cedar Falls (B.A., 1998) and in earth and planetary sciences at Washington Univ., St. Louis (M.A., 2001; Ph.D., 2003). He has been associated with the University's Laboratory for Atmospheric and Space Physics (LASP) since 2003 as a Research Associate. In 2007, he joined the Department of Geological Sciences faculty at the Univ. of Colorado, as an asst. professor and was promoted to assoc. professor in 2013. He has also been appointed Director of CU Center of Astrobiology (2013). His recent research has focused on the geologic, geochemical, hydrologic, and climatic evolutions of the planet Mars. He has been studying the Meridiani hematite site and other regional layered deposits that contain sulfate minerals and their astrobiological potential. Brian conducts Mars analog work on acid-sulfate systems including within active volcanoes in Central America, Iceland, and Hawaii and laboratory experiments and modeling to help constrain the natural environment. He also has research interests in Martian drainage morphometry, the thermophysical properties of Mars, impact craters, and the physics of volcanic eruptions on Earth and other planets. Brian teaches undergraduate and graduate courses at the University of Colorado covering topics such as the geology of the solar system, astrobiology, and geographic information systems.

Kenneth Charles Jezek (1951–), b. Chicago, of Czech ancestry, is a geologist. He was trained as a geophysicist at Univ. of Wisconsin (M.S., 1977; Ph.D., 1980). He held post-doctoral positions at The Ohio State University and the University of Wisconsin which resulted in research work at the South Pole and the East Antarctic Plateau. He joined the U.S. Army Cold Regions Research and Engineering Laboratory in 1983 where he conducted seismic and laser scattering experiments as well as investigated high-frequency acoustic-wave propagation beneath the icy canopy of the Arctic Ocean. For two years, Jezek was detailed to NASA Headquarters in Washington D.C. where he served as the manager of NASA's polar oceans and ice sheets program. Jezek rejoined the Ohio State University as director of the Byrd Polar Research Center in 1989. During his 10-year tenure as director, he led the science team which supported the Office of Naval Research Accelerated Research Initiative on sea ice remote sensing. He also led the NASA-sponsored Radarsat Antarctic Mapping Project which resulted in the first, high-resolution radar map of the southern continent. From 2007–2010, he was the co-lead of an International Polar Year project to monitor high latitudes using the international constellation of satellites. Jezek is now a professor emeritus of the Byrd Polar Research Center and the School of Environmental Sciences at OSU. He is actively involved in the development of new radar technology for imaging the land surface buried beneath the Greenland and Antarctic Ice Sheets. He is also pursuing novel, ice-sheet thermometry measurements using airborne and spaceborne radiometers. His research has been featured in the popular press and his radar image-mosaic of Antarctica was published as a map by the National Geographic Society Magazine and by the US Geological Survey.

Peter Alfons Ježek (1948–), b. Prague, Czech., holds a double B.A. degree geology & geosciences from the University of New Hampshire, and a Ph.D. in geology from the University of Massachusetts. He specializes in geology, petrology and volcanology. He has served as lecturer at the University of Massachusetts, the Massachusetts Maritime Academy, Cal State University and the Graduate School of Management, UC Davis. He received the Smithsonian Institution Award in recognition of distinguished accomplishments in higher education and research. He contributed more than 30 years of experience in the field developing power sector and infrastructure projects, primarily in the Muslim world. Ježek has extensive international private and government experience working in the natural resource and power industries. He holds the position of director of infrastructure with Moseley Horizon, Inc. - Energy and international Development, with headquarters in Washington, DC. His working relationship with M. Charles Moseley dates back to the early 1980s. Most recently, Ježek and Mr. Moseley worked together in Afghanistan creating, structuring, and managing the USAID/Afghanistan Office of Infrastructure, Energy and Engineering (OIEE). Dr. Jezek served as Deputy Director of OIEE until early 2006, and is well respected throughout Afghanistan, especially among key decision makers.

Vladimír Jindřich (1934–), b. Prague, Czech., was trained as a marine geologist at State Univ. of New York, Binghamton. He has been with State Univ. of New York, Binghamton (s. 1969), asst. prof. of geology (s. 1971). He is a specialist on structure and development of coral reefs.

Zdeněk Václav Jizba (1927–), b. Prague, Czech., was trained as a geologist at Univ. of Wisconsin (Ph.D., 1953). He was with Chevron Res. Co. (1955–67); and as sr. res. assoc. with Chevron Oil Field Res. Co., Standard Oil Co., CA (1967–87). He is a specialist on mathematical geology, man-machine interactions to solve geological problems, computer applications in geology.

Zdeněk Kalenský (1931–) b. Strakonice, Czech., graduated from Forestry School in Písek (Vyšší odborná škola lesnická) and then studied geodesy at Czech Technical Univ. in Prague. He emigrated to Canada in 1968. He joined the Forest Management Inst. and then taught, as asst. professor of remote sensing, for a year (1970–71) at Laval Univ., Quebec, Canada. Subsequently, he joined FAO and in later years he was assigned to Rome (1980–94).

Katharine Marie Kanak (1965–), b. St. Louis, MO, of Czech ancestry, was trained as a meteorologist at Univ. of Oklahoma (B.S., 1987; Ph.D., 1999) and Univ. of Wisconsin, Madison (M.S., 1990). She has been associated with the Univ. of Oklahoma, first as a res. scientist at the Cooperative Inst. of Mesoscale Meteorological Studies (2001–07), before joining the School of Meteorology as an adjunct assoc. professor (2007–12). She retired in 1012. Dr. Kanak's main research interests are in turbulent atmospheric boundary structures, in particular, vertical structures on both Earth and Mars. Her methodologies are numerical Large Eddy Simulation (LES), numerical modeling, and observational. She also conducts research on tornadogenesis, hurricanes, cloud physics, mammatus clouds, and idealized convective elements. Her accomplishments include the Schwerdtfeger Award for academic excellence, the Lettau award for best Master's thesis while a student at the University of Wisconsin-Madison. While a student at the University of Oklahoma she received the University of Oklahoma Graduate Teaching Assistant Award.

William M. Kaula (1926–2000), b. Sydney, Australia, of Czech American descent, is a geodesist, and geophysicist, who is considered the father of space-based geodesy. He was a graduate of US Military Academy, West Point, (B.S., 1948) and then attended Ohio State University, Columbus, OH (M.S., 1953). He started his career as a geodesist (1957–58) and chief, Division of Geodesy (1958–60) Army Map Service, US Army. This led to him becoming Geophysicist and Geodesist, Celestial Mechanics and Planetary Interiors, Goddard Space Flight Center, NASA (1960–63). Subsequently, he became Professor of Geophysics, Institute for Geophysics and Planetary Physics, University of California, Los Angeles (1963–92), while simultaneously being Chief, National Geodetic Survey, NOAA (1984–87). He is a member of NAS. Kaula was most notable for using early earth satellites to produce maps of Earth. He was a participant in several NASA missions, as a team leader on Apollos 15, 16, and 17. The National Academies Press called Kaula "the father of space-based geodesy".

Dennis V. Kent (1946–), b. Prague, Czech., graduated from City College of New York, majoring in geology (B.S., 1968) and studied marine geology and geophysics at Columbia Univ. (Ph.D., 1974). He holds the position of Board of Governors Distinguished Professor of Geology at Rutgers Univ. (s. 2007). He is also adjunct senior research scientist at Lamont-Doherty Earth Observatory. His research interests are in the area of paleomagnetism, geomagnetism, and rock magnetism, and their application to geologic problems. His current interests include Cenozoic and Mesozoic magnetostratigraphy and geomagnetic polarity time scales, paleoclimatology, paleogeography and the long-term carbon cycle, and the magnetic recording properties of sediments. He is Fellow of the Geological Society of America, American Geophysical Union, American Association for the Advancement of Science, American Academy of Arts & Sciences and a member of the National Academy of Sciences.

Karl Walter Klement (1931–1982), b. Aš, Czech., was trained as a paleontologist at Univ. of Tübingen. He was associated with Texas Tech Univ.; with Univ. of Texas, El Paso (s. 1969), where he held the position of prof. of geology and dept. chair. He was a specialist on paleontology, geology, recent and fossil microplankton and internationally recognized authority on carbonate petrography and petrology.

Vít Klemeš (1932–2010), b. Podivín, Czech., was a Canadian hydrologist. He received a Civil Engineering degree (Ing.) from the Brno University of Technology, Moravia, a CSc./Ph.D. degree in hydrology and water resources from the Slovak Technical University in Bratislava and a DrSc. degree from the Czech Technical University in Prague. Following the Soviet-led invasion of Czechoslovakia, Klemeš and his family came to Canada in September 1968. There he obtained the position of associate professor at the University of Toronto, first in the Department of Mechanical Engineering and later in the Institute of Environmental Sciences and Engineering. In 1972, he was appointed research hydrologist at the National Hydrology Research Institute of Environment Canada, a position he held for 17 years; after the institute's move from Ottawa to Saskatoon, he also served as its chief scientist. From 1990 to 1999, he was a water resources consultant in Victoria, British Columbia where he continued to live after his retirement until his death. During his career Klemeš, has authored about 150 scientific and technical publications, lectured extensively on all five continents, was visiting professor at the California Institute of Technology (Caltech), the Swiss Federal Institute of Technology (ETH) in Zurich, Monash University in Melbourne, Agricultural University (BOKU) in Vienna, the University of Karlsruhe, and in 1994, was appointed Invited Professor at Institut National de la Recherche Scientifique of Universite du Quebec. In 1987, he was elected president of the International Association of Hydrological Sciences (IAHS) and his work has been recognized by a number of awards; among other, he received a Gold Medal from the

Slovak Academy of Sciences (1993), the International Hydrology Prize from the IAHS (1994), the Ray K. Linsley Award from the American Institute of Hydrology (1995) and the Ven Te Chow Award from the American Society of Civil Engineering (1998).

Stephen B. Konarik (1982–), b. Granger, TX, of Czech ancestry, spent most of his childhood in Taylor, TX. He attended Iowa State University where he received Bachelor of Science degree in meteorology and environmental studies in 2004. He then went on to earn a Master of Science in atmospheric science from North Carolina State University in 2006. Mr. Konarik's research emphasis in graduate school was air quality forecasting, and he studied and presented a thesis on the impacts of agricultural ammonia emissions on the state of North Carolina and greater southeastern United States. Since 2012, Konarik is a senior forecaster at the Miami Weather Forecast office of the National Weather Service. Konarik develops forecasts for weather conditions in Southern Florida. He issues weather watches, warnings, and advisories for hazardous and severe weather. In addition, Konarik provides meteorological forecasts to the aviation community and marine weather information for customers in portions of the Gulf of Mexico and Atlantic Ocean. His specialty is severe weather, and he helps to educate co-workers on the predictability of large hail, damaging winds, and tornadoes. Prior to working at the Miami Weather Forecast Office, Mr. Konarik was a general forecaster at the National Weather Service's Baltimore-Washington, DC Forecast Office.

George Jiří Kukla (1930–), b. Prague, Czech., was trained as a paleoclimatologist at Charles Univ. He is a senior research scientist at the Lamont-Doherty Earth Observatory of Columbia University, with which he has been associated (s. 1971). In 1972, he became a central figure in convincing the US government to take the dangers of climate change seriously.

Edward Henry Kraus (1875–1973), b. Syracuse, NY, of Bohemian ancestry (having descended from Daniel Kraus (1818–1979) of Kbely, Bohemia, was a geologist and mineralogist. After training in the high school of Syracuse, he entered Syracuse University, from which he was graduated with a Bachelor of Science in 1896. During the following year, he was a graduate student at that university and was also an assistant in chemistry and German. He received the degree of Master of Science at the end of the year. For two years (1897–99), he was an instructor in German and mineralogy at Syracuse. During 1899–1901, he studied at the University of Munich, and at the end of the period received the degree of Doctor of Philosophy magna cum laude. His major study was mineralogy with chemistry and geology as minors. He returned to Syracuse University for one year, first as an instructor in mineralogy and then as an associate professor of the same subject. During 1902–1904, he was head of the department of science at the Syracuse High School, and in the summer sessions of Syracuse University of 1903 and 1904, he was a professor of chemistry and geology. Dr. Kraus was a Fellow of the Geological Society of America, a member of the American Chemical Society, the American Association for the Advancement of Science, and other scientific organizations. For two years, 1903 to 1904, he was president of the Onondaga Academy of Science. In the fall of 1904, he was called to the University of Michigan as Assistant Professor of Mineralogy, and in 1906 he became Junior Professor. In 1907, he was made Junior Professor of Mineralogy and Petrography, and Director of the Mineralogical Laboratory, and, in 1908, he was granted a full professorship in Mineralogy and Petrography. From 1908 to 1910, he was Secretary, and since 1911, Acting Dean of the Summer Session. From 1908 to 1912, he also served as Secretary of the Graduate School. He published Essentials of Crystallography (1906), Descriptive Mineralogy and, with W. F. Hunt, Tables for the Determination of Minerals (1911).

Eric B. Kraus (1913–2003), b. Liberec, Bohemia, was trained as a geophysicist at Charles Univ. He was with Woods Hole Oceanographic Inst. (1960–66); then became prof. of meteorology at Univ. of Miami (s. 1966), as dir. of Meteorological Inst. (s. 1967), and as div. chair of atmospheric sciences (s. 1969). He was a specialist on thermodynamics, dynamic climatology and climatic change, hydro-meteorology, engineering applications of meteorology, air-sea interactions.

Jiří Krupička (1913–), b. Prague, Bohemia, was trained as a geologist at Charles Univ. He was associated with Univ. of Alberta, Edmonton where he held the position of prof. of geology until his retirement in 1988. He specialized in metamorphic petrology with emphasis on the Canadian Shield (surface and basement) and the Western Cordillera of North America.

Paul Russell Krutak (1934–2016), b. Pueblo, CO, of Slovak descent, was an eminent American micropaleontologist. He received his Bachelor's and Master's degrees in geology at Louisiana State University (LSU) in Baton Rouge, as well as a Ph.D. in geology at LSU in 1963. He was a Professor of Geology at Eastern New Mexico University, Ball State University, and the University of Nebraska-Lincoln. After leaving the University of Nebraska in 1982, Krutak worked as a consulting geologist for ARCO Oil Company, primarily in Lafayette, Louisiana, with some time spent on the North Slope in Alaska. Following his stint at ARCO, Krutak finished his formal teaching career as a Professor of Geology and Chairman of the Geology Department at Fort Hays State University. In 1997, he received the President's Distinguished Scholar Award. He was a Fellow of the Geological Society of America.

Denise Kay Kulhanek (1975–), b. Lincoln, NE, of Czech ancestry, studied geology (B.S., 1997) and geosciences (M.S., 2000) at Univ. of Nebraska, Lincoln. She worked as a biostratigrapher at BP in Houston, Texas (2000–03) before returning to university to study geological sciences (Ph.D., 2009) at Florida State Univ., Tallahassee. After post-doctoral research at Yamagata Univ., Japan (2010) and at GNS Science, Lower Hutt, New Zealand (2011–13), she joined Texas A&M Univ. as a staff scientist and expedition project manager in the International Ocean Discovery Program (s. 2013). In her research, she uses microfossils, sediments/rocks, and geochemical proxies to address paleooceanographic, paleoclimatic and biostratigraphic questions covering a wide span of geologic time. Currently her main interest is Paleogene hyperthermals as an analogue for future warming. She also studies the development of the Antarctic Circumpolar Current as Antarctica became progressively isolated during the Cenozoic and the role this had in the transition from Greenhouse to Icehouse conditions. She uses samples from cores collected through the International Ocean Discovery Program (IODP) and its predecessor programs, drilling programs around Antarctica, and samples collected from outcrops of marine rocks.

Jan Kutina (1924–2008), b. Prague, Czech., was trained as a geologist at Charles Univ. (RNDr., 1949) and at ČSAV (CSc./Ph.D., 1957). Since 1980 Jan Kutina was a research professor at the American University (s. 1976), where he taught earth sciences and developed a Laboratory of Global Tectonics and Metallogeny within the Chemistry Department. Jan Kutina compiled mineral prognosis maps for parts of twenty countries; two of these maps helped in new mineral discoveries, the first a nickel deposit in Burundi, and the second a Cu-Mo porphyry discovery in Nevada.

Peter Láznička (1936–), b. Prague, Czech., was educated at Charles Univ. and upon his emigration to Canada, he received Master's degree (1968) and Ph.D. (1971) from Univ. of Manitoba. He joined the Univ. of Manitoba, as asst. professor geology and mineral resources (1972–75), assoc. professor (1975–88), as full professor (s. 1988). Later, he relocated to Adelaide, Australia to co-found the Data Metallogenica information system on mineral deposits (1999–2005), supported by an extensive collection of miniaturized rock and sample sets from 3,500 mineral deposits in 86 countries. He consulted and lectured for mineral industry, government departments and universities, followed/combined with field work in 100+ countries. He published 7 substantial (largest: 1,600 pages) technical books in English with major international publishers about global metallogeny and ore distribution: Empirical and Precambrian Empirical Metallogeny (1985, 1993); Breccias and Coarse Fragmentites (1988); Giant Metallic Deposits (2nd ed., 2010).

George Losonsky (ca. 1958–), studied geology at Oberlin Coll. (B.A., 1980) a, physical and chemical processes of geology (M.S., 1983) and hydrology and sedimentology (Ph.D., 1992) at Univ. of Cincinnati. He has been president of Losonsky and Associates, Greencastle, IN (s. 2005) and vice president and principal scientist at Directional Technologies (s. 2007).

Dr. Losonsky has 20 years of experience in environmental problem solving and management. He has developed and managed soil and groundwater remediation programs at military bases, chemical plants, dry cleaning facilities, petrochemical refineries, fuel storage facilities, hazardous waste landfills, food processing plants, pharmaceutical industry facilities, and steel manufacturing factories. He has assisted in the development of state and regional environmental assessment, remediation, and risk evaluation programs for the dry cleaning and retail petroleum industries. Losonsky is serving on the Board of Commissioners of the Southeast Louisiana Flood Protection Authority-East. He is a recognized expert in groundwater remediation using directional drilling technology, has published numerous technical papers and taught seminars on this subject, and is a founding member of the Horizontal Environmental Technical Committee of the National Ground Water Association.

Ivo Lucchita (1937–), b. České Budějovice, succeeded in getting out from Czechoslovakia during the time of the Nazi occupation and eventually emigrated to the US, settling in Pasadena, CA, where he studied as an undergraduate student at the California Institute of Technology (Caltech), majoring in geology (B.Sc., 1961). He continued his studies in geology at Pennsylvania State Univ. (Ph.D., 1966). His study area was at the mouth of the Grand Canyon and focused on the geologic history of the Colorado River and Grand Canyon. He joined the US Geological Survey Center for Astrogeology in Flagstaff, Arizona, as a research geologist. He stayed at this Center for his entire career, from 1966 until retirement in 1995. From 1966 to 1972, he was engaged in the Apollo Program of Manned Lunar Exploration throughout the various Apollo missions. After 1972, he returned to his first love, terrestrial geology seen from a field perspective. He has done research on many places in the western US and Alaska. He was the first to propose that the Grand Canyon is less than 6 million years old, thus far younger than previously thought. During his tenure at the USGS, he served as director of the Center for three years in the mid-80s. It was then that he started the Flagstaff Festival of Science, a well-regarded annual event now celebrating its 35th year. His scientific output consists of about 150 research papers and one book, *Hiking Arizona's Geology*, which was runner-up in a national competition for books in its class published by independent publishers.

Jeffrey Masek (1967–), b. La Jolla, CA, of Czech ancestry, received a B.A. in geology from Haverford College (1989) and a Ph.D. in geological sciences from Cornell University (1994). At first, he held research positions at the University of Maryland, and Hughes Information Systems. Since 2001, he has been a member of the Biospheric Sciences Laboratory at NASA GSFC, as a research scientist and since 2014, chief of the Laboratory. His research interests include mapping land-cover change in temperate environments, application of advanced computing to remote sensing, and satellite remote sensing techniques. He has recently been involved in several projects quantifying forest disturbance across North America using time-series satellite data, and serves as a co-investigator on the NASA Carbon Monitoring System Project and as the NASA Landsat project scientist.

Robert 'Rob' Moucha (ca. 1975-), b. Prague, Czech., escaped from the communist Czechoslovakia in 1983 and immigrated to Canada. He graduated from Univ. of Waterloo, majoring in physics (B.Sc., 1997). He then moved to Toronto to continue his studies in physics at Univ. of Toronto (M.Sc., 1998; Ph.D., 2003). Subsequently, he went to Univ. of Quebec, Montreal. to do research in the Earth System Program, on a postdoctoral fellowship from the Canadian Inst. for Advanced Research. He associated with Syracuse Univ., where he holds the position of asst. professor of earth sciences. A key ingredient of his research is the incorporation of observational constraints from varying fields such as seismology, geodesy, sedimentology, geochemistry, structural geology and geomorphology. This extensive list is made possible through a number of key collaborations across different fields that have formed over the past few years. His current projects are: geodynamic and geomorphologic evolution of the southwestern US, African topography throughout the Cenozoic, coupling of surface processes with mantle dynamics, long-term sea-level change; the role of mantle and lithospheric dynamics, and numerical modeling of mantle and lithospheric dynamics.

John L. Nábělek (1952-), b. Prague, Czech., was trained as a geologist and geophysicist at MIT and Woods Hole Oceanographic Inst. He now holds the position of professor of geology and geophysics at College of Oceanography, Oregon State University, Corvallis. OR. He specializes in applied and theoretical seismology, faulting processes of large earthquakes; tectonics of mid-ocean ridges, island arcs, and regions of continental extension.

Peter Igor Nábělek (1955-), b. Prague, Czech., was trained as a geologist at the University of Tennessee. He now serves as a professor of igneous and metamorphic petrology, dept. of Geology, University of Missouri, Colombia, MO. He specializes in igneous and metamorphic petrology and geochemistry, volcanology, and environmental geology.

Michael J. Novacek (1948-), b. Evanston, IL, probably of Czech ancestry, studied zoology at UCLA (A.B., 1971), biology at San Diego State Univ. (M.A., 1973) and paleontology at Univ. of California, Berkeley (Ph.D., 1978). He was with San Diego State Univ., as asst. professor (1977-79), as assoc. professor (1979-82) as full professor (s. 1982). He has been adj. professor, Dept. of biology, CUNY (s. 1987) and at the Center for Environmental Research and Conservation, Columbia Univ. (s. 1995). Presently, he is associated with the American Museum of Natural History, Smithsonian Inst., Washington, DC, where he holds the position vice president and Provost of Science and curator of Paleontology Division and professor at

Richard Glider Graduate School. Dr. Novacek's studies concern patterns of evolution and relationships among organisms, particularly mammals. His interests have ranged from paleontological evidence to new data on DNA sequences. He has led paleontological expeditions to Baja California, Mexico; the Andes Mountains of Chile; and the Yemen Arab Republic in search of fossil mammals and dinosaurs. He also is one of the team leaders of the joint American Museum of Natural History/Mongolian Academy of Sciences ongoing expeditions to the Gobi Desert, begun in 1990. The Mongolian expeditions marked the first return of a Western scientific team to the country in over sixty years and have received worldwide scientific and public attention for their spectacular findings. In 1993, Dr. Novacek was one of the discoverers of the Gobi's Ukhaa Tolgod, the richest Cretaceous fossil vertebrate site in the world. In 1999, he started a series of expeditions to Patagonia, Argentina, to research dinosaurs, mammals, and other fossils. He was instrumental in establishing the Museum's Center for Biodiversity and Conservation, Sackler Institute for Comparative Genomics, and research program in astrophysics.

Eldon Joseph Parizek (1920–), b. Iowa City, IA, of Czech ancestry, was trained as a geologist at Univ. of Iowa. He was associated with the Univ. of Missouri (s. 1957), as professor of geology (s. 1963), as dept. chmn. (s. 1974), as Dean of College of Arts and Sciences (1978–85). His interests include general geology of southeast Missouri, metamorphic and igneous geology of east central Georgia Piedmont and structural geology.

Richard R. Parizek (1934–), b. Stafford Springs, CT, of Czech ancestry, studied geology at Univ. of Connecticut (N.S., 1956) and at Univ. of Illinois (M.S., 1960; Ph.D., 1961). He began teaching in 1961 as assistant professor of geology and geophysics at the Pennsylvania State University and became a full professor in 1971 and continues to teach in the Department of Geosciences, as professor of geology and geoenvironmental engineering. He is also president of Richard R. Parizek and Associates, consulting hydrogeologists and environmental geologists and a registered professional geologist. On February 11, 1997, President Bill Clinton appointed Richard Parizek to the Nuclear Waste Technical Review Board. Parizek also has been a visiting scientist with the U.S. Geological Survey and a visiting scholar at Stanford University, the Desert Research Institute, Changchun College of Geology and the Institute of Karst Geology in the Peoples' Republic of China, and National Cheng Kung University in Taiwan. His research interests include the hydrogeology of karst, fractured rock, and glaciated terranes; factors controlling groundwater occurrence and movement; and the relationship between land use and groundwater pollution resulting from disposal of nuclear waste and other hazardous substances.

Alvin Joseph Peterka (1911–1983), b. Cleveland, OH, of Czech ancestry, was a hydrologist. He graduated from Case Institute of Technology, Cleveland, OH (1934) and added graduate work at the Universities of Tennessee and Colorado. From 1936 to 1946, he was on the staff of the Tennessee Valley Authority (TVA), then joined the US Bureau of Reclamation (USBR), Denver, CO, eventually heading the Special Investigations Sections of the USBR Hydraulic Laboratory. Peterka retired from this activity in 1968 to become a consultant. In 1946, he reported on a tunnel spillway, which was later adopted also for the Glen Canyon Spillway, and on flip buckets. He developed into an expert on high-speed flows, co-authoring the 1948 paper on frictional effects of tunnel flows. This paper was awarded the 1949 ASCE James Laurie Prize. He also was the first to analyze the effect of air entrained on the reduction of cavitation damage in 1953. In 1954, now with USBR, he presented an important study on shaft spillways, an alternative to the standard spillway, thereby investigating both free and submerged flow conditions. At the vertical shaft base, the flow is horizontally deflected to the outlet structure. The so-called morning spillway is a standard today provided the free surface flow is maintained from the inlet to the outlet. Peterka's name has become known for his 1958 publication on the design of stilling basins, a notable research campaign undertaken during the 1950s in collaboration with Joseph N. Bradley (1903–1993). Ten different basins are model-tested, and designs were proposed that have remained a standard.

Josef Podzimek (1923–2007), b. Brandýs n/L, Czech., was trained as a physicist and meteorologist at Charles Univ. He was sr. investigator, Grad. Center of Cloud Physics Research and prof. of mechanical engineering at Univ. of Missouri, Rolla (s. 1970). He specialized in cloud and aerosol physics, aerodynamics of precipitation elements, and formation of precipitation elements.

John Pojeta, Jr. (1935–2017), b. New York, NY, of Czech ancestry, has been an active paleontologist since 1957. He is a scientist emeritus with the U.S. Geological Survey (USGS) and a Research Associate with the Department of Paleobiology, Smithsonian Institution. He earned his B.S. degree (1957) at Capital University, Bexley, OH, majoring in biology and chemistry and earned his M.S. (1961) and Ph.D. (1963) degrees from the University of Cincinnati, majoring in geology and paleontology. In 1963, he joined the USGS, Branch of Paleontology and Stratigraphy, where he spent his career. His research has centered on early Paleozoic mollusks, and has taken him to many American states, Antarctica, Australia, Canada, China, the Czech Republic, Senegal, Sweden, and the United Kingdom, and elsewhere. He has been Secretary and President of The Paleontological Society; President of the Paleontological Research Institution; Chief, Branch of Paleontology and Stratigraphy, USGS; and a member of the National Academy of Sciences Committee on Paleontological Collecting.

Leo Wenzel Pollak (1888-1964), b. Prague, Bohemia, was trained as a physicist at Univ. of Prague. He was a chief investigator on contracts with US Army and USAF; consultant with General Electric, Schenectady (1958-64); and served as res. prof. in atmospheric sciences, State Univ. of New York Res. Ctr. (1963-64). He was a specialist on development of meteorological instruments; he introduced punch card method for weather data, developed photoelectric condensation counter for measurement of fog density, and air pollution.

John James Prucha (1924-2012), b. River Falls, WI, of Czech ancestry, earned his Ph.B. and M.Ph. from the University of Wisconsin in 1945 and 1946 respectively. He continued his education at Princeton University earning his M.A. and Ph.D. in 1948 and 1950. During his graduate study he was an instructor of geology at Rutgers University and was assistant professor of geology there from 1949-1951. He was senior geologist with the New York State Geological Survey from 1951-1956 and then spent seven years as a research geologist with Shell Development Company in Houston, Texas. His fields of specialization included structural geology, tectonophysics, basement tectonics and regional tectonics of North America. He joined the faculty of the College of Arts and Sciences at Syracuse University in 1963 as professor of geology and chair of the department. He served two terms as department chair from 1963 to 1970 and in 1988 to 1989. He was appointed dean of the college in 1970 serving until his appointment as vice chancellor for academic affairs in 1972. In 1985, he returned to the faculty in geology and spent a year as adjunct professor of geology at Texas A&M University. In 1990, he retired from active service to the University and continued his professional involvement in the field of geology as a consultant.

Carol J. Ptacek (1959-), b. Milwaukee, WI, of Czech ancestry, was trained in geology and earth sciences at Univ. of Windsor (B.S.) and in contaminant hydrogeology and geochemistry at Univ. of Waterloo (Ph.D.). Dr. Carol Ptacek is a professor in the Department of Earth Sciences, University of Waterloo (s. 2006). She conducts research on a variety of topics in Contaminant Hydrogeology and Geochemistry, including studies on mechanisms controlling the fate and transport of metals, nutrients, pathogens, organic compounds in groundwater, and the development of passive methods for remediating contaminated groundwater. She conducts field and laboratory studies and complements these with numerical modeling techniques. Her current research focuses on passive groundwater remediation technologies, the release and transport of metals at northern mine sites, the fate of wastewater contaminants in shallow sand aquifers, and the fate of emerging contaminants in the environment. She was a recipient of Synergy.

John F. Rakovan (1964-), b. Buffalo, NY, of Czech ancestry, studied geology (B.S., 1988) and clay mineralogy/crystallography (M.S., 1990) at Univ. of Illinois, Urbana and mineralogy/geochemistry (Ph.D., 1996) at State Univ. of New York, Stony Brook. He has been a guest researcher at Brookhaven National Lab. (s. 1991) and at Argonne National Laboratory (s. 1998). He has held an academic appointment with the dept. of geology at the Univ. of Miami, as asst. professor (1998-2004), as assoc. professor (2004-11) and as professor (s. 2011). His research interests involve the integration of mineralogy and low temperature geochemistry in the study of crystal surfaces and water-rock interactions found in natural systems. In particular, he is interested in environmentally significant processes such as crystal growth, metal sorption, trace element partitioning and other surface mediated reactions. His research also addresses the structural response of minerals to substituent elements, especially lanthanides and actinides in apatite group minerals. Another growing area of his research interest is the formation, mineralogy and geochemistry of hydrothermal ore deposits. He has served as executive editor of *Rocks and Minerals* (s. 2001) and assoc. editor of *American Mineralogist* (s. 2002).

David William Schindler (1940-), b. Fargo, ND, of Czech ancestry, is an American/Canadian limnologist. He holds the Killam Memorial Chair and is a professor of ecology in the Department of Biological Sciences at the University of Alberta in Edmonton, Canada. After completing his Bachelor's degree in zoology from North Dakota State University (B.S., 1962), he studied aquatic ecology at Oxford University as a Rhodes Scholar. He worked first under Nikolaas Tinbergen (Ph.D., 1966). In 1966, he took a teaching position at Trent University. Trent recruited him as part of an international team of young scientists to begin a series of whole lake studies. Starting in 1968, he worked with the Freshwater Institute (FWI) of the University of Manitoba. He was the founding director of the FWI's Experimental Lakes Area freshwater research program in northwestern Ontario. Schindler left the FWI for the University of Alberta in 1989. He is notable for 'innovative large-scale experiments' on whole lakes which proved that phosphorus controls the eutrophication of temperate lakes leading to the banning of harmful phosphates in detergents. He is also known for his research on acid rain. Dr. Schindler continued his research at the University of Alberta in Edmonton (s. 1989), with studies into fresh water shortages and the effects of climate change on Canada's alpine and northern boreal ecosystems. He remains on faculty there as Killam Memorial Chair and a professor of ecology. Schindler has earned numerous national and international awards, including the Gerhard Herzberg Gold Medal, the First Stockholm Water Prize (1991), the Volvo Environment Prize (1998), and the Tyler Prize for Environmental Achievement (2006). He is a member of NAS.

Zdeněk Sekera (1905-1973), b. Tábor, Bohemia, was trained as meteorologist and physicist at Charles Univ. He was with Univ. of California, Los Angeles (s. 1949), as prof. of meteorology (1955-78), as dept. chair (1962-67). He specialized in dynamic and theoretical meteorology, atmospheric optics and radiation, problems of scattering sky light polarization, and radioactive transfer in planetary atmospheres

Jiří 'Jirka' Šimůnek (1959–), b. Teplice, Czech., studied civil engineering, specializing in water management and construction, at Czech Technical Univ. (M.Sc., 1984) and water management at ČSAV (Ph.D., 1993). He was first employed by the Research Inst. of Soil Amelioration, Prague (1984–90). After spending two years as a postdoctoral soil scientist at Univ. of California, Riverside (1990–92) and a research scientist at Research Inst. of Soil Protection, Prague (1993–94), he joined the dept. of environmental sciences at Univ. of California, Riverside, as asst. research scientist (1995–2000), assoc. research scientist (2001–03) and professor and hydrologist (s. 2004). His main interests are in the areas of numerical modeling of various equilibrium and nonequilibrium water flow, heat and solute transport processes in variably saturated porous media in one, two, and/or three dimensions. Specific interests are in the areas of carbon dioxide transport and production, virus and colloid transport, multicomponent transport of major ions involving both equilibrium and nonequilibrium kinetic reactions, and nonlinear non-equilibrium transport of multiple solutes involved in first-order decay reactions. He was a recipient of Don and Betty Kirkham Award (2005) and was elected Soil Science Society of America Fellow and American Geophysical Union Fellow (2012).

Katherine Skalak (ca. 1979–), b. possibly of Czech ancestry, studied environmental science at St. Joseph's Univ., Philadelphia (B.S., 2001), geology at Univ. of Delaware (M.S., 2004) and geological sciences, also at Univ. of Delaware (Ph.D., 2009). She has been associated with US Geological Survey, National Research Program, first as a post-doctoral fellow (2009–11) and now as a research hydrologist (s. 2011). Katherine Skalak studies landscape dynamics and fluvial geomorphology, focused on understanding and predicting changes in the patterns and functions of landforms in response to human impacts and restoration efforts. In particular, dynamics of fine sediment and particle associated nutrients and contaminants on varying temporal and spatial scales, flow and vegetation effects, and disturbance.

John P. Smol (1955–), b. Montreal, Quebec, Canada, of Slovak descent, is a Canadian ecologist, limnologist, and paleolimnologist who holds the Canada Research Chair in Environmental Change in the Department of Biology at Queen's University, Kingston, Ontario. He founded and co-directs the Paleoecological Environmental Assessment and Research Lab (PEARL). Smol was educated at McGill University (B.Sc.), Brock University (M.Sc.), and Queen's University (Ph.D.). Smol works on a diverse range of subjects, most of which focus on using lake sediments to reconstruct past environmental trends. Topics include: Lake Acidification caused by acid rain, sewage input and fertilizer runoff (eutrophication), studies of nutrient and contaminant transport by birds and other biovectors, and a large program on climatic change. He is an author or editor of 21 books and over 620 journal publications and book chapters. Smol is an international lecturer and media commentator on a variety of topics, but most dealing with environmental issues. From 1987 to 2007, he edited the *Journal of Paleolimnology*. Since 2004, he has been editor of the journal Environmental Reviews. He is the series editor of the *Developments in Paleoenvironmental Research* book series. He held the Chair of the International Paleolimnology Association for two three-year terms ending in August 2018, and he is currently President (2019-2022) of the Academy of Science, Royal Society of Canada.

Peter Sonnenfeld (1922-2004), b. Berlin, of Czech ancestry, was trained as a geologist at Charles Univ. He was the founder of the Geology Department, University of Windsor, and Canada. He taught there for many years until he retired in 1989. He came to Windsor in 1966 with the express purpose of establishing the geology department at the University which came officially into being in 1967. Peter Sonnenfeld became the first head of the department until 1973. He was also instrumental in establishing the Geological Engineering Program. He was an international authority on salt evaporates and has written a book on the subject in 1988.

Jerry Michael Straka (1961-), b. Milwaukee, WI, of Czech ancestry, is an American atmospheric scientist with expertise in microphysics of clouds, cloud modeling, and dynamics of severe convection in conjunction with weather radar. Straka earned a B.S. and M.S. in 1984 and 1986, respectively, from the University of Wisconsin Milwaukee. His Master's dissertation was "A Mesoscale Numerical Study of Environmental Conditions Preceding the 08 June 1984 Tornado Outbreak over South Central Wisconsin." Straka earned a Ph.D. in meteorology from the University of Wisconsin-Madison in 1989 with the Doctoral dissertation, "Hail Growth in a Highly Glaciated Central High Plains Multi-cellular Hailstorm." He has been associated with the Univ. of Oklahoma in Norman (s. 1990), where he advanced from asst. professor (1990-96) to assoc. professor (1996-2010) and full professor (s. 2010). He incorporates numerical/computational and observational methods to study tornado formation, precipitation formation, and the rapid intensification of hurricanes. He also has interests in radar and observational meteorology. Dr. Straka has been a leader and participant in several major field experiments and has been an author of 74 peer-review journal articles and nearly 125 conference papers. As a student at the University of Wisconsin-Madison, he won the Schwerdtfeger Award for academic excellence.

William H. Streeruwitz (1833-1916), b. Stříbro, Bohemia, studied mining at Univ. of Prague. He was employed as a mining engineer in the coal fields of Pennsylvania for some nine years before he arrived in Houston, Texas, in 1876. Presumably, he also served as professor. civ. and mech. eng., at Western Univ. PA (1863-73). In Houston, he became acquainted with Edwin Theodore Dumble and published articles in the Geological and Scientific Bulletin. He was a Fellow of the Texas Academy of Sciences from 1892 to 1899, became a member of the Houston Natural History Society, and was a charter member of the Texas Geological and Scientific Association. When Dumble became director of the Geological and Mineral Survey of Texas, he appointed Wilhelm von Streeruwitz as one of the geologists for the Trans-Pecos District. The Dumble Survey first completely described the basic geology of Texas, and the Trans-Pecos part of this work is largely that of Wilhelm von Streeruwitz.

Petr Vaníček (1935-), b. Sušice, Czech., was trained as a geodesist at Czech Technical Univ. and ČSAV. He has been with Univ. of New Brunswick (s. 1971), as prof. geodesy (s. 1978), and as prof. emer. of geodesy and geomatics engineering (s. 2001). One of his main contributions of general relevance is least-squares spectral analysis, also called the Vaníček method, frequency spectrum computation method published in 1969 and 1971. His res. interests include: geodesy, earth tides, crystal movements and mean sea level, applied mathematics, and spectral analysis and mechanics. He initiated the establishing of the Canadian Geophysical Union in 1974, and served as the Union's president between 1986 and 1988. He was the first chairman of the United Nations Committee for Geodetic Aspects of the Law of the Sea (GALOS), founded in Edinburgh, Scotland by the International Association of Geodesy (IAG) in 1989. His book *Geodesy: The Concepts* (3rd ed., 1986), translated into several languages, is a standard text for both undergraduate and graduate courses in geodesy worldwide. He also served as editor-in-chief and a reviewer for several scientific journals as well as on numerous scientific boards and committees.

Martin J. Vitousek (1924-1999), b. Honolulu, HI, of Czech ancestry, was an oceanographer and inventor, who flew his own airplane and sailed his schooner *Fiesta*. He studied mathematics and geophysics at Stanford Univ. He was with the Univ. of Hawaii at Manoa (s. 1974), as a specialist on oceanography instruments, Hawaiian Inst. of Geophysics, Univ. Hawaii (1974-90). The longtime University of Hawaii researcher, who moved to Kona after retirement, achieved one of the first advances in a tsunami warning system with the development of ocean gauges to measure tides and waves in the 1960s. He headed a UH research outpost on Fanning Island, 1,200 miles from Hawaii, and was field chief of the Line Island scientific program during the International Geophysical Year. His research interests were in the area of applied mathematics, solid earth geophysics and oceanography, long-period ocean waves, instrumentation and analysis.

Barry Voight (1937–), b. US, of Slovak descent; brother of actor Jon Voight, is an American geologist, volcanologist, author, and engineer. He attended the University of Notre Dame (B.S., 1959; B.S.C.E., 1960; M.S.C.E., 1961). After earning his Ph.D. at Columbia University (1965), Voight worked as a professor of geology at several universities, including Pennsylvania State University, where he taught from 1964 until his retirement in 2005. Voight's publications on landslides and avalanches and other mass movements attracted the attention of Rocky Crandell of the United States Geological Survey (USGS), who asked him to look at a growing bulge on the Mount St. Helens volcano in the state of Washington. Voight foresaw the collapse of the mountain's north flank as well as a powerful eruption. His predictions came true when St. Helens erupted in May 1980; Voight was then hired by the USGS to investigate the debris avalanche that initiated the eruption. After his work at Mount St. Helens brought him international recognition, Voight continued researching and guiding monitoring efforts at several active volcanoes throughout his career, including Nevado del Ruiz in Colombia, Mount Merapi in Indonesia, and Soufrière Hills, a volcano on the Caribbean Island of Montserrat.

Zdenka Saba Willis (1959–), b. Washington, DC, of Czech ancestry, received her Bachelor's Degree in marine science from the University of South Carolina, in 1981. She received a Master's degree in meteorology and oceanography from the Naval Postgraduate in 1987, and a Master's Degree in national strategy from the Industrial College of the Armed Forces in 1989. She is a member of the Senior Executive Service. From 2007 to the present, she has been the director of the US Integrated Ocean Observing System (U.S. IOOS). The US IOOS, led by the National Oceanic and Atmospheric Administration (NOAA), is a coordinated network of people and technology that work together to generate and disseminate continuous data on our coastal waters, Great Lakes, and oceans. From 2006 to 2007, she was the director of NOAA's National Oceanographic Data Center. She was commissioned an ensign in the United States Navy in 1981 and retired with the rank of Captain in 2006, serving as a Meteorology and Oceanography officer. Willis has a background in the collection of oceanographic data onboard the USNS Harkness and USNS Maury survey vessels and in electronic navigational charting as deputy navigator of the Navy. Her other relevant Naval positions are the director of the Strategic Policy Forum (Congressional and Executive Branch crisis simulation for Members of Congress, senior Executive branch officials, and military leaders) and adjunct professor in the Strategic Leadership Department at the Industrial College for the Armed Forces.

Paul M. Yaniga (1950–2012), b. Houlton, MA, of Slovak ancestry was a geologist and hydrologist. He spent his childhood and early years in Nesquehoning, Pennsylvania. He was a graduate of Bloomsburg State College (B.A., 1972), majoring in Earth Sciences and continued his studies in Geologic Sciences at Lehigh University (M.A., 1974). He was a co-founder of Groundwater Technology, Inc., a multinational, publicly traded $200 million environmental consulting and remediation firm that later merged with Fluor Daniel Corp. Mr. Yaniga was co-founder and developer of Novitrek, a joint venture for downhole selective oil recovery in the Samara, Oblast, Russia. Novitrek ultimately became part of Yukos Oil, one of Russia's leading oil companies. Mr. Yaniga also co-founded RPT, a Rome, Italy-based equipment and service company providing solutions to the petrochemical industry of southern and central Europe. He was a past director of SECOR, a multinational industrial service company in the petrochemical marketplace and a past director of EEE, a leading-edge continuing education organization for advanced solutions for soil and geologic environments. He was a technical advisor and instructor for the Department of Defense and the National Groundwater Association. More recently, Paul Yaniga was President of WISE, Ltd, an international environmental consulting company, a director of BEDCO, a US-based oil/gas field tool developer, and director of TAIC, information, and Technology Company servicing the DOD and Fortune 500 companies. He instructed in colleges and Universities and presented professional papers and oral presentations, including an appearance before US Congress, all related to his expertise in subsurface geological matters.

D. Social Sciences

Lotte Bailyn (née Lazarsfeld) (1930-), b. Vienna, of Moravian ancestry (daughter of Paul Lazarsfeld and Marie Jahoda), is a social psychologist trained from Harvard/Radcliffe. She is the T. Wilson Professor of Management, and emerita at the MIT Sloan School of Management. For the period 1997-99 she was Chair of the MIT faculty, and during 1995-97 she was the Matina S. Horner Distinguished Visiting Professor at Radcliffe's Public Policy Institute. Her research investigates how institutional and organizational processes intersect with people's lives, with special emphasis on the dynamics of gender and diversity in business organizations and academia.

Louis M. Baska (1888-1973), b. Kansas City, of Slovak descent a R.C. priest, O.S.B., was professor of economics, Sr. Benedictine's College, Atchison, KS. Charles Sokol Bednar (1928-), b. New York, NY, of Slovak descent, is a political scientist. He was professor, Muhlenberg College, Allentown, PA.

Edward (Louis James) Bernays (1891-1995), b. Vienna, the son of Anna Freud (1858-1955), from Příbor, Moravia, and Ely Bernays, was an American pioneer in the field of public relations and propaganda, referred to in his obituary as "the father of public relations". Bernays was named one of the 100 most influential Americans of the 20th century by *Life*. He was the subject of a full-length biography by Larry Tye called *The Father of Spin* (1999) and later an award-winning 2002 documentary for the BBC by Adam Curtis called *The Century of the Self*. His best-known campaigns include a 1929 effort to promote female smoking by branding cigarettes as feminist "Torches of Freedom", and his work for the United Fruit Company in the 1950s, connected with the CIA-orchestrated overthrow of the democratically elected Guatemalan government in 1954. He worked for dozens of major American corporations including Procter & Gamble and General Electric, and for government agencies, politicians, and non-profit organizations. In 1912, he graduated from Cornell University with a degree in agriculture but chose journalism as his first career. After graduating from Cornell, Bernays wrote for the *National Nurseryman* journal. Then he worked at the New York City Produce Exchange, where his father was a grain exporter. He went to Paris and worked for Louis Dreyfus and Company, reading grain cables. By December 1912, he had returned to New York.

Roger H. Bezdek (1945–), b. Berwyn, IL, received his Ph.D. in economics from the University of Illinois, Urbana. He is an internationally recognized expert in energy market analysis, R&D assessment, and energy forecasting. He is the founder and president of Management Information Services, Inc. – a Washington, DC-based economic and energy research firm. He has served as Corporate Director, Corporate President, and CEO, University Professor, Research Director in Energy Research and Development Administration (Department of Energy), Special Advisor on Energy in the Office of the Secretary of the Treasury. He has served as a consultant to the White House, Federal and State government agencies, and various corporations and research organizations, including the National Academies of Science, the National Science Foundation, NASA, DOE, DOD, EPA, IBM, Raytheon, Lockheed Martin, etc. He is the author of four books and of 200 articles in scientific and technical journals and serves as an editorial board member for various professional publications. He is the recipient of numerous honors and awards (including awards from the White House, the Energy Department, the Treasury Department, and the National Science Foundation).

Ruth Leah Bunzel (1898-1990), b. New York, NY, of Bohemian ancestry, was an anthropologist of note, who was an authority on the Zuni Indians and who learned their language. She was associated with Columbia Univ. as an adjunct professor.

Stella M. Capek (1953–), b. Minneapolis, MN, the daughter of Milič Čapek, who was from Třebechovice, Moravia, is a sociologist. She graduated from Boston Univ. (B.A. 1975) and studied sociology at Univ. of Texas, Austin (M.A., 1981; Ph.D., 1985). She is associated with Hendrix College, Conway, AZ, where she holds the position of professor of sociology. She teaches courses on environmental sociology, social change/social movements, medical sociology, urban/community sociology, images of the city, gender and family in a cross-cultural perspective, sociological theory, food/culture/nature and exploring nature writing. She has also team-taught student-faculty travel seminars in Costa Rica and in the U.S. Southwest. She is interested in interdisciplinary environmental studies, sustainable community design, social justice issues, and creative writing. She has published articles on environmental justice, tenants' rights and housing issues, urban/community dynamics, grassroots movements, and women's health issues. She has co-authored two books, *Community Versus Commodity: Tenants and the American City* (1992) and *Come Lovely and Soothing Death: The Right to Die Movement in the United States* (1999). She also authored a history and social change guide for the Endometriosis Association (*Building Partnerships That Work: Grassroots, Science, and Social Change. The Endometriosis Association Story*, 2006). She is married to anthropologist Hans Baer (1944–).

Michael Lewis Cepek (1973–), b. Hinsdale, Il, of Czech ancestry, studied anthropology at Univ. of Illinois, Urbana (B.A., 1996) and at Univ. of Chicago (M.A., 1999; Ph.D., 2006). After completion of his Mellon Postgraduate Fellowship at Macalester Coll. (2006–07), he joined Univ. of Texas at San Antonio, as asst. professor (2007–13), as assoc. professor (s. 2013). Since 2007, he has also been Action Fellow of the Division of Environment, Culture and Conservation, Field Museum of Natural History. He also works as book review editor for *Environment and Society: Advances in Research*, a publication affiliated with the Earth Institute at Columbia University. His research explores the relationship between socioecological crisis, cultural difference, and directed change at the margins of global orders. In his studies with indigenous Cofán people in the lowland forests, Andean foothills, and capital city of Ecuador, he investigated environmentally oriented political movements from the perspective of longstanding concerns in social theory and emerging debates in South American ethnology. In his current project, he is producing a critical phenomenology of the oil-related transformation of Cofán lands, which lie at the epicenter of Ecuador's petroleum industry. In all his work, he employs an immersed ethnographic standpoint to develop new perspectives on the forces that trouble us, whether ecological disasters, specters of cultural loss, or enduring constraints on human agency. He uses this viewpoint to contribute to broader discussions in environmental anthropology, political economy, science and technology studies, conservation policy and practice, and collaborative filmmaking and activism with indigenous peoples and other subaltern groups.

Milan Jaques Dluhy (1942-2015), b. Chicago, IL, of Slovak ancestry, was professor of political science and public administration, University of North Carolina, Wilmington, NC.

George John Dudycha (1903-1971), b. Cedar Rapids, IA, of Czech ancestry, studied at Coe Coll. (B.A., 1925), State Univ. of Iowa (M.A., 1926) and at Columbia Univ. (Ph.D., 1936). He was associated with Ripon College, WI, where he rose from instructor to professor psychology (1926–50); and served as registrar (1936–40), director student personnel (1944–50). Subsequently, he joined Wittenberg Univ., as professor of psychology (1950–70) and dept. chair (1950–60). He was the author of *Psychology for Law Enforcement Officers* (1955) and *Learn More with Less Effort* (1957) and *Applied Psychology* (1963).

Marianne Abeles Ferber (1923–2013), b. Mirkov, Bohemia, was an economist trained at Univ. of Chicago (Ph.D.). Her husband, Robert Ferber, was hired by the University of Illinois to teach in the economics department in 1948, but strict nepotism rules at Illinois prevented her from being hired as a full-time professor. Yet, the economics department did hire her on a semester-by-semester basis because of a severe teacher shortage (s. 1956). In 1971, she was promoted from lecturer to assistant professor. In 1979, she became a full professor. She was an American feminist economist and the author of many books and articles on the subject of women's work, the family, and the construction of gender. She was most noted for her work as coeditor with Julie A. Nelson of the influential anthology *Beyond Economic Man: Feminist Theory and Economics* and her book *The Economics of Women, Men and Work*, co-authored with Francine D. Blau and Anne Winkler. She was one of the first people to confront Gary Becker's work on economics and the family. She and Robert Ferber (1922–1981) had 2 children.

Erna Mary Furman (1926–2002), b. Vienna, of Czech descent, when she was twelve years old, her family having Czech citizenship fled to Czechoslovakia to escape the Nazis. Unfortunately, this did not save her from being sent to a concentration camp after the Nazis occupied Czechoslovakia. Fortunately, she survived the Holocaust. In 1945, Anna Freud took a small group of Terezín children to England, Erna being one of them, and they were taken care of under Anna Freud's supervision. A graduate of the Child Therapy Training Program offered by Anna Freud in Hampstead following World War II, Erna Furman was a child psychoanalyst, a licensed psychologist, and a teacher. She immigrated to the United States with the help of Anny Katan in the 1950s. Erna Furman specialized in children and how children process grief. Of particular importance was her evidence that children as young as three essentially process grief no differently than adults and her insistence that children not be misled or deceived when a parent dies. She practiced at the Hanna Perkins Center for Child Development and also saw patients in her Cleveland Heights home. She was a prolific writer; over the years she received extensive accolades for her contributions to psychoanalysis. She was made an honorary member of the American Psychoanalytic Association in 1999.

Bertram Myron Gross (1912–1997) b. Philadelphia, CA, of Czechoslovak Jewish immigrant parents, was an American social scientist, Federal bureaucrat and Professor of Political Science at Hunter College (CUNY). He is known from his book *Friendly Fascism: The New Face* of Power in America from 1980. He played an important role in crafting policies and legislation that were cornerstones of the New Deal. From 1941 to 1945, he served on the staffs of a number of Senate committees. In that capacity, he wrote the Roosevelt Truman full employment bills of 1944 and 1945, legislation that articulated for the first time that full employment at a living wage should be a national priority. This legislation also created the President's Council of Economic Advisers, and from 1946 to 1952 Mr. Gross served as its first executive secretary, an administrative post. In the 1950s, he moved with his family to Israel where he served as an economic advisor in the Prime Minister's Office and as a Visiting Professor at the Hebrew University, where he established their program in Public Administration. He returned in the 1960s and joined the faculty of Syracuse University in the Maxwell School. In 1961-62, he was a Fellow at the Center for Advanced Studies in the Behavioral Sciences, Palo Alto, and in 1962-63, he was the Leatherbee Lecturer at the Harvard Business School. In 1970, Bertram Gross was president of the Society for General Systems Research. In the 1980s, he became Distinguished Professor of Political Science and Urban Affairs at Hunter College and the CUNY Graduate Center.

Eric Hanushek (1943–), b. Lakewood, OH, of Czech ancestry, was a distinguished graduate of US Air Force Academy (B.S., 1965), who studied economics at MIT (Ph.D., 1968). He was first associated with US Air Force Academy, as asst. professor of economics (1969-71), and as assoc. professor (1971-73), before joining Yale Univ. as assoc. professor of economics (1975-78). Subsequently, he joined Univ. of Rochester, as professor of economics and political science (1978-2000), as chairman of dept. of economics (1982-87, 1988-90, 1991-93), as director of W. Allen E Wallis Inst. of Political Economy (1991-99), and as professor of public policy (1992-2000). Currently, he holds the position of Paul and Jean Hanna Senior Fellow at Hoover Inst., Stanford Univ. (s. 2000) and professor of education (by courtesy) (s. 2001) and professor of economics (by courtesy) (s. 2004). Government service includes being Deputy Director of the Congressional Budget Office, Senior Staff Economist at the Council of Economic Advisers, and Senior Economist at the Cost of Living Council. He has been a leader in the development of economic analysis of educational issues. He has authored numerous, highly cited studies on the effects of class size reduction, high stakes accountability, value-added assessments of teacher quality, and other education related topics. His pioneering analysis measuring teacher quality through the growth in student achievement forms the basis for current research into the value added of teachers and schools. He is chairman of the Executive Committee for the Texas Schools Project at the University of Texas at Dallas, a research associate of the National Bureau of Economic Research, and a member of the Koret Task Force on K-12 Education. He recently served as a commissioner on the Equity and Excellence Commission of the U.S. Department of Education. He was chair of the Board of Directors of the National Board for Education

Sciences during 2008–2010. He is currently the Area Coordinator for Economics of Education of the CESifo Research Network. He was awarded the Fordham Prize for Distinguished Scholarship in 2004.

Friedrich August von Hayek (1899–1992), b. Vienna, of Czech ancestry, was raised and educated in Austria and taught at the London School of Economics in the 1930s, where he gained attention for his criticism of Keynes. He expressed his commitment to free markets and his aversion to government intervention in *The Road to Serfdom* (1944). The economic policies of former British Prime Minister Margaret Thatcher were significantly influenced by his ideas. Hayek branched out into the fields of philosophy, psychology, and epistemology. He was awarded the Nobel Memorial Prize in Economic Sciences in 1974. In 1950, Hayek left the London School of Economics for the University of Chicago, where he became a professor in the Committee on Social Thought. His first class at Chicago was a faculty seminar on the philosophy of science attended by many of the University's most notable scientists of the time, including Enrico Fermi, Sewall Wright and Leó Szilárd. During his time at Chicago, Hayek worked on the philosophy of science, economics, political philosophy, and the history of ideas. Hayek's economics notes from this period have yet to be published. Hayek received a Guggenheim Fellowship in 1954. After editing a book on John Stuart Mill's letters, he planned to publish two books on the liberal order, *The Constitution of Liberty* and "The Creative Powers of a Free Civilization" (eventually the title for the second chapter of The Constitution of Liberty). He completed *The Constitution of Liberty* in May 1959, with publication in February 1960.

Katherine 'Katie' Rose Hejtmanek (1978–), b. Nucla, CO, of Czech ancestry, earned her Bachelor of Arts degree (2000) from the University of Wyoming with honors in 2-and-a-half years. In 2002, she began graduate school at Washington University in Saint Louis where she earned her Master of Arts in 2004. In 2010 she successfully defended her dissertation on cultural aspects of institutionalized mental health treatment in the United States and earned her Doctor of Philosophy (Ph.D.) degree. That same year she was hired by Brooklyn College of the City University of New York as an assistant professor in the children and youth studies program in the Department of Anthropology and Archaeology. Hejtmanek has also served as the director of the Children and Youth Studies Program. She is a cultural anthropologist. Her research focus is on psychiatry, race, and the processes by which young people heal from trauma and social marginalization and oppression. She has been particularly interested in the ways African American men challenge psychiatry's power to moralize and control them, especially those in state psychiatric custody. The National Science Foundation has generously supported her research. She has also conducted research in Rwanda with orphans from the genocide and Uganda with child soldiers. Presently she is part of a large research team that works in Barbuda, on the effects of climate change on small island communities. Dr. Hejtmanek has presented her research nationally and internationally, in both oral and written formats. In fall 2013, she earned a prestigious teaching award that allowed her to work on her book manuscript based on her dissertation research. It is set to be published in fall 2015 under the title *Mad Love: Perspectives on Custodial Psychiatry from African American Men*.

Mary Therese Henle (1913-2007), b. Cleveland, OH, daughter of Pearl A. Hahn (1880?) of Bohemian ancestry, was a psychologist, most notably known for her contributions to Gestalt psychology and for her involvement in the American Psychological Association. Henle also taught at the New School of Social Research in New York; she was involved in the writing of eight book publications and also helped develop the first psychology laboratory manual in 1948 based on the famous works of Kurt Lewin. She got her Ph.D. at Bryn Mawr College where she was hired as an assistant for Harry Helson. Under Helson's watch, she was able to get a solid education in experimental methods. Henle completed her doctorate in 1939, followed by being a research assistant at Swarthmore College to Robert B. MacLeod. In 1941, Henle worked as a professor at the University of Delaware for one year until war efforts opened many jobs for psychologists. In 1942, Harry Helson called Henle back to Bryn Mawr, where she first taught psychology to graduate students. After two years of teaching, Henle was appointed to the psychological institute of Sarah Lawrence College (1944-46). In 1946, Solomon Asch invited Henle, on Köhler's recommendation, to become a professor at the New School for Social Research in New York. She remained there for the rest of her career (1946-1983), where she published empirical research and claimed herself as a Gestalt psychologist. Henle's legacy includes writing eight books, her presidency of the American Psychological Association's (APA) Division of the History of Psychology (1971-72), presidency of the APA's division Philosophical Psychology (1974-95), and as the president of the Eastern Psychological Association (1981-82).

Melville J. Herskovits (1895-1963), b. Bellefontaine, OH, of Slovak ancestry, was anthropologist. He served in the United States Army Medical Corps in France during World War I. Afterward, he went to college, earning a Bachelor of Philosophy at the University of Chicago in 1923. He went to New York City for graduate work, earning his M.A. and Ph.D. in anthropology from Columbia University under the guidance of the anthropologist Franz Boas. In 1927, Herskovits moved to Northwestern University in Evanston, Illinois as a full-time anthropologist. He helped establish African and African American studies in American academia. He is known for exploring the cultural continuity from African cultures as expressed in African American communities. He worked with his wife Frances (Shapiro) Herskovits, also an anthropologist, in the field in South America, the Caribbean and Africa. They jointly wrote several books and monographs.

Marie Jahoda (1907-2001), b. Vienna, of Bohemian ancestry, was a social psychologist. She contributed significantly to the analysis of the authoritarian personality. Between 1958 and 1965, at what is now Brunel University, she was involved in establishing the Psychology degree programs, including the unique four-year, 'thin-sandwich' degree.

Peter Rudolph Hruby (1921-2017), b. Prague, Czech., was a political scientist and writer. After the Czechoslovak coup d'état of 1948, he exiled himself to Geneva. While there he founded the monthly journal Skutecnost (Reality), which he edited for two years. In 1969, Peter Hruby received an MA in International Relations from the Graduate Institute of International Studies in Geneva. He worked as an editor and writer for Radio Free Europe in Munich from 1951 to 1957. In 1957, he immigrated to the United States and worked for Radio Free Europe as a senior editor and writer until 1964. In the evenings, he attended Columbia University and obtained an MA in Eastern European Studies. From 1965-68, Peter Hruby taught for the University of Maryland, Overseas Divisions, then moved to Perth, Western Australia where he worked at Curtin University and then also from 1971 until 1999. He returned to Geneva in 1978 to defend his Ph.D. dissertation, entitled "Czechoslovakia between the West and the East: The Changing Role of Communist Intellectuals." He was a visiting professor at Carleton University in 1985. In 2000, he moved back to Prague and taught at Charles University (2001-07). In 2007, he moved to Annapolis, MD with his younger daughter and her family. Peter Hruby published three books: *Fools and Heroes: The Changing Role of Communist Intellectuals in Czechoslovakia, Daydreams and Nightmares: Czech Communist and Ex-Communist Literature*, and *Dangerous Dreamers: The Australian Anti Democratic Left and Czechoslovak Agents*.

Ivan Kalmar (1948-), b. Prague, Czech., is a Canadian professor. His family moved to Komárno, and later to Bratislava. When he was seventeen, he left what was then Czechoslovakia, and eventually arrived in the United States, settling in Philadelphia. Kalmar attended The University of Pennsylvania. There he received his undergraduate degree. Moving to Toronto during the Vietnam War, he took up study at The University of Toronto, where he received both a Master's degree and a Ph.D. in anthropology. Kalmar is currently a Professor of Anthropology at the University of Toronto. He is a faculty member of the Munk School of Global Affairs, and a fellow of Victoria College. In his recent research, the focus has been on western Christian views of Jews and Muslims. Currently, Kalmar is working on illiberalism and populism in the eastern, formerly communist-ruled areas of the European Union.

Norbert John 'Jack' Kanak (1936-2013), b. Atwood, KS, of Czech ancestry, earned a B.A. in sociology with minors in psychology and philosophy in 1961 from St. Benedict's College in Atchison, Kansas. He earned a Master of Science in 1964 and a Ph.D. in 1967, both in experimental psychology from Saint Louis University. In August of 1967, he accepted a position as psychology professor at the University of Oklahoma. In 1969, he became chairman of the Psychology Department serving for a total of 14 years and led the department's graduate program to national research recognition. His early career research was on learning and memory, and later he focused on the influences of culture on learning and education. As a professor, Dr. Kanak mentored 15 Doctoral dissertations and 19 Masters theses. Shortly after retiring in 1998 as professor emeritus, he was asked to return to teach his award-winning course, 'Prejudice and the Civil Rights Movement' through the spring of 2011. While at the University of Oklahoma, he received the Oklahoma Psychological Association Leadership Award, 'Distinguished AMOCO Foundation Good Teaching Award Administrative Service Citation,' the Rev. Martin Luther King Big Eight Student Leaders Award, and University of Oklahoma Black Student Association Best Professor Award. He was a fellow of the American Psychological Association. Listed in *Lisa Birnbach's College Book*, as 'Best Professor,' Dr. Kanak is one of only seven to be so named. His name is listed on the Wall of Tolerance, Civil Rights Memorial Center, Montgomery, AL.

Eric Peter Kaufmann (1970-), b. Hong Kong, of Moravian Jewish grandfather, is a Canadian professor of politics at Birkbeck, University of London. He is a specialist on Orangeism in Northern Ireland, nationalism, political demography, and religious demography. He has authored, co-authored, and edited multiple books on these subjects. He was raised in Vancouver, BC, Canada, and Japan. He received his BA from the University of Western Ontario in 1991 and his MA from the London School of Economics in 1994 where he subsequently also completed his Ph.D. in 1998. Kaufmann was a lecturer in comparative politics at the University of Southampton from 1999 to 2003. He was a fellow at the Belfer Center, Kennedy School of Government, Harvard University, for the 2008-09 academic year. Kaufmann joined Birkbeck College, University of London, in 2003. He became professor of politics there in 2011.

Eric M. Klinenberg (1970-), b. Chicago, IL, to Czech Jewish parents, is an American sociologist and a scholar of urban studies, culture, and media. He is best known for his contributions as a public sociologist. He attended the Francis W. Parker School and later earned a bachelor of arts degree from Brown University (1993), master's degree (1997) and Ph.D. (2000) from the University of California, Berkeley. He is currently a Professor of Sociology, Public Policy, and Media, Culture, and Communication at New York University, as well as the editor of the journal *Public Culture*. In 2012, Klinenberg became the director of the Institute for Public Knowledge at New York University. In 2013, he was appointed research director of the Rebuild by Design competition.

Thomas R. Kratochwill (1946–), Madison, WI, of Czech ancestry, received training in educational psychology at Univ. of Wisconsin, Madison (M.S., Ph.D., 1973). He was associated with the dept, of educational psychology at Univ. of Arizona, Tucson, as asst. professor (s. 1974), as assoc. professor (s. 1977), as a professor (1981–83). Subsequently, he joined the dept. of educational psychology at the Univ. of Wisconsin, Madison, as a full professor (s. 1983). He holds the position of Sears Roebuck Foundation-Bascom Professor and Director of the School Psychology Program, a Principal Investigator in the Wisconsin Center for Education Research, and is a licensed psychologist in Wisconsin. Kratochwill is the author of over 200 journal articles and book chapters. He has written or edited over 30 books and has made over 300 professional presentations. In 1977, he received the Lightner Witmer Award from Division 16 of the American Psychological Association (APA). In 1981, he received the Outstanding Research Contributions Award from the Arizona State Psychological Association and an award for Outstanding Contributions to the Advancement of Scientific Knowledge in Psychology from the Wisconsin Psychological Association in 1995. Since then, he received many other awards.

Mark Jerome Krejci (1959–), b. Grand Forks, ND, of Czech ancestry, earned his B.S. degree in psychology from the University of North Dakota in 1982, and his M.A. in 1985 and Ph.D. in 1987 in counseling psychology from the University of Notre Dame. He is a licensed psychologist in Minnesota, acquiring his license in 1992. Dr. Krejci has been employed at Concordia College in Moorhead, Minnesota since 1987. After 17 years in the Psychology Department, rising to the rank of professor in 2000, he was appointed as vice-president for academic affairs and dean of the College at Concordia. After serving in that role from 2004 to 2013, he returned to the Psychology Department at Concordia. His research interests fall in the area of the psychology of religion and treatment-related articles in this area. He served as the editor of the *Psychology of Religion Newsletter* from 1998 to 2002.

Charles J. Ksir (1945–), b. Albuquerque, NM of Czech ancestry, received his Bachelor's degree in psychology from the University of Texas at Austin, and his Ph.D. from Indiana University in Bloomington. Following his postdoctoral training in neurobiology at the Worcester Foundation in Massachusetts, he began a 34-year career in teaching and research at the University of Wyoming, where he also served in a variety of administrative positions. Now professor emeritus, he focuses his efforts on teaching and textbook writing. He has taught the psychology course Drugs and Behavior to over three thousand students since 1972 and has received several teaching awards. He held the position of dean, College of Education (1997–2001). He is a specialist on psychopharmacology and drug policy. His areas of interest include: substance use, abuse, and dependence drug policy and medications for behavioral disorders. He is the author of *Drugs, Society and Human Behavior* (10th ed., 2004) and *Fix Until Broken: A Guide to Destructive Leadership* (2004).

Lars Krutak (1971-), b. Lincoln, NE, of Slovak descent, was an American anthropologist, photographer, and writer known for his research about tattoo and its cultural background. Between 1999-2002 and 2010-2014, Krutak worked as an archaeologist and Repatriation Case Officer at the National Museum of the American Indian and National Museum of Natural History, facilitating the return of human remains, funerary objects, sacred and ceremonial objects. Today, he is a Research Associate at the Museum of International Folk Art.

Gregor Lazarčík (1923-2013), b. Horná Streda, Czech., was an economist. He was a professor of economics, from the State University of New York, Geneseo, NY (s. 1968). He also studied the demographic structure and ethnic change of Los Angeles and conducted studies of Jewish populations throughout the United States. His behavioral research was conducted in banks and savings institutions, manufacturing, and social welfare systems in the United States and overseas: Japan, Germany, Austria and Hungary, Switzerland, the United Kingdom, Ireland, Nepal and India. His 1961 book, *Leadership and Organization: A Behavioral Science Approach* was significant in making the academic and practical argument for the use of group dynamics in developing leaders and teaching them how to operate effectively.

Paul Felix Lazarsfeld (1901-1976), b. Vienna, of Moravian ancestry, was a pioneering sociologist, who founded Columbia University's Bureau of Applied Social Research. He attended schools in Vienna, eventually receiving a Doctorate in applied mathematics (his Doctoral dissertation dealt with mathematical aspects of Einstein's gravitational theory). A Rockefeller Foundation grant for psychological research enabled Lazarsfeld to come to the United States in 1933. He served as director of the Office of Radio Research, a Rockefeller project at Princeton University (1937-40), and, when the project was transferred to Columbia University in 1940 (it was later renamed the Bureau of Applied Social Research), he continued as its director and was appointed to the sociology department of that university. Under his leadership (1940-50), the Bureau became a well-known laboratory for empirical social research. He remained a professor at Columbia until 1970. Lazarsfeld addressed a great variety of topics in his research. Chief among them was his use of statistical means to determine the impact of radio and the print media on Americans' voting habits and preferences. He conducted large-scale studies on the effect of newspapers, magazines, radio, and motion pictures on society, and he carried out particularly detailed investigations of the radio-listening habits of the American public with his associates, the psychologist Hadley Cantril and Frank Stanton, the then-head of research for the CBS broadcasting company. Among Lazarsfeld's more important works are *Radio and the Printed Page* (1940); *The People's Choice* (1944), *Voting* (1954), and the textbook *An Introduction to Applied Sociology* (1975).

John Meisel (1923-), b. Vienna, of Czech ancestry, is a Canadian political scientist, educated at the Univ. of Toronto and the Univ. of London. He is the Sir Edward Peacock Professor of Political Science Emeritus at Queen's University and is also senior research fellow in the Centre for the Study of Public Opinion at Queen's University. He has written extensively on various aspects of politics, notably on parties, elections, ethnic relations, politics and leisure culture and international politics.

Ilse Schüller Mintz (née Schueller) (1904–1978), b. Vienna, the daughter of the economist Richard Schüller, a native of Brno, Moravia, and Emma Rosenthal from Hohenems. She studied economics in Vienna and married the lawyer Maximilian Mintz in 1926. Together with their children Walter and Gabriele, they fled to Zurich via Feldkirch in March 1938. In July of the same year, they emigrated to the USA, where they settled in Riverdale, north of New York. Ilse Mintz remained active as a national economist in the USA. She continued her business studies at Columbia University, where she received her Ph.D. in 1945, and began teaching at Columbia University. In addition to her professorship, Ilse Schüller worked for the National Bureau of Economic Research in New York, for which she conducted numerous studies on the influence of foreign bonds and foreign trade on economic cycles. In 1968, she moved with her husband to Washington, where she taught at Catholic University.

Walter Mintz (1929–2004), b. Vienna, the son of Ilse Schüller (1904–1978) of Moravian ancestry, and Maximilian (Moses) Mintz, came to the United States with his family in 1938. After attending public schools in the Bronx, he graduated from Reed College in Portland, Oregon in 1950, and then did post-graduate work in economics at Columbia University. He was an associate editor at Barron's before he began his career in the investment business at Shearson Hammill Co. in 1956. There, he was the Director of Research, 1962–69, and Executive Vice President of their Investment Division, 1965–70. In 1970, he co-founded Cumberland Associates, an investment management company in New York. He retired as a Managing partner from that firm in 1982, remaining a special limited partner. Mr. Mintz was a Trustee of Reed College for 33 years, from 1971–2003. He was Vice-Chairman of the Board of Trustees, 1991–98, and Chairman 1998–2002. He established the Walter Mintz Economics Scholarship for students and co-sponsored a Chair in Economic History. In New York, he was a Trustee of The Manhattan Institute, 1990–2003, and served as Vice Chairman, 1994–2003. He was also on the Boards of Merrill Lynch Phoenix Fund and Federal Security Trust, 1982–2001; on the Board of the Citizen's Union Foundation, 1985–2003, and was a member of the N.Y. Society of Security Analysts, where he served on their Board of Directors, 1969–75.

Jiří Nehněvajsa (1925-1996), b. Dyjákovice, Czech., was a sociologist. In June 1944, under the Nazi occupation, he graduated from high school in Brno, Czechoslovakia. Being deeply opposed to the Nazis, he somehow managed to cross Europe amidst the raging War to join the Royal Air Force, Czechoslovak Section in England for training in the United Kingdom until the end of the War. After his return to Moravia, he studied at Masaryk University (1945-48). In 1948, he escaped from Communist Czechoslovakia to Switzerland, where he studied sociology at the University of Lausanne (1948-49) and then at Zürich, where he completed his Doctorate in Zürich (Ph.D., 1953) under Rene König. In January 1951, he came to the United States under the Displaced Persons Act of 1948. He was with Univ. of Colorado (1951-56) and then with Univ. of Pittsburgh, where he was prof. of sociology (196l-), dept. chair (1962-66, 1994-95), and prof. of economic and social development (s.1964). His other appointments included Research director, Inter-University Program in Institution Building Research (s. 1966). He was an authority on research methods, socio-economic development, political sociology, public opinion, and disaster research. His sociological work was strongly grounded in empirical research. He co-authored *Sociometry Reader* (1961) and co-edited *Message Diffusion* (1956).

Richard Elliot Neustadt (1919-2003), b. Philadelphia, PA, of Czech ancestry, received a BA in history from the University of California, Berkeley in 1939, followed by an M.A. degree from Harvard University in 1941. After a short stint as an economist in the Office of Price Administration, he joined the US Navy in 1942, where he was a supply officer in the Aleutian Islands and stayed until 1946. He then went to the Bureau of Budget, while working on his Harvard Ph.D., which he received in 1951. He was the Special Assistant of the White House Office from 1950-53 under President Harry S. Truman. During the following year, he was a professor of public administration at Cornell, then from 1954-64, taught government at Columbia University, where he received a Woodrow Wilson Foundation Award in 1961. Neustadt later founded the Kennedy School of Government at Harvard, where he taught as a popular professor for more than two decades, officially retiring in 1989, but continuing to teach there for years thereafter. Neustadt also served as the first director of the Harvard Institute of Politics (IOP), which was founded as "a living memorial to President John F. Kennedy that engages young people in politics and public service." He was an authority on presidential power. His most influential work on the presidency was first published in 1960 under the title *Presidential Power*.

Nora S. Newcombe (1951-), b. Toronto, Ont., Canada, daughter of Hanna Hammerschlag (1922-2011), a native of Prague, Czech., and Alan George Newcombe, is the Laura H. Carnell Professor of Psychology and the James H. Glackin Distinguished Faculty Fellow at Temple University. She is a Canadian American researcher in cognitive development, cognitive psychology, and cognitive science, working on the development of spatial thinking and reasoning and on the development of episodic memory. She was the principal investigator of the Spatial Intelligence and Learning Center, one of six NSF-funded Science of Learning Centers. Newcombe received her Ph.D. from Harvard University in 1976. She has served as the Chair of the Cognitive Science Society Board, President of the Cognitive Development Society, Division 7 (Developmental) of the American Psychological Association, the Eastern Psychological Association and as Chair of the Board of Scientific Affairs of the American Psychological Association.

Gustav F. Papanek (1926–), b. Vienna, of Bohemian ancestry, studied agricultural economics at Cornell Univ. (B.S.) and economics at Harvard Univ. (A.M., Ph.D.). He was associated with Boston Univ., as professor and chair of the dept. of economics (1974–83), as professor of economics and director, Center for Asian Development Studies/Asian Program (1983–92); Gustav F. Papanek has been president of the Boston Institute for Developing Economies (BIDE) (s. 1987) and professor of economics emeritus at Boston University (s. 1997). For the last five decades, he has been considered one of the outstanding development economists, as exemplified by his leadership of the Harvard University Development Advisory Service (then the HIID); the Boston University Economics Department; BIDE; and several AID, World Bank, ADB and Harvard University advisory and research teams. He has provided economic advice to prime ministers, presidents, ministers, central bank governors and senior officials in: Indonesia, Pakistan, Bangladesh, Sri Lanka, India, Micronesia, Malaysia, Egypt, Korea, Nepal, Iran, Ghana, Greece, Colombia, Liberia, Guinea, Ethiopia, Venezuela, and Argentina. He has written or edited 8 books, including *Pakistan's Development: Social Goals and Private Incentives* (1967), *Development Strategy, Growth, Equity and the Political Process in Southern Asia* (1986).

Karl Paul Polanyi (1886–1964), b. Vienna, of Slovak ancestry, was an economic historian, anthropologist and sociologist, political economist, social philosopher. In college in Budapest Polanyi founded the radical Club Galilei, which would have far-reaching effects on Hungarian intellectual life. He qualified as a lawyer in 1912 and served as a cavalry officer during World War I. Once back home he founded the Radical Citizens Party of Hungary. He then had to leave Hungary for political reasons. After working in Vienna as an economic journalist (1924–33), he moved to England and then, in 1940, to the United States. He was professor of economics at Columbia University (1947–53). Polanyi was not a conventional economist but was instead concerned with the development of an overall view of the functioning of economic relationships within different social frameworks. He is best known for his book *The Great Transformation*, which argues against self-regulating markets. In the book, he advances the concept of the Double Movement, which refers to the dialectical process of marketization and push for social protection against that marketization.

Leopold J. Pospíšil (1923–2021), b. Olomouc, Czech., received his undergraduate education in that city before moving to Prague to obtain a degree in law. After a year of studying philosophy in Germany, he immigrated to the United States where his interest in the social sciences led him to complete a second undergraduate degree in Sociology at Willamette University and a Master's degree in anthropology from the University of Oregon. Finally, in 1952, he arrived at Yale University where he obtained a Ph.D. in anthropology four years later. Leopold Pospíšil pioneered the anthropological study of law and his three books *Kapauku Papuans and Their Law*, *Anthropology of Law*, and *The Ethnology of Law*, along with the students he trained at Yale, are largely responsible for establishing this area of research as a flourishing subfield of anthropology. Deeply committed to developing a scientific approach to ethnography, he carried out a quantitative study of highland New Guinea agriculture, published under the title of *Kapauku Papuan Economy*, that set new standards for research in economic anthropology. Pospíšil, like Malinowski, studied a range of the world's cultures. Besides his distinguished fieldwork in Melanasia, he also worked among the Hopi people of Arizona, the Nunamiut Eskimo of Alaska and the Tirolean peasants of Obernberg Valley in Austria. An unforgettable lecturer, Leopold Pospíšil has influenced generations of students in the Department of Anthropology and Law School and, as curator of anthropology in the Yale Peabody Museum of Natural History, he helped to create many outstanding exhibits. As director of the Division of Anthropology in the Peabody since 1966, he labored tirelessly to protect, preserve, and expand Yale's unique collections.

Zora Prochazka Pryor (née Prochazka) (1926–2008), b. Prague, Czech., was an economist. She studied economics at Univ. Paris (dipl., 1951), Radcliffe Coll. (M.A., 1956) and at Harvard Univ. (Ph.D., 1960). She began her career in Washington, D.C., working on the economics of Eastern Europe, first for the Census Bureau and later at the Research Analysis Corporation, a research branch of the U.S. Army. In 1964, she married a fellow specialist on East Europe, moved to New Haven, Connecticut and thence to Swarthmore. For several years she taught economics, first at Temple University and later for many years at St. Joseph's University. During her academic career, she published a number of scholarly articles and short monographs on the economic history and current economic problems of East European nations. She was married to economist Frederic LeRoy Pryor (1933–2019).

Elizabeth Brandeis Raushenbush (1896–1980), b. Boston, MA, of Bohemian ancestry (daughter of Supreme Court Justice Louis Brandeis), was trained as an economist at Univ. of Wisconsin. (Ph.D., 1928). She was an economics professor who used her scholarly understanding of labor issues as a public advocate. She taught in the Economics Department at the University of Wisconsin for over 40 years. As an academic, Raushenbush studied the economic, sociological, and political implications of unregulated working conditions. Her greatest achievement as an advocate was leading the successful fight for the implementation of unemployment insurance in Wisconsin. The resulting law, called the Groves Bill, was fashioned after a model law that she had developed. It was the first law of its kind in the United States, providing the foundation for the Social Security Act of the New Deal.

Beardsley Ruml (1894-1960), b. Cedar Rapids, IA, of Czech immigrant father, studied at Univ. of Chicago. He became Dir. of Laura Spelman Rockefeller Memorial (1922-29); Dean of social sciences and prof. of education, Univ. of Chicago (1931-34); treas., R.H. Macy & Co., Inc., NYC (s. 1934), chairman of the Board (1945-); dir. of Federal Reserve Bank of NY (s. 1937), chairman of the Board and Federal Reserve agent of NY district (1941-46). Ruml's studies of economics and fiscal problems led him to propose publicly (1942), as a substitute for the government's costly and complicated method of collecting individual income taxes on wages and salaries, a plan to collect such taxes at their source by means of a payroll deduction system, on a pay as you go basis. US Congress several times evaded his proposal, but public opinion approved it so overwhelmingly that it was finally written into the nation's tax structure signed by Pres. Roosevelt in 1943. Ruml also played a prominent role at the Bretton Woods Conference of monetary experts which led to the establishment of the International Monetary Fund and the International Bank for Reconstruction and Development, popularly known as the World Bank.

Edgar Schein (1928-), b. Zurich, Switzerland, of Slovak ancestry, was a social psychologist. He was professor at MIT.

Joseph Alois Schumpeter (1853-1950), b. Třešť, Moravia, was a notable economist trained at Univ. of Vienna. He was prof. of economics, Harvard Univ. (1932-50). He was a pioneer in the field of econometrics and specialist in the history of economic theory and economic development, including studies of business cycles, capitalism, and socialism in economic and sociological perspective. He was the author of *Business Cycles: A Theoretical Historical and Statistical Analysis of the Capitalistic Process* (1939, 2 vols.).

Joseph Senko (1935-), b. Pittsburgh, PA, of Slovak descent, was a certified public accountant. He was a tax law specialist for the Internal Revenue Service and Adjunct Professor of income taxes at Duquesne, and a board member of various nonprofit and civic associations. He also worked for an international accounting firm, before starting his own accounting firm of McKeever Varka & Senko.

Herbert Alexander Simon (1916-2001), b. Milwaukee, WI, the son of Edna Marguerite Merkel (1888-1969) of Czech ancestry on her mother's side, and Arthur Carl Simon, was an American political scientist, economist, sociologist, psychologist, and professor, most notably at Carnegie Mellon University, whose research ranged across the fields of cognitive psychology, cognitive science, computer science, public administration, economics, management, philosophy of science, sociology, and political science. With almost a thousand very highly cited publications, he was one of the most influential social scientists of the twentieth century. Simon was among the founding fathers of several of today's important scientific domains, including artificial intelligence, information processing, decision-making, problem-solving, attention economics, organization theory, complex systems, and computer simulation of scientific discovery. He coined the terms "bounded rationality" and "satisficing" and was the first to analyze the architecture of complexity and to propose a preferential attachment mechanism to explain power law distributions. He also received many top-level honors later in life. These include: becoming a fellow of the American Academy of Arts and Sciences in 1959; election to the National Academy of Sciences in 1967; the ACM's Turing Award for making "basic contributions to artificial intelligence, the psychology of human cognition, and list processing" (1975); the Nobel Memorial Prize in Economics "for his pioneering research into the decision-making process within economic organizations" (1978); the National Medal of Science (1986); and the APA's Award for Outstanding Lifetime Contributions to Psychology (1993). As a testament to his interdisciplinary approach, Simon was affiliated with such varied Carnegie Mellon departments as the School of Computer Science, Tepper School of Business, departments of Philosophy, Social and Decision Sciences, and Psychology. Simon received an honorary Doctor of Political science degree from University of Pavia in 1988 and an honorary Doctor of Laws (LL.D.) degree from Harvard University in 1990.

Jody L. Sindelar (1951–), b. Oak Park IL, of Czech ancestry, studied economics at Stanford Univ. (M.A., 1974; Ph.D., 1980), with additional training, as a postdoctoral fellow, at Univ. of Chicago (1978–80). She was an asst. professor of business economics (1980–84) at the Univ. of Chicago, before joining Yale School of Public Health, Yale School of Medicine. Starting as asst. professor (1984–89), she advanced to assoc. professor (1989–2004) and then to full professor (s. 2004). In 1995–97, she served as assoc. dean of the Yale School of Public Health and in 2005, she was appointed head of the Division of Health Policy and Management in the School. In addition, Dr. Sindelar is a Research Associate at the National Bureau Economic Research; Research Fellow at IZA (Institute for the Study of Labor); and Associated Faculty at the Institution for Social and Policy Studies (ISPS) at Yale. Dr. Sindelar is an expert on the economics of substance abuse, including tobacco, illicit drugs and alcoholism, as well as obesity. Her studies include lost productivity, cost effectiveness of treatments, social costs, and policy. She has published over 100 papers and studies on the impacts of substance abuse on productivity, educational attainment, gender differences, regulation and taxation of tobacco and related policy issues in economics, policy, addiction, health and medical journals. She has served on numerous editorial, review, advisory and other Boards and committees, and has presented her research at seminars and conferences both nationally and internationally. She has two sons, Tyler Ibbotson-Sindelar and Tim Ibbotson-Sindelar, who are both economists.

Michael Sumichrast (1921-2007), b. Trenčín, Czech., was an internationally known housing economist. He was chief economist for the National Association of Home Builders in Washington for more than 20 years and was considered one of the most-quoted people in the housing industry. He was also author of several number of books on housing and finance. Sumichrast joined the underground resistance against the Nazis during World War II. He was captured by the Gestapo in 1944 but escaped a prison camp and helped drive the Nazis from Bratislava. After the Communists took over in 1948, Sumichrast was on an arrest list and he and two friends paddled a canoe across Danube River to Austria. In 1955, he immigrated to the United States. He earned a Doctorate in economics in 1962 at Ohio State University and shortly afterward became an economist at the National Association of Home Builders where he was an adviser to several presidents and several Fed chairmen.

Jan Švejnar (1952-), b. Prague, Czech., received his training in economics at Princeton Univ. (M.A., Ph.D.). He was associated with Cornell Univ. (1978-83) before joining the Univ. of Pittsburgh as professor of economics (1987-93, becoming distinguished service professor (1993-96). Since 1996, he has held the position of professor of economics and Everet E. Berg Professor of Business Administration at Univ. of Michigan (1996-2012), while also holding the position of Professor of Public Policy (2005-12). In 2012, he assumed the James T. Shotwell Professorship of Global Political Economy and also became the Founding Director of the Center on Global Economic Governance at the School of International and Public Affairs at Columbia University. His areas of interest include economic development and transition, labor economics, and behavior of the firm. Professor Svejnar works as an advisor to governments, non-profit organizations and firms, and he serves as Chairman of the Supervisory Board of CSOB Bank and co-editor of Economics of Transition. He was an advisor to President Havel, consultant to World Bank, EBRD, etc. He was an unsuccessful candidate for the 2008 election of the President of the Czech Republic.

Zdeněk Ludvík Suda (1920-2015), b. Pelhřimov, Czech., was trained as sociologist at Charles Univ. Suda played a key early organizing role in the United Europe Movement — the precursor of the present European Union — in Paris, France, from 1949 to 1953. From 1954 to 1968, he worked as a journalist on the Czechoslovak Desk of the US Government-sponsored news agency, Radio Free Europe, broadcasting daily news reports and topics of cultural interest from a wide range of non-political sources to radio audiences in then-Czechoslovakia who otherwise had no alternative source of news other than what the Soviet-aligned Communist government of Czechoslovakia permitted to be broadcast. From 1968 to 1985, Mr. Suda was a professor of sociology at the University of Pittsburgh, where he rose to full prof. of sociology. Following his retirement from the University in 1985, until 2009 he continued as professor emeritus to advance landmark scholarly research into comparative politics and history, primarily focused on Eastern Europe in the post-World War II era. He was the author of several notable works on a wide range of topics, including the political economy of the Soviet bloc and an in-depth history of the Czechoslovak Communist Party. He was a specialist on social change, political sociology, sociology of work, sociology of education.

Frank William Taussig (1859–1940), b. St. Louis, MO, of Czech ancestry, was trained as an economist at Harvard Univ. He was with Harvard Univ. (s. 1882), as prof. of political economy (1892–1901), as Henry Lee prof. (1901–35). He was Chairman of US Tariff Commission (1917–19). He was an authority on questions of international commerce, esp. US tariff. He developed import-export theory and wage-fund theory; applied economics to public policy; co-founder of School of School of Business Administration at Harvard.

Marc A. Weiss (1950–), b. Chicago, IL, of Bohemian ancestry, was trained as an urban and regional planner at the University of California at Berkeley. He is Chairman and CEO of Global Urban Development, an international policy organization and professional network of 600 leaders and experts in 60 countries, with offices in Barcelona, Beijing, Curitiba, Hong Kong, Istanbul, London, Porto Alegre, Prague, Rehoboth, San Francisco Bay Area, Singapore, Sydney, Toronto, and Washington DC. He serves as Adjunct Professor of International and Public Affairs at Columbia University, executive editor of *GUD Magazine*, and as a Steering Committee member of the UN Sustainable Development Knowledge Partnership, UN Habitat World Urban Campaign and Best Practices Program, and Atlantic Council Urban World 2030.

Edith Weisskopf (1910–1983), b. Vienna, the daughter of Emil Weisskopf of Sušice, Bohemia, was a psychologist. She earned a Doctorate in psychology at University of Vienna and in 1939, immigrated to the US. Weisskopf pursued her career in psychology at several prominent universities, including Briarcliff College in New York, Indiana University, Purdue and Duke University, and finally the University of Georgia. She also served as a clinical consultant for the state of Indiana. While teaching at Purdue University, she contracted tuberculosis and was admitted to the hospital for treatment during 1962–1964. During this time, she began experiencing symptoms of schizophrenia. Despite this development, she taught at St. Mary-in-the-Woods College in Terre Haute for one year. She kept a diary of her madness, and that diary became a book, *Father, Have I Kept My Promise?* published posthumously in 1988 by Purdue University. After her release from a mental hospital in 1966, she returned to teaching and continued her distinguished academic career. Weisskopf retired from the University of Georgia in 1978 and died in

1983 of cardiac arrest. She was married to social psychologist Gustav Ichheiser (1897–1969) but the marriage lasted only two years. In I951, Edith Weisskopf married her long-term partner, engineer and businessman Michael Joelson, who was born in Riga/Latvia, but the marriage also failed (in 1961) and she was finally divorced in 1972.

Max Wertheimer (1880–1943), b. Prague, Bohemia, received his training at Univ. of Prague, Berlin and Würzburg. He held the position of prof. of philosophy and psychology at New School for Social Research, NY (1933–43), becoming the first immigrant psychologist there. He was editor of (1934–43) and member of Commission for Displaced Foreign Psychologists. He was the founder of 'Gestalt School for Psychology' and promoter of application of Gestalt methodology to other social sciences. He stressed importance of wholes in learning and problem solving; discovered phi phenomenon concerning illusion of motion in perception.

Martha Wolfenstein (1911–1976), b. Cleveland, OH, of Bohemian ancestry, was a child psychologist and psychoanalyst. She graduated from Radcliffe Coll., and then earned an M.A. in psychology and a Ph.D. in aesthetics from Columbia University. She was analyzed by the art historian and lay analyst Ernst Kris and attended classes at the New York Psychoanalytic Institute between 1948 and 1953. A lay psychoanalyst, she was not a member of a society belonging to the American Psychoanalytic Association, but nonetheless was a widely admired teacher and supervisor in New York City. She was a specialist on child psychology. Wolfenstein books include *Movies* (1950), *Children's Humor* (1954), and *Disaster* (1957), a seminal analysis of the impact of catastrophic events on individuals. With the anthropologist Margaret Mead, she edited *Childhood in Contemporary Cultures* (1955). Wolfenstein's books and essays are exemplary for their use of psychoanalytic insights as a prism with which to illuminate and connect the origins and vicissitudes of cultural values and attitudes to psychological imperatives. She was married to political scientist Nathan Constantin Leites (1912–1987) but they eventually divorced.

Philip Joseph Zuckerman (1969–), b. Los Angeles, CA, of Czech Jewish parents, is a professor of sociology and secular studies at Pitzer College in Claremont, California. He specializes in the sociology of substantial secularity. He is the author of several books, including *Living the Secular Life* (2014), *What It Means to be Moral* (2019) and *Society Without God* (2008) for which he won ForeWord Magazine's silver book of the year award, and *Faith No More* (2011).

XI. Technology

A. Engineering

Jerry (Jaromir) Astl (1922–2017), Most, Czech., was a Czechoslovak aeronautical engineer and explosive engineer who helped design the American Project Orion nuclear propulsion spacecraft in the 1950s and 1960s.

Edward Michael Buyer (1921–2012), b. NYC, son of Dr. Edith Selma Michael (1894–1960) of Czech descent, and Samuel Buyer, was an electrical engineer, who trained at Columbia University (B.S., 1943) and Brooklyn Polytechnic (M.S.). He flew with the 493rd Bombardment Group, Tenth Air Force in India and Burma. He worked as an electrical engineer who helped pioneer the development of electronic reconnaissance. With his wife Marilyn Patterson Stier, they had 3 children.

Royal Samuel Buyer (1922–2017), b. NYC, son of Dr. Edith Selma Michael (1894–1960) of Czech descent, and Samuel Buyer, was a mechanical engineer. He graduated from SUNY in Syracuse with a degree in forestry in 1943 with a mechanical engineering degree in 1953. He moved to Washington area in 1966 and worked for the US Navy Department. He was instrumental in recommending that the Navy use the General Electric LM2500, which is still used today on the majority of Navy destroyers and cruisers. In the later 1970s, until his retirement in 1988, he worked on a program to develop a prototype reverse osmosis plant for shipboard freshwater production to replace the Navy's steam, distilling freshwater plants. That prototype RO plant led to the production version that is in use in today's Navy destroyers. With his wife, Marjory Allewelt Buyer, they had 5 children.

Jerry George Capka (1922–1978), b. Middletown, PA, of Slovak descent, was a civil engineer. He was with US Army. In 1961-64, he was the area engineer for the US Engineer Group in Turkey, where he received the Legion of Merit. After retiring in 1969, he joined Kaiser Engineers where he was based in London, where he responsible for project development in Europe, Africa and the Middle East. He then went to Seoul and established Korea-Kaiser Engineering Company, Ltd. He was US Army Lieutenant Colonel, recipient of Legion of Merit for action during Vietnam War (1965).

Harry George Drickamer (orig. Weidenthal) (1918–2002), b. Cleveland, OH, of Bohemian ancestry, received training in chemical engineering at Univ. of Michigan. Drickamer joined the Univ. of Illinois at Urbana-Champaign, where he subsequently remained for his entire professional career. After his initial appointment as an assistant professor of chemical engineering in 1946, he was promoted to assoc. professor in 1949 and to full professor in 1953. In 1958 he was appointed professor of chemical engineering and physical chemistry, and in 1983, he became professor of chemical engineering, chemistry, and physics. Drickamer's work led to advances in the understanding of the molecular, atomic, and electronic properties of matter, and provided the tools to study these properties with greater detail and precision. He was the first to use infrared and UV-vis spectroscopy to study matter at high pressure, thereby discovering that high pressure perturbs different types of electronic orbitals to different degrees. He discovered a wide variety of electronic transitions in solids and molecules and the optical, electrical, chemical, and magnetic consequences thereof.

Jessica Fridrich (1964–), b. Ostrava, Czech., is a professor at Binghamton University, who specializes in data hiding applications in digital imagery. She is also known for documenting and popularizing the CFOP method (sometimes referred to as the "Fridrich method"), one of the most commonly used methods for speedsolving the Rubik's Cube, also known as speedcubing. She is considered one of the pioneers of speedcubing, along with Lars Petrus. Nearly all of the fastest speedcubers have based their methods on Fridrich's, usually referred to as CFOP (Cross, First 2 Layers, Orient Last Layer, Permute Last Layer). Jessica Fridrich works as a professor at the Department of Electrical and Computer Engineering at Binghamton University and specializes in digital watermarking and forensics. She received her MS degree in applied mathematics from the Czech Technical University in Prague in 1987, and her Ph.D. in systems science from Binghamton University in 1995.

Ivan A. Getting (1912–2003), b. New York, NY, of Slovak ancestry, was an electrical engineer and physicist, credited (along with Roger L. Easton and Bradford Parkinson) with the development of the Global Positioning System (GPS). He was the co-leader (the other being Louis Ridenour) of the research group which developed the SCR-584, an automatic microwave tracking fire-control system, which enabled anti-aircraft guns to destroy a significant percentage of the German V-1 flying bombs launched against London late in the Second World War. He attended the Massachusetts Institute of Technology (MIT) as an Edison Scholar (S.B. Physics, 1933); and Merton College, Oxford as a Graduate Rhodes Scholar (D.Phil., 1935) in astrophysics. He then worked at Harvard University on nuclear instrumentation and cosmic rays (Junior Fellow, 1935-1940) and the MIT Radiation Laboratory (1940-1950; Director of the Division on Fire Control and Army Radar, Associate Professor 1945; Professor 1946). During the Second World War, he was a special consultant to Secretary of War Henry L. Stimson on the Army's use of radar. He also served as head of the Naval Fire Control Section of the Office of Scientific Research and Development, member of the Combined Chiefs of Staff Committee on Searchlight and Fire Control, and head of the Radar Panel of the Research and Development Board of the Department of Defense. In 1950, during the Korean War, Getting became Assistant for Development Planning, Deputy Chief of Staff, United States Air Force; and in 1951, Vice President for

Engineering and Research at the Raytheon Corporation (1951-1960). While at Raytheon, Getting also served on the Undersea Warfare Committee of the National Research Council. In 1960 Getting became the founding President of The Aerospace Corporation (1960-1977).

Mark Donald Gross (1961-), b. US, son of Sonja Osaki Keller (1926-1992), a native of Trutnov, Czech., and the physicist Eugene Paul Gross, is a professor of computer science and director of the ATLAS Institute at the University of Colorado, Boulder, an interdisciplinary institute for radical creativity and invention with academic programs in the College of Engineering and Applied Science. Gross has served on the faculties of Carnegie Mellon University and the University of Washington, Seattle and worked at Atari Cambridge Research, Logo Computer Systems Incorporated and Kurzweil Computer Products. With former students he co-founded Boulder companies Modular Robotics Incorporated and Blank Slate Systems LLC, and is a partner in Momotone, Inc. Gross' research interests include design methods, modular robotics, computationally enhanced construction toys and crafts, design software for digital fabrication, and the internet of things. He earned BS and Ph.D. degrees from the Massachusetts Institute of Technology.

Theodore von Kármán (1881-1963), b. Budapest, Hungary, son of Helen Kohn (1853-1941) of Bohemian descent, and Moriz Kármán (orig. Kleinmann), was an aerospace engineer, physicist and mathematician, who was active primarily in the fields of aeronautics and astronautics. He is responsible for many key advances in aerodynamics, notably his work on supersonic and hypersonic airflow characterization. He is regarded as the outstanding aerodynamic theoretician of the twentieth century. He received a Ph.D. in engineering at the University of Göttingen in Germany in 1908. Von Kármán worked in a variety of academic posts, was in the Austro-Hungarian Army during World War I, worked in private industry doing research, and built a world-renowned reputation by lecturing extensively in various countries. He was invited to the United States by Robert A. Millikan to advise California Institute of Technology (Caltech) engineers on the design of a wind tunnel. After the wind tunnel was completed in 1928, von Kármán stayed on to join Caltech's newly established Guggenheim Aeronautical Laboratory (GALCIT). In 1930, he became Director of GALCIT. In 1942, von Kármán and five other scientists formed Aerojet Engineering Corporation, to accept contracts for building jet engines. In 1949, he resigned from Caltech and JPL to work at the Pentagon where he chaired the Air Force Scientific Advisory Board until 1954. In March 1952, he became the chair of the NATO Advisory Group for Aeronautical Research and Development (AGARD). In 1954, he received the Astronautics Engineer Achievement Award and in 1960, he received the Goddard Memorial Medal for liquid rocket work. In 1963, President John F. Kennedy presented him with the first National Medal of Science.

XI. TECHNOLOGY

Andrej Karpathy (1986–), b. Czech., moved with his family to Toronto, Canada when he was 15. He is the director of artificial intelligence and Autopilot Vision at Tesla. He specializes in deep learning and computer vision.

Edward George Keshock (1935–2010), b. Campbell, OH, of Slovak descent, was a mechanical engineer. He had been professor and chairperson at Cleveland State University, Cleveland, OH. He also served as the Honorary Consul of the Slovak Republic for the State of Ohio.

Daniel John Kisha (1937–2016), b. Johnstown, PA, of Slovak descent, was a chemical and industrial engineer. He graduated from Johnstown Central High School in 1955, and received B.S. degree from University of Pittsburgh and M.S. degree in chemical engineering from MIT. He was president of Kisha Engineering, Inc., Pensacola, FL. Previously was employed by Exxon, Fluor and James Chemical Engineering. He also owned and operated Slovak Import (2000–2016). He resided in Johnstown, PA.

Edward S. Kolesar, Jr. (1950–2009), b. Canton, OH, of Slovak descent, as an electrical engineer. He taught at Air Force Institute of Technology (AFIT) (for 8 years), before accepting the newly established Montecrief Professor of Engineering chair at the Texas Christian University.

Raymond 'Ray' Kurzweil (1948–), b. Queens, NYC, of Moravian ancestry, is a computer scientist, inventor, and futurist. Kurzweil is a public advocate for the futurist and transhumanist movements and gives public talks to share his optimistic outlook on life extension technologies and the future of nanotechnology, robotics, and biotechnology. Kurzweil received the 1999 National Medal of Technology and Innovation, the United States' highest honor in technology, from President Clinton in a White House ceremony. He was the recipient of the $500,000 Lemelson-MIT Prize for 2001. He was elected a member of the National Academy of Engineering in 2001 for the application of technology to improve human-machine communication. In 2002, he was inducted into the National Inventors Hall of Fame, established by the U.S. Patent Office. He has received 21 honorary doctorates, and honors from three U.S. presidents. The Public Broadcasting Service (PBS) included Kurzweil as one of 16 "revolutionaries who made America" along with other inventors of the past two centuries. *Inc.* magazine ranked him #8 among the "most fascinating" entrepreneurs in the United States and called him "Edison's rightful heir."

Harold Alvin Levey (1889–1987), b. New Orleans, LA, son of Bella Pokorny (1864–1944), whose father was from Moravia, and Moses Edmond Levey, was an engineer. He obtained a Master's degree in chemistry at the University of Illinois in 1916. From 1911, he had worked as a mechanical and electrical engineer, before becoming a chemical engineer at Mariner and Hoskins in Chicago. He founded the company American Products Manufacturing in

1919, and the same year founded Harold A. Levey Incorporated, a consulting engineering firm. He specialized in the production of plastic packaging and sheeting. His honors included the Honor Scroll Award from the American Institute of Chemists in 1956. He also established the Harold A. Levey Award at Tulane University.

James Arthur Lovell (1928–), b. Cleveland, OH, the son of Blanche Masek (1895–1973), of Czech ancestry, and James Arthur Lovell, was mechanical engineer, US Navy captain and NASA astronaut. In 1968, as command module pilot of Apollo 8, he became one of the first three humans to fly to and orbit the Moon. He then commanded the 1970 Apollo 13 lunar mission which, after a critical failure en route, circled around the Moon and returned safely to Earth through the efforts of the crew and mission control. Lovell had previously flown on two Gemini missions, Gemini 7 in 1965 and Gemini 12 in 1966. He was the first person to fly into space four times. He is one of 24 people to have flown to the Moon, Lovell was the first person to fly to it twice. He is a recipient of the Congressional Space Medal of Honor and the Presidential Medal of Freedom (in 1970, as one of 17 recipients in the Space Exploration group, and co-author of the 1994 book *Lost Moon*, on which the 1995 film *Apollo 13* was based.

Vlado Meller (1947–), b. Czech., is an audio mastering engineer, currently with Vlado Meller Mastering in Charleston, South Carolina. Meller works across many genres of music, with credits on rock, hip-hop, pop, jazz, metal, dance, opera, Broadway, and classical albums over 50+ year career. Albums that he engineered have won two Grammy Awards.

Rudolf Glenn Minarik (1907–1993), b. Cleveland, OH, of Slovak descent, was a mechanical engineer. He was professor of mechanical engineering at Syracuse University (1943–45), and president of The Integral Engineering Services Co. (s. 1947).

Elizabeth Podlaha-Murphy (née Podlaha) (1964–), a native of New York, NY, of Czech ancestry, was an engineer. She studied chemical engineering at Univ. of Connecticut, Storrs (B.S., 1986) and at Columbia Univ. (Ph.D., 1992). She is a professor of interior chemical engineering at Northeastern Univ., Boston, MA (2007–present) with expertise in electrochemical phenomena. She was formerly employed at Louisiana State Univ. (LSU) as an assistant and tenured associate professor in chemical engineering (1998–2007) and completed a postdoctoral appointment at the Ecole Polytechnique Fédérale de Lausanne, Department of Materials Science, Lausanne, Switzerland. As part of NSF, DOE and DARPA funded projects, Podlaha has directed research in the development and discovery of electrodeposited alloys and composite thin films and nanostructured materials. Applications of these materials are diverse, spanning from everyday uses, such as to improve corrosion resistance films for surface finishers, to high tech adaptation of nanowires for biosensors. Podlaha's research lab has helped over 25 students complete their graduate degrees and has had over 20 undergraduate students participate in electrochemical research. She has been the recipient of the noteworthy NSF-Career award and the LSU Alumni Association Faculty Excellence Award. She has authored or co-authored over 60 reviewed journal papers, 1 book chapter and 20 proceedings papers. She is married to mechanical engineer Michael C. Murphy (1955–).

Emanuel A. Salma (1908–1989), b. US, of Slovak descent, was a mechanical engineer. He served as Associate Dean of the College of Engineering and Science at New York University.

Charles Susskind (1919–2004), b. Prague, Czech., earned his Bachelor's degree in electrical engineering at the California Institute of Technology in 1948, and his Ph.D. in electrical engineering at Yale University in 1951. He was associated with University of California, Berkeley, where he held the position of professor of electrical engineering and where he was a co-founder of bioengineering studies. Susskind's work on the intersection of engineering with biological sciences became a driving force for his advocacy of a bioengineering program at UC Berkeley. Working with Irving Fatt, at the time a UC Berkeley professor of mechanical engineering, Susskind organized the campus's first bioengineering graduate training program and later helped expand it to an undergraduate curriculum. Their efforts formed the foundation for the Joint UC Berkeley/UC San Francisco Graduate Group in Bioengineering in 1982, and the Department of Bioengineering in 1999.

Frank Toepfer (orig. Franz Hrncir) (1845–1902), b. Sázava, Bohemia, was a Czech-American machinist, engineer, and businessman in Milwaukee, Wisconsin. He constructed two self-powered carriages before being involved in making the first gasoline-driven vehicle in the United States. He immigrated to the US at 22 in 1867. Milwaukee dentist Christian Linger in 1889 ordered two hand-propelled "horseless carriages" from Toepfer to build at his machine shop at 460 National Avenue on the south side of the city. The reason Linger wanted such a vehicle was to attract attention to be able to sell a medical ointment he manufactured. Toepfer, part-owner and a machinist at the shop, designed and constructed the vehicles. One of the carriages was pumped like a railway handcar for its forward locomotion power and another one was powered by a person that rocked back and forth on a movable chair mechanism built on a horseless carriage and that was mechanically attached to a crankshaft device that was linked to the wheels of a carriage for its propulsion. The hand-powered vehicles were successful and the dentist became known as the "Penny Doctor" when he would throw out pennies as he traveled along on the streets in his vehicles to attract attention. Toepfer then worked with Gottfried Schloemer, a coppersmith at the shop, in constructing a horseless carriage that would have a gasoline engine to power it, making it the first gas-driven vehicle in the United States.

Bohumil Voleský (1939–), b. Prague, Czech., received training in mechanical and food engineering at Czech Technical Univ. (Ing./M.S., 1962) and in bioengineering at Univ. of Western Ontario, London, Canada (Ph.D., 1971). He has been associated with McGill Univ. (s. 1973), as prof. of biochemical engineering (s. 2003). His res. interests are in fermentation process engineering, microbial product process development, biosorbent detoxification, industrial effluents, biosorbent recovery of nuclear fuel and metallic elements, development of new biosorbent materials, and industrial water pollution control.

B. Invention

Jerry (Jaromir) Astl (1922–2017), Most, Czech., was a Czechoslovak aeronautical engineer and explosive engineer who helped design the American Project Orion nuclear propulsion spacecraft in the 1950s and 1960s.

Edward Michael Buyer (1921–2012), b. NYC, son of Dr. Edith Selma Michael (1894–1960) of Czech descent, and Samuel Buyer, was an electrical engineer, who trained at Columbia University (B.S., 1943) and Brooklyn Polytechnic (M.S.). He flew with the 493rd Bombardment Group, Tenth Air Force in India and Burma. He worked as an electrical engineer who helped pioneer the development of electronic reconnaissance. With his wife Marilyn Patterson Stier, they had 3 children.

Anton Bakovský (fl. 1857), b. of Czech descent, according to Thomas Čapek, invented the sleeper car, which he constructed for St. Joseph and Hannibal Railroad in 1857.

Stefan Banič (1870–1941), b. Jánostelek, Slovakia, was a Slovak inventor who patented an early parachute design. Banič immigrated to the United States and worked as a coal miner in Greenville, Pennsylvania. After witnessing a plane crash in 1912, Banič constructed a prototype of a parachute, and on August 25, 1914 was granted a US patent. The design which was radically different from others – it was a type of umbrella attached to the body, but it is claimed that he successfully tested it in Washington, D.C. jumping first from a 15-story building and subsequently from an airplane in 1914. He sold his patent to the U.S. Army, although there is no evidence that it was ever used.

Itzhak Bentov (1923–1979), b. Humenné, Czech., was an Israeli American scientist, inventor, mystic and author. His many inventions, including the steerable cardiac catheter, helped pioneer the biomedical engineering industry. Despite not having a university degree, Bentov joined the Israeli Science Corps, which David Ben-Gurion incorporated into the Israeli Defense Forces one month before Israel declared statehood in 1948. The Science Corps became a military branch known by the Hebrew acronym HEMED. Bentov designed Israel's first rocket for the War of Independence. HEMED was forced to make improvised weapons as there was a worldwide embargo on selling weapons to the Jewish state. Bentov immigrated to the United States in 1954, and settled in Massachusetts.

Rudolph Thomas Bozak (1910–1982), b. Uniontown, PA, of Bohemian immigrant parentage, was an audio electronics and acoustics designer and engineer in the field of sound reproduction. Bozak studied at Milwaukee School of Engineering; in 1981, the school awarded him an honorary doctorate in engineering. Fresh out of college in 1933, Rudy Bozak began working for Allen-Bradley, an electronics manufacturer based in Milwaukee, Wisconsin. Bozak moved to the East Coast in 1935 to work for Cinaudagraph out of Stamford, Connecticut. Two years later he was chief engineer. At the 1939 New York World's Fair, a tower topped with a cluster of eight 27" Cinaudagraph loudspeakers in 30" frames with huge 450 lb. field coil magnets covered low frequency duties for a 2-way PA system at Flushing Meadows. The loudspeakers were mounted into horns with 14' wide mouths and were each driven by a 500-watt amplifier derived from a high-power radio broadcast tube. In June 1940, *Electronics* magazine published an article that Bozak had written about the design of the 27" loudspeaker. During World War II, Bozak worked with Lincoln Walsh at Dinion Coil Company in Caledonia, New York developing very high voltage power supplies for radar. Bozak joined C.G. Conn in 1944 to help them develop an electronic organ. Bozak is often remembered today for his advanced designs of DJ mixers which allowed the development of the concept of disc jockey mixing and 'discotheques'.

Royal Samuel Buyer (1922–2017), b. NYC, son of Dr. Edith Selma Michael (1894–1960) of Czech descent, and Samuel Buyer, was a mechanical engineer. He graduated from SUNY in Syracuse with a degree in forestry in 1943 with a mechanical engineering degree in 1953. He moved to Washington area in 1966 and worked for the US Navy Department. He was instrumental in recommending that the Navy use the General Electric LM2500, which is still used today on the majority of Navy destroyers and cruisers. In the later 1970s, until his retirement in 1988, he worked on a program to develop a prototype reverse osmosis plant for shipboard freshwater production to replace the Navy's steam, distilling freshwater plants. That prototype RO plant led to the production version that is in use in today's Navy destroyers. With his wife, Marjory Allewelt Buyer, they had 5 children.

Jan Vratislav Čapek (1842–1909), b. Chrastovovice, Bohemia, a journalist and publicist, toward the end of his life, he devoted his energy to inventions relating to electricity and chemistry.

Jerry George Capka (1922–1978), b. Middletown, PA, of Slovak descent, was a civil engineer. He was with US Army. In 1961-64, he was the area engineer for the US Engineer Group in Turkey, where he received the Legion of Merit. After retiring in 1969, he joined

Kaiser Engineers where he was based in London, where he responsible for project development in Europe, Africa and the Middle East. He then went to Seoul and established Korea-Kaiser Engineering Company, Ltd. He was US Army Lieutenant Colonel, recipient of Legion of Merit for action during Vietnam War (1965).

William Cermak (1886–1907), b. Kasejovice, Blatná, Czech., a master potter, came to the US in 1886 at age of 30. William Cermak headed General Electric's porcelain factory that moved from New York City to Schenectady, NY in 1889. Cermak found he had trouble creating high quality porcelain insulators through the dry process (granulated clay pressed dry in molds). Cermak, along with his team of engineers, developed the petticoated insulator (insulator that increases length of electricity passage on the surface and continuously keeps a part of the path dry) that could withstand 10,000 volts. Cermak continued his work on porcelain insulators with General Electric. William lived on the East Side in New York City in a cold water flat, one bathroom to each floor. He found work at a foundry or pottery in the lower east side, and sent for his wife and three sons, Frank, Edward, and Charles. They lived somewhere in or near downtown Schenectady. Up through the early 1890s, electrical insulators were made of glass, which was fragile and not capable of withstanding high voltages. In 1893, William Cermak, working with his subordinate John J. Kraus, developed the "petticoated" porcelain insulator usable with 10,000-volt transmission lines, a breakthrough that enabled the rapid growth of electrification in the United States. In 1904, after the Cermaks moved to Fourth Ave in Schenectady's Mont Pleasant area, a neighborhood where many other Czechs lived, William was appointed Alderman for the Ninth Ward. At the time, Frank was 24 and working at General Electric, learning from his father and helping him. He later became an Alderman himself, and his son, also named Frank, was a Councilman in the Schenectady County Town of Niskayuna at the time of his death in 1971.

Emil Czapek (1891–1959), b. Vrutice, Bohemia, a chemical engineer, developed a new commercial process for the manufacture of cellophane as well as designing equipment used in the process. Later on, he developed another process for manufacturing cellulose based on the use of cuprammonium cellulose which was adopted in a number of countries.

Zola Gotthard Deutsch (1899–1965), b. Cincinnati, OH, of Bohemian ancestry, a chemical engineer, was an inventor of improvements in multiple effect evaporation, in gas concentrators of stills and in interchange of steam and electric power.

John Dopyera (orig. Ján Dopjera) (1893–1988), b. Šaštín-Stráže, Slovakia, was a Slovak-American inventor and entrepreneur, and a maker of stringed instruments. His inventions include the resonator guitar and important contributions in the early development of the electric guitar.

XI. TECHNOLOGY

Philip Drinker (1893–1972), b. Haverford, PA, of Moravian ancestry, a chemical engineer, was an inventor of the Drinker respirator, popularly known as the 'iron lung,' a device that induced artificial respiration. It came into use in 1929 for maintaining life of patients suffering from respiratory paralysis caused principally by poliomyelitis. Another of his inventions was the use of helium air mixture for deep diving purposes which made possible for the escape of the crew of the disabled submarine *Squalus* in 1939. He developed many new protective devices, such as dust and fume masks.

August Dvorak (1894–1975), b. Glencoe, MN, of Czech ancestry, an educational psychologist, designed a more keystroke-efficient keyboard, an alternative to the standard 'QWERTY' arrangement of keys.

Ernst Eger (1892–ca. 1984), b. Kroměříž, Moravia, a mechanical engineer, was holder of some 50 patents in rubber, including rubber cutting machines, liquid weighing device, Eger valve of vented tubes and rubber valves, steel grip airplane tires, non-metallic replacements for sheet aluminum. His greatest invention for war efforts was the development of self-sealing gas tanks designed to withstand machine gun bullets.

Otto Eisenschiml (1880–1963), b. Vienna, Aust., of Czech ancestry, a chemist, devised one of the earliest deodorants, transparent window envelopes, oiled baseball gloves, rust proof barbed wire (originally used in Flanders during World War I) and dozens of other useful contributions which have flowed unheralded into the stream of our necessities.

Paul Eisler (1907–1992), b. Vienna, of Bohemian ancestry, an engineer, was an inventor. Among his innovations was the printed circuit board. He was responsible for a number of other popular developments, including the rear windscreen heater, heated clothes and also a pizza warmer, to enable a customer to keep his takeout pizza warm by plugging the box into a battery powered by the car. In 2012, *Printed Circuit Design & Fab* magazine named its Hall of Fame after Eisler.

Martin Fleischmann (1927–2012), b. Karlovy Vary, Czech., an electrochemist, is best known for his controversial work with his former graduate student Stanley Pons on cold fusion, in the 1980s and '90s. On March 23, 1989, while Pons was a researcher at the University of Utah, he and Fleischmann announced the experimental production of cold fusion – a result previously thought to be unattainable. After a short period of public acclaim, the pair was attacked widely for sloppy, unreproducible research and inaccurate results, as Fleischmann predicted they would be. Fleischmann, Pons and the researchers who replicated the effect remain convinced the effect is real, but skeptics who oppose them are convinced it is not. In 1992, Fleischmann moved to France with Pons, to work at the IMRA laboratory (part of Technova Corporation, a subsidiary of Toyota). The pair parted ways in 1995, and

Fleischmann returned to Southampton, where he remained as of 1999. In 2006, Fleischmann joined the San Francisco company D2Fusion.

Jessica Fridrich (1964–), b. Ostrava, Czech., is a professor at Binghamton University, who specializes in data hiding applications in digital imagery. She is also known for documenting and popularizing the CFOP method (sometimes referred to as the "Fridrich method"), one of the most commonly used methods for speed solving the Rubik's Cube, also known as speed cubing. She is considered one of the pioneers of speed cubing, along with Lars Petrus. Nearly all of the fastest speedcubers have based their methods on Fridrich's, usually referred to as CFOP (Cross, First 2 Layers, Orient Last Layer, Permute Last Layer). Jessica Fridrich works as a professor at the Department of Electrical and Computer Engineering at Binghamton University and specializes in digital watermarking and forensics. She received her MS degree in applied mathematics from the Czech Technical University in Prague in 1987, and her Ph.D. in systems science from Binghamton University in 1995.

Rudolf Gaertner (1873–1930), b. Prague, Bohemia, a ceramic chemist, trained at Liberec Polytechnicum, invented a jet-black glaze for hard feldspar china, an incandescent lamp refractor, and china insulators with inserted glaze lamelles for electric currents up to 50,000 volts. He established his own decalcomania plant at Mt. Vernon, NY which developed into one of the largest enterprises of its kind in the world.

William Ganz (1919–2009), b. Czech., a physician, was a co-inventor of Swan-Ganz catheter – a thin flexible, flow-directed catheter with a terminal inflatable balloon. It is inserted through the right atrium and ventricle into the pulmonary artery. The balloon is then inflated sufficiently to block the flow of blood from the right heart to the lung. This allows the back pressure in the pulmonary artery distal to the balloon to be recorded. This pressure reflects the pressure transmitted back from the left atrial chamber of the heart.

Ivan A. Getting (1912–2003), b. New York, NY, of Slovak ancestry, was an electrical engineer and physicist, credited (along with Roger L. Easton and Bradford Parkinson) with the development of the Global Positioning System (GPS). He was the co-leader (the other being Louis Ridenour) of the research group which developed the SCR 584, an automatic microwave tracking fire-control system, which enabled anti-aircraft guns to destroy a significant percentage of the German V-1 flying bombs launched against London late in the Second World War. He attended the Massachusetts Institute of Technology (MIT) as an Edison Scholar (B.S. Physics, 1933); and Merton College, Oxford as a Graduate Rhodes Scholar (D.Phil., 1935) in astrophysics. He then worked at Harvard University on nuclear instrumentation and cosmic rays (Junior Fellow, 1935–1940) and the MIT Radiation Laboratory (1940–1950); Director of the Division on Fire Control and Army Radar, Associate

Professor 1945; Professor 1946). During the Second World War, he was a special consultant to Secretary of War Henry L. Stimson on the Army's use of radar. He also served as head of the Naval Fire Control Section of the Office of Scientific Research and Development, member of the Combined Chiefs of Staff Committee on Searchlight and Fire Control, and head of the Radar Panel of the Research and Development Board of the Department of Defense. In 1950, during the Korean War, Getting became Assistant for Development Planning, Deputy Chief of Staff, United States Air Force; and in 1951, Vice President for Engineering and Research at the Raytheon Corporation (1951-1960). While at Raytheon, Getting also served on the Undersea Warfare Committee of the National Research Council. In 1960, Getting became the founding President of The Aerospace Corporation (1960-1977).

Frank Gollan (1909-1988), b. Brno, Moravia, a physician and physiologist, was an inventor of a simple heart-lung machine for use in open-heart surgery.

Herbert Graf (1903-1973), b. Vienna, Aust., of Czech ancestry, an opera director and producer, was a holder of US patents for combined axial theater and arena and theater with TV.

Herbert Hans Greger (1900-1972), b. Turnov, Bohemia, a ceramics and chemical engineer and business executive, trained at Univ. of Leipzig and Mining Academy of Freiburg, received some 50 patents for various inventions, e.g. for processes for the production of electricity by means of a fuel cell, for an electric cell and methods for decolorizing sulphur, and the production of sulphur and fertilizers, aluminum phosphates, bonded materials, a process for manufacturing chinaware, a rotary fast bed kiln, air setting plastic refractories, process of making ferrites, apparatus for pressure sintering ceramic material, process for making high temperature ceramics, the flat press, etc.

Mark Donald Gross (1961-), b. US, son of Sonja Osaki Keller (1926-1992), a native of Trutnov, Czech., and the physicist Eugene Paul Gross, is a professor of computer science and director of the ATLAS Institute at the University of Colorado, Boulder, an interdisciplinary institute for radical creativity and invention with academic programs in the College of Engineering and Applied Science. Gross has served on the faculties of Carnegie Mellon University and the University of Washington, Seattle and worked at Atari Cambridge Research, Logo Computer Systems Incorporated and Kurzweil Computer Products. With former students, he co-founded Boulder companies Modular Robotics Incorporated and Blank Slate Systems LLC, and is a partner in Momotone, Inc. Gross' research interests include design methods, modular robotics, computationally enhanced construction toys and crafts, design software for digital fabrication, and the internet of things. He earned B.S. and Ph.D. degrees from the Massachusetts Institute of Technology.

Raymond Richard Halik (1917-2001), Kilkenny, MN, of Czech ancestry, graduated B.S. in chemical engineering from the University of Minnesota with honors including membership in the honor societies: Tau Beta Pi and Phi Lambda Epsilon. His graduate work at Carnegie Mellon earned him a Ph.D. degree in 1948. He spent almost 40 years in the chemical and petroleum industries before retiring as a consulting engineer from Mobil Oil Co in 1981. During this time, he was active (including officer positions) in many technical societies (National Society of Professional Engineers, American Chemical Society, American Institute of Chemical Engineers), as well as several civic and religious organizations. He was the holder of 17 patents.

Frank Hamachek (1853-1935), b. Bohemia, a manufacturer, was an inventor of stump puller, the feed cutter, giant feed mill, ideal pea harvester, ideal viner feeder, viners, ideal chain adjusters. He was granted over 30 patents.

William Joseph Hammer (1858-1934), b. Cressona, PA, of Moravian ancestry, became assistant in lab. of Thomas A. Edison, Menlo Park, NJ and later chief engr., Edison Lamp Works and chief inspector of central stations, Edison Elect. Lab. Co. In London, he established first central station in world for incandescent electric lighting. He invented radium luminous preparations used for watches, clocks, airplane and automobile instruments, etc. He first suggested and used radium for cancer and tumor treatment. He was an inventor of motor driven flashing electric signs. He was a recipient of John Scott Legacy medal and premium from Franklin Inst.: grand prize, St. Louis exposition (1904); gold medal, St. Louis exposition and Elliot Cresson Gold Medal from Franklin Inst. (1906).

John J. Hanacek (1902-2003), b. Ružomberok, Slovakia, was instrumental designer biological science dept., Univ. of Chicago. He was self-taught artist, musician, astronomer, inventor, collector, and outdoorsman. Designed and built his own log cabin in Michigan, Upper Peninsula and called it his "U.P. Topia."

Edward Hanak (1872-1948), b. San Francisco, CA, of Czech ancestry, a mining engineer, turned his talents to invention. By 1930, he held 58 patents. In 1886, he originated the first coin in the slot pay telephone device. He sold this invention for $7,000 to a man who received for it $40,000. He later invented an automatic scale on which he held a number of patents. He built and patented the Hanak conveyor which could negotiate great distances, carrying freight of all kinds, including those for unloading ships. He also invented and patented small passenger elevators for use in private homes.

Rochus Heinisch (1801-1874), b. Litoměřice, Bohemia, a surgical instrument maker, was a successful inventor, his most prominent achievement having been the invention of the tailors' shears, which have since found a market in nearly every part of Europe and America.

Milo P. Hnilicka (1912–1998), b. Prague, Czech., graduated from the University of Prague in 1929 with a degree in mechanical and electrical engineering. Two years later, he received a degree in chemical technology, also from the University of Prague. In Czechoslovakia, he oversaw the operation and management of the power plant in Ostrava, the country's largest. He served in the Czech Army during the Nazi invasion of Czechoslovakia and during World War II. In 1948, he and his family escaped Czechoslovakia into Western Germany and came to the U.S. in 1949. Dr. Hnilicka went on to become chief scientist at National Research Corp. in Cambridge, Mass., USA, which later became Norton Company. He was a patentee in field invention of super insulation for cryonic and space technology.

Josef L. Hůrka (1925–2005), b. Radnice, Czech., was a Czech resistance fighter and later US spy, worked as an engineer with the Warner Electric Brake and Clutch Company in Beloit Wisconsin, and with the USM Corporation in Beverly, Massachusetts. In the late nineteen-sixties and early nineteen-seventies, was the president of the Graves Ski Corporation, in Newburyport, MA, and then ran his own consulting firm for many years. He was the inventor of the fiberglass ski and other revolutionary items for the ski and boating industries: the first foam core and molded edges in skis were his creation, as well as some of the first synthetic paddles and oars used in kayaking and rowing. He invented winches for the European communications industry made of Kevlar and urethane, and furniture (molded from a combination of sawdust and fiberglass) used in major restaurant chains. He gave numerous lectures on his work as an inventor and engineer. During his retirement, he was a ski instructor at the Killington Ski Resort, in Killington, Vermont.

Karl Guthe Jansky (1905–1950), b. Norman, OK, of Bohemian ancestry, an American physicist and radio engineer, in 1931, first discovered radio waves emanating from the Milky Way. He is considered one of the founding figures of radio astronomy.

Ferdinand Nickolas 'Ferd' Kahler, Sr. (1864–1927), b. Bohemia, was an American inventor, entrepreneur and automobile pioneer who founded The Kahler Co. in New Albany, Indiana. He was a manufacturer of wood and lumber products, founded two early American automobile companies and was granted patents by the United States Patent and Trademark Office for his inventions.

Jeffrey Kapec (1950–), b. Jersey City, NJ, of Czech ancestry, an industrial designer, is a primary inventor and co-inventor of some 50 US utility patents and 10 international utility patents, including orthopedic instrument design and other surgical instruments, medical diagnostic equipment, pharmaceutical packaging, drug delivery systems, technical instruments, office equipment, office furniture design, and consumer products.

John Karmazin (1884–1977), b. Tmaň, Bohemia, a mechanical engineer, obtained patents for major improvements to the automobile radiator cap. With royalties earned from General Motors for his radiator cap patent, he founded the Karmazin Products Corporation in Wyandotte, Michigan in 1946. Most of the company's products were based on patents obtained by Karmazin who was awarded more than 50 patents by the U.S. Patent and Trademark Office during his lifetime.

Joseph John Kaspar (1883–d.), b. Omaha, NE of Czech ancestry, a construction engineer, was an inventor of Kaspar process of direct conversion of iron to steel.

Erick Kauders (1907–1995), b. Prague, Bohemia, an engineer, was a co-inventor of Bazooka gun.

Anton Tiberius Kliegl (1872–1927), b. Bad Kissingen, Bavaria, of Bohemian ancestry, was an American businessman and inventor. In 1911, Kliegl invented the carbon arc lamp still known as Klieg light, which produced double the brightness with the same energy needs as contemporary lamps of that time and was specifically used for stage lighting and filming.

Tobias Kohn (1817–1898), b. Prague, Bohemia, was a developer of the silk manufacturing process by loom. It was due to his invention that the silk industry in Patterson, NJ came into being.

Henry Kolm (1924–2010), b. Vienna, of Bohemian ancestry, a physicist and industrialist, is a holder of more than 30 patents. Kolm developed world record electromagnets (both pulsed and continuous), designed the MIT National Magnet Laboratory, and initiated its programs of high field applications. He built the first in-situ niobium-tin superconducting magnet, the first closed-loop supercritical helium cooling system, the first pulsed field metal forming system, and the first superconducting maglev system. He invented high gradient magnetic separation and filtration, the Magneplane system of magnetically levitated transportation (with Richard Thornton), and developed the first practical synchronous electromagnetic aircraft catapults and projectile launchers.

Joseph Kubka (?–1955), b. Strašice, presumably was an inventor of a cigarette lighter in 1933. He founded Kem Lighter Manufacturing Co. and earned around $2 million annually.

XI. TECHNOLOGY

Andrej Karpathy (1986–), b. Czech., moved with his family to Toronto, Canada when he was 15. He is the director of artificial intelligence and Autopilot Vision at Tesla. He specializes in deep learning and computer vision.

Edward George Keshock (1935–2010), b. Campbell, OH, of Slovak descent, was a mechanical engineer. He had been professor and chairperson at Cleveland State University, Cleveland, OH. He also served as the Honorary Consul of the Slovak Republic for the State of Ohio.

Daniel John Kisha (1937–2016), b. Johnstown, PA, of Slovak descent, was a chemical and industrial engineer. He graduated from Johnstown Central High School in 1955 and received a B.S. degree from the University of Pittsburgh and M.S. degree in chemical engineering from MIT. He was president of Kisha Engineering, Inc., Pensacola, FL. Previously was employed by Exxon, Fluor and James Chemical.

Edward S. Kolesar, Jr. (1950–2009), b. Canton, OH, of Slovak descent, as an electrical engineer. He taught at Air Force Institute of Technology (AFIT) for 8 years before accepting the newly established Montecrief Professor of Engineering chair at the Texas Christian University.

Raymond 'Ray' Kurzweil (1948–), b. Queens, NYC, of Moravian ancestry, is a computer scientist, inventor, and futurist. Kurzweil is a public advocate for the futurist and transhumanist movements and gives public talks to share his optimistic outlook on life extension technologies and the future of nanotechnology, robotics, and biotechnology. Kurzweil received the 1999 National Medal of Technology and Innovation, the United States' highest honor in technology, from President Clinton in a White House ceremony. He was the recipient of the $500,000 Lemelson-MIT Prize for 2001. He was elected a member of the National Academy of Engineering in 2001 for the application of technology to improve human-machine communication. In 2002, he was inducted into the National Inventors Hall of Fame, established by the U.S. Patent Office. He has received 21 honorary doctorates, and honors from three U.S. presidents. The Public Broadcasting Service (PBS) included Kurzweil as one of 16 "revolutionaries who made America" along with other inventors of the past two centuries. *Inc.* magazine ranked him #8 among the "most fascinating" entrepreneurs in the United States and called him "Edison's rightful heir."

Ernst A. Lederer (1895–d.), b. Prague, Bohemia, an electrical engineer, developed a passion for technology early in life, and counted Abraham Lincoln and Thomas Edison among his heroes. After an unsuccessful foray into independent inventing, he served in World War I as an educator. After the War, Lederer accepted an offer from Westinghouse to work on lamp filament research. He later became one of the company's leading researchers in vacuum tubes. After working briefly for National Union, he took a job in the vacuum tube research department of Radio Corporation of America. Lederer contributed substantially to the design and manufacture of special tubes for British and American radar systems. During World War II, he traveled in Britain as a consultant of vacuum tube manufacturers and returned after 1945 to accept a position at Westinghouse. There, he worked on the development of television tubes.

Kurt Lehovec (1918–2012), b. Ledvice, Bohemia, is one of the pioneers of the integrated circuit (1959). He innovated the concept of p-n junction isolation used in every circuit element with a guard ring: a p-n junction surrounding the planar periphery of that element. This patent was assigned to Sprague Electric.

Harold Alvin Levey (1889–1987), b. New Orleans, LA, son of Bella Pokorny (1864–1944), whose father was from Moravia, and Moses Edmond Levey, was an engineer. He obtained a Master's degree in chemistry at the University of Illinois in 1916. From 1911, he had worked as a mechanical and electrical engineer, before becoming a chemical engineer at Mariner and Hoskins in Chicago. He founded the company American Products Manufacturing in 1919, and the same year founded Harold A. Levey Incorporated, a consulting engineering firm. He specialized in the production of plastic packaging and sheeting. His honors included the Honor Scroll Award from the American Institute of Chemists in 1956. He also established the Harold A. Levey Award at Tulane University.

Louis Edward Levy (1846–1919), b. Stenovice, Bohemia, invented a photo-chemical engraving process 'levy-type,' which was patented in 1874. He also invented an etching machine by which etching could be produced by the application of a spray of acid forced upward against horizontal metal plate by an air blast. For his invention, he received the Elliot Cresson Medal of the Franklin Institute in 1889. His last invention was a device for applying powdered resin to plates preparatory to the etching process. For this he received the Elliot Cresson Medal in 1907.

Lionel Faraday Levy (1884–1978), b. Philadelphia, PA, of Bohemian ancestry, received training in chemical engineering at the Univ. of Pennsylvania. After graduation he worked successively as an engineer for the Graphic Arts Co., the Herald Publication Co. and the Repro Art Machinery Co., all in Philadelphia. He joined the latter in 1915 and later was elected its president and technical director, positions he held till 1968. This business was a subsidiary of Max Levy Co., a firm that he bought in 1926 and of which he was president to 1968 and chairman of the Board thereafter to his death. Lionel Levy invented special appliances for photo technique processes. He was also director of the Erie National Bank, Philadelphia from 1927 to 1947. Long interested in the affairs of the Franklin Inst., Philadelphia, he was a trustee and member of the Board of managers and a member of its science and arts committee after 1916. During World War I he was affiliated with the corps of engineers of the PA National Guard.

Max Levy (1857-1926), b. Detroit, MI, of Bohemian ancestry, invented, jointly with his brother Louis, the Levy half tone screen, an etched glass grating which they patented in 1893. For this invention, they received the John Scott Legacy Medal. Max then engaged in the manufacture of half tone screens and photographic plate holders and camera diaphragms of his own invention for photoengraver's use. He also patented the hemocytometer in 1917.

James Arthur Lovell (1928-), b. Cleveland, OH, the son of Blanche Masek (1895-1973), of Czech ancestry, and James Arthur Lovell, was mechanical engineer, US Navy captain and NASA astronaut. In 1968, as command module pilot of Apollo 8, he became one of the first three humans to fly to and orbit the Moon. He then commanded the 1970 Apollo 13 lunar mission which, after a critical failure enroute, circled around the Moon and returned safely to Earth through the efforts of the crew and mission control. Lovell had previously flown on two Gemini missions, Gemini 7 in 1965 and Gemini 12 in 1966. He was the first person to fly into space four times. He is one of 24 people to have flown to the Moon, Lovell was the first person to fly to it twice. He is a recipient of the Congressional Space Medal of Honor and the Presidential Medal of Freedom in 1970, as one of 17 recipients in the Space Exploration group, and co-author of the 1994 book *Lost Moon*, on which the 1995 film *Apollo 13* was based.

Matthew Luckiesh (1889-1967), b. Maquoketa, IA, of Czech ancestry, an electrical engineer and physicist, pioneered artificial sunlight development and invented 'Mazda' daylight lamp. He was awarded the Longstreth Medal by Franklin Inst. for work on visibility of airplanes and gold medal by Optometry Foundation for research in seeing medal from Illuminating Engineering Soc.

Mike Machacek (1872-1956), b. Wheatland Twp., MN, of Czech ancestry, a manufacturer and inventor, had many US patents granted, e.g. application of hydraulics to machinery and several patents relative to foundry practice.

Joseph Mahler (1899-1981), b. Czech., a physicist, was an inventor of vectographs, polarizers, and stereoscopic viewers.

Louise Mannheimer (1845-1920), b. Prague, Bohemia. Teacher by profession, was the inventor of Pureairin Patent Ventilator.

Miroslav Marek, b. Prague, Czech., was trained as a chemical engineer at Czech Technical Univ. and a metallurgist at Georgia Tech. He held the position as assoc. professor of chemical engineering at Georgia Inst. of Technology and later that of professor and associate director of the School of Materials Engineering. Marek has been recognized for his corrosion research of medical and dental metals. Dr. Marek was the first to show that mercury is released from dental amalgam as a dissolution process, as well as a corrosion phenomenon. He has had influence on establishing the need to elucidate the corrosion mechanisms of dental metals to promote their biocompatible use.

Vlado Meller (1947–), b. Humenné, Czech., is an American Slovak audio mastering engineer. He studied electrical engineering at the Czech Technical University in Prague. After the Soviet Union invaded Czechoslovakia in 1968, Meller was a refugee in Austria and Italy before emigrating to the United States. In December 1969, he obtained an entry-level job at CBS Records in New York, and later received training in audio mastering. He worked with Sony/CBS for 38 years, and then joined Universal Mastering Studios in 2007 as senior mastering engineer. He later spent a short time at Masterdisk, then relocated to Charleston, South Carolina where he opened his own facility, Vlado Meller Mastering, in 2014. Albums engineered by Meller have been nominated for seven Grammy Awards and have won two Latin Grammy Awards.

Rudolf Glenn Minarik (1907–1993), b. Cleveland, OH, of Slovak descent, was a mechanical engineer. He was a professor of mechanical engineering at Syracuse University (1943–45), and president of The Integral Engineering Services Co. (s. 1947).

Jozef Murgaš (1864–1929), b. Tajov, Slovakia, was a Slovak inventor, architect, botanist, painter, and Roman Catholic priest. He contributed to radio development, which at the time was commonly known as "wireless telegraphy." Murgaš was nicknamed the Radio Priest and deemed a Renaissance man. From his youth he was bright, skillful and good at painting and electrotechnology. Due to permanent conflicts with the bishop's secretary, Rev. Murgaš had to emigrate to the United States in 1896, where he was assigned a Slovak parish in the city of Wilkes-Barre, Pennsylvania. Having no possibility for painting, he started to deal with natural sciences again, especially electrotechnology. He established a laboratory in Wilkes-Barre, in which he primarily investigated radiotelegraphy. His article in the *Tovaryšstvo* magazine of 1900 shows that his radiotelegraphy studies had achieved a high level. In 1904, he received his first two US patents: the Apparatus for wireless telegraphy and the way of transmitted messages by wireless telegraphy. Fifteen additional patents followed between 1907 and 1916. Based on the first two patents, he created the Universal Aether Telegraph Co., which organized a public test of Murgaš's transmitting and receiving facilities in September 1905.

XI. TECHNOLOGY

Frederick George Novy (1864-1951), b. Chicago, IL, of Czech ancestry, a bacteriologist, was an inventor of Novy jar and other laboratory equipment.

John Oster (1891-1963), b. Červenka, Czech., a manufacturer in Racine, WI, was an inventor of the Osterizer blender.

Frank Pařízek (1880-d.), b. Bohemia, a manufacturer, invented superior automobile wind shields which were manufactured by his Universal Wind Shield Co. in Chicago. He was also the inventor of the Illinois automotive wind-shield hinge for use on limousines, coupes, and automobile trucks. The superiority of this device had gained the inventor a national reputation.

Vladimír S. Pavlečka (1901-1980), b. Charvatce, Bohemia, developed a wind motor rotor having substantially constant pressure and relative velocity for airflow there through, i.e., a method of generating power from wind providing a turbine in an airstream with the turbine having a rotor with a plurality of blades and a stator with a plurality of blades upstream of the rotor.

John Valentine Pliška (1879-1956), b. Týn, Moravia, was a mechanical genius who made and flew first locally owned aircraft. He came with parents to Texas, and after 1903 followed the blacksmith trade in Midland. He built (1912) and flew at intervals up to 15 minutes an airplane of his own invention (plane now in museum at Midland-Odessa air terminal). Pliska was a master blacksmith. Gen. John J. Pershing had US Army horses shod here during border trouble prior to World War I. Branding irons for a large west Texas area were also made there.

Elizabeth Podlaha-Murphy (née Podlaha) (1964-), a native of New York, NY, of Czech ancestry, was an engineer. She studied chemical engineering at Univ. of Connecticut, Storrs (B.S., 1986) and at Columbia Univ. (Ph.D., 1992). She is a professor of interior chemical engineering at Northeastern Univ., Boston, MA (2007-present) with expertise in electrochemical phenomena. She was formerly employed at Louisiana State Univ. (LSU) as an assistant and tenured associate professor in chemical engineering (1998-2007) and completed a postdoctoral appointment at the Ecole Polytechnique Fédérale de Lausanne, Department of Materials Science, Lausanne, Switzerland. As part of NSF, DOE, and DARPA-funded projects, Podlaha has directed research in the development and discovery of electrodeposited alloys and composite thin films and nanostructured materials. Applications of these materials are diverse, spanning from everyday uses, such as to improve corrosion resistance films for surface finishers, to high tech adaptation of nanowires for biosensors. Podlaha's research lab has helped over 25 students complete their graduate degrees and has had over 20 undergraduate students participate in electrochemical research. She has been the recipient of the noteworthy NSF-Career award and the LSU Alumni Association Faculty Excellence Award. She has authored or co-authored over 60 reviewed journal papers, 1 book chapter and 20 proceedings papers. She is married to mechanical engineer Michael C. Murphy (1955–).

Emil Podlesak (1875–1962), b. Exeter, NE, of Czech ancestry, was nicknamed 'Tesla' after Nicola Tesla, the electrical wizard of that time whose electrical inventions were recognized for their brilliance and practicality. He and his brother were constantly experimenting with homemade gadgets and on their farm, they wired several buildings in order for them to transmit sound and to be heard over the wire some distance from the speaker. This continued experimentation with electricity resulted in the brothers perfecting a gadget that developed the 'make and break' spark used in the Webster magnet and spark plug which led to the breakthrough in developing the internal combustion engine used even now. Emil also designed and supervised the construction of the barge and conduit used in the Kingsley Dam which reduced greatly the cost of the dam. He was always inspired to attempt what was considered impossible. He was among the twenty men cited by the U.S. Government for his electronic development for the Navy during World War I. During World War II he worked as a designer, draftsman and consultant in Toledo, Ohio to improve the Willy's jeep, enabling it to travel and start in water beyond the jeep's depth.

Thomas G. Polanyi (1918–2007), b. of Slovak grandfather, in US s. 1943, was a physicist, inventor, residing in Bolkon, MA. He patented a carbon dioxide surgical laser system. A micro-surgical laser system wherein a carbon dioxide (CO_2) laser is fixedly attached to the freely positionable combination of an operation or surgical microscope and a stereo laser endoscope. This arrangement completely eliminates the need for a bulky and/or complex laser-beam-guiding articulated arm apparatus. The laser features novel and light-weight construction, and novel means for heat exchanging.

Svante Procházka (1928–), b. Prague, Czech., a chemist, is an inventor and a holder of a number of patents.

Václav Rejsek (1874–1962), b. Dneboh, Bohemia, came to U.S. in 1904 and settled in New York, in 1905, invented a self-packing cigarette machine and, to introduce his invention, he traveled throughout the world. He was editor of *Volné Listy*, a semimonthly radical newspaper for 25 years. In 1947, he returned to Czechoslovakia.

Edward Rondthaler (1905–2009), b. Bethlehem, PA, of Moravian ancestry, was a typographer, as well as a simplified spelling champion, and chairman of the American Literacy Council. He received his first small printing press at the age of 5, thus starting his career in the graphic arts. Working in New York in the 1930s, he associated with Harold

Horman of the Rutherford Machinery Co. Together they adapted a step-and-repeat machine (for texture and metal printing) for photographic lettering, and in 1936 founded Photo Lettering Inc. In 1969, Rondthaler associated with Aaron Burns and Herb Lubalin in founding the International Typeface Corporation. For several decades, ITC furnished manufacturers of photographic, electronic and laser equipment, a plethora of superb typefaces. In later life, Rondthaler became interested in promoting the spelling reform of the English language as a means of fighting illiteracy. He was also an avid historian.

Nathan Rosewater (1854-1926), b. Buchovany, Bohemia, a pharmacist by training, developed and published many formulae for Vaseline preparations, some of which were exhibited at the Paris Exposition of 1889 and won prizes there. He also perfected mineral oil for general use. As a chief chemist at New York Hospital, he invented the first antiseptic surgical dressings to be used in the US. He later invented and patented a percolator for making extracts from herbs, a device which bears his name and is still used by pharmacists all over the world.

Emanuel A. Salma (1908-1989), b. US, of Slovak descent, was a mechanical engineer. He served as Associate Dean of the College of Engineering and Science at New York University.

Franz Charles Schmelkes (1899-1942), b. Prague, Bohemia, a chemist, was best known for his discovery of azochloramid, used to sterilize wounds and burns. This compound is also known by the name chlorazodin, but its formal name is 1-(amino-chloroimino-methyl) imino-2-chloro-guanidine.

Peter C. Schultz (1942-), b. New York, NY, of Czech ancestry on his mother's side, is known for being the co-inventor of the optical fiber. In 1972, Dr. Schultz and his colleagues at Corning made the discovery and invention of the optical fiber. Since then, the invention has had a major impact on the world of telecommunications, including making the high-speed data transmission capability of the internet possible. Today's fiber optic cables can send 65,000 times as much data over a similar sized copper cable. Dr. Schultz was inducted into the Inventors Hall of Fame in 1993 and received the National Medal of Technology in 2000.

Paul Schwarzkopf (1886-1970), b. Prague, Bohemia, developed physical purification method for molybdenum based on distillation of the volatile molybdenum oxide which he patented in 1927. He also developed the multi carbide tool materials (1929) which revolutionized machining technique by permitting the high-speed machining of steel. He also developed copper filtrated iron and steel and initiated and directed research which led to development of refractory borides for service at extremely high temperatures.

Karel Jan Staller (1896–1975), b. Velká Biteš, Moravia, an engineer trained at Czech Technical Univ. was associated with Zbrojovka, Brno, rising to the level of gen. director in 1939. After the communist takeover in 1948, he fled the country and, in 1951, immigrated to the US. He was first employed at Wright Air Force Base and later at ITT, Nutley, NJ. While still in Zbrojovka, he was responsible for perfecting the famous machine gun BREN-GUN. He owned some 150 patents.

Sigmund Strauss (1875–1942), b. Znojmo, Moravia, participated in the invention of the radio amplifier tube and is credited for inventing the feedback. Both inventions were fundamental in the development of the European radio industry. He also developed medical instruments including the so called mecapion, an integrating measuring device for the medical application of X rays and the so called cardiotron which indicates the respiration, blood pressure and pulse frequency of a patient during an operation. After coming to the US, he obtained a patent for a new X ray apparatus to make photographic images of the movement in the human body.

Robert Anthony Suczek (1883–1955), b. Vsetín, Moravia, invented and designed the radojet ejector type vacuum pump, the first of its kind for use in the US Navy and Merchant Marine 1917 through 1940. He also did considerable work in research and design of hydraulic torque converters. During his career, he received more than 200 US patents including patents for radojet pump, independent wheel suspensions for vehicles and universal joints. He was awarded the Edward Longreth Medal of Merit by the Franklin Institute in 1920 for his invention of the radojet pump.

Michael Sveda (1912–1990), b. West Ashford, CT, of Czech immigrant parents, a chemist, was a discoverer of cyclamates, an artificial noncaloric sweetener that was widely used in diet soft drinks and desserts before being banned by the Department of Health, Education, and Welfare as a possible carcinogen in 1969. He also invented method for production of pyrosulfyl chloride, thionyl chloride, vapor phase sulfonation hydrocarbons, with sulphur trioxide, method for separating two forms of DDT, first polymerization of silicon.

Frank Toepfer (orig. Franz Hrncir) (1845–1902), b. Sázava, Bohemia, was a Czech American machinist, engineer, and businessman in Milwaukee, Wisconsin. He constructed two self-powered carriages before being involved in making the first gasoline-driven vehicle in the United States. He immigrated to the US at 22 in 1867. Milwaukee dentist Christian Linger in 1889 ordered two hand propelled "horseless carriages" from Toepfer to build at his machine shop at 460 National Avenue on the south side of the city. The reason Linger wanted such a vehicle was to attract attention to be able to sell a medical ointment he manufactured. Toepfer, part owner and a machinist at the shop, designed and constructed the vehicles. One of the carriages was pumped like a railway handcar for its forward locomotion power and another one was powered by a person that rocked back and forth on a movable chair mechanism built on a horseless carriage and that was mechanically attached to a crankshaft device that was linked to the wheels of a carriage for its propulsion. The hand-powered vehicles were successful and the dentist became known as the "Penny Doctor" when he would throw out pennies as he traveled along on the streets in his vehicles to attract attention. Toepfer then worked with Gottfried Schloemer, a coppersmith at the shop, in constructing a horseless carriage that would have a gasoline engine to power it, making it the first gas driven vehicle in the United States.

Hans Tropsch (1889–1935), b. Plana, Bohemia, chemist, along with Franz Fischer, was responsible for the development of the Fischer-Tropsch process. It is a collection of chemical reactions that converts a mixture of carbon monoxide and hydrogen into liquid hydrocarbons. The process, a key component of gas to liquids technology, produces a synthetic lubrication oil and synthetic fuel, typically from coal, natural gas, or biomass. The Fischer-Tropsch process has received intermittent attention as a source of low-sulfur diesel fuel and to address the supply or cost of petroleum-derived hydrocarbons.

Arthur Uhlir, Jr. (1926–2016), b. Chicago, IL, of Czech ancestry, a physicist and electrical engineer, was a discoverer of porous silicon. After high school he earned his bachelor's degree, and while working at the Armour Research Foundation, his master's degree, both from the Illinois Institute of Technology in chemical engineering. He then completed his education at the University of Chicago with another master's degree and a Ph.D. degree in physics. Arthur then joined the staff of Bell Laboratories in Murray Hill, New Jersey after which he became the Director of Research at Microwave Associates. In 1970, Arthur began his academic career when he joined the Tufts University faculty as the chairman of electrical engineering. He was a fixture at Tufts for over twenty years where he served as Dean of the College from 1973 through 1980. He was an innovative educator, an active researcher, and a model mentor to both the student body and faculty.

Bohumil Vančo (1907–1990), b. Madunice, Slovakia, was a writer, photographer and psychologist. He immigrated to Brazil and resided in Sao Paulo. In 1964, he moved to the US. He worked in optics and photography, areas in which he received several patents for his inventions. He was the inventor of stereoscopy.

Theodore von Kármán (1881–1963), b. Budapest, Hungary, son of Helen Kohn (1853–1941) of Bohemian descent, and Moriz Kármán (orig. Kleinmann), was an aerospace engineer, physicist and mathematician, who was active primarily in the fields of aeronautics and astronautics. He is responsible for many key advances in aerodynamics, notably his work on supersonic and hypersonic airflow characterization. He is regarded as the outstanding aerodynamic theoretician of the twentieth century. He received a Ph.D. in engineering at the University of Göttingen in Germany in 1908. Von Kármán worked in a variety of academic posts, was in the Austro-Hungarian Army during World War I, worked in private industry doing research, and built a world-renowned reputation by lecturing extensively in various countries. He was invited to the United States by Robert A. Millikan to advise California Institute of Technology (Caltech) engineers on the design of a wind tunnel. After the wind tunnel was completed in 1928, von Kármán stayed on to join Caltech's newly established Guggenheim Aeronautical Laboratory (GALCIT). In 1930, he became Director of GALCIT. In 1942, von Kármán and five other scientists formed Aerojet Engineering Corporation, to accept contracts for building jet engines. In 1949, he resigned from Caltech and JPL to work at the Pentagon where he chaired the Air Force Scientific Advisory Board until 1954. In March 1952, he became the chair of the NATO Advisory Group for Aeronautical Research and Development (AGARD). In 1954, he received the Astronautics Engineer Achievement Award and in 1960, he received the Goddard Memorial Medal for liquid rocket work. In 1963, President John F. Kennedy presented him with the first National Medal of Science.

Philip Van Horn Weems (1889–1979), b. TN, desc. f. Frederick Philipse, internationally known air navigator, before the invention of the GPS, Weems modernized the art of celestial navigation by simplifying techniques and inventing time saving methods. He attended Walnut Grove Country School in Montgomery County and Branham and Hughes School in Spring Hill before receiving an appointment to the U.S. Naval Academy at Annapolis in 1908. He graduated in 1912 and was commissioned an ensign in the U.S. Navy. In 1927, Weems served with the Aircraft Squadron Battle Fleet, began research in air navigation, and published *Line of Position Book*. From 1928 to 1930, he served as executive officer on USS *Cuyama* and wrote the textbook *Air Navigation* (1931), which received international acclaim and won a gold medal awarded by the Aero Club of France. In addition to his military career, Weems established with his wife the Weems School of Navigation (1927). He perfected his air navigation system by simplifying the method of determining latitude and longitude by aerial observations, improving sextants, and adapting chronometers to air use. He taught air navigation to Charles Lindbergh and assisted in the aviator's global flight to determine commercial airways for Pan American Airways. In 1933, Weems went on the naval retired list and devoted his energies to further perfecting his navigation system. That year he designed the first Air Almanac. Two years later, he patented the Mark II Plotter and published *Marine Navigation* and *Star Altitude Curves*.

Howard Lawrence Wenberger (1927-2009), b. New York city, of Slovak descent, attended Townsend-Harris High School, NYC and Columbia University. He developed missile systems and communication satellites for Hughes Aircraft. Sailed with Fairwind Yacht Club in Marina del Rey, and, an avid cycler, took many bicycle trips in the US, and overseas. Together with his wife Maureen traveled to the "ends of the earth" enjoying many parts of France, the Silk Road, as well as Japan, China, Australia and many other countries.

Lewis Weiner (1910-2003), b. Klatovy, Bohemia, a mechanical engineer by avocation, was a holder of over 30 patents in dye casting, packaging, shuttles loom, slider assembly machines, zipper, chain machines, film projection and film camera.

Arnold Weissberger (1898-1984), b. Chemnitz, Saxony, of Bohemian ancestry, a chemist, formulated and developed many of the organic compounds used in the color process photography, and was holder of more than 100 US and foreign patents.

Alexander Jay Wurts (1862-1932), b. Carbondale, PA, desc. f. F. Philipse, a mechanical and electrical engineer, was a discoverer of nonarcing metals.

Paul C. Zamecnik (1912-2009), b. Cleveland, OH, of Bohemian ancestry, a medical researcher, was a co-discovered tRNA, and was later credited as the inventor of antisense therapeutics. Zamecnik earned over a dozen US patents for his therapeutic techniques.

John Zeleny (1897-1945), b. Racine, WI, of Czech ancestry, a physicist, invented the Zeleny electroscope.

C. Computing

Franz Leopold Alt (1910-2011), b. Vienna, of Moravian ancestry, was trained at Univ. of Vienna as a mathematician. He was with National Bureau of Standards (1948-67); dept. dir. of information div., Am. Inst. of Physics (s. 1967). He was a specialist on numerical computation, using high speed computing devices, information retrieval, statistical methods of business forecasting, foundations of geometry. He is best known as one of the founders of the Association for Computing Machinery, having served as its president from 1950 to 1952; he also wrote one of the first books on digital computers, *Electronic Digital Computers* (1958).

Robert C. Bedichek (1958-), b. US, of Bohemian ancestry, holds a Ph.D. in computer science and engineering, University of Washington, and a Master's and B.A. in computer science from Cornell University. Currently he is vice president of engineering at Transmeta Corp. He has 30 years of software, hardware, and architectural design experience. He was formerly VP of engineering at VaST Systems Technologies, a Fellow at Advanced Micro

Devices, director of Software Products at Transmeta Corporation, a researcher in MIT's Computer Architecture Group, a computer architect at Intel Corporation, as well as doing extensive work in embedded systems. He developed high speed simulation techniques in the 1980's that were widely used by the mid-1990's by many processor design companies. His work at AMD included managing the logic design, architecture, and performance modeling teams for the AMD Opteron/Athlon (also known as the "K8").

George Albert Bekey (1928–), b. Bratislava, Czech., was originally named Juraj, but after the family moved to Prague, his name was changed to Jiří. In 1939, the family moved to Bolivia and in 1945 to Los Angeles. He received training in electrical engineering at Univ. of California, Berkley (B.S., 1950) and in in engineering at Univ. of California, Los Angeles (Ph.D., 1962). He is professor emeritus of computer science, electrical engineering and biomedical engineering at the University of Southern California, research scholar and adjunct professor of biomedical engineering, California Polytechnic State University, San Luis Obispo, CA. He specializes in human robot interaction, robot ethics, medical and rehabilitation robotics. Dr. George A. Bekey's career of more than 40 years has significantly advanced the art of robotics and automation. His groundbreaking research and teaching in biomedical engineering, robotics and system identification have greatly influenced the direction of such areas as humanoid development, human-robot interaction, and coordination and control of multiple robots. He is a member of the National Academy of Engineering and a Fellow in various professional societies. Bekey is best known for his achievements across multiple technical fields, for which he was designated a USC University Professor, which honors the university's most accomplished, multi-disciplinary faculty.

Miroslav Benda (1944–), b. Uherské Hradiště, Czech., was trained at Univ. of Wisconsin as mathematician and computer scientist (M.A., 1969; Ph.D., 1970). He was asst. professor of mathematics at Univ. of Washington, Seattle (1972-80), before joining Boeing Computer Service in Seattle as a modeling analyst (1980-99). He has then served as a sr. research Fellow at Innovation Creativity & Capital Ints., University of Texas (s. 2007). He is a specialist on theory of models, optimization, and computer simulation.

Joyce Arlene Bischoff (1938–), b. Chicago, IL, of Czech ancestry, studied mathematics at IL Inst. of Technology (B.S., 1959). She became a programmer and analyst with Inst. of Gas Technology, Chicago (1959-60) and then was employed by the Univ. of Ghent, Belgium (1960-61). After raising two children, she went back to school, to the Univ. of Delaware between 1977 and 1979 to become updated in the computer field and completed a Certificate in Computer Technology at the University of Delaware in 1979 and returned to the work force. She became database administrator, Med. Center Delaware, Wilmington (1979-84); then sr. database administrator, ICI Ams, Wilmington (1984-87); and sr. consultant with CSC

Printers, Malvern, PA (1987-90). Afterwards she opened her own firm, Bischoff Co., Inc., Hockessin, DE (s. 1990), of which she is president. From 1997-99, she was an Executive Consultant with IBM and from 1999-2001, she was Vice President of First USA Bank (which became Chase Bank). She then went back to her own consulting business, Bischoff Consulting, Inc. She is an internationally known author, lecturer, and consultant in the field of data warehousing, now called Big Data. She is a contributing author to the *Handbook of Data Management* (1993), and the lead author *of Data Warehouse: Practical Advice from the Experts* (1997), and co-author of *Impossible Data Warehouse Situations with Solutions from the Experts* (2003). Since she retired, she has been very active in the University of Delaware's Osher Lifelong Learning Institute. She has taught classes there in genealogy and also initiated a course in 'Creating Your Family History' that she has taught several times.

Lubomír Blažek (1933-), b. Prague, Czech., was trained at Charles Univ. He has been on technical staff of International Planning, AT&T Bell Labs., Holmdel, NJ. He is specialist on computer technology, operations research, telecommunications traffic engineering and network planning.

Daniel Brand (1949-), b. Prague, Czech., studied mathematics and physics at Charles Univ. (dipl., 1968) and computer science at Univ. of Toronto (B.Sc., 1972; M.Sc., 1973; Ph.D., 1976). He has been associated, as a research staff member, with the IBM T.J. Watson Research, in New York City area (s. 1976). His experience includes being a research staff member of IBM Rueschlikon Res. Lab. (1979-80); visiting researcher at Beijing Inst. of Aeronautics and Astronautics (1982); and visiting researcher at Kyushu Inst. of Technology (1990). He works in the area of research and development of design tools for both software and hardware, his specialties being: software correctness, algorithms for analysis, and interaction with users.

Václav 'Vašek' Chvátal (1946-), b. Prague, Czech., was educated in mathematics at Charles University in Prague. He completed his Ph.D. in mathematics at the University of Waterloo, in only one year. Subsequently, he took positions at McGill University, the Université de Montréal, Stanford University, and Rutgers University, where he remained for 18 years before returning to Canada for his position at Concordia Univ., Montreal. There he is a professor in the Department of Computer Science and Software Engineering, in addition to holding the Canada Research Chair in Combinatorial Optimization. Chvátal has published extensively on topics in graph theory, combinatorics, and combinatorial optimization. While at Rutgers, Chvátal, in 1988, received the Alexander von Humboldt Distinguished Senior Scientist Award and, in 2000, the Beale-Orchard-Hays Prize for Excellence in Computational Mathematical Programming.

Karel Čulík (1926–2002), b. Skalice, Czech., studied mathematics at Charles Univ. (dipl. 1953) and computer science at Masaryk Univ., Brno (CSc./Ph.D., 1956). After some political difficulties, he eventually was named professor at Charles Univ. In 1976, he was allowed to leave for the US. He taught for a year at Univ. of Massachusetts, Amherst; two years at Penn State Univ., before his appointment as professor at Wayne State Univ. (s. 1979). He remained in that position until 1986 when he suffered a stroke. His research interests were in the area of formal languages and automata theory parallel computing, cellular automata, image generation, compression and manipulation.

Karel Čulík II (1934–), b. Prague, Czech., was trained as a theoretical computer scientist at Charles Univ. (dipl., 1957; RNDr., 1967) and at ČSAV (CSc./Ph.D., 1966). He has been associated with the Univ. of Waterloo, Can., where he advanced from asst. professor to professor (1969–87); with Univ. of South Carolina, as professor of computer science (s. 1987). His interests are in the area of decomposition of automata and note on their analysis, construction of the automation mapping.

Herman M. Dolezal, b. Prague, Czech, studied at Fordham University (B.S.) and at Stevens Institute of Technology (M.S., Ph.D.) He is an instructional specialist in the dept. of computer science at Montclair State Univ., NJ and an adjunct professor in School of Business, St. Thomas Aquinas College, Sparkill, NY.

Frantisek Fiala, b. Czech., received his training in Brno. He was prof. of mathematics, in the Computer Science Dept. at Carleton Univ. He was also associate director and undergraduate adviser of the dept. He was co-editor of *Lecture Notes in Computer Science* (1987).

František Franěk (1947–), b. Prague, Czech., after initial political problems in communist Czechoslovakia, he was allowed to complete his studies in theoretical cybernetics at Charles Univ. (RNDr., 1976). After being asked to join the Communist Party in 1977, rather than joining the Party, he and his wife defected to Canada. There he worked as a computer programmer at Zurich Insurance Co. till January 1979, when he started a doctoral program in pure mathematics in the dept. of mathematics at University of Toronto (Ph.D., 1983). Subsequently, he accepted a prestigious two-year position as 'Wesley Young Researcher' at the dept. of mathematics and computer science at Dartmouth College (1983–85). During the stay at Dartmouth College, he switched his interests from set theory to computer science and his next position was as an assistant professor of computer science at Columbia University (1985–86). He then decided to return to Canada, where he joined the dept. of computer science at McMaster Univ., as an asst. professor (1986–92), advancing to assoc. professor (1992–98) and full professor of computer science and mathematics (s. 1998). His research interests are in the area of computer science (string algorithms, compilers, databases); combinatorics (design theory, graph theory); and set theory (Boolean algebras, dynamical systems).

Jan Gecsei (1934–), b. Košice, Czech, received his M.Sc. (electrical engineering) and Ph.D. (computer science) degrees from the Czech Technical University in Prague. Until 1966, he worked at the Research Institute for Computers in Prague; then until 1973 at IBM Corp. in San Jose, Cal. From 1974 he is professor of computer science at the Université de Montréal. His main research interests are in the area of distributed multimedia systems, the management of quality of service and computer architecture.

Richard H. Gallagher (1927–1997), b. New York City, of Czech ancestry on his mother's side, was an American civil and structural engineer. He was one of the originators of the finite element method (FEM), an engineering computation technique that is now widely used in the design of aircraft, buildings, and ships, and in the study of electrical phenomena. He also made noteworthy research contributions to computational mechanics, coupled problems, and finite elements in flow problems.

Henry Gladney (1938–), b. Prague, Czech, studied physics and chemistry at Univ. of Toronto (B.A. 1960) and chemical physics at Princeton Univ. (M.A., 1962; Ph.D., 1963). He has been associated with IBM (s. 1963), as tech. asst. to VP (1968–70), manager of research computer facility (1970–72, 1975–79), as manager of chemical dynamics (1972–75), as res. staff, computer science (1979–91, 1991–94), retiring (s. 2000). From 1963 to 1980, he was involved in chemical physics research and computing service management and from 1980 to 2000, he was in computer science research, i.e., large distributed data systems, digital libraries, security, and intellectual property management. His consulting specialties include enterprise digital document management, especially long-term digital preservation, document security, authenticity, trust, from strategic business assessment to bit-level software design, and intellectual property law and management. He published some 80 papers and is holder of 11 patents. He was elected American Physical Society Fellow in 1978.

Philip Heidelberger (1951–), b. of Bohemian ancestry, received a Doctorate in operations research from Stanford University. He has been a research staff member at the IBM Thomas J. Watson Research Center since 1978. His research interests include modeling and analysis of computer performance, probabilistic aspects of discrete event simulations, parallel simulation, and parallel computer architectures. Heidelberger has served as editor-in-chief of the *ACM Transactions on Modeling and Computer Simulation*. He is currently the vice president of ACM Sigmetrics.

Randall E. Henzlik (1951–2011), b. Muncie, IN, probably of Czech ancestry, attended Purdue and Northwestern Universities. Randy moved to Chicago in 1970, to start work in the rapidly developing computer industry. Later he worked for RealCom, an IBM Company in Chicago. From 1985-1992, Randall served as President of the Chicago-based Henzlik Institute of Cognitive Development working with Dr. Wilma B. Henzlik. The institute specialized in cultivating intelligence in young children and presented seminars at Elmhurst College and Barat College in Lake Forest. At the time of his death, he was the managing partner and a trading system developer at Chicago Market Science Group, LLC. He was an entrepreneur and a self-taught scholar, but a tenacious researcher into investment market dynamics (thus the "market science" in the business name).

Hynek Heřmanský (1946-), b. Nové Město na Moravě, Czech., received his electrical engineering training at Brno Univ. of Technology and at Univ. of Tokyo. He was with Oregon Grad. Institute of Science and Tech., Beaverton (s. 1993), as prof. (1995-2003); as prof. at Swiss Fed. Inst. of Technology (2003-05). Since 2008, he has been with Johns Hopkins Univ., where he holds the position of the Julian S. Smith Professor of the Electrical and Computer Engineering and the Director of the Center for Language and Speech Processing. His current research aims at a design and development of systems that would reliably detect, identify, classify, and transmit information in speech.

Natalie Hruska (1975-), b. Phoenix, AZ, of Czech ancestry, received her training in information technology at Capella Univ. (M.S., 2006) and management at Walden Univ. (Ph.D., 2012). She has been associated with the Design and Interactive Media Faculty at the Art Inst. of Pittsburgh OnLine Div. (s. 2006). Her specialty is the use of the Internet and World Wide Web to meet important social needs in areas like education, employment, and health.

Devlin J. Hyna (1972-), b. Chicago, of Czech ancestry, studied computer science (B.S., 2000; M.S., 2010) and linguistics (M.A., 2006), all at Northeastern Illinois Univ., Chicago. He has been associated with Northeastern Illinois Univ., as an information systems specialist (s. 2001) and computer science instructor (s. 2010). His professional interests are in database development and administration. His research and teaching interests are in computer programming.

Paul Janecek (ca. 1967-), b. possibly of Czech ancestry, graduated from West Point in electrical engineering (B.Sc., 1989) and studied computer science at Univ. of London (M.Sc., 1996) and at Swiss Federal Inst. of Technology (EPFL) (Ph.D., 2004). He was asst. professor at Asian Inst. of Technology (2005-11) and then chief architect with Spyglass Technologies, Inc. (2011-13). Currently he is the founder and CEO of Thin Blu Data, based in Thailand (s. 2012).

Frederick Jelínek (1932-2010), b. Kladno, Czech., was a pioneer of statistical methods in computational linguistics. His research focus was on information theory, automatic speech recognition, and natural language processing. He studied engineering at the Massachusetts Institute of Technology (S.B., 1956; S.M., 1958; Ph.D., 1962) and taught for 10 years at Cornell University before being offered a job at IBM Research. There his team essentially revolutionized approaches to computer speech recognition and machine translation. After IBM, he went to head the Center for Language and Speech Processing at Johns Hopkins University for 17 years.

Christopher 'Chris' A. Kadlec (1966–), from Oxford, MS, of Bohemian ancestry, received his Bachelor of Science from the University of Mississippi. After graduation, he implemented a computer helpdesk at the University of Mississippi, supporting desktop computing for the campus (1994–96). He accepted a position at the University of Georgia, supporting the Terry College of Business in their computing needs (1996–2000). He was technical lead for a distance learning MBA program when he began work on a Ph.D. (dipl., 2000). Currently, he holds the position of assoc. professor in the dept. of information technology at Georgia Southern Univ., Statesboro, GA (s. 2007). His research interests are in the area of technology mediated learning, end-user and IS professional training, network security/disaster recovery, collaboration technology and telecommunication database management.

Kevin Karplus (1954–), b. Chicago, IL, of Moravian ancestry, studied mathematics at Michigan State Univ. (B.S., 1974) and at Stanford Univ. (M.S., 1976). He then pursued his studies in computer science, also at Stanford Univ. (Ph.D., 1983). He was asst. professor of computer science and electrical engineering at Cornell Univ. (1982–86), before joining Univ. of California, Santa Cruz (s. 1986), as asst. professor of computer engineering (1986–93), as assoc. professor (1993–2000) and as professor (2000–04), as professor of biomolecular engineering (s. 2004). His specialties included computer science, bioinformatics, and protein-structure prediction. He is probably best known for work he did as a computer science graduate student at Stanford University on the Karplus-Strong string synthesis algorithm. He taught VLSI design and computer engineering for several years, helping create the Computer Engineering Department at University of California, Santa Cruz. He made some contributions to VLSI CAD, particularly to logic minimization, where he invented the if-then-else DAG (a generalization of the binary decision diagram) and a canonical form for it, before changing to protein structure prediction and bioinformatics in 1995. He has participated in CASP (Critical Assessment of Techniques for Protein Structure Prediction) since CASP2 in 1996. He served on the Board of Directors for the International Society for Computational Biology (2005–11).

Ladislav Kavan (1980–), b. Prague, Czech., received training in computer science at Charles Univ. (Mgr., 2003) and the Czech Technical Univ., Prague (Ph.D., 2007). After his fellowship at the Trinity Coll., Dublin (2007–09), he became research scientist at Disney Interactive Studios,

Salt Lake City (2009-11), and then senior research scientist at ETH Zürich, Switzerland (2011-12). Subsequently, he joined the Univ. of Pennsylvania as an asst. professor (s. 2013). His research interests include: computer graphics and animation, deformation modeling, medical applications, numerical methods, physics-based simulation, combining data and physics, applied geometry, real-time rendering. He has been associate editor for ACM Transactions on Graphics (s. 2013) and Graphical Models (s. 2012).

George J. Klir (1932-2016), b. Prague, Czech., received his diploma in electrical engineering from the Czech Technical University in Prague in 1957 and Ph.D. degree in computer engineering from ČSAV in 1964. He is also a graduate of the IBM System Research Institute in 1969. After immigrating to the United States in 1966, he held academic positions at UCLA (1966-68), Fairleigh Dickinson University (1968-69), and the State University of New York at Binghamton (1969-2008), where he served as chairman of the Department of Systems Science (1978-94) and director of the Center for Intelligent Systems (1994-2000). He retired in 2008. He has also worked part time for IBM, Sandia Laboratories, Bell Laboratories, and Canadian Government, and taught summer courses at the University of Colorado, Portland State University in Oregon, and Rutgers University. During the earlier stages of his professional career, Dr. Klir conducted research in the areas of systems theory, systems modeling and simulation, computer architecture and design, and discrete mathematics. His current research interests include the areas of generalized theories of uncertainty and information (including the various theories of imprecise probabilities), soft computing and intelligent systems, fuzzy set theory and fuzzy logic, and generalized measure theory. He is the author of well over three hundred research papers, holds a number of patents, and is an author or co-author of 19 books. Dr. Klir has been editor-in-chief of the *International Journal of General Systems* since 1974 and the *International Book Series on Systems Science and Engineering* (Springer) since 1985. He was president of the Society for General Systems Research (SGSR) (1981-82), the founding president of the International Federation for Systems Research (IFSR) (1980-84), president of the North American Fuzzy Information Processing Society (NAFIPS) (1988-1991), and president of the International Fuzzy Systems Association (IFSA) (1993-1995).

Alfred Kobsa (1956-), b. Linz, of Moravian ancestry, received training in computer science at Univ. of Linz (M.S., 1981; Ph.D., 1985). He was associated with Univ. of Vienna (1982-84), Univ. of Saarbrucken (1985-91); and then became assoc. professor in the dept, of computer science at the Univ. of Konstanz (1991-95). He then joined Univ. of Essen as professor in the dept. of computer science (1995-2000). After moving to the US, he accepted the position of assoc. professor at Univ. of California, Irvine (2000-03), advancing to full professor (s. 2003). He had several visiting professorship appointments in between. Alfred Kobsa is a professor in the Donald Bren School of Information and

Computer Sciences. His research lies in the areas of user modeling and personalized systems, privacy, and support for personal health maintenance. He is the editor of *User Modeling and User-Adapted Interaction: The Journal of Personalization Research*, and edited several books and authored numerous publications in the areas of user-adaptive systems, privacy, human-computer interaction and knowledge representation.

Ladislav J. Kohout (1941–2009), b. Prague, Czech., studied electrical engineering at the Czech Technical Univ. (M.S.E.E., 1963). After graduation, he worked for 5 years as an interdisciplinary researcher at ČSAV in Prague. When Czechoslovakia was invaded by the Soviet Union in 1968, he managed to escape. For several years, he worked in the areas of medical computing and bioengineering at the Medical School of the Univ. of London and, at the same time, he pursued Doctoral studies in the area of man-machine studies at the Univ. of Essex in Colchester (Ph.D., 1978). He then joined the Dept. of Computer Science at Brunel Univ. in West London, as a lecturer, and then as a reader. In 1988, he immigrated to the US and joined the Florida State Univ. Tallahassee as professor of computer science. He remained there until his untimely death in 2009. Professor Kohout was internationally recognized as one of the major contributors in fuzzy sets, in particular in theory and applications of crisp and fuzzy relations. BK-relational products, which he co-invented with Wyllis Bandler, play a major role in development of relational computational methods in the field of intelligent systems and elsewhere.

Miloš Konopásek (1931–2002), b. Pardubice, Czech., was a mechanical engineer best known as the creator of TK!Solver, an iterative, constraint-based declarative environment for the numerical solution of systems of equations. He graduated from the Leningrad Textile Institute, Leningrad, USSR, and received the Ph.D. and D.Sc. degrees from the University of Manchester, England. His career included management, research, and teaching positions in Czechoslovakia, United Kingdom, and the United States, including the Georgia Institute of Technology and North Carolina State University. At Manchester in the late 1960s and early 1970s, he developed a system called 'Question Answering System on mathematical models' (QAS). He expected his system to be used by a broad range of non-computer professionals and non-mathematicians who apply math to their fields. Konopasek recognized that the new personal computer was an ideal vehicle for bringing his concept to the masses and developed a version of his system for them in 1977. In 1982, Software Arts commercialized TK!Solver based on his work. Konopasek was senior scientist at Software Arts while holding a visiting faculty position in the Department of Mechanical Engineering at M.I.T. When TK!Solver was sold to Universal Technical Systems (Rockford, Illinois), he continued as vice president of UTS. Most of his research interests and contributions were in textile engineering, applied mechanics, operations research, and computer science, in areas as diverse as CAD/CAM, large deflection analysis of slender bodies, topology of line structures, and language design. Konopasek was a member of the ACM and the IEEE Computer Society.

Danny Kopec (1954–) b. Kfar Saba, Israel, of Czechoslovak ancestry, received Ph.D. in machine intelligence at Edinburgh Univ. He was associated with Univ. of Maine as asst. prof. (1986–92); assoc. prof. of computer science, US Coast Guard Academy (1993–96); sr. lect. at Am. International Univ. in London (1997–99); and presently holds the position of assoc. prof. at Brooklyn Coll. (s. 1999). His areas of specialization include: artificial intelligence, cognitive science, knowledge representation, problem solving methods, interactive teaching and learning systems and computer science education.

Sandra Kopecky (1966–), b. New York, NY, of Czech ancestry, was trained in computer science at New York Inst. of Technology (B.S., 1988; M.S., 2011). As part of her work on Master's degree, Sandra was among a handful of students, who were working on Motorola's Golden-i, the world's first hands-free wireless headset computer. Golden-i puts just under the user's eye a tiny screen that gives the equivalent of a 15-inch adjustable display. Sandra worked developing barcode and QR scanner applications for the Golden-i. The applications would help users easily navigate areas and identify items and people associated with a database. She was self-employed, working as a software developer under contract (1997–2002); on staff of Cache Cloud, East Meadow, NY (s. 2012), as an Oracle database administrator (s. 2012); and Big Data Analyst (s. 2014). She has also been on the adjunct faculty of New York Inst. of Technology (s. 2012), teaching undergraduate courses in database management systems.

Lukáš Kroc (1979–), b. Domažlice, Czech., was trained in computer science at Charles Univ. (MSc., 2004) and at Cornell Univ. (Ph.D., 2009) with focus on artificial intelligence techniques. He spent a year as a post-doc at Los Alamos National Laboratory. In 2010, he was awarded a Computing Innovation Fellowship and became a research assistant professor at Claremont Graduate University (CGU), working with Allon Percus at CGU and Jeremy Frank at NASA Ames Research Center. Since 2012, he has been working as a software engineer at Space Exploration Technologies (SpaceX) in Los Angeles, CA.

Miroslav Kubát (1958–), b. Prague, Czech., studied electrical engineering at the Technical University of Brno (dipl., 1982; Ph.D., 1990). He was sr. research Fellow at Univ. of Ottawa (1995–97), before becoming assoc. professor at Univ. of Louisiana, Lafayette (1998–2001). Subsequently, he joined Univ. of Miami, as assoc. professor in the dept. of electrical and computer engineering. He specializes in machine learning, neural network and artificial intelligence. He published more than 100 scientific papers, and co-edited or co-authored three books: *Machine Learning and Data Mining* (1998), *Machines that Learn to Play Games* (2001) and *Induction-Based Approach to Personalized Search Engines* (2009).

George Eric Lasker (1935–), b. Prague, Czech. was trained as a clinical psychologists and a computer scientist at Czech Tech. University and Charles Univ. He was with Univ. of Saskatchewan (1965–66); as assoc. prof. of computer science with Univ. of Manitoba (1966–68); with Univ. of Windsor (s. 1968), as professor of computer science (s. 1972). He is currently IIAS-Distinguished Professor of Psychosomatic Medicine at the International Institute for Advanced Studies in Systems Research and Cybernetics. Dr. Lasker has been editor-in-chief of the IIAS-*International Journal on Systems Research and Cybernetics* and *Acta Systemica* and editor of the International Online IIAS E-Journal on Systems Research.

Ondřej Lhoták (1977–), b. Prague, Czech, was trained in computer science at Univ. of Waterloo (B.Math., 2001) and at McGill Univ.(Ph.D., 2006). His team (with Jeff Shute and Donny Cheung) was the world champion in the ACM International Collegiate Programming Contest in 1999. He was an assistant professor (2006–11) and associate professor (s. 2011) in the Programming Languages Group, David R. Cheriton School of Computer Science, Univ. of Waterloo. Professor Lhoták's research interests are generally in the area of programming languages, compilers, and program analysis, with a specific focus on object-oriented languages. He received the 2013 Outstanding Young Computer Science Researcher Award from the Canadian Association of Computer Science.

Egon Ezriel Loebner (1924–1989), b. Plzeň, Czech., was trained as a physicist at Univ. of Buffalo. He was with RCA Labs. (1955–61); with Hewlett-Packard Co, CA (s. 1961), as head, special projects dept., Solid State Lab (1965–73), as res. adv. (1973–74); with US Embassy, Moscow (1974–76); with Hewlett-Packard Co. (s. 1976), as head, section data base management systems, Computer Research Lab. (1977–81), as head, dept cognitive interface computer science lab., Computer Research Center (1981–). He is a specialist on computer science, system intelligence, solid state, optoelectronic phenomena materials, devices, image sensing, display and processing.

Kurt Maly (1944–), b. Mödling, of Bohemian ancestry, received training in computer science at New York Univ. (Ph.D., 1973). He has been associated with Univ. of Minnesota, starting as asst. professor (1972–78), becoming assoc. professor (1978–85) and head of computer science dept. (1982–85). Subsequently, he joined Old Dominion Univ., Norfolk, VA, as a professor (s. 1985) and chair of Computer Science Dept. (1985–2007), as eminent scholar (s. 1989), as Kaufman Professor (s. 1991). As a co-founder of the OpenArchive Initiative (OAI), he is an expert on harvesting information from the web and taking advantage of the community's interest and willingness to help in furthering dissemination of scientific information. In OAI, he developed a process that started with a serious problem in science, found technical solutions, developed standards and proselytized the community to participate in the collaborative solution.

Jeff Matocha (ca. 1970–), b. possibly of Czech ancestry, studied computer science at Univ. of Central Arkansas (B.S., 1992), Louisiana Tech. Univ. (M.S., 1955) and at Univ. of Alabama (Ph.D., 1998). He joined Ouachita Baptist Univ. (OBU) in 2008, where he now holds the position of assoc. professor of computer science. He teaches all levels of computer science courses and maintains the department's triple-boot iMac lab.

Karel Matouš (ca. 1974–), b. Czech., was trained at the Czech Technical Univ. in the theoretical and applied mechanics (M.S.; Ph.D., 2000). He is an associate professor in the aerospace and mechanical engineering department at the University of Notre Dame. He leads the Computational Physics Team and is the software architect for the Center for Shock Wave-processing of Advanced Reactive that has been established as one of six NNSA's center of Excellence whose primary focus is on the emerging field of predictive science. His research group focuses on computational mechanics and physics, computational science and engineering, computational materials science, advanced numerical methods, microtomography-based computational and experimental modeling of heterogeneous materials, and multiscale/multitime/multiphysics modeling of complex heterogeneous nonlinear materials and systems. He is involved in several interdisciplinary research programs with funding from various agencies and private companies. Dr. Matouš received the Rector's Award for the best Ph.D. students from the Czech Technical University in Prague.

David W Matula (ca. 1937–), b. possibly of Czech ancestry, was trained in engineering science at Univ. of California, Berkeley. Since 1974, he has served as professor of computer science and engineering at SMU. His research focuses on the foundations and applications of algorithm engineering with specific emphasis on computer arithmetic and graph/network algorithms. He has published over one hundred archival publications. Two-thirds of his publications focus on computer arithmetic and have appeared primarily in the IEEE and computer science literature. He holds numerous patents.

Gernot Metze (1930–), b. Šumperk, Czech., is Univ. of Illinois trained electrical engineer and computer scientist. He has been with Univ. of Illinois, Urbana (s. 1959), as res. prof. of electrical engineering (1970–), as prof. emer. of electrical and computer engineering (s. 2001). His res. interests include digital systems design, fault-tolerant computing, sequential machine theory, computer arithmetic.

Hans P. Moravec (1948–), b. Kautzen, of Moravian ancestry, received training in computer science at Stanford Univ. (M.Sc., 1971; Ph.D., 1980). Subsequently, he has been associated with the Carnegie Mellon Univ. (CMU), where he held the position of res. professor and directed the Mobile Robot Lab. He received his Doctorate for a TV-equipped robot, remote controlled by a large computer that negotiated cluttered obstacle courses, taking about five hours. Since 1980, his Mobile Robot Lab at CMU has discovered more effective approaches for robot spatial representation, notably 3D occupancy grids that, with newly available computer power, promise commercial free-ranging mobile robots within a decade. In 2003, he co-founded Seegrid Corp. to undertake this commercialization, while retaining an adjunct professor position at CMU. He is chief scientist of Seegrid Corporation, maker of vision-guided industrial mobile robots. He has been thinking about machines thinking since he was a child in the 1950s, building his first robot, a construct of tin cans, batteries, lights and a motor, at age ten. In high school, he won two science fair prizes for a light-following electronic turtle and a tape-controlled robot hand. As an undergraduate he designed a computer to control fancier robots, and experimented with learning and automatic programming on commercial machines. During his Master's work he built a small robot with whiskers and photoelectric eyes controlled by a minicomputer, and wrote a thesis on a computer language for artificial intelligence. His books, *Mind Children: the Future of Robot and Human Intelligence* (1988), and *Robot: Mere Machine to Transcendent Mind* (1998), consider the implications of evolving robot intelligence. He has also published papers and articles in robotics, computer graphics, multiprocessors, space travel and other speculative areas.

Jiří Navrátil (1971–), b. Hodonín, Czech., studied electrical engineering at the Ilmenau Technical University, Thuringia, Germany (Ing., 1994; Dr. Ing., 1998). He then joined the IBM Thomas J. Watson Research Center, Yorktown Heights, NY, as a member of the Conversational Biometrics Group in the Human Language Technologies Department. He is currently involved in research efforts in the area of statistical question answering (DeepQA). Previously at IBM Jiří worked on machine translation, voice-based authentication technologies, and spoken language recognition technologies. He has published more than 50 conference and journal papers, and filed 15 patent applications. Dr. Navrátil is recipient of the 1999 Johann-Philipp-Reis prize awarded by the German Association for Electrical, Electronic & Information Technologies VDE, the Deutsche Telecom, and the cities of Friedrichsdorf and Gelnhausen, for outstanding contributions to the field of language recognition. He received multiple invention achievement awards and technical group awards from IBM. In 2004–2006, Jiří served as the Watson chair of the User Interface Technologies interest area.

Stephen Nemecek (ca. 1957–), b. Norman, OK, was trained as a computer scientist at Univ. of Louisiana, Lafayette (Ph.D., 1983). He was with Univ. Arkansas, as asst. professor of computer science (1984–91); with Elizabeth City State Univ., Univ. of North Carolina System NC, as assoc. prof., (1991–97); with Univ. Tennessee, as assoc. professor (2000–02); with Southern Univ., Baton Rouge, as assoc. professor (2002–04); besides being consultant for individual firm, such as US Army, Marriott, DOD Health Systems, Environmental Protection

Agency, Kaiser Permanente, America OnLine, etc. Since 2004, he has served as a private consultant, providing services in these areas: computer systems design, feasibility studies, legacy systems evaluation, professional project leadership and management, project evaluation, requirements analysis, software architecture design, software development, test planning and design and training.

Gordon Shaw Novak, Jr. (1948-), b. CO, of Czech ancestry, studied electrical engineering B.S., with highest honors, 1969) and computer sciences (B.A., 1971; Ph.D., 1976), at Univ. of Texas, Austin. He has been associated with Univ. of Texas, Austin, as asst. professor (1978-81, 1983-84), as assoc. professor (1984-98), as full professor (s. 1998); as director of Artificial Intelligence Lab. (1984-99). His areas of interest include automatic programming by reuse of generic algorithms, automatic solution of physics problems, artificial intelligence, compilers, Lisp.

George J. Nožička (1937-), b. Prague, Czech., studied at Catholic Univ. (M.S.) and at American Univ. (Ph.D., 1979), where he majored in science policy analysis. He was president and CEO of Quantum Res. Corp., Washington, DC. for 18 years (1982-2000). Currently, he is the owner and president of GJN Enterprises (s. 2010), based in Sarasota, FL. His interests are in computer science and design and development of science policy research databases.

Jaroslav Opatrný (1946-), b. Plzeň, Czech., was trained as a computer scientist at Charles Univ. and Univ. of Waterloo. He has been with Univ. of Alberta (1975-77), as assoc. prof. (1977-85); as prof. of computer science, Concordia Univ. (s. 2002). His res. interests are in network models for ad-hoc or mobile networks.

Michael 'Misha' Pavel (1946-), b. Teplice, Czech., studied electrical engineering at Polytechnic Inst. Brooklyn (B.S., 1970) and at Stanford Univ. (M.S., 1971), and experimental psychology at New York Univ. (Ph.D., 1980). Pavel was a member of the technical staff at Bell Laboratories in early 1970s, where his research included network analysis and modeling, and later at AT&T Laboratories with focus on mobile and Internet-based technologies. He started his academic career at New York Univ. (1980-83) and at Stanford (1983-90). Returning shortly to New York Univ., as assoc. professor of psychology (1990-94), before joining Oregon Graduate Inst. of Sciences, as director of the Center of Information Technology (1995-98) and professor of electric and computer engineering (1998-2001) and biomedical engineering (2001-13), and as chair of biomedical engineering 2010-13). In the period of 2010-14, he served as program director of Smart Health and Wellbeing, and Computer and Information Science and Engineering at the National Science Foundation. Currently, he holds the position of professor of practice, jointly appointed between College of Computer and Information Sciences and the Bouvé College of Health Sciences at

Northeastern University. He has written numerous publications in his field and is a holder of a number of patents.

Jiří Pochobradský (1940–), b. Polná, Czech., studied physics at Charles Univ. (dipl., 1962) and at American Univ. (Ph.D., 1973). His interests are in the area of medical physics, applied mathematics, and computer science. He resided in Switzerland.

Vladimír Pochop (1946–), Lázně Bělohrad, Czech., studied computer science at Czech Technical Univ. in Prague (Ing., 1969) and numerical mathematics at Charles Univ. (RNDr., 1976). He immigrated to US in 1982, settling in California. He eventually found a job as a senior scientist at Autodesk, a software company in Rafael, CA (1984–89) and then with another software company, Multigen, Inc. at San Jose (1999–2006). Currently he is associated as senior scientist with Total Immersion and Total Immersion Software, located in San Francisco Area, CA (s. 2006). His specialties are in the area of computational geometry, geometric modeling, CAD/CAM, and 3D user interfaces. He and his family lives in Concord, CA.

Raymond Peter Polivka (1929–), b. US, studied mathematics at North Central College, Naperville, IL (A.B., 1951; M.S., 1953) and at Univ. of Illinois (Ph.D., 1958). He was assoc. prof., North Central Coll. Illinois (1965–66); instructor and educator, with IBM Corp. System Group (1958–93). While at IBM, he was responsible for its company-wide APL education. Subsequently, he established his own computer software company, Polivka Associates, specializing in interactive information and data visualization applications (1993–2010). He has co-authored three APL textbooks: *APL: The Language and Its Usage* (1975), *APL2 at a Glance* (1988), *APL2 in Depth* (1995). His research interests were in system programming, and engineering analysis.

Aurelius Prochazka (1969–), b. Ohio, of Czech ancestry, was trained as an aeronautical engineer at California Inst. of Technology (M.S., 1992; Ph.D., 1997). He was a co-founder and programmer of Creative Internet Design, Pasadena, CA (1995–97); co-founder and vice president of ArsDigita Corp. (1998–2001); founder and consultant of Aurelius Productions, LLC, Pasadena (2001–08); and principal scientist at Cool Earth Solar, Livermore, CA (2007–11). His specialties include recruiting and building teams of software engineers, software and system design, data modeling, user interface design, multimedia applications, and educational software. He co-authored the book *RailsSpace: Building a Social Networking Website with Ruby on Rails* (2007) and developed and narrated the video series *RailsSpace Ruby on Rails Tutorial*.

Václav Rajlich (1939–), b. Prague, Czech, received training in mechanical engineering at Czech Technical Univ. (dipl., 1963) and in mathematics (automata and formal languages) at

Case Western Reserve University (Ph.D., 1971). He held the position of manager of the dept. of algorithms and languages at the Research Inst. for Mathematical Machines in Prague (1974-79) and various visiting professorships in the US. He then became an associate professor of computer science and engineering, at University of Michigan (1982-85). Subsequently, he joined Wayne State Univ. as prof., Dept. of Computer Science (s. 1985), as dept. chair (1985-90). His academic interests are in the areas of software engineering, software evolution, and program comprehension. He is the founder of IEEE International Conference on Program Comprehension (ICPC). His research focuses on process of software change and as-needed comprehension of complex program, including feature location and impact analysis. He is the author of *Software Engineering: The Current Practice* (2012).

Daniel R. Rehak (ca. 1955–), b. presumably of Hungarian, but more likely of Czech ancestry, was awarded a Ph.D. in civil engineering from the University of Illinois at Urbana-Champaign in 1981 and earned both M.S. and B.S., both in civil engineering, from the Carnegie Institute of Technology at Carnegie Mellon University. He was with Carnegie-Mellon Univ. (s. 1986), as prof., dept of civil and environmental engineering (s. 1990), as tech. dir., Learning Systems Architecture Lab. (s. 2000). In 2006, Dr. Rehak joined the University of Memphis' Herff College of Engineering as a visiting professor in the Department of Electrical and Computer Engineering. He served as the co-director of the Workforce Advanced Distributed Learning (ADL) Co-Laboratory and technical director of the Learning Systems Architecture Laboratory (LSAL), a research unit within the Institute for Intelligent Systems. His professional career has been devoted to the research, design and development of large scale, interdisciplinary engineering computer systems, general-purpose engineering software tools and support environments, technology-enhanced education, and engineering application programs.

John Henry Reif (1951–), b. Madison, WI, of Moravian ancestry, studied applied mathematics and computer science at Tufts Univ. (B.S., 1973) and applied mathematics at Harvard Univ. (M.A., 1975; Ph.D., 1977). He started as asst professor at Univ. of Rochester (1977-78), prior to moving to Harvard Univ., as asst. professor (1979-83) and assoc. professor (1983-86). Subsequently, he joined Duke University, as professor (s. 1986) and as Hollis Edens Distinguished Professor of Computer Science (s. 2003). His research interests include: DNA nanostructures, molecular computation, efficient algorithms, parallel computation, robotic motion planning, and optical computing. He is also president of Eagle Eye Research, Inc., which specializes in defense applications of DNA biotechnology.

Adam Sadílek (ca. 1986–), b. Czech., was trained in computer science at Czech Technical Univ. (B.S., 2008) and at Univ. of Rochester (M.Sc., 2010; Ph.D., 2012). He remained another year at Univ. of Rochester as a postdoctoral Fellow (2012-13). He was CEO and co-founder of Fount.in (2012-13). Subsequently, he joined Google X, Mountain View, CA, as data scientist (s. 2013).

Bruno Otto Schubert (ca. 1937-), was trained at Czech Technical Univ. in Prague (Ing., 1960), at Charles Univ. (PhDr., 1964) and Stanford Univ. (Ph.D., 1968). He was assoc. prof. of operations research and systems analysis, Naval Postgrad. School, Monterey.

Robert W. Sebesta (1942-), b. Sioux Falls, SD, of Czech ancestry, received training in applied mathematics at Univ. of Colorado, Boulder (B.S., 1969) and in computer science at Pennsylvania State Univ. (M.S., 1970; Ph.D., 1974). He was associated with the Computer Science Dept. at the State University of New York College at Oswego, as asst. professor (1974-77), as assoc. professor (1978-81), as a chairman of the computer science Dept. (1978-81). He then joined the Univ. of Colorado, Colorado Springs, as assoc. professor (1981-2005), as chair of computer science dept. (1987-2001). He has taught computer science for more than 38 years. His professional interests are the design and evaluation of programming languages. He is the author *Concepts of Programming Languages* (now in 10th edition, 2012), *Programming the World Wide Web* (7th edition, 2012), *Concepts of Programming Languages* (9th edition, 2009), *VAX: Structured Assembly Language Programming* (2000), *Structured Assembly Language Programming (Benjamin/Cummings Series in Structured Programming* (1984) and *Computer Concepts, Structured Programming, and Interactive BASIC* (1982).

David Bingham Skalak (ca. 1954-), b. possibly of Czech ancestry, studied mathematics at Union Coll. (B.S., summa cum laude, 1976) and at Dartmouth Coll. (M.A., 1979), and then computer science at Univ. of Massachusetts (M.S., 1989; Ph.D., 1997). He also studied law at Harvard Law School (J.D., 1982). He was a Senior Data Mining Analyst with IBM (1997-2005). Since then, he has been self-employed (s. 2005), as securities trading system developer and trader. He is the owner of Highgate Predictions, LLC in Ithaca, NY. His current research interests include instance-based and local learning algorithms, classifier combination, case-based reasoning, artificial intelligence and law, and the application of machine learning algorithms and knowledge discovery methods to equity selection, money.

Vladimír Slámečka (1928-2006), b. Brno, Czech., was trained as a chemical engineer and librarian. He became the first director of Georgia Tech's School of Information and Computer Science in the fall of 1964 and as a pioneer of the Information Age. Under his direction, the school grew into one of the largest in the Institute. It became the College of Computing in 1990.

Nova Spivack (1969-), b. Boston, MA, of Bohemian ancestry (the eldest grandson of Peter F. Drucker, widely considered 'the father of modern management'), is a technology entrepreneur. Presently CEO of Bottlenose, a Los Angeles-based company that provides social search, listening and analytic tools for marketers. He is also a co-founder and investor in several other ventures, including Live Matrix, which was sold to OVGuide in 2012, The *Daily Dot* which provides an online newspaper about Web culture, and was the first outside investor in Klout, which measures social influence. In 1994, he co-founded EarthWeb, Inc., one of the first Internet companies, which later spun off Dice.com. He founded Lucid Ventures in 2001 and the semantic web venture Radar Networks in 2003. Spivack is an active angel investor and advisor to startups including Cambrian Genomics, Sensentia, Publish This, WhoKnows.com, NextIT, Chronos Trading and Energy Magnification Corporation. He is on the Board of Directors of the Common Crawl Foundation which provides a free and open 5-billion-page search index of the Web. Spivack was founder and CEO of Radar Networks, the makers of Twine.com and is considered a leading pioneer in semantic web technology. Nova Spivack writes about the future of the Internet and topics concerning search, social media, personalization, information filtering, entrepreneurship, Web technology and Web applications.

Peter A. Stark (1938-), b. Prague, Czech., was trained at New York Univ. He is now prof. of computer science, at CUNY, Queensborough Community Coll., Queens.

Steven Stepanek (1951-), b. Van Nuys, California, of Czech ancestry, received his B.A. in mathematics in 1974 and his M.S. in computer science in 1980 from California State University, Northridge. At CSU, Northridge he was an academic consultant and an operating systems analyst at the campus Computer Center (1972-1978). With the formation of computer science as an academic discipline at CSU, Northridge, he became a computer science lecturer (1976-1981), assistant professor (1981-1985), tenured in 1984, associate professor (1985-1993) and full professor (s. 1993). His research interests are in the areas of operating systems, object-oriented programming and the use of technology in course pedagogy. He was a lecturer at UCLA (1984-1990) and a computing consultant to major corporations including CADAM, Control Data Corporation, Honeywell, IBM, Litton, NASA, Rand Corporation and Teradyne (1978-1987). At CSU, Northridge, he chaired the computer science department (1999-2014), and served as faculty president (2010-14). He was a recipient of numerous awards. In 2013, the Governor of the State of California appointed Professor Stepanek to the position of Faculty Trustee on the California State University Board of Trustees.

Petr Švec (1980-), b. Znojmo, Czech., is a trained roboticist who specializes in research in robot motion planning, machine learning, and artificial intelligence. He is currently an Assistant Research Scientist in the Department of Mechanical Engineering at the University of Maryland, College Park. He is also a member of the Maryland Robotics Center. He was trained in computer science (M.S., 2003) and in mechanical engineering with a focus on robot motion planning (Ph.D., 2007) at the Brno University of Technology. Due to his preparation for interdisciplinary research in robotics by simultaneously studying computer science and mechanical engineering at two universities, he also received a Bachelor's degree in computer science from the Faculty of Informatics, Masaryk University in 2004 and a second Master's degree in 2006 from the same institute.

Antonín Svoboda (1907–1980), b. Prague, Bohemia, was trained as an electrical engineer at Czech Inst. of Technology and experimental physicist at Charles Univ. During the World War II, he was on staff of Radiation Lab at MIT. After the War, he went back to Czechoslovakia and became one of the pioneers in the development of digital computers. The Research Inst. of Mathematical Machines, which he headed, became the center of computer research in East Europe. In 1965, he returned to U.S. and joined the faculty of Univ. of California, Los Angeles where he taught logic design and computer architecture.

Líba Svobodová (1946–), b. Prague, Czech., was trained as a computer scientist at ČVUT and Stanford Univ. She held faculty positions at Columbia University in New York and the Massachusetts Institute of Technology / Laboratory for Computer Science, where she did pioneering work in the area of resilient distributed systems. In 1982, she joined the IBM Zurich Research Laboratory in Rüschlikon, Switzerland. Over many years she managed research projects in the areas of computer networks and distributed systems, security, and network services and applications.

Jaroslav 'Jerry' Sychra (1939–), b. Přívrat, Czech., was trained as a physicist at Charles Univ. (M.S., 1962; RNDr., 1968; CSc./Ph.D., 1969). He was associated with Univ. of Chicago, as a research associate (1971–75) and as an assistant professor (1975–80). He then worked for Monsanto, St., Louis, MO (1980–81) and Schlumberger, Houston, TX (1981–83). Subsequently, he joined dept. of radiology at Univ. of Chicago, where he held the position of assoc. professor (1983–2000) and director of Medical Imaging an Artificial Intelligence Lab. After his retirement, he became director of research and development at Zero Maintenance International Inc., Chicago (2000–03), and consultant and, currently, is adjunct professor in the math. dept. at Roosevelt University (s. 2000). His research interests were in the area of artificial intelligence, pattern recognition, medical diagnosis by computer analysis of medical images.

Bruce Tesar (1966–), b. Kalamazoo, MI, of Czech ancestry, was trained as a computer scientist and mathematician at Western Michigan University (B.S., summa cum laude, 1990) and in computer science at Univ., of Colorado, Boulder (M.S., 1992; Ph.D., 1995). He has been with Rutgers Univ. (s. 1995), as asst. professor at the Center for Cognitive Science and the Department of Linguistics (1998-2003) and as assoc. professor (s. 2003). He specializes in computational linguistics. He has been on the editorial Board of *Cognition* (1999-2002) and *Journal of Cognition and Culture* (s. 2001).

Martin Thoma (1968-), Czech., studied applied mathematics at Czech Technical Univ. in Prague (M.Sc., 1991) and mathematical physics at McGill Univ. (Ph.D., 1997). He holds the position of systems and software architect at Utica First Insurance Co., Utica, NY.

Ivan Tomek (1939-), b. Prague, Czech., was trained in mechanical engineering at the Technical University of Liberec (Ing., 1966), and in electrical engineering at Univ. of Alberta (Ph.D., 1971). After working on computer applications in medicine at the University of Alberta for four years, he accepted a position at Acadia University, Wolfville, Nova Scotia, Canada in 1975. He then worked at Acadia University for 30 years, as asst. professor (1975-79), as assoc. professor (1979-84), and professor (1984-2005), teaching courses in a variety of areas, and supervising 24 M.Sc. students. He published numerous articles in areas ranging from computer architecture, pattern recognition, programming languages, biomedical applications, support for geographically dispersed work teams, and Information Technology (IT) use in education in refereed journals, presented papers at conferences, wrote five books in the area of computer science, served on editorial boards of two journals, and presided over six international conferences in IT use in education. He is now retired, holds the title of professor emeritus at Acadia University, and participates in academic activities occasionally. His main research interests have lately been centered on support for geographically dispersed work teams, in particular software development teams, interactive software development environments, object-oriented programming and development methodologies, collaborative learning, and collaborative virtual environments.

Thomas Vachuska (1963-), b. Ostrov, Czech., was trained as a mathematician and software engineer at Charles Univ. (1981-82) and at California State Univ., Sacramento (B.A., 1994). He has a solid background in object-oriented system design and architecture of distributed software systems. He is avid proponent of agile development processes, remains familiar with a wide field of evolving technologies and software development tools. Thomas is an unceasing advocate for elegant simplicity, a self-driven learner, up-front & open communicator, creative pragmatist, a mentor, and is consistently ranked as top performer. He was employed as a software engineer, first with Hewlett-Packard Server and Workstation Manufacturing (1988-95); with HP Workgroup Network Division (1996-98); and with Storage Area Networks Management Group (1998-2005). Subsequently, he became software architect with HP Information Group (2005-08); then with HP Networking (2009-14); and currently he holds the position of chief architect with Open Networking Lab (s.

2014), a non-profit organization, where he leads a team developing a next-generation SDN (software-defined networking) controller. He is a principal author of several patents.

Miroslav Valach (1926–), b. Hnúšťa, Czech., was trained as a computer scientist at Czech Technical Univ. & ČSAV. He was with General Electric Co, AZ (1965–69); as professor of information and computer science, Georgia Inst. Technology (1969–74); as research director, Karsten Mfg. Corp. (1974–80); with Friday Compute Inc (s. 1980). He is a specialist on switching theory, cybernetics, artificial intelligence, computer hardware, linguistics.

Roman Vichr (ca. 1965–), b. Czech., was trained at Inst. of Chemical Technology in Prague, where he majored in mechanical engineering (Ing., 1987; Ph.D., 1992). He has 16 years of international software development, system and database engineering experience. He specializes in software development, database, IT architecture blueprints and system engineering services for software development firms and government agencies. His experience includes numerous projects for Fortune 100 companies and government bodies at the federal and state level. He also worked on Mantas related projects focusing on high data ingestion processing, scenario mapping, system tuning and adjustments. In 2004, Roman founded RDMaX, a consulting firm with a focus on technology consulting to judicial and financial institutions in the public and private sector. He serves as its president and chief technology officer. He has designed case management, allocation, and tracking systems for over two hundred jurisdictions in the United States. Internationally, he has designed IT systems for the Rwandan Ministry of Justice and the Court of Bosnia and Herzegovina.

Peter Weverka (1958–), likely of Czech ancestry, is the author of 17 computer books, including *Dummies 101: Microsoft Office 2000 for Windows* and *Money 99 for Dummies*, both published by IDG Books Worldwide, Inc. His humorous articles and stories (none related to computers) have appeared in *Harper's* and *SPY* magazine. He is also an editor. He has polished, cleaned up, and actually read over 80 computer books on topics ranging from word processing to desktop publishing to the Internet. He edited about 50 of those books online with Microsoft Word. Peter believes that the goal of all computing is to help you get your work done faster so you don't have to sit in front of the computer anymore.

Eric Zelenka (1975–), b. Czech., is a senior manager for Mac OS X Worldwide Product Marketing at Apple Computer. Eric participated in the marketing, design and development of Mac OS X and is now managing Apple's server, storage and desktop management products including Mac OS X Server, Vsan, Apple Remote Desktop, and technologies including iCal Server, Open directory, Podcast Producer, iChat Server and Xgrid. At Apple's Worldwide Developers Conf. in 2004, Steve Jobs mentioned Eric as having participated in the world's first in-air commercial video conference using uChat AV. Eric Zelenka initiated the video conference while returning to San Francisco from Munich, using Lufthansa's new wireless high-speed broadband connection service. Prior to joining Apple, Eric managed the product marketing and development of WebSTAR, originally by StarNine Technologies and later bought by Quarterdeck Software (now part of Symantec Corporation).

Maria Zemánková (1951–), b. Uherský Brod, Czech, studied at a computer programmer and operator school (1970–71) and mathematics at Masaryk University in Brno (1971–72). She moved to Egypt where she received her B.S. (with highest honors) in mathematics and computing with minor in psychology from the American University in Cairo in 1977. Since 1977, she has lived in the US and received M.S. and Ph.D. in computer science from the Florida State University in 1979 and 1983, respectively. From 1983–84, she was a developer in a database start-up company, she was on faculty of the Department of Computer Science at the University of Tennessee, Knoxville 1984–88, collaborated with researchers at the Oakridge National Laboratory and held a visiting position at the University of Illinois Urbana-Champaign 1986–87. Maria Zemánková joined the National Science Foundation as a program director in the Information and Intelligent Systems (IIS) Division in 1988. She has been instrumental in developing initiatives on Scientific Databases, Digital Libraries, and Biodiversity and Ecosystem Informatics, and has been active in cross-disciplinary initiatives, including Information Technology Research, Wireless Information Systems, Science of Design, Cyber Trust, Cyber-enabled Discovery and Innovation, Research Infrastructure, INSPIRE, Smart Health and Big Data. In addition, she has been involved in programs aimed at supporting technology transfer, Small Business Innovation Research and Grant Opportunities for Academic Liaison and in educational programs, Research Experience for Undergraduates and Graduate STEM Fellows in K-12 Education, and served on interagency working group for Global Change Data & Information Systems and international organization Global Biodiversity Information Facility (GBIF). Her research interests include intelligent information systems; information/knowledge organization and evolution, management of uncertainty (fuzzy logic), knowledge discovery environments, data mining, privacy/security, visualization, information retrieval, text mining, social media, multimedia systems, spatio-temporal systems (GIS), scientific databases and process modeling. Maria Zemánková was a founding co-editor-in-chief of the *Journal of Intelligent Information Systems*, served as the associate editor of the *International Journal of Approximate Reasoning*, and has been on program or organizing committees of numerous conferences and workshops.

D. Artificial Intelligence

Růžena Bajcsy (1933–), b. Bratislava, Czech., is a Slovak American engineer and computer scientist who specializes in robotics. She is professor of electrical engineering and computer sciences at the University of California, Berkeley, where she is also director emerita of CITRIS (the Center for Information Technology Research in the Interest of Society). She was previously professor and chair of computer science and engineering at the University of Pennsylvania, where she was the founding director of the University of Pennsylvania's General Robotics and Active Sensory Perception (GRASP) Laboratory, and a member of the Neurosciences Institute in the School of Medicine. She has also been head of the National Science Foundation's Computer and Information Science and Engineering Directorate, with authority over a $500 million budget. She supervised at least 26 doctoral students at the University of Pennsylvania.

Andrej Karpathy (1986–), b. Czech., moved with his family to Toronto, Canada when he was 15. He is the director of artificial intelligence and Autopilot Vision at Tesla. He specializes in deep learning and computer vision.

Raymond Kurzweil (1948–), b. New York, of Czech ancestry, is an American computer scientist, author, inventor, and futurist. He is involved in fields such as optical character recognition (OCR), text-to-speech synthesis, speech recognition technology and electronic keyboard instruments. He has written books on health technology, artificial intelligence (AI), transhumanism, the technological singularity, and futurism. Kurzweil is a public advocate for the futurist and transhumanist movements and gives public talks to share his optimistic outlook on life extension technologies and the future of nanotechnology, robotics, and biotechnology. Kurzweil received the 1999 National Medal of Technology and Innovation, the United States' highest honor in technology, from then President Bill Clinton in a White House ceremony.

Hans Peter Moravec (1948–), Kautzen, Austria, only a few miles from the Moravian border, probably of Czech ancestry, is an adjunct faculty member at the Robotics Institute of Carnegie Mellon University in Pittsburgh, USA. He is known for his work on robotics, artificial intelligence, and writings on the impact of technology. Moravec also is a futurist with many of his publications and predictions focusing on transhumanism. Moravec developed techniques in computer vision for determining the region of interest (ROI) in a scene.

John 'Jack' E. Rechcigl (1960–), b., Washington, DC, of Czech ancestry, has been praised as a visionary leader by the media. He is a notable soil scientist and horticulturist, with a professorship at the University of Florida and directorship of two UF Research and Education Centers, one in Balm (GCREC) and the other in Ft. Lauderdale. Under his leadership, robotics has already been used in some of the research. It was also on his initiative that UF/IFAS decided to build now a new Center for Applied Artificial Intelligence in Agriculture at GCREC. The 35,000 square-foot center is envisioned as a facility for scientists across Florida to collaborate to solve problems plaguing growers and to do so in a relatively short amount of time, using AI technology. The University of Florida is making artificial intelligence the centerpiece of a major, long-term initiative that combines world-class research infrastructure, cutting-edge research and a transformational approach to curriculum. Hearing about the UF efforts, a delegation of the White House officials came down and toured the UF/IFAS Gulf Coast Research and Education Center to see for themselves what was going on. Jack Rechcigl briefed them on various AI-related research by GCREC faculty. At the end, the members of the delegation were truly amazed and impressed by how the GCREC is using AI to help agricultural producers already.

Herbert Alexander Simon (1916–2001), b. Milwaukee, WI, of Bohemian ancestry, was an American political scientist whose work also influenced the fields of computer science, economics, and cognitive psychology. He is considered one of the founding fathers of artificial intelligence. His primary research interest was decision-making within organizations and he is best known for the theories of "bounded rationality" and "satisficing". He received the Nobel Memorial Prize in Economic Sciences in 1978 and the Turing Award in computer science in 1975. His research was noted for its interdisciplinary nature, spanning the fields of cognitive science, computer science, public administration, management, and political science. He was at Carnegie Mellon University for most of his career, from 1949 to 2001, where he helped found the Carnegie Mellon School of Computer Science, one of the first such departments in the world. Notably, Simon was among the pioneers of several modern-day scientific domains such as artificial intelligence, information processing, decision-making, problem-solving, organization theory, and complex systems. He was among the earliest to analyze the architecture of complexity and to propose a preferential attachment mechanism to explain power law distributions.

REFERENCES

A. Business

"Czech American Tradesmen: Masters of their Profession," in: *Beyond the Sea of Beer*. By Miloslav Rechcigl, Jr. Bloomington, IN: AuthorHouse, 2017, pp. 436-441.

First Bohemian Businessmen in America," in: *Beyond the Sea of Beer*. By Miloslav Rechcigl, Jr. Bloomington, IN: AuthorHouse, 2017, pp. 441-449.

"Businesspersons & Entrepreneurs," in: *Notable Czech and Slovak Americans. From Explorers and Pioneer Colonists through Activists to Public Figures, Diplomats, Professionals, and Sports Competitors*. By Miloslav Rechcigl, Jr. Bloomington, IN: AuthorHouse, 2021, pp. 500-644.

B. Religion

"American Czechs and their Religious Beliefs," in: *Beyond the Sea of Beer*. By Miloslav Rechcigl, Jr. Bloomington, IN: AuthorHouse, 2017, pp. 384-393.

"Clergy," in: *Notable Czech and Slovak Americans. From Explorers and Pioneer Colonists through Activists to Public Figures, Diplomats, Professionals, and Sports Competitors*. By Miloslav Rechcigl, Jr. Bloomington, IN: AuthorHouse, 2021, pp. 263-370.

C. Government & Politics

US Legislators with Czechoslovak Roots from Colonial Times to Present. With Genealogical Lineages. By Miloslav Rechcigl, Jr. Washington, DC: SVU Press, 1987. 65p.

"Political Life of Czech Americans," in: *Beyond the Sea of Beer*. By Miloslav Rechcigl, Jr. Bloomington, IN: AuthorHouse, 2017, pp. 402-406.

"Government Officials & Politicians," in: *Notable Czech and Slovak Americans. From Explorers and Pioneer Colonists through Activists to Public Figures, Diplomats, Professionals, and Sports Competitors*. By Miloslav Rechcigl, Jr. Bloomington, IN: AuthorHouse, 2021, pp. 645-803.

D. Military

"Czechs in the US Military," by Miloslav Rechcigl, Jr. Kosmas 27, No. 1 (Fall 2013), pp. 49-78.

"Czechs in the US Military," in: *Beyond the Sea of Beer*. By Miloslav Rechcigl, Jr. Bloomington, IN: AuthorHouse, 2017, pp. 506-531.

"Military Notables," in: *Notable Czech and Slovak Americans. From Explorers and Pioneer Colonists through Activists to Public Figures, Diplomats, Professionals, and Sports Competitors*. By Miloslav Rechcigl, Jr. Bloomington, IN: AuthorHouse, 2021, pp. 804–843.

E. Activism

"From Socialism to Anarchism to Rationalism," in: *Beyond the Sea of Beer*. By Miloslav Rechcigl, Jr. Bloomington, IN: AuthorHouse, 2017, pp. 398–401.

"Activists, Reformers, Archivists," in: *Notable Czech and Slovak Americans. From Explorers and Pioneer Colonists through Activists to Public Figures Diplomats, Professionals, and Sports Competitors*. By Miloslav Rechcigl, Jr. Bloomington, IN: AuthorHouse, 2021, pp. 85–182.

"Leaders," in: *Notable Czech and Slovak Americans. From Explorers and Pioneer Colonists through Activists to Public Figures Diplomats, Professionals, and Sports Competitors*. By Miloslav Rechcigl, Jr. Bloomington, IN: AuthorHouse, 2021, pp. 183–262.

F. Law & Jurisprudence

"First Czech Physicians and Lawyers in America," in: *Beyond the Sea of Beer*. By Miloslav Rechcigl, Jr. Bloomington, IN: AuthorHouse, 2017, pp. 469–475.

"Lawyers," in: *Notable Czech and Slovak Americans. From Explorers and Pioneer Colonists through Activists to Public Figures Diplomats, Professionals, and Sports Competitors*. By Miloslav Rechcigl, Jr. Bloomington, IN: AuthorHouse, 2021, pp. 371–499.

G. Medicine

"First Czech Physicians and Lawyers in America," in: *Beyond the Sea of Beer*. By Miloslav Rechcigl, Jr. Bloomington, IN: AuthorHouse, 2017, pp. 469–475.

"Medicine," in: *American Men and Women in Medicine, Applied Sciences and Engineering with Roots in Czechoslovakia*. By Miloslav Rechcigl, Jr. Bloomington, IN: AuthorHouse, 2021, pp. 1–358.

"Allied Health Sciences and Social Services," in: *American Men and Women in Medicine, Applied Sciences and Engineering with Roots in Czechoslovakia*. By Miloslav Rechcigl, Jr. Bloomington, IN: AuthorHouse, 2021, pp. 359–451.

REFERENCES

H. Agriculture & Food

"Czech Farmer and Agribusinessman in America." In: *Beyond the Sea of Beer.* By Miloslav Rechcigl, Jr. Bloomington, IN: Author House, 2017, pp. 429–436.

"Agriculture and Food Science," in: *American Men and Women in Medicine, Applied Sciences and Engineering with Roots in Czechoslovakia.* By Miloslav Rechcigl, Jr. Bloomington, IN: AuthorHouse, 2021, pp. 452–508

I. Earth Sciences

"Exile Scientists and Engineers from Communist Czechoslovakia," in: *Beyond the Sea of Beer.* By Miloslav Rechcigl, Jr. Bloomington, IN: AuthorHouse, 2017, pp. 628-660.

"Earth and Environmental Science," in: *American Men and Women in Medicine, Applied Sciences and Engineering with Roots in Czechoslovakia.* By Miloslav Rechcigl, Jr. Bloomington, IN: AuthorHouse, 2021, pp. 509–560.

J. Visual Art

"First Czech Artists in America," in: *Beyond the Sea of Beer.* By Miloslav Rechcigl, Jr. Bloomington, IN: AuthorHouse, 2017, pp. 450–459.

"Visual Art," in: *Notable Americans of Czechoslovak Ancestry in Arts and Letters and in Education.* By Miloslav Rechcigl, Jr. Bloomington, IN: AuthorHouse, pp. 1–189.

K. Dramatic Art

"Dramatic Arts," in: *Beyond the Sea of Beer.* By Miloslav Rechcigl, Jr. Bloomington, IN: AuthorHouse, 2017, pp. 459–462.

"Dramatic Art," in: *Notable Americans of Czechoslovak Ancestry in Arts and Letters and in Education.* By Miloslav Rechcigl, Jr. Bloomington, IN: AuthorHouse, pp. 190–374.

L. Music

"The Czech the Musician," in: *Beyond the Sea of Beer.* By Miloslav Rechcigl, Jr. Bloomington, IN: AuthorHouse, 2017, pp. 447–449.

"Music," in: *Notable Americans of Czechoslovak Ancestry in Arts and Letters and in Education.* By Miloslav Rechcigl.

M. Creative Writing

"Writers of Fiction and Non-Fiction," in: *Beyond the Sea of Beer*. By Miloslav Rechcigl, Jr. Bloomington, IN: AuthorHouse, 2017, pp. 462–469.

"Creative Writing," in: *Notable Americans of Czechoslovak Ancestry in Arts and Letters and in Education*. By Miloslav Rechcigl, Jr. Bloomington, IN: AuthorHouse, pp. 629–802.

N. Media

Beginnings of the Czech Press in America," in: *Beyond the Sea of Beer*. By Miloslav Rechcigl, Jr. Bloomington, IN: AuthorHouse, 2017, pp. 380–384.

"Journalists," in: *Notable Americans of Czechoslovak Ancestry in Arts and Letters and in Education*. By Miloslav Rechcigl, Jr. Bloomington, IN: AuthorHouse, IN, 2021, pp. 731–783.

"Radio & TV Journalists & Broadcasters," in: *Notable Americans of Czechoslovak Ancestry in Arts and Letters and in Education*. By Miloslav Rechcigl, Jr. Bloomington, IN: AuthorHouse, IN, 2021, pp.783–802.

O. Publishing

"Publishing, Printing, Bookselling, Librarianship," in: *Notable Americans of Czechoslovak Ancestry in Arts and Letters and in Education*. By Miloslav Rechcigl, Jr. Bloomington, IN: AuthorHouse, pp. 804–867.

P. Education

Educators with Czechoslovak Roots. A US and Canada Faculty MILOSLAV RECHCIGL, JR. 1998 Roster. By Miloslav Rechcigl, Jr. Washington, DC: SVU Press, 1980. 122 pp.

"Education and Learning," in: *Notable Americans of Czechoslovak Ancestry in Arts and Letters and in Education*. By Miloslav Rechcigl, Jr. Bloomington, IN: AuthorHouse, 2021, pp. 868–1010.

Q. Humanities

"First Czech Scholars and Social Scientists in America," in: *Beyond the Sea of Beer*. By Miloslav Rechcigl, Jr. Bloomington, IN: AuthorHouse, 2017, pp. 487–505.

REFERENCES

"Czech Intellectual Refugees from Nazism in the US - in Humanities and the Arts and Letters," in: *Beyond the Sea of Beer*. By Miloslav Rechcigl, Jr. Bloomington, IN: AuthorHouse, 2017, pp. 602.

"Scholars," in: *American Learned Men and Women with Czechoslovak Roots*. By Miloslav Rechcigl, Jr. Bloomington, IN: AuthorHouse, 2020, pp. 14–272.

R. Social Sciences

"First Czech Scholars and Social Scientists in America," in: *Beyond the Sea of Beer*. By Miloslav Rechcigl, Jr. Bloomington, IN: AuthorHouse, 2017, pp. 487–505.

"Czech Intellectual Refugees from Nazism in the US - Natural and Social Sciences," in: *Beyond the Sea of Beer*. By Miloslav Rechcigl, Jr. Bloomington, IN: AuthorHouse, 2017, pp. 549–578.

"Social Scientists," in: *American Learned Men and Women with Czechoslovak Roots*. By Miloslav Rechcigl, Jr. Bloomington, IN: AuthorHouse, 2020, pp. pp. 273–529

S. Natural Sciences

"First Czech Scientists and Engineers in America," in: *Beyond the Sea of Beer*. By Miloslav Rechcigl, Jr. Bloomington, IN: AuthorHouse, 2017, pp. 476–487.

"Czech Intellectual Refugees from Nazism in the US - Natural and Social Sciences," in: *Beyond the Sea of Beer*. By Miloslav Rechcigl, Jr. Bloomington, IN: AuthorHouse, 2017, pp. 549–578.

"Exile Scientists and Engineers from Communist Czechoslovakia," in: *Beyond the Sea of Beer*. By Miloslav Rechcigl, Jr. Bloomington, IN: AuthorHouse, 2017, pp. 628–660.

"Biological Scientists," in: *American Learned Men and Women with Czechoslovak Roots*. By Miloslav Rechcigl, Jr. Bloomington, IN: AuthorHouse, 2020, pp. 530–720.

"Physical Scientists," in: *American Learned Men and Women with Czechoslovak Roots*. By Miloslav Rechcigl, Jr. Bloomington, IN: AuthorHouse, 2020, pp. 721–929.

T. Engineering & Technology

"First Czech Scientists and Engineers in America," in: *Beyond the Sea of Beer*. By Miloslav Rechcigl, Jr. Bloomington, IN: AuthorHouse, 2017, pp. 476–487.

"Exile Scientists and Engineers from Communist Czechoslovakia," in: *Beyond the Sea of Beer*. By Miloslav Rechcigl, Jr. Bloomington, IN: AuthorHouse, 2017, pp. 628–660.

"Engineering," in: *American Men and Women in Medicine, Applied Sciences and Engineering with Roots in Czechoslovakia*. By Miloslav Rechcigl, Jr. Bloomington, IN: AuthorHouse, 2021, pp. 561–810.

ABOUT THE AUTHOR

Miloslav 'Míla' Rechcígl, Jr., a notable biochemist and science administrator at DHEW, US Department of State and the US Agency for International Development, where he managed research for some 27 years, and after retirement in 1996, becoming a bona fide full-fledged non-fiction writer, having reached the venerable age of 94, on July 30, 2024, is still fully engrossed in full-time work. He is a true visionary and activist, spending all his energy and stamina in writing scholarly books, sometime as many as two a year, in his capacity as SVU Scholar- in-Residence.

Above all, he has always maintained his role as an activist on behalf of Czechoslovakia and its Successor States and on Czech American relations. As the past Czech Ambassador to the USA, H.E. Dr. Hynek Kmoníček wrote in his Foreword for one of Mila's books, "It was my personal pleasure to award him on his 90th birthday the highest diplomatic award, which the Minister of Foreign Affairs of the Czech Republic could bestow upon hm, The Medal of Merit in Diplomacy. Rechcigl never entered foreign service. However, through his life and chairmanship of the Czechoslovak Society of Arts and Sciences, as well as through his books and interactions with Americans, he did as much for the diplomacy of the Czech state as career ambassadors have, if not more."

'Mila', as he likes to be called, is one of the founders, and past President, of many years of the Czechoslovak Society of Arts and Sciences (SVU), an international professional organization based in Washington, DC. Born in Czechoslovakia to a son of the youngest member of the Czechoslovak Parliament, he spent the War years under Nazi occupation and after the Communist's coup d'état escaped to the West and in 1950 immigrated to the US. After receiving a scholarship, he went to Cornell University where he studied from 1951-58, receiving his B.S., M.N.S., and Ph.D. degrees there, specializing in biochemistry, nutrition, physiology, and food science.

He then spent two years conducting research at the National Institutes of Health as a postdoctoral research fellow. Subsequently he was appointed to the staff of the Laboratory of Biochemistry at the National Cancer Institute (NCI). For some 10 years, while he was at NCI, he conducted extensive research relating to cancer biochemistry and enzyme turnover *in vivo*.

During 1968-69, he was selected for one year of training in a special USPHS executive program in research management, grants administration, and science policy. This led to his appointment as Special Assistant for Nutrition and Health in the Health Services and Mental

Health Administration. In 1970, he joined the Agency for International Development (AID), US Department of State, as Nutrition Advisor and soon after was promoted to the position of Chief of Research and Institutional Grants Division. Later he became a Director with the responsibility for reviewing, administering and managing AID research.

He is the author or editor of over 30 books and handbooks in the field of biochemistry, physiology, nutrition, food science and technology, agriculture, and international development, in addition to a large number of peer-reviewed original scientific articles and book chapters.

Apart from his purely scientific endeavors, as a researcher and science administrator, Dr. Rechcigl devoted over 50 years of his life to the Czechoslovak Society of Arts and Sciences (SVU). In 1960-62 he served as Executive Secretary of the SVU Washington DC Chapter. He was responsible for the first two Society's World Congresses, both of which were a great success, which put the Society on the world map. For a number of years, he then directed the publication program of the Society.

He also edited the Congress lectures and arranged for their publication, under the title *The Czechoslovak Contribution to World Culture* (1964, 682 p.) and *Czechoslovakia Past and Present* (1968, 2 volumes, 1900 p.). The publications received acclaim in the American academic circles and greatly contributed to the growing prestige of the Society worldwide.

Dr. Rechcigl was also involved, one way or another, with most of the subsequent SVU World Congresses, including the SVU Congresses in Prague, Brno, Bratislava, Washington, Plzeň, Olomouc and České Budějovice.

Prior to his last term as the SVU President (2004-06), he held similar posts during 1974-76, 1976-78, and again in 1994-96, 1996-98, 1998-2000, 2000-02, and 2002-04.

Together with his devoted wife Eva, he published eight editions of the *SVU Biographical Directory*, the last of which was printed in Prague in 2003. He was instrumental in launching a new English periodical *Kosmas - Czechoslovak and Central European Journal*. It was his idea to establish the SVU Research Institute and to create the SVU Commission for Cooperation with Czechoslovakia, and its Successor States, which played an important role in the first years after the Velvet Revolution of 1989. Under the sponsorship of the SVU Research Institute, he and his colleagues conducted a series of seminars about research management and the art of 'grantsmanship' for scientists and scholars, as well as for the administrators, and science policy makers, at Czech and Slovak universities, the Academies of Sciences and the Government.

ABOUT THE AUTHOR

He was also instrumental in establishing the National Heritage Commission with the aim of preserving Czech and Slovak cultural heritage in America. Under its aegis, he has undertaken a comprehensive survey of Czech-related historic sites and archival materials in the US. Based on this survey, he has prepared a detailed listing, *Czech-American Historic Sites, Monuments, and Memorials,* which was published through the courtesy of Palacký University in Olomouc (2004). The second part of the survey, bearing the title *Czechoslovak American Archivalia,* was also published by Palacký University (2004).

In this connection, he also organized several important conferences, one in Texas in 1997, the second in Minnesota (1999), the third in Nebraska (2001), and the fourth in Iowa (2003). Through his initiative, a special Working Conference on 'Czech & Slovak American Materials and their Preservation' was also held at the Czech and Slovak Embassies in Washington, DC in November 2003. It was an exceptionally successful conference which led to the establishment of the new Czech & Slovak American Archival Consortium (CSAAC). Later, he also organized, jointly with the ACSCC of North Miami, a conference on 'Czech and Slovak Heritage on Both Sides of the Atlantic', 17-20 March 2005. The conference was co-sponsored by the US Commission for the Preservation of America's Heritage Abroad, under the aegis of both Presidents of the Czech and Slovak Republics.

For a number of years, Mila also held the position of SVU Archivist. In this capacity, he had organized the Society's fairly complete archival collection, which he then had deposited in several prestigious depositories, i.e., University of Minnesota's Immigration History Research Center (IHRC), University of Nebraska, Palacký University in Olomouc, Czech Republic, and most recently, at the National Archives in Prague, Náprstek Museum in Prague and the National Czech & Slovak Museum & Library in Cedar Rapids, IA. The latter dedicated, on September 21,2024, a special Research Room, containing his books and archival collection that bears his name and that of his late wife Eva, as their joint legacy.

Among historians, Dr. Rechcigl is well known for his studies on history, genealogy, and bibliography of American Czechs and Slovaks. A number of his publications deal with the early immigrants from the Czechlands and Slovakia, including the migration of Moravian Brethren to America. In subsequent years, he has been working on the cultural contributions of American Czechs and Slovaks, including Bohemian Jews.

A selection of his biographical portraits of prominent Czech Americans from the 17th century to date had been published in Prague, under the title *Postavy naší Ameriky* (Personalities of our America) (2000; 350 p.) On the occasion of his 75th birthday, SVU published a collection of his essays, under the title *Czechs and Slovaks in America* (2005; 316 p.). Three years later, he published a voluminous monograph, *On Behalf of their Homeland:*

Fifty Years of SVU, an eyewitness account of the history of the Czechoslovak Society of Arts and Sciences (2008; 671 p, 28 p. ill.). The Czech version was published in Prague by Academia, under the title *Pro vlast. Padesát let Společnosti pro vědy a umění* (2012), with the Foreword by President of the Academy of the Czech Republic Václav Pačes, and the Epilogue by H.E. Czech Ambassador to the US Petr Kolář.

On the occasion of his 80th birthday, the SVU published his personal memoir, *Czechmate, From Bohemian Paradise to America Haven* (2011). In the same year, Rechcigl published his unique *Czech American Bibliography. A Comprehensive Listing with Focus on the US and with Appendices on Czechs in Canada and Latin America* (2011). In 2013, he published *Czech American Timeline. Chronology of Milestones in the History of Czechs in America* and, in 2015, *Czech It Out. Czech American Biography Sourcebook*. The latter, which has been patterned after the *Almanac of Famous People* (2011), provides a wealth of information on a variety of sources relating to biographical information about notable Czech Americans, including individual biographies, major national and local biographical compendia, ethnic sources and subject compendia, and finally family histories and genealogies.

In 2016, he wrote a 3-volume monumental comprehensive *Encyclopedia of Bohemian and Czech American Biography* (2016), covering a universe, starting soon after the discovery of the New World, through the escapades and significant contributions of Bohemian Jesuits and Moravian Brethren in the 17th and 18th centuries, and the mass migration of the Czechs after the Revolutionary Year of 1848, up to the early years of the 20th century, and the influx of refugees from Nazism and Communism. As the Czech Ambassador to the US, H.E. Petr Gandalovič noted in his Foreword to this book, Mila Rechcigl has written a monumental work, representing a culmination of his life achievement as a historian of Czech America. He compares him to the famed Thomas Čapek, who wrote his classical books about Czech immigrants in America, almost a century ago, whom he may have surpassed.

One of his latest endeavors has been a history of Czech Americans, under the title *Beyond the Sea of Beer or Czech America as Few People Know It* (2017), published in Bloomington, IN, by AuthorHouse. It is a comprehensive history of emigrants from the Historic Lands of the Bohemian Crown and its successor States, including Czechoslovakia and the Czech Republic, based on the painstaking lifetime research of the author. The reader will find lots of new information in this book that is not available elsewhere. The title of the book comes from a popular song of the famous Czech artistic duo, Voskovec & Werich, who described America in those words when they lived here, reflecting on their love for this country. It covers the period starting soon after the discovery of the New World to date. The emphasis is on the US, although Canada and Latin America are also covered. It covers the arrival and the settlement of the immigrants in various states and regions of America, their harsh beginnings, the establishment of their communities, and their organization. A separate section is devoted to the contributions of notable individuals in different areas of human endeavor, including Bohemians, Moravians, Bohemian Jews, and the Slovaks. The Czech version of the book was published under the title, *Za tím mořem piva* (2019) by Palacký University in Olomouc.. Nothing like this has ever been published since the time Thomas Čapek wrote his classic *The Čechs (Bohemians) in America* some one hundred years ago.

In 2018, he authored *Czechs Won't Get lost in the World, Let Alone in America* (2018), featuring a panorama of selected personalities, whose roots had origin in the Czech Lands and who, in the US, reached extraordinary success and who, with their activities, substantially influenced the growth and development of their new homeland. It is a saga of plain, as well as powerful, people whose influence and importance often exceeded the borders of the US. A great portion of included individuals may be unknown to readers since it concerns persons whose Czech origin was usually not known. The book was published in Bloomington, IN by AuthorHouse. The Czech version of the book, under the title, *Češi se ve svetě neztratí, natož v Americe* (2010) was published by Palacký University in Olomouc.

This was followed by another first, *American Jews with Czechoslovak Roots* (2018), also published by AuthorHouse, a pioneering, comprehensive bibliography, bio-bibliography and historiography of writings relating to American Jews with ancestry in the former Czechoslovakia and its Successor States, the Czech and the Slovak Republics, which has never before been attempted. As the reader will find out, the listed individuals have been involved, practically, in every field of human endeavor, in numbers that surprise.

His next two books bear the titles *Notable Americans with Slovak Roots* (2019) and *Notable American Women with Czechoslovak Roots* (2019). The purpose of these two monographs has been to correct some of the shortcomings that have existed in literature. No comprehensive study about the American Slovaks nor about the American Women of Czechoslovak ancestry has ever been attempted before. As these books demonstrate, the lack of existing information has. not at all been a reflection of the paucity of work done by these individuals. Their contributions have been distinctive and truly remarkable.

And to crown it all, a new extraordinary book appeared soon after. In contrast to American ethnic literature that usually relates to immigrants, this monograph's focus is on Americans who married them, specifically to American men whose spouses were women with Czech or Bohemian roots. Czech women, apart from being beautiful and charming, are known for their extraordinary distinctive character, i.e., independent spirit and nonconforming behavior. And, Lest we Forget, their cuisine art has no equal. It is for these reasons, why the Americans like to marry them. The book, to which Czech Ambassador

Kmoníček wrote a complimentary Foreword, is appropriately titled: *Celebrities and Less Famed Americans Married to Women of Bohemian and Czech Ancestry and their Progeny* (2020).

However, that was not the end of it. *American Learned Men and Women with Czechoslovak Roots* (2020), *American Men and Women in Medicine, Applied Sciences and Engineering* (2021), *Notable Americans of Czechoslovak Ancestry in Arts and Letters; and in Education* (2021), and *Notable Czech and Slovak Americans . From Explorers and Pioneer Colonists through Activists to Public Figures, Diplomats, Professionals, Entrepreneurs and Sports Competitors*, followed soon after (2021).

Believe it or not, additional Mila's scholarly books have come later.

The large monograph, *The Rechcigl Genealogy* (2021) published by the Author's Tranquility Press in Atlanta, GA, is not a typical family genealogy but a comprehensive genealogy consisting of a plethora of individual genealogies related to all allied or related family histories.

Canceled Czechs and Oher Uncovered Americans with Czechoslovak Roots (2022) encompass notable Czech and Slovak Americans, Bohemian Jews and their descendants. Many of them may be heretofore unknown, or ignored, forgotten, obscured, concealed or snubbed. A number of these individuals may not even be aware of their ancestry. This unique monograph has been also published by the Author's Tranquility Press in Atlanta, GA.

Keep Them in Czech (2022) is a composite and comprehensive overview of the life and achievements of immigrants to the New World (the USA, Latin America and Canada) from their ancestral home in the Kingdom of Bohemia and its Successor States. The compendium, coming in 2 volumes, comprises three major sections: the Czechs, the Slovaks and the Jews. The fourth section deals with the Yuppies, the upwardly mobile professionals of promise.

Two more books to be published by the Atlanta, GA publisher, Author's Tranquility Press, are in process. Mila Rechcigl's 2nd volume of his personal memoir, under the title *A Sequel to Czechmate* will soon be reissued, still in 2024. Another unique noteworthy book, *New World Visionaries, Seekers, and Creators with Czechoslovak Roots* is in press.

In 1970, the International College of Applied Nutrition presented Dr. Rechcigl an Honor Scroll, in recognition of his contributions to their scientific program and progress. In 1978, SVU recognized his contributions to natural sciences, by bestowing on him its highest award, the Honorary Membership in the Society. In 1991, on the occasion of its 100th anniversary, the Czechoslovak Academy of Sciences awarded him the Hlávka

ABOUT THE AUTHOR

Memorial Medal. Subsequently, he was also given the Bolzano and the Comenius Medals. In 1998 he received a newly established prize "*Gratias agit*" from the Czech Minister of Foreign Affairs, in addition to receiving a special award from the Ambassador of Czech Republic in the US, Alexander Vondra, for his tireless contribution to the Celebration of the 80th Anniversary of the founding of the Independent Czechoslovak State. In 1999, he received from the hands of President Václav Havel a Memorial Presidential Medal. More recently, he was given an honorary title 'Admiral of the Nebraska Navy' by the Governor of Nebraska and the key to the Capital of Nebraska by the Mayor of Lincoln and the SVU Prague Chapter awarded him '2002 Praha SVU Award'. In 2002, on the occasion of SVU World Congress in Plzeň, Prof. Ing. Zdeněk Vostracký, DrSc., Rector of the University of West Bohemia, presented him a special commendation for the "development of academic, cultural and social relations between the Czech Republic and the expatriate communities." In 2005, the Minister of Foreign Affairs of the Czech Republic honored him by awarding him Jan Masaryk Medal for his contributions in preserving and fostering relations between the Czech Republic and the United States. In February 2010, President of the Senate of the Parliament of the Czech Republic presented him a Silver Medal of the Senate for his efforts on behalf of Czechs abroad and for fostering a good name and the traditions of the Czech Republic. In 2012 he was awarded by the Minister of Interior of the Czech Republic Jan Kubice a medal for his lifetime contributions to Czech archival science. In 2020, he was recipient of the Czech Ministry of Foreign Affairs' Medal of Merit in Diplomacy, for his lifetime contribution to the advancement of Czech American Relations.

Since 1953, Mila has been married to his devoted wife Eva, who has been a strong supporter of her husband in all his endeavors. She passed away on January 24, 2024.They are parents of two highly successful children, Jack E. Rechcigl and Karen Rechcigl Kollecas. Jack is Professor Soil Science with Directorships of two Research & Education Centers at the University of Florida, while Karen is Territory Account Executive for DS Services Crystal Springs. Mila and Eva have 5 grandchildren: Greg Rechcigl, Kevn Rechcigl, Lindsey Rechcigl and 2 great-grandchildren: James Rechcigl and Evelyn Rechcigl.

NAME INDEX

A

Abbick, Rev. John F. 870
Abbott, Monika 657
Abeles, Sara Rebecca 568
Ackermann, Manfred 336
Acosta, Abilio James 'Jim' 35
Adam, Gustav 385
Adam, Johann R. 79
Adamec, Austin Mark 419
Adamová, Jiřina 336
Adkins, Olga Maria Bibza 602
Adler, David 753, 777
Adler, Egon 657
Adler, Friedrich 336
Adler, Kurt 385
Adler, Kurt Herbert 385
Adler, Leopold 79
Adler, Margot Susanna 35
Adler, Peter Herman 385
Adler, Solomon 125
Adren, Robert Lyman 'Bob' 24
Akahoshi, Iris 326
Albieri, Pavel 369
Albright, Madeleine 242, 249
Aleman, Andrés 63
Alexander, Franz Gabriel 221
Alexander, June Granatir 808
Alexander, Lidye Bauer 776
Al-Hilali, Neda 741
Alkhateeb, Sharifa 330
Allers, Franz 385
Alleyn, Kamila 790
Alschuler, Samuel 265
Alt, Franz Leopold 1021
Altmann, Alexander 172, 845
Altmann, Maria 805
Altmanová, Irena 657
Amann, Paul 896
Ambros, Veronika 903
Ambrose, Anton Štefan 17, 24
Ambrosi, Anton Štefan 17, 24
Ambruš, OBE, Ján 280
Ambrusova, Katarina 620
Amsel, Leila Leah 811
Amsel, Pearl 730
Ančerl, Karel 386
Anderle, Josef 808
Anderle, Martin 887
Anderle, Richard J. 955
Andic, Martin F. 846
Anger, Maurice 478
Antheil, George 419, 577
Appel, Karen 207
Appel, Nina 189
Aragón, Angélica 527
Archer, Anne 538, 554, 581
Arlet, Stanislaus (Stanislav) 65
Arnall, Roland E. 126, 250
Arnold, Herbert Anton 887
Arnold, Robert Karl 887
Arnstein, Helen 685
Arnstein, Karl 104
Aronson, Lisa 645
Ascher, Leo 386
Astaire, Adele 603
Astaire, Fred 603
Astl, Jerry (Jaromir) 996, 1002
Aterman, Peter 528
Attl, Kajetán Antonín 419
Attl, Vojmír 419
Auerbach, Norbert 622
Augenfeld, Felix 753

NAME INDEX

Austerlitz, Adele Marie 603
Austerlitz, Frederick 603
Avni, Abraham Albert 870

B

Babbitt, Art 777
Babbitt, Dina 657
Babitsky, Arthur Harold 777
Babka, John Joseph 255
Bača, Frank J. 386
Backer, Julia Nessy 478
Bacon, Isaac 921
Bader, Franz 1
Badnarik, Michael 337
Baeck, Leo 172, 185
Baer, Buddy 554
Baer, Jr., Max 555
Baerwald, Leo 172
Baikal, John L. 250
Bailyn, John Frederick 921
Bailyn, Lotte 976
Bajcsy, Růžena 1043
Bajus, Jozef 779
Baker, Blanche 555
Baker, Herschel Clay 870
Bakovský, Anton 1002
Bakula, Scott Stewart 555
Bala, Nicholas 'Nick' 189
Balatka, Christian Ferdinand 419
Balatka, Hans (Jan) 80, 386
Ballard, Ernesta Drinker 323
Bandas, Rudolph G. 149
Banerjee, Maria Němcová 903
Banič, Stefan 1002
Barber, Elinor G. 808
Bareither, George 420
Bareither, Jacob 420
Baring, Jr., Walter Stephan 255
Barna-Gulanich, Luba 904, 922
Barsch, Wulf 727

Bartík, Otokar 603
Bartók, Béla 387, 436, 476
Bartos, Michael William 870
Bartusek-Brown, Libushka 420
Baska, Louis M. 976
Bassett, Richard 255, 265, 268, 281
Baťka, Bedřich 642
Baťa, Jan Antonín 126
Baťa, Thomas J. 126
Batka, Fred 'Béďa' 642
Batla, Jr., Raymond 190
Baucke, Florián 71
Bauer, František 71
Bauer, Peter 741
Baum, Hedwig 382
Baum, Kurt 478
Baum, Robert 366
Baum, Solomon 173, 494
Baum, Vicki 382
Baumgartner, Ingeborg H. 887
Baumrucker, Dr. George O. 221
Bauska, Barry Arnold 870
Bayard, Alexis I. du Pont 268
Bayard, Jr., James Asheton 256
Bayard, Jr., Thomas Francis 256
Bayard, Richard Henry 250, 256, 272
Bayard, Thomas F. 242, 666
Bayard, Thomas Francis 250, 256
Baycura, David Peter 754
Beaver, Olga 'Ollie' 944
Becher, Gustavus 281
Beck, 3rd, James Montgomery 126
Beck, Abraham Reinke 117
Beck, Erich 846
Beck, James M. 256
Beck, James Montgomery 126, 242
Beck, James Nathan 50
Beck, John 50, 73, 117
Beck, Martin 622, 637, 857
Beck, Maximilian 846

1050

Beck, Prof. Paul Eugene	420
Beck, Věra Fischer	896
Becka, Richard Marion	846
Becka, Tom	36
Becker, Marion Rombauer	362, 373
BecVar, Arthur Nicholas	710
Bedichek, Donald	871
Bedichek, Robert C.	1021
Beerman, Tibor (Eliahu)	754
Begich, Mark Peter	256
Behaim, Martin	59
Behensky, Rosemarie 'Rosie'	843
Behr, Jan	387
Behul, Julius	17
Bejcek, Joseph C.	420
Bekey, George Albert	1022
Belejcak, Adalbert Thomas	373
Bell, Susan Groag	808
Bell, Thomas	373
Bella, Igor Vladimir	161
Bella, Julius Igor Constantine	161
Belohlavek, Charles (Karol)	17
Bělonoha, Markéta	615
Belton, Betty Rose Kepka	741
Benatzky, Ralph	387
Benca, Adolf	657
Bencůr, Matej	372
Benda, Harry Jindřich	809
Benda, Miroslav	1022
Benda, Stan D.	190
Bendáková, Růžena	483
Bender, George Harrison	256
Benes, Barton Lidice	730
Beneš, Jan	369
Beneš, Miroslava M.	754, 790
Beneš, W. Dominick	754
Benesch, Alfred Abraham	190
Benesch, Susan	191
Benischek, Brad	698
Benishek, Dan	257
Bennes, John Virginius	755
Benovský, Móric	61, 107
Bentley, Peter John Gerald	126
Bentov, Itzhak	1002
Benyovszky, Móric	61, 107
Beranek, Christian	698
Beranek, Luke	955
Berchtold, Bedřich Všemír	94
Bercik, William	272
Berger, Augustin	603
Berger, Dr. Frank M.	221
Berger, Johann	61
Berger, Meyer	25
Berger, Oscar	698
Berger, Rudolf	478
Berger, Victor L.	257
Bergmann, Michael	623
Bernal, Olga	896
Bernardiová, Karla	486
Bernays, Anne	374
Bernays, Edward (Louis James)	976
Bérová, Olinka	591
Berryman, Michael John	556
Bertolotti, Brittany Anne	582
Bervida, Jan	281
Bettelheim, Aaron Albert Siegfried	173
Bettelheim, Bernard Jean	161
Bettelheim, Samuel	350
Bey, Turhan	556
Bezdek, Roger H.	977
Bialik, Mayim Hoya	557
Bicha, Karel D.	809
Bicondova, Camren	557
Biddle, Francis	265
Biddle, Francis Beverley	242
Biddle, Gorge	658
Biddle, Michael John	727
Biederman, Charles	730
Biederman, Joseph	127
Biel, Jessica	557

Bielek, Ivan 18, 127
Bielo, Henry 420, 421
Bielo, Julius 420, 421
Bila, William 326
Bily, Frank 742
Bily, Joseph 742
Bingham Skalak, David 1037
Biřkov, Václav Šašek of 60
Birnbaum, William Franklin 'Frank' 478
Bischoff, Franz A 658
Bischoff, Joyce Arlene 1022
Bischoff, Juan Xavier 65
Biskup, George Joseph 149
Bittman, Ladislav 113
Bittner, Bartoš 8, 321
Bitton-Jackson, Livia 809
Black, Karen Blanche 528, 558
Blackburn, Tyler Jordon 558
Blaha, John 102
Bláha, Louis M. 387
Blahnik, Gary 846
Blahous, 3rd, Charles Paul 242
Blau, Eve 790, 809
Blau, George Erwin 810
Blau, Helen M. 934
Blažek, Lubomír 1023
Blezek, J. W. 272
Bloch, Albert 658
Bloch, Benjamin C. 755
Bloch, Charles Edward 50
Bloch, Claude Charles 282
Bloch, Edward 51
Bloch, Henry W. 127
Bloch, Herbert 867
Bloch, Jacob 173
Bloch, Maria Victoria 805
Block, Abraham 282
Block, Abram 227
Block, Daniel 173
Blonsky, Nicole 'Nikki' Margaret 559

Bloomfield, Leonard 922
Bloomfield-Zeisler, Fannie 476
Blucas, Marcus Paul 'Marc' 559
Blum, Sara (Abeles) 350
Bobinet, Kyra J. 221
Bobula, Titus de 755
Bodanzky, Arthur 387
Bodiford, William M. 188, 919
Bodnar, John 810
Bodner, Joseph 658
Boehm, Carl 559
Boehm, Jacob 61
Boehm, Karl 559
Bohacek, Stuart J. 243
Bohm, Henry Victor 944
Böhm, Karl August Leopold 387
Böhm, Karlheinz 559
Bohmann, Joseph 522
Bohmer, Alois 191
Bohůnek, Rudolf 658
Boková, Jana 623
Bolchazy, Ladislaus Joseph 51
Boldizar, Darina 659
Bolech, William Emanuel 388
Bolehovská, Helena 603
Bolerjack, Craig 36
Boleska, William Emanuel 388
Bolona, Melissa 560
Bon Jovi, Jon 500
Bondi, August 80, 107, 282, 319
Bondi, Jonas (ben Abraham) 25, 51, 173
Bondy, Heinz Erie 117
Bondy, Max 117, 123, 124
Bondy, William 265
Bondy-Charvát, Richard 755
Bongiovi, Jr., John Francis 500
Bor, Ján E. 18
Bordley, John Beale 227, 659
Boreanaz, David 560
Borecký, Miloš 916

Bories, Herman 174
Borinie, Franciscus 66
Bořkovec, Věra Žanda 904
Borsody, Stephen 810
Boruhradský, Šimon 66
Borůvka, Radmila 940
Boryně, František 66
Bosak, Edita 810
Bosbyshell, Oliver C. 283
Bottom, Joaquin Rafael 586
Bottom, River Jude 586
Bouchal, John L. 250
Bouché, René Robert 693
Bouchet, Barbara 561
Boudník, Jiří W. 755
Bouldin, James Wood 257
Bouldin, Thomas Tyler 257
Bouska, Adam 712
Bozak, Rudolph Thomas 1003
Bozek, Phillip Edward 871
Brabec, Harry J. 421
Bradac, Thomas F. 649
Brand, Daniel 1023
Brand, Jiří 66
Brandeis, Adele 790
Brandeis, Adolph 80, 81, 227
Brandeis, Alfred F. 228
Brandeis, Alice Goldmark 82, 326, 330, 337
Brandeis, Arthur D. 127
Brandeis, Fanny 508
Brandeis, Frederick 421
Brandeis, Louis D. 80, 81, 82, 191, 215, 227, 265, 326, 336, 337, 508, 790
Brandeis, Otto 487
Brandeis, Rabbi Louis D. 351
Brandesky, Joseph 650
Braun, Maurice 659
Braunfeld, Fritz 192
Braunfeld, Peter George 118

Brazda, Bozidor 750
Brázda-Jankovský, Andrej 371, 750
Brecher, Egon 529
Brecht-Schall, Barbara 529
Breckinridge, John Bayne 257
Breiner, Peter 388
Breitenfeld, Paul Emil 424
Břeský, Dushan 896
Brestovansky, Marta 659
Breuer, Miles J. 374
Brewerton, George Douglas 283
Brewster, David Baugh 257
Brezik, Victor Benjamin 847
Březina, Jiří 955
Brice, 3rd, John 272
Brice, James 269, 272
Brice, James E. 250
Brod, Fritzi 703
Brodenová, Lída 478
Brody, Adrien 561
Brolin, Talisman 713
Brom, Libor 904
Bronner, Leila Leah 811
Brosch, Jimmy 388
Broshek, Joseph John 284
Brouk, Frank 421
Brown, Gail 561
Brown, John Marshall 284
Brožík, Jaroslav 708, 727
Bruchac, Joseph 374
Bruckman, Henrietta 323
Bruml, Charles (Karel) 703
Brůžek, John Frank 272
Bryan, 3rd, John Steuart 51
Bryan, David Tennant 51
Bryan, Henry 284
Bryan, John Stewart 51
Bryce, Lloyd S. 250
Bryce, Lloyd Stephens 257
Brymová, Ester 623

Brzezinski, Emilie Beneš 730
Brzezinski, Mark Francis 250
Brzorad, Nina 604
Bubenik, Andrea 791
Bubeník, Vít 922
Buberl, Casper 730
Büch, Laszlo 128
Buchanan, George Wesley 162
Buchar, Joseph 389
Buchar, Robert 642
Buchstein, Robert August 693
Buchta, William Carl 272
Bučil, Milan Bohumil 421
Buck, Leslie 128
Buckingham, Carmel 495
Buckingham, Celeste 495
Buergenthal, Thomas 192
Bugas, Jack 109
Bugas, John Stephen 109
Bullaty, Sonja 713
Bulova, Arde 128
Buňata, Joseph 8
Bunzel, Gertrude 605
Bunzel, Ruth Leah 977
Bunzl, Julius 228
Burda, Pavel 421
Burda, Robert Warren 871
Bures, Charles Edwin 847
Bureš, Václav 45
Buresch, Joe E. 699
Buresch, Zdenka 659
Burger, Hanuš 624
Burger, Jiří 66
Burian, Jarka Marsano 650
Burian, Karel 479
Burian, Laura 811, 919
Burian, Peter 811, 867
Burian, Richard Martin 847
Buřík, Paul 756
Burka, Jan 703

Burkvíz, Marcus Thiel of 65
Busch, Isidor 81, 228, 319, 337
Bušek, Vratislav 193
Bush, Barbara 73, 243
Bush, George W. 39, 212, 242, 243, 251,
    268, 269, 376, 578, 752
Bush, Isidor 81, 228, 319, 337
Bush, John Ellis 'Jeb' 269
Bush, Lauren Pierce 578, 752
Bush, Lewis 284
Bush, Mathias 61, 284, 331
Bush, Solomon 284
Buyer, Edward Michael 996, 1002
Buyer, Royal Samuel 996, 1003

C

Čada, Joseph 813
Čadek, Joseph Ottokar 422
Cadek, Ottokar Theodore 422
Calhoun, Alice 561
Callies, David Lee 193
Callies, Sarah Anne Wayne 561
Cancelmi, Annie 585
Cantrell, Jr., Jerry (Fulton) 495
Čapek, Dr. Radan 222
Čapek, Jan Vratislav 8, 1003
Čapek, John 495
Čapek, Joseph Horymír 423
Čapek, Mája V. 162
Čapek, Milič 848, 977
Capek, Stella M. 977
Čapek, Thomas 240, 700, 812, 1002
Capka, Jerry George 285, 996, 1003
Cardew, Angelika 887
Carol, Sue 562
Carroll, Margaret Deutsch 791
Carroll, Samuel Sprigg 285
Carson, Hunter 562
Cartwright, Katherine 163
Cary, Claiborne 529

Caviezel, Jim	563
Cech, John O.	871
Čech-Colini, Vojen W.	659
Čechová, A.	9
Cejka, Mike	36
Cekota, Antonín	9
Čelovský, Bořivoj (Boris)	812
Cenker, Robert J.	102
Cenkl, Pavel	872
Cepak, William	52
Cepek, Michael Lewis	978
Ceplecha, Christian William	813
Cepuran, Edward	389
Čermák, Albina Rose	338
Čermák, Anton	338
Čermák, Anton Joseph	272
Čermák, Lily	678
Čermák, Vladimír	956
Cermak, William	1004
Čermáková, Leokadia	678
Cernan, Eugene	102
Cernik, Eva	605
Černý, Albert Vojtěch 'Vojta'	422
Cerny, Charlene Ann	791
Černý, Daniel	149
Cerny, Edward A.	149
Cerny, JoBe (or Jo Be)	563
Cerny, Joseph G.	273
Cerny, Milada	422
Černý, Petr	956
Cerny, Robert George	756
Cerny, William	422
Červená, Soňa	479
Cervenik, William R.	273
Cervenka, Christene Lee	496
Cervenka, Exene	496
Cervenka, O.P., Barbara	660
Cerveny, George Robert	872
Cesnakova, Eva M.	163
Chaback, Michael J.	149
Chada, Joseph	813
Chalmers, Ariana Margaretta Jekyll	315
Chaloupka, Vladimír	713
Chalupa, Cynthia S.	887
Chalupa, Frederico Abel	897
Chalupa, William Victor	934
Chambers, Ezekiel Forman	257, 285
Chance, Greyson Michael	496
Chando, Alexandra	563
Chapek, Joseph Edward	423
Chapek, Joseph Horymír	423
Chapman, John Jay	193, 331
Charmatz, Jan Paul	194
Charvát, Otakar	9
Chase, Stephanie Ann	423
Cheever, Benjamin	375
Cheever, Mary (Watson)	375
Cheever, Susan	375
Chekova, Josepha	479
Chernosky, Jr., Joseph V.	956
Cherny, Andrei	339
Cherny, Andrei Hugo	194, 331
Cherny, Robert	813
Chihuly, Dale	742
Chlumská, Renata	107
Chlumsky, Anna	563
Chorvat, Scarlett	615
Chorvathova-Conant, Verona	905
Chotek, Hugo	369
Chow, Kelsey Asbille	564
Chrisman, Václav	66
Christensen, Raylin	615
Christman, Václav	66
Chudoba, Bohdan	813
Chvala, Joe	530, 605
Chvatal, Janet Marie	479
Chvátal, Václav 'Vašek'	1023
Chvostek, Annabelle	496
Chýlek, Petr	956
Chytka, Tony	731

Chytry, Joseph 814
Cieker, John 18
Cíger, Jozef 371
Cíger-Hronský, Jozef 371
Cihlář, Tomáš 222
Cihlář, Vlasta 704
Čimera, Jaroslav 423
Cincík, Jozef G. 780
Činčura, Andrew 905
Cipra, Winslow 52
Ciprisová, Hanička 384
Cisar, George 564
Cisar, John L. 934
Cizek, Eugene 756
Cizek, Katerina 624
Clagett, John Rozier 285
Clagett, Marshall 814
Clark, Charlotte H. 888
Clarkson, Jesse D. 815
Clarkson, Matthew 286
Clayton, Joshua 228
Clayton, Thomas 258
Closs, Hannah Margaret Mary 369
Cmarada, Claudine 263
Coates, Grace Stone 369
Coblentz, Dorothy Wormser 757
Cohn, Dorrit 888
Cohn, Richard 509
Cohn, Steven 52
Colhoun, Edmund Ross 286
Colhoun, Samuel Reed 286
Collier, Henry Watkins 269
Columbus, Chris 625
Comrada, Norma 905
Connell, Gaelan Alexander 564
Constable, Albert 258
Coon, Carrie 530
Cope, Lída 922
Cope, Lída Dutková 872
Copjec, Joan 651, 848

Coufal, Edward A. 273
Craig, Charlotte M. 888
Crisler, Matthias 63
Critz, Mark 258
Cuculinus, Matthias 66
Čulen, Konštantin 815
Čulík II, Karel 1024
Čulík, Karel 1024
Čupková, Dana 757
Curtis, Jamie Lee 564
Curtis, Tony 564
Cushing, Howard Gardiner 660
Cushing, Lily Dulany 660
Cvancara, Alan Milton 957
Cykler, Edmund 509
Czada, Friederike 608
Czapek, Emil 1004
Czerny, Henry 565

D

d'Harnoncourt, Anne 791
d'Harnoncourt, Everard 652
Daddario, Alexandra Anna 565
Daddario, Matthew 565
Dafčík, Ján Marian 651
Damberger, Heinz H. 957
Daněk, Jaromir 849
Daneš, Jiří 94
Daneš, Zdenko Frankenberger 957
Daniel, Jr., Robert Williams 243, 258
Dano, Paul Franklin 530
Dano, Sarah Ann Courtney 751
Darvaš, Lydia 660
Daugherty, Brant 565
David, Christian 73, 78
David, Zdeněk 815
Davis, Ruth 332
de Peyster, John Watts 286, 287
de Peyster, Johnston Livingston 287
de Peyster, Jr., Frederick 287

de Peyster, Jr., John Watts	287
Deák, František	637
DeCoutere, Lucy	565
DeFore, Donald John 'Don'	565
Deitch, Gene	694
Dembitz, Fredericka	81
Dembitz, Lewis N.	339
Dembitz, Lewis Naphtali	319
Demetz, Peter	889
Demuth, Charles	660
Demuth, Christoph	73
Demuth, Gotthard	73
Demuth, Gottlieb	73
Demuth, Oliver J.	273
Den, Petr	370
Denďúr, John	18, 49
Derham, Katarina Van	620
Dershowitz, Zvi	174
Desmond, John Jacob	757
Desmond, John Michael	757
Desmond, Paul	424
Destinn, Emmy	479
Deutsch, Ernst	531
Deutsch, Ernst Robert	957
Deutsch, Friedrich	509
Deutsch, Gotthard	174, 815
Deutsch, Kurt	114
Deutsch, Ruth	889
Deutsch, Sender	34, 174
Deutsch, Zola Gotthard	1004
Diakité, Jason Michael Bosak	507
Diamond, Skin	615
Díaz, Federico	788
Dibelka, James B.	758, 759
Dieska, Jozef	849
Digital, Lord	365
Dignowity, Anthony Michael	287, 319
Dilong, Rudolf	18, 372
Diskay, Joseph	480
Ditko, Stephen J.	702
Dittrich, Francis J.	758
Divina, Vaclav	389
Divisek, Fred J.	423
Dluhy, Milan Jaques	978
Dober, Charles Christian	74
Dober, John Leonard	74
Döbereiner, Johanna	935
Dobesh, Elsa Lee	481
Dobias, Charles	424
Dobozy, Péter Pál	81, 288
Dobrík, David	621
Dobrizhoffer, Martin	67
Dobrý, Anton F.	228
Doe, Sandra Lee Maresh	872
Dojc, Yuri	713
Dokoupil, Tony	36
Dokulíková, Lída	478
Dolejsi, Robert	424
Dolejska, Frank	661
Dolezal, Darry	424
Dolezal, George E.	273
Dolezal, Herman M.	1024
Dolezal, Natasha	195
Doležel, Lubomír	905
Doleželová-Velingerová, Milena	920
Dolný, Ján	149
Donato, Anthony	509
Dongres, Ludvík W.	9
Donohue, Agnes McNeill	873
Doolittle, Hilda	375
Dopjera, Ján	523, 1004
Dopyera, John	523, 1004
Dorian, Ernest	531
Dorian, Frederick	509
Dorian, Paul (Deutsch)	389
Dostál, Antonin F.	923
Dostál, Hynek	9
Dostál, Jaroslav	957
Dostál, Joseph O.	228
Dostal, Jr., Lumir E.	229

NAME INDEX

Dostal, Lumir 229
Dostal, Robert J. 849
Dostálová, Anna 9
Dostálová-Busick, Alice M. 196
Doubrava, Jan 661
Drabek, Matthew L. 850
Drac, John Francis 196
Drapell, Joseph 661
Drasdil, Anna 480
Drazdil, Anna 480
Drdlík, Frank J. 645
Drechsler, Sigmund 174
Dreiser, Paul 497
Dreiser, Theodore 375
Dresser, Paul 497
Drickamer, Harry George 996
Drickamer, Jewel 6
Drinker, Jr., Henry Sandwith 510
Drinker, Philip 1005
Drizhal, Luděk 389
Drmola, Evžen 652
Drozd, Andrew M. 906
Drtina, Richard L. 850
Drvota, Mojmír 652
du Pont, Jean Kane Foulke 323
Duane, James Chatham 288
Duben, Vojtěch 9
Ducháček, Helena Kolda 713
Duda, Andrew 229
Duda, Michael 118
Dudek, Les 425
Dudycha, George John 978
Dufek, Anthony V. 273
Dufek, George John 104, 288
Dunn, Helena T. 776
Duras, Victor Hugo 251, 266
Durik, Joseph E. 288
Durovičová, Nataša 652, 873
Dusatko, Tomas (John George) 389
Dusay, Debra 566
Dusay, Marj 566
Dušek, Ivan 653
Dusek, Joe 230
Dusek, Rudolph Valentin 850
Dvonch, Frederick R. 390
Dvorak, Ann 566
Dvořák, Antonín 390, 402, 418, 439, 441, 451, 452, 453, 471
Dvorak, August 118, 1005
Dvorak, Geraldine 566
Dvorak, Jeraldine Matilda 566
Dvorak, John C. 37
Dvorak, Raymond Francis 390
Dvorak, Robert C. 52
Dvorak, Vernon F. 958
Dvořáková, Ludmila 480
Dvorník, Francis 815
Dworak, James Joseph 273
Dworschak, Baldwin 150
Dworschak, Leo Ferdinand 150
Dworshak, Henry Clarence 52, 258

E

Eakin, Květa (Marie) 119
Eckels, Steve 425
Eckels, Steven Zdenek 425
Eckert, Eva 923
Eder, Doris Leonora 873
Eger, Ernst 1005
Ehrenberg, Herman 288
Ehrenfeld, Shmuel 175
Eidlitz, Cyrus Lazelle Warner 758
Eidlitz, Leopold 758
Eidlitz, Robert James 758
Eins, Stefan 789
Eisen, Max 375
Eisen, Norman L. 251
Eisenschiml, Alexander 81, 107, 289
Eisenschiml, Otto 944, 1005
Eisler, Elfriede 109, 338

Eisler, Eva (Tlustá) 780
Eisler, Hanns 390
Eisler, Martin 759
Eisler, Paul 1005
Eisner, Breck 625
Eisner, Sigmund 128, 873
Eisner, Will 694, 699, 702
Eitner, Lorenz E. A. 792
Elias, Frank 425
Elias, Fred 425
Eliáš, Ján 18
Elkins, Frances Adler 777
Elliott, Gertrude 531
Elliott, Maxine 531
Ellmers, Renee 258
Elsik, William Clinton 958
Ember-Spitz, Oskar 661
Engelmann, Michael 704
Englund, Anabel 497
Enzer, Trudy 952
Epstein, Helen 26
Ernst, John L. 129
Ernst, Richard C. 129, 196
Ernst, Roger 251
Erst, Stephen A. 425
Esten, Charles 'Chip' 566
Esterka, Petr 150
Esteyneffer, Juan de 67
Estin, Peter George 699
Estocin, Michael J. 289
Ettrich, Rudi H. 945
Eustache, Elena 532
Evancho, Jacqueline Marie 480, 497
Evans, Hedda Graab 480
Exner, Max Vernon 390
Eymer, Wenceslao (Václav) 67
Ezarik, Breanne 621
Ezarik, Jenna 621
Ezarik, Justine 622

F

Faber, Maurice 175
Fabian, Patrick Joseph 566
Fabian-Reihs, Eva 426
Fabritius, Jacobus 61
Fabry, Jaro 694
Fabry, Jr., Alois 661
Fabry, Marion Leona 426
Fadhli, Amy 615
Fakhri, Nargis 616
Falk, Eugene H. 897
Falk, Peter 566
Fall, Richard 391
Fallat, Paul (Pavol) C. 661
Fallik, Ferdiand 733
Falta, Josef 10
Falteisek, Chris 426
Falteisek, Edwin Francis 150
Faltis, Vincenc František 426
Fanderlík, Velen 662
Fanderlik, Velenka 662
Fanderlíková, Stanislava Eliška 662
Farge, Oliver Hazard Perry La 334
Farkas, Philip 421, 426
Farsky, Aldrich Otto 662
Farsky, Edward Aldrich 662
Farský, Oldřich 662
Faul, Jan 714
Fegley, Oakes 567
Feher, Hans 567
Fehl, Fred 714, 792
Fehl, Philipp 792, 793
Fehl, Raina 792
Feigl, Fred (Bedřich) 663
Feigl, Herbert 851
Feigl, Hugo 793, 806
Feldman, Tibor 567
Fencl, Brian 663
Ferber, Marianne Abeles 979
Feriencik, John Adolf 18

Ferko, Joseph Aloysius 391
Fery, John 663
Fiala, Anthony..94
Fiala, Frantisek..1024
Fiala, Ján..289
Fiala, Robert Dennis..816
Fiala-Zedníček, Irena 664
Ficek-Swenson, Bernice 727
Fiebeger, Gustav Joseph 289
Fierlinger, Paul 778
Figner, Frederico..129
Figuli, František Samuel......................................82
Filas, Francis Lad 150
Filek, Jozef 19
Fincke, Michael..103
Firkušný, Leoš 483, 510, 520
Firkušný, Rudolf 426, 510, 520
Fischbach, Elias Beck 427
Fischer, Irene 958
Fischer, Jenna..567
Fischer, Juliana 776
Fischer, Regina Marie 567
Fischer, Ruth 109, 338
Fischl, Hanna...894
Fischler, Alexander 897
Fischmann, Zdenka E.......................................510
Fišera, František 10
Fišerová, Martina 497
Fisher, Harrison...694
Fisher, Hugo Anton 664
Fisher, Hugo Melville...664
Fisher, Jiří 637
Fisk, Schuyler Elizabeth 498
Flaks, Francis Augustus 759
Fleischmann, Charles Louis 129
Fleischmann, Julius..273
Fleischmann, Martin.............................. 945, 1005
Fleischmann, Peter F. 53
Fleming, Renée 480
Flexner, Abraham..119

Flexner, Bernard 196
Flexner, Charles William 222
Flexner, Eleanor...817
Flexner, James Thomas.......................... 376, 817
Flexner, Jennie Mass 6
Flexner, Louis Barkhouse 222
Flexner, Simon 223
Flexner, Washington 53
Fodor, Eugene..53, 110
Fogl, Alois 523, 524, 527
Folda, 3rd, Jaroslav Thayer 793
Folda, Jr., Jaroslav Thayer 289
Folta, George W...266
Folta, George William..290
Foltin, Lore Barbara 890
Ford, Morgan...266
Forges, Alison L. Des...327
Forman, Gen. Thomas Marsh...........................290
Forman, Miloš 13, 549, 587, 625, 630, 644
Fornet, Cornelius 290
Fornét, Kornél (Cornelius) 82
Fousek, Albert Joseph.......................................274
Fousek, Frank Daniel 665
Fousek, John 817
Fousek, Marianka S................................. 163, 818
Fradel, Juriaen 61
Francisci, Miloslav...391
Francken, Ruth..780
Franěk, František 1024
Frank, Oskar Benjamin.......................................31
Frank, Pamela...427
Frankfurter, Felix 197, 266
Frankl, Oscar Benjamin........................... 851, 890
Frankl, Paul.. 530, 793
Frankl, Viktor Emil 851
Franko, Frank R. 274
Franta, Petr 759
František Choura, ...356
Franz, Dennis..567
Franzl, Josef 427

Fraser, Brendan James 568
Freedle, Frank 714
Freilich, Samuel 175
Freiman, Mark 480
Frel, Jiří 794
Frenkel, Vera 780
Freund, Edward J. 427
Freund, Karl 642
Freund, Paul Abraham 197
Frey, Sigmund 175
Fric, Alberto Vojtěch 94
Fridrich, Jessica 997, 1006
Fried, Alexander 818
Fried, Charles 197, 243
Fried, Maru Prokop 665
Friedländer, Saul 818
Friedmann, David 665
Friedmann, Elli L. 809
Fries, Adelaide 1
Fries, Adelaide Lisetta 819
Friese, Alfred 427
Friesleben, Daniel N. 230
Friml, Jr., Rudolf 568
Friml, Rudolf 391, 568
Frind, Anni 481
Frinta, Dagmar 781
Frinta, Mojmír Svatopluk 794
Fritz, Samuel 67, 71, 95
Frolík, Josef 110
Frolik, Lawrence A. 198
Froula, Anna Katherine 874
Froula, Christine 874
Fryščák, Milan 923
Fuchs, Ewald 523, 527
Fuerst, Moritz 742
Fuka, Eva 714
Fuller, Joseph 760
Furdek, Stephen 49
Furman, Erna 223
Furman, Erna Mary 979

Fürth, Ernestine 324
Fürth, Victor 760

G

G, Hanka 498
G'Vera, Ivan 569
Gabanek, Joseph 665
Gabánková, Maria 665
Gabriny, John Gustav 760
Gaertner, Rudolf 945, 1006
Gág, Anton 666
Gág, Wanda Hazel 694
Gajdusek, Daniel Carleton 224
Gálfy-Gállik, Andrew 82, 290
Galla, Roxanne 616
Gallagher, Richard H. 1025
Gallatin, Albert Eugene 794
Gamble, Eugenia A. 163
Gans, Joachim 62
Gans, Louis 129
Ganter, Bernard J. 150
Ganz, Peter 224
Ganz, William 1006
Garfein, Blanche 555
Garfein, Herschel 391
Garfein, Jack 532
Garson, Willie 568
Gartner, Hana 37
Garvin, Paul Lucian 924
Gasparik, Tibor 714
Gatterman, Antone 231
Gavencky, Frank John 666
Gavenda, Rev. Joseph John 151
Gaydos, Joseph M. 259
Geber, Hana 731
Gecsei, Jan 1025
Geiger, Bernhard 917
Gelbart, Petra 511
Gelley, Alexander 875
Gelley, Zachariah 175

NAME INDEX

Gellhorn, Edna Fischel 324
Gellhorn, Martha 26
Gellhorn, Walter Fischel 198
Genuth, David L. 176
Georgevich, Maria Mattei 481
Geringer, August 16, 45, 321
Geringer, Vladimir A. 251
Gernreich, Rudi 751
Gerster, Anthony (Antal) 82, 291
Gerster, Etelka 481
Gessman, Albert Miloslav 868, 924
Getting, Ivan A. 997, 1006
Getting, Milan Alexander 19, 49
Gibian, George 906
Gibian, Peter 875
Giger, Maryellen Lissak 946
Gilbert, Sara 568
Gilfert, Charles 638
Gilfond, Elsie 481
Gilg, Adam 68
Gilinsky, Jack 498, 568
Gimbel, Peter R. 625
Ginter, Anthony 511
Gintzel, Jan 68
Ginzel, Nicola 731, 781
Gladis, Michael 568
Gladney, Henry 1025
Gleiman, Lubomír 852
Glenn, Otis Ferguson 259
Glos, George Ernest 199
Glover, Bruce Herbert 568
Glover, Crispin Hellion 569
Glücksmann, Heinrich 31
Goetzl, Anselm 392
Goetz-Stankiewicz, Markéta 890
Golden, Arthur 376
Goldman, Ernest 428
Goldmark, Josephine Clara 332
Goldmark, Pauline Dorothea 324, 332
Goldmark, Regina 82

Goldschmied, Gertrude 605
Goldstein, Otto Herman 291
Goldzier, Julius 259
Gollan, Frank 1007
Gompers, Heinrich 852
Gonosová, Anna 794
Gosz, Roman 'Romy' Louis 392
Gottlieb, Eugene 925
Gottliebová, Dina 657
Grab, Alexander 820
Grab, Hedda Graab 480
Grab, Hermann 511
Graf, Herbert 1007
Graf, Max 521
Grandillo, Sean 533
Gratz, Bernard 62
Gratz, Michael 62
Gratz, Rebecca 119
Gray, Clayland Boyden 251
Gray, Ray Weld 760
Green, Adam 498
Greenfield, Irene 681
Greenfield, Martin 130
Greenfield, Samuel 176
Greenhut, Benedict Joseph 130
Greenhut, Joseph Benedict 130, 291
Greger, Herbert Hans 1007
Gregor, Helen Frances 743
Gregušová, Hanka 498
Greil, Jacob 130, 291
Grenchik, Joseph 274
Greytak, John Joseph 292
Gries, Moses J. 176
Gries, Roger 151
Grippando, James 376
Gross, Ariela 199
Gross, Bertram Myron 979
Gross, David Jonathan 946
Gross, Mark Donald 998, 1007
Gross, Samuel R. 199

Gross-Bettelheim, Jolán 658
Grossman, George 498
Grosz, Anita H. 714
Gruen, Victor 760
Grünbaum, Victor 760
Grund, Francis 26
Grund, Francis Joseph 251
Grünfeld, Paul Stefan 518
Grünzweig, Bedřich 715
Grymes, Oliver Smith 610
Grymes, Susannah Beverley 315
Gschwind, Kamil Stephen 760
Guderna, Ladislav 666, 733, 784
Guermonprez, Trude 743
Guerrini, Stella Eugenia
 Hammerschlag 199
Guinzburg, Aaron 176
Guinzburg, Frederick Victor 731
Guinzburg, Harold Kleinert 54
Guinzburg, Henry Aaron 339
Guinzburg, Kate 626
Guinzburg, Ralph Kleinert 131
Gulíšek, Tomáš 760
Gulovich, Maria 110
Gunn, Anna 569
Gunter, Jr., Carl Newton 339
Gurewich, Marinka 482, 653
Gutsler, Barbara 561

H

Haas, Arthur Gustav 820
Haas, Gaby (Gabriel) 428
Haas, Hugo 569
Haas, Jean Tachau 605
Haas, Otto Henry 958
Haberecht, Gottlieb 74
Haberman, Gustav 356
Hacaj, Lydia 660
Hackenschmied, Alexandr 715
Hadraba, Theodore Joseph 251

Haenke, Thaddeus (Tadeáš) 96
Hager, Dagmar Regine 578
Hahn, Aaron 177
Hahn, Fred 820
Haidušek, August 274
Haidušek, Augustin 339
Hain, Frank J. 428
Hajda, Jr., John 511
Hajicek, James 716
Halama, Maria 482
Halata, Mark 429
Halik, Raymond Richard 1008
Halko, Arlene A. 946
Halm, Teo Lucas 533
Hamachek, Frank 1008
Hamáchek, Frank 231
Hamachek, Matthew 645
Hamerschlag, Arthur Arton 119
Hammer, Jan 392, 506
Hammer, William Joseph 1008
Hammerschlag, Hanna 343
Hampl, Patricia 376
Hanacek, John J. 1008
Hanak, Edward 1008
Hanák, Miroslav John 897
Hanak, Walter Karl 820
Hanatschek, Herman Carl 666
Haněl, Olaf 666
Hanka, Ladislav R. 728
Hanket, Arthur 292, 533
Hanna, Gabrielle Jeannette 621
Hannah-Jones, Nikole Sheri 26
Hanover, Donna 37
Hanslik, Adolph Rudolph 232
Hanus, George 151
Hanus, Jerome 151
Hanushek, Eric 980
Hanzelka, Richard L. 875
Hanzlik, Louis 429
Hanzlik, Rayburn D. 244

NAME INDEX

Hardon, John 151
Harmon, Tony 429
Harnisch, Wolf 569
Harnyak, Thomas B. 19
Hartford, Henrietta 131
Hartford, Juliet 570, 667
Hartmann, Joseph S. 131
Harvanek, Robert Francis 852
Harzer, Edeltraud 917
Hasalová, Dagmar 493
Hašek, Eliška 244
Hašek, John Henry George 292
Hassaurek, Friedrich 82
Hatala, Želmíra 704
Hatcher, Teri Lynn 570
Hauner, Magdalena 920
Hauner, Milan L. 820
Hauptmann, Henry George 62
Hauserová, Božena 113
Havel, Brian F. 200
Havel, Dan 731
Havel, Hippolyte 365
Havel, Joseph 732
Havel, Martin Victor 274
Havel, Richard W. 200
Havelka, Maria Ludmila 482
Havelka, Václav 533
Haven, James 570
Havlasa, Jan 95, 370
Havlicek, Charles (Karel) 430
Havlicek, Lumir C. 392
Havran, Martin Joseph 821
Hayek, Emil J. 200
Hayek, Julie Lynne 570
Hayek, Matthew 'Matt' J. 274
Headly, Glenne 570
Hearn, Jana Srba 821
Hecht, Margaret Maria 482
Hecht, Sigmund 177
Heckewalder, Christian Renatus 74

Heckewelder, John E. G. 74
Heckewelder, John G. E. 96, 110
Heidelberger, Philip 1025
Heinisch, Rochus 131, 224, 292, 1008
Heinrich, Anthony Philip 393
Heinrich, Rudolph 743
Heinz, Hans Joachim 482
Heiskell, Marian Sulzberger Dryfoos 363
Heisner, Beverly F. 794
Hejduk, John Quentin 761
Hejduk, Renata 795
Hejtmanek, Katherine 'Katie' Rose 981
Hekelová, Drahomíra Lea 739
Helclová-Snížková, Božena 533
Heller, Bernhard 232
Heller, Erich 890
Heller, James Gutheim 177, 393
Heller, Maximilian H. 177
Heller, Mildred Grey 483
Heller, Otto 890
Heller, Rabbi James G. 351
Heller, Rabbi Maximilian H. 351
Helms, Mark 293
Helmschmied, Carl V. 744
Henderson, Logan Phillip 571
Henle, Mary Therese 982
Henle, Paul William 852
Henreid, Paul 571
Henshel, Harry Bulova 131
Henzl, Věra M. 925
Henzlik, Randall E. 1025
Hepburn, Audrey 571
Herc, Bernard 356
Herda, Frank A. 293
Hering, Oswald Constantin 761
Heritesová-Kohn, Maria 430
Herlinger, Růžena G. 483
Heřman, Augustine 5, 51, 62, 107, 227,
    228, 242, 243, 246, 247, 249, 250, 255,
    256, 257, 258, 259, 260, 261, 262, 263,

264, 265, 267, 268, 269, 270, 271, 272, 277, 281, 283, 284, 285, 286, 288, 290, 296, 301, 304, 307, 308, 313, 315, 317, 318, 324, 610, 658, 659, 660, 727, 765, 814, 870, 877, 899

Heřman, John 83
Heřmanská, Hanička 384
Heřmanský, Hynek 1026
Herskovits, Jean Frances 821
Herskovits, Melville J. 821, 982
Herskowitz, Milton Leon 'Mickey' 376
Hertz, John D. 132
Herz, Otto 430
Herzigová, Eva 616
Herzog, Elsie Wise Gross 777
Herzog, Fred 201
Hesse-Sprotte, Mme. 483
Hessoun, Joseph 10
Heyberger, Anna 897
Heying, Andrew Keegan 574
Heying, Casey Keegan 574
Heythum, Antonin 710
Hilles, Florence Bayard 324
Hinlicky, Paul 164
Hirsch, Helen Kotas 430
Hirsch, Ruth Weir 925
Hirschberger, Fritz 667
Hladis, Iva 667
Hladky, James Robert 431
Hlava, Francisco 68
Hlaváček, Frank 356
Hlaváček, Frank J. 10
Hlubek, David Lawrence 499
Hlubůček, Jiří 45
Hnilicka, Milo P. 1009
Hochman, Jiří 11
Hochwald, Ruth 332
Hodek, Frank W. 393
Hodous, Edward Joseph 152
Hodous, Lewis 164

Hoffman, Harold Giles 269, 274
Hoffman, Martin Hermanzen 62
Hoffman, Philip 626
Hofner, Emil 'Bash' 431
Holick, Joseph 393
Holick, Michael F. 935
Holik, Joseph 393
Holliday, Ashley 572
Holmberg, Ruth Sulzberger 54
Holub, Leo Millard 716
Holub, Martin 761
Holubar, Allen J. 626
Holý, Alfred 431
Homolka, Oskar 572
Homolka, Robert 'Bill' 274
Honner, John 37
Honsa, Vladimír 898, 926
Hora, John C. 643
Horacek, Leo 512
Horack, Hugo Claude 201
Horack, Jr., Frank Edward 201
Horak, Jan-Christopher 795
Hořáková-Firkušná, Růžena 483
Horecký, Paul 1, 6
Hořejš, Vít 638
Hornak, Ian 781
Hornak, Mark R. 201, 266
Horner, Anton 431
Horner, Christopher 646
Horner, Harry 393, 646
Horner, Henry 132, 269
Horner, James Roy 393
Horner, Joseph P. 431
Hornig, Leslie Elizabeth 935
Hornig, Lili 946
Hornig, Lilli 324
Horsák, Beda 152
Horsky, Charles A. 244
Horsky, Edward 274
Horsky, Emery Donaldson 668

Horský, John 132, 232
Hoschna, Karl 394
Hošek, Chaviva Milada 325
Hosken, Fran 325
Hosken, Franziska 761
Hospodský, John A. 46
Hossaini, Ali 782
Hostinský, Jiří 69
Hostovský, Egon 49, 370
Houda, Bohumil 96
Houdek, Joseph 432
Houdek, Robert G. 251
Houska, Charles 668
Hovadik, Jaroslav 782
Hovorka, Susan D. 958
Hrachovský, Frank M. 761
Hrádek, J. W. 762
Hradilák, Karel 588
Hradílek, Henry 762
Hrbek, Greg 376
Hrbková, Šárka B. 907
Hrdlicka, Ales 936
Hrdlicka, Clement Lewis 868
Hrdlík, Miloslav 432
Hrdy, Olinka 668, 782
Hreha, Stefan 19
Hridel, Anna C. 37
Hrncir, Franz 1001, 1018
Hrobak, Philip Anthony 19
Hromádka, John M. 141
Hromádka, Joseph Lukl 165
Hron, František 959
Hron, Vince 668
Hronek, John 432
Hrousek, Oldřich 432
Hrubý, Antonín 891
Hruby, Edward J. 432
Hruby, Frank M. 512, 521
Hruby, John Franklin 653
Hruby, Peter Rudolph 983

Hruby, Sr., Frank 394
Hruby, William 432, 454
Hrunek, Patricia Betsy 585
Hruska, Natalie 1026
Hruska, Roman Lee 259
Hubacek, William 669
Hubenka, Lloyd John 875
Hudec, Ladislav 762
Hudec, Robert Emil 202
Hudeček, Antonín 669
Hudek, Prokop 83
Huebsch, Adolph 83, 177
Huebsch, Benjamin 54
Hulčr, Jiří 936
Humpal-Zeman, Josephine 11, 325
Hupka, Robert 716
Huppert, George 822
Hůrka, Josef L. 110, 1009
Hurka, Thomas 852
Husa, Karel 394
Husak, Douglas N. 853
Hušek, Joseph 19
Husek, Stephanie Olga 822
Huska, Stephen 19
Husserl, Gerhart 202
Huta, Jaroslav F. 732
Hyna, Devlin J. 1026
Hyna, Otto 433
Hynek, Brian Michael 959
Hynous, David Matthew 152

I

Icahn, Brett 132
Ichida, Audrey 605
Ickovic, Paul 717
Iggers, Wilma Abeles 891
Ihnat, Steve 572
iJustine, ... 622
Illowy, Bernard 177
Iltis, Fred 717

Indichova, Julia 327
Ingerle, Rudolph Frank 669
Ingriš, Eduard 96, 394, 643
Irglová, Marketa 499
Iseman, Matt 534
Iška, Frank (František) 321
Issa, Darrell Edward 259
Ivanec, Teresa 'Terri' 20
Ivanec, Thomas 606

J

Jablonski, Wanda 27
Jablonský, Milan 572
Jacisin, Renee 258
Jacoby, Emil 351
Jaeger, Charles Nepomucene 152
Jaeschke, Juliana 75
Jahoda, Marie 219, 976, 983
Jahoda, Rosa 938
Jahoda, Rosi 342
Jahoda, Susan E. 782
Jakeš, Miroslav 96
Jakl, Miloš B. 762
Jakobson, Roman 908, 926
Jakub, Lisa 572
Jakubovics, Emil 351
Jakubovits, Oskar 822
Jalowetz, Gertrud 743
Jalowetz, Heinrich 512
Jalowetz, Lisa 645
Janac, John Rudolph 524
Janáček, Pavel 669
Janacek, Robert 'Bob' 165
Janacek, Robert Norman 152
Janauschek, Fanny 534
Janček, Jr., Ján 20
Janda, Frank 274
Janda, Laura A. 927
Janda, Richard 927
Jandak, Patrik 717

Jandasek, Francesca 606
Janeček, Helen Hájnik 483
Janeček, Mirko 46
Janecek, Paul 1026
Janega, Ann 202
Jangl, Otto 232
Janik, Del Ivan 875
Janike, Edward W. E. 936
Jankola, Matúš 20
Jankovsky, Michael 732
Janos, James George 271
Janovsky, Felix Bohumil 251
Janowitz, Albert F. 762
Janowitz, Walter 573
Jánská, Markéta 616
Jansky, Karl Guthe 947, 1009
Jansky, Nelson Moreau 512, 521
Jantoška, Jozef 606
Janura, Anton 274
Januschke, Daniel 69
Januška, Daniel 69
Janvier, Catherine Drinker 669
Jarmusch, Jim 626
Jaros, Anne 752
Jasmin, Pierre 433
Jasný, Vojtěch 627
Jason, Sonya 376
Jászi, Oskar 822
Javor, Ken 433
Jay, John ... 193, 202, 245, 251, 259, 266, 269, 280, 320, 331
Jay, Peter Augustus 252
Jay, William 202, 293, 320, 331
Jaymes, Jessica 573
Jebo, Cameron 573
Jecelin, William R. 293
Jedlica, Justin 617
Jedličková, Marie 484
Jekyll, Ariana Margaretta 315
Jelen, Ben 499

Jelik, Andrew 63, 107
Jelínek, Frederick 1026
Jelinek, Hans.. 670, 704
Jelinek, Jerome M. 'Jerry' 433
Jelinek, John Peter................................853
Jelinek, Joseph R. 293
Jelinek, Lawrence James......................822
Jelinek, Stephen (Štěpán)......................433
Jelinek, Stephen H.................................274
Jelinek, Yeshayahu A. 822
Jellinek, Oskar 382
Jeníček, Jana 670
Jenteal, ...573
Jerabek, Esther 6
Jeritza, Maria 484
Jesenský, J. 20
Jesenský, Marcel 823
Ježek, Jaroslav 394, 416, 552
Jezek, Kenneth Charles........................959
Ježek, Peter Alfons 960
Jicha, Jon..704
Jícha, Joseph W. 670
Jilka, Alan...275
Jindřich, Vladimír 960
Jinek, Eva 37
Jirák, Karel Boleslav 395, 417, 512
Jiran, Joseph 524
Jiranek, Leo A. 711
Jirouch, Frank L. 733
Jirousek, Olda 434
Jirousek, Peter.......................................434
Jirovec, Joseph Frank 434
Jiskra, Václav................................ 434, 435
Jizba, Zdeněk Václav 961
John, Jan..69
Jolie, Angelina.......................................573
Jonas, Benjamin Franklin............ 259, 294
Jonáš, Charles (Karel)....... 11, 83, 252, 269, 321, 340
Jonas, Charles H....................................294

Jonas, Charles Raper............................. 203
Jones, January Kristen.......................... 574
Jordan, Frances Ruml 119
Jorissen, Burger...................................... 63
Jorissen, Citizen 63
Joseffy, Rafael 395
Joseph, 4th, Corin Nemec 583
Juhn, Erich 639
Jumba-Lipchick, Angela M. 608
Jung, Leo 177, 178, 853
Jung, Moses 177, 178
Jungk, Robert... 366
Jurasik, Peter 534
Jurásková, Kateřina 434
Jurco, Olga... 266
Jurečka, Cyril 733
Jurena, John A. 435
Juricek, John T. 823
Jurka, Blanche 554
Justman, Zuzana................................... 627

K

Kabat, Timothy 'Tim' 275
Kabeš, Otilia Marie................................ 927
Kacer, Kathy 377
Kadár, Ján 627
Kadavy, Timothy J. 295
Kaderabek, Frank John......................... 435
Kaderavek, Milan 396
Kadlec, Christopher 'Chris' A............... 1027
Kadlec, Dušan 670
Kadler, Eric H... 898
Kafka, Hugo... 762
Kahler, Erich 823, 891
Kahler, Sr., Ferdinand Nickolas 'Ferd' 1009
Kahn, Arthur.. 341
Kahn, Henrietta 323
Kaiser, Alois 178, 494, 495
Kaiser, Christopher Barina (Bařina) 166
Kaiser, Helen Beneš 937

Kajlich, Bianca 574
Kajlik, Vladimír 928
Kalabza, Albert P. 133
Kalanick, Travis 133
Kalas, Clementine 484
Kalas, Gregor 795
Kalas, Harry Norbert 37
Kalas, Jan 435
Kalas, Todd Harry 38
Kalašová, Klementina 484
Kalenčík, Rudolf 372
Kalenský, Zdeněk 961
Kalina, Alois 275
Kalina, Anthony S. 824
Kalina, Vladimír 435
Kall, Adamus 69
Kaller, Adamus 69
Kallik, Ferdinand 670
Kallir, Lilian 436
Kalmar, Ivan 983
Kalnoky, Tomas 500
Kalvoda, Josef 824
Kamen, Michael (Arnold) 396
Kanak, Katharine Marie 961
Kanak, Norbert John 'Jack' 983
Kane, Jerry 232
Kane, Sam 232, 233
Kann, Frederick 671
Kantor, Alfred 671
Kantor-Berg, Friedrich 383
Kapaun, Emil Joseph 294
Kapec, Jeffrey 711, 1009
Kaplan, Ladislav 524
Kaplíř ze Sulevic, Jiří Kryštof 63
Karas, Joža 436
Karch, John 252
Karel, David Gordon 796
Karel, John C. 252
Karel, Leon Charles 513, 521
Karembeu, Adriana 617

Karger, George 671
Karlíček, Martin 436
Karlik, John R. 245
Karlovský, Jaroslav 436
Karmazin, John 133, 1010
Karpathy, Andrej 999, 1011, 1043
Karpeles, Leopold 295
Karpiscak, Adeline Lee 796
Karplus, Arnold 762
Karplus, Gerhard Emanuel 762
Karplus, Kevin 1027
Karplus, Ruth 685
Kasal, Bradley 295
Kasala, Stephen 672
Kasich, John Richard 260, 270
Kasinec, Edward 6
Kaspar, John Wenceslaus 437
Kaspar, Joseph John 1010
Kasparek, Jerry Lewis 868
Kastner, Martin 783
Katko, John 260
Katz, Jane Lobman 341
Katz, Leo 672
Katzer, Frederick Xavier 153
Kauder, Hugo 396
Kauders, Erick 1010
Kaufman, Alexander 178
Kaufman, Enit 672
Kaufmann, Charles B. 717
Kaufmann, Eric Peter 984
Kaufmann, Felix 203
Kaufmann, Walter 397
Kaula, William Jurian 672
Kaula, William M. 961
Kaus, Otto Michael 203
Kaus, Peter Edward 947
Kaus, Regina 'Gina' 377
Kautsky, Catherine C. 437
Kavan, Albia 606
Kavan, Ladislav 1027

Kaye, Sammy 397
Kayser, Jiří (George) 672
Keane, John F. 252
Kebrdle, John 744
Kebrle, John 744
Kebrle, Jr., John 744
Kec, Václav Ignác 437
Keegan, Andrew 574
Keegan, Casey 574
Keller, Ignacius Xavier 70
Keller, Sonja Osaki 937, 998, 1007
Kellner, Charles H. 673
Kellner, Tatana 709, 783
Kellner, Tatana 'Tana' 709
Kelsen, Hans 204
Kelton, Kate 574
Kenny, Anne Marie 484, 500
Kent, Dennis V. 962
Kenton, Christina 733, 784
Keown, Anne Stepan 928
Keppler, Joseph 699
Kern, Jerome David 397, 501
Kernaghan, Charles 333
Kerner, Jr., Otto 266, 270
Kerner, Robert Joseph 824
Kerner, Sr., Otto 266
Kerry, Alexandra Forbes 628
Kerry, John Forbes 260, 628
Kerry, Richard John 252
Keshock, Edward George 999, 1011
Kessler, Alice 825
Kessler-Harris, Alice 825
Khuner, Felix 437
Khyl, Helen Sadilek 437
Kiesler, Hedwig Eva Maria 577
Kiihnl, Herman Willard 295
Kimbrell, Kaiulani 501
Kimbrell, Markéta 535, 575
Kinzek, Charles 907
Kirs, Rudolf 438

Kisch, Egon Erwin 32
Kisch, Ernestine 324
Kisch, Guido 204
Kisha, Daniel John 999, 1011
Kistler, Věra Polenová 397
Kitlová, Emmy 479
Klácel, Ladimír 11, 322, 333, 357, 853
Klamar, Joe 673
Klamár, Joe (Jozef) 718
Klapka, Jerome Jaroslav 673
Klauber, Adolph 639, 649
Klauber, Alice Ellen 673
Klauber, Amy Salz 673
Klauber, Edward 718
Klauber, Edward V. 38
Klauber, Leda Josephine 673
Klecanda, Jan 95, 370
Klecka, August 341
Klein, Alex 438
Klein, David 179
Klein, Henry 179
Klein, Jacob 179
Klein, Jan 224
Klein, Klára Katherina 738
Klein, Philip 179
Klein-Pejšová, Rebekah 825
Klema, Martin 524
Klement, Karl Walter 962
Klemeš, Vít 962
Klemperer, Werner 535
Klenha, Joseph Z. 275
Kliegl, Anton Tiberius 1010
Klier, Robert 438
Klika, Russell Lee 718
Klima, Edward Stephen 928
Klima, John 438, 789
Klimek, Kimberley 'Kim' 825
Kliment, Robert Michael 762
Kliment, Stephen Alexander 763
Klinenberg, Eric M. 984

Kling, Paul	438	Kohn, Charles	233
Klir, George J.	1028	Kohn, Eugene	179
Klumpar, Vladimíra	733, 747	Kohn, Fritz Nathan	536
Klutschak, Heinrich Wenzel	97	Kohn, Hans	826
Kmetz, John T.	245	Kohn, Jacob	179
Kneisel, Franz	439	Kohn, Karl	764
Knerr, Harold Hering	700	Kohn, Tobias	1010
Knight, Frances Gladys	245	Kohn, Tobiáš	134
Knížek, Charles	907	Kohner, Frederick	377
Knoflicek, Agnes	439	Kohner, Pancho	628
Knoller, Mark	39	Kohner, Paul	134, 657
Knop, Karen	204	Kohner, Paul Julius	628
Knott, John Francis	700	Kohner, Susan	575, 636
Kober, Leo	673	Kohner, Walter	657
Kobler, Franz	825	Kohout z Lichtenfeldu, Šimon	63
Kobsa, Alfred	1028	Kohout, Alois	676
Kobza, Dennis	763	Kohout, Jára	535
Kocábová, Natálie	501	Kohout, Ladislav J.	1029
Kocak, Matej	295	Kolar, Rev. Basil Charles	868
Kocán, Štefan	485	Kolar, Rob	501
Kocandrle, Jaromir 'Mirek'	439	Kolar, Roger H.	764
Kochalka, James	702	Kolar, Victor	439
Kochman, Leopold	12	Kolarik, Ruth	797
Kochmann, Leo	356, 357	Kolesar, Jr., Edward S.	999, 1011
Kocián, Jaroslav	439	Kolin, Philip C.	876
Kocianová, Michaela	617	Kolisch, Rudolf	440
Kocourek, Albert	204	Koller, Karl	224
Kocourek, Estanislao	763	Kollisch, Eva	327, 342
Kocourek, Roman Anthony	854	Kollisch, Eva-Maria	341
Kocourek, Rostislav	928	Kollisch, Otto	764
Kodjak, Andrej	907	Kolm, Henry	1010
Koecher, Karel	111	Kolský, Thomas	826
Koechlin, Carl	764	Komara, Ondrej E.	20
Koehler, Herman	233	Komarek, Ed	363
Koerner, John Michael Anthony	673, 784	Komarek, Thomas C.	245
Kofnovec, Donna Ann	37	Komárková, Věra	97
Kofránek, Jan Jaroslav	764	Komonchak, Joseph Andrew	153
Kohák, Erazim Václav	854	Komorous, Rudolf	397
Kohlbeck, Valentine	12, 153	Konarik, Stephen B.	963
Kohler, Frederick	275	Koncelik, Joseph	711

Kondorossy, Leslie	398
Koníček, Zdeněk	440
Konkolski, Richard	97
Konop, Matt	296
Konop, Thomas F.	260
Konop, Thomas Frank	205
Konopasek, Lenka	674
Konopásek, Miloš	1029
Konstantin, Leopoldine	536
Konuš, Jozef J.	928
Kopanic, Jr., Michael J.	827
Kopec, Danny	1030
Kopecky, Frank	205
Kopecky, Joe	440
Kopecky, Sandra	1030
Kopecky, William	440
Kopf, Maxim	674
Kopfstein, Mayer	180
Kopta, Václav Jan	440
Kopunek, Martin	20
Korbel, Francis	233
Korbel, Francis (František) J.	83
Korbel, Francis J.	134
Korbel, Mario	733
Korbelová, Madeleine	242, 249
Korcek, Katarina	502
Kordule, Jindřich	70
Korinek, Valerie Joyce	827
Kořízek, Frank	11, 46, 321
Korn, Philip	84
Körner, Stephen	855
Kornfeld, Joseph Saul	180
Korngold, Erich Wolfgang	398, 513
Korngold, Julius Leopold	513
Korponay, Gábor	606
Korponay, Gabriel de	606
Kortner, Fritz	536
Kosa, Jr., Emil	646
Kosa, Sr., Emil	646
Kosco, George F.	98
Košice, Gyula	733
Kosiczky, Karl	592
Kositchek, Jr., Robert Jay	643, 719
Košler, Zdeněk	398
Kossuth, Lajos	84
Kostal, Irwin	398
Kostal, Rande W.	205
Kostoryz, Stanley L.	46
Kostroun, Daniella Jane	827
Košút, Ludevít	84
Kotalik, Elizabeth 'Liz'	38
Kotas, Helen	421, 430, 440
Koterba, Arthur G.	441
Koterba, Edward Victor	27
Koterba, Jeffrey	700
Kotík, Jan Jakub	789
Kotík, Petr	441, 789
Kotík, Tom	734
Koubek, Vlastimil	764
Koudelka, George John	441
Koudelka, Joseph Maria	153
Kouma, Ernest Richard	296
Kousal, Matthew	674
Koutsky, Frank	275
Kovac, Edward	21
Kovac, John D.	166
Kovac, John Michael	947
Kovacik, Andrew S.	275
Kovacik, John	21
Kovacs, Ernie	536
Kovalik, Peter	675
Kovalik, Tibor	675
Kovály, Pavel	855
Kovanda, Anna R.	325
Kovanda, Vlastimil	399
Kovařík, Jan Josef	441
Kovarik, Terry	39
Kovárna, František	797
Kozak, Harley Jane	575
Kozauer, Nikolaus	828

Kozelnicky, George 'Koz'	937
Kozlay, Eugene Arthur	296
Kozlík, Luděk Alois	907
Krainik, Ardis	485
Krajcik, Josh	502
Krajicek, David	27
Krajsa, Joseph Charles	21
Krakora, Joseph J.	797
Kral, Irene	502
Král, Ivan	399
Král, Josef Jiří	12
Krall, Diana	502
Kramer, Leopold	441
Kramrisch, Stella	798
Krásný, Anton	84
Krásová, Marta	485
Kratina, Joseph M.	734
Kratochvíl, Antonín	719
Kratochvil, Stephen	675
Kratochwill, Thomas R.	985
Kraus, Edward Henry	963
Kraus, Eric B.	964
Kraus, Hana	731
Kraus, Hans Peter	2, 806
Kraus, Jr., Hans P.	806
Kraus, Lily	441
Kraus, Milton	260
Kraushaar, Karoly	410
Krauskopf, Marcus	180
Krausová, Eliška	898
Kravjanský, Mikuláš	675
Krčméry, Jozef Borivoj	21
Krebs, Nita	576
Kreisler, Georg	502
Kreisler, Matthias	63
Krejcar, Jan	399, 442
Krejci, Mark Jerome	985
Krejci, Matthew	442
Krejčí, Rudolph	855
Křenek, Ernst	400
Kreutz, Arthur R.	400
Kreutz, Robert Edward	400
Kreutzberg, Harold	606
Krieglstein, Werner Josef	856
Krieglstein, William George	442
Křikava, Joseph	84
Kris, Ernst Walter	798
Kristufek, Otto	442, 456
Krivak, Andrew	377
Kříž, Milan	734
Kříž, Pavel	576
Kriz, Robert L.	275
Kriz, Tony	166
Kříž, Vilém Francis	719
Kriza, John	607
Krizek, Donald Thomas	938
Kroc, Lukáš	1030
Kroc, Ray	134
Krommer, Anna	32
Krommer, Helmut	675
Krondl, Michael	734
Kronik, John William	898
Kroslak, Candace	576
Kroupa, Antonín	84
Kroupa, Bohuslav	98
Kroupa, Patrick K.	365
Kroutil, John Francis	234
Kroužilka, William (Vilém)	358
Krukar, Jo Ann	245
Kruliš-Randová, Angelika	887
Krupička, Jiří	964
Krusenstiern, Alfred V.	32
Kruta, David	720
Krutak, Lars	986
Krutak, Paul	948
Krutak, Paul Russell	964
Krykorka, Vladyana Langer	695
Kryl, Bohumír	400
Kryl, Frank	421, 430, 442
Kryzan, Frank X.	275

Ksir, Charles J.	985
Kubal, David L.	876
Kubálek, Antonín	442, 666
Kubásek, Helena M.	689
Kubát, Miroslav	1030
Kubelík, Jan	391, 439, 443, 453
Kubelik, Rafael	401, 464
Kubelka, Johanna	935
Kubena, Keith	443
Kubik, Gail Thompson	401
Kubik, Jr., Henry Hank	443
Kubík, Kamil	675
Kubík, Ladislav	401
Kubik, Milo	639
Kubinec, John C.	296
Kubínek, Tomáš	537
Kubitschek, Ernest L.	443
Kubka, Joseph	1010
Kubricht, Paul	828
Kucera, 3rd, William John	39
Kucera, Bedrich 'Ben' Fred	276
Kucera, Daniel Jerome	205
Kucera, Daniel W.	154
Kucera, Ernie	401
Kučera, Henry	928
Kucera, Karil	799
Kucera, Louis Benedict	154
Kuchačevič ze Schluderpacheru, Herbert Charles Angelo	579
Kucharek, Wilma	167
Kuchyňka, Frank	443
Kuchynka, Julius Victor	877
Kudelka, James	607
Kudlata, Václav	358
Kudlich, Hans	85
Kuerti, Anton Emil	444, 938
Kuerti, Julian Andreas	444
Kuerti, Rosa	938
Kuerti, Rosi	342
Kugler, Victor	327
Kuh, Anton	32
Kukalova, Jarmila	948
Kukalova-Peck, Jarmila	948
Kukla, George Jiří	367, 963
Kukučín, Martin	372
Kukulín, Matthias	66
Kulhan, John	342
Kulhanek, Denise Kay	964
Kulich, Vladimír	576
Kumin, Maxine	377
Kun, Joseph	524, 525
Kuntz, Benjamin Putnam	877
Kunzer, Ruth Goldsmith	352, 917
Kupcek, Joseph R.	907
Kurath, Gertrude Prokosch	513, 607
Kurka, Robert	402
Kurka, Robert C.	167
Kurková, Karolina	617
Kurzweil, Raymond	1043
Kurzweil, Raymond 'Ray'	367, 999, 1011
Kushner, Eva Dubská	120, 898
Kuska, George	764
Kuska, Gerhard F.	245
Kuska, James J.	765
Kussi, Peter	907
Kussy, Sarah	352
Kuták, Frank Jaroslav	12
Kutina, Jan	965
Kutka, Anne	675, 680
Kutscherra, Elise	485
Kuzelka, Robert	765
Kvapil, Diane L.	653
Kvapil, Jay	745
Kymlička, Milan	402
Kymlicka, Will	856
Kyncl, Robert	134

L

La Farge, Jr., Christopher	765
Laadt, Anton	135

Labitzky, Wilhelm 402	Lauder, Jane 136
Lach, John J. 50	Lauder, Ronald 135, 136, 342
Lada, Anton 445	Lauder, Ronald Stephen 246, 252
Ladd, Alana 576	Lauersdorf, Mark Richard 929
Ladd, Carol Lee 576	Lauren, Lauren Bush 578, 752
Ladd, David Alan 628	Laurin, Anne 32
Ladd, Jordan Elizabeth 576	Laurin, Arne 27
Ladd, Shane 577	Lawatsch, Andreas Anton 75
Ladocha, Jiří 675	Lax, Thomas 728
Laisner, George Alois Frederick 784	Lazarčík, Gregor 986
Lakin, Christine 577	Lazarsfeld, Lotte 976
Laksar, Václav 445	Lazarsfeld, Paul Felix 986
Lamar, 2nd, Lucius Quintus Cincinnatus 246	Láznička, Peter 965
Lamar, Lucius Quintus Cincinnatus 246, 260, 267, 296	Le Clercq, Jaques J. C. 899
	Leachman, Claiborne 529
Lamar, William Bailey 261	Leachman, Cloris 497, 529, 537
Lamarr, Hedy 577	Lebduska, Lawrence 676
Lamberg, Robert Felix 33	Lebedová, Karla 486
Lamm, Max Robert 445	Lebovics, Herman 829
Landa, Louis A. 877	Lecoque, Alois 676
Landau, Moses M. 180	Ledecky, Jonathan Joseph 136
Landsberger, Benno 917	Lederer, Doris 446
Lang, Fritz 538, 629	Lederer, Ernst A. 1011
Lang, June 577	Lederer, Evelyn L Jeanette 562
Langer, Joseph J. 252	Lederer, Francis 578
Langer, William 261, 266, 270	Lederer, George 639
Laník-Gabanek, Antonia 676	Lederer, Henry B. 297
Lanner, Max Robert 445	Lederer, Josephine Rose 579
Lapka, Eva 745	Lederer, Max M. 234
Lapka, Milan 745	Lederer, Otto 578
Lashanska, Hulda 485	Lederer, Pepi 579
Láska, Věra 828	Ledvina, Emmanuel Boleslaus 154
Lasker, George Eric 1031	Ledyard, Henry Brockhorst 252, 276
Lassak, Francis W. 135	Lee, Ryan Scott 579
Lassander, Dagmar 578	Lefkowitz, David 180, 181
Latzgo, Roger L. 445	Lefkowitz, Jr., David 181
Laucik, Michal 21	Lehár, Franz 402, 484, 507
Lauder, Aerin 135	Lehovec, Kurt 1012
Lauder, Estée 135	Lehovec, Linda 608
	Lehr, Anna 579

NAME INDEX

Leichter, Otto 33
Lemsky, Frederick 108
Lemský, Frederick 297
Lenhoff, Arthur 205
Leopold, Isaiah Edwin 553
Leopold, John 112
Lerando, Lev Zelenka 446
Lerch, Tosca 676
Leskanich, Katrina Elizabeth 503
Lešovský, Adolf 647, 677
Lesznai, Anna 677, 705
Letňanová, Elena 446
Letovský, Jan Bárta 11, 12, 46
Letovský, Jan Milostín Bárta 47
Letovsky, Stanislav Jan 403
Letovsky, Stanley Barta 445
Levey, Harold Alvin 999, 1012
Levey, Ralph Pokorney 136
Levi, Adolph 235
Levitský, Alexander 908
Levy, Henry L. 677
Levy, Jr., Nathan 206
Levy, Lionel Faraday 1012
Levy, Louis Edward 948, 1012
Levy, Max 765, 948, 1012, 1013
Levy, Nathan 206, 235
Levy, Solomon 235
Lewellen, Anne Preucil 446
Lewi, Isidor 27
Lewi, Josef 85
Ley-Piscator, Maria 608
Lhota, Joseph J. 'Joe' 342
Lhoták, Ondřej 1031
Lhotský, Antonín 644
Liberato, Liana Daine 579
Lichtenberg, Lenka 494, 503
Lidinsky, Jr., Richard A. 246
Liebling, Terry Hamlisch 629
Liebman, Joshua Loth 181
Liehm, Antonín J. 12

Lihani, John 899
Liháni, Pavel 705
Lihani, Terezka 503
Líková, Eva 486
Lilienthal, David Eli 246
Liman, Anthony (Antonín) V. 920
Linck, Wenceslao 70, 98
Linder, Barbara Pejsar 677
Linhart, Frank 447
Link, Arthur Albert 261, 270
Link, Wenceslao 70, 98
Lipchick, Angie 608
Liptak, Vanessa 543, 589
Liška, Alexander 98
Lissak, Maryellen 946
Liszewski, Jessica Lee 580
Livingston, Goodhue 766
Livingston, Henry Brockholst 267, 298
Lizoň, Peter 766
Lizoň, Tatiana Krizová 746
Lobkowicz, Nicholas 857
Lockridge, Oksana Maslivec 939
Loebl, Greta 746
Loebner, Egon Ezriel 1031
Loeffler, William 276
Loewenbach, Jan 521
Lojan, Radoslav 154
Lojeková, Florentina 609
Lom, Herbert 579
Lonek, Adolph 766
Long, Fern 6
Lord, Marjorie 538
Loree, Renata 785
Lorenz, Francisco Valdomiro 921
Lorenz, František 921
Lorre, Peter 538
Losonsky, George 965
Lothar, Ernst 383
Lotter, Frederic August 98
Loupal, Milan 908

Lovell, James Arthur 1000, 1013
Lovell, Jr., James 'Jim' A. 103
Lovsky, Celia 579
Low, George David 103
Low, George Michael 120, 246
Low, George Wilhelm 120, 246
Lowenfeld, Viktor 799
Löwenstein, László 538
Löwy, Arthur 205
Lowy, George 678
Lowy, Otto 40
Lowy, Sir Frank P. 137
Luba, George Stephen 21
Lucas, George (Gary) 503
Lucas, Heidi 580
Lucas, Michael 343
Lucchita, Ivo 966
Luckiesh, Matthew 1013
Ludvík, František 539, 640
Ludvik, Karel Martin 486
Ludvíková, Bohumila 539
Ludwig, Oscar 447
Luka, Milo 487
Lukachko, Andrew Leonard 678
Lukas, Jan 720
Lukas, Paul 560, 580
Lukash, William N. 298
Lukes, Edward J. 276
Lukeš, Igor 829
Lukeš, William F. 298
Lupo, Janet Paula 617
Lurie, Robert Alfred 137
Lusk, George 678
Lusk, Marie Koupal 678
Lusk, Milan 447
Lustig, Arnošt 370
Lustig, Josef 'Pepi' 653
Lutovsky, Charles 276
Luttwak, Dalya 735
Luža, Radomir 829

Lyda, Grady (Gray) 700, 702
Lyons, Bridget Gellert 877
Lyons, William 137

M

Mácal, Zdeněk 403
Macalík, Miroslav J. 766
Macallan, Jes 580
Macejko, Jr., Theodore 206
Mach, Jr., Frank J. 448
Mach, Peter 525
Machacek, Mike 1013
Machan, Benjamin A. 403
Machatý, Gustav 629
Machlica, 3rd, Frank J. 766
Mackenzie, Jr., Alexander Slidell 299
Mackenzie, Morris Robinson Slidell 299
Mackenzie, Ronald Slidell 299
Macko, Hubert 21
Macků, Pina 735
Mahler, Anna Justine 'Gucki' 735
Mahler, Gustav 387, 403, 413, 428, 513,
    518, 521, 603, 735, 948
Mahler, Joseph 948, 1013
Mahone, Austin 504
Mahoney, Daniela 746
Mahoney, Marjorie Ellen Pivonka 566
Mahoney, Teresa 27
Mahr, Paula (Marie) 940
Maier, Vivian 720
Majthenyi, Joseph 85, 299
Majthenyi, Theodore 299
Makarska-Čermák, Leokadia 678
Makovsky, Bohumil 'Boh' 404
Malac, Deborah R. 252
Malachowski, Ricardo de Jaxa 766
Malcolm, Janet 28
Malden, Karl 580
Malek, Frederic Vincent 246
Málek, Ottokar 448

NAME INDEX

Malik, Hana Mrázová 678
Malik, Jr., Joe 908
Malina, Frank 777
Malinak, Edward M. 899
Mallin, John A. 679
Maly, Eugene H. 154
Maly, Kurt 1031
Malý, Winslow 300
Malyshev, Alexy N. 830
Mamatey, Victor S. 830
Manchin, 3rd, Joseph 270
Manchin, Joe 261
Manda, Albert Anthony 235
Mandel, Rabbi Morris 352
Mandl, Otto William 891
Mandl, Sigmund S. 137
Mann, Joseph F. 448
Mann, Jr., Thomas Randall 580
Manner, Jane 654
Mannheimer, Eugene Max 181
Mannheimer, Jennie 654
Mannheimer, Leo 181
Mannheimer, Louise 1013
Mannheimer, Louise Herschman 120
Mantegna, Gina 'Gia' Cristine 581
Manuel, Jay 618
Mařák, Otakar 411, 487
Marcinko, Nadia 105
Marcus, Maria Lenhoff 206
Marden, Charles Carroll 899
Marek, Miroslav 1013
Marek, Vladimír 609
Mares, Jan W. 247
Mares, Jr., Joseph E. 448
Mares, Sr., Joseph E. 448
Maresh, Ferdinand 448
Marešová, Markéta 43
Maretzek, Max 85, 404
Margules, Gabriele Ella 679
Marks, Annalaina 618

Marley, Florence 581
Maršall-Petrovský, Gustáv 372
Marshall, Jonathan 54
Marshall, Lenore Guinzburg ..334, 343, 378
Martin, Bernard 857
Martin, Susan K. 7
Martin-Bittman, Lawrence 113
Martinek, Frank V. 700
Martínek, Joseph 13, 358
Martinka, David 448
Martinů, Alena 13
Martinů, Bohuslav 404, 436, 521
Marton, Bernard Dov 181
Marton, Jiřina 695, 701
Marzik, Thomas D. 830
Masacek, Edward William 449
Masek, Douglas 449
Masek, Jeffrey 966
Mašek, Matěj 300
Mašek, Vojta 13, 85
Maser, Edward A. 799
Masheck, Joseph Daniel 800
Maslivec, Oksana 939
Mason, Luba 539, 581
Massary, Fritzi 487
Massaryk, Frederike 487
Mastics, Marianne Matousek 449
Mastný, Vojtěch 830
Matějček, Jan (Vladimír) 521
Matejicka, Deb 40
Matejka, Jerry Vrchlický 300
Matějka, John V. 13
Matějka, Ladislav 908
Matejka, Mark 'Sparky' 449
Matey, Sr., Thomas W. 138
Mathews, Nancy Mowll 800
Matlocha, John 21, 50
Matocha, Jeff 1032
Matouš, František 11, 322, 333, 357, 853
Matouš, Karel 1032

Matula, David W	1032
Matulka, Jan	679
Matuška, Waldemar	504
Matuštík, Martin Beck	857
Maxa, Jr., Rudolph 'Rudy' Joseph	28, 40
May, Karl	679
Mayda, Jaro	206
Mayer, Anka	680
Mayercak, Zdeno	736
Mazanec, Jerry	404
McAtee, Allison	539
McCartan, Ryan	539
McCosh, Anne Kutka	680
McGrath), Margaret	363
McGraw, Mark	581
McGraw, Samuel Timothy 'Tim'	504
McIntosh, Margaret Millicent Carey	326
McIntosh, Milicent Carey	120
McKim, Anna	566
McMillan, Gloria Ptacek	877
McNeill, Donald 'Don'	40
Mečiar, Stanislav	22
Med, Bohumil	449
Medlin, Wenzel	235
Mehok, Rev. Edward E.	878
Meilbek, Leo	359
Meisel, John	987
Meissner, Margit	120
Meizlik, Aranka	380
Melichar, Donald	878
Melichar, James A.	450
Meller, Vlado	1000, 1014
Mendlowitz, Shmuel	182
Mendlowitz, Shraga Feivel	182
Mentzer, Estée	135
Merced, Isabela	582
Mermall, Thomas	900
Messer, Thomas M.	800
Metze, Gernot	1032
Metzl, Ervine	680, 705
Meyer, Edward C	301
Meyerhoefer, Wilhelm	86
Meyers, Joshua Dylan 'Josh'	540
Meyers, Seth Adam	582
Meyerstein, Goldie Piroch	929
Mica, Daniel	261
Mica, John L.	261
Míček, Eduard	909
Michaels, Bret	504
Michálek, Anthony	261
Michalek, Bohumil	450
Michalek, Chris 'Buddha'	450
Michalek, Joseph James	451
Michalicka, Vaclav	155
Michalovič, Géza	301
Michals, Duane	720
Michna, Marienka	451
Michney, Todd Michael	831
Michnik, Nathan	182
Mihalótzy, Géza	301
Mihalotzy-Mikulas, Gejza	301
Mihok, Dashiell 'Dash'	582
Mikolanda, Jacob	359
Mikova, Marie	451
Mikula, Susan	831
Mikulak, Maxim William	831
Mikuš, Joseph A	832
Mikuska, Frank	680
Mikuska, Vincent	680
Mikuta, Rudolf	766
Miller, Martin	582
Milý, Edward	359
Minarik, Rudolf Glenn	1000, 1014
Miniberger, Václav J.	13, 370
Mintz, Gabriele	879
Mintz, Ilse Schüller	987
Mintz, Walter	987
Mischka, Joseph	451
Mitchell, George Edward	261, 301
Mitermiler, Andrew Robert	766

Mládek, Meda Sokolová 806
Mladen, Leo Mucha 832
Mladova, Milada 609
Mlynarovich, Clement K. 372
Moffat, J. Pierrepoint 253
Mokrejs, John 405
Molitor, Joseph 767
Molitor, Joseph W. 720
Molnar, Enrico Selley 167
Molzer, August 405, 451
Molzer, Victor Joseph 405
Moner, Isabela 582
Morales, Andrés Morav 63
Morando, Otto 487
Morav, Andrés 63
Morava, Jack Johnson 949
Moravčík, Milica (Hasalová) 610
Moravec, Bedřich 370
Moravec, František 113
Moravec, Hans P. 1032
Moravec, Hans Peter 1043
Moravec, Josef 680
Moravec, Paul 405
Morawetz, Albert Richard 253
Morawetz, Oskar 405, 666
Morawetz, Victor 206
Morkovsky, Alois J. 155
Morkovsky, John Louis 155
Morkovsky, Sister Mary Christine 858
Moschcowitz, Paul 680
Moses, Emile Phillips 301
Moskowitz, Amália J. 677, 705
Moss, Irene 681
Mottl, Ronald M. 262
Moucha, Robert 'Rob' 967
Mourek, Joseph E. 452
Mráček, Franta Rostislav 86
Mráček, František 14
Mracek, Jaroslav 514
Mraz, Annabelle Milada 609

Mraz, J. Gerald 452
Mraz, Jason Thomas 504
Mraz, Magda 785
Mráz, Magdalena 'Magda' 681
Mrázek, Josef M. 767
Mrázek, Joseph 746
Mrazek, Robert J. 262
Mrázek, Rudolf 832
Mucek, Jan 369
Mucha, Alphonse 646, 681, 696, 705
Mudroch, Václav 832
Mueller, Ernst 383
Mueller, Ignatius 182
Mueller, Reinhold Christopher 832
Muhlenberg, Francis Swaine 262
Muhlenberg, Frederick Augustus 262
Muhlenberg, Frederick Augustus
   Conrad 262
Muhlenberg, Henry Augustus Philip 262
Muhlenberg, John Peter Gabriel 262
Müller, Jan 681
Muller, Rudolph 582
Munck, Noah 582
Munk, Peter 138
Műnzer, Zdenka 801
Murgaš, Jozef 1014
Murin, Charles (aka Karol) 858
Murphy, Brittany Anne 582
Murphy, Donna 540
Musil, Ferdinand L. 14
Muska, Mark H. 167
Muzik, Claire 618
Myers, Baruch 182
Myzet, Rudolf 583

N

Nábělek, John L. 967
Nábělek, Peter Igor 967
Nádherný, Emanuel Václav 695
Nadherny, Joseph Jerome 767

Nagel, Ernest	858	Neumark, David	858
Nagy, Elemer Joseph	868	Neuspiel, Jiří George	207
Napravilová, Josefina	327	Neustadt, Richard Elliot	988
Naprstek, Joel F.	702	Neustadtl, Isaac	87
Náprstek, Vojtěch 'Vojta'	14, 322	Neutra, Dion	768
Natonek, Hans	383	Neutra, Richard	768
Navrátil, Jiří	1033	Neuzil, Mark R.	28
Nechodoma, Antonín	767	Neužil, Procopius	47
Nedbal, Martin	514	Neužil, Procopius Charles	155
Nedela, Frank	405	Nevlud, Vojtěch	9
Nedvěd, Rudolph James	767	Newcombe, Hanna	343
Negri, Pola	541	Newcombe, Nora S.	988
Nehněvajsa, Jiří	988	Newfield, Morris	182
Neisser, Augustine	75	Newman, Elinor 'Nell' Teresa	363, 583
Neisser, George	76	Newman, Eugenia Fichtenová	452
Nejdl, Marjorie 'Marj' A. Kopecek	747	Newman, Melissa 'Lissy'	583
Nekola, Anna	514	Newman, Paul	363, 583, 584
Nelhýbel, Václav	405	Newman, Scott	584
Němcová, Petra	618	Newton, Becki	584
Nemec, 3rd, Joseph C.	647	Newton, Matt	584
Nemec, Anastacia Carmel	583	Nikodem, Vera Marie	939
Nemec, Corin	583	Nitschmann, Anna Caritas	76
Nemec, John William	920	Nitschmann, David	74, 76, 78, 168
Němec, Ludvík	833	Nitschmann, David the 'Syndic'	76
Nemecek, Stephen	1033	Nitschmann, John	168
Němeček, Zdeněk	370	Nitschová, Markéta	535, 575
Nemeth, Joseph	87, 302	Noga, Francis R. E.	681
Nepomucký, Bohumír	492	Nohel, Arthur	236
Netolička, Karel	452	Nosco, Beatrice M.	909
Nettl, Bruno	515	Nosek, Z. Vlasta	681
Nettl, Paul	515	Novacek, John	452
Nettl-Fiol, Rebecca	610	Novacek, Michael J.	967
Neudorfl, Marie L.	833	Nováček, Ottokar Eugen	406
Neumann, Frederick	515	Novacek, Stephanie	487
Neumann, John Nepomucene	155	Novak, Alfred	155
Neumann, Joseph	70	Novák, Anton	47
Neumann, Karel	541	Novak, Arthur Francis	938
Neumann, Robert G.	253	Novák, Dagobert	47
Neumann, Ronald E.	253	Novak, Eva	584
Neumann, Walter Friedrich	891	Novak, Jane	584, 590

Novak, John 406
Novak, John K. 515
Novak, Jr., Frank Joseph 452
Novak, Jr., Gordon Shaw 1034
Novak, Kim 584
Novak, Louis 728
Novak, Maximillian E. 878
Novak, Michael 859
Novak, Olivia Darvaš 682
Novak, Vincent Michael 155
Novotná, Jarmila 488
Novotný, Anthony 'Tony 359
Novotný, Antonin 14
Novotný, Daniel D. 859
Novotny, Elmer Ladislaw 682
Novotny, Frank 276
Novotný, Frank 729
Novotny, George P. 302
Novotný, Joseph 168
Novotny, Monica 41
Novotny, Vincent A. 682
Novy, Donald Andrew 453
Novy, Frederick George 939, 1015
Novy, Joseph F. 453
Novy, Marianne 878
Nowotny, Jr., George Edward 344
Nowotný, Vincent C. 453
Nožička, George J. 1034
Nýdrle, Peter 630
Nykl, Alois Richard 921
Nykl, David 584

O

O'Keefe, Jodi Lyn 585
O'Toole, Annette 585
Obdrzalek, Suzanne 860
Oberwesier, Edward Andrew 138
Obsitnik, Steve 139
Obsitnik, Vincent 253
Ocasek, Oliver Robert 344

Ochs, Effie Wise 649
Odložilík, Otakar 833
Oesterreicher, John Maria 156
Okáľ, Ján 22
Oktávec, Mája V. 162
Oktávec, William Anton 682
Oliverius, Jan A. 14
Oliveroff, Andre 610
Olšanský, Klement 683
Omundson, Timothy 585
Ondrák, Ambrose 334
Ondrak, Ambrose Leo 156
Ondrasik, 3rd, Vladimir John 504
Ondrejkovic, Joseph 640
Ondříček, Emanuel 453
Ondříček, Karel 453
Ondříček, Miroslav 644
Opatrný, Jaroslav 1034
Oppenheim, Adolf Leo 918
Oravec, Christian Robert 156
Oravec, Věra 828
Oros, Nadia 610
Orowan, Susan K. 7
Osborne, Mark Randolph 630
Osheroff, Douglas (Dean) 949
Oshman, Karen Appel 207
Oskerova, Lucia 618
Oster, John 1015
Ostrovsky, Erika 900
Otcasek, Christopher 505
Otcasek, Eron 585
Otcasek, Richard Theodore 505
Otenášek, Mildred 344
Ott, Emiline Royco 722
Ott, Peterpaul 736
Ott, Philip 63
Otten, Anna 900
Ottendorfer, Oswald 33, 58, 87
Oulanoff, Hongor 909
Oumiroff, Bogea 492

P

Pabisch, Franz Josef 87
Pabisch, Franz Joseph 157
Pabst, Georg Wilhelm 630
Pačes, Joseph (Josef) 360
Pache, Joseph 406
Pachner, Ann 786
Pachner, William 683
Paclt, Čeněk 108
Paclt, Čeněk 302
Page, Alex R. 879
Page, Angelica 541
Page, Max 801
Paidar, Rose 488
Paige, Diane M. 516
Palatas, Cameron 585
Palatas, Nick 585
Palda, Leo (Lev) J. 361
Palda, Lev J. 15, 334
Paleček, James (Václav) 453
Palek, Shawn 683
Palickar, Stephen J. 22
Palka, John 939
Pálka, John 939
Palmedo, Lillian Gaertner 683
Palmer, Betsy 585
Pancella, Phyllis 488
Panek, Hana E. 768
Pánek, Hana E. 683
Panek, Jennifer 879
Panenka, Ernst 453
Pangborn, Robert 454
Pankratz, George 276
Pankúch, Ján 22, 50
Panuch, Joseph Anthony 247
Papanek, Ernst 121, 335
Papanek, Gustav F. 989
Papanek, Victor 768
Papin, Joseph 157
Parada, Peter 'Pete' 454

Parazaider, Walter 454
Parisse, Annie 585
Parizek, Eldon Joseph 968
Pařízek, Frank 1015
Parizek, Richard R. 968
Pascheles, Wolfgang Ernst 949
Pašek, Thomas 406
Pashkus, Theodore 454
Passer, Ivan 630
Pastor, Josef 15
Pastor, Joseph 322
Pastrick, Robert A. 276
Paszaman, William Garson 568
Patek, John 407
Patek, Joseph 407
Patek, Sheila N. 939
Paterek, Joe Pat 455
Paternostrová, Zuzana Trepková 802
Paucke, Florián 71
Paučo, Draga 22
Paučo, Joseph 50
Pauer, Francisco Xavier 71
Paukert, Karel 407
Pauli, Wolfgang Ernst 949
Paulu, Burton 41
Pauly, Rose 489
Pavel, Michael 'Misha' 1034
Pavelka, Jacob 'Jake' Lynn 586
Pavlechko, Thomas 407
Pavlečka, Vladimír S. 1015
Pavlík, Michael 747
Payer, Ernst Denis 768
Payer, Harry Franklin 247
Pazdernik, Charles Frederick 868
Pech, Stanley Zdeněk 833
Pecha, Pamela 455
Pechacek, Emil Frank 276
Pechacek, Jr., Major Frank Fred 304
Pěchota, Vratislav 207
Pecka, Josef Boleslav 15

Pecka, Joseph Boleslav	361
Pejskar, Jožka	15
Pekarek, Neyla	455
Pekárková, Iva	370
Pelich, Joseph Roman	768
Pelikan, Jaroslav	169
Pelikan, Lisa	542
Pelikan, Sr., Jaroslav John	22
Pell, Julia Lorillard Wampage	328
Penkava, Francis	188
Perchlik, Richard	277
Pergler, Charles (aka Karel)	208
Peřina, Peter	640, 654
Peřina, Rudolf V.	253
Perk, Ralph	277, 345
Perl, John Ignatius	684
Perl, William R.	328, 352
Perlman, Anne S.	378
Perlman, Fredy	365
Perloff, Marjorie	879
Perloff-Giles, Alexandra	208
Perloff-Giles, Nicholas	505
Perman, Dagmar Horna	821, 834
Peroutka, Ferdinand	15
Peroutka, Michael Anthony	345
Peschel, Lisa A.	654
Peštová, Daniela	619
Peter, John Frederick	456
Peterik, James 'Jim' Michael	505
Peterka, Alvin Joseph	968
Peters, Gordon B.	456
Petkoff, Robert	542
Petrák, Miloš	456
Petrak, Rudolf	489
Petran, Dušan	748
Petrasek, David	209
Petrik, Michael T.	209
Petro, Peter	910
Petrovská, Marija	900
Petrtýl, August	695
Petschek, George	209
Peukert, Josef	345, 365
Pflanzer, Vilém	88, 98
Philipi, John J.	302
Philipse Robinson of Nashwaaksis, Frederick	317
Philipse, 3rd, Frederick	315
Philipse, Frederick	64, 193, 202, 219, 245, 251, 252, 259, 264, 266, 267, 269, 276, 284, 285, 286, 287, 293, 298, 299, 305, 314, 315, 316, 317, 318, 320, 331, 334, 766, 794, 812, 815, 1020
Philipse, Mary	316
Philipse, Susannah	316, 317
Phillips, Barnet	29
Phillips, Henry Myer	262
Phoenix, Joan of Arc	586
Phoenix, Joaquin	586
Phoenix, Liberty	586
Phoenix, Rain	586
Phoenix, River	586
Phoenix, Summer	586
Picha, Jr., Kenneth G.	247
Pichel, Irving	631
Pichlíková-Burke, Lenka	543
Píchová, Hana	910
Pick, Adolf	408
Pick, Ernest	901
Pick, Zuzana	627
Pierce, Adele	684
Pies, Beata	786
Piesch, Anna Johanna	77
Pietsch, Coral Wong	267, 303
Pinkava, Jan Jaroslav	778
Pintauro, Danny	587
Pipal, Krystof	456
Pique, Edward	457
Pisk, George Michael	880
Pisk, Paul Amadeus	408, 417, 516
Pistorius, George (Jiří)	901

Pitelka, Kazi 457	Pojman, Ruth Freedom 329, 345
Pitelka, Vince 748	Pokorny, Gene 457
Pitha-Rowe, Paula (Marie) 940	Pokorny, Henry A. 277
Pitlik, Edward 457	Pokorný, Jan Hird 769
Pitlik, Noam 631	Pokorny, Wilma 43
Pitzinger, Gertrude 489	Polakovič, Štefan 861
Placek, Emil Edwin 277	Polanyi, John C. 950
Plachy, Sylvia 561, 721	Polanyi, Karl Paul 989
Placzek, Adolf K. 2, 7	Polanyi, Laura Matild 834
Placzek, Roman 408	Polanyi, Thomas G. 1016
Planer, Franz 644	Polášek, Albin 736
Plank, Emma Karoline 'Nuschi' 121	Polerecky, John L. 108
Plavcan, Joseph 684	Polerecký, John L. 64, 303
Pletnev, Rostislav V. 910	Politzer, Heinz 891
Plicka, Joseph 'Joe' Benjamin 880	Politzer, Hugh David 950
Pliška, John Valentine 1015	Polivka, Raymond Peter 1035
Ploszek, Pete 587	Polivka, Vladimír 457
Pluhar, Werner S. 860	Pollacsek, John C. 950
Pochobradský, Jiří 1035	Pollak, Felix 7
Pochop, Jana 505	Pollak, Gustav 2
Pochop, Vladimír 1035	Pollak, Leo Wenzel 970
Podany, Jerry Charles 802	Pollak, Louis Heilprin 210, 267
Podany, Nicholas Anton 543	Pollak, Max 685
Podešvová, Eva 714	Pollak, Rose 489
Podivinský, Ina 769	Pollatschek, John H. 901
Podlaha, Elizabeth 1000, 1015	Pollitzer, Anita 326
Podlaha-Murphy, Elizabeth 1000, 1015	Pollitzer, Anita Lily 721
Podlesak, Emil 1016	Pollitzer, Carrie T. 122
Podoski, Barbara Hauserová 303	Pollitzer, Gustave M. 236
Podoski, Barbara Lauewers 113	Pollitzer, Henrietta 131
Poduska, Donald Miles 869	Pollitzer, Mabel L. 122
Podzimek, Josef 969	Pollitzer, Moritz 236
Pohanka, Frank S. 139	Poloka, Dean 610
Pohl, Johann Baptist Emanuel 99	Poloka, Jack 611
Pohl, Václav 88	Polt, John H. 901
Pohlad, Bill 631	Pomahač, Bohdan 225
Pojar, Břetislav 778	Pomykal, Ann 277
Pojeta, Jr., John 969	Ponicsan, Darryl 378
Pojman, Louis Paul 329, 345, 860, 861	Popelka, Ashley 572
Pojman, Paul Theodore 861	Popp, Lucia 489

Popper, Erna Mary 223
Popper, Jan 409
Popper, Nicholas S. 834
Popper, Sir Karl Raimund 862
Popper, William 918
Porges, Franziska 761
Porges, Frederick 33
Porges, Maria 736
Porges, Paul Peter 701
Porges, Walter Rudolf 41
Pořízková, Paulina 591, 619
Porubský, John 22
Pošíval, Marek 632
Pospishil, Božena B. 910
Pospíšil, Leopold J. 990
Pospisil, Miroslava 'Mira' 611
Pospíšil, Zdenka 802
Potuckova, Kristina 802
Povolný, Josef 409
Powolny, Frank 721
Pratt, Katherine Eunice
    Schwarzenegger 380
Praver, Tori 619
Prchal, Tim 880
Preisler, Ernst 769
Preisner, Rio 892
Preiss, Eduard 88
Preissig, Vojtěch 705
Preucil, Walter 457, 458
Preucil, William 458
Preucil, Zachary 458
Pribic, Elizabeth 929
Pribram, Aurora 951
Pribram-Jones, Aurora 951
Priebsch, Hannah Margaret Mary 369
Příhoda, Váša 409
Přikryl, Jana 378
Printz, Alexander 139
Pritzker, Daniel 139
Pritzker, John A. 140

Pritzker, Thomas 140
Probasco, Juriaen 64
Prochaska, David 835
Prochaska, Frank 835
Procházka, Adolf 210
Prochazka, Aurelius 1035
Procházka, Denisa 737
Procházka, Jiří 769
Procházka, Ludmila 737, 748
Procházka, Svante 951, 1016
Prochazka, Zora 990
Prochotsky, Irena 611
Prokop, George (Jiří) 543
Prokop, Matthew 'Matt' 587
Prokosch, Eduard 513, 929
Prokosch, Edward 892
Prokosch, Frederic 379, 892, 929
Prokosch, Walther 769
Prucha, Francis Paul 835
Prucha, John James 970
Prucha, Mallory 752
Průchová, Vlasta 506
Prusak, Lyuba Durdakova 737
Pryor, Zora Prochazka 990
Pšenička, Rudolf Jaromír 15, 371
Pšenka, Rudolf Jaromír 15, 371
Psota, Ivo Váňa 611
Ptacek, Carol J. 970
Ptacek, Fatima 587
Ptacek, Kathryn 379
Ptacek, Rainer 506
Ptacek, Robin Louis 802
Ptacek, Russ 41
Ptak, Tom 458
Pucelik, Thomas M. 157
Pucher-Čiernovodský, František 22
Puchmajer, George J. 769
Puchmajer, Liba 706
Puchmajerová-Girsová, Libuše 706
Pucholt, Vladimír 587

Pulitzer, 3rd, Joseph 55
Pulitzer, Joseph 55, 56, 262
Pulitzer, Jr., Joseph 55
Pulitzer, Ralph 56
Pumberton, Ida Hrubesky 685
Pummer, Reinhard Erich 188
Purgina, Emil 685
Pustejovsky, James D. 929
Pustejovsky, John 892
Pustejovsky, Luke 140
Putti, Lya De 565
Pyro, Hana 7

Q
Quigley, Fannie 108

R
Raba, Ernest Aloysius 211
Raba, Ernst 721
Rabb, Theodore K. 836
Rabinowicz, Oskar K. 353, 836
Rabinowicz, Theodore K. 836
Racek, Edward 277
Radilak, Charles H. 588
Radimský, Ladislav 370
Radnich, Emeric (Imre) 88
Radnich, István 89
Radnich, Stephen 89
Rado, Ladislav 770
Radok, Emil 632
Radvanovsky, Sondra 490
Rady, Michael 587
Ragan, James 379
Raikow, Radmila B. 940
Rajlich, Václav 1035
Rajskub, Mary Lynn 588
Rakovan, John F. 970
Rakušan, Jaromíra 910
Rakušan, Zdenko 770
Ralston, Rudy 632

Ralston, Věra Hrubá 588
Rambousek, Ota 114
Ramsey, Dylan 588
Randa, Josef 737
Randák, Frank 770
Randolph, Ariana Jennings 317
Randolph, Edmund Jennings 247, 262, 270, 277, 304, 317
Randolph, Payton 271
Randolph, Susannah Beverley 315
Raushenbush, Elizabeth Brandeis 335, 990
Raushenbush, Walter Brandeis 211
Ray, Vanessa 543, 589
Raymond, Antonín 770
Rebec, George 862
Rechcigl, John 'Jack' E. 940, 1043
Rechcigl, Miloslav 'Mila' 3, 247, 837
Rechcygl, Dennis 738
Redlich, Joseph 211
Reguly, Robert 29
Rehak, Daniel R. 1036
Rehr, Jan 72
Reich, Siegmund Moses 183
Reichart, Walter Albert 893
Reichenthal, Frank 685
Reichsman, Andrew 633
Reif, Elsie Mary 'Peggy' 382
Reif, John Henry 1036
Reif, Paul 409
Reindl, Miloš 706, 750
Reinfeld, Barbara Kimmel 837
Reinhardt, Gottfried 633
Reinhardt, Max 488, 531, 536, 544, 571, 606, 608, 633, 635, 636, 640, 646
Reinhardt, Stephen Roy 267
Reiser, Alois 409
Reistetter, Stephen 22
Reisz, Karel 633
Reitman, Catherine 589

NAME INDEX

Reitman, Ivan 589, 633
Reitman, Jason 633
Rejsek, Václav 1016
Remes, J. J. 277
Remetta, John J. 305
Renský, Miroslav 881, 930
Resek, Carl Peter 838
Resko, John Allen 941
Ressel, Fred (Ferdinand) Anton 458
Revész, Marinka 482, 653
Rezac, Richard 738
Rezny, James B. 770
Rich, Morris 140, 141
Rich, Richard H. 141
Richman, Julia 122
Richter, Francis Xavier 237
Richter, Henricus (Jindřich Václav) 71
Richter, Jr., Francis Xavier (Frank) 346
Ridge, Tom 263, 271
Riha, Frank J. 47
Říha, Thomas 838
Říhová, Blanka 941
Ringsmuth, František K. 16
Riška, Augustin C. 862
Ritchson, Alan Michael 589
Ritter, Frederick (Fritz) 893
Ritter, Frederick 'Fritz' 544
Rittig, Johann 90, 320
Riva, David 633
Riva, J. Michael 647
Riva, J. Paul 648
Riva, Maria (Sieber) 589
Robel, John Michael 409
Robel, Jolly Jack 409
Roberts, Charles J. 410
Roberts, Jr., John (Glover) 211
Roberts, Jr., John Glover 267
Robey, Ken 640
Robinson, Hon. William Henry 318
Robinson, John 317, 318

Robinson, Lt. Col. Beverley 317
Robinson, Sir Frederick Philipse ... 305, 317
Robitschek, Kurt 640
Rochac, John R. 770
Rockart, John R. 770
Rockefeller, Margaret 363
Roden, Karel 589
Roeper, Annemarie Bondy 123
Roezl, Benedikt 99
Rogers-Altmann, Ruth 685
Rohlík, Josef 212
Röhr, Jan 72
Rollerová, Věra Marie 16
Romadka, John M. 141
Roman, Stephen Boleslav 142
Romanov, Stephanie 619
Rombauer, Johann Theodore (Tivadar) . 89
Rombauer, Koerner 237
Rombauer, Raphael Guido 305
Rombauer, Richard 89
Rombauer, Robert Julius 90, 306
Rombauer, Roderick 90
Rombauer, Roderick E. 306
Rombauer, Roland 306
Romig, Joseph Herman 278
Rondthaler, Edward 1016
Ronell, Avital 862
Rosa, Peter 75, 76
Rose, Jeanne Preucil 458
Rosenbaum, Hulda 485
Rosenberg, Imrich Vitzak 354
Rosenblatt, Samuel 183, 918
Rosenheim, Richard H. 141
Rosewater, Edward 29, 48, 56
Rosewater, Nathan 225, 1017
Rosewater, Victor 346
Rosická, Rose 16
Rosický, John 48
Rosicky, Rose 16
Ross, David 263, 307

NEW WORLD VISIONARIES, SEEKERS, AND CREATORS WITH CZECHOSLOVAK ROOTS

Rossi, Reanna Lynn 573
Rössler, Ernestine 490
Rostinský, Josef 910
Roth, Emery 771
Roth, Feri 459
Roth, Julian 771
Roth, Richard 771
Roubicek, Dorothy 381
Roubíčková, Zdenka 801
Roubik, Rev. Joseph Charles 838
Rouse, Benjamin Irving 838
Rouse, Pete 247
Roux, Nicholas 'Nick' Edward 590
Rovnianek, Peter Víťazoslav 22
Royco, Emil 771
Rozsa, Johnny 722
Rozsafy, Matthias Ernest 90, 307
Rozsypal, Anton J. 930
Rubeš, Jan 490, 544
Rubeš, Susan Douglas 544
Rubovits, Edward R. 354
Rucka, Gregory A. 379
Rudavská, Zuzana 786
Rudavský, Ondrej 786
Rudofský, Bernard 771
Rudolph, Joseph 90
Ruml, 2nd, Treadwell 881
Ruml, Beardsley 119, 881, 991
Ruppe, Philip 263
Ruscha, 4th, Edward Joseph 750
Ruston, Audrey Kathleen 571
Ruta, Sebastian 278
Ruth, Jan De 660
Růžička, Drahomír 722
Ruzicka, Francis (Frank) A. 712
Ruzicka, Francis William 237
Růžička, Joseph F 237
Ruzicka, Maria 346
Růžička, Rudolph 709, 729
Ruzicka, Stephen Quade 839

Ruzicska, Matthias Ernest 90, 307
Rybáčková, Jiřina 3
Rybak, Christopher 'Chris' Lee 459
Rybak, Jr., Raymond Thomas 'R. T.' 278
Rybka, Frank A. 278
Rybovich, Jr., John 142
Rychlik, Charles Vaclav 410
Rychtařík, Richard 648
Rydlo, Dagmar 459
Rysanek, Leonie 490

S

Sabath, Adolph Joachim 263
Sabathil, Sigurd 525
Sabathil, Simon 526
Sabato, Jr., Antonio 619
Sabla, Peter 506
Sablica, Rev. Michael John 863
Sabo, Gerald J. 911
Sachs, Adam Ehrlich 379
Sadek, George 706
Sadílek, Adam 1036
Sadler, Bernard 183
Safar, Peter 225
Šafránek, Vincent Frank 411
Sahanek, Tatjana 7
Sahultavy, Turhan Gilbert Selahattin .. 556
Salak, Kira 99
Sales, James B. 212
Salivarová, Zdena Josefa 48
Salma, Emanuel A. 1001, 1017
Salmson, Axel Jakob 729, 748
Salva, Fedor Ivan 23
Salva, Karol 23, 50
Salz, Helen A. 685
Salzer, Felix 517
Samstag, Gordon 685, 787
Šándor, Andrej 373
Šároši, Izák 64
Sarosy, Anne Dolores Zvara 460

NAME INDEX

Šarošy, Isaac Ferdinand 64
Šašek, Miroslav 695
Sasko, Vladimir G. 411
Šašková-Pierce, Míla 911
Saunders, John Simcoe 318
Savant, Marilyn vos 31
Saxl, Eva 951
Scarborough, Mika (Emilie Leonia)
   Brzezinski 42
Schacht, Cornelia Ludmila 42
Schaefer, Anne 590
Schaeffer, Francis B. 307
Schalek, Alice 723
Schamschula, Walter 911
Schanzer, George Oswald 902
Schapiro, Andrew 213, 254
Schapiro, Tamar 863
Schauffler, Robert Haven 460
Schein, Edgar 991
Schejbal, Jaroslav 881
Schenk, Frederick 213
Schenk, Lynn 214, 263
Schermer, Fritzi 703
Schick, Frederick 863
Schick, Nina 189
Schienle, Martin James Pflieger ...594
Schiffer, William 'Bill' 749
Schildkraut, Joseph 544
Schiller, Andrew 930
Schimmel, Fredolin 526
Schimmerling, Hanuš A. 411
Schindler, David William 971
Schindler, Rudolph Michael 772
Schlachta, Dennis Franz 567
Schleisner, William 723
Schlesinger, Joe 42
Schlesinger, Libor Alois 91
Schlesinger, Max 183
Schlesinger, Rudolph Michael 772
Schling, Jr., Max 238

Schling, Maximillian 'Max' 238
Schmausová, Helena 603
Schmelkes, Franz Charles 952, 1017
Schmolka, Walter 43
Schnabel, Lola Montes 590, 685
Schnabel, Stefan 545
Schnabel, Stella Madrid 590
Schnabel, Vito Maria 807
Schneider, Clara Tesar 460
Schneider, Claudine 263
Schneiderová-Zubaníková, Marie 772
Schoberová, Olga 591
Schoenberg, Arnold 214, 404, 412, 418,
   437, 512, 516, 518
Schoenberg, Barbara Zeisl 894
Schoenberg, Randol 214, 894
Schoenbrun, Emanuel 183
Scholzová-Železná, Helene 740
Schottertova, Viera 620
Schramek, Thomas (Tomáš) 611
Schreiber, Emanuel 183
Schreyer, Greta Loebl 746
Schubert, Bruno Otto 1037
Schubert, Orlando V. 686
Schubert, Peter Zdeněk 911
Schubert, Richard Francis 248
Schüller, Ilse 987
Schultz, Peter C. 1017
Schumann-Heink, Ernestine 490
Schumpeter, Joseph Alois 991
Schűtz, Alfred 864
Schwanda, Benedict 142
Schwanda, Tom 169
Schwartz, Bernard 564
Schwartz, Růžena G. 483
Schwartz-Markovič, Edward 23, 50
Schwarz, Heinrich 803
Schwarzenegger, Arnold Alois 271, 591
Schwarzenegger, Katherine 380
Schwarzkopf, Paul 143, 952, 1017

Schweinburg, Raina	792
Schwelb, Frank (František) E.	268
Schwenk, Lilli	324
Schwenková, Lili Hornig	946
Sciranka, John C.	23
Scott, Lizabeth	545
Scott, Stefanie Noelle	591
Scott, Věra Prášilová	723
Sealsfield, Charles	383
Sebak, Rick	633
Sebek, Barbara	881
Sebesta, Edward H.	347
Sebesta, Robert W.	1037
Sebranek, Joseph G.	942
Sebranek, Patrick 'Pat'	881
Seckar, Alvena Vajda	686
Secor, Martin Mathias	143
Secor, Mathias M.	278
Sedivy, Edmund P.	412
Sedivy, Edmund Premysl	278
Šedivý, Julie	930
Sedlacek, Frances	108
Sedlacek, Milo J.	278
Sedlon, Richard	686
Seeman, Murray	143
Segert, Eva	215
Segert, Stanislav	919, 931
Segert-Tauger, Eva	215
Seidel, Adolph	591
Seidel, Anna Johanna	77
Seidel, Nathaniel	77
Seifert, Anton	78
Šejna, Jan	114
Šejnoha, Jaroslav	686
Sekera, Zdeněk	971
Sekula-Gibbs, Shelley	263
Selleck, Thomas 'Tom' William	591
Selye, Hans	225
Semancik, Joseph Stephen	942
Semrad, John A.	238
Semsey, Károly	91, 307
Seng, Michael P.	215
Senko, Joseph	991
Senko, Michael J.	254
Sepeshy, Zoltan Leslie	686
Serger, Frederick B.	686
Serkin, Peter	460
Serkin, Rudolf	444, 460, 461, 485, 518, 736
Serly, Tibor	412
Sernett, Milton C.	839
Sersen, Fred	648
Sessler, Morris	184
Sestak, Joe	263
Settlemire, Chris	602
Seventy, Steve	461
Sever, Klára Katherina	738
Severa, Václav F.	143
Shake, Christi	620
Sharoshi, Isaacus	64
Shary, John H.	238
Shober, Francis Edwin	263
Shober, Francis Emanuel	264
Shober, Gottlieb	77
Shulze, John Andrew	271
Siakel, Jaroslav	634
Siegal, Aranka	380
Sikela, John	701
Sima, Thomas W.	308
Sima, William R.	412
Simak, Clifford D.	380
Simanek, Robert Ernest	308
Simecek, John Dana	882
Simek Sr., Joseph 'Pep'	143
Šimek, Štěpán	640
Simon, Herbert Alexander	991, 1044
Simon, T. F.	729
Šimončič, Klement	912
Simor, Suzanna	803
Simpson, Daniela	144
Šimůnek, Jiří 'Jirka'	972

Šimunek, Květa (Marie) 119
Sinaiberger, Frederick B........................686
Sindelar, Jody L.......................................992
Sindelar, Thomas A. 696
Singer, Kurt D..114
Šípková, Daniela 746
Sís, Peter 696
Šiškovský, Jaroslav 461
Sisolak, Steve..271
Sitka, Emil 592
Sivek, Marketa 687
Sixta, George 701
Sjögren, Tina 100
Skala, Libby...545
Skala, Lilia 546, 772
Skalak, Katherine 972
Skalicky, Jan 753
Skalicky, Mary Elizabeth 461
Skalník, Pavel 687
Škarda, Frank (František)........................362
Škarda, František 48
Skarda, Patricia Lyn 883
Skinker, Alexander Rives 308
Sklenar, Frederick A................................701
Sklenar, Frederick J.................................696
Sklenar, Robert John...............................869
Sklenaříková, Adriana 617
Skluzacek, Valentine...............................157
Skodik, Antonín C....................................738
Skrivanek, John Marion..........................912
Skuta, Ernie 461
Škvařil, Joseph 772
Škvorecký, Josef............... 371, 655, 656, 908
Slabý, Luis 461
Slade, Isaac 506
Sladky, Mathias 'Math' J.........................413
Slámečka, Vladimír................................1037
Slavíková, Magdalena 920
Slepčíková-Resovská, Markéta 43
Šlesinger, Libor Alois 91

Slezak, Erika Alena 546
Slezák, John.. 248
Slezák, Leo 491, 546
Slezak, Walter.. 546
Slipka, Yvonne 687
Slivka, Meyer Benjamin 462
Slovak, Mira 105
Slovenský, Ján 'Janko' 23
Slover, Karl 592
Smékalová, Hana................................... 581
Smetak, Walter...................................... 413
Smetana, František................................ 462
Smietanka, John 268
Smil, Václav 368
Smisek, Anita M. 522
Smith, Trudy Enzer 952
Smith, Wilma... 43
Smithin, Hanička 384
Šmok, Pavel 612
Smol, John P... 972
Smutný, Joseph S. 687
Smutny, Robert Jaroslav....................... 869
Smykal, Richard 308
Šnajdr, Václav 16, 322
Sobota, Jan Bohuslav 709
Sobotka, Ruth A..................................... 612
Sobotka, Walter S.................................. 772
Sochor, Božena 687
Sofer, Lilia 546, 772
Sojka, Trude (Gertrud) 687
Sokol, Anthony E.................................... 839
Sokol, Elena.. 912
Sokol, F.J. 278
Sokol, Jennifer 462
Sokol, John A. 239
Sokol, Koloman 688, 706
Sokol, Kyle.. 462
Sokol, Mark 462
Sökol, Sasha 506
Sokol, Vilém... 463

Sokol-Elliott, Paula 463
Solar-Kinderman, Eva 463
Šolc, Josef.. 169
Solomon(s), Ezekiel.................................... 64
Solomon, William.................................... 309
Sonja, Magda 567, 592
Sonnenfeld, Peter.................................... 973
Sonneschein, Rosa 29, 56, 354
Sonneschein, Solomon H. 184
Sopko, John 310
Sosel, Josef.. 91
Soucek, Apollo 105, 106, 309
Soucek, Brian 215
Soucek, Leo Eugene 309
Soucek, Zeus.. 106
Soukupová, Hana 620
Soul, Maelcum 592
Soul, Patricia Ann 592
Sovák, Jan 696
Sovik, Thomas Paul................................. 517
Sovinec, Carl Richard 952
Spacek, Arnold A..................................... 278
Spacek, Mary Elizabeth 'Sissy' 593
Špaček, Otto 310
Spain, Dagmar 613
Sparks, Nicholas (Charles) 380
Spencer, Hanna 894
Spencer, John 593
Spenser, Daniela 840
Speshock, John 593
Spevak, John 50
Spiegel, Thomas 144
Spielberg, Erika 900
Spielberg, Peter 883
Spilka, Mark 883
Spinka, Matthew 170, 840
Spira, Emma Karoline 'Nuschi' 121
Spira, Thomas 841
Spitz, Tibor 787
Spivack, Nova 1037

Splavcová-Stropnická, Otilie 546
Šplíchal, Ivan.. 569
Spravka-Oumiroff, Ella 464
Šprinc, Mikuláš 372
Sprotte, Anna Růžena 483, 491
Sramek, Joseph 841
Šrámek, Paul S... 279
Sramek, Peter 723
Šroubek, Otakar C................................... 464
Sršeň, Fred... 648
Stach, Matthew 78
Stadler, Eva Maria 902
Stádníková, Hana....................................... 7
Stafford, Frederick 594
Stafford, John 347
Stahura, Joseph 279
Staller, Karel Jan 1018
Stalmach, Adele 684
Štalmach, Frank (František) 773
Stanek, Richard W. 347
Staňková, Maruška.................................. 547
Stansel, Valentin 72
Stark, Peter A. 1038
Starosta, Stanley 931
Starr, Martin 594
Staša, Josef... 773
Staško, Joseph 23
Staško, Jozef... 8
Stassen, Glen Harold 170
Stassen, Harlod Edward........................ 348
Stassen, Harold 170, 248, 271
Stassen, William A.................................. 279
Stastny, Anthony J................................... 522
Stavan, Henry Anthony 902
Stavovčík, Jiří 688
Stedronsky, George 279
Steele, Henry Bernard 144
Steele, Maurice Bernard........................ 144
Steele, Samuel Bernard 144
Steele, Sarah Jane 594

NAME INDEX

Stefan, Charles G.	254
Štefan, Karl	43, 264
Stefan, Paul	518
Stefanský, George	895
Steffanina, Matt	613
Steffel, Mathias	72
Stefl, Jerry	803
Steiger, John Stephen	65
Stein, Adolf	239
Stein, Clarence	773
Stein, Eric	216
Stein, Julian H.	723
Stein, Simon Leonard	723
Steiner, Andrew	774
Steiner, Edward Alfred	170
Steiner, Gitta Hana	413
Steiner, Linda	29
Steiner, Peter	913
Steiner, Ralph	724
Steiner, Robert Eugene	310
Steiner-Prag, Hugo	688, 706
Steinhardt, Melanie Kent	787
Steinhöffer, Jan	67
Stein-Kubin, Daniel	689
Stejskal, Jiří	913
Sten, Suzanne	491
Stendal, Ian	724
Stepanek, Brian	547
Stepanek, Orin	913
Stepanek, Steven	1038
Stepanek, William Henry	279
Štěrba, Antonín	689
Sterba, James P.	864
Sterba, Lydia Smutny	464
Sterba, Wendy	655
Štěrbák, Jana	739
Stern, Jan Peter	739
Stern, Lynn	724
Stern, Miroslava	595
Sternberg, Eugene	774
Sternberger, Jakob	91
Sternfeld, Frederick William	518
Šternová, Miroslava	595
Sternstein, Malynne	913
Stiedry, Fritz	413
Stika, Joseph Edward	310
Stika, Richard	158
Štipl, Richard	739
Štípl, Richard	689
Stockar, Helena M.	689
Stöhr, Richard	518
Stoklas, George	724
Stoklasa, Mike	30
Stolarik, M. Mark	4, 841
Stolz, Robert E.	507
Stone, Grace	369
Stonier, Tom	368
Straka, Emil	465
Straka, Jerry Michael	973
Straka, Michael 'Mike'	44
Strand, Paul	724
Strank, Michael	311
Stransky, Angélica Espinoza	527
Stransky, Charles	547
Stránský, Hugo	184
Stránský, Josef	413
Stransky, Paul	724
Strasak, Henry	115
Strauss, Sigmund	1018
Stražnický, Edward R.	92
Strážnický, Edward R.	8
Streeruwitz, William H.	973
Strelka, Joseph Peter	895
Stříbrná, Irene Olga	777
Strmeň, Karol	373
Strnad, Frank	519
Strnad, Jan Steven	703
Strnad, Jeff	216
Stroheim, Erich Oswald	635
Štrupl, Miloš	171

Stuart, Carol Lee	576
Stuchlik, Joshua	864
Stupka, Ladislav 'Laddie'	311
Štupl, Antonín	724
Sturm, Rudolf	914
Styer, Henry Delp	311, 312
Styer, Wilhelm D.	312
Stypeck, Allan J.	4
Suchy-Pilalis, Jessica	465
Sucsy, Michael	634
Suczek, Robert Anthony	1018
Suda, Zdeněk Ludvík	993
Suhany, Adalbert B.	465
Sulak, Louis J.	48, 56
Šulc, Miroslav	774
Sulzberger, Arthur Hays	54, 56
Sulzberger, Arthur Ochs 'Punch'	56
Sulzberger, Iphigene Ochs	57, 364
Sulzberger, Jr., Arthur Ochs	57
Sulzberger, Judith	30
Sulzberger, Judith Peixotto	30
Sumichrast, Michael	993
Supa, Joseph	158
Suppetius, Andreas (Ondřej)	72
Surovy, Nicolas	547, 548
Surovy, Walter	548
Susskind, Charles	1001
Susskind, Jan Walter	414
Süsskind, Nathan	932
Sutherland, Anna Chladek	23
Sutherland, Anthony X.	23
Sutnar, Ladislav	707
Sutnar, Radoslav Ladislav	775
Šuvadová, Silvia	595
Šváb, Zdeněk	465
Svasek, Albert F.	725
Švec, Petr	1038
Sveda, Michael	953, 1018
Švehla, Antonín	690
Švehla, Antonín (Tony)	690
Švehla, Frank	48
Svehla, Henry	312
Švejda, George J.	842
Svejda, Jim	44
Svejkovský, František	914
Švejnar, Jan	993
Sviták, Ivan	864
Svoboda, Antonín	1039
Svoboda, Charles Vincent	239
Svoboda, Edward E.	414
Svoboda, Erin	466, 467
Svoboda, F. H.	49
Svoboda, Frank J.	49
Svoboda, Frederic Joseph	884
Svoboda, George	466
Svoboda, George Jiří	914
Svoboda, John	466
Svoboda, Josef Čestmír	690, 696
Svoboda, Josef G.	5
Svoboda, Ralph Edward	216
Svoboda, Richard	466, 467
Svoboda, Tomáš	414
Svoboda, Vincent A.	701
Svobodová, Líba	1039
Svojger, Jr., Joseph	314
Swoboda, A. J.	171
Swoboda, Henry	414
Swoboda, William J.	279
Sychak, Bret Michael	504
Sychra, Jaroslav 'Jerry'	1039
Sýkora, Bohumil	467
Sýkora, Frank	467
Szekely, Rudolph Rezso	491
Szell, George	414, 452
Szold, Benjamin	92, 184
Szold, Henrietta	355
Sztacho, Jiřina Anna	902
Szurovy, Walter	548

NAME INDEX

T

Tabor, Edward Otto 216
Tabor, John K. 248
Táborský, Václav 634
Tachau, Eric S. 330
Tachau, Jean Brandeis 336
Tachau, Katherine H. 842
Tachau, William Gabriel 775
Talackova, Jenna 620
Talafous, Joseph J. 216
Tanneberger, David 78, 526
Tannenberg, David 78
Tanzer, Lester 30
Tausky, Thomas E. 884
Taussig, Arthur 725
Taussig, Charles William 145, 248
Taussig, Edward David 313
Taussig, Francis Brewster 57
Taussig, Frank William 248, 994
Taussig, Hans 803
Taussig, Hans Karl 804
Taussig, Harry A. 725
Taussig, Helen Brooke 225
Taussig, Isaac William 279
Taussig, James 92, 320, 348
Taussig, John Joseph 145
Taussig, Joseph Knefler 313
Taussig, Jr., Joseph K. 249
Taussig, Louis 145, 240
Taussig, Michael 842
Taussig, Michael K. 842
Taussig, Peter Elyakim 415
Taussig, Ralph J. 145
Taussig, Samuel 145, 240
Taussig, Walter 415
Taussig, Walter M. 279
Taussig, William 145, 279
Taussky, Olga 953
Taussky-Todd, Olga 953
Taylor, Chip 507

Teller, Edward 953
Tenney, Emerson 595
Teply, Lee 519
Terzaghi, Margaret 942
Terzaghi-Howe, Margaret 942
Tesar, Bruce 1039
Tesar, Clara Schneider 468
Tesar, Paul 775
Tholt-Veľkoštiavnický, Adalbert 23
Thoma, Martin 1040
Thomas, Robin 953
Thompson, Dennis 468
Thompson, John Dockery 313
Thorson, Victoria 739
Tietze, Andreas 919
Tietze, Hans 803
Tietze, Hans Karl 804
Tietze-Conrat, Erica 803
Till, Jacob C. 468
Till, Johann Christian 468
Timbuktu, ... 507
Tintner, Benjamin Abner 184
Tintner, Moritz 184
Tirsch, Ignác 72
Tkach, Stephen J. 24
Tkach, Walter Robert 313
Tkacik, Arnold John 158
Tobias, Joseph F. 279
Toepfer, Frank 1001, 1018
Toman, Jindřich 915
Toman, Jiří 217
Tomanek, Godfrey Bohumir Antonin ... 469
Tománek, Joseph 690
Tomanek, Rita Svoboda 690
Tománek, Thomas J. 902
Tomanová, Marie 725
Tomas, Vincent Anthony 864
Tomascik, Joseph G. 217
Tomasek, Kathryn 843
Tomasko, Matthew Wayne 551

Tomek, Ivan 1040
Tomich, Dennis A. 468
Tong, Rosemarie 'Rosie' 843
Topferová, Marta 507
Topinka, Judy Baar 330
Torberg, Friedrich 383
Torn, Angelica 541
Torn, Elmore Rual 'Rip' 548
Torovský, Adolph 415
Torovsky, Rudolph Adams 726
Toth, Carl 527
Toth, Jerry (Jaroslav) 469
Toth, Tony 469
Totushek, John 313
Totushek, Ken 508
Touchet, Jaques 65
Touchet, Wilson 415
Traficant, James 264
Trahan, Elisabeth 895
Trahan, Jennifer 218
Traugott, Elizabeth Closs 843, 932
Traxler, Jiří (George) 416
Trenský, Pavel I. 656
Trier, Walter 697
Trimbur, Angela 595
Triner, Václav 146
Tříska, Jan 548
Trlica, John Paul 726
Trnka, Alois 469
Trnka, Alois C. 470
Trnka, Karla 932
Trnka, Peter 865
Troller, Georg Stefan 34
Troller, Norbert 775
Trombley, Laura Skandera 123, 884
Tropsch, Hans 953, 1019
Trump, Eric (Frederick) 146
Trump, Ivana 620
Trump, Ivanka Marie 147, 249
Trump, Jr., Donald (John) 146

Trumpel, Hans 65
Tuček, Jaques 65
Tugendhat, Ernst 865
Tuleya, Edward Andrew 843
Tuma, Keith 885
Tuma, Mym 691
Tumlir, Jan 804
Tupa, Julius Victor 522
Tupy, Leslie T. 218
Turek, Jiří 726
Turnau, Josef 491
Tuska, John Regis 788
Tutzek, Jaques 65
Tuzar, Georgia 492
Tybor, Sister M. Martina 8
Tydings, Joseph Davies 264
Tylka, Wendel 24
Týnek, Dušan 613

U

Uhde, Jan 656
Uhlir, Jr., Arthur 1019
Újházy, Laszlo 92
Újházy, László 254
Ullmann, Walter P. 843
Ulmer, Arianne 596
Ulmer, Edgar G. 596, 635
Umirov, Boža 492
Ungar, Sanford 'Sandy' J. 249
Unkrich, Lee 645
Urban, George John 279
Urban, Joseph 527, 683, 775
Urbanovsky, Elo John 776
Urbis, Richard J. 470
Urich, Justin 596
Urich, Robert 549, 596
Urich, Ryan 596
Urich, Tom 596
Urzidil, Johannes 383

V

Vacek, Edward 158
Vacek, Joseph J. 218
Vachuska, Thomas 1040
Vacin, Emil 279
Vaculík, Jan 49, 57
Vaget, Hans Rudolph 896
Vajda, Jaroslav 416
Valach, Miroslav 1041
Valášek, Otakar 702
Valášek, Sharon K. 147
Valasek, Thomas 656
Valenta, Joseph A. 158
Valenta, Yaroslav (Jaroslav) Henry 691
Valert, František 644
Valigursky, Edward 'Ed' Ignatius 697
Valko, Andrew 692
Vallila, Marja 788
Vančo, Bohumil 1019
Vancura, Rev. Leo C. 885
Vanek, Al. 470
Vanek, Betty Rose Kepka 741
Vanek, Miroslav 776
Vanhara, John 147
Vaníček, Petr 974
Vanik, Charles Albert 264
Vaňková, Jana 'Jaja' 614
Vano, Robert 726
Vanous, Lucky Joseph 620
Váňová, Apollonia 596
Vařeková, Veronika 621
Varn, Johann Peter 65
Varzaly, Stephen 24
Vasa, Robert Francis 158
Vašák, Jetta Marie 348
Vasek, Leslie J. 159
Vasicek, John 635
Váška, Bedřich 471
Vašut, Marek 596
Vaváková, Ivana 707
Vaverka, Anton 597
Vaverka, Julie 471
Vavřinová, Milena 492
Vavruska, Frank 692
Vejtasa, Stanley 'Swede' 313
Vejvoda, Kathleen 885
Velan, Karel Adolf 147
Velinger, George (Jiří) 805
Velinský, Ludmila Ondrujová 902
Veninger, Ingrid 597
Ventura, Jesse 271
Verchota, Joseph John 280
Vesely, Bohumir C. 471
Veselý, Frank 280
Veselý, Godfrey Francis 692
Vesely, Jr., Stanley 'Stan' J. 471
Vesely, O.S.B., Sister Charlotte 495
Vichr, Roman 1041
Vilček, Jan 226
Vilim, Joseph Alois 471
Vilim, Mark Washington 471
Vilim, Richard 472
Vinecká, Ludmila 472
Visclosky, Peter John 264
Vitek, William 'Bill' 866
Vitouš, Miroslav Ladislav 416
Vitousek, Martin J. 974
Vivot, Lea 739
Vlach, Anton James 280
Vlach, Robert 371, 915
Vlasák, František 135
Vlasak, Lavínia Gutmann 597
Vlasek, Winifred June 577
Vlazny, John George 159
Vlk, Paul 381
Vltchek, André 30
Vodicka, Ruth 740
Voegele, Kate Elizabeth 508
Vogelstein, Hermann 185
Vogelstein, Ludwig 148

Vogelstein, Max 185
Vogl-Garrett, Edith 519
Voight, Angelina Jolie 573
Voight, Barry 975
Voight, James Haven 570
Voight, James Wesley 507
Voight, Jon 507, 570, 597, 975
Vojan, Jaroslav E. S. 16
Vojta, Jiří Theodor 843
Vojtěch, Anna 697
Vojtěch, Václav 100
Vojtko, Margaret Mary 902
Volavka, Zdenka 805
Volavý, Marguerite 472
Volek, Emil 902
Voleský, Bohumil 1002
Volková, Bronislava 371, 915
von Benedikt, Wulf Erich Barsch 727
von Dohnanyi, Ernst 416
von Friedrichsthal, Emanuel 95
von Hayek, Friedrich August 981
von Kármán, Theodore 998, 1019
von Kuneš, Karen 915
von Payer, Julius 100, 106
von Stein, Friedrich Strobel 594
von Stroheim, Erich 635
von Watteville, Benigna 123
von Watteville, Henrietta Benigna Justine
    Zinzendorf 79
Vondracek, Felix John 843
Vondrous, John C. 730
Vonesh, Raymond James 159
Vopat, Mark C. 866
Vopička, Charles J. 240, 254
Voska, Emanuel Viktor 115
Voskovec, George (Jiří) 549
Vostrovsky, Jerome 240
Votapek, Ralph 472
Votipka, Thelma 492
Votruba, Martin 916

Vožech, Anthony 740
Vrana, Albert S. 740
Vrana, John George 159
Vrana, Sydney 472
Vrana, Vlasta 598
Vráz, Enrique Stanko 101, 921
Vrba, Čeněk 473
Vrhel, James 473
Vrtis, Robert 641
Vyhlidal, Mark 473
Vyoral, Rev. Alois 866
Vysekal, Edouard Antonín 692
Vytlacil, Václav 692

W

Wachal, Robert S. 932
Wachs, Ruby 550
Wachsmann, George (Jiří) 549
Wadina, Sidonka 749
Wainwright, Jonathan Mayhew ... 249, 264, 314
Waldes, Heinrich (Jindřich) 807
Waldes, Henry 148
Waldstein, Sonja 692
Walker, Scott Kevin 271
Walter, Arnold M. 520
Walter, Johann Nepomuk 73
Warhol, Andy 751
Warhola, Andrew 751
Warhola, James 698
Warsh, Jane Lauder 136
Wasicsko, Nick 280
Waskey, Frank Hinman 265
Waskovich, George 844
Wattawa, John 219, 280
Watts, Jon 635
Wax, Ruby 550
Wayne, Matt 551
Wcela, Emil Aloysius 159
Weatherly, Albert 474

NAME INDEX

Weatherly, Jr., Albert 474
Weatherly, Robert 474
Wechsberg, Joseph 381
Wechsler, Morris 185
Wedeles, Emil 146, 240
Weems, Philip Van Horn 314, 1020
Wehle, Charles 93
Wehle, Gottlieb 93
Wehle, Harry Brandeis 805
Wehle, Louis Brandeis 254
Wehle, Regina 82
Weicher, John 451, 475
Weidenthal, Harry George 996
Weidenthal, Jewel 6
Weidenthal, Leo 31
Weidenthal, Maurice 57
Weiener, Thomas G. 932
Weigel, Helene 529, 551
Weinberg, Norbert 185
Weinberg, William (Wilhelm) 185
Weinberg, Zvi 355
Weinberger, Caspar Willard 249
Weinberger, Jacob 268
Weinberger, Jaromír 416
Weiner, Lewis 1021
Weinfeld, Edward 268
Weinmann, Charles Alfred 148
Weisgall, Hugo David 417
Weiskopf, Franz Carl 384
Weiss, Emil 698, 994
Weiss, Isaac Mayer 124, 186
Weiss, Jiří 636
Weiss, Marc A. 994
Weiss, Stephen Samuel 187
Weissberger, Arnold 954, 1021
Weisskopf, Edith 994
Weisskopf, Karen 125
Weisskopf, Victor 'Viki' Frederick 954
Weisz, Cornel 552
Weitz, Chris 575, 636
Weitz, Paul John 636
Wellek, René 886
Wellwarth, George E. 656
Wels, Charles 475
Welt, Elisabeth 895
Weltsch, Samuel 495
Welzl, Jan Eskymo 101
Wenberger, Howard Lawrence 1021
Wendel, Elmarie Louise 551
Wendel, Jennifer J. C. 598
Werba, Henry C. 932
Werbesik, Giselle 551
Werbezirk, Gisela 551
Werfel, Franz 383, 384, 890, 892
Werich, Jan 395, 550, 552, 779
Werkheiser, Devon 599
Wertheimer, Max 995
Weselak, Anton Bernard 349
Wesely, Don 280
Weverka, Peter 1041
Wexler, Tanya 599
White, Alex W. 707
White, Dagmar 493
White, Jan V. 707
Wickes, Joseph Augustus 219
Wiener, Adolf 34
Wiener, Gertrud 117, 123, 124
Wiener, Jan 844
Wierer, Otto 8
Wiesel, Alexander Sandor 186
Wiesner, Adolf 34
Wilde, Cornel 552
Wildfang, Johannes 65
Wilfahrt, John Anthony 475
Wilfer, Anton 523, 527
Wilimovsky, Charles A. 693, 700
Wilkes, Helen Waldstein 903
Wilkes, Paul 381
Williams, John Skelton 249
Williams, Murat Willis 255

Williams, Rosemary 'Rosie'	475
Willis, Zdenka Saba	975
Winkler, Mayer	186
Winner, Thomas G.	932
Winner, Thomas Gustav	916
Winokur, Maxine	377
Winter, Andrew Jan	255
Winter, John F.	903
Winterhalt, Keala Wayne	599
Winternitz, Emanuel	520
Winternitz, Felix	475, 599
Winternitz, Mary (Watson)	375
Winters, Ben H.	381
Winters, Benjamin Allen H.	381
Winters, Roland	476, 599
Wirtschafter, David	186
Wise, Aaron	186
Wise, Isaac Mayer	124, 186
Wise, Jonah Bondi	187
Wise, Leo	57
Wise, Stephen S.	355
Wise, Stephen Samuel	187
Wisocky, Rebecca	553
Witek, Anton	476
Wittgenstein, Paul	476
Wodicka, Virgil Orville	240
Wojatsek, Charles	844
Wolf, Frederick C.	44
Wolf, Henry	708
Wolf, Július	24, 50
Wolfenstein, Martha	381, 995
Wolfenstein, Samuel	188
Wollenberg, Marjorie	538
Woodic, Emanuel	240, 314
Woolfolk, Dorothy	381
Woolley, Victor Baynard	268
Wopat, Tom	599
ormeley, Katharine Prescott	5
mser, Amy Josephine Klauber	693
ser, Ella Klauber	693
Worth, Karen	125
Wozniak, John Keith	508
Wright, Trevor	600
Wurts, Alexander Jay	1021
Wurts, John	219
Wyman, Charles Alfred	148
Wyman, Thomas G.	249
Wynn, Ed	553
Wynn, Keenan	554, 601
Wynn, Ned	601

Y

Yaniga, Paul M.	975
Yanosky, Thomas R.	788
Yarabek, Stefan Andrew	776
Yoková, Betty	753
Yosowitz, Philip	417
Yuhaus, Cassian	159
Yurka, Blanche	554

Z

Z., Charlie	477
Zabka, Stanley 'Stan' William	636
Zabka, William 'Billy'	601
Zabransky, Joseph	280
Zacek, Dennis	641
Zacek, Joseph Frederick	844
Zach, Jan	740
Zachar, Jacob	601
Zaeske, Jr., Louis W.	349
Zahorec, Joseph John	280
Zahradníček, Petr	614
Zajíček, Jeronym	417
Zajick, Dolora	493
Žák-Marušiak, Jozef	24
Zalom, Frank	942
Zamecnik, John Stepan	418
Zamecnik, Paul C.	1021
Zamecnik, Paul Charles	943
Zarechnak, Michael	933

Žarnov, Andrej 373
Zathureczky, Ede 476
Žatko, Dr. Ernest 18
Zátková, Irena 903
Zavadil, Joseph B. 886
Zbinovsky, Vladimir 944
Zbořílek, Vladimír 916
Zdechlik, John 418
Zdenek, Joseph William 903
Zdrůbek, F. B. 17
Zdrůbek, František Boleslav 323
ze Lhoty, František Boryně 94
Zeisberger, David 74, 78, 101
Zeisberger, Jr., David 78
Zeisel, Eva Striker 712
Zeisel, Hans 219
Zeisl, Eric 214, 418, 894
Zeisler, Sigmund 220, 336
Žekulin, Gleb N. 916
Zelenka, Eric 1041
Zeleny, Charlie 477
Zeleny, Jeff 45
Zeleny, Jeffrey 'Jeff' Dean 31
Zeleny, John 1021
Zeleny, Jon 954
Zeleny, Robert Owen 5
Zelezny, Helen 740
Zellen, Jan 477
Zelníčková, Ivana Marie 620
Zeman, Francis 160
Zeman, Jarold Knox 171
Zeman, Ludmila 779
Zeman, Vladimír 866
Zemánková, Maria 1042
Zenisek, Chad 220
Zenkl, Radim 477

Zerzan, John 366
Zetek, Jaroslav 693
Zezula, Jindřich 903
Zgusta, Ladislav 933
Ziegler, Elsie Mary 'Peggy' 382
Ziegler, Gail 561
Ziegler, Karen Blanche 528, 558
Zieglerová, Klára 648
Zika, Mathias M. 278
Zika, Rosemary 'Rosie' 475
Zimbler, Liane 776
Zimmerman, Zora Devrnja 887
Zinner, Peter 636
Zinterhofer, Aerin Rebecca Lauder 135
Zinzendorf, Count Nicholaus Ludwig 79
Zinzendorf, Countess Benigna 79
Žiškovský, Alois 160
Žiškovský, George Joseph 160
Žižka, Jan 477
Zmrhal, Jaroslav 125
Zoli, Winter Ave 602
Zona, Stephen A. 280
Žorna-Horský, Julius 24
Zoula, Norbert 362
Zúbek, Theodore Joseph 160
Zucker, Dorrit 888
Zuckerman, Philip Joseph 995
Zupko, Ronald Edward 845
Zurek, Patrick 161
Zvetina, John Adam 220
Zvonický, Gorazd 373
Zwach, Sr., John Matthew 265
Zwara, John 693
Zweig, Fritz 418
Zweig, Stefan ....
Zylka, Chris ....

1102

Milton Keynes UK
Ingram Content Group UK Ltd.
UKHW052028231124
451424UK00006B/56